Sports Collectors Digest

1887–1947
BASEBALL CARD
PRICE GUIDE

Edited By Jeff Kurowski

Published by

**krause
publications**

700 E. State Street • Iola, WI 54990-0001
Telephone: 715/445-2214

Library of Congress Number 93-77550
ISBN: 0-87341-262-1
Printed in the United States of America

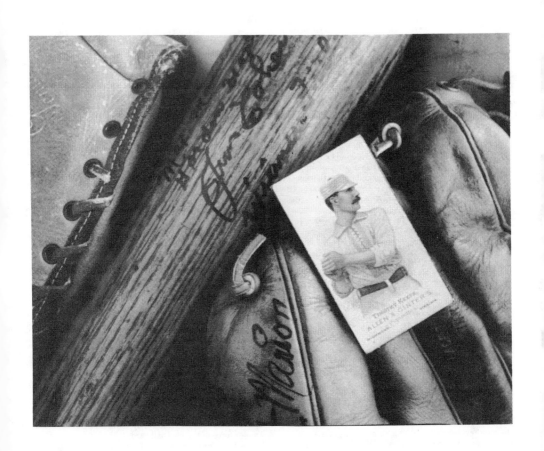

BASEBALL CARD HISTORY

In 1887 — over 100 years ago — the first nationally distributed baseball cards were issued by Goodwin & Co. of New York City. The 1½" x 2½" cards featured posed studio photographs glued to stiff cardboard. They were inserted into cigarette packages with such exotic brand names as Old Judge, Gypsy Queen and Dog's Head. Poses were formal, with artificial backgrounds and bare-handed players fielding balls suspended on strings to simulate action.

Then, as now, baseball cards were intended to stimulate product sales. What could be more American than using the diamond heroes of the national pastime to gain an edge on the competition? It is a tradition that has continued virtually unbroken for a century.

Following Goodwin's lead a year later, competitors began issuing baseball cards with their cigarettes, using full-color lithography to bring to life painted portraits of the era's top players.

After a few short years of intense competition, the cigarette industry's leading firms formed a monopoly and cornered the market. By the mid-1980s there was little competition, and no reason to issue baseball cards. The first great period of baseball card issues came to an end.

The importing of Turkish tobaccos in the years just prior to 1910 created a revolution in American smoking habits. With dozens of new firms entering the market, the idea of using baseball cards to boost sales was revived.

In the years from 1909-1912, dozens of different sets of cards were produced to be given away in cigarette packages. There was a greater than ever variety in sizes, shapes and designs, from the extremely popular 1½" x 2⅝" color lithographed set of 500+ players which collectors call T206, to the large (5" x 8") Turkey Red brand cards. There were double folders, featuring two players on the same card, and triple folders, which had two player portraits and an action scene. Gold ink and embossed designs were also tried to make competing companies' cards attractive and popular.

It was this era that saw the issue of the king of baseball cards, the T206 Honus Wagner card, worth $400,000.

The zeal with which America's youngsters pursued their fathers, uncles, and neighbors for cigarette cards in the years just prior to World War I convinced the nation's confectioners that baseball cards could also be used to boost candy sales.

While baseball cards had been produced by candy companies on a limited basis as far back as the 1880s, by the early 1920s the concept was being widely used in the industry. The highly competitive caramel business was a major force in this new marketing strategy, offering a baseball card in each package of candy. Not to be outdone, Cracker Jack began including baseball cards in each box. The 1914-1915 Cracker Jack cards are important because they were the most popular of the candy cards to include players from a short-lived third major league, the Federal League.

Generally, candy cards of the era were not as colorful or well-printed as the earlier tobacco cards, due to the shortage of paper and ink-making ingredients caused by World War I.

The association of bubble gum and baseball cards is a phenomenon of only the past half-century. In the early 1930s techniques were developed using rubber tree products to give the elasticity necessary for blowing bubbles.

During this era the standard method of selling a slab of bubble gum and a baseball card in a colorfully wax-wrapped 1-cent package was developed. Bubble gum — and baseball card — production in this era was centered in Massachusetts, where National Chicle Co. (Cambridge) and Goudey Gum Co. (Boston) were headquartered.

Most bubble gum cards produced in the early 1930s featured a roughly square (about 2½") format, with players depicted in colorful paintings. For the first time, considerable attention was paid to the backs of the cards, where biographical details, career highlights and past season statistics were presented.

In 1939, a new company entered the baseball card market — Gum Inc., of Philadelphia. Its "Play Ball" gum was the major supplier of baseball cards until 1941, when World War II caused a shortage of the materials necessary both for the production of bubble gum and the printing of baseball cards.

Three years after the end of World War II baseball cards returned on a national scale, with two companies competing for the bubble gum market. In Philadelphia, the former Gum Inc. reappeared on the market as Bowman Gum Inc.

Bowman's first baseball card set appeared in 1948, very similar in format to the cards which had existed prior to the war, black-and-white player photos on nearly square (2" x 2½") cardboard. The 1948 Bowman effort was modest, with only 48 cards. The following year, color was added to the photos. For 1950, Bowman replaced the retouched photos with original color paintings of players, many of which were repeated a year later in the 1951 issue. Also new for 1951 was a larger card size, 2" x 3⅛".

Bowman had little national competition in this era. In 1948-1949, Leaf Gum in Chicago produced a 98-card set that is the only bubble gum issue of the era to include a Joe DiMaggio card.

While Bowman dominated the post-war era through 1951, in that year Topps began production of its first baseball cards, issuing three different small sets of cards and serving warning that it was going to become a major force in the baseball card field.

In 1952, Brooklyn-based Topps entered the baseball card market in a big way. Not only was its 407-card set the largest single-year issue ever produced, but its 2⅝" x 3¾" format was the largest-sized baseball card ever offered for over-the-counter sale. Other innovations in Topps' premiere issue for 1952 included the first-ever use of team logos in card design, and on the back of the card, the first use of line statistics to document the player's previous year and career performance. By contrast, Bowman's set for 1952 remained in the smaller format, had 72 fewer cards and showed little change in design from 1951.

Just as clearly as Topps won the 1952 baseball card battle, Bowman came back in 1953 with what is often considered the finest baseball card set ever produced. For the first time ever, actual color photographs were reproduced on baseball cards in Bowman's 160-card set. To allow the full impact of the new technology, there were no other design elements on the front of the card and Bowman adopted a larger format, 2½" x 3¾".

And so the competition went for five years, with each

company trying to gain an edge by signing players to exclusive contracts and creating new and exciting card designs each year. Gradually, Topps became the dominant force in the baseball card market. In late 1955, Bowman admitted defeat and the company was sold to Topps.

Baseball cards entered a new era in 1957. After years of intense competition, Topps enjoyed a virtual monopoly that was rarely seriously challenged in the next 25 years. One such challenge in the opening years of the 1960s came from Post cereal, which from 1961-1963 issued 200-card sets on the backs of its cereal boxes.

In 1957, Topps' baseball cards were issued in a new size — 2½" x 3½" — that would become the industrywide standard that prevails to this day. It was also the year that Topps first used full-color photographs for its cards, rather than paintings or retouched black-and-white photos. Another innovation in the 1957 set was the introduction of complete major/and or minor league statistics on the card backs. This feature quickly became a favorite with youngsters and provided fuel for endless schoolyard debates about whether one player was better than another.

In the ensuing five years, major league baseball underwent monumental changes. In 1958, the Giants and Dodgers left New York for California. In 1961-1962 expansion came to the major leagues, with new teams springing up from coast to coast and border to border.

The Topps baseball cards of the era preserve those days when modern baseball was in its formative stages.

In 1963, for the first time in seven years, it looked as if there might once again be two baseball card issues to choose from. After three years of issuing "old-timers" card sets, Fleer issued a 66-card set of current players. Topps took Fleer to court, where the validity of Topps' exclusive contracts with baseball players to appear on bubble gum cards was upheld. It was the last major challenge to Topps for nearly 20 years.

The 1960s offered baseball card collecting at its traditional finest. Youngsters would wait and worry through the long winter, watching candy store shelves for the first appearance of the brightly colored 5-cent card packs in the spring. A cry of "They're in!" could empty a playground in seconds as youngsters rushed to the corner store to see what design innovations Topps had come up with for the new year. Then, periodically during the summer, new series would be released, offering a new challenge to complete. As the seasons wore down, fewer and fewer stores carried the final few series, and it became a real struggle to complete the "high numbers" from a given year's set. But it was all part of the fun of buying baseball cards in the 1960s.

The early 1970s brought some important changes to the baseball card scene. The decade's first two Topps issues were stunning in that the traditional white border was dropped in favor of gray in 1970, and black in 1971. In 1972, Topps' card design was absolutely psychedelic, with brightly colored frames around the player photos, and comic book typography popping out all over. The design for the 1973 cards was more traditional, but the photos were not. Instead of close-up portraits or posed "action" shots, many cards in the 1973 Topps set featured actual game action photos. Unfortunately, too many of those photos made it hard to tell which player was which, and the set was roundly panned by collectors.

But most significantly, 1973 marked the last year in which baseball cards were issued by series through the course of the summer. On the positive side, this eliminated the traditional scarce "high numbers" produced

toward the end of the season. On the negative side, it meant players who had been traded in the pre-season could no longer be shown in their correct uniforms, and outstanding new players had to wait a full year before their rookie cards would debut.

This marketing change made a significant impact on the hobby and helped spur a tremendous growth period in the late 1970s. By offering all of the cards at once, Topps made it easy for baseball card dealers to offer complete sets early in the year. Previously, collectors had to either assemble their sets by buying packs of cards, or wait until all series had been issued to buy a set from a dealer. It was in this era that many of today's top baseball card dealers got their start or made the switch to baseball cards a full-time business.

During this era, the first significant national competition to Topps' baseball card monopoly in many years was introduced. Hostess, a bakery products company, began distributing baseball cards printed on the bottoms of packages of its snack cakes, while the Kellogg's company distributed simulated 3-D cards in boxes of its cereals. The eagerness with which collectors gobbled up these issues showed that the hobby was ready for a period of unprecedented growth.

The baseball card hobby literally boomed in 1981. A federal court broke Topps' monopoly on the issue of baseball cards with bubble gum, and Fleer, from Philadelphia, and Donruss, of Memphis, entered the field as the first meaningful competition in nearly 20 years.

That same year also marked a beginning of the resurgence in the number of regional baseball card issues. Over the next few years, dozens of such sets came onto the market, helping to boost sales of everything from snack cakes to soda pop and police public relations. By 1984, more than half of the teams in the major leagues were issuing some type of baseball cards on a regional basis. The hobby had not enjoyed such diversity of issues since the mid-1950s.

While yet another court decision cost Fleer and Donruss the right to sell their baseball cards with bubble gum, both companies remained in the market and gained strength.

Topps' major contribution in this era was the introduction of annual "Traded" sets which offered cards of the year's new rookies as well as cards of traded players in their correct uniforms.

The mid-1980s showed continued strong growth in the number of active baseball card collectors, as well as the number of new baseball card issues. Topps, still the industry's leader, expanded the number and variety of its baseball issues with many different test issues and on-going speciality sets, including oversize cards, 3-D plastic cards, metal "cards" and much more.

After three years of over-production of its baseball card sets, Donruss, in 1984, significantly limited the number of cards printed, creating a situation in which demand exceeded supply, causing the value of Donruss cards to rise above Topps for the first time.

In 1984, Fleer followed Topps' lead and produced a season's-end "Update" set. Because the quantity of sets printed was extremely limited, and because it contains many of today's hottest young players, the 1984 Fleer Update set has become the most valuable baseball card issue produced in recent times.

In 1986, a fourth company joined the baseball card wars. Called "Sportflics," the cards were produced by a subsidiary of the Wrigley Gum Co., and featured three different photos on each card in a simulated 3-D effect. For 1987, a fourth national baseball card set, called Score, entered the scene. A fifth national baseball card set, Upper Deck, was created in 1989.

HOW TO USE THIS CATALOG

This catalog has been uniquely designed to serve the needs of beginning and advanced collectors. It provides a comprehensive guide to more than 100 years of baseball card issues, arranged so that even the most novice collector can consult it with confidence and ease.

The following explanations summarize the general practices used in preparing this catalog's listings. However, because of specialized requirements which may vary from card set to card set, these must not be considered ironclad. Where these standards have been set aside, appropriate notations are incorporated.

ARRANGEMENT

Because the most important feature in identifying, and pricing, a baseball card is its set of origin, this catalog has been alphabetically arranged according to the name by which the set is most popularly known to collectors.

Those sets that were issued for more than one year are then listed chronologically, from earliest to most recent.

Within each set, the cards are listed by their designated card number, or in the absence of card numbers, alphabetically according to the last name of the player pictured.

IDENTIFICATION

While most modern baseball cards are well identified on front, back or both, as to date and issue, such has not always been the case. In general, the back of the card is more useful in identifying the set of origin than the front. The issuer or sponsor's name will usually appear on the back since, after all, baseball cards were first issued as a promotional item to stimulate sales of other products. As often as not, that issuer's name is the name by which the set is known to collectors and under which it will be found listed in this catalog.

Virtually every set listed in this catalog is accompanied by a photograph of a representative card. If all else fails, a comparison of an unknown card with the photos in this book will usually produce a match.

As a special feature, each set listed in this catalog has been cross-indexed by its date of issue. This will allow identification in some difficult cases because a baseball card's general age, if not specific year of issue, can usually be fixed by studying the biographical or statistical information on the back of the card. The last year mentioned in either the biography or stats is usually the year which preceded the year of issue.

PHOTOGRAPHS

A photograph on the front and back of at least one representative card from virtually every set listed in this catalog has been incorporated into the listings to aid in identification.

Photographs have been printed in reduced size. The actual size of cards in each set is given in the introductory text preceding its listing.

DATING

The dating of baseball cards by year of issue on the front or back of the card itself is a relatively new phenomenon. In most cases, to accurately determine a date of issue for an unidentified card, it must be studied for clues. As mentioned, the biography, career summary or statistics on the back of the card are the best way to pinpoint a year of issue. In most cases, the year of issue will be the year after the last season mentioned on the card.

Luckily for today's collector, earlier generations have done much of the research in determining year of issue for those cards which bear no clues. The painstaking task of matching players' listed and/or pictured team against their career records often allowed an issue date to be determined.

In some cases, particular cards sets were issued over a period of more than one calendar year, but since they are collected together as a single set, their specific year of issue is not important. Such sets will be listed with their complete known range of issue years.

NUMBERING

While many baseball card issues as far back as the 1880s have contained card numbers assigned by the issuer, to facilitate the collecting of a compete set, the practice has by no means been universal. Even today, not every set bears card numbers.

Logically, those baseball cards which were numbered by their manufacturer are presented in that numerical order within the listings of this catalog. The many unnumbered issues, however, have been assigned *Sports Collectors Digest Baseball Card Price Guide* numbers to facilitate their universal identification within the hobby, especially when buying and selling by mail. In all cases, numbers which have been assigned, or which otherwise do not appear on the card through error or by design, are shown in this catalog within parentheses. In virtually all cases, unless a more natural system suggested itself by the unique nature of a particular set, the assignment of *Sports Collectors Digest Baseball Card Price Guide* numbers by the cataloging staff has been done by alphabetical arrangement of the player's last names or the card's principal title.

Significant collectible variations of any particular card are noted within the listings by the application of a suffix letter within parentheses. In instances of variations, the suffix "a" is assigned to the variation which was created first.

NAMES

The identification of a player by full name on the front of his baseball card has been a common practice only since the 1920s. Prior to that, the player's last name and team were the usual information found on the card front.

As a standard practice, the listings in the *Sports Collectors Digest Baseball Card Price Guide* present the player's name exactly as it appears on the front of the card, if his full name is given there. If the player's full name only appears on the back, rather than the front of the card, the listing corresponds to that designation.

In cases where only the player's last name is given on the card, the cataloging staff has included the first name by which he was most often known for ease of identification.

Cards which contain misspelled first or last names, or even wrong initials, will have included in their listings the incorrect information, with a correction accompanying in parentheses. This extends, also, to cases where the name on the card does not correspond to the player actually pictured.

GRADING

It is necessary that some sort of card grading standard be used so that buyer and seller (especially when dealing by mail) may reach an informed agreement on the value of a card. Each card set's listings are priced in the three grades of preservation in which those cards are most commonly encountered in the daily buying and selling of the hobby marketplace.

Older cards are listed in grades of Near Mint (NR MT), Excellent (EX) and Very Good (VG), reflecting the basic fact that few cards were able to survive for 25, 50 or even 100 years in close semblance to the condition of their issue. The pricing of cards in these three conditions will allow readers to accurately price cards which fall in intermediate grades, such as EX-MT, or VG-EX.

More recent issues, which have been preserved in top condition in considerable number, are listed in the grades of Mint (MT), Near Mint and Excellent, reflective of the fact that there exists in the current market little or no demand for cards of the recent past in grades below Excellent.

In general, although grades below Very Good are not priced in this catalog, close approximations of low-grade card values may figure on the following formula: Good condition cards are valued at about 50% of VG price, with Fair cards priced about 50% of Good. Cards in Poor condition have no market value except in the cases of the rarest and most expensive cards. In such cases, value has to be negotiated individually.

For the benefit of the reader, we present herewith the grading guide which was orginally formulated by *Baseball Cards* magazine and *Sports Collectors Digest* in 1981, and has been continually refined since that time. These grading definitions have been used in the pricing of cards in this) catalog, but they are by no means a universally accepted grading standard. The potential buyer of a baseball card should keep that in mind when encountering cards of nominally the same grade, but at a price which differs widely from that quoted in this book. Ultimately, the collector himself must formulate his own personal grading standards in deciding whether cards available for purchase meet the needs of his own collection.

No collector or dealer is required to adhere to the grading standards presented herewith — or to any other published grading standards — but all are invited to do so. The editors of the *Sports Collectors Digest Baseball Card Price Guide* are eager to work toward the development of a standardized system of card grading that will be consistent with the realities of the hobby marketplace. Contact the editors.

Mint (MT): A perfect card. Well-centered, with parallel borders which appear equal to the naked eye. Four sharp, square corners. No creases, edge dents, surface scratches, paper flaws, loss of luster, yellowing or fading, regardless of age. No imperfectly printed card — out of register, badly cut or ink flawed — or card stained by contact with gum, wax or other substances can be considered truly Mint, even if new out of the pack.

Near Mint (NR MT): A nearly perfect card. At first glance, a Near Mint card appears perfect; upon closer examination, however, a minor flaw will be discovered. On well-centered cards, three of the four corners must be perfectly sharp; only one corner shows a minor imperfection upon close inspection. A slightly off-center card with one or more borders being noticeably unequal — but still present — would also fit this grade.

Excellent (EX): Corners are still fairly sharp with only moderate wear. Card borders may be off center. No creases. May have very minor gum, wax or product stains, front or back. Surfaces may show slight loss of luster from rubbing across other cards.

Very Good (VG): Shows obvious handling. Corners rounded and/or perhaps showing minor creases. Other minor creases may be visible. Surfaces may exhibit loss of luster, but all printing is intact. May show major gum, wax or other packaging stains. No major creases, tape marks or extraneous markings or writing. Exhibit honest wear.

Good (G): A well-worn card, but exhibits no intentional damage or abuse. May have major or multiple creases. Corners rounded well beyond the border.

Fair (F): Shows excessive wear, along with damage or abuse. Will show all the wear characteristics of a Good card, along with such damage as thumb tack holes in or near margins, evidence of having been taped or pasted, perhaps small tears around the edges, or creases so heavy as to break the cardboard. Backs may show minor added pen or pencil writing, or be missing small bits of paper. Still, a basically complete card.

Poor: A card that has been tortured to death. Corners or other areas may be torn off. Card may have been trimmed, show holes from paper punch or have been used for BB gun practice. Front may have extraneous pen or pencil writing, or other defacement. Major portions of front or back design may be missing. Not a pretty sight.

In addition to these seven widely-used terms, collectors will often encounter intermediate grades, such as VG-EX (Very Good to Excellent), EX-MT (Excellent to Mint), or NR MT-MT (Near Mint to Mint). Persons who describe a card with such grades are usually trying to convey that the card has all the characteristics of the lower grade, with enough of the higher grade to merit mention. Such cards are usually priced at a point midway between the two grades.

VALUATIONS

Values quoted in this book represent the current retail market and are compiled from recommendations provided and verified through the author's daily involvement in the publication of the hobby's leading advertising periodicals, as well as the input of specialized consultants.

It should be stressed, however, that this book is intended to serve only as an aid in evaluating cards; actual market conditions are constantly changing. This is especially true of the cards of current players, whose on-field performance during the course of a season can greatly affect the value of their cards — upwards or downwards.

Publication of this catalog is not intended as a solicitation to buy or sell the listed cards by the editors, publishers or contributors.

Again, the values here are retail prices — what a collector can expect to pay when buying a card from a dealer. The wholesale price, that which a collector can expect to receive from a dealer when selling cards, will be significantly lower. Most dealers operate on a 100% mark-up, generally paying about 50% of a card's retail value. On some high-demand cards, dealers will pay up to 75% or even 100% or more of retail value, anticipating continued price increases. Conversely, for may low-demand cards, such as common player's cards of recent years, dealers may pay 25% or even less of retail.

It should also be noted that with several hundred thousand valuations quoted in this book, there are bound to be a few compilations or typographical errors which will creep into the final product, a fact readers should remember if they encounter a listing at a fraction of, or several times, the card's actual current retail price. The editors welcome the correction of any such errors discovered. Write: *Sports Collectors Digest Baseball Card Price Guide*, 700 E. State St., Iola, Wis. 54990.

SETS

Collectors may note that the complete set prices for newer issues quoted in these listings are usually significantly lower than the total of the value of the individual cards which comprise the set.

This reflects two factors in the baseball card market. First, a seller is often willing to take a lower composite price for a complete set as a "volume discount" and to avoid inventorying a large number of common player or other lower-demand cards.

Second, to a degree, the value of common cards can be said to be inflated as a result of having a built-in overhead charge to justify the dealer's time in sorting cards, carrying them in stock and filling orders. This accounts for the fact that even brand new baseball cards, which cost the dealer around 1 cent each when bought in bulk, carry individual price tags of 3 cents or higher.

ERRORS/VARIATIONS

It is often hard for the beginning collector to understand that an error on a baseball card, in and of itself, does not usually add premium value to that card. It is usually only when the correcting of an error in the subsequent printing creates a variation that premium value attaches to an error.

Minor errors, such as wrong stats or personal data, create a variation that premium value attaches to an error. Misspellings, inconsistencies, etc. — usually affecting the back of the card — are very common, especially in recent years. Unless a corrected variation was also printed, these errors are not noted in the listings of this book because they are not generally perceived by collectors to have premium value.

On the other hand, major effort has been expended to include the most complete listings ever for collectible variation cards. Many scarce and valuable variations — dozens of them never before cataloged — are included in these listings because they are widely collected and often have significant premium value.

COUNTERFEITS/REPRINTS

As the value of baseball cards has risen in the past 10-20 years, certains cards and sets have become too expensive for the average collector to obtain. This, along with changes in the technology of color printing, has given rise to increasing numbers of counterfeit and reprint cards.

While both terms describe essentially the same thing — a modern copy which attempts to duplicate as closely as possible an original baseball card — there are differences which are important to the collector.

Generally, a counterfeit is made with the intention of deceiving somebody into believing it is genuine, and thus paying large amounts of money for it. The counterfeiter takes every pain to try to make his fakes look as authentic as possible. In recent years, the 1963 Pete Rose, 1984 Donruss Don Mattingly and more than 30 superstar cards of the late 1960s-early 1980s have been counterfeited — all were quickly detected because of the differences in quality of cardboard on which they were printed.

A reprint, on the other hand, while it may have been made to look as close as possible to an original card, is made with the intention of allowing collectors to buy them as substitutes for cards they may never be otherwise able to afford. The big difference is that a reprint is generally marked as such, usually on the back of the card. In other cases, like the Topps 1952 reprint set, the replicas are printed in a size markedly different from the originals.

Collectors should be aware, however, that unscrupulous persons will sometimes cut off or otherwise obliterate the distinguishing word — "Reprint," "Copy," — or modern copyright date on the back of a reprint card in an attempt to pass it as genuine.

A collector's best defense against reprints and counterfeits is to acquire a knowledge of the look and feel of genuine baseball cards of various eras and issues.

UNLISTED CARDS

Readers who have cards or sets which are not covered in this edition are invited to correspond with the editor for purposes of adding to the compilation work now in progress. Address: *Sports Collectors Digest Baseball Card Price Guide*, 700 E. State St., Iola, Wis. 54990.

Contributors will be acknowledged in future editions.

COLLECTORS ISSUES

There exists within the hobby a great body of cards which do not fall under the scope of this catalog by virtue of their nature of having been issued solely for the collector market. Known as "collector issues," these cards and sets are distinguished from "legitimate" issues in not having been created as a sales promotional item for another product or service — bubble gum, soda, snack cakes, dog food, cigarettes, gasoline, etc.

By their nature, and principally because the person issuing them is always free to print and distribute more of the same if they should ever attain any real value, collector issues are generally regarded by collectors as having little or no premium value.

NEW ISSUES

Because new baseball cards are being issued all the time, the cataloging of them remains an on-going challenge. The editor will attempt to keep abreast of new issues so that they may be added to future editions of this book.

Readers are invited to submit news of new issues, especially limited-edition or regionally issued cards to the editors. Address: *Sports Collectors Digest Baseball Card Price Guide*, 700 E. State St., Iola, Wis. 54990.

Common Hobby Terms & Definitions

A

Airbrushing — An artist's technique used on baseball cards in which logos on uniforms or hats are altered or eliminated.

All-Star card (AS) — A card which denotes a player's selection to the previous year's All-Star Team.

Autographed card — Card which was personally autographed by the player depicted. Cards with facsimile signatures that are printed on many cards as part of the design, are not considered autographed cards.

Autograph guest — A current or former ball player or other celebrity who attends a card convention for the purpose of signing autographs for fans. Usually a fee is charged for the autograph, ranging from a few dollars to more than $30 for HOF players.

B

Baseball's Best — A set made by Donruss in 1988 and 1989. Also the name of a boxed set made by Fleer in 1987 and 1988, and the name of the set of insert cards made by *Baseball Cards* magazine in 1989 and 1990.

Bazooka cards — Cards issued with boxes of Bazooka Bubblegum (1959-1971, 1988-1990).

Big cards — Name for Topps' large, glossy-finish card issues produced in 1988-present. Cards reminiscent of Topps' cards from the 1950s.

Blank backs — A card that has a blank card back. Most collectors feel these cards are merely damaged, with a lower value than correctly-printed specimens, though some collectors will pay premiums on superstars or rookies.

Blanket — An early 20th-century collectible consisting of a square piece of felt or other fabric depicting a baseball player. Most popular are the 5'' by 5'' B-18 "blankets" from 1914, so-called because they were sometimes sewn together to form a blanket.

Blister pack — A blister pack is a method of card packaging in which cards are packaged in hard plastic on a cardboard backing, with three to four pockets of cards. Donruss (1987-present).

Borders — The portion of a card which surrounds the picture. They are usually white, but are sometimes other colors. Border condition is very important to the card's grade and value.

Bowman (B) — Sportscard manufacturer (1948-1955) bought out by Topps in 1956. Topps issued baseball sets under the Bowman name (1989-present).

Boxed sets — These are sets produced by one of the major card companies, usually in conjunction with a business, such as K-Mart or Walgreens. Boxed sets usually contain fewer than 60 cards, most of which are star players.

Box panel cards — Bonus cards which are featured on a panel of wax boxes of the major card companies. The idea was originated by Donruss in 1985. Complete sets range from four to 16 cards, and feature star players.

Brick — A "brick" of cards is any group of cards with similar characteristics, such as a 100-card brick of 1975 Topps cards. Bricks usually contain common cards.

Buy price — The price a dealer will to pay for cards or memorabilia.

Burger King cards (BK) — Cards issued in conjunction with Burger King (1977-1987).

C

Cabinet card — A large card from the 19th or early 20th centuries, usually issued on heavy cardboard.

Card lot — A "lot" of cards is the same card, such as a 1988 Topps Don Mattingly card, sold in a lot or "grouping" of five, 25, 50, 100 or whatever number of cards. A collector purchasing a "lot" of cards, gets the cards at a discounted price, as opposed to buying a single card. Example: a single Mattingly card costs $1, but 100 Mattingly cards cost $75 or 75-cents apiece.

Case — A sealed case containing wax boxes or other product units which card companies sell at wholesale to dealers or retail stores. For instance, a 1991 Topps "wax case" is made up of 20 "wax boxes."

Cello pack — A package of about 30 cards wrapped in a printed cellophane wrapper that allows you to see the top and bottom cards. There are usually 24 cello packs to a cello box, and 16 cello boxes to a cello case. Cello packs retail between for around $1. Issued by Topps, Fleer and Donruss.

Checklist (CL) — A list of every card in a particular set, usually with space allowing the collector to check whether or not he has the card. A checklist can appear on a card(s), in a book or elsewhere.

Classic cards — Baseball cards made by Game Time, Ltd., to go with its "Classic Baseball" trivia game (1987-present).

Coin — Can refer to an actual coin struck to commemorate an achievement made by a team or player; also, a collectible made soley from or with a combination of plastic, paper or metal, issued as a set, such as the 1988 Topps Coin set.

Collation — The act of putting cards in order, by hand or machine, usually numerically.

Collector issue — A set of cards produced primarily to be sold to collectors and not issued as a premium to be given away or sold with a commercial product.

Common card — A card which carries no premium value in a set. "Common" is a blunt way of saying the player depicted is not a star.

Convention — Also known as a "baseball card show" or "trading card show." A gathering of anywhere from one to 600 or more card dealers at a single location (convention center, hotel, school auditoriums or gymnasiums) for the purpose of buying, selling or trading cards.

Counterfeit cards — Cards made to look like original cards, and distributed with the intention of fooling a buyer. High-demand cards are the most likely to be counterfeited.

D

Dealer — A person who buys, sells and trades baseball cards and other memorabilia for profit. A dealer may be full-time, part-time, own a shop, operate a mail-order business from his home, deal at baseball card shows on weekends, or any combination of the above.

Die-cut card — A baseball card in which the player's outline has been partially separated from the background, enabling the card to be folded into a "stand-up" figure. Die-cut cards that have never been folded are worth more to collectors.

Disc — Circular-shaped card.

Donruss (D) — Baseball card manufacturer (1981-present).

Donruss Rookies (DR) — 56-card post-season set issued by Donruss which includes rookie players (1986-present). Sold exclusively through hobby dealers in separate box.

Double print (DP) — A card printed twice on the same sheet, making it twice as common as other cards on the sheet. Topps double-printed cards in virtually every set from 1952 to 1981. This was done to accomodate the year's set size on standard company printing sheets.

Drakes — Ohio-based bakery which made baseball cards in the 1950s, and again from 1981-1988.

E

Error — An error is usually found on card backs in the statistical or personal information, and sometimes on the card front (such as a reversed negative). If an error is not corrected, the error adds nothing to the value of the card. If the error is corrected, it is called a "variation" card.

Exhibit card — Postcard-size cards picturing baseball players and other celebrities and sold in penny-arcade machines. Exhibit cards were produced from the 1920s to the 1960s.

F

Factory set (F or FAC.) — A complete set collated (packaged) by the card producing company. Issued by all companies.

First card (FC) — Price guide designation which refers to the first appearance of a player in the major card sets.

Fleer (F) — Baseball card manufacturer (1959-1963, 1981-present).

Fleer Glossy Tin (FG) — Limited edition set produced by Fleer, which features the year's regular issue set in a high gloss finish and sold in a tin box (1987-present). Fleer Update sets also done in glossy style.

Fleer Update (FU) -— 132-card post-season set from Fleer which includes players traded to other teams during the season, and rookies (1984-present). Sold exclusively through hobby dealers in its own separate box.

Food issue — A set of baseball cards or related memorabilia which was issued in conjunction with a food product, such as Post cereal or Hostess snack cakes.

G

Gallery of Champions — Trade name for a set of metallic reproductions of Topps cards made and sold by Topps from 1986-1988. The metals used were bronze, aluminum, pewter and silver.

Goudey — Baseball card manufacturer (1933-1936, 1938, 1941).

Grades — The physical state or condition of a card.

H

Hand collated set (H or HC) — A complete set put together by hand using cards from wax, cello, rack or vending boxes.

High-numbers — A term used to describe the final series in a particular set of cards. "High numbers" were generally produced in smaller quantities than other series and are, therefore, scarcer and more valuable.

Hall of Famer (HOFer) - A card picturing a member of the Baseball Hall of Fame, in Cooperstown, N.Y. Hall of Famer cards almost always command a premium over other cards.

Hartland statues — Wisconsin plastics company which produced, among other things, statues of baseball players in the late 1950s and early 1960s. Company reproduced the set in 1989 as Hartland's 25th Anniversary Commemorative Edition. Original statues very collectible.

I

In Action card (IA) — A card featuring a star player, designated with the words "In Action" on the card front. Most notably from the 1972 and 1982 Topps sets.

Inserts — A collectible included inside a regular pack of baseball cards to boost sales. Inserts have included posters, coins, stamps, tatoos, special cards, etc.

J

Jell-O cards — Cards sold as premiums with Jell-O packages (1962-1963).

K

Kellog's cards — Simulated three-dimensional cards given away in cereal boxes or via a mail-in offer (1970-1983).

Key cards — The most important (valuable) cards in a set, such as the Mickey Mantle card, a "key" card in the 1952 Topps set.

L

Last card — The final regular card issued for a player, such as Hank Aaron's "last" card was in the 1976 Topps set. No particular extra value is added for last cards.

Leaf-Donruss — Baseball cards produced by Donruss specifically for the Canadian market (1985-1988). Leaf issued its own set in 1990.

Legitimate issue — A card set issued as a premium with a commerical product to increase sales; not a "collector issue."

Letter of authenticity — A letter stating that a certain piece of memorabilia, like a uniform, is authentic.

Lithograph — A high-quality art print made in limited quantities.

M

MVP — Most Valuable Player award.

Mail-bid auction — An auction where bids are sent through the mail, with the highest bidder winning the merchandise.

Major set — A large, nationally-distributed set produced by a major card maker like Topps, Fleer, Donruss, Score, Sportflics or Upper Deck.

Megalot — A megalot describes a group of cards, usually 1,000 or more of the same player, purchased for investment or speculation.

Memorabilia — Refers to items other than cards, such as uniforms, bats, autographed baseballs, magazines, scorecards, pins, statues and the like.

Minis — Cards which resemble the regular issue cards in every way, except they are smaller in size. Most noteable are the 1975 Topps Minis.

Minor league cards — A card depicting a player from the minor leagues. Minor league sets are a fast-growing segment of the hobby.

Mother's cards — An Oakland, (Calif.)-based cookie company which produces popular high quality glossy finish regional sets (1982-present).

Multi-player card — A card picturing more than one player.

N

Non-sport card — A trading card or bubblegum card picturing a subject other than sports. Non-sports cards have depicted movie stars, television shows, moments in history and other subjects.

O

Obverse — The front of the card displaying the picture.

O-Pee-Chee (OPC) — Canadian card producing company (1965-present). O-Pee-Chee is Topps' official Canadian licensee, and O-Pee-Chee cards are almost identical to Topps' issues of the same year.

P

Panel — A strip of two or more uncut cards. Some card sets are issued in "panels."

Phone auction — An auction where bids for baseball cards or other memorabilia are taken over the phone, with the highest bidder getting the merchandise.

Plastic sheet — A polyethelyne or polyvinyl sheet designed to store baseball cards, the most common being the nine-pocket sheet (which fits today's standard-sized cards). The sheets have pre-punched holes on the left side which allows them to be placed in a three-ring binder.

Play Ball — Name of baseball cards produced by Gum, Inc., (1939-1941).

Police/Fire/Safety sets — Card sets sponsored by public law enforcement or fire fighting agencies and a major or minor league team. Card backs usually contain anti-drug messages, fire prevention tips or other safety messages.

Post cards — Cards sold as premiums on boxes of Post cereal (1960-1963, 1990).

Pre-rookie card — Name given to a major league player's minor league cards.

Price guide — A periodical or book which contains checklists of cards, sets and other memorabilia and their values in varying conditions.

Price on request (POR) — A dealer will advertise a card P.O.R. if he believes the card will fluctuate in price from the time he places his ad until the time the ad is seen by the public.

Promotional cards — Cards produced by the card companies which serve as a marketing tool for their upcoming cards. Promotional or "promo" cards are often sent to dealers to entice them to order cards. Promo cards have limited distribution and can be very expensive.

Proof card — A card produced by the card companies prior to printing their sets, which is "proofed" for errors, and checked for card design, photography, colors, statisical accuracy and so on. Proof cards are not distributed and a few of the older proof cards on the hobby market can be quite expensive.

PPD — Postage Paid.

R

Rack pack — A three-sectioned card package with about 14-16 cards per section. There are usually 24 rack packs to a rack box, and six rack boxes to a rack case. Topps, Fleer, Donruss, Score.

Rare — Difficult to obtain and limited in number. See "Scarce."

Rated Rookie (RR) — Donruss subset featuring young players the company feels are the top rookie players from a particular year (1984-present).

Record Breaker card (RB) — A special Topps card found in a regular issue set which commemorates a record-breaking performance by a player from the previous season.

Regional set — A card set distributed in one geographical area. Regional sets often depict players from one team.

Regular issue set — See "Major set."

Reprint cards — Cards reprinted to closely match original cards, made with the intention of allowing collectors to buy them as substitutes for cards they could not ever afford. Reprints are usually labled — but not always — "reprint."

Reverse — The back of a card.

Rookie card (R or RC) — The first appearance of a player in one of the major sets (Topps, Fleer, etc.), excluding update and traded sets. It may or may not be issued during the player's actual rookie season.

S

SASE — Self-Addressed Stamped Envelope.

Score (S or SC) — Brand name of sports cards (1988-present). Major League Marketing is the manufacturer.

Score Traded (ScTr) - 110-card post-season set issued by Score to include players traded during the season, as well as rookie players. Sold exclusively by hobby dealers in its own separate box.

Second-year card — The second card of a player issued in the major sets. Usually, a second-year card is the most expensive card of a player, next to the rookie card.

Sell price — The price a dealer sells a card.

Series — A group of cards that is part of a set, and was issued at one time. The term usually applied to Topps sets from 1952-1973, when sets were issued in various "series." Cards of different series are valued at different prices since some series are scarcer than others.

Set — A complete run of cards, including one number of each card issued by a particular manufacturer in a particular year; for example, a 1985 Fleer "set."

Set case — Companies sell their factory sets in sealed cases containing 8 to 16 sets per case, depending on the company. Issued by all major companies.

Skip-numbered — A set of cards not numbered in exact sequence. Some manufacturers have issued "skip-numbered" sets to trick collectors into buying more cards, looking for card numbers that didn't exist. Other sets became skip-numbered when one or more players were dropped from the set at the last minute and were not replaced with another.

Sleeve — A specially-designed, plastic wrapper used to house and protect individual baseball cards.

Special card — A card in a set that depicts something other than a single player; for example a checklist card, All-Star card, team card or leaders card.

Sportflics — Brand name of baseball cards (1986-present). Major League Marketing is the manufacturer.

SCD — *Sports Collectors Digest.*

Standard size card — A card which measures 2½" wide by 3½" tall. In 1957, Topps baseball cards were produced in the 2½" by 3½" size, which set the standard for modern baseball cards.

Star card — Card featuring a star player, but not one of "superstar" caliber. The term "minor star" may also be used to differentiate between levels of skill and popularity. In terms of value, "star" cards fall between "commons" and "superstars."

Starter lot — A group of cards from the same set, usually more than 100, which serves as a starting point for a hobbyist to begin putting a set together. Starter lots usually contain common players. Also known as a "starter set."

Starting Lineup — A line of plastic sports statues produced by Kenner (1988-present). Also, the name for a computer-based baseball game from Parker Brothers.

Sticker — An adhesive-backed baseball card. Stickers can be card-size or smaller. Topps, Fleer and Panini have issued major baseball sticker sets over the past years. Stickers are not overly popular with older collectors, though younger collectors seem to enjoy them.

Subset — A set of cards with the same theme within a larger set. Examples: Donruss Diamond Kings are a "subset" of the Donruss set; or Topps All-Star cards are a subset of the Topps set.

Super card — A designation referring to the physical size of a card. Generally, any card postcard-size or larger is referred to as a "super."

Superstar card — A card picturing a true "superstar," a player of Hall of Fame caliber, like Mike Schmidt.

Stock — Refers to the type of paper or cardboard used on a baseball card.

Swap Meet — Term used to describe early baseball card shows where most of the cards were traded between hobbyists.

T

Team card — Card which depicts an entire team.

Team set — A set which includes all cards relating to a certain team from a particular year, by a particular manufacturer.

Team issued set — A set produced to be sold or given away by a baseball team.

Test issue — A set of cards test-marketed on a small scale in a limited geographic areas of the country. Topps test-marketed a variety of items from the 1950s-1980s.

Tobacco cards — Cards issued in the late 19th and early 20th centuries as premiums with cigarettes or other tobacco products.

Topps (T) — Sports card company (1951-present).

Topps Tiffany (TTF) — Limited edition set produced by Topps, featuring the year's regular complete set in a high gloss finish (1984-present). Topps Traded sets also done in this style.

Topps Traded (TT or TTR) — 132-card post-season set which includes players traded to other teams during the year, as well as rookie players (1981-present). Sold mainly through hobby dealers.

Traded set — An auxiliary set of cards issued toward the end of the season to reflect trades made after the printing of the regular set. Also called "Update" sets, they may also include rookies not included in the regular set.

U

Uncut sheet — A full sheet of baseball cards that has never been cut into individual cards.

Upper Deck (UD) — Sportscard company (1989-present).

Upper Deck High Numbers (UDH) — 100-card set featuring players traded during the season, as well as rookie players. This set was sold through hobby dealers and in Upper Deck foil packs, similar to the way cards before 1974 were released.

V

Variation — A variation is the result of a card company correcting a previous mistake on a card, resulting in two or more variations of the same card. Some variations have increased in value, if they were produced in lesser quantities.

Vending box — Vending boxes contain 500 cards per box. There are 24 vending boxes per vending case, for a total of 12,000 cards. Topps.

W

Want list — A collector's or dealer's list of items he is wishing to buy. Often, a collector will send a dealer a "want" list, and the dealer will try to locate the items on the list.

1910 All Star Base-Ball

LEFT FIELD
Sheckard, Chicago Nat'l.

Issued circa 1910, this rare 12-card set was issued by candy maker J.H. Dockman & Son. The cards, measuring approximately 1-7/8" by 3-3/8", were printed on the front and back of boxes of candy sold as "All Star Base-Ball Package." There are two players on each box - one on the front, the other on the back - but the cards consist of crude drawings that actually bear no resemblance to the player named below the drawing.

		NR MT	EX	VG
Complete Set:		1500.00	750.00	450.00
Common Player:		60.00	30.00	15.00
(1)	Heinie Beckendorf	60.00	30.00	15.00
(2)	Roger Bresnahan	100.00	50.00	30.00
(3)	Al Burch	60.00	30.00	15.00
(4)	Frank Chance	150.00	75.00	45.00
(5)	Wid Conroy	60.00	30.00	15.00
(6)	Jack Coombs	60.00	30.00	15.00
(7)	George Gibson	60.00	30.00	15.00
(8)	Dick Hoblitzel	60.00	30.00	15.00
(9)	Johnny Kling	60.00	30.00	15.00
(10)	Frank LaPorte	60.00	30.00	15.00
(11)	Connie Mack	200.00	100.00	60.00
(12)	Christy Mathewson	300.00	150.00	90.00
(13)	Matty McIntyre	60.00	30.00	15.00
(14)	Jimmy Sheckard	60.00	30.00	15.00
(15)	Al Schweitzer	60.00	30.00	15.00
(16)	Harry Wolter	60.00	30.00	15.00

1955 Armour Coins

In 1955, Armour inserted a plastic "coin" in their packages of hot dogs. A raised profile of a ballplayer is on the front of each coin along with the player's name, position, birthplace and date, batting and throwing preference, and 1954 hitting or pitching record. The coins, which measure 1-1/2" in diameter and are unnumbered, came in a variety of colors.

Common colors are aqua, dark blue, light green, orange, red and yellow. Scarce colors are black, pale blue, lime green, very dark green, gold, pale orange, pink, silver, and tan. Scarce colors are double the value of the coins listed in the checklist that follows. Twenty-four different players are included in the set. Variations can be found for the Kuenn and Mantle coins. The Kuenn coin comes with the letters in his name bunched closely together (condensed) or spread apart (spaced). The Mantle coin can be found with his last name spelled correctly or misspelled "Mantel." The complete set price includes the two variations.

		NR MT	EX	VG
Complete Set:		1000.00	500.00	300.00
Common Player:		12.00	6.00	3.50
(1)	John "Johnny" Antonelli	15.00	7.50	4.50
(2)	Larry "Yogi" Berra	60.00	30.00	18.00
(3)	Delmar "Del" Crandall	15.00	7.50	4.50
(4)	Lawrence "Larry" Doby	18.00	9.00	5.50
(5)	James "Jim" Finigan	12.00	6.00	3.50
(6)	Edward "Whitey" Ford	60.00	30.00	18.00
(7)	James "Junior" Gilliam	20.00	10.00	6.00
(8)	Harvey "Kitten" Haddix	12.00	6.00	3.50
(9)	Ranson "Randy" Jackson (name actually Ransom)	20.00	10.00	6.00
(10)	Jack "Jackie" Jensen	18.00	9.00	5.50
(11)	Theodore "Ted" Kluszewski	18.00	9.00	5.50
(12a)	Harvey E. Kuenn (spaced letters in name)	25.00	12.50	7.50
(12b)	Harvey E. Kuenn (condensed letters in name)	40.00	20.00	12.00
(13a)	Charles "Mickey" Mantel (incorrect spelling)	150.00	75.00	45.00
(13b)	Charles "Mickey" Mantle (correct spelling)	400.00	200.00	125.00
(14)	Donald "Don" Mueller	20.00	10.00	6.00
(15)	Harold "Pee Wee" Reese	40.00	20.00	12.00
(16)	Allie P. Reynolds	18.00	9.00	5.50
(17)	Albert "Flip" Rosen	18.00	9.00	5.50
(18)	Curtis "Curt" Simmons	12.00	6.00	3.50
(19)	Edwin "Duke" Snider	60.00	30.00	18.00
(20)	Warren Spahn	40.00	20.00	12.00
(21)	Frank J. Thomas	35.00	17.50	10.50
(22)	Virgil "Fire" Trucks	12.00	6.00	3.50
(23)	Robert "Bob" Turley	18.00	9.00	5.50
(24)	James "Mickey" Vernon	12.00	6.00	3.50

1959 Armour Coins

After a three-year layoff, Armour once again inserted plastic baseball "coins" into their hot dog packages. The coins retained their 1-1/2" size but did not include as much detailed information as in 1955. Missing from the coins' backs is information such as birthplace and date, team, and batting and throwing preference. The fronts contain the player's name and, unlike 1955, only the team nickname is given. The set consists of 20 coins which come in a myriad of colors. Common colors are navy blue, royal blue, dark green, orange, red, and pale yellow. Scarce colors are pale blue, cream, grey-green, pale green, dark or light pink, pale red, tan, and translucent coins of any color with or without multi-colored flecks in the plastic mix. Scarce colors are double the value listed for coins in the checklist that follows. In 1959,

Armour had a write-in offer of ten coins for one dollar. The same ten players were part of the write-in offer, accounting for why half of the coins in the set are much more plentiful than the other.

		NR MT	EX	VG
Complete Set:		400.00	200.00	125.00
Common Player:		7.00	3.50	2.00
(1)	Hank Aaron	40.00	20.00	12.00
(2)	John Antonelli	15.00	7.50	4.50
(3)	Richie Ashburn	15.00	7.50	4.50
(4)	Ernie Banks	40.00	20.00	12.00
(5)	Don Blasingame	7.00	3.50	2.00
(6)	Bob Cerv	7.00	3.50	2.00
(7)	Del Crandall	15.00	7.50	4.50
(8)	Whitey Ford	35.00	17.50	10.50
(9)	Nellie Fox	12.00	6.00	3.50
(10)	Jackie Jensen	25.00	12.50	7.50
(11)	Harvey Kuenn	15.00	7.50	4.50
(12)	Frank Malzone	7.00	3.50	2.00
(13)	Johnny Podres	15.00	7.50	4.50
(14)	Frank Robinson	20.00	10.00	6.00
(15)	Roy Sievers	7.00	3.50	2.00
(16)	Bob Skinner	7.00	3.50	2.00
(17)	Frank Thomas	15.00	9.00	4.50
(18)	Gus Triandos	7.00	3.50	2.00
(19)	Bob Turley	18.00	9.00	5.50
(20)	Mickey Vernon	15.00	9.00	4.50

1960 Armour Coins

The 1960 Armour coin issue is identical in number and·style to the 1959 set. The unnumbered coins, which measure 1-1/2" in diameter, once again came in a variety of colors. Common colors for 1960 are dark blue, light blue, dark green, light green, red-orange, dark red, and light yellow. Scarce colors are aqua, grey-blue, cream, tan, and dark yellow. Scarce colors are double the value of the coins in the checklist that follows. The Daley coin is very scarce, although it is not exactly known why. Theories for the scarcity center on broken printing molds, contract disputes, and that the coin was only inserted in a test product that quickly proved to be unsuccessful. As in 1959, a mail-in offer for ten free coins was made available by Armour. The set price for the 1960 Armour set does not include the three more difficult variations.

		NR MT	EX	VG
Complete Set:		1200.00	600.00	350.00
Common Player:		7.00	3.50	2.00
(1a)	Hank Aaron (Braves)	40.00	20.00	12.00
(1b)	Hank Aaron (Milwaukee Braves)	70.00	35.00	21.00
(2)	Bob Allison	12.00	6.00	3.50
(3)	Ernie Banks	15.00	7.50	4.50
(4)	Ken Boyer	10.00	5.00	3.00
(5)	Rocky Colavito	12.00	6.00	3.50
(6)	Gene Conley	10.00	5.00	3.00
(7)	Del Crandall	10.00	5.00	3.00
(8)	Bud Daley	750.00	375.00	225.00
(9a)	Don Drysdale (L.A condensed)	20.00	10.00	6.00
(9b)	Don Drysdale (space between L. and A.)	25.00	12.50	7.50
(10)	Whitey Ford	15.00	7.50	4.50
(11)	Nellie Fox	10.00	5.00	3.00

		NR MT	EX	VG
(12)	Al Kaline	25.00	12.50	7.50
(13a)	Frank Malzone (Red Sox)	7.00	3.50	2.00
(13b)	Frank Malzone (Boston Red Sox)	25.00	12.50	7.50
(14)	Mickey Mantle	100.00	50.00	30.00
(15)	Ed Mathews	25.00	12.50	7.50
(16)	Willie Mays	40.00	20.00	12.00
(17)	Vada Pinson	10.00	5.00	3.00
(18)	Dick Stuart	10.00	5.00	3.00
(19)	Gus Triandos	7.00	3.50	2.00
(20)	Early Wynn	20.00	10.00	6.00

1914 B18 Blankets

These 5-1/4" flannels were issued in 1914 with several popular brands of tobacco. The flannels, whose ACC designation is B18, picked up the nickname blankets because many of the square pieces of cloth were sewn together to form pillow covers or bed spreads. Different color combinations on the flannels exist for all ten teams included in the set. The complete set price in the checklist that follows does not include higher priced variations.

		NR MT	EX	VG
Complete Set:		4000.00	2000.00	1200.
Common Player:		20.00	10.00	6.00
(1a)	Babe Adams (purple pennants)	40.00	20.00	12.00
(1b)	Babe Adams (red pennants)	45.00	22.00	13.50
(2a)	Sam Agnew (purple basepaths)	40.00	20.00	12.00
(2b)	Sam Agnew (red basepaths)	45.00	22.00	13.50
(3a)	Eddie Ainsmith (green pennants)	20.00	10.00	6.00
(3b)	Eddie Ainsmith (brown pennants)	20.00	10.00	6.00
(4a)	Jimmy Austin (purple basepaths)	40.00	20.00	12.00
(4b)	Jimmy Austin (red basepaths)	45.00	22.00	13.50
(5a)	Del Baker (white infield)	20.00	10.00	6.00
(5b)	Del Baker (brown infield)	75.00	37.00	22.00
(5c)	Del Baker (red infield)	275.00	137.00	82.00
(6a)	Johnny Bassler (purple pennants)	40.00	20.00	12.00
(6b)	Johnny Bassler (yellow pennants)	75.00	37.00	22.00
(7a)	Paddy Bauman (Baumann) (white infield)	20.00	10.00	6.00
(7b)	Paddy Bauman (Baumann) (brown infield)	75.00	37.00	22.00
(7c)	Paddy Bauman (Baumann) (red infield)	275.00	137.00	82.00
(8a)	Luke Boone (blue infield)	20.00	10.00	6.00
(8b)	Luke Boone (green infield)	20.00	10.00	6.00
(9a)	George Burns (brown basepaths)	20.00	10.00	6.00
(9b)	George Burns (green basepaths)	20.00	10.00	6.00
(10a)	Tioga George Burns (white infield)	20.00	10.00	6.00
(10b)	Tioga George Burns (brown infield)	75.00	37.00	22.00
(11a)	Max Carey (purple pennants)	75.00	37.00	22.00
(11b)	Max Carey (red pennants)	100.00	50.00	30.00
(12a)	Marty Cavanaugh (Kavanagh) (white infield)	20.00	10.00	6.00
(12b)	Marty Cavanaugh (Kavanagh) (brown infield)	125.00	62.00	37.00
(12c)	Marty Cavanaugh (Kavanagh) (red infield)	275.00	137.00	82.00

Card	NR MT	EX	VG
(12d) Marty Kavanaugh (Kavanagh)	20.00	10.00	6.00
(13a) Frank Chance (green infield)	40.00	20.00	12.00
(13b) Frank Chance (brown pennants, infield)	40.00	20.00	12.00
(13c) Frank Chance (yellow pennants, blue infield)	275.00	137.00	82.00
(14a) Ray Chapman (purple pennants)	40.00	20.00	12.00
(14b) Ray Chapman (yellow pennants)	75.00	37.00	22.00
(15a) Ty Cobb (white infield)	275.00	137.00	82.00
(15b) Ty Cobb (brown infield)	600.00	300.00	180.00
(15c) Ty Cobb (red infield)	2500.00	1250.00	750.00
(16a) King Cole (blue infield)	20.00	10.00	6.00
(16b) King Cole (green infield)	20.00	10.00	6.00
(17a) Joe Connolly (white infield)	20.00	10.00	6.00
(17b) Joe Connolly (brown infield)	75.00	37.00	22.00
(18a) Harry Coveleski (white infield)	20.00	10.00	6.00
(18b) Harry Coveleski (brown infield)	75.00	37.00	22.00
(19a) George Cutshaw (blue infield)	20.00	10.00	6.00
(19b) George Cutshaw (green infield)	20.00	10.00	6.00
(20a) Jake Daubert (blue infield)	25.00	12.50	7.50
(20b) Jake Daubert (green infield)	25.00	12.50	7.50
(21a) Ray Demmitt (white infield)	20.00	10.00	6.00
(21b) Ray Demmitt (brown infield)	75.00	37.00	22.00
(22a) Bill Doak (purple pennants)	40.00	20.00	12.00
(22b) Bill Doak (yellow pennants)	75.00	37.00	22.00
(23a) Cozy Dolan (purple pennants)	40.00	20.00	12.00
(23b) Cozy Dolan (yellow pennants)	75.00	37.00	22.00
(24a) Larry Doyle (brown basepaths)	25.00	12.50	7.50
(24b) Larry Doyle (green basepaths)	25.00	12.50	7.50
(25a) Art Fletcher (brown basepaths)	20.00	10.00	6.00
(25b) Art Fletcher (green basepaths)	20.00	10.00	6.00
(26a) Eddie Foster (brown pennants)	20.00	10.00	6.00
(26b) Eddie Foster (green pennants)	20.00	10.00	6.00
(27a) Del Gainor (white infield)	20.00	10.00	6.00
(27b) Del Gainor (brown infield)	75.00	37.00	22.00
(28a) Chick Gandil (brown pennants)	25.00	12.50	7.50
(28b) Chick Gandil (green pennants)	25.00	12.50	7.50
(29a) George Gibson (purple pennants)	40.00	20.00	12.00
(29b) George Gibson (red pennants)	45.00	22.00	13.50
(30a) Hank Gowdy (white infield)	20.00	10.00	6.00
(30b) Hank Gowdy (brown infield)	75.00	37.00	22.00
(30c) Hank Gowdy (red infield)	275.00	137.00	82.00
(31a) Jack Graney (purple pennants)	40.00	20.00	12.00
(31b) Jack Graney (yellow pennants)	75.00	37.00	22.00
(32a) Eddie Grant (brown basepaths)	20.00	10.00	6.00
(32b) Eddie Grant (green basepaths)	20.00	10.00	6.00
(33a) Tommy Griffith (white infield, green pennants)	20.00	10.00	6.00
(33b) Tommy Griffith (white infield, red pennants)	275.00	137.00	82.00
(33c) Tommy Griffith (brown infield)	75.00	37.00	22.00
(34a) Earl Hamilton (purple basepaths)	40.00	20.00	12.00
(34b) Earl Hamilton (red basepaths)	45.00	22.00	13.50
(35a) Roy Hartzell (blue infield)	20.00	10.00	6.00
(35b) Roy Hartzell (green infield)	20.00	10.00	6.00
(36a) Miller Huggins (purple pennants)	75.00	37.00	22.00
(36b) Miller Huggins (yellow pennants)	150.00	75.00	45.00
(37a) John Hummel (brown infield)	20.00	10.00	6.00
(37b) John Hummel (green infield)	20.00	10.00	6.00
(38a) Ham Hyatt (purple pennants)	40.00	20.00	12.00
(38b) Ham Hyatt (yellow pennants)	45.00	22.00	13.50
(39a) Shoeless Joe Jackson (purple pennants)	1200.00	600.00	350.00
(39b) Shoeless Joe Jackson (yellow pennants)	1500.00	750.00	450.00
(40a) Bill James (white infield)	20.00	10.00	6.00
(40b) Bill James (brown infield)	75.00	37.00	22.00
(41a) Walter Johnson (brown pennants)	275.00	137.00	82.00
(41b) Walter Johnson (green pennants)	275.00	137.00	82.00
(42a) Ray Keating (blue infield)	20.00	10.00	6.00
(42b) Ray Keating (green infield)	20.00	10.00	6.00
(43a) Joe Kelley (Kelly) (purple pennants)	75.00	37.00	22.00
(43b) Joe Kelley (Kelly) (red pennants)	100.00	50.00	30.00
(44a) Ed Konetchy (purple pennants)	40.00	20.00	12.00
(44b) Ed Konetchy (red pennants)	45.00	22.00	13.50
(45a) Nemo Leibold (purple pennants)	40.00	20.00	12.00
(45b) Nemo Leibold (yellow pennants)	75.00	37.00	22.00
(46a) Fritz Maisel (blue infield)	20.00	10.00	6.00
(46b) Fritz Maisel (green infield)	20.00	10.00	6.00
(47a) Les Mann (white infield)	20.00	10.00	6.00
(47b) Les Mann (brown infield)	75.00	37.00	22.00
(48a) Rabbit Maranville (white infield)	45.00	22.00	13.50
(48b) Rabbit Maranville (brown infield)	150.00	75.00	45.00
(48c) Rabbit Maranville (red infield)	350.00	175.00	105.00
(49a) Bill McAllister (McAllester) (purple pennants)	40.00	20.00	12.00
(49b) Bill McAllister (McAllester) (red pennants)	45.00	22.00	13.50
(50a) George McBride (brown pennants)	20.00	10.00	6.00
(50b) George McBride (green pennants)	20.00	10.00	6.00
(51a) Chief Meyers (brown basepaths)	20.00	10.00	6.00
(51b) Chief Meyers (green basepaths)	20.00	10.00	6.00
(52a) Clyde Milan (brown pennants)	20.00	10.00	6.00
(52b) Clyde Milan (green pennants)	20.00	10.00	6.00
(53a) Dots Miller (purple pennants)	40.00	20.00	12.00
(53b) Dots Miller (yellow pennants)	75.00	37.00	22.00
(54a) Otto Miller (blue infield)	20.00	10.00	6.00
(54b) Otto Miller (green infield)	20.00	10.00	6.00
(55a) Willie Mitchell (purple pennants)	40.00	20.00	12.00
(55b) Willie Mitchell (yellow pennants)	75.00	37.00	22.00
(56a) Danny Moeller (brown pennants)	20.00	10.00	6.00
(56b) Danny Moeller (green pennants)	20.00	10.00	6.00
(57a) Ray Morgan (brown pennants)	20.00	10.00	6.00
(57b) Ray Morgan (green pennants)	20.00	10.00	6.00
(58a) George Moriarty (white infield)	20.00	10.00	6.00
(58b) Geroge Moriarty (brown infield)	75.00	37.00	22.00
(58c) Geroge Moriarty (red infield)	275.00	137.00	82.00
(59a) Mike Mowrey (purple pennants)	40.00	20.00	12.00
(59b) Mike Mowrey (red pennants)	45.00	22.00	13.50
(60a) Red Murray (brown basepaths)	20.00	10.00	6.00
(60b) Red Murray (green basepaths)	20.00	10.00	6.00
(61a) Ivy Olson (purple pennants)	40.00	20.00	12.00
(61b) Ivy Olson (yellow pennants)	75.00	37.00	22.00
(62a) Steve O'Neill (purple pennants)	40.00	20.00	12.00
(62b) Steve O'Neill (red pennants)	75.00	37.00	22.00
(63a) Marty O'Toole (purple pennants)	40.00	20.00	12.00
(63b) Marty O'Toole (red pennants)	45.00	22.00	13.50
(64a) Roger Peckinpaugh (blue infield)	25.00	12.50	7.50
(64b) Roger Peckinpaugh (green infield)	25.00	12.50	7.50
(65a) Hub Perdue (white infield)	20.00	10.00	6.00
(65b) Hub Perdue (brown infield)	75.00	37.00	22.00
(66a) Del Pratt (purple pennants)	40.00	20.00	12.00
(66b) Del Pratt (yellow pennants)	45.00	22.00	13.50
(67a) Hank Robinson (purple pennants)	40.00	20.00	12.00
(67b) Hank Robinson (yellow pennants)	75.00	37.00	22.00
(68a) Nap Rucker (blue infield)	20.00	10.00	6.00
(68b) Nap Rucker (green infield)	20.00	10.00	6.00
(69a) Slim Sallee (purple pennants)	40.00	20.00	12.00
(69b) Slim Sallee (yellow pennants)	75.00	37.00	22.00
(70a) Howard Shanks (brown pennants)	20.00	10.00	6.00
(70b) Howard Shanks (green pennants)	20.00	10.00	6.00
(71a) Burt Shotton (purple basepaths)	40.00	20.00	12.00
(71b) Burt Shotton (red basepaths)	45.00	22.00	13.50
(72a) Red Smith (blue infield)	20.00	10.00	6.00
(72b) Red Smith (green infield)	20.00	10.00	6.00
(73a) Fred Snodgrass (brown basepaths)	25.00	12.50	7.50
(73b) Fred Snodgrass (green basepaths)	25.00	12.50	7.50
(74a) Bill Steele (purple pennants)	40.00	20.00	12.00
74b Bill Steele (yellow pennants)	75.00	37.00	22.00
(75a) Casey Stengel (blue infield)	125.00	62.00	37.00
(75b) Casey Stengel (green infield)	125.00	62.00	37.00
(76a) Jeff Sweeney (blue infield)	20.00	10.00	6.00
(76b) Jeff Sweeney (green infield)	20.00	10.00	6.00
(77a) Jeff Tesreau (brown basepaths)	20.00	10.00	6.00
(77b) Jeff Tesreau (green basepaths)	20.00	10.00	6.00
(78a) Terry Turner (purple pennants)	40.00	20.00	12.00
(78b) Terry Turner (yellow pennants)	75.00	37.00	22.00
(79a) Lefty Tyler (white infield)	20.00	10.00	6.00
(79b) Lefty Tyler (brown infield)	75.00	37.00	22.00
(79c) Lefty Tyler (red infield)	275.00	137.00	82.00
(80a) Jim Viox (purple pennants)	40.00	20.00	12.00
(80b) Jim Viox (red pennants)	45.00	22.00	13.50
(81a) Bull Wagner (blue infield)	20.00	10.00	6.00
(81b) Bull Wagner (green infield)	20.00	10.00	6.00
(82a) Bobby Wallace (purple basepaths)	75.00	37.00	22.00
(82b) Bobby Wallace (red basepaths)	75.00	37.00	22.00
(83a) Dee Walsh (purple basepaths)	40.00	20.00	12.00
(83b) Dee Walsh (red basepaths)	45.00	22.00	13.50
(84a) Jimmy Walsh (blue infield)	20.00	10.00	6.00
(84b) Jimmy Walsh (green infield)	20.00	10.00	6.00
(85a) Bert Whaling (white infield)	20.00	10.00	6.00
(85b) Bert Whaling (brown infield)	75.00	37.00	22.00
(85c) Bert Whaling (red infield)	275.00	137.00	82.00

		NR MT	EX	VG
(86a)	Zach Wheat (blue infield)	75.00	37.00	22.00
(86b)	Zach Wheat (green infield)	75.00	37.00	22.00
(87a)	Possum Whitted (purple pennants)	40.00	20.00	12.00
(87b)	Possum Whitted (yellow pennants)	75.00	37.00	22.00
(88a)	Gus Williams (purple basepaths)	40.00	20.00	12.00
(88b)	Gus Williams (red basepaths)	45.00	22.00	13.50
(89a)	Owen Wilson (purple pennants)	40.00	20.00	12.00
(89b)	Owen Wilson (yellow pennants)	75.00	37.00	22.00
(90a)	Hooks Wiltse (brown basepaths)	20.00	10.00	6.00
(90b)	Hooks Wiltse (green basepaths)	20.00	10.00	6.00

1916 BF2 Felt Pennants

Issued circa 1916, this unnumbered set consists of 94 felt pennants with a small black and white player photo glued to each one. The triangular pennants measure approximately 8-1/4" long, while the photos are 1-3/4" by 1-1/4" and appear to be identical to photos used for The Sporting News issues of the same period. The pennants list the player's name and team.

		NR MT	EX	VG
Complete Set:		7500.00	3750.00	2250.
Common Player:		40.00	20.00	12.00
(1)	Grover Alexander	125.00	62.00	37.00
(2)	Jimmy Archer	40.00	20.00	12.00
(3)	Home Run Baker	125.00	62.00	37.00
(4)	Dave Bancroft	60.00	30.00	18.00
(5)	Jack Barry	40.00	20.00	12.00
(6)	Chief Bender	125.00	62.00	37.00
(7)	Joe Benz	40.00	20.00	12.00
(8)	Mordecai Brown	100.00	50.00	30.00
(9)	George J. Burns	40.00	20.00	12.00
(10)	Donie Bush	40.00	20.00	12.00
(11)	Hick Cady	40.00	20.00	12.00
(12)	Max Carey	40.00	20.00	12.00
(13)	Ray Chapman	50.00	25.00	15.00
(14)	Ty Cobb	500.00	250.00	150.00
(15)	Eddie Collins	125.00	62.00	37.00
(16)	Shano Collins	40.00	20.00	12.00
(17)	Commy Comiskey	125.00	62.00	37.00
(18)	Harry Coveleskie (Coveleski)	40.00	20.00	12.00
(19)	Gavvy Cravath	45.00	22.00	13.50
(20)	Sam Crawford	100.00	50.00	30.00
(21)	Jake Daubert	45.00	22.00	13.50
(22)	Josh Devore	40.00	20.00	12.00
(23)	Red Dooin	40.00	20.00	12.00
(24)	Larry Doyle	40.00	20.00	12.00
(25)	Jean Dubuc	40.00	20.00	12.00
(26)	Johnny Evers	125.00	62.00	37.00
(27)	Red Faber	100.00	50.00	30.00
(28)	Eddie Foster	40.00	20.00	12.00
(29)	Del Gainer (Gainor)	40.00	20.00	12.00
(30)	Chick Gandil	50.00	25.00	15.00
(31)	Joe Gedeon	40.00	20.00	12.00
(32)	Hank Gowdy	40.00	20.00	12.00
(33)	Earl Hamilton	40.00	20.00	12.00
(34)	Claude Hendrix	40.00	20.00	12.00
(35)	Buck Herzog	40.00	20.00	12.00
(36)	Harry Hooper	60.00	30.00	18.00
(37)	Miller Huggins	60.00	30.00	18.00
(38)	Shoeless Joe Jackson	700.00	350.00	200.00
(39)	Seattle Bill James	40.00	20.00	12.00
(40)	Hugh Jennings	60.00	30.00	18.00
(41)	Walter Johnson	300.00	150.00	90.00
(42)	Fielder Jones	40.00	20.00	12.00

		NR MT	EX	VG
(43)	Joe Judge	40.00	20.00	12.00
(44)	Benny Kauff	40.00	20.00	12.00
(45)	Bill Killefer	40.00	20.00	12.00
(46)	Nap Lajoie	200.00	100.00	60.00
(47)	Jack Lapp	40.00	20.00	12.00
(48)	Doc Lavan	40.00	20.00	12.00
(49)	Jimmy Lavender	40.00	20.00	12.00
(50)	Dutch Leonard	40.00	20.00	12.00
(51)	Duffy Lewis	40.00	20.00	12.00
(52)	Hans Lobert	40.00	20.00	12.00
(53)	Fred Luderus	40.00	20.00	12.00
(54)	Connie Mack	150.00	75.00	45.00
(55)	Sherry Magee	45.00	22.00	13.50
(56)	Al Mamaux	40.00	20.00	12.00
(57)	Rabbit Maranville	100.00	50.00	30.00
(58)	Rube Marquard	100.00	50.00	30.00
(59)	George McBride	40.00	20.00	12.00
(60)	John McGraw	75.00	37.00	22.00
(61)	Stuffy McInnes (McInnis)	40.00	20.00	12.00
(62)	Fred Merkle	45.00	22.00	13.50
(63)	Chief Meyers	40.00	20.00	12.00
(64)	Clyde Milan	40.00	20.00	12.00
(65)	Otto Miller	40.00	20.00	12.00
(66)	Pat Moran	40.00	20.00	12.00
(67)	Ray Morgan	40.00	20.00	12.00
(68)	Guy Morton	40.00	20.00	12.00
(69)	Eddie Murphy	40.00	20.00	12.00
(70)	Rube Oldring	40.00	20.00	12.00
(71)	Dode Paskert	40.00	20.00	12.00
(72)	Wally Pipp	60.00	30.00	18.00
(73)	Pants Rowland	40.00	20.00	12.00
(74)	Nap Rucker	40.00	20.00	12.00
(75)	Dick Rudolph	40.00	20.00	12.00
(76)	Reb Russell	40.00	20.00	12.00
(77)	Vic Saier	40.00	20.00	12.00
(78)	Slim Sallee	40.00	20.00	12.00
(79)	Ray Schalk	100.00	50.00	30.00
(80)	Wally Schang	40.00	20.00	12.00
(81)	Wildfire Schulte	40.00	20.00	12.00
(82)	Jim Scott	40.00	20.00	12.00
(83)	George Sisler	125.00	62.00	37.00
(84)	George Stallings	40.00	20.00	12.00
(85)	Oscar Stanage	40.00	20.00	12.00
(86)	Jeff Tesreau	40.00	20.00	12.00
(87)	Joe Tinker	125.00	62.00	37.00
(88)	Lefty Tyler	40.00	20.00	12.00
(89)	Hippo Vaughn	40.00	20.00	12.00
(90)	Bobby Veach	40.00	20.00	12.00
(91)	Honus Wagner	300.00	150.00	90.00
(92)	Ed Walsh	100.00	50.00	30.00
(93)	Buck Weaver	60.00	30.00	18.00
(94)	Ivy Wingo	40.00	20.00	12.00
(95)	Joe Wood	50.00	25.00	15.00
(96)	Ralph Young	40.00	20.00	12.00
(97)	Heinie Zimmerman	40.00	20.00	12.00

1937 BF3 Felt Pennants Type I

The checklist for this obscure set of felt pennants issued circa 1936-1937 is not complete, and new examples are still being reported. The pennants do not carry any manufacturer's name and their method of distribution is not certain, although it is believed they were issued as a premium with candy or gum. The pennants vary in size slightly but generally measure approximately 2-1/2" by 4-1/2" and were issued in various styles and colors, including red, yellow, white, blue, green, purple, black and brown.

Most of the printing is white, although some pennants have been found with red or black printing, and the same pennant is often found in more than one color combination. The pennants feature both individual players and teams, including some minor league clubs. Advanced collectors have categorized the BF3 pennants into the following 11 design types, depending on what elements are included on the pennant: Type I: Player's name and figure. Type II: Player's name, team nickname and figure. Type III: Player's name and team nickname and figure. Type IV: Team nickname and figure. Type V: Team nickname with emblem. Type VI: Team nickname only. Type VII: Player's name and team nickname on two-tailed pennant displayed inside the BF3 pennant. Type VIII: Player's name, year, and team nickname on ball. Type IX: Player's name, year on ball and team nickname. Type X: Team nickname and year. Type XI: Minor league and team.

	NR MT	EX	VG
Complete Set:	4000.00	2000.00	1250.
Common Player: Type I	15.00	7.50	4.50
Common Player: Type II	15.00	7.50	4.50
Common Player: Type III	15.00	7.50	4.50
Common Team: Type IV	15.00	7.50	4.50
Common Team: Type V	15.00	7.50	4.50
Common Team: Type VI	15.00	7.50	4.50
Common Player: Type VII	15.00	7.50	4.50
Common Player: Type VIII	15.00	7.50	4.50
Common Player: Type IX	15.00	7.50	4.50
Common Team: Type X	15.00	7.50	4.50
Common Team: Type XI	15.00	7.50	4.50

		NR MT	EX	VG
(1)	Luke Appling (batting)	25.00	12.50	7.50
(2)	Wally Berger (fielding)	15.00	7.50	4.50
(3)	Zeke Bonura (fielding ground ball)			
		15.00	7.50	4.50
(4)	Dolph Camilli (fielding)	15.00	7.50	4.50
(5)	Ben Chapman (batting)	15.00	7.50	4.50
(6)	Mickey Cochrane (catching)	25.00	12.50	7.50
(7)	Rip Collins (batting)	15.00	7.50	4.50
(8)	Joe Cronin (batting)	25.00	12.50	7.50
(9)	Kiki Cuyler (running)	25.00	12.50	7.50
(10)	Dizzy Dean (pitching)	40.00	20.00	12.50
(11)	Frank Demaree (batting)	15.00	7.50	4.50
(12)	Paul Derringer (pitching)	15.00	7.50	4.50
(13)	Bill Dickey (catching)	35.00	17.50	10.50
(14)	Jimmy Dykes (fielding)	15.00	7.50	4.50
(15)	Bob Feller (pitching)	35.00	17.50	10.50
(16)	Wes Ferrell (running)	15.00	7.50	4.50
(17)	Jimmy Foxx (batting)	35.00	17.50	10.50
(18)	Larry French (batting)	15.00	7.50	4.50
(19)	Franky Frisch (running)	25.00	12.50	7.50
(20)	Lou Gehrig (fielding at 1st base)			
		150.00	75.00	45.00
(21)	Charles Gehringer (running)	25.00	12.50	7.50
(22)	Lefty Gomez (pitching)	25.00	12.50	7.50
(23)	Goose Goslin (batting)	25.00	12.50	7.50
(24)	Hank Greenberg (fielding)	25.00	12.50	7.50
(25)	Charlie Grimm (running)	18.00	9.00	5.50
(26)	Lefty Grove (pitching)	25.00	12.50	7.50
(27)	Gabby Hartnett (catching)	25.00	12.50	7.50
(28)	Rollie Hemsley (catching)	15.00	7.50	4.50
(29)	Billy Herman (fielding at 1st base)			
		25.00	12.50	7.50
(30)	Frank Higgins (fielding)	15.00	7.50	4.50
(31)	Rogers Hornsby (batting)	25.00	12.50	7.50
(32)	Carl Hubbell (pitching)	25.00	12.50	7.50
(33)	Chuck Klein (throwing)	25.00	12.50	7.50
(34)	Tony Lazzeri (batting)	15.00	7.50	4.50
(35)	Hank Leiber (fielding ground ball)			
		15.00	7.50	4.50
(36)	Ernie Lombardi (catching)	25.00	12.50	7.50
(37)	Al Lopez (throwing)	25.00	12.50	7.50
(38)	Gus Mancuso (running)	15.00	7.50	4.50
(39)	Heinie Manush (batting)	25.00	12.50	7.50
(40)	Pepper Martin (batting)	18.00	9.00	5.50
(41)	Joe McCarthy (kneeling)	25.00	12.50	7.50
(42)	Wally Moses (running)	15.00	7.50	4.50
(43)	Van Mungo (standing)	15.00	7.50	4.50
(44)	Mel Ott (throwing)	35.00	17.50	10.50
(45)	Schoolboy Rowe (pitching)	18.00	9.00	5.50
(46)	Babe Ruth (batting)	250.00	125.00	75.00
(47)	George Selkirk (batting)	15.00	7.50	4.50
(48)	Luke Sewell (sliding)	15.00	7.50	4.50
(49)	Joe Stripp (batting)	15.00	7.50	4.50
(50)	Hal Trosky (fielding)	15.00	7.50	4.50
(51)	Floyd Vaughan (running, script signature)			
		25.00	12.50	7.50

		NR MT	EX	VG
(52)	Floyd Vaughan (running, not script signature)			
		25.00	12.50	7.50
(53)	Paul Waner (batting)	25.00	12.50	7.50
(54)	Lon Warneke (pitching)	15.00	7.50	4.50
(55)	Jimmy Wilson (fielding ground ball)			
		15.00	7.50	4.50
(56)	Joe Vosmik (running)	15.00	7.50	4.50

1937 BF3 Felt Pennants
Type II

		NR MT	EX	VG
(1)	Luke Appling (batting)	25.00	12.50	7.50
(2)	Zeke Bonura (batting)	15.00	7.50	4.50
(3)	Dolph Camilli (batting)	15.00	7.50	4.50
(4)	Dizzy Dean (batting)	40.00	20.00	12.50
(5)	Frank Demaree (batting)	15.00	7.50	4.50
(6)	Bob Feller (pitching)	40.00	20.00	12.50
(7)	Wes Ferrell (throwing)	15.00	7.50	4.50
(8)	Frank Frisch (fielding)	25.00	12.50	7.50
(9)	Lou Gehrig (batting)	90.00	45.00	27.50
(10)	Lou Gehrig (fielding)	90.00	45.00	27.50
(11)	Hank Greenberg (throwing)	25.00	12.50	7.50
(12)	Charlie Grimm (fielding)	12.00	6.00	3.50
(13)	Charlie Grimm (throwing)	12.00	6.00	3.50
(14)	Lefty Grove (pitching)	25.00	12.50	7.50
(15)	Gabby Hartnett (batting)	25.00	12.50	7.50
(16)	Billy Herman (batting)	25.00	12.50	7.50
(17)	Tony Lazzeri (running)	20.00	10.00	6.00
(18)	Tony Lazzeri (throwing)	20.00	10.00	6.00
(19)	Hank Leiber (batting)	15.00	7.50	4.50
(20)	Ernie Lombardi (batting)	25.00	12.50	7.50
(21)	Ducky Medwick (batting)	25.00	12.50	7.50
(22)	Joe Stripp (batting)	15.00	7.50	4.50
(23)	Floyd Vaughan (batting)	25.00	12.50	7.50
(24)	Joe Vosmik (throwing)	15.00	7.50	4.50
(25)	Paul Waner (batting)	25.00	12.50	7.50
(26)	Lon Warneke (batting)	15.00	7.50	4.50
(27)	Lon Warneke (pitching)	15.00	7.50	4.50

1937 BF3 Felt Pennants
Type III

		NR MT	EX	VG
(1)	Zeke Bonura	15.00	7.50	4.50
(2)	Dolph Camilli	15.00	7.50	4.50
(3)	Ben Chapman	15.00	7.50	4.50
(4)	Dizzy Dean	40.00	20.00	12.50
(5)	Bill Dickey	35.00	17.50	10.50
(6)	Joe DiMaggio (name in script)	150.00	75.00	45.00
(7)	Bob Feller (name in script)	35.00	17.50	10.50
(8)	Wes Ferrell	15.00	7.50	4.50
(9)	Lou Gehrig (name in script)	150.00	75.00	45.00
(10)	Charles Gehringer	25.00	12.50	7.50
(11)	Lefty Grove	25.00	12.50	7.50
(12)	Billy Herman (name in script)	25.00	12.50	7.50
(13)	Carl Hubbell	25.00	12.50	7.50
(14)	Chuck Klein	25.00	12.50	7.50
(15)	Tony Lazzeri	20.00	10.00	6.00
(16)	Al Lopez	25.00	12.50	7.50
(17)	Johnny Marcum	15.00	7.50	4.50
(18)	Pepper Martin	15.00	7.50	4.50
(19)	Van Lingo Mungo	15.00	7.50	4.50
(20)	Schoolboy Rowe	15.00	7.50	4.50
(21)	George Selkirk	15.00	7.50	4.50
(22)	Bill Terry	25.00	12.50	7.50
(23)	Hal Trosky	15.00	7.50	4.50
(24)	Floyd Vaughan	25.00	12.50	7.50
(25)	Lon Warneke	15.00	7.50	4.50

1937 BF3 Felt Pennants
Type IV

		NR MT	EX	VG
(1)	Athletics (fielder)	15.00	7.50	4.50
(2)	Browns (catcher)	15.00	7.50	4.50
(3)	Cubs (batter)	15.00	7.50	4.50
(4)	Dodgers (batter)	15.00	7.50	4.50
(5)	Dodgers (fielder)	15.00	7.50	4.50
(6)	Giants (standing by base)	15.00	7.50	4.50

		NR MT	EX	VG
(7)	Giants (two players)	15.00	7.50	4.50
(8)	Phillies (pitcher)	15.00	7.50	4.50
(9)	Reds (batter)	15.00	7.50	4.50
(10)	Reds (pitcher)	15.00	7.50	4.50
(11)	White Sox (batter)	15.00	7.50	4.50
(12)	White Sox (catcher)	15.00	7.50	4.50
(13)	White Sox (pitcher)	15.00	7.50	4.50
(14)	Yankees (batter)	25.00	12.50	7.50
(15)	Yankees (fielding ball, from waist up)	25.00	12.50	7.50

1937 BF3 Felt Pennants
Type V

		NR MT	EX	VG
(1)	Athletics (bat)	15.00	7.50	4.50
(2)	Athletics (elephant)	15.00	7.50	4.50
(3)	Bees (bee)	15.00	7.50	4.50
(4)	Browns (bat)	15.00	7.50	4.50
(5)	Cardinals (bat)	15.00	7.50	4.50
(6)	Cardinals (cardinal)	15.00	7.50	4.50
(7)	Cardinals (four birds flying)	15.00	7.50	4.50
(8)	Cubs (cub)	15.00	7.50	4.50
(9)	Cubs (cub's head)	15.00	7.50	4.50
(10)	Dodgers (ball, bat and glove)	15.00	7.50	4.50
(11)	Dodgers (ball)	15.00	7.50	4.50
(12)	Indians (Indian)	15.00	7.50	4.50
(13)	Indians (Indian's head)	15.00	7.50	4.50
(14)	Indians (Indian's head with hat)	15.00	7.50	4.50
(15)	Phillies (Liberty Bell)	15.00	7.50	4.50
(16)	Pirates (skull and crossbones)	15.00	7.50	4.50
(17)	Red Sox (ball and bat)	15.00	7.50	4.50
(18)	Red Sox (bat)	15.00	7.50	4.50
(19)	Reds (ball)	15.00	7.50	4.50
(20)	Senators (ball)	15.00	7.50	4.50
(21)	Senators (Capitol building)	15.00	7.50	4.50
(22)	Tigers (cap)	15.00	7.50	4.50
(23)	Tigers (tiger)	15.00	7.50	4.50

1937 BF3 Felt Pennants
Type VI

		NR MT	EX	VG
(1)	Cardinals	15.00	7.50	4.50
(2)	Cubs	15.00	7.50	4.50
(3)	Dodgers	15.00	7.50	4.50
(4)	Giants	15.00	7.50	4.50
(5)	Indians	15.00	7.50	4.50
(6)	Phillies (Phillies on spine)	15.00	7.50	4.50
(7)	Pirates (Pirates on spine)	15.00	7.50	4.50
(8)	Pirates (no Pirates on spine)	15.00	7.50	4.50
(9)	Yankees	25.00	12.50	7.50

1937 BF3 Felt Pennants
Type VII

		NR MT	EX	VG
(1)	Earl Grace	15.00	7.50	4.50
(2)	Al Lopez	25.00	12.50	7.50

1937 BF3 Felt Pennants
Type VIII

		NR MT	EX	VG
(1)	Larry French	15.00	7.50	4.50

1937 BF3 Felt Pennants
Type IX

		NR MT	EX	VG
(1)	Clay Bryant	15.00	7.50	4.50
(2)	Tex Carleton	15.00	7.50	4.50
(3)	Phil Cavaretta (Cavarretta)	15.00	7.50	4.50
(4)	Irving Cherry	15.00	7.50	4.50
(5)	Ripper Collins	15.00	7.50	4.50
(6)	Curt Davis	15.00	7.50	4.50
(7)	Vince DiMaggio	18.00	9.00	5.50
(8)	Frank Demaree	15.00	7.50	4.50
(9)	Wes Flowers	15.00	7.50	4.50
(10)	Larry French	15.00	7.50	4.50
(11)	Linus Frey	15.00	7.50	4.50
(12)	Augie Galan	15.00	7.50	4.50
(13)	Charlie Grimm	18.00	9.00	5.50
(14)	Stan Hack	15.00	7.50	4.50
(15)	Gabby Hartnett	25.00	12.50	7.50
(16)	Billy Herman	25.00	12.50	7.50
(17)	Walt Higbee	15.00	7.50	4.50
(18)	Billy Jurges	15.00	7.50	4.50
(19)	Andy Lotshaw	15.00	7.50	4.50
(20)	Henry Majeski	15.00	7.50	4.50
(21)	Joe Marty	15.00	7.50	4.50
(22)	Tony Piet	15.00	7.50	4.50
(23)	Chas. Root	15.00	7.50	4.50
(24)	Tuck Stainback	15.00	7.50	4.50

1937 BF3 Felt Pennants
Type X

		NR MT	EX	VG
(1)	Yankees (1936 Champions)	25.00	12.50	7.50

1937 BF3 Felt Pennants
Type XI

		NR MT	EX	VG
(1)	Barons (Southern Association)	15.00	7.50	4.50
(2)	Bears (International League)	15.00	7.50	4.50
(3)	Blues (American Association)	15.00	7.50	4.50
(4)	Brewers (American Association)	15.00	7.50	4.50
(5)	Chicks (Southern Association)	15.00	7.50	4.50
(6)	Colonels (American Association)	15.00	7.50	4.50
(7)	Giants (International League)	15.00	7.50	4.50
(8)	Maple Leafs (International League)	15.00	7.50	4.50
(9)	Millers (American Association)	15.00	7.50	4.50
(10)	Mud Hens (American Association)	15.00	7.50	4.50
(11)	Orioles (International League)	15.00	7.50	4.50
(12)	Red Birds (American Association)	15.00	7.50	4.50
(13)	Saints (American Association)	15.00	7.50	4.50
(14)	Smokies (Southern Association)	15.00	7.50	4.50
(15)	Travelers (Southern Association)	15.00	7.50	4.50

1948 Babe Ruth Story

The Philadelphia Gum Co., in 1948, created a card set about the movie "The Babe Ruth Story", which starred William Bendix and Claire Trevor. The set, whose American Card Catalog designation is R421, contains 28 black and white, numbered cards which measure 2" by 2-1/2". The Babe Ruth Story set was originally intended to consist of sixteen cards. Twelve additional cards (#'s 17-28) were added when Ruth died before the release of the film. The card backs include a offer for an autographed photo of William Bendix, starring as the Babe, for five Swell Bubble Gum wrappers and five cents.

No. 1
"THE BABE RUTH STORY"
IN THE MAKING

Babe Ruth gives William Bendix some fine pointers in the art of hitting home runs.

Bendix enacts the part of the Bombing in the film's glorification of Ruth's dramatic life, an Allied Artists picture produced by Roy Del Ruth.

As bat boy for the Yankees Ruth was Bendix's idol years ago. Little did he think that more than 20 years later he would be selected to play the Sultan of Swat in the motion picture "The Babe Ruth Story."

Send us 5 Swell Bubble Gum wrappers and 1c for a large autographed picture of William Bendix, starring as Babe Ruth.

SWELL BUBBLE GUM
Philadelphia Chewing Gum Corporation
Havertown, Pa.

	NR MT	EX	VG
Complete Set:	1200.00	600.00	360.00
Common Player: 1-16	13.00	6.50	4.00
Common Player: 17-28	40.00	20.00	12.00

		NR MT	EX	VG
1	"The Babe Ruth Story" In The Making	75.00	38.00	23.00
2	Bat Boy Becomes the Babe... William Bendix	13.00	6.50	4.00
3	Claire Hodgson...Claire Trevor	13.00	6.50	4.00
4	Babe Ruth and Claire Hodgson	13.00	6.50	4.00
5	Brother Matthias...Charles Bickford	13.00	6.50	4.00
6	Phil Conrad...Sam Levene	13.00	6.50	4.00
7	Night Club Singer...Gertrude Niesen	13.00	6.50	4.00
8	Baseball's Famous Deal...Jack Dunn (William Frawley)	13.00	6.50	4.00
9	Mr. & Mrs. Babe Ruth	13.00	6.50	4.00
10	Babe Ruth, Claire Ruth, and Brother Matthias	13.00	6.50	4.00
11	Babe Ruth and Miller Huggins (Fred Lightner)	13.00	6.50	4.00
12	Babe Ruth At Bed Of Ill Boy Johnny Sylvester (Gregory Marshall)	13.00	6.50	4.00
13	Sylvester Family Listening To Game	13.00	6.50	4.00
14	"When A Feller Needs a Friend" (With Dog At Police Station)	13.00	6.50	4.00

		NR MT	EX	VG
15	Dramatic Home Run	13.00	6.50	4.00
16	The Homer That Set the Record (#60)	13.00	6.50	4.00
17	"The Slap That Started Baseball's Famous Career"	40.00	20.00	12.00
18	The Babe Plays Santa Claus	40.00	20.00	12.00
19	Meeting Of Owner And Manager	40.00	20.00	12.00
20	"Broken Window Paid Off"	40.00	20.00	12.00
21	Babe In A Crowd Of Autograph Collectors	40.00	20.00	12.00
22	Charley Grimm And William Bendix	40.00	20.00	12.00
23	Ted Lyons And William Bendix	50.00	25.00	15.00
24	Lefty Gomez, William Bendix, And Bucky Harris	50.00	25.00	15.00
25	Babe Ruth and William Bendix	115.00	57.00	34.00
26	Babe Ruth And William Bendix	115.00	57.00	34.00
27	Babe Ruth And Claire Trevor	115.00	57.00	34.00
28	William Bendix, Babe Ruth, And Claire Trevor	115.00	57.00	34.00

1911 Baseball Bats

---

25 Most Valuable Cards

1. 1909-11 T206 Honus Wagner — $300,000

2. 1909-11 T206 Joe Doyle — $30,000

3. 1909-11 T206 Sherry Magie — $30,000

4. 1933 Goudey Nap Lajoie — $30,000

5. 1952 Topps Mickey Mantle — $30,000

6. 1909-11 T206 Eddie Plank — $25,000

7. 1932 U.S. Caramel Lindy Lindstrom — $25,000

8. 1933 Goudey Benny Bengough — $12,000

9. 1909 E90-1 American Caramel Mike Mitchell — $10,000

10. 1888 N-403 Yum Yum Tobacco Cap Anson — $10,000

11. 1951 Topps Current All-Stars Robin Roberts — $9,500

12. 1951 Bowman Mickey Mantle — $9,000

13. 1951 Topps Current All-Stars Eddie Stanky — $8,500

14. 1951 Topps Current All-Stars Jim Kostanty — $8,500

15. 1909 T204 Ramly Walter Johnson — $8,500

16. 1911 T3 Turkey Reds Ty Cobb — $8,500

17. 1914 Cracker Jack Joe Jackson — $8,000

18. E90-1 American Caramel Joe Jackson — $8,000

19. 1911 T205 Ty Cobb — $7,500

20. 1909-11 T206 Ray Demmitt — $7,500

21. 1909-11 T206 Bill O'Hara — $7,500

22. 1911 T5 Pinkerton Joe Jackson — $7,500

23. 1915 Cracker Jack Joe Jackson — $7,000

24. 1888 E223 G & B Chewing Gum Cap Anson — $6,000

25. 1910 E-98 Ty Cobb — $5,700

Issued circa 1911, cards in this rare 47-card issue were printed on the back panel of "Baseball Bats" penny candy. The cards themselves measure approximately 1-3/8" by 2-3/8" and feature a black and white player photo surrounded by an orange or white border. The player's name and team are printed in small, black capital letters near the bottom of the photo.

		NR MT	EX	VG
Complete Set:		8000.00	4000.00	2400.
Common Player:		100.00	50.00	30.00
(1)	Red Ames	100.00	50.00	30.00
(2)	Home Run Baker	175.00	87.00	52.00
(3)	Jack Barry	100.00	50.00	30.00
4	Ginger Beaumont	175.00	87.00	52.00
(5)	Chief Bender	175.00	87.00	52.00
(6)	Al Bridwell	100.00	50.00	30.00
(7)	Mordecai Brown	175.00	87.00	52.00
(8)	Bill Corrigan (Carrigan)	100.00	50.00	30.00
(9)	Frank Chance	150.00	75.00	45.00
(10)	Hal Chase	125.00	62.00	37.00
(11)	Ed Cicotte	125.00	62.00	37.00
(12)	Fred Clark (Clarke)	175.00	87.00	52.00
(13)	Ty Cobb	800.00	400.00	240.00
(14)	King Cole	100.00	50.00	30.00
(15)	Eddie Collins	200.00	100.00	60.00
(16)	Sam Crawford	175.00	87.00	52.00
(17)	Lou Criger	100.00	50.00	30.00
(18)	Harry Davis	100.00	50.00	30.00
(19)	Jim Delehanty	100.00	50.00	30.00
(20)	Art Devlin	100.00	50.00	30.00
(21)	Josh Devore	100.00	50.00	30.00
(22)	Wild Bill Donovan	100.00	50.00	30.00
(23)	Larry Doyle	110.00	55.00	33.00
(24)	Johnny Evers	175.00	87.00	52.00
(25)	John Flynn	100.00	50.00	30.00
26	George Gibson	175.00	87.00	52.00
(27)	Solly Hoffman (Hofman)	100.00	50.00	30.00
(28)	Walter Johnson	300.00	150.00	90.00
(29)	Johnny Kling	100.00	50.00	30.00
(30)	Nap Lajoie	250.00	125.00	75.00
(31)	Matty McIntyre	100.00	50.00	30.00
(32)	Fred Merkle	110.00	55.00	33.00
(33)	Tom Needham	100.00	50.00	30.00
(34)	Rube Oldring	100.00	50.00	30.00
(35)	Wildfire Schulte	100.00	50.00	30.00
(36)	Cy Seymour	100.00	50.00	30.00
(37)	Jimmy Sheckard	100.00	50.00	30.00
(38)	Tris Speaker	250.00	125.00	75.00
(39)	Oscar Stanage (batting - front view)			
		100.00	50.00	30.00
(40)	Oscar Stanage (batting - side view)			
		100.00	50.00	30.00
(41)	Ira Thomas	100.00	50.00	30.00
(42)	Joe Tinker	175.00	87.00	52.00
(43)	Heinie Wagner	100.00	50.00	30.00
(44)	Honus Wagner	400.00	200.00	120.00
(45)	Ed Walsh	175.00	87.00	52.00
(46)	Art Wilson	100.00	50.00	30.00
(47)	Owen Wilson	100.00	50.00	30.00

A player's name in *italic* indicates a rookie card. An (FC) indicates a player's first card for that particular card company.

1934 Batter-Up

National Chicle's 192-card "Batter-Up" set was issued from 1934 through 1936. The blank-backed cards are die-cut, enabling collectors of the era to fold the top of the card over so that it could stand upright on its own support. The cards can be found in black and white or a variety of color tints. Card numbers 1-80 measure 2-3/8" by 3-1/4" in size, while the high-numbered cards (#'s 81-192) measure

1/4" smaller in width. The high-numbered cards are significantly more difficult to find than the lower numbers. The set's ACC designation is R318.

		NR MT	EX	VG
Complete Set:		32500.00	16250.00	9750.
Common Player: 1-80		75.00	35.00	15.00
Common Player: 81-192		150.00	70.00	25.00
1	Wally Berger	150.00	50.00	15.00
2	Ed Brandt	75.00	35.00	15.00
3	Al Lopez	150.00	70.00	25.00
4	Dick Bartell	75.00	35.00	15.00
5	Carl Hubbell	200.00	100.00	35.00
6	Bill Terry	200.00	100.00	35.00
7	Pepper Martin	75.00	35.00	15.00
8	Jim Bottomley	150.00	70.00	25.00
9	Tommy Bridges	75.00	35.00	15.00
10	Rick Ferrell	125.00	50.00	15.00
11	Ray Benge	75.00	35.00	15.00
12	Wes Ferrell	75.00	35.00	15.00
13	Bill Cissell	75.00	35.00	15.00
14	Pie Traynor	175.00	80.00	30.00
15	Roy Mahaffey	75.00	35.00	15.00
16	Chick Hafey	150.00	75.00	25.00
17	Lloyd Waner	150.00	75.00	25.00
18	Jack Burns	75.00	35.00	15.00
19	Buddy Myer	75.00	35.00	15.00
20	Bob Johnson	75.00	35.00	15.00
21	Arky Vaughn (Vaughan)	125.00	55.00	28.00
22	Red Rolfe	75.00	35.00	15.00
23	Lefty Gomez	250.00	125.00	40.00
24	Earl Averill	125.00	55.00	20.00
25	Mickey Cochrane	150.00	75.00	30.00
26	Van Mungo	75.00	35.00	15.00
27	Mel Ott	275.00	125.00	50.00
28	Jimmie Foxx	300.00	150.00	50.00
29	Jimmy Dykes	75.00	35.00	15.00
30	Bill Dickey	275.00	125.00	55.00
31	Lefty Grove	250.00	125.00	35.00
32	Joe Cronin	150.00	75.00	28.00
33	Frankie Frisch	200.00	100.00	35.00
34	Al Simmons	150.00	70.00	25.00
35	Rogers Hornsby	400.00	200.00	75.00
36	Ted Lyons	175.00	80.00	25.00
37	Rabbit Maranville	175.00	80.00	25.00
38	Jimmie Wilson	75.00	35.00	15.00
39	Willie Kamm	75.00	35.00	15.00
40	Bill Hallahan	75.00	35.00	15.00
41	Gus Suhr	75.00	35.00	15.00
42	Charlie Gehringer	250.00	125.00	40.00
43	Joe Heving	75.00	35.00	15.00
44	Adam Comorosky	75.00	35.00	15.00
45	Tony Lazzeri	150.00	70.00	25.00
46	Sam Leslie	75.00	35.00	15.00
47	Bob Smith	75.00	35.00	15.00
48	Willis Hudlin	75.00	35.00	15.00
49	Carl Reynolds	75.00	35.00	15.00
50	Fred Schulte	75.00	35.00	15.00
51	Cookie Lavagetto	75.00	35.00	15.00
52	Hal Schumacher	75.00	35.00	15.00
53	Doc Cramer	75.00	35.00	15.00
54	Si Johnson	75.00	35.00	15.00
55	Ollie Bejma	75.00	35.00	15.00
56	Sammy Byrd	75.00	35.00	15.00
57	Hank Greenberg	250.00	125.00	40.00
58	Bill Knickerbocker	75.00	35.00	15.00
59	Billy Urbanski	75.00	35.00	15.00
60	Ed Morgan	75.00	35.00	15.00
61	Eric McNair	75.00	35.00	15.00
62	Ben Chapman	75.00	35.00	15.00

		NR MT	EX	VG
63	Roy Johnson	75.00	35.00	15.00
64	"Dizzy" Dean	650.00	300.00	100.00
65	Zeke Bonura	75.00	35.00	15.00
66	Firpo Marberry	75.00	35.00	15.00
67	Gus Mancuso	75.00	35.00	15.00
68	Joe Vosmik	75.00	35.00	15.00
69	Earl Grace	75.00	35.00	15.00
70	Tony Piet	75.00	35.00	15.00
71	Rollie Hemsley	75.00	35.00	15.00
72	Fred Fitzsimmons	75.00	35.00	15.00
73	Hack Wilson	300.00	150.00	50.00
74	Chick Fullis	75.00	35.00	15.00
75	Fred Frankhouse	75.00	35.00	15.00
76	Ethan Allen	75.00	35.00	15.00
77	Heinie Manush	125.00	50.00	18.00
78	Rip Collins	75.00	35.00	15.00
79	Tony Cuccinello	75.00	35.00	15.00
80	Joe Kuhel	75.00	35.00	15.00
81	Thomas Bridges	150.00	70.00	25.00
82	Clinton Brown	150.00	70.00	25.00
83	Albert Blanche	150.00	70.00	25.00
84	"Boze" Berger	150.00	70.00	25.00
85	Goose Goslin	400.00	200.00	65.00
86	Vernon Gomez	550.00	275.00	110.00
87	Joe Glen (Glenn)	150.00	70.00	25.00
88	"Cy" Blanton	150.00	70.00	25.00
89	Tom Carey	150.00	70.00	25.00
90	Ralph Birkhofer	150.00	70.00	25.00
91	Frank Gabler	150.00	70.00	25.00
92	Dick Coffman	150.00	70.00	25.00
93	Ollie Bejma	150.00	70.00	25.00
94	Leroy Earl Parmalee	150.00	70.00	25.00
95	Carl Reynolds	150.00	70.00	25.00
96	Ben Cantwell	150.00	70.00	25.00
97	Curtis Davis	150.00	70.00	25.00
98	Wallace Moses, Billy Webb	150.00	70.00	25.00
99	Ray Benge	150.00	70.00	25.00
100	"Pie" Traynor	400.00	200.00	75.00
101	Phil. Cavarretta	150.00	70.00	25.00
102	"Pep" Young	150.00	70.00	25.00
103	Willis Hudlin	150.00	70.00	25.00
104	Mickey Haslin	150.00	70.00	25.00
105	Oswald Bluege	150.00	70.00	25.00
106	Paul Andrews	150.00	70.00	25.00
107	Edward A. Brandt	150.00	70.00	25.00
108	Dan Taylor	150.00	70.00	25.00
109	Thornton T. Lee	150.00	70.00	25.00
110	Hal Schumacher	150.00	70.00	25.00
111	Minter Hayes, Ted Lyons	450.00	225.00	135.00
112	Odell Hale	150.00	70.00	25.00
113	Earl Averill	300.00	150.00	50.00
114	Italo Chelini	150.00	70.00	25.00
115	Ivy Andrews, Jim Bottomley	450.00	225.00	135.00
116	Bill Walker	150.00	70.00	25.00
117	Bill Dickey	550.00	275.00	115.00
118	Gerald Walker	150.00	70.00	25.00
119	Ted Lyons	300.00	150.00	50.00
120	Elden Auker (Eldon)	150.00	70.00	25.00
121	Wild Bill Hallahan	150.00	70.00	25.00
122	Freddy Lindstrom	350.00	175.00	65.00
123	Oral C. Hildebrand	150.00	70.00	25.00
124	Luke Appling	350.00	175.00	65.00
125	"Pepper" Martin	175.00	80.00	30.00
126	Rick Ferrell	350.00	175.00	65.00
127	Ival Goodman	150.00	70.00	25.00
128	Joe Kuhel	150.00	70.00	25.00
129	Ernest Lombardi	350.00	175.00	65.00
130	Charles Gehringer	450.00	225.00	135.00
131	Van L. Mungo	175.00	80.00	30.00
132	Larry French	150.00	70.00	25.00
133	"Buddy" Myer	150.00	70.00	25.00
134	Mel Harder	150.00	70.00	25.00
135	Augie Galan	150.00	70.00	25.00
136	"Gabby" Hartnett	350.00	175.00	65.00
137	Stan Hack	150.00	70.00	25.00
138	Billy Herman	350.00	175.00	65.00
139	Bill Jurges	150.00	70.00	25.00
140	Bill Lee	150.00	70.00	25.00
141	"Zeke" Bonura	150.00	70.00	25.00
142	Tony Piet	150.00	70.00	25.00
143	Paul Dean	250.00	125.00	50.00
144	Jimmy Foxx	700.00	300.00	115.00
145	Joe Medwick	350.00	175.00	65.00
146	Rip Collins	150.00	70.00	25.00
147	Melo Almada	150.00	70.00	25.00
148	Allan Cooke	150.00	70.00	25.00
149	Moe Berg	150.00	70.00	25.00
150	Adolph Camilli	150.00	70.00	25.00
151	Oscar Melillo	150.00	70.00	25.00
152	Bruce Campbell	150.00	70.00	25.00
153	Lefty Grove	600.00	275.00	115.00

		NR MT	EX	VG
154	John Murphy	150.00	70.00	25.00
155	Luke Sewell	150.00	70.00	25.00
156	Leo Durocher	350.00	175.00	65.00
157	Lloyd Waner	350.00	175.00	65.00
158	Guy Bush	150.00	70.00	25.00
159	Jimmy Dykes	150.00	70.00	25.00
160	Steve O'Neill	150.00	70.00	25.00
161	Gen. Crowder	150.00	70.00	25.00
162	Joe Cascarella	150.00	70.00	25.00
163	"Bud" Hafey	150.00	70.00	25.00
164	"Gilly" Campbell	150.00	70.00	25.00
165	Ray Hayworth	150.00	70.00	25.00
166	Frank Demaree	150.00	70.00	25.00
167	John Babich	150.00	70.00	25.00
168	Marvin Owen	150.00	70.00	25.00
169	Ralph Kress	150.00	70.00	25.00
170	"Mule" Haas	150.00	70.00	25.00
171	Frank Higgins	150.00	70.00	25.00
172	Walter Berger	150.00	70.00	25.00
173	Frank Frisch	400.00	200.00	75.00
174	Wess Ferrell (Wes)	150.00	70.00	25.00
175	Pete Fox	150.00	70.00	25.00
176	John Vergez	150.00	70.00	25.00
177	William Rogell	150.00	70.00	25.00
178	"Don" Brennan	150.00	70.00	25.00
179	James Bottomley	250.00	125.00	50.00
180	Travis Jackson	350.00	175.00	65.00
181	Robert Rolfe	175.00	80.00	30.00
182	Frank Crosetti	275.00	135.00	50.00
183	Joe Cronin	350.00	175.00	65.00
184	"Schoolboy" Rowe	175.00	80.00	30.00
185	"Chuck" Klein	350.00	175.00	65.00
186	Lon Warneke	150.00	70.00	25.00
187	Gus Suhr	150.00	70.00	25.00
188	Ben Chapman	200.00	90.00	30.00
189	Clint. Brown	180.00	85.00	35.00
190	Paul Derringer	250.00	125.00	40.00
191	John Burns	300.00	150.00	45.00
192	John Broaca	450.00	225.00	135.00

1958 Bell Brand Dodgers

Celebrating the Dodgers first year of play in Los Angeles, Bell Brand inserted ten different unnumbered cards in their bags of potato chips and corn chips. The cards, which measure 3" by 4", have a sepia-colored photo inside a 1/4" green woodgrain border. The card backs feature statistical and biographical information and include the Bell Brand logo. Roy Campanella is included in the set despite a career-ending car wreck that prevented him from ever playing in Los Angeles.

		NR MT	EX	VG
Complete Set:		1200.00	600.00	360.00
Common Player:		40.00	20.00	12.00
1	Roy Campanella	150.00	75.00	45.00
2	Gino Cimoli	125.00	62.00	37.00
3	Don Drysdale	90.00	45.00	27.00
4	Junior Gilliam	40.00	20.00	12.00
5	Gil Hodges	90.00	45.00	27.00
6	Sandy Koufax	150.00	75.00	45.00
7	Johnny Podres	125.00	62.00	37.00
8	Pee Wee Reese	90.00	45.00	27.00
9	Duke Snider	300.00	150.00	90.00
10	Don Zimmer	40.00	20.00	12.00

1960 Bell Brand Dodgers

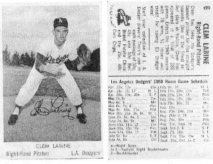

CLEM LABINE
Right-Hand Pitcher   L.A. Dodgers

Bell Brand returned with a baseball card set in 1960 that was entirely different in style to their previous effort. The cards, which measure 2-1/2" by 3-1/2", feature beautiful, full-color photos. The backs carry a short player biography, the 1960 Dodgers home schedule, and the Bell Brand logo. Twenty different numbered cards were inserted in various size bags of potato chips and corn chips. Although sealed in cellophane, the cards were still subject to grease stains. Cards #'s 6, 12 and 18 are the scarcest in the set.

		NR MT	EX	VG
Complete Set:		700.00	350.00	210.00
Common Player:		20.00	10.00	6.00
1	Norm Larker	20.00	10.00	6.00
2	Duke Snider	70.00	35.00	21.00
3	Danny McDevitt	20.00	10.00	6.00
4	Jim Gilliam	25.00	12.50	7.50
5	Rip Repulski	20.00	10.00	6.00
6	Clem Labine	100.00	50.00	30.00
7	John Roseboro	20.00	10.00	6.00
8	Carl Furillo	25.00	12.50	7.50
9	Sandy Koufax	125.00	62.00	37.00
10	Joe Pignatano	20.00	10.00	6.00
11	Chuck Essegian	20.00	10.00	6.00
12	John Klippstein	80.00	40.00	25.00
13	Ed Roebuck	20.00	10.00	6.00
14	Don Demeter	20.00	10.00	6.00
15	Roger Craig	30.00	15.00	9.00
16	Stan Williams	20.00	10.00	6.00
17	Don Zimmer	25.00	12.50	7.50
18	Walter Alston	125.00	62.00	37.00
19	Johnny Podres	25.00	12.50	7.50
20	Maury Wills	30.00	15.00	9.00

1961 Bell Brand Dodgers

NORM LARKER
INFIELDER   L.A. DODGERS

The 1961 Bell Brand set is identical in format to the previous year, although printed on thinner stock. Cards can be distinguished from the 1960 set by the 1961 schedule on the backs. The cards, which

measure 2-7/16" by 3-1/2", are numbered by the player's uniform number. Twenty different cards were inserted into various size potato chip and corn chip packages, each card being sealed in a cellophane wrapper.

		NR MT	EX	VG
Complete Set:		375.00	185.00	110.00
Common Player:		12.00	6.00	3.50
3	Willie Davis	15.00	7.50	4.50
4	Duke Snider	60.00	30.00	18.00
5	Norm Larker	12.00	6.00	3.50
8	John Roseboro	12.00	6.00	3.50
9	Wally Moon	12.00	6.00	3.50
11	Bob Lillis	12.00	6.00	3.50
12	Tom Davis	12.00	6.00	3.50
14	Gil Hodges	30.00	15.00	9.00
16	Don Demeter	12.00	6.00	3.50
19	Jim Gilliam	15.00	7.50	4.50
22	John Podres	15.00	7.50	4.50
24	Walter Alston	30.00	15.00	9.00
30	Maury Wills	30.00	15.00	9.00
32	Sandy Koufax	80.00	40.00	25.00
34	Norm Sherry	12.00	6.00	3.50
37	Ed Roebuck	12.00	6.00	3.50
38	Roger Craig	15.00	7.50	4.50
40	Stan Williams	12.00	6.00	3.50
43	Charlie Neal	12.00	6.00	3.50
51	Larry Sherry	12.00	6.00	3.50

1962 Bell Brand Dodgers

WALLY MOON
OUTFIELDER   L.A. DODGERS

The 1962 Bell Brand set is identical in style to the previous two years and cards can be distinguished by the 1962 Dodgers schedule on the back. The set consists of 20 cards, each measuring 2-7/16" by 3-1/2" and numbered by the player's uniform number. Printed on glossy stock, the 1962 set was less susceptible to grease stains.

		NR MT	EX	VG
Complete Set:		375.00	185.00	110.00
Common Player:		12.00	6.00	3.50
3	Willie Davis	15.00	7.50	4.50
4	Duke Snider	60.00	30.00	18.00
6	Ron Fairly	12.00	6.00	3.50
8	John Roseboro	12.00	6.00	3.50
9	Wally Moon	12.00	6.00	3.50
12	Tom Davis	12.00	6.00	3.50
16	Ron Perranoski	12.00	6.00	3.50
19	Jim Gilliam	15.00	7.50	4.50
20	Daryl Spencer	12.00	6.00	3.50
22	John Podres	15.00	7.50	4.50
24	Walter Alston	30.00	15.00	9.00
25	Frank Howard	15.00	7.50	4.50
30	Maury Wills	30.00	15.00	9.00
32	Sandy Koufax	80.00	40.00	25.00
34	Norm Sherry	12.00	6.00	3.50
37	Ed Roebuck	12.00	6.00	3.50
40	Stan Williams	12.00	6.00	3.50
51	Larry Sherry	12.00	6.00	3.50
53	Don Drysdale	50.00	25.00	15.00
56	Lee Walls	12.00	6.00	3.50

1951 Berk Ross

Entitled "Hit Parade of Champions," the 1951 Berk Ross set features 72 stars of various sports. The cards, which measure 2-1/16" by 2-1/2" and have tinted color photographs, were issued in boxes containing two-card panels. The issue is divided into four subsets with the first ten players of each series being baseball players. Only the baseball players are listed in the checklist that follows. Complete panels are valued 50 per cent higher than the sum of the individual cards.

		NR MT	EX	VG
Complete Set:		1200.00	600.00	360.00
Common Player:		12.00	6.00	3.50
1-1	Al Rosen	20.00	10.00	6.00
1-2	Bob Lemon	20.00	10.00	6.00
1-3	Phil Rizzuto	50.00	25.00	15.00
1-4	Hank Bauer	30.00	15.00	9.00
1-5	Billy Johnson	13.00	6.50	4.00
1-6	Jerry Coleman	13.00	6.50	4.00
1-7	Johnny Mize	30.00	15.00	7.50
1-8	Dom DiMaggio	30.00	15.00	9.00
1-9	Richie Ashburn	15.00	7.50	4.50
1-10	Del Ennis	13.00	6.50	4.00
2-1	Stan Musial	300.00	150.00	90.00
2-2	Warren Spahn	30.00	15.00	9.00
2-3	Tommy Henrich	15.00	7.50	4.50
2-4	Larry "Yogi" Berra	225.00	112.00	67.00
2-5	Joe DiMaggio	400.00	200.00	120.00
2-6	Bobby Brown	15.00	7.50	4.50
2-7	Granville Hamner	12.00	6.00	3.50
2-8	Willie Jones	12.00	6.00	3.50
2-9	Stanley Lopata	12.00	6.00	3.50
2-10	Mike Goliat	12.00	6.00	3.50
3-1	Ralph Kiner	30.00	15.00	9.00
3-2	Billy Goodman	12.00	6.00	3.50
3-3	Allie Reynolds	15.00	7.50	4.50
3-4	Vic Raschi	15.00	7.50	4.50
3-5	Joe Page	13.00	6.50	4.00
3-6	Eddie Lopat	15.00	7.50	4.50
3-7	Andy Seminick	12.00	6.00	3.50
3-8	Dick Sisler	12.00	6.00	3.50
3-9	Eddie Waitkus	12.00	6.00	3.50
3-10	Ken Heintzelman	12.00	6.00	3.50
4-1	Gene Woodling	15.00	7.50	4.50
4-2	Cliff Mapes	13.00	6.50	4.00
4-3	Fred Sanford	13.00	6.50	4.00
4-4	Tommy Bryne	13.00	6.50	4.00
4-5	Eddie (Whitey) Ford	125.00	62.00	37.00
4-6	Jim Konstanty	13.00	6.50	4.00
4-7	Russ Meyer	12.00	6.00	3.50
4-8	Robin Roberts	30.00	15.00	9.00
4-9	Curt Simmons	13.00	6.50	4.00
4-10	Sam Jethroe	30.00	15.00	9.00

1952 Berk Ross

Although the card size is different (2" by 3"), the style of the fronts and backs of the 1952 Berk Ross set is similar to the previous year's effort. Seventy-two unnumbered cards make up the set. Rizzuto is included in the set and the Blackwell and Fox cards have transposed backs. The cards were issued individually rather than as two-card panels like in 1951.

		NR MT	EX	VG
Complete Set:		4500.00	2250.00	1350.
Common Player:		12.00	6.00	3.50
(1)	Richie Ashburn	30.00	15.00	9.00
(2)	Hank Bauer	18.00	9.00	5.50
(3)	Larry "Yogi" Berra	100.00	50.00	30.00
(4)	Ewell Blackwell (photo actually Nelson Fox)	18.00	9.00	5.50
(5)	Bobby Brown	18.00	9.00	5.50
(6)	Jim Busby	12.00	6.00	3.50
(7)	Roy Campanella	125.00	56.00	35.00
(8)	Chico Carrasquel	12.00	6.00	3.50
(9)	Jerry Coleman	15.00	7.50	4.50
(10)	Joe Collins	15.00	7.50	4.50
(11)	Alvin Dark	15.00	7.50	4.50
(12)	Dom DiMaggio	18.00	9.00	5.50
(13)	Joe DiMaggio	700.00	350.00	200.00
(14)	Larry Doby	18.00	9.00	5.50
(15)	Bobby Doerr	35.00	17.50	10.50
(16)	Bob Elliot (Elliott)	12.00	6.00	3.50
(17)	Del Ennis	12.00	6.00	3.50
(18)	Ferris Fain	12.00	6.00	3.50
(19)	Bob Feller	75.00	38.00	23.00
(20)	Nelson Fox (photo actually Ewell Blackwell)	18.00	9.00	5.50
(21)	Ned Garver	12.00	6.00	3.50
(22)	Clint Hartung	12.00	6.00	3.50
(23)	Jim Hearn	12.00	6.00	3.50
(24)	Gil Hodges	50.00	30.00	15.00
(25)	Monte Irvin	30.00	15.00	9.00
(26)	Larry Jansen	12.00	6.00	3.50
(27)	George Kell	25.00	12.50	7.50
(28)	Sheldon Jones	12.00	6.00	3.50
(29)	Monte Kennedy	12.00	6.00	3.50
(30)	Ralph Kiner	40.00	20.00	12.00
(31)	Dave Koslo	12.00	6.00	3.50
(32)	Bob Kuzava	15.00	7.50	4.50
(33)	Bob Lemon	30.00	15.00	9.00
(34)	Whitey Lockman	12.00	6.00	3.50
(35)	Eddie Lopat	18.00	9.00	5.50
(36)	Sal Maglie	15.00	7.50	4.50
(37)	Mickey Mantle	1200.00	600.00	360.00
(38)	Billy Martin	50.00	30.00	15.00
(39)	Willie Mays	500.00	250.00	150.00
(40)	Gil McDougal (McDougald)	18.00	9.00	5.50
(41)	Orestes Minoso	15.00	7.50	4.50
(42)	Johnny Mize	40.00	20.00	12.00
(43)	Tom Morgan	15.00	7.50	4.50
(44)	Don Mueller	12.00	6.00	3.50
(45)	Stan Musial	400.00	200.00	120.00
(46)	Don Newcombe	18.00	9.00	5.50
(47)	Ray Noble	12.00	6.00	3.50
(48)	Joe Ostrowski	15.00	7.50	4.50
(49)	Mel Parnell	12.00	6.00	3.50
(50)	Vic Raschi	18.00	9.00	5.50
(51)	Pee Wee Reese	65.00	33.00	20.00
(52)	Allie Reynolds	18.00	9.00	5.50
(53)	Bill Rigney	12.00	6.00	3.50
(54)	Phil Rizzuto (bunting)	55.00	28.00	16.50
(55)	Phil Rizzuto (swinging)	55.00	28.00	16.50
(56)	Robin Roberts	30.00	15.00	9.00
(57)	Eddie Robinson	12.00	6.00	3.50
(58)	Jackie Robinson	200.00	100.00	60.00
(59)	Elwin "Preacher" Roe	15.00	7.50	4.50
(60)	Johnny Sain	15.00	7.50	4.50
(61)	Albert "Red" Schoendienst	30.00	15.00	9.00
(62)	Duke Snider	125.00	56.00	35.00
(63)	George Spencer	12.00	6.00	3.50
(64)	Eddie Stanky	15.00	7.50	4.50
(65)	Henry Thompson	12.00	6.00	3.50
(66)	Bobby Thomson	18.00	9.00	5.50
(67)	Vic Wertz	12.00	6.00	3.50

		NR MT	EX	VG
(68)	Waldon Westlake	12.00	6.00	3.50
(69)	Wes Westrum	12.00	6.00	3.50
(70)	Ted Williams	400.00	200.00	120.00
(71)	Gene Woodling	18.00	9.00	5.50
(72)	Gus Zernial	12.00	6.00	3.50

1911 Big Eater

This very rare set was issued circa 1911 and includes only members of the Pacific Coast League Sacramento Solons. The black and white cards measure 2-1/8" by 4" and feature action photos. The lower part of the card contains a three-line caption that includes the player's last name, team designation (abbreviated to "Sac'to), and the promotional line: "He Eats 'Big Eaters'." (Although the exact origin is undetermined, it is believed that "Big Eaters" were a candy novelty.)

		NR MT	EX	VG
Complete Set:		2750.00	1375.00	825.00
Common Player:		110.00	55.00	33.00
(1)	Arellanes	110.00	55.00	33.00
(2)	Baum	110.00	55.00	33.00
(3)	Byram	110.00	55.00	33.00
(4)	Danzig	110.00	55.00	33.00
(5)	Fitzgerald	110.00	55.00	33.00
(6)	Gaddy	110.00	55.00	33.00
(7)	Heister	110.00	55.00	33.00
(8)	Hunt	110.00	55.00	33.00
(9)	Kerns	110.00	55.00	33.00
(10)	LaLonge	110.00	55.00	33.00
(11)	Lerchen	110.00	55.00	33.00
(12)	Lewis	110.00	55.00	33.00
(13)	Mahoney	110.00	55.00	33.00
(14)	Nebinger	110.00	55.00	33.00
(15)	O'Rourke	110.00	55.00	33.00
(16)	Shinn	110.00	55.00	33.00
(17)	Thomas	110.00	55.00	33.00
(18)	Thompson	110.00	55.00	33.00
(19)	Thornton	110.00	55.00	33.00
(20)	Van Buren	110.00	55.00	33.00

1948 Bowman

Bowman Gum Co.'s premiere set was produced in 1948, making it one of the first major issues of the post-war period. Forty-eight black and white cards comprise the set, with each card measuring 2-1/16" by 2-1/2" in size. The card backs, printed in black ink on grey stock, include the card number and the player's name, team, position, and a short biography. Twelve cards (#'s 7, 8, 13, 16, 20, 22, 24, 26, 29, 30 and 34) were printed in short supply when they were removed from the 36-card printing sheet to make room for the set's high numbers (#'s 37-48). These 24 cards command a higher price than the remaining cards in the set.

		NR MT	EX	VG
Complete Set:		3500.00	1750.00	1050.
Common Player: 1-36		20.00	10.00	6.00
Common Player: 37-48		25.00	12.50	7.50
1	Bob Elliott	100.00	35.00	15.00
2	Ewell (The Whip) Blackwell	25.00	12.50	7.50
3	Ralph Kiner	200.00	100.00	60.00
4	Johnny Mize	110.00	55.00	33.00
5	Bob Feller	225.00	112.00	67.00
6	Larry (Yogi) Berra	600.00	300.00	180.00
7	Pete (Pistol Pete) Reiser	60.00	30.00	18.00
8	Phil (Scooter) Rizzuto	225.00	112.00	67.00
9	Walker Cooper	20.00	10.00	6.00
10	Buddy Rosar	20.00	10.00	6.00
11	Johnny Lindell	20.00	10.00	6.00
12	Johnny Sain	25.00	12.50	7.50
13	Willard Marshall	30.00	15.00	9.00
14	Allie Reynolds	30.00	15.00	9.00
15	Eddie Joost	20.00	10.00	6.00
16	Jack Lohrke	30.00	15.00	9.00
17	Enos (Country) Slaughter	100.00	50.00	30.00
18	Warren Spahn	300.00	150.00	90.00
19	Tommy (The Clutch) Henrich	25.00	12.50	7.50
20	Buddy Kerr	30.00	15.00	9.00
21	Ferris Fain	20.00	10.00	6.00
22	Floyd (Bill) Bevins (Bevens)	40.00	20.00	12.00
23	Larry Jansen	20.00	10.00	6.00
24	Emil (Dutch) Leonard	40.00	20.00	12.00
25	Barney McCoskey (McCosky)	20.00	10.00	6.00
26	Frank Shea	40.00	20.00	12.00
27	Sid Gordon	20.00	10.00	6.00
28	Emil (The Antelope) Verban	30.00	15.00	9.00
29	Joe Page	55.00	33.00	18.00
30	"Whitey" Lockman	40.00	20.00	12.00
31	Bill McCahan	20.00	10.00	6.00
32	Bill Rigney	20.00	10.00	6.00
33	Bill (The Bull) Johnson	20.00	10.00	6.00
34	Sheldon (Available) Jones	30.00	15.00	9.00
35	George (Snuffy) Stirnweiss	20.00	10.00	6.00
36	Stan Musial	900.00	450.00	275.00
37	Clint Hartung	25.00	12.50	7.50
38	Al "Red" Schoendienst	175.00	87.00	52.00
39	Augie Galan	25.00	12.50	7.50
40	Marty Marion	80.00	40.00	25.00
41	Rex Barney	25.00	12.50	7.50
42	Ray Poat	25.00	12.50	7.50
43	Bruce Edwards	25.00	12.50	7.50
44	Johnny Wyrostek	25.00	12.50	7.50
45	Hank Sauer	25.00	12.50	7.50
46	Herman Wehmeier	25.00	12.50	7.50
47	Bobby Thomson	80.00	40.00	25.00
48	George "Dave" Koslo	70.00	20.00	10.00

1949 Bowman

In 1949, Bowman increased the size of its issue to 240 numbered cards. The cards, which measure 2-1/16" by 2-1/2", are black and white photos overprinted with various pastel colors. Beginning with card #109 in the set, Bowman inserted the player's names on the card fronts. Twelve cards (#'s 4, 78, 83, 85, 88, 98, 109, 124, 127, 132 and 143), which were produced in the first four series of printings, were reprinted in the seventh series with either a card front or back modification. These variations are noted in the checklist that follows. Card #'s 1-3 and 5-73 can be found with either white or grey backs. The complete set of value in the following checklist does not include the higher priced variation cards.

		NR MT	EX	VG
Complete Set:		16500.00	8250.00	4900.
Common Player: 1-36		15.00	7.50	4.50
Common Player: 37-73		18.00	9.00	5.50
Common Player: 74-144		15.00	7.50	4.50
Common Player: 145-240		70.00	35.00	21.00
1	Vernon Bickford	100.00	30.00	15.00
2	Carroll "Whitey" Lockman	18.00	9.00	5.50
3	Bob Porterfield	18.00	9.00	5.50
4a	Jerry Priddy (no name on front)	18.00	9.00	5.50
4b	Jerry Priddy (name on front)	40.00	20.00	12.00
5	Hank Sauer	15.00	7.50	4.50
6	Phil Cavarretta	20.00	10.00	6.00
7	Joe Dobson	15.00	7.50	4.50
8	Murry Dickson	15.00	7.50	4.50
9	Ferris Fain	18.00	9.00	5.50
10	Ted Gray	15.00	7.50	4.50
11	Lou Boudreau	60.00	30.00	18.00
12	Cass Michaels	15.00	7.50	4.50
13	Bob Chesnes	15.00	7.50	4.50
14	Curt Simmons	35.00	17.50	10.50
15	Ned Garver	15.00	7.50	4.50
16	Al Kozar	15.00	7.50	4.50
17	Earl Torgeson	15.00	7.50	4.50
18	Bobby Thomson	35.00	17.50	10.50
19	Bobby Brown	60.00	30.00	18.00
20	Gene Hermanski	18.00	9.00	5.50
21	Frank Baumholtz	15.00	7.50	4.50
22	Harry "P-Nuts" Lowrey	15.00	7.50	4.50
23	Bobby Doerr	70.00	35.00	21.00
24	Stan Musial	600.00	300.00	180.00
25	Carl Scheib	15.00	7.50	4.50
26	George Kell	60.00	30.00	18.00
27	Bob Feller	150.00	75.00	45.00
28	Don Kolloway	15.00	7.50	4.50
29	Ralph Kiner	90.00	45.00	27.00
30	Andy Seminick	15.00	7.50	4.50
31	Dick Kokos	15.00	7.50	4.50
32	Eddie Yost	15.00	7.50	4.50
33	Warren Spahn	175.00	87.00	52.00
34	Dave Koslo	15.00	7.50	4.50
35	Vic Raschi	20.00	10.00	6.00
36	Harold "Peewee" Reese	200.00	100.00	60.00
37	John Wyrostek	18.00	9.00	5.50
38	Emil "The Antelope" Verban	18.00	9.00	5.50
39	Bill Goodman	18.00	9.00	5.50
40	George "Red" Munger	18.00	9.00	5.50
41	Lou Brissie	18.00	9.00	5.50
42	Walter "Hoot" Evers	18.00	9.00	5.50
43	Dale Mitchell	18.00	9.00	5.50
44	Dave Philley	18.00	9.00	5.50
45	Wally Westlake	18.00	9.00	5.50
46	Robin Roberts	275.00	137.00	82.00
47	Johnny Sain	18.00	9.00	5.50
48	Willard Marshall	18.00	9.00	5.50
49	Frank Shea	18.00	9.00	5.50
50	Jackie Robinson	900.00	450.00	275.00
51	Herman Wehmeier	18.00	9.00	5.50
52	Johnny Schmitz	18.00	9.00	5.50
53	Jack Kramer	18.00	9.00	5.50
54	Marty "Slats" Marion	20.00	10.00	6.00
55	Eddie Joost	18.00	9.00	5.50
56	Pat Mullin	18.00	9.00	5.50
57	Gene Bearden	18.00	9.00	5.50
58	Bob Elliott	18.00	9.00	5.50
59	Jack "Lucky" Lohrke	18.00	9.00	5.50
60	Larry "Yogi" Berra	300.00	150.00	90.00
61	Rex Barney	20.00	10.00	6.00
62	Grady Hatton	18.00	9.00	5.50
63	Andy Pafko	20.00	10.00	6.00
64	Dom "The Little Professor" DiMaggio	30.00	15.00	9.00
65	Enos "Country" Slaughter	75.00	37.00	23.00
66	Elmer Valo	18.00	9.00	5.50
67	Alvin Dark	30.00	15.00	9.00
68	Sheldon "Available" Jones	18.00	9.00	5.50
69	Tommy "The Clutch" Henrich	25.00	12.50	7.50
70	Carl Furillo	60.00	30.00	18.00
71	Vern "Junior" Stephens	18.00	9.00	5.50
72	Tommy Holmes	20.00	10.00	6.00
73	Billy Cox	20.00	10.00	6.00
74	Tom McBride	15.00	7.50	4.50
75	Eddie Mayo	15.00	7.50	4.50
76	Bill Nicholson	15.00	7.50	4.50
77	Ernie (Jumbo and Tiny) Bonham	15.00	7.50	4.50
78a	Sam Zoldak (no name on front)	18.00	9.00	5.50
78b	Sam Zoldak (name on front)	40.00	20.00	12.00
79	Ron Northey	15.00	7.50	4.50
80	Bill McCahan	15.00	7.50	4.50
81	Virgil "Red" Stallcup	15.00	7.50	4.50
82	Joe Page	20.00	10.00	6.00
83a	Bob Scheffing (no name on front)	18.00	9.00	5.50
83b	Bob Scheffing (name on front)	40.00	20.00	12.00
84	Roy Campanella	800.00	400.00	250.00
85a	Johnny "Big John" Mize (no name on front)	75.00	37.00	23.00
85b	Johnny "Big John" Mize (name on front)	125.00	62.00	37.00
86	Johnny Pesky	18.00	9.00	5.50
87	Randy Gumpert	15.00	7.50	4.50
88a	Bill Salkeld (no name on front)	18.00	9.00	5.50
88b	Bill Salkeld (name on front)	40.00	20.00	12.00
89	Mizell "Whitey" Platt	15.00	7.50	4.50
90	Gil Coan	15.00	7.50	4.50
91	Dick Wakefield	15.00	7.50	4.50
92	Willie "Puddin-Head" Jones	15.00	7.50	4.50
93	Ed Stevens	15.00	7.50	4.50
94	James "Mickey" Vernon	18.00	9.00	5.50
95	Howie Pollett	15.00	7.50	4.50
96	Taft Wright	15.00	7.50	4.50
97	Danny Litwhiler	15.00	7.50	4.50
98a	Phil Rizzuto (no name on front)	100.00	50.00	30.00
98b	Phil Rizzuto (name on front)	200.00	100.00	60.00
99	Frank Gustine	15.00	7.50	4.50
100	Gil Hodges	200.00	100.00	60.00
101	Sid Gordon	15.00	7.50	4.50
102	Stan Spence	15.00	7.50	4.50
103	Joe Tipton	15.00	7.50	4.50
104	Ed Stanky	18.00	9.00	5.50
105	Bill Kennedy	15.00	7.50	4.50
106	Jake Early	15.00	7.50	4.50
107	Eddie Lake	15.00	7.50	4.50
108	Ken Heintzelman	15.00	7.50	4.50
109a	Ed Fitzgerald (Fitz Gerald) (script name on back)	18.00	9.00	5.50
109b	Ed Fitzgerald (Fitz Gerald) (printed name on back)	40.00	20.00	12.00
110	Early Wynn	125.00	62.00	37.00
111	Al "Red" Schoendienst	80.00	40.00	25.00
112	Sam Chapman	15.00	7.50	4.50
113	Ray Lamanno	15.00	7.50	4.50
114	Allie Reynolds	30.00	15.00	9.00
115	Emil "Dutch" Leonard	15.00	7.50	4.50
116	Joe Hatten	18.00	9.00	5.50
117	Walker Cooper	15.00	7.50	4.50
118	Sam Mele	15.00	7.50	4.50
119	Floyd Baker	15.00	7.50	4.50
120	Cliff Fannin	15.00	7.50	4.50
121	Mark Christman	15.00	7.50	4.50
122	George Vico	15.00	7.50	4.50
123	Johnny Blatnick	15.00	7.50	4.50
124a	Danny Murtaugh (script name on back)	18.00	9.00	5.50
124b	Danny Murtaugh (printed name on back)	40.00	20.00	12.00
125	Ken Keltner	18.00	9.00	5.50
126a	Al Brazle (script name on back)	18.00	9.00	5.50
126b	Al Brazle (printed name on back)	40.00	20.00	12.00
127a	Henry "Heeney" Majeski (script name on back)	18.00	9.00	5.50
127b	Henry "Heeney" Majeski (printed name on back)	40.00	20.00	12.00
128	Johnny Vander Meer	20.00	10.00	6.00
129	Bill "The Bull" Johnson	20.00	10.00	6.00
130	Harry "The Hat" Walker	18.00	9.00	5.50
131	Paul Lehner	15.00	7.50	4.50
132a	Al Evans (script name on back)	18.00	9.00	5.50
132b	Al Evans (printed name on back)	40.00	20.00	12.00
133	Aaron Robinson	15.00	7.50	4.50
134	Hank Borowy	15.00	7.50	4.50
135	Stan Rojek	15.00	7.50	4.50
136	Henry "Hank" Edwards	15.00	7.50	4.50
137	Ted Wilks	15.00	7.50	4.50
138	Warren "Buddy" Rosar	15.00	7.50	4.50
139	Hank "Bow-Wow" Arft	15.00	7.50	4.50

		NR MT	EX	VG
140	Rae Scarborough (Ray)	15.00	7.50	4.50
141	Ulysses "Tony" Lupien	15.00	7.50	4.50
142	Eddie Waitkus	15.00	7.50	4.50
143a	Bob Dillinger (script name on back)			
		18.00	9.00	5.50
143b	Bob Dillinger (printed name on back)			
		40.00	20.00	12.00
144	Milton "Mickey" Haefner	15.00	7.50	4.50
145	Sylvester "Blix" Donnelly	70.00	35.00	21.00
146	Myron "Mike" McCormick	75.00	37.00	22.00
147	Elmer "Bert" Singleton	70.00	35.00	21.00
148	Bob Swift	70.00	35.00	21.00
149	Roy Partee	75.00	37.00	22.00
150	Alfred "Allie" Clark	70.00	35.00	21.00
151	Maurice "Mickey" Harris	70.00	35.00	21.00
152	Clarence Maddern	70.00	35.00	21.00
153	Phil Masi	70.00	35.00	21.00
154	Clint Hartung	70.00	35.00	21.00
155	Fermin "Mickey" Guerra	70.00	35.00	21.00
156	Al "Zeke" Zarilla	70.00	35.00	21.00
157	Walt Masterson	70.00	35.00	21.00
158	Harry "The Cat" Brecheen	70.00	35.00	21.00
159	Glen Moulder	70.00	35.00	21.00
160	Jim Blackburn	70.00	35.00	21.00
161	John "Jocko" Thompson	70.00	35.00	21.00
162	Elwin "Preacher" Roe	150.00	75.00	50.00
163	Clyde McCullough	70.00	35.00	21.00
164	Vic Wertz	110.00	55.00	33.00
165	George "Snuffy" Stirnweiss	70.00	35.00	21.00
166	Mike Tresh	70.00	35.00	21.00
167	Boris "Babe" Martin	70.00	35.00	21.00
168	Doyle Lade	70.00	35.00	21.00
169	Jeff Heath	70.00	35.00	21.00
170	Bill Rigney	75.00	37.00	22.00
171	Dick Fowler	70.00	35.00	21.00
172	Eddie Pellagrini	70.00	35.00	21.00
173	Eddie Stewart	70.00	35.00	21.00
174	Terry Moore	75.00	37.00	22.00
175	Luke Appling	125.00	62.00	37.00
176	Ken Raffensberger	70.00	35.00	21.00
177	Stan Lopata	70.00	35.00	21.00
178	Tommy Brown	75.00	37.00	22.00
179	Hugh Casey	75.00	37.00	22.00
180	Connie Berry	70.00	35.00	21.00
181	Gus Niarhos	70.00	35.00	21.00
182	Hal Peck	70.00	35.00	21.00
183	Lou Stringer	70.00	35.00	21.00
184	Bob Chipman	70.00	35.00	21.00
185	Pete Reiser	75.00	37.00	22.00
186	John "Buddy" Kerr	70.00	35.00	21.00
187	Phil Marchildon	70.00	35.00	21.00
188	Karl Drews	70.00	35.00	21.00
189	Earl Wooten	70.00	35.00	21.00
190	Jim Hearn	70.00	35.00	21.00
191	Joe Haynes	70.00	35.00	21.00
192	Harry Gumbert	70.00	35.00	21.00
193	Ken Trinkle	70.00	35.00	21.00
194	Ralph Branca	110.00	55.00	33.00
195	Eddie Bockman	70.00	35.00	21.00
196	Fred Hutchinson	75.00	37.00	22.00
197	Johnny Lindell	70.00	35.00	21.00
198	Steve Gromek	70.00	35.00	21.00
199	Cecil "Tex" Hughson	70.00	35.00	21.00
200	Jess Dobernic	70.00	35.00	21.00
201	Sibby Sisti	70.00	35.00	21.00
202	Larry Jansen	70.00	35.00	21.00
203	Barney McCosky	70.00	35.00	21.00
204	Bob Savage	70.00	35.00	21.00
205	Dick Sisler	70.00	35.00	21.00
206	Bruce Edwards	75.00	37.00	22.00
207	Johnny "Hippity" Hopp	70.00	35.00	21.00
208	Paul "Dizzy" Trout	75.00	37.00	22.00
209	Charlie "King Kong" Keller	100.00	50.00	30.00
210	Joe "Flash" Gordon	75.00	37.00	22.00
211	Dave "Boo" Ferris	70.00	35.00	21.00
212	Ralph Hamner	70.00	35.00	21.00
213	Charles "Red" Barrett	70.00	35.00	21.00
214	*Richie Ashburn*	550.00	275.00	165.00
215	Kirby Higbe	70.00	35.00	21.00
216	Lynwood "Schoolboy" Rowe	70.00	35.00	21.00
217	Marino Pieretti	70.00	35.00	21.00
218	Dick Kryhoski	70.00	35.00	21.00
219	Virgil "Fire" Trucks	75.00	37.00	22.00
220	Johnny McCarthy	70.00	35.00	21.00
221	Bob Muncrief	70.00	35.00	21.00
222	Alex Kellner	70.00	35.00	21.00
223	Bob Hoffman (Hofman)	70.00	35.00	21.00
224	*Leroy "Satchel" Paige*	1200.00	600.00	350.00
225	Gerry Coleman	100.00	50.00	30.00
226	Edwin "Duke" Snider	1200.00	600.00	350.00
227	Fritz Ostermueller	70.00	35.00	21.00

		NR MT	EX	VG
228	Jackie Mayo	70.00	35.00	21.00
229	Ed Lopat	125.00	60.00	40.00
230	Augie Galan	70.00	35.00	21.00
231	Earl Johnson	70.00	35.00	21.00
232	George McQuinn	70.00	35.00	21.00
233	*Larry Doby*	175.00	87.00	52.00
234	Truett "Rip" Sewell	75.00	37.00	22.00
235	Jim Russell	70.00	35.00	21.00
236	Fred Sanford	70.00	35.00	21.00
237	Monte Kennedy	70.00	35.00	21.00
238	Bob Lemon	250.00	125.00	75.00
239	Frank McCormick	70.00	35.00	21.00
240	Norman "Babe" Young (photo actually			
	Bobby Young)	150.00	75.00	45.00

1949 Bowman
Pacific Coast League

One of the scarcest issues of the post-war period, the 1949 Bowman PCL set was issued only on the West Coast. Like the 1949 Bowman regular issue, the cards contain black and white photos overprinted with various pastel colors. Thirty-six cards, which measure 2-1/16" by 2-1/2", make up the set. It is believed that the cards may have been issued only in sheets and not sold in gum packs.

		NR MT	EX	VG
	Complete Set:	5500.00	2750.00	1650.
	Common Player:	150.00	75.00	45.00
1	Lee Anthony	150.00	75.00	45.00
2	George Metkovich	150.00	75.00	45.00
3	Ralph Hodgin	150.00	75.00	45.00
4	George Woods	150.00	75.00	45.00
5	Xavier Rescigno	150.00	75.00	45.00
6	Mickey Grasso	150.00	75.00	45.00
7	Johnny Rucker	150.00	75.00	45.00
8	Jack Brewer	150.00	75.00	45.00
9	Dom D'Allessandro	150.00	75.00	45.00
10	Charlie Gassaway	150.00	75.00	45.00
11	Tony Freitas	150.00	75.00	45.00
12	Gordon Maltzberger	150.00	75.00	45.00
13	John Jensen	150.00	75.00	45.00
14	Joyner White	150.00	75.00	45.00
15	Harvey Storey	150.00	75.00	45.00
16	Dick Lajeski	150.00	75.00	45.00
17	Albie Glossop	150.00	75.00	45.00
18	Bill Raimondi	150.00	75.00	45.00
19	Ken Holcombe	150.00	75.00	45.00
20	Don Ross	150.00	75.00	45.00
21	Pete Coscarart	150.00	75.00	45.00
22	Tony York	150.00	75.00	45.00
23	Jake Mooty	150.00	75.00	45.00
24	Charles Adams	150.00	75.00	45.00
25	Les Scarsella	150.00	75.00	45.00
26	Joe Marty	150.00	75.00	45.00
27	Frank Kelleher	150.00	75.00	45.00
28	Lee Handley	150.00	75.00	45.00
29	Herman Besse	150.00	75.00	45.00
30	John Lazor	150.00	75.00	45.00
31	Eddie Malone	150.00	75.00	45.00
32	Maurice Van Robays	150.00	75.00	45.00
33	Jim Tabor	150.00	75.00	45.00
34	Gene Handley	150.00	75.00	45.00
35	Tom Seats	150.00	75.00	45.00

		NR MT	EX	VG
36	Ora Burnett	150.00	75.00	45.00

1950 Bowman

The quality of the 1950 Bowman issue showed a marked improvement over the company's previous efforts. The cards are beautiful color art reproductions of actual photographs and measure 2-1/16" by 2-1/2" in size. The card backs include the same type of information as found in the previous year's issue but are designed in a horizontal format. Cards found in the first two series of the set (#'s 1-72) are the scarcest in the issue. The backs of the final 72 cards in the set (#'s 181-252) can be found with or without the copyright line at the bottom of the card, the "without" version being the less common.

	NR MT	EX	VG
Complete Set:	10000.00	5000.00	3000.
Common Player: 1-72	50.00	25.00	15.00
Common Player: 73-252	16.00	8.00	4.75

		NR MT	EX	VG
1	Mel Parnell	200.00	25.00	8.00
2	Vern Stephens	50.00	25.00	15.00
3	Dom DiMaggio	60.00	30.00	18.00
4	Gus Zernial	50.00	25.00	15.00
5	Bob Kuzava	50.00	25.00	15.00
6	Bob Feller	200.00	100.00	60.00
7	Jim Hegan	50.00	25.00	15.00
8	George Kell	100.00	50.00	30.00
9	Vic Wertz	50.00	25.00	15.00
10	Tommy Henrich	60.00	30.00	18.00
11	Phil Rizzuto	150.00	75.00	45.00
12	Joe Page	50.00	25.00	15.00
13	Ferris Fain	50.00	25.00	15.00
14	Alex Kellner	50.00	25.00	15.00
15	Al Kozar	50.00	25.00	15.00
16	*Roy Sievers*	50.00	25.00	15.00
17	Sid Hudson	50.00	25.00	15.00
18	Eddie Robinson	50.00	25.00	15.00
19	Warren Spahn	200.00	100.00	60.00
20	Bob Elliott	50.00	25.00	15.00
21	Harold Reese	200.00	100.00	60.00
22	Jackie Robinson	700.00	350.00	200.00
23	*Don Newcombe*	150.00	75.00	50.00
24	Johnny Schmitz	50.00	25.00	15.00
25	Hank Sauer	50.00	25.00	15.00
26	Grady Hatton	50.00	25.00	15.00
27	Herman Wehmeier	50.00	25.00	15.00
28	Bobby Thomson	70.00	35.00	21.00
29	Ed Stanky	50.00	25.00	15.00
30	Eddie Waitkus	50.00	25.00	15.00
31	Del Ennis	50.00	25.00	15.00
32	Robin Roberts	150.00	75.00	45.00
33	Ralph Kiner	125.00	62.00	37.00
34	Murry Dickson	50.00	25.00	15.00
35	Enos Slaughter	100.00	50.00	30.00
36	Eddie Kazak	50.00	25.00	15.00
37	Luke Appling	70.00	35.00	21.00
38	Bill Wight	50.00	25.00	15.00
39	Larry Doby	60.00	30.00	18.00
40	Bob Lemon	100.00	50.00	30.00
41	Walter "Hoot" Evers	50.00	25.00	15.00
42	Art Houtteman	50.00	25.00	15.00
43	Bobby Doerr	80.00	40.00	25.00
44	Joe Dobson	50.00	25.00	15.00
45	Al "Zeke" Zarilla	50.00	25.00	15.00

		NR MT	EX	VG
46	Larry "Yogi" Berra	400.00	200.00	125.00
47	Jerry Coleman	55.00	27.00	16.50
48	Leland "Lou" Brissie	50.00	25.00	15.00
49	Elmer Valo	50.00	25.00	15.00
50	Dick Kokos	50.00	25.00	15.00
51	Ned Garver	50.00	25.00	15.00
52	Sam Mele	50.00	25.00	15.00
53	Clyde Vollmer	50.00	25.00	15.00
54	Gil Coan	50.00	25.00	15.00
55	John "Buddy" Kerr	50.00	25.00	15.00
56	*Del Crandell (Crandall)*	70.00	35.00	21.00
57	Vernon Bickford	50.00	25.00	15.00
58	Carl Furillo	70.00	35.00	21.00
59	Ralph Branca	60.00	30.00	18.00
60	Andy Pafko	50.00	25.00	15.00
61	Bob Rush	50.00	25.00	15.00
62	Ted Kluszewski	70.00	35.00	21.00
63	Ewell Blackwell	50.00	25.00	15.00
64	Alvin Dark	50.00	25.00	15.00
65	Dave Koslo	50.00	25.00	15.00
66	Larry Jansen	50.00	25.00	15.00
67	Willie Jones	50.00	25.00	15.00
68	Curt Simmons	50.00	25.00	15.00
69	Wally Westlake	50.00	25.00	15.00
70	Bob Chesnes	50.00	25.00	15.00
71	Al Schoendienst	100.00	50.00	30.00
72	Howie Pollet	50.00	25.00	15.00
73	Willard Marshall	16.00	8.00	4.75
74	*Johnny Antonelli*	16.00	8.00	4.75
75	Roy Campanella	300.00	150.00	90.00
76	Rex Barney	16.00	8.00	4.75
77	Edwin "Duke" Snider	300.00	150.00	90.00
78	Mickey Owen	16.00	8.00	4.75
79	Johnny Vander Meer	16.00	8.00	4.75
80	Howard Fox	16.00	8.00	4.75
81	Ron Northey	16.00	8.00	4.75
82	Carroll Lockman	16.00	8.00	4.75
83	Sheldon Jones	16.00	8.00	4.75
84	Richie Ashburn	75.00	38.00	23.00
85	Ken Heintzelman	16.00	8.00	4.75
86	Stan Rojek	16.00	8.00	4.75
87	Bill Werle	16.00	8.00	4.75
88	Marty Marion	16.00	8.00	4.75
89	George Munger	16.00	8.00	4.75
90	Harry Brecheen	16.00	8.00	4.75
91	Cass Michaels	16.00	8.00	4.75
92	Hank Majeski	16.00	8.00	4.75
93	Gene Bearden	16.00	8.00	4.75
94	Lou Boudreau	50.00	25.00	15.00
95	Aaron Robinson	16.00	8.00	4.75
96	Virgil "Fire" Trucks	16.00	8.00	4.75
97	Maurice McDermott	16.00	8.00	4.75
98	Ted Williams	800.00	400.00	250.00
99	Billy Goodman	16.00	8.00	4.75
100	Vic Raschi	20.00	10.00	6.00
101	Bobby Brown	20.00	10.00	6.00
102	Billy Johnson	16.00	8.00	4.75
103	Eddie Joost	16.00	8.00	4.75
104	Sam Chapman	16.00	8.00	4.75
105	Bob Dillinger	16.00	8.00	4.75
106	Cliff Fannin	16.00	8.00	4.75
107	Sam Dente	16.00	8.00	4.75
108	Rae Scarborough (Ray)	16.00	8.00	4.75
109	Sid Gordon	16.00	8.00	4.75
110	Tommy Holmes	16.00	8.00	4.75
111	Walker Cooper	16.00	8.00	4.75
112	Gil Hodges	80.00	40.00	24.00
113	Gene Hermanski	16.00	8.00	4.75
114	Wayne Terwilliger	16.00	8.00	4.75
115	Roy Smalley	16.00	8.00	4.75
116	Virgil "Red" Stallcup	16.00	8.00	4.75
117	Bill Rigney	16.00	8.00	4.75
118	Clint Hartung	16.00	8.00	4.75
119	Dick Sisler	16.00	8.00	4.75
120	John Thompson	16.00	8.00	4.75
121	Andy Seminick	16.00	8.00	4.75
122	Johnny Hopp	16.00	8.00	4.75
123	Dino Restelli	16.00	8.00	4.75
124	Clyde McCullough	16.00	8.00	4.75
125	Del Rice	16.00	8.00	4.75
126	Al Brazle	16.00	8.00	4.75
127	Dave Philley	16.00	8.00	4.75
128	Phil Masi	16.00	8.00	4.75
129	Joe "Flash" Gordon	16.00	8.00	4.75
130	Dale Mitchell	16.00	8.00	4.75
131	Steve Gromek	16.00	8.00	4.75
132	James Vernon	16.00	8.00	4.75
133	Don Kolloway	16.00	8.00	4.75
134	Paul "Dizzy" Trout	16.00	8.00	4.75
135	Pat Mullin	16.00	8.00	4.75
136	Warren Rosar	16.00	8.00	4.75

		NR MT	EX	VG
137	Johnny Pesky	16.00	8.00	4.75
138	Allie Reynolds	60.00	30.00	18.00
139	Johnny Mize	60.00	30.00	18.00
140	Pete Suder	16.00	8.00	4.75
141	Joe Coleman	16.00	8.00	4.75
142	*Sherman Lollar*	16.00	8.00	4.75
143	Eddie Stewart	16.00	8.00	4.75
144	Al Evans	16.00	8.00	4.75
145	Jack Graham	16.00	8.00	4.75
146	Floyd Baker	16.00	8.00	4.75
147	*Mike Garcia*	16.00	8.00	4.75
148	Early Wynn	70.00	35.00	21.00
149	Bob Swift	16.00	8.00	4.75
150	George Vico	16.00	8.00	4.75
151	Fred Hutchinson	16.00	8.00	4.75
152	Ellis Kinder	16.00	8.00	4.75
153	Walt Masterson	16.00	8.00	4.75
154	Gus Niarhos	16.00	8.00	4.75
155	Frank "Spec" Shea	16.00	8.00	4.75
156	Fred Sanford	16.00	8.00	4.75
157	Mike Guerra	16.00	8.00	4.75
158	Paul Lehner	16.00	8.00	4.75
159	Joe Tipton	16.00	8.00	4.75
160	Mickey Harris	16.00	8.00	4.75
161	Sherry Robertson	16.00	8.00	4.75
162	Eddie Yost	16.00	8.00	4.75
163	Earl Torgeson	16.00	8.00	4.75
164	Sibby Sisti	16.00	8.00	4.75
165	Bruce Edwards	16.00	8.00	4.75
166	Joe Hatten	16.00	8.00	4.75
167	Elwin Roe	60.00	30.00	18.00
168	Bob Scheffing	16.00	8.00	4.75
169	Hank Edwards	16.00	8.00	4.75
170	Emil Leonard	16.00	8.00	4.75
171	Harry Gumbert	16.00	8.00	4.75
172	Harry Lowrey	16.00	8.00	4.75
173	Lloyd Merriman	16.00	8.00	4.75
174	Henry Thompson	16.00	8.00	4.75
175	Monte Kennedy	16.00	8.00	4.75
176	Sylvester Donnelly	16.00	8.00	4.75
177	Hank Borowy	16.00	8.00	4.75
178	Eddy Fitzgerald (Fitz Gerald)	16.00	8.00	4.75
179	Charles Diering	16.00	8.00	4.75
180	Harry Walker	16.00	8.00	4.75
181	Marino Pieretti	16.00	8.00	4.75
182	Sam Zoldak	16.00	8.00	4.75
183	Mickey Haefner	16.00	8.00	4.75
184	Randy Gumpert	16.00	8.00	4.75
185	Howie Judson	16.00	8.00	4.75
186	Ken Keltner	16.00	8.00	4.75
187	Lou Stringer	16.00	8.00	4.75
188	Earl Johnson	16.00	8.00	4.75
189	Owen Friend	16.00	8.00	4.75
190	Ken Wood	16.00	8.00	4.75
191	Dick Starr	16.00	8.00	4.75
192	Bob Chipman	16.00	8.00	4.75
193	Harold "Pete" Reiser	16.00	8.00	4.75
194	Billy Cox	16.00	8.00	4.75
195	Phil Cavaretta (Cavarretta)	16.00	8.00	4.75
196	Doyle Lade	16.00	8.00	4.75
197	Johnny Wyrostek	16.00	8.00	4.75
198	Danny Litwhiler	16.00	8.00	4.75
199	Jack Kramer	16.00	8.00	4.75
200	Kirby Higbe	16.00	8.00	4.75
201	Pete Castiglione	16.00	8.00	4.75
202	Cliff Chambers	16.00	8.00	4.75
203	Danny Murtaugh	16.00	8.00	4.75
204	Granville Hamner	16.00	8.00	4.75
205	Mike Goliat	16.00	8.00	4.75
206	Stan Lopata	16.00	8.00	4.75
207	Max Lanier	16.00	8.00	4.75
208	Jim Hearn	16.00	8.00	4.75
209	Johnny Lindell	16.00	8.00	4.75
210	Ted Gray	16.00	8.00	4.75
211	Charlie Keller	16.00	8.00	4.75
212	Gerry Priddy	16.00	8.00	4.75
213	Carl Scheib	16.00	8.00	4.75
214	Dick Fowler	16.00	8.00	4.75
215	Ed Lopat	20.00	10.00	6.00
216	Bob Porterfield	16.00	8.00	4.75
217	Casey Stengel	150.00	75.00	45.00
218	Cliff Mapes	16.00	8.00	4.75
219	*Hank Bauer*	70.00	35.00	20.00
220	Leo Durocher	60.00	30.00	18.00
221	Don Mueller	16.00	8.00	4.75
222	Bobby Morgan	16.00	8.00	4.75
223	Jimmy Russell	16.00	8.00	4.75
224	Jack Banta	16.00	8.00	4.75
225	Eddie Sawyer	16.00	8.00	4.75
226	Jim Konstanty	16.00	8.00	4.75
227	Bob Miller	16.00	8.00	4.75

		NR MT	EX	VG
228	Bill Nicholson	16.00	8.00	4.75
229	Frank Frisch	60.00	30.00	18.00
230	Bill Serena	16.00	8.00	4.75
231	Preston Ward	16.00	8.00	4.75
232	*Al "Flip" Rosen*	70.00	35.00	21.00
233	Allie Clark	16.00	8.00	4.75
234	*Bobby Shantz*	25.00	12.50	7.50
235	Harold Gilbert	16.00	8.00	4.75
236	Bob Cain	16.00	8.00	4.75
237	Bill Salkeld	16.00	8.00	4.75
238	Vernal Jones	16.00	8.00	4.75
239	Bill Howerton	16.00	8.00	4.75
240	Eddie Lake	16.00	8.00	4.75
241	Neil Berry	16.00	8.00	4.75
242	Dick Kryhoski	16.00	8.00	4.75
243	Johnny Groth	16.00	8.00	4.75
244	Dale Coogan	16.00	8.00	4.75
245	Al Papai	16.00	8.00	4.75
246	*Walt Dropo*	25.00	12.50	7.50
247	Irv Noren	16.00	8.00	4.75
248	*Sam Jethroe*	16.00	8.00	4.75
249	George Stirnweiss	16.00	8.00	4.75
250	Ray Coleman	16.00	8.00	4.75
251	John Lester Moss	16.00	8.00	4.75
252	Billy DeMars	100.00	50.00	30.00

1951 Bowman

In 1951, Bowman increased the numbers of cards in its set for the third consecutive year when it issued 324 cards. The cards are, like 1950, color art reproductions of actual photographs but now measured 2-1/16" by 3-1/8" in size. The player's name is situated in a small, black box on the card front. Several of the card fronts are enlargements of the 1950 version. The high-numbered series of the set (#'s 253-324), which includes the rookie cards of Mantle and Mays, are the scarcest of the issue.

		NR MT	EX	VG
Complete Set:		22500.00	11250.00	6600.
Common Player: 1-36		20.00	10.00	6.00
Common Player: 37-252		14.00	7.00	4.25
Common Player: 253-324		60.00	30.00	18.00
1	*Ed Ford*	1300.00	575.00	300.00
2	Larry "Yogi" Berra	450.00	225.00	135.00
3	Robin Roberts	80.00	40.00	25.00
4	Del Ennis	20.00	10.00	6.00
5	Dale Mitchell	20.00	10.00	6.00
6	Don Newcombe	35.00	17.50	10.50
7	Gil Hodges	90.00	45.00	27.00
8	Paul Lehner	20.00	10.00	6.00
9	Sam Chapman	20.00	10.00	6.00
10	Al "Red" Schoendienst	80.00	40.00	25.00
11	George "Red" Munger	20.00	10.00	6.00
12	Hank Majeski	20.00	10.00	6.00
13	Ed Stanky	20.00	10.00	6.00
14	Alvin Dark	22.00	11.00	6.50
15	Johnny Pesky	20.00	10.00	6.00
16	Maurice McDermott	20.00	10.00	6.00
17	Pete Castiglione	20.00	10.00	6.00
18	Gil Coan	20.00	10.00	6.00
19	Sid Gordon	20.00	10.00	6.00
20	Del Crandall	20.00	10.00	6.00
21	George "Snuffy" Stirnweiss	20.00	10.00	6.00
22	Hank Sauer	20.00	10.00	6.00

#	Name	NR MT	EX	VG
23	Walter "Hoot" Evers	20.00	10.00	6.00
24	Ewell Blackwell	20.00	10.00	6.00
25	Vic Raschi	30.00	15.00	9.00
26	Phil Rizzuto	100.00	50.00	30.00
27	Jim Konstanty	20.00	10.00	6.00
28	Eddie Waitkus	20.00	10.00	6.00
29	Allie Clark	20.00	10.00	6.00
30	Bob Feller	125.00	62.00	37.00
31	Roy Campanella	260.00	130.00	78.00
32	Duke Snider	250.00	125.00	75.00
33	Bob Hooper	20.00	10.00	6.00
34	Marty Marion	20.00	10.00	6.00
35	Al Zarilla	20.00	10.00	6.00
36	Joe Dobson	20.00	10.00	6.00
37	Whitey Lockman	14.00	7.00	4.25
38	Al Evans	14.00	7.00	4.25
39	Ray Scarborough	14.00	7.00	4.25
40	Dave "Gus" Bell	20.00	10.00	6.00
41	Eddie Yost	20.00	10.00	6.00
42	Vern Bickford	14.00	7.00	4.25
43	Billy DeMars	14.00	7.00	4.25
44	Roy Smalley	14.00	7.00	4.25
45	Art Houtteman	14.00	7.00	4.25
46	George Kell	65.00	32.50	19.50
47	Grady Hatton	14.00	7.00	4.25
48	Ken Raffensberger	14.00	7.00	4.25
49	Jerry Coleman	20.00	10.00	6.00
50	Johnny Mize	60.00	30.00	18.00
51	Andy Seminick	14.00	7.00	4.25
52	Dick Sisler	14.00	7.00	4.25
53	Bob Lemon	50.00	25.00	15.00
54	Ray Boone	20.00	10.00	6.00
55	Gene Hermanski	20.00	10.00	6.00
56	Ralph Branca	30.00	15.00	9.00
57	Alex Kellner	14.00	7.00	4.25
58	Enos Slaughter	60.00	30.00	18.00
59	Randy Gumpert	14.00	7.00	4.25
60	Alfonso Carrasquel	14.00	7.00	4.25
61	Jim Hearn	14.00	7.00	4.25
62	Lou Boudreau	55.00	27.50	16.50
63	Bob Dillinger	14.00	7.00	4.25
64	Bill Werle	14.00	7.00	4.25
65	Mickey Vernon	20.00	10.00	6.00
66	Bob Elliott	14.00	7.00	4.25
67	Roy Sievers	20.00	10.00	6.00
68	Dick Kokos	14.00	7.00	4.25
69	Johnny Schmitz	14.00	7.00	4.25
70	Ron Northey	14.00	7.00	4.25
71	Jerry Priddy	14.00	7.00	4.25
72	Lloyd Merriman	14.00	7.00	4.25
73	Tommy Byrne	20.00	10.00	6.00
74	Billy Johnson	20.00	10.00	6.00
75	Russ Meyer	14.00	7.00	4.25
76	Stan Lopata	14.00	7.00	4.25
77	Mike Goliat	14.00	7.00	4.25
78	Early Wynn	60.00	30.00	18.00
79	Jim Hegan	14.00	7.00	4.25
80	Harold "Peewee" Reese	150.00	75.00	50.00
81	Carl Furillo	40.00	20.00	12.00
82	Joe Tipton	14.00	7.00	4.25
83	Carl Scheib	14.00	7.00	4.25
84	Barney McCosky	14.00	7.00	4.25
85	Eddie Kazak	14.00	7.00	4.25
86	Harry Brecheen	20.00	10.00	6.00
87	Floyd Baker	14.00	7.00	4.25
88	Eddie Robinson	14.00	7.00	4.25
89	Henry Thompson	14.00	7.00	4.25
90	Dave Koslo	14.00	7.00	4.25
91	Clyde Vollmer	14.00	7.00	4.25
92	Vern "Junior" Stephens	20.00	10.00	6.00
93	Danny O'Connell	14.00	7.00	4.25
94	Clyde McCullough	14.00	7.00	4.25
95	Sherry Robertson	14.00	7.00	4.25
96	Sandalio Consuegra	14.00	7.00	4.25
97	Bob Kuzava	14.00	7.00	4.25
98	Willard Marshall	14.00	7.00	4.25
99	Earl Torgeson	14.00	7.00	4.25
100	Sherman Lollar	20.00	10.00	6.00
101	Owen Friend	14.00	7.00	4.25
102	Emil "Dutch" Leonard	14.00	7.00	4.25
103	Andy Pafko	20.00	10.00	6.00
104	Virgil "Fire" Trucks	20.00	10.00	6.00
105	Don Kolloway	14.00	7.00	4.25
106	Pat Mullin	14.00	7.00	4.25
107	Johnny Wyrostek	14.00	7.00	4.25
108	Virgil Stallcup	14.00	7.00	4.25
109	Allie Reynolds	40.00	20.00	12.00
110	Bobby Brown	40.00	20.00	12.00
111	Curt Simmons	20.00	10.00	6.00
112	Willie Jones	14.00	7.00	4.25
113	Bill "Swish" Nicholson	14.00	7.00	4.25

#	Name	NR MT	EX	VG
114	Sam Zoldak	14.00	7.00	4.25
115	Steve Gromek	14.00	7.00	4.25
116	Bruce Edwards	20.00	10.00	6.00
117	Eddie Miksis	20.00	10.00	6.00
118	Preacher Roe	40.00	20.00	12.00
119	Eddie Joost	14.00	7.00	4.25
120	Joe Coleman	14.00	7.00	4.25
121	Gerry Staley	14.00	7.00	4.25
122	Joe Garagiola	150.00	75.00	45.00
123	Howie Judson	14.00	7.00	4.25
124	Gus Niarhos	14.00	7.00	4.25
125	Bill Rigney	20.00	10.00	6.00
126	Bobby Thomson	30.00	15.00	9.00
127	Sal Maglie	50.00	25.00	15.00
128	Ellis Kinder	14.00	7.00	4.25
129	Matt Batts	14.00	7.00	4.25
130	Tom Saffell	14.00	7.00	4.25
131	Cliff Chambers	14.00	7.00	4.25
132	Cass Michaels	14.00	7.00	4.25
133	Sam Dente	14.00	7.00	4.25
134	Warren Spahn	110.00	55.00	33.00
135	Walker Cooper	14.00	7.00	4.25
136	Ray Coleman	14.00	7.00	4.25
137	Dick Starr	14.00	7.00	4.25
138	Phil Cavarretta	20.00	10.00	6.00
139	Doyle Lade	14.00	7.00	4.25
140	Eddie Lake	14.00	7.00	4.25
141	Fred Hutchinson	20.00	10.00	6.00
142	Aaron Robinson	14.00	7.00	4.25
143	Ted Kluszewski	40.00	20.00	12.00
144	Herman Wehmeier	14.00	7.00	4.25
145	Fred Sanford	20.00	10.00	6.00
146	Johnny Hopp	20.00	10.00	6.00
147	Ken Heintzelman	14.00	7.00	4.25
148	Granny Hamner	14.00	7.00	4.25
149	Emory "Bubba" Church	14.00	7.00	4.25
150	Mike Garcia	20.00	10.00	6.00
151	Larry Doby	25.00	12.50	7.50
152	Cal Abrams	20.00	10.00	6.00
153	Rex Barney	20.00	10.00	6.00
154	Pete Suder	14.00	7.00	4.25
155	Lou Brissie	14.00	7.00	4.25
156	Del Rice	14.00	7.00	4.25
157	Al Brazle	14.00	7.00	4.25
158	Chuck Diering	14.00	7.00	4.25
159	Eddie Stewart	14.00	7.00	4.25
160	Phil Masi	14.00	7.00	4.25
161	Wes Westrum	20.00	10.00	6.00
162	Larry Jansen	14.00	7.00	4.25
163	Monte Kennedy	14.00	7.00	4.25
164	Bill Wight	14.00	7.00	4.25
165	Ted Williams	700.00	350.00	215.00
166	Stan Rojek	14.00	7.00	4.25
167	Murry Dickson	14.00	7.00	4.25
168	Sam Mele	14.00	7.00	4.25
169	Sid Hudson	14.00	7.00	4.25
170	Sibby Sisti	14.00	7.00	4.25
171	Buddy Kerr	14.00	7.00	4.25
172	Ned Garver	14.00	7.00	4.25
173	Hank Arft	14.00	7.00	4.25
174	Mickey Owen	14.00	7.00	4.25
175	Wayne Terwilliger	14.00	7.00	4.25
176	Vic Wertz	20.00	10.00	6.00
177	Charlie Keller	20.00	10.00	6.00
178	Ted Gray	14.00	7.00	4.25
179	Danny Litwhiler	14.00	7.00	4.25
180	Howie Fox	14.00	7.00	4.25
181	Casey Stengel	100.00	50.00	30.00
182	Tom Ferrick	20.00	10.00	6.00
183	Hank Bauer	40.00	20.00	12.00
184	Eddie Sawyer	14.00	7.00	4.25
185	Jimmy Bloodworth	14.00	7.00	4.25
186	Richie Ashburn	60.00	30.00	18.00
187	Al "Flip" Rosen	25.00	12.50	7.50
188	Roberto Avila	20.00	10.00	6.00
189	Erv Palica	20.00	10.00	6.00
190	Joe Hatten	20.00	10.00	6.00
191	Billy Hitchcock	14.00	7.00	4.25
192	Hank Wyse	14.00	7.00	4.25
193	Ted Wilks	14.00	7.00	4.25
194	Harry "Peanuts" Lowrey	14.00	7.00	4.25
195	Paul Richards	30.00	15.00	9.00
196	Bill Pierce	20.00	10.00	6.00
197	Bob Cain	14.00	7.00	4.25
198	Monte Irvin	100.00	50.00	30.00
199	Sheldon Jones	14.00	7.00	4.25
200	Jack Kramer	14.00	7.00	4.25
201	Steve O'Neill	14.00	7.00	4.25
202	Mike Guerra	14.00	7.00	4.25
203	Vernon Law	20.00	10.00	6.00
204	Vic Lombardi	14.00	7.00	4.25

		NR MT	EX	VG
205	Mickey Grasso	14.00	7.00	4.25
206	Conrado Marrero	14.00	7.00	4.25
207	Billy Southworth	14.00	7.00	4.25
208	Blix Donnelly	14.00	7.00	4.25
209	Ken Wood	14.00	7.00	4.25
210	Les Moss	14.00	7.00	4.25
211	Hal Jeffcoat	14.00	7.00	4.25
212	Bob Rush	14.00	7.00	4.25
213	Neil Berry	14.00	7.00	4.25
214	Bob Swift	14.00	7.00	4.25
215	Kent Peterson	14.00	7.00	4.25
216	Connie Ryan	14.00	7.00	4.25
217	Joe Page	20.00	10.00	6.00
218	Ed Lopat	20.00	10.00	6.00
219	Gene Woodling	40.00	20.00	12.00
220	Bob Miller	14.00	7.00	4.25
221	Dick Whitman	14.00	7.00	4.25
222	Thurman Tucker	14.00	7.00	4.25
223	Johnny Vander Meer	20.00	10.00	6.00
224	Billy Cox	20.00	10.00	6.00
225	Dan Bankhead	20.00	10.00	6.00
226	Jimmy Dykes	20.00	10.00	6.00
227	Bobby Schantz (Shantz)	20.00	10.00	6.00
228	Cloyd Boyer	14.00	7.00	4.25
229	Bill Howerton	14.00	7.00	4.25
230	Max Lanier	14.00	7.00	4.25
231	Luis Aloma	14.00	7.00	4.25
232	Nelson Fox	125.00	67.00	37.00
233	Leo Durocher	60.00	30.00	18.00
234	Clint Hartung	14.00	7.00	4.25
235	Jack "Lucky" Lohrke	14.00	7.00	4.25
236	Warren "Buddy" Rosar	14.00	7.00	4.25
237	Billy Goodman	14.00	7.00	4.25
238	Pete Reiser	20.00	10.00	6.00
239	Bill MacDonald	14.00	7.00	4.25
240	Joe Haynes	14.00	7.00	4.25
241	Irv Noren	14.00	7.00	4.25
242	Sam Jethroe	20.00	10.00	6.00
243	John Antonelli	20.00	10.00	6.00
244	Cliff Fannin	14.00	7.00	4.25
245	John Berardino	20.00	10.00	6.00
246	Bill Serena	14.00	7.00	4.25
247	Bob Ramazotti	14.00	7.00	4.25
248	*Johnny Klippstein*	20.00	10.00	6.00
249	Johnny Groth	14.00	7.00	4.25
250	Hank Borowy	14.00	7.00	4.25
251	Willard Ramsdell	14.00	7.00	4.25
252	Homer "Dixie" Howell	14.00	7.00	4.25
253	*Mickey Mantle*	9000.00	4500.00	2750.
254	*Jackie Jensen*	100.00	50.00	30.00
255	Milo Candini	60.00	30.00	18.00
256	Ken Silvestri	60.00	30.00	18.00
257	Birdie Tebbetts	60.00	30.00	18.00
258	*Luke Easter*	60.00	30.00	18.00
259	Charlie Dressen	60.00	30.00	18.00
260	Carl Erskine	90.00	45.00	27.00
261	Wally Moses	60.00	30.00	18.00
262	Gus Zernial	60.00	30.00	18.00
263	Howie Pollett (Pollet)	60.00	30.00	18.00
264	Don Richmond	60.00	30.00	18.00
265	Steve Bilko	60.00	30.00	18.00
266	Harry Dorish	60.00	30.00	18.00
267	Ken Holcombe	60.00	30.00	18.00
268	Don Mueller	60.00	30.00	18.00
269	Ray Noble	60.00	30.00	18.00
270	Willard Nixon	60.00	30.00	18.00
271	Tommy Wright	60.00	30.00	18.00
272	Billy Meyer	60.00	30.00	18.00
273	Danny Murtaugh	60.00	30.00	18.00
274	George Metkovich	60.00	30.00	18.00
275	Bucky Harris	60.00	30.00	18.00
276	Frank Quinn	60.00	30.00	18.00
277	Roy Hartsfield	60.00	30.00	18.00
278	Norman Roy	60.00	30.00	18.00
279	Jim Delsing	60.00	30.00	18.00
280	Frank Overmire	60.00	30.00	18.00
281	Al Widmar	60.00	30.00	18.00
282	Frank Frisch	80.00	40.00	25.00
283	Walt Dubiel	60.00	30.00	18.00
284	Gene Bearden	60.00	30.00	18.00
285	Johnny Lipon	60.00	30.00	18.00
286	Bob Usher	60.00	30.00	18.00
287	Jim Blackburn	60.00	30.00	18.00
288	Bobby Adams	60.00	30.00	18.00
289	Cliff Mapes	60.00	30.00	18.00
290	Bill Dickey	175.00	70.00	44.00
291	Tommy Henrich	70.00	35.00	20.00
292	Eddie Pellagrini	60.00	30.00	18.00
293	Ken Johnson	60.00	30.00	18.00
294	Jocko Thompson	60.00	30.00	18.00
295	Al Lopez	90.00	45.00	25.00

		NR MT	EX	VG
296	Bob Kennedy	60.00	30.00	18.00
297	Dave Philley	60.00	30.00	18.00
298	Joe Astroth	60.00	30.00	18.00
299	Clyde King	60.00	30.00	18.00
300	Hal Rice	60.00	30.00	18.00
301	Tommy Glaviano	60.00	30.00	18.00
302	Jim Busby	60.00	30.00	18.00
303	Marv Rotblatt	60.00	30.00	18.00
304	Allen Gettel	60.00	30.00	18.00
305	*Willie Mays*	3500.00	1750.00	1050.
306	*Jim Piersall*	110.00	55.00	33.00
307	Walt Masterson	60.00	30.00	18.00
308	Ted Beard	60.00	30.00	18.00
309	Mel Queen	60.00	30.00	18.00
310	Erv Dusak	60.00	30.00	18.00
311	Mickey Harris	60.00	30.00	18.00
312	Gene Mauch	60.00	30.00	18.00
313	Ray Mueller	60.00	30.00	18.00
314	Johnny Sain	60.00	30.00	18.00
315	Zack Taylor	60.00	30.00	18.00
316	Duane Pillette	60.00	30.00	18.00
317	*Forrest Burgess*	70.00	35.00	20.00
318	Warren Hacker	60.00	30.00	18.00
319	Red Rolfe	60.00	30.00	18.00
320	Hal White	60.00	30.00	18.00
321	Earl Johnson	60.00	30.00	18.00
322	Luke Sewell	60.00	30.00	18.00
323	*Joe Adcock*	100.00	50.00	30.00
324	Johnny Pramesa	110.00	40.00	15.00

1952 Bowman

Bowman reverted back to a 252-card set in 1952, but retained the card size (2-1/16" by 3-1/8") employed the preceding year. The cards, which are color art reproductions of actual photographs, feature a facsimile autograph on the fronts. Artwork for 15 cards that were never issued was uncovered several years ago and a set featuring those cards was subsequently made available to the collecting public.

		NR MT	EX	VG
Complete Set:		9500.00	4500.00	2750.
Common Player: 1-36		18.00	9.00	5.50
Common Player: 37-216		18.00	9.00	5.50
Common Player: 217-252		30.00	15.00	9.00
1	Larry "Yogi" Berra	600.00	250.00	100.00
2	Bobby Thomson	30.00	10.00	6.00
3	Fred Hutchinson	18.00	9.00	5.50
4	Robin Roberts	60.00	30.00	18.00
5	*Orestes Minoso*	100.00	50.00	30.00
6	Virgil "Red" Stallcup	18.00	9.00	5.50
7	Mike Garcia	18.00	9.00	5.50
8	Harold "Pee Wee" Reese	100.00	50.00	30.00
9	Vern Stephens	18.00	9.00	5.50
10	Bob Hooper	18.00	9.00	5.50
11	Ralph Kiner	60.00	30.00	18.00
12	Max Surkont	18.00	9.00	5.50
13	Cliff Mapes	18.00	9.00	5.50
14	Cliff Chambers	18.00	9.00	5.50
15	Sam Mele	18.00	9.00	5.50
16	Omar Lown	18.00	9.00	5.50
17	Ed Lopat	32.00	16.00	9.50
18	Don Mueller	18.00	9.00	5.50
19	Bob Cain	18.00	9.00	5.50
20	Willie Jones	18.00	9.00	5.50
21	Nelson Fox	50.00	25.00	15.00

#	Player	NR MT	EX	VG
22	Willard Ramsdell	18.00	9.00	5.50
23	Bob Lemon	40.00	20.00	12.00
24	Carl Furillo	30.00	15.00	9.00
25	Maurice McDermott	18.00	9.00	5.50
26	Eddie Joost	18.00	9.00	5.50
27	Joe Garagiola	70.00	35.00	23.00
28	Roy Hartsfield	18.00	9.00	5.50
29	Ned Garver	18.00	9.00	5.50
30	Al "Red" Schoendienst	60.00	30.00	18.00
31	Eddie Yost	18.00	9.00	5.50
32	Eddie Miksis	18.00	9.00	5.50
33	*Gil McDougald*	70.00	35.00	20.00
34	Al Dark	20.00	10.00	6.00
35	Gran Hamner	18.00	9.00	5.50
36	Cass Michaels	18.00	9.00	5.50
37	Vic Raschi	20.00	10.00	6.00
38	Whitey Lockman	18.00	9.00	5.50
39	Vic Wertz	18.00	9.00	5.50
40	Emory Church	18.00	9.00	5.50
41	Chico Carrasquel	18.00	9.00	5.50
42	Johnny Wyrostek	18.00	9.00	5.50
43	Bob Feller	125.00	67.00	37.00
44	Roy Campanella	200.00	100.00	60.00
45	Johnny Pesky	18.00	9.00	5.50
46	Carl Scheib	18.00	9.00	5.50
47	Pete Castiglione	18.00	9.00	5.50
48	Vern Bickford	18.00	9.00	5.50
49	Jim Hearn	18.00	9.00	5.50
50	Gerry Staley	18.00	9.00	5.50
51	Gil Coan	18.00	9.00	5.50
52	Phil Rizzuto	80.00	40.00	25.00
53	Richie Ashburn	50.00	25.00	15.00
54	Billy Pierce	18.00	9.00	5.50
55	Ken Raffensberger	18.00	9.00	5.50
56	Clyde King	18.00	9.00	5.50
57	Clyde Vollmer	18.00	9.00	5.50
58	Hank Majeski	18.00	9.00	5.50
59	Murray Dickson (Murry)	18.00	9.00	5.50
60	Sid Gordon	18.00	9.00	5.50
61	Tommy Byrne	18.00	9.00	5.50
62	Joe Presko	18.00	9.00	5.50
63	Irv Noren	18.00	9.00	5.50
64	Roy Smalley	18.00	9.00	5.50
65	Hank Bauer	30.00	15.00	9.00
66	Sal Maglie	30.00	15.00	9.00
67	Johnny Groth	18.00	9.00	5.50
68	Jim Busby	18.00	9.00	5.50
69	Joe Adcock	30.00	15.00	9.00
70	Carl Erskine	30.00	15.00	9.00
71	Vernon Law	18.00	9.00	5.50
72	Earl Torgeson	18.00	9.00	5.50
73	Jerry Coleman	18.00	9.00	5.50
74	Wes Westrum	18.00	9.00	5.50
75	George Kell	40.00	20.00	12.00
76	Del Ennis	18.00	9.00	5.50
77	Eddie Robinson	18.00	9.00	5.50
78	Lloyd Merriman	18.00	9.00	5.50
79	Lou Brissie	18.00	9.00	5.50
80	Gil Hodges	80.00	40.00	25.00
81	Billy Goodman	18.00	9.00	5.50
82	Gus Zernial	18.00	9.00	5.50
83	Howie Pollet	18.00	9.00	5.50
84	Sam Jethroe	18.00	9.00	5.50
85	Marty Marion	18.00	9.00	5.50
86	Cal Abrams	18.00	9.00	5.50
87	Mickey Vernon	18.00	9.00	5.50
88	Bruce Edwards	18.00	9.00	5.50
89	Billy Hitchcock	18.00	9.00	5.50
90	Larry Jansen	18.00	9.00	5.50
91	Don Kolloway	18.00	9.00	5.50
92	Eddie Waitkus	18.00	9.00	5.50
93	Paul Richards	18.00	9.00	5.50
94	Luke Sewell	18.00	9.00	5.50
95	Luke Easter	18.00	9.00	5.50
96	Ralph Branca	18.00	9.00	5.50
97	Willard Marshall	18.00	9.00	5.50
98	Jimmy Dykes	18.00	9.00	5.50
99	Clyde McCullough	18.00	9.00	5.50
100	Sibby Sisti	18.00	9.00	5.50
101	Mickey Mantle	2500.00	1250.00	750.00
102	Peanuts Lowrey	18.00	9.00	5.50
103	Joe Haynes	18.00	9.00	5.50
104	Hal Jeffcoat	18.00	9.00	5.50
105	Bobby Brown	20.00	10.00	6.00
106	Randy Gumpert	18.00	9.00	5.50
107	Del Rice	18.00	9.00	5.50
108	George Metkovich	18.00	9.00	5.50
109	Tom Morgan	15.00	7.50	4.50
110	Max Lanier	18.00	9.00	5.50
111	Walter "Hoot" Evers	18.00	9.00	5.50
112	Forrest "Smokey" Burgess	18.00	9.00	5.50
113	Al Zarilla	18.00	9.00	5.50
114	Frank Hiller	18.00	9.00	5.50
115	Larry Doby	30.00	15.00	9.00
116	Duke Snider	200.00	100.00	60.00
117	Bill Wight	18.00	9.00	5.50
118	Ray Murray	18.00	9.00	5.50
119	Bill Howerton	18.00	9.00	5.50
120	Chet Nichols	18.00	9.00	5.50
121	Al Corwin	18.00	9.00	5.50
122	Billy Johnson	18.00	9.00	5.50
123	Sid Hudson	18.00	9.00	5.50
124	George Tebbetts	18.00	9.00	5.50
125	Howie Fox	18.00	9.00	5.50
126	Phil Cavarretta	18.00	9.00	5.50
127	Dick Sisler	18.00	9.00	5.50
128	Don Newcombe	30.00	15.00	9.00
129	Gus Niarhos	18.00	9.00	5.50
130	Allie Clark	18.00	9.00	5.50
131	Bob Swift	18.00	9.00	5.50
132	Dave Cole	18.00	9.00	5.50
133	Dick Kryhoski	18.00	9.00	5.50
134	Al Brazle	18.00	9.00	5.50
135	Mickey Harris	18.00	9.00	5.50
136	Gene Hermanski	18.00	9.00	5.50
137	Stan Rojek	18.00	9.00	5.50
138	Ted Wilks	18.00	9.00	5.50
139	Jerry Priddy	18.00	9.00	5.50
140	Ray Scarborough	18.00	9.00	5.50
141	Hank Edwards	18.00	9.00	5.50
142	Early Wynn	40.00	20.00	12.00
143	Sandalio Consuegra	18.00	9.00	5.50
144	Joe Hatten	18.00	9.00	5.50
145	Johnny Mize	50.00	30.00	15.00
146	Leo Durocher	35.00	17.50	10.50
147	Marlin Stuart	18.00	9.00	5.50
148	Ken Heintzelman	18.00	9.00	5.50
149	Howie Judson	18.00	9.00	5.50
150	Herman Wehmeier	18.00	9.00	5.50
151	Al "Flip" Rosen	30.00	15.00	9.00
152	Billy Cox	18.00	9.00	5.50
153	Fred Hatfield	18.00	9.00	5.50
154	Ferris Fain	18.00	9.00	5.50
155	Billy Meyer	18.00	9.00	5.50
156	Warren Spahn	110.00	55.00	33.00
157	Jim Delsing	18.00	9.00	5.50
158	Bucky Harris	30.00	15.00	9.00
159	Dutch Leonard	18.00	9.00	5.50
160	Eddie Stanky	18.00	9.00	5.50
161	Jackie Jensen	32.00	16.00	9.50
162	Monte Irvin	50.00	25.00	15.00
163	Johnny Lipon	18.00	9.00	5.50
164	Connie Ryan	18.00	9.00	5.50
165	Saul Rogovin	18.00	9.00	5.50
166	Bobby Adams	18.00	9.00	5.50
167	Bob Avila	18.00	9.00	5.50
168	Preacher Roe	32.00	16.00	9.50
169	Walt Dropo	18.00	9.00	5.50
170	Joe Astroth	18.00	9.00	5.50
171	Mel Queen	18.00	9.00	5.50
172	Ebba St. Claire	18.00	9.00	5.50
173	Gene Bearden	18.00	9.00	5.50
174	Mickey Grasso	18.00	9.00	5.50
175	Ransom Jackson	18.00	9.00	5.50
176	Harry Brecheen	18.00	9.00	5.50
177	Gene Woodling	30.00	15.00	9.00
178	Dave Williams	18.00	9.00	5.50
179	Pete Suder	18.00	9.00	5.50
180	Eddie Fitzgerald (Fitz Gerald)	18.00	9.00	5.50
181	Joe Collins	15.00	7.50	4.50
182	Dave Koslo	18.00	9.00	5.50
183	Pat Mullin	18.00	9.00	5.50
184	Curt Simmons	18.00	9.00	5.50
185	Eddie Stewart	18.00	9.00	5.50
186	Frank Smith	18.00	9.00	5.50
187	Jim Hegan	18.00	9.00	5.50
188	Charlie Dressen	15.00	7.50	4.50
189	Jim Piersall	18.00	9.00	5.50
190	Dick Fowler	18.00	9.00	5.50
191	*Bob Friend*	15.00	7.50	4.50
192	John Cusick	18.00	9.00	5.50
193	Bobby Young	18.00	9.00	5.50
194	Bob Porterfield	18.00	9.00	5.50
195	Frank Baumholtz	18.00	9.00	5.50
196	Stan Musial	550.00	275.00	165.00
197	Charlie Silvera	15.00	7.50	4.50
198	Chuck Diering	18.00	9.00	5.50
199	Ted Gray	18.00	9.00	5.50
200	Ken Silvestri	18.00	9.00	5.50
201	Ray Coleman	18.00	9.00	5.50
202	Harry Perkowski	18.00	9.00	5.50
203	Steve Gromek	18.00	9.00	5.50

		NR MT	EX	VG
204	Andy Pafko	18.00	9.00	5.50
205	Walt Masterson	18.00	9.00	5.50
206	Elmer Valo	18.00	9.00	5.50
207	George Strickland	18.00	9.00	5.50
208	Walker Cooper	18.00	9.00	5.50
209	Dick Littlefield	18.00	9.00	5.50
210	Archie Wilson	18.00	9.00	5.50
211	Paul Minner	18.00	9.00	5.50
212	Solly Hemus	18.00	9.00	5.50
213	Monte Kennedy	18.00	9.00	5.50
214	Ray Boone	18.00	9.00	5.50
215	Sheldon Jones	18.00	9.00	5.50
216	Matt Batts	18.00	9.00	5.50
217	Casey Stengel	150.00	75.00	45.00
218	Willie Mays	1300.00	650.00	375.00
219	Neil Berry	32.00	16.00	9.50
220	Russ Meyer	32.00	16.00	9.50
221	Lou Kretlow	32.00	16.00	9.50
222	Homer "Dixie" Howell	32.00	16.00	9.50
223	Harry Simpson	32.00	16.00	9.50
224	Johnny Schmitz	32.00	16.00	9.50
225	Del Wilber	32.00	16.00	9.50
226	Alex Kellner	32.00	16.00	9.50
227	Clyde Sukeforth	32.00	16.00	9.50
228	Bob Chipman	32.00	16.00	9.50
229	Hank Arft	32.00	16.00	9.50
230	Frank Shea	32.00	16.00	9.50
231	Dee Fondy	32.00	16.00	9.50
232	Enos Slaughter	90.00	45.00	25.00
233	Bob Kuzava	32.00	16.00	9.50
234	Fred Fitzsimmons	32.00	16.00	9.50
235	Steve Souchock	32.00	16.00	9.50
236	Tommy Brown	32.00	16.00	9.50
237	Sherman Lollar	32.00	16.00	9.50
238	*Roy McMillan*	32.00	16.00	9.50
239	Dale Mitchell	32.00	16.00	9.50
240	*Billy Loes*	40.00	20.00	12.50
241	Mel Parnell	32.00	16.00	9.50
242	Everett Kell	32.00	16.00	9.50
243	George "Red" Munger	32.00	16.00	9.50
244	*Lew Burdette*	70.00	35.00	21.00
245	George Schmees	32.00	16.00	9.50
246	Jerry Snyder	32.00	16.00	9.50
247	John Pramesa	32.00	16.00	9.50
248	Bill Werle	32.00	16.00	9.50
249	Henry Thompson	32.00	16.00	9.50
250	Ivan Delock	32.00	16.00	9.50
251	Jack Lohrke	32.00	12.50	7.50
252	Frank Crosetti	150.00	50.00	20.00

1953 Bowman Color

The first set of current major league players featuring actual color photographs, the 160-card 1953 Bowman Color set remains one of the most popular issues of the post-war era. The set is greatly appreciated for its uncluttered look; card fronts that contain no names, teams or facsimile autographs. Bowman increased the size of their cards to a 2-1/2" by 3-3/4" size in order to better compete with Topps Chewing Gum. Bowman copied an idea from the 1952 Topps set and developed card backs that gave player career and previous year statistics. The high-numbered cards (#'s 113-160) are the scarcest of the set, with #'s 113-128 being exceptionally difficult to find.

		NR MT	EX	VG
Complete Set:		12000.00	6000.00	3500.
Common Player: 1-112		30.00	15.00	9.00
Common Player: 113-128		40.00	20.00	12.00
Common Player: 129-160		40.00	20.00	12.00
1	Davey Williams	100.00	25.00	12.00
2	Vic Wertz	30.00	15.00	9.00
3	Sam Jethroe	30.00	15.00	9.00
4	Art Houtteman	30.00	15.00	9.00
5	Sid Gordon	30.00	15.00	9.00
6	Joe Ginsberg	30.00	15.00	9.00
7	Harry Chiti	30.00	15.00	9.00
8	Al Rosen	40.00	20.00	12.00
9	Phil Rizzuto	110.00	55.00	33.00
10	Richie Ashburn	85.00	42.00	26.00
11	Bobby Shantz	30.00	15.00	9.00
12	Carl Erskine	50.00	30.00	15.00
13	Gus Zernial	30.00	15.00	9.00
14	Billy Loes	30.00	15.00	9.00
15	Jim Busby	30.00	15.00	9.00
16	Bob Friend	30.00	15.00	9.00
17	Gerry Staley	30.00	15.00	9.00
18	Nelson Fox	75.00	38.00	23.00
19	Al Dark	30.00	15.00	9.00
20	Don Lenhardt	30.00	15.00	9.00
21	Joe Garagiola	80.00	40.00	25.00
22	Bob Porterfield	30.00	15.00	9.00
23	Herman Wehmeier	30.00	15.00	9.00
24	Jackie Jensen	40.00	20.00	12.00
25	Walter "Hoot" Evers	30.00	15.00	9.00
26	Roy McMillan	30.00	15.00	9.00
27	Vic Raschi	40.00	20.00	12.00
28	Forrest "Smoky" Burgess	30.00	15.00	9.00
29	Roberto Avila	30.00	15.00	9.00
30	Phil Cavarretta	30.00	15.00	9.00
31	Jimmy Dykes	30.00	15.00	9.00
32	Stan Musial	550.00	275.00	165.00
33	Harold "Peewee" Reese	450.00	225.00	135.00
34	Gil Coan	30.00	15.00	9.00
35	Maury McDermott	30.00	15.00	9.00
36	Orestes Minoso	50.00	30.00	15.00
37	Jim Wilson	30.00	15.00	9.00
38	Harry Byrd	30.00	15.00	9.00
39	Paul Richards	30.00	15.00	9.00
40	Larry Doby	40.00	20.00	12.00
41	Sammy White	30.00	15.00	9.00
42	Tommy Brown	30.00	15.00	9.00
43	Mike Garcia	30.00	15.00	9.00
44	Hank Bauer, Yogi Berra, Mickey Mantle	400.00	200.00	125.00
45	Walt Dropo	30.00	15.00	9.00
46	Roy Campanella	250.00	125.00	75.00
47	Ned Garver	30.00	15.00	9.00
48	Hank Sauer	30.00	15.00	9.00
49	Eddie Stanky	30.00	15.00	9.00
50	Lou Kretlow	30.00	15.00	9.00
51	Monte Irvin	50.00	25.00	15.00
52	Marty Marion	30.00	15.00	9.00
53	Del Rice	30.00	15.00	9.00
54	Chico Carrasquel	30.00	15.00	9.00
55	Leo Durocher	60.00	30.00	18.00
56	Bob Cain	30.00	15.00	9.00
57	Lou Boudreau	50.00	25.00	15.00
58	Willard Marshall	30.00	15.00	9.00
59	Mickey Mantle	2600.00	1300.00	750.00
60	Granny Hamner	30.00	15.00	9.00
61	George Kell	30.00	15.00	9.00
62	Ted Kluszewski	50.00	25.00	15.00
63	Gil McDougald	50.00	25.00	15.00
64	Curt Simmons	30.00	15.00	9.00
65	Robin Roberts	70.00	35.00	21.00
66	Mel Parnell	30.00	15.00	9.00
67	Mel Clark	30.00	15.00	9.00
68	Allie Reynolds	50.00	25.00	15.00
69	Charlie Grimm	30.00	15.00	9.00
70	Clint Courtney	30.00	15.00	9.00
71	Paul Minner	30.00	15.00	9.00
72	Ted Gray	30.00	15.00	9.00
73	Billy Pierce	30.00	15.00	9.00
74	Don Mueller	30.00	15.00	9.00
75	Saul Rogovin	30.00	15.00	9.00
76	Jim Hearn	30.00	15.00	9.00
77	Mickey Grasso	30.00	15.00	9.00
78	Carl Furillo	50.00	25.00	15.00
79	Ray Boone	30.00	15.00	9.00
80	Ralph Kiner	80.00	40.00	25.00
81	Enos Slaughter	70.00	35.00	21.00
82	Joe Astroth	30.00	15.00	9.00
83	Jack Daniels	30.00	15.00	9.00
84	Hank Bauer	50.00	25.00	15.00
85	Solly Hemus	30.00	15.00	9.00

		NR MT	EX	VG
86	Harry Simpson	30.00	15.00	9.00
87	Harry Perkowski	30.00	15.00	9.00
88	Joe Dobson	30.00	15.00	9.00
89	Sandalio Consuegra	30.00	15.00	9.00
90	Joe Nuxhall	30.00	15.00	9.00
91	Steve Souchock	30.00	15.00	9.00
92	Gil Hodges	110.00	55.00	33.00
93	Billy Martin, Phil Rizzuto	200.00	100.00	60.00
94	Bob Addis	30.00	15.00	9.00
95	Wally Moses	30.00	15.00	9.00
96	Sal Maglie	45.00	23.00	13.50
97	Eddie Mathews	200.00	100.00	60.00
98	Hector Rodriquez	30.00	15.00	9.00
99	Warren Spahn	175.00	87.00	52.00
100	Bill Wight	30.00	15.00	9.00
101	Al "Red" Schoendienst	80.00	40.00	25.00
102	Jim Hegan	30.00	15.00	9.00
103	Del Ennis	30.00	15.00	9.00
104	Luke Easter	30.00	15.00	9.00
105	Eddie Joost	30.00	15.00	9.00
106	Ken Raffensberger	30.00	15.00	9.00
107	Alex Kellner	30.00	15.00	9.00
108	Bobby Adams	30.00	15.00	9.00
109	Ken Wood	30.00	15.00	9.00
110	Bob Rush	30.00	15.00	9.00
111	Jim Dyck	30.00	15.00	9.00
112	Toby Atwell	30.00	15.00	9.00
113	Karl Drews	40.00	20.00	12.00
114	Bob Feller	300.00	150.00	90.00
115	Cloyd Boyer	40.00	20.00	12.00
116	Eddie Yost	40.00	20.00	12.00
117	Duke Snider	600.00	300.00	175.00
118	Billy Martin	300.00	150.00	90.00
119	Dale Mitchell	40.00	20.00	12.00
120	Marlin Stuart	40.00	20.00	12.00
121	Yogi Berra	500.00	250.00	150.00
122	Bill Serena	40.00	20.00	12.00
123	Johnny Lipon	40.00	20.00	12.00
124	Charlie Dressen	45.00	23.00	13.50
125	Fred Hatfield	40.00	20.00	12.00
126	Al Corwin	40.00	20.00	12.00
127	Dick Kryhoski	40.00	20.00	12.00
128	Whitey Lockman	40.00	20.00	12.00
129	Russ Meyer	50.00	25.00	15.00
130	Cass Michaels	40.00	20.00	12.00
131	Connie Ryan	40.00	20.00	12.00
132	Fred Hutchinson	50.00	25.00	15.00
133	Willie Jones	40.00	20.00	12.00
134	Johnny Pesky	50.00	25.00	15.00
135	Bobby Morgan	50.00	25.00	15.00
136	Jim Brideweser	40.00	20.00	12.00
137	Sam Dente	40.00	20.00	12.00
138	Bubba Church	40.00	20.00	12.00
139	Pete Runnels	50.00	25.00	15.00
140	Alpha Brazle	40.00	20.00	12.00
141	Frank "Spec" Shea	40.00	20.00	12.00
142	Larry Miggins	40.00	20.00	12.00
143	Al Lopez	60.00	30.00	18.00
144	Warren Hacker	40.00	20.00	12.00
145	George Shuba	50.00	25.00	15.00
146	Early Wynn	125.00	62.00	40.00
147	Clem Koshorek	40.00	20.00	12.00
148	Billy Goodman	40.00	20.00	12.00
149	Al Corwin	40.00	20.00	12.00
150	Carl Scheib	40.00	20.00	12.00
151	Joe Adcock	40.00	20.00	12.00
152	Clyde Vollmer	40.00	20.00	12.00
153	Ed "Whitey" Ford	450.00	225.00	135.00
154	Omar "Turk" Lown	40.00	20.00	12.00
155	Allie Clark	40.00	20.00	12.00
156	Max Surkont	40.00	20.00	12.00
157	Sherman Lollar	50.00	25.00	15.00
158	Howard Fox	40.00	20.00	12.00
159	Mickey Vernon (Photo actually Floyd Baker)	40.00	17.50	10.50
160	Cal Abrams	90.00	30.00	15.00

1953 Bowman
Black & White

The 1953 Bowman Black and White set is similar in all respects to the 1953 Bowman Color set, except that it lacks color. Purportedly, high costs in producing the color series forced Bowman to issue the set in black and white. Sixty-four cards, which measure 2-1/2" by 3-3/4", comprise the set.

		NR MT	EX	VG
Complete Set:		2500.00	1250.00	700.00
Common Player:		30.00	15.00	9.00
1	Gus Bell	125.00	55.00	35.00
2	Willard Nixon	32.00	11.00	6.50
3	Bill Rigney	32.00	16.00	9.50
4	Pat Mullin	30.00	15.00	9.00
5	Dee Fondy	30.00	15.00	9.00
6	Ray Murray	30.00	15.00	9.00
7	Andy Seminick	30.00	15.00	9.00
8	Pete Suder	30.00	15.00	9.00
9	Walt Masterson	30.00	15.00	9.00
10	Dick Sisler	30.00	15.00	9.00
11	Dick Gernert	30.00	15.00	9.00
12	Randy Jackson	30.00	15.00	9.00
13	Joe Tipton	30.00	15.00	9.00
14	Bill Nicholson	30.00	15.00	9.00
15	Johnny Mize	125.00	67.00	37.00
16	Stu Miller	30.00	15.00	9.00
17	Virgil Trucks	32.00	16.00	9.50
18	Billy Hoeft	30.00	15.00	9.00
19	Paul LaPalme	30.00	15.00	9.00
20	Eddie Robinson	30.00	15.00	9.00
21	Clarence "Bud" Podbielan	30.00	15.00	9.00
22	Matt Batts	30.00	15.00	9.00
23	Wilmer Mizell	30.00	15.00	9.00
24	Del Wilber	30.00	15.00	9.00
25	John Sain	60.00	30.00	18.00
26	Preacher Roe	60.00	30.00	18.00
27	Bob Lemon	125.00	67.00	37.00
28	Hoyt Wilhelm	125.00	67.00	37.00
29	Sid Hudson	30.00	15.00	9.00
30	Walker Cooper	30.00	15.00	9.00
31	Gene Woodling	50.00	25.00	15.00
32	Rocky Bridges	30.00	15.00	9.00
33	Bob Kuzava	32.00	16.00	9.50
34	Ebba St. Clair (St. Claire)	30.00	15.00	9.00
35	Johnny Wyrostek	30.00	15.00	9.00
36	Jim Piersall	50.00	25.00	15.00
37	Hal Jeffcoat	30.00	15.00	9.00
38	Dave Cole	30.00	15.00	9.00
39	Casey Stengel	300.00	150.00	90.00
40	Larry Jansen	30.00	15.00	9.00
41	Bob Ramazotti	30.00	15.00	9.00
42	Howie Judson	30.00	15.00	9.00
43	Hal Bevan	30.00	15.00	9.00
44	Jim Delsing	30.00	15.00	9.00
45	Irv Noren	32.00	16.00	9.50
46	Bucky Harris	50.00	25.00	15.00
47	Jack Lohrke	30.00	15.00	9.00
48	Steve Ridzik	30.00	15.00	9.00
49	Floyd Baker	30.00	15.00	9.00
50	Emil "Dutch" Leonard	30.00	15.00	9.00
51	Lou Burdette	50.00	25.00	15.00
52	Ralph Branca	40.00	20.00	12.00
53	Morris Martin	30.00	15.00	9.00
54	Bill Miller	32.00	16.00	9.50
55	Don Johnson	30.00	15.00	9.00
56	Roy Smalley	30.00	15.00	9.00
57	Andy Pafko	30.00	15.00	9.00
58	Jim Konstanty	30.00	15.00	9.00
59	Duane Pillette	30.00	15.00	9.00
60	Billy Cox	40.00	20.00	12.00
61	Tom Gorman	32.00	16.00	9.50
62	Keith Thomas	30.00	15.00	9.00
63	Steve Gromek	32.00	16.00	9.50
64	Andy Hansen	50.00	25.00	15.00
81	Joe Black	50.00	25.00	15.00

1954 Bowman

Bowman's 1954 set consists of 224 full-color cards that measure 2-1/2" by 3-3/4". It is believed that contractual problems caused the pulling of card #66 (Ted Williams) from the set, creating one of the most sought-after scarcities of the post-war era. The Williams card was replaced by Jim Piersall (who is also #210) in subsequent print runs. The set contains over 40 variations, most involving statistical errors on the card backs that were corrected. Neither variation carries a premium value as both varieties appear to have been printed in equal amounts. The complete set price that follows does not include all variations or #66 Williams.

		NR MT	EX	VG
Complete Set:		4500.00	2250.00	1350.
Common Player: 1-112		8.00	4.00	2.50
Common Player:113-224		10.00	5.00	3.00
1	Phil Rizzuto	150.00	50.00	21.00
2	Jack Jensen	15.00	7.50	4.50
3	Marion Fricano	8.00	4.00	2.50
4	Bob Hooper	8.00	4.00	2.50
5	William Hunter	8.00	4.00	2.50
6	Nelson Fox	25.00	12.50	7.50
7	Walter Dropo	8.00	4.00	2.50
8	James F. Busby	8.00	4.00	2.50
9	Dave Williams	8.00	4.00	2.50
10	Carl Daniel Erskine	12.00	6.00	3.50
11	Sid Gordon	8.00	4.00	2.50
12a	Roy McMillan (551/1290 At Bat)	8.00	4.00	2.50
12b	Roy McMillan (557/1296 At Bat)	8.00	4.00	2.50
13	Paul Minner	8.00	4.00	2.50
14	Gerald Staley	8.00	4.00	2.50
15	Richie Ashburn	35.00	17.50	10.50
16	Jim Wilson	8.00	4.00	2.50
17	Tom Gorman	8.00	4.00	2.50
18	Walter "Hoot" Evers	8.00	4.00	2.50
19	Bobby Shantz	8.00	4.00	2.50
20	Artie Houtteman	8.00	4.00	2.50
21	Victor Wertz	8.00	4.00	2.50
22a	Sam Mele (213/1661 Putouts)	8.00	4.00	2.50
22b	Sam Mele (217/1665 Putouts)	8.00	4.00	2.50
23	*Harvey Kuenn*	35.00	17.50	10.50
24	Bob Porterfield	8.00	4.00	2.50
25a	Wes Westrum (1.000/.987 Field Avg.)	8.00	4.00	2.50
25b	Wes Westrum (.982/.986 Field Avg.)	8.00	4.00	2.50
26a	Billy Cox (1.000/.960 Field Avg.)	8.00	4.00	2.50
26b	Billy Cox (.972/.960 Field Avg.)	8.00	4.00	2.50
27	Richard Roy Cole	8.00	4.00	2.50
28a	Jim Greengrass (Birthplace Addison, N.J.)	8.00	4.00	2.50
28b	Jim Greengrass (Birthplace Addison, N.Y.)	8.00	4.00	2.50
29	Johnny Klippstein	8.00	4.00	2.50
30	Delbert Rice Jr.	8.00	4.00	2.50
31	"Smoky" Burgess	8.00	4.00	2.50
32	Del Crandall	8.00	4.00	2.50
33a	Victor Raschi (no traded line)	12.00	6.00	3.50
33b	Victor Raschi (with traded line)	30.00	15.00	9.00
34	Sammy White	8.00	4.00	2.50
35a	Eddie Joost (quiz answer is 8)	8.00	4.00	2.50
35b	Eddie Joost (quiz answer is 33)	8.00	4.00	2.50
36	George Strickland	8.00	4.00	2.50
37	Dick Kokos	8.00	4.00	2.50

		NR MT	EX	VG
38a	Orestes Minoso (.895/.961 Field Avg.)	8.00	4.00	2.50
38b	Orestes Minoso (.963/.963 Field Avg.)	8.00	4.00	2.50
39	Ned Garver	8.00	4.00	2.50
40	Gil Coan	8.00	4.00	2.50
41a	Alvin Dark (.986/.960 Field Avg.)	8.00	4.00	2.50
41b	Alvin Dark (.968/.960 Field Avg.)	8.00	4.00	2.50
42	Billy Loes	8.00	4.00	2.50
43a	Robert B. Friend (20 shutouts in quiz question)	8.00	4.00	2.50
43b	Robert B. Friend (16 shutouts in quiz question)	8.00	4.00	2.50
44	Harry Perkowski	8.00	4.00	2.50
45	Ralph Kiner	40.00	20.00	12.00
46	Eldon Repulski	8.00	4.00	2.50
47a	Granville Hamner (.970/.953 Field Avg.)	8.00	4.00	2.50
47b	Granville Hamner (.953/.951 Field Avg.)	8.00	4.00	2.50
48	Jack Dittmer	8.00	4.00	2.50
49	Harry Byrd	8.00	4.00	2.50
50	George Kell	25.00	12.50	7.50
51	Alex Kellner	8.00	4.00	2.50
52	Myron N. Ginsberg	8.00	4.00	2.50
53a	Don Lenhardt (.969/.984 Field Avg.)	8.00	4.00	2.50
53b	Don Lenhardt (.966/.983 Field Avg.)	8.00	4.00	2.50
54	Alfonso Carrasquel	8.00	4.00	2.50
55	Jim Delsing	8.00	4.00	2.50
56	Maurice M. McDermott	8.00	4.00	2.50
57	Hoyt Wilhelm	30.00	15.00	9.00
58	"Pee Wee" Reese	70.00	35.00	21.00
59	Robert D. Schultz	8.00	4.00	2.50
60	Fred Baczewski	8.00	4.00	2.50
61a	Eddie Miksis (.954/.962 Field Avg.)	8.00	4.00	2.50
61b	Eddie Miksis (.954/.961 Field Avg.)	8.00	4.00	2.50
62	Enos Slaughter	40.00	20.00	12.00
63	Earl Torgeson	8.00	4.00	2.50
64	Ed Mathews	60.00	30.00	18.00
65	Mickey Mantle	1000.00	500.00	300.00
66a	Ted Williams	5000.00	2500.00	1500.
66b	Jimmy Piersall	100.00	50.00	30.00
67a	Carl Scheib (.306 Pct. with two lines under bio)	8.00	4.00	2.50
67b	Carl Scheib (.306 Pct. with one line under bio)	8.00	4.00	2.50
67c	Carl Scheib (.300 Pct.)	8.00	4.00	2.50
68	Bob Avila	8.00	4.00	2.50
69	Clinton Courtney	8.00	4.00	2.50
70	Willard Marshall	8.00	4.00	2.50
71	Ted Gray	8.00	4.00	2.50
72	Ed Yost	8.00	4.00	2.50
73	Don Mueller	8.00	4.00	2.50
74	James Gilliam	20.00	10.00	6.00
75	Max Surkont	8.00	4.00	2.50
76	Joe Nuxhall	8.00	4.00	2.50
77	Bob Rush	8.00	4.00	2.50
78	Sal A. Yvars	8.00	4.00	2.50
79	Curt Simmons	8.00	4.00	2.50
80a	John Logan (106 Runs)	8.00	4.00	2.50
80b	John Logan (100 Runs)	8.00	4.00	2.50
81a	Jerry Coleman (1.000/.975 Field Avg.)	8.00	4.00	2.50
81b	Jerry Coleman (.952/.975 Field Avg.)	8.00	4.00	2.50
82a	Bill Goodman (.965/.986 Field Avg.)	8.00	4.00	2.50
82b	Bill Goodman (.972/.985 Field Avg.)	8.00	4.00	2.50
83	Ray Murray	8.00	4.00	2.50
84	Larry Doby	12.00	6.00	3.50
85a	Jim Dyck (.926/.956 Field Avg.)	8.00	4.00	2.50
85b	Jim Dyck (.947/.960 Field Avg.)	8.00	4.00	2.50
86	Harry Dorish	8.00	4.00	2.50
87	Don Lund	8.00	4.00	2.50
88	Tommy Umphlett	8.00	4.00	2.50
89	Willie May (Mays)	400.00	200.00	125.00
90	Roy Campanella	150.00	60.00	38.00
91	Cal Abrams	8.00	4.00	2.50
92	Kenneth David Raffensberger	8.00	4.00	2.50
93a	Bill Serena (.983/.966 Field Avg.)	8.00	4.00	2.50
93b	Bill Serena (.977/.966 Field Avg.)	8.00	4.00	2.50
94a	Solly Hemus (476/1343 Assists)	8.00	4.00	2.50
94b	Solly Hemus (477/1343 Assists)	8.00	4.00	2.50
95	Robin Roberts	40.00	20.00	12.00
96	Joe Adcock	8.00	4.00	2.50
97	Gil McDougald	15.00	7.50	4.50

		NR MT	EX	VG
98	Ellis Kinder	8.00	4.00	2.50
99a	Peter Suder (.985/.974 Field Avg.)			
		8.00	4.00	2.50
99b	Peter Suder (.978/.974 Field Avg.)			
		8.00	4.00	2.50
100	Mike Garcia	8.00	4.00	2.50
101	*Don James Larsen*	45.00	23.00	13.50
102	Bill Pierce	8.00	4.00	2.50
103a	Stephen Souchock (144/1192 Putouts)			
		8.00	4.00	2.50
103b	Stephen Souchock (147/1195 Putouts)			
		8.00	4.00	2.50
104	Frank Spec Shea	8.00	4.00	2.50
105a	Sal Maglie (quiz answer is 8)	8.00	4.00	2.50
105b	Sal Maglie (quiz answer is 1904)	8.00	4.00	2.50
106	"Clem" Labine	8.00	4.00	2.50
107	Paul E. LaPalme	8.00	4.00	2.50
108	Bobby Adams	8.00	4.00	2.50
109	Roy Smalley	8.00	4.00	2.50
110	Al Schoendienst	35.00	17.50	10.50
111	Murry Monroe Dickson	8.00	4.00	2.50
112	Andy Pafko	8.00	4.00	2.50
113	Allie Reynolds	12.00	6.00	3.50
114	Willard Nixon	12.00	6.00	3.50
115	Don Bollweg	12.00	6.00	3.50
116	Luscious Luke Easter	12.00	6.00	3.50
117	Dick Kryhoski	12.00	6.00	3.50
118	Robert R. Boyd	12.00	6.00	3.50
119	Fred Hatfield	12.00	6.00	3.50
120	Mel Hoderlein	12.00	6.00	3.50
121	Ray Katt	12.00	6.00	3.50
122	Carl Furillo	15.00	7.50	4.50
123	Toby Atwell	12.00	6.00	3.50
124a	Gus Bell (15/27 Errors)	12.00	6.00	3.50
124b	Gus Bell (11/26 Errors)	12.00	6.00	3.50
125	Warren Hacker	12.00	6.00	3.50
126	Cliff Chambers	12.00	6.00	3.50
127	Del Ennis	12.00	6.00	3.50
128	Ebba St Claire	12.00	6.00	3.50
129	Hank Bauer	20.00	10.00	6.00
130	Milt Bolling	12.00	6.00	3.50
131	Joe Astroth	12.00	6.00	3.50
132	Bob Feller	100.00	50.00	30.00
133	Duane Pillette	12.00	6.00	3.50
134	Luis Aloma	12.00	6.00	3.50
135	Johnny Pesky	12.00	6.00	3.50
136	Clyde Vollmer	12.00	6.00	3.50
137	Elmer N. Corwin Jr.	12.00	6.00	3.50
138a	Gil Hodges (.993/.991 Field Avg.)			
		50.00	25.00	15.00
138b	Gil Hodges (.992/.991 Field Avg.)			
		55.00	28.00	16.50
139a	Preston Ward (.961/.992 Field Avg.)			
		12.00	6.00	3.50
139b	Preston Ward (.990/.992 Field Avg.)			
		12.00	6.00	3.50
140a	Saul Rogovin (7-12 Won/Lost with 2 Strikeouts)	12.00	6.00	3.50
140b	Saul Rogovin (7-12 Won/Lost with 62 Strikeouts)	12.00	6.00	3.50
140c	Saul Rogovin (8-12 Won/Lost)	12.00	6.00	3.50
141	Joe Garagiola	45.00	23.00	13.50
142	Al Brazle	12.00	6.00	3.50
143	Puddin Head Jones	12.00	6.00	3.50
144	Ernie Johnson	12.00	6.00	3.50
145a	Billy Martin (.985/.983 Field Avg.)			
		50.00	25.00	15.00
145b	Billy Martin (.983/.982 Field Avg.)			
		60.00	30.00	18.00
146	Dick Gernert	12.00	6.00	3.50
147	Joe DeMaestri	12.00	6.00	3.50
148	Dale Mitchell	12.00	6.00	3.50
149	Bob Young	12.00	6.00	3.50
150	Cass Michaels	12.00	6.00	3.50
151	Patrick J. Mullin	12.00	6.00	3.50
152	Mickey Vernon	12.00	6.00	3.50
153a	Whitey Lockman (100/331 Assists)			
		12.00	6.00	3.50
153b	Whitey Lockman (102/333 Assists)			
		12.00	6.00	3.50
154	Don Newcombe	25.00	12.50	7.50
155	*Frank J. Thomas*	12.00	6.00	3.50
156a	Everett Lamar Bridges (320/467 Assists)			
		12.00	6.00	3.50
156b	Everett Lamar Bridges (328/475 Assists)			
		12.00	6.00	3.50
157	Omar Lown	12.00	6.00	3.50
158	Stu Miller	12.00	6.00	3.50
159	John Lindell	12.00	6.00	3.50
160	Danny O'Connell	12.00	6.00	3.50
161	Yogi Berra	175.00	87.00	52.00
162	Ted Lepcio	12.00	6.00	3.50
163a	Dave Philley (152 Games with no traded line)	12.00	6.00	3.50
163b	Dave Philley (152 Games with traded line)	25.00	12.50	7.50
163c	Dave Philley (157 Games with traded line)	12.00	6.00	3.50
164	Early "Gus" Wynn	40.00	20.00	12.50
165	Johnny Groth	12.00	6.00	3.50
166	Sandalio Consuegra	12.00	6.00	3.50
167	Bill Hoeft	12.00	6.00	3.50
168	Edward Fitzgerald (Fitz Gerald)	12.00	6.00	3.50
169	Larry Jansen	12.00	6.00	3.50
170	Edwin D. Snider	175.00	87.00	52.00
171	Carlos Bernier	12.00	6.00	3.50
172	Andy Seminick	12.00	6.00	3.50
173	Dee V. Fondy Jr.	12.00	6.00	3.50
174a	Peter Paul Castiglione (.966/.959 Field Avg.)	12.00	6.00	3.50
174b	Peter Paul Castiglione (.970/.959 Field Avg.)	12.00	6.00	3.50
175	Melvin E. Clark	12.00	6.00	3.50
176	Vernon Bickford	12.00	6.00	3.50
177	Edward Ford	110.00	55.00	33.00
178	Del Wilber	12.00	6.00	3.50
179a	Morris Martin (44 ERA)	12.00	6.00	3.50
179b	Morris Martin (4.44 ERA)	12.00	6.00	3.50
180	Joe Tipton	12.00	6.00	3.50
181	Lester Moss	12.00	6.00	3.50
182	Sherman Lollar	12.00	6.00	3.50
183	Matt Batts	12.00	6.00	3.50
184	Mickey Grasso	12.00	6.00	3.50
185a	*Daryl Spencer* (.941/.944 Field Avg.)			
		12.00	6.00	3.50
185b	*Daryl Spencer* (.933/.936 Field Avg.)			
		12.00	6.00	3.50
186	Russell Meyer	12.00	6.00	3.50
187	Verne Law (Vern)	12.00	6.00	3.50
188	Frank Smith	12.00	6.00	3.50
189	Ransom Jackson	12.00	6.00	3.50
190	Joe Presko	12.00	6.00	3.50
191	Karl A. Drews	12.00	6.00	3.50
192	Selva L. Burdette	12.00	6.00	3.50
193	Eddie Robinson	12.00	6.00	3.50
194	Sid Hudson	12.00	6.00	3.50
195	Bob Cain	12.00	6.00	3.50
196	Bob Lemon	35.00	17.50	10.50
197	Lou Kretlow	12.00	6.00	3.50
198	Virgil Trucks	12.00	6.00	3.50
199	Steve Gromek	12.00	6.00	3.50
200	C. Marrero	12.00	6.00	3.50
201	Bob Thomson	12.00	6.00	3.50
202	George Shuba	12.00	6.00	3.50
203	Vic Janowicz	12.00	6.00	3.50
204	Jack Collum	12.00	6.00	3.50
205	Hal Jeffcoat	12.00	6.00	3.50
206	Steve Bilko	12.00	6.00	3.50
207	Stan Lopata	12.00	6.00	3.50
208	Johnny Antonelli	12.00	6.00	3.50
209	Gene Woodling (photo reversed)	12.00	6.00	3.50
210	Jimmy Piersall	20.00	10.00	6.00
211	Alfred James Robertson Jr.	12.00	6.00	3.50
212a	Owen L. Friend (.964/.957 Field Avg.)			
		12.00	6.00	3.50
212b	Owen L. Friend (.967/.958 Field Avg.)			
		12.00	6.00	3.50
213	Dick Littlefield	12.00	6.00	3.50
214	Ferris Fain	12.00	6.00	3.50
215	Johnny Bucha	12.00	6.00	3.50
216a	Jerry Snyder (.988/.988 Field Avg.)			
		12.00	6.00	3.50
216b	Jerry Snyder (.968/.968 Field Avg.)			
		12.00	6.00	3.50
217a	Henry Thompson (.956/.951 Field Avg.)			
		12.00	6.00	3.50
217b	Henry Thompson (.958/.952 Field Avg.)			
		12.00	6.00	3.50
218	Preacher Roe	12.00	6.00	3.50
219	Hal Rice	12.00	6.00	3.50
220	Hobie Landrith	12.00	6.00	3.50
221	Frank Baumholtz	12.00	6.00	3.50
222	Memo Luna	12.00	6.00	3.50
223	Steve Ridzik	12.00	6.00	3.50
224	William Bruton	30.00	9.00	4.00

1955 Bowman

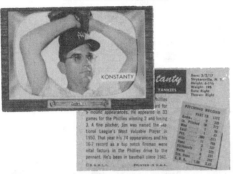

Bowman produced its final baseball card set in 1955, a popular issue which has player photographs placed inside a television set design. The set consists of 320 cards that measure 2-1/2" by 3-3/4" in size. The high-numbered cards (#'s 225-320) are scarcest in the set and include 31 umpire cards.

		NR MT	EX	VG
Complete Set:		5000.00	2500.00	1500.
Common Player: 1-224		9.00	4.50	2.75
Common Player: 225-320		25.00	12.50	7.50
1	Hoyt Wilhelm	100.00	20.00	12.00
2	Al Dark	10.00	5.00	3.00
3	Joe Coleman	9.00	4.50	2.75
4	Eddie Waitkus	9.00	4.50	2.75
5	Jim Robertson	9.00	4.50	2.75
6	Pete Suder	9.00	4.50	2.75
7	Gene Baker	9.00	4.50	2.75
8	Warren Hacker	9.00	4.50	2.75
9	Gil McDougald	12.00	6.00	3.50
10	Phil Rizzuto	50.00	25.00	15.00
11	Billy Bruton	9.00	4.50	2.75
12	Andy Pafko	10.00	5.00	3.00
13	Clyde Vollmer	9.00	4.50	2.75
14	Gus Keriazakos	9.00	4.50	2.75
15	*Frank Sullivan*	10.00	5.00	3.00
16	Jim Piersall	9.00	4.50	2.75
17	Del Ennis	10.00	5.00	3.00
18	Stan Lopata	9.00	4.50	2.75
19	Bobby Avila	9.00	4.50	2.75
20	Al Smith	9.00	4.50	2.75
21	Don Hoak	9.00	4.50	2.75
22	Roy Campanella	100.00	50.00	30.00
23	Al Kaline	150.00	75.00	45.00
24	Al Aber	9.00	4.50	2.75
25	Orestes "Minnie" Minoso	25.00	12.50	7.50
26	Virgil Trucks	10.00	5.00	3.00
27	Preston Ward	9.00	4.50	2.75
28	Dick Cole	9.00	4.50	2.75
29	Al "Red" Schoendienst	30.00	15.00	10.50
30	Bill Sarni	9.00	4.50	2.75
31	Johnny Temple	9.00	4.50	2.75
32	Wally Post	9.00	4.50	2.75
33	Nelson Fox	20.00	10.00	6.00
34	Clint Courtney	9.00	4.50	2.75
35	Bill Tuttle	9.00	4.50	2.75
36	Wayne Belardi	9.00	4.50	2.75
37	Harold "Pee Wee" Reese	80.00	40.00	25.00
38	Early Wynn	20.00	10.00	6.00
39	Bob Darnell	10.00	5.00	3.00
40	Vic Wertz	10.00	5.00	3.00
41	Mel Clark	9.00	4.50	2.75
42	Bob Greenwood	9.00	4.50	2.75
43	Bob Buhl	10.00	5.00	3.00
44	Danny O'Connell	9.00	4.50	2.75
45	Tom Umphlett	9.00	4.50	2.75
46	Mickey Vernon	10.00	5.00	3.00
47	Sammy White	9.00	4.50	2.75
48a	Milt Bolling (Frank Bolling back)	10.00	5.00	3.00
48b	Milt Bolling (Milt Bolling back)	25.00	12.50	7.50
49	Jim Greengrass	9.00	4.50	2.75
50	Hobie Landrith	9.00	4.50	2.75
51	Elvin Tappe	9.00	4.50	2.75
52	Hal Rice	9.00	4.50	2.75
53	Alex Kellner	9.00	4.50	2.75
54	Don Bollweg	9.00	4.50	2.75
55	Cal Abrams	9.00	4.50	2.75

		NR MT	EX	VG
56	Billy Cox	9.00	4.50	2.75
57	Bob Friend	10.00	5.00	3.00
58	Frank Thomas	9.00	4.50	2.75
59	Ed "Whitey" Ford	75.00	38.00	23.00
60	Enos Slaughter	30.00	15.00	9.00
61	Paul LaPalme	9.00	4.50	2.75
62	Royce Lint	9.00	4.50	2.75
63	Irv Noren	10.00	5.00	3.00
64	Curt Simmons	10.00	5.00	3.00
65	*Don Zimmer*	25.00	12.50	7.50
66	George Shuba	10.00	5.00	3.00
67	Don Larsen	20.00	10.00	6.00
68	*Elston Howard*	70.00	35.00	21.00
69	Bill Hunter	10.00	5.00	3.00
70	Lou Burdette	9.00	4.50	2.75
71	Dave Jolly	9.00	4.50	2.75
72	Chet Nichols	9.00	4.50	2.75
73	Eddie Yost	9.00	4.50	2.75
74	Jerry Snyder	9.00	4.50	2.75
75	Brooks Lawrence	9.00	4.50	2.75
76	Tom Poholsky	9.00	4.50	2.75
77	Jim McDonald	9.00	4.50	2.75
78	Gil Coan	9.00	4.50	2.75
79	Willie Miranda	9.00	4.50	2.75
80	Lou Limmer	9.00	4.50	2.75
81	Bob Morgan	9.00	4.50	2.75
82	Lee Walls	9.00	4.50	2.75
83	Max Surkont	9.00	4.50	2.75
84	George Freese	9.00	4.50	2.75
85	Cass Michaels	9.00	4.50	2.75
86	Ted Gray	9.00	4.50	2.75
87	Randy Jackson	9.00	4.50	2.75
88	Steve Bilko	9.00	4.50	2.75
89	Lou Boudreau	20.00	10.00	6.00
90	Art Ditmar	9.00	4.50	2.75
91	Dick Marlowe	9.00	4.50	2.75
92	George Zuverink	9.00	4.50	2.75
93	Andy Seminick	9.00	4.50	2.75
94	Hank Thompson	9.00	4.50	2.75
95	Sal Maglie	12.00	6.00	3.50
96	Ray Narleski	9.00	4.50	2.75
97	John Podres	20.00	10.00	6.00
98	James "Junior" Gilliam	12.00	6.00	3.50
99	Jerry Coleman	10.00	5.00	3.00
100	Tom Morgan	10.00	5.00	3.00
101a	Don Johnson (Ernie Johnson (Braves) on front)	10.00	5.00	3.00
101b	Don Johnson (Don Johnson (Orioles) on front)	25.00	12.50	7.50
102	Bobby Thomson	12.00	6.00	3.50
103	Eddie Mathews	60.00	30.00	18.00
104	Bob Porterfield	9.00	4.50	2.75
105	Johnny Schmitz	9.00	4.50	2.75
106	Del Rice	9.00	4.50	2.75
107	Solly Hemus	9.00	4.50	2.75
108	Lou Kretlow	9.00	4.50	2.75
109	Vern Stephens	9.00	4.50	2.75
110	Bob Miller	9.00	4.50	2.75
111	Steve Ridzik	9.00	4.50	2.75
112	Gran Hamner	9.00	4.50	2.75
113	Bob Hall	9.00	4.50	2.75
114	Vic Janowicz	9.00	4.50	2.75
115	Roger Bowman	9.00	4.50	2.75
116	Sandalio Consuegra	9.00	4.50	2.75
117	Johnny Groth	9.00	4.50	2.75
118	Bobby Adams	9.00	4.50	2.75
119	Joe Astroth	9.00	4.50	2.75
120	Ed Burtschy	9.00	4.50	2.75
121	Rufus Crawford	9.00	4.50	2.75
122	Al Corwin	9.00	4.50	2.75
123	Marv Grissom	9.00	4.50	2.75
124	Johnny Antonelli	10.00	5.00	3.00
125	Paul Giel	9.00	4.50	2.75
126	Billy Goodman	9.00	4.50	2.75
127	Hank Majeski	9.00	4.50	2.75
128	Mike Garcia	10.00	5.00	3.00
129	Hal Naragon	9.00	4.50	2.75
130	Richie Ashburn	25.00	12.50	7.50
131	Willard Marshall	9.00	4.50	2.75
132a	Harvey Kueen (incorrect spelling on back)	10.00	5.00	3.00
132b	Harvey Kuenn (correct spelling on back)	30.00	15.00	9.00
133	Charles King	9.00	4.50	2.75
134	Bob Feller	60.00	30.00	18.00
135	Lloyd Merriman	9.00	4.50	2.75
136	Rocky Bridges	9.00	4.50	2.75
137	Bob Talbot	9.00	4.50	2.75
138	Davey Williams	9.00	4.50	2.75
139	Billy & Bobby Shantz	9.00	4.50	2.75
140	Bobby Shantz	10.00	5.00	3.00

		NR MT	EX	VG
141	Wes Westrum	10.00	5.00	3.00
142	Rudy Regalado	9.00	4.50	2.75
143	Don Newcombe	25.00	12.50	7.50
144	Art Houtteman	9.00	4.50	2.75
145	Bob Nieman	9.00	4.50	2.75
146	Don Liddle	9.00	4.50	2.75
147	Sam Mele	9.00	4.50	2.75
148	Bob Chakales	9.00	4.50	2.75
149	Cloyd Boyer	9.00	4.50	2.75
150	Bill Klaus	9.00	4.50	2.75
151	Jim Brideweser	9.00	4.50	2.75
152	Johnny Klippstein	9.00	4.50	2.75
153	Eddie Robinson	10.00	5.00	3.00
154	*Frank Lary*	9.00	4.50	2.75
155	Gerry Staley	9.00	4.50	2.75
156	Jim Hughes	10.00	5.00	3.00
157a	Ernie Johnson (Don Johnson (Orioles) picture on front)	10.00	5.00	3.00
157b	Ernie Johnson (Ernie Johnson (Braves) picture on front)	18.00	9.00	5.50
158	Gil Hodges	40.00	20.00	12.00
159	Harry Byrd	9.00	4.50	2.75
160	Bill Skowron	25.00	12.50	7.50
161	Matt Batts	9.00	4.50	2.75
162	Charlie Maxwell	9.00	4.50	2.75
163	Sid Gordon	9.00	4.50	2.75
164	Toby Atwell	9.00	4.50	2.75
165	Maurice McDermott	9.00	4.50	2.75
166	Jim Busby	9.00	4.50	2.75
167	Bob Grim	10.00	5.00	3.00
168	Larry "Yogi" Berra	110.00	55.00	33.00
169	Carl Furillo	25.00	12.50	7.50
170	Carl Erskine	15.00	7.50	4.50
171	Robin Roberts	30.00	15.00	9.00
172	Willie Jones	9.00	4.50	2.75
173	Al "Chico" Carrasquel	9.00	4.50	2.75
174	Sherman Lollar	10.00	5.00	3.00
175	Wilmer Shantz	9.00	4.50	2.75
176	Joe DeMaestri	9.00	4.50	2.75
177	Willard Nixon	9.00	4.50	2.75
178	Tom Brewer	9.00	4.50	2.75
179	Hank Aaron	250.00	125.00	75.00
180	Johnny Logan	9.00	4.50	2.75
181	Eddie Miksis	9.00	4.50	2.75
182	Bob Rush	9.00	4.50	2.75
183	Ray Katt	9.00	4.50	2.75
184	Willie Mays	250.00	125.00	75.00
185	Vic Raschi	10.00	5.00	3.00
186	Alex Grammas	9.00	4.50	2.75
187	Fred Hatfield	9.00	4.50	2.75
188	Ned Garver	9.00	4.50	2.75
189	Jack Collum	9.00	4.50	2.75
190	Fred Baczewski	9.00	4.50	2.75
191	Bob Lemon	25.00	12.50	7.50
192	George Strickland	9.00	4.50	2.75
193	Howie Judson	9.00	4.50	2.75
194	Joe Nuxhall	10.00	5.00	3.00
195a	Erv Palica (no traded line on back)	9.00	4.50	2.75
195b	Erv Palica (traded line on back)	25.00	12.50	7.50
196	Russ Meyer	10.00	5.00	3.00
197	Ralph Kiner	35.00	17.50	10.50
198	Dave Pope	9.00	4.50	2.75
199	Vernon Law	10.00	5.00	3.00
200	Dick Littlefield	9.00	4.50	2.75
201	Allie Reynolds	25.00	12.50	7.50
202	Mickey Mantle	500.00	250.00	150.00
203	Steve Gromek	9.00	4.50	2.75
204a	*Frank Bolling* (Milt Bolling back)	10.00	5.00	3.00
204b	*Frank Bolling* (Frank Bolling back)	20.00	10.00	6.00
205	Eldon "Rip" Repulski	9.00	4.50	2.75
206	Ralph Beard	9.00	4.50	2.75
207	Frank Shea	9.00	4.50	2.75
208	Eddy Fitzgerald (Fitz Gerald)	9.00	4.50	2.75
209	Forrest "Smoky" Burgess	10.00	5.00	3.00
210	Earl Torgeson	9.00	4.50	2.75
211	John "Sonny" Dixon	9.00	4.50	2.75
212	Jack Dittmer	9.00	4.50	2.75
213	George Kell	25.00	12.50	7.50
214	Billy Pierce	10.00	5.00	3.00
215	Bob Kuzava	9.00	4.50	2.75
216	Preacher Roe	10.00	5.00	3.00
217	Del Crandall	10.00	5.00	3.00
218	Joe Adcock	10.00	5.00	3.00
219	Whitey Lockman	9.00	4.50	2.75
220	Jim Hearn	9.00	4.50	2.75
221	Hector "Skinny" Brown	9.00	4.50	2.75
222	Russ Kemmerer	9.00	4.50	2.75
223	Hal Jeffcoat	9.00	4.50	2.75
224	Dee Fondy	9.00	4.50	2.75

		NR MT	EX	VG
225	Paul Richards	16.00	8.00	4.75
226	W.F. McKinley (umpire)	25.00	12.50	7.50
227	Frank Baumholtz	15.00	7.50	4.50
228	John M. Phillips	15.00	7.50	4.50
229	Jim Brosnan	16.00	8.00	4.75
230	Al Brazle	15.00	7.50	4.50
231	Jim Konstanty	25.00	12.50	7.50
232	Birdie Tebbetts	15.00	7.50	4.50
233	Bill Serena	15.00	7.50	4.50
234	Dick Bartell	15.00	7.50	4.50
235	J.A. Paparella (umpire)	25.00	12.50	7.50
236	Murray Dickson (Murry)	15.00	7.50	4.50
237	Johnny Wyrostek	15.00	7.50	4.50
238	Eddie Stanky	16.00	8.00	4.75
239	Edwin A. Rommel (umpire)	25.00	12.50	7.50
240	Billy Loes	16.00	8.00	4.75
241	John Pesky	16.00	8.00	4.75
242	Ernie Banks	400.00	200.00	125.00
243	Gus Bell	16.00	8.00	4.75
244	Duane Pillette	15.00	7.50	4.50
245	Bill Miller	15.00	7.50	4.50
246	Hank Bauer	30.00	15.00	9.00
247	Dutch Leonard	15.00	7.50	4.50
248	Harry Dorish	15.00	7.50	4.50
249	Billy Gardner	15.00	7.50	4.50
250	Larry Napp (umpire)	25.00	12.50	7.50
251	Stan Jok	15.00	7.50	4.50
252	Roy Smalley	15.00	7.50	4.50
253	Jim Wilson	15.00	7.50	4.50
254	Bennett Flowers	15.00	7.50	4.50
255	Pete Runnels	16.00	8.00	4.75
256	Owen Friend	15.00	7.50	4.50
257	Tom Alston	15.00	7.50	4.50
258	John W. Stevens (umpire)	25.00	12.50	7.50
259	*Don Mossi*	25.00	12.50	7.50
260	Edwin H. Hurley (umpire)	25.00	12.50	7.50
261	Walt Moryn	16.00	8.00	4.75
262	Jim Lemon	16.00	8.00	4.75
263	Eddie Joost	15.00	7.50	4.50
264	Bill Henry	15.00	7.50	4.50
265	Albert J. Barlick (umpire)	80.00	40.00	25.00
266	Mike Fornieles	15.00	7.50	4.50
267	George (Jim) Honochick (umpire)	80.00	40.00	25.00
268	Roy Lee Hawes	15.00	7.50	4.50
269	Joe Amalfitano	15.00	7.50	4.50
270	Chico Fernandez	16.00	8.00	4.75
271	Bob Hooper	15.00	7.50	4.50
272	John Flaherty (umpire)	25.00	12.50	7.50
273	Emory "Bubba" Church	15.00	7.50	4.50
274	Jim Delsing	15.00	7.50	4.50
275	William T. Grieve (umpire)	25.00	12.50	7.50
276	Ivan Delock	15.00	7.50	4.50
277	Ed Runge (umpire)	25.00	12.50	7.50
278	*Charles Neal*	25.00	12.50	7.50
279	Hank Soar (umpire)	25.00	12.50	7.50
280	Clyde McCullough	15.00	7.50	4.50
281	Charles Berry (umpire)	25.00	12.50	7.50
282	Phil Cavarretta	16.00	8.00	4.75
283	Nestor Chylak (umpire)	25.00	12.50	7.50
284	William A. Jackowski (umpire)	25.00	12.50	7.50
285	Walt Dropo	16.00	8.00	4.75
286	Frank E. Secory (umpire)	25.00	12.50	7.50
287	Ron Mrozinski	15.00	7.50	4.50
288	Dick Smith	15.00	7.50	4.50
289	Arthur J. Gore (umpire)	25.00	12.50	7.50
290	Hershell Freeman	15.00	7.50	4.50
291	Frank Dascoli (umpire)	25.00	12.50	7.50
292	Marv Blaylock	15.00	7.50	4.50
293	Thomas D. Gorman (umpire)	25.00	12.50	7.50
294	Wally Moses	15.00	7.50	4.50
295	E. Lee Ballanfant (umpire)	25.00	12.50	7.50
296	*Bill Virdon*	40.00	20.00	12.00
297	L.R. "Dusty" Boggess (umpire)	25.00	12.50	7.50
298	Charlie Grimm	25.00	12.50	7.50
299	Lonnie Warneke (umpire)	25.00	12.50	7.50
300	Tommy Byrne	16.00	8.00	4.75
301	William R. Engeln (umpire)	25.00	12.50	7.50
302	*Frank Malzone*	30.00	15.00	9.00
303	J.B. "Jocko" Conlan (umpire)	100.00	50.00	30.00
304	Harry Chiti	15.00	7.50	4.50
305	Frank Umont (umpire)	25.00	12.50	7.50
306	Bob Cerv	25.00	12.50	7.50
307	R.A. "Babe" Pinelli (umpire)	25.00	12.50	7.50
308	Al Lopez	40.00	20.00	12.00
309	Hal H. Dixon (umpire)	25.00	12.50	7.50
310	Ken Lehman	16.00	8.00	4.75
311	Lawrence J. Goetz (umpire)	25.00	12.50	7.50
312	Bill Wight	15.00	7.50	4.50
313	A.J. Donatelli (umpire)	25.00	12.50	7.50
314	Dale Mitchell	15.00	7.50	4.50

		NR MT	EX	VG
315	Cal Hubbard (umpire)	100.00	50.00	30.00
316	Marion Fricano	15.00	7.50	4.50
317	Wm. R. Summers (umpire)	25.00	12.50	7.50
318	Sid Hudson	15.00	7.50	4.50
319	Albert B. Schroll	25.00	12.50	7.50
320	George D. Susce, Jr.	60.00	30.00	18.00

1954 Briggs Meats

The Briggs Meat set was issued over a two-year span (1953-54) and features 26 players from the Washington Senators and 12 from the New York City area baseball teams. The set was issued in two-card panels on hot dog packages sold in the Washington, D.C. vicinity. The color cards, which are blank-backed and measure 2-1/4" by 3-1/2", are printed on waxed cardboard. The style of the Senators cards in the set differs from that of the New York players. Poses for the New York players can also be found on cards in the 1954 Dan-Dee Potato Chips and 1953-1955 Stahl-Meyer Franks sets.

		NR MT	EX	VG
	Complete Set	8000.00	4000.00	2500.
	Common Player	100.00	50.00	30.00
(1)	Hank Bauer	150.00	75.00	45.00
(2)	James Busby	100.00	50.00	30.00
(3)	Tommy Byrne	100.00	50.00	30.00
(4)	John Dixon	100.00	50.00	30.00
(5)	Carl Erskine	150.00	75.00	45.00
(6)	Edward Fitzgerald (Fitz Gerald)	100.00	50.00	30.00
(7)	Newton Grasso	100.00	50.00	30.00
(8)	Melvin Hoderlein	100.00	50.00	30.00
(9)	Gil Hodges	250.00	125.00	75.00
(10)	Monte Irvin	175.00	87.00	52.00
(11)	Whitey Lockman	100.00	50.00	30.00
(12)	Mickey Mantle	2200.00	1100.00	660.00
(13)	Conrado Marrero	100.00	50.00	30.00
(14)	Walter Masterson	100.00	50.00	30.00
(15)	Carmen Mauro	100.00	50.00	30.00
(16)	Willie Mays	1000.00	500.00	300.00
(17)	Mickey McDermott	100.00	50.00	30.00
(18)	Gil McDougald	150.00	75.00	45.00
(19)	Julio Moreno	100.00	50.00	30.00
(20)	Don Mueller	100.00	50.00	30.00
(21)	Don Newcombe	150.00	75.00	45.00
(22)	Robert Oldis	100.00	50.00	30.00
(23)	Erwin Porterfield	100.00	50.00	30.00
(24)	Phil Rizzuto	250.00	125.00	75.00
(25)	James Runnels	100.00	50.00	30.00
(26)	John Schmitz	100.00	50.00	30.00
(27)	Angel Scull	100.00	50.00	30.00
(28)	Frank Shea	100.00	50.00	30.00
(29)	Albert Sima	100.00	50.00	30.00
(30)	Duke Snider	500.00	250.00	150.00
(31)	Charles Stobbs	100.00	50.00	30.00
(32)	Willard Terwilliger	100.00	50.00	30.00
(33)	Joe Tipton	100.00	50.00	30.00
(34)	Thomas Umphlett	100.00	50.00	30.00
(35)	Gene Verble	100.00	50.00	30.00
(36)	James Vernon	125.00	62.00	37.00
(37)	Clyde Volmer (Vollmer)	100.00	50.00	30.00
(38)	Edward Yost	100.00	50.00	30.00

1947 Bond Bread
Jackie Robinson

The major league's first black player, Jackie Robinson, was featured in a 13-card set issued by Bond Bread in 1947. The cards, which measure 2-1/4" by 3-1/2", are black and white photos of Robinson in various action and portrait poses. The unnumbered cards bear three different backs which contain advertising for Bond Bread. Four of the 13 cards make use of a horizontal format. Card #6 in the checklist below is believed to have been issued in greater quantities and perhaps was a promotional card. The back of this card is the only one in the set containing a short biography of Jackie. The ACC designation for the set is D302.

		NR MT	EX	VG
	Complete Set:	4500.00	2250.00	1350.
	Common Player:	250.00	125.00	75.00
(1)	Batting (awaiting pitch)	375.00	187.00	112.00
(2)	Batting Follow-Thru (white shirtsleeves)			
		375.00	187.00	112.00
(3)	Batting Follow-Thru (no shirtsleeves)			
		375.00	187.00	112.00
(4)	Leaping (scoreboard in background)			
		375.00	187.00	112.00
(5)	Leaping (no scoreboard)	375.00	187.00	112.00
(6)	Portrait (facsimile autograph)	250.00	125.00	75.00
(7)	Portrait (holding glove in air)	375.00	187.00	112.00
(8)	Running (down the baseline)	375.00	187.00	112.00
(9)	Running (about to catch ball)	375.00	187.00	112.00
(10)	Sliding (umpire in picture)	375.00	187.00	112.00
(11)	Stretching For Throw (ball in glove)			
		375.00	187.00	112.00
(12)	Stretching For Throw (no ball visible)			
		375.00	187.00	112.00
(13)	Throwing (ball in hand)	375.00	187.00	112.00

1933 Butter Cream

The 1933 Butter Cream set consists of 30 unnumbered, black and white cards which measure 1-1/4" by 3-1/2" in size. The card backs feature a contest sponsored by the Butter Cream Confectionary Corp. in which the collector was to estimate the players' statistics by a specific date. Two different backs are known: 1) Estimate through Sept. 1 and no company address, and 2) Estimate through Oct. 1 with the Butter Cream address. The ACC designation for the set is R306.

		NR MT	EX	VG
Complete Set:		11000.00	5500.00	3300.
Common Player:		225.00	112.00	67.00
(1)	Earl Averill	350.00	175.00	105.00
(2)	Ed. Brandt	225.00	112.00	67.00
(3)	Guy T. Bush	225.00	112.00	67.00
(4)	Gordon Cochrane	400.00	200.00	120.00
(5)	Joe Cronin	400.00	200.00	120.00
(6)	George Earnshaw	225.00	112.00	67.00
(7)	Wesley Ferrell	225.00	112.00	67.00
(8)	"Jimmy" E. Foxx	600.00	300.00	175.00
(9)	Frank C. Frisch	400.00	200.00	120.00
(10)	Charles M. Gelbert	225.00	112.00	67.00
(11)	"Lefty" Robert M. Grove	450.00	225.00	135.00
(12)	Leo Charles Hartnett	350.00	175.00	105.00
(13)	"Babe" Herman	225.00	112.00	67.00
(14)	Charles Klein	350.00	175.00	105.00
(15)	Ray Kremer	225.00	112.00	67.00
(16)	Fred C. Linstrom (Lindstrom)	350.00	175.00	105.00
(17)	Ted A. Lyons	350.00	175.00	105.00
(18)	"Pepper" John L. Martin	225.00	112.00	67.00
(19)	Robert O'Farrell	225.00	112.00	67.00
(20)	Ed. A. Rommel	225.00	112.00	67.00
(21)	Charles Root	225.00	112.00	67.00
(22)	Harold "Muddy" Ruel (Herold)	225.00	112.00	67.00
(23)	Babe Ruth	2500.00	1250.00	750.00
(24)	"Al" Simmons	350.00	175.00	105.00
(25)	"Bill" Terry	400.00	200.00	120.00
(26)	George E. Uhle	225.00	112.00	67.00
(27)	Lloyd J. Waner	350.00	175.00	105.00
(28)	Paul G. Waner	350.00	175.00	105.00
(29)	"Hack" Wilson	350.00	175.00	105.00
(30)	Glen. Wright	225.00	112.00	67.00

1912 C46

This minor league set, issued in 1912 by the Imperial Tobacco Company, is the only tobacco baseball set issued in Canada. Designated as C46 in the American Card Catalog, each sepia-toned card measures 1-1/2" by 2-5/8" and features a distinctive card design that pictures the player inside an oval surrounded by a simulated woodgrain background featuring a bat, ball and glove in the borders. The player's last name appears in capital letters in a panel beneath the oval. (An exception is the card of James Murray, whose caption includes both first and last names.) The backs include the player's name and team at the top, followed by a brief biography. The 90 subjects in the set are members of the eight teams in the Eastern League (Rochester, Toronto, Buffalo, Newark, Providence, Baltimore, Montreal and Jersey City), even though the card backs refer to it as the International League. Although a minor league issue, the C46 set contains many players with major league experience, including Hall of Famers Joe Kelley and Joe "Iron Man" McGinnity.

		NR MT	EX	VG
Complete Set:		4200.00	2100.00	1260.
Common Player:		35.00	17.50	10.50
1	William O'Hara	100.00	50.00	30.00
2	James McGinley	50.00	25.00	15.00
3	"Frenchy" LeClaire	35.00	17.50	10.50
4	John White	35.00	17.50	10.50
5	James Murray	35.00	17.50	10.50
6	Joe Ward	35.00	17.50	10.50
7	"Whitey" Alperman	35.00	17.50	10.50
8	"Natty" Nattress	35.00	17.50	10.50
9	Fred Sline	35.00	17.50	10.50
10	Royal Rock	35.00	17.50	10.50
11	Ray Demmitt	35.00	17.50	10.50
12	"Butcher Boy" Schmidt	35.00	17.50	10.50
13	Samuel Frock	35.00	17.50	10.50
14	Fred Burchell	35.00	17.50	10.50
15	Jack Kelley	35.00	17.50	10.50
16	Frank Barberich	35.00	17.50	10.50
17	Frank Corridon	35.00	17.50	10.50
18	"Doc" Adkins	35.00	17.50	10.50
19	Jack Dunn	35.00	17.50	10.50
20	James Walsh	35.00	17.50	10.50
21	Charles Hanford	35.00	17.50	10.50
22	Dick Rudolph	35.00	17.50	10.50
23	Curt Elston	35.00	17.50	10.50
24	Silton	35.00	17.50	10.50
25	Charlie French	35.00	17.50	10.50
26	John Ganzel	35.00	17.50	10.50
27	Joe Kelley	200.00	100.00	60.00
28	Benny Meyers	35.00	17.50	10.50
29	George Schirm	35.00	17.50	10.50
30	William Purtell	35.00	17.50	10.50
31	Bayard Sharpe	35.00	17.50	10.50
32	Tony Smith	35.00	17.50	10.50
33	John Lush	35.00	17.50	10.50
34	William Collins	35.00	17.50	10.50
35	Art Phelan	35.00	17.50	10.50
36	Edward Phelps	35.00	17.50	10.50
37	"Rube" Vickers	35.00	17.50	10.50
38	Cy Seymour	35.00	17.50	10.50
39	"Shadow" Carroll	35.00	17.50	10.50
40	Jake Gettman	35.00	17.50	10.50
41	Luther Taylor	35.00	17.50	10.50
42	Walter Justis	35.00	17.50	10.50
43	Robert Fisher	35.00	17.50	10.50
44	Fred Parent	35.00	17.50	10.50
45	James Dygert	35.00	17.50	10.50
46	Johnnie Butler	35.00	17.50	10.50
47	Fred Mitchell	35.00	17.50	10.50
48	Heinie Batch	35.00	17.50	10.50
49	Michael Corcoran	35.00	17.50	10.50
50	Edward Doescher	35.00	17.50	10.50
51	Wheeler	35.00	17.50	10.50
52	Elijah Jones	35.00	17.50	10.50
53	Fred Truesdale	35.00	17.50	10.50
54	Fred Beebe	35.00	17.50	10.50
55	Louis Brockett	35.00	17.50	10.50
56	Wells	35.00	17.50	10.50
57	"Lew" McAllister	35.00	17.50	10.50
58	Ralph Stroud	35.00	17.50	10.50
59	Manser	35.00	17.50	10.50
60	"Ducky" Holmes	35.00	17.50	10.50
61	Rube Dessau	35.00	17.50	10.50
62	Fred Jacklitsch	35.00	17.50	10.50
63	Graham	35.00	17.50	10.50
64	Noah Henline	35.00	17.50	10.50
65	"Chick" Gandil	50.00	25.00	15.00
66	Tom Hughes	35.00	17.50	10.50
67	Joseph Delehanty	35.00	17.50	10.50
68	Pierce	35.00	17.50	10.50
69	Gaunt	35.00	17.50	10.50
70	Edward Fitzpatrick	35.00	17.50	10.50
71	Wyatt Lee	35.00	17.50	10.50
72	John Kissinger	35.00	17.50	10.50
73	William Malarkey	35.00	17.50	10.50
74	William Byers	35.00	17.50	10.50
75	George Simmons	35.00	17.50	10.50
76	Daniel Moeller	35.00	17.50	10.50
77	Joseph McGinnity	200.00	100.00	60.00
78	Alex Hardy	35.00	17.50	10.50
79	Bob Holmes	35.00	17.50	10.50
80	William Baxter	35.00	17.50	10.50
81	Edward Spencer	35.00	17.50	10.50
82	Bradley Kocher	35.00	17.50	10.50
83	Robert Shaw	35.00	17.50	10.50
84	Joseph Yeager	35.00	17.50	10.50
85	Carlo	35.00	17.50	10.50

		NR MT	EX	VG
86	William Abstein	35.00	17.50	10.50
87	Tim Jordan	35.00	17.50	10.50
88	Dick Breen	35.00	17.50	10.50
89	Tom McCarty	50.00	25.00	15.00
90	Ed Curtis	100.00	50.00	30.00

A player's name in italic indicates a rookie card. An (FC) indicates a player's first card for that particular card company.

1956 Carling Indians

This 10-card set was sponsored by Carling Black Label Beer. The oversized cards feature black and white posed photos with the plyers' name and a Carling ad at the bottom of the card front.

		NR MT	EX	VG
	Complete Set:	50.00	25.00	15.00
	Common Player:	3.00	1.50	.90
(1)	Bob Feller	20.00	10.00	6.00
(2)	Mike Garcia	3.00	1.50	.90
(3)	Jim Hegan	3.00	1.50	.90
(4)	Art Houtteman	3.00	1.50	.90
(5)	Bob Lemon	10.00	5.00	3.00
(6)	Al Rosen	6.00	3.00	1.75
(7)	Herb Score	7.00	3.50	2.00
(8)	Al Smith	3.00	2.25	1.25
(9)	George Strickland	3.00	2.25	1.25
(10)	Early Wynn	10.00	5.00	3.00

1932 Charles Denby Cigars Cubs

Actually a series of postcards, this Chicago Cubs set issued by the Charles Denby Company in 1932 is the last known tobacco issue produced before World War II. The cards are a standard postcard size (5-1/4" by 3-3/8") and feature a glossy black and white player photo with a facsimile autograph. In typical postcard style, the back of the card is divided in half, with a printed player profile on the left and room for the mailing address on the right. The back also includes an advertisement for Charles Denby Cigars, the mild five-cent cigar "for men who like to inhale". Only five different subjects have been reported to date, but there is speculation that more probably exist.

		NR MT	EX	VG
	Complete Set:	500.00	250.00	150.00
	Common Player:	80.00	40.00	24.00
(1)	Elwood English	80.00	40.00	24.00
(2)	Charles J. Grimm	110.00	55.00	33.00
(3)	William Herman	175.00	87.00	52.00
(4)	William F. Jurges	80.00	40.00	24.00
(5)	Lonnie Warneke	80.00	40.00	24.00

1914 D303

Hartzell, c. f. N. Y. Americans

COMPLIMENTS OF

GENERAL BAKING CO.

UNTIL SEPTEMBER 1ST. WRAPPED IN

STAR BREAD FRENCH BREAD LITTLE GENERAL BREAD

Issued in 1914 by the General Baking Company, these unnumbered cards measure 1-1/2" by 2-3/4". The player photos and fronts of the cards are identical to the E106 set, but the D303 cards are easily identified by the advertisement for General Baking on the back.

		NR MT	EX	VG
	Complete Set:	10000.00	5000.00	3000.
	Common Player:	80.00	40.00	24.00
(1)	Jack Barry	80.00	40.00	24.00
(2)	Chief Bender (blue background)			
		200.00	100.00	60.00
(3)	Chief Bender (green background)			
		200.00	100.00	60.00
(4a)	Bob Bescher (New York)	80.00	40.00	24.00
(4b)	Bob Bescher (St. Louis)	80.00	40.00	24.00
(5)	Roger Bresnahan	200.00	100.00	60.00
(6)	Al Bridwell	80.00	40.00	24.00
(7)	Donie Bush	80.00	40.00	24.00
(8)	Hal Chase (catching)	90.00	45.00	27.00
(9)	Hal Chase (portrait)	90.00	45.00	27.00
(10)	Ty Cobb (batting, front view)	1000.00	500.00	300.00
(11)	Ty Cobb (batting, side view)	1000.00	500.00	300.00
(12)	Eddie Collins	200.00	100.00	60.00
(13)	Sam Crawford	200.00	100.00	60.00
(14)	Ray Demmitt	80.00	40.00	24.00
(15)	Wild Bill Donovan	80.00	40.00	24.00
(16)	Red Dooin	80.00	40.00	24.00
(17)	Mickey Doolan	80.00	40.00	24.00
(18)	Larry Doyle	80.00	40.00	24.00
(19)	Clyde Engle	80.00	40.00	24.00
(20)	Johnny Evers	200.00	100.00	60.00
(21)	Art Fromme	80.00	40.00	24.00
(22)	George Gibson (catching, back view)			
		80.00	40.00	24.00
(23)	George Gibson (catching, front view)			
		80.00	40.00	24.00
(24)	Roy Hartzell	80.00	40.00	24.00
(25)	Fred Jacklitsch	80.00	40.00	24.00
(26)	Hugh Jennings	200.00	100.00	60.00
(27)	Otto Knabe	80.00	40.00	24.00
(28)	Nap Lajoie	300.00	150.00	90.00
(29)	Hans Lobert	80.00	40.00	24.00
(30)	Rube Marquard	200.00	100.00	60.00
(31)	Christy Mathewson	600.00	300.00	180.00
(32)	John McGraw	250.00	125.00	75.00
(33)	George McQuillan	80.00	40.00	24.00

		NR MT	EX	VG
(34)	Dots Miller	80.00	40.00	24.00
(35)	Danny Murphy	80.00	40.00	24.00
(36)	Rebel Oakes	80.00	40.00	24.00
(37a)	Eddie Plank (no position on front)			
		200.00	100.00	60.00
(37b)	Eddie Plank (position on front)	200.00	100.00	60.00
(38)	Germany Schaefer	80.00	40.00	24.00
(39)	Boss Smith (Schmidt)	80.00	40.00	24.00
(40)	Tris Speaker	250.00	125.00	75.00
(41)	Oscar Stanage	80.00	40.00	24.00
(42)	George Stovall	80.00	40.00	24.00
(43)	Jeff Sweeney	80.00	40.00	24.00
(44)	Joe Tinker (batting)	200.00	100.00	60.00
(45)	Joe Tinker (portrait)	200.00	100.00	60.00
(46)	Honus Wagner (batting)	600.00	300.00	180.00
(47)	Honus Wagner (throwing)	600.00	300.00	180.00
(48)	Hooks Wiltse	80.00	40.00	24.00
(49)	Heinie Zimmerman	80.00	40.00	24.00

1911 D304

This unnumbered 25-card set, issued in 1911, is similar in design to the tobacco and candy company issues of the same period, but is different in size, measuring 1-3/4" by 2-1/2". The fronts of the cards feature a color lithograph with the player's name and team below in capital letters. The backs advertise various breads produced by the General Baking Company in the Buffalo, N.Y. area. The bottom of the back notes that "There are 25 subjects in this set/One with each loaf of the above breads."

		NR MT	EX	VG
Complete Set:		5000.00	2500.00	1500.
Common Player:		50.00	25.00	15.00
(1)	J. Frank Baker	125.00	62.00	37.00
(2)	Jack Barry	50.00	25.00	15.00
(3)	George Bell	50.00	25.00	15.00
(4)	Charles Bender	125.00	62.00	37.00
(5)	Frank Chance	125.00	62.00	37.00
(6)	Hal Chase	75.00	38.00	23.00
(7)	Ty Cobb	900.00	450.00	270.00
(8)	Eddie Collins	125.00	62.00	37.00
(9)	Otis Crandall	50.00	25.00	15.00
(10)	Sam Crawford	125.00	62.00	37.00
(11)	John Evers	125.00	62.00	37.00
(12)	Arthur Fletcher	50.00	25.00	15.00
(13)	Charles Herzog	50.00	25.00	15.00
(14)	M. Kelly	50.00	25.00	15.00
(15)	Napoleon Lajoie	200.00	100.00	60.00
(16)	Rube Marquard	125.00	62.00	37.00
(17)	Christy Mathewson	375.00	187.00	115.00
(18)	Fred Merkle	50.00	25.00	15.00
(19)	"Chief" Meyers	50.00	25.00	15.00
(20)	Marty O'Toole	50.00	25.00	15.00
(21)	Nap. Rucker	50.00	25.00	15.00
(22)	Arthur Shafer	50.00	25.00	15.00
(23)	Fred Tenny (Tenney)	50.00	25.00	15.00
(24)	Honus Wagner	600.00	300.00	180.00
(25)	Cy Young	375.00	187.00	112.00

NOTE: A card number in parentheses ( ) indicates the set is unnumbered.

A player's name in *italic* indicates a rookie card. An (FC) indicates a player's first card for that particular card company.

1916 D381 Fleischman Bread

		NR MT	EX	VG
Complete Set:		1200.00	600.00	325.00
Common Player:				

(1)	Grover Alexander (pitcher)
(2)	Fred Anderson (pitcher)
(3)	Dave Bancroft (shortstop)
(4)	Beals Becker (right field)
(5)	Eddie Burns (catcher)
(6)	R.B. Caldwell (pitcher)
(7)	James J. Callahan (Mgr., catcher)
(8)	William Carrigan (Mgr.)
(9)	Tom Clark (catcher)
(10)	Ray W. Collins (pitcher)
(11)	Wm. E. Donovan (Mgr.)
(12)	Larry Doyle (second base)
(13)	Bobby Dyrne (third base)
(14)	Johnny Evers (second base)
(15)	Harry Gardner (third base)
(16)	Larry Gilbert (outfielder)
(17)	Frank Gilhooley (right field)
(18)	Heinie Groh (third base)
(19)	Claude Hendrix (pitcher)
(20)	Dick Hoblitzell (first base)
(21)	Chas. Hoerzog (Mgr., shortstop)
(22)	H.H. Hunter (first base)
(23)	Harold Janvrin (shortstop)
(24)	Erving L. Kantlehner (pitcher)
(25)	R.H. Keating (pitcher)
(26)	Wade Killifer (center field)
(27)	Fred Landerus (first base)
(28)	H.B. Leonard (pitcher)
(29)	Duffy Lewis (second base)
(30)	Ed H. Love (pitcher)
(31)	Albert L. Mamaux (pitcher)
(32)	Christopher Matthewson (pitcher)
(33)	W.B. McKechnie (third base)
(34)	Chief Meyer (catcher)
(35)	Dan Murphy (catcher)
(36)	Rube Oldring (left field)
(37)	'Dode' Paskert (center field)
(38)	Wm. Rodgers (second base)
(39)	Edw. F. Rousch (right field)
(40)	Pete Schneider (pitcher)
(41)	Ernie Shore (pitcher)
(42)	Fred Snodgrass (center field)
(43)	Tris Speaker (center field)
(44)	George T. Stallings (Manager)
(45)	C.D. Stengle (right field)
(46)	Amos Strunk (center field)
(47)	Chas. Tesreau (pitcher)
(48)	Chester D. Thomas (catcher)
(49)	Chester D. Thomas (catcher)
(50)	John P. Wagner (shortstop)
(51)	George Whitten (center field)
(52)	Arthur Wilson (catcher)
(53)	Ivy Wingo (catcher)

1954 Dan-Dee Potato Chips

Issued in bags of potato chips, the cards in this 29-card set are commonly found with grease stains despite their waxed surface. The unnumbered cards, which measure 2-1/2" by 3-5/8", feature full-color

AL LOPEZ

photos. The card backs contain player statistical and biographical information. The set consists mostly of players from the Indians and Pirates. Photos of the Yankees players were also used for the Briggs Meats and Stahl-Meyer Franks sets. Cooper and Smith are the scarcest cards in the set.

		NR MT	EX	VG
Complete Set		4500.00	2250.00	1350.
Common Player		60.00	30.00	18.00
(1)	Bob Avila	60.00	30.00	18.00
(2)	Hank Bauer	80.00	40.00	24.00
(3)	Walker Cooper	350.00	175.00	105.00
(4)	Larry Doby	90.00	45.00	27.00
(5)	Luke Easter	60.00	30.00	18.00
(6)	Bob Feller	200.00	100.00	60.00
(7)	Bob Friend	60.00	30.00	18.00
(8)	Mike Garcia	60.00	30.00	18.00
(9)	Sid Gordon	60.00	30.00	18.00
(10)	Jim Hegan	60.00	30.00	18.00
(11)	Gil Hodges	150.00	75.00	45.00
(12)	Art Houtteman	60.00	30.00	18.00
(13)	Monte Irvin	100.00	50.00	30.00
(14)	Paul LaPalm (LaPalme)	60.00	30.00	18.00
(15)	Bob Lemon	110.00	55.00	33.00
(16)	Al Lopez	90.00	45.00	27.00
(17)	Mickey Mantle	1500.00	750.00	450.00
(18)	Dale Mitchell	60.00	30.00	18.00
(19)	Phil Rizzuto	125.00	62.00	37.00
(20)	Curtis Roberts	60.00	30.00	18.00
(21)	Al Rosen	80.00	40.00	24.00
(22)	Red Schoendienst	110.00	55.00	33.00
(23)	Paul Smith	450.00	225.00	135.00
(24)	Duke Snider	225.00	112.00	67.00
(25)	George Strickland	60.00	30.00	18.00
(26)	Max Surkont	60.00	30.00	18.00
(27)	Frank Thomas	125.00	62.00	37.00
(28)	Wally Westlake	60.00	30.00	18.00
(29)	Early Wynn	110.00	55.00	33.00

1933 Delong

HAROLD (PIE) TRAYNOR
PITTSBURGH PIRATES

The DeLong Gum Company of Boston, Mass. was among the first to sell baseball cards with gum. It issued a set of 24 cards in 1933, the same year the Goudey Gum Co. issued its premiere set, making both companies pioneers in the field. The DeLong cards

measure 2" by 3" and feature black and white player photos on a color background. The photos show the players in various action poses and positions them in the middle of a miniature stadium setting so that they appear to be giant in size. Most of the cards in the set are vertically designed, but a few are horizontal. The backs of the cards, written by Austen Lake, editor of the Boston Transcript, contain a series of sports tips to help youngsters become better ballplayers. Lake later wrote the tips that appeared on the backs of the Diamond Stars cards issued by National Chicle from 1934-1936. The ACC designation for this set is R333. The checklist below gives the players' names exactly as they appear on the fronts of the cards.

		NR MT	EX	VG
Complete Set:		10500.00	5250.00	3150.00
Common Player:		200.00	100.00	60.00
1	"Marty" McManus	200.00	100.00	60.00
2	Al Simmons	275.00	137.00	75.00
3	Oscar Melillo	200.00	100.00	60.00
4	William (Bill) Terry	400.00	200.00	125.00
5	Charlie Gehringer	400.00	200.00	125.00
6	Gordon (Mickey) Cochrane	400.00	200.00	125.00
7	Lou Gehrig	3500.00	1750.00	1050.
8	Hazen S. (Kiki) Cuyler	300.00	150.00	90.00
9	Bill Urbanski	200.00	100.00	60.00
10	Frank J. (Lefty) O'Doul	200.00	100.00	60.00
11	Freddie Lindstrom	250.00	125.00	70.00
12	Harold (Pie) Traynor	300.00	150.00	90.00
13	"Rabbit" Maranville	300.00	150.00	90.00
14	Vernon "Lefty" Gomez	300.00	150.00	90.00
15	Riggs Stephenson	200.00	100.00	60.00
16	Lon Warneke	200.00	100.00	60.00
17	Pepper Martin	200.00	100.00	60.00
18	Jimmy Dykes	200.00	100.00	60.00
19	Chick Hafey	300.00	150.00	90.00
20	Joe Vosmik	200.00	100.00	60.00
21	Jimmy Foxx	600.00	300.00	175.00
22	Charles (Chuck) Klein	300.00	150.00	90.00
23	Robert (Lefty) Grove	500.00	250.00	150.00
24	"Goose" Goslin	300.00	150.00	90.00

1909 Derby Cigars

Although there is no advertising on these cards to indicate their origin, it is generally accepted that this 1909 set was issued by Derby Cigars, a product of the American Tobacco Co. A dozen different subjects, all members of the New York Giants, have been found. Much uncertainty still surrounds this obscure set, but it is believed that the cards, which measure 1-3/4" by 2-3/4", were inserted in boxes of Derby "Little Cigars." The cards feature a player portrait inside an oval with the player's name and position at the bottom.

		NR MT	EX	VG
Complete Set:		800.00	400.00	250.00
Common Player:		40.00	20.00	12.00
(1)	Josh Devore	40.00	20.00	12.00
(2)	Larry Doyle	50.00	25.00	15.00
(3)	Art Fletcher	40.00	20.00	12.00
(4)	Buck Herzog	40.00	20.00	12.00
(5)	Rube Marquard	100.00	50.00	30.00
(6)	Christy Mathewson	225.00	112.00	67.00
(7)	Fred Merkle	50.00	25.00	15.00

		NR MT	EX	VG
(8)	Chief Meyers	40.00	20.00	12.00
(9)	Red Murray	40.00	20.00	12.00
(10)	John McGraw	100.00	50.00	30.00
(11)	Fred Snodgrass	50.00	25.00	15.00
(12)	Hooks Wiltse	40.00	20.00	12.00

1900 Diamond Stars

Issued from 1934 through 1936, the Diamond Stars set (ACC designation R327) consists of 108 cards. Produced by National Chicle, the numbered cards measure 2-3/8" by 2-7/8" and are color art reproductions of actual photographs. The year of issue can be determined by the player's statistics found on the reverse of the card. The backs feature either a player biography or a baseball playing tip. Some cards can be found with either green or blue printing on the backs. Artwork for 12 cards that were never issued was uncovered several years ago and a set featuring those cards was subsequently made available to the collecting public. The complete set price does not include the higher priced variations.

	NR MT	EX	VG
Complete Set:	20500.00	10250.00	6150.
Common Player: 1-31	90.00	45.00	27.00
Common Player: 32-72	70.00	35.00	21.00
Common Player: 73-84	75.00	38.00	23.00
Common Player: 85-96	125.00	62.00	37.00
Common Player: 97-108	350.00	175.00	105.00

		NR MT	EX	VG
1a	"Lefty" Grove (1934 green back)	1300.00	650.00	390.00
1b	"Lefty" Grove (1935 green back)	1300.00	650.00	390.00
2a	Al Simmons (1934 green back)	200.00	100.00	60.00
2b	Al Simmons (1935 green back)	200.00	100.00	60.00
2c	Al Simmons (1936 blue back)	225.00	112.00	67.00
3a	"Rabbit" Maranville (1934 green back)	100.00	50.00	30.00
3b	"Rabbit" Maranville (1935 green back)	100.00	50.00	30.00
4a	"Buddy" Myer (1934 green back)	90.00	45.00	27.00
4b	"Buddy" Myer (1935 green back)	90.00	45.00	27.00
4c	"Buddy" Myer (1936 blue back)	90.00	45.00	27.00
5a	Tom Bridges (1934 green back)	90.00	45.00	27.00
5b	Tom Bridges (1935 green back)	90.00	45.00	27.00
5c	Tom Bridges (1936 blue back)	90.00	45.00	27.00
6a	Max Bishop (1934 green back)	90.00	45.00	27.00
6b	Max Bishop (1935 green back)	90.00	45.00	27.00
7a	Lew Fonseca (1934 green back)	90.00	45.00	27.00
7b	Lew Fonseca (1935 green back)	90.00	45.00	27.00
8a	Joe Vosmik (1934 green back)	90.00	45.00	27.00
8b	Joe Vosmik (1935 green back)	90.00	45.00	27.00
8c	Joe Vosmik (1936 blue back)	90.00	45.00	27.00
9a	"Mickey" Cochrane (1934 green back)	225.00	112.00	67.00
9b	"Mickey" Cochrane (1935 green back)	225.00	112.00	67.00
9c	"Mickey" Cochrane (1936 blue back)	225.00	112.00	67.00
10a	Roy Mahaffey (1934 green back)	90.00	45.00	27.00
10b	Roy Mahaffey (1935 green back)	90.00	45.00	27.00

		NR MT	EX	VG
10c	Roy Mahaffey (1936 blue back)	90.00	45.00	27.00
11a	Bill Dickey (1934 green back)	275.00	137.00	82.00
11b	Bill Dickey (1935 green back)	275.00	137.00	82.00
12a	"Dixie" Walker (1934 green back)	90.00	45.00	27.00
12b	"Dixie" Walker (1935 green back)	90.00	45.00	27.00
12c	"Dixie" Walker (1936 blue back)	90.00	45.00	27.00
13a	George Blaeholder (1934 green back)	90.00	45.00	27.00
13b	George Blaeholder (1935 green back)	90.00	45.00	27.00
14a	Bill Terry (1934 green back)	110.00	55.00	33.00
14b	Bill Terry (1935 green back)	110.00	55.00	33.00
15a	Dick Bartell (1934 green back)	90.00	45.00	27.00
15b	Dick Bartell (1935 green back)	90.00	45.00	27.00
16a	Lloyd Waner (1934 green back)	125.00	62.00	37.00
16b	Lloyd Waner (1935 green back)	125.00	62.00	37.00
16c	Lloyd Waner (1936 blue back)	125.00	62.00	37.00
17a	Frankie Frisch (1934 green back)	110.00	55.00	33.00
17b	Frankie Frisch (1935 green back)	110.00	55.00	33.00
18a	"Chick" Hafey (1934 green back)	100.00	50.00	30.00
18b	"Chick" Hafey (1935 green back)	100.00	50.00	30.00
19a	Van Mungo (1934 green back)	90.00	45.00	27.00
19b	Van Mungo (1935 green back)	90.00	45.00	27.00
20a	"Shanty" Hogan (1934 green back)	90.00	45.00	27.00
20b	"Shanty" Hogan (1935 green back)	90.00	45.00	27.00
21a	Johnny Vergez (1934 green back)	90.00	45.00	27.00
21b	Johnny Vergez (1935 green back)	90.00	45.00	27.00
22a	Jimmy Wilson (1934 green back)	90.00	45.00	27.00
22b	Jimmy Wilson (1935 green back)	90.00	45.00	27.00
22c	Jimmy Wilson (1936 blue back)	90.00	45.00	27.00
23a	Bill Hallahan (1934 green back)	90.00	45.00	27.00
23b	Bill Hallahan (1935 green back)	90.00	45.00	27.00
24a	"Sparky" Adams (1934 green back)	90.00	45.00	27.00
24b	"Sparky" Adams (1935 green back)	90.00	45.00	27.00
25	Walter Berger	100.00	50.00	30.00
26a	"Pepper" Martin (1935 green back)	100.00	50.00	30.00
26b	"Pepper" Martin (1936 blue back)	100.00	50.00	30.00
27	"Pie" Traynor	225.00	112.00	67.00
28	"Al" Lopez	225.00	112.00	67.00
29	Robert Rolfe	90.00	45.00	27.00
30a	"Heinie" Manush (1935 green back)	125.00	62.00	37.00
30b	"Heinie" Manush (1936 blue back)	150.00	75.00	45.00
31a	"Kiki" Cuyler (1935 green back)	125.00	62.00	37.00
31b	"Kiki" Cuyler (1936 blue back)	125.00	62.00	37.00
32	Sam Rice	125.00	62.00	37.00
33	"Schoolboy" Rowe	90.00	45.00	27.00
34	Stanley Hack	90.00	45.00	27.00
35	Earle Averill	125.00	62.00	37.00
36a	Earnie Lombardi	200.00	100.00	60.00
36b	Ernie Lombardi	150.00	75.00	45.00
37	"Billie" Urbanski	70.00	35.00	21.00
38	Ben Chapman	90.00	45.00	27.00
39	Carl Hubbell	110.00	55.00	33.00
40	"Blondy" Ryan	70.00	35.00	21.00
41	Harvey Hendrick	70.00	35.00	21.00
42	Jimmy Dykes	90.00	45.00	27.00
43	Ted Lyons	100.00	50.00	30.00
44	Rogers Hornsby	350.00	175.00	105.00
45	"Jo Jo" White	70.00	35.00	21.00
46	"Red" Lucas	70.00	35.00	21.00
47	Cliff Bolton	70.00	35.00	21.00
48	"Rick" Ferrell	125.00	62.00	37.00
49	"Buck" Jordan	70.00	35.00	21.00
50	"Mel" Ott	275.00	137.00	82.00
51	John Whitehead	70.00	35.00	21.00
52	George Stainback	70.00	35.00	21.00
53	Oscar Melillo	70.00	35.00	21.00
54a	"Hank" Greenburg	400.00	200.00	120.00
54b	"Hank" Greenberg	250.00	125.00	75.00
55	Tony Cuccinello	70.00	35.00	21.00
56	"Gus" Suhr	70.00	35.00	21.00

		NR MT	EX	VG
57	"Cy" Blanton	70.00	35.00	21.00
58	Glenn Myatt	70.00	35.00	21.00
59	Jim Bottomley	125.00	62.00	37.00
60	Charley "Red" Ruffing	100.00	50.00	30.00
61	"Billie" Werber	70.00	35.00	21.00
62	Fred M. Frankhouse	70.00	35.00	21.00
63	"Stonewall" Jackson	125.00	62.00	37.00
64	Jimmie Foxx	350.00	175.00	105.00
65	"Zeke" Bonura	70.00	35.00	21.00
66	"Ducky" Medwick	100.00	50.00	30.00
67	Marvin Owen	70.00	35.00	21.00
68	"Sam" Leslie	70.00	35.00	21.00
69	Earl Grace	70.00	35.00	21.00
70	"Hal" Trosky	70.00	35.00	21.00
71	"Ossie" Bluege	70.00	35.00	21.00
72	"Tony" Piet	70.00	35.00	21.00
73a	"Fritz" Ostermueller (1935 green back)	75.00	38.00	23.00
73b	"Fritz" Ostermueller (1935 blue back)	75.00	38.00	23.00
73c	"Fritz" Ostermueller (1936 blue back)	75.00	38.00	23.00
74a	Tony Lazzeri (1935 green back)	125.00	62.00	37.00
74b	Tony Lazzeri (1935 blue back)	125.00	62.00	37.00
74c	Tony Lazzeri (1936 blue back)	125.00	62.00	37.00
75a	Irving Burns (1935 green back)	75.00	38.00	23.00
75b	Irving Burns (1935 blue back)	75.00	38.00	23.00
75c	Irving Burns (1936 blue back)	75.00	38.00	23.00
76a	Bill Rogell (1935 green back)	75.00	38.00	23.00
76b	Bill Rogell (1935 blue back)	75.00	38.00	23.00
76c	Bill Rogell (1936 blue back)	75.00	38.00	23.00
77a	Charlie Gehringer (1935 green back)	150.00	75.00	45.00
77b	Charlie Gehringer (1935 blue back)	150.00	75.00	45.00
77c	Charlie Gehringer (1936 blue back)	150.00	75.00	45.00
78a	Joe Kuhel (1935 green back)	75.00	38.00	23.00
78b	Joe Kuhel (1935 blue back)	75.00	38.00	23.00
78c	Joe Kuhel (1936 blue back)	75.00	38.00	23.00
79a	Willis Hudlin (1935 green back)	75.00	38.00	23.00
79b	Willis Hudlin (1935 blue back)	75.00	38.00	23.00
79c	Willis Hudlin (1936 blue back)	75.00	38.00	23.00
80a	Louis Chiozza (1935 green back)	75.00	38.00	23.00
80b	Louis Chiozza (1935 blue back)	75.00	38.00	23.00
80c	Louis Chiozza (1936 blue back)	75.00	38.00	23.00
81a	Bill DeLancey (1935 green back)	75.00	38.00	23.00
81b	Bill DeLancey (1935 blue back)	75.00	38.00	23.00
81c	Bill DeLancey (1936 blue back)	75.00	38.00	23.00
82a	John Babich (1935 green back)	100.00	50.00	30.00
82b	John Babich (1935 blue back)	100.00	50.00	30.00
82c	John Babich (1936 blue back)	100.00	50.00	30.00
83a	Paul Waner (1935 green back)	200.00	100.00	60.00
83b	Paul Waner (1935 blue back)	200.00	100.00	60.00
83c	Paul Waner (1936 blue back)	200.00	100.00	60.00
84a	Sam Byrd (1935 green back)	75.00	38.00	23.00
84b	Sam Byrd (1935 blue back)	75.00	38.00	23.00
84c	Sam Byrd (1936 blue back)	75.00	38.00	23.00
85	Julius Solters	125.00	62.00	37.00
86	Frank Crosetti	200.00	100.00	60.00
87	Steve O'Neil (O'Neill)	125.00	62.00	37.00
88	Geo. Selkirk	100.00	50.00	30.00
89	Joe Stripp	125.00	62.00	37.00
90	Ray Hayworth	125.00	62.00	37.00
91	Bucky Harris	150.00	75.00	45.00
92	Ethan Allen	125.00	62.00	37.00
93	Alvin Crowder	125.00	62.00	37.00
94	Wes Ferrell	125.00	62.00	37.00
95	Luke Appling	275.00	137.00	82.00
96	Lew Riggs	125.00	62.00	37.00
97	"Al" Lopez	500.00	250.00	150.00
98	"Schoolboy" Rowe	350.00	175.00	105.00
99	"Pie" Traynor	600.00	300.00	180.00
100	Earle Averill (Earl)	500.00	250.00	150.00
101	Dick Bartell	350.00	175.00	105.00
102	Van Mungo	350.00	175.00	105.00
103	Bill Dickey	800.00	400.00	250.00
104	Robert Rolfe	350.00	175.00	105.00
105	"Ernie" Lombardi	500.00	250.00	150.00
106	"Red" Lucas	350.00	175.00	105.00
107	Stanley Hack	350.00	175.00	105.00
108	Walter Berger	350.00	175.00	105.00

NOTE: A card number in parentheses ( ) indicates the set is unnumbered.

1924 Diaz Cigarettes

Because they were printed in Cuba and feature only pitchers, the 1924 Diaz Cigarette cards are among the rarest and most intriguing of all tobacco issues. Produced in Havana for the Diaz brand, the black and white cards measure 1-3/4" by 2-1/2" and were printed on a glossy-type stock. The player's name and position are listed at the bottom of the card, while his team and league appear at the top. According to the card backs, printed in Spanish, the set consists of 136 cards - all major league pitchers. But to date only the 12 cards checklisted here have been discovered.

		NR MT	EX	VG
Complete Set:		3500.00	1750.00	1050.
Common Player:		225.00	112.00	67.00
2	Waite C. Hoyt	400.00	200.00	120.00
12	Curtis Fullerton	225.00	112.00	67.00
14	George Walberg	225.00	112.00	67.00
40	A. Wilbur Cooper	225.00	112.00	67.00
51	Roy Meeker	225.00	112.00	67.00
58	Sam Gray	225.00	112.00	67.00
96	Philip B. Weinart	225.00	112.00	67.00
105	Hubert F. Pruett	225.00	112.00	67.00
121	Bert Cole	225.00	112.00	67.00
——	Leslie J. Bush	225.00	112.00	67.00
——	Wm. Piercy	225.00	112.00	67.00
——	Arnold E. Stone	225.00	112.00	67.00

1937 Dixie Lids

This unnumbered set of Dixie cup ice cream lids was issued in 1937 and consists of 24 different lids, although only six picture sports stars - four of whom are baseball stars. The lids are found in two different sizes, either 2-11/16" in diameter or 2-5/16" in diameter. The 1937 Dixie Lids were printed in black or dark red. The lids must have the small tab still intact to command top value.

		NR MT	EX	VG
Complete Set:		400.00	200.00	120.00
Common Player:		75.00	38.00	23.00
(1)	Charles Gehringer	110.00	55.00	33.00
(2)	Charles ("Gabby") Hartnett	110.00	55.00	33.00
(3)	Carl Hubbell	125.00	62.00	37.00
(4)	Joe Medwick	75.00	38.00	23.00

1937 Dixie Lids Premiums

Issued as a premium offer in conjunction with the 1937 Dixie lids, this unnumbered set of color 8" by 10" pictures was printed on heavy paper and features the same subjects as the Dixie Lids set. The 1937 Dixie premiums have a distinctive dark green band along the left margin containing the player's name. The back has smaller photos of the player in action with a large star at the top and a player write-up.

		NR MT	EX	VG
Complete Set:		400.00	200.00	120.00
Common Player:		75.00	38.00	23.00
(1)	Charles Gehringer	110.00	55.00	33.00
(2)	Charles (Gabby) Hartnett	110.00	55.00	33.00
(3)	Carl Hubbell	125.00	62.00	37.00
(4)	Joe (Ducky) Medwick	75.00	38.00	23.00

1938 Dixie Lids

Similar to its set of the previous year, the 1938 Dixie Lids set is a 24-subject set that includes six sports stars - four of whom are baseball players. The lids are found in two sizes, either 2 11/16" in diameter or 2-5/16" in diameter. The 1938 Dixie lids are printed in blue ink. Dixie lids must have the small tab still intact to command top value.

		NR MT	EX	VG
Complete Set:		375.00	187.00	112.00
Common Player:		50.00	25.00	15.00
(1)	Bob Feller	110.00	55.00	33.00
(2)	Jimmie Foxx	110.00	55.00	33.00
(3)	Carl Hubbell	110.00	55.00	33.00
(4)	Wally Moses	50.00	25.00	15.00

1938 Dixie Lids Premiums

Issued in conjunction with the 1938 Dixie cup lids, this unnumbered set of 8" x 10" pictures contains the same subjects and is printed on surrounding the entire picture with the player's name to the left. The

back contains smaller photos of the player in action with his name in script at the top and a short write-up.

		NR MT	EX	VG
Complete Set:		300.00	150.00	90.00
Common Player:		50.00	25.00	15.00
(1)	Bob Feller	100.00	50.00	30.00
(2)	Jimmy Foxx	80.00	40.00	24.00
(3)	Carl Hubbell	80.00	40.00	24.00
(4)	Wally Moses	50.00	25.00	15.00

1952 Dixie Lids

After a 14-year break, another Dixie lid set, featuring 24 baseball players, appeared in 1952. The unnumbered lids measure 2-11/16" in diameter and were printed with a blue tint. The Dixie lids of the 1950s can be distinguished from earlier issues because the bottom of the photo is squared off to accomodate the player's name. Dixie lids must contain the small tab to command top value.

		NR MT	EX	VG
Complete Set:		3500.00	1750.00	1050.00
Common Player:		140.00	70.00	42.00
(1)	Richie Ashburn	175.00	87.00	52.00
(2)	Tommy Byrne	140.00	70.00	42.00
(3)	Chico Carrasquel	140.00	70.00	42.00
(4)	Pete Castiglione	140.00	70.00	42.00
(5)	Walker Cooper	140.00	70.00	42.00
(6)	Billy Cox	140.00	70.00	42.00
(7)	Ferris Fain	140.00	70.00	42.00
(8)	Bobby Feller	250.00	125.00	75.00
(9)	Nelson Fox	175.00	87.00	52.00
(10)	Monte Irvin	200.00	100.00	60.00
(11)	Ralph Kiner	200.00	100.00	60.00
(12)	Cass Michaels	140.00	70.00	42.00
(13)	Don Mueller	140.00	70.00	42.00
(14)	Mel Parnell	140.00	70.00	42.00
(15)	Allie Reynolds	175.00	87.00	52.00
(16)	Preacher Roe	175.00	87.00	52.00
(17)	Connie Ryan	140.00	70.00	42.00
(18)	Hank Sauer	140.00	70.00	42.00
(19)	Al Schoendienst	175.00	87.00	52.00
(20)	Andy Seminick	140.00	70.00	42.00
(21)	Bobby Shantz	150.00	75.00	45.00
(22)	Enos Slaughter	200.00	100.00	60.00
(23)	Virgil Trucks	140.00	70.00	42.00
(24)	Gene Woodling	150.00	75.00	45.00

1952 Dixie Lids Premiums

This unnumbered set of 24 player photos was issued as a premium in conjunction with the 1952 Dixie cup lids and features the same subjects. The player's team and facsimile autograph appear along the bottom of the 8" by 10" blank-backed photo, which was printed on heavy paper. The 1952 Dixie premiums show the player's 1951 season statistics in the lower right corner.

		NR MT	EX	VG
Complete Set:		600.00	300.00	180.00
Common Player:		30.00	15.00	9.00
(1)	Richie Ashburn	35.00	17.50	10.50
(2)	Tommy Byrne	30.00	15.00	9.00
(3)	Chico Carrasquel	30.00	15.00	9.00
(4)	Pete Castiglione	30.00	15.00	9.00
(5)	Walker Cooper	30.00	15.00	9.00
(6)	Billy Cox	30.00	15.00	9.00
(7)	Ferris Fain	30.00	15.00	9.00
(8)	Bob Feller	75.00	37.00	22.00
(9)	Nelson Fox	35.00	17.50	10.50
(10)	Monte Irvin	40.00	20.00	12.00
(11)	Ralph Kiner	45.00	22.00	13.50
(12)	Cass Michaels	30.00	15.00	9.00
(13)	Don Mueller	30.00	15.00	9.00
(14)	Mel Parnell	30.00	15.00	9.00
(15)	Allie Reynolds	35.00	17.50	10.50
(16)	Preacher Roe	35.00	17.50	10.50
(17)	Connie Ryan	30.00	15.00	9.00
(18)	Hank Sauer	30.00	15.00	9.00
(19)	Al Schoendienst	35.00	17.50	10.50
(20)	Andy Seminick	30.00	15.00	9.00
(21)	Bobby Shantz	35.00	17.50	10.50
(22)	Enos Slaughter	45.00	22.00	13.50
(23)	Virgil Trucks	30.00	15.00	9.00
(24)	Gene Woodling	35.00	17.50	10.50

1953 Dixie Lids

The 1953 Dixie Lids set again consists of 24 unnumbered players and is identical in design to the 1953 set. Each lid measures 2-11/16"in diameter and must include the small tab to command top value.

		NR MT	EX	VG
Complete Set:		1500.00	750.00	450.00
Common Player:		35.00	17.50	10.50
(1)	Richie Ashburn	40.00	20.00	12.00
(2)	Chico Carrasquel	35.00	17.50	10.50
(3)	Billy Cox	35.00	17.50	10.50
(4)	Ferris Fain	35.00	17.50	10.50
(5)	Nelson Fox	40.00	20.00	12.00
(6a)	Sid Gordon (Boston)	70.00	35.00	20.00
(6b)	Sid Gordon (Milwaukee)	35.00	17.50	10.50
(7)	Warren Hacker	35.00	17.50	10.50
(8)	Monte Irvin	60.00	30.00	18.00
(9)	Jackie Jensen	40.00	20.00	12.00
(10a)	Ralph Kiner (Pittsburgh)	100.00	50.00	30.00
(10b)	Ralph Kiner (Chicago)	60.00	30.00	18.00
(11)	Ted Kluszewski	40.00	20.00	12.00
(12)	Bob Lemon	60.00	30.00	18.00
(13)	Don Mueller	35.00	17.50	10.50
(14)	Mel Parnell	35.00	17.50	10.50
(15)	Jerry Priddy	35.00	17.50	10.50
(16)	Allie Reynolds	40.00	20.00	12.00
(17)	Preacher Roe	40.00	20.00	12.00
(18)	Hank Sauer	35.00	17.50	10.50
(19)	Al Schoendienst	40.00	20.00	12.00
(20)	Bobby Shantz	40.00	20.00	12.00
(21)	Enos Slaughter	60.00	30.00	18.00
(22a)	Warren Spahn (Boston)	150.00	75.00	45.00
(22b)	Warren Spahn (Milwaukee)	75.00	38.00	23.00
(23a)	Virgil Trucks (Chicago)	75.00	38.00	23.00
(23b)	Virgil Trucks (St. Louis)	35.00	17.50	10.50
(24)	Gene Woodling	40.00	20.00	12.00

1953 Dixie Lids Premiums

heavy paper. The 1938 Dixie Lids Premiums have a light green border This set of 24 8" by 10" photos was issued as a premium in conjunction with the 1953 Dixie Lids set and includes the same subjects. The player's team and facsimile autograph are at the bottom of the unnumbered, blank-backed photos. His 1952 season stats are shown in the lower right corner.

		NR MT	EX	VG
Complete Set:		700.00	350.00	210.00
Common Player:		20.00	10.00	6.00
(1)	Richie Ashburn	25.00	12.50	7.50
(2)	Chico Carrasquel	20.00	10.00	6.00
(3)	Billy Cox	20.00	10.00	6.00
(4)	Ferris Fain	20.00	10.00	6.00
(5)	Nelson Fox	25.00	12.50	7.50
(6)	Sid Gordon	20.00	10.00	6.00
(7)	Warren Hacker	20.00	10.00	6.00
(8)	Monte Irvin	25.00	12.50	7.50
(9)	Jack Jensen	25.00	12.50	7.50
(10)	Ralph Kiner	30.00	15.00	9.00
(11)	Ted Kluszewski	25.00	12.50	7.50
(12)	Bob Lemon	30.00	15.00	9.00
(13)	Don Mueller	20.00	10.00	6.00
(14)	Mel Parnell	20.00	10.00	6.00
(15)	Jerry Priddy	20.00	10.00	6.00
(16)	Allie Reynolds	25.00	12.50	7.50
(17)	Preacher Roe	25.00	12.50	7.50
(18)	Hank Sauer	20.00	10.00	6.00
(19)	Al Schoendienst	25.00	12.50	7.50
(20)	Bobby Shantz	20.00	10.00	6.00
(21)	Enos Slaughter	30.00	15.00	9.00
(22)	Warren Spahn	40.00	20.00	12.00
(23)	Virgil Trucks	20.00	10.00	6.00
(24)	Gene Woodling	25.00	12.50	7.50

1954 Dixie Lids

The 1954 Dixie Lids set consists of 18 players, and the lids are usually found with a gray tint. The lids usually measure 2-11/16" in diameter, although two other sizes also exist (2-1/4" in diameter and 3-3/16" in diameter), which are valued at about twice the prices listed. The 1953 Dixie Lids are similar to earlier issues, except they carry an offer for a "3-D Starviewer" around the outside edge. The small tabs must be attached to command top value. The lids are unnumbered.

		NR MT	EX	VG
Complete Set:		600.00	300.00	180.00
Common Player:		25.00	12.50	7.50
(1)	Richie Ashburn	30.00	15.00	9.00
(2)	Clint Courtney	25.00	12.50	7.50
(3)	Sid Gordon	25.00	12.50	7.50
(4)	Billy Hoeft	25.00	12.50	7.50
(5)	Monte Irvin	35.00	17.50	10.50
(6)	Jackie Jensen	30.00	15.00	9.00
(7)	Ralph Kiner	40.00	20.00	12.00
(8)	Ted Kluszewski	30.00	15.00	9.00
(9)	Gil McDougald	30.00	15.00	9.00
(10)	Minny Minoso	30.00	15.00	9.00
(11)	Danny O'Connell	25.00	12.50	7.50
(12)	Mel Parnell	25.00	12.50	7.50
(13)	Preacher Roe	30.00	15.00	9.00
(14)	Al Rosen	30.00	15.00	9.00
(15)	Al Schoendienst	30.00	15.00	9.00
(16)	Enos Slaughter	40.00	20.00	12.00
(17)	Gene Woodling	30.00	15.00	9.00
(18)	Gus Zernial	25.00	12.50	7.50

1941 Double Play

Issued by Gum, Inc., this set includes 75 numbered cards (two consecutive numbers per card) featuring 150 baseball players. The cards, which are blank-backed and measure 2-1/2" by 3-1/8", contain sepia-tone photos of two players. Action and portrait poses are found in the set, with card designs on either a vertical or horizontal format. The last fifty cards are the scarcest of the set. Cards cut to form two single cards have little value.

		NR MT	EX	VG
Complete Set:		6500.00	3300.00	2000.
Common Player: 1-100		35.00	17.50	10.50
Common Player: 101-150		50.00	25.00	15.00
1	Larry French			
2	Vance Page	75.00	38.50	23.00
3	Billy Herman			
4	Stanley Hack	50.00	25.00	15.00
5	Linus Frey			
6	John Vander Meer	45.00	23.00	13.50
7	Paul Derringer			
8	Bucky Walters	35.00	17.50	10.50
9	Frank McCormick			
10	Bill Werber	35.00	17.50	10.50
11	Jimmy Ripple			
12	Ernie Lombardi	60.00	30.00	18.00
13	Alex Kampouris			
14	John Wyatt	35.00	17.50	10.50
15	Mickey Owen			
16	Paul Waner	60.00	30.00	18.00
17	Harry Lavagetto			
18	Harold Reiser	45.00	22.00	13.50
19	Jimmy Wasdell			
20	Dolph Camilli	45.00	22.00	13.50
21	Dixie Walker			
22	Ducky Medwick	60.00	30.00	18.00
23	Harold Reese			
24	Kirby Higbe	225.00	112.00	70.00
25	Harry Danning			
26	Cliff Melton	35.00	17.50	10.50
27	Harry Gumbert			
28	Burgess Whitehead	35.00	17.50	10.50
29	Joe Orengo			
30	Joe Moore	35.00	17.50	10.50
31	Mel Ott			
32	Babe Young	90.00	45.00	27.00
33	Lee Handley			
34	Arky Vaughan	60.00	30.00	18.00
35	Bob Klinger			
36	Stanley Brown	35.00	17.50	10.50
37	Terry Moore			
38	Gus Mancuso	35.00	17.50	10.50
39	Johnny Mize			
40	Enos Slaughter	100.00	50.00	30.00
41	John Cooney			
42	Sibby Sisti	35.00	17.50	10.50
43	Max West			
44	Carvel Rowell	35.00	17.50	10.50
45	Dan Litwhiler			
46	Merrill May	35.00	17.50	10.50
47	Frank Hayes			
48	Al Brancato	35.00	17.50	10.50
49	Bob Johnson			
50	Bill Nagel	35.00	17.50	10.50
51	Buck Newsom			
52	Hank Greenberg	90.00	45.00	27.00
53	Barney McCosky			
54	Charley Gehringer	90.00	45.00	27.00
55	Pinky Higgins			
56	Dick Bartell	35.00	17.50	10.50
57	Ted Williams			
58	Jim Tabor	600.00	300.00	180.00
59	Joe Cronin			
60	Jimmy Foxx	175.00	90.00	50.00
61	Lefty Gomez			
62	Phil Rizzuto	250.00	125.00	70.00
63	Joe DiMaggio			
64	Charley Keller	700.00	350.00	210.00
65	Red Rolfe			
66	Bill Dickey	125.00	62.00	37.00
67	Joe Gordon			
68	Red Ruffing	75.00	37.00	22.00
69	Mike Tresh			
70	Luke Appling	60.00	30.00	18.00
71	Moose Solters			
72	John Rigney	35.00	17.50	10.50
73	Buddy Meyer			
74	Ben Chapman	35.00	17.50	10.50
75	Cecil Travis			
76	George Case	35.00	17.50	10.50
77	Joe Krakauskas			
78	Bob Feller	150.00	75.00	45.00
79	Ken Keltner			
80	Hal Trosky	35.00	17.50	10.50
81	Ted Williams			
82	Joe Cronin	600.00	300.00	175.00
83	Joe Gordon			
84	Charley Keller	45.00	22.00	13.50
85	Hank Greenberg			
86	Red Ruffing	90.00	45.00	27.00
87	Hal Trosky			
88	George Case	35.00	17.50	10.50

		NR MT	EX	VG
89	Mel Ott			
90	Burgess Whitehead	90.00	45.00	27.00
91	Harry Danning			
92	Harry Gumbert	35.00	17.50	10.50
93	Babe Young			
94	Cliff Melton	35.00	17.50	10.50
95	Jimmy Ripple			
96	Bucky Walters	35.00	17.50	10.50
97	Stanley Hack			
98	Bob Klinger	35.00	17.50	10.50
99	Johnny Mize			
100	Dan Litwhiler	60.00	30.00	20.00
101	Dominic Dallessandro			
102	Augie Galan	50.00	25.00	15.00
103	Bill Lee			
104	Phil Cavarretta	50.00	25.00	15.00
105	Lefty Grove			
106	Bobby Doerr	150.00	70.00	45.00
107	Frank Pytlak			
108	Dom DiMaggio	60.00	30.00	20.00
109	Gerald Priddy			
110	John Murphy	60.00	30.00	20.00
111	Tommy Henrich			
112	Marius Russo	75.00	37.00	22.00
113	Frank Crosetti			
114	John Sturm	75.00	37.00	22.00
115	Ival Goodman			
116	Myron McCormick	50.00	25.00	15.00
117	Eddie Joost			
118	Ernest Koy	50.00	25.00	15.00
119	Lloyd Waner			
120	Henry Majeski	75.00	37.00	22.00
121	Buddy Hassett			
122	Eugene Moore	50.00	25.00	15.00
123	Nick Etten			
124	John Rizzo	50.00	25.00	15.00
125	Sam Chapman			
126	Wally Moses	50.00	25.00	15.00
127	John Babich			
128	Richard Siebert	50.00	25.00	15.00
129	Nelson Potter			
130	Benny McCoy	50.00	25.00	15.00
131	Clarence Campbell			
132	Louis Boudreau	75.00	37.00	22.00
133	Rolly Hemsley			
134	Mel Harder	50.00	25.00	15.00
135	Gerald Walker			
136	Joe Heving	50.00	25.00	15.00
137	John Rucker			
138	Ace Adams	50.00	25.00	15.00
139	Morris Arnovich			
140	Carl Hubbell	125.00	62.00	37.00
141	Lew Riggs			
142	Leo Durocher	75.00	37.00	22.00
143	Fred Fitzsimmons			
144	Joe Vosmik	50.00	25.00	15.00
145	Frank Crespi			
146	Jim Brown	50.00	25.00	15.00
147	Don Heffner			
148	Harland Clift (Harlond)	50.00	25.00	15.00
149	Debs Garms			
150	Elbert Fletcher	80.00	40.00	24.00

1950 Drake's

Entitled "TV Baseball Series", the 1950 Drake's Bakeries set pictures 36 different players on a television screen format. The cards, which measure 2-1/2" by 2-1/2", contain black and white photos surrounded by a black border. The card backs carry a player biography plus an advertisement advising collectors to look for the cards in packages of Oatmeal or Jumble cookies. The ACC designation for the set is D358.

		NR MT	EX	VG
Complete Set:		5000.00	3000.00	1500.
Common Player:		50.00	25.00	15.00
1	Elwin "Preacher" Roe	100.00	50.00	30.00
2	Clint Hartung	50.00	25.00	15.00
3	Earl Torgeson	50.00	25.00	15.00
4	Leland "Lou" Brissie	50.00	25.00	15.00
5	Edwin "Duke" Snider	350.00	175.00	100.00
6	Roy Campanella	400.00	200.00	125.00
7	Sheldon "Available" Jones	50.00	25.00	15.00
8	Carroll "Whitey" Lockman	50.00	25.00	15.00
9	Bobby Thomson	80.00	40.00	25.00
10	Dick Sisler	50.00	25.00	15.00
11	Gil Hodges	200.00	100.00	60.00
12	Eddie Waitkus	50.00	25.00	15.00
13	Bobby Doerr	150.00	75.00	45.00
14	Warren Spahn	250.00	125.00	75.00
15	John "Buddy" Kerr	50.00	25.00	15.00
16	Sid Gordon	50.00	25.00	15.00
17	Willard Marshall	50.00	25.00	15.00
18	Carl Furillo	90.00	45.00	25.00
19	Harold "Pee Wee" Reese	300.00	150.00	90.00
20	Alvin Dark	70.00	35.00	20.00
21	Del Ennis	50.00	25.00	15.00
22	Ed Stanky	70.00	35.00	20.00
23	Tommy "Old Reliable" Henrich	90.00	45.00	25.00
24	Larry "Yogi" Berra	400.00	200.00	125.00
25	Phil "Scooter" Rizzuto	275.00	150.00	100.00
26	Jerry Coleman	70.00	35.00	20.00
27	Joe Page	70.00	35.00	20.00
28	Allie Reynolds	90.00	45.00	25.00
29	Ray Scarborough	50.00	25.00	15.00
30	George "Birdie" Tebbetts	50.00	25.00	15.00
31	Maurice "Lefty" McDermott	50.00	25.00	15.00
32	Johnny Pesky	70.00	35.00	20.00
33	Dom "Little Professor" DiMaggio	80.00	40.00	25.00
34	Vern "Junior" Stephens	50.00	25.00	15.00
35	Bob Elliott	50.00	25.00	15.00
36	Enos "Country" Slaughter	250.00	125.00	75.00

1900 E90-1

The E90-1 set was issued by the American Caramel Co. from 1909 through 1911, with the bulk of the set being produced in the first year. The cards, which measure 1-1/2" by 2-3/4" in size and were issued with sticks of caramel candy, are color reproductions of actual photographs. The card backs state that 100 subjects are included in the set though more actually do exist. There are several levels of scarcity in the set, those levels being mostly determined by the year the cards were issued. Mitchell (Cincinnati), Clarke (Pittsburg), Graham, and Sweeney (Boston) are the most difficult cards in the set to obtain. For the collector's convenience, the players' first names have been added in the checklist that follows. The complete set price includes all variations.

		NR MT	EX	VG
Complete Set:		85000.00	35000.00	13500.
Common Player:		125.00	62.00	37.00
(1)	Bill Bailey	125.00	62.00	37.00
(2)	Home Run Baker	550.00	220.00	105.00
(3)	Jack Barry	125.00	62.00	37.00
(4)	George Bell	125.00	62.00	37.00
(5)	Harry Bemis	225.00	100.00	50.00
(6)	Chief Bender	450.00	180.00	95.00
(7)	Bob Bescher	175.00	75.00	40.00
(8)	Cliff Blankenship	125.00	62.00	37.00
(9)	John Bliss	125.00	62.00	37.00
(10)	Bill Bradley	125.00	62.00	37.00
(11)	Kitty Bransfield ("P" on shirt)	125.00	62.00	37.00
(12)	Kitty Bransfield (no "P" on shirt)			
		175.00	75.00	40.00
(13)	Roger Bresnahan	500.00	250.00	125.00
(14)	Al Bridwell	125.00	62.00	37.00
(15)	Buster Brown (Boston)	125.00	62.00	37.00
(16)	Mordecai Brown (Chicago)	650.00	275.00	150.00
(17)	Donie Bush	125.00	62.00	37.00
(18)	John Butler	125.00	62.00	37.00
(19)	Howie Camnitz	125.00	62.00	37.00
(20)	Frank Chance	550.00	225.00	105.00
(21)	Hal Chase	150.00	70.00	30.00
(22a)	Fred Clarke (Philadelphia)	450.00	180.00	95.00
(22b)	Fred Clarke (Pittsburgh)	1500.00	750.00	335.00
(23)	Wally Clement	175.00	75.00	40.00
(24)	Ty Cobb	4500.00	2000.00	900.00
(25)	Eddie Collins	550.00	220.00	105.00
(26)	Sam Crawford	500.00	200.00	100.00
(27)	Frank Corridon	125.00	62.00	37.00
(28)	Lou Criger	125.00	62.00	37.00
(29)	George Davis	125.00	62.00	37.00
(30)	Harry Davis	125.00	62.00	37.00
(31)	Ray Demmitt	375.00	150.00	60.00
(32)	Mike Donlin	125.00	62.00	37.00
(33)	Wild Bill Donovan	125.00	62.00	37.00
(34)	Red Dooin	125.00	62.00	37.00
(35)	Patsy Dougherty	225.00	100.00	50.00
(36)	Hugh Duffy	1800.00	900.00	400.00
(37)	Jimmy Dygert	125.00	62.00	37.00
(38)	Rube Ellis	125.00	62.00	37.00
(39)	Clyde Engle	125.00	62.00	37.00
(40)	Art Fromme	450.00	200.00	75.00
(41)	George Gibson (back view)	600.00	250.00	100.00
(42)	George Gibson (front view)	125.00	62.00	37.00
(43)	Peaches Graham	2200.00	1000.00	600.00
(44)	Eddie Grant	125.00	62.00	37.00
(45)	Dolly Gray	125.00	62.00	37.00
(46)	Bob Groom	125.00	62.00	37.00
(47)	Charley Hall	125.00	62.00	37.00
(48)	Roy Hartzell (fielding)	125.00	62.00	37.00
(49)	Roy Hartzell (batting)	125.00	62.00	37.00
(50)	Heinie Heitmuller	125.00	62.00	37.00
(51)	Harry Howell (follow thru)	125.00	62.00	37.00
(52)	Harry Howell (windup)	175.00	75.00	40.00
(53)	Tex Irwin (Erwin)	125.00	62.00	37.00
(54)	Frank Isbell	125.00	62.00	37.00
(55)	Shoeless Joe Jackson	7500.00	3500.00	1600.
(56)	Hughie Jennings	500.00	250.00	100.00
(57)	Buck Jordon (Jordan)	125.00	62.00	37.00
(58)	Addie Joss (portrait)	500.00	250.00	100.00
(59)	Addie Joss (pitching)	1650.00	825.00	350.00
(60)	Ed Karger	1650.00	825.00	350.00
(61a)	Willie Keeler (portrait, pink background)			
		550.00	225.00	125.00
(61b)	Willie Keeler (portrait, red background)			
		1650.00	825.00	375.00
(62)	Willie Keeler (throwing)	2000.00	1000.00	500.00
(63)	John Knight	125.00	62.00	37.00
(64)	Harry Krause	125.00	62.00	37.00
(65)	Nap Lajoie	775.00	350.00	175.00
(66)	Tommy Leach (throwing)	125.00	62.00	37.00
(67)	Tommy Leach (batting)	125.00	62.00	37.00
(68)	Sam Leever	125.00	62.00	37.00
(69)	Hans Lobert	1000.00	400.00	245.00
(70)	Harry Lumley	125.00	62.00	37.00
(71)	Rube Marquard	500.00	200.00	100.00
(72)	Christy Matthewson (Mathewson)			
		1000.00	500.00	225.00
(73)	Stuffy McInnes (McInnis)	125.00	62.00	37.00
(74)	Harry McIntyre	125.00	62.00	37.00
(75)	Larry McLean	225.00	100.00	40.00
(76)	George McQuillan	125.00	62.00	37.00

		NR MT	EX	VG
(77)	Dots Miller	125.00	62.00	37.00
(78)	Fred Mitchell (New York)	125.00	62.00	37.00
(79)	Mike Mitchell (Cincinnati)	10000.00	5000.00	2250.
(80)	George Mullin	125.00	62.00	37.00
(81)	Rebel Oakes	125.00	62.00	37.00
(82)	Paddy O'Connor	125.00	62.00	37.00
(83)	Charley O'Leary	125.00	62.00	37.00
(84)	Orval Overall	1000.00	475.00	235.00
(85)	Jim Pastorius	125.00	62.00	37.00
(86)	Ed Phelps	125.00	62.00	37.00
(87)	Eddie Plank	900.00	450.00	200.00
(88)	Lew Richie	125.00	62.00	37.00
(89)	Germany Schaefer	125.00	62.00	37.00
(90)	Biff Schlitzer	175.00	75.00	35.00
(91)	Johnny Seigle (Siegle)	225.00	100.00	40.00
(92)	Dave Shean	175.00	75.00	35.00
(93)	Jimmy Sheckard	175.00	75.00	35.00
(94)	Tris Speaker	2000.00	900.00	400.00
(95)	Jake Stahl	1650.00	825.00	375.00
(96)	Oscar Stanage	125.00	62.00	37.00
(97)	George Stone (no hands visible)			
		125.00	62.00	37.00
(98)	George Stone (left hand visible)			
		125.00	62.00	37.00
(99)	George Stovall	125.00	62.00	37.00
(100)	Ed Summers	125.00	62.00	37.00
(101)	Bill Sweeney (Boston)	1800.00	900.00	400.00
(102)	Jeff Sweeney (New York)	125.00	62.00	37.00
(103)	Jesse Tannehill (Chicago A.L.)	125.00	62.00	37.00
(104)	Lee Tannehill (Chicago N.L.)	125.00	62.00	37.00
(105)	Fred Tenney	125.00	62.00	37.00
(106)	Ira Thomas (Philadelphia)	125.00	62.00	37.00
(107)	Roy Thomas (Boston)	125.00	62.00	37.00
(108)	Joe Tinker	500.00	225.00	100.00
(109)	Bob Unglaub	125.00	62.00	37.00
(110)	Jerry Upp	125.00	62.00	37.00
(111)	Honus Wagner (batting)	1500.00	750.00	300.00
(112)	Honus Wagner (throwing)	1500.00	750.00	300.00
(113)	Bobby Wallace	400.00	175.00	90.00
(114)	Ed Walsh	1750.00	875.00	500.00
(115)	Vic Willis	125.00	62.00	37.00
(116)	Hooks Wiltse	225.00	100.00	35.00
(117)	Cy Young (Cleveland)	900.00	450.00	225.00
(118)	Cy Young (Boston)	750.00	375.00	200.00

1910 E90-2

MADDOX, Pittsburg

Closely related to the E90-1 American Caramel set, the E90-2 set consists of 11 cards featuring members of the 1909 champion Pittsburgh Pirates. The cards measure 1-1/2" by 2-3/4" and display a color lithograph on the front with a solid color background of either red, green blue or pink. The player's name and "Pittsburg" appear in blue capital letters in the border beneath the portrait. The backs are identical to those in the E90-1 set, depicting a drawing of a ball, glove and crossed bats with the words "Base Ball Caramels" and a reference to "100 Subjects." The set includes Hall of Famers Honus Wagner and Fred Clarke.

		NR MT	EX	VG
Complete Set:		5000.00	2500.00	1000.
Common Player:		175.00	87.00	52.00
(1)	Babe Adams	175.00	87.00	52.00
(2)	Fred Clarke	500.00	225.00	100.00
(3)	George Gibson	175.00	87.00	52.00
(4)	Ham Hyatt	175.00	87.00	52.00

		NR MT	EX	VG
(5)	Tommy Leach	175.00	87.00	52.00
(6)	Sam Leever	175.00	87.00	52.00
(7)	Nick Maddox	175.00	87.00	52.00
(8)	Dots Miller	175.00	87.00	52.00
(9)	Deacon Phillippe	175.00	87.00	52.00
(10)	Honus Wagner	2000.00	900.00	400.00
(11)	Owen Wilson	175.00	87.00	52.00

1910 E90-3

Schulte, r. f. Cubs

Similar in size (1-1/2" by 2-3/4") and style to the more popular E90-1 set, the E90-3 set was issued by the American Caramel Co. in 1910. The 20-card, color lithograph set includes 11 Chicago Cubs and nine White Sox. The fronts of the cards have a similar design to the E90-1 set, although different photos were used. The backs can be differentiated by two major changes: The bottom of the card indicates the American Caramel Co. of "Chicago," rather than Philadelphia, and the top of the card contains the phrase "All The Star Players," rather than "100 Subjects." The E90-3 cards are generally more scarce than those in the E90-1 set.

		NR MT	EX	VG
Complete Set:		8500.00	4000.00	2200.
Common Player:		200.00	100.00	60.00
(1)	Jimmy Archer	200.00	100.00	60.00
(2)	Lena Blackburne	200.00	100.00	60.00
(3)	Mordecai Brown	600.00	300.00	150.00
(4)	Frank Chance	900.00	450.00	200.00
(5)	King Cole	200.00	100.00	60.00
(6)	Patsy Dougherty	200.00	100.00	60.00
(7)	Johnny Evers	600.00	300.00	150.00
(8)	Chick Gandil	300.00	150.00	75.00
(9)	Ed Hahn	200.00	100.00	60.00
(10)	Solly Hofman	200.00	100.00	60.00
(11)	Orval Overall	200.00	100.00	60.00
(12)	Fred Payne	200.00	100.00	60.00
(13)	Billy Purtell	200.00	100.00	60.00
(14)	Wildfire Schulte	200.00	100.00	60.00
(15)	Jimmy Sheckard	200.00	100.00	60.00
(16)	Frank Smith	200.00	100.00	60.00
(17)	Harry Steinfeldt	250.00	125.00	50.00
(18)	Joe Tinker	600.00	300.00	150.00
(19)	Ed Walsh	600.00	300.00	150.00
(20)	Rollie Zeider	200.00	100.00	60.00

1908 E91 - Set A

JAMES COLLINS

Issued by Philadelphia's American Caramel Company from 1908 through 1910, the E91 set of Base Ball Caramels is generally not popular with collectors because the color drawings show "generic" players, rather than actual major leaguers. In other words, the exact same drawing was used to depict two or three different players. For this reason, the set is sometimes referred to as "Fake Design". The player's name, position and team appear below the color drawing on the front of the card. The cards measure approximately 1-1/2" by 2-3/4" and were issued in three separate series. They can be differentiated by their backs, which checklist the cards. Set A backs list the Athletics in the upper left, the Giants in the upper right and the Cubs below. Set B backs list the Cubs and Athletics on top with the Giants below, and Set C backs list Pittsburg and Washington on top with Boston below. A line indicating the cards were "Manufactured Only by the American Caramel Co." appears at the bottom.

		NR MT	EX	VG
Complete Set:		4500.00	2250.00	1500.
Common Player:		50.00	25.00	15.00
(1)	Charles Bender	200.00	100.00	35.00
(2)	Roger Bresnahan	200.00	100.00	35.00
(3)	Albert Bridwell	50.00	25.00	15.00
(4)	Mordecai Brown	200.00	100.00	35.00
(5)	Frank Chance	250.00	125.00	40.00
(6)	James Collins	200.00	100.00	35.00
(7)	Harry Davis	50.00	25.00	15.00
(8)	Arthur Devlin	50.00	25.00	15.00
(9)	Michael Donlin	50.00	25.00	15.00
(10)	John Evers	200.00	100.00	35.00
(11)	Frederick L. Hartsel	50.00	25.00	15.00
(12)	John Kling	50.00	25.00	15.00
(13)	Christopher Matthewson (Mathewson)	350.00	175.00	75.00
(14)	Joseph McGinnity	200.00	100.00	35.00
(15)	John J McGraw	250.00	125.00	40.00
(16)	Daniel F Murphy	50.00	25.00	15.00
(17)	Simon Nicholls	50.00	25.00	15.00
(18)	Reuben Oldring	50.00	25.00	15.00
(19)	Orvill Overall (Orval)	50.00	25.00	15.00
(20)	Edward S. Plank	300.00	150.00	60.00
(21)	Edward Reulbach	50.00	25.00	15.00
(22)	James Scheckard (Sheckard)	50.00	25.00	15.00
(23)	Osee Schreckengost (Ossee)	50.00	25.00	15.00
(24)	Ralph O. Seybold	50.00	25.00	15.00
(25)	J. Bentley Seymour	50.00	25.00	15.00
(26)	Daniel Shay	50.00	25.00	15.00
(27)	Frank Shulte (Schulte)	50.00	25.00	15.00
(28)	James Slagle	50.00	25.00	15.00
(29)	Harry Steinfeldt	60.00	30.00	18.00
(30)	Luther H. Taylor	50.00	25.00	15.00
(31)	Fred Tenney	50.00	25.00	15.00
(32)	Joseph B. Tinker	200.00	100.00	35.00
(33)	George Edward Waddell	200.00	100.00	35.00

1909 E91 - Set B

FRANK BAKER

		NR MT	EX	VG
Complete Set:		4300.00	2100.00	1450.
Common Player:		50.00	25.00	15.00
(1)	James Archer	50.00	25.00	15.00
(2)	Frank Baker	200.00	100.00	35.00
(3)	John Barry	50.00	25.00	15.00
(4)	Charles Bender	250.00	125.00	35.00

		NR MT	EX	VG
(5)	Albert Bridwell	50.00	25.00	15.00
(6)	Mordecai Brown	200.00	100.00	35.00
(7)	Frank Chance	250.00	100.00	40.00
(8)	Edw. Collins	200.00	100.00	35.00
(9)	Harry Davis	50.00	25.00	15.00
(10)	Arthur Devlin	50.00	25.00	15.00
(11)	Michael Donlin	50.00	25.00	15.00
(12)	Larry Doyle	50.00	25.00	15.00
(13)	John Evers	200.00	100.00	35.00
(14)	Robt. Ganley	50.00	25.00	15.00
(15)	Frederick L. Hartsel	50.00	25.00	15.00
(16)	Arthur Hoffman (Hofman)	50.00	25.00	15.00
(17)	Harry Krause	50.00	25.00	15.00
(18)	Rich. W. Marquard	200.00	100.00	35.00
(19)	Christopher Matthewson (Mathewson)			
		350.00	175.00	75.00
(20)	John J. McGraw	250.00	125.00	40.00
(21)	J.T. Meyers	50.00	25.00	15.00
(22)	Dan Murphy	50.00	25.00	15.00
(23)	Jno. J. Murray	50.00	25.00	15.00
(24)	Orvill Overall (Orval)	50.00	25.00	15.00
(25)	Edward S. Plank	300.00	150.00	50.00
(26)	Edward Reulbach	50.00	25.00	15.00
(27)	James Scheckard (Sheckard)	50.00	25.00	15.00
(28)	J. Bentley Seymour	50.00	25.00	15.00
(29)	Harry Steinfeldt	60.00	30.00	18.00
(30)	Frank Shulte (Schulte)	60.00	30.00	18.00
(31)	Fred Tenney	50.00	25.00	15.00
(32)	Joseph B Tinker	200.00	100.00	35.00
(33)	Ira Thomas	50.00	25.00	15.00

1909 E91 - Set C

Base Ball Caramels.

THIS CARD IS ONE OF A SET OF THIRTY THREE BASE BALL PLAYERS, CONSISTING OF PITTS-BURG, WASHINGTON AND BOSTON BASE BALL TEAMS, ONE OF WHICH IS WRAPPED WITH EVERY BASE BALL CARAMEL.

WID CONROY
3 b   Washington (A. L.)

Manufactured only by the
AMERICAN CARAMEL CO.

		NR MT	EX	VG
Complete Set:		4000.00	2000.00	1200.
Common Player:		50.00	25.00	15.00
(1)	W.J. Barbeau	50.00	25.00	15.00
(2)	Geo. Brown	50.00	25.00	15.00
(3)	Robt. Check (Charles Chech)	50.00	25.00	15.00
(4)	Fred Clarke	225.00	112.50	37.50
(5)	Wid Conroy	50.00	25.00	15.00
(6)	James Delehanty	50.00	25.00	15.00
(7)	Jon A. Donohue (Donahue)	50.00	25.00	15.00
(8)	P. Donahue	50.00	25.00	15.00
(9)	Geo. Gibson	50.00	25.00	15.00
(10)	Robt. Groom	50.00	25.00	15.00
(11)	Harry Hooper	200.00	100.00	35.00
(12)	Tom Hughes	50.00	25.00	15.00
(13)	Walter Johnson	500.00	225.00	100.00
(14)	Edwin Karger	50.00	25.00	15.00
(15)	Tommy Leach	50.00	25.00	15.00
(16)	Sam'l Leever	50.00	25.00	15.00
(17)	Harry Lord	50.00	25.00	15.00
(18)	Geo. F. McBride	50.00	25.00	15.00
(19)	Ambr. McConnell	50.00	25.00	15.00
(20)	Clyde Milan	50.00	25.00	15.00
(21)	J.B. Miller	50.00	25.00	15.00
(22)	Harry Niles	50.00	25.00	15.00
(23)	Chas. Phillipi (Phillippe)	50.00	25.00	15.00
(24)	T.H. Speaker	350.00	175.00	75.00
(25)	Jacob Stahl	50.00	25.00	15.00
(26)	Chas. E. Street	50.00	25.00	15.00
(27)	Allen Storke	50.00	25.00	15.00
(28)	Robt. Unglaub	50.00	25.00	15.00
(29)	C. Wagner	50.00	25.00	15.00
(30)	Hans Wagner	500.00	250.00	110.00
(31)	Victor Willis	50.00	25.00	15.00

		NR MT	EX	VG
(32)	Owen Wilson	50.00	25.00	15.00
(33)	Jos. Wood	75.00	35.00	18.00

1909 E92 Croft's Candy

Wagner, s.s. Pittsburg Nat'l.

CANDY
CROFT'S
CROFT
AND
ALLEN CO.
Philadelphia, Pa.

		NR MT	EX	VG
Complete Set:		15000.00	7500.00	4500.
Common Player:		150.00	75.00	45.00
(1)	Jack Barry	450.00	225.00	100.00
(2)	Harry Bemis	150.00	75.00	45.00
(3)	Chief Bender (striped cap)	700.00	325.00	150.00
(4)	Chief Bender (white cap)	450.00	225.00	100.00
(5)	Bill Bergen	150.00	75.00	45.00
(6)	Bob Bescher	150.00	75.00	45.00
(7)	Al Bridwell	150.00	75.00	45.00
(8)	Doc Casey	150.00	75.00	45.00
(9)	Frank Chance	450.00	225.00	100.00
(10)	Hal Chase	200.00	100.00	50.00
(11)	Ty Cobb	4500.00	2200.00	1000.
(12)	Eddie Collins	850.00	400.00	200.00
(13)	Sam Crawford	400.00	200.00	100.00
(14)	Harry Davis	150.00	75.00	45.00
(15)	Art Devlin	150.00	75.00	45.00
(16)	Wild Bill Donovan	150.00	75.00	45.00
(17)	Red Dooin	350.00	175.00	75.00
(18)	Mickey Doolan	150.00	75.00	45.00
(19)	Patsy Dougherty	150.00	75.00	45.00
(20)	Larry Doyle (throwing)	150.00	75.00	45.00
(21)	Larry Doyle (with bat)	150.00	75.00	45.00
(22)	Johnny Evers	1000.00	500.00	200.00
(23)	George Gibson	150.00	75.00	45.00
(24)	Topsy Hartsel	150.00	75.00	45.00
(25)	Fred Jacklitsch	350.00	175.00	75.00
(26)	Hugh Jennings	400.00	200.00	100.00
(27)	Red Kleinow	150.00	75.00	45.00
(28)	Otto Knabe	350.00	175.00	75.00
(29)	Jack Knight	350.00	175.00	75.00
(30)	Nap Lajoie	700.00	350.00	200.00
(31)	Hans Lobert	150.00	75.00	45.00
(32)	Sherry Magee	150.00	75.00	45.00
(33)	Christy Matthewson (Mathewson)			
		1200.00	600.00	275.00
(34)	John McGraw	550.00	275.00	150.00
(35)	Larry McLean	150.00	75.00	45.00
(36)	Dots Miller (batting)	150.00	75.00	45.00
(37)	Dots Miller (fielding)	350.00	175.00	75.00
(38)	Danny Murphy	150.00	75.00	45.00
(39)	Bil O'Hara	150.00	75.00	45.00
(40)	Germany Schaefer	150.00	75.00	45.00
(41)	Admiral Schlei	150.00	75.00	45.00
(42)	Boss Schmidt	150.00	75.00	45.00
(43)	Johnny Seigle (Siegle)	150.00	75.00	45.00
(44)	Dave Shean	150.00	75.00	45.00
(45)	Boss Smith (Schmidt)	150.00	75.00	45.00
(46)	Joe Tinker	450.00	225.00	110.00
(47)	Honus Wagner (batting)	1000.00	500.00	275.00
(48)	Honus Wagner (throwing)	1000.00	500.00	275.00
(49)	Cy Young	900.00	450.00	250.00
(50)	Heinie Zimmerman	150.00	75.00	45.00

NOTE: A card number in parentheses ( ) indicates the set is unnumbered.

1909 E92 Croft's Cocoa

		NR MT	EX	VG
Complete Set:		27500.00	15000.00	6500.
Common Player:		150.00	75.00	45.00
(1)	Jack Barry	450.00	225.00	100.00
(2)	Harry Bemis	150.00	75.00	45.00
(3)	Chief Bender (striped hat)	700.00	325.00	150.00
(4)	Chief Bender (white hat)	450.00	225.00	100.00
(5)	Bill Bergen	150.00	75.00	45.00
(6)	Bob Bescher	150.00	75.00	45.00
(7)	Al Bridwell	150.00	75.00	45.00
(8)	Doc Casey	150.00	75.00	45.00
(9)	Frank Chance	450.00	225.00	100.00
(10)	Hal Chase	200.00	100.00	50.00
(11)	Ty Cobb	4500.00	2200.00	1000.
(12)	Eddie Collins	850.00	400.00	200.00
(13)	Sam Crawford	400.00	200.00	100.00
(14)	Harry Davis	150.00	75.00	45.00
(15)	Art Devlin	150.00	75.00	45.00
(16)	Wild Bill Donovan	150.00	75.00	45.00
(17)	Red Dooin	350.00	175.00	75.00
(18)	Mickey Doolan	150.00	75.00	45.00
(19)	Patsy Dougherty	150.00	75.00	45.00
(20)	Larry Doyle (throwing)	150.00	75.00	45.00
(21)	Larry Doyle (with bat)	150.00	75.00	45.00
(22)	Johnny Evers	1000.00	500.00	200.00
(23)	George Gibson	150.00	75.00	45.00
(24)	Topsy Hartsel	150.00	75.00	45.00
(25)	Fred Jacklitsch	350.00	175.00	75.00
(26)	Hugh Jennings	400.00	200.00	100.00
(27)	Red Kleinow	150.00	75.00	45.00
(28)	Otto Knabe	350.00	175.00	75.00
(29)	Jack Knight	350.00	175.00	75.00
(30)	Nap Lajoie	700.00	350.00	200.00
(31)	Hans Lobert	150.00	75.00	45.00
(32)	Sherry Magee	150.00	75.00	30.00
(33)	Christy Matthewson (Mathewson)			
		1200.00	600.00	275.00
(34)	John McGraw	550.00	275.00	150.00
(35)	Larry McLean	150.00	75.00	45.00
(36)	Dots Miller (batting)	150.00	75.00	45.00
(37)	Dots Miller (fielding)	350.00	175.00	75.00
(38)	Danny Murphy	150.00	75.00	45.00
(39)	Bill O'Hara	150.00	75.00	45.00
(40)	Germany Schaefer	150.00	75.00	45.00
(41)	Admiral Schlei	150.00	75.00	45.00
(42)	Boss Schmidt	150.00	75.00	45.00
(43)	Johnny Seigle (Siegle)	150.00	75.00	45.00
(44)	Dave Shean	150.00	75.00	45.00
(45)	Boss Smith (Schmidt)	150.00	75.00	45.00
(46)	Joe Tinker	450.00	225.00	110.00
(47)	Honus Wagner (batting)	1000.00	500.00	275.00
(48)	Honus Wagner (throwing)	1000.00	500.00	275.00
(49)	Cy Young	900.00	450.00	250.00
(50)	Heinie Zimmerman	150.00	75.00	45.00

1909 E92 Dockman

Designated in the American Card Catalog as the E92 set, this 1910 issue which is similar in size (1-1/2" by 2-3/4") and style to the E101 set, could actually be considered four separate sets, depending on the back design. The fronts of the cards are nearly identical to the more popular E90-1 American Caramels. The four different backs included under the E92 designation advertise Croft's Candy, Croft's Cocoa, Nadja Caramels, and John H.

Dockman and Sons Base Ball Gum. The basic set consists of 50 cards picturing 45 different players (five players are shown on two cards each). However, only 40 cards are known to exist with the Dockman back, and eight additional cards have been found only with the Nadja back and are considered very rare.

		NR MT	EX	VG
Complete Set:		13500.00	7500.00	3000.
Common Player:		125.00	62.00	37.00
(1)	Harry Bemis	125.00	62.00	37.00
(2)	Chief Bender	350.00	175.00	75.00
(3)	Bill Bergen	125.00	62.00	37.00
(4)	Bob Bescher	125.00	62.00	37.00
(5)	Al Bridwell	125.00	62.00	37.00
(6)	Doc Casey	125.00	62.00	37.00
(7)	Frank Chance	350.00	175.00	75.00
(8)	Hal Chase	125.00	50.00	25.00
(9)	Sam Crawford	300.00	150.00	50.00
(10)	Harry Davis	125.00	62.00	37.00
(11)	Art Devlin	125.00	62.00	37.00
(12)	Wild Bill Donovan	125.00	62.00	37.00
(13)	Mickey Doolan	125.00	62.00	37.00
(14)	Patsy Dougherty	125.00	62.00	37.00
(15)	Larry Doyle (throwing)	125.00	62.00	37.00
(16)	Larry Doyle (with bat)	125.00	62.00	37.00
(17)	George Gibson	125.00	62.00	37.00
(18)	Topsy Hartsel	125.00	62.00	37.00
(19)	Hugh Jennings	350.00	175.00	75.00
(20)	Red Kleinow	125.00	62.00	37.00
(21)	Nap Lajoie	500.00	250.00	100.00
(22)	Hans Lobert	125.00	62.00	37.00
(23)	Sherry Magee	125.00	62.00	37.00
(24)	Christy Matthewson (Mathewson)			
		900.00	450.00	200.00
(25)	John McGraw	400.00	200.00	85.00
(26)	Larry McLean	125.00	62.00	37.00
(27)	Dots Miller	125.00	62.00	37.00
(28)	Danny Murphy	125.00	62.00	37.00
(29)	Bill O'Hara	125.00	62.00	37.00
(30)	Germany Schaefer	125.00	62.00	37.00
(31)	Admiral Schlei	125.00	62.00	37.00
(32)	Boss Schmidt	125.00	62.00	37.00
(33)	Johnny Seigle	125.00	62.00	37.00
(34)	Dave Shean	125.00	62.00	37.00
(35)	Boss Smith (Schmidt)	125.00	62.00	37.00
(36)	Joe Tinker	350.00	175.00	75.00
(37)	Honus Wagner (batting)	700.00	350.00	150.00
(38)	Honus Wagner (throwing)	700.00	350.00	150.00
(39)	Cy Young	600.00	300.00	135.00
(40)	Heinie Zimmerman	125.00	62.00	37.00

1909 E92 Najda

		NR MT	EX	VG
Complete Set:		15500.00	7500.00	4000.
Common Player:		200.00	100.00	60.00
(1)	Bill Bailey	200.00	100.00	60.00
(2)	Rube Ellis	2500.00	1250.00	500.00
(3)	Roy Hartzell (batting)	200.00	100.00	60.00
(4)	Roy Hartzell (fielding)	200.00	100.00	60.00
(5)	Harry Howell (ready to pitch)	200.00	100.00	60.00
(6)	Harry Howell (follow-thru)	200.00	100.00	60.00
(7)	Eddie Phelps	200.00	100.00	60.00
(8)	George Stone (Blue Background)			
		1000.00	500.00	300.00

		NR MT	EX	VG
(9)	George Stone (Green Background)			
		1500.00	750.00	450.00
(10)	Bobby Wallace	1000.00	500.00	200.00
(11)	Roger Bresnahan	2500.00	1250.00	500.00
(12)	Rebel Oakes	400.00	200.00	100.00

1910 E93

This 30-card set issued in 1910 by Standard Caramel Co. of Lancaster, Pa., is closely related to several other candy sets from this period which share the same format and, in many cases, the same player poses. The cards measure 1-1/2" by 2-3/4" and contain tinted black and white player photos. The back of each card contains an alphabetical checklist of the set plus a line indicating it was manufactured by Standard Caramel Co., Lancaster, Pa. The set carries the ACC designation of E93.

		NR MT	EX	VG
Complete Set:		18000.00	9000.00	5400.
Common Player:		150.00	75.00	45.00
(1)	Red Ames	150.00	75.00	45.00
(2)	Chief Bender	500.00	225.00	100.00
(3)	Mordecai Brown	500.00	225.00	100.00
(4)	Frank Chance	550.00	250.00	115.00
(5)	Hal Chase	250.00	100.00	50.00
(6)	Fred Clarke	500.00	225.00	100.00
(7)	Ty Cobb	4500.00	2000.00	1150.
(8)	Eddie Collins	500.00	225.00	100.00
(9)	Harry Coveleskie (Coveleski)	150.00	75.00	45.00
(10)	Jim Delehanty	150.00	75.00	45.00
(11)	Wild Bill Donovan	150.00	75.00	45.00
(12)	Red Dooin	150.00	75.00	45.00
(13)	Johnny Evers	500.00	225.00	100.00
(14)	George Gibson	150.00	75.00	45.00
(15)	Clark Griffith	500.00	225.00	100.00
(16)	Hugh Jennings	500.00	225.00	100.00
(17)	Davy Jones	150.00	75.00	45.00
(18)	Addie Joss	500.00	225.00	100.00
(19)	Nap Lajoie	750.00	350.00	150.00
(20)	Tommy Leach	150.00	75.00	45.00
(21)	Christy Mathewson	1000.00	450.00	200.00
(22)	John McGraw	600.00	250.00	115.00
(23)	Jim Pastorious	150.00	75.00	45.00
(24)	Deacon Phillippi (Phillippe)	150.00	75.00	45.00
(25)	Eddie Plank	650.00	300.00	130.00
(26)	Joe Tinker	500.00	225.00	100.00
(27)	Honus Wagner	1500.00	700.00	300.00
(28)	Rube Waddell	500.00	225.00	100.00
(29)	Hooks Wiltse	150.00	75.00	45.00
(30)	Cy Young	1000.00	450.00	200.00

1911 E94

This 30-card set, issued in 1911, is nearly identical to several early candy and caramel sets of the same period. The set was apparently issued by the George Close Candy Co. of Cambridge, Mass., however, many of the cards found contain no indication of who produced them. The cards measure 1-1/2" by 2-3/4" and feature tinted black and white player photos. The back of each card, printed in gray, carries a checklist of the 30 cards in the set. Eight different back cariations are known to exist. One variation contains just the checklist without any advertising, while seven other variations include overprinted backs advertising various candy products manufactured by the George Close Company. The set carries the ACC designation E94.

		NR MT	EX	VG
Complete Set:		16000.00	8000.00	4800.
Common Player:		185.00	92.00	55.00
(1)	Jimmy Austin	185.00	92.00	55.00
(2)	Johnny Bates	185.00	92.00	55.00
(3)	Bob Bescher	185.00	92.00	55.00
(4)	Bobby Byrne	185.00	92.00	55.00
(5)	Frank Chance	550.00	225.00	100.00
(6)	Ed Cicotte	225.00	112.50	50.00
(7)	Ty Cobb	4500.00	2000.00	1000.
(8)	Sam Crawford	500.00	250.00	100.00
(9)	Harry Davis	185.00	92.00	55.00
(10)	Art Devlin	185.00	92.00	55.00
(11)	Josh Devore	185.00	92.00	55.00
(12)	Mickey Doolan	185.00	92.00	55.00
(13)	Patsy Dougherty	185.00	92.00	55.00
(14)	Johnny Evers	500.00	250.00	100.00
(15)	Eddie Grant	185.00	92.00	55.00
(16)	Hugh Jennings	500.00	250.00	100.00
(17)	Kleinow	185.00	92.00	55.00
(18)	Joe Lake	185.00	92.00	55.00
(19)	Nap Lajoie	800.00	400.00	200.00
(20)	Tommy Leach	185.00	92.00	55.00
(21)	Hans Lobert	185.00	92.00	55.00
(22)	Harry Lord	185.00	92.00	55.00
(23)	Sherry Magee	200.00	100.00	50.00
(24)	John McGraw	575.00	287.00	150.00
(25)	Earl Moore	185.00	92.00	55.00
(26)	Red Murray	185.00	92.00	55.00
(27)	Tris Speaker	900.00	450.00	250.00
(28)	Turner	185.00	92.00	55.00
(29)	"Hans" Wagner	1500.00	750.00	400.00
(30)	Cy (Old) Young	1000.00	500.00	225.00

1909 E95

Similar in style to the many other early candy and caramel cards, the set designated as E95 by the American Card Catalog is a 25-card issue produced by the Philadelphia Caramel Co. (actually of Camden, N.J.) in 1909. The cards measure approximately 2-5/8" by 1-1/2" and contain a full-color player drawing. The back, which differentiates the set from other similar issues, checklists the 25 players in black

ink and displays the Philadelphia Caramel Co. name at the bottom.

		NR MT	EX	VG
Complete Set:		16000.00	8000.00	4800.
Common Player:		150.00	75.00	45.00
(1)	Chief Bender	500.00	250.00	110.00
(2)	Bill Carrigan	150.00	75.00	45.00
(3)	Frank Chance	550.00	275.00	125.00
(4)	Ed Cicotte	225.00	112.50	65.00
(5)	Ty Cobb	5000.00	2500.00	210.00
(6)	Eddie Collins	500.00	250.00	135.00
(7)	Sam Crawford	500.00	250.00	135.00
(8)	Art Devlin	150.00	75.00	45.00
(9)	Larry Doyle	150.00	75.00	45.00
(10)	Johnny Evers	500.00	250.00	135.00
(11)	Solly Hoffman (Hofman)	150.00	75.00	45.00
(12)	Harry Krause	150.00	75.00	45.00
(13)	Tommy Leach	150.00	75.00	45.00
(14)	Harry Lord	150.00	75.00	45.00
(15)	Nick Maddox	150.00	75.00	45.00
(16)	Christy Matthewson (Mathewson)	1500.00	750.00	350.00
(17)	Matty McIntyre	150.00	75.00	45.00
(18)	Fred Merkle	250.00	125.00	75.00
(19)	Cy Morgan	150.00	75.00	45.00
(20)	Eddie Plank	650.00	325.00	200.00
(21)	Ed Reulbach	150.00	75.00	45.00
(22)	Honus Wagner	1800.00	900.00	450.00
(23)	Ed Willetts (Willett)	150.00	75.00	45.00
(24)	Vic Willis	150.00	75.00	45.00
(25)	Hooks Wiltse	150.00	75.00	45.00

1910 E96

This set of 30 subjects, known by the ACC designation E96, was issued in 1910 by the Philadelphia Caramel Co. as a continuation of the E95 set of the previous year. The front design remained the same, but the two issues can be identified by the backs. The backs of the E96 cards are printed in red and carry a checklist of 30 players. There is also a line at the bottom advising "Previous series 25, making total issue 55 cards." Just below that appears "Philadelphia Caramel Co./Camden, N.J."

		NR MT	EX	VG
Complete Set:		8000.00	4000.00	2400.
Common Player:		150.00	75.00	45.00
(1)	Babe Adams	150.00	75.00	45.00
(2)	Red Ames	150.00	75.00	45.00
(3)	Frank Arrelanes (Arellanes)	150.00	75.00	45.00
(4)	Home Run Baker	550.00	275.00	150.00
(5)	Mordecai Brown	500.00	250.00	100.00
(6)	Fred Clark (Clarke)	500.00	250.00	100.00
(7)	Harry Davis	150.00	75.00	45.00
(8)	Wild Bill Donovan	150.00	75.00	45.00
(9)	Jim Delehanty	150.00	75.00	45.00
(10)	Red Dooin	150.00	75.00	45.00
(11)	George Gibson	150.00	75.00	45.00
(12)	Buck Herzog	150.00	75.00	45.00
(13)	Hugh Jennings	500.00	250.00	100.00
(14)	Ed Karger	150.00	75.00	45.00
(15)	Johnny Kling	150.00	75.00	45.00
(16)	Ed Konetchy	150.00	75.00	45.00
(17)	Nap Lajoie	800.00	400.00	200.00
(18)	Connie Mack	900.00	450.00	215.00
(19)	Rube Marquard	500.00	250.00	100.00
(20)	George McQuillan	150.00	75.00	45.00
(21)	Chief Meyers	150.00	75.00	45.00
(22)	Mike Mowrey	150.00	75.00	45.00
(23)	George Mullin	150.00	75.00	45.00
(24)	Red Murray	150.00	75.00	45.00
(25)	Jack Pfister (Pfiester)	150.00	75.00	45.00
(26)	Nap Rucker	150.00	75.00	45.00
(27)	Claude Rossman	150.00	75.00	45.00
(28)	Tubby Spencer	150.00	75.00	45.00
(29)	Ira Thomas	150.00	75.00	45.00
(30)	Joe Tinker	500.00	250.00	100.00

1909 E97

Measuring approximately 1-1/2" by 2-3/4", this 30-card set is nearly identical to several other candy issues of the same period. Designated as E97 in the American Card Catalog, the set was issued in 1909-1910 by C.A. Briggs Co., Lozenge Makers of Boston, Mass. The front of the card shows a tinted black and white player photo, with the player's last name, position and team printed below. The backs of the cards are printed in brown type and checklist the 30 players in the set alphabetically. The C.A. Briggs Co. name appears at the bottom. Black and white examples of this set have also been found on a thin paper stock with blank backs and are believed to be "proof cards." Four variations are also found in the set. The more expensive variations are not included in the complete set price.

		NR MT	EX	VG
Complete Set:		18000.00	9000.00	5400.
Common Player:		200.00	100.00	60.00
(1)	Jimmy Austin	200.00	100.00	60.00
(2)	Joe Birmingham	200.00	100.00	60.00
(3)	Bill Bradley	200.00	100.00	60.00
(4)	Kitty Bransfield	200.00	100.00	60.00
(5)	Howie Camnitz	200.00	100.00	60.00
(6)	Bill Carrigan	200.00	100.00	60.00
(7)	Harry Davis	200.00	100.00	60.00
(8)	Josh Devore	200.00	100.00	60.00
(9)	Mickey Doolan	200.00	100.00	60.00
(10)	Bull Durham	200.00	100.00	60.00

		NR MT	EX	VG
(11)	Jimmy Dygert	200.00	100.00	60.00
(12)	Topsy Hartsell (Hartsel)	200.00	100.00	60.00
(13)	Bill Heinchman (Hinchman)	200.00	100.00	60.00
(14)	Charlie Hemphill	200.00	100.00	60.00
(15)	Wee Willie Keeler	1000.00	500.00	225.00
(16)	Joe Kelly (Kelley)	900.00	450.00	200.00
(17)	Red Kleinow	200.00	100.00	60.00
(18)	Rube Kroh	200.00	100.00	60.00
(19)	Matty McIntyre	200.00	100.00	60.00
(20)	Amby McConnell	200.00	100.00	60.00
(21)	Chief Meyers	200.00	100.00	60.00
(22)	Earl Moore	200.00	100.00	60.00
(23)	George Mullin	200.00	100.00	60.00
(24)	Red Murray	200.00	100.00	60.00
(25a)	Simon Nichols (Nicholls) (Philadelphia)			
		550.00	275.00	150.00
(25b)	Simon Nichols (Nicholls) (Cleveland)			
		200.00	100.00	60.00
(26)	Claude Rossman	200.00	100.00	60.00
(27)	Admiral Schlei	200.00	100.00	60.00
(28a)	Harry Steinfeld (name incorrect)			
		200.00	100.00	60.00
(28b)	Harry Steinfeldt (name correct)			
		550.00	275.00	150.00
(29a)	Dennis Sullivan (Chicago)	200.00	100.00	60.00
(29b)	Dennis Sullivan (Boston)	3500.00	1500.00	675.00
(30a)	Cy. Young (Cleveland)	1800.00	900.00	400.00
(30b)	Cy. Young (Boston)	1500.00	700.00	325.00

		NR MT	EX	VG
(25)	Fred Tenny (Tenney)	150.00	75.00	45.00
(26)	Joe Tinker	650.00	325.00	200.00
(27)	Hippo Vaughn	150.00	75.00	45.00
(28)	Hans Wagner	2000.00	1000.00	500.00
(29)	Ed Walsh	700.00	350.00	225.00
(30)	Cy Young	1000.00	500.00	250.00

1910 E99

Briggs, c. f. Sacramento

The first of two obscure sets produced by the Los Angeles candy maker Bishop & Co., this 30-card set was issued in 1910 and depicts players from the Pacific Coast League, showing five players from each of the six teams. The cards measure approximately 1-1/2" by 2-3/4" and feature black and white player photos with colored backgrounds (either green, blue, purple or yellow). The player's last name, position and team appear along the bottom, The backs of the cards contain the complete checklist in groups of five, according to team, with each name indented slightly more than the name above. Cards in the set, which has been designated E99 by the ACC, do not contain the name "Bishop & Company, California" along the bottom on the back.

1910 E98

This set of 30 subjects was issued in 1910 and is closely related to several other early candy issues. that art nearly identical. The cards measure 1-1/2" by 2-3/4" and feature tinted black and white player photos. The backs, printed in brown, contain a checklist of the set but no advertising or other information indicating the manufacturer. The set is assigned the designation of E98 by the ACC.

		NR MT	EX	VG
Complete Set:		22000.00	11000.00	6600.
Common Player:		150.00	75.00	45.00
(1)	Chief Bender	650.00	325.00	200.00
(2)	Roger Bresnahan	650.00	325.00	200.00
(3)	Al Bridwell	150.00	75.00	45.00
(4)	Miner Brown	600.00	300.00	150.00
(5)	Frank Chance	700.00	350.00	215.00
(6)	Hal Chase	300.00	150.00	75.00
(7)	Fred Clarke	650.00	325.00	200.00
(8)	Ty Cobb	5500.00	2250.00	1500.
(9)	Eddie Collins	600.00	300.00	150.00
(10)	Jack Coombs	250.00	125.00	70.00
(11)	Bill Dahlen	150.00	75.00	45.00
(12)	Harry Davis	150.00	75.00	45.00
(13)	Red Dooin	150.00	75.00	45.00
(14)	Johnny Evers	650.00	325.00	200.00
(15)	Russ Ford	150.00	75.00	45.00
(16)	Hughey Jennings	650.00	325.00	200.00
(17)	Johnny Kling	150.00	75.00	45.00
(18)	Nap Lajoie	1000.00	500.00	225.00
(19)	Connie Mack	1000.00	500.00	225.00
(20)	Christy Mathewson	1500.00	750.00	325.00
(21)	John McGraw	850.00	425.00	240.00
(22)	Larry McLean	150.00	75.00	45.00
(23)	Chief Meyers	150.00	75.00	45.00
(24)	George Mullin	150.00	75.00	45.00

		NR MT	EX	VG
Complete Set:		10000.00	4500.00	2500.
Common Player:		250.00	125.00	75.00
(1)	Bodie	350.00	175.00	95.00
(2)	N. Brashear	250.00	125.00	75.00
(3)	Briggs	250.00	125.00	75.00
(4)	Byones (Byrnes)	250.00	125.00	75.00
(5)	Cameron	250.00	125.00	75.00
(6)	Casey	250.00	125.00	75.00
(7)	Cutshaw	250.00	125.00	75.00
(8)	Delmas	250.00	125.00	75.00
(9)	Dillon	250.00	125.00	75.00
(10)	Hasty	250.00	125.00	75.00
(11)	Hitt	250.00	125.00	75.00
(12)	Hap. Hogan	250.00	125.00	75.00
(13)	Hunt	250.00	125.00	75.00
(14)	Krapp	250.00	125.00	75.00
(15)	Lindsay	250.00	125.00	75.00
(16)	McArdle	250.00	125.00	75.00
(17)	McCredie (McCreedle)	250.00	125.00	75.00
(18)	Maggert	250.00	125.00	75.00
(19)	Melchoir	250.00	125.00	75.00
(20)	Mohler	250.00	125.00	75.00
(21)	Nagle	250.00	125.00	75.00
(22)	Nelson	250.00	125.00	75.00
(23)	Nourse	250.00	125.00	75.00
(24)	Olsen	250.00	125.00	75.00
(25)	Raymer	250.00	125.00	75.00
(26)	Smith	250.00	125.00	75.00
(27)	Tennent (Tennant)	250.00	125.00	75.00
(28)	Thorsen	250.00	125.00	75.00
(29)	Van Buren	250.00	125.00	75.00
(30)	Wolverton	250.00	125.00	75.00

NOTE: A card number in parentheses ( ) indicates the set is unnumbered.

1909 E100 - Type 1

This picture is one of a set of
30 BASEBALL PLAYERS in
the COAST LEAGUE, as follows
Seaton, Portland
Steen, Portland
Rapps, Portland
Peckinpaugh, Portland
McCreedie, Portland
Tozer, Los Angeles
Delhi, Los Angeles
Daley, Los Angeles
Delmas, Los Angeles
Moore, Los Angeles
Tennant, San Francisco
Mohler, San Francisco
Powell, San Francisco
Suter, San Francisco
Weaver, San Francisco
Hap Hogan, Vernon
Burrell, Vernon
Carlisle, Vernon
Hitt, Vernon
Patterson, Vernon
Pfyle, Oakland
Cutshaw, Oakland
Nelson, Oakland
Pearce, Oakland
Wares, Oakland
Baum, Sacramento
Danzig, Sacramento
O'Rourke, Sacramento
Thomas, Sacramento
Lerchen, Sacramento
Bishop & Company, California

Suter, p. San Francisco

		NR MT	EX	VG
Complete Set:		82000.00	41000.00	24600.
Common Player:		250.00	125.00	75.00
(1)	Spider Baum	250.00	125.00	75.00
(2)	Burrell	250.00	125.00	75.00
(3)	Carlisle	250.00	125.00	75.00
(4)	Cutshaw	250.00	125.00	75.00
(5)	Pete Daley	250.00	125.00	75.00
(6)	Danzig	250.00	125.00	75.00
(7)	Delhi	250.00	125.00	75.00
(8)	Delmas	250.00	125.00	75.00
(9)	Hitt	250.00	125.00	75.00
(10)	Hap Hogan (actually Walter Bray)	250.00	125.00	75.00
(11)	Lerchen	250.00	125.00	75.00
(12)	McCreddie (McCreedie)	250.00	125.00	75.00
(13)	Mohler	250.00	125.00	75.00
(14)	Moore	250.00	125.00	75.00
(15)	Slim Nelson	250.00	125.00	75.00
(16)	P. O'Rourke	250.00	125.00	75.00
(17)	Patterson	250.00	125.00	75.00
(18)	Bunny Pearce	250.00	125.00	75.00
(19)	Peckinpaugh	250.00	125.00	60.00
(20)	Monte Pfyle (Pfyl)	250.00	125.00	75.00
(21)	Powell	250.00	125.00	75.00
(22)	Rapps	250.00	125.00	75.00
(23)	Seaton	250.00	125.00	75.00
(24)	Steen	250.00	125.00	75.00
(25)	Suter	250.00	125.00	75.00
(26)	Tennant	250.00	125.00	75.00
(27)	Thomas	250.00	125.00	75.00
(28)	Tozer	250.00	125.00	75.00
(29)	Clyde Wares	250.00	125.00	75.00
(30)	Weaver	500.00	200.00	100.00

1911 E100 - Type 2

Sutor, p., Frisco.

This 30-card set, designated E100 by the ACC, was issued in 1911 by the California confectioner Bishop & Company of Los Angeles, which had produced a similar set a year earlier. Both set showcased star players from the Pacific Coast League. The cards measure approximately 1-1/2" by 2-3/4" and feature black and white photos with a background of

either green, blue, yellow or red. The backs contain the complete checklist of the set, listing the players in groups of five by team, with one line indented slightly more than the previous one. In addition to the checklist, the 1911 set can be differentiated from the previous year because the line "Bishop & Company, California" appears along the bottom, The Type II E100's are blank-backed and are enlarged Type I photos. Variations have been discovered in recent years for many of the cards in the E100 set. The variations, known as "Type II" have either orange backgrounds or green backgrounds with more tightly cropped photos and blank backs.

		NR MT	EX	VG
Complete Set:		4750.00	2375.00	1425.
Common Player:		225.00	112.00	67.00
(1)	Burrell	225.00	112.00	67.00
(2)	Danzig	225.00	112.00	67.00
(3)	Delhi	225.00	112.00	67.00
(4)	Hitt	225.00	112.00	67.00
(5)	Lerchen	225.00	112.00	67.00
(6)	McCreddie	225.00	112.00	67.00
(7)	Slim Nelson	225.00	112.00	67.00
(8)	P. O'Rourke	225.00	112.00	67.00
(9)	Patterson	225.00	112.00	67.00
(10)	Bunny Pearce	225.00	112.00	67.00
(11)	Monte Pfyle	225.00	112.00	67.00
(12)	Rapps	225.00	112.00	67.00
(13)	Seaton	225.00	112.00	67.00
(14)	Steen	225.00	112.00	67.00
(15)	Suter	225.00	112.00	67.00
(16)	Tennant	225.00	112.00	67.00
(17)	Weaver	400.00	200.00	100.00

1909 E101

THIS CARD IS ONE OF A SET OF 50 Base Ball Players PROMINENT MEMBERS OF NATIONAL AND AMERICAN LEAGUES,

Collins, 2b. Phila. Am.

This 50-card set, issued in 1910, is closely related to the E92 set and is sometimes collected as part of that set. The fronts of the E101 cards are identical to the E92 set, but the back is an "anonymous" one, containing no advertising or any other information regarding the set's sponsor. The backs read simply "This card is one of a set of 50 Base Ball Players/Prominent Members of National and American Leagues."

		NR MT	EX	VG
Complete Set:		16000.00	8000.00	4800.
Common Player:		150.00	75.00	45.00
(1)	Jack Barry	150.00	75.00	45.00
(2)	Harry Bemis	150.00	75.00	45.00
(3)	Chief Bender (white hat)	600.00	300.00	150.00
(4)	Chief Bender (striped hat)	600.00	300.00	150.00
(5)	Bill Bergen	150.00	75.00	45.00
(6)	Bob Bescher	150.00	75.00	45.00
(7)	Al Bridwell	150.00	75.00	45.00
(8)	Doc Casey	150.00	75.00	45.00
(9)	Frank Chance	600.00	300.00	180.00
(10)	Hal Chase	350.00	175.00	80.00
(11)	Ty Cobb	4500.00	2250.00	1350.
(12)	Eddie Collins	600.00	300.00	180.00
(13)	Sam Crawford	600.00	300.00	180.00
(14)	Harry Davis	150.00	75.00	45.00

		NR MT	EX	VG
(15)	Art Devlin	150.00	75.00	45.00
(16)	Wild Bill Donovan	150.00	75.00	45.00
(17)	Red Dooin	150.00	75.00	45.00
(18)	Mickey Doolan	150.00	75.00	45.00
(19)	Patsy Dougherty	150.00	75.00	45.00
(20)	Larry Doyle (with bat)	150.00	75.00	45.00
(21)	Larry Doyle (throwing)	150.00	75.00	45.00
(22)	Johnny Evers	600.00	300.00	150.00
(23)	George Gibson	150.00	75.00	45.00
(24)	Topsy Hartsel	150.00	75.00	45.00
(25)	Fred Jacklitsch	150.00	75.00	45.00
(26)	Hugh Jennings	550.00	275.00	115.00
(27)	Red Kleinow	550.00	275.00	115.00
(28)	Otto Knabe	550.00	275.00	115.00
(29)	Jack Knight	550.00	275.00	115.00
(30)	Nap Lajoie	1000.00	500.00	250.00
(31)	Hans Lobert	150.00	75.00	45.00
(32)	Sherry Magee	200.00	100.00	50.00
(33)	Christy Matthewson (Mathewson)			
		1400.00	700.00	300.00
(34)	John McGraw	500.00	250.00	150.00
(35)	Larry McLean	150.00	75.00	45.00
(36)	Dots Miller (batting)	150.00	75.00	45.00
(37)	Dots Miller (fielding)	150.00	75.00	45.00
(38)	Danny Murphy	150.00	75.00	45.00
(39)	Bill O'Hara	150.00	75.00	45.00
(40)	Germany Schaefer	150.00	75.00	45.00
(41)	Admiral Schlei	150.00	75.00	45.00
(42)	Boss Schmidt	150.00	75.00	45.00
(43)	Johnny Seigle	150.00	75.00	45.00
(44)	Dave Shean	150.00	75.00	45.00
(45)	Boss Smith (Schmidt)	150.00	75.00	45.00
(46)	Joe Tinker	600.00	300.00	150.00
(47)	Honus Wagner (batting)	1000.00	500.00	300.00
(48)	Honus Wagner (throwing)	1000.00	500.00	300.00
(49)	Cy Young	1000.00	500.00	225.00
(50)	Heinie Zimmerman	150.00	75.00	45.00

		NR MT	EX	VG
(9)	Patsy Dougherty	200.00	100.00	60.00
(10)	Larry Doyle (batting)	200.00	100.00	60.00
(11)	Larry Doyle (throwing)	200.00	100.00	60.00
(12)	Johnny Evers	600.00	300.00	150.00
(13)	Red Kleinow	200.00	100.00	60.00
(14)	Otto Knabe	200.00	100.00	60.00
(15)	Nap Lajoie	1200.00	600.00	275.00
(16)	Hans Lobert	200.00	100.00	60.00
(17)	Sherry Magee	250.00	125.00	60.00
(18)	Christy Matthewson (Mathewson)			
		1500.00	750.00	375.00
(19)	Dots Miller (batting)	200.00	100.00	60.00
(20)	Dots Miller (fielding)	1900.00	800.00	450.00
(21)	Danny Murphy	200.00	100.00	60.00
(22)	Germany Schaefer	200.00	100.00	60.00
(23)	Boss Schmidt	200.00	100.00	60.00
(24)	Dave Shean	200.00	100.00	60.00
(25)	Boss Smith (Schmidt)	200.00	100.00	60.00
(26)	Joe Tinker	600.00	300.00	150.00
(27)	Honus Wagner (batting)	1500.00	750.00	450.00
(28)	Honus Wagner (fielding)	1500.00	750.00	450.00
(29)	Heinie Zimmerman	200.00	100.00	60.00

1908 E102

Dooin, c. Phila. Nat.

One of many similar early candy card sets, this set - designated as E102 in the American Card Catalog - was distributed around 1910, although the producer of the set is unknown. Measuring approximately 1-1/2" by 2-3/4", the set is almost identical in design to the E101 set and other closely related issues, The set consists of 25 players, which are checklisted on the back of the card. Three of the players have been found in two poses, resulting in 28 different cards. Because there is no advertising on the cards, the set can best be identified by the words - "This Picture is one of a Set of Twenty-five Base Ball Players, as follows" - which appears at the top of the back of each card.

		NR MT	EX	VG
Complete Set:		25000.00	12000.00	6000.
Common Player:		200.00	100.00	60.00
(1)	Chief Bender	600.00	300.00	150.00
(2)	Bob Bescher	200.00	100.00	60.00
(3)	Hal Chase	350.00	175.00	75.00
(4)	Ty Cobb	5500.00	2750.00	1650.
(5)	Eddie Collins	600.00	300.00	150.00
(6)	Sam Crawford	600.00	300.00	150.00
(7)	Wild Bill Donovan	200.00	100.00	60.00
(8)	Red Dooin	200.00	100.00	60.00

1910 E103

FRED TENNY, 1st B., N. Y.
The Williams Caramel Co. Oxford, Pa.

This 30-card set issued by the Williams Caramel Co. of Oxford, Pa., in 1910 can be differentiated from other similar sets because it was printed on a thin paper stock rather than cardboard. Measuring approximately 1-1/2" by 2-3/4", each card features a player portrait set against a red background. The bottom of the card lists the player's last name, position and team, followed by a line reading "The Williams Caramel Co. Oxford Pa." Nearly all of the photos in the set, which is designated E103 by the ACC, are identical to those in the M116 Sporting Life set.

		NR MT	EX	VG
Complete Set:		18000.00	9000.00	5400.
Common Player:		200.00	100.00	60.00
(1)	Chas. Bender	700.00	350.00	210.00
(2)	Roger Bresnahan	700.00	350.00	210.00
(3)	Mordecai Brown	700.00	350.00	210.00
(4)	Frank Chance	700.00	350.00	210.00
(5)	Hal Chase	500.00	250.00	125.00
(6)	Ty Cobb	5000.00	2500.00	1500.
(7)	Edward Collins	700.00	350.00	210.00
(8)	Sam Crawford	700.00	350.00	210.00
(9)	Harry Davis	200.00	100.00	60.00
(10)	Arthur Devlin	200.00	100.00	60.00
(11)	William Donovan	200.00	100.00	60.00
(12)	Chas. Dooin	200.00	100.00	60.00
(13)	L. Doyle	200.00	100.00	60.00
(14)	John Ewing	200.00	100.00	60.00
(15)	George Gibson	200.00	100.00	60.00
(16)	Hugh Jennings	700.00	350.00	210.00
(17)	David Jones	200.00	100.00	60.00
(18)	Tim Jordan	200.00	100.00	60.00
(19)	N. Lajoie	1500.00	750.00	300.00
(20)	Thomas Leach	200.00	100.00	60.00
(21)	Harry Lord	200.00	100.00	60.00
(22)	Chris. Mathewson	2500.00	1200.00	500.00
(23)	John McLean	200.00	100.00	60.00
(24)	Geo. W. McQuillan	200.00	100.00	60.00
(25)	Pastorius	200.00	100.00	60.00

		NR MT	EX	VG
(26)	N. Rucker	200.00	100.00	60.00
(27)	Fred Tenny (Tenney)	200.00	100.00	60.00
(28)	Ira Thomas	200.00	100.00	60.00
(29)	Hans Wagner	3500.00	1750.00	750.00
(30)	Robert Wood	200.00	100.00	60.00

1910 E104 - Type 1

Although advanced collectors usually refer to this set as "Nadjas," because of the ad for Nadja Caramels on some of the backs, examples are also found with blank backs. (In fact, the blank backs are more common.) Issued in 1910-1911, the cards measure 2-5/8" by 1-1/2" and feature player portraits with the player's name and team printed below in blue capital letters. Three distinct types exist. Type I, an 18-card series picturing members of the 1910 World Champion Philadelphia Athletics, is nearly identical in appearance to the T208 Fireside set. Type II is an 11-card series similar to the E90-2 set of Pittsburgh Pirates; and Type III is a 30-card series featuring original artwork. Cards in all three types can be found either with the Nadja back or with blank backs. Collectively, these cards have been designated by the American Card Catalog. Complete set prices for all three types di not include the higher priced variations.

		NR MT	EX	VG
Complete Set:		8000.00	4000.00	2400.
Common Player:		125.00	62.00	37.00
(1a)	Home Run Baker (no "World's Champions" at top)	225.00	112.00	67.00
(1b)	Home Run Baker ("World's Champions" at top)	275.00	137.00	82.00
(2a)	Jack Barry (no "World's Champions" at top)	125.00	62.00	37.00
(2b)	Jack Barry ("World's Champions" at top)	150.00	75.00	45.00
(3a)	Chief Bender (no "World's Champions" at top)	225.00	112.00	67.00
(3b)	Chief Bender ("World's Champions" at top)	275.00	137.00	82.00
(4a)	Eddie Collins (no "World's Champions" at top)	225.00	112.00	67.00
(4b)	Eddie Collins ("World's Champions" at top)	275.00	137.00	82.00
(5a)	Harry Davis (no "World's Champions" at top)	125.00	62.00	37.00
(5b)	Harry Davis ("World's Champions" at top)	150.00	75.00	45.00
(6a)	Jimmy Dygert (no "World's Champions" at top)	125.00	62.00	37.00
(6b)	Jimmy Dygert ("World's Champions" at top)	150.00	75.00	45.00
(6c)	Jimmy Dygert (Nadja ad on back)	150.00	75.00	45.00
(7a)	Topsy Hartsel (no "World's Champions" at top)	125.00	62.00	37.00
(7b)	Topsy Hartel ("World's Champions" at top)	150.00	75.00	45.00
(7c)	Topsy Hartslet (Nadja ad on back)	150.00	75.00	45.00
(8a)	Harry Krause (no "World's Champions" at top)	125.00	62.00	37.00

		NR MT	EX	VG
(8b)	Harry Krause ("World's Champions" at top)	150.00	75.00	45.00
(9a)	Jack Lapp (no "World's Champions" at top)	125.00	62.00	37.00
(9b)	Jack Lapp ("World's Champions" at top)	150.00	75.00	45.00
(10a)	Paddy Livingstone (Livingston) (no "World's Champions" at top)	125.00	62.00	37.00
(10b)	Paddy Livingstone (Livingston) ("World's Champions" at top)	150.00	75.00	45.00
(11a)	Bris Lord (no "World's Champions" at top)	125.00	62.00	37.00
(11b)	Bris Lord ("World's Champions" at top)	150.00	75.00	45.00
(12a)	Connie Mack (no "World's Champions" at top)	275.00	137.00	82.00
(12b)	Connie Mack ("World's Champions" at top)	350.00	175.00	105.00
(12c)	Connie Mack (Nadja ad on back)	350.00	175.00	105.00
(13a)	Cy Morgan (no "World's Champions" at top)	125.00	62.00	37.00
(13b)	Cy Morgan ("World's Champions" at top)	150.00	75.00	45.00
(13c)	Cy Morgan (Nadja ad on back)	150.00	75.00	45.00
(14a)	Danny Murphy (no "World's Champions" at top)	125.00	62.00	37.00
(14b)	Danny Murphy ("World's Champions" at top)	150.00	75.00	45.00
(15a)	Rube Oldring (no "World's Champions" at top)	125.00	62.00	37.00
(15b)	Rube Oldring ("World's Champions" at top)	150.00	75.00	45.00
(16a)	Eddie Plank (no "World's Champions" at top)	225.00	112.00	67.00
(16b)	Eddie Plank ("World's Champions" at top)	275.00	137.00	82.00
(16c)	Eddie Plank (Nadja ad on back)	275.00	137.00	82.00
(17a)	Amos Strunk (no "World's Champions" at top)	125.00	62.00	37.00
(17b)	Amos Strunk ("World's Champions" at top)	150.00	75.00	45.00
(18a)	Ira Thomas (no "World's Champions" at top)	125.00	62.00	37.00
(18b)	Ira Thomas ("World's Champions" at top)	150.00	75.00	45.00

1910 E104 - Type 2

		NR MT	EX	VG
Complete Set:		6000.00	3000.00	1800.
Common Player:		125.00	62.00	37.00
(1a)	Babe Adams (no ad on back)	125.00	62.00	37.00
(1b)	Babe Adams (Nadja ad on back)	125.00	62.00	37.00
(2)	Fred Clarke	300.00	150.00	90.00
(3a)	George Gibson (no ad on back)	125.00	62.00	37.00
(3b)	George Gibson (Nadja ad on back)	125.00	62.00	37.00
(4a)	Ham Hyatt (no ad on back)	125.00	62.00	37.00
(4b)	Ham Hyatt (Nadja ad on back)	125.00	62.00	37.00
(5)	Tommy Leach	125.00	62.00	37.00
(6)	Sam Leever	125.00	62.00	37.00
(7)	Nick Maddox	125.00	62.00	37.00
(8)	Dots Miller	125.00	62.00	37.00
(9)	Deacon Phillippe	125.00	62.00	37.00
(10a)	Honus Wagner (no ad on back)	800.00	400.00	240.00

		NR MT	EX	VG
(10b)	Honus Wagner (Nadja ad on back)			
		800.00	400.00	240.00
(11a)	Owen Wilson (no ad on back)	125.00	62.00	37.00
(11b)	Owen Wilson (Nadja ad on back)			
		125.00	62.00	37.00

1910 E104 - Type 3

		NR MT	EX	VG
Complete Set:		10000.00	5000.00	3000.
Common Player:		175.00	87.00	52.00
(1)	Bill Abstein	175.00	87.00	52.00
(2)	Red Ames	175.00	87.00	52.00
(3)	Johnny Bates	175.00	87.00	52.00
(4a)	Kitty Bransfield (blank back)	175.00	87.00	52.00
(4b)	Kitty Bransfield (Nadja back)	200.00	100.00	60.00
(5a)	Al Bridwell (blank back)	175.00	87.00	52.00
(5b)	Al Bridwell (Nadja back)	200.00	100.00	60.00
(6)	Doc Crandall	175.00	87.00	52.00
(7)	Sam Crawford	400.00	200.00	120.00
(8)	Jim Delehanty	175.00	87.00	52.00
(9)	Larry Doyle	175.00	87.00	52.00
(10a)	Eddie Grant (blank back)	175.00	87.00	52.00
(10b)	Eddie Grant (Nadja back)	200.00	100.00	60.00
(11)	Fred Jacklitsch	175.00	87.00	52.00
(12)	Hugh Jennings	400.00	200.00	120.00
(13)	Davy Jones	175.00	87.00	52.00
(14)	Tom Jones	175.00	87.00	52.00
(15a)	Otto Knabe (blank back)	175.00	87.00	52.00
(15b)	Otto Knabe (Nadja back)	200.00	100.00	60.00
(16)	John McGraw	450.00	225.00	135.00
(17)	Matty McIntyre	175.00	87.00	52.00
(18)	Earl Moore	175.00	87.00	52.00
(19)	Pat Moren (Moran)	175.00	87.00	52.00
(20)	George Moriarity	175.00	87.00	52.00
(21)	George Mullin	175.00	87.00	52.00
(22)	Red Murray	175.00	87.00	52.00
(23)	Simon Nicholls	175.00	87.00	52.00
(24)	Charley O'Leary	175.00	87.00	52.00
(25a)	Admiral Schlei (blank back)	175.00	87.00	52.00
(25b)	Admiral Schlei (Nadja back)	200.00	100.00	60.00
(26a)	Cy Seymore (Seymour) (blank back)			
		175.00	87.00	52.00
(26b)	Cy Seymore (Seymour) (Nadja back)			
		200.00	100.00	60.00
(27)	Tully Sparks	175.00	87.00	52.00
(28)	Ed Summers	175.00	87.00	52.00
(29a)	Ed Willetts (Willetts) (blank back)			
		175.00	87.00	52.00
(29b)	Ed Willetts (Willetts) (Nadja back)			
		200.00	100.00	60.00
(30)	Vic Willis	175.00	87.00	52.00

1910 E105

Issued circa 1910 by Smith's Mello-Mint, "The Texas Gum", this set of 50 cards shares the same checklist and artwork as the better known E101 set. The Mello-Mint cards, however, are slightly smaller, measuring approximately 2-5/8" by 1-3/8", and were printed on thin paper, making them difficult to find in top condition. The backs contain an advertisement for Mello-Mint Gum. The set carries

an ACC designation of E105.

		NR MT	EX	VG
Complete Set:		18000.00	9000.00	5400.
Common Player:		150.00	75.00	45.00
(1)	Jack Barry	150.00	75.00	45.00
(2)	Harry Bemis	150.00	75.00	45.00
(3)	Chief Bender (white hat)	300.00	150.00	90.00
(4)	Chief Bender (striped hat)	300.00	150.00	90.00
(5)	Bill Bergen	150.00	75.00	45.00
(6)	Bob Bescher	150.00	75.00	45.00
(7)	Al Bridwell	150.00	75.00	45.00
(8)	Doc Casey	150.00	75.00	45.00
(9)	Frank Chance	400.00	200.00	120.00
(10)	Hal Chase	250.00	125.00	75.00
(11)	Ty Cobb	2000.00	1000.00	600.00
(12)	Eddie Collins	300.00	150.00	90.00
(13)	Sam Crawford	300.00	150.00	90.00
(14)	Harry Davis	150.00	75.00	45.00
(15)	Art Devlin	150.00	75.00	45.00
(16)	Wild Bill Donovan	150.00	75.00	45.00
(17)	Red Dooin	150.00	75.00	45.00
(18)	Mickey Doolan	150.00	75.00	45.00
(19)	Patsy Dougherty	150.00	75.00	45.00
(20)	Larry Doyle (with bat)	150.00	75.00	45.00
(21)	Larry Doyle (throwing)	150.00	75.00	45.00
(22)	Johnny Evers	300.00	150.00	90.00
(23)	George Gibson	150.00	75.00	45.00
(24)	Topsy Hartsel	150.00	75.00	45.00
(25)	Fred Jacklitsch	150.00	75.00	45.00
(26)	Hugh Jennings	300.00	150.00	90.00
(27)	Red Kleinow	150.00	75.00	45.00
(28)	Otto Knabe	150.00	75.00	45.00
(29)	Jack Knight	150.00	75.00	45.00
(30)	Nap Lajoie	600.00	300.00	180.00
(31)	Hans Lobert	150.00	75.00	45.00
(32)	Sherry Magee	150.00	75.00	45.00
(33)	Christy Matthewson (Mathewson)			
		1000.00	500.00	300.00
(34)	John McGraw	350.00	175.00	105.00
(35)	Larry McLean	150.00	75.00	45.00
(36)	Dots Miller (batting)	150.00	75.00	45.00
(37)	Dots Miller (fielding)	150.00	75.00	45.00
(38)	Danny Murphy	150.00	75.00	45.00
(39)	Bill O'Hara	150.00	75.00	45.00
(40)	Germany Schaefer	150.00	75.00	45.00
(41)	Admiral Schlei	150.00	75.00	45.00
(42)	Boss Schmidt	150.00	75.00	45.00
(43)	Johnny Seigle	150.00	75.00	45.00
(44)	Dave Shean	150.00	75.00	45.00
(45)	Boss Smith (Schmidt)	150.00	75.00	45.00
(46)	Joe Tinker	300.00	150.00	90.00
(47)	Honus Wagner (batting)	1200.00	600.00	360.00
(48)	Honus Wagner (throwing)	1200.00	600.00	360.00
(49)	Cy Young	600.00	300.00	180.00
(50)	Heinie Zimmerman	150.00	75.00	45.00

1915 E106

This 48-card set, designated E106 by the American Card Catalog, was produced by the American Caramel Company of York, Pa., in 1915 and includes players from the National, American and Federal Leagues. The cards measure 1-1/2" by 2-3/4". The set is related to the E90-1 and E92 sets, from which the artwork is taken. The American Caramel cards,

Chase, 1b. Buffalo Feds

This card is one of a set of forty-eight leading Baseball Players in the National, American and Federal Leagues. One card is given with every piece of Baseball Caramel manufactured by the

AMERICAN CARAMEL CO.

YORK PA

UNDER THE FAMOUS BRAND OF THE

P. C. W.

however, have a glossy coating, which makes them very susceptible to cracking. The backs of the cards advise that the card is "one of a set of forty-eight leading Baseball Players" and identifies the American Caramel Co. as the manufacturer.

		NR MT	EX	VG
Complete Set:		25000.00	12500.00	7500.
Common Player:		150.00	75.00	45.00
(1)	Jack Barry	150.00	75.00	45.00
(2)	Chief Bender (white hat)	400.00	200.00	120.00
(3)	Chief Bender (striped hat)	400.00	200.00	120.00
(4)	Bob Bescher	150.00	75.00	45.00
(5)	Roger Bresnahan	400.00	200.00	120.00
(6)	Al Bridwell	150.00	75.00	45.00
(7)	Donie Bush	150.00	75.00	45.00
(8)	Hal Chase (portrait)	250.00	125.00	75.00
(9)	Hal Chase (catching)	250.00	125.00	75.00
(10)	Ty Cobb (batting, facing front)	6000.00	3000.00	1200.
(11)	Ty Cobb (batting, facing to side)	6500.00	3250.00	2000.
(12)	Eddie Collins	350.00	175.00	105.00
(13)	Sam Crawford	350.00	175.00	105.00
(14)	Ray Demmitt	150.00	75.00	45.00
(15)	Wild Bill Donovan	150.00	75.00	45.00
(16)	Red Dooin	150.00	75.00	45.00
(17)	Mickey Doolan	150.00	75.00	45.00
(18)	Larry Doyle	150.00	75.00	45.00
(19)	Clyde Engle	150.00	75.00	45.00
(20)	Johnny Evers	350.00	175.00	105.00
(21)	Art Fromme	150.00	75.00	45.00
(22)	George Gibson (catching, back view)	150.00	75.00	45.00
(23)	George Gibson (catching, front view)	150.00	75.00	45.00
(24)	Roy Hartzell	150.00	75.00	45.00
(25)	Fred Jacklitsch	150.00	75.00	45.00
(26)	Hugh Jennings	350.00	175.00	105.00
(27)	Otto Knabe	150.00	75.00	45.00
(28)	Nap Lajoie	900.00	450.00	270.00
(29)	Hans Lobert	150.00	75.00	45.00
(30)	Rube Marquard	350.00	175.00	105.00
(31)	Christy Matthewson (Mathewson)	1000.00	500.00	300.00
(32)	John McGraw	850.00	400.00	250.00
(33)	George McQuillan	150.00	75.00	45.00
(34)	Dots Miller	150.00	75.00	45.00
(35)	Danny Murphy	150.00	75.00	45.00
(36)	Rebel Oakes	150.00	75.00	45.00
(37)	Eddie Plank	900.00	425.00	255.00
(38)	Germany Schaefer	150.00	75.00	45.00
(39)	Tris Speaker	1000.00	450.00	225.00
(40)	Oscar Stanage	150.00	75.00	45.00
(41)	George Stovall	150.00	75.00	45.00
(42)	Jeff Sweeney	150.00	75.00	45.00
(43)	Joe Tinker (portrait)	400.00	200.00	120.00
(44)	Joe Tinker (batting)	400.00	200.00	120.00
(45)	Honus Wagner (batting)	3000.00	1250.00	500.00
(46)	Honus Wagner (throwing)	3000.00	1250.00	500.00
(47)	Hooks Wiltse	150.00	75.00	45.00
(48)	Heinie Zimmerman	150.00	75.00	45.00

A player's name in *italic type* indicates a rookie card. An (FC) indicates a player's first card for that particular card company.

1903 E107 - Type 1

W. GLEASON, 2 B, Phila, N

One of a hundred and fifty prominent Baseball players

Identified by the American Card Catalog as E107, this circa 1903 set is very significant because it was the first major baseball card set since the days of the Old Judge issues in the 1880's, and it established the pattern for most of the tobacco and candy sets that were to follow over the next two decades. Measuring approximately 1-3/8" by 2-5/8", the cards feature black and white player photos with the name, position and team along the bottom. The back states simply "One of a hundred and fifty prominent Baseball players," although blank-backed varieties of this set are fairl common. Also found have been cards with a diagonal overprint stating "The Breisch-Williams Co." establishing the producer of the set. The Type I set consists of 147 different players although 11 additional variations can be found. The Type III cards are thicker than those in Type I and may have been cut from an advertising piece. The Keeler and Delehanty cards have captions different from those found in Type I. The 11 variations found in Type I are not included in the complete set price. Many of the photos were used in other sets, like T206 and M116 Sporting Life.

		NR MT	EX	VG
Complete Set:		45000.00	22500.00	13500.
Common Player:		150.00	75.00	45.00
(1a)	John Anderson (New York)	150.00	75.00	45.00
(1b)	John Anderson (St. Louis)	150.00	75.00	45.00
(2)	Jimmy Barret (Barrett)	150.00	75.00	45.00
(3)	Ginger Beaumont	150.00	75.00	45.00
(4)	Fred Beck	150.00	75.00	45.00
(5)	Jake Beckley	600.00	300.00	180.00
(6)	Harry Bemis	150.00	75.00	45.00
(7)	Chief Bender	500.00	250.00	150.00
(8)	Bill Bernhard	150.00	75.00	45.00
(9)	Harry Bey (Bay)	150.00	75.00	45.00
(10)	Bill Bradley	150.00	75.00	45.00
(11)	Fritz Buelow	150.00	75.00	45.00
(12)	Nixey Callahan	150.00	75.00	45.00
(13)	Scoops Carey	500.00	250.00	150.00
(14)	Charley Carr	150.00	75.00	45.00
(15)	Bill Carrick	150.00	75.00	45.00
(16)	Doc Casey	150.00	75.00	45.00
(17)	Frank Chance	500.00	250.00	150.00
(18)	Jack Chesbro	500.00	250.00	150.00
(19)	Boileryard Clark (Clarke)	150.00	75.00	45.00
(20)	Fred Clarke	600.00	300.00	180.00
(21)	Jimmy Collins	600.00	300.00	180.00
(22)	Duff Cooley	150.00	75.00	45.00
(23)	Tommy Corcoran	150.00	75.00	45.00
(24)	Bill Coughlan (Coughlin)	150.00	75.00	45.00
(25)	Lou Criger	150.00	75.00	45.00
(26)	Lave Cross	150.00	75.00	45.00
(27)	Monte Cross	150.00	75.00	45.00
(28)	Bill Dahlen	150.00	75.00	45.00
(29)	Tom Daly	150.00	75.00	45.00
(30)	George Davis	150.00	75.00	45.00
(31)	Harry Davis	150.00	75.00	45.00
(32)	Ed Delehanty	700.00	350.00	210.00
(33)	Gene DeMont (DeMontreville)	150.00	75.00	45.00
(34a)	Pop Dillon (Detroit)	150.00	75.00	45.00
(34b)	Pop Dillon (Brooklyn)	150.00	75.00	45.00
(35)	Bill Dineen (Dinneen)	150.00	75.00	45.00

		NR MT	EX	VG
(36)	Jiggs Donahue	150.00	75.00	45.00
(37)	Mike Donlin	150.00	75.00	45.00
(38)	Patsy Donovan	150.00	75.00	45.00
(39)	Patsy Dougherty	150.00	75.00	45.00
(40)	Klondike Douglass	150.00	75.00	45.00
(41a)	Jack Doyle (Brooklyn)	150.00	75.00	45.00
(41b)	Jack Doyle (Philadelphia)	150.00	75.00	45.00
(42)	Lew Drill	150.00	75.00	45.00
(43)	Jack Dunn	150.00	75.00	45.00
(44a)	Kid Elberfield (Elberfeld) (Detroit)			
		150.00	75.00	45.00
(44b)	Kid Elberfield (Elberfeld) (no team designation)	150.00	75.00	45.00
(45)	Duke Farrell	150.00	75.00	45.00
(46)	Hobe Ferris	150.00	75.00	45.00
(47)	Elmer Flick	600.00	300.00	180.00
(48)	Buck Freeman	150.00	75.00	45.00
(49)	Bill Freil (Friel)	150.00	75.00	45.00
(50)	Dave Fultz	150.00	75.00	45.00
(51)	Ned Garvin	150.00	75.00	45.00
(52)	Billy Gilbert	150.00	75.00	45.00
(53)	Harry Gleason	150.00	75.00	45.00
(54a)	Kid Gleason (New York)	150.00	75.00	45.00
(54b)	Kid Gleason (Philadelphia)	150.00	75.00	45.00
(55)	John Gochnauer (Gochnaur)	150.00	75.00	45.00
(56)	Danny Green	150.00	75.00	45.00
(57)	Noodles Hahn	150.00	75.00	45.00
(58)	Bill Hallman	150.00	75.00	45.00
(59)	Ned Hanlon	150.00	75.00	45.00
(60)	Dick Harley	150.00	75.00	45.00
(61)	Jack Harper	150.00	75.00	45.00
(62)	Topsy Hartsell (Hartsel)	150.00	75.00	45.00
(63)	Emmet Heidrick	150.00	75.00	45.00
(64)	Charlie Hemphill	150.00	75.00	45.00
(65)	Weldon Henley	150.00	75.00	45.00
(66)	Piano Legs Hickman	150.00	75.00	45.00
(67)	Harry Howell	150.00	75.00	45.00
(68)	Frank Isabel (Isbell)	150.00	75.00	45.00
(69)	Fred Jacklitzch (Jacklitsch)	150.00	75.00	45.00
(70)	Fielder Jones (Chicago)	150.00	75.00	45.00
(71)	Charlie Jones (Boston)	150.00	75.00	45.00
(72)	Addie Joss	600.00	300.00	180.00
(73)	Mike Kahoe	150.00	75.00	45.00
(74)	Wee Willie Keeler	600.00	300.00	180.00
(75)	Joe Kelley	600.00	300.00	180.00
(76)	Brickyard Kennedy	150.00	75.00	45.00
(77)	Frank Kitson	150.00	75.00	45.00
(78a)	Malachi Kittredge (Boston)	150.00	75.00	45.00
(78b)	Malachi Kittredge (Washington)	150.00	75.00	45.00
(79)	Candy LaChance	150.00	75.00	45.00
(80)	Nap Lajoie	700.00	350.00	200.00
(81)	Tommy Leach	150.00	75.00	45.00
(82a)	Watty Lee (Washington)	150.00	75.00	45.00
(82b)	Watty Lee (Pittsburg)	150.00	75.00	45.00
(83)	Sam Leever	150.00	75.00	45.00
(84)	Herman Long	150.00	75.00	45.00
(85a)	Billy Lush (Detroit)	150.00	75.00	45.00
(85b)	Billy Lush (Cleveland)	150.00	75.00	45.00
(86)	Christy Mathewson	1400.00	700.00	420.00
(87)	Sport McAllister	150.00	75.00	45.00
(88)	Jack McCarthy	150.00	75.00	45.00
(89)	Barry McCormick	150.00	75.00	45.00
(90)	Ed McFarland (Chicago)	150.00	75.00	45.00
(91)	Herm McFarland (New York)	150.00	75.00	45.00
(92)	Joe McGinnity	600.00	300.00	180.00
(93)	John McGraw	600.00	300.00	180.00
(94)	Deacon McGuire	150.00	75.00	45.00
(95)	Jock Menefee	150.00	75.00	45.00
(96)	Sam Mertes	150.00	75.00	45.00
(97)	Roscoe Miller	150.00	75.00	45.00
(98)	Fred Mitchell	150.00	75.00	45.00
(99)	Earl Moore	150.00	75.00	45.00
(100)	Danny Murphy	150.00	75.00	45.00
(101)	Jack O'Connor	150.00	75.00	45.00
(102)	Al Orth	150.00	75.00	45.00
(103)	Dick Padden	150.00	75.00	45.00
(104)	Freddy Parent	150.00	75.00	45.00
(105)	Roy Patterson	150.00	75.00	45.00
(106)	Heinie Peitz	150.00	75.00	45.00
(107)	Deacon Phillipi (Phillippe)	150.00	75.00	45.00
(108)	Wiley Piatt	150.00	75.00	45.00
(109)	Ollie Pickering	150.00	75.00	45.00
(110)	Eddie Plank	600.00	300.00	175.00
(111a)	Ed Poole (Cincinnati)	150.00	75.00	45.00
(111b)	Ed Poole (Brooklyn)	150.00	75.00	45.00
(112a)	Jack Powell (St. Louis)	150.00	75.00	45.00
(112b)	Jack Powell (New York)	150.00	75.00	45.00
(113)	Mike Powers	150.00	75.00	45.00
(114)	Claude Ritchie (Ritchey)	150.00	75.00	45.00
(115)	Jimmy Ryan	150.00	75.00	45.00

		NR MT	EX	VG
(116)	Ossee Schreckengost	150.00	75.00	45.00
(117)	Kip Selbach	150.00	75.00	45.00
(118)	Socks Seybold	150.00	75.00	45.00
(119)	Jimmy Sheckard	150.00	75.00	45.00
(120)	Ed Siever	150.00	75.00	45.00
(121)	Harry Smith	150.00	75.00	45.00
(122)	Tully Sparks	150.00	75.00	45.00
(123)	Jake Stahl	150.00	75.00	45.00
(124)	Harry Steinfeldt	175.00	87.00	52.00
(125)	Sammy Strang	150.00	75.00	45.00
(126)	Willie Sudhoff	150.00	75.00	45.00
(127)	Joe Sugden	150.00	75.00	45.00
(128)	Billy Sullivan	150.00	75.00	45.00
(129)	Jack Taylor	150.00	75.00	45.00
(130)	Fred Tenney	150.00	75.00	45.00
(131)	Ira Thomas	150.00	75.00	45.00
(132a)	Jack Thoney (Cleveland)	150.00	75.00	45.00
(132b)	Jack Thoney (New York)	150.00	75.00	45.00
(133)	Jack Townsend	150.00	75.00	45.00
(134)	George Van Haltren	150.00	75.00	45.00
(135)	Rube Waddell	600.00	300.00	180.00
(136)	Honus Wagner	2000.00	1000.00	600.00
(137)	Bobby Wallace	600.00	300.00	180.00
(138)	Jack Warner	150.00	75.00	45.00
(139)	Jimmy Wiggs	150.00	75.00	45.00
(140)	Jimmy Williams	150.00	75.00	45.00
(141)	Vic Willis	150.00	75.00	45.00
(142)	Snake Wiltse	150.00	75.00	45.00
(143)	George Winters (Winter)	150.00	75.00	45.00
(144)	Bob Wood	150.00	75.00	45.00
(145)	Joe Yeager	150.00	75.00	45.00
(146)	Cy Young	1200.00	600.00	360.00
(147)	Chief Zimmer	150.00	75.00	45.00

1903 E107 - Type 2

DELAHANTY, Fielder, Wash.

		NR MT	EX	VG
Complete Set:		2300.00	1150.00	690.00
Common Player:		300.00	150.00	90.00
(1)	Ed Delehanty	750.00	375.00	225.00
(2)	Jack Doyle	300.00	150.00	90.00
(3)	Wee Willie Keeler	750.00	375.00	225.00
(4)	Tommy Leach	300.00	150.00	90.00
(5)	Socks Seybold	300.00	150.00	90.00
(6)	Fred Tenney	300.00	150.00	90.00

1922 E120 American Caramel

One of the most popular of the "E" issues, the 1922 E120 set was produced by the American Caramel Co. in 1922 and distributed with sticks of caramel candy. The unnumbered cards measure 2" by 3-1/2" in size. Cards depicting players from the American League are printed in brown ink on yellow, while the National Leaguers are printed in green on a blue-green background. The card reverses carry team checklists Many of the E120 photos were used in other sets such as E121, W572, W573 and V61.

		NR MT	EX	VG
Complete Set:		18000.00	9000.00	5400.
Common Player:		40.00	20.00	12.00
(1)	Charles (Babe) Adams	40.00	20.00	12.00
(2)	Eddie Ainsmith	40.00	20.00	12.00
(3)	Vic Aldridge	40.00	20.00	12.00
(4)	Grover C. Alexander	150.00	75.00	45.00
(5)	Jim Bagby	40.00	20.00	12.00
(6)	Frank (Home Run) Baker	150.00	75.00	45.00
(7)	Dave (Beauty) Bancroft	100.00	50.00	30.00
(8)	Walt Barbare	40.00	20.00	12.00
(9)	Turner Barber	40.00	20.00	12.00
(10)	Jess Barnes	40.00	20.00	12.00
(11)	Clyde Barnhart	40.00	20.00	12.00
(12)	John Bassler	40.00	20.00	12.00
(13)	Will Bayne	40.00	20.00	12.00
(14)	Walter (Huck) Betts	40.00	20.00	12.00
(15)	Carson Bigbee	40.00	20.00	12.00
(16)	Lu Blue	40.00	20.00	12.00
(17)	Norman Boeckel	40.00	20.00	12.00
(18)	Sammy Bohne	40.00	20.00	12.00
(19)	George Burns	40.00	20.00	12.00
(20)	George Burns	40.00	20.00	12.00
(21)	"Bullet Joe" Bush	40.00	20.00	12.00
(22)	Leon Cadore	40.00	20.00	12.00
(23)	Marty Callaghan	40.00	20.00	12.00
(24)	Frank Calloway (Callaway)	40.00	20.00	12.00
(25)	Max Carey	100.00	50.00	30.00
(26)	Jimmy Caveney	40.00	20.00	12.00
(27)	Virgil Cheeves	40.00	20.00	12.00
(28)	Vern Clemons	40.00	20.00	12.00
(29)	Ty Cobb (Cobb)	1000.00	500.00	300.00
(30)	Bert Cole	40.00	20.00	12.00
(31)	Eddie Collins	150.00	75.00	45.00
(32)	John (Shano) Collins	40.00	20.00	12.00
(33)	T.P. (Pat) Collins	40.00	20.00	12.00
(34)	Wilbur Cooper	40.00	20.00	12.00
(35)	Harry Courtney	40.00	20.00	12.00
(36)	Stanley Coveleskie (Coveleski)	100.00	50.00	30.00
(37)	Elmer Cox	40.00	20.00	12.00
(38)	Sam Crane	40.00	20.00	12.00
(39)	Walton Cruise	40.00	20.00	12.00
(40)	Bill Cunningham	40.00	20.00	12.00
(41)	George Cutshaw	40.00	20.00	12.00
(42)	Dave Danforth	40.00	20.00	12.00
(43)	Jake Daubert	40.00	20.00	12.00
(44)	George Dauss	40.00	20.00	12.00
(45)	Frank (Dixie) Davis	40.00	20.00	12.00
(46)	Hank DeBerry	40.00	20.00	12.00
(47)	Albert (Lou) Devormer (DeVormer)			
		40.00	20.00	12.00
(48)	Bill Doak	40.00	20.00	12.00
(49)	Pete Donohue	40.00	20.00	12.00
(50)	"Shufflin" Phil Douglas	40.00	20.00	12.00
(51)	Joe Dugan	40.00	20.00	12.00
(52)	Louis (Pat) Duncan	40.00	20.00	12.00
(53)	Jimmy Dykes	40.00	20.00	12.00
(54)	Howard Ehmke	40.00	20.00	12.00
(55)	Frank Ellerbe	40.00	20.00	12.00
(56)	Urban (Red) Faber	100.00	50.00	30.00
(57)	Bib Falk (Bibb)	40.00	20.00	12.00
(58)	Dana Fillingim	40.00	20.00	12.00
(59)	Max Flack	40.00	20.00	12.00
(60)	Ira Flagstead	40.00	20.00	12.00
(61)	Art Fletcher	40.00	20.00	12.00
(62)	Horace Ford	40.00	20.00	12.00
(63)	Jack Fournier	40.00	20.00	12.00
(64)	Frank Frisch	150.00	75.00	45.00
(65)	Ollie Fuhrman	40.00	20.00	12.00
(66)	Clarence Galloway	40.00	20.00	12.00
(67)	Larry Gardner	40.00	20.00	12.00
(68)	Walter Gerber	40.00	20.00	12.00
(69)	Ed Gharrity	40.00	20.00	12.00
(70)	John Gillespie	40.00	20.00	12.00
(71)	Chas. (Whitey) Glazner	40.00	20.00	12.00
(72)	Johnny Gooch	40.00	20.00	12.00
(73)	Leon Goslin	100.00	50.00	30.00
(74)	Hank Gowdy	40.00	20.00	12.00

		NR MT	EX	VG
(75)	John Graney	40.00	20.00	12.00
(76)	Tom Griffith	40.00	20.00	12.00
(77)	Burleigh Grimes	100.00	50.00	30.00
(78)	Oscar Ray Grimes	40.00	20.00	12.00
(79)	Charlie Grimm	40.00	20.00	12.00
(80)	Heinie Groh	40.00	20.00	12.00
(81)	Jesse Haines	100.00	50.00	30.00
(82)	Earl Hamilton	40.00	20.00	12.00
(83)	Gene (Bubbles) Hargrave	40.00	20.00	12.00
(84)	Bryan Harris (Harriss)	40.00	20.00	12.00
(85)	Joe Harris	40.00	20.00	12.00
(86)	Stanley Harris	40.00	20.00	12.00
(87)	Chas. (Dowdy) Hartnett	150.00	75.00	45.00
(88)	Bob Hasty	40.00	20.00	12.00
(89)	Joe Hauser	40.00	20.00	12.00
(90)	Clif Heathcote (Cliff)	40.00	20.00	12.00
(91)	Harry Heilmann	100.00	50.00	30.00
(92)	Walter (Butch) Henline	40.00	20.00	12.00
(93)	Clarence (Shovel) Hodge	40.00	20.00	12.00
(94)	Walter Holke	40.00	20.00	12.00
(95)	Charles Hollocher	40.00	20.00	12.00
(96)	Harry Hooper	100.00	50.00	30.00
(97)	Rogers Hornsby	250.00	125.00	75.00
(98)	Waite Hoyt	100.00	50.00	30.00
(99)	Wilbur Hubbell (Wilbert)	40.00	20.00	12.00
(100)	Bernard (Bud) Hungling	40.00	20.00	12.00
(101)	Will Jacobson	40.00	20.00	12.00
(102)	Charlie Jamieson	40.00	20.00	12.00
(103)	Ernie Johnson	40.00	20.00	12.00
(104)	Sylvester Johnson	40.00	20.00	12.00
(105)	Walter Johnson	500.00	250.00	150.00
(106)	Jimmy Johnston	40.00	20.00	12.00
(107)	W.R. (Doc) Johnston	40.00	20.00	12.00
(108)	"Deacon" Sam Jones	40.00	20.00	12.00
(109)	Bob Jones	40.00	20.00	12.00
(110)	Percy Jones	40.00	20.00	12.00
(111)	Joe Judge	40.00	20.00	12.00
(112)	Ben Karr	40.00	20.00	12.00
(113)	Johnny Kelleher	40.00	20.00	12.00
(114)	George Kelly	100.00	50.00	30.00
(115)	Lee King	40.00	20.00	12.00
(116)	Wm (Larry) Kopff (Kopf)	40.00	20.00	12.00
(117)	Marty Krug	40.00	20.00	12.00
(118)	Johnny Lavan	40.00	20.00	12.00
(119)	Nemo Leibold	40.00	20.00	12.00
(120)	Roy Leslie	40.00	20.00	12.00
(121)	George Leverette (Leverett)	40.00	20.00	12.00
(122)	Adolfo Luque	40.00	20.00	12.00
(123)	Walter Mails	40.00	20.00	12.00
(124)	Al Mamaux	40.00	20.00	12.00
(125)	"Rabbit" Maranville	100.00	50.00	30.00
(126)	Cliff Markle	40.00	20.00	12.00
(127)	Richard (Rube) Marquard	150.00	75.00	45.00
(128)	Carl Mays	60.00	30.00	18.00
(129)	Hervey McClellan (Harvey)	40.00	20.00	12.00
(130)	Austin McHenry	40.00	20.00	12.00
(131)	"Stuffy" McInnis	40.00	20.00	12.00
(132)	Martin McManus	40.00	20.00	12.00
(133)	Mike McNally	40.00	20.00	12.00
(134)	Hugh McQuillan	40.00	20.00	12.00
(135)	Lee Meadows	40.00	20.00	12.00
(136)	Mike Menosky	40.00	20.00	12.00
(137)	Bob (Dutch) Meusel	60.00	30.00	18.00
(138)	Emil (Irish) Meusel	40.00	20.00	12.00
(139)	Clyde Milan	40.00	20.00	12.00
(140)	Edmund (Bing) Miller	40.00	20.00	12.00
(141)	Elmer Miller	40.00	20.00	12.00
(142)	Lawrence (Hack) Miller	40.00	20.00	12.00
(143)	Clarence Mitchell	40.00	20.00	12.00
(144)	George Mogridge	40.00	20.00	12.00
(145)	Roy Moore	40.00	20.00	12.00
(146)	John L. Mokan	40.00	20.00	12.00
(147)	John Morrison	40.00	20.00	12.00
(148)	Johnny Mostil	40.00	20.00	12.00
(149)	Elmer Myers	40.00	20.00	12.00
(150)	Hy Myers	40.00	20.00	12.00
(151)	Roliene Naylor (Roleine)	40.00	20.00	12.00
(152)	Earl (Greasy) Neale	60.00	30.00	18.00
(153)	Art Nehf	40.00	20.00	12.00
(154)	Les Nunamaker	40.00	20.00	12.00
(155)	Joe Oeschger	40.00	20.00	12.00
(156)	Bob O'Farrell	40.00	20.00	12.00
(157)	Ivan Olson	40.00	20.00	12.00
(158)	George O'Neil	40.00	20.00	12.00
(159)	Steve O'Neill	40.00	20.00	12.00
(160)	Frank Parkinson	40.00	20.00	12.00
(161)	Roger Peckinpaugh	40.00	20.00	12.00
(162)	Herb Pennock	100.00	50.00	30.00
(163)	Ralph (Cy) Perkins	40.00	20.00	12.00
(164)	Will Pertica	40.00	20.00	12.00
(165)	Jack Peters	40.00	20.00	12.00

		NR MT	EX	VG
(166)	Tom Phillips	40.00	20.00	12.00
(167)	Val Picinich	40.00	20.00	12.00
(168)	Herman Pillette	40.00	20.00	12.00
(169)	Ralph Pinelli	40.00	20.00	12.00
(170)	Wallie Pipp	50.00	25.00	15.00
(171)	Clark Pittenger (Clarke)	40.00	20.00	12.00
(172)	Raymond Powell	40.00	20.00	12.00
(173)	Derrill Pratt	40.00	20.00	12.00
(174)	Jack Quinn	40.00	20.00	12.00
(175)	Joe (Goldie) Rapp	40.00	20.00	12.00
(176)	John Rawlings	40.00	20.00	12.00
(177)	Walter (Dutch) Reuther (Ruether)			
		40.00	20.00	12.00
(178)	Sam Rice	100.00	50.00	30.00
(179)	Emory Rigney	40.00	20.00	12.00
(180)	Jimmy Ring	40.00	20.00	12.00
(181)	Eppa Rixey	100.00	50.00	30.00
(182)	Charles Robertson	40.00	20.00	12.00
(183)	Ed Rommel	40.00	20.00	12.00
(184)	Eddie Roush	100.00	50.00	30.00
(185)	Harold (Muddy) Ruel (Herold)	40.00	20.00	12.00
(186)	Babe Ruth	2000.00	1000.00	600.00
(187)	Ray Schalk	100.00	50.00	30.00
(188)	Wallie Schang	40.00	20.00	12.00
(189)	Ray Schmandt	40.00	20.00	12.00
(190)	Walter Schmidt	40.00	20.00	12.00
(191)	Joe Schultz	40.00	20.00	12.00
(192)	Everett Scott	40.00	20.00	12.00
(193)	Henry Severeid	40.00	20.00	12.00
(194)	Joe Sewell	150.00	75.00	45.00
(195)	Howard Shanks	40.00	20.00	12.00
(196)	Bob Shawkey	40.00	20.00	12.00
(197)	Earl Sheely	40.00	20.00	12.00
(198)	Will Sherdel	40.00	20.00	12.00
(199)	Ralph Shinners	40.00	20.00	12.00
(200)	Urban Shocker	40.00	20.00	12.00
(201)	Charles (Chick) Shorten	40.00	20.00	12.00
(202)	George Sisler	175.00	87.00	52.00
(203)	Earl Smith	40.00	20.00	12.00
(204)	Earl Smith	40.00	20.00	12.00
(205)	Elmer Smith	40.00	20.00	12.00
(206)	Jack Smith	40.00	20.00	12.00
(207)	Sherrod Smith	40.00	20.00	12.00
(208)	Colonel Snover	40.00	20.00	12.00
(209)	Frank Snyder	40.00	20.00	12.00
(210)	Al Sothoron	40.00	20.00	12.00
(211)	Bill Southworth	40.00	20.00	12.00
(212)	Tris Speaker	350.00	175.00	105.00
(213)	Arnold Statz	40.00	20.00	12.00
(214)	Milton Stock	40.00	20.00	12.00
(215)	Amos Strunk	40.00	20.00	12.00
(216)	Jim Tierney	40.00	20.00	12.00
(217)	John Tobin	40.00	20.00	12.00
(218)	Fred Toney	40.00	20.00	12.00
(219)	George Toporcer	40.00	20.00	12.00
(220)	Harold (Pie) Traynor	100.00	50.00	30.00
(221)	George Uhle	40.00	20.00	12.00
(222)	Elam Vangilder	40.00	20.00	12.00
(223)	Bob Veach	40.00	20.00	12.00
(224)	Clarence (Tillie) Walker	40.00	20.00	12.00
(225)	Curtis Walker	40.00	20.00	12.00
(226)	Al Walters	40.00	20.00	12.00
(227)	Bill Wambsganss	40.00	20.00	12.00
(228)	Aaron (Erin) Ward	40.00	20.00	12.00
(229)	John Watson	40.00	20.00	12.00
(230)	Frank Welch	40.00	20.00	12.00
(231)	Zach Wheat	150.00	75.00	45.00
(232)	Fred (Cy) Williams	40.00	20.00	12.00
(233)	Kenneth Williams	40.00	20.00	12.00
(234)	Ivy Wingo	40.00	20.00	12.00
(235)	Joe Wood	40.00	20.00	12.00
(236)	Lawrence Woodall	40.00	20.00	12.00
(237)	Russell Wrightstone	40.00	20.00	12.00
(238)	Everett Yaryan	40.00	20.00	12.00
(239)	Ross Young (Youngs)	150.00	75.00	45.00
(240)	J.T. Zachary	40.00	20.00	12.00

1921 E121 American Caramel Series Of 80

Issued circa 1921, the E121 Series of 80 is designated as such because of the card reverses which indicate the player pictured is just one of 80 baseball stars in the set. The figure of 80 supplied by the American Caramel Co. is incorrect as over 100 different pictures do exist. The unnumbered cards,

DUFFY LEWIS
L. F. Washington Americans

which measure 2" by 3-1/2", feature black and white photos. Two different backs exist for the Series of 80. The common back variation has the first line ending with the word "the," while the scarcer version ends with the word "eighty." The complete set price does not include the variations.

		NR MT	EX	VG
Complete Set:		12000.00	6000.00	3600.
Commmon Player:		25.00	12.50	7.50
(1)	G.C. Alexander (arms above head)			
		150.00	75.00	45.00
(2)	Grover Alexander	150.00	75.00	45.00
(3)	Jim Bagby	25.00	12.50	7.50
(4a)	J. Franklin Baker	150.00	75.00	45.00
(4b)	Frank Baker	150.00	75.00	45.00
(5)	Dave Bancroft (batting)	80.00	40.00	24.00
(6)	Dave Bancroft (leaping)	80.00	40.00	24.00
(7)	Ping Bodie	25.00	12.50	7.50
(8)	George Burns	25.00	12.50	7.50
(9)	Geo. J. Burns	25.00	12.50	7.50
(10)	Owen Bush	25.00	12.50	7.50
(11)	Max Carey (batting)	80.00	40.00	24.00
(12)	Max Carey (hands at hips)	80.00	40.00	24.00
(13)	Cecil Causey	25.00	12.50	7.50
(14)	Ty Cobb (throwing, looking front)			
		700.00	350.00	210.00
(15a)	Ty Cobb (throwing, looking right, Mgr. on front)			
		700.00	350.00	210.00
(15b)	Ty Cobb (throwing, looking right, Manager on front)			
		700.00	350.00	210.00
(16)	Eddie Collins	150.00	75.00	45.00
(17)	"Rip" Collins	25.00	12.50	7.50
(18)	Jake Daubert	50.00	25.00	15.00
(19)	George Dauss	25.00	12.50	7.50
(20)	Charles Deal (dark uniform)	25.00	12.50	7.50
(21)	Charles Deal (white uniform)	25.00	12.50	7.50
(22)	William Doak	25.00	12.50	7.50
(23)	Bill Donovan	25.00	12.50	7.50
(24)	"Phil" Douglas	50.00	25.00	15.00
(25a)	Johnny Evers (Manager)	80.00	40.00	24.00
(25b)	Johnny Evers (Mgr.)	80.00	40.00	24.00
(26)	Urban Faber (dark uniform)	80.00	40.00	24.00
(27)	Urban Faber (white uniform)	80.00	40.00	24.00
(28)	William Fewster (first name actually Wilson)	25.00	12.50	7.50
(29)	Eddie Foster	25.00	12.50	7.50
(30)	Frank Frisch	70.00	35.00	21.00
(31)	W.L. Gardner	25.00	12.50	7.50
(32a)	Alexander Gaston (no position on front)			
		25.00	12.50	7.50
(32b)	Alexander Gaston (position on front)			
		25.00	12.50	7.50
(33)	"Kid" Gleason	25.00	12.50	7.50
(34)	"Mike" Gonzalez	25.00	12.50	7.50
(35)	Hank Gowdy	25.00	12.50	7.50
(36)	John Graney	25.00	12.50	7.50
(37)	Tom Griffith	25.00	12.50	7.50
(38)	Heinie Groh	50.00	25.00	15.00
(39)	Harry Harper	25.00	12.50	7.50
(40)	Harry Heilman (Heilmann)	80.00	40.00	24.00
(41)	Walter Holke (portrait)	25.00	12.50	7.50
(42)	Walter Holke (throwing)	25.00	12.50	7.50
(43)	Charles Hollacher (Hollocher)	25.00	12.50	7.50
(44)	Harry Hooper	80.00	40.00	24.00
(45)	Rogers Hornsby	200.00	100.00	60.00
(46)	Waite Hoyt	80.00	40.00	24.00
(47)	Miller Huggins	80.00	40.00	24.00
(48)	Wm. C. Jacobson	25.00	12.50	7.50

		NR MT	EX	VG
(49)	Hugh Jennings	80.00	40.00	24.00
(50)	Walter Johnson (throwing)	275.00	137.00	82.00
(51)	Walter Johnson (hands at chest)			
		275.00	137.00	82.00
(52)	James Johnston	25.00	12.50	7.50
(53)	Joe Judge	25.00	12.50	7.50
(54)	George Kelly	80.00	40.00	24.00
(55)	Dick Kerr	25.00	12.50	7.50
(56)	P.J. Kilduff	25.00	12.50	7.50
(57a)	Bill Killifer (incorrect name)	50.00	25.00	15.00
(57b)	Bill Killefer (correct name)	50.00	25.00	15.00
(58)	John Lavan	25.00	12.50	7.50
(59)	"Nemo" Leibold	25.00	12.50	7.50
(60)	Duffy Lewis	50.00	25.00	15.00
(61)	Al. Mamaux	25.00	12.50	7.50
(62)	"Rabbit" Maranville	80.00	40.00	24.00
(63a)	Carl May (incorrect name)	80.00	40.00	24.00
(63b)	Carl Mays (correct name)	50.00	25.00	15.00
(64)	John McGraw	150.00	75.00	45.00
(65)	Jack McInnis	25.00	12.50	7.50
(66)	M.J. McNally	25.00	12.50	7.50
(67)	Emil Muesel (Photo actually Lou DeVormer)	50.00	25.00	15.00
(68)	R. Meusel	40.00	20.00	12.00
(69)	Clyde Milan	25.00	12.50	7.50
(70)	Elmer Miller	25.00	12.50	7.50
(71)	Otto Miller	25.00	12.50	7.50
(72)	Guy Morton	25.00	12.50	7.50
(73)	Eddie Murphy	25.00	12.50	7.50
(74)	"Hy" Myers	25.00	12.50	7.50
(75)	Arthur Nehf	25.00	12.50	7.50
(76)	Steve O'Neill	25.00	12.50	7.50
(77a)	Roger Peckinbaugh (incorrect name)	50.00	25.00	15.00
(77b)	Roger Peckinpaugh (correct name)	50.00	25.00	15.00
(78a)	Jeff Pfeffer (Brooklyn)	25.00	12.50	7.50
(78b)	Jeff Pfeffer (St. Louis)	25.00	12.50	7.50
(79)	Walter Pipp	40.00	20.00	12.00
(80)	Jack Quinn	25.00	12.50	7.50
(81)	John Rawlings	25.00	12.50	7.50
(82)	E.C. Rice	80.00	40.00	24.00
(83)	Eppa Rixey, Jr.	80.00	40.00	24.00
(84)	Robert Roth	25.00	12.50	7.50
(85a)	Ed. Roush (C.F.)	80.00	40.00	24.00
(85b)	Ed. Roush (L.F.)	70.00	35.00	21.00
(86a)	Babe Ruth	1500.00	750.00	450.00
(86b)	"Babe" Ruth	1500.00	750.00	450.00
(86c)	George Ruth	1500.00	750.00	450.00
(87)	"Bill" Ryan	25.00	12.50	7.50
(88)	"Slim" Sallee (glove showing)	25.00	12.50	7.50
(89)	"Slim" Sallee (no glove showing)	25.00	12.50	7.50
(90)	Ray Schalk	80.00	40.00	24.00
(91)	Walter Schang	25.00	12.50	7.50
(92a)	Fred Schupp (name incorrect)	50.00	25.00	15.00
(92b)	Ferd Schupp (name correct)	50.00	25.00	15.00
(93)	Everett Scott	25.00	12.50	7.50
(94)	Hank Severeid	25.00	12.50	7.50
(95)	Robert Shawkey	50.00	25.00	15.00
(96a)	Pat Shea	50.00	25.00	15.00
(96b)	"Pat" Shea	25.00	12.50	7.50
(97)	George Sisler (batting)	70.00	35.00	21.00
(98)	George Sisler (throwing)	70.00	35.00	21.00
(99)	Earl Smith	25.00	12.50	7.50
(100)	Frank Snyder	25.00	12.50	7.50
(101a)	Tris Speaker (Mgr.)	200.00	100.00	60.00
(101b)	Tris Speaker (Manager - large projection)	200.00	100.00	60.00
(101c)	Tris Speaker (Manager - small projection)	200.00	100.00	60.00
(102)	Milton Stock	25.00	12.50	7.50
(103)	Amos Strunk	25.00	12.50	7.50
(104)	Zeb Terry	25.00	12.50	7.50
(105)	Chester Thomas	25.00	12.50	7.50
(106)	Fred Toney (trees in background)	25.00	12.50	7.50
(107)	Fred Toney (no trees in background)	25.00	12.50	7.50
(108)	George Tyler	25.00	12.50	7.50
(109)	Jim Vaughn (dark hat)	25.00	12.50	7.50
(110)	Jim Vaughn (white hat)	25.00	12.50	7.50
(111)	Bob Veach (glove in air)	25.00	12.50	7.50
(112)	Bob Veach (arms crossed)	25.00	12.50	7.50
(113)	Oscar Vitt	25.00	12.50	7.50
(114)	W. Wambsganss (photo actually Fred Coumbe)	50.00	25.00	15.00
(115)	Aaron Ward	25.00	12.50	7.50
(116)	Zach Wheat	150.00	75.00	45.00
(117)	George Whitted	25.00	12.50	7.50
(118)	Fred Williams	50.00	25.00	15.00
(119)	Ivy B. Wingo	25.00	12.50	7.50

		NR MT	EX	VG
(120)	Joe Wood	50.00	25.00	15.00
(121)	"Pep" Young	25.00	12.50	7.50

1922 E121 American Caramel Series Of 120

Produced by the American Caramel Co. circa 1922, the E121 Series of 120 is labeled as such by the company's claim that the set contained 120 subjects. Identical in design to the E121 Series of 80 set except for the card backs, the cards measure 2" by 3-1/2" in size. Numerous variations are found in the set, most involving a change in the player's name, team or position. The complete set price does not include variations.

		NR MT	EX	VG
Complete Set:		15000.00	7500.00	4500.
Common Player:		30.00	15.00	9.00
(1)	Chas. "Babe" Adams	30.00	15.00	9.00
(2)	G.C. Alexander	150.00	75.00	45.00
(3)	Jim Bagby	30.00	15.00	9.00
(4)	Dave Bancroft	100.00	50.00	30.00
(5)	Turner Barber	30.00	15.00	9.00
(6a)	Carlson Bigbee (correct name Carson L. Bigbee)	35.00	17.50	10.50
(6b)	Carlson L. Bigbee	30.00	15.00	9.00
(6c)	Corson L. Bigbee	35.00	17.50	10.50
(6d)	L. Bigbee	30.00	15.00	9.00
(7)	"Bullet Joe" Bush	30.00	15.00	9.00
(8)	Max Carey	100.00	50.00	30.00
(9)	Cecil Causey	30.00	15.00	9.00
(10)	Ty Cobb (batting)	700.00	350.00	210.00
(11)	Ty Cobb (throwing)	700.00	350.00	210.00
(12)	Eddie Collins	150.00	75.00	45.00
(13)	A. Wilbur Cooper	30.00	15.00	9.00
(14)	Stanley Coveleskie (Coveleski)	100.00	50.00	30.00
(15)	Dave Danforth	30.00	15.00	9.00
(16)	Jake Daubert	30.00	15.00	9.00
(17)	George Dauss	30.00	15.00	9.00
(18)	"Dixie" Davis	30.00	15.00	9.00
(19)	Lou DeVormer	30.00	15.00	9.00
(20)	William Doak	30.00	15.00	9.00
(21)	Phil Douglas	30.00	15.00	9.00
(22)	Urban Faber	100.00	50.00	30.00
(23)	Bib Falk (Bibb)	30.00	15.00	9.00
(24)	Wm: Fewster (first name actually Wilson)	30.00	15.00	9.00
(25)	Max Flack	30.00	15.00	9.00
(26)	Ira Falgstead (Flagstead)	30.00	15.00	9.00
(27)	Frank Frisch	150.00	75.00	45.00
(28)	W.L. Gardner	30.00	15.00	9.00
(29)	Alexander Gaston	30.00	15.00	9.00
(30)	E.P. Gharrity	30.00	15.00	9.00
(31)	George Gibson	30.00	15.00	9.00
(32)	Chas. "Whitey" Glazner	30.00	15.00	9.00
(33)	"Kid" Gleason	30.00	15.00	9.00
(34)	Hank Gowdy	30.00	15.00	9.00
(35)	John Graney	30.00	15.00	9.00
(36)	Tom Griffith	30.00	15.00	9.00
(37)	Chas. Grimm	35.00	17.50	10.50
(38)	Heine Groh	30.00	15.00	9.00
(39)	Jess Haines	100.00	50.00	30.00
(40)	Harry Harper	30.00	15.00	9.00
(41a)	Harry Heilman (name incorrect)	150.00	75.00	45.00

		NR MT	EX	VG
(41b)	Harry Heilmann (name correct)			
		100.00	50.00	30.00
(42)	Clarence Hodge	30.00	15.00	9.00
(43)	Walter Holke (portrait)	35.00	17.50	10.50
(44)	Walter Holke (throwing)	30.00	15.00	9.00
(45)	Charles Hollocher	30.00	15.00	9.00
(46)	Harry Hooper	100.00	50.00	30.00
(47a)	Rogers Hornsby (2B.)	200.00	100.00	60.00
(47b)	Rogers Hornsby (O.F.)	200.00	100.00	60.00
(48)	Waite Hoyt	100.00	50.00	30.00
(49)	Miller Huggins	100.00	50.00	30.00
(50)	Walter Johnson	400.00	200.00	120.00
(51)	Joe Judge	30.00	15.00	9.00
(52)	George Kelly	100.00	50.00	30.00
(53)	Dick Kerr	30.00	15.00	9.00
(54)	P.J. Kilduff	30.00	15.00	9.00
(55)	Bill Killifer (Killefer) (batting)	30.00	15.00	9.00
(56)	Bill Killifer (Killefer) (throwing)	30.00	15.00	9.00
(57)	John Lavan	30.00	15.00	9.00
(58)	Walter Mails	30.00	15.00	9.00
(59)	"Rabbit" Maranville	100.00	50.00	30.00
(60)	Elwood Martin	30.00	15.00	9.00
(61)	Carl Mays	35.00	17.50	10.50
(62)	John J. McGraw	125.00	62.00	37.00
(63)	Jack McInnis	30.00	15.00	9.00
(64)	M.J. McNally	30.00	15.00	9.00
(65)	Emil Meusel (photo actually Lou DeVormer)			
		30.00	15.00	9.00
(66)	R. Meusel	40.00	20.00	12.00
(67)	Clyde Milan	30.00	15.00	9.00
(68)	Elmer Miller	30.00	15.00	9.00
(69)	Otto Miller	30.00	15.00	9.00
(70)	Johnny Mostil	30.00	15.00	9.00
(71)	Eddie Mulligan	30.00	15.00	9.00
(72a)	Hy Myers	30.00	15.00	9.00
(72b)	"Hy" Myers	35.00	17.50	10.50
(73)	Earl Neale	40.00	20.00	12.00
(74)	Arthur Nehf	30.00	15.00	9.00
(75)	Leslie Nunamaker	30.00	15.00	9.00
(76)	Joe Oeschger	30.00	15.00	9.00
(77)	Chas. O'Leary	35.00	17.50	10.50
(78)	Steve O'Neill	30.00	15.00	9.00
(79)	D.B. Pratt	30.00	15.00	9.00
(80a)	John Rawlings (2B.)	30.00	15.00	9.00
(80b)	John Rawlings (Utl.)	30.00	15.00	9.00
(81)	E.S. Rice (intials actually E.C.)	100.00	50.00	30.00
(82)	Eppa J. Rixey	100.00	50.00	30.00
(83)	Eppa Rixey, Jr.	100.00	50.00	30.00
(84)	Wilbert Robinson	100.00	50.00	30.00
(85)	Tom Rogers	30.00	15.00	9.00
(86a)	Ed Rounnel	30.00	15.00	9.00
(86b)	Ed. Rommel	30.00	15.00	9.00
(87)	Ed Roush	100.00	50.00	30.00
(88)	"Muddy" Ruel	30.00	15.00	9.00
(89)	Walter Ruether	30.00	15.00	9.00
(90a)	Babe Ruth (photo montage)	1500.00	750.00	450.00
(90b)	"Babe" Ruth (photo montage)	1500.00	750.00	450.00
(91a)	Babe Ruth (holding bird)	1500.00	750.00	450.00
(91b)	"Babe" Ruth (holding bird)	1500.00	750.00	450.00
(92)	"Babe" Ruth (holding ball)	1500.00	750.00	450.00
(93)	Bill Ryan	30.00	15.00	9.00
(94)	Ray Schalk (catching)	100.00	50.00	30.00
(95)	Ray Schalk (batting)	100.00	50.00	30.00
(96)	Wally Schang	24.00	12.00	7.25
(97)	Ferd Schupp	35.00	17.50	10.50
(98)	Everett Scott	30.00	15.00	9.00
(99)	Joe Sewell	150.00	75.00	45.00
(100)	Robert Shawkey	30.00	15.00	9.00
(101)	Pat Shea	30.00	15.00	9.00
(102)	Earl Sheely	30.00	15.00	9.00
(103)	Urban Schocker	30.00	15.00	9.00
(104)	George Sisler (batting)	150.00	75.00	45.00
(105)	George Sisler (throwing)	75.00	37.00	22.00
(106)	Earl Smith	30.00	15.00	9.00
(107)	Elmer Smith	30.00	15.00	9.00
(108)	Frank Snyder	30.00	15.00	9.00
(109)	Bill Southworth	30.00	15.00	9.00
(110a)	Tris Speaker (large projection)	200.00	100.00	60.00
(110b)	Tris Speaker (small projection)	200.00	100.00	60.00
(111a)	Milton Stock	35.00	17.50	10.50
(111b)	Milton J. Stock	30.00	15.00	9.00
(112)	Amos Strunk	30.00	15.00	9.00
(113)	Zeb Terry	30.00	15.00	9.00
(114)	Fred Toney	30.00	15.00	9.00
(115)	George Topocer (Toporcer)	30.00	15.00	9.00
(116)	Bob Veach	30.00	15.00	9.00
(117)	Oscar Vitt	30.00	15.00	9.00
(118)	Curtis Walker	30.00	15.00	9.00
(119)	W. Wambsganss (photo actually Fred Coumbe)			
		30.00	15.00	9.00
(120)	Aaron Ward	30.00	15.00	9.00
(121)	Zach Wheat	40.00	20.00	12.00

		NR MT	EX	VG
(122a)	George Whitted (Pittsburgh)	30.00	15.00	9.00
(122b)	George Whitted (Brooklyn)	30.00	15.00	9.00
(123)	Fred Williams	30.00	15.00	9.00
(124)	Ivy B. Wingo	30.00	15.00	9.00
(125)	Ross Young (Youngs)	150.00	75.00	45.00

1922 E122

"RABBIT" MARANVILLE
S. S.—Pittsburgh Nationals

This set consists of pictures of 120 of the leading BASE BALL STARS —of the— AMERICAN AND NATIONAL LEAGUES —Made only by— AMERICAN CARAMEL COMPANY, LANCASTER AND YORK, PENNA.

Known as E122 in the American Card Catalog, this set is actually a subset of the E121 American Caramel set. The cards are nealy identical to E121's "Series of 80," except the player's name, position and team are printed inside a gray rectangle at the bottom of the card, and the photos have a more coarse appearance.

		NR MT	EX	VG
Complete Set:		8000.00	4000.00	2400.
Common Player:		40.00	20.00	12.00
(1)	Grover Alexander	125.00	62.00	37.00
(2)	Jim Bagby	40.00	20.00	12.00
(3)	J. Franklin Baker	150.00	75.00	45.00
(4)	Dave Bancroft	150.00	75.00	45.00
(5)	Ping Bodie	40.00	20.00	12.00
(6)	George Burns	40.00	20.00	12.00
(7)	Geo. J. Burns	40.00	20.00	12.00
(8)	Owen Bush	40.00	20.00	12.00
(9)	Max Carey	150.00	75.00	45.00
(10)	Cecil Causey	40.00	20.00	12.00
(11)	Ty Cobb	1000.00	500.00	300.00
(12)	Eddie Collins	150.00	75.00	45.00
(13)	Jake Daubert	50.00	25.00	15.00
(14)	George Dauss	40.00	20.00	12.00
(15)	Charles Deal	40.00	20.00	12.00
(16)	William Doak	40.00	20.00	12.00
(17)	Bill Donovan	40.00	20.00	12.00
(18)	Johnny Evers	150.00	75.00	45.00
(19)	Urban Faber	150.00	75.00	45.00
(20)	Eddie Foster	40.00	20.00	12.00
(21)	W.L. Gardner	40.00	20.00	12.00
(22)	"Kid" Gleason	40.00	20.00	12.00
(23)	Hank Gowdy	40.00	20.00	12.00
(24)	John Graney	40.00	20.00	12.00
(25)	Tom Griffith	40.00	20.00	12.00
(26)	Harry Heilman (Heilmann)	150.00	75.00	45.00
(27)	Walter Holke	40.00	20.00	12.00
(28)	Charles Hollacher (Hollocher)	40.00	20.00	12.00
(29)	Harry Hooper	150.00	75.00	45.00
(30)	Rogers Hornsby	200.00	100.00	60.00
(31)	Wm. C. Jacobson	40.00	20.00	12.00
(32)	Walter Johnson	300.00	150.00	90.00
(33)	James Johnston	40.00	20.00	12.00
(34)	Joe Judge	40.00	20.00	12.00
(35)	George Kelly	150.00	75.00	45.00
(36)	Dick Kerr	40.00	20.00	12.00
(37)	P.J. Kilduff	40.00	20.00	12.00
(38)	Bill Killefer	40.00	20.00	12.00
(39)	John Lavan	40.00	20.00	12.00
(40)	Duffy Lewis	40.00	20.00	12.00
(41)	Perry Lipe	40.00	20.00	12.00
(42)	Al. Mamaux	40.00	20.00	12.00
(43)	"Rabbit" Maranville	150.00	75.00	45.00
(44)	Carl May (Mays)	60.00	30.00	18.00
(45)	John McGraw	125.00	62.00	37.00
(46)	Jack McInnis	40.00	20.00	12.00
(47)	Clyde Milan	40.00	20.00	12.00
(48)	Otto Miller	40.00	20.00	12.00

		NR MT	EX	VG
(49)	Guy Morton	40.00	20.00	12.00
(50)	Eddie Murphy	40.00	20.00	12.00
(51)	"Hy" Myers	40.00	20.00	12.00
(52)	Steve O'Neill	40.00	20.00	12.00
(53)	Roger Peckinbaugh (Peckinpaugh)			
		40.00	20.00	12.00
(54)	Jeff Pfeffer	40.00	20.00	12.00
(55)	Walter Pipp	75.00	37.00	22.00
(56)	E.C. Rice	150.00	75.00	45.00
(57)	Eppa Rixey, Jr.	150.00	75.00	45.00
(58)	Babe Ruth	1000.00	500.00	300.00
(59)	"Slim" Sallee	40.00	20.00	12.00
(60)	Ray Schalk	150.00	75.00	45.00
(61)	Walter Schang	40.00	20.00	12.00
(62a)	Fred Schupp (name incorrect)	40.00	20.00	12.00
(62b)	Ferd Schupp (name correct)	40.00	20.00	12.00
(63)	Everett Scott	40.00	20.00	12.00
(64)	Hank Severeid	40.00	20.00	12.00
(65)	George Sisler (batting)	150.00	75.00	45.00
(66)	George Sisler (throwing)	150.00	75.00	45.00
(67)	Tris Speaker	150.00	75.00	45.00
(68)	Milton Stock	40.00	20.00	12.00
(69)	Amos Strunk	40.00	20.00	12.00
(70)	Chester Thomas	40.00	20.00	12.00
(71)	George Tyler	40.00	20.00	12.00
(72)	Jim Vaughn	40.00	20.00	12.00
(73)	Bob Veach	40.00	20.00	12.00
(74)	W. Wambsganss	60.00	30.00	18.00
(75)	Zach Wheat	150.00	75.00	45.00
(76)	Fred Williams	50.00	25.00	15.00
(77)	Ivy B. Wingo	40.00	20.00	12.00
(78)	Joe Wood	60.00	30.00	18.00
(79)	Pep Young	40.00	20.00	12.00

1923 E123

This set, identified in the ACC as E123, was issued in 1923 by the Curtis Ireland Candy Corporation of St. Louis and was distributed with Ireland's "All Star Bars." Except for the backs, the Ireland set is identical to the Willard Chocolate V100 set of the same year. Measuring 3-1/4" by 2-1/16", the cards feature sepia-toned photos with the player's name in script on the front. The backs advertise a contest which required the collector to mail in the cards in exchange for prizes, which probably explains their relative scarcity today.

		NR MT	EX	VG
	Complete Set:	15000.00	7500.00	4500.
	Common Player:	30.00	15.00	9.00
(1)	Chas. B Adams	30.00	15.00	9.00
(2)	Grover C. Alexander	175.00	87.00	52.00
(3)	J.P. Austin	30.00	15.00	9.00
(4)	J.C. Bagby	30.00	15.00	9.00
(5)	J. Franklin Baker	125.00	62.00	37.00
(6)	David J. Bancroft	125.00	62.00	37.00
(7)	Turner Barber	30.00	15.00	9.00
(8)	Jesse L. Barnes	30.00	15.00	9.00
(9)	J.C. Bassler	30.00	15.00	9.00
(10)	L.A. Blue	30.00	15.00	9.00
(11)	Norman D. Boeckel	30.00	15.00	9.00
(12)	F.L. Brazil (Brazill)	30.00	15.00	9.00
(13)	G.H. Burns	30.00	15.00	9.00
(14)	Geo. J. Burns	30.00	15.00	9.00
(15)	Leon Cadore	30.00	15.00	9.00

		NR MT	EX	VG
(16)	Max G. Carey	125.00	62.00	37.00
(17)	Harold G. Carlson	30.00	15.00	9.00
(18)	Lloyd R. Christenberry (Christenbury)			
		30.00	15.00	9.00
(19)	Vernon J.. Clemons	30.00	15.00	9.00
(20)	T.R. Cobb	800.00	400.00	250.00
(21)	Bert Cole	30.00	15.00	9.00
(22)	John F. Collins	30.00	15.00	9.00
(23)	S. Coveleskie (Coveleski)	125.00	62.00	37.00
(24)	Walton E. Cruise	30.00	15.00	9.00
(25)	G.W. Cutshaw	30.00	15.00	9.00
(26)	Jacob E. Daubert	35.00	17.50	10.50
(27)	Geo. Dauss	30.00	15.00	9.00
(28)	F.T. Davis	30.00	15.00	9.00
(29)	Chas. A. Deal	30.00	15.00	9.00
(30)	William L. Doak	30.00	15.00	9.00
(31)	William E. Donovan	30.00	15.00	9.00
(32)	Hugh Duffy	125.00	62.00	37.00
(33)	J.A. Dugan	35.00	17.50	10.50
(34)	Louis B. Duncan	30.00	15.00	9.00
(35)	James Dykes	35.00	17.50	10.50
(36)	H.J. Ehmke	30.00	15.00	9.00
(37)	F.R. Ellerbe	30.00	15.00	9.00
(38)	E.G. Erickson	30.00	15.00	9.00
(39)	John J. Evers	125.00	62.00	37.00
(40)	U.C. Faber	125.00	62.00	37.00
(41)	B.A. Falk	30.00	15.00	9.00
(42)	Max Flack	30.00	15.00	9.00
(43)	Lee Fohl	30.00	15.00	9.00
(44)	Jacques F. Fournier	30.00	15.00	9.00
(45)	Frank F. Frisch	125.00	62.00	37.00
(46)	C.E. Galloway	30.00	15.00	9.00
(47)	W.C. Gardner	30.00	15.00	9.00
(48)	E.P. Gharrity	30.00	15.00	9.00
(49)	Geo. Gibson	30.00	15.00	9.00
(50)	Wm. Gleason	30.00	15.00	9.00
(51)	William Gleason	30.00	15.00	9.00
(52)	Henry M. Gowdy	30.00	15.00	9.00
(53)	I.M. Griffin	30.00	15.00	9.00
(54)	Griffith	125.00	62.00	37.00
(55)	Burleigh A. Grimes	125.00	62.00	37.00
(56)	Charles J. Grimm	35.00	17.50	10.50
(57)	Jesse J. Haines	125.00	62.00	37.00
(58)	S.R. Harris	125.00	62.00	37.00
(59)	W.B. Harris	30.00	15.00	9.00
(60)	R.K. Hasty	30.00	15.00	9.00
(61)	H.E. Heilman (Heilmann)	125.00	62.00	37.00
(62)	Walter J. Henline	30.00	15.00	9.00
(63)	Walter L. Holke	30.00	15.00	9.00
(64)	Charles J. Hollocher	30.00	15.00	9.00
(65)	H.B. Hooper	125.00	62.00	37.00
(66)	Rogers Hornsby	125.00	62.00	37.00
(67)	W.C. Hoyt	125.00	62.00	37.00
(68)	Miller Huggins	125.00	62.00	37.00
(69)	W.C. Jacobsen (Jacobson)	30.00	15.00	9.00
(70)	C.D. Jamieson	30.00	15.00	9.00
(71)	Ernest Johnson	30.00	15.00	9.00
(72)	W.P. Johnson	400.00	200.00	125.00
(73)	James H. Johnston	30.00	15.00	9.00
(74)	R.W. Jones	30.00	15.00	9.00
(75)	Samuel Pond Jones	30.00	15.00	9.00
(76)	J.I. Judge	30.00	15.00	9.00
(77)	James W. Keenan	30.00	15.00	9.00
(78)	Geo. L. Kelly	125.00	62.00	37.00
(79)	Peter J. Kilduff	30.00	15.00	9.00
(80)	William Killefer	30.00	15.00	9.00
(81)	Lee King	30.00	15.00	9.00
(82)	Ray Kolp	30.00	15.00	9.00
(83)	John Lavan	30.00	15.00	9.00
(84)	H.L. Leibold	30.00	15.00	9.00
(85)	Connie Mack	500.00	250.00	150.00
(86)	J.W. Mails	30.00	15.00	9.00
(87)	Walter J. Maranville	125.00	62.00	37.00
(88)	Richard W. Marquard	125.00	62.00	37.00
(89)	C.W. Mays	35.00	17.50	10.50
(90)	Geo. F. McBride	30.00	15.00	9.00
(91)	H.M. McClellan	30.00	15.00	9.00
(92)	John J. McGraw	450.00	225.00	135.00
(93)	Austin B. McHenry	30.00	15.00	9.00
(94)	J. McInnis	30.00	15.00	9.00
(95)	Douglas McWeeney (McWeeny)	30.00	15.00	9.00
(96)	M. Menosky	30.00	15.00	9.00
(97)	Emil F. Meusel	30.00	15.00	9.00
(98)	R. Meusel	35.00	17.50	10.50
(99)	Henry W. Meyers	30.00	15.00	9.00
(100)	J.C. Milan	30.00	15.00	9.00
(101)	John K. Miljus	30.00	15.00	9.00
(102)	Edmund J. Miller	30.00	15.00	9.00
(103)	Elmer Miller	30.00	15.00	9.00
(104)	Otto L. Miller	30.00	15.00	9.00
(105)	Fred Mitchell	30.00	15.00	9.00

		NR MT	EX	VG
(106)	Geo. Mogridge	30.00	15.00	9.00
(107)	Patrick J. Moran	30.00	15.00	9.00
(108)	John D. Morrison	30.00	15.00	9.00
(109)	J.A. Mostil	30.00	15.00	9.00
(110)	Clarence F. Mueller	30.00	15.00	9.00
(111)	A. Earle Neale	35.00	17.50	10.50
(112)	Joseph Oeschger	30.00	15.00	9.00
(113)	Robert J. O'Farrell	30.00	15.00	9.00
(114)	J.C. Oldham	30.00	15.00	9.00
(115)	I.M. Olson	30.00	15.00	9.00
(116)	Geo. M. O'Neil	30.00	15.00	9.00
(117)	S.F. O'Neill	30.00	15.00	9.00
(118)	Frank J. Parkinson	30.00	15.00	9.00
(119)	Geo. H. Paskert	30.00	15.00	9.00
(120)	R.T. Peckinpaugh	30.00	15.00	9.00
(121)	H.J. Pennock	125.00	62.00	37.00
(122)	Ralph Perkins	30.00	15.00	9.00
(123)	Edw. J. Pfeffer	30.00	15.00	9.00
(124)	W.C. Pipp	250.00	125.00	75.00
(125)	Charles Elmer Ponder	30.00	15.00	9.00
(126)	Raymond R. Powell	30.00	15.00	9.00
(127)	D.B. Pratt	30.00	15.00	9.00
(128)	Joseph Rapp	30.00	15.00	9.00
(129)	John H. Rawlings	30.00	15.00	9.00
(130)	E.S. Rice (should be E.C.)	125.00	62.00	37.00
(131)	Rickey	200.00	100.00	60.00
(132)	James J. Ring	30.00	15.00	9.00
(133)	Eppa J. Rixey	125.00	62.00	37.00
(134)	Davis A. Robertson	30.00	15.00	9.00
(135)	Edwin Rommel	30.00	15.00	9.00
(136)	Edd J. Roush	125.00	62.00	37.00
(137)	Harold Ruel (Herold)	30.00	15.00	9.00
(138)	Allen Russell	30.00	15.00	9.00
(139)	G.H. Ruth	1000.00	500.00	300.00
(140)	Wilfred D. Ryan	30.00	15.00	9.00
(141)	Henry F. Sallee	30.00	15.00	9.00
(142)	W.H. Schang	30.00	15.00	9.00
(143)	Raymond H. Schmandt	30.00	15.00	9.00
(144)	Everett Scott	30.00	15.00	9.00
(145)	Henry Severeid	30.00	15.00	9.00
(146)	Jos. W. Sewell	125.00	62.00	37.00
(147)	Howard S. Shanks	30.00	15.00	9.00
(148)	E.H. Sheely	30.00	15.00	9.00
(149)	Ralph Shinners	30.00	15.00	9.00
(150)	U.J. Shocker	30.00	15.00	9.00
(151)	G.H. Sisler	125.00	62.00	37.00
(152)	Earl L. Smith	30.00	15.00	9.00
(153)	Earl S. Smith	30.00	15.00	9.00
(154)	Geo. A. Smith	30.00	15.00	9.00
(155)	J.W. Smith	30.00	15.00	9.00
(156)	Tris E. Speaker	250.00	125.00	75.00
(157)	Arnold Staatz	30.00	15.00	9.00
(158)	J.R. Stephenson	30.00	15.00	9.00
(159)	Milton J. Stock	30.00	15.00	9.00
(160)	John L. Sullivan	30.00	15.00	9.00
(161)	H.F. Tormahlen	30.00	15.00	9.00
(162)	Jas. A. Tierney	30.00	15.00	9.00
(163)	J.T. Tobin	30.00	15.00	9.00
(164)	Jas. L. Vaughn	30.00	15.00	9.00
(165)	R.H. Veach	30.00	15.00	9.00
(166)	C.W. Walker	30.00	15.00	9.00
(167)	A.L. Ward	30.00	15.00	9.00
(168)	Zack D. Wheat	125.00	62.00	37.00
(169)	George B. Whitted	30.00	15.00	9.00
(170)	Irvin K. Wilhelm	30.00	15.00	9.00
(171)	Roy H. Wilkinson	30.00	15.00	9.00
(172)	Fred C. Williams	35.00	17.50	10.50
(173)	K.R. Williams	30.00	15.00	9.00
(174)	Sam'l W. Wilson	30.00	15.00	9.00
(175)	Ivy B. Wingo	30.00	15.00	9.00
(176)	L.W. Witt	30.00	15.00	9.00
(177)	Joseph Wood	35.00	17.50	10.50
(178)	E. Yaryan	30.00	15.00	9.00
(179)	R.S. Young	30.00	15.00	9.00
(180)	Ross Young (Youngs)	125.00	62.00	37.00

the checklists, the set would be complete at 41 cards (including two separate poses of Honus Wagner), but to date only about 20 different cards have been found. The set is designated as E125.

		NR MT	EX	VG
Complete Set:		40000.00	20000.00	12000.
Common Player:		750.00	375.00	225.00
(1)	Babe Adams	750.00	375.00	225.00
(2)	Red Ames	750.00	375.00	225.00
(3)	Home Run Baker	2000.00	1000.00	600.00
(4)	Jack Barry	750.00	375.00	225.00
(5)	Chief Bender	2000.00	1000.00	600.00
(6)	Al Bridwell	750.00	375.00	225.00
(7)	Bobby Byrne	750.00	375.00	225.00
(8)	Bill Carrigan	750.00	375.00	225.00
(9)	Ed Cicotte	1500.00	750.00	450.00
(10)	Fred Clark (Clarke)	2000.00	1000.00	600.00
(11)	Eddie Collins	3500.00	1750.00	1050.
(12)	Harry Davis	750.00	375.00	225.00
(13)	Art Devlin	750.00	375.00	225.00
(14)	Josh Devore	750.00	375.00	225.00
(15)	Larry Doyle	750.00	375.00	225.00
(16)	John Flynn	750.00	375.00	225.00
(17)	George Gibson	750.00	375.00	225.00
(18)	Topsy Hartsell (Hartsel)	750.00	375.00	225.00
(19)	Harry Hooper	2000.00	1000.00	600.00
(20)	Harry Krause	750.00	375.00	225.00
(21)	Tommy Leach	750.00	375.00	225.00
(22)	Harry Lord	750.00	375.00	225.00
(23)	Christy Mathewson	6500.00	3250.00	1950.
(24)	Amby McConnell	750.00	375.00	225.00
(25)	Fred Merkle	750.00	375.00	225.00
(26)	Dots Miller	750.00	375.00	225.00
(27)	Danny Murphy	750.00	375.00	225.00
(28)	Red Murray	750.00	375.00	225.00
(29)	Harry Niles	750.00	375.00	225.00
(30)	Rube Oldring	750.00	375.00	225.00
(31)	Eddie Plank	3500.00	1750.00	1050.
(32)	Cy Seymour	750.00	375.00	225.00
(33)	Tris Speaker	4000.00	2000.00	1200.
(34)	Jake Stahl	750.00	375.00	225.00
(35)	Ira Thomas	750.00	375.00	225.00
(36)	Heinie Wagner	750.00	375.00	225.00
(37)	Honus Wagner (batting)	6500.00	3250.00	1950.
(38)	Honus Wagner (throwing)	6500.00	3250.00	1950.
(39)	Art Wilson	750.00	375.00	225.00
(40)	Owen Wilson	750.00	375.00	225.00
(41)	Hooks Wiltse	750.00	375.00	225.00

1910 E125

Issued circa 1910 by the American Caramel Company, this set of die-cut cards is so rare that it wasn't even known to exist until the late 1960s. Apparently inserted in boxes of caramels, these cards, which are die-cut figures of baseball players, vary in size but are all relatively large - some measuring 7" high and 4" wide. Players from the Athletics, Red Sox, Giants and Pirates are known with a team checklist appearing on the back. According to

1927 E126

Issued in 1927 by the American Caramel Company of Lancaster, Pa., this obscure 60-card set was one of the last of the caramel card issues. Measuring 2" by 3-1/4", the cards differ from most sets of the period because they are numbered. The back of each card includes an offer for an album to house the 60-card set which includes players from all 16 major league teams, but to date no such album has been found. The set has been given the designation E126.

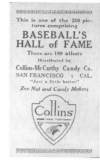

	NR MT	EX	VG
Complete Set:	15000.00	6200.00	3500.00
Common Player:	75.00	37.00	22.00

		NR MT	EX	VG
1	John Gooch	200.00	100.00	60.00
2	Clyde L. Barnhart	75.00	37.00	22.00
3	Joe Busch (Bush)	100.00	50.00	30.00
4	Lee Meadows	75.00	37.00	22.00
5	E.T. Cox	75.00	37.00	22.00
6	"Red" Faber	200.00	100.00	60.00
7	Aaron Ward	75.00	37.00	22.00
8	Ray Schalk	200.00	100.00	60.00
9	"Specs" Toporcer ("Specs")	75.00	37.00	22.00
10	Bill Southworth	75.00	37.00	22.00
11	Allen Sothoron	75.00	37.00	22.00
12	Will Sherdel	75.00	37.00	22.00
13	Grover Alexander	250.00	125.00	75.00
14	Jack Quinn	75.00	37.00	22.00
15	C. Galloway	75.00	37.00	22.00
16	"Eddie" Collins	275.00	130.00	50.00
17	"Ty" Cobb	1500.00	700.00	250.00
18	Percy Jones	75.00	37.00	22.00
19	Chas. Grimm	100.00	50.00	30.00
20	"Bennie" Karr	75.00	37.00	22.00
21	Charlie Jamieson	75.00	37.00	22.00
22	Sherrod Smith	75.00	37.00	22.00
23	Virgil Cheeves	75.00	37.00	22.00
24	James Ring	75.00	37.00	22.00
25	"Muddy" Ruel	75.00	37.00	22.00
26	Joe Judge	75.00	37.00	22.00
27	Tris Speaker	400.00	200.00	125.00
28	Walter Johnson	600.00	300.00	150.00
29	E.C. "Sam" Rice	200.00	100.00	60.00
30	Hank DeBerry	75.00	37.00	22.00
31	Walter Henline	75.00	37.00	22.00
32	Max Carey	200.00	100.00	60.00
33	Arnold J. Statz	75.00	37.00	22.00
34	Emil Meusel	75.00	37.00	22.00
35	T.P. "Pat" Collins	75.00	37.00	22.00
36	Urban Shocker	75.00	37.00	22.00
37	Bob Shawkey	100.00	50.00	30.00
38	"Babe" Ruth	2500.00	1000.00	450.00
39	Bob Meusel	100.00	40.00	16.00
40	Alex Ferguson	75.00	37.00	22.00
41	"Stuffy" McInnis	75.00	37.00	22.00
42	"Cy" Williams	100.00	40.00	16.00
43	Russel Wrightstone (Russell)	75.00	37.00	22.00
44	John Tobin	75.00	37.00	22.00
45	Wm. C. Jacobson	75.00	37.00	22.00
46	Bryan "Slim" Harriss	75.00	37.00	22.00
47	Elam Vangilder	75.00	37.00	22.00
48	Ken Williams	75.00	37.00	22.00
49	Geo. R. Sisler	200.00	100.00	60.00
50	Ed Brown	75.00	37.00	22.00
51	Jack Smith	75.00	37.00	22.00
52	Dave Bancroft	200.00	100.00	60.00
53	Larry Woodall	75.00	37.00	22.00
54	Lu Blue	75.00	37.00	22.00
55	Johnny Bassler	75.00	37.00	22.00
56	"Jakie" May	75.00	37.00	22.00
57	Horace Ford	75.00	37.00	22.00
58	"Curt" Walker	75.00	37.00	22.00
59	"Artie" Nehf	75.00	37.00	22.00
60	Geo. Kelly	250.00	125.00	75.00

1916 E135

Produced by the Collins-McCarthy Candy Co. of San Francisco, the 200-card, black and white set represents the company's only venture into issuing non-Pacific Coast League players. The cards, which are numbered alphabetically, measure 2" by 3-1/4" in size and are printed on think stock. Though the set is entitled "Baseball's Hall of Fame," many nondescript players appear in the issue. The complete set price does not include the more expensive variations.

		NR MT	EX	VG
Complete Set:		30000.00	15000.00	9000.
Common Player:		60.00	30.00	18.00

		NR MT	EX	VG
1	Sam Agnew	60.00	30.00	18.00
2	Grover Alexander	250.00	125.00	75.00
3	W.S. Alexander (initials actually W.E.)	60.00	30.00	18.00
4	Leon Ames	60.00	30.00	18.00
5	Fred Anderson	60.00	30.00	18.00
6	Ed Appleton	60.00	30.00	18.00
7	Jimmy Archer	60.00	30.00	18.00
8	Jimmy Austin	60.00	30.00	18.00
9	Jim Bagby	60.00	30.00	18.00
10	H.D. Baird	60.00	30.00	18.00
11	J. Franklin Baker	250.00	125.00	75.00
12	Dave Bancroft	250.00	125.00	75.00
13	Jack Barry	60.00	30.00	18.00
14	Joe Benz	60.00	30.00	18.00
15	Al Betzel	60.00	30.00	18.00
16	Ping Bodie	60.00	30.00	18.00
17	Joe Boehling	60.00	30.00	18.00
18	Eddie Burns	60.00	30.00	18.00
19	George Burns	60.00	30.00	18.00
20	Geo. J. Burns	80.00	30.00	18.00
21	Joe Bush	80.00	40.00	24.00
22	Owen Bush	60.00	30.00	18.00
23	Bobby Byrne	60.00	30.00	18.00
24	Forrest Cady	60.00	30.00	18.00
25	Max Carey	250.00	125.00	75.00
26	Ray Chapman	45.00	20.00	12.00
27	Larry Cheney	60.00	30.00	18.00
28	Eddie Cicotte	100.00	50.00	30.00
29	Tom Clarke	60.00	30.00	18.00
30	Ty Cobb	2000.00	1000.00	600.00
31	Eddie Collins	250.00	125.00	75.00
32	"Shauno" Collins (Shano)	60.00	30.00	18.00
33	Fred Coumbe	60.00	30.00	18.00
34	Harry Coveleskie (Coveleski)	60.00	30.00	18.00
35	Gavvy Cravath	80.00	40.00	24.00
36	Sam Crawford	250.00	125.00	75.00
37	Geo. Cutshaw	60.00	30.00	18.00
38	Jake Daubert	80.00	40.00	24.00
39	Geo. Dauss	60.00	30.00	18.00
40	Charles Deal	60.00	30.00	18.00
41	"Wheezer" Dell	60.00	30.00	18.00
42	William Doak	60.00	30.00	18.00
43	Bill Donovan	60.00	30.00	18.00
44	Larry Doyle	80.00	40.00	24.00
45	Johnny Evers	250.00	125.00	75.00
46	Urban Faber	250.00	125.00	75.00
47	"Hap" Felsch	80.00	40.00	24.00
48	Bill Fischer	60.00	30.00	18.00
49	Ray Fisher	60.00	30.00	18.00
50	Art Fletcher	60.00	30.00	18.00
51	Eddie Foster	60.00	30.00	18.00
52	Jacques Fournier	60.00	30.00	18.00
53	Del Gainer (Gainor)	60.00	30.00	18.00
54	Bert Gallia	60.00	30.00	18.00
55	"Chic" Gandil (Chick)	55.00	22.00	13.50
56	Larry Gardner	60.00	30.00	18.00
57	Joe Gedeon	60.00	30.00	18.00

		NR MT	EX	VG
58	Gus Getz	60.00	30.00	18.00
59	Frank Gilhooley	60.00	30.00	18.00
60	Wm. Gleason	60.00	30.00	18.00
61	M.A. Gonzales (Gonzalez)	60.00	30.00	18.00
62	Hank Gowdy	60.00	30.00	18.00
63	John Graney	60.00	30.00	18.00
64	Tom Griffith	60.00	30.00	18.00
65	Heinie Groh	80.00	40.00	24.00
66	Bob Groom	60.00	30.00	18.00
67	Louis Guisto	60.00	30.00	18.00
68	Earl Hamilton	60.00	30.00	18.00
69	Harry Harper	60.00	30.00	18.00
70	Grover Hartley	60.00	30.00	18.00
71	Harry Heilmann	250.00	125.00	75.00
72	Claude Hendrix	60.00	30.00	18.00
73	Olaf Henriksen	60.00	30.00	18.00
74	John Henry	60.00	30.00	18.00
75	"Buck" Herzog	60.00	30.00	18.00
76a	Hugh High (white stockings, photo actually Claude Williams)	250.00	125.00	75.00
76b	Hugh High (black stockings, correct photo)	80.00	40.00	24.00
77	Dick Hoblitzell	60.00	30.00	18.00
78	Walter Holke	60.00	30.00	18.00
79	Harry Hooper	250.00	125.00	75.00
80	Rogers Hornsby	400.00	200.00	120.00
81	Ivan Howard	60.00	30.00	18.00
82	Joe Jackson	5000.00	2500.00	1500.
83	Harold Janvrin	60.00	30.00	18.00
84	William James	60.00	30.00	18.00
85	C. Jamieson	60.00	30.00	18.00
86	Hugh Jennings	250.00	125.00	75.00
87	Walter Johnson	1000.00	500.00	300.00
88	James Johnston	60.00	30.00	18.00
89	Fielder Jones	60.00	30.00	18.00
90a	Joe Judge (bat on right shoulder, photo actually Ray Morgan)	250.00	125.00	75.00
90b	Joe Judge (bat on left shoulder, correct photo)	80.00	40.00	24.00
91	Hans Lobert	60.00	30.00	18.00
92	Benny Kauff	60.00	30.00	18.00
93	Wm. Killefer Jr.	60.00	30.00	18.00
94	Ed. Konetchy	60.00	30.00	18.00
95	John Lavan	60.00	30.00	18.00
96	Jimmy Lavender	60.00	30.00	18.00
97	"Nemo" Leibold	60.00	30.00	18.00
98	H.B. Leonard	60.00	30.00	18.00
99	Duffy Lewis	80.00	40.00	24.00
100	Tom Long	60.00	30.00	18.00
101	Wm. Louden	60.00	30.00	18.00
102	Fred Luderus	60.00	30.00	18.00
103	Lee Magee	60.00	30.00	18.00
104	Sherwood Magee	80.00	40.00	24.00
105	Al Mamaux	60.00	30.00	18.00
106	Leslie Mann	60.00	30.00	18.00
107	"Rabbit" Maranville	250.00	125.00	75.00
108	Rube Marquard	250.00	125.00	75.00
109	Armando Marsans	60.00	30.00	18.00
110	J. Erskine Mayer	60.00	30.00	18.00
111	George McBride	60.00	30.00	18.00
112	Lew McCarty	60.00	30.00	18.00
113	John J. McGraw	300.00	150.00	90.00
114	Jack McInnis	60.00	30.00	18.00
115	Lee Meadows	60.00	30.00	18.00
116	Fred Merkle	80.00	40.00	24.00
117	"Chief" Meyers	60.00	30.00	18.00
118	Clyde Milan	60.00	30.00	18.00
119	Otto Miller	60.00	30.00	18.00
120	Clarence Mitchell	60.00	30.00	18.00
121a	Ray Morgan (bat on right shoulder, photo actually Joe Judge)	250.00	125.00	75.00
121b	Ray Morgan (bat on left shoulder, correct photo)	80.00	40.00	24.00
122	Guy Morton	60.00	30.00	18.00
123	"Mike" Mowrey	60.00	30.00	18.00
124	Elmer Myers	60.00	30.00	18.00
125	"Hy" Myers	60.00	30.00	18.00
126	A.E. Neale	100.00	50.00	30.00
127	Arthur Nehf	60.00	30.00	18.00
128	J.A. Niehoff	60.00	30.00	18.00
129	Steve O'Neill	60.00	30.00	18.00
130	"Dode" Paskert	60.00	30.00	18.00
131	Roger Peckinpaugh	80.00	40.00	24.00
132	"Pol" Perritt	60.00	30.00	18.00
133	"Jeff" Pfeffer	60.00	30.00	18.00
134	Walter Pipp	150.00	75.00	45.00
135	Derril Pratt (Derrill)	60.00	30.00	18.00
136	Bill Rariden	60.00	30.00	18.00
137	E.C. Rice	250.00	125.00	75.00
138	Wm. A. Ritter (actually Wm. H.)	60.00	30.00	18.00
139	Eppa Rixey	250.00	125.00	75.00

		NR MT	EX	VG
140	Davey Robertson	60.00	30.00	18.00
141	"Bob" Roth	60.00	30.00	18.00
142	Ed. Roush	250.00	125.00	75.00
143	Clarence Rowland	60.00	30.00	18.00
144	Dick Rudolph	60.00	30.00	18.00
145	William Rumler	60.00	30.00	18.00
146a	Reb Russell (pitching follow-thru, photo actually Mellie Wolfgang)	250.00	125.00	75.00
146b	Reb Russell (hands at side, correct photo)	1000.00	500.00	300.00
147	"Babe" Ruth	3500.00	1750.00	1050.
148	Vic Saier	60.00	30.00	18.00
149	"Slim" Sallee	60.00	30.00	18.00
150	Ray Schalk	250.00	125.00	75.00
151	Walter Schang	60.00	30.00	18.00
152	Frank Schulte	60.00	30.00	18.00
153	Ferd Schupp	60.00	30.00	18.00
154	Everett Scott	60.00	30.00	18.00
155	Hank Severeid	60.00	30.00	18.00
156	Howard Shanks	60.00	30.00	18.00
157	Bob Shawkey	80.00	40.00	24.00
158	Jas. Sheckard	60.00	30.00	18.00
159	Ernie Shore	60.00	30.00	18.00
160	C.H. Shorten	60.00	30.00	18.00
161	Burt Shotton	60.00	30.00	18.00
162	Geo. Sisler	250.00	125.00	75.00
163	Elmer Smith	60.00	30.00	18.00
164	J. Carlisle Smith	60.00	30.00	18.00
165	Fred Snodgrass	60.00	30.00	18.00
166	Tris Speaker	400.00	200.00	120.00
167	Oscar Stanage	60.00	30.00	18.00
168	Charles Stengel	600.00	300.00	180.00
169	Milton Stock	60.00	30.00	18.00
170	Amos Strunk	60.00	30.00	18.00
171	"Zeb" Terry	60.00	30.00	18.00
172	"Jeff" Tesreau	60.00	30.00	18.00
173	Chester Thomas	60.00	30.00	18.00
174	Fred Toney	60.00	30.00	18.00
175	Terry Turner	60.00	30.00	18.00
176	George Tyler	60.00	30.00	18.00
177	Jim Vaughn	60.00	30.00	18.00
178	Bob Veach	60.00	30.00	18.00
179	Oscar Vitt	60.00	30.00	18.00
180	Hans Wagner	2000.00	1000.00	600.00
181	Clarence Walker	60.00	30.00	18.00
182	Jim Walsh	60.00	30.00	18.00
183	Al Walters	60.00	30.00	18.00
184	W. Wambsganss	80.00	40.00	24.00
185	Buck Weaver	100.00	50.00	30.00
186	Carl Weilman	60.00	30.00	18.00
187	Zack Wheat	250.00	125.00	75.00
188	Geo. Whitted	60.00	30.00	18.00
189	Joe Wilhoit	60.00	30.00	18.00
190a	Claude Williams (black stockings, photo actually Hugh High)	250.00	125.00	75.00
190b	Claude Williams (white stockings, correct photo)	100.00	50.00	30.00
191	Fred Williams	80.00	40.00	24.00
192	Art Wilson	60.00	30.00	18.00
193	Lawton Witt	60.00	30.00	18.00
194	Joe Wood	80.00	40.00	24.00
195	William Wortman	60.00	30.00	18.00
196	Steve Yerkes	60.00	30.00	18.00
197	Earl Yingling	60.00	30.00	18.00
198	"Pep" Young (photo actually Ralph Young)	60.00	30.00	18.00
199	Rollie Zeider	60.00	30.00	18.00
200	Henry Zimmerman	60.00	30.00	18.00

1911 E136 Zeenut

Produced for 28 straight years, these Pacific Coast League cards were among the longest-running and most popular baseball issues ever to appear on the West Coast. Issued by the Collins-McCarthy Candy Co. (later known as the Collins-Hencke Candy Co. and then simply the Collins Candy Co.) of San Francisco Zeenut cards were inserted in boxes of the company's products: Zeenuts, Ruf-Neks and Home Run Kisses. All Zeenut cards issued from 1913 to 1937 included a half-inch coupon at the bottom that coudl be redeemed for various prizes. Since most of these coupons were removed (and many not too carefully) Zeenuts are difficult to find in top condition today, and only a very small percentage survived with the coupon intact. (The sizes listed in the following descriptions are for cards without coupons.) Over the 28-year span, it is estimated that nearly 3,700 different cards were issued as part of the Zeenuts series, but new discoveries are still being made, and the checklist continues to grow. It is sometimes difficult to differentiate one year from another after 1930. Because it is so rare to find Zeenuts cards with the coupon still attached, values listed are for cards without the coupon. Cards with the coupon still intact will generally command an additional 25-35 percent premium. The first Zeenut cards measure 2-1/8" by 4" and feature a sepia-toned photo on a brown background surrounded by an off-white border. The backs of the cards are blank. Although the 1911 cards did not include the coupon bottom, some cards have been found with punch holes, indicating they may have also been used for premiums. A total of 122 different players have been found.

		NR MT	EX	VG
Complete Set:		2700.00	1350.00	800.00
Common Player:		18.00	9.00	5.50
(1)	Abbott	18.00	9.00	5.50
(2)	Ables	18.00	9.00	5.50
(3a)	Agnew (large pose)	18.00	9.00	5.50
(3b)	Agnew (small pose)	18.00	9.00	5.50
(4a)	Akin (large pose)	18.00	9.00	5.50
(4b)	Akin (small pose)	18.00	9.00	5.50
(5)	Arellanes	18.00	9.00	5.50
(6a)	Arlett (large pose)	18.00	9.00	5.50
(6b)	Arlett (middle size pose)	18.00	9.00	5.50
(6c)	Arlett (small pose)	18.00	9.00	5.50
(7)	Barry	18.00	9.00	5.50
(8)	Baum	18.00	9.00	5.50
(9)	Bernard	18.00	9.00	5.50
(10)	Berry	18.00	9.00	5.50
(11)	Bohen	18.00	9.00	5.50
(12)	Brackenridge	18.00	9.00	5.50
(13)	Brashear	18.00	9.00	5.50
(14a)	Brown (large pose)	18.00	9.00	5.50
(14b)	Brown (small pose)	18.00	9.00	5.50
(15)	Browning	18.00	9.00	5.50
(16a)	Burrell (large pose)	18.00	9.00	5.50
(16b)	Burrell (small pose)	18.00	9.00	5.50
(17)	Byram	18.00	9.00	5.50
(18)	Carlisle	18.00	9.00	5.50
(19)	Carman	18.00	9.00	5.50
(20a)	Carson (large pose)	18.00	9.00	5.50
(20b)	Carson (middle size pose)	18.00	9.00	5.50
(20c)	Carson (small pose)	18.00	9.00	5.50
(21)	Castleton	18.00	9.00	5.50
(22)	Chadbourne	18.00	9.00	5.50
(23)	Christian	18.00	9.00	5.50
(24)	Couchman	18.00	9.00	5.50
(25)	Coy	18.00	9.00	5.50
(26)	Criger	18.00	9.00	5.50
(27)	Cutshaw	18.00	9.00	5.50
(28)	Daley	18.00	9.00	5.50
(29)	Danzig	18.00	9.00	5.50
(30)	Delhi	18.00	9.00	5.50
(31a)	Delmas (large pose)	18.00	9.00	5.50
(31b)	Delmas (small pose)	18.00	9.00	5.50
(32)	Dillon	18.00	9.00	5.50
(33a)	Discoll (name incorrect)	18.00	9.00	5.50
(33b)	Driscoll (name correct)	18.00	9.00	5.50
(34)	Dulin	18.00	9.00	5.50
(35)	Fanning	18.00	9.00	5.50
(36)	Fitzgerald	18.00	9.00	5.50
(37)	Flater	18.00	9.00	5.50
(38)	French	18.00	9.00	5.50

		NR MT	EX	VG
(39)	Fullerton	18.00	9.00	5.50
(40)	Gleason	18.00	9.00	5.50
(41)	Gregory	18.00	9.00	5.50
(42)	Halla	18.00	9.00	5.50
(43)	Harkness	18.00	9.00	5.50
(44a)	Heitmuller (large pose)	18.00	9.00	5.50
(44b)	Heitmuller (small pose)	18.00	9.00	5.50
(45)	Henley	18.00	9.00	5.50
(46)	Hetling	18.00	9.00	5.50
(47)	Hiester	18.00	9.00	5.50
(48a)	Hitt (large pose)	18.00	9.00	5.50
(48b)	Hitt (small pose)	18.00	9.00	5.50
(50)	Hoffman	18.00	9.00	5.50
(51)	Hogan	18.00	9.00	5.50
(52a)	Holland (large pose)	18.00	9.00	5.50
(52b)	Holland (small pose)	18.00	9.00	5.50
(53)	Hosp	18.00	9.00	5.50
(54a)	Howard (large pose)	18.00	9.00	5.50
(54b)	Howard (small pose)	18.00	9.00	5.50
(55)	Kane	18.00	9.00	5.50
(56)	Kerns	18.00	9.00	5.50
(57)	Kilroy	18.00	9.00	5.50
(58)	Knight	18.00	9.00	5.50
(59)	Koestner	18.00	9.00	5.50
(60)	Krueger	18.00	9.00	5.50
(61)	Kuhn	18.00	9.00	5.50
(62)	LaLonge	18.00	9.00	5.50
(63)	Lerchen	18.00	9.00	5.50
(64)	Leverenz	18.00	9.00	5.50
(65)	Lewis	18.00	9.00	5.50
(66)	Lindsay	18.00	9.00	5.50
(67)	Lober	18.00	9.00	5.50
(68)	Madden	18.00	9.00	5.50
(69)	Maggert	18.00	9.00	5.50
(70)	Mahoney	18.00	9.00	5.50
(71)	Martinoni	18.00	9.00	5.50
(72)	McArdle	18.00	9.00	5.50
(73)	McCredie	18.00	9.00	5.50
(74)	McDonnell	18.00	9.00	5.50
(75a)	McKune (large pose)	18.00	9.00	5.50
(75b)	McKune (middle size pose)	18.00	9.00	5.50
(75c)	McKune (small pose)	18.00	9.00	5.50
(76)	Meikle	18.00	9.00	5.50
(77)	Melchoir	18.00	9.00	5.50
(78)	Metzger	18.00	9.00	5.50
(79)	Miller	18.00	9.00	5.50
(80)	Mitze	18.00	9.00	5.50
(81)	Mohler	18.00	9.00	5.50
(82a)	Moore (large pose)	18.00	9.00	5.50
(82b)	Moore (small pose)	18.00	9.00	5.50
(83a)	Moskiman (lettering size large)	18.00	9.00	5.50
(83b)	Moskiman (lettering size small)	18.00	9.00	5.50
(84)	Murray	18.00	9.00	5.50
(85)	Naylor	18.00	9.00	5.50
(86)	Nebinger	18.00	9.00	5.50
(87)	Nourse	18.00	9.00	5.50
(88a)	Noyes (large pose)	18.00	9.00	5.50
(88b)	Noyes (small pose)	18.00	9.00	5.50
(89)	O'Rourke	18.00	9.00	5.50
(90)	Patterson (Oakland)	18.00	9.00	5.50
(91)	Patterson (Vernon)	18.00	9.00	5.50
(92)	Pearce	18.00	9.00	5.50
(93)	Peckinpaugh	30.00	15.00	9.00
(94)	Pernoll	18.00	9.00	5.50
(95)	Pfyl	18.00	9.00	5.50
(96)	Powell	18.00	9.00	5.50
(97a)	Raleigh (large pose)	18.00	9.00	5.50
(97b)	Raleigh (small pose)	18.00	9.00	5.50
(98)	Rapps	18.00	9.00	5.50
(99)	Rodgers	18.00	9.00	5.50
(100a)	Ryan (Portland, box around name and team)	25.00	12.50	7.50
(100b)	Ryan (Portland, no box around name and team)	18.00	9.00	5.50
(101)	Ryan (San Francisco)	18.00	9.00	5.50
(102)	Seaton	18.00	9.00	5.50
(103)	Shaw	18.00	9.00	5.50
(104)	Sheehan	18.00	9.00	5.50
(105)	Shinn	18.00	9.00	5.50
106a	Smith (Los Angeles, large pose)	18.00	9.00	5.50
(106b)	Smith (Los Angeles, small pose)	18.00	9.00	5.50
(107a)	Smith (San Francisco, large pose)	18.00	9.00	5.50
(107b)	Smith (San Francisco, small pose)	18.00	9.00	5.50
(108)	Steen	18.00	9.00	5.50
(109)	Stewart	18.00	9.00	5.50
(110a)	Stinson (large pose)	18.00	9.00	5.50
(110b)	Stinson (small pose)	18.00	9.00	5.50
(111)	Sutor	18.00	9.00	5.50
(112)	Tennant	18.00	9.00	5.50

		NR MT	EX	VG
(113)	Thomas	18.00	9.00	5.50
(114)	Thompson	18.00	9.00	5.50
(115)	Thornton	18.00	9.00	5.50
(116)	Tiedeman	18.00	9.00	5.50
(117)	Van Buren	18.00	9.00	5.50
(118)	Vitt	18.00	9.00	5.50
(119)	Wares	18.00	9.00	5.50
(120)	Weaver	75.00	38.00	23.00
(121)	Wolverton	18.00	9.00	5.50
(122)	Zacher	18.00	9.00	5.50
(123)	Zamloch	18.00	9.00	5.50

1912 E136 Home Run Kisses

Save HOME RUN KISSES Pictures
for valuable premiums
List will be issued July 15, 1912
COLLINS-McCARTHY CANDY CO.
San Francisco, Cal.

This 90-card set of Pacific Coast League players, known by the ACC designation E136, was produced in 1912 by the San Francisco candy company of Collins-McCarthy. Each card measures a large 2-1/4" by 4-1/4" and features sepia-toned player photos surrounded by an ornate frame. The front of the card has the words "Home Run Kisses" above the player's name. Most cards found are blank-backed, but others exist with a back that advises "Save Home Run Kisses Pictures for Valuable Premiums" along with other details of the Collins-McCarthy promotion.

		NR MT	EX	VG
Complete Set:		7000.00	3500.00	2100.
Common Player:		80.00	40.00	24.00
(1)	Ables	80.00	40.00	24.00
(2)	Agnew	80.00	40.00	24.00
(3)	Altman	80.00	40.00	24.00
(4)	Arrelanes	80.00	40.00	24.00
(5)	Auer	80.00	40.00	24.00
(6)	Bancroft	175.00	87.00	52.00
(7)	Bayless	80.00	40.00	24.00
(8)	Berry	80.00	40.00	24.00
(9)	Boles	80.00	40.00	24.00
(10)	Brashear	80.00	40.00	24.00
(11)	Brooks (Los Angeles)	80.00	40.00	24.00
(12)	Brooks (Oakland)	80.00	40.00	24.00
(13)	Brown	80.00	40.00	24.00
(14)	Burrell	80.00	40.00	24.00
(15)	Butler	80.00	40.00	24.00
(16)	Carlisle	90.00	45.00	27.00
(17)	Carson	80.00	40.00	24.00
(18)	Castleton	80.00	40.00	24.00
(19)	Chadbourne	80.00	40.00	24.00
(20)	Check	80.00	40.00	24.00
(21)	Core	80.00	40.00	24.00
(22)	Corhan	80.00	40.00	24.00
(23)	Coy	80.00	40.00	24.00
(24)	Daley	80.00	40.00	24.00
(25)	Dillon	80.00	40.00	24.00
(26)	Doane	80.00	40.00	24.00
(27)	Driscoll	90.00	45.00	27.00
(28)	Fisher	80.00	40.00	24.00
(29)	Flater	80.00	40.00	24.00
(30)	Gaddy	80.00	40.00	24.00
(31)	Gregg	80.00	40.00	24.00
(32)	Gregory	80.00	40.00	24.00
(33)	Harkness	80.00	40.00	24.00
(34)	Heitmuller	80.00	40.00	24.00
(35)	Henley	80.00	40.00	24.00
(36)	Hiester	80.00	40.00	24.00
(37)	Hoffman	80.00	40.00	24.00

		NR MT	EX	VG
(38)	Hogan	80.00	40.00	24.00
(39)	Hosp	80.00	40.00	24.00
(40)	Howley	80.00	40.00	24.00
(41)	Ireland	80.00	40.00	24.00
(42)	Johnson	80.00	40.00	24.00
(43)	Kane	80.00	40.00	24.00
(44)	Klawitter	80.00	40.00	24.00
(45)	Kreitz	80.00	40.00	24.00
(46)	Krueger	80.00	40.00	24.00
(47)	Leard	80.00	40.00	24.00
(48)	Leverencz	90.00	45.00	27.00
(49)	Lewis	80.00	40.00	24.00
(50)	Lindsay	80.00	40.00	24.00
(51)	Litschi	80.00	40.00	24.00
(52)	Lober	80.00	40.00	24.00
(53)	Malarkey	80.00	40.00	24.00
(54)	Martinoni	80.00	40.00	24.00
(55)	McArdle	80.00	40.00	24.00
(56)	McCorry	80.00	40.00	24.00
(57)	McDowell	80.00	40.00	24.00
(58)	McIver	80.00	40.00	24.00
(59)	Metzger	90.00	45.00	27.00
(60)	Miller	80.00	40.00	24.00
(61)	Mundorf	80.00	40.00	24.00
(62)	Nagle	80.00	40.00	24.00
(63)	Noyes	80.00	40.00	24.00
(64)	Olmstead	80.00	40.00	24.00
(65)	O'Rourke	80.00	40.00	24.00
(66)	Page	80.00	40.00	24.00
(67)	Parkins	80.00	40.00	24.00
(68)	Patterson (Oakland)	80.00	40.00	24.00
(69)	Patterson (Vernon)	80.00	40.00	24.00
(70)	Pernoll	80.00	40.00	24.00
(71)	Powell	80.00	40.00	24.00
(72)	Price	80.00	40.00	24.00
(73)	Raftery	80.00	40.00	24.00
(74)	Raleigh	80.00	40.00	24.00
(75)	Rogers	80.00	40.00	24.00
(76)	Schmidt	80.00	40.00	24.00
(77)	Schwenk	80.00	40.00	24.00
(78)	Sheehan	80.00	40.00	24.00
(79)	Shinn	80.00	40.00	24.00
(80)	Slagle	80.00	40.00	24.00
(81)	Smith	80.00	40.00	24.00
(82)	Stone	80.00	40.00	24.00
(83)	Swain	80.00	40.00	24.00
(84)	Taylor	80.00	40.00	24.00
(85)	Tiedeman	80.00	40.00	24.00
(86)	Toner	80.00	40.00	24.00
(87)	Tozer	80.00	40.00	24.00
(88)	Van Buren	80.00	40.00	24.00
(89)	Williams	80.00	40.00	24.00
(90)	Zacher	80.00	40.00	24.00

1912 E136 Zeenut

The second series of Zeenut cards measure 2-1/8" by 4-2/8" and featured sepia-toned photographs on a brown background with no border. Most cards have blank backs, but some have been found with printing advising collectors to "Save Zeenut pictures for valuable premiums." The checklist consists of 158 subjects, but more cards are still being discovered.

	NR MT	EX	VG
Complete Set:	2875.00	1425.00	850.00
Common Player:	18.00	9.00	5.50

		NR MT	EX	VG
(1)	Abbott	18.00	9.00	5.50
(2)	Ables	18.00	9.00	5.50
(3)	Agnew	18.00	9.00	5.50
(4)	Altman	18.00	9.00	5.50
(5)	Arellanes	18.00	9.00	5.50
(6)	Auer	18.00	9.00	5.50
(7)	Baker (horizontal pose)	18.00	9.00	5.50
(8)	Baker (vertical pose)	18.00	9.00	5.50
(9)	Bancroft	50.00	25.00	15.00
(10)	Baum	18.00	9.00	5.50
(11)	Bayless	18.00	9.00	5.50
(12)	Berger	18.00	9.00	5.50
(13)	Berry	18.00	9.00	5.50
(14)	Bohen	18.00	9.00	5.50
(15)	Boles	18.00	9.00	5.50
(16)	Bonner			
(17)	Boone	18.00	9.00	5.50
(18)	Brackenridge	18.00	9.00	5.50
(19)	Brashear	18.00	9.00	5.50
(20)	Breen			
(21)	Brooks (Los Angeles)	18.00	9.00	5.50
(22)	Brooks (Oakland)	18.00	9.00	5.50
(23)	Brown	18.00	9.00	5.50
(24)	Burch	18.00	9.00	5.50
(25)	Burrell	18.00	9.00	5.50
(26)	Butcher	18.00	9.00	5.50
(27)	Butler	18.00	9.00	5.50
(28)	Byram	18.00	9.00	5.50
(29)	Carlisle	18.00	9.00	5.50
(30)	Carson	18.00	9.00	5.50
(31)	Castleton	18.00	9.00	5.50
(32)	Chadbourne	18.00	9.00	5.50
(33)	Chech	18.00	9.00	5.50
(34)	Cheek	18.00	9.00	5.50
(35)	Christian	18.00	9.00	5.50
(36)	Cook	18.00	9.00	5.50
(37)	Core	18.00	9.00	5.50
(38)	Corhan	18.00	9.00	5.50
(39)	Coy	18.00	9.00	5.50
(40)	Daley	18.00	9.00	5.50
(41)	Delhi	18.00	9.00	5.50
(42)	Dillon	18.00	9.00	5.50
(43)	Doane	18.00	9.00	5.50
(44)	Driscoll	18.00	9.00	5.50
(45)	Durbin	18.00	9.00	5.50
(46)	Fanning	18.00	9.00	5.50
(47)	Felts	18.00	9.00	5.50
(48)	Fisher	18.00	9.00	5.50
(49)	Fitzgerald	18.00	9.00	5.50
(50)	Flater	18.00	9.00	5.50
(51)	Frick	18.00	9.00	5.50
(52)	Gaddy	18.00	9.00	5.50
(53)	Gedeon	18.00	9.00	5.50
(54)	Gilligan	18.00	9.00	5.50
(55)	Girot	18.00	9.00	5.50
(56)	Gray	18.00	9.00	5.50
(57)	Gregg	18.00	9.00	5.50
(58)	Gregory	18.00	9.00	5.50
(59)	Halla	18.00	9.00	5.50
(60)	Hamilton (Oakland)	18.00	9.00	5.50
(61)	Hamilton (San Francisco)	18.00	9.00	5.50
(62)	Harkness	18.00	9.00	5.50
(63)	Hartley	18.00	9.00	5.50
(64)	Heitmuller	18.00	9.00	5.50
(65)	Henley	18.00	9.00	5.50
(66)	Hetling (glove open)	18.00	9.00	5.50
(67)	Hetling (glove closed)	18.00	9.00	5.50
(68)	Hiester	18.00	9.00	5.50
(69)	Higginbottom	18.00	9.00	5.50
(70)	Hitt	18.00	9.00	5.50
(71)	Hoffman	18.00	9.00	5.50
(72)	Hogan	18.00	9.00	5.50
(73)	Hosp	18.00	9.00	5.50
(74)	Howard	18.00	9.00	5.50
(75)	Howley	18.00	9.00	5.50
(76)	Ireland	18.00	9.00	5.50
(77)	Jackson	18.00	9.00	5.50
(78)	Johnson	18.00	9.00	5.50
(79)	Kane	18.00	9.00	5.50
(80)	Killilay	18.00	9.00	5.50
(81)	Klawitter	18.00	9.00	5.50
(82)	Knight	18.00	9.00	5.50
(83)	Koestner ("P" visible)	18.00	9.00	5.50
(84)	Koestner (no "P" visible)	18.00	9.00	5.50
(85)	Kreitz	18.00	9.00	5.50
(86)	Krueger	18.00	9.00	5.50
(87)	LaLonge	18.00	9.00	5.50
(88)	Leard	18.00	9.00	5.50
(89)	Leverenz	18.00	9.00	5.50
(90)	Lewis	18.00	9.00	5.50
(91)	Lindsay	18.00	9.00	5.50
(92)	Litschi	18.00	9.00	5.50
(93)	Lober	18.00	9.00	5.50
(94)	Madden	18.00	9.00	5.50
(95)	Mahoney	18.00	9.00	5.50
(96)	Malarkey	18.00	9.00	5.50
(97)	Martinoni	18.00	9.00	5.50
(98)	McArdle	18.00	9.00	5.50
(99)	McAvoy	18.00	9.00	5.50
(100)	McCorrey	18.00	9.00	5.50
(101)	McCredie	18.00	9.00	5.50
(102)	McDonald	18.00	9.00	5.50
(103)	McDowell	18.00	9.00	5.50
(104)	McIver	18.00	9.00	5.50
(105)	Meikle	18.00	9.00	5.50
(106)	Metzger	18.00	9.00	5.50
(107)	Miller (Sacramento)	18.00	9.00	5.50
(108)	Miller (San Francisco)	18.00	9.00	5.50
(109)	Mitze	18.00	9.00	5.50
(110)	Mohler	18.00	9.00	5.50
(111)	Moore	18.00	9.00	5.50
(112)	Mundorf (batting)	18.00	9.00	5.50
(113)	Mundorf (fielding)	18.00	9.00	5.50
(114)	Nagle	18.00	9.00	5.50
(115)	Noyes	18.00	9.00	5.50
(116)	O'Rourke	18.00	9.00	5.50
(117)	Olmstead	18.00	9.00	5.50
(118)	Orr	18.00	9.00	5.50
(119)	Page	18.00	9.00	5.50
(120)	Parkins	18.00	9.00	5.50
(121)	Patterson (Oakland)	18.00	9.00	5.50
(122)	Patterson (Vernon)	18.00	9.00	5.50
(123)	Pernol	18.00	9.00	5.50
(124)	Pope	18.00	9.00	5.50
(125)	Powell	18.00	9.00	5.50
(126)	Price	18.00	9.00	5.50
(127)	Raftery	18.00	9.00	5.50
(128)	Raleigh	18.00	9.00	5.50
(129)	Rapps ("P" visible)	18.00	9.00	5.50
(130)	Rapps (no "P" visible)	18.00	9.00	5.50
(131)	Reidy	18.00	9.00	5.50
(132)	Rodgers	18.00	9.00	5.50
(133)	Rohrer	18.00	9.00	5.50
(134)	Schmidt	18.00	9.00	5.50
(135)	Schwenk	18.00	9.00	5.50
(136)	Sharpe	18.00	9.00	5.50
(137)	Sheehan	18.00	9.00	5.50
(138)	Shinn	18.00	9.00	5.50
(139)	Slagle	18.00	9.00	5.50
(140)	Smith	18.00	9.00	5.50
(141)	Stewart	18.00	9.00	5.50
(142)	Stinson	18.00	9.00	5.50
(143)	Stone	18.00	9.00	5.50
(144)	Sullivan	18.00	9.00	5.50
(145)	Swain	18.00	9.00	5.50
(146)	Taylor	18.00	9.00	5.50
(147)	Temple	18.00	9.00	5.50
(148)	Tiedeman	18.00	9.00	5.50
(149)	Toner	18.00	9.00	5.50
(150)	Tozer	18.00	9.00	5.50
(151)	Van Buren	18.00	9.00	5.50
(152)	Wagner	18.00	9.00	5.50
(153)	Whalen	18.00	9.00	5.50
(154)	Williams (Sacramento)	18.00	9.00	5.50
(155)	Williams (San Francisco)	18.00	9.00	5.50
(156)	Joe Williams	18.00	9.00	5.50
(157)	Wuffli	18.00	9.00	5.50
(158)	Zacher	18.00	9.00	5.50
(159)	Zimmerman	18.00	9.00	5.50

1913 E136 Zeenut

The first year to include the coupon bottom, the 1913 Zeenuts measure 2" by 3-1/4" without the coupon. The sepia-toned photos are printed on a yellow background that contains the words "P.C. League/Season 1913." This series is the only Zeenut set printed prior to 1931 that does not have the words "Zeenut Series" on the front. The backs of the cards are blank.

		NR MT	EX	VG
Complete Set:		2700.00	1350.00	800.00
Common Player:		18.00	9.00	5.50

		NR MT	EX	VG
(1)	Abbott	18.00	9.00	5.50
(2)	Ables	18.00	9.00	5.50
(3)	Arelanes	18.00	9.00	5.50
(4)	Arlett	18.00	9.00	5.50
(5)	Baker	18.00	9.00	5.50
(6)	Baum	18.00	9.00	5.50
(7)	Bayless	18.00	9.00	5.50
(8)	Becker	18.00	9.00	5.50
(9)	Berry	18.00	9.00	5.50
(10)	Bliss	18.00	9.00	5.50
(11)	Boles	18.00	9.00	5.50
(12)	Brackenridge	18.00	9.00	5.50
(13)	Brashear	18.00	9.00	5.50
(14)	Brooks	18.00	9.00	5.50
(15)	Byrnes	18.00	9.00	5.50
(16)	Cadreau	18.00	9.00	5.50
(17)	Carlisle	18.00	9.00	5.50
(18)	Carson	18.00	9.00	5.50
(19)	Cartwright	18.00	9.00	5.50
(20)	Chadbourne	18.00	9.00	5.50
(21)	Charles	18.00	9.00	5.50
(22)	Cheek	18.00	9.00	5.50
(23)	Christian	18.00	9.00	5.50
(24)	Clarke	18.00	9.00	5.50
(25)	Clemons	18.00	9.00	5.50
(26)	Cook	18.00	9.00	5.50
(27)	Corhan	18.00	9.00	5.50
(28)	Coy	18.00	9.00	5.50
(29)	Crabb	18.00	9.00	5.50
(30)	Crisp	18.00	9.00	5.50
(31)	Derrick	18.00	9.00	5.50
(32)	DeCanniere	18.00	9.00	5.50
(33)	Dillon	18.00	9.00	5.50
(34)	Doane	18.00	9.00	5.50
(35)	Douglass	18.00	9.00	5.50
(36)	Downs	18.00	9.00	5.50
(37)	Driscoll	18.00	9.00	5.50
(38)	Drucke	18.00	9.00	5.50
(39)	Elliott	18.00	9.00	5.50
(40)	Ellis	18.00	9.00	5.50
(41)	Fanning	18.00	9.00	5.50
(42)	Fisher	18.00	9.00	5.50
(43)	Fitzgerald	18.00	9.00	5.50
(44)	Gardner	18.00	9.00	5.50
(45)	Gill	18.00	9.00	5.50
(46)	Goodwin	18.00	9.00	5.50
(47a)	Gregory (large pose)	18.00	9.00	5.50
(47b)	Gregory (small pose)	18.00	9.00	5.50
(48)	Grey	18.00	9.00	5.50
(49)	Guest	18.00	9.00	5.50
(50)	Hagerman	18.00	9.00	5.50
(51)	Halla	18.00	9.00	5.50
(52)	Hallinan	18.00	9.00	5.50
(53)	Heilmann	100.00	50.00	30.00
(54)	Henley	18.00	9.00	5.50
(55)	Hetling	18.00	9.00	5.50
(56)	Higginbotham	18.00	9.00	5.50
(57)	Hitt	18.00	9.00	5.50
(58)	Hoffman	18.00	9.00	5.50
(59)	Hogan (San Francisco)	18.00	9.00	5.50
(60)	Hogan (Vernon)	18.00	9.00	5.50
(61)	Hosp	18.00	9.00	5.50
(62)	Howard (Los Angeles)	18.00	9.00	5.50
(63)	Howard (San Francisco)	18.00	9.00	5.50
(64)	Hughes	18.00	9.00	5.50
(65)	Jackson	18.00	9.00	5.50
(66)	James	18.00	9.00	5.50
(67)	Johnson	18.00	9.00	5.50
(68)	Johnston	18.00	9.00	5.50
(69)	Kane	18.00	9.00	5.50
(70)	Kaylor	18.00	9.00	5.50
(71)	Kenworthy	18.00	9.00	5.50
(72)	Killilay	18.00	9.00	5.50
(73)	Klawitter	18.00	9.00	5.50
(74)	Koestner	18.00	9.00	5.50
(75)	Kores	18.00	9.00	5.50
(76)	Krapp	18.00	9.00	5.50
(77)	Kreitz	18.00	9.00	5.50
(78)	Krause	18.00	9.00	5.50
(79)	Krueger	18.00	9.00	5.50
(80)	Leard	18.00	9.00	5.50

		NR MT	EX	VG
(81)	Leifield	18.00	9.00	5.50
(82)	Lewis	18.00	9.00	5.50
(83)	Lindsay	18.00	9.00	5.50
(84)	Litschi	18.00	9.00	5.50
(85)	Lively	18.00	9.00	5.50
(86)	Lober	18.00	9.00	5.50
(87)	Lohman	18.00	9.00	5.50
(88)	Maggart	18.00	9.00	5.50
(89)	Malarky	18.00	9.00	5.50
(90)	McArdle	18.00	9.00	5.50
(91)	McCarl	18.00	9.00	5.50
(92)	McCormick	18.00	9.00	5.50
(93)	McCorry	18.00	9.00	5.50
(94)	McCredie	18.00	9.00	5.50
(95)	McDonnell	18.00	9.00	5.50
(96)	Meloan	18.00	9.00	5.50
(97)	Metzger	18.00	9.00	5.50
(98)	Miller	18.00	9.00	5.50
(99)	Mitze	18.00	9.00	5.50
(100)	Moore	18.00	9.00	5.50
(101)	Moran	18.00	9.00	5.50
(102)	Mundorf	18.00	9.00	5.50
(103)	Munsell	18.00	9.00	5.50
(104)	Ness	18.00	9.00	5.50
(105)	O'Rourke	18.00	9.00	5.50
(106)	Overall	18.00	9.00	5.50
(107)	Page	18.00	9.00	5.50
(108)	Parkin	18.00	9.00	5.50
(109)	Patterson	18.00	9.00	5.50
(110)	Pearce	18.00	9.00	5.50
(111)	Pernoll	18.00	9.00	5.50
(112)	Perritt	18.00	9.00	5.50
(113)	Pope	18.00	9.00	5.50
(114)	Pruitt	18.00	9.00	5.50
(115)	Raleigh	18.00	9.00	5.50
(116)	Reitmyer	18.00	9.00	5.50
(117)	Riordan	18.00	9.00	5.50
(118)	Rodgers	18.00	9.00	5.50
(119)	Rogers	18.00	9.00	5.50
(120)	Rohrer	18.00	9.00	5.50
(121)	Ryan	18.00	9.00	5.50
(122)	Schaller	18.00	9.00	5.50
(123)	Schirm	18.00	9.00	5.50
(124)	Schmidt	18.00	9.00	5.50
(125)	Schulz	18.00	9.00	5.50
(126)	Sepulveda	18.00	9.00	5.50
(127)	Shinn	18.00	9.00	5.50
(128)	Spenger	18.00	9.00	5.50
(129)	Stanley	18.00	9.00	5.50
(130)	Stanridge	18.00	9.00	5.50
(131)	Stark	18.00	9.00	5.50
(132)	Sterritt	18.00	9.00	5.50
(133)	Stroud	18.00	9.00	5.50
(134)	Tennant	18.00	9.00	5.50
(135)	Thomas	18.00	9.00	5.50
(136)	Todd	18.00	9.00	5.50
(137)	Tonneman	18.00	9.00	5.50
(138)	Tozer	18.00	9.00	5.50
(139)	Van Buren	18.00	9.00	5.50
(140)	Wagner	18.00	9.00	5.50
(141)	West	18.00	9.00	5.50
(142)	Williams	18.00	9.00	5.50
(143)	Wolverton	18.00	9.00	5.50
(144)	Wotell	18.00	9.00	5.50
(145)	Wuffli	18.00	9.00	5.50
(146)	Young	18.00	9.00	5.50
(147)	Zacher	18.00	9.00	5.50
(148)	Zimmerman	18.00	9.00	5.50

1914 E136 Zeenut

The 1914 Zeenut cards measure 2" by 3-1/2" without the coupon, and feature black and white photos on a gray, borderless background. To date, 146 different poses have been found. The backs are blank.

		NR MT	EX	VG
Complete Set:		2200.00	1100.00	700.00
Common Player:		15.00	7.50	4.50
(1)	Ables	15.00	7.50	4.50
(2)	Abstein	15.00	7.50	4.50
(3)	Alexander	15.00	7.50	4.50
(4)	Arbogast	15.00	7.50	4.50
(5)	Arlett	15.00	7.50	4.50
(6)	Arrelanes	15.00	7.50	4.50
(7)	Bancroft	75.00	38.00	23.00
(8)	Barham	15.00	7.50	4.50
(9)	Barrenkamp	15.00	7.50	4.50
(10)	Barton	15.00	7.50	4.50
(11)	Baum	15.00	7.50	4.50
(12)	Bayless	15.00	7.50	4.50
(13a)	Bliss (large pose)	15.00	7.50	4.50
(13b)	Bliss (small pose)	15.00	7.50	4.50
(14)	Boles	15.00	7.50	4.50
(15)	Borton	15.00	7.50	4.50
(16)	Brashear	15.00	7.50	4.50
(17)	Brenegan	15.00	7.50	4.50
(18)	Brooks	15.00	7.50	4.50
(19)	Brown	15.00	7.50	4.50
(20)	Butler	15.00	7.50	4.50
(21)	Calvo	15.00	7.50	4.50
(22)	Carlisle	15.00	7.50	4.50
(23)	Cartwright	15.00	7.50	4.50
(24)	Charles	15.00	7.50	4.50
(25)	Chech	15.00	7.50	4.50
(26)	Christian	15.00	7.50	4.50
(27)	Clarke	15.00	7.50	4.50
(28)	Colligan	15.00	7.50	4.50
(29)	Cook	15.00	7.50	4.50
(31)	Coy	15.00	7.50	4.50
(32)	Crabb	15.00	7.50	4.50
(33)	Davis	15.00	7.50	4.50
(34)	Derrick	15.00	7.50	4.50
(35)	Devlin	15.00	7.50	4.50
(36)	DeCannier	15.00	7.50	4.50
(37)	Dillon	15.00	7.50	4.50
(38)	Doane	15.00	7.50	4.50
(39)	Downs	15.00	7.50	4.50
(40)	Ehmke	12.00	6.00	3.50
(41)	Ellis	15.00	7.50	4.50
(42)	Evans	15.00	7.50	4.50
(43)	Fanning	15.00	7.50	4.50
(44)	Fisher	15.00	7.50	4.50
(45)	Fitzgerald	15.00	7.50	4.50
(46)	Fleharty	15.00	7.50	4.50
(47)	Frambach	15.00	7.50	4.50
(48)	Gardner	15.00	7.50	4.50
(49)	Gedeon	15.00	7.50	4.50
(50)	Geyer	15.00	7.50	4.50
(51)	Gianini	15.00	7.50	4.50
(52)	Gregory	15.00	7.50	4.50
(53)	Guest	15.00	7.50	4.50
(54)	Hallinan	15.00	7.50	4.50
(55)	Hannah	15.00	7.50	4.50
(56)	Harkness (batting)	15.00	7.50	4.50
(57)	Haworth (batting)	15.00	7.50	4.50
(58)	Haworth (catching)	15.00	7.50	4.50
(59)	Henderson	15.00	7.50	4.50
(60)	Henley	15.00	7.50	4.50
(61)	Hern	15.00	7.50	4.50
(62)	Hettling	15.00	7.50	4.50
(63)	Higginbotham	15.00	7.50	4.50
(64)	Hitt	15.00	7.50	4.50
(65)	Hogan	15.00	7.50	4.50
(66a)	Hosp (large pose)	15.00	7.50	4.50
(66b)	Hosp (small pose)	15.00	7.50	4.50
(67)	Howard	15.00	7.50	4.50
(68)	Hughes (Los Angeles)	15.00	7.50	4.50
(69)	Hughes (San Francisco)	15.00	7.50	4.50
(70)	Johnson	15.00	7.50	4.50
(71)	Kane	15.00	7.50	4.50
(72)	Kaylor	15.00	7.50	4.50
(73)	Killilay	15.00	7.50	4.50
(74)	Klawitter	15.00	7.50	4.50
(75)	Klepfler	15.00	7.50	4.50
(76)	Kores	15.00	7.50	4.50
(77)	Kramer	15.00	7.50	4.50
(78)	Krause	15.00	7.50	4.50
(79a)	Leard (large pose)	15.00	7.50	4.50
(79b)	Leard (small pose)	15.00	7.50	4.50

		NR MT	EX	VG
(80)	Liefeld	15.00	7.50	4.50
(81)	Litschi	15.00	7.50	4.50
(82)	Lober	15.00	7.50	4.50
(83)	Loomis	15.00	7.50	4.50
(84)	Love	15.00	7.50	4.50
(85)	Lynn	15.00	7.50	4.50
(86)	Maggart	15.00	7.50	4.50
(87)	Malarkey	15.00	7.50	4.50
(88)	Martinoni	15.00	7.50	4.50
(89)	McArdle	15.00	7.50	4.50
(90)	McCredie	15.00	7.50	4.50
(91)	McDonald	15.00	7.50	4.50
(92)	Meek	15.00	7.50	4.50
(93)	Meloan	15.00	7.50	4.50
(94)	Menges	15.00	7.50	4.50
(95)	Metzger	15.00	7.50	4.50
(96)	Middleton	15.00	7.50	4.50
(97)	Mitze	15.00	7.50	4.50
(98)	Mohler	15.00	7.50	4.50
(99)	Moore	15.00	7.50	4.50
(100)	Moran	15.00	7.50	4.50
(101)	Mundorf	15.00	7.50	4.50
(102)	Murphy	15.00	7.50	4.50
(103)	Musser	15.00	7.50	4.50
(104)	Ness	15.00	7.50	4.50
(105)	O'Leary	15.00	7.50	4.50
(106)	Orr	15.00	7.50	4.50
(107)	Page	15.00	7.50	4.50
(108)	Pape	15.00	7.50	4.50
(109)	Parkin	15.00	7.50	4.50
(110a)	Peet (large pose)	15.00	7.50	4.50
(110b)	Peet (small pose)	15.00	7.50	4.50
(111)	Perkins	15.00	7.50	4.50
(112)	Pernoll	15.00	7.50	4.50
(113)	Perritt	15.00	7.50	4.50
(114)	Powell	15.00	7.50	4.50
(115)	Prough	15.00	7.50	4.50
(116)	Pruiett	15.00	7.50	4.50
(117)	Quinlan	15.00	7.50	4.50
(118a)	Raney (incorrect spelling)	15.00	7.50	4.50
(118b)	Ramey (correct spelling)	15.00	7.50	4.50
(119)	Rieger	15.00	7.50	4.50
(120)	Rodgers	15.00	7.50	4.50
(121)	Rogers	15.00	7.50	4.50
(122)	Rohrer	15.00	7.50	4.50
(123)	Ryan	15.00	7.50	4.50
(124)	Ryan	15.00	7.50	4.50
(125)	Sawyer	15.00	7.50	4.50
(126)	Schaller	15.00	7.50	4.50
(127)	Schmidt	15.00	7.50	4.50
(128)	Sepulveda	15.00	7.50	4.50
(129)	Shinn	15.00	7.50	4.50
(130)	Slagle	15.00	7.50	4.50
(131)	Speas	15.00	7.50	4.50
(132)	Stanridge	15.00	7.50	4.50
(133)	Stroud	15.00	7.50	4.50
(134)	Tennant	15.00	7.50	4.50
(135)	Tobin	15.00	7.50	4.50
(136)	Tozer	15.00	7.50	4.50
(137)	Van Buren	15.00	7.50	4.50
(138)	West	15.00	7.50	4.50
(139)	White	15.00	7.50	4.50
(140)	Wolter	15.00	7.50	4.50
(141)	Wolverton	15.00	7.50	4.50
(142)	Yantz	15.00	7.50	4.50
(143)	Young	15.00	7.50	4.50
(144)	Zacher	15.00	7.50	4.50
(145)	Zumwalt	15.00	7.50	4.50

1915 E137 Zeenut

The 1915 Zeenut cards are dated on the front, making identification very easy. They measure 2" 3-1/8" without the coupon and feature a black and white photo on a light background. To date 141 different cards are known to exist. This year is among the toughest of all Zeenuts to find.

		NR MT	EX	VG
	Complete Set:	2600.00	1300.00	775.00
	Common Player:	18.00	9.00	5.50
(1)	Ables	18.00	9.00	5.50
(2)	Abstein	18.00	9.00	5.50
(3)	Alcock	18.00	9.00	5.50
(4)	Arbogast	18.00	9.00	5.50
(5)	Baerwald	18.00	9.00	5.50
(6)	Barbour	18.00	9.00	5.50
(7)	Bates	18.00	9.00	5.50
(8)	Baum	18.00	9.00	5.50
(9)	Bayless	18.00	9.00	5.50
(10)	Beatty	18.00	9.00	5.50
(11)	Beer	18.00	9.00	5.50
(12)	Benham	18.00	9.00	5.50
(13)	Berger	18.00	9.00	5.50
(14)	Beumiller	18.00	9.00	5.50
(15)	Blankenship	18.00	9.00	5.50
(16)	Block	18.00	9.00	5.50
(17)	Bodie	25.00	12.50	7.50
(18)	Boles	18.00	9.00	5.50
(19)	Boyd	18.00	9.00	5.50
(20)	Bromley	18.00	9.00	5.50
(21)	Brown	18.00	9.00	5.50
(22)	Burns	18.00	9.00	5.50
(23)	Carlisle	18.00	9.00	5.50
(24)	Carrisch	18.00	9.00	5.50
(25)	Charles	18.00	9.00	5.50
(26)	Chech	18.00	9.00	5.50
(27)	Christian	18.00	9.00	5.50
(28)	Clarke	18.00	9.00	5.50
(29)	Couch	18.00	9.00	5.50
(30)	Covaleski (Coveleski)	40.00	20.00	12.00
(31)	Daniels	18.00	9.00	5.50
(32)	Davis	18.00	9.00	5.50
(33)	DeCanniere	18.00	9.00	5.50
(34)	Dent	18.00	9.00	5.50
(35)	Derrick	18.00	9.00	5.50
(36)	Dillon	18.00	9.00	5.50
(37)	Doane	18.00	9.00	5.50
(38)	Downs	18.00	9.00	5.50
(39)	Elliott	18.00	9.00	5.50
(40)	F. Elliott	18.00	9.00	5.50
(41)	Ellis	18.00	9.00	5.50
(42)	Evans	18.00	9.00	5.50
(43)	Fanning	18.00	9.00	5.50
(44)	Faye	18.00	9.00	5.50
(45)	Fisher	18.00	9.00	5.50
(46)	Fittery	18.00	9.00	5.50
(47)	Fitzgerald	18.00	9.00	5.50
(48)	Fromme	18.00	9.00	5.50
(49)	Gardiner	18.00	9.00	5.50
(50)	Gedeon	18.00	9.00	5.50
(51)	Gleischmann	18.00	9.00	5.50
(52)	Gregory	18.00	9.00	5.50
(53)	Guest	18.00	9.00	5.50
(54)	Hall	18.00	9.00	5.50
(55)	Halla	18.00	9.00	5.50
(56)	Hallinan	18.00	9.00	5.50
(57)	Hannah	18.00	9.00	5.50
(58)	Harper	18.00	9.00	5.50
(59)	Heilmann	75.00	38.00	23.00
(60)	Henley	18.00	9.00	5.50
(61)	Hetling	18.00	9.00	5.50
(62)	Higginbotham	18.00	9.00	5.50
(63)	Hilliard	18.00	9.00	5.50
(64)	Hitt (winding up)	18.00	9.00	5.50
(65)	Hitt (throwing)	18.00	9.00	5.50
(66)	Hogan	18.00	9.00	5.50
(67)	Hosp	18.00	9.00	5.50
(68)	Howard	18.00	9.00	5.50
(69)	Hughes	18.00	9.00	5.50
(70)	Johnson	18.00	9.00	5.50
(71)	Jones	18.00	9.00	5.50
(72)	Kahler	18.00	9.00	5.50
(73)	Kane	18.00	9.00	5.50
(74)	Karr	18.00	9.00	5.50
(75)	Killilay	18.00	9.00	5.50
(76)	Klawitter	18.00	9.00	5.50
(77)	Koerner	18.00	9.00	5.50
(78)	Krause	18.00	9.00	5.50
(79)	Kuhn	18.00	9.00	5.50
(80)	LaRoy	18.00	9.00	5.50

		NR MT	EX	VG
(81)	Leard	18.00	9.00	5.50
(82)	Lindsay	18.00	9.00	5.50
(83)	Litschi	18.00	9.00	5.50
(84)	Lober	18.00	9.00	5.50
(85)	Love	18.00	9.00	5.50
(86)	Lush	18.00	9.00	5.50
(87)	Maggart	18.00	9.00	5.50
(88)	Malarkey	18.00	9.00	5.50
(89)	Manda	18.00	9.00	5.50
(90)	Marcan	18.00	9.00	5.50
(91)	Martinoni	18.00	9.00	5.50
(92)	McAvoy	18.00	9.00	5.50
(93)	McCredie	18.00	9.00	5.50
(94)	McDonell	18.00	9.00	5.50
(95)	McMullen	75.00	38.00	23.00
(96)	Meek	18.00	9.00	5.50
(97)	Meloan	18.00	9.00	5.50
(98)	Metzger	18.00	9.00	5.50
(99)	Middleton	18.00	9.00	5.50
(100)	Mitchell	18.00	9.00	5.50
(101)	Mitze	18.00	9.00	5.50
(102)	Morgan	18.00	9.00	5.50
(103)	Mundorff	18.00	9.00	5.50
(104)	Murphy	18.00	9.00	5.50
(105)	Ness	18.00	9.00	5.50
(106)	Nutt	18.00	9.00	5.50
(107)	Orr	18.00	9.00	5.50
(108)	Pernoll	18.00	9.00	5.50
(109)	Perritt	18.00	9.00	5.50
(110)	Piercey	18.00	9.00	5.50
(111)	Price	18.00	9.00	5.50
(112)	Prough	18.00	9.00	5.50
(113)	Prueitt	18.00	9.00	5.50
(114)	Purtell	18.00	9.00	5.50
(115)	Reed	18.00	9.00	5.50
(116)	Reisigl	18.00	9.00	5.50
(117)	Remneas	18.00	9.00	5.50
(118)	Risberg	75.00	38.00	23.00
(119)	Rohrer	18.00	9.00	5.50
(120)	Russell	18.00	9.00	5.50
(121)	Ryan (Los Angeles)	18.00	9.00	5.50
(122)	Ryan	18.00	9.00	5.50
(123)	Schaller	18.00	9.00	5.50
(124)	Schmidt	18.00	9.00	5.50
(125)	Scoggins	18.00	9.00	5.50
(126)	Sepulveda	18.00	9.00	5.50
(127)	Shinn	18.00	9.00	5.50
(128)	Smith	18.00	9.00	5.50
(129)	Speas	18.00	9.00	5.50
(130)	Spencer	18.00	9.00	5.50
(132)	Tennant	18.00	9.00	5.50
(133)	Terry	18.00	9.00	5.50
(134)	Tobin	18.00	9.00	5.50
(135)	West	18.00	9.00	5.50
(136)	White	18.00	9.00	5.50
(137)	C. Williams	75.00	38.00	23.00
(138)	J. Williams	18.00	9.00	5.50
(139)	Wolter	18.00	9.00	5.50
(140)	Wolverton	18.00	9.00	5.50
(141)	Zacher	18.00	9.00	5.50

1916 E137 Zeenut

The 1916 Zeenuts measure 2" by 3-1/8" without the coupon and are dated on the front (some cards were misdated 1916, however). The card fronts feature black and white photos on a blue background. There are 144 known subjects. The 1916 series was among the more difficult.

		NR MT	EX	VG
Complete Set:		2200.00	1100.00	625.00
Common Player:		15.00	7.50	4.50
(1)	Autrey	15.00	7.50	4.50
(2)	Barbeau	15.00	7.50	4.50
(3)	Barry	15.00	7.50	4.50
(4)	Bassler	15.00	7.50	4.50
(5)	Bates	15.00	7.50	4.50
(6)	Baum	15.00	7.50	4.50
(7)	Bayless	15.00	7.50	4.50
(8)	Beer	15.00	7.50	4.50
(9)	Berg	15.00	7.50	4.50
(10)	Berger	15.00	7.50	4.50
(11)	Blankenship	15.00	7.50	4.50
(12)	Block	15.00	7.50	4.50
(13)	Bodie	20.00	10.00	6.00
(14)	Bohne	15.00	7.50	4.50
(15)	Boles	15.00	7.50	4.50
(16)	Boyd	15.00	7.50	4.50
(17)	Brief	15.00	7.50	4.50
(18)	Brooks	15.00	7.50	4.50
(19)	Brown	15.00	7.50	4.50
(20)	Butler	15.00	7.50	4.50
(21)	Callahan	15.00	7.50	4.50
(22)	Carrisch	15.00	7.50	4.50
(23)	Chance	75.00	38.00	23.00
(24)	Claxton	100.00	50.00	30.00
(25)	Coffey	15.00	7.50	4.50
(26)	Cook	15.00	7.50	4.50
(27)	Corbett	15.00	7.50	4.50
(28)	Couch	15.00	7.50	4.50
(29)	Crandall	15.00	7.50	4.50
(30)	Dalton	15.00	7.50	4.50
(31)	Davis	15.00	7.50	4.50
(32)	Derrick	15.00	7.50	4.50
(33)	Doane	15.00	7.50	4.50
(34)	Downs	15.00	7.50	4.50
(35)	Dugan	15.00	7.50	4.50
(36)	Eldred	15.00	7.50	4.50
(37)	F. Elliott	15.00	7.50	4.50
(38)	H. Elliott	15.00	7.50	4.50
(39)	Ellis	15.00	7.50	4.50
(40)	Erickson	15.00	7.50	4.50
(41)	Fanning	15.00	7.50	4.50
(42)	Fisher	15.00	7.50	4.50
(43)	Fittery	15.00	7.50	4.50
(44)	Fitzgerald	15.00	7.50	4.50
(45)	Fromme	15.00	7.50	4.50
(46)	Galloway	15.00	7.50	4.50
(47)	Gardner	15.00	7.50	4.50
(48)	Gay	15.00	7.50	4.50
(49)	Gleischmann	15.00	7.50	4.50
(50)	Griffith	15.00	7.50	4.50
(51)	Griggs	15.00	7.50	4.50
(52)	Guisto	15.00	7.50	4.50
(53)	Hagerman	15.00	7.50	4.50
(54)	Hall	15.00	7.50	4.50
(55)	Hallinan	15.00	7.50	4.50
(56)	Hannah	15.00	7.50	4.50
(57)	Harstadt	15.00	7.50	4.50
(58)	Haworth	15.00	7.50	4.50
(59)	Hess	15.00	7.50	4.50
(60)	Higginbotham	15.00	7.50	4.50
(61)	Hitt	15.00	7.50	4.50
(62)	Hogg	15.00	7.50	4.50
(63)	Hollocher	15.00	7.50	4.50
(64)	Horstman	15.00	7.50	4.50
(65)	Houck	15.00	7.50	4.50
(66)	Howard	15.00	7.50	4.50
(67)	Hughes	15.00	7.50	4.50
(68)	E. Johnston	15.00	7.50	4.50
(69)	G. Johnston	15.00	7.50	4.50
(70)	Jones	15.00	7.50	4.50
(71)	Kahler	15.00	7.50	4.50
(72)	Kane	15.00	7.50	4.50
(73)	Kelly	15.00	7.50	4.50
(74)	Kenworthy	15.00	7.50	4.50
(75)	Klawitter	15.00	7.50	4.50
(76)	Klein	15.00	7.50	4.50
(77)	Koerner	15.00	7.50	4.50
(78)	Krause	15.00	7.50	4.50
(79)	Kuhn	15.00	7.50	4.50
(80)	Lane	15.00	7.50	4.50
(81)	Larsen	15.00	7.50	4.50
(82)	Lush	15.00	7.50	4.50
(83)	Machold	15.00	7.50	4.50
(84)	Maggert	15.00	7.50	4.50
(85)	Manser	15.00	7.50	4.50
(86)	Martin	15.00	7.50	4.50
(87)	Mattick	15.00	7.50	4.50
(88)	McCredie	15.00	7.50	4.50

		NR MT	EX	VG
(89)	McGaffigan	15.00	7.50	4.50
(90)	McLarry	15.00	7.50	4.50
(91)	Menges	15.00	7.50	4.50
(92)	Middleton	15.00	7.50	4.50
(93)	Mitchell	15.00	7.50	4.50
(94)	Mitze	15.00	7.50	4.50
(95)	Munsell	15.00	7.50	4.50
(96)	Murphy	15.00	7.50	4.50
(97)	Nixon	15.00	7.50	4.50
(98)	Noyes	15.00	7.50	4.50
(99)	Nutt	15.00	7.50	4.50
(100)	O'Brien	15.00	7.50	4.50
(101)	Oldham	15.00	7.50	4.50
(102)	Orr	15.00	7.50	4.50
(103)	Patterson	15.00	7.50	4.50
(104)	Perritt	15.00	7.50	4.50
(105)	Prough	15.00	7.50	4.50
(106)	Prueitt	15.00	7.50	4.50
(107)	Quinlan	15.00	7.50	4.50
(108)	Quinn (Portland)	15.00	7.50	4.50
(109)	Quinn (Vernon)	15.00	7.50	4.50
(110)	Rader	15.00	7.50	4.50
(111)	Randall	15.00	7.50	4.50
(112)	Rath	15.00	7.50	4.50
(113)	Reisegl	15.00	7.50	4.50
(114)	Reuther	15.00	7.50	4.50
(115)	Risberg	75.00	38.00	23.00
(116)	Roche	15.00	7.50	4.50
(117)	Ryan	15.00	7.50	4.50
(118)	Ryan	15.00	7.50	4.50
(119)	Scoggins	15.00	7.50	4.50
(120)	Sepulveda	15.00	7.50	4.50
(121)	Schaller	15.00	7.50	4.50
(122)	Sheehan	15.00	7.50	4.50
(123)	Shinn	15.00	7.50	4.50
(124)	Smith	15.00	7.50	4.50
(125)	Sothoron	15.00	7.50	4.50
(126)	Southworth	15.00	7.50	4.50
(127)	Speas	15.00	7.50	4.50
(128)	Spencer	15.00	7.50	4.50
(129)	Standridge	15.00	7.50	4.50
(130)	Steen	15.00	7.50	4.50
(131)	Stumpf	15.00	7.50	4.50
(132)	Vann	15.00	7.50	4.50
(133)	Vaughn	15.00	7.50	4.50
(134)	Ward	15.00	7.50	4.50
(135)	Whalling	15.00	7.50	4.50
(136)	Wilie	15.00	7.50	4.50
(137)	Williams	15.00	7.50	4.50
(138)	Wolverton	15.00	7.50	4.50
(139)	Wuffli	15.00	7.50	4.50
(140)	Zabel	15.00	7.50	4.50
(141)	Zacher	15.00	7.50	4.50
(142)	Zimmerman	15.00	7.50	4.50

1917 E137 Zeenut

The 1917 Zeenuts measure 1-3/4" by 3-1/2" and feature black and white photos on a light background. They are dated on the front and have blank backs. An advertising poster has been found listing 119 players (two pose variations brings the total to 121), but to date, six players on the list have not been found.

		NR MT	EX	VG
Complete Set:		1800.00	900.00	550.00
Common Player:		15.00	7.50	4.50

		NR MT	EX	VG
(1)	Arlett	15.00	7.50	4.50
(2)	Arrelanes	15.00	7.50	4.50
(3)	Baker (catching)	15.00	7.50	4.50
(4)	Baker (throwing)	15.00	7.50	4.50
(5)	Baldwin	15.00	7.50	4.50
(6)	Bassler	15.00	7.50	4.50
(7)	Baum	15.00	7.50	4.50
(8)	Beer	15.00	7.50	4.50
(9)	Bernhard	15.00	7.50	4.50
(10)	Bliss	15.00	7.50	4.50
(11)	Boles	15.00	7.50	4.50
(12)	Brenton	15.00	7.50	4.50
(13)	Brief	15.00	7.50	4.50
(14)	Brown	15.00	7.50	4.50
(15)	Burns	15.00	7.50	4.50
(16)	Callahan	15.00	7.50	4.50
(17)	Callan	15.00	7.50	4.50
(18)	Calvo	15.00	7.50	4.50
(19)	Chadbourne	15.00	7.50	4.50
(20)	Chance	75.00	38.00	23.00
(21)	Coltrin	15.00	7.50	4.50
(22)	Connifer	15.00	7.50	4.50
(23)	Corhan	15.00	7.50	4.50
(24)	Crandall (Los Angeles)	15.00	7.50	4.50
(25)	Crandall (Salt Lake)	15.00	7.50	4.50
(26)	Cress	15.00	7.50	4.50
(27)	Davis	15.00	7.50	4.50
(28)	DeCanniere	15.00	7.50	4.50
(29)	Doane	15.00	7.50	4.50
(30)	Dougan	15.00	7.50	4.50
(31)	Dougherty	15.00	7.50	4.50
(32)	Downs	15.00	7.50	4.50
(33)	Dubuc	15.00	7.50	4.50
(34)	Ellis	15.00	7.50	4.50
(35)	Erickson	15.00	7.50	4.50
(36)	Evans	15.00	7.50	4.50
(37)	Farmer	15.00	7.50	4.50
(38)	Fincher	15.00	7.50	4.50
(39)	Fisher	15.00	7.50	4.50
(40)	Fitzgerald	15.00	7.50	4.50
(41)	Fournier	15.00	7.50	4.50
(42)	Fromme	15.00	7.50	4.50
(43)	Galloway	15.00	7.50	4.50
(44)	Gislason	15.00	7.50	4.50
(45)	Goodbred	15.00	7.50	4.50
(46)	Griggs	15.00	7.50	4.50
(47)	Groehling	15.00	7.50	4.50
(48)	Hall (Los Angeles)	15.00	7.50	4.50
(49)	Hall (San Francisco)	15.00	7.50	4.50
(50)	Hannah	15.00	7.50	4.50
(51)	Harstad	15.00	7.50	4.50
(52)	Helfrich	15.00	7.50	4.50
(53)	Hess	15.00	7.50	4.50
(54)	Hitt	15.00	7.50	4.50
(55)	Hoff	15.00	7.50	4.50
(56)	Hollacher	15.00	7.50	4.50
(57)	Hollywood	15.00	7.50	4.50
(58)	Houck	15.00	7.50	4.50
(59)	Howard	15.00	7.50	4.50
(60)	Hughes	15.00	7.50	4.50
(61)	Johnson	15.00	7.50	4.50
(62)	Kilhullen	15.00	7.50	4.50
(63)	Killiffer	15.00	7.50	4.50
(64)	Koerner	15.00	7.50	4.50
(65)	Krause	15.00	7.50	4.50
(66)	Lane	15.00	7.50	4.50
(67)	Lapan	15.00	7.50	4.50
(68)	Leake	15.00	7.50	4.50
(69)	Lee	15.00	7.50	4.50
(70)	Leverenz	15.00	7.50	4.50
(71)	Maggert	15.00	7.50	4.50
(72)	Maisel	15.00	7.50	4.50
(73)	Mattick	15.00	7.50	4.50
(74)	McCreedie	15.00	7.50	4.50
(75)	McLarry	15.00	7.50	4.50
(76)	Mensor	15.00	7.50	4.50
(77)	Meusel	12.00	6.00	3.50
(78)	Middleton	15.00	7.50	4.50
(79)	Miller (batting)	15.00	7.50	4.50
(80)	Miller (throwing)	15.00	7.50	4.50
(81)	Mitchell	15.00	7.50	4.50
(82)	Mitze	15.00	7.50	4.50
(83)	Murphy	15.00	7.50	4.50
(84)	Murray	15.00	7.50	4.50
(85)	O'Brien	15.00	7.50	4.50
(86)	O'Mara	15.00	7.50	4.50
(87)	Oldham	15.00	7.50	4.50
(88)	Orr	15.00	7.50	4.50
(89)	Penelli	15.00	7.50	4.50
(90)	Penner	15.00	7.50	4.50
(91)	Pick	15.00	7.50	4.50

		NR MT	EX	VG
(92)	Prough	15.00	7.50	4.50
(93)	Pruiett	15.00	7.50	4.50
(94)	Quinlan	15.00	7.50	4.50
(95)	Quinn	15.00	7.50	4.50
(96)	Rath	15.00	7.50	4.50
(97)	Roche	15.00	7.50	4.50
(98)	Ryan (Los Angeles)	15.00	7.50	4.50
(99)	Ryan (Salt Lake)	15.00	7.50	4.50
(100)	Schaller	15.00	7.50	4.50
(101)	Schinkle	15.00	7.50	4.50
(102)	Schultz	15.00	7.50	4.50
(103)	Sheehan	15.00	7.50	4.50
(104)	Sheeley	15.00	7.50	4.50
(105)	Shinn	15.00	7.50	4.50
(106)	Siglin	15.00	7.50	4.50
(107)	Simon	15.00	7.50	4.50
(108)	Smith	15.00	7.50	4.50
(109)	Snyder	15.00	7.50	4.50
(110)	Stanridge	15.00	7.50	4.50
(111)	Steen	15.00	7.50	4.50
(112)	Stovall	15.00	7.50	4.50
(113)	Stumpf	15.00	7.50	4.50
(114)	Sullivan	15.00	7.50	4.50
(115)	Terry	15.00	7.50	4.50
(116)	Tobin	15.00	7.50	4.50
(117)	Valencia	15.00	7.50	4.50
(118)	Vaughn	15.00	7.50	4.50
(119)	Whalling	15.00	7.50	4.50
(120)	Wilie	15.00	7.50	4.50
(121)	Wolverton	15.00	7.50	4.50

1918 E137 Zeenut

The 1918 Zeenuts are among the most distinctive because of their red borders surrounding the photos. They measure 1-3/4" by 3-1/8" and are among the more difficult years to find.

		NR MT	EX	VG
Complete Set:		2000.00	1000.00	600.00
Common Player:		18.00	9.00	5.50
(1)	Alcock	18.00	9.00	5.50
(2)	Arkenburg	18.00	9.00	5.50
(3)	A. Arlett	18.00	9.00	5.50
(4)	Baum	18.00	9.00	5.50
(5)	Boles	18.00	9.00	5.50
(6)	Borton	18.00	9.00	5.50
(7)	Brenton	18.00	9.00	5.50
(8)	Bromley	18.00	9.00	5.50
(9)	Brooks	18.00	9.00	5.50
(10)	Brown	18.00	9.00	5.50
(11)	Caldera	18.00	9.00	5.50
(12)	Camm	18.00	9.00	5.50
(13)	Chadbourne	18.00	9.00	5.50
(14)	Chappell	18.00	9.00	5.50
(15)	Codington	18.00	9.00	5.50
(16)	Conwright	18.00	9.00	5.50
(17)	Cooper	18.00	9.00	5.50
(18)	Cox	18.00	9.00	5.50
(19)	Crandall (Los Angeles)	18.00	9.00	5.50
(20)	Crandall (Salt Lake)	18.00	9.00	5.50
(21)	Crawford	18.00	9.00	5.50
(22)	Croll	18.00	9.00	5.50
(23)	Davis	18.00	9.00	5.50
(24)	DeVormer	18.00	9.00	5.50
(25)	Dobbs	18.00	9.00	5.50
(26)	Downs	18.00	9.00	5.50

		NR MT	EX	VG
(27)	Dubuc	18.00	9.00	5.50
(28)	Dunn	18.00	9.00	5.50
(29)	Easterly	18.00	9.00	5.50
(30)	Eldred	18.00	9.00	5.50
(31)	Elliot	18.00	9.00	5.50
(32)	Ellis	18.00	9.00	5.50
(33)	Essick	18.00	9.00	5.50
(34)	Farmer	18.00	9.00	5.50
(35)	Fisher	18.00	9.00	5.50
(36)	Fittery	18.00	9.00	5.50
(37)	Forsythe	18.00	9.00	5.50
(38)	Fournier	18.00	9.00	5.50
(39)	Fromme	18.00	9.00	5.50
(40)	Gardner (Oakland)	18.00	9.00	5.50
(41)	Gardner (Sacramento)	18.00	9.00	5.50
(42)	Goldie	18.00	9.00	5.50
(43)	Griggs	18.00	9.00	5.50
(44)	Hawkes	18.00	9.00	5.50
(45)	Hollander	18.00	9.00	5.50
(46)	Hosp	18.00	9.00	5.50
(47)	Howard	18.00	9.00	5.50
(48)	Hummel	18.00	9.00	5.50
(49)	Hunter	18.00	9.00	5.50
(50)	Johnson	18.00	9.00	5.50
(51)	G. Johnson	18.00	9.00	5.50
(52)	Kantlehner	18.00	9.00	5.50
(53)	Killefer	18.00	9.00	5.50
(54)	Koerner	18.00	9.00	5.50
(55)	Konnick	18.00	9.00	5.50
(56)	Kremer	18.00	9.00	5.50
(57)	Lapan	18.00	9.00	5.50
(58)	Leake	18.00	9.00	5.50
(59)	Leathers	18.00	9.00	5.50
(60)	Leifer	18.00	9.00	5.50
(61)	Leverenz	18.00	9.00	5.50
(62)	Llewlyn	18.00	9.00	5.50
(63)	Martin	18.00	9.00	5.50
(64)	McCabe	18.00	9.00	5.50
(65)	McCredie	18.00	9.00	5.50
(66)	McKee	18.00	9.00	5.50
(67)	McNulty	18.00	9.00	5.50
(68)	Mensor	18.00	9.00	5.50
(69)	Middleton	18.00	9.00	5.50
(70)	Miller (Oakland)	18.00	9.00	5.50
(71)	Miller (Salt Lake)	18.00	9.00	5.50
(72)	J. Mitchell	18.00	9.00	5.50
(73)	R. Mitchell	18.00	9.00	5.50
(74)	Mitze	18.00	9.00	5.50
(75)	Moore	18.00	9.00	5.50
(76)	Morton	18.00	9.00	5.50
(77)	Murray	18.00	9.00	5.50
(78)	O'Doul	75.00	38.00	23.00
(79)	Orr	18.00	9.00	5.50
(80)	Pepe	18.00	9.00	5.50
(81)	Pertica	18.00	9.00	5.50
(82)	Phillips	18.00	9.00	5.50
(83)	Pick	18.00	9.00	5.50
(84)	Pinelli	35.00	17.50	10.50
(85)	Prentice	18.00	9.00	5.50
(86)	Prough	18.00	9.00	5.50
(87)	Quinlan	18.00	9.00	5.50
(88)	Ritchie	18.00	9.00	5.50
(89)	Rogers	18.00	9.00	5.50
(90)	Ryan	18.00	9.00	5.50
(91)	Sand	18.00	9.00	5.50
(92)	Shader	18.00	9.00	5.50
(93)	Sheely	18.00	9.00	5.50
(94)	Siglin	18.00	9.00	5.50
(95)	Smale	18.00	9.00	5.50
(96)	Smith	18.00	9.00	5.50
(97)	Smith	18.00	9.00	5.50
(98)	Stanbridge	18.00	9.00	5.50
(99)	Terry	18.00	9.00	5.50
(100)	Valencia	18.00	9.00	5.50
(101)	West	18.00	9.00	5.50
(102)	Wilie	18.00	9.00	5.50
(103)	Williams	18.00	9.00	5.50
(104)	Wisterzill	18.00	9.00	5.50

1919 E137 Zeenut

The 1919-1921 Zeenuts cards were dated on the front and measure 1-3/4" by 3-1/8". They featured borderless, sepia-toned photos. To date, 144 subjects exist in the 1919 series; 151 have been found for 1920; and 168 different subjects have been discovered for 1921 (even though a promotional flier indicates 180 players).

		NR MT	EX	VG
Complete Set:		1450.00	725.00	425.00
Common Player:		10.00	5.00	3.00
(1)	Ally	10.00	5.00	3.00
(2)	Fatty Arbuckle	60.00	30.00	18.00
(3)	A. Arlett	10.00	5.00	3.00
(4)	R. Arlett	10.00	5.00	3.00
(5)	Baker	10.00	5.00	3.00
(6)	Baldwin	10.00	5.00	3.00
(7)	Baum	10.00	5.00	3.00
(8)	Beck	10.00	5.00	3.00
(9)	Bigbee	10.00	5.00	3.00
(10)	Blue	10.00	5.00	3.00
(11)	Bohne	10.00	5.00	3.00
(12)	Boles	10.00	5.00	3.00
(13)	Borton	10.00	5.00	3.00
(14)	Bowman	10.00	5.00	3.00
(15)	Brooks	10.00	5.00	3.00
(16)	Brown	10.00	5.00	3.00
(17)	Byler	10.00	5.00	3.00
(18)	Caldera	10.00	5.00	3.00
(19)	Cavaney	10.00	5.00	3.00
(20)	Chadbourne	10.00	5.00	3.00
(21)	Chech	10.00	5.00	3.00
(22)	Church	10.00	5.00	3.00
(23)	Clymer	10.00	5.00	3.00
(24)	Coleman	10.00	5.00	3.00
(25)	Compton	10.00	5.00	3.00
(26)	Conkwright	10.00	5.00	3.00
(27)	Connolly	10.00	5.00	3.00
(28)	Cook	10.00	5.00	3.00
(29)	Cooper (Los Angeles)	10.00	5.00	3.00
(30)	Cooper (Oakland)	10.00	5.00	3.00
(31)	Cooper (Portland)	10.00	5.00	3.00
(32)	Corhan	10.00	5.00	3.00
(33)	Couch	10.00	5.00	3.00
(34)	Cox	10.00	5.00	3.00
(35)	Crandall (Los Angeles)	10.00	5.00	3.00
(36)	Crandall (San Francisco)	10.00	5.00	3.00
(37)	Crespi	10.00	5.00	3.00
(38)	Croll	10.00	5.00	3.00
(39)	Cunningham	10.00	5.00	3.00
(40)	Dawson	10.00	5.00	3.00
(41)	Dell	10.00	5.00	3.00
(42)	DeVormer	10.00	5.00	3.00
(43)	Driscoll	10.00	5.00	3.00
(44)	Eastley	10.00	5.00	3.00
(45)	Edington	10.00	5.00	3.00
(46)	Eldred	10.00	5.00	3.00
(47)	Elliott	10.00	5.00	3.00
(48)	Ellis	10.00	5.00	3.00
(49)	Essick	10.00	5.00	3.00
(50)	Fabrique	10.00	5.00	3.00
(51)	Falkenberg	10.00	5.00	3.00
(52)	Fallentine	10.00	5.00	3.00
(53)	Finneran	10.00	5.00	3.00
(54)	Fisher (Sacramento)	10.00	5.00	3.00
(55)	Fisher (Vernon)	10.00	5.00	3.00
(56)	Fitzgerald	10.00	5.00	3.00
(57)	Flannigan	10.00	5.00	3.00
(58)	Fournier	10.00	5.00	3.00
(59)	French	10.00	5.00	3.00
(60)	Fromme	10.00	5.00	3.00
(61)	Gibson	10.00	5.00	3.00
(62)	Griggs	10.00	5.00	3.00
(63)	Haney	9.00	4.50	2.75
(64)	Harper	10.00	5.00	3.00
(65)	Henkle	10.00	5.00	3.00

		NR MT	EX	VG
(66)	Herr	10.00	5.00	3.00
(67)	Hickey	10.00	5.00	3.00
(68)	High	10.00	5.00	3.00
(69)	Holling	10.00	5.00	3.00
(70)	Hosp	10.00	5.00	3.00
(71)	Houck	10.00	5.00	3.00
(72)	Howard	10.00	5.00	3.00
(73)	Kamm	10.00	5.00	3.00
(74)	Kenworthy	10.00	5.00	3.00
(75)	Killefer	10.00	5.00	3.00
(76)	King	10.00	5.00	3.00
(77)	Koehler	10.00	5.00	3.00
(78)	Koerner	10.00	5.00	3.00
(79)	Kramer (Oakland)	10.00	5.00	3.00
(80)	Kramer (San Francisco)	10.00	5.00	3.00
(81)	Land	10.00	5.00	3.00
(82)	Lane	10.00	5.00	3.00
(83)	Lapan	10.00	5.00	3.00
(84)	Larkin	10.00	5.00	3.00
(85)	Lee	10.00	5.00	3.00
(86)	Long	10.00	5.00	3.00
(87)	Mails	10.00	5.00	3.00
(88)	Mains	10.00	5.00	3.00
(89)	Maisel	10.00	5.00	3.00
(90)	Mathes	10.00	5.00	3.00
(91)	McCredie	10.00	5.00	3.00
(92)	McGaffigan	10.00	5.00	3.00
(93)	McHenry	10.00	5.00	3.00
(94)	McNulty	10.00	5.00	3.00
(95)	Meusel	12.00	6.00	3.50
(96)	Middleton	10.00	5.00	3.00
(97)	Mitchell	10.00	5.00	3.00
(98)	Mitze	10.00	5.00	3.00
(99)	Mulory	10.00	5.00	3.00
(100)	Murphy	10.00	5.00	3.00
(101)	Murray	10.00	5.00	3.00
(102)	Niehoff (Los Angeles)	10.00	5.00	3.00
(103)	Niehoff (Seattle)	10.00	5.00	3.00
(104)	Norse	10.00	5.00	3.00
(105)	Oldham	10.00	5.00	3.00
(106)	Orr	10.00	5.00	3.00
(107)	Penner	10.00	5.00	3.00
(108)	Pennington	10.00	5.00	3.00
(109)	Piercy	10.00	5.00	3.00
(110)	Pinelli	15.00	7.50	4.50
(111)	Prough	10.00	5.00	3.00
(112)	Rader	10.00	5.00	3.00
(113)	Reiger	10.00	5.00	3.00
(114)	Ritchie	10.00	5.00	3.00
(115)	Roach	10.00	5.00	3.00
(116)	Rodgers	10.00	5.00	3.00
(117)	Rumler	10.00	5.00	3.00
(118)	Sands	10.00	5.00	3.00
(119)	Schick	10.00	5.00	3.00
(120)	Schultz	10.00	5.00	3.00
(121)	Scott	10.00	5.00	3.00
(122)	Seaton	10.00	5.00	3.00
(123)	Sheely	10.00	5.00	3.00
(124)	Siglin	10.00	5.00	3.00
(125)	Smith	10.00	5.00	3.00
(126)	Bill Smith	10.00	5.00	3.00
(127)	Snell	10.00	5.00	3.00
(128)	Spangler	10.00	5.00	3.00
(129)	Speas	10.00	5.00	3.00
(130)	Spencer	10.00	5.00	3.00
(131)	Starasenich	10.00	5.00	3.00
(132)	Stumpf	10.00	5.00	3.00
(133)	Sutherland	10.00	5.00	3.00
(134)	Vance	10.00	5.00	3.00
(135)	Walker	10.00	5.00	3.00
(136)	Walsh	10.00	5.00	3.00
(137)	Ware	10.00	5.00	3.00
(138)	Weaver	10.00	5.00	3.00
(139)	Westerzil	10.00	5.00	3.00
(140)	Wilhoit	10.00	5.00	3.00
(141)	Wilie	10.00	5.00	3.00
(142)	Willets	10.00	5.00	3.00
(143)	Zamloch	10.00	5.00	3.00
(144)	Zweifel	10.00	5.00	3.00

1920 E137 Zeenut

	NR MT	EX	VG
Complete Set:	1500.00	750.00	450.00
Common Player:	10.00	5.00	3.00

		NR MT	EX	VG
(1)	Adams	10.00	5.00	3.00
(2)	Agnew	10.00	5.00	3.00
(3)	Alcock	10.00	5.00	3.00
(4)	Aldrige	10.00	5.00	3.00
(5)	Andrews	10.00	5.00	3.00
(6)	Anfinson	10.00	5.00	3.00
(7)	A. Arlett	10.00	5.00	3.00
(8)	R. Arlett	9.00	4.50	2.75
(9)	Baker	10.00	5.00	3.00
(10)	Baldwin	10.00	5.00	3.00
(11)	Bassler	10.00	5.00	3.00
(12)	Baum	10.00	5.00	3.00
(13)	Blue	10.00	5.00	3.00
(14)	Bohne	10.00	5.00	3.00
(15)	Brenton	10.00	5.00	3.00
(16)	Bromley (dark hat)	10.00	5.00	3.00
(17)	Bromley (light hat)	10.00	5.00	3.00
(18)	Brown	10.00	5.00	3.00
(19)	Butler	10.00	5.00	3.00
(20)	Caveney	10.00	5.00	3.00
(21)	Chadbourne	10.00	5.00	3.00
(22)	Compton	10.00	5.00	3.00
(23)	Connolly	10.00	5.00	3.00
(24)	Cook	10.00	5.00	3.00
(25)	Corhan	10.00	5.00	3.00
(26)	Cox	10.00	5.00	3.00
(27)	K. Crandall	10.00	5.00	3.00
(28)	O. Crandall	10.00	5.00	3.00
(29)	Crawford	10.00	5.00	3.00
(30)	Cullop	10.00	5.00	3.00
(31)	Cunningham	10.00	5.00	3.00
(32)	DeVitalis	10.00	5.00	3.00
(33)	DeVormer	10.00	5.00	3.00
(34)	Dooley	10.00	5.00	3.00
(35)	Dorman	10.00	5.00	3.00
(36)	Dumovich	10.00	5.00	3.00
(37)	Dylar	10.00	5.00	3.00
(38)	Edington	10.00	5.00	3.00
(39)	Eldred	10.00	5.00	3.00
(40)	Ellis	10.00	5.00	3.00
(41)	Essick	10.00	5.00	3.00
(42)	Fisher	10.00	5.00	3.00
(43)	Fitzgerald	10.00	5.00	3.00
(44)	Fromme	10.00	5.00	3.00
(45)	Gardner	10.00	5.00	3.00
(46)	Ginglardi	10.00	5.00	3.00
(47)	Gough	10.00	5.00	3.00
(48)	Griggs	10.00	5.00	3.00
(49)	Guisto	10.00	5.00	3.00
(50)	Hamilton	10.00	5.00	3.00
(51)	Hanicy	10.00	5.00	3.00
(52)	Hartford	10.00	5.00	3.00
(53)	High	10.00	5.00	3.00
(54)	Hill	10.00	5.00	3.00
(55)	Hodges	10.00	5.00	3.00
(56)	Howard	10.00	5.00	3.00
(57)	James	10.00	5.00	3.00
(58)	Jenkins	10.00	5.00	3.00
(59)	Johnson (Portland)	10.00	5.00	3.00
(60)	Johnson (Salt Lake)	10.00	5.00	3.00
(61)	Jones	10.00	5.00	3.00
(62)	Juney	10.00	5.00	3.00
(63)	Kallio	10.00	5.00	3.00
(64)	Kamm	10.00	5.00	3.00
(65)	Keating	10.00	5.00	3.00
(66)	Kenworthy	10.00	5.00	3.00
(67)	Killeen	10.00	5.00	3.00
(68)	Killefer	10.00	5.00	3.00
(69)	Kingdon	10.00	5.00	3.00
(70)	Knight	10.00	5.00	3.00
(71)	Koehler	10.00	5.00	3.00
(72)	Koerner	10.00	5.00	3.00

		NR MT	EX	VG
(73)	Kopp	10.00	5.00	3.00
(74)	Kremer	10.00	5.00	3.00
(75)	Krug	10.00	5.00	3.00
(76)	Kunz	10.00	5.00	3.00
(77)	Lambert	10.00	5.00	3.00
(78)	Lane	10.00	5.00	3.00
(79)	Larkin	10.00	5.00	3.00
(80)	Leverenz	10.00	5.00	3.00
(81)	Long	10.00	5.00	3.00
(82)	Love	10.00	5.00	3.00
(83)	Maggart	10.00	5.00	3.00
(84)	Mails	10.00	5.00	3.00
(85)	Maisel	10.00	5.00	3.00
(86)	Matterson	10.00	5.00	3.00
(87)	Matteson	10.00	5.00	3.00
(88)	McAuley	10.00	5.00	3.00
(89)	McCredie	10.00	5.00	3.00
(90)	McGaffigan	10.00	5.00	3.00
(91)	McHenry	10.00	5.00	3.00
(92)	McQuaid	10.00	5.00	3.00
(93)	Miller	10.00	5.00	3.00
(94)	Mitchell	10.00	5.00	3.00
(95)	J. Mitchell	10.00	5.00	3.00
(96)	Mitchell	10.00	5.00	3.00
(97)	Mitze	10.00	5.00	3.00
(98)	Moffitt	10.00	5.00	3.00
(99)	Mollwitz	10.00	5.00	3.00
(100)	Morse	10.00	5.00	3.00
(101)	Mulligan	10.00	5.00	3.00
(102)	Murphy	10.00	5.00	3.00
(103)	Niehoff	10.00	5.00	3.00
(104)	Nixon	10.00	5.00	3.00
(105)	O'Shaughnessy	10.00	5.00	3.00
(106)	Orr	10.00	5.00	3.00
(107)	Paull	10.00	5.00	3.00
(108)	Penner	10.00	5.00	3.00
(109)	Pertica	10.00	5.00	3.00
(110)	Peterson	10.00	5.00	3.00
(111)	Polson	10.00	5.00	3.00
(112)	Prough	10.00	5.00	3.00
(113)	Reagan	10.00	5.00	3.00
(114)	Reiger	10.00	5.00	3.00
(115)	Reilly	10.00	5.00	3.00
(116)	Rheinhart	10.00	5.00	3.00
(117)	Rodgers	10.00	5.00	3.00
(118)	Ross	10.00	5.00	3.00
(119)	Rumler	10.00	5.00	3.00
(120)	Russell	10.00	5.00	3.00
(121)	Sands	10.00	5.00	3.00
(122)	Schaller	10.00	5.00	3.00
(123)	Schang	10.00	5.00	3.00
(124)	Schellenback	10.00	5.00	3.00
(125)	Schick	10.00	5.00	3.00
(126)	Schorr	10.00	5.00	3.00
(127)	Schroeder	10.00	5.00	3.00
(128)	Scott	10.00	5.00	3.00
(129)	Seaton	10.00	5.00	3.00
(130)	Sheely	10.00	5.00	3.00
(131)	Siebold	10.00	5.00	3.00
(132)	Siglin	10.00	5.00	3.00
(133)	Smith	10.00	5.00	3.00
(134)	G. Smith	10.00	5.00	3.00
(135)	Spellman	10.00	5.00	3.00
(136)	Spranger	10.00	5.00	3.00
(137)	Stroud	10.00	5.00	3.00
(138)	Stumpf	10.00	5.00	3.00
(139)	Sullivan	10.00	5.00	3.00
(140)	Sutherland	10.00	5.00	3.00
(141)	Thurston (dark hat)	10.00	5.00	3.00
(142)	Thurston (light hat)	10.00	5.00	3.00
(143)	Walsh	10.00	5.00	3.00
(144)	Wares	10.00	5.00	3.00
(145)	Weaver	10.00	5.00	3.00
(146)	Willie	10.00	5.00	3.00
(147)	Winn	10.00	5.00	3.00
(148)	Wisterzill	10.00	5.00	3.00
(149)	Worth	10.00	5.00	3.00
(150)	Yelle	10.00	5.00	3.00
(151)	Zamlock	10.00	5.00	3.00
(152)	Zeider	10.00	5.00	3.00

1921 E137 Zeenut

	NR MT	EX	VG
Complete Set:	1750.00	875.00	500.00
Common Player:	10.00	5.00	3.00

		NR MT	EX	VG
(1)	Adams	10.00	5.00	3.00
(2)	Alcock	10.00	5.00	3.00
(3)	Aldridge	10.00	5.00	3.00
(4)	Alton	10.00	5.00	3.00
(5)	Anfinson	10.00	5.00	3.00
(6)	Arlett	9.00	4.50	2.75
(7)	Baker	10.00	5.00	3.00
(8)	Baldwin	10.00	5.00	3.00
(9)	Bates	10.00	5.00	3.00
(10)	Berry	10.00	5.00	3.00
(11)	Blacholder	10.00	5.00	3.00
(12)	Blossom	10.00	5.00	3.00
(13)	Bourg	10.00	5.00	3.00
(14)	Brinley	10.00	5.00	3.00
(15)	Bromley	10.00	5.00	3.00
(16)	Brown	10.00	5.00	3.00
(17)	Brubaker	10.00	5.00	3.00
(18)	Butler	10.00	5.00	3.00
(19)	Byler	10.00	5.00	3.00
(20)	Carroll	10.00	5.00	3.00
(21)	Casey	10.00	5.00	3.00
(22)	Cather	10.00	5.00	3.00
(23)	Caveney	10.00	5.00	3.00
(24)	Chadbourne	10.00	5.00	3.00
(25)	Compton	10.00	5.00	3.00
(26)	Connel	10.00	5.00	3.00
(27)	Cook	10.00	5.00	3.00
(28)	Cooper	10.00	5.00	3.00
(29)	Couch	10.00	5.00	3.00
(30)	Cox	10.00	5.00	3.00
(31)	Crandall	10.00	5.00	3.00
(32)	Cravath	10.00	5.00	3.00
(33)	Crawford	75.00	38.00	23.00
(34)	Crumpler	10.00	5.00	3.00
(35)	Cunningham	10.00	5.00	3.00
(36)	Daley	10.00	5.00	3.00
(37)	Dell	10.00	5.00	3.00
(38)	Demaree	10.00	5.00	3.00
(39)	Douglas	10.00	5.00	3.00
(40)	Dumovich	10.00	5.00	3.00
(41)	Elliott	10.00	5.00	3.00
(42)	Ellis	10.00	5.00	3.00
(43)	Ellison	10.00	5.00	3.00
(44)	Essick	10.00	5.00	3.00
(45)	Faeth	10.00	5.00	3.00
(46)	Fisher	10.00	5.00	3.00
(47)	Fittery	10.00	5.00	3.00
(48)	Fitzgerald	10.00	5.00	3.00
(49)	Flaherty	10.00	5.00	3.00
(50)	Francis	10.00	5.00	3.00
(51)	French	10.00	5.00	3.00
(52)	Fromme	10.00	5.00	3.00
(53)	Gardner	10.00	5.00	3.00
(54)	Geary	10.00	5.00	3.00
(55)	Gennin	10.00	5.00	3.00
(56)	Gorman	10.00	5.00	3.00
(57)	Gould	10.00	5.00	3.00
(58)	Griggs	10.00	5.00	3.00
(59)	Hale	10.00	5.00	3.00
(60)	Hannah	10.00	5.00	3.00
(61)	Hansen	10.00	5.00	3.00
(62)	Hesse	10.00	5.00	3.00
(63)	High	10.00	5.00	3.00
(64)	Hughes	10.00	5.00	3.00
(65)	Hyatt	10.00	5.00	3.00
(66)	Jackson	10.00	5.00	3.00
(67)	Jacobs	10.00	5.00	3.00
(68)	Jacobs	10.00	5.00	3.00
(69)	Jenkins	10.00	5.00	3.00
(70)	Johnson	10.00	5.00	3.00
(71)	Jones	10.00	5.00	3.00
(72)	Jourden	10.00	5.00	3.00

		NR MT	EX	VG
(73)	Kallio	10.00	5.00	3.00
(74)	Kamm	10.00	5.00	3.00
(75)	Kearns	10.00	5.00	3.00
(76)	Kelly	10.00	5.00	3.00
(77)	Kersten	10.00	5.00	3.00
(78)	Kifer	10.00	5.00	3.00
(79)	Killefer	10.00	5.00	3.00
(80)	King	10.00	5.00	3.00
(81)	Kingdon	10.00	5.00	3.00
(82)	Knight	10.00	5.00	3.00
(83)	Koehler	10.00	5.00	3.00
(84)	Kopp	10.00	5.00	3.00
(85)	Krause	10.00	5.00	3.00
(86)	Kremer	10.00	5.00	3.00
(87)	Krug	10.00	5.00	3.00
(88)	Kunz	10.00	5.00	3.00
(89)	Lane	10.00	5.00	3.00
(90)	Leverenz	10.00	5.00	3.00
(91)	Lewis	10.00	5.00	3.00
(92)	Lindimore	10.00	5.00	3.00
(93)	Love	10.00	5.00	3.00
(94)	Ludolph	10.00	5.00	3.00
(95)	Lynn	10.00	5.00	3.00
(96)	Lyons	10.00	5.00	3.00
(97)	McAuley	10.00	5.00	3.00
(98)	McCredie	10.00	5.00	3.00
(99)	McGaffigan	10.00	5.00	3.00
(100)	McGraw	10.00	5.00	3.00
(101)	McQuaid	10.00	5.00	3.00
(102)	Merritt	10.00	5.00	3.00
(103)	Middleton	10.00	5.00	3.00
(104)	Miller	10.00	5.00	3.00
(105)	Mitchell	10.00	5.00	3.00
(106)	Mitze	10.00	5.00	3.00
(107)	Mollwitz	10.00	5.00	3.00
(108)	Morse	10.00	5.00	3.00
(109)	Murphy (Seattle)	10.00	5.00	3.00
(110)	Murphy (Vernon)	10.00	5.00	3.00
(111)	Mustain	10.00	5.00	3.00
(112)	Nickels	10.00	5.00	3.00
(113)	Niehaus	10.00	5.00	3.00
(114)	Niehoff	10.00	5.00	3.00
(115)	Nofziger	10.00	5.00	3.00
(116)	O'Connell	10.00	5.00	3.00
(117)	O'Doul	40.00	20.00	12.00
(118)	O'Malia	10.00	5.00	3.00
(119)	Oldring	10.00	5.00	3.00
(120)	Oliver	10.00	5.00	3.00
(121)	Orr	10.00	5.00	3.00
(122)	Paton	10.00	5.00	3.00
(123)	Penner	10.00	5.00	3.00
(124)	Pick	10.00	5.00	3.00
(125)	Pillette	10.00	5.00	3.00
(126)	Pinelli	10.00	5.00	3.00
(127)	Polson	10.00	5.00	3.00
(128)	Poole	10.00	5.00	3.00
(129)	Prough	10.00	5.00	3.00
(130)	Rath	10.00	5.00	3.00
(131)	Read	10.00	5.00	3.00
(132)	Reinhardt	10.00	5.00	3.00
(133)	Rieger	10.00	5.00	3.00
(134)	Rogers	10.00	5.00	3.00
(135)	Rose (Sacramento)	10.00	5.00	3.00
(136)	Rose (Salt Lake)	10.00	5.00	3.00
(137)	Ross (Portland)	10.00	5.00	3.00
(138)	Ross (Sacramento)	10.00	5.00	3.00
(139)	Ryan	10.00	5.00	3.00
(140)	Sand	10.00	5.00	3.00
(141)	Schick	10.00	5.00	3.00
(142)	Schneider	10.00	5.00	3.00
(143)	Scott	10.00	5.00	3.00
(144)	Shang	10.00	5.00	3.00
(145)	Sheehan	10.00	5.00	3.00
(146)	Shore	10.00	5.00	3.00
(147)	Shorr	10.00	5.00	3.00
(148)	Shultis	10.00	5.00	3.00
(149)	Siebold	10.00	5.00	3.00
(150)	Siglin	10.00	5.00	3.00
(151)	Smallwood	10.00	5.00	3.00
(152)	Smith	10.00	5.00	3.00
(153)	Spencer	10.00	5.00	3.00
(154)	Stanage	10.00	5.00	3.00
(155)	Statz	10.00	5.00	3.00
(156)	Stumph	10.00	5.00	3.00
(157)	Thomas	10.00	5.00	3.00
(158)	Thurston	10.00	5.00	3.00
(159)	Tyrrell	10.00	5.00	3.00
(160)	Van Osdoll	10.00	5.00	3.00
(161)	Walsh	10.00	5.00	3.00
(162)	White	10.00	5.00	3.00
(163)	Wilhoit	10.00	5.00	3.00

		NR MT	EX	VG
(164)	Wilie	10.00	5.00	3.00
(165)	Winn	10.00	5.00	3.00
(166)	Wolfer	10.00	5.00	3.00
(167)	Yelle	10.00	5.00	3.00
(168)	Young	10.00	5.00	3.00
(169)	Zeider	10.00	5.00	3.00

1922 E137 Zeenut

The 1922 Zeenuts are dated on the front, measure 1-7/8" by 3-1/8" and feature black and white photos with sepia highlights. There are 162 subjects, and four of them (Koehler, Williams, Gregg and Schneider) have been found with variations in color tones.

		NR MT	EX	VG
Complete Set:		3500.00	1750.00	1050.
Common Player:		10.00	5.00	3.00
(1)	J. Adams	10.00	5.00	3.00
(2)	S. Adams	10.00	5.00	3.00
(3)	Agnew	10.00	5.00	3.00
(4)	Anfinson	10.00	5.00	3.00
(5)	Arlett	9.00	4.50	2.75
(6)	Baldwin	10.00	5.00	3.00
(7)	Barney	10.00	5.00	3.00
(8)	Bell	10.00	5.00	3.00
(9)	Blaeholder	10.00	5.00	3.00
(10)	Bodie	12.00	6.00	3.50
(11)	Brenton	10.00	5.00	3.00
(12)	Bromley	10.00	5.00	3.00
(13)	Brovold	10.00	5.00	3.00
(14)	Brown	10.00	5.00	3.00
(15)	Brubaker	10.00	5.00	3.00
(16)	Burger	10.00	5.00	3.00
(17)	Byler	10.00	5.00	3.00
(18)	Canfield	10.00	5.00	3.00
(19)	Carroll	10.00	5.00	3.00
(20)	Cartwright	10.00	5.00	3.00
(21)	Chadbourne	10.00	5.00	3.00
(22)	Compton	10.00	5.00	3.00
(23)	Connolly	10.00	5.00	3.00
(24)	Cook	10.00	5.00	3.00
(25)	Cooper	10.00	5.00	3.00
(26)	Coumbe	10.00	5.00	3.00
(27)	Cox	10.00	5.00	3.00
(28)	Crandall	10.00	5.00	3.00
(29)	Crumpler	10.00	5.00	3.00
(30)	Cueto	10.00	5.00	3.00
(31)	Dailey	10.00	5.00	3.00
(32)	Daly	10.00	5.00	3.00
(33)	Deal	10.00	5.00	3.00
(34)	Dell	10.00	5.00	3.00
(35)	Doyle	10.00	5.00	3.00
(36)	Dumovich	10.00	5.00	3.00
(37)	Eldred	10.00	5.00	3.00
(38)	Eller	10.00	5.00	3.00
(39)	Elliott	10.00	5.00	3.00
(40)	Ellison	10.00	5.00	3.00
(41)	Essick	10.00	5.00	3.00
(42)	Finneran	10.00	5.00	3.00
(43)	Fittery	10.00	5.00	3.00
(44)	Fitzgerald	10.00	5.00	3.00
(45)	Freeman	10.00	5.00	3.00
(46)	French	10.00	5.00	3.00
(47)	Gardner	10.00	5.00	3.00
(48)	Geary	10.00	5.00	3.00

		NR MT	EX	VG
(49)	Gibson	10.00	5.00	3.00
(50)	Gilder	10.00	5.00	3.00
(51)	Gould	10.00	5.00	3.00
(52)	Gregg	10.00	5.00	3.00
(53)	Gressett	10.00	5.00	3.00
(54)	Griggs	10.00	5.00	3.00
(55)	Hampton	10.00	5.00	3.00
(56)	Hannah	10.00	5.00	3.00
(57)	Hawks	10.00	5.00	3.00
(58)	Henke	10.00	5.00	3.00
(59)	High (Portland)	10.00	5.00	3.00
(60)	High (Vernon)	10.00	5.00	3.00
(61)	Houck	10.00	5.00	3.00
(62)	Howard	10.00	5.00	3.00
(63)	Hughes	10.00	5.00	3.00
(64)	Hyatt	10.00	5.00	3.00
(65)	Jacobs	10.00	5.00	3.00
(66)	James	10.00	5.00	3.00
(67)	Jenkins	10.00	5.00	3.00
(68)	Jones	10.00	5.00	3.00
(69)	Kallio	10.00	5.00	3.00
(70)	Kamm	10.00	5.00	3.00
(71)	Keiser	10.00	5.00	3.00
(72)	Kelly	10.00	5.00	3.00
(73)	Kenworthy	10.00	5.00	3.00
(74)	Kilduff	10.00	5.00	3.00
(75)	Killefer	10.00	5.00	3.00
(76)	Killhullen	10.00	5.00	3.00
(77)	King	10.00	5.00	3.00
(78)	Knight	10.00	5.00	3.00
(79)	Koehler	10.00	5.00	3.00
(80)	Kremer	10.00	5.00	3.00
(81)	Kunz	10.00	5.00	3.00
(82)	Lafayette	10.00	5.00	3.00
(83)	Lane	10.00	5.00	3.00
(84)	Lazzeri	60.00	30.00	18.00
(85)	Lefevre	10.00	5.00	3.00
(86)	D. Lewis	15.00	7.50	4.50
(87)	S. Lewis	10.00	5.00	3.00
(88)	Lindimore	10.00	5.00	3.00
(89)	Locker	10.00	5.00	3.00
(90)	Lyons	10.00	5.00	3.00
(91)	Mack	10.00	5.00	3.00
(92)	Marriott	10.00	5.00	3.00
(93)	May	10.00	5.00	3.00
(94)	McAuley	10.00	5.00	3.00
(95)	McCabe	10.00	5.00	3.00
(96)	McCann	10.00	5.00	3.00
(97)	McCredie	10.00	5.00	3.00
(98)	McNeely	10.00	5.00	3.00
(99)	McQuaid	10.00	5.00	3.00
(100)	Miller	10.00	5.00	3.00
(101)	Mitchell	10.00	5.00	3.00
(102)	Mitze	10.00	5.00	3.00
(103)	Mollwitz	10.00	5.00	3.00
(104)	Monahan	10.00	5.00	3.00
(105)	Murphy (Seattle)	10.00	5.00	3.00
(106)	Murphy (Vernon)	10.00	5.00	3.00
(107)	Niehaus	10.00	5.00	3.00
(108)	O'Connell	10.00	5.00	3.00
(109)	Orr	10.00	5.00	3.00
(110)	Owen	10.00	5.00	3.00
(111)	Pearce	10.00	5.00	3.00
(112)	Pick	10.00	5.00	3.00
(113)	Ponder	10.00	5.00	3.00
(114)	Poole	10.00	5.00	3.00
(115)	Prough	10.00	5.00	3.00
(116)	Read	10.00	5.00	3.00
(117)	Richardson	10.00	5.00	3.00
(118)	Rieger	10.00	5.00	3.00
(119)	Ritchie	10.00	5.00	3.00
(120)	Ross	10.00	5.00	3.00
(121)	Ryan	10.00	5.00	3.00
(122)	Sand	10.00	5.00	3.00
(123)	Sargent	10.00	5.00	3.00
(124)	Sawyer	10.00	5.00	3.00
(125)	Schang	10.00	5.00	3.00
(126)	Schick	10.00	5.00	3.00
(127)	Schneider	10.00	5.00	3.00
(128)	Schorr	10.00	5.00	3.00
(129)	Schulte (Oakland)	10.00	5.00	3.00
(130)	Schulte (Seattle)	10.00	5.00	3.00
(131)	Scott	10.00	5.00	3.00
(132)	See	10.00	5.00	3.00
(133)	Shea	10.00	5.00	3.00
(134)	Sheehan	10.00	5.00	3.00
(135)	Siglin	10.00	5.00	3.00
(136)	Smith	10.00	5.00	3.00
(137)	Soria	10.00	5.00	3.00
(138)	Spencer	10.00	5.00	3.00
(139)	Stanage	10.00	5.00	3.00

		NR MT	EX	VG
(140)	Strand	10.00	5.00	3.00
(141)	Stumpf	10.00	5.00	3.00
(142)	Sullivan	10.00	5.00	3.00
(143)	Sutherland	10.00	5.00	3.00
(144)	Thomas	10.00	5.00	3.00
(145)	Thorpe	2000.00	1000.00	600.00
(146)	Thurston	10.00	5.00	3.00
(147)	Tobin	10.00	5.00	3.00
(148)	Turner	10.00	5.00	3.00
(149)	Twombly	10.00	5.00	3.00
(150)	Valla	10.00	5.00	3.00
(151)	Vargas	10.00	5.00	3.00
(152)	Viveros	10.00	5.00	3.00
(153)	Wallace	10.00	5.00	3.00
(154)	Walsh	10.00	5.00	3.00
(155)	Wells	10.00	5.00	3.00
(156)	Westersil	10.00	5.00	3.00
(157)	Wheat	10.00	5.00	3.00
(158)	Wilhoit	10.00	5.00	3.00
(159)	Wilie	10.00	5.00	3.00
(160)	Williams	10.00	5.00	3.00
(161)	Yelle	10.00	5.00	3.00
(162)	Zeider	10.00	5.00	3.00

1923 E137 Zeenut

This is the only year that Zeenuts cards were issued in two different sizes. Cards in the "regular" series measure 1-7/8" by 3", feature black and white photos and are dated 1923. A second series, containing just 24 cards (all San Francisco and Oakland players), were actually re0issues of the 1922 series with a "1923" date.

		NR MT	EX	VG
Complete Set:		2100.00	1050.00	650.00
Common Player:		10.00	5.00	3.00
(1)	Agnew (1923 photo)	10.00	5.00	3.00
(2)	Agnew (1922 photo re-dated)	20.00	10.00	6.00
(3)	Alten	10.00	5.00	3.00
(4)	Anderson	10.00	5.00	3.00
(5)	Anfinson	10.00	5.00	3.00
(6)	Arlett	9.00	4.50	2.75
(7)	Baker	10.00	5.00	3.00
(8)	Baldwin	10.00	5.00	3.00
(9)	Barney	10.00	5.00	3.00
(10)	Blake	10.00	5.00	3.00
(11)	Bodie	7.00	3.50	2.00
(12)	Brazil	10.00	5.00	3.00
(13)	Brenton	11.00	5.50	3.25
(14)	Brown (Oakland)	11.00	5.50	3.25
(15)	Brown (Sacramento)	10.00	5.00	3.00
(16)	Brubaker	10.00	5.00	3.00
(17)	Buckley	10.00	5.00	3.00
(18)	Canfield	10.00	5.00	3.00
(19)	Carroll	10.00	5.00	3.00
(20)	Cather	10.00	5.00	3.00
(21)	Chadbourne	10.00	5.00	3.00
(22)	Charvez	10.00	5.00	3.00
(23)	Cochrane	10.00	5.00	3.00
(24)	Colwell	10.00	5.00	3.00
(25)	Compton	10.00	5.00	3.00
(26)	Cook	10.00	5.00	3.00
(27)	Cooper (1923 photo)	10.00	5.00	3.00
(28)	Cooper (1922 photo re-date)	20.00	10.00	6.00
(29)	Coumbe	10.00	5.00	3.00
(30)	Courtney	10.00	5.00	3.00

		NR MT	EX	VG
(31)	Crandall	10.00	5.00	3.00
(32)	Crane	10.00	5.00	3.00
(33)	Crowder	7.00	3.50	2.00
(34)	Crumpler	10.00	5.00	3.00
(35)	Daly (Los Angeles)	10.00	5.00	3.00
(36)	Daly (Portland)	10.00	5.00	3.00
(37)	Deal	10.00	5.00	3.00
(38)	Doyle	10.00	5.00	3.00
(39)	Duchalsky	10.00	5.00	3.00
(40)	Eckert	10.00	5.00	3.00
(41)	Eldred	10.00	5.00	3.00
(42)	Eley	10.00	5.00	3.00
(43)	Eller	11.00	5.50	3.25
(44)	Ellison (1923 photo)	10.00	5.00	3.00
(45)	Ellison (1922 photo re-dated)	20.00	10.00	6.00
(46)	Essick	10.00	5.00	3.00
(47)	Fittery	10.00	5.00	3.00
(48)	Flashkamper	10.00	5.00	3.00
(49)	Frederick	10.00	5.00	3.00
(50)	French	10.00	5.00	3.00
(51)	Geary (1923 photo)	10.00	5.00	3.00
(52)	Geary (1922 photo re-dated)	20.00	10.00	6.00
(53)	Gilder	10.00	5.00	3.00
(54)	Golvin	10.00	5.00	3.00
(55)	Gorman	10.00	5.00	3.00
(56)	Gould	10.00	5.00	3.00
(57)	Gressett	10.00	5.00	3.00
(58)	Griggs	10.00	5.00	3.00
(59)	Hannah (Los Angeles)	10.00	5.00	3.00
(60)	Hannah (Vernon)	10.00	5.00	3.00
(61)	Hemingway	10.00	5.00	3.00
(62)	Hendryx	10.00	5.00	3.00
(63)	High	10.00	5.00	3.00
(64)	H. High	10.00	5.00	3.00
(65)	Hodge	10.00	5.00	3.00
(66)	Hood	10.00	5.00	3.00
(67)	Houghs	10.00	5.00	3.00
(68)	Howard (1923 photo)	10.00	5.00	3.00
(69)	Howard (1922 photo re-date)	20.00	10.00	6.00
(70)	Del Howard	10.00	5.00	3.00
(71)	Jacobs	10.00	5.00	3.00
(72)	James	10.00	5.00	3.00
(73)	Johnson	10.00	5.00	3.00
(74)	Johnston	10.00	5.00	3.00
(75)	Jolly	10.00	5.00	3.00
(76)	Jones (Los Angeles)	10.00	5.00	3.00
(77)	Jones (Oakland)	11.00	5.50	3.25
(78)	Jones (Portland)	10.00	5.00	3.00
(79)	Kallio	10.00	5.00	3.00
(80)	Kearns	10.00	5.00	3.00
(81)	Keiser	10.00	5.00	3.00
(82)	Keller	10.00	5.00	3.00
(83)	Kelly (San Francisco)	10.00	5.00	3.00
(84)	Kelly (Seattle)	10.00	5.00	3.00
(85)	Kenna	10.00	5.00	3.00
(86)	Kilduff	10.00	5.00	3.00
(87)	Killifer	10.00	5.00	3.00
(88)	King	10.00	5.00	3.00
(89)	Knight (1923 photo)	10.00	5.00	3.00
(90)	Knight (1922 photo re-dated)	11.00	5.50	3.25
(91)	Koehler	10.00	5.00	3.00
(92)	Kopp	10.00	5.00	3.00
(93)	Krause	10.00	5.00	3.00
(94)	Kremer	10.00	5.00	3.00
(95)	Krug	10.00	5.00	3.00
(96)	Lafayette (1923 photo)	10.00	5.00	3.00
(97)	Lafayette (1922 photo re-dated)	11.00	5.50	3.25
(98)	Lane	10.00	5.00	3.00
(99)	Lefevre	20.00	10.00	6.00
(100)	Leslie	10.00	5.00	3.00
(101)	Levere	10.00	5.00	3.00
(102)	Leverenz	10.00	5.00	3.00
(103)	Lewis	10.00	5.00	3.00
(104)	Lindimore	10.00	5.00	3.00
(105)	Locker	10.00	5.00	3.00
(106)	Lyons	10.00	5.00	3.00
(107)	Maderas	10.00	5.00	3.00
(108)	Mails	10.00	5.00	3.00
(109)	Marriott	20.00	10.00	6.00
(110)	Matzen	10.00	5.00	3.00
(111)	McAuley	10.00	5.00	3.00
(112)	McAuliffe	10.00	5.00	3.00
(113)	McCabe (Los Angeles)	10.00	5.00	3.00
(114)	McCabe (Salt Lake)	10.00	5.00	3.00
(115)	McCann	10.00	5.00	3.00
(116)	McGaffigan	10.00	5.00	3.00
(117)	McGinnis	10.00	5.00	3.00
(118)	McNeilly	10.00	5.00	3.00
(119)	McWeeney	10.00	5.00	3.00
(120)	Middleton	10.00	5.00	3.00

		NR MT	EX	VG
(121)	Miller	10.00	5.00	3.00
(122)	Mitchell (1922 photo)	20.00	10.00	6.00
(123)	Mitchell (1922 photo re-date)	20.00	10.00	6.00
(124)	Mitze	11.00	5.50	3.25
(125)	Mulligan	10.00	5.00	3.00
(126)	Murchio	10.00	5.00	3.00
(127)	D. Murphy	10.00	5.00	3.00
(128)	R. Murphy	10.00	5.00	3.00
(129)	Noack	10.00	5.00	3.00
(130)	O'Brien	10.00	5.00	3.00
(131)	Onslow	10.00	5.00	3.00
(132)	Orr	10.00	5.00	3.00
(133)	Pearce	10.00	5.00	3.00
(134)	Penner	10.00	5.00	3.00
(135)	Peters	10.00	5.00	3.00
(136)	Pick	10.00	5.00	3.00
(137)	Pigg	10.00	5.00	3.00
(138)	Plummer	10.00	5.00	3.00
(139)	Ponder	10.00	5.00	3.00
(140)	Poole	10.00	5.00	3.00
(141)	Ramage	10.00	5.00	3.00
(142)	Read (1923 photo)	10.00	5.00	3.00
(143)	Read (1922 photo re-dated)	20.00	10.00	6.00
(144)	Rhyne	10.00	5.00	3.00
(145)	Ritchie	10.00	5.00	3.00
(146)	Robertson	10.00	5.00	3.00
(147)	Rohwer (Sacramento)	10.00	5.00	3.00
(148)	Rohwer (Seattle)	10.00	5.00	3.00
(149)	Ryan	10.00	5.00	3.00
(150)	Sawyer	10.00	5.00	3.00
(151)	Schang	10.00	5.00	3.00
(152)	Schneider	10.00	5.00	3.00
(153)	Schroeder	10.00	5.00	3.00
(154)	Scott	10.00	5.00	3.00
(155)	See	20.00	10.00	6.00
(156)	Shea	10.00	5.00	3.00
(157)	M. Shea	10.00	5.00	3.00
(158)	Spec Shea	10.00	5.00	3.00
(159)	Sheehan	10.00	5.00	3.00
(160)	Shellenback	10.00	5.00	3.00
(161)	Siglin	10.00	5.00	3.00
(162)	Singleton	10.00	5.00	3.00
(163)	Smith	10.00	5.00	3.00
(164)	M.H. Smith	10.00	5.00	3.00
(165)	Stanton	10.00	5.00	3.00
(166)	Strand	10.00	5.00	3.00
(167)	Stumpf	10.00	5.00	3.00
(168)	Sutherland	10.00	5.00	3.00
(169)	Tesar	10.00	5.00	3.00
(170)	Thomas (Los Angeles)	10.00	5.00	3.00
(171)	Thomas (Oakland)	10.00	5.00	3.00
(172)	Tobin	10.00	5.00	3.00
(173)	Twombly	10.00	5.00	3.00
(174)	Valla	10.00	5.00	3.00
(175)	Vargas	11.00	5.50	3.25
(176)	Vitt	10.00	5.00	3.00
(177)	Wallace	10.00	5.00	3.00
(178)	Walsh (San Francisco)	10.00	5.00	3.00
(179)	Walsh (Seattle)	10.00	5.00	3.00
(180)	Waner	75.00	38.00	23.00
(181)	Wells (Oakland)	10.00	5.00	3.00
(182)	Wells (San Francisco)	11.00	5.50	3.25
(183)	Welsh	10.00	5.00	3.00
(184)	Wilhoit	10.00	5.00	3.00
(185)	Wilie (1923 photo)	10.00	5.00	3.00
(186)	Wilie (1922 photo re-dated)	11.00	5.50	3.25
(187)	Williams	10.00	5.00	3.00
(188)	Witzel	10.00	5.00	3.00
(189)	Wolfer	10.00	5.00	3.00
(190)	Wolverton	10.00	5.00	3.00
(191)	Yarrison	10.00	5.00	3.00
(192)	Yaryan	10.00	5.00	3.00
(193)	Yelle (1923 photo)	10.00	5.00	3.00
(194)	Yelle (1922 photo re-dated)	11.00	5.50	3.25
(195)	Yellowhorse	9.00	4.50	2.75
(196)	Zeider	10.00	5.00	3.00

1924 E137 Zeenut

Zeenut cards in 1924 and 1925 measure 1-3/4" by 2-7/8" and display the date on the front. The cards include a full photographic background. There are 144 subjects known in the 1924 series and 162 known for 1925.

	NR MT	EX	VG
Complete Set:	1500.00	750.00	450.00
Common Player:	10.00	5.00	3.00

		NR MT	EX	VG
(1)	Adams	10.00	5.00	3.00
(2)	Agnew	10.00	5.00	3.00
(3)	Arlett	9.00	4.50	2.75
(4)	Baker	10.00	5.00	3.00
(5)	E. Baldwin	10.00	5.00	3.00
(6)	T. Baldwin	10.00	5.00	3.00
(7)	Beck	10.00	5.00	3.00
(8)	Benton	10.00	5.00	3.00
(9)	Bernard	10.00	5.00	3.00
(10)	Bigbee	10.00	5.00	3.00
(11)	Billings	10.00	5.00	3.00
(12)	Blakesly	10.00	5.00	3.00
(13)	Brady	10.00	5.00	3.00
(14)	Brazil	10.00	5.00	3.00
(15)	Brown	10.00	5.00	3.00
(16)	Brubaker	10.00	5.00	3.00
(17)	Buckley	10.00	5.00	3.00
(18)	Burger	10.00	5.00	3.00
(19)	Byler	10.00	5.00	3.00
(20)	Cadore	10.00	5.00	3.00
(21)	Cather	10.00	5.00	3.00
(22)	Chadbourne	10.00	5.00	3.00
(23)	Christian	10.00	5.00	3.00
(24)	Cochrane (Portland)	75.00	38.00	23.00
(25)	Cochrane (Sacramento)	10.00	5.00	3.00
(26)	Cooper	10.00	5.00	3.00
(27)	Coumbe	10.00	5.00	3.00
(28)	Cox	10.00	5.00	3.00
(29)	Crandall	10.00	5.00	3.00
(30)	Daly	10.00	5.00	3.00
(31)	Deal	10.00	5.00	3.00
(32)	Distel	10.00	5.00	3.00
(33)	Durst	10.00	5.00	3.00
(34)	Eckert	10.00	5.00	3.00
(35)	Eldred	10.00	5.00	3.00
(36)	Ellison	10.00	5.00	3.00
(37)	Essick	10.00	5.00	3.00
(38)	Flashkamper	10.00	5.00	3.00
(39)	Foster	10.00	5.00	3.00
(40)	Fredericks	10.00	5.00	3.00
(41)	Geary	10.00	5.00	3.00
(42)	Goebel	10.00	5.00	3.00
(43)	Golvin	10.00	5.00	3.00
(44)	Gorman	10.00	5.00	3.00
(45)	Gould	10.00	5.00	3.00
(46)	Gressett	10.00	5.00	3.00
(47)	Griffin (San Francisco)	10.00	5.00	3.00
(48)	Griffin (Vernon)	10.00	5.00	3.00
(49)	Guisto	10.00	5.00	3.00
(50)	Gunther	10.00	5.00	3.00
(51)	Hall	10.00	5.00	3.00
(52)	Hannah	10.00	5.00	3.00
(53)	Hendryx	10.00	5.00	3.00
(54)	High	10.00	5.00	3.00
(55)	Hodge	10.00	5.00	3.00
(56)	Hood	10.00	5.00	3.00
(57)	Ivan Howard	10.00	5.00	3.00
(58)	Hughes (Los Angeles)	10.00	5.00	3.00
(59)	Hughes (Sacramento)	10.00	5.00	3.00
(60)	Jacobs	10.00	5.00	3.00
(61)	James	10.00	5.00	3.00
(62)	Jenkins	10.00	5.00	3.00
(63)	Johnson	10.00	5.00	3.00
(64)	Jones	10.00	5.00	3.00
(65)	Keck	10.00	5.00	3.00
(66)	Kelley	10.00	5.00	3.00
(67)	Kenworthy	10.00	5.00	3.00
(68)	Kilduff	10.00	5.00	3.00
(69)	Killifer	10.00	5.00	3.00
(70)	Kimmick	10.00	5.00	3.00

		NR MT	EX	VG
(71)	Kopp	10.00	5.00	3.00
(72)	Krause	10.00	5.00	3.00
(73)	Krug	10.00	5.00	3.00
(74)	Kunz	10.00	5.00	3.00
(75)	Lafayette	10.00	5.00	3.00
(76)	Lennon	10.00	5.00	3.00
(77)	Leptich	10.00	5.00	3.00
(78)	Leslie	10.00	5.00	3.00
(79)	Leverenz	10.00	5.00	3.00
(80)	Lewis	10.00	5.00	3.00
(81)	Maderas	10.00	5.00	3.00
(82)	Mails	10.00	5.00	3.00
(83)	McAuley	10.00	5.00	3.00
(84)	McCann	10.00	5.00	3.00
(85)	McDowell	10.00	5.00	3.00
(86)	McNeely	10.00	5.00	3.00
(87)	Menosky	10.00	5.00	3.00
(88)	Meyers	10.00	5.00	3.00
(89)	Miller	10.00	5.00	3.00
(90)	Mitchell	10.00	5.00	3.00
(91)	Mulligan	10.00	5.00	3.00
(92)	D. Murphy	10.00	5.00	3.00
(93)	R. Murphy	10.00	5.00	3.00
(94)	Osborne	10.00	5.00	3.00
(95)	Paynter	10.00	5.00	3.00
(96)	Penner	10.00	5.00	3.00
(97)	Peters (Sacramento)	10.00	5.00	3.00
(98)	Peters (Salt Lake)	10.00	5.00	3.00
(99)	Pick	10.00	5.00	3.00
(100)	Pillette	10.00	5.00	3.00
(101)	Poole	10.00	5.00	3.00
(102)	Prough	10.00	5.00	3.00
(103)	Querry	10.00	5.00	3.00
(104)	Read	10.00	5.00	3.00
(105)	Rhyne	10.00	5.00	3.00
(106)	Ritchie	10.00	5.00	3.00
(107)	Root	12.00	6.00	3.50
(108)	Rowher	10.00	5.00	3.00
(109)	Schang	10.00	5.00	3.00
(110)	Schneider	10.00	5.00	3.00
(111)	Schorr	10.00	5.00	3.00
(112)	Schroeder	10.00	5.00	3.00
(113)	Scott	10.00	5.00	3.00
(114)	Sellers	10.00	5.00	3.00
(115)	"Speck" Shay	10.00	5.00	3.00
(116)	Shea (Sacramento)	10.00	5.00	3.00
(117)	Shea (San Francisco)	10.00	5.00	3.00
(118)	Shellenback	10.00	5.00	3.00
(119)	Siebold	10.00	5.00	3.00
(120)	Siglin	10.00	5.00	3.00
(121)	Slade	10.00	5.00	3.00
(122)	Smith (Sacramento)	10.00	5.00	3.00
(123)	Smith (San Francisco)	10.00	5.00	3.00
(124)	Stanton	10.00	5.00	3.00
(125)	Tanner	10.00	5.00	3.00
(126)	Twomley	10.00	5.00	3.00
(127)	Valla	10.00	5.00	3.00
(128)	Vargas	10.00	5.00	3.00
(129)	Vines	10.00	5.00	3.00
(130)	Vitt	10.00	5.00	3.00
(131)	Wallace	10.00	5.00	3.00
(132)	Walsh	10.00	5.00	3.00
(133)	Waner	75.00	38.00	23.00
(134)	Warner (fielding)	10.00	5.00	3.00
(135)	Warner (throwing)	10.00	5.00	3.00
(136)	Welsh	10.00	5.00	3.00
(137)	Wetzel	10.00	5.00	3.00
(138)	Whalen	10.00	5.00	3.00
(139)	Wilhoit	10.00	5.00	3.00
(140)	Williams (San Francisco)	10.00	5.00	3.00
(141)	Williams (Seattle)	10.00	5.00	3.00
(142)	Wolfer	10.00	5.00	3.00
(143)	Yelle	10.00	5.00	3.00
(144)	Yellowhorse	9.00	4.50	2.75

1925 E137 Zeenut

		NR MT	EX	VG
Complete Set:		1700.00	850.00	500.00
Common Player:		10.00	5.00	3.00
(1)	Adeylatte	10.00	5.00	3.00
(2)	Agnew	10.00	5.00	3.00
(3)	Arlett	12.00	6.00	3.50
(4)	Bagby	10.00	5.00	3.00
(5)	Bahr	10.00	5.00	3.00

		NR MT	EX	VG
(75)	Keating	10.00	5.00	3.00
(76)	Keefe	10.00	5.00	3.00
(77)	Kelly	10.00	5.00	3.00
(78)	Kilduff	10.00	5.00	3.00
(79)	Kohler	10.00	5.00	3.00
(80)	Kopp	10.00	5.00	3.00
(81)	Krause	10.00	5.00	3.00
(82)	Krug	10.00	5.00	3.00
(83)	Kunz	10.00	5.00	3.00
(84)	Lafayette	10.00	5.00	3.00
(85)	Lazzeri	60.00	30.00	18.00
(86)	Leslie	10.00	5.00	3.00
(87)	Leverenz	10.00	5.00	3.00
(88)	Duffy Lewis	15.00	7.50	4.50
(89)	Lindemore	10.00	5.00	3.00
(90)	Ludolph	10.00	5.00	3.00
(91)	Makin	10.00	5.00	3.00
(92)	Martin (Sacramento)	10.00	5.00	3.00
(93)	Martin (Portland)	10.00	5.00	3.00
(94)	McCabe	10.00	5.00	3.00
(95)	McCann	10.00	5.00	3.00
(96)	McCarren	10.00	5.00	3.00
(97)	McDonald	10.00	5.00	3.00
(98)	McGinnis (Portland)	10.00	5.00	3.00
(99)	McGinnis (Sacramento)	10.00	5.00	3.00
(100)	McLaughlin	10.00	5.00	3.00
(101)	Milstead	10.00	5.00	3.00
(102)	Mitchell	10.00	5.00	3.00
(103)	Moudy	10.00	5.00	3.00
(104)	Mulcahy	10.00	5.00	3.00
(105)	Mulligan	10.00	5.00	3.00
(106)	O'Doul	40.00	20.00	12.00
(107)	O'Neil	10.00	5.00	3.00
(108)	Ortman	10.00	5.00	3.00
(109)	Pailey	10.00	5.00	3.00
(110)	Paynter	10.00	5.00	3.00
(111)	Peery	10.00	5.00	3.00
(112)	Penner	10.00	5.00	3.00
(113)	Pfeffer	10.00	5.00	3.00
(114)	Phillips	10.00	5.00	3.00
(115)	Pickering	10.00	5.00	3.00
(116)	Piercy	10.00	5.00	3.00
(117)	Pillette	10.00	5.00	3.00
(118)	Plummer	10.00	5.00	3.00
(119)	Ponder	10.00	5.00	3.00
(120)	Pruett	10.00	5.00	3.00
(121)	Rawlings	10.00	5.00	3.00
(122)	Read	10.00	5.00	3.00
(123)	Reese	12.00	6.00	3.50
(124)	Rhyne	10.00	5.00	3.00
(125)	Riconda	10.00	5.00	3.00
(126)	Ritchie	10.00	5.00	3.00
(127)	Rohwer	10.00	5.00	3.00
(128)	Rowland	10.00	5.00	3.00
(129)	Ryan	10.00	5.00	3.00
(130)	Sandberg	10.00	5.00	3.00
(131)	Schang	10.00	5.00	3.00
(132)	Shea	10.00	5.00	3.00
(133)	M. Shea	10.00	5.00	3.00
(134)	Shellenbach	10.00	5.00	3.00
(135)	Sherling	10.00	5.00	3.00
(136)	Siglin	10.00	5.00	3.00
(137)	Slade	10.00	5.00	3.00
(138)	Spencer	10.00	5.00	3.00
(139)	Steward	10.00	5.00	3.00
(140)	Stivers	10.00	5.00	3.00
(141)	Suhr	10.00	5.00	3.00
(142)	Sutherland	10.00	5.00	3.00
(143)	Thomas (Portland)	10.00	5.00	3.00
(144)	Thomas (Vernon)	10.00	5.00	3.00
(145)	Thompson	10.00	5.00	3.00
(146)	Tobin	10.00	5.00	3.00
(147)	Twombly	10.00	5.00	3.00
(148)	Valla	10.00	5.00	3.00
(149)	Vinci	10.00	5.00	3.00
(150)	O. Vitt	10.00	5.00	3.00
(151)	Wachenfeld	10.00	5.00	3.00
(152)	Waner	75.00	38.00	23.00
(153)	L. Waner	75.00	38.00	23.00
(154)	Warner	10.00	5.00	3.00
(155)	Watson	10.00	5.00	3.00
(156)	Weinert	10.00	5.00	3.00
(157)	Whaley	10.00	5.00	3.00
(158)	Whitney	10.00	5.00	3.00
(159)	Williams	10.00	5.00	3.00
(160)	Winters	10.00	5.00	3.00
(161)	Wolfer	10.00	5.00	3.00
(162)	Woodring	10.00	5.00	3.00
(163)	Yeargin	10.00	5.00	3.00
(164)	Yelle	10.00	5.00	3.00

		NR MT	EX	VG
(6)	Baker	10.00	5.00	3.00
(7)	E. Baldwin	10.00	5.00	3.00
(8)	Barfoot	10.00	5.00	3.00
(9)	Beck	10.00	5.00	3.00
(10)	Becker	10.00	5.00	3.00
(11)	Blakesley	10.00	5.00	3.00
(12)	Boehler	10.00	5.00	3.00
(13)	Brady	10.00	5.00	3.00
(14)	Brandt	10.00	5.00	3.00
(15)	Bratcher	10.00	5.00	3.00
(16)	Brazil	10.00	5.00	3.00
(17)	Brower	10.00	5.00	3.00
(18)	Brown	10.00	5.00	3.00
(19)	Brubaker	10.00	5.00	3.00
(20)	Bryan	10.00	5.00	3.00
(21)	Canfield	10.00	5.00	3.00
(22)	W. Canfield	10.00	5.00	3.00
(23)	Cather	10.00	5.00	3.00
(24)	Chavez	10.00	5.00	3.00
(25)	Christain	10.00	5.00	3.00
(26)	Cochrane	10.00	5.00	3.00
(27)	Connolly	10.00	5.00	3.00
(28)	Cook	10.00	5.00	3.00
(29)	Cooper	10.00	5.00	3.00
(30)	Coumbe	10.00	5.00	3.00
(31)	Crandall	10.00	5.00	3.00
(32)	Crane	10.00	5.00	3.00
(33)	Crockett	10.00	5.00	3.00
(34)	Crosby	10.00	5.00	3.00
(35)	Cutshaw	10.00	5.00	3.00
(36)	Daly	10.00	5.00	3.00
(37)	Davis	10.00	5.00	3.00
(38)	Deal	10.00	5.00	3.00
(39)	Delaney	10.00	5.00	3.00
(40)	Dempsey	10.00	5.00	3.00
(41)	Dumovich	10.00	5.00	3.00
(42)	Eckert	10.00	5.00	3.00
(43)	Eldred	10.00	5.00	3.00
(44)	Elliott	10.00	5.00	3.00
(45)	Ellison	10.00	5.00	3.00
(46)	Emmer	10.00	5.00	3.00
(47)	Ennis	10.00	5.00	3.00
(48)	Essick	10.00	5.00	3.00
(49)	Finn	10.00	5.00	3.00
(50)	Flowers	10.00	5.00	3.00
(51)	Frederick	10.00	5.00	3.00
(52)	Fussell	10.00	5.00	3.00
(53)	Geary	10.00	5.00	3.00
(54)	Gorman	10.00	5.00	3.00
(55)	Griffin (San Francisco)	10.00	5.00	3.00
(56)	Griffin (Vernon)	10.00	5.00	3.00
(57)	Grimes	10.00	5.00	3.00
(58)	Guisto	10.00	5.00	3.00
(59)	Hannah	10.00	5.00	3.00
(60)	Haughy	10.00	5.00	3.00
(61)	Hemingway	10.00	5.00	3.00
(62)	Hendryx	10.00	5.00	3.00
(63)	Herman	15.00	7.50	4.50
(64)	High	10.00	5.00	3.00
(65)	Hoffman	10.00	5.00	3.00
(66)	Hood	10.00	5.00	3.00
(67)	Horan	10.00	5.00	3.00
(68)	Horton	10.00	5.00	3.00
(69)	Howard	10.00	5.00	3.00
(70)	Hughes	10.00	5.00	3.00
(71)	Hulvey	10.00	5.00	3.00
(72)	Hunnefield	10.00	5.00	3.00
(73)	Jacobs	10.00	5.00	3.00
(74)	James	10.00	5.00	3.00

1926 E137 Zeenut

Except for their slightly smaller size (1-3/4" by 2-3/4"), the 1926 Zeenut cards are nearly identical to the previous years. Considered more difficult than other Zeenuts series of this era, the 1926 set consists of 71 known subjects.

		NR MT	EX	VG
Complete Set:		1800.00	900.00	550.00
Common Player:		10.00	5.00	3.00
(1)	Agnew	10.00	5.00	3.00
(2)	Allen	10.00	5.00	3.00
(3)	Alley	10.00	5.00	3.00
(4)	Averill	25.00	12.50	7.50
(5)	Bagwell	10.00	5.00	3.00
(6)	Baker	10.00	5.00	3.00
(7)	T. Baldwin	10.00	5.00	3.00
(8)	Berry	10.00	5.00	3.00
(9)	Bool	10.00	5.00	3.00
(10)	Boone	10.00	5.00	3.00
(11)	Boyd	10.00	5.00	3.00
(12)	Brady	10.00	5.00	3.00
(13)	Brazil	10.00	5.00	3.00
(14)	Brower	10.00	5.00	3.00
(15)	Brubaker	10.00	5.00	3.00
(16)	Bryan	10.00	5.00	3.00
(17)	Burns	10.00	5.00	3.00
(18)	C. Canfield	10.00	5.00	3.00
(19)	W. Canfield	10.00	5.00	3.00
(20)	Carson	10.00	5.00	3.00
(21)	Christian	10.00	5.00	3.00
(22)	Cole	10.00	5.00	3.00
(23)	Connolly	10.00	5.00	3.00
(24)	Cook	10.00	5.00	3.00
(25)	Couch	10.00	5.00	3.00
(26)	Coumbe	10.00	5.00	3.00
(27)	Crockett	10.00	5.00	3.00
(28)	Cunningham	10.00	5.00	3.00
(29)	Cutshaw	10.00	5.00	3.00
(30)	Daglia	10.00	5.00	3.00
(31)	Danning	10.00	5.00	3.00
(32)	Davis	10.00	5.00	3.00
(33)	Delaney	10.00	5.00	3.00
(34)	Eckert	10.00	5.00	3.00
(35)	Eldred	10.00	5.00	3.00
(36)	Elliott	10.00	5.00	3.00
(37)	Ellison	10.00	5.00	3.00
(38)	Ellsworth	10.00	5.00	3.00
(39)	Elsh	10.00	5.00	3.00
(40)	Fenton	10.00	5.00	3.00
(41)	Finn	10.00	5.00	3.00
(42)	Flashkamper	10.00	5.00	3.00
(43)	Fowler	10.00	5.00	3.00
(44)	Frederick	10.00	5.00	3.00
(45)	Freeman	10.00	5.00	3.00
(46)	French	10.00	5.00	3.00
(47)	Garrison	10.00	5.00	3.00
(48)	Geary	10.00	5.00	3.00
(49)	Gillespie	10.00	5.00	3.00
(50)	Glazner	10.00	5.00	3.00
(51)	Gould	10.00	5.00	3.00
(52)	Governor	10.00	5.00	3.00
(53)	Griffin (Missions)	10.00	5.00	3.00
(54)	Griffin (San Francisco)	10.00	5.00	3.00
(55)	Guisto	10.00	5.00	3.00
(56)	Hamilton	10.00	5.00	3.00
(57)	Hannah	10.00	5.00	3.00
(58)	Hansen	10.00	5.00	3.00

		NR MT	EX	VG
(59)	Hasty	10.00	5.00	3.00
(60)	Hemingway	10.00	5.00	3.00
(61)	Hendryx	10.00	5.00	3.00
(62)	Hickok	10.00	5.00	3.00
(63)	Hillis	10.00	5.00	3.00
(64)	Hoffman	10.00	5.00	3.00
(65)	Hollerson	10.00	5.00	3.00
(66)	Holmes	10.00	5.00	3.00
(67)	Hood	10.00	5.00	3.00
(68)	Howard	10.00	5.00	3.00
(69)	Hufft	10.00	5.00	3.00
(70)	Hughes	10.00	5.00	3.00
(71)	Hulvey	10.00	5.00	3.00
(72)	Hurst	10.00	5.00	3.00
(73)	R. Jacobs	10.00	5.00	3.00
(74)	Jahn	10.00	5.00	3.00
(75)	Jenkins	10.00	5.00	3.00
(76)	Johnson	10.00	5.00	3.00
(77)	Jolly	10.00	5.00	3.00
(78)	Jones	10.00	5.00	3.00
(79)	Kallio	10.00	5.00	3.00
(80)	Keating	10.00	5.00	3.00
(81)	Kerr (Hollywood)	10.00	5.00	3.00
(82)	Kerr (San Francisco)	10.00	5.00	3.00
(83)	Kilduff	10.00	5.00	3.00
(84)	Killefer	10.00	5.00	3.00
(85)	Knight	10.00	5.00	3.00
(86)	Koehler	10.00	5.00	3.00
(87)	Kopp	10.00	5.00	3.00
(88)	Krause	10.00	5.00	3.00
(89)	Krug	10.00	5.00	3.00
(90)	Kunz	10.00	5.00	3.00
(91)	Lafayette	10.00	5.00	3.00
(92)	Lane	10.00	5.00	3.00
(93)	Lang	10.00	5.00	3.00
(94)	Lary	10.00	5.00	3.00
(95)	Leslie	10.00	5.00	3.00
(96)	Lindemore	10.00	5.00	3.00
(97)	Ludolph	10.00	5.00	3.00
(98)	Makin	10.00	5.00	3.00
(99)	Mangum	10.00	5.00	3.00
(100)	Martin	10.00	5.00	3.00
(101)	McCredie	10.00	5.00	3.00
(102)	McDowell	10.00	5.00	3.00
(103)	McKenry	10.00	5.00	3.00
(104)	McLoughlin	10.00	5.00	3.00
(105)	McNally	10.00	5.00	3.00
(106)	McPhee	10.00	5.00	3.00
(107)	Meeker	10.00	5.00	3.00
(108)	Metz	10.00	5.00	3.00
(109)	Miller	10.00	5.00	3.00
(110)	Mitchell (Los Angeles)	10.00	5.00	3.00
(111)	Mitchell (San Francisco)	10.00	5.00	3.00
(112)	Monroe	10.00	5.00	3.00
(113)	Moudy	10.00	5.00	3.00
(114)	Mulcahy	10.00	5.00	3.00
(115)	Mulligan	10.00	5.00	3.00
(116)	Murphy	10.00	5.00	3.00
(117)	O'Doul	40.00	20.00	12.50
(118)	O'Neill	10.00	5.00	3.00
(119)	Oeschger	9.00	4.50	2.75
(120)	Oliver	10.00	5.00	3.00
(121)	Ortman	10.00	5.00	3.00
(122)	Osborn	10.00	5.00	3.00
(123)	Paynter	10.00	5.00	3.00
(124)	Peters	10.00	5.00	3.00
(125)	Pfahler	10.00	5.00	3.00
(126)	Pillette	10.00	5.00	3.00
(127)	Plummer	10.00	5.00	3.00
(128)	Prothro	10.00	5.00	3.00
(129)	Pruett	10.00	5.00	3.00
(130)	Rachac	10.00	5.00	3.00
(131)	Ramsey	10.00	5.00	3.00
(132)	Rathjen	10.00	5.00	3.00
(133)	Read	10.00	5.00	3.00
(134)	Redman	10.00	5.00	3.00
(135)	Reese	12.00	6.00	3.50
(136)	Rodda	10.00	5.00	3.00
(137)	Rohwer	10.00	5.00	3.00
(138)	Ryan	10.00	5.00	3.00
(139)	Sandberg	10.00	5.00	3.00
(140)	Sanders	10.00	5.00	3.00
(141)	E. Shea	10.00	5.00	3.00
(142)	M. Shea	10.00	5.00	3.00
(143)	Sheehan	10.00	5.00	3.00
(144)	Shellenbach	10.00	5.00	3.00
(145)	Sherlock	10.00	5.00	3.00
(146)	Siglin	10.00	5.00	3.00
(147)	Slade	10.00	5.00	3.00
(148)	E. Smith	10.00	5.00	3.00
(149)	M. Smith	10.00	5.00	3.00

		NR MT	EX	VG
(150)	Staley	10.00	5.00	3.00
(151)	Statz	10.00	5.00	3.00
(152)	Stroud	10.00	5.00	3.00
(153)	Stuart	10.00	5.00	3.00
(154)	Suhr	10.00	5.00	3.00
(155)	Swanson	10.00	5.00	3.00
(156)	Sweeney	10.00	5.00	3.00
(157)	Tadevich	10.00	5.00	3.00
(158)	Thomas	10.00	5.00	3.00
(159)	Thompson	10.00	5.00	3.00
(160)	Tobin	10.00	5.00	3.00
(161)	Valla	10.00	5.00	3.00
(162)	Vargas	10.00	5.00	3.00
(163)	Vinci	10.00	5.00	3.00
(164)	Walters	10.00	5.00	3.00
(165)	Waner	75.00	38.00	23.00
(166)	Weis	10.00	5.00	3.00
(167)	Whitney	10.00	5.00	3.00
(168)	Williams	10.00	5.00	3.00
(169)	Wright	10.00	5.00	3.00
(170)	Yelle	10.00	5.00	3.00
(171)	Zaeffel	10.00	5.00	3.00
(172)	Zoellers	10.00	5.00	3.00

1927 E137 Zeenut

The 1927 Zeenuts are the same size and color as the 1926 issue, except the year is expressed in just two digits (27), a practice that continued through 1930. There are 144 subjects known.

		NR MT	EX	VG
Complete Set:		1500.00	750.00	450.00
Common Player:		10.00	5.00	3.00
(1)	Agnew	10.00	5.00	3.00
(2)	Arlett	12.00	6.00	3.50
(3)	Averill	25.00	12.50	7.50
(4)	Backer	10.00	5.00	3.00
(5)	Bagwell	10.00	5.00	3.00
(6)	Baker	10.00	5.00	3.00
(7)	D. Baker	10.00	5.00	3.00
(8)	Ballenger	10.00	5.00	3.00
(9)	Baumgartner	10.00	5.00	3.00
(10)	Bigbee	10.00	5.00	3.00
(11)	Boehler	10.00	5.00	3.00
(12)	Bool	10.00	5.00	3.00
(13)	Borreani	10.00	5.00	3.00
(14)	Brady	10.00	5.00	3.00
(15)	Bratcher	10.00	5.00	3.00
(16)	Brett	10.00	5.00	3.00
(17)	Brown	10.00	5.00	3.00
(18)	Brubaker	10.00	5.00	3.00
(19)	Bryan	10.00	5.00	3.00
(20)	Callaghan	10.00	5.00	3.00
(21)	Caveney	10.00	5.00	3.00
(22)	Christian	10.00	5.00	3.00
(23)	Cissell	10.00	5.00	3.00
(24)	Cook	10.00	5.00	3.00
(25)	Cooper (Oakland)	10.00	5.00	3.00
(26)	Cooper (Sacramento)	10.00	5.00	3.00
(27)	Cox	10.00	5.00	3.00
(28)	Cunningham	10.00	5.00	3.00
(29)	Daglia	10.00	5.00	3.00
(30)	Dickerman	10.00	5.00	3.00
(31)	Dumovitch	10.00	5.00	3.00
(32)	Eckert	10.00	5.00	3.00
(33)	Eldred	10.00	5.00	3.00

		NR MT	EX	VG
(34)	Ellison	10.00	5.00	3.00
(35)	Fenton	10.00	5.00	3.00
(36)	Finn	10.00	5.00	3.00
(37)	Fischer	10.00	5.00	3.00
(38)	Frederick	10.00	5.00	3.00
(39)	French	10.00	5.00	3.00
(40)	Fullerton	10.00	5.00	3.00
(41)	Geary	10.00	5.00	3.00
(42)	Gillespie	10.00	5.00	3.00
(43)	Gooch	10.00	5.00	3.00
(44)	Gould	10.00	5.00	3.00
(45)	Governor	10.00	5.00	3.00
(46)	Guisto	10.00	5.00	3.00
(47)	Hannah	10.00	5.00	3.00
(48)	Hasty	10.00	5.00	3.00
(49)	Hemingway	10.00	5.00	3.00
(50)	Hoffman	10.00	5.00	3.00
(51)	Hood	10.00	5.00	3.00
(52)	Hooper	75.00	38.00	23.00
(53)	Hudgens	10.00	5.00	3.00
(54)	Hufft	10.00	5.00	3.00
(55)	Hughes	10.00	5.00	3.00
(56)	Jahn	10.00	5.00	3.00
(57)	Johnson (Portland)	10.00	5.00	3.00
(58)	Johnson (Seals)	10.00	5.00	3.00
(59)	Jolly	10.00	5.00	3.00
(60)	Jones	10.00	5.00	3.00
(61)	Kallio	10.00	5.00	3.00
(62)	Keating	10.00	5.00	3.00
(63)	Keefe	10.00	5.00	3.00
(64)	Killifer	10.00	5.00	3.00
(65)	Kimmick	10.00	5.00	3.00
(66)	Kinney	10.00	5.00	3.00
(67)	Knight	10.00	5.00	3.00
(68)	Koehler	10.00	5.00	3.00
(69)	Kopp	10.00	5.00	3.00
(70)	Krause	10.00	5.00	3.00
(71)	Krug	10.00	5.00	3.00
(72)	Kunz	10.00	5.00	3.00
(73)	Lary	10.00	5.00	3.00
(74)	Leard	10.00	5.00	3.00
(75)	Lingrel	10.00	5.00	3.00
(76)	Ludolph	10.00	5.00	3.00
(77)	Mails	10.00	5.00	3.00
(78)	Makin	10.00	5.00	3.00
(79)	Martin	10.00	5.00	3.00
(80)	May	10.00	5.00	3.00
(81)	McCabe	10.00	5.00	3.00
(82)	McCurdy	10.00	5.00	3.00
(83)	McDaniel	10.00	5.00	3.00
(84)	McGee	10.00	5.00	3.00
(85)	McLaughlin	10.00	5.00	3.00
(86)	McMurtry	10.00	5.00	3.00
(87)	Metz	10.00	5.00	3.00
(88)	Miljus	10.00	5.00	3.00
(89)	Mitchell	10.00	5.00	3.00
(90)	Monroe	10.00	5.00	3.00
(91)	Moudy	10.00	5.00	3.00
(92)	Mulligan	10.00	5.00	3.00
(93)	Murphy	10.00	5.00	3.00
(94)	O'Brien	10.00	5.00	3.00
(95)	O'Doul	40.00	20.00	12.00
(96)	Oliver	10.00	5.00	3.00
(97)	Osborn	10.00	5.00	3.00
(98)	Parker (Missions, batting)	10.00	5.00	3.00
(99)	Parker (Missions, throwing)	10.00	5.00	3.00
(100)	Parker (Portland)	10.00	5.00	3.00
(101)	Peters	10.00	5.00	3.00
(102)	Pillette	10.00	5.00	3.00
(103)	Ponder	10.00	5.00	3.00
(104)	Prothro	10.00	5.00	3.00
(105)	Rachac	10.00	5.00	3.00
(106)	Ramsey	10.00	5.00	3.00
(107)	Read	10.00	5.00	3.00
(108)	Reese	12.00	6.00	3.50
(109)	Rodda	10.00	5.00	3.00
(110)	Rohwer	10.00	5.00	3.00
(111)	Rose	10.00	5.00	3.00
(112)	Ryan	10.00	5.00	3.00
(113)	Sandberg	10.00	5.00	3.00
(114)	Sanders	10.00	5.00	3.00
(115)	Severeid	10.00	5.00	3.00
(116)	Shea	10.00	5.00	3.00
(117)	Sheehan (Hollywood)	10.00	5.00	3.00
(118)	Sheehan (Seals)	10.00	5.00	3.00
(119)	Sherlock	10.00	5.00	3.00
(120a)	Shinners (date is "1927")	25.00	12.50	7.50
(120b)	Shinners (date is "27")	10.00	5.00	3.00
(121)	Singleton	10.00	5.00	3.00
(122)	Slade	10.00	5.00	3.00
(123)	E. Smith	10.00	5.00	3.00

		NR MT	EX	VG
(124)	Sparks	10.00	5.00	3.00
(125)	Stokes	10.00	5.00	3.00
(126)	J. Storti	10.00	5.00	3.00
(127)	L. Storti	10.00	5.00	3.00
(128)	Strand	10.00	5.00	3.00
(129)	Suhr	10.00	5.00	3.00
(130)	Sunseri	10.00	5.00	3.00
(131)	Swanson	10.00	5.00	3.00
(132)	Tierney	10.00	5.00	3.00
(133)	Valla	10.00	5.00	3.00
(134)	Vargas	10.00	5.00	3.00
(135)	Vitt	10.00	5.00	3.00
(136)	Weinert	10.00	5.00	3.00
(137)	Weis	10.00	5.00	3.00
(138)	Wendell	10.00	5.00	3.00
(139)	Whitney	10.00	5.00	3.00
(140)	Williams	10.00	5.00	3.00
(141)	Guy Williams	10.00	5.00	3.00
(142)	Woodson	10.00	5.00	3.00
(143)	Wright	10.00	5.00	3.00
(144)	Yelle	10.00	5.00	3.00

1928 E137 Zeenut

Zeenut cards from 1928 through 1930 maintain the same size and style as the 1927 series. The 1928 and 1929 series consist of 168 known subjects, while the 1930 series has 186. There are some lettering variations in the 1930 series.

		NR MT	EX	VG
Complete Set:		1700.00	850.00	500.00
Common Player:		10.00	5.00	3.00
(1)	Agnew	10.00	5.00	3.00
(2)	Averill	25.00	12.50	7.50
(3)	Backer	10.00	5.00	3.00
(4)	Baker	10.00	5.00	3.00
(5)	Baldwin	10.00	5.00	3.00
(6)	Barfoot	10.00	5.00	3.00
(7)	Bassler	10.00	5.00	3.00
(8)	Berger	10.00	5.00	3.00
(9)	Bigbee (Los Angeles)	10.00	5.00	3.00
(10)	Bigbee (Portland)	10.00	5.00	3.00
(11)	Bodie	12.00	6.00	3.50
(12)	Boehler	10.00	5.00	3.00
(13)	Bool	10.00	5.00	3.00
(14)	Boone	10.00	5.00	3.00
(15)	Borreani	10.00	5.00	3.00
(16)	Bratcher	10.00	5.00	3.00
(17)	Brenzel	10.00	5.00	3.00
(18)	Brubaker	10.00	5.00	3.00
(19)	Bryan	10.00	5.00	3.00
(20)	Burkett	10.00	5.00	3.00
(21)	Camilli	12.00	6.00	3.50
(22)	W. Canfield	10.00	5.00	3.00
(23)	Caveney	10.00	5.00	3.00
(24)	Cohen	10.00	5.00	3.00
(25)	Cook	10.00	5.00	3.00
(26)	Cooper	10.00	5.00	3.00
(27)	Craghead	10.00	5.00	3.00
(28)	Crosetti	20.00	10.00	6.00
(29)	Cunningham	10.00	5.00	3.00
(30)	Daglia	10.00	5.00	3.00
(31)	Davis	10.00	5.00	3.00
(32)	Dean	10.00	5.00	3.00
(33)	Dittmar	10.00	5.00	3.00
(34)	Donovan	10.00	5.00	3.00

		NR MT	EX	VG
(35)	Downs	10.00	5.00	3.00
(36)	Duff	10.00	5.00	3.00
(37)	Eckert	10.00	5.00	3.00
(38)	Eldred	10.00	5.00	3.00
(39)	Ellsworth	10.00	5.00	3.00
(40)	Fenton	10.00	5.00	3.00
(41)	Finn	10.00	5.00	3.00
(42)	Fitterer	10.00	5.00	3.00
(43)	Flynn	10.00	5.00	3.00
(44)	Frazier	10.00	5.00	3.00
(45)	French (Portland)	10.00	5.00	3.00
(46)	French (Sacramento)	10.00	5.00	3.00
(47)	Fullerton	10.00	5.00	3.00
(48)	Gabler	10.00	5.00	3.00
(49)	Gomes	10.00	5.00	3.00
(50)	Gooch	10.00	5.00	3.00
(51)	Gould	10.00	5.00	3.00
(52)	Governor	10.00	5.00	3.00
(53)	Graham ("S" on uniform)	10.00	5.00	3.00
(54)	Graham (no "S" on uniform)	10.00	5.00	3.00
(55)	Guisto	10.00	5.00	3.00
(56)	Hannah	10.00	5.00	3.00
(57)	Hansen	10.00	5.00	3.00
(58)	Harris	10.00	5.00	3.00
(59)	Hasty	10.00	5.00	3.00
(60)	Heath	10.00	5.00	3.00
(61)	Hoffman	10.00	5.00	3.00
(62)	Holling	10.00	5.00	3.00
(63)	Hood	10.00	5.00	3.00
(64)	House	10.00	5.00	3.00
(65)	Howard	10.00	5.00	3.00
(66)	Hudgens	10.00	5.00	3.00
(67)	Hufft	10.00	5.00	3.00
(68)	Hughes	10.00	5.00	3.00
(69)	Hulvey	10.00	5.00	3.00
(70)	Jacobs	10.00	5.00	3.00
(71)	Johnson (Portland)	10.00	5.00	3.00
(72)	Johnson (San Francisco)	10.00	5.00	3.00
(73)	Jolley	10.00	5.00	3.00
(74)	Jones (batting)	10.00	5.00	3.00
(75)	Jones (throwing)	10.00	5.00	3.00
(76)	Kallio	10.00	5.00	3.00
(77)	Keating	10.00	5.00	3.00
(78)	Keefe	10.00	5.00	3.00
(79)	Keesey	10.00	5.00	3.00
(80)	Kerr	10.00	5.00	3.00
(81)	Killifer	10.00	5.00	3.00
(82)	Kinney	10.00	5.00	3.00
(83)	Knight	10.00	5.00	3.00
(84)	Knothe	10.00	5.00	3.00
(85)	Koehler	10.00	5.00	3.00
(86)	Kopp	10.00	5.00	3.00
(87)	Krause	10.00	5.00	3.00
(88)	Krug	10.00	5.00	3.00
(89)	Lary	10.00	5.00	3.00
(90)	LeBourveau	10.00	5.00	3.00
(91)	Lee	10.00	5.00	3.00
(92)	Lombardi	50.00	25.00	15.00
(93)	Mails	10.00	5.00	3.00
(94)	Martin (Missions)	10.00	5.00	3.00
(95)	Martin (Seattle)	10.00	5.00	3.00
(96)	May	10.00	5.00	3.00
(97)	McCabe	10.00	5.00	3.00
(98)	McCrea	10.00	5.00	3.00
(99)	McDaniel	10.00	5.00	3.00
(100)	McLaughlin	10.00	5.00	3.00
(101)	McNulty	10.00	5.00	3.00
(102)	Mellano	10.00	5.00	3.00
(103)	Muesel (Meusel)	9.00	4.50	2.75
(104)	Middleton	10.00	5.00	3.00
(105)	Mishkin	10.00	5.00	3.00
(106)	Mitchell	10.00	5.00	3.00
(107)	Monroe	10.00	5.00	3.00
(108)	Moudy	10.00	5.00	3.00
(109)	Mulcahy	10.00	5.00	3.00
(110)	Muller	10.00	5.00	3.00
(111)	Mulligan	10.00	5.00	3.00
(112)	W. Murphy	10.00	5.00	3.00
(113)	Nance	10.00	5.00	3.00
(114)	Nelson	10.00	5.00	3.00
(115)	Osborn	10.00	5.00	3.00
(116)	Osborne	10.00	5.00	3.00
(117)	Parker	10.00	5.00	3.00
(118)	Peters	10.00	5.00	3.00
(119)	Pillette	10.00	5.00	3.00
(120)	Pinelli	10.00	5.00	3.00
(121)	Plitt	10.00	5.00	3.00
(122)	Ponder	10.00	5.00	3.00
(123)	Rachac	10.00	5.00	3.00
(124)	Read	10.00	5.00	3.00
(125)	Reed	10.00	5.00	3.00

		NR MT	EX	VG
(126)	Reese	12.00	6.00	3.50
(127)	Rego	10.00	5.00	3.00
(128)	Rhodes	10.00	5.00	3.00
(129)	Rhyne	10.00	5.00	3.00
(130)	Rodda	10.00	5.00	3.00
(131)	Rohwer	10.00	5.00	3.00
(132)	Rose	10.00	5.00	3.00
(133)	Roth	10.00	5.00	3.00
(134)	Ruble	10.00	5.00	3.00
(135)	Ryan	10.00	5.00	3.00
(136)	Sandberg	10.00	5.00	3.00
(137)	Schulmerich	10.00	5.00	3.00
(138)	Severeid	10.00	5.00	3.00
(139)	Shea	10.00	5.00	3.00
(140)	Sheely	10.00	5.00	3.00
(141)	Shellenback	10.00	5.00	3.00
(142)	Sherlock	10.00	5.00	3.00
(143)	Sigafoos	10.00	5.00	3.00
(144)	Singleton	10.00	5.00	3.00
(145)	Slade	10.00	5.00	3.00
(146)	Smith	10.00	5.00	3.00
(147)	Sprinz	10.00	5.00	3.00
(148)	Staley	10.00	5.00	3.00
(149)	Suhr	10.00	5.00	3.00
(150)	Sunseri	10.00	5.00	3.00
(151)	Swanson	10.00	5.00	3.00
(152)	Sweeney	10.00	5.00	3.00
(153)	Teachout	10.00	5.00	3.00
(154)	Twombly	10.00	5.00	3.00
(155)	Vargas	10.00	5.00	3.00
(156)	Vinci	10.00	5.00	3.00
(157)	Vitt	10.00	5.00	3.00
(158)	Warhop	10.00	5.00	3.00
(159)	Weathersby	10.00	5.00	3.00
(160)	Weiss	10.00	5.00	3.00
(161)	Welch	10.00	5.00	3.00
(162)	Wera	10.00	5.00	3.00
(163)	Wetzel	10.00	5.00	3.00
(164)	Whitney	10.00	5.00	3.00
(165)	Williams	10.00	5.00	3.00
(166)	Wilson	10.00	5.00	3.00
(167)	Wolfer	10.00	5.00	3.00
(168)	Yerkes	10.00	5.00	3.00

1929 E137 Zeenut

		NR MT	EX	VG
Complete Set:		1700.00	850.00	500.00
Common Player:		10.00	5.00	3.00
(1)	Albert	10.00	5.00	3.00
(2)	Almada	10.00	5.00	3.00
(3)	Anderson	10.00	5.00	3.00
(4)	Anton	10.00	5.00	3.00
(5)	Backer	10.00	5.00	3.00
(6)	Baker	10.00	5.00	3.00
(7)	Baldwin	10.00	5.00	3.00
(8)	Barbee	10.00	5.00	3.00
(9)	Barfoot	10.00	5.00	3.00
(10)	Bassler	10.00	5.00	3.00
(11)	Bates	10.00	5.00	3.00
(12)	Berger	10.00	5.00	3.00
(13)	Boehler	10.00	5.00	3.00
(14)	Boone	10.00	5.00	3.00
(15)	Borreani	10.00	5.00	3.00
(16)	Brenzel	10.00	5.00	3.00
(17)	Brooks	10.00	5.00	3.00
(18)	Brubaker	10.00	5.00	3.00

		NR MT	EX	VG
(19)	Bryan	10.00	5.00	3.00
(20)	Burke	10.00	5.00	3.00
(21)	Burkett	10.00	5.00	3.00
(22)	Burns	10.00	5.00	3.00
(23)	Bush	10.00	5.00	3.00
(24)	Butler	10.00	5.00	3.00
(25)	Camilli	12.00	6.00	3.50
(26)	Carlyle	10.00	5.00	3.00
(27)	Carlyle	10.00	5.00	3.00
(28)	Cascarella	10.00	5.00	3.00
(29)	Caveney	10.00	5.00	3.00
(30)	Childs	10.00	5.00	3.00
(31)	Christensen	10.00	5.00	3.00
(32)	Cole	10.00	5.00	3.00
(33)	Collard	10.00	5.00	3.00
(34)	Cooper	10.00	5.00	3.00
(35)	Couch	10.00	5.00	3.00
(36)	Cox	10.00	5.00	3.00
(37)	Craghead	10.00	5.00	3.00
(38)	Crandall	10.00	5.00	3.00
(39)	Cronin	10.00	5.00	3.00
(40)	Crosetti	20.00	10.00	6.00
(41)	Daglia	10.00	5.00	3.00
(42)	Davis	10.00	5.00	3.00
(43)	Dean	10.00	5.00	3.00
(44)	Dittmar	10.00	5.00	3.00
(45)	Donovan	10.00	5.00	3.00
(46)	Dumovich	10.00	5.00	3.00
(47)	Eckardt	10.00	5.00	3.00
(48)	Ellsworth	10.00	5.00	3.00
(49)	Fenton	10.00	5.00	3.00
(50)	Finn	10.00	5.00	3.00
(51)	Fisch	10.00	5.00	3.00
(52)	Flynn	10.00	5.00	3.00
(53)	Frazier	10.00	5.00	3.00
(54)	Freitas	10.00	5.00	3.00
(55)	French	10.00	5.00	3.00
(56)	Gabler	10.00	5.00	3.00
(57)	Glynn	10.00	5.00	3.00
(58)	Gomez	50.00	25.00	15.00
(59)	Gould	10.00	5.00	3.00
(60)	Governor	10.00	5.00	3.00
(61)	Graham	10.00	5.00	3.00
(62)	Hand	10.00	5.00	3.00
(63)	Hannah	10.00	5.00	3.00
(64)	Harris	10.00	5.00	3.00
(65)	Heath	10.00	5.00	3.00
(66)	Heatherly	10.00	5.00	3.00
(67)	Hepting	10.00	5.00	3.00
(68)	Hillis	10.00	5.00	3.00
(69)	Hoffman	10.00	5.00	3.00
(70)	Holling	10.00	5.00	3.00
(71)	Hood	10.00	5.00	3.00
(72)	House	10.00	5.00	3.00
(73)	Howard	10.00	5.00	3.00
(74)	Hubbell	10.00	5.00	3.00
(75)	Hufft	10.00	5.00	3.00
(76)	Hurst	10.00	5.00	3.00
(77)	Jacobs (Los Angeles)	10.00	5.00	3.00
(78)	Jacobs (San Francisco)	10.00	5.00	3.00
(79)	Jahn	10.00	5.00	3.00
(80)	Jeffcoat	10.00	5.00	3.00
(81)	Johnson	10.00	5.00	3.00
(82)	Jolley	10.00	5.00	3.00
(83)	Jones	10.00	5.00	3.00
(84)	Jones	10.00	5.00	3.00
(85)	Kallio	10.00	5.00	3.00
(86)	Kasich	10.00	5.00	3.00
(87)	Keane	10.00	5.00	3.00
(88)	Keating	10.00	5.00	3.00
(89)	Keesey	10.00	5.00	3.00
(90)	Killifer	10.00	5.00	3.00
(91)	Knight	10.00	5.00	3.00
(92)	Knothe	10.00	5.00	3.00
(93)	Knott	10.00	5.00	3.00
(94)	Koehler	10.00	5.00	3.00
(95)	Krasovich	10.00	5.00	3.00
(96)	Krause	10.00	5.00	3.00
(97)	Krug (Hollywood)	10.00	5.00	3.00
(98)	Krug (Los Angeles)	10.00	5.00	3.00
(99)	Kunz	10.00	5.00	3.00
(100)	Langford	10.00	5.00	3.00
(101)	Lee	10.00	5.00	3.00
(102)	Lombardi	50.00	25.00	15.00
(103)	Mahaffey	10.00	5.00	3.00
(104)	Mails	10.00	5.00	3.00
(105)	Maloney	10.00	5.00	3.00
(106)	McCabe	10.00	5.00	3.00
(107)	McDaniel	10.00	5.00	3.00
(108)	McEvoy	10.00	5.00	3.00
(109)	McIssacs	10.00	5.00	3.00

		NR MT	EX	VG
(110)	McQuaid	10.00	5.00	3.00
(111)	Miller	10.00	5.00	3.00
(112)	Monroe	10.00	5.00	3.00
(113)	Muller	10.00	5.00	3.00
(114)	Mulligan	10.00	5.00	3.00
(115)	Nance	10.00	5.00	3.00
(116)	Nelson	10.00	5.00	3.00
(117)	Nevers	10.00	5.00	3.00
(118)	Oana	10.00	5.00	3.00
(119)	Olney	10.00	5.00	3.00
(120)	Ortman	10.00	5.00	3.00
(121)	Osborne	10.00	5.00	3.00
(122)	Ostenberg	10.00	5.00	3.00
(123)	Peters	10.00	5.00	3.00
(124)	Pillette	10.00	5.00	3.00
(125)	Pinelli	12.00	6.50	3.50
(126)	Pipgras	10.00	5.00	3.00
(127)	Plitt	10.00	5.00	3.00
(128)	Polvogt	10.00	5.00	3.00
(129)	Rachac	10.00	5.00	3.00
(130)	Read	10.00	5.00	3.00
(131)	Reed	10.00	5.00	3.00
(132)	Reese	12.00	6.50	3.50
(133)	Rego	10.00	5.00	3.00
(134)	Ritter	10.00	5.00	3.00
(135)	Roberts	10.00	5.00	3.00
(136)	Rodda	10.00	5.00	3.00
(137)	Rodgers	10.00	5.00	3.00
(138)	Rohwer	10.00	5.00	3.00
(139)	Rollings	10.00	5.00	3.00
(140)	Rumler	10.00	5.00	3.00
(141)	Ryan	10.00	5.00	3.00
(142)	Sandberg	10.00	5.00	3.00
(143)	Schino	10.00	5.00	3.00
(144)	Schmidt	10.00	5.00	3.00
(145)	Schulmerich	10.00	5.00	3.00
(146)	Scott	10.00	5.00	3.00
(147)	Severeid	10.00	5.00	3.00
(148)	Shanklin	10.00	5.00	3.00
(149)	Sherlock	10.00	5.00	3.00
(150)	Slade	10.00	5.00	3.00
(151)	Staley	10.00	5.00	3.00
(152)	Statz	10.00	5.00	3.00
(153)	Steinecke	10.00	5.00	3.00
(154)	Suhr	10.00	5.00	3.00
(155)	Taylor	10.00	5.00	3.00
(156)	Thurston	10.00	5.00	3.00
(157)	Tierney	10.00	5.00	3.00
(158)	Tolson	10.00	5.00	3.00
(159)	Tomlin	10.00	5.00	3.00
(160)	Vergez	10.00	5.00	3.00
(161)	Vinci	10.00	5.00	3.00
(162)	Volkman	10.00	5.00	3.00
(163)	Walsh	10.00	5.00	3.00
(164)	Warren	10.00	5.00	3.00
(165)	Webb	10.00	5.00	3.00
(166)	Weustling	10.00	5.00	3.00
(167)	Williams	10.00	5.00	3.00
(168)	Wingo	10.00	5.00	3.00

1930 E137 Zeenut

		NR MT	EX	VG
Complete Set:		1200.00	600.00	360.00
Common Player:		10.00	5.00	3.00
(1)	Allington	10.00	5.00	3.00
(2)	Almada	10.00	5.00	3.00

		NR MT	EX	VG
(3)	Andrews	10.00	5.00	3.00
(4)	Anton	10.00	5.00	3.00
(5)	Arlett	12.00	6.00	3.50
(6)	Backer	10.00	5.00	3.00
(7)	Baecht	10.00	5.00	3.00
(8)	Baker	10.00	5.00	3.00
(9)	Baldwin	10.00	5.00	3.00
(10)	Ballou	10.00	5.00	3.00
(11)	Barbee	10.00	5.00	3.00
(12)	Barfoot	10.00	5.00	3.00
(13)	Bassler	10.00	5.00	3.00
(14)	Bates	10.00	5.00	3.00
(15)	Beck	10.00	5.00	3.00
(16)	Boone	10.00	5.00	3.00
(17)	Bowman	10.00	5.00	3.00
(18)	Brannon	10.00	5.00	3.00
(19)	Brenzel	10.00	5.00	3.00
(20)	Brown	10.00	5.00	3.00
(21)	Brubaker	10.00	5.00	3.00
(22)	Brucker	10.00	5.00	3.00
(23)	Bryan	10.00	5.00	3.00
(24)	Burkett	10.00	5.00	3.00
(25)	Burns	10.00	5.00	3.00
(26)	Butler	10.00	5.00	3.00
(27)	Camilli	12.00	6.00	3.50
(28)	Carlyle	10.00	5.00	3.00
(29)	Caster	10.00	5.00	3.00
(30)	Caveney	10.00	5.00	3.00
(31)	Chamberlain	10.00	5.00	3.00
(32)	Chatham	10.00	5.00	3.00
(33)	Childs	10.00	5.00	3.00
(34)	Christensen	10.00	5.00	3.00
(35)	Church	10.00	5.00	3.00
(36)	Cole	10.00	5.00	3.00
(37)	Coleman	10.00	5.00	3.00
(38)	Collins	10.00	5.00	3.00
(39)	Coscarart	10.00	5.00	3.00
(40)	Cox	10.00	5.00	3.00
(41)	Coyle	10.00	5.00	3.00
(42)	Craghead	10.00	5.00	3.00
(43)	Cronin	10.00	5.00	3.00
(44)	Crosetti	20.00	10.00	6.00
(45)	Daglia	10.00	5.00	3.00
(46)	Davis	10.00	5.00	3.00
(47)	Dean	10.00	5.00	3.00
(48)	DeViveiros	10.00	5.00	3.00
(49)	Dittmar	10.00	5.00	3.00
(50)	Donovan	10.00	5.00	3.00
(51)	Douglas	10.00	5.00	3.00
(52)	Dumovich	10.00	5.00	3.00
(53)	Edwards	10.00	5.00	3.00
(54)	Ellsworth	10.00	5.00	3.00
(55)	Falk	10.00	5.00	3.00
(56)	Fisch	10.00	5.00	3.00
(57)	Flynn	10.00	5.00	3.00
(58)	Freitas	10.00	5.00	3.00
(59)	French (Portland)	10.00	5.00	3.00
(60)	French (Sacramento)	10.00	5.00	3.00
(61)	Gabler	10.00	5.00	3.00
(62)	Gaston	10.00	5.00	3.00
(63)	Gazella	10.00	5.00	3.00
(64)	Gould	10.00	5.00	3.00
(65)	Governor	10.00	5.00	3.00
(66)	Green	10.00	5.00	3.00
(67)	Griffin	10.00	5.00	3.00
(68)	Haney	9.00	4.50	2.75
(69)	Hannah	10.00	5.00	3.00
(70)	Harper	10.00	5.00	3.00
(71)	Heath	10.00	5.00	3.00
(72)	Hillis	10.00	5.00	3.00
(73)	Hoag	10.00	5.00	3.00
(74)	Hoffman	10.00	5.00	3.00
(75)	Holland	10.00	5.00	3.00
(76)	Hollerson	10.00	5.00	3.00
(77)	Holling	10.00	5.00	3.00
(78)	Hood	10.00	5.00	3.00
(79)	Horn	10.00	5.00	3.00
(80)	House	10.00	5.00	3.00
(81)	Hubbell	10.00	5.00	3.00
(82)	Hufft	10.00	5.00	3.00
(83)	Hurst	10.00	5.00	3.00
(84)	Jacobs (Los Angeles)	10.00	5.00	3.00
(85)	Jacobs (Oakland)	10.00	5.00	3.00
(86)	Jacobs	10.00	5.00	3.00
(87)	Jahn	10.00	5.00	3.00
(88)	Jeffcoat	10.00	5.00	3.00
(89)	Johns	10.00	5.00	3.00
(90)	Johnson (Portland)	10.00	5.00	3.00
(91)	Johnson (Seattle)	10.00	5.00	3.00
(92)	Joiner	10.00	5.00	3.00
(93)	Kallio	10.00	5.00	3.00

		NR MT	EX	VG
(94)	Kasich	10.00	5.00	3.00
(95)	Keating	10.00	5.00	3.00
(96)	Kelly	10.00	5.00	3.00
(97)	Killifer	10.00	5.00	3.00
(98)	Knight	10.00	5.00	3.00
(99)	Knothe	10.00	5.00	3.00
(100)	Koehler	10.00	5.00	3.00
(101)	Kunz	10.00	5.00	3.00
(102)	Lamanski	10.00	5.00	3.00
(103)	Lawrence	10.00	5.00	3.00
(104)	Lee	10.00	5.00	3.00
(105)	Leishman	10.00	5.00	3.00
(106)	Lelivelt	10.00	5.00	3.00
(107)	Lieber	10.00	5.00	3.00
(108)	Lombardi	50.00	25.00	15.00
(109)	Mails	10.00	5.00	3.00
(110)	Maloney	10.00	5.00	3.00
(111)	Martin	10.00	5.00	3.00
(112)	McDougal	10.00	5.00	3.00
(113)	McLaughlin	10.00	5.00	3.00
(114)	McQuaide	10.00	5.00	3.00
(115)	Mellana	10.00	5.00	3.00
(116)	Miljus ("S" on uniform)	10.00	5.00	3.00
(117)	Miljus ("Seals" on uniform)	10.00	5.00	3.00
(118)	Monroe	10.00	5.00	3.00
(119)	Montgomery	10.00	5.00	3.00
(120)	Moore	10.00	5.00	3.00
(121)	Mulana	10.00	5.00	3.00
(122)	Muller	10.00	5.00	3.00
(123)	Mulligan	10.00	5.00	3.00
(124)	Nelson	10.00	5.00	3.00
(125)	Nevers	10.00	5.00	3.00
(126)	Odell	10.00	5.00	3.00
(127)	Olney	10.00	5.00	3.00
(128)	Osborne	10.00	5.00	3.00
(129)	Page	10.00	5.00	3.00
(130)	Palmisano	10.00	5.00	3.00
(131)	Parker	10.00	5.00	3.00
(132)	Pasedel	10.00	5.00	3.00
(133)	Pearson	10.00	5.00	3.00
(134)	Penebskey	10.00	5.00	3.00
(135)	Perry	10.00	5.00	3.00
(136)	Peters	10.00	5.00	3.00
(137)	Petterson	10.00	5.00	3.00
(138)	H. Pillette	10.00	5.00	3.00
(139)	T. Pillette	10.00	5.00	3.00
(140)	Pinelli	12.00	6.00	3.50
(141)	Pipgrass	10.00	5.00	3.00
(142)	Porter	10.00	5.00	3.00
(143)	Powles	10.00	5.00	3.00
(144)	Read	10.00	5.00	3.00
(145)	Reed	10.00	5.00	3.00
(146)	Rehg	10.00	5.00	3.00
(147)	Ricci	10.00	5.00	3.00
(148)	Roberts	10.00	5.00	3.00
(149)	Rodda	10.00	5.00	3.00
(150)	Rohwer	10.00	5.00	3.00
(151)	Rosenberg	10.00	5.00	3.00
(152)	Rumler	10.00	5.00	3.00
(153)	Ryan	10.00	5.00	3.00
(154)	Schino	10.00	5.00	3.00
(155)	Severeid	10.00	5.00	3.00
(156)	Shanklin	10.00	5.00	3.00
(157)	Sheely	10.00	5.00	3.00
(158)	Sigafoos	10.00	5.00	3.00
(159)	Statz	10.00	5.00	3.00
(160)	Steinbacker	10.00	5.00	3.00
(161)	Stevenson	10.00	5.00	3.00
(162)	Sulik	10.00	5.00	3.00
(163)	Taylor	10.00	5.00	3.00
(164)	Thomas (Sacramento)	10.00	5.00	3.00
(165)	Thomas (San Francisco)	10.00	5.00	3.00
(166)	Trembly	10.00	5.00	3.00
(167)	Turner	10.00	5.00	3.00
(168)	Turpin	10.00	5.00	3.00
(169)	Uhalt	10.00	5.00	3.00
(170)	Vergez	10.00	5.00	3.00
(171)	Vinci	10.00	5.00	3.00
(172)	Vitt	10.00	5.00	3.00
(173)	Wallgren	10.00	5.00	3.00
(174)	Walsh	10.00	5.00	3.00
(175)	Ward	10.00	5.00	3.00
(176)	Warren	10.00	5.00	3.00
(177)	Webb	10.00	5.00	3.00
(178)	Wetzell	10.00	5.00	3.00
(179)	F. Wetzel	10.00	5.00	3.00
(180)	Williams	10.00	5.00	3.00
(181)	Wilson	10.00	5.00	3.00
(182)	Wingo	10.00	5.00	3.00
(183)	Wirts	10.00	5.00	3.00
(184)	Woodall	10.00	5.00	3.00

		NR MT	EX	VG
(185)	Zamlack	10.00	5.00	3.00
(186)	Zinn	10.00	5.00	3.00

1931 E137 Zeenut

Beginning in 1931, Zeenuts cards were no longer dated on the front, and cards without the coupon are very difficult to date. The words "Zeenuts Series" was also dropped form the front and replaced with just the words "Coast League." Zeenut cards in 1931 and 1932 measure 1-3/4" by 2-3/4".

		NR MT	EX	VG
Complete Set:		1200.00	600.00	350.00
Common Player:		10.00	5.00	3.00
(1)	Abbott	10.00	5.00	3.00
(2)	Andrews	10.00	5.00	3.00
(3)	Anton	10.00	5.00	3.00
(4)	Backer	10.00	5.00	3.00
(5)	Baker	10.00	5.00	3.00
(6)	Baldwin	10.00	5.00	3.00
(7)	Barbee	10.00	5.00	3.00
(8)	Barton	10.00	5.00	3.00
(9)	Bassler	10.00	5.00	3.00
(10)	Berger (Missions)	10.00	5.00	3.00
(11)	Berger (Portland)	10.00	5.00	3.00
(12)	Biggs	10.00	5.00	3.00
(13)	Bowman	10.00	5.00	3.00
(14)	Brenzel	10.00	5.00	3.00
(15)	Bryan	10.00	5.00	3.00
(16)	Burns	10.00	5.00	3.00
(17)	Camilli	12.00	6.00	3.50
(18)	Campbell	10.00	5.00	3.00
(19)	Carlyle	10.00	5.00	3.00
(20)	Caveney	10.00	5.00	3.00
(21)	Chesterfield	10.00	5.00	3.00
(22)	Cole	10.00	5.00	3.00
(23)	Coleman	10.00	5.00	3.00
(24)	Coscarart	10.00	5.00	3.00
(25)	Crosetti	20.00	10.00	6.00
(26)	Davis	10.00	5.00	3.00
(27)	DeBerry	10.00	5.00	3.00
(28)	Demaree	10.00	5.00	3.00
(29)	Dean	10.00	5.00	3.00
(30)	Delaney	10.00	5.00	3.00
(31)	Dondero	10.00	5.00	3.00
(32)	Donovan	10.00	5.00	3.00
(33)	Douglas	10.00	5.00	3.00
(34)	Ellsworth	10.00	5.00	3.00
(35)	Farrell	10.00	5.00	3.00
(36)	Fenton	10.00	5.00	3.00
(37)	Fitzpatrick	10.00	5.00	3.00
(38)	Flagstead	10.00	5.00	3.00
(39)	Flynn	10.00	5.00	3.00
(40)	Frazier	10.00	5.00	3.00
(41)	Freitas	10.00	5.00	3.00
(42)	French	10.00	5.00	3.00
(43)	Fullerton	10.00	5.00	3.00
(44)	Gabler	10.00	5.00	3.00
(45)	Gazella	10.00	5.00	3.00
(46)	Hale	10.00	5.00	3.00
(47)	Hamilton	10.00	5.00	3.00
(48)	Haney	9.00	4.50	2.75
(49)	Hannah	10.00	5.00	3.00
(50)	Harper	10.00	5.00	3.00
(51)	Henderson	10.00	5.00	3.00
(52)	Herrmann	10.00	5.00	3.00

		NR MT	EX	VG
(53)	Hoffman	10.00	5.00	3.00
(54)	Holland	10.00	5.00	3.00
(55)	Holling	10.00	5.00	3.00
(56)	Hubbell	10.00	5.00	3.00
(57)	Hufft	10.00	5.00	3.00
(58)	Hurst	10.00	5.00	3.00
(59)	Jacobs	10.00	5.00	3.00
(60)	Kallio	10.00	5.00	3.00
(61)	Keating	10.00	5.00	3.00
(62)	Keesey	10.00	5.00	3.00
(63)	Knothe	10.00	5.00	3.00
(64)	Knott	10.00	5.00	3.00
(65)	Kohler	10.00	5.00	3.00
(66)	Lamanski	10.00	5.00	3.00
(67)	Lee	10.00	5.00	3.00
(68)	Lelivelt	10.00	5.00	3.00
(69)	Lieber	10.00	5.00	3.00
(70)	Lipanovic	10.00	5.00	3.00
(71)	McDonald	10.00	5.00	3.00
(72)	McDougall	10.00	5.00	3.00
(73)	McLaughlin	10.00	5.00	3.00
(74)	Monroe	10.00	5.00	3.00
(75)	Moss	10.00	5.00	3.00
(76)	Mulligan	10.00	5.00	3.00
(77)	Ortman	10.00	5.00	3.00
(78)	Orwoll	10.00	5.00	3.00
(79)	Parker	10.00	5.00	3.00
(80)	Penebskey	10.00	5.00	3.00
(81)	H. Pillette	10.00	5.00	3.00
(82)	T. Pillette	10.00	5.00	3.00
(83)	Pinelli	12.00	6.00	3.50
(84)	Pool	10.00	5.00	3.00
(85)	Posedel	10.00	5.00	3.00
(86)	Powers	10.00	5.00	3.00
(87)	Read	10.00	5.00	3.00
(88)	Reese	12.00	6.00	3.50
(89)	Rhiel	10.00	5.00	3.00
(90)	Ricci	10.00	5.00	3.00
(91)	Rohwer	10.00	5.00	3.00
(92)	Ryan	10.00	5.00	3.00
(93)	Schino	10.00	5.00	3.00
(94)	Schulte	10.00	5.00	3.00
(95)	Severeid	10.00	5.00	3.00
(96)	Sharpe	10.00	5.00	3.00
(97)	Shellenback	10.00	5.00	3.00
(98)	Simas	10.00	5.00	3.00
(99)	Steinbacker	10.00	5.00	3.00
(100)	Summa	10.00	5.00	3.00
(101)	Tubbs	10.00	5.00	3.00
(102)	Turner	10.00	5.00	3.00
(103)	Turpin	10.00	5.00	3.00
(104)	Uhalt	10.00	5.00	3.00
(105)	Vinci	10.00	5.00	3.00
(106)	Vitt	10.00	5.00	3.00
(107)	Wade	10.00	5.00	3.00
(108)	Walsh	10.00	5.00	3.00
(109)	Walters	10.00	5.00	3.00
(110)	Wera	10.00	5.00	3.00
(111)	Wetzel	10.00	5.00	3.00
(112)	Williams (Portland)	10.00	5.00	3.00
(113)	Williams (San Francisco)	10.00	5.00	3.00
(114)	Wingo	10.00	5.00	3.00
(115)	Wirts	10.00	5.00	3.00
(116)	Wise	10.00	5.00	3.00
(117)	Woodall	10.00	5.00	3.00
(118)	Yerkes	10.00	5.00	3.00
(119)	Zamlock	10.00	5.00	3.00
(120)	Zinn	10.00	5.00	3.00

1932 E137 Zeenut

CUT **COUPON** HERE
GOOD FOR VALUABLE PREMIUMS
ASK YOUR DEALER FOR LIST.
This offer expires April 1st, 1932

		NR MT	EX	VG
Complete Set:		1200.00	600.00	350.00
Common Player:		10.00	5.00	3.00
(1)	Abbott	10.00	5.00	3.00
(2)	Almada	10.00	5.00	3.00
(3)	Anton	10.00	5.00	3.00
(4)	Babich	10.00	5.00	3.00
(5)	Backer	10.00	5.00	3.00
(6)	Baker	10.00	5.00	3.00
(7)	Ballou	10.00	5.00	3.00
(8)	Bassler	10.00	5.00	3.00
(9)	Berger	10.00	5.00	3.00
(10)	Blackerby	10.00	5.00	3.00
(11)	Bordagaray	10.00	5.00	3.00
(12)	Brannon	10.00	5.00	3.00
(13)	Briggs	10.00	5.00	3.00
(14)	Brubaker	10.00	5.00	3.00
(15)	Callaghan	10.00	5.00	3.00
(16)	Camilli	12.00	6.00	3.50
(17)	Campbell	10.00	5.00	3.00
(18)	Carlyle	10.00	5.00	3.00
(19)	Caster	10.00	5.00	3.00
(20)	Caveney	10.00	5.00	3.00
(21)	Chamberlain	10.00	5.00	3.00
(22)	Cole	10.00	5.00	3.00
(23)	Collard	10.00	5.00	3.00
(24)	Cook	10.00	5.00	3.00
(25)	Coscarart	10.00	5.00	3.00
(26)	Cox	10.00	5.00	3.00
(27)	Cronin	10.00	5.00	3.00
(28)	Daglia	10.00	5.00	3.00
(29)	Dahlgren	12.00	6.00	3.50
(30)	Davis	10.00	5.00	3.00
(31)	Dean	10.00	5.00	3.00
(32)	Delaney	10.00	5.00	3.00
(33)	Demaree	10.00	5.00	3.00
(34)	Devine	10.00	5.00	3.00
(35)	DeViveiros	10.00	5.00	3.00
(36)	Dittmar	10.00	5.00	3.00
(37)	Donovan	10.00	5.00	3.00
(38)	Ellsworth	10.00	5.00	3.00
(39)	Fitzpatrick	10.00	5.00	3.00
(40)	Frazier	10.00	5.00	3.00
(41)	Freitas	10.00	5.00	3.00
(42)	Garibaldi	10.00	5.00	3.00
(43)	Gaston	10.00	5.00	3.00
(44)	Gazella	10.00	5.00	3.00
(45)	Gillick	10.00	5.00	3.00
(46)	Hafey	10.00	5.00	3.00
(47)	Haney	9.00	4.50	2.75
(48)	Hannah	10.00	5.00	3.00
(49)	Henderson	10.00	5.00	3.00
(50)	Herrmann	10.00	5.00	3.00
(51)	Hipps	10.00	5.00	3.00
(52)	Hofman	10.00	5.00	3.00
(53)	Holland	10.00	5.00	3.00
(54)	House	10.00	5.00	3.00
(55)	Hufft	10.00	5.00	3.00
(56)	Hunt	10.00	5.00	3.00
(57)	Hurst	10.00	5.00	3.00
(58)	Jacobs	10.00	5.00	3.00
(59)	Johns	10.00	5.00	3.00
(60)	Johnson (Missions)	10.00	5.00	3.00
(61)	Johnson (Portland)	10.00	5.00	3.00
(62)	Johnson (Seattle)	10.00	5.00	3.00
(63)	Joiner	10.00	5.00	3.00
(64)	Kallio	10.00	5.00	3.00
(65)	Kasich	10.00	5.00	3.00
(66)	Keesey	10.00	5.00	3.00
(67)	Kelly	10.00	5.00	3.00
(68)	Koehler	10.00	5.00	3.00
(69)	Lee	10.00	5.00	3.00
(70)	Lieber	10.00	5.00	3.00
(71)	Mailho	10.00	5.00	3.00
(72)	Martin (Oakland)	10.00	5.00	3.00
(73)	Martin (San Francisco)	10.00	5.00	3.00
(74)	McNeely	10.00	5.00	3.00
(75)	Miljus	10.00	5.00	3.00
(76)	Monroe	10.00	5.00	3.00
(77)	Mosolf	10.00	5.00	3.00
(78)	Moss	10.00	5.00	3.00
(79)	Muller	10.00	5.00	3.00
(80)	Mulligan	10.00	5.00	3.00
(81)	Oana	10.00	5.00	3.00
(82)	Osborn	10.00	5.00	3.00
(83)	Page	10.00	5.00	3.00
(84)	Penebsky	10.00	5.00	3.00
(85)	H. Pillette	10.00	5.00	3.00
(86)	Pinelli	12.00	6.00	3.50
(87)	Poole	10.00	5.00	3.00
(88)	Quellich	10.00	5.00	3.00

		NR MT	EX	VG
(89)	Read	10.00	5.00	3.00
(90)	Ricci	10.00	5.00	3.00
(91)	Salvo	10.00	5.00	3.00
(92)	Sankey	10.00	5.00	3.00
(93)	Sheehan	10.00	5.00	3.00
(94)	Shellenback	10.00	5.00	3.00
(95)	Sherlock (Hollywood)	10.00	5.00	3.00
(96)	Sherlock (Missions)	10.00	5.00	3.00
(97)	Shores	10.00	5.00	3.00
(98)	Simas	10.00	5.00	3.00
(99)	Statz	10.00	5.00	3.00
(100)	Steinbacker	10.00	5.00	3.00
(101)	Sulik	10.00	5.00	3.00
(102)	Summa	10.00	5.00	3.00
(103)	Thomas	10.00	5.00	3.00
(104)	Uhalt	10.00	5.00	3.00
(105)	Vinci	10.00	5.00	3.00
(106)	Vitt	10.00	5.00	3.00
(107)	Walsh (Missions)	10.00	5.00	3.00
(108)	Walsh (Oakland)	10.00	5.00	3.00
(109)	Walters	10.00	5.00	3.00
(110)	Ward	10.00	5.00	3.00
(111)	Welsh	10.00	5.00	3.00
(112)	Wera	10.00	5.00	3.00
(113)	Williams	10.00	5.00	3.00
(114)	Willoughby	10.00	5.00	3.00
(115)	Wirts	10.00	5.00	3.00
(116)	Wise	10.00	5.00	3.00
(117)	Woodall	10.00	5.00	3.00
(118)	Yde	10.00	5.00	3.00
(119)	Zahniser	10.00	5.00	3.00
(120)	Zamloch	10.00	5.00	3.00

		NR MT	EX	VG
(12)	Chozen	10.00	5.00	3.00
(13)	Cole	10.00	5.00	3.00
(14)	Cronin	10.00	5.00	3.00
(15)	Dahlgren	12.00	6.00	3.50
(16)	Donovan	10.00	5.00	3.00
(17)	Douglas	10.00	5.00	3.00
(18)	Flynn	10.00	5.00	3.00
(19)	French	10.00	5.00	3.00
(20)	Frietas	10.00	5.00	3.00
(21)	Galan	10.00	5.00	3.00
(22)	Hofmann	10.00	5.00	3.00
(23)	Kelman	10.00	5.00	3.00
(24)	Lelivelt	10.00	5.00	3.00
(25)	Ludolph	10.00	5.00	3.00
(26)	McDonald	10.00	5.00	3.00
(27)	McNeely	10.00	5.00	3.00
(28)	McQuaid	10.00	5.00	3.00
(29)	Moncrief	10.00	5.00	3.00
(30)	Nelson	10.00	5.00	3.00
(31)	Osborne	10.00	5.00	3.00
(32)	Petersen	10.00	5.00	3.00
(33)	Reeves	10.00	5.00	3.00
(34)	Scott	10.00	5.00	3.00
(35)	Shellenback	10.00	5.00	3.00
(36)	J. Sherlock	10.00	5.00	3.00
(37)	V. Sherlock	10.00	5.00	3.00
(38)	Steinbacker	10.00	5.00	3.00
(39)	Stine	10.00	5.00	3.00
(40)	Strange	10.00	5.00	3.00
(41)	Sulik	10.00	5.00	3.00
(42)	Sweetland	10.00	5.00	3.00
(43)	Uhalt	10.00	5.00	3.00
(44)	Vinci	10.00	5.00	3.00
(45)	Vitt	10.00	5.00	3.00
(46)	Wetzel	10.00	5.00	3.00
(47)	Woodall	10.00	5.00	3.00
(48)	Zinn	10.00	5.00	3.00

1933 E137 Zeenut

This is the most confusing era for Zeenut cards. The cards in all three years are nearly identical, displaying the words, "Coast League" in a small rectangle (with rounded corners), along with the player's name and team. The photos were black and white (except 1933 Zeenuts have also been found with sepia photos). Because no date appears on the photos, cards from these years are impossible to tell apart without the coupon bottom that lists an expiration date. To date 161 subjects have been found, with some known to exist in all four years There are cases where the exact same photo was used from one year to the next (sometimes with minor cropping differences). All cards of Joe and Vince DiMaggio have their last name misspelled "DeMaggio."

		NR MT	EX	VG
Complete Set:		475.00	235.00	135.00
Common Player:		10.00	5.00	3.00
(1)	L. Almada	10.00	5.00	3.00
(2)	Anton	10.00	5.00	3.00
(3)	Bassler	10.00	5.00	3.00
(4)	Bonnelly	10.00	5.00	3.00
(5)	Bordagary	10.00	5.00	3.00
(6)	Bottarini	10.00	5.00	3.00
(7)	Brannan	10.00	5.00	3.00
(8)	Brubaker	10.00	5.00	3.00
(9)	Bryan	10.00	5.00	3.00
(10)	Burns	10.00	5.00	3.00
(11)	Camilli	12.00	6.00	3.50

1933 E137 Zeenut
Black And White

		NR MT	EX	VG
Complete Set:		6000.00	3000.00	1800.
Common Player:		10.00	5.00	3.00
(1a)	Almada (large pose)	10.00	5.00	3.00
(1b)	Almada (small pose)	10.00	5.00	3.00
(2a)	Anton (large pose)	10.00	5.00	3.00
(2b)	Anton (small pose)	10.00	5.00	3.00
(3)	Babich	10.00	5.00	3.00
(4)	Backer	10.00	5.00	3.00
(5)	Ballou (black stockings)	10.00	5.00	3.00
(6a)	Ballou (stockings with band, large pose)			
		10.00	5.00	3.00
(6b)	Ballou (stockings with band, small pose)			
(7)	Barath	10.00	5.00	3.00
(8)	Beck	10.00	5.00	3.00
(9)	C. Beck	10.00	5.00	3.00
(10)	W. Beck	10.00	5.00	3.00
(11)	Becker	10.00	5.00	3.00
(12)	Biongovanni	10.00	5.00	3.00
(13)	Blackerby	10.00	5.00	3.00
(14)	Blakely	10.00	5.00	3.00
(15)	Borja (Sacramento)	10.00	5.00	3.00
(16)	Borja (Seals)	10.00	5.00	3.00
(17)	Brundin	10.00	5.00	3.00

		NR MT	EX	VG
(18)	Carlyle	10.00	5.00	3.00
(19a)	Caveney (name incorrect)	10.00	5.00	3.00
(19b)	Cavaney (name correct)	10.00	5.00	3.00
(20)	Chelini	10.00	5.00	3.00
(21)	Cole (with glove)	10.00	5.00	3.00
(22)	Cole (no glove)	10.00	5.00	3.00
(23)	Connors	10.00	5.00	3.00
(24)	Coscarart (Missions)	10.00	5.00	3.00
(25)	Coscarart (Seattle)	10.00	5.00	3.00
(26)	Cox	10.00	5.00	3.00
(27)	Davis	10.00	5.00	3.00
(28)	J. DeMaggio (DiMaggio) (batting)	2000.00	1000.00	600.00
(29)	J. DeMaggio (DiMaggio) (throwing)	2000.00	1000.00	600.00
(30)	V. DeMaggio (DiMaggio)	400.00	200.00	120.00
(31)	DeViveiros	10.00	5.00	3.00
(32)	Densmore	10.00	5.00	3.00
(33)	Dittmar	10.00	5.00	3.00
(34)	Donovan	10.00	5.00	3.00
(35)	Douglas (Oakland)	10.00	5.00	3.00
(36)	Douglas (Seals)	10.00	5.00	3.00
(37a)	Duggan (large pose)	10.00	5.00	3.00
(37b)	Duggan (small pose)	10.00	5.00	3.00
(38)	Durst	10.00	5.00	3.00
(39a)	Eckhardt (large pose)	10.00	5.00	3.00
(39b)	Eckhardt (small pose)	10.00	5.00	3.00
(40)	Ellsworth	10.00	5.00	3.00
(41)	Fenton	10.00	5.00	3.00
(42)	Fitzpatrick	10.00	5.00	3.00
(43)	Francovich	10.00	5.00	3.00
(44)	Funk	10.00	5.00	3.00
(45a)	Garibaldi (large pose)	10.00	5.00	3.00
(45b)	Garibaldi (small pose)	10.00	5.00	3.00
(46)	Gibson (black sleeves)	10.00	5.00	3.00
(47)	Gibson (white sleeves)	10.00	5.00	3.00
(48)	Gira	10.00	5.00	3.00
(49)	Glaister	10.00	5.00	3.00
(50)	Graves	10.00	5.00	3.00
(51a)	Hafey (Missions, large pose)	10.00	5.00	3.00
(51b)	Hafey (Missions, middle-size pose)	10.00	5.00	3.00
(51c)	Hafey (Missions, small pose)	10.00	5.00	3.00
(52)	Hafey (Sacramento)	10.00	5.00	3.00
(53)	Haid (Oakland)	10.00	5.00	3.00
(54)	Haid (Seattle)	10.00	5.00	3.00
(55)	Haney	9.00	4.50	2.75
(56a)	Hartwig (Sacramento, large pose)	10.00	5.00	3.00
(56b)	Hartwig (Sacramento, small pose)	10.00	5.00	3.00
(57)	Hartwig (Seals)	10.00	5.00	3.00
(58)	Henderson	10.00	5.00	3.00
(59)	Herrmann	10.00	5.00	3.00
(60)	B. Holder	10.00	5.00	3.00
(61)	Holland	10.00	5.00	3.00
(62)	Horne	10.00	5.00	3.00
(63)	House	10.00	5.00	3.00
(64)	Hunt	10.00	5.00	3.00
(65)	A.E. Jacobs	10.00	5.00	3.00
(66)	Johns	10.00	5.00	3.00
(67)	D. Johnson	10.00	5.00	3.00
(68)	L. Johnson	10.00	5.00	3.00
(69)	Joiner	10.00	5.00	3.00
(70)	Jolly, Jorgensen	10.00	5.00	3.00
(71)	Joost, Kallio	10.00	5.00	3.00
(74)	Kamm	10.00	5.00	3.00
(75)	Kampouris	10.00	5.00	3.00
(76)	E. Kelly (Oakland)	10.00	5.00	3.00
(77)	E. Kelly (Seattle)	10.00	5.00	3.00
(78)	Kenna	10.00	5.00	3.00
(79)	Kintana	10.00	5.00	3.00
(80)	Lahman	10.00	5.00	3.00
(81)	Lieber	10.00	5.00	3.00
(82)	Ludolph	10.00	5.00	3.00
(83)	Mailho	10.00	5.00	3.00
(84a)	Mails (large pose)	10.00	5.00	3.00
(84b)	Mails (small pose)	10.00	5.00	3.00
(85)	Marty (black sleeves)	10.00	5.00	3.00
(86)	Marty (white sleeves)	10.00	5.00	3.00
(87)	Massuci (different pose)	10.00	5.00	3.00
(88)	Masucci (different pose)	10.00	5.00	3.00
(89a)	McEvoy (large pose)	10.00	5.00	3.00
(89b)	McEvoy (small pose)	10.00	5.00	3.00
(90)	McIsaacs	10.00	5.00	3.00
(91)	McMullen (Oakland)	10.00	5.00	3.00
(92)	McMullen (Seals)	10.00	5.00	3.00
(93)	Mitchell	10.00	5.00	3.00
(94a)	Monzo (large pose)	10.00	5.00	3.00
(94b)	Monzo (small pose)	10.00	5.00	3.00
(95)	Mort (throwing)	10.00	5.00	3.00

		NR MT	EX	VG
(96)	Mort (batting)	10.00	5.00	3.00
(97a)	Muller (Oakland, large pose)	10.00	5.00	3.00
(97b)	Muller (Oakland, small pose)	10.00	5.00	3.00
(98)	Muller (Seattle)	10.00	5.00	3.00
(99)	Mulligan (hands showing)	10.00	5.00	3.00
(100)	Mulligan (hands not showing)	10.00	5.00	3.00
(101)	Newkirk	10.00	5.00	3.00
(102)	Nicholas	10.00	5.00	3.00
(103)	Nitcholas	10.00	5.00	3.00
(103a)	Norbert (large pose)	10.00	5.00	3.00
(103b)	Norbert (small pose)	10.00	5.00	3.00
(105)	O'Doul (black sleeves)	40.00	20.00	12.00
(106)	O'Doul (white sleeves)	40.00	20.00	12.00
(107)	Oglesby	10.00	5.00	3.00
(108)	Ostenberg	10.00	5.00	3.00
(109)	Outen (throwing)	10.00	5.00	3.00
(110)	Outen (batting)	10.00	5.00	3.00
(111)	Page (Hollywood)	10.00	5.00	3.00
(112)	Page (Seattle)	10.00	5.00	3.00
(113)	Palmisano	10.00	5.00	3.00
(114)	Parker	10.00	5.00	3.00
(115)	Phebus	10.00	5.00	3.00
(116)	T. Pillette	10.00	5.00	3.00
(117)	Pool	10.00	5.00	3.00
(118)	Powers	10.00	5.00	3.00
(119)	Quellich	10.00	5.00	3.00
(120)	Radonitz	10.00	5.00	3.00
(121a)	Raimondi (large pose)	10.00	5.00	3.00
(121b)	Raimondi (small pose)	10.00	5.00	3.00
(122a)	Reese (large pose)	12.00	6.00	3.50
(122b)	Reese (small pose)	12.00	6.00	3.50
(123)	Rego	10.00	5.00	3.00
(124)	Rhyne (front)	10.00	5.00	3.00
(125)	Rosenberg	10.00	5.00	3.00
(126)	Salinsen	10.00	5.00	3.00
(127)	Salkeld	10.00	5.00	3.00
(128)	Salvo	10.00	5.00	3.00
(129)	Sever	10.00	5.00	3.00
(130)	Sheehan (black sleeves)	10.00	5.00	3.00
(131)	Sheehan (white sleeves)	10.00	5.00	3.00
(132a)	Sheely (large pose)	10.00	5.00	3.00
(132b)	Sheely (small pose)	10.00	5.00	3.00
(134)	Sprinz	10.00	5.00	3.00
(135)	Starritt	10.00	5.00	3.00
(136)	Statz	10.00	5.00	3.00
(137a)	Steinbacker (large pose)	10.00	5.00	3.00
(137b)	Steinbacker (small pose)	10.00	5.00	3.00
(138)	Stewart	10.00	5.00	3.00
(139)	Stitzel (Los Angeles)	10.00	5.00	3.00
(140)	Stitzel (Missions)	10.00	5.00	3.00
(141)	Stitzel (Seals)	10.00	5.00	3.00
(142)	Stoneham	10.00	5.00	3.00
(143)	Street	10.00	5.00	3.00
(144)	Stroner	10.00	5.00	3.00
(145)	Stutz	10.00	5.00	3.00
(146)	Sulik	10.00	5.00	3.00
(147a)	Thurston (Mission)	10.00	5.00	3.00
(147b)	Thurston (Missions)	10.00	5.00	3.00
(148)	Vitt (Hollywood)	10.00	5.00	3.00
(149)	Vitt (Oakland)	10.00	5.00	3.00
(150)	Wallgren	10.00	5.00	3.00
(151)	Walsh	10.00	5.00	3.00
(152)	Walters	10.00	5.00	3.00
(153)	West	10.00	5.00	3.00
(154a)	Wirts (large pose)	10.00	5.00	3.00
(154b)	Wirts (small pose)	10.00	5.00	3.00
(155)	Woodall (batting)	10.00	5.00	3.00
(156)	Woodall (throwing)	10.00	5.00	3.00
(157)	Wright (facing to front)	10.00	5.00	3.00
(158)	Wright (facing to left)	10.00	5.00	3.00
(159)	Zinn	10.00	5.00	3.00

1937 E137 Zeenut

The 1937 and 1938 Zeenuts are similar to the 1933-1936 issues, except the black rectangle containing the player's name and team has square (rather than rounded) corners. Again, it is difficult to distinguish between the two years. In 1938, Zeenuts elimintaed the coupon bottom and began including a separate coupon in the candy package along with the baseball card. The final two years of the Zeenuts issues, the 1937 and 1938 cards, are among the more difficult to find.

		NR MT	EX	VG
Complete Set:		2100.00	1050.00	630.00
Common Player:		18.00	9.00	5.50
(1)	Annunzio	18.00	9.00	5.50
(2)	Baker	18.00	9.00	5.50
(3)	Ballou	18.00	9.00	5.50
(4)	C. Beck			
(5)	W. Beck	18.00	9.00	5.50
(6)	Bolin	18.00	9.00	5.50
(7)	Bongiavanni	18.00	9.00	5.50
(8)	Boss	18.00	9.00	5.50
(9)	Carson	18.00	9.00	5.50
(10)	Clabaugh	12.00	6.00	3.50
(11)	Clifford	18.00	9.00	5.50
(12)	B. Cole	18.00	9.00	5.50
(13)	Coscarart	18.00	9.00	5.50
(14)	Cronin	18.00	9.00	5.50
(15)	Cullop	18.00	9.00	5.50
(16)	Daglia	18.00	9.00	5.50
(17)	D. DeMaggio (DiMaggio)	400.00	200.00	120.00
(18)	Douglas	18.00	9.00	5.50
(19)	Frankovich	18.00	9.00	5.50
(20)	Frazier	18.00	9.00	5.50
(21)	Fredericks	18.00	9.00	5.50
(22)	Freitas	18.00	9.00	5.50
(23)	Gabrielson (Oakland)	18.00	9.00	5.50
(24)	Gabrielson (Seattle)	18.00	9.00	5.50
(25)	Garibaldi	18.00	9.00	5.50
(26)	Gibson	18.00	9.00	5.50
(27)	Gill	18.00	9.00	5.50
(28)	Graves	18.00	9.00	5.50
(29)	Guay	18.00	9.00	5.50
(30)	Gudat	18.00	9.00	5.50
(31)	Haid	18.00	9.00	5.50
(32)	Hannah	18.00	9.00	5.50
(33)	Hawkins	18.00	9.00	5.50
(34)	Herrmann	18.00	9.00	5.50
(35)	Holder	18.00	9.00	5.50
(36)	Jennings	18.00	9.00	5.50
(37)	Judnich	18.00	9.00	5.50
(38)	Klinger	18.00	9.00	5.50
(39)	Koenig	18.00	9.00	5.50
(40)	Koupal	18.00	9.00	5.50
(41)	Koy	18.00	9.00	5.50
(42)	Lamanski	18.00	9.00	5.50
(43)	Leishman (Oakland)	18.00	9.00	5.50
(44)	Leishman (Seattle)	18.00	9.00	5.50
(45)	G. Lillard	18.00	9.00	5.50
(46)	Mann	18.00	9.00	5.50
(47)	Marble (Hollywood)	18.00	9.00	5.50
(49)	Miller	18.00	9.00	5.50
(50)	Mills	18.00	9.00	5.50
(51)	Monzo	18.00	9.00	5.50
(52)	B. Mort (Hollywood)	18.00	9.00	5.50
(53)	B. Mort (Missions)	18.00	9.00	5.50
(54)	Muller	18.00	9.00	5.50
(55)	Murray	18.00	9.00	5.50
(56)	Newsome	18.00	9.00	5.50
(57)	Nitcholas	18.00	9.00	5.50
(58)	Olds	18.00	9.00	5.50
(59)	Orengo	18.00	9.00	5.50
(60)	Osborne	18.00	9.00	5.50
(61)	Outen	18.00	9.00	5.50
(62)	C. Outen (Hollywood)	18.00	9.00	5.50
(63)	C. Outen (Missions)	18.00	9.00	5.50
(64)	Pippin	18.00	9.00	5.50
(65)	Powell	18.00	9.00	5.50
(66)	Radonitz	18.00	9.00	5.50
(67)	Raimondi (Oakland)	18.00	9.00	5.50
(68)	Raimondi (San Francisco)	18.00	9.00	5.50
(69)	A. Raimondi	18.00	9.00	5.50
(70)	W. Raimondi	18.00	9.00	5.50
(71)	Rhyne	18.00	9.00	5.50
(72)	Rosenberg (Missions)	18.00	9.00	5.50
(73)	Rosenberg (Portland)	18.00	9.00	5.50
(74)	Sawyer	18.00	9.00	5.50
(75)	Seats	18.00	9.00	5.50
(76)	Sheehan (Oakland)	18.00	9.00	5.50

		NR MT	EX	VG
(77)	Sheehan (San Francisco)	18.00	9.00	5.50
(78)	Shores	18.00	9.00	5.50
(79)	Slade (Hollywood)	18.00	9.00	5.50
(80)	Slade (Missions)	18.00	9.00	5.50
(81)	Sprinz (Missions)	18.00	9.00	5.50
(82)	Sprinz (San Francisco)	18.00	9.00	5.50
(83)	Statz	18.00	9.00	5.50
(84)	Storey	18.00	9.00	5.50
(85)	Stringfellow	18.00	9.00	5.50
(86)	Stutz	18.00	9.00	5.50
(87)	Sweeney	18.00	9.00	5.50
(88)	Thomson	18.00	9.00	5.50
(89)	Tost (Hollywood)	18.00	9.00	5.50
(90)	Tost (Missions)	18.00	9.00	5.50
(91)	Ulrich	18.00	9.00	5.50
(92)	Vergez	18.00	9.00	5.50
(93)	Vezelich	18.00	9.00	5.50
(94)	Vitter (Hollywood)	18.00	9.00	5.50
(95)	Vitter (San Francisco)	18.00	9.00	5.50
(96)	West	18.00	9.00	5.50
(97)	Wilson	18.00	9.00	5.50
(98)	Woodall	18.00	9.00	5.50
(99)	Wright	18.00	9.00	5.50

1927 E210-1

Issued in 1927 by the York Caramel Co. of York, Pa., these black and white cards are among the last of the caramel issues. Measuring 1-3/8" by 2-1/2", they are similar in appearance to earlier candy and tobacco cards. The front of the card carries the player's name in capital letters beneath the photo preceded by a number in parenthesis. The back also lists the player's name in capital letters, along with a brief phrase describing him and the line "This is one of a series of sixty of the most prominent stars in baseball." The bottom of the cards reads "York Caramel Co. York, Pa." The set includes several variations and is desginated in the ACC as E210. It is closely related to the W502 set of the same year. The E210-2s differ from the E210-1s in that the card stock is close to being glossy as opposed to the dull appearance of E210-1.

		NR MT	EX	VG
Complete Set:		5000.00	2500.00	1500.
Common Player:		32.00	16.00	9.50
1	Burleigh Grimes	125.00	35.00	21.00
2	Walter Reuther (Ruether)	32.00	16.00	9.50
3	Joe Duggan (Dugan)	40.00	20.00	12.00
4	Red Faber	70.00	35.00	21.00
5	Gabby Hartnett	70.00	35.00	21.00
6	Babe Ruth	1200.00	600.00	360.00
7	Bob Meusel	40.00	20.00	12.00
8	Herb Pennock	70.00	35.00	21.00
9	George Burns	32.00	16.00	9.50
10	Joe Sewell	70.00	35.00	21.00
11	George Uhle	32.00	16.00	9.50
12	Bob O'Farrel (O'Farrell)	32.00	16.00	9.50
13	Rogers Hornsby	125.00	62.00	37.00
14	Pie Traynor	70.00	35.00	21.00
15	Clarence Mitchell	32.00	16.00	9.50
16	Eppa Jepha Rixey (Jeptha)	70.00	35.00	21.00
17	Carl Mays	40.00	20.00	12.00
18	Adolph Luque (Adolfo)	32.00	16.00	9.50

		NR MT	EX	VG
19	Dave Bancroft	70.00	35.00	21.00
20	George Kelly	70.00	35.00	21.00
21	Ira Flagstead	32.00	16.00	9.50
22	Harry Heilmann	70.00	35.00	21.00
23	Raymond W. Shalk (Schalk)	70.00	35.00	21.00
24	Johnny Mostil	32.00	16.00	9.50
25	Hack Wilson (photo actually Art Wilson)			
		70.00	35.00	21.00
26	Tom Zachary	32.00	16.00	9.50
27	Ty Cobb	800.00	400.00	240.00
28	Tris Speaker	90.00	45.00	27.00
29	Ralph Perkins	32.00	16.00	9.50
30	Jess Haines	70.00	35.00	21.00
31	Sherwood Smith (photo actually Jack			
	Coombs)	32.00	16.00	9.50
32	Max Carey	70.00	35.00	21.00
33	Eugene Hargraves	32.00	16.00	9.50
34	Miguel L. Gonzales	32.00	16.00	9.50
35a	Clifton Heathcot (incorrect spelling)			
		32.00	16.00	9.50
35b	Clifton Heathcote (correct spelling)			
		32.00	16.00	9.50
36	E.C. (Sam) Rice	70.00	35.00	21.00
37	Earl Sheely	32.00	16.00	9.50
38	Emory E. Rigney	32.00	16.00	9.50
39	Bib A. Falk (Bibb)	32.00	16.00	9.50
40	Nick Altrock	32.00	16.00	9.50
41	Stanley Harris	70.00	35.00	21.00
42	John J. McGraw	80.00	40.00	24.00
43	Wilbert Robinson	70.00	35.00	21.00
44	Grover Alexander	80.00	40.00	24.00
45	Walter Johnson	150.00	75.00	45.00
46	William H. Terry (photo actually Zeb			
	Terry)	90.00	45.00	27.00
47	Edward Collins	70.00	35.00	21.00
48	Marty McManus	32.00	16.00	9.50
49	Leon (Goose) Goslin	70.00	35.00	21.00
50	Frank Frisch	70.00	35.00	21.00
51	Jimmie Dykes	35.00	17.50	10.50
52	Fred (Cy) Williams	35.00	17.50	10.50
53	Eddie Roush	70.00	35.00	21.00
54	George Sisler	70.00	35.00	21.00
55	Ed Rommel	32.00	16.00	9.50
56	Rogers Peckinpaugh (Roger)	35.00	17.50	10.50
57	Stanley Coveleskie (Coveleski)	70.00	35.00	21.00
58	Clarence Gallaway (Galloway)	32.00	16.00	9.50
59	Bob Shawkey	35.00	17.50	10.50
60	John P. McInnis	75.00	16.00	9.50

		NR MT	EX	VG
31	Sherwood Smith (photo actually Jack			
	Coombs)	50.00	25.00	15.00
32	Max Carey	90.00	45.00	27.00
33	Eugene Hargrave (Hargraves)	50.00	25.00	15.00
34	Miguel L. Gonzales	50.00	25.00	15.00
35	Joe Judge	50.00	25.00	15.00
40	Willie Kamm	50.00	25.00	15.00
43	Artie Nehf	50.00	25.00	15.00
46	William H. Terry (photo actually Zeb			
	Terry)	110.00	55.00	33.00
51	Joe Harris	50.00	25.00	15.00
54	George Sisler	90.00	45.00	27.00
55	Ed Rommel	50.00	25.00	15.00
57	Stanley Coveleskie (Coveleski)	90.00	45.00	27.00
58	Lester Bell	75.00	25.00	15.00

1921 E220

Issued circa 1921 to 1923, this 120-card set is sometimes confused with the E121 or E122 sets, but is easy to identify because of the words "Made only by National Caramel Company" on the back. It is the only baseball card set issued by National Caramel of Lancaster, Pa. The cards measure 2" by 3-1/4" and feature black and white photos with the player's name, position and team at the bottom. In addition to the line indicating the manufacturer, the backs read "This set consists of pictures of 120 of the leading Base Ball Stars of the American and National Leagues". There are 115 different players included in the set, with five players shown on two cards each. About half of the photos in the set are identical to those used in either the E120 or E121 sets, leading to some confusion regarding the three sets.

		NR MT	EX	VG
Complete Set:		12000.00	6000.00	3600.
Common Player:		45.00	22.00	13.50
(1)	Charles "Babe" Adams	45.00	22.00	13.50
(2)	G.C. Alexander	150.00	75.00	45.00
(3)	James Austin	45.00	22.00	13.50
(4)	Jim Bagbyk (Bagby)	45.00	22.00	13.50
(5)	Franklin "Home Run Baker"	150.00	75.00	45.00
(6)	Dave Bancroft	150.00	75.00	45.00
(7)	Turner Barber	45.00	22.00	13.50
(8)	George Burns (Cincinnati)	45.00	22.00	13.50
(9)	George Burns (Cleveland)	45.00	22.00	13.50
(10)	Joe Bush	50.00	25.00	15.00
(11)	Leon Cadore	45.00	22.00	13.50
(12)	Max Carey	150.00	75.00	45.00
(13)	Ty Cobb	800.00	400.00	240.00
(14)	Eddie Collins	150.00	75.00	45.00
(15)	John Collins	45.00	22.00	13.50
(16)	Wilbur Cooper	45.00	22.00	13.50
(17)	S. Coveleskie (Coveleski)	150.00	75.00	45.00
(18)	Walton Cruise	45.00	22.00	13.50
(19)	Wm. Cunningham	45.00	22.00	13.50
(20)	George Cutshaw	45.00	22.00	13.50
(21)	Jake Daubert	50.00	25.00	15.00
(22)	Chas. A. Deal	45.00	22.00	13.50
(23)	Bill Doak	45.00	22.00	13.50
(24)	Joe Dugan	60.00	30.00	18.00
(25)	Jimmy Dykes (batting)	50.00	25.00	15.00
(26)	Jimmy Dykes (fielding)	50.00	25.00	15.00
(27)	"Red" Faber	150.00	75.00	45.00
(28)	"Chick" Fewster	45.00	22.00	13.50

1927 E210-2

(3) JOE DUGAN

JOE DUGAN — Joe — A great third baseman. This is one of a series of sixty of the most prominent stars in baseball. York Caramel Co. York, Pa.

		NR MT	EX	VG
Complete Set:		3800.00	1900.00	1140.
Common Player:		50.00	25.00	15.00
1	Burleigh Grimes	125.00	45.00	27.00
2	Walter Reuther (Ruether)	50.00	25.00	15.00
3	Joe Dugan	60.00	30.00	18.00
6	Babe Ruth	1200.00	600.00	360.00
12	Bob O'Farrell	50.00	25.00	15.00
14	Pie Traynor	90.00	45.00	27.00
16	Eppa Rixey	90.00	45.00	27.00
18	Adolfo Luque	50.00	25.00	15.00
22	Harry Heilmann	90.00	45.00	27.00
23	Ray W. Schalk	90.00	45.00	27.00
24	Johnny Mostil	50.00	25.00	15.00
27	Ty Cobb	800.00	400.00	240.00
29	Tony Lazzeri	75.00	37.00	22.50

		NR MT	EX	VG
(29)	Wilson Fewster	45.00	22.00	13.50
(30)	Ira Flagstead	45.00	22.00	13.50
(31)	Arthur Fletcher	45.00	22.00	13.50
(32)	Frank Frisch	150.00	75.00	45.00
(33)	Larry Gardner	45.00	22.00	13.50
(34)	Walter Gerber	45.00	22.00	13.50
(35)	Charles Glazner	45.00	22.00	13.50
(36)	Hank Gowdy	45.00	22.00	13.50
(37)	J.C. Graney (should be J.G.)	45.00	22.00	13.50
(38)	Tommy Griffith	45.00	22.00	13.50
(39)	Charles Grimm	50.00	25.00	15.00
(40)	Heinie Groh	45.00	22.00	13.50
(41)	Byron Harris	45.00	22.00	13.50
(42)	Sam Harris (Stanley or Bucky)	150.00	75.00	45.00
(43)	Harry Heilman (Heilmann)	150.00	75.00	45.00
(44)	Claude Hendrix	45.00	22.00	13.50
(45)	Walter Henline	45.00	22.00	13.50
(46)	Chas. Hollocher	45.00	22.00	13.50
(47)	Harry Hooper	150.00	75.00	45.00
(48)	Rogers Hornsby	200.00	100.00	60.00
(49)	Waite Hoyt	150.00	75.00	45.00
(50)	Wilbert Hubbell	45.00	22.00	13.50
(51)	Wm. Jacobson	45.00	22.00	13.50
(52)	Walter Johnson	400.00	200.00	120.00
(53)	Jimmy Johnston	45.00	22.00	13.50
(54)	Joe Judge	45.00	22.00	13.50
(55)	Geo. "Bingo" Kelly	150.00	75.00	45.00
(56)	Dick Kerr	45.00	22.00	13.50
(57)	Pete Kilduff (bending)	45.00	22.00	13.50
(58)	Pete Kilduff (leaping)	45.00	22.00	13.50
(59)	Larry Kopf	45.00	22.00	13.50
(60)	H.B. Leonard	45.00	22.00	13.50
(61)	Harry Liebold (Leibold)	45.00	22.00	13.50
(62)	Walter "Buster" Mails ("Duster")	45.00	22.00	13.50
(63)	Walter "Rabbit" Maranville	150.00	75.00	45.00
(64)	Carl Mays	50.00	25.00	15.00
(65)	Lee Meadows	45.00	22.00	13.50
(66)	Bob Meusel	60.00	30.00	18.00
(67)	Emil Meusel	45.00	22.00	13.50
(68)	J.C. Milan	45.00	22.00	13.50
(69)	Earl Neale	60.00	30.00	18.00
(70)	Albert Nehf (Arthur)	45.00	22.00	13.50
(71)	Robert Nehf (Arthur)	45.00	22.00	13.50
(72)	Bernie Neis	45.00	22.00	13.50
(73)	Joe Oeschger	45.00	22.00	13.50
(74)	Robert O'Farrell	45.00	22.00	13.50
(75)	Ivan Olson	45.00	22.00	13.50
(76)	Steve O'Neill	45.00	22.00	13.50
(77)	Geo. Paskert	45.00	22.00	13.50
(78)	Roger Peckinpaugh	50.00	25.00	15.00
(79)	Herb Pennock	150.00	75.00	45.00
(80)	Ralph "Cy" Perkins	45.00	22.00	13.50
(81)	Scott Perry (photo actually Ed Rommel)	45.00	22.00	13.50
(82)	Jeff Pfeffer	45.00	22.00	13.50
(83)	V.J. Picinich	45.00	22.00	13.50
(84)	Walter Pipp	75.00	37.00	22.00
(85)	Derrill Pratt	45.00	22.00	13.50
(86)	Goldie Rapp	45.00	22.00	13.50
(87)	Edgar Rice	150.00	75.00	45.00
(88)	Jimmy Ring	45.00	22.00	13.50
(89)	Eddie Rousch (Roush)	150.00	75.00	45.00
(90)	Babe Ruth	2500.00	1250.00	750.00
(91)	Raymond Schmandt	45.00	22.00	13.50
(92)	Everett Scott	50.00	25.00	15.00
(93)	Joe Sewell	150.00	75.00	45.00
(94)	Wally Shang (Schang)	45.00	22.00	13.50
(95)	Maurice Shannon	45.00	22.00	13.50
(96)	Bob Shawkey	50.00	25.00	15.00
(97)	Urban Shocker	45.00	22.00	13.50
(98)	George Sisler	150.00	75.00	45.00
(99)	Earl Smith	45.00	22.00	13.50
(100)	John Smith	45.00	22.00	13.50
(101)	Sherrod Smith	45.00	22.00	13.50
(102)	Frank Snyder (crouching)	45.00	22.00	13.50
(103)	Frank Snyder (standing)	45.00	22.00	13.50
(104)	Tris Speaker	150.00	75.00	45.00
(105)	Vernon Spencer	45.00	22.00	13.50
(106)	Chas. "Casey" Stengle (Stengel)	275.00	137.00	82.00
(107)	Milton Stock (batting)	45.00	22.00	13.50
(108)	Milton Stock (fielding)	45.00	22.00	13.50
(109)	James Vaughn	45.00	22.00	13.50
(110)	Robert Veach	45.00	22.00	13.50
(111)	Wm. Wambsgauss (Wambsganss)	50.00	25.00	15.00
(112)	Aaron Ward	45.00	22.00	13.50
(113)	Zach Wheat	150.00	75.00	45.00
(114)	George Whitted (batting)	45.00	22.00	13.50
(115)	George Whitted (fielding)	45.00	22.00	13.50
(116)	Fred C. Williams	50.00	25.00	15.00
(117)	Arthur Wilson	45.00	22.00	13.50

		NR MT	EX	VG
(118)	Ivy Wingo	45.00	22.00	13.50
(119)	Lawton Witt	45.00	22.00	13.50
(120)	"Pep" Young (photo actually Ralph Young)	45.00	22.00	13.50
(121)	Ross Young (Youngs)	150.00	75.00	45.00

1910 E221

A very rare issue, this series of team pictures of clubs in the Pacific Coast League, was distributed by Bishop & Company of Los Angeles in 1910. The team photos were printed on a thin, newsprint-type paper that measures an elongated 2-3/4" by 10". Although there were six teams in the PCL at the time, only five clubs have been found - Los Angeles, San Francisco, Portland, Vernon and Oakland. The sixth team, Sacramento, was apparently never issued. The cards indicate that they were issued with five-cent packages of Bishop's Milk Chocolate and that the photos wre taken by the Los Angeles Examiner. The black and white team photos are found with either a red or green background. The set has been designated E221.

		NR MT	EX	VG
Complete Set:		6000.00	3000.00	1800.
Common Team:		1200.00	600.00	360.00
(1)	Los Angeles	1200.00	600.00	360.00
(2)	Oakland	1200.00	600.00	360.00
(3)	Portland	1200.00	600.00	360.00
(4)	San Francisco	1200.00	600.00	360.00
(5)	Vernon	1200.00	600.00	360.00

1910 E222

TITMAN, Richmond

A.W.H. BRAND CARAMELS
Base Ball Series
Va State League
Fulton Press - Richmond Va.

This rare set of cards picturing players from the Virginia League was issued by the A.W.H. Caramel Company in 1910. The cards measure 1-1/2" by 2-3/4" and feature player portraits in either red, black, brown, or blue and white. To date examples of 10 different cards have been found. The set carries the ACC designation of E222. The front of the card displays the player's last name and team below his photo. The back states "A.W.H. Brand Caramels" in large letters with "Base Ball Series/Va. State League" below.

	NR MT	EX	VG
Complete Set:	5000.00	2500.00	1500.
Common Player:	450.00	225.00	135.00
(1) Guiheen	450.00	225.00	135.00
(2) Hooker	450.00	225.00	135.00
(3) Ison	450.00	225.00	135.00
(4) McCauley	450.00	225.00	135.00
(5) Otey	450.00	225.00	135.00
(6) Revelle	450.00	225.00	135.00
(7) Ryan	450.00	225.00	135.00
(8) Shaugnessy	450.00	225.00	135.00
(9) Sieber	450.00	225.00	135.00
(10) Smith	450.00	225.00	135.00
(11) Titman	450.00	225.00	135.00

1888 E223 G & B Chewing Gum

This set, issued with G&B Chewing Gum, is the first baseball card issued with candy or gum and the only 19th Century candy issue. The cards in the G&B set are small, measuring just 1" by 2-1/8". The cards are very similar in design to the August Beck Yum Yum issue (N403) and many of the photos appear have been to borrowed from that set. The player's name and position appear in thin capital letters below the photo, followed by either "National League" or "American League" (actually referring to the American Association.) At the very bottom of the card, the manufacturer, "G&B N.Y." is indicated. (Some of the "National League" cards also include the words "Chewing Gum" after the league designation.) THe set has been assigned the ACC number E223.

	NR MT	EX	VG
Complete Set:	80000.00	40000.00	25000.
Common Player:	500.00	250.00	150.00
(1) Cap Anson	5000.00	2500.00	1500.
(2) Fido Baldwin (bat at side)	500.00	250.00	150.00
(3) Fido Baldwin (portrait)	1000.00	500.00	300.00
(4) Lady Baldwin (Detroit)	500.00	250.00	150.00
(5) Stephen Brady	1000.00	500.00	300.00
(6) Bill Brown (portrait)	1000.00	500.00	300.00
(7) Bill Brown (standing)	500.00	250.00	150.00
(8) Charles Buffington (Buffinton)	500.00	250.00	150.00
(9) Thomas Burns	1000.00	500.00	300.00
(10) John Clarkson	2000.00	1000.00	360.00
(11) John Coleman	1000.00	500.00	300.00
(12) Commy Comiskey	2000.00	1000.00	600.00
(13) Roger Connor (batting)	1000.00	500.00	300.00
(14) Roger Connor (portrait)	2000.00	1000.00	600.00
(15) Con Daily	1000.00	500.00	300.00
(16) Tom Deasley	1000.00	500.00	300.00
(17) Dude Esterbrook	1000.00	500.00	300.00
(18) Buck Ewing (batting)	1000.00	500.00	300.00
(19) Buck Ewing (portrait)	2000.00	1000.00	600.00
(20) Charlie Ferguson	500.00	250.00	150.00
(21) Silver Flint	1000.00	500.00	300.00
(22) Charlie Getzein	500.00	250.00	150.00

	NR MT	EX	VG
(23) Will Gleason	500.00	250.00	150.00
(24) Frank Hankinson	1000.00	500.00	300.00
(25) Pete Hotaling	500.00	250.00	150.00
(26) Spud Johnson	500.00	250.00	150.00
(27) Tim Keefe (batting)	1000.00	500.00	300.00
(28) Tim Keefe (throwing)	1000.00	500.00	300.00
(29) Tim Keefe (portrait)	2000.00	1000.00	600.00
(30) King Kelly (batting)	1000.00	500.00	300.00
(31) King Kelly (standing by urn)	2500.00	1250.00	750.00
(32) Gus Krock	1000.00	500.00	300.00
(33) Connie Mack	2500.00	1250.00	750.00
(34) Doggie Miller	500.00	250.00	150.00
(35) Honest John Morrill	500.00	250.00	150.00
(36) James Mutrie	1000.00	500.00	300.00
(37) Little Nick Nicoll (Nicol)	1000.00	500.00	300.00
(38) Tip O'Neill	1000.00	500.00	300.00
(39) Orator Jim O'Rourke	2000.00	1000.00	600.00
(40) Fred Pfeffer	500.00	250.00	150.00
(41) Henry Porter	500.00	250.00	150.00
(42) Danny Richardson (batting)	500.00	250.00	150.00
(43) Danny Richardson (portrait)	1000.00	500.00	300.00
(44) Chief Roseman	1000.00	500.00	300.00
(45) Jimmy Ryan (portrait)	1000.00	500.00	300.00
(46) Jimmy Ryan (throwing)	500.00	250.00	150.00
(47) Little Bill Sowders (throwing)	500.00	250.00	150.00
(48) Marty Sullivan	1000.00	500.00	300.00
(49) Billy Sunday (fielding)	900.00	450.00	275.00
(50) Billy Sunday (portrait)	2000.00	1000.00	600.00
(51) Ezra Sutton	500.00	250.00	150.00
(52) Silent Mike Tiernan (batting)	500.00	250.00	150.00
(53) Silent Mike Tiernan (portrait)	1000.00	500.00	300.00
(54) Big Sam Thompson	1000.00	500.00	300.00
(55) Larry Twitchell	1000.00	500.00	300.00
(56) Rip Van Haltren	1000.00	500.00	300.00
(57) Monte Ward	2000.00	1000.00	600.00
(58) Smiling Mickey Welch (pitching)	1000.00	500.00	300.00
(59) Smiling Mickey Welch (portrait)	2000.00	1000.00	600.00
(60) Curt Welsh (Welch)	1000.00	500.00	300.00
(61) Grasshopper Whitney	1000.00	500.00	300.00
(62) Pete Wood	500.00	250.00	150.00

1914 E224 - Type 1

Little is known about the origin of this 50-card set issued in 1914 and designated as E224 in the American Card Catalog. Measuring 2-3/8" by 3-1/2", the front of the cards feature sepia-toned action photos with the player's name in capital letters and his team below in parenthesis. The back carries a rather lengthy player biography and most cards, although not all, include year-by-year statistics at the bottom. The words "Texas Tommy" appear at the top, apparently referring to the sponsor of the set, although it is still unclear who or what "Texas Tommy" was, and despite its name, most examples of this set have been found in northern California. There is also a second variety of the set, smaller in size (1-7/8" by 3"), which are borderless pictures with a glossy finish.

	NR MT	EX	VG
Complete Set:	30000.00	15000.00	9000.
Common Player:	225.00	112.00	67.00
(1) Jimmy Archer	225.00	112.00	67.00

		NR MT	EX	VG
(2)	Jimmy Austin	225.00	112.00	67.00
(3)	Home Run Baker	800.00	400.00	240.00
(4)	Chief Bender	800.00	400.00	240.00
(5)	Bob Bescher	225.00	112.00	67.00
(6)	Ping Bodie	225.00	112.00	67.00
(7)	Donie Bush	225.00	112.00	67.00
(8)	Bobby Byrne	225.00	112.00	67.00
(9)	Nixey Callanan (Callahan)	225.00	112.00	67.00
(10)	Howie Camnitz	225.00	112.00	67.00
(11)	Frank Chance	800.00	400.00	240.00
(12)	Hal Chase	500.00	250.00	150.00
(13)	Ty Cobb	3500.00	1750.00	1050.
(14)	Jack Coombs	225.00	112.00	67.00
(15)	Sam Crawford	800.00	400.00	240.00
(16)	Birdie Cree	225.00	112.00	67.00
(17)	Al DeMaree	225.00	112.00	67.00
(18)	Red Dooin	225.00	112.00	67.00
(19)	Larry Doyle	225.00	112.00	67.00
(20)	Johnny Evers	800.00	400.00	240.00
(21)	Vean Gregg	225.00	112.00	67.00
(22)	Bob Harmon	225.00	112.00	67.00
(23)	Shoeless Joe Jackson	3500.00	1750.00	1050.
(24)	Walter Johnson	1250.00	625.00	375.00
(25)	Otto Knabe	225.00	112.00	67.00
(26)	Nap Lajoie	1000.00	500.00	300.00
(27)	Harry Lord	225.00	112.00	67.00
(28)	Connie Mack	850.00	425.00	255.00
(29)	Armando Marsans	225.00	112.00	67.00
(30)	Christy Mathewson	1200.00	600.00	360.00
(31)	George McBride	225.00	112.00	67.00
(32)	John McGraw	800.00	400.00	240.00
(33)	Stuffy McInnis	225.00	112.00	67.00
(34)	Chief Meyers	225.00	112.00	67.00
(35)	Earl Moore	225.00	112.00	67.00
(36)	Mike Mowrey	225.00	112.00	67.00
(37)	Marty O'Toole	225.00	112.00	67.00
(38)	Eddie Plank	800.00	400.00	240.00
(39)	Bud Ryan	225.00	112.00	67.00
(40)	Tris Speaker	1000.00	500.00	300.00
(41)	Jake Stahl	225.00	112.00	67.00
(42)	Oscar Strange (Stanage)	225.00	112.00	67.00
(43)	Bill Sweeney	225.00	112.00	67.00
(44)	Honus Wagner	2000.00	1000.00	600.00
(45)	Ed Walsh	800.00	400.00	240.00
(46)	Zach Wheat	800.00	400.00	240.00
(47)	Harry Wolter	225.00	112.00	67.00
(48)	Joe Wood	450.00	225.00	135.00
(49)	Steve Yerkes	225.00	112.00	67.00
(50)	Heinie Zimmerman	225.00	112.00	67.00

		NR MT	EX	VG
(13)	Joe Wood	275.00	137.00	82.00
(14)	Steve Yerkes	250.00	125.00	75.00

1921 E253

SPEAKER, CLEVELAND

THE following star baseball players of both major leagues make up the complete set of lithographed cards, one of which is wrapped with each piece of caramel. These cards are reproduced solely for the OXFORD CONFECTIONERY CO., OXFORD, PA.

EDDIE COLLINS, White Sox
WALTER JOHNSON, Washington
ROUSCH, Cincinnati
ALEXANDER, Chicago Nat.
SPEAKER, Cleveland
BANCROFT, Giants
"BILL" HOLKE, Boston Nat.
SISLER, St. Louis Amer.
PRATT, Boston Amer.
COBB, Detroit
"BABE" RUTH, Yankees
WITT, Athletics
FRISCH, Giants
LEE MEADOWS, Phillies
CY WILLIAMS, Phillies
CAREY, Pittsburg
RAY SCHALK, White Sox
GRIMES, Brooklyn
CY PERKINS, Athletics
HORNSBY, St. Louis Nat.

Issued in 1921 by Oxford Confectionary of Oxford, Pa., this 2-card set was printed on thin paper and distributed with caramels. Each card measures 1-5/8" by 2-3/4" and features a black and white player photo with the player's name and team printed in a white band along the bottom. The back carries the Oxford Confectionary name and a checklist of the 20 major leaguers in the set, 14 of whom are now in the Hall of Fame. The set is designated as E253 in the ACC.

		NR MT	EX	VG
Complete Set:		6000.00	3000.00	1800.
Common Player:		75.00	37.00	22.00
(1)	Grover Alexander	200.00	100.00	60.00
(2)	Dave Bancroft	150.00	75.00	45.00
(3)	Max Carey	150.00	75.00	45.00
(4)	Ty Cobb	1500.00	750.00	450.00
(5)	Eddie Collins	150.00	75.00	45.00
(6)	Frankie Frisch	150.00	75.00	45.00
(7)	Burleigh Grimes	150.00	75.00	45.00
(8)	"Bill" Holke (Walter)	75.00	37.00	22.00
(9)	Rogers Hornsby	300.00	150.00	90.00
(10)	Walter Johnson	500.00	250.00	150.00
(11)	Lee Meadows	75.00	37.00	22.00
(12)	Cy Perkins	75.00	37.00	22.00
(13)	Derrill Pratt	75.00	37.00	22.00
(14)	Ed Rousch (Roush)	150.00	75.00	45.00
(15)	"Babe" Ruth	2000.00	1000.00	600.00
(16)	Ray Schalk	150.00	75.00	45.00
(17)	George Sisler	150.00	75.00	45.00
(18)	Tris Speaker	200.00	100.00	60.00
(19)	Cy Williams	75.00	37.00	22.00
(20)	Whitey Witt	75.00	37.00	22.00

1914 E224 - Type 2

MATHEWSON

		NR MT	EX	VG
Complete Set:		9000.00	4500.00	2700.
Common Player:		250.00	125.00	75.00
(1)	Ping Bodie	250.00	125.00	75.00
(2)	Larry Doyle	250.00	125.00	75.00
(3)	Vean Gregg	250.00	125.00	75.00
(4)	Harry Hooper	700.00	350.00	210.00
(5)	Walter Johnson	1250.00	625.00	375.00
(6)	Connie Mack	900.00	450.00	270.00
(7)	Rube Marquard	700.00	350.00	210.00
(8)	Christy Mathewson	1000.00	500.00	300.00
(9)	John McGraw	750.00	375.00	225.00
(10)	Chief Meyers	250.00	125.00	75.00
(11)	Jake Stahl	250.00	125.00	75.00
(12)	Honus Wagner	2000.00	1000.00	600.00

1909 E254

LUDWIG MILWAUKEE

STARS OF THE DIAMOND
ONE IN EVERY 5c PACKAGE OF
COLGAN'S
Violet Chips
and
Mint Chips
BEWARE OF IMITATIONS.
THE GUM THAT'S ROUND

This unusual set of round cards, each measuring 1-1/2" in diameter, was issued over a three-year period from 1909 to 1911 by the Colgan Gum

Company of Louisville, Ky. The cards were printed on paper and inserted in five-cent cannisters of Colgan's Mint Chips and Violet Chips. The broderless cards include a player portrait on the front along with the player's last name, team and league. The back identifies the set as "Stars of teh Diamond" and carries advertising for Colgan's Gum. A total of 235 different players were pictures over the three-year period, but because of team changes and other variations, more than 300 different cards exist. The set, designated as E254, is closely related to the E270 Red Border and E270 Tin Tops sets of the same period. The complete set price does not include all variations.

		NR MT	EX	VG
Complete Set:		31500.00	15750.00	9450.
Common Player:		60.00	30.00	18.00
(1)	Ed Abbaticchio	60.00	30.00	18.00
(2)	Fred Abbott	60.00	30.00	18.00
(3a)	Bill Abstein (Pittsburg)	60.00	30.00	18.00
(3b)	Bill Abstein (Jersey City)	60.00	30.00	18.00
(4)	Babe Adams	60.00	30.00	18.00
(5)	Doc Adkins	60.00	30.00	18.00
(6)	Joe Agler	60.00	30.00	18.00
(7a)	Dave Altizer (Cincinnati)	60.00	30.00	18.00
(7b)	Dave Altizer (Minneapolis)	60.00	30.00	18.00
(8)	Nick Altrock	60.00	30.00	18.00
(9)	Red Ames	60.00	30.00	18.00
(10)	Jimmy Archer	60.00	30.00	18.00
(11a)	Jimmy Austin (New York)	60.00	30.00	18.00
(11b)	Jimmy Austin (St. Louis)	60.00	30.00	18.00
(12a)	Charlie Babb (Memphis)	60.00	30.00	18.00
(12b)	Charlie Babb (Norfolk)	60.00	30.00	18.00
(13)	Baerwald	60.00	30.00	18.00
(14)	Bill Bailey	60.00	30.00	18.00
(15)	Home Run Baker	150.00	75.00	45.00
(16)	Jack Barry	60.00	30.00	18.00
(17a)	Bill Bartley (curved letters)	60.00	30.00	18.00
(17b)	Bill Bartley (horizontal letters)	60.00	30.00	18.00
(18a)	Johnny Bates (Cincinnati)	60.00	30.00	18.00
(18b)	Johnny Bates (Philadelphia, black letters)			
		60.00	30.00	18.00
(18c)	Johnny Bates (Philadelphia, white letters)			
		60.00	30.00	18.00
(19)	Dick Bayless	60.00	30.00	18.00
(20a)	Ginger Beaumont (Boston)	60.00	30.00	18.00
(20b)	Ginger Beaumont (Chicago)	60.00	30.00	18.00
(20c)	Ginger Beaumont (St. Paul)	60.00	30.00	18.00
(21)	Beals Becker	60.00	30.00	18.00
(22)	George Bell	60.00	30.00	18.00
(23a)	Harry Bemis (Cleveland)	60.00	30.00	18.00
(23b)	Harry Bemis (Columbus)	60.00	30.00	18.00
(24a)	Heinie Berger (Cleveland)	60.00	30.00	18.00
(24b)	Heinie Berger (Columbus)	60.00	30.00	18.00
(25)	Bob Bescher	60.00	30.00	18.00
(26)	Beumiller	60.00	30.00	18.00
(27)	Joe Birmingham	60.00	30.00	18.00
(28)	Kitty Bransfield	60.00	30.00	18.00
(29)	Roger Bresnahan	150.00	75.00	45.00
(30)	Al Bridwell	60.00	30.00	18.00
(31)	Lew Brockett	60.00	30.00	18.00
(32)	Al Burch	60.00	30.00	18.00
(33a)	Burke (Ft. Wayne)	60.00	30.00	18.00
(33b)	Burke (Indianapolis)	60.00	30.00	18.00
(34)	Donie Bush	60.00	30.00	18.00
(35)	Bill Byers	60.00	30.00	18.00
(36)	Howie Cammitz (Camnitz)	60.00	30.00	18.00
(37a)	Charlie Carr (Indianapolis)	60.00	30.00	18.00
(37b)	Charlie Carr (Utica)	60.00	30.00	18.00
(38)	Frank Chance	175.00	87.00	52.00
(39)	Hal Chase	100.00	50.00	30.00
(40)	Bill Clancy (Clancey)	60.00	30.00	18.00
(41a)	Fred Clarke (Pittsburg)	150.00	75.00	45.00
(41b)	Fred Clarke (Pittsburgh)	150.00	75.00	45.00
(42)	Tommy Clarke (Cincinnati)	60.00	30.00	18.00
(43)	Bill Clymer	60.00	30.00	18.00
(44a)	Ty Cobb (no team on uniform)	1200.00	600.00	250.00
(44b)	Ty Cobb (team name on uniform))			
		1500.00	750.00	300.00
(45)	Eddie Collins	150.00	75.00	45.00
(46)	Bunk Congalton	60.00	30.00	18.00
(47)	Wid Conroy	60.00	30.00	18.00
(48)	Ernie Courtney	60.00	30.00	18.00
(49a)	Harry Coveleski (Cincinnati)	60.00	30.00	18.00
(49b)	Harry Coveleski (Chattanooga)	60.00	30.00	18.00
(50)	Doc Crandall	60.00	30.00	18.00
(51)	Gavvy Cravath	60.00	30.00	18.00
(52)	Dode Criss	60.00	30.00	18.00

		NR MT	EX	VG
(53)	Bill Dahlen	60.00	30.00	18.00
(54a)	Jake Daubert (Memphis)	60.00	30.00	18.00
(54b)	Jake Daubert (Brooklyn)	60.00	30.00	18.00
(55)	Harry Davis (Philadelphia)	60.00	30.00	18.00
(56)	Davis (St. Paul)	60.00	30.00	18.00
(57)	Frank Delahanty	60.00	30.00	18.00
(58a)	Ray Demmett (Demmitt) (New York)			
		60.00	30.00	18.00
(58b)	Ray Demmett (Demmitt) (Montreal)			
		60.00	30.00	18.00
(58c)	Ray Demmett (Demmitt) (St. Louis)			
		60.00	30.00	18.00
(59)	Art Devlin	60.00	30.00	18.00
(60)	Wild Bill Donovan	60.00	30.00	18.00
(61)	Mickey Doolin (Doolan)	60.00	30.00	18.00
(62)	Patsy Dougherty	60.00	30.00	18.00
(63)	Tom Downey	60.00	30.00	18.00
(64)	Larry Doyle	60.00	30.00	18.00
(65)	Jack Dunn	60.00	30.00	18.00
(66)	Dick Eagan (Egan)	60.00	30.00	18.00
(67a)	Kid Elberfield (Elberfeld) (Washington)			
		60.00	30.00	18.00
(67b)	Kid Elberfield (Elberfeld) (New York)			
		60.00	30.00	18.00
(68)	Rube Ellis	60.00	30.00	18.00
(69a)	Clyde Engle (New York)	60.00	30.00	18.00
(69b)	Clyde Engle (Boston)	60.00	30.00	18.00
(70a)	Steve Evans (curved letters)	60.00	30.00	18.00
(70b)	Steve Evans (horizontal letters)	60.00	30.00	18.00
(71)	Johnny Evers	150.00	75.00	45.00
(72)	Cecil Ferguson	60.00	30.00	18.00
(73)	Hobe Ferris	60.00	30.00	18.00
(74)	Field	60.00	30.00	18.00
(75)	Fitzgerald	60.00	30.00	18.00
(76a)	Patsy Flaherty (Kansas City)	60.00	30.00	18.00
(76b)	Patsy Flaherty (Atlanta)	60.00	30.00	18.00
(77)	Jack Flater	60.00	30.00	18.00
(78a)	Elmer Flick (Cleveland)	150.00	75.00	45.00
(78b)	Elmer Flick (Toledo)	150.00	75.00	45.00
(79a)	James Freck (Frick) (Baltimore)	60.00	30.00	18.00
(79b)	James Freck (Frick) (Toronto)	60.00	30.00	18.00
(80)	Jerry Freeman (photo actually Buck Freeman)	60.00	30.00	18.00
(81)	Art Froome (Fromme)	60.00	30.00	18.00
(82a)	Larry Gardner (Boston)	60.00	30.00	18.00
(82b)	Larry Gardner (New York)	60.00	30.00	18.00
(83)	Harry Gaspar	60.00	30.00	18.00
(84a)	Gus Getz	60.00	30.00	18.00
(84b)	Gus Getz	60.00	30.00	18.00
(85)	George Gibson	60.00	30.00	18.00
(86a)	Moose Grimshaw (Toronto)	60.00	30.00	18.00
(86b)	Moose Grimshaw (Louisville)	60.00	30.00	18.00
(87)	Ed Hahn	60.00	30.00	18.00
(88)	John Halla	60.00	30.00	18.00
(89)	Ed Hally (Holly)	60.00	30.00	18.00
(90)	Charlie Hanford	60.00	30.00	18.00
(91)	Topsy Hartsel	60.00	30.00	18.00
(92a)	Roy Hartzell (St. Louis)	60.00	30.00	18.00
(92b)	Roy Hartzell (New York)	60.00	30.00	18.00
(93)	Weldon Henley	60.00	30.00	18.00
(94)	Harry Hinchman	60.00	30.00	18.00
(95)	Solly Hofman	60.00	30.00	18.00
(96a)	Harry Hooper (Boston Na'l)	150.00	75.00	45.00
(96b)	Harry Hooper (Boston Am. L.)	150.00	75.00	45.00
(97)	Howard	60.00	30.00	18.00
(98a)	Hughes (no team name on uniform)			
		60.00	30.00	18.00
(98b)	Hughes (team name on uniform)			
		60.00	30.00	18.00
(99a)	Rudy Hulswilt (St. Louis, name incorrect)			
		60.00	30.00	18.00
(99b)	Rudy Hulswitt (St. Louis, name correct)			
		60.00	30.00	18.00
(99c)	Rudy Hulswitt (Chattanooga)	60.00	30.00	18.00
(100)	John Hummel	60.00	30.00	18.00
(101)	George Hunter	60.00	30.00	18.00
(102)	Shoeless Joe Jackson	3500.00	1750.00	1050.
(103)	Hugh Jennings	150.00	75.00	45.00
(104)	Davy Jones	60.00	30.00	18.00
(105)	Tom Jones	60.00	30.00	18.00
(106a)	Tim Jordon (Jordan) (Brooklyn)	60.00	30.00	18.00
(106b)	Tim Jordon (Jordan) (Atlanta)	60.00	30.00	18.00
(106c)	Tim Jordon (Jordan) (Louisville)	60.00	30.00	18.00
(107)	Addie Joss	200.00	100.00	60.00
(108)	Al Kaiser	60.00	30.00	18.00
(109)	Wee Willie Keeler	150.00	75.00	45.00
(110)	Joe Kelly (Kelley)	150.00	75.00	45.00
(111)	Bill Killefer	60.00	30.00	18.00
(112a)	Ed Killian (Detroit)	60.00	30.00	18.00
(112b)	Ed Killian (Toronto)	60.00	30.00	18.00
(113)	Johnny Kling	60.00	30.00	18.00

	NR MT	EX	VG
(114) Otto Knabe	60.00	30.00	18.00
(115) Jack Knight	60.00	30.00	18.00
(116) Ed Konetchy	60.00	30.00	18.00
(117) Rube Kroh	60.00	30.00	18.00
(118) James Lafitte	60.00	30.00	18.00
(119) Nap Lajoie	400.00	200.00	90.00
(120) Lakoff	60.00	30.00	18.00
(121) Frank Lange	60.00	30.00	18.00
(122a)Frank LaPorte (St. Louis)	60.00	30.00	18.00
(122b)Frank LaPorte (New York)	60.00	30.00	18.00
(123) Tommy Leach	60.00	30.00	18.00
(124) Jack Lelivelt	60.00	30.00	18.00
(125a)Jack Lewis (Milwaukee)	60.00	30.00	18.00
(125b)Jack Lewis (Indianapolis)	60.00	30.00	18.00
(126a)Vive Lindaman (Boston)	60.00	30.00	18.00
(126b)Vive Lindaman (Louisville)	60.00	30.00	18.00
(126c)Vive Lindaman (Indianapolis)	60.00	30.00	18.00
(127) Bris Lord	60.00	30.00	18.00
(128a)Harry Lord (Boston)	60.00	30.00	18.00
(128b)Harry Lord (Chicago)	60.00	30.00	18.00
(129a)Bill Ludwig (Milwaukee)	60.00	30.00	18.00
(129b)Bill Ludwig (St. Louis)	60.00	30.00	18.00
(130) Madden	60.00	30.00	18.00
(131) Nick Maddox	60.00	30.00	18.00
(132a)Manser (Jersey City)	60.00	30.00	18.00
(132b)Manser (Rochester)	60.00	30.00	18.00
(133) Rube Marquard	150.00	75.00	45.00
(134) Al Mattern	60.00	30.00	18.00
(135) Bill Matthews	60.00	30.00	18.00
(136) George McBride	60.00	30.00	18.00
(137) McCathy	60.00	30.00	18.00
(138) McConnell	60.00	30.00	18.00
(139) Moose McCormick	60.00	30.00	18.00
(140) Dan McGann	60.00	30.00	18.00
(141) Jim McGinley	60.00	30.00	18.00
(142) Iron Man McGinnity	150.00	75.00	45.00
(143a)Matty McIntyre (Detroit)	60.00	30.00	18.00
(143b)Matty McIntyre (Chicago)	60.00	30.00	18.00
(144) Larry McLean	60.00	30.00	18.00
(145) Fred Merkle	60.00	30.00	18.00
(146a)Merritt (Buffalo)	60.00	30.00	18.00
(146b)Merritt (Jersey City)	60.00	30.00	18.00
(147a)Meyer (Newark, name correct)	60.00	30.00	18.00
(147b)Meyers (Newark, name incorrect)	60.00	30.00	18.00
(148) Chief Meyers (New York)	60.00	30.00	18.00
(149) Clyde Milan	60.00	30.00	18.00
(150) Dots Miller	60.00	30.00	18.00
(151) Mike Mitchell	60.00	30.00	18.00
(152) Moran	60.00	30.00	18.00
(153a)Bill Moriarty (Louisville)	60.00	30.00	18.00
(153b)Bill Moriarty (Omaha)	60.00	30.00	18.00
(154) George Moriarty	60.00	30.00	18.00
(155a)George Mullen (name incorrect)	60.00	30.00	18.00
(155b)George Mullin (name correct)	60.00	30.00	18.00
(156a)Simmy Murch (Chattanooga)	60.00	30.00	18.00
(156b)Simmy Murch (Indianapolis)	60.00	30.00	18.00
(157) Danny Murphy	60.00	30.00	18.00
(158a)Red Murray (New York, white letters)	60.00	30.00	18.00
(158b)Red Murray (New York, black letters)	60.00	30.00	18.00
(158c)Red Murray (St. Paul)	60.00	30.00	18.00
(159) Billy Nattress	60.00	30.00	18.00
(160a)Red Nelson (St. Louis)	60.00	30.00	18.00
(160b)Red Nelson (Toledo)	60.00	30.00	18.00
(161) Rebel Oakes	60.00	30.00	18.00
(162) Fred Odwell	60.00	30.00	18.00
(163) O'Rourke	60.00	30.00	18.00
(164a)Al Orth (New York)	60.00	30.00	18.00
(164b)Al Orth (Indianapolis)	60.00	30.00	18.00
(165) Fred Osborn	60.00	30.00	18.00
(166) Orval Overall	60.00	30.00	18.00
(167) Owens	60.00	30.00	18.00
(168) Fred Parent	60.00	30.00	18.00
(169a)Dode Paskert (Cincinnati)	60.00	30.00	18.00
(169b)Dode Paskert (Philadelphia)	60.00	30.00	18.00
(170) Heinie Peitz	60.00	30.00	18.00
(171) Bob Peterson	60.00	30.00	18.00
(172) Jake Pfeister	60.00	30.00	18.00
(173) Deacon Phillipe (Phillippe)	60.00	30.00	18.00
(174a)Ollie Pickering (Louisville)	60.00	30.00	18.00
(174b)Ollie Pickering (Minneapolis)	60.00	30.00	18.00
(174c)Ollie Pickering (Omaha)	60.00	30.00	18.00
(175a)Billy Purtell (Chicago)	60.00	30.00	18.00
(175b)Billy Purtell (Boston)	60.00	30.00	18.00
(176) Bugs Raymond	60.00	30.00	18.00
(177) Pat Regan (Ragan)	60.00	30.00	18.00
(178) Barney Reilly	60.00	30.00	18.00
(179) Duke Reilly (Reilley)	60.00	30.00	18.00
(180) Ed Reulbach	60.00	30.00	18.00

	NR MT	EX	VG
(181) Ritchery	60.00	30.00	18.00
(182) Lou Ritter	60.00	30.00	18.00
(183) Robinson	60.00	30.00	18.00
(184) Rock	60.00	30.00	18.00
(185a)Jack Rowan (Cincinnati)	60.00	30.00	18.00
(185b)Jack Rowan (Philadelphia)	60.00	30.00	18.00
(186) Nap Rucker	60.00	30.00	18.00
(187a)Dick Rudolph (New York)	60.00	30.00	18.00
(187b)Dick Rudolph (Toronto)	60.00	30.00	18.00
(188) Ryan	60.00	30.00	18.00
(189) Slim Sallee	60.00	30.00	18.00
(190a)Bill Schardt (Birmingham)	60.00	30.00	18.00
(190b)Bill Schardt (Milwaukee)	60.00	30.00	18.00
(191) Jimmy Scheckard (Sheckard)	60.00	30.00	18.00
(192a)George Schirm (Birmingham)	60.00	30.00	18.00
(192b)George Schirm (Buffalo)	60.00	30.00	18.00
(193) Larry Schlafly	60.00	30.00	18.00
(194) Wildfire Schulte	60.00	30.00	18.00
(195a)James Seabaugh (looking to left, photo actually Julius Weisman)	60.00	30.00	18.00
(195b)James Seabaugh (looking straight ahead, correct photo)	60.00	30.00	18.00
(196) Selby	60.00	30.00	18.00
(197a)Cy Seymour (New York)	60.00	30.00	18.00
(197b)Cy Seymour (Baltimore)	60.00	30.00	18.00
(198) Hosea Siner	60.00	30.00	18.00
(199) G. Smith	60.00	30.00	18.00
(200a)Sid Smith (Atlanta)	60.00	30.00	18.00
(200b)Sid Smith (Buffalo)	60.00	30.00	18.00
(201) Fred Snodgrass	60.00	30.00	18.00
(202a)Bob Spade (Cincinnati)	60.00	30.00	18.00
(202b)Bob Spade (Newark)	60.00	30.00	18.00
(203a)Tully Sparks (Philadelphia)	60.00	30.00	18.00
(203b)Tully Sparks (Richmond)	60.00	30.00	18.00
(204a)Tris Speaker (Boston Nat'l)	275.00	125.00	55.00
(204b)Tris Speaker (Boston Am.)	275.00	125.00	55.00
(205) Tubby Spencer	60.00	30.00	18.00
(206) Jake Stahl	60.00	30.00	18.00
(207) John Stansberry (Stansbury)	60.00	30.00	18.00
(208) Harry Steinfeldt	35.00	17.50	10.50
(209) George Stone	60.00	30.00	18.00
(210) George Stovall	60.00	30.00	18.00
(211) Gabby Street	60.00	30.00	18.00
(212a)Sullivan (Louisville)	60.00	30.00	18.00
(212b)Sullivan (Omaha)	60.00	30.00	18.00
(213) Ed Summers	60.00	30.00	18.00
(214) Lee Tannehill	60.00	30.00	18.00
(215) Taylor	60.00	30.00	18.00
(216) Joe Tinker	150.00	75.00	45.00
(217) John Titus	60.00	30.00	18.00
(218) Terry Turner	60.00	30.00	18.00
(219a)Bob Unglaub (Washington)	60.00	30.00	18.00
(219b)Bob Unglaub (Lincoln)	60.00	30.00	18.00
(220a)Rube Waddell (St. Louis)	150.00	75.00	45.00
(220b)Rube Waddell (Minneapolis)	150.00	75.00	45.00
(220c)Rube Waddell (Newark)	150.00	75.00	45.00
(221a)Honus Wagner (Pittsburg, curved letters)	900.00	400.00	150.00
(221b)Honus Wagner (Pittsburg, horizontal letters)	900.00	400.00	150.00
(221c)Honus Wagner (Pittsburgh)	900.00	400.00	150.00
(222) Walker	60.00	30.00	18.00
(223) Waller	60.00	30.00	18.00
(224) Clarence Wauner (Wanner)	60.00	30.00	18.00
(225a)Julius Wiesman (name incorrect)	60.00	30.00	18.00
(225b)Julius Weisman (name correct)	60.00	30.00	18.00
(226) Jack White (Buffalo)	60.00	30.00	18.00
(227) Kirby White (Boston)	60.00	30.00	18.00
(228) Ed Willett	60.00	30.00	18.00
(229a)Otto Williams (Indianapolis)	60.00	30.00	18.00
(229b)Otto Williams (Minneapolis)	60.00	30.00	18.00
(230) Owen Wilson	60.00	30.00	18.00
(231) Hooks Wiltse	60.00	30.00	18.00
(232a)Orville Woodruff (Indianapolis)	60.00	30.00	18.00
(232b)Orville Woodruff (Louisville)	60.00	30.00	18.00
(233) Woods	60.00	30.00	18.00
(234) Cy Young	500.00	250.00	135.00
(235) Bill Zimmerman	60.00	30.00	18.00
(236) Heinie Zimmerman	60.00	30.00	18.00

1912 E270 Red Border

This set, issued in 1912 by Colgan Gum Company of Louisville Ky., is very similar to the E254 Colgan's Chips set. Measuring 1-1/2" in diameter, these round, paper player photos were inserted in cannisters of Colgan's Mint and Violet Chips.

They are differentiated from other similar issues by their distinctive red borders and by the back of the cards, which advises collectors to "Send 25 Box Tops" for a photo of the "World's Pennant Winning Team." THe set is designated as the E270 Red Border set.

		NR MT	EX	VG
	Complete Set:	14000.00	7000.00	4200.
	Common Player:	75.00	37.00	22.00
(1)	Ed Abbaticchio	75.00	37.00	22.00
(2)	Fred Abbott	75.00	37.00	22.00
(3)	Babe Adams	75.00	37.00	22.00
(4)	Red Ames	75.00	37.00	22.00
(5)	Charlie Babb	75.00	37.00	22.00
(6)	Bill Bailey	75.00	37.00	22.00
(7)	Home Run Baker	200.00	100.00	60.00
(8)	Jack Barry	75.00	37.00	22.00
(9)	Johnny Bates	75.00	37.00	22.00
(10)	Dick Bayless	75.00	37.00	22.00
(11)	Beals Becker	75.00	37.00	22.00
(13)	Heinie Berger	75.00	37.00	22.00
(14)	Beumiller	75.00	37.00	22.00
(15)	Joe Birmingham	75.00	37.00	22.00
(16)	Kitty Bransfield	75.00	37.00	22.00
(17)	Roger Bresnahan	200.00	100.00	60.00
(18)	Lew Brockett	75.00	37.00	22.00
(19)	Al Burch	75.00	37.00	22.00
(20)	Donie Bush	75.00	37.00	22.00
(21)	Bill Byers	75.00	37.00	22.00
(22)	Howie Cammitz (Camnitz)	75.00	37.00	22.00
(23)	Charlie Carr	75.00	37.00	22.00
(24)	Frank Chance	135.00	67.00	40.00
(25)	Fred Clarke (Pittsburg)	200.00	100.00	60.00
(26)	Tommy Clarke (Cincinnati)	75.00	37.00	22.00
(27)	Bill Clymer	75.00	37.00	22.00
(28)	Ty Cobb	1500.00	750.00	450.00
(29)	Eddie Collins	200.00	100.00	60.00
(30)	Wid Conroy	75.00	37.00	22.00
(31)	Harry Coveleski	75.00	37.00	22.00
(32)	Gavvy Cravath	65.00	32.00	19.50
(33)	Dode Criss	75.00	37.00	22.00
(34)	Harry Davis (Philadelphia)	75.00	37.00	22.00
(35)	Davis (St. Paul)	75.00	37.00	22.00
(36)	Frank Delahanty	75.00	37.00	22.00
(37)	Ray Demmett (Demmitt)	75.00	37.00	22.00
(38)	Art Devlin	75.00	37.00	22.00
(39)	Wild Bill Donovan	75.00	37.00	22.00
(40)	Mickey Doolan	75.00	37.00	22.00
(41)	Patsy Dougherty	75.00	37.00	22.00
(42)	Tom Downey	75.00	37.00	22.00
(43)	Larry Doyle	75.00	37.00	22.00
(44)	Jack Dunn	75.00	37.00	22.00
(45)	Dick Eagan (Egan)	75.00	37.00	22.00
(46)	Kid Elberfield (Elberfeld)	75.00	37.00	22.00
(47)	Rube Ellis	75.00	37.00	22.00
(48)	Steve Evans	75.00	37.00	22.00
(49)	Johnny Evers	200.00	100.00	60.00
(50)	Cecil Ferguson	75.00	37.00	22.00
(51)	Hobe Ferris	75.00	37.00	22.00
(52)	Fitzgerald	75.00	37.00	22.00
(53)	Fisher	200.00	100.00	60.00
(54)	Elmer Flick	200.00	100.00	60.00
(55)	James Freck (Frick)	75.00	37.00	22.00
(56)	Art Froome (Fromme)	75.00	37.00	22.00
(57)	Harry Gaspar	75.00	37.00	22.00
(58)	George Gibson	75.00	37.00	22.00
(59)	Moose Grimshaw	75.00	37.00	22.00
(60)	John Halla	75.00	37.00	22.00

		NR MT	EX	VG
(61)	Ed Hally (Holly)	75.00	37.00	22.00
(62)	Charlie Hanford	75.00	37.00	22.00
(63)	Topsy Hartsel	75.00	37.00	22.00
(64)	Roy Hartzell	75.00	37.00	22.00
(65)	Weldon Henley	75.00	37.00	22.00
(66)	Harry Hinchman	75.00	37.00	22.00
(67)	Solly Hofman	75.00	37.00	22.00
(68)	Harry Hooper	200.00	100.00	60.00
(69)	Howard	75.00	37.00	22.00
(70)	Hughes	75.00	37.00	22.00
(71)	Rudy Hulswitt	75.00	37.00	22.00
(72)	John Hummel	75.00	37.00	22.00
(73)	George Hunter	75.00	37.00	22.00
(74)	Hugh Jennings	200.00	100.00	60.00
(75)	Davy Jones	75.00	37.00	22.00
(76)	Tim Jordon (Jordan)	75.00	37.00	22.00
(77)	Bill Killefer	75.00	37.00	22.00
(78)	Ed Killian	75.00	37.00	22.00
(79)	Otto Knabe	75.00	37.00	22.00
(80)	Jack Knight	75.00	37.00	22.00
(81)	Ed Konetchy	75.00	37.00	22.00
(82)	Rube Kroh	75.00	37.00	22.00
(83)	LaCrosse (photo actually Bill Schardt)			
		75.00	37.00	22.00
(84)	Tommy Leach	75.00	37.00	22.00
(85)	Jack Lelivelt	75.00	37.00	22.00
(86)	Jack Lewis	75.00	37.00	22.00
(87)	Vive Lindaman	75.00	37.00	22.00
(88)	Bris Lord	75.00	37.00	22.00
(89)	Bill Ludwig	75.00	37.00	22.00
(90)	Harry Lord	75.00	37.00	22.00
(91)	Nick Maddox	75.00	37.00	22.00
(92)	Al Mattern	75.00	37.00	22.00
(93)	George McBride	75.00	37.00	22.00
(94)	McCathy	75.00	37.00	22.00
(95)	McConnell	75.00	37.00	22.00
(96)	Moose McCormick	75.00	37.00	22.00
(97)	Jim McGinley	75.00	37.00	22.00
(98)	Iron Man McGinnity	200.00	100.00	60.00
(99)	Matty McIntyre	75.00	37.00	22.00
(100)	Fred Merkle	65.00	32.00	19.50
(101)	Merritt	75.00	37.00	22.00
(102)	Chief Meyers	75.00	37.00	22.00
(103)	Clyde Milan	75.00	37.00	22.00
(104)	Dots Miller	75.00	37.00	22.00
(105)	Mike Mitchell	75.00	37.00	22.00
(106)	Bill Moriarty (Omaha)	75.00	37.00	22.00
(107)	George Moriarty (Detroit)	75.00	37.00	22.00
(108)	George Mullen	75.00	37.00	22.00
(109)	Simmy Murch	75.00	37.00	22.00
(110)	Danny Murphy	75.00	37.00	22.00
(111)	Red Murray	75.00	37.00	22.00
(112)	Red Nelson	75.00	37.00	22.00
(113)	Rebel Oakes	75.00	37.00	22.00
(114)	Orval Overall	75.00	37.00	22.00
(115)	Owens	75.00	37.00	22.00
(116)	Fred Parent	75.00	37.00	22.00
(117)	Dode Paskert	75.00	37.00	22.00
(118)	Heinie Peitz (Pietz)	75.00	37.00	22.00
(119)	Bob Peterson	75.00	37.00	22.00
(120)	Ollie Pickering	75.00	37.00	22.00
(121)	Bugs Raymond	75.00	37.00	22.00
(122)	Pat Regan (Ragan)	75.00	37.00	22.00
(123)	Robinson	75.00	37.00	22.00
(124)	Rock	75.00	37.00	22.00
(125)	Jack Rowan	75.00	37.00	22.00
(126)	Nap Rucker	75.00	37.00	22.00
(127)	Dick Rudolph	75.00	37.00	22.00
(128)	Slim Sallee	75.00	37.00	22.00
(129)	Jimmy Scheckard (Sheckard)	75.00	37.00	22.00
(130)	George Schirm	75.00	37.00	22.00
(131)	Wildfire Schulte	75.00	37.00	22.00
(132)	James Seabaugh	75.00	37.00	22.00
(133)	Selby	75.00	37.00	22.00
(134)	Hosea Siner	75.00	37.00	22.00
(135)	Sid Smith	75.00	37.00	22.00
(136)	Fred Snodgrass	65.00	32.00	19.50
(137)	Bob Spade	75.00	37.00	22.00
(138)	Tully Sparks	75.00	37.00	22.00
(139)	Tris Speaker	350.00	175.00	105.00
(140)	Tubby Spencer	75.00	37.00	22.00
(141)	George Stone	75.00	37.00	22.00
(142)	George Stovall	75.00	37.00	22.00
(143)	Gabby Street	75.00	37.00	22.00
(144)	Sullivan (Omaha)	75.00	37.00	22.00
(145)	John Sullivan (Louisville)	75.00	37.00	22.00
(146)	Ed Summers	75.00	37.00	22.00
(147)	Joe Tinker	200.00	100.00	60.00
(148)	John Titus	75.00	37.00	22.00
(149)	Rube Waddell	200.00	100.00	60.00
(150)	Walker	75.00	37.00	22.00

		NR MT	EX	VG
(151)	Waller	75.00	37.00	22.00
(152)	Julius Wiesman (Weisman)	75.00	37.00	22.00
(153)	Jack White	75.00	37.00	22.00
(154)	Otto Williams	75.00	37.00	22.00
(155)	Hooks Wiltse	75.00	37.00	22.00
(156)	Orville Woodruff	75.00	37.00	22.00
(157)	Woods	75.00	37.00	22.00
(158)	Cy Young	600.00	300.00	180.00
(159)	Heinie Zimmerman	75.00	37.00	22.00

1912 E270 Tin Tops

Except for the backs, these round, paper cards (Measuring 1-1/2" in diameter) are identical to the E254 Colgan's Chips issue, and were inserted in tin cannisters of Colgan's Mint Chips and Violet Chips. The front contains a player portrait photo along with the player's last name, team and league. The back advises collectors to "Send 25 Tin Tops" and a two-cent stamp to receive a photo of the "World's Pennant Winning Team." THe set carries the designation E270 Tin Tops.

		NR MT	EX	VG
Complete Set:		18000.00	9000.00	5400.
Common Player:		85.00	42.00	25.00
(1)	Doc Adkins	85.00	42.00	25.00
(2)	Whitey Alperman	85.00	42.00	25.00
(3a)	Red Ames (New York)	85.00	42.00	25.00
(3b)	Red Ames (Cincinnati)	85.00	42.00	25.00
(4a)	Tommy Atkins (Atlanta)	85.00	42.00	25.00
(4b)	Tommy Atkins (Ft. Wayne)	85.00	42.00	25.00
(5)	Jake Atz	85.00	42.00	25.00
(6)	Jimmy Austin	85.00	42.00	25.00
(7)	Home Run Baker	175.00	87.00	52.00
(8)	Johnny Bates	85.00	42.00	25.00
(9)	Beebe	85.00	42.00	25.00
(10)	Harry Bemis	85.00	42.00	25.00
(11)	Bob Bescher	85.00	42.00	25.00
(12)	Joe Birmingham	85.00	42.00	25.00
(13)	Roger Bresnahan	175.00	87.00	52.00
(14)	George Brown (Browne)	85.00	42.00	25.00
(15)	Al Burch	85.00	42.00	25.00
(16)	Burns	85.00	42.00	25.00
(17)	Donie Bush	85.00	42.00	25.00
(18)	Bobby Byrne	85.00	42.00	25.00
(19)	Nixey Callahan	85.00	42.00	25.00
(20)	Billy Campbell	85.00	42.00	25.00
(21)	Charlie Carr	85.00	42.00	25.00
(22)	Jay Cashion	85.00	42.00	25.00
(23)	Frank Chance	175.00	87.00	52.00
(24)	Hal Chase	110.00	55.00	33.00
(25)	Ed Cicotte	90.00	45.00	27.00
(26)	Clarke (Indianapolis)	85.00	42.00	25.00
(27)	Fred Clarke (Pittsburg)	175.00	87.00	52.00
(28)	Tommy Clarke (Cincinnati)	85.00	42.00	25.00
(29)	Clemons	85.00	42.00	25.00
(30)	Bill Clymer	85.00	42.00	25.00
(31)	Ty Cobb	1200.00	600.00	360.00
(32)	Eddie Collins	175.00	87.00	52.00
(33a)	Bunk Congalton (Omaha)	85.00	42.00	25.00
(33b)	Bunk Congalton (Toledo)	85.00	42.00	25.00
(34)	Cook	85.00	42.00	25.00
(35)	Jack Coombs	85.00	42.00	25.00
(36)	Corcoran	85.00	42.00	25.00
(37)	Sam Crawford	175.00	87.00	52.00

		NR MT	EX	VG
(38)	Bert Daniels	85.00	42.00	25.00
(39)	Jake Daubert	80.00	40.00	24.00
(40a)	Josh Devore	85.00	42.00	25.00
(40b)	Josh Devore	85.00	42.00	25.00
(41)	Mike Donlin	85.00	42.00	25.00
(42)	Red Dooin	85.00	42.00	25.00
(43)	Mickey Doolan	85.00	42.00	25.00
(44)	Larry Doyle	85.00	42.00	25.00
(45)	Delos Drake	85.00	42.00	25.00
(46)	Kid Elberfield (Elberfeld)	85.00	42.00	25.00
(47)	Roy Ellam	85.00	42.00	25.00
(48)	Elliott	85.00	42.00	25.00
(49)	Rube Ellis	85.00	42.00	25.00
(50)	Elwert	85.00	42.00	25.00
(51)	Clyde Engle	85.00	42.00	25.00
(52)	Jimmy Esmond	85.00	42.00	25.00
(53)	Steve Evans	85.00	42.00	25.00
(54)	Johnny Evers	175.00	87.00	52.00
(55)	Hobe Ferris	85.00	42.00	25.00
(56)	Russ Ford	85.00	42.00	25.00
(57)	Ed Foster	85.00	42.00	25.00
(58)	Friel	85.00	42.00	25.00
(59)	John Frill	85.00	42.00	25.00
(60)	Art Froome (Fromme)	85.00	42.00	25.00
(61)	Gus Getz	85.00	42.00	25.00
(62)	George Gibson	85.00	42.00	25.00
(63)	Graham	85.00	42.00	25.00
(64a)	Eddie Grant (Cincinnati)	85.00	42.00	25.00
(64b)	Eddie Grant (New York)	85.00	42.00	25.00
(65)	Grief	85.00	42.00	25.00
(66)	Bob Grom (Groom)	85.00	42.00	25.00
(67)	Charlie Hanford	85.00	42.00	25.00
(68)	Topsy Hartsel	85.00	42.00	25.00
(69)	Harry Hinchman	85.00	42.00	25.00
(70)	Dick Hoblitzell	85.00	42.00	25.00
(71)	Happy Hogan (St. Louis)	85.00	42.00	25.00
(72)	Happy Hogan (San Francisco)	85.00	42.00	25.00
(73)	Harry Hooper	175.00	87.00	52.00
(74)	Miller Huggins	175.00	87.00	52.00
(75a)	Hughes (Milwaukee)	85.00	42.00	25.00
(75b)	Hughes (Rochester)	85.00	42.00	25.00
(76)	Rudy Hulswitt	85.00	42.00	25.00
(77)	John Hummel	85.00	42.00	25.00
(78)	Hugh Jennings	175.00	87.00	52.00
(79)	Pete Johns	85.00	42.00	25.00
(80)	Davy Jones	85.00	42.00	25.00
(81)	Tim Jordan	85.00	42.00	25.00
(82)	Bob Keefe	85.00	42.00	25.00
(83)	Wee Willie Keeler	175.00	87.00	52.00
(84)	Joe Kelly (Kelley)	175.00	87.00	52.00
(85)	Bill Killefer	85.00	42.00	25.00
(86)	Ed Killian	85.00	42.00	25.00
(87)	Klipfer	85.00	42.00	25.00
(88)	Otto Knabe	85.00	42.00	25.00
(89)	Jack Knight	85.00	42.00	25.00
(90)	Ed Konetchy	85.00	42.00	25.00
(91)	Paul Krichell	85.00	42.00	25.00
(92)	James Lafitte	85.00	42.00	25.00
(93)	Nap Lajoie	200.00	100.00	60.00
(94)	Frank Lange	85.00	42.00	25.00
(95)	Lee	85.00	42.00	25.00
(96)	Jack Lewis	85.00	42.00	25.00
(97)	Harry Lord	85.00	42.00	25.00
(98)	Johnny Lush	85.00	42.00	25.00
(99)	Madden	85.00	42.00	25.00
(100)	Nick Maddox	85.00	42.00	25.00
(101)	Sherry Magee	80.00	40.00	24.00
(102)	Manser	85.00	42.00	25.00
(103)	McAllister	85.00	42.00	25.00
(104)	McCathy	85.00	42.00	25.00
(105)	McConnell	85.00	42.00	25.00
(106)	Larry McLean	85.00	42.00	25.00
(107)	Fred Merkle	75.00	37.00	22.00
(108)	Chief Meyers	85.00	42.00	25.00
(109)	Miller (Columbus)	85.00	42.00	25.00
(110)	Dots Miller (Pittsburg)	85.00	42.00	25.00
(111)	Clarence Mitchell	85.00	42.00	25.00
(112)	Mike Mitchell	85.00	42.00	25.00
(113)	Roy Mitchell	85.00	42.00	25.00
(114)	Carlton Molesworth	85.00	42.00	25.00
(115)	Herbie Moran	85.00	42.00	25.00
(116)	George Moriarty	85.00	42.00	25.00
(117)	Danny Murphy	85.00	42.00	25.00
(118)	Jim Murray	85.00	42.00	25.00
(119)	Jake Northrop	85.00	42.00	25.00
(120)	Rube Oldring	85.00	42.00	25.00
(121)	Steve O'Neil (O'Neill)	85.00	42.00	25.00
(122)	O'Rourke	85.00	42.00	25.00
(123)	Larry Pape	85.00	42.00	25.00
(124)	Fred Parent	85.00	42.00	25.00
(125)	Perry	85.00	42.00	25.00

		NR MT	EX	VG
(126)	Billy Purtell	85.00	42.00	25.00
(127)	Bill Rariden	85.00	42.00	25.00
(128)	Morrie Rath	85.00	42.00	25.00
(129)	Dick Rudolph	85.00	42.00	25.00
(130)	Bud Ryan	85.00	42.00	25.00
(131)	Slim Sallee	85.00	42.00	25.00
(132)	Ray Schalk	85.00	42.00	25.00
(133)	Jimmy Scheckard (Sheckard)	85.00	42.00	25.00
(134)	Bob Shawkey	85.00	42.00	25.00
(135)	Skeeter Shelton	85.00	42.00	25.00
(136)	Smith (Montreal)	85.00	42.00	25.00
(137a)	Sid Smith (Atlanta)	85.00	42.00	25.00
(137b)	Sid Smith (Newark)	85.00	42.00	25.00
(138)	Fred Snodgrass	85.00	42.00	25.00
(139)	Tris Speaker	175.00	87.00	52.00
(140)	Jake Stahl	85.00	42.00	25.00
(141)	John Stansberry (Stansbury)	85.00	42.00	25.00
(142)	Amos Strunk	85.00	42.00	25.00
(143)	Sullivan	85.00	42.00	25.00
(144)	Harry Swacina	85.00	42.00	25.00
(145)	Bill Sweeney	85.00	42.00	25.00
(146)	Jeff Sweeney	85.00	42.00	25.00
(147)	Taylor	85.00	42.00	25.00
(148)	Jim Thorpe	2500.00	1250.00	750.00
(149)	Joe Tinker	175.00	87.00	52.00
(150)	John Titus	85.00	42.00	25.00
(151)	Terry Turner	85.00	42.00	25.00
(152)	Bob Unglaub	85.00	42.00	25.00
(153)	Viebahn	85.00	42.00	25.00
(154)	Rube Waddell	175.00	87.00	52.00
(155)	Honus Wagner	500.00	250.00	150.00
(156)	Bobby Wallace	175.00	87.00	52.00
(157)	Ed Walsh	175.00	87.00	52.00
(158)	Jack Warhop	85.00	42.00	25.00
(159)	Zach Wheat	175.00	87.00	52.00
(160)	Kaiser Wilhelm	85.00	42.00	25.00
(161)	Ed Willett	85.00	42.00	25.00
(162)	Owen Wilson	85.00	42.00	25.00
(163)	Hooks Wiltse	85.00	42.00	25.00
(164)	Joe Wood	80.00	40.00	24.00
(165)	Orville Woodruff	85.00	42.00	25.00
(166)	Joe Yeager	85.00	42.00	25.00
(167)	Bill Zimmerman	85.00	42.00	25.00

		NR MT	EX	VG
(6)	Mordicai Brown (Mordecai)	800.00	400.00	240.00
(7)	"Eddie" Cicotte	650.00	325.00	195.00
(8)	Fred Clark (Clarke)	800.00	400.00	240.00
(9)	Ty. Cobb	2500.00	1250.00	750.00
(10)	King Cole	400.00	200.00	120.00
(11)	E. Collins	800.00	400.00	240.00
(12)	Wid Conroy	400.00	200.00	120.00
(13)	"Sam" Crawford	800.00	400.00	240.00
(14)	Bill Dahlin (Dahlen)	400.00	200.00	120.00
(15)	Bill Donovan	400.00	200.00	120.00
(16)	"Pat" Dougherty	400.00	200.00	120.00
(17)	Kid Elberfeld	400.00	200.00	120.00
(18)	"Johnny" Evers	800.00	400.00	240.00
(19)	Charlie Herzog	400.00	200.00	120.00
(20)	Walter Johnson	1500.00	750.00	450.00
(21)	Ed Konetchy	400.00	200.00	120.00
(22)	Tommy Leach	400.00	200.00	120.00
(23)	Fred Luderous (Luderus)	400.00	200.00	120.00
(24)	"Mike" Mowery	400.00	200.00	120.00
(25)	Jack Powell	400.00	200.00	120.00
(26)	Slim Sallee	400.00	200.00	120.00
(27)	James Scheckard (Sheckard)	400.00	200.00	120.00
(28)	Walter Snodgrass	400.00	200.00	120.00
(29)	"Tris" Speaker	1000.00	500.00	300.00
(30)	Charlie Suggs	400.00	200.00	120.00
(31)	Fred Tenney	400.00	200.00	120.00
(32)	"Hans" Wagner	2000.00	1000.00	600.00

1933 E285

Designed to resemble a set of playing cards, this set, issued circa 1933 by the Rittenhouse Candy Company of Philadelphia, carries the ACC designation E285 and is generally considered to be the last of the E-card issues. Each card measures 2-1/4" by 1-7/16" and features a small player photo in the center of the playing card design. The backs of the cards usually consist of just one large letter and were part of a promotion in which collectors were instructed to find enough different letters to spell "Rittenhouse Candy Co." Other backs explaining the contest and the prizes available have also been found. Because it was designed as a deck of playing cards, the set is complete at 52 cards, featuring 46 different players (six are pictured on two cards each). Cards have been found in red, green and blue.

1910 E271

Designated as E271 by the ACC, the 1910 Darby Chocolates cards are among the rarest of all candy cards. The cards were printed on boxes of Darby's "Pennant" Chocolates, two players per box - one on the front of the box, the other on the back. The cards feature black and white player silhouettes outlined with a thick dark line. The cards are accented with orange or green tinting. Most of the 32 known examples of this set were not found until 1982, and there is speculation that the checklist is still not complete.

		NR MT	EX	VG
Complete Set:		35000.00	17500.00	10500.
Common Player:		400.00	200.00	120.00
(1)	Jimmy Archer	400.00	200.00	120.00
(2)	Chief Bender	800.00	400.00	240.00
(3)	"Bob" Bescher	400.00	200.00	120.00
(4)	Roger Bresnahan	800.00	400.00	240.00
(5)	Al Bridwell	400.00	200.00	120.00

		NR MT	EX	VG
Complete Set:		7500.00	3750.00	2250.
Common Player:		50.00	25.00	15.00
(1)	Dick Bartell	50.00	25.00	15.00
(2)	Walter Berger	50.00	25.00	15.00
(3)	Max Bishop	50.00	25.00	15.00
(4)	James Bottomley	100.00	50.00	30.00
(5)	Fred Brickell	50.00	25.00	15.00
(6)	Sugar Cain	50.00	25.00	15.00
(7)	Ed. Cihocki	50.00	25.00	15.00
(8)	Phil Collins	50.00	25.00	15.00
(9)	Roger Cramer	50.00	25.00	15.00
(10)	Hughie Critz	50.00	25.00	15.00
(11)	Joe Cronin	110.00	55.00	33.00
(12)	Hazen (Kiki) Cuyler	100.00	50.00	30.00
(13)	Geo. Davis	50.00	25.00	15.00
(14)	Spud Davis	50.00	25.00	15.00
(15)	Jimmy Dykes	55.00	27.00	16.50
(16)	George Earnshaw	50.00	25.00	15.00

		NR MT	EX	VG
(17)	Jumbo Elliot	50.00	25.00	15.00
(18)	Lou Finney	50.00	25.00	15.00
(19)	Jimmy Foxx	150.00	75.00	45.00
(20)	Frankie Frisch (3 of Spades)	100.00	50.00	30.00
(21)	Frankie Frisch (7 of Spades)	100.00	50.00	30.00
(22)	Robert (Lefty) Grove	125.00	62.00	37.00
(23)	Mule Haas	50.00	25.00	15.00
(24)	Chick Hafey	100.00	50.00	30.00
(25)	Chas. Leo Hartnett	100.00	50.00	30.00
(26)	Babe Herman	55.00	27.00	16.50
(27)	Wm. Herman	100.00	50.00	30.00
(28)	Kid Higgins	50.00	25.00	15.00
(29)	Rogers Hornsby	125.00	62.00	37.00
(30)	Don Hurst (Jack of Diamonds)	50.00	25.00	15.00
(31)	Don Hurst (6 of Spades)	50.00	25.00	15.00
(32)	Chuck Klein	100.00	50.00	30.00
(33)	Leroy Mahaffey	50.00	25.00	15.00
(34)	Gus Mancuso	50.00	25.00	15.00
(35)	Rabbit McNair	50.00	25.00	15.00
(36)	Bing Miller	50.00	25.00	15.00
(37)	Frank (Lefty) O'Doul	60.00	30.00	18.00
(38)	Mel Ott	110.00	55.00	33.00
(39)	Babe Ruth (Ace of Spades)	1000.00	500.00	300.00
(40)	Babe Ruth (King of Clubs)	1000.00	500.00	300.00
(41)	Al Simmons	100.00	50.00	30.00
(42)	Bill Terry	110.00	55.00	33.00
(43)	Pie Traynor	100.00	50.00	30.00
(44)	Rube Wallberg (Walberg)	50.00	25.00	15.00
(45)	Lloyd Waner	100.00	50.00	30.00
(46)	Paul Waner	100.00	50.00	30.00
(47)	Lloyd Warner (Waner)	100.00	50.00	30.00
(48)	Paul Warner (Warner)	100.00	50.00	30.00
(49)	Pinkey Whitney	50.00	25.00	15.00
(50)	Dib Williams	50.00	25.00	15.00
(51)	Hack Wilson (9 of Spades)	100.00	50.00	30.00
(52)	Hack Wilson (9 of Clubs)	100.00	50.00	30.00

		NR MT	EX	VG
(14)	Bill Dahlen	250.00	125.00	75.00
(15)	Bert Daniels	250.00	125.00	75.00
(16)	Harry Davis	250.00	125.00	75.00
(17)	Larry Doyle	250.00	125.00	75.00
(18)	Rube Ellis	250.00	125.00	75.00
(19)	Cecil Ferguson	250.00	125.00	75.00
(20)	Russ Ford	250.00	125.00	75.00
(21)	Bob Harnion (Harmon)	250.00	125.00	75.00
(22)	Ham Hyatt	250.00	125.00	75.00
(23)	Red Kellifer (Killifer)	250.00	125.00	75.00
(24)	Art Kruger (Krueger)	250.00	125.00	75.00
(25)	Tommy Leach	250.00	125.00	75.00
(26)	Harry Lumley	250.00	125.00	75.00
(27)	Christy Mathewson	800.00	400.00	240.00
(28)	John McGraw	800.00	400.00	240.00
(29)	Deacon McGuire	250.00	125.00	75.00
(30)	Chief Meyers	250.00	125.00	75.00
(31)	Otto Miller	250.00	125.00	75.00
(32)	Charlie Mullen	250.00	125.00	75.00
(33)	Tom Needham	250.00	125.00	75.00
(34)	Rube Oldring	250.00	125.00	75.00
(35)	Barney Pelty	250.00	125.00	75.00
(36)	Ed Reulbach	250.00	125.00	75.00
(37)	Jack Rowan	250.00	125.00	75.00
(38)	Dave Shean	250.00	125.00	75.00
(39)	Tris Speaker	850.00	425.00	255.00
(40)	Jeff Sweeney	250.00	125.00	75.00
(41)	Honus Wagner	2000.00	1000.00	600.00
(42)	Ed Walsh	500.00	250.00	150.00
(43)	Kirby White	250.00	125.00	75.00
(44)	Ralph Works	250.00	125.00	75.00
(45)	Elmer Zacher	250.00	125.00	75.00

1910 E286

Issued in 1910 with Ju Ju Drum Candy, this extremely rare set of circular baseball cards is very similar in design to the more common Colgan's Chips cards. About the size of a silver dollar (1-7/16" in diameter) the cards display a player photo on the front with the player's name and team printed below in a semi-circle design. The backs carry advertising for Ju Ju Drums. The checklist contains 45 different players to datem but the issue - known as E286 in the American Card Catalog - is so rare that others are likely to exist.

		NR MT	EX	VG
Complete Set:		20000.00	10000.00	6000.
Common Player:		250.00	125.00	75.00
(1)	Eddie Ainsmith	250.00	125.00	75.00
(2)	Jimmy Austin	250.00	125.00	75.00
(3)	Chief Bender	500.00	250.00	150.00
(4)	Bob Bescher	250.00	125.00	75.00
(5)	Bruno Bloch (Block)	250.00	125.00	75.00
(6)	Frank Burke	250.00	125.00	75.00
(7)	Donie Bush	250.00	125.00	75.00
(8)	Frank Chance	500.00	250.00	150.00
(9)	Harry Cheek	250.00	125.00	75.00
(10)	Ed Cicotte	300.00	150.00	90.00
(11)	Ty Cobb	2500.00	1250.00	750.00
(12)	King Cole	250.00	125.00	75.00
(13)	Jack Coombs	250.00	125.00	75.00

1912 E300

DELEHANTY
DETROIT AMERICANS

An extremely rare candy issue, cards in this 1912 set measures 3" by 4" and feature sepia-toned photos surrounded by a rather wide border. The player's name and team appear in the border below the photo, while the words "Plow's Candy Collection" appear at the top. The backs are blank. Not even known to exist until the late 1960s, this set has been assigned the designation of E300.

		NR MT	EX	VG
Complete Set:		25000.00	12500.00	7500.
Common Player:		300.00	150.00	90.00
(1)	Babe Adams	300.00	150.00	90.00
(2)	Home Run Baker	750.00	375.00	225.00
(3)	Cy Barger	300.00	150.00	90.00
(4)	Jack Barry	300.00	150.00	90.00
(5)	Johnny Bates	300.00	150.00	90.00
(7)	Joe Benz	300.00	150.00	90.00
(8)	Cy Berger (Barger)	300.00	150.00	90.00
(9)	Roger Bresnahan	750.00	375.00	225.00
(10)	Mordecai Brown	750.00	375.00	225.00
(11)	Donie Bush	300.00	150.00	90.00
(12)	Bobby Byrne	300.00	150.00	90.00
(13)	Nixey Callahan	300.00	150.00	90.00
(14)	Hal Chase	500.00	250.00	150.00
(15)	Fred Clarke	750.00	375.00	225.00
(16)	Ty Cobb	3000.00	1500.00	900.00
(17)	King Cole	300.00	150.00	90.00
(18)	Eddie Collins	800.00	400.00	240.00
(19)	Jack Coombs	300.00	150.00	90.00
(20)	Bill Dahlen	300.00	150.00	90.00
(21)	Bert Daniels	300.00	150.00	90.00

		NR MT	EX	VG
(22)	Harry Davis	300.00	150.00	90.00
(23)	Jim Delehanty	300.00	150.00	90.00
(24)	Josh Devore	300.00	150.00	90.00
(25)	Wild Bill Donovan	300.00	150.00	90.00
(26)	Red Dooin	300.00	150.00	90.00
(27)	Johnny Evers	750.00	375.00	225.00
(28)	Russ Ford	300.00	150.00	90.00
(29)	Del Gainor	300.00	150.00	90.00
(30)	Vean Gregg	300.00	150.00	90.00
(31)	Bob Harmon	300.00	150.00	90.00
(32)	Arnold Hauser	300.00	150.00	90.00
(33)	Dick Hoblitzelle (Hoblitzell)	300.00	150.00	90.00
(34)	Solly Hofman	300.00	150.00	90.00
(35)	Miller Huggins	750.00	375.00	225.00
(36)	John Hummel	300.00	150.00	90.00
(37)	Walter Johnson	1500.00	750.00	450.00
(38)	Johnny Kling	300.00	150.00	90.00
(39)	Nap Lajoie	1200.00	600.00	360.00
(40)	Jack Lapp	300.00	150.00	90.00
(41)	Fred Luderus	300.00	150.00	90.00
(42)	Sherry Magee	300.00	150.00	90.00
(43)	Rube Marquard	750.00	375.00	225.00
(44)	Christy Mathewson	1500.00	750.00	450.00
(45)	Stuffy McInnes (McInnis)	300.00	150.00	90.00
(46)	Larry McLean	300.00	150.00	90.00
(47)	Fred Merkle	300.00	150.00	90.00
(48)	Cy Morgan	300.00	150.00	90.00
(49)	George Moriarty	300.00	150.00	90.00
(50)	Mike Mowrey	300.00	150.00	90.00
(51)	Chief Myers (Meyers)	300.00	150.00	90.00
(52)	Rube Oldring	300.00	150.00	90.00
(53)	Marty O'Toole	300.00	150.00	90.00
(54)	Nap Rucker	300.00	150.00	90.00
(55)	Slim Sallee	300.00	150.00	90.00
(56)	Boss Schmidt	300.00	150.00	90.00
(57)	Jimmy Sheckard	300.00	150.00	90.00
(58)	Tris Speaker	850.00	425.00	255.00
(59)	Billy Sullivan	300.00	150.00	90.00
(60)	Ira Thomas	300.00	150.00	90.00
(61)	Joe Tinker	750.00	375.00	225.00
(62)	John Titus	300.00	150.00	90.00
(63)	Hippo Vaughan (Vaughn)	300.00	150.00	90.00
(64)	Honus Wagner	2500.00	1250.00	750.00
(65)	Ed Walsh	750.00	375.00	225.00
(66)	Bob Williams	300.00	150.00	90.00

1888 E.R. Williams Card Game

This 1889 set of 52 playing cards came packed in its own box that advertised the set as the "Egerton R. Williams Popular Indoor Base Ball Game." Designed to look like a conventional deck of playing cards, the set included various players from the National League and the American Association. Although the set contains 52 cards (like a typical deck of playing cards) only 19 actually feature color drawings of players. Each of these cards pictures two different players (one at the top and a second at the bottom, separated by sepia-colored crossed bats in the middle), resulting in 38 different players. The remaining 33 cards in the deck are strictly game cards showing a specific baseball play (such as "Batter Out on Fly" or "Two Base Hit," etc.) The cards have green-tinted backs and measure 2-7/16" by 3-1/2". Each one carries an 1889 copyright line by E.R. Williams.

		NR MT	EX	VG
Complete Set:		10000.00	5000.00	3000.
Common Player:		250.00	125.00	75.00
(1)	Cap Anson, Buck Ewing	700.00	350.00	210.00
(2)	Dan Brouthers, Arlie Latham	375.00	187.00	112.00
(3)	Charles Buffinton, Parisian Bob Carruthers	250.00	125.00	75.00
(4)	Hick Carpenter, Cliff Carroll	250.00	125.00	75.00
(5)	Charles Comiskey, Roger Connor	500.00	250.00	150.00
(6)	Pop Corkhill, Jim Fogarty	250.00	125.00	75.00
(7)	John Clarkson, Tim Keefe	500.00	250.00	150.00
(8)	Jerry Denny, Silent Mike Tiernan	250.00	125.00	75.00
(9)	Dave Foutz, King Kelly	400.00	200.00	120.00
(10)	Pud Galvin, Dave Orr	375.00	187.00	112.00
(11)	Pebbly Jack Glasscock, Foghorn Tucker	250.00	125.00	75.00
(12)	Mike Griffin, Ed McKean	250.00	125.00	75.00
(13)	Dummy Hoy, Long John Reilley (Reilly)	250.00	125.00	75.00
(14)	Arthur Irwin, Ned Williamson	250.00	125.00	75.00
(15)	Silver King, John Tener	250.00	125.00	75.00
(16)	Al Myers, Cub Stricker	250.00	125.00	75.00
(17)	Fred Pfeffer, Chicken Wolf	250.00	125.00	75.00
(18)	Toad Ramsey, Gus Weyhing	250.00	125.00	75.00
(19)	Monte Ward, Curt Welch	375.00	187.00	112.00

1954 Esskay Hot Dogs Orioles

Measuring 2-1/4" by 3-1/2", the 1954 Esskay Hot Dogs set features the Baltimore Orioles. The unnumbered color cards were issued in panels of two on packages of hot dogs and are usually found with grease stains. The cards have waxed fronts with blank backs on a white stock. Complete boxes of Esskay Hot Dogs are scarce and command a price of 2-3 times greater than the single card values.

		NR MT	EX	VG
Complete Set:		3300.00	1650.00	990.00
Common Player:		90.00	45.00	27.00
(1)	Neil Berry	90.00	45.00	27.00
(2)	Michael Blyzka	90.00	45.00	27.00
(3)	Harry Brecheen	90.00	45.00	27.00
(4)	Gil Coan	90.00	45.00	27.00
(5)	Joe Coleman	90.00	45.00	27.00
(6)	Clinton Courtney	90.00	45.00	27.00
(7)	Charles E. Diering	90.00	45.00	27.00
(8)	Jimmie Dykes	100.00	50.00	30.00
(9)	Frank J. Fanovich	90.00	45.00	27.00
(10)	Howard Fox	90.00	45.00	27.00
(11)	Jim Fridley	90.00	45.00	27.00
(12)	Vinicio "Chico" Garcia	90.00	45.00	27.00
(13)	Jehosie Heard	90.00	45.00	27.00
(14)	Darrell Johnson	90.00	45.00	27.00
(15)	Bob Kennedy	90.00	45.00	27.00
(16)	Dick Kokos	90.00	45.00	27.00
(17)	Dave Koslo	90.00	45.00	27.00
(18)	Lou Kretlow	90.00	45.00	27.00
(19)	Richard D. Kryhoski	90.00	45.00	27.00
(20)	Don Larsen	100.00	50.00	30.00
(21)	Donald E. Lenhardt	90.00	45.00	27.00
(22)	Richard Littlefield	90.00	45.00	27.00
(23)	Sam Mele	90.00	45.00	27.00
(24)	Les Moss	90.00	45.00	27.00
(25)	Ray L. Murray	90.00	45.00	27.00

		NR MT	EX	VG
(26a)	"Bobo" Newsom (no stadium lights in background)	125.00	62.00	37.00
(26b)	"Bobo" Newson (stadium lights in background)	125.00	62.00	37.00
(27)	Tom Oliver	90.00	45.00	27.00
(28)	Duane Pillette	90.00	45.00	27.00
(29)	Francis M. Skaff	90.00	45.00	27.00
(30)	Marlin Stuart	90.00	45.00	27.00
(31)	Robert L. Turley	150.00	75.00	45.00
(32)	Eddie Waitkus	90.00	45.00	27.00
(33)	Vic Wertz	110.00	55.00	33.00
(34)	Robert G. Young	90.00	45.00	27.00

1955 Esskay Hot Dogs Orioles

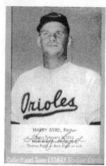

For the second consecutive year, Esskay Meats placed two baseball cards of Orioles players on their boxes of hot dogs. The unnumbered, color cards measure 2-1/4" by 3-1/2" and can be distinguished from the previous year by unwaxed fronts and grey backs. Many of the same photos from 1954 were used with only minor picture-cropping differences.

		NR MT	EX	VG
Complete Set:		2400.00	1200.00	720.00
Common Player:		90.00	45.00	27.00
(1)	Cal Abrams	90.00	45.00	27.00
(2)	Robert S. Alexander	90.00	45.00	27.00
(3)	Harry Byrd	90.00	45.00	27.00
(4)	Gil Coan	90.00	45.00	27.00
(5)	Joseph P. Coleman	90.00	45.00	27.00
(6)	William R. Cox	90.00	45.00	27.00
(7)	Charles E. Diering	90.00	45.00	27.00
(8)	Walter A. Evers	90.00	45.00	27.00
(9)	Don Johnson	90.00	45.00	27.00
(10)	Robert D. Kennedy	90.00	45.00	27.00
(11)	Lou Kretlow	90.00	45.00	27.00
(12)	Robert L. Kuzava	90.00	45.00	27.00
(13)	Fred Marsh	90.00	45.00	27.00
(14)	Charles Maxwell	90.00	45.00	27.00
(15)	Jimmie McDonald	90.00	45.00	27.00
(16)	Bill Miller	90.00	45.00	27.00
(17)	Willy Miranda	90.00	45.00	27.00
(18)	Raymond L. Moore	90.00	45.00	27.00
(19)	John Lester Moss	90.00	45.00	27.00
(20)	"Bobo" Newsom	100.00	50.00	30.00
(21)	Duane Pillette	90.00	45.00	27.00
(22)	Edward S. Waitkus	90.00	45.00	27.00
(23)	Harold W. Smith	90.00	45.00	27.00
(24)	Gus Triandos	110.00	55.00	33.00
(25)	Eugene R. Woodling	110.00	55.00	33.00
(26)	Robert G. Young	90.00	45.00	27.00

1921 Exhibits - 1921

The Exhibit Supply Company of Chicago issued the first in a long series of postcard-size baseball cards in 1921. The Exhibit cards were commonly sold in "penny arcade" vending machines. The 1921 series consists of 64 cards and includes four players from each of the 16 major league teams. The cards feature black and white photos with the player's name printed in a fancy script. The player's position and team appear below the name in small, hand-lettered capital letters. American League is designated as "AM.L.," which can help differentiate the 1921 series from future years. Some of the cards contain white borders, while others do not. All have blank backs. There are various spelling errors in the picture legends.

		NR MT	EX	VG
Complete Set:		2500.00	1250.00	750.00
Common Player:		15.00	7.50	4.50
(1)	Chas. B. Adams	15.00	7.50	4.50
(2)	Grover C. Alexander	15.00	7.50	4.50
(3)	David Bancroft	40.00	20.00	12.00
(4)	Geo. J. Burns	15.00	7.50	4.50
(5)	Owen Bush	15.00	7.50	4.50
(6)	Max J. Carey	40.00	20.00	12.00
(7)	Ty Cobb	300.00	150.00	90.00
(8)	Eddie T. Collins	40.00	20.00	12.00
(9)	John Collins	15.00	7.50	4.50
(10)	Stanley Coveleskie (Coveleski)	40.00	20.00	12.00
(11)	Walton E. Cruse (Cruise)	15.00	7.50	4.50
(12)	Jacob E. Daubert	18.00	9.00	5.50
(13)	George Dauss	15.00	7.50	4.50
(14)	Charles A. Deal	15.00	7.50	4.50
(15)	Joe A. Dugan	20.00	10.00	6.00
(16)	James Dykes	18.00	9.00	5.50
(17)	U.C. "Red" Faber	40.00	20.00	12.00
(18)	J.F. Fournier	15.00	7.50	4.50
(19)	Frank F. Frisch	40.00	20.00	12.00
(20)	W.L. Gardner	15.00	7.50	4.50
(21)	H.M. "Hank" Gowdy	15.00	7.50	4.50
(22)	Burleigh Grimes	40.00	20.00	12.00
(23)	Heinie Groh	15.00	7.50	4.50
(24)	Jesse Haines	40.00	20.00	12.00
(25)	Sam Harris (Stanley)	40.00	20.00	12.00
(26)	Walter L. Holke	15.00	7.50	4.50
(27)	Charles J. Hollicher (Hollocher)	15.00	7.50	4.50
(28)	Rogers Hornsby	60.00	30.00	18.00
(29)	James H. Johnson (Johnston)	15.00	7.50	4.50
(30)	Walter P. Johnson	150.00	75.00	45.00
(31)	Sam P. Jones	15.00	7.50	4.50
(32)	Geo. L. Kelly	40.00	20.00	12.00
(33)	Dick Kerr	15.00	7.50	4.50
(34)	William L. Killifer	15.00	7.50	4.50
(35)	Ed Konetchy	15.00	7.50	4.50
(36)	John "Doc" Lavan	15.00	7.50	4.50
(37)	Walter J. Maranville	40.00	20.00	12.00
(38)	Carl W. Mays	18.00	9.00	5.50
(39)	J. "Stuffy" McInnis	15.00	7.50	4.50
(40)	Rollie C. Naylor	15.00	7.50	4.50
(41)	A. Earl Neale (Earle)	20.00	10.00	6.00
(42)	Ivan M. Olsen	15.00	7.50	4.50
(43)	S.F. "Steve" O'Neil (O'Neill)	15.00	7.50	4.50
(44)	Robert Peckinpaugh	18.00	9.00	5.50
(45)	Ralph "Cy" Perkins	15.00	7.50	4.50
(46)	Raymond R. Powell	15.00	7.50	4.50
(47)	Joe "Goldie" Rapp	15.00	7.50	4.50
(48)	Edgar S. Rice	40.00	20.00	12.00
(49)	Jimmy Ring	15.00	7.50	4.50
(50)	Geo. H. "Babe" Ruth	500.00	250.00	150.00
(51)	Ray W. Schalk	40.00	20.00	12.00
(52)	Wallie Schang	15.00	7.50	4.50
(53)	Everett Scott	15.00	7.50	4.50
(54)	H.S. Shanks (photo actually Wally Schang)	15.00	7.50	4.50
(55)	Urban Shocker	15.00	7.50	4.50
(56)	Geo. J. Sisler	40.00	20.00	12.00
(57)	Tris Speaker	150.00	75.00	45.00

		NR MT	EX	VG
(58)	John Tobin	15.00	7.50	4.50
(59)	Robt. Veach	15.00	7.50	4.50
(60)	Zack D. Wheat	40.00	20.00	12.00
(61)	Geo. B. Whitted	15.00	7.50	4.50
(62)	Cy Williams	18.00	9.00	5.50
(63)	Kenneth R. Williams	18.00	9.00	5.50
(64)	Ivy B. Wingo	15.00	7.50	4.50

1922 Exhibits - 1922

The Exhibit Supply Company continued the same format in 1922 but doubled the number of cards in the series to 128, including eight players from each team. All but nine of the players who appeared in the 1921 series are pictured in the 1922 set, along with 74 new players. The cards again display black and white photos with blank backs. Some of the photos have white borders. The player's name appears in a plain script with the postition and team below in small capital letters. American League is designated as "A.L." Again, there are several spelling errors and incorrect player identifications. In early printings the Earl Smith card actually pictured Brad Kocher. Only the 74 new additions are included in the checklist that follows.

		NR MT	EX	VG
Complete Set:		2000.00	1000.00	600.00
Common Player:		20.00	10.00	6.00
(1)	J. Frank Baker	35.00	17.50	10.50
(2)	Jin Bagby	20.00	10.00	6.00
(3)	Walter Barbare	20.00	10.00	6.00
(4)	Turner Barber	20.00	10.00	6.00
(5)	John Bassler	20.00	10.00	6.00
(6)	Carlson L. Bigbee (Carson)	20.00	10.00	6.00
(7)	Sam Bohne	20.00	10.00	6.00
(8)	Geo. Burns	20.00	10.00	6.00
(9)	George Burns	20.00	10.00	6.00
(10)	Jeo Bush (Joe)	22.00	11.00	6.50
(11)	Leon Cadore	20.00	10.00	6.00
(12)	Jim Caveney	20.00	10.00	6.00
(13)	Wilbur Cooper	20.00	10.00	6.00
(14)	Dave Danforth	20.00	10.00	6.00
(15)	George Cutshaw	20.00	10.00	6.00
(16)	Bill Doak	20.00	10.00	6.00
(17)	Joe Dugan	25.00	12.50	7.50
(18)	Pat Duncan	20.00	10.00	6.00
(19)	Howard Emke (Ehmke)	20.00	10.00	6.00
(20)	Wm. Evans (umpire)	35.00	17.50	10.50
(21)	Bib Falk (Bibb)	20.00	10.00	6.00
(22)	Dana Fillingin (Fillingim)	20.00	10.00	6.00
(23)	Ira Flagstead	20.00	10.00	6.00
(24)	Fletcher	20.00	10.00	6.00
(25)	Gerber	20.00	10.00	6.00
(26)	Ray Grimes	20.00	10.00	6.00
(27)	Hildebrand (umpire)	20.00	10.00	6.00
(28)	Harry Heilman (Heilmann)	35.00	17.50	10.50
(29)	Wibur Hubbell (Wilbert)	20.00	10.00	6.00
(30)	Bill Jacobson	20.00	10.00	6.00
(31)	E.R. Johnson	20.00	10.00	6.00
(32)	Joe Judge	20.00	10.00	6.00
(33)	Bill Klem (umpire)	35.00	17.50	10.50
(34)	Harry Liebold (Leibold)	20.00	10.00	6.00
(35)	Walter Mails	20.00	10.00	6.00
(36)	Geo. Maisel	20.00	10.00	6.00
(37)	Lee Meadows	20.00	10.00	6.00

		NR MT	EX	VG
(38)	Clyde Milam (Milan)	20.00	10.00	6.00
(39)	Ed (Bing) Miller	20.00	10.00	6.00
(40)	Hack Miller	20.00	10.00	6.00
(41)	Moriarty (umpire)	20.00	10.00	6.00
(42)	Robert Muesel (Meusel)	25.00	12.50	7.50
(43)	Harry Myers	20.00	10.00	6.00
(44)	Arthur Nehf	20.00	10.00	6.00
(45)	Joe Oeschger	20.00	10.00	6.00
(46)	Geo. O'Neil	20.00	10.00	6.00
(47)	Roger Peckinpaugh	22.00	11.00	6.50
(48)	Val Picinich	20.00	10.00	6.00
(49)	Bill Piercy	20.00	10.00	6.00
(50)	Derrill Pratt	20.00	10.00	6.00
(51)	Jack Quinn	20.00	10.00	6.00
(52)	Walter Reuther (Ruether)	20.00	10.00	6.00
(53)	Rigler	20.00	10.00	6.00
(54)	Eppa Rixey	35.00	17.50	10.50
(55)	Chas. Robertson	20.00	10.00	6.00
(56)	Everett Scott	20.00	10.00	6.00
(57)	Earl Sheely	20.00	10.00	6.00
(58)	Earl Smith (portrait)	20.00	10.00	6.00
(59)	Earl Smith (standing) (photo actually Brad Kocher)	20.00	10.00	6.00
(60)	Elmer Smith	20.00	10.00	6.00
(61)	Jack Smith (photo actually Jimmy Smith)	20.00	10.00	6.00
(62)	Sherrod Smith	20.00	10.00	6.00
(63)	Frank Snyder	20.00	10.00	6.00
(64)	Allan Sothoron	20.00	10.00	6.00
(65)	Arnold Statz	20.00	10.00	6.00
(66)	Milton Stock	20.00	10.00	6.00
(67)	James Tierney	20.00	10.00	6.00
(68)	George Toporcer	20.00	10.00	6.00
(69)	Clarence (Tilly) Walker	20.00	10.00	6.00
(70)	Curtis Walker	20.00	10.00	6.00
(71)	Aaron Ward	20.00	10.00	6.00
(72)	Joe Wood	22.00	11.00	6.50
(73)	Moses Yellowhorse	22.00	11.00	6.50
(74)	Ross Young (Youngs)	35.00	17.50	10.50

A player's name in *italic* indicates a rookie card. An (FC) indicates a player's first card for that particular card company.

1923 Exhibits - 1923-1924

The Exhibit cards for 1923 and 1924 are generally collected as a single 128-card series. The format remained basically the same as the previous year, with black and white photos (some surrounded by a white border) and blank backs. The player's name is again shown in a plain script with the position and team printed below in a small, square-block type style. Many of the same photos were used from previous years, although some are cropped differently, and some players have new team designations, background changes, team emblems removed, borders added or taken away, and other minor changes. Fifty-eight new cards are featured, including 38 players pictured for the first time in an Exhibit set. Only the 58 new cards are included in the checklist that follows.

		NR MT	EX	VG
Complete Set:		2300.00	1150.00	690.00
Common Player:		25.00	12.50	7.50
(1)	Clyde Barnhart	25.00	12.50	7.50
(2)	Ray Blades	25.00	12.50	7.50
(3)	James Bottomley	40.00	20.00	12.00
(4)	George Burns	25.00	12.50	7.50

		NR MT	EX	VG
(5)	Dan Clark	25.00	12.50	7.50
(6)	Bill Doak	25.00	12.50	7.50
(7)	Joe Dugan	25.00	12.50	7.50
(8)	Howard J. Ehmke	25.00	12.50	7.50
(9)	Ira Flagstead	25.00	12.50	7.50
(10)	J.F. Fournier	25.00	12.50	7.50
(11)	Howard Freigan (Freigau)	25.00	12.50	7.50
(12)	C.E. Galloway	25.00	12.50	7.50
(13)	Joe Genewich	25.00	12.50	7.50
(14)	Mike Gonzales	25.00	12.50	7.50
(15)	H.M. "Hank" Gowdy	25.00	12.50	7.50
(16)	Charles Grimm	28.00	14.00	8.50
(17)	Heinie Groh	25.00	12.50	7.50
(18)	Chas. L. Harnett (Hartnett)	60.00	30.00	18.00
(19)	George Harper	25.00	12.50	7.50
(20)	Slim Harris (Harriss)	25.00	12.50	7.50
(21)	Clifton Heathcote	25.00	12.50	7.50
(22)	Andy High	25.00	12.50	7.50
(23)	Walter L. Holke	25.00	12.50	7.50
(24)	Charles D. Jamieson	25.00	12.50	7.50
(25)	Willie Kamm	25.00	12.50	7.50
(26)	Tony Kaufmann	25.00	12.50	7.50
(27)	Dudley Lee	25.00	12.50	7.50
(28)	Harry Liebold (Leibold)	25.00	12.50	7.50
(29)	Aldofo Luque	25.00	12.50	7.50
(30)	W.C. (Wid) Matthews	25.00	12.50	7.50
(31)	John J. McGraw	80.00	40.00	24.00
(32)	J. "Stuffy" McInnis	25.00	12.50	7.50
(33)	Johnny Morrison	25.00	12.50	7.50
(34)	John A. Mostil	25.00	12.50	7.50
(35)	J.F. O'Neill (should be S.F.)	25.00	12.50	7.50
(36)	Ernest Padgett	25.00	12.50	7.50
(37)	Val Picinich	25.00	12.50	7.50
(38)	Bill Piercy	25.00	12.50	7.50
(39)	Herman Pillette	25.00	12.50	7.50
(40)	Wallie Pipp	30.00	15.00	9.00
(41)	Raymond R. Powell	25.00	12.50	7.50
(42)	Del. Pratt	25.00	12.50	7.50
(43)	E.E. Rigney	25.00	12.50	7.50
(44)	Eddie Rommel	25.00	12.50	7.50
(45)	Geo. H. "Babe" Ruth	500.00	250.00	150.00
(46)	Muddy Ruel	25.00	12.50	7.50
(47)	J.H. Sand	25.00	12.50	7.50
(48)	Henry Severeid	25.00	12.50	7.50
(49)	Joseph Sewell	70.00	35.00	20.00
(50)	Al. Simmons	40.00	20.00	12.00
(51)	R.E. Smith	25.00	12.50	7.50
(52)	Sherrod Smith	25.00	12.50	7.50
(53)	Casey Stengel	125.00	62.00	37.00
(54)	J.R. Stevenson (Stephenson)	25.00	12.50	7.50
(55)	James Tierney	25.00	12.50	7.50
(56)	Robt. Veach	25.00	12.50	7.50
(57)	L. Woodall	25.00	12.50	7.50
(58)	Russell G. Wrighstone	25.00	12.50	7.50

1925 Exhibits - 1925

The 1925 series of Exhibits contains 128 unnumbered cards, each measuring 3-3/8" by 5-3/8". The player's name (in all capital letters), position and team (along with a line reading "Made in U.S.A.) are printed in a small white box in a lower corner of the card. Most of the photos are vertical, however a few are horizontal. There are several misspellings in the set, and the card of Robert Veach actually pictures Ernest Vache. The cards are listed here in alphabetical order.

		NR MT	EX	VG
Complete Set:		6000.00	3000.00	1800.
Common Player:		28.00	14.00	8.50
(1)	Sparky Adams	28.00	14.00	8.50
(2)	Grover C. Alexander	100.00	50.00	30.00
(3)	David Bancroft	45.00	22.00	13.50
(4)	Jesse Barnes	28.00	14.00	8.50
(5)	John Bassler	28.00	14.00	8.50
(6)	Lester Bell	28.00	14.00	8.50
(7)	Lawrence Benton	28.00	14.00	8.50
(8)	Carson Bigbee	28.00	14.00	8.50
(9)	Max Bishop	28.00	14.00	8.50
(10)	Raymond Blates (Blades)	28.00	14.00	8.50
(11)	Oswald Bluege	28.00	14.00	8.50
(12)	James Bottomly (Bottomley)	45.00	22.00	13.50
(13)	Raymond Bressler	28.00	14.00	8.50
(14)	John Brooks	28.00	14.00	8.50
(15)	Maurice Burrus	28.00	14.00	8.50
(16)	Max Carey	45.00	22.00	13.50
(17)	Tyrus Cobb	600.00	300.00	180.00
(18)	Eddie Collins	35.00	17.50	10.50
(19)	Stanley Coveleski	35.00	17.50	10.50
(20)	Hugh M. Critz	28.00	14.00	8.50
(21)	Hazen Cuyler	35.00	17.50	10.50
(22)	George Dauss	28.00	14.00	8.50
(23)	I.M. Davis	28.00	14.00	8.50
(24)	John H. DeBerry	28.00	14.00	8.50
(25)	Decatur	28.00	14.00	8.50
(26)	Peter Donohue	28.00	14.00	8.50
(27)	Charles Dressen	30.00	15.00	9.00
(28)	James J. Dykes	30.00	15.00	9.00
(29)	Howard Ehmke	28.00	14.00	8.50
(30)	Bib Falk (Bibb)	28.00	14.00	8.50
(31)	Wilson Fewster	28.00	14.00	8.50
(32)	Max Flack	28.00	14.00	8.50
(33)	Ira Flagstead	28.00	14.00	8.50
(34)	Jacques F. Fournier	28.00	14.00	8.50
(35)	Howard Freigau	28.00	14.00	8.50
(36)	Frank Frisch	35.00	17.50	10.50
(37)	Henry L. Gehrig	600.00	300.00	180.00
(38)	Joseph Genewich	28.00	14.00	8.50
(39)	Walter Gerber	28.00	14.00	8.50
(40)	Frank Gibson	28.00	14.00	8.50
(41)	Leon Goslin	35.00	17.50	10.50
(42)	George Grantham	28.00	14.00	8.50
(43)	Samuel Gray	28.00	14.00	8.50
(44)	Burleigh A. Grimes	35.00	17.50	10.50
(45)	Charles Grimm	30.00	15.00	9.00
(46)	Heine Groh (Heinie)	28.00	14.00	8.50
(47)	Samuel Hale	28.00	14.00	8.50
(48)	George Harper	28.00	14.00	8.50
(49)	David Harris	28.00	14.00	8.50
(50)	Stanley Harris	45.00	22.00	13.50
(51)	Leo Hartnett	45.00	22.00	13.50
(52)	Nelson Hawks	28.00	14.00	8.50
(53)	Harry Heilmann	45.00	22.00	13.50
(54)	Walter Henline	28.00	14.00	8.50
(55)	Walter Holke	28.00	14.00	8.50
(56)	Harry Hooper	45.00	22.00	13.50
(57)	Rogers Hornsby	90.00	45.00	27.00
(58)	Wilbur Hubbell	28.00	14.00	8.50
(59)	Travis C. Jackson	45.00	22.00	13.50
(60)	William Jacobson	28.00	14.00	8.50
(61)	Charles Jamieson	28.00	14.00	8.50
(62)	James H. Johnson (Johnston)	28.00	14.00	8.50
(63)	Walter Johnson	100.00	50.00	30.00
(64)	Joseph Judge	28.00	14.00	8.50
(65)	Willie Kamm	28.00	14.00	8.50
(66)	Ray Kremer	28.00	14.00	8.50
(67)	Walter Lutzke	28.00	14.00	8.50
(68)	Walter Maranville	45.00	22.00	13.50
(69)	John ("Stuffy") McInnes (McInnis)			
		28.00	14.00	8.50
(70)	Martin McManus	28.00	14.00	8.50
(71)	Earl McNeely	28.00	14.00	8.50
(72)	Emil Meusel	28.00	14.00	8.50
(73)	Edmund (Bing) Miller (Bing)	28.00	14.00	8.50
(74)	John Mokan	28.00	14.00	8.50
(75)	Clarence Mueller	28.00	14.00	8.50
(76)	Robert W. Muesel (Meusel)	35.00	17.50	10.50
(77)	Glenn Myatt	28.00	14.00	8.50
(78)	Arthur Nehf	28.00	14.00	8.50
(79)	George O'Neil	28.00	14.00	8.50
(80)	Frank O'Rourke	28.00	14.00	8.50
(81)	Ralph Perkins	28.00	14.00	8.50
(82)	Valentine Picinich	28.00	14.00	8.50
(83)	Walter C. Pipp	35.00	17.50	10.50
(84)	John Quinn	28.00	14.00	8.50
(85)	Emory Rigney	28.00	14.00	8.50
(86)	Eppa Rixey	45.00	22.00	13.50
(87)	Edwin Rommel	28.00	14.00	8.50

		NR MT	EX	VG
(88)	Ed Roush	45.00	22.00	13.50
(89)	Harold Ruel (Herold)	28.00	14.00	8.50
(90)	Charles Ruffing	45.00	22.00	13.50
(91)	George H. "Babe" Ruth	750.00	375.00	225.00
(92)	John Sand	28.00	14.00	8.50
(93)	Henry Severid (Severeid)	28.00	14.00	8.50
(94)	Joseph Sewell	45.00	22.00	13.50
(95)	Ray Shalk (Schalk)	45.00	22.00	13.50
(96)	Walter H. Shang (Schang)	28.00	14.00	8.50
(97)	J.R. Shawkey	30.00	15.00	9.00
(98)	Earl Sheely	28.00	14.00	8.50
(99)	William Sherdell (Sherdel)	28.00	14.00	8.50
(100)	Urban J. Shocker	28.00	14.00	8.50
(101)	George Sissler (Sisler)	45.00	22.00	13.50
(102)	Earl Smith	28.00	14.00	8.50
(103)	Sherrod Smith	28.00	14.00	8.50
(104)	Frank Snyder	28.00	14.00	8.50
(105)	Wm. H. Southworth	28.00	14.00	8.50
(106)	Tristram Speaker	55.00	27.00	16.50
(107)	Milton J. Stock	28.00	14.00	8.50
(108)	Homer Summa	28.00	14.00	8.50
(109)	William Terry	60.00	30.00	18.00
(110)	Hollis Thurston	28.00	14.00	8.50
(111)	John Tobin	28.00	14.00	8.50
(112)	Philip Todt	28.00	14.00	8.50
(113)	George Torporcer (Toporcer)	28.00	14.00	8.50
(114)	Harold Traynor	45.00	22.00	13.50
(115)	A.C. "Dazzy" Vance	45.00	22.00	13.50
(116)	Robert Veach	28.00	14.00	8.50
(117)	William Wambsganss	30.00	15.00	9.00
(118)	Aaron Ward	28.00	14.00	8.50
(119)	A.J. Weis	28.00	14.00	8.50
(120)	Frank Welch	28.00	14.00	8.50
(121)	Zack Wheat	45.00	22.00	13.50
(122)	Fred Williams	30.00	15.00	9.00
(123)	Kenneth Williams	30.00	15.00	9.00
(124)	Ernest Wingard	28.00	14.00	8.50
(125)	Ivy Wingo	28.00	14.00	8.50
(126)	Al Wings (Wingo)	28.00	14.00	8.50
(127)	Larry Woodall	28.00	14.00	8.50
(128)	Glen Wright (Glenn)	28.00	14.00	8.50

1926 Exhibits - 1926

The 1926 Exhibit cards are the same size (3-3/8" by 5-3/8") as previous Exhibit issues but are easily distinguished because of their blue-gray color. The set consists of 128 cards, 91 of which are identical to the photos in the 1925 series. The 37 new photos do not include the boxed caption used in 1925. There are several errors in the 1926 set: The photos of Hunnefield and Thomas are transposed; Bischoff's card identifies him as playing for Boston, N.L. (rather than A.L.) and the photo of Galloway is reversed. The cards are unnumbered and are listed here alphabetically.

		NR MT	EX	VG
Complete Set:		6000.00	3000.00	1800.
Common Player:		28.00	14.00	8.50
(1)	Sparky Adams	28.00	14.00	8.50
(2)	David Bancroft	45.00	22.00	13.50
(3)	John Bassler	28.00	14.00	8.50
(4)	Lester Bell	28.00	14.00	8.50
(5)	John M. Bentley	28.00	14.00	8.50
(6)	Lawrence Benton	28.00	14.00	8.50

		NR MT	EX	VG
(7)	Carson Bigbee	28.00	14.00	8.50
(8)	George Bischoff	28.00	14.00	8.50
(9)	Max Bishop	28.00	14.00	8.50
(10)	J. Fred Blake	28.00	14.00	8.50
(11)	Ted Blankenship	28.00	14.00	8.50
(12)	Raymond Blates (Blades)	28.00	14.00	8.50
(13)	Lucerne A. Blue (Luzerne)	28.00	14.00	8.50
(14)	Oswald Bluege	28.00	14.00	8.50
(15)	James Bottomly (Bottomley)	45.00	22.00	13.50
(16)	Raymond Bressler	28.00	14.00	8.50
(17)	Geo. H. Burns	28.00	14.00	8.50
(18)	Maurice Burrus	28.00	14.00	8.50
(19)	John Butler	28.00	14.00	8.50
(20)	Max Carey	45.00	22.00	13.50
(21)	Tyrus Cobb	600.00	300.00	180.00
(22)	Eddie Collins	45.00	22.00	13.50
(23)	Patrick T. Collins	28.00	14.00	8.50
(24)	Earl B. Combs (Earle)	45.00	22.00	13.50
(25)	James E. Cooney	28.00	14.00	8.50
(26)	Stanley Coveleski	45.00	22.00	13.50
(27)	Hugh M. Critz	28.00	14.00	8.50
(28)	Hazen Cuyler	45.00	22.00	13.50
(29)	George Dauss	28.00	14.00	8.50
(30)	Peter Donohue	28.00	14.00	8.50
(31)	Charles Dressen	30.00	15.00	9.00
(32)	James J. Dykes	28.00	14.00	8.50
(33)	Bib Falk (Bibb)	28.00	14.00	8.50
(34)	Edward S. Farrell	28.00	14.00	8.50
(35)	Wilson Fewster	28.00	14.00	8.50
(36)	Ira Flagstead	28.00	14.00	8.50
(37)	Howard Freigau	28.00	14.00	8.50
(38)	Bernard Friberg	28.00	14.00	8.50
(39)	Frank Frisch	45.00	22.00	13.50
(40)	Jacques F. Furnier (Fournier)	28.00	14.00	8.50
(41)	Joseph Galloway (Clarence)	28.00	14.00	8.50
(42)	Henry L. Gehrig	600.00	300.00	180.00
(43)	Charles Gehringer	45.00	22.00	13.50
(44)	Joseph Genewich	28.00	14.00	8.50
(45)	Walter Gerber	28.00	14.00	8.50
(46)	Leon Goslin	45.00	22.00	13.50
(47)	George Grantham	28.00	14.00	8.50
(48)	Burleigh A. Grimes	45.00	22.00	13.50
(49)	Charles Grimm	28.00	14.00	8.50
(50)	Fred Haney	28.00	14.00	8.50
(51)	Wm. Hargrave	28.00	14.00	8.50
(52)	George Harper	28.00	14.00	8.50
(53)	Stanley Harris	45.00	22.00	13.50
(54)	Leo Hartnett	45.00	22.00	13.50
(55)	Joseph Hauser	30.00	15.00	9.00
(56)	C.E. Heathcote	28.00	14.00	8.50
(57)	Harry Heilmann	45.00	22.00	13.50
(58)	Walter Henline	28.00	14.00	8.50
(59)	Ramon Herrera	28.00	14.00	8.50
(60)	Andrew A. High	28.00	14.00	8.50
(61)	Rogers Hornsby	100.00	50.00	30.00
(62)	Clarence Huber	28.00	14.00	8.50
(63)	Wm. Hunnefield (photo actually Tommy Thomas)	28.00	14.00	8.50
(64)	William Jacobson	28.00	14.00	8.50
(65)	Walter Johnson	100.00	50.00	30.00
(66)	Joseph Judge	28.00	14.00	8.50
(67)	Willie Kamm	28.00	14.00	8.50
(68)	Ray Kremer	28.00	14.00	8.50
(69)	Anthony Lazzeri	35.00	17.50	10.50
(70)	Frederick Lindstrom	45.00	22.00	13.50
(71)	Walter Lutzke	28.00	14.00	8.50
(72)	John Makan (Mokan)	28.00	14.00	8.50
(73)	Walter Maranville	45.00	22.00	13.50
(74)	Martin McManus	28.00	14.00	8.50
(75)	Earl McNeely	28.00	14.00	8.50
(76)	Hugh A. McQuillan	28.00	14.00	8.50
(77)	Douglas McWeeny	28.00	14.00	8.50
(78)	Oscar Melillo	28.00	14.00	8.50
(79)	Edmund (Bind) Miller (Bing)	28.00	14.00	8.50
(80)	Clarence Mueller	28.00	14.00	8.50
(81)	Robert W. Muesel (Meusel)	35.00	17.50	10.50
(82)	Joseph W. Munson	28.00	14.00	8.50
(83)	Emil Musel (Meusel)	28.00	14.00	8.50
(84)	Glenn Myatt	28.00	14.00	8.50
(85)	Bernie F. Neis	28.00	14.00	8.50
(86)	Robert O'Farrell	28.00	14.00	8.50
(87)	George O'Neil	28.00	14.00	8.50
(88)	Frank O'Rourke	28.00	14.00	8.50
(89)	Ralph Perkins	28.00	14.00	8.50
(90)	Walter C. Pipp	35.00	17.50	10.50
(91)	Emory Rigney	28.00	14.00	8.50
(92)	James J. Ring	28.00	14.00	8.50
(93)	Eppa Rixey	45.00	22.00	13.50
(94)	Edwin Rommel	28.00	14.00	8.50
(95)	Ed. Roush	45.00	22.00	13.50
(96)	Harold Ruel (Herold)	28.00	14.00	8.50

		NR MT	EX	VG
(97)	Charles Ruffing	45.00	22.00	13.50
(98)	Geo. H. "Babe" Ruth	750.00	375.00	225.00
(99)	John Sand	28.00	14.00	8.50
(100)	Joseph Sewell	45.00	22.00	13.50
(101)	Ray Shalk (Schalk)	45.00	22.00	13.50
(102)	J.R. Shawkey	28.00	14.00	8.50
(103)	Earl Sheely	28.00	14.00	8.50
(104)	William Sherdell (Sherdel)	28.00	14.00	8.50
(105)	Urban J. Shocker	28.00	14.00	8.50
(106)	George Sissler (Sisler)	45.00	22.00	13.50
(107)	Earl Smith	28.00	14.00	8.50
(108)	Sherrod Smith	28.00	14.00	8.50
(109)	Frank Snyder	28.00	14.00	8.50
(110)	Tristram Speaker	50.00	25.00	15.00
(111)	Fred Spurgeon	28.00	14.00	8.50
(112)	Homer Summa	28.00	14.00	8.50
(113)	Edward Taylor	28.00	14.00	8.50
(114)	J. Taylor	28.00	14.00	8.50
(115)	William Terry	50.00	25.00	15.00
(116)	Hollis Thurston	28.00	14.00	8.50
(117)	Philip Todt	28.00	14.00	8.50
(118)	George Torporcer (Toporcer)	28.00	14.00	8.50
(119)	Harold Traynor	45.00	22.00	13.50
(120)	Wm. Wambsganss	28.00	14.00	8.50
(121)	John Warner	28.00	14.00	8.50
(122)	Zach Wheat	45.00	22.00	13.50
(123)	Kenneth Williams	28.00	14.00	8.50
(124)	Ernest Wingard	28.00	14.00	8.50
(125)	Fred Wingfield	28.00	14.00	8.50
(126)	Ivy Wingo	28.00	14.00	8.50
(127)	Glen Wright (Glenn)	28.00	14.00	8.50
(128)	Russell Wrightstone	28.00	14.00	8.50

1927 Exhibits - 1927

The Exhibit Supply Company issued a set of 64 cards in 1927, each measuring 3-3/8" by 5-3/8". The set can be identified from earlier issues by its light green tint. The player's name and team appear in capital letters in one lower corner, while "Ex. Sup. Co., Chgo." and "Made in U.S.A." appear in the other. All 64 photos used in the 1927 set were borrowed from previous issues, but 13 players are listed with new teams. There are several misspellings and other labeling errors in the set. The unnumbered cards are listed here in alphabetical order.

		NR MT	EX	VG
Complete Set:		3500.00	1750.00	1050.
Common Player:		20.00	10.00	6.00
(1)	Sparky Adams	20.00	10.00	6.00
(2)	Grover C. Alexander	45.00	22.00	13.50
(3)	David Bancroft	35.00	17.50	10.50
(4)	John Bassler	20.00	10.00	6.00
(5)	John M. Bentley (middle initial actually N.)			
		20.00	10.00	6.00
(6)	Fred Blankenship (Ted)	20.00	10.00	6.00
(7)	James Bottomly (Bottomley)	35.00	17.50	10.50
(8)	Raymond Bressler	20.00	10.00	6.00
(9)	Geo. H. Burns	20.00	10.00	6.00
(10)	John Buttler (Butler)	20.00	10.00	6.00
(11)	Tyrus Cobb	400.00	200.00	120.00
(12)	Eddie Collins	35.00	17.50	10.50
(13)	Hazen Cuyler	35.00	17.50	10.50
(14)	George Daus (Dauss)	20.00	10.00	6.00
(15)	A.R. Decatur	20.00	10.00	6.00

		NR MT	EX	VG
(16)	Wilson Fewster	20.00	10.00	6.00
(17)	Ira Flagstead	20.00	10.00	6.00
(18)	Henry L. Gehrig	400.00	200.00	120.00
(19)	Charles Gehringer	35.00	17.50	10.50
(20)	Joseph Genewich	20.00	10.00	6.00
(21)	Leon Goslin	35.00	17.50	10.50
(22)	Burleigh A. Grimes	35.00	17.50	10.50
(23)	Charles Grimm	22.00	11.00	6.50
(24)	Fred Haney	22.00	11.00	6.50
(25)	Wm. Hargrave	20.00	10.00	6.00
(26)	George Harper	20.00	10.00	6.00
(27)	Leo Hartnett	35.00	17.50	10.50
(28)	Clifton Heathcote	20.00	10.00	6.00
(29)	Harry Heilman (Heillmann)	35.00	17.50	10.50
(30)	Walter Henline	20.00	10.00	6.00
(31)	Andrew High	20.00	10.00	6.00
(32)	Rogers Hornsby	100.00	50.00	30.00
(33)	Wm. Hunnefield (photo actually Tommy Thomas)			
		20.00	10.00	6.00
(34)	Walter Johnson	100.00	50.00	30.00
(35)	Willie Kamm	20.00	10.00	6.00
(36)	Ray Kremer	20.00	10.00	6.00
(37)	Anthony Lazzeri	30.00	15.00	9.00
(38)	Fredrick Lindstrom (Frederick)	35.00	17.50	10.50
(39)	Walter Lutzke	20.00	10.00	6.00
(40)	John "Stuffy" McInnes (McInnis)	20.00	10.00	6.00
(41)	John Mokan	20.00	10.00	6.00
(42)	Robert W. Muesel (Meusel)	25.00	12.50	7.50
(43)	Glenn Myatt	20.00	10.00	6.00
(44)	Bernie Neis	20.00	10.00	6.00
(45)	Robert O'Farrell	20.00	10.00	6.00
(46)	Walter C. Pipp	30.00	15.00	9.00
(47)	Eppa Rixey	35.00	17.50	10.50
(48)	Harold Ruel (Herold)	20.00	10.00	6.00
(49)	Geo. H. "Babe" Ruth	600.00	300.00	180.00
(50)	Ray Schalk	35.00	17.50	10.50
(51)	George Sissler (Sisler)	35.00	17.50	10.50
(52)	Earl Smith	20.00	10.00	6.00
(53)	Wm. H. Southworth	20.00	10.00	6.00
(54)	Tristam Speaker (Tristram)	100.00	50.00	30.00
(55)	J. Taylor	20.00	10.00	6.00
(56)	Philip Todt	20.00	10.00	6.00
(57)	Harold Traynor	35.00	17.50	10.50
(58)	William Wambsganns (Wambsganss)			
		22.00	11.00	6.50
(59)	Zach Wheat	35.00	17.50	10.50
(60)	Kenneth Williams	22.00	11.00	6.50
(61)	Ernest Wingard	20.00	10.00	6.00
(62)	Fred Wingfield	20.00	10.00	6.00
(63)	Ivy Wingo	20.00	10.00	6.00
(64)	Russell Wrightstone	20.00	10.00	6.00

1928 Exhibits - 1928

The Exhibit Supply Company switched to a blue tint for the photos in its 64-card set in 1928. There are 36 new photos in the set, including 24 new players. Four players from the previous year are shown with new teams and 24 of the cards are identical to the 1927 series, except for the color of the card. Cards are found with either blank backs or postcard backs. The photos are captioned in the same style as the 1927 set. The set again includes some misspelling and incorrect labels. The cards are unnumbered and are listed here in alphabetical order.

	NR MT	EX	VG
Complete Set:	3250.00	1625.00	975.00
Common Player:	20.00	10.00	6.00
(1) Grover C. Alexander	70.00	35.00	20.00
(2) David Bancroft	20.00	10.00	6.00
(3) Virgil Barnes	20.00	10.00	6.00
(4) Francis R. Blades	20.00	10.00	6.00
(5) L.A. Blue	20.00	10.00	6.00
(6) Edward W. Brown	20.00	10.00	6.00
(7) Max G. Carey	35.00	17.50	10.50
(8) Chalmer W. Cissell	20.00	10.00	6.00
(9) Gordon S. Cochrane	35.00	17.50	10.50
(10) Pat Collins	20.00	10.00	6.00
(11) Hugh M. Critz	20.00	10.00	6.00
(12) Howard Ehmke	20.00	10.00	6.00
(13) E. English	20.00	10.00	6.00
(14) Bib Falk (Bibb)	20.00	10.00	6.00
(15) Ira Flagstead	20.00	10.00	6.00
(16) Robert Fothergill	20.00	10.00	6.00
(17) Frank Frisch	35.00	17.50	10.50
(18) Lou Gehrig	600.00	300.00	180.00
(19) Leon Goslin	35.00	17.50	10.50
(20) Eugene Hargrave	20.00	10.00	6.00
(21) Charles R. Hargraves (Hargreaves)	20.00	10.00	6.00
(22) Stanley Harris	35.00	17.50	10.50
(23) Bryan "Slim" Harriss	20.00	10.00	6.00
(24) Leo Hartnett	35.00	17.50	10.50
(25) Joseph Hauser	20.00	10.00	6.00
(26) Fred Hoffman (Hofmann)	20.00	10.00	6.00
(27) J. Francis Hogan	20.00	10.00	6.00
(28) Rogers Hornsby	100.00	50.00	30.00
(29) Chas. Jamieson	20.00	10.00	6.00
(30) Sam Jones	20.00	10.00	6.00
(31) Ray Kremer	20.00	10.00	6.00
(32) Fred Leach	20.00	10.00	6.00
(33) Fredrick Lindstrom (Frederick)	35.00	17.50	10.50
(34) Adolph Luque (Adolfo)	20.00	10.00	6.00
(35) Theodore Lyons	35.00	17.50	10.50
(36) Harry McCurdy	20.00	10.00	6.00
(37) Glenn Myatt	20.00	10.00	6.00
(38) John Ogden (photo actually Warren Ogden)	20.00	10.00	6.00
(39) James Ring	20.00	10.00	6.00
(40) A.C. Root (should be C.H.)	20.00	10.00	6.00
(41) Edd. Roush	35.00	17.50	10.50
(42) Harold Ruel (Herold)	20.00	10.00	6.00
(43) Geo. H. "Babe" Ruth	750.00	375.00	225.00
(44) Henry Sand	20.00	10.00	6.00
(45) Joseph Sewell	35.00	17.50	10.50
(46) Walter Shang (Schang)	20.00	10.00	6.00
(47) Urban J. Shocker	20.00	10.00	6.00
(48) Al. Simmons	60.00	30.00	18.00
(49) Earl Smith	20.00	10.00	6.00
(50) Robert Smith	20.00	10.00	6.00
(51) Fred Schulte	20.00	10.00	6.00
(52) Jack Tavener	20.00	10.00	6.00
(53) J. Taylor	20.00	10.00	6.00
(54) Philip Todt	20.00	10.00	6.00
(55) Geo. Uhle	20.00	10.00	6.00
(56) Arthur "Dazzy" Vance	35.00	17.50	10.50
(57) Paul Waner	35.00	17.50	10.50
(58) Earl G. Whitehill (middle intial actually O.)	20.00	10.00	6.00
(59) Fred Williams	22.00	11.00	6.50
(60) James Wilson	20.00	10.00	6.00
(61) L.R. (Hack) Wilson	35.00	17.50	10.50
(62) Lawrence Woodall	20.00	10.00	6.00
(63) Glen Wright (Glen)	20.00	10.00	6.00
(64) William A. Zitzman (Zitzmann)	20.00	10.00	6.00

		NR MT	EX	VG
1	"Buzz" Arlett	70.00	35.00	20.00
2	Earl Averill	150.00	75.00	45.00
3	Carl Berger (Walter)	70.00	35.00	20.00
4	"Ping" Bodie	60.00	30.00	18.00
5	Carl Dittmar	40.00	20.00	12.00
6	Jack Fenton	40.00	20.00	12.00
7	Neal "Mickey" Finn (Cornelius)	40.00	20.00	12.00
8	Ray French	40.00	20.00	12.00
9	Tony Governor	40.00	20.00	12.00
10	"Truck" Hannah	40.00	20.00	12.00
11	Mickey Heath	40.00	20.00	12.00
12	Wally Hood	40.00	20.00	12.00
13	"Fuzzy" Hufft	40.00	20.00	12.00
14	Snead Jolly (Smead)	40.00	20.00	12.00
15	Bobby "Ducky" Jones	40.00	20.00	12.00
16	Rudy Kallio	40.00	20.00	12.00
17	Ray Keating	40.00	20.00	12.00
18	Johnny Kerr	40.00	20.00	12.00
19	Harry Krause	40.00	20.00	12.00
20	Lynford H. Larry (Lary)	40.00	20.00	12.00
21	Dudley Lee	40.00	20.00	12.00
22	Walter "Duster" Mails	40.00	20.00	12.00
23	Jimmy Reese	50.00	25.00	15.00
24	"Dusty" Rhodes	40.00	20.00	12.00
25	Hal Rhyne	40.00	20.00	12.00
26	Hank Severied (Severeid)	40.00	20.00	12.00
27	Earl Sheely	40.00	20.00	12.00
28	Frank Shellenback	40.00	20.00	12.00
29	Gordon Slade	40.00	20.00	12.00
30	Hollis Thurston	40.00	20.00	12.00
31	"Babe" Twombly	40.00	20.00	12.00
32	Earl "Tex" Weathersby	40.00	20.00	12.00

1929 Exhibits
Four-On-One 1929-1930

1928 Exhibits
Pacific Coast League

This regional series of 32 cards pictures players from the six California teams in the Pacific Coast League. Like the 1928 major league Exhibits, the PCL cards have a blue tint and are not numbered. They are blank-backed and measure 3-3/8" by 5-3/8". The set includes several misspellings. Cards are occasionally found with a corner clipped, the card corner to be used as a coupon with redemption value.

	NR MT	EX	VG
Complete Set:	1500.00	750.00	450.00
Common Player:	40.00	20.00	12.00

Although the size of the card remained the same, the Exhibit Supply Company of Chicago began putting four players' pictures on each card in 1929 - a practice that would continue for the next decade. Known as "four-on-one" cards, the players are identified by name and team at the bottom of the photos, which are separated by borders. The 32 cards in the 1929-30 series have postcard backs and were printed in a wide range of color combinations including: black on orange, black on blue, brown on orange, blue on green, black on red, black on white, blue on white, black on yellow, brown on white, brown on yellow and red on yellow. Most of the backs are uncolored, however, cards with a black on red front have been seen with red backs, and cards with blue on yellow fronts have been seen with yellow backs. There are numerous spelling and caption errors in the set, and the player identified as Babe Herman is actually Jesse Petty.

	NR MT	EX	VG
Complete Set:	2500.00	1250.00	750.00
Common Player:	35.00	17.50	10.50

	NR MT	EX	VG
(1) Earl J. Adams, R. Bartell, Earl Sheely, Harold Traynor	45.00	22.00	13.50
(2) Dale Alexander, C. Gehringer, G.F. McManus (should be M.J.), H.F. Rice	45.00	22.00	13.50
(3) Grover C. Alexander, James Bottomly (Bottomley), Frank Frisch, James Wilson	70.00	35.00	20.00
(4) Martin G. Autrey (Autry), Alex Metzler, Carl Reynolds, Alphonse Thomas	35.00	17.50	10.50
(5) Earl Averill, B.A. Falk, K. Holloway, L. Sewell	45.00	22.00	13.50
(6) David Bancroft, Del L. Bisonette (Bissonette), John H. DeBerry, Floyd C. Herman (photo actually Jesse Petty)	45.00	22.00	13.50
(7) C.E. Beck, Leo Hartnett, Rogers Hornsby, L.R. (Hack) Wilson	90.00	45.00	27.00
(8) Ray Benge, Lester L. Sweetland, A.C. Whitney, Cy. Williams	35.00	17.50	10.50
(9) Benny Bengough, Earl B. Coombs (Combs), Waite Hoyt, Anthony Lazzeri	50.00	25.00	15.00
(10) L. Benton, Melvin Ott, Andrew Reese, William Terry	45.00	22.00	13.50
(11) Max Bishop, James Dykes, Samuel Hale, Homer Summa	35.00	17.50	10.50
(12) L.A. Blue, O. Melillo, F.O. Rourke (Frank O'Rourke), F. Schulte	35.00	17.50	10.50
(13) Oswald Bluege, Leon Goslin, Joseph Judge, Harold Ruel (Herold)	45.00	22.00	13.50
(14) Chalmer W. Cissell, John W. Clancy, Willie Kamm, John L. Kerr	35.00	17.50	10.50
(15) Gordon S. Cochrane, Jimmy Foxx, Robert M. Grove, George Haas	100.00	50.00	30.00
(16) Pat Collins, Joe Dugan, Edward Farrel (Farrell), George Sisler	45.00	22.00	13.50
(17) H.M. Critz, G.L. Kelly, V.J. Picinich, W.C. Walker	45.00	22.00	13.50
(18) Nick Cullop, D'Arcy Flowers, Harvey Hendrick, Arthur "Dazzy" Vance	45.00	22.00	13.50
(19) Hazen Cuyler, E. English, C.J. Grimm, C.H. Root	45.00	22.00	13.50
(20) Taylor Douthit, Chas. M. Gilbert (Gelbert), Chas. J. Hafey, Fred G. Haney	45.00	22.00	13.50
(21) Leo Durocher, Henry L. Gehrig, Mark Koenig, Geo. H. "Babe" Ruth	1000.00	500.00	300.00
(22) L.A. Fonseca, Carl Lind, J. Sewell, J. Tavener	45.00	22.00	13.50
(23) H.E. Ford, C.F. Lucas, C.A. Pittenger, E.V. Purdy	35.00	17.50	10.50
(24) Bernard Friberg, Donald Hurst, Frank O'Doul, Fresco Thompson	35.00	17.50	10.50
(25) S. Gray, R. Kress, H. Manush, W.H. Shang (Schang)	45.00	22.00	13.50
(26) Charles R. Hargreaves, Ray Kremer, Lloyd Waner, Paul Waner	45.00	22.00	13.50
(27) George Harper, Fred Maguire, Lance Richbourg, Robert Smith	35.00	17.50	10.50
(28) Jack Hayes, Sam P. Jones, Chas. M. Myer, Sam Rice	45.00	22.00	13.50
(29) Harry E. Heilman (Heilmann), C.N. Richardson, M.J. Shea, G.E. Uhle	45.00	22.00	13.50
(30) J.A. Heving, R.R. Reeves (should be R.E.), J. Rothrock, C.H. Ruffing	45.00	22.00	13.50
(31) J.F. Hogan, T.C. Jackson, Fred Lindstrom, J.D. Welsh	45.00	22.00	13.50
(32) W.W. Regan, H. Rhyne, D. Taitt, P.J. Todt	35.00	17.50	10.50

NOTE: A card number in parentheses ( ) indicates the set is unnumbered.

1931 Exhibits
Four-On-One 1931-1932

The 1931-1932 series issued by the Exhibit Company again consisted of 32 cards, each picturing four players. The series can be differentiated from the previous year by the coupon backs. which list various premiums available (including kazoos, toy pistols and other prizes). The cards again were printed in various color combinations, including; black on green, blue on green, black on orange, black on red, blue on white and black on yellow. There are numerous spelling and caption errors in the series. The Babe Herman/Jesse Petty error of the previous year was still not corrected, and the card of Rick Ferell not only misspells his name ("Farrel"), but also pictures the wrong player (Edward Farrell).

	NR MT	EX	VG
Complete Set:	3500.00	1750.00	1050.
Common Player:	40.00	20.00	12.00

	NR MT	EX	VG
(1) Earl J. Adams, James Bottomly (Bottomley), Frank Frisch, James Wilson	55.00	27.00	16.50
(2) Dale Alexander, C. Gehringer, G.F. McManus (should be M.J.), G.E. Uhle	55.00	27.00	16.50
(3) L.L. Appling (should be L.B.), Chalmer W. Cissell, Willie Kamm, Ted Lyons	55.00	27.00	16.50
(4) Buzz Arlett, Ray Benge, Chuck Klein, A.C. Whitney	55.00	27.00	16.50
(5) Earl Averill, B.A. Falk, L.A. Fonseca, L. Sewell	55.00	27.00	16.50
(6) Richard Bartell, Bernard Friberg, Donald Hurst, Harry McCurdy	40.00	20.00	12.00
(7) Walter Berger, Fred Maguire, Lance Richbourg, Earl Sheely	40.00	20.00	12.00
(8) Chas. Berry, Robt. Reeves, R.R. Reeves (should be R.E.), J. Rothrock	40.00	20.00	12.00
(9) Del L. Bisonette (Bissonette), Floyd C. Herman (photo - J. Petty), Jack Quinn, Glenn Wright	40.00	20.00	12.00
(10) L.A. Blue, Smead Jolley, Carl Reynolds, Henry Tate	40.00	20.00	12.00
(11) O. Bluege, Joe Judge, Chas. M. Myer, Sam Rice	55.00	27.00	16.50
(12) John Boley, James Dykes, E.J. Miller, Al. Simmons	55.00	27.00	16.50
(13) Gordon S. Chochrane, Jimmy Foxx, Robert M. Grove, George Haas	150.00	75.00	45.00
(14) Adam Comorosky, Gus Suhr, T.J. Thevenow, Harold Traynor	55.00	27.00	16.50
(15) Earl B. Coombs (Combs), W. Dickey, Anthony Lazzeri, H. Pennock	150.00	75.00	45.00
(16) H.M. Critz, J.F. Hogan, T.C. Jackson, Fred Lindstrom	55.00	27.00	16.50
(17) Joe Cronin, H. Manush, F. Marberry, Roy Spencer	55.00	27.00	16.50
(18) Nick Cullop, Les Durocher (Leo), Harry Heilmann, W.C. Walker	55.00	27.00	16.50
(19) Hazen Cuyler, E. English, C.J. Grimm, C.H. Root	55.00	27.00	16.50
(20) Taylor Douthit, Chas. M. Gilbert (Gelbert), Chas. J. Hafey, Bill Hallahan	40.00	20.00	12.00
(21) Richard Farrel (Ferrell), S. Gray, R. Kress, W. Stewart	50.00	25.00	15.00
(22) W. Ferrell, J. Goldman, Hunnefield, Ed Morgan	40.00	20.00	12.00
(23) Fred Fitzsimmons, Robert O'Farrell, Melvin Ott, William Terry	55.00	27.00	16.50
(24) D'Arcy Flowers, Frank O'Doul, Fresco Thompson, Arthur "Dazzy" Vance	55.00	27.00	16.50
(25) H.E. Ford (should be H.H.), Gooch, C.F. Lucas, W. Roettger	40.00	20.00	12.00
(26) E. Funk, W. Hoyt, Mark Koenig, Wallie Schang	55.00	27.00	16.50
(27) Henry L. Gehrig, Lyn Lary, James Reese, Geo. H. "Babe" Ruth	1000.00	500.00	300.00
(28) George Grantham, Ray Kremer, Lloyd Waner, Paul Waner	55.00	27.00	16.50
(29) Leon Goslin, O. Melillo, F.O. Rourke (Frank O'Rourke), F. Schulte	55.00	27.00	16.50

	NR MT	EX	VG
(30) Leo Hartnett, Rogers Hornsby, J.R. Stevenson (Stephenson), L.R. (Hack) Wilson	90.00	45.00	27.00
(31) D. MacFayden, H. Rhyne, Bill Sweeney, E.W. Webb	40.00	20.00	12.00
(32) Walter Maranville, Randolph Moore, Alfred Spohrer, J.T. Zachary	55.00	27.00	16.50

1933 Exhibits
Four-On-One 1933

The 1933 series of four-on-one Exhibits consists of 16 cards with blank backs. Color combinations include: blue on green, black on orange, black on red, blue on white and black on yellow. Most have a plain, white back, although the black on yellow cards are also found with a yellow back. Most of the pictures used are reprinted from previous series, and there are some spelling and caption errors, including the Richard Ferrell/Edward Farrel mixup from the previous year. Al Lopez is shown as "Vincent" Lopez.

	NR MT	EX	VG
Complete Set:	2250.00	1125.00	675.00
Common Player:	40.00	20.00	12.00

	NR MT	EX	VG
(1) Earl J. Adams, Frank Frisch, Chas. Gilbert (Gelbert), Bill Hallahan	55.00	27.00	16.50
(2) Earl Averill, W. Ferrell, Ed Morgan, L. Sewell	55.00	27.00	16.50
(3) Richard Bartell, Ray Benge, Donald Hurst, Chuck Klein	55.00	27.00	16.50
(4) Walter Berger, Walter Maranville, Alfred Spohrer, J.T. Zachary	55.00	27.00	16.50
(5) Charles Berry, L.A. Blue, Ted Lyons, Bob Seeds	55.00	27.00	16.50
(6) Chas. Berry, D. MacFayden, H. Rhyne, E.W. Webb	40.00	20.00	12.00
(7) Mickey Cochrane, Jimmy Foxx, Robert M. Grove, Al. Simmons	200.00	100.00	60.00
(8) H.M. Critz, Fred Fitzsimmons, Fred Lindstrom, Robert O'Farrell	55.00	27.00	16.50
(9) W. Dickey, Anthony Lazzeri, H. Pennock, George H. "Babe" Ruth	1000.00	500.00	300.00
(10) Taylor Douthit, George Grantham, Chas. J. Hafey, C.F. Lucas	55.00	27.00	16.50
(11) E. English, C.J. Grimm, C.H. Root, J.R. Stevenson (Stephenson)	40.00	20.00	12.00
(12) Richard Farrel (Farrell), Leon Goslin, S. Gray, O. Melillo	55.00	27.00	16.50
(13) C. Gehringer, "Muddy" Ruel, Jonathan Stone (first name - John), G.E. Uhle	55.00	27.00	16.50
(14) Joseph Judge, H. Manush, F. Marberry, Roy Spencer	55.00	27.00	16.50
(15) Vincent Lopez (Al), Frank O'Doul, Arthur "Dazzy" Vance, Glenn Wright	55.00	27.00	16.50
(16) Gus Suhr, Tom J. Thevenow, Lloyd Waner, Paul Waner	55.00	27.00	16.50

1934 Exhibits
Four-On-One 1934

This 16-card series issued by the Exhibit Co. in 1934 is again blank-backed and continues the four-on-one format. The 1934 series can be differentiated from previous years by the more subdued color combinations of the cards, which include lighter shades of blue, brown, green and violet - all printed on white card stock. Many new photos were also used in the 1934 series. Of the 64 players included, 25 appear for the first time and another 16 were given new poses. Spelling was improved, but Al Lopez is still identified as "Vincent."

	NR MT	EX	VG
Complete Set:	2000.00	1000.00	600.00
Common Player:	35.00	17.50	10.50

	NR MT	EX	VG
(1) Luke Appling, George Earnshaw, Al Simmons, Evar Swanson	45.00	22.00	13.50
(2) Earl Averill, W. Ferrell, Willie Kamm, Frank Pytlak	45.00	22.00	13.50
(3) Richard Bartell, Donald Hurst, Wesley Schulmerich, Jimmy Wilson	35.00	17.50	10.50
(4) Walter Berger, Ed Brandt, Frank Hogan, Bill Urbanski	35.00	17.50	10.50
(5) Jim Bottomley, Chas. J. Hafey, Botchi Lombardi, Tony Piet	45.00	22.00	13.50
(6) Irving Burns, Irving Hadley, Rollie Hemsley, O. Melillo	35.00	17.50	10.50
(7) Bill Cissell, Rick Ferrell, Lefty Grove, Roy Johnson	45.00	22.00	13.50
(8) Mickey Cochrane, C. Gehringer, Goose Goslin, Fred Marberry	70.00	35.00	20.00
(9) George Cramer (Roger), Jimmy Foxx, Frank Higgins, Slug Mahaffey	70.00	35.00	20.00
(10) Joe Cronin, Alvin Crowder, Joe Kuhel, H. Manush	45.00	22.00	13.50
(11) W. Dickey, Lou Gehrig, Vernon Gomez, Geo. H. "Babe" Ruth	1000.00	500.00	300.00
(12) E. English, C.J. Grimm, Chas. Klein, Lon Warneke	45.00	22.00	13.50
(13) Frank Frisch, Bill Hallahan, Pepper Martin, John Rothrock	45.00	22.00	13.50
(14) Carl Hubbell, Mel Ott, Blondy Ryan, Bill Terry	70.00	35.00	20.00
(15) Leonard Koenecke, Sam Leslie, Vincent Lopez (Al), Glenn Wright	40.00	20.00	12.00
(16) T.J. Thevenow, Pie Traynor, Lloyd Waner, Paul Waner	65.00	33.00	20.00

1935 Exhibits
Four-On-One 1935

Continuing with the same four-on-one format, the Exhibit Supply Co. issued another 16-card series in 1935. All cards were printed in a slate-blue color with a plain, blank back. Seventeen of the players included in the 1935 series appear for the first time. while another 11 are shown with new poses. There are several spelling and caption errors. Babe Ruth appears in a regular Exhibit issue for the last time.

	NR MT	EX	VG
Complete Set:	2750.00	1375.00	825.00
Common Player:	30.00	15.00	9.00

	NR MT	EX	VG
(1) Earl Averill, Mel Harder, Willie Kamm, Hal Trosky	45.00	22.00	13.50
(2) Walter Berger, Ed Brandt, Frank Hogan, "Babe" Ruth	900.00	450.00	270.00
(3) Henry Bonura, Jimmy Dykes, Ted Lyons, Al Simmons	45.00	22.00	13.50
(4) Jimmy Bottomley, Paul Derringer, Chas. J. Hafey, Botchi Lombardi	65.00	33.00	20.00
(5) Irving Burns, Rollie Hemsley, O. Melillo, L.N. Newson	30.00	15.00	9.00
(6) Guy Bush, Pie Traynor, Floyd Vaughn (Vaughan), Paul Waner	65.00	33.00	20.00

	NR MT	EX	VG
(7) Mickey Cochrane, C. Gehringer, Goose Goslin, Linwood Rowe (Lynwood)	65.00	33.00	20.00
(8) Phil Collins, John "Blondy" Ryan, Geo. Watkins, Jimmy Wilson	30.00	15.00	9.00
(9) George Cramer (Roger), Jimmy Foxx, Bob Johnson, Slug Mahaffey	65.00	33.00	20.00
(10) Hughie Critz, Carl Hubbell, Mel Ott, Bill Terry	70.00	35.00	21.00
(11) Joe Cronin, Rick Ferrell, Lefty Grove, Billy Werber	65.00	33.00	20.00
(12) Tony Cuccinello, Vincent Lopez (Al), Van Mungo, Dan Taylor	40.00	20.00	12.00
(13) Jerome "Dizzy" Dean, Paul Dean, Frank Frisch, Pepper Martin	150.00	75.00	45.00
(14) W. Dickey, Lou Gehrig, Vernon Gomez, Tony Lazzeri	900.00	450.00	270.00
(15) C.J. Grimm, Gabby Hartnett, Chas. Klein, Lon Warneke	45.00	22.00	13.50
(16) H. Manush, Buddy Meyer (Myer), Fred Schulte, Earl Whitehill	45.00	22.00	13.50

1936 Exhibits
Four-On-One 1936

The 1936 series of four-on-one cards again consisted of 16 cards in either green or slate blue with plain, blank backs. The series can be differentiated from the previous year's Exhibit cards by the line "PTD. IN U.S.A." at the bottom. Of the 64 players pictured, 16 appear for the first time and another nine are shown in new poses. The series is again marred by several spelling and caption errors.

	NR MT	EX	VG
Complete Set:	2000.00	1000.00	600.00
Common Player:	35.00	17.50	10.50
(1) Paul Andrews, Harland Clift (Harland), Rollie Hemsley, Sammy West	35.00	17.50	10.50
(2) Luke Appling, Henry Bonura, Jimmy Dykes, Ted Lyons	45.00	22.00	13.50
(3) Earl Averill, Mel Harder, Hal Trosky, Joe Vosmik	45.00	22.00	13.50
(4) Walter Berger, Danny MacFayden, Bill Urbanski, Pinky Whitney	35.00	17.50	10.50
(5) Charles Berry, Frank Higgins, Bob Johnson, Puccinelli	35.00	17.50	10.50
(6) Ossie Bluege, Buddy Meyer (Myer), L.N. Newsom, Earl Whitehill	35.00	17.50	10.50
(7) Stan. Bordagaray, Dutch Brandt, Fred Lindstrom, Van Mungo	45.00	22.00	13.50
(8) Guy Bush, Pie Traynor, Floyd Vaughn (Vaughan), Paul Waner	60.00	30.00	18.00
(9) Dolph Camilli, Curt Davis, Johnny Moore, Jimmy Wilson	35.00	17.50	10.50
(10) Mickey Cochrane, C. Gehringer, Goose Goslin, Linwood Rowe (Lynwood)	60.00	30.00	18.00
(11) Joe Cronin, Rick Ferrell, Jimmy Foxx, Lefty Grove	75.00	38.00	23.00
(12) Jerome "Dizzy" Dean, Paul Dean, Frank Frisch, Joe "Ducky" Medwick	150.00	75.00	45.00

	NR MT	EX	VG
(13) Paul Derringer, Babe Herman, Alex Kampouris, Botchi Lombardi	45.00	22.00	13.50
(14) Augie Galan, Gabby Hartnett, Billy Herman, Lon Warneke	45.00	22.00	13.50
(15) Lou Gehrig, Vernon Gomez, Tony Lazzeri, Red Ruffing	800.00	400.00	240.00
(16) Carl Hubbell, Gus Mancuso, Mel Ott, Bill Terry	65.00	33.00	20.00

1937 Exhibits
Four-On-One 1937

The 1937 four-on-one Exhibit cards were printed in either green or bright blue. The backs are again blank. The 1937 cards are difficult to distinguish from the 1936 series, because both contain the "PTD. IN U.S.A." line along the bottom. Of the 64 photos, 47 are re-issues from previous series.

	NR MT	EX	VG
Complete Set:	2000.00	1000.00	600.00
Common Player:	35.00	17.50	10.50
(1) Earl Averill, Bob Feller, Frank Pytlak, Hal Trosky	75.00	38.00	23.00
(2) Luke Appling, Henry Bonura, Jimmy Dykes, Vernon Kennedy	45.00	22.00	13.50
(3) Walter Berger, Alfonso Lopez, Danny MacFayden, Bill Urbanski	40.00	20.00	12.00
(4) Cy Blanton, Gus Suhr, Floyd Vaughn (Vaughan), Paul Waner	45.00	22.00	13.50
(5) Dolph Camilli, Johnny Moore, Wm. Walters, Pinky Whitney	35.00	17.50	10.50
(6) Harland Clift (Harlond), Rollie Hemsley, Orval Hildebrand (Oral), Sammy West	35.00	17.50	10.50
(7) Mickey Cochrane, C. Gehringer, Goose Goslin, Linwood Rowe (Lynwood)	60.00	30.00	18.00
(8) Joe Cronin, Rick Ferrell, Jimmy Foxx, Lefty Grove	75.00	38.00	23.00
(9) Jerome "Dizzy" Dean, Stuart Martin, Joe "Ducky" Medwick, Lon Warneke	110.00	55.00	33.00
(10) Paul Derringer, Botchi Lombardi, Lew Riggs, Phil Weintraub	45.00	22.00	13.50
(11) Joe DiMaggio, Lou Gehrig, Vernon Gomez, Tony Lazzeri	1000.00	500.00	300.00
(12) F. English, Johnny Moore, Van Mungo, Gordon Phelps	35.00	17.50	10.50
(13) Augie Galan, Gabby Hartnett, Billy Herman, Bill Lee	45.00	22.00	13.50
(14) Carl Hubbell, Sam Leslie, Gus. Mancuso, Mel Ott	45.00	22.00	13.50
(15) Bob Johnson, Harry Kelly (Kelley), Wallace Moses, Billy Weber (Werber)	35.00	17.50	10.50
(16) Joe Kuhel, Buddy Meyer (Myer), L.N. Newsom, Jonathan Stone (first name actually John)	35.00	17.50	10.50

1938 Exhibits
Four-On-One 1938

The Exhibit Co. used its four-on-one format for the final time in 1938, issuing another 16-card series. the cards feature brown printing on white stock with the line "MADE IN U.S.A." appearing along the bottom. The backs are blank. Twelve players appeared for the first time and three others are shown in new poses. Again, there are several spelling and caption mistakes.

are unnumbered and blank-backed. Most exhibits were sold through vending machines for a penny. The complete set price includes all variations.

	NR MT	EX	VG
Complete Set:	2000.00	1000.00	600.00
Common Player:	35.00	17.50	10.50

		NR MT	EX	VG
(1)	Luke Appling, Mike Kreevich, Ted Lyons, L. Sewell	45.00	22.00	13.50
(2)	Morris Arnovich, Chas. Klein, Wm. Walters, Pinky Whitney	45.00	22.00	13.50
(3)	Earl Averill, Bob Feller, Odell Hale, Hal Trosky	75.00	38.00	23.00
(4)	Beau Bell, Harland Clift (Harlond), L.N. Newsom, Sammy West	35.00	17.50	10.50
(5)	Cy Blanton, Gus Suhr, Floyd Vaughn (Vaughan), Paul Waner	45.00	22.00	13.50
(6)	Tom Bridges, C. Gehringer, Hank Greenberg, Rudy York	45.00	22.00	13.50
(7)	Dolph Camilli, Leo Durocher, Van Mungo, Gordon Phelps	40.00	20.00	12.00
(8)	Joe Cronin, Jimmy Foxx, Lefty Grove, Joe Vosmik	65.00	33.00	20.00
(9)	Tony Cuccinello, Vince DiMaggio, Roy Johnson, Danny MacFayden	35.00	17.50	10.50
(10)	Jerome "Dizzy" Dean, Augie Galan, Gabby Hartnett, Billy Herman	100.00	50.00	30.00
(11)	Paul Derringer, Ival Goodman, Botchi Lombardi, Lew Riggs	45.00	22.00	13.50
(12)	W. Dickey, Joe DiMaggio, Lou Gehrig, Vernon Gomez	1000.00	500.00	300.00
(13)	Rick Ferrell, W. Ferrell, Buddy Meyer (Myer), Jonathan Stone (first name actually John)	45.00	22.00	13.50
(14)	Carl Hubbell, Hank Leiber, Mel Ott, Jim Ripple	60.00	30.00	18.00
(15)	Bob Johnson, Harry Kelly (Kelley), Wallace Moses, Billy Weber (Werber)	35.00	17.50	10.50
(16)	Stuart Martin, Joe "Ducky" Medwick, Johnny Mize, Lon Warneke	45.00	22.00	13.50

1900 Exhibits - Salutation

Referred to as "Exhibits" because they were issued by the Exhibit Supply Co. of Chicago, Ill., this group was produced over an 8-year span. They are frequently called "Salutations" because of the personalized greeting found on the card. The black and white cards, which measure 3-3/8" by 5-3/8",

		NR MT	EX	VG
Complete Set:		4750.00	2375.00	1425.
Common Player:		5.00	2.50	1.50

		NR MT	EX	VG
(1a)	Luke Appling ("Made In U.S.A." in left corner)	12.00	6.00	3.50
(1b)	Luke Appling ("Made In U.S.A." in right corner)	7.00	3.50	2.00
(2)	Earl Averill	375.00	175.00	100.00
(3)	Charles "Red" Barrett	5.00	2.50	1.50
(4)	Henry "Hank" Borowy	5.00	2.50	1.50
(5)	Lou Boudreau	8.00	4.00	2.50
(6)	Adolf Camilli	25.00	12.50	7.50
(7)	Phil Cavarretta	6.00	3.00	1.75
(8)	Harland Clift (Harlond)	12.00	6.00	3.50
(9)	Tony Cuccinello	25.00	12.50	7.50
(10)	Dizzy Dean	80.00	40.00	24.00
(11)	Paul Derringer	5.00	2.50	1.50
(12a)	Bill Dickey ("Made In U.S.A." in left corner)	25.00	12.50	7.50
(12b)	Bill Dickey ("Made In U.S.A." in right corner)	25.00	12.50	7.50
(13)	Joe DiMaggio	35.00	17.50	10.50
(14)	Bob Elliott	5.00	2.50	1.50
(15)	Bob Feller (portrait)	100.00	50.00	30.00
(16)	Bob Feller (pitching)	30.00	15.00	9.00
(17)	Dave Ferriss	5.00	2.50	1.50
(18)	Jimmy Foxx	100.00	50.00	30.00
(19)	Lou Gehrig	1000.00	500.00	300.00
(20)	Charlie Gehringer	125.00	56.00	35.00
(21)	Vernon Gomez	180.00	90.00	55.00
(22a)	Joe Gordon (Cleveland)	25.00	12.50	7.50
(22b)	Joe Gordon (New York)	6.00	3.00	1.75
(23)	Hank Greenberg (Truly yours)	20.00	10.00	6.00
(24)	Hank Greenberg (Very truly yours)	80.00	40.00	24.00

(21) IRA FLAGSTEAD

		NR MT	EX	VG
(25)	Robert Grove	50.00	25.00	15.00
(26)	Gabby Hartnett	275.00	150.00	80.00
(27)	Buddy Hassett	15.00	7.50	4.50
(28a)	Jeff Heath (large projection)	25.00	12.50	7.50
(28b)	Jeff Heath (small projection)	5.00	2.50	1.50
(29)	Kirby Higbe	15.00	7.50	4.50
(30a)	Tommy Holmes (Yours truly)	5.00	2.50	1.50
(30b)	Tommy Holmes (Sincerely yours)	125.00	60.00	40.00
(31)	Carl Hubbell	25.00	12.50	7.50
(32)	Bob Johnson	15.00	7.50	4.50
(33)	Charles Keller	5.00	2.50	1.50
(34)	Ken Keltner	25.00	12.50	7.50
(35)	Chuck Klein	175.00	90.00	50.00
(36)	Mike Kreevich	80.00	40.00	24.00
(37)	Joe Kuhel	20.00	10.00	6.00
(38)	Bill Lee	20.00	10.00	6.00
(39)	Ernie Lombardi (Cordially)	200.00	100.00	60.00
(40)	Ernie Lombardi (Cordially yours)	8.00	4.00	2.50
(41a)	Martin Marion ("Made in U.S.A." in left corner)	5.00	2.50	1.50
(41b)	Martin Marion ("Made in U.S.A." in right corner)	5.00	2.50	1.50
(42)	Merrill May	20.00	10.00	6.00
(43a)	Frank McCormick ("Made In U.S.A." in left corner)	20.00	10.00	6.00
(43b)	Frank McCormick ("Made In U.S.A." in right corner)	6.00	3.00	1.75
(44a)	George McQuinn ("Made In U.S.A." in left corner)	20.00	10.00	6.00
(44b)	George McQuinn ("Made In U.S.A." in right corner)	6.00	3.00	1.75
(45)	Joe Medwick	30.00	15.00	9.00
(46a)	Johnny Mize ("Made In U.S.A." in left corner)	25.00	12.50	7.50
(46b)	Johnny Mize ("Made In U.S.A." in right corner)	15.00	7.50	4.50
(47)	Hugh Mulcahy	80.00	40.00	24.00
(48)	Hal Newhouser	5.00	2.50	1.50
(49)	Buck Newson (Newsom)	175.00	90.00	50.00
(50)	Louis (Buck) Newsom	5.00	2.50	1.50
(51a)	Mel Ott ("Made In U.S.A." in left corner)	50.00	25.00	15.00
(51b)	Mel Ott ("Made In U.S.A." in right corner)	25.00	12.50	7.50
(52a)	Andy Pafko ("C" on cap)	5.00	2.50	1.50
(52b)	Andy Pafko (plain cap)	5.00	2.50	1.50
(53)	Claude Passeau	6.00	3.00	1.75
(54a)	Howard Pollet ("Made In U.S.A." in left corner)	11.00	5.50	3.25
(54b)	Howard Pollet ("Made In U.S.A." in right corner)	5.00	2.50	1.50
(55a)	Pete Reiser ("Made In U.S.A." in left corner)	80.00	40.00	24.00
(55b)	Pete Reiser ("Made In U.S.A." in right corner)	5.00	2.50	1.50
(56)	Johnny Rizzo	90.00	45.00	27.00
(57)	Glenn Russell	90.00	45.00	27.00
(58)	George Stirnweiss	5.00	2.50	1.50
(59)	Cecil Travis	15.00	7.50	4.50
(60)	Paul Trout	5.00	2.50	1.50
(61)	Johnny Vander Meer	40.00	20.00	12.00
(62)	Arky Vaughn (Vaughan)	20.00	10.00	6.00
(63a)	Fred "Dixie" Walker ("D" on cap)	5.00	2.50	1.50
(63b)	Louis "Dixie" Walker ("D" blanked out)	25.00	12.50	7.50
(64)	"Bucky" Walters	5.00	2.50	1.50
(65)	Lon Warneke	6.50	3.25	2.00
(66)	Ted Williams (#9 shows)	350.00	175.00	105.00
(67)	Ted Williams (#9 not showing)	40.00	20.00	12.00
(68)	Rudy York	5.00	2.50	1.50

1900 Exhibits - 1947-1966

Called "Exhibits" as they were produced by the Exhibit Supply Co. of Chicago, Ill., this group covers a span of twenty years. Each unnumbered, black and white card, printed on heavy stock, measures 3-3/8" by 5-3/8" and is blank-backed. The Exhibit Supply Co. issued new sets each year, with many players being repeated year after year. Other players appeared in only one or two years, thereby creating levels of scarcity. Many variations of the same basic pose are found in the group. Those cards are listed in the checklist that follows with an "a", "b", etc. following the assigned card number. The complete set includes all variations.

		NR MT	EX	VG
Complete Set:		5000.00	2500.00	1500.
Common Player:		4.00	2.00	1.25
(1)	Hank Aaron	30.00	15.00	9.00
(2a)	Joe Adcock (script signature)	4.00	2.00	1.25
(2b)	Joe Adcock (plain signature)	5.00	2.50	1.50
(3)	Max Alvis	25.00	12.50	7.50
(4)	Johnny Antonelli (Braves)	4.00	2.00	1.25
(5)	Johnny Antonelli (Giants)	5.00	2.50	1.50
(6)	Luis Aparicio (portrait)	7.00	3.50	2.00
(7)	Luis Aparicio (batting)	25.00	12.50	7.50
(8)	Luke Appling	7.00	3.50	2.00
(9a)	Ritchie Ashburn (Phillies, first name incorrect)	5.00	2.50	1.50
(9b)	Richie Ashburn (Phillies, first name correct)	7.00	3.50	2.00
(10)	Richie Ashburn (Cubs)	13.00	6.50	4.00
(11)	Bob Aspromonte	4.00	2.00	1.25
(12)	Toby Atwell	4.00	2.00	1.25
(13)	Ed Bailey (with cap)	5.00	2.50	1.50
(14)	Ed Bailey (no cap)	4.00	2.00	1.25
(15)	Gene Baker	4.00	2.00	1.25
(16a)	Ernie Banks (bat on shoulder, script signature)	25.00	12.50	7.50
(16b)	Ernie Banks (bat on shoulder, plain signature)	10.00	5.00	3.00
(17)	Ernie Banks (portrait)	25.00	12.50	7.50
(18)	Steve Barber	4.00	2.00	1.25
(19)	Earl Battey	5.00	2.50	1.50
(20)	Matt Batts	4.00	2.00	1.25
(21a)	Hank Bauer (N.Y. cap)	5.00	2.50	1.50
(21b)	Hank Bauer (plain cap)	7.00	3.50	2.00
(22)	Frank Baumholtz	4.00	2.00	1.25
(23)	Gene Bearden	4.00	2.00	1.25
(24)	Joe Beggs	12.00	6.00	3.50
(25)	Larry "Yogi" Berra	30.00	15.00	9.00
(26)	Yogi Berra	10.00	5.00	3.00
(27)	Steve Bilko	5.00	2.50	1.50
(28)	Ewell Blackwell (pitching)	7.00	3.50	2.00
(29)	Ewell Blackwell (portrait)	4.00	2.00	1.25
(30a)	Don Blasingame (St. Louis cap)	4.00	2.00	1.25
(30b)	Don Blasingame (plain cap)	6.00	3.00	1.75
(31)	Ken Boyer	7.00	3.50	2.00
(32)	Ralph Branca	7.00	3.50	2.00
(33)	Jackie Brandt	50.00	25.00	15.00
(34)	Harry Brecheen	4.00	2.00	1.25
(35)	Tom Brewer	12.00	6.00	3.50
(36)	Lou Brissie	5.00	2.50	1.50
(37)	Bill Bruton	4.00	2.00	1.25
(38)	Lew Burdette (pitching, side view)	4.00	2.00	1.25
(39)	Lew Burdette (pitching, front view)	6.00	3.00	1.75
(40)	Johnny Callison	7.00	3.50	2.00
(41)	Roy Campanella	13.00	6.50	4.00
(42)	Chico Carrasquel (portrait)	13.00	6.50	4.00
(43)	Chico Carrasquel (leaping)	4.00	2.00	1.25
(44)	George Case	12.00	6.00	3.50
(45)	Hugh Casey	5.00	2.50	1.50
(46)	Norm Cash	7.00	3.50	2.00
(47)	Orlando Cepeda (portrait)	7.00	3.50	2.00
(48)	Orlando Cepeda (batting)	7.00	3.50	2.00
(49a)	Bob Cerv (A's cap)	7.00	3.50	2.00
(49b)	Bob Cerv (plain cap)	16.00	8.00	4.75
(50)	Dean Chance	4.00	2.00	1.25
(51)	Spud Chandler	12.00	6.00	3.50
(52)	Tom Cheney	4.00	2.00	1.25
(53)	Bubba Church	5.00	2.50	1.50
(54)	Roberto Clemente	30.00	15.00	9.00
(55)	Rocky Colavito (portrait)	30.00	15.00	9.00
(56)	Rocky Colavito (batting)	7.00	3.50	2.00
(57)	Choo Choo Coleman	13.00	6.50	4.00
(58)	Gordy Coleman	25.00	12.50	7.50
(59)	Jerry Coleman	5.00	2.50	1.50

		NR MT	EX	VG
(60)	Mort Cooper	12.00	6.00	3.50
(61)	Walker Cooper	4.00	2.00	1.25
(62)	Roger Craig	12.00	6.00	3.50
(63)	Delmar Crandall	4.00	2.00	1.25
(64)	Joe Cunningham (batting)	30.00	15.00	9.00
(65)	Joe Cunningham (portrait)	7.00	3.50	2.00
(66)	Guy Curtwright (Curtright)	5.00	2.50	1.50
(67)	Bud Daley	35.00	17.50	10.50
(68a)	Alvin Dark (Braves)	7.00	3.50	2.00
(68b)	Alvin Dark (Giants)	5.00	2.50	1.50
(69)	Alvin Dark (Cubs)	7.00	3.50	2.00
(70)	Murray Dickson (Murry)	5.00	2.50	1.50
(71)	Bob Dillinger	7.00	3.50	2.00
(72)	Dom DiMaggio	18.00	9.00	5.50
(73)	Joe Dobson	7.00	3.50	2.00
(74)	Larry Doby	4.00	2.00	1.25
(75)	Bobby Doerr	12.00	6.00	3.50
(76)	Dick Donovan (plain cap)	7.00	3.50	2.00
(77)	Dick Donovan (Sox cap)	4.00	2.00	1.25
(78)	Walter Dropo	4.00	2.00	1.25
(79)	Don Drysdale (glove at waist)	30.00	15.00	9.00
(80)	Don Drysdale (portrait)	30.00	15.00	9.00
(81)	Luke Easter	5.00	2.50	1.50
(82)	Bruce Edwards	5.00	2.50	1.50
(83)	Del Ennis	4.00	2.00	1.25
(84)	Al Evans	4.50	2.25	1.25
(85)	Walter Evers	4.00	2.00	1.25
(86)	Ferris Fain (fielding)	7.00	3.50	2.00
(87)	Ferris Fain (portrait)	4.00	2.00	1.25
(88)	Dick Farrell	4.00	2.00	1.25
(89)	Ed "Whitey" Ford	15.00	7.50	4.50
(90)	Whitey Ford (pitching)	10.00	5.00	3.00
(91)	Whitey Ford (portrait)	60.00	30.00	17.50
(92)	Dick Fowler	7.00	3.50	2.00
(93)	Nelson Fox	5.00	2.50	1.50
(94)	Tito Francona	4.00	2.00	1.25
(95)	Bob Friend	4.00	2.00	1.25
(96)	Carl Furillo	7.00	3.50	2.00
(97)	Augie Galan	7.00	3.50	2.00
(98)	Jim Gentile	4.00	2.00	1.25
(99)	Tony Gonzalez	4.00	2.00	1.25
(100)	Billy Goodman (leaping)	4.00	2.00	1.25
(101)	Billy Goodman (batting)	7.00	3.50	2.00
(102)	Ted Greengrass (Jim)	4.00	2.00	1.25
(103)	Dick Groat	7.00	3.50	2.00
(104)	Steve Gromek	4.00	2.00	1.25
(105)	Johnny Groth	4.00	2.00	1.25
(106)	Orval Grove	13.00	6.50	4.00
(107a)	Frank Gustine (Pirates uniform)	5.00	2.50	1.50
(107b)	Frank Gustine (plain uniform)	5.00	2.50	1.50
(108)	Berthold Haas	13.00	6.50	4.00
(109)	Grady Hatton	5.00	2.50	1.50
(110)	Jim Hegan	4.00	2.00	1.25
(111)	Tom Henrich	7.00	3.50	2.00
(112)	Ray Herbert	25.00	12.50	7.50
(113)	Gene Hermanski	4.50	2.25	1.25
(114)	Whitey Herzog	7.00	3.50	2.00
(115)	Kirby Higbe	13.00	6.50	4.00
(116)	Chuck Hinton	4.00	2.00	1.25
(117)	Don Hoak	13.00	6.50	4.00
(118a)	Gil Hodges ("B" on cap)	9.00	4.50	2.75
(118b)	Gil Hodges ("LA" on cap)	9.00	4.50	2.75
(119)	Johnny Hopp	12.00	6.00	3.50
(120)	Elston Howard	4.00	2.00	1.25
(121)	Frank Howard	7.00	3.50	2.00
(122)	Ken Hubbs	35.00	17.50	10.50
(123)	Tex Hughson	12.00	6.00	3.50
(124)	Fred Hutchinson	4.50	2.25	1.25
(125)	Monty Irvin	7.00	3.50	2.00
(126)	Joey Jay	4.00	2.00	1.25
(127)	Jackie Jensen	30.00	15.00	9.00
(128)	Sam Jethroe	5.00	2.50	1.50
(129)	Bill Johnson	5.00	2.50	1.50
(130)	Walter Judnich	12.00	6.00	3.50
(131)	Al Kaline (kneeling)	30.00	15.00	9.00
(132)	Al Kaline (portrait)	30.00	15.00	9.00
(133)	George Kell	7.00	3.50	2.00
(134)	Charley Keller	4.50	2.25	1.25
(135)	Alex Kellner	4.00	2.00	1.25
(136)	Kenn Keltner (Ken)	5.00	2.50	1.50
(137)	Harmon Killebrew (batting)	30.00	15.00	9.00
(138)	Harmon Killebrew (throwing)	30.00	15.00	9.00
(139)	Harmon Killibrew (Killebrew) (portrait)	30.00	15.00	9.00
(140)	Ellis Kinder	4.00	2.00	1.25
(141)	Ralph Kiner	6.00	3.00	1.75
(142)	Billy Klaus	25.00	12.50	7.50
(143)	Ted Kluzewski (Kluszewski) (batting)	5.00	2.50	1.50
(144a)	Ted Kluzewski (Kluszewski) (Pirates uniform)	5.00	2.50	1.50
(144b)	Ted Kluzewski (Kluszewski) (plain uniform)	13.00	6.50	4.00
(145)	Don Kolloway	7.00	3.50	2.00
(146)	Jim Konstanty	5.00	2.50	1.50
(147)	Sandy Koufax	25.00	12.50	7.50
(148)	Ed Kranepool	50.00	25.00	15.00
(149a)	Tony Kubek (light background)	7.00	3.50	2.00
(149b)	Tony Kubek (dark background)	5.00	2.50	1.50
(150a)	Harvey Kuenn ("D" on cap)	12.00	6.00	3.50
(150b)	Harvey Kuenn (plain cap)	13.00	6.50	4.00
(151)	Harvey Kuenn ("SF" on cap)	7.00	3.50	2.00
(152)	Kurowski (Whitey)	4.50	2.25	1.25
(153)	Eddie Lake	5.00	2.50	1.50
(154)	Jim Landis	4.00	2.00	1.25
(155)	Don Larsen	4.00	2.00	1.25
(156)	Bob Lemon (glove not visible)	7.00	3.50	2.00
(157)	Bob Lemon (glove partially visible)	30.00	15.00	9.00
(158)	Buddy Lewis	12.00	6.00	3.50
(159)	Johnny Lindell	25.00	12.50	7.50
(160)	Phil Linz	25.00	12.50	7.50
(161)	Don Lock	25.00	12.50	7.50
(162)	Whitey Lockman	4.00	2.00	1.25
(163)	Johnny Logan	4.00	2.00	1.25
(164)	Dale Long ("P" on cap)	4.00	2.00	1.25
(165)	Dale Long ("C" on cap)	7.00	3.50	2.00
(166)	Ed Lopat	5.00	2.50	1.50
(167a)	Harry Lowery (name misspelled)	5.00	2.50	1.50
(167b)	Harry Lowrey (name correct)	5.00	2.50	1.50
(168)	Sal Maglie	4.00	2.00	1.25
(169)	Art Mahaffey	5.00	2.50	1.50
(170)	Hank Majeski	4.00	2.00	1.25
(171)	Frank Malzone	4.00	2.00	1.25
(172)	Mickey Mantle (batting, pinstriped uniform)	100.00	50.00	30.00
(173a)	Mickey Mantle (batting, no pinstripes, first name outlined in white)	75.00	38.00	23.00
173b	Mickey Mantle (batting, no pinstripes, first name not outlined in white)	75.00	38.00	23.00
(174)	Mickey Mantle (portrait)	400.00	200.00	120.00
(175)	Martin Marion	7.00	3.50	2.00
(176)	Roger Maris	25.00	12.50	7.50
(177)	Willard Marshall	5.00	2.50	1.50
(178a)	Eddie Matthews (name incorrect)	12.00	6.00	3.50
(178b)	Eddie Mathews (name correct)	13.00	6.50	4.00
(179)	Ed Mayo	5.00	2.50	1.50
(180)	Willie Mays (batting)	18.00	9.00	5.50
(181)	Willie Mays (portrait)	25.00	12.50	7.50
(182)	Bill Mazeroski (portrait)	7.00	3.50	2.00
(183)	Bill Mazeroski (batting)	7.00	3.50	2.00
(184)	Ken McBride	4.00	2.00	1.25
(185a)	Barney McCaskey (McCosky)	13.00	6.50	4.00
(185b)	Barney McCoskey (McCosky)	90.00	45.00	27.00
(186)	Lindy McDaniel	4.00	2.00	1.25
(187)	Gil McDougald	4.00	2.00	1.25
(188)	Albert Mele	13.00	6.50	4.00
(189)	Sam Mele	5.00	2.50	1.50
(190)	Orestes Minoso ("C" on cap)	7.00	3.50	2.00
(191)	Orestes Minoso (Sox on cap)	4.00	2.00	1.25
(192)	Dale Mitchell	4.00	2.00	1.25
(193)	Wally Moon	7.00	3.50	2.00
(194)	Don Mueller	5.00	2.50	1.50
(195)	Stan Musial (kneeling)	15.00	7.50	4.50
(196)	Stan Musial (batting)	35.00	17.50	10.50
(197)	Charley Neal	18.00	9.00	5.50
(198)	Don Newcombe (shaking hands)	7.00	3.50	2.00
(199a)	Don Newcombe (Dodgers on jacket)	5.00	2.50	1.50
(199b)	Don Newcombe (plain jacket)	5.00	2.50	1.50
(200)	Hal Newhouser	4.00	2.00	1.25
(201)	Ron Northey	12.00	6.00	3.50
(202)	Bill O'Dell	4.00	2.00	1.25
(203)	Joe Page	12.00	6.00	3.50
(204)	Satchel Paige	35.00	17.50	10.50
(205)	Milt Pappas	4.00	2.00	1.25
(206)	Camilo Pascual	4.00	2.00	1.25
(207)	Albie Pearson	25.00	12.50	7.50
(208)	Johnny Pesky	4.00	2.00	1.25
(209)	Gary Peters	25.00	12.50	7.50
(210)	Dave Philley	4.00	2.00	1.25
(211)	Billy Pierce	4.00	2.00	1.25
(212)	Jimmy Piersall	16.00	8.00	4.75
(213)	Vada Pinson	7.00	3.50	2.00
(214)	Bob Porterfield	4.00	2.00	1.25
(215)	John "Boog" Powell	35.00	17.50	10.50
(216)	Vic Raschi	4.50	2.25	1.25
(217a)	Harold "Peewee" Reese (fielding, ball partially visible)	10.00	5.00	3.00
(217b)	Harold "Peewee" Reese (fielding, ball not visible)	10.00	5.00	3.00

	NR MT	EX	VG
(218) Del Rice	4.00	2.00	1.25
(219) Bobby Richardson	55.00	28.00	16.50
(220) Phil Rizzuto	6.00	3.00	1.75
(221a) Robin Roberts (script signature)	12.00	6.00	3.50
(221b) Robin Roberts (plain signature)	6.00	3.00	1.75
(222) Brooks Robinson	30.00	15.00	9.00
(223) Eddie Robinson	4.00	2.00	1.25
(224) Floyd Robinson	25.00	12.50	7.50
(225) Frankie Robinson	18.00	9.00	5.50
(226) Jackie Robinson	30.00	15.00	9.00
(227) Preacher Roe	4.50	2.25	1.25
(228) Bob Rogers (Rodgers)	25.00	12.50	7.50
(229) Richard Rollins	25.00	12.50	7.50
(230) Pete Runnels	12.00	6.00	3.50
(231) John Sain	5.00	2.50	1.50
(232) Ron Santo	6.00	3.00	1.75
(233) Henry Sauer	5.00	2.50	1.50
(234a) Carl Sawatski ("M" on cap)	4.00	2.00	1.25
(234b) Carl Sawatski ("P" on cap)	4.00	2.00	1.25
(234c) Carl Sawatski (plain cap)	13.00	6.50	4.00
(235) Johnny Schmitz	5.00	2.50	1.50
(236a) Red Schoendeinst (Schoendienst) (fielding, name in white)	5.00	2.50	1.50
(236b) Red Schoendeinst (Schoendienst) (fielding, name in red-brown)	7.00	3.50	2.00
(237) Red Schoendinst (Schoendienst) (batting)	4.00	2.00	1.25
(238a) Herb Score ("C" on cap)	5.00	2.50	1.50
(238b) Herb Score (plain cap)	12.00	6.00	3.50
(239) Andy Seminick	4.00	2.00	1.25
(240) Rip Sewell	7.00	3.50	2.00
(241) Norm Siebern	4.00	2.00	1.25
(242) Roy Sievers (batting)	5.00	2.50	1.50
(243a) Roy Sievers (portrait, "W" on cap, light background)	7.00	3.50	2.00
(243b) Roy Sievers (portrait, "W" on cap, dark background)	5.00	2.50	1.50
(243c) Roy Sievers (portrait, plain cap)	4.50	2.25	1.25
(244) Curt Simmons	5.00	2.50	1.50
(245) Dick Sisler	5.00	2.50	1.50
(246) Bill Skowron	5.00	2.50	1.50
(247) Bill "Moose" Skowron	55.00	28.00	16.50
(248) Enos Slaughter	7.00	3.50	2.00
(249a) Duke Snider ("B" on cap)	8.50	4.25	2.50
(249b) Duke Snider ("LA" on cap)	18.00	9.00	5.50
(250a) Warren Spahn ("B" on cap)	10.00	5.00	3.00
(250b) Warren Spahn ("M" on cap)	12.00	6.00	3.50
(251) Stanley Spence	13.00	6.50	4.00
(252) Ed Stanky (plain uniform)	5.00	2.50	1.50
(253) Ed Stanky (Giants uniform)	5.00	2.50	1.50
(254) Vern Stephens (batting)	5.00	2.50	1.50
(255) Vern Stephens (portrait)	5.00	2.50	1.50
(256) Ed Stewart	5.00	2.50	1.50
(257) Snuffy Stirnweiss	13.00	6.50	4.00
(258) George "Birdie" Tebbetts	12.00	6.00	3.50
(259) Frankie Thomas (photo actually Bob Skinner)	30.00	15.00	9.00
(260) Frank Thomas (portrait)	13.00	6.50	4.00
(261) Lee Thomas	4.00	2.00	1.25
(262) Bobby Thomson	7.00	3.50	2.00
(263a) Earl Torgeson (Braves uniform)	4.00	2.00	1.25
(263b) Earl Torgeson (plain uniform)	5.00	2.50	1.50
(264) Gus Triandos	7.00	3.50	2.00
(265) Virgil Trucks	4.00	2.00	1.25
(266) Johnny Vandermeer (VanderMeer)	13.00	6.50	4.00
(267) Emil Verban	7.00	3.50	2.00
(268) Mickey Vernon (throwing)	4.00	2.00	1.25
(269) Mickey Vernon (batting)	4.00	2.00	1.25
(270) Bill Voiselle	7.00	3.50	2.00
(271) Leon Wagner	4.00	2.00	1.25
(272a) Eddie Waitkus (throwing, Chicago uniform)	7.00	3.50	2.00
(272b) Eddie Waitkus (throwing, plain uniform)	5.00	2.50	1.50
(273) Eddie Waitkus (portrait)	13.00	6.50	4.00
(274) Dick Wakefield	5.00	2.50	1.50
(275) Harry Walker	7.00	3.50	2.00
(276) Bucky Walters	4.50	2.25	1.25
(277) Pete Ward	30.00	15.00	9.00
(278) Herman Wehmeier	5.00	2.50	1.50
(279) Vic Wertz (batting)	4.00	2.00	1.25
(280) Vic Wertz (portrait)	4.00	2.00	1.25
(281) Wally Westlake	5.00	2.50	1.50
(282) Wes Westrum	13.00	6.50	4.00
(283) Billy Williams	13.00	6.50	4.00
(284) Maurice Wills	12.00	6.00	3.50
(285a) Gene Woodling (script signature)	4.00	2.00	1.25
(285b) Gene Woodling (plain signature)	7.00	3.50	2.00
(286) Taffy Wright	5.00	2.50	1.50
(287) Carl Yastrazemski (Yastrzemski)	175.00	90.00	50.00

	NR MT	EX	VG
(288) Al Zarilla	5.00	2.50	1.50
(289a) Gus Zernial (script signature)	4.00	2.00	1.25
(289b) Gus Zernial (plain signature)	7.00	3.50	2.00
(290) Braves Team - 1948	18.00	9.00	5.50
(291) Dodgers Team - 1949	25.00	12.50	7.50
(292) Dodgers Team - 1952	25.00	12.50	7.50
(293) Dodgers Team - 1955	25.00	12.50	7.50
(294) Dodgers Team - 1956	25.00	12.50	7.50
(295) Giants Team - 1951	18.00	9.00	5.50
(296) Giants Team - 1954	18.00	9.00	5.50
(297) Indians Team - 1948	18.00	9.00	5.50
(298) Indians Team - 1954	18.00	9.00	5.50
(299) Phillies Team - 1950	18.00	9.00	5.50
(300) Yankees Team - 1949	30.00	15.00	9.00
(301) Yankees Team - 1950	30.00	15.00	9.00
(302) Yankees Team - 1951	30.00	15.00	9.00
(303) Yankees Team - 1952	30.00	15.00	9.00
(304) Yankees Team - 1955	30.00	15.00	9.00
(305) Yankees Team - 1956	30.00	15.00	9.00

1948 Exhibits
Baseball's Great Hall Of Fame

Titled "Baseball's Great Hall of Fame," this 32-player set features black and white player photos against a gray background. The photos are accented by Greek columns on either side with brief player information printed at the bottom. The blank-backed cards are unnumbered and are listed here alphabetically. The cards measure 3-3/8" by 5-3/8". Collectors should be aware that 24 of the cards in this set were reprinted on white stock in the mid-1970s.

	NR MT	EX	VG
Complete Set:	550.00	275.00	165.00
Common Player:	4.00	2.00	1.25
(1) Grover Cleveland Alexander	7.00	3.50	2.00
(2) Roger Bresnahan	4.00	2.00	1.25
(3) Frank Chance	5.00	2.50	1.50
(4) Jack Chesbro	4.00	2.00	1.25
(5) Fred Clarke	4.00	2.00	1.25
(6) Ty Cobb	50.00	25.00	15.00
(7) Mickey Cochrane	5.00	2.50	1.50
(8) Eddie Collins	4.00	2.00	1.25
(9) Hugh Duffy	4.00	2.00	1.25
(10) Johnny Evers	4.00	2.00	1.25
(11) Frankie Frisch	4.00	2.00	1.25
(12) Lou Gehrig	50.00	25.00	15.00
(13) Clark Griffith	4.00	2.00	1.25
(14) Robert "Lefty" Grove	6.00	3.00	1.75
(15) Rogers Hornsby	10.00	5.00	3.00
(16) Carl Hubbell	5.00	2.50	1.50
(17) Hughie Jennings	4.00	2.00	1.25
(18) Walter Johnson	15.00	7.50	4.50
(19) Willie Keeler	4.00	2.00	1.25
(20) Napolean Lajoie	7.00	3.50	2.00
(21) Connie Mack	7.00	3.50	2.00
(22) Christy Matthewson (Mathewson)	15.00	7.50	4.50
(23) John J. McGraw	5.00	2.50	1.50
(24) Eddie Plank	4.00	2.00	1.25
(25) Babe Ruth (batting)	75.00	37.00	22.00
(26) Babe Ruth (standing with bats)	200.00	100.00	60.00
(27) George Sisler	5.00	2.50	1.50

		NR MT	EX	VG
(28)	Tris Speaker	7.00	3.50	2.00
(29)	Joe Tinker	4.00	2.00	1.25
(30)	Rube Waddell	4.00	2.00	1.25
(31)	Honus Wagner	15.00	7.50	4.50
(32)	Ed Walsh	4.00	2.00	1.25
(33)	Cy Young	9.00	4.50	2.75

1953 Exhibits - Canadian

This Canadian-issued set consists of 64 cards and includes both major leaguers and player from the Montreal Royals of the International League. The cards are slightly smaller than the U.S. exhibit cards, measuring 3-1/4" by 5-1/4", and are numbered. The blank-backed cards were printed on gray stock. Card numbers 1-32 have a green or red tint, while card numbers 33-64 have a blue or reddish-brown tint.

		NR MT	EX	VG
	Complete Set:	1300.00	650.00	390.00
	Common Player: 1-32	6.00	3.00	1.75
	Common Player: 33-64	4.00	2.00	1.25
1	Preacher Roe	9.00	4.50	2.75
2	Luke Easter	6.00	3.00	1.75
3	Gene Bearden	6.00	3.00	1.75
4	Chico Carrasquel	6.00	3.00	1.75
5	Vic Raschi	9.00	4.50	2.75
6	Monty Irvin	18.00	9.00	5.50
7	Henry Sauer	6.00	3.00	1.75
8	Ralph Branca	9.00	4.50	2.75
9	Ed Stanky	7.00	3.50	2.00
10	Sam Jethroe	6.00	3.00	1.75
11	Larry Doby	7.00	3.50	2.00
12	Hal Newhouser	6.00	3.00	1.75
13	Gil Hodges	25.00	12.50	7.50
14	Harry Brecheen	6.00	3.00	1.75
15	Ed Lopat	9.00	4.50	2.75
16	Don Newcombe	9.00	4.50	2.75
17	Bob Feller	35.00	17.50	10.50
18	Tommy Holmes	6.00	3.00	1.75
19	Jackie Robinson	110.00	55.00	33.00
20	Roy Campanella	110.00	55.00	33.00
21	Harold "Peewee" Reese	30.00	15.00	9.00
22	Ralph Kiner	25.00	12.50	7.50
23	Dom DiMaggio	8.00	4.00	2.50
24	Bobby Doerr	18.00	9.00	5.50
25	Phil Rizzuto	25.00	12.50	7.50
26	Bob Elliott	6.00	3.00	1.75
27	Tom Henrich	9.00	4.50	2.75
28	Joe DiMaggio	350.00	175.00	105.00
29	Harry Lowery (Lowrey)	6.00	3.00	1.75
30	Ted Williams	150.00	75.00	45.00
31	Bob Lemon	20.00	10.00	6.00
32	Warren Spahn	30.00	15.00	9.00
33	Don Hoak	5.00	2.50	1.50
34	Bob Alexander	4.00	2.00	1.25
35	Simmons	4.00	2.00	1.25
36	Steve Lembo	4.00	2.00	1.25
37	Norman Larker	4.50	2.25	1.25
38	Bob Ludwick	4.00	2.00	1.25
39	Walter Moryn	4.00	2.00	1.25
40	Charlie Thompson	4.00	2.00	1.25
41	Ed Roebuck	4.50	2.25	1.25
42	Rose	4.00	2.00	1.25
43	Edmundo Amoros	4.50	2.25	1.25
44	Bob Milliken	4.00	2.00	1.25

		NR MT	EX	VG
45	Art Fabbro	4.00	2.00	1.25
46	Jacobs	4.00	2.00	1.25
47	Mauro	4.00	2.00	1.25
48	Walter Fiala	4.00	2.00	1.25
49	Rocky Nelson	4.00	2.00	1.25
50	Tom La Sorda (Lasorda)	40.00	20.00	12.00
51	Ronnie Lee	4.00	2.00	1.25
52	Hampton Coleman	4.00	2.00	1.25
53	Frank Marchio	4.00	2.00	1.25
54	Sampson	4.00	2.00	1.25
55	Gil Mills	4.00	2.00	1.25
56	Al Ronning	4.00	2.00	1.25
57	Stan Musial	70.00	35.00	21.00
58	Walker Cooper	4.50	2.25	1.25
59	Mickey Vernon	5.00	2.50	1.50
60	Del Ennis	5.00	2.50	1.50
61	Walter Alston	20.00	10.00	6.00
62	Dick Sisler	4.50	2.25	1.25
63	Billy Goodman	4.50	2.25	1.25
64	Alex Kellner	4.00	2.00	1.25

F

1939 Father & Son Shoes Phillies

Chuck Klein, outfielder, Phillies
Compliments Father & Son Shoes

This 25-card set featuring members of the Phillies was distributed in the Philadelphia area in 1939 by Father & Son Shoes stores. The unnumbered black and white cards measure 3" by 4". The player's name, position and team (Phillies) appear below the photo, along with the line "Compliments of Fathers & Son Shoes." The backs are blank. The only player of note in the set is Hall of Famer Chuck Klein.

		NR MT	EX	VG
	Complete Set:	725.00	362.00	217.00
	Common Player:	35.00	17.50	10.50
(1)	Morrie Arnovich	35.00	17.50	10.50
(2)	Earl Brucker	35.00	17.50	10.50
(3)	George Caster	35.00	17.50	10.50
(4)	Spud Davis	35.00	17.50	10.50
(5)	Gantenbein	35.00	17.50	10.50
(6)	Bob Johnson	45.00	22.00	13.50
(7)	Merrill May	35.00	17.50	10.50
(8)	Claude Passeau	35.00	17.50	10.50
(9)	Sam Chapman	35.00	17.50	10.50
(10)	Chuck Klein	150.00	75.00	45.00
(11)	Herschel Martin	35.00	17.50	10.50
(12)	Wally Moses	45.00	22.00	13.50
(13)	Hugh Mulcahy	35.00	17.50	10.50
(14)	Skeeter Newsome	35.00	17.50	10.50
(15)	George Scharien	35.00	17.50	10.50
(16)	Dick Siebert	35.00	17.50	10.50

NOTE: A card number in parentheses ( ) indicates the set is unnumbered.

1951 Fischer Baking Labels

This set of end-labels from loaves of bread consists of 32 player photos, each measuring approximately 2-3/4" square. The labels include the player's name, team and position, along with a few words about him. The bakery's slogan "Bread For Energy" appears in a dark band along the bottom. The set, which is unnumbered, was distributed in the Northeast.

		NR MT	EX	VG
Complete Set:		2300.00	1150.00	690.00
Common Player:		60.00	30.00	18.00
(1)	Vern Bickford	60.00	30.00	18.00
(2)	Ralph Branca	65.00	32.00	19.50
(3)	Harry Brecheen	60.00	30.00	18.00
(4)	"Chico" Carrasquel	60.00	30.00	18.00
(5)	Cliff Chambers	60.00	30.00	18.00
(6)	"Hoot" Evers	60.00	30.00	18.00
(7)	Ned Garver	60.00	30.00	18.00
(8)	Billy Goodman	60.00	30.00	18.00
(9)	Gil Hodges	90.00	45.00	27.00
(10)	Larry Jansen	60.00	30.00	18.00
(11)	Willie Jones	60.00	30.00	18.00
(12)	Eddie Joost	60.00	30.00	18.00
(13)	George Kell	85.00	42.00	25.00
(14)	Alex Kellner	60.00	30.00	18.00
(15)	Ted Kluszewski	80.00	40.00	24.00
(16)	Jim Konstanty	60.00	30.00	18.00
(17)	Bob Lemon	85.00	42.00	25.00
(18)	Cass Michaels	60.00	30.00	18.00
(19)	Johnny Mize	85.00	42.00	25.00
(20)	Irv Noren	60.00	30.00	18.00
(21)	Joe Page	65.00	32.00	19.50
(22)	Andy Pafko	65.00	32.00	19.50
(23)	Mel Parnell	60.00	30.00	18.00
(24)	Johnny Sain	65.00	32.00	19.50
(25)	"Red" Schoendienst	80.00	40.00	24.00
(26)	Roy Sievers	60.00	30.00	18.00
(27)	Roy Smalley	60.00	30.00	18.00
(28)	Herman Wehmeier	60.00	30.00	18.00
(29)	Bill Werle	60.00	30.00	18.00
(30)	Wes Westrum	60.00	30.00	18.00
(31)	Early Wynn	85.00	42.00	25.00
(32)	Gus Zernial	60.00	30.00	18.00

1959 Fleer Ted Williams

This 80-card 1959 Fleer set tells of the life of baseball great Ted Williams, from his childhood years

up to 1958. The full-color cards measure 2-1/2" by 3-1/2" in size and make use of both horizontal and vertical formats. The card backs, all designed horizontally, contain a continuing biography of Williams. Card #68 was withdrawn from the set early in production and is scarce. Counterfeit cards of #68 have been produced and can be distinguished by a cross-hatch pattern which appears over the photo on the card fronts.

		NR MT	EX	VG
Complete Set:		1000.00	500.00	300.00
Common Player:		5.00	2.50	1.50
1	The Early Years	25.00	12.50	7.50
2	Ted's Idol - Babe Ruth	25.00	12.50	7.50
3	Practice Makes Perfect	5.00	2.50	1.50
4	1934 - Ted Learns The Fine Points			
		5.00	2.50	1.50
5	Ted's Fame Spreads - 1935-36	5.00	2.50	1.50
6	Ted Turns Professional	5.00	2.50	1.50
7	1936 - From Mound To Plate	5.00	2.50	1.50
8	1937 - First Full Season	5.00	2.50	1.50
9	1937 - First Step To The Majors	5.00	2.50	1.50
10	1938 - Gunning As A Pastime	5.00	2.50	1.50
11	1938 - First Spring Training	4.00	2.00	1.25
12	1939 - Burning Up The Minors	5.00	2.50	1.50
13	1939 - Ted Shows He Will Stay	5.00	2.50	1.50
14	Outstanding Rookie of 1939	5.00	2.50	1.50
15	1940 - Williams Licks Sophomore Jinx			
		5.00	2.50	1.50
16	1941 - Williams' Greatest Year	5.00	2.50	1.50
17	1941 - How Ted Hit .400	5.00	2.50	1.50
18	1941 - All-Star Hero	5.00	2.50	1.50
19	1942 - Ted Wins Triple Crown	5.00	2.50	1.50
20	1942 - On To Naval Training	5.00	2.50	1.50
21	1943 - Honors For Williams	5.00	2.50	1.50
22	1944 - Ted Solos	5.00	2.50	1.50
23	1944 - Williams Wins His Wings	5.00	2.50	1.50
24	1945 - Sharpshooter	5.00	2.50	1.50
25	1945 - Ted Is Discharged	5.00	2.50	1.50
26	1946 - Off To A Flying Start	5.00	2.50	1.50
27	July 9, 1946 - One Man Show	5.00	2.50	1.50
28	July 14, 1946 - The Williams Shift	5.00	2.50	1.50
29	July 21, 1946, Ted Hits For The Cycle			
		5.00	2.50	1.50
30	1946 - Beating The Williams Shift	5.00	2.50	1.50
31	Oct. 1946 - Sox Lose The Series	5.00	2.50	1.50
32	1946 - Most Valuable Player	5.00	2.50	1.50
33	1947 - Another Triple Crown For Ted			
		5.00	2.50	1.50
34	1947 - Ted Sets Runs-Scored Record			
		5.00	2.50	1.50
35	1948 - The Sox Miss The Pennant	5.00	2.50	1.50
36	1948 - Banner Year For Ted	5.00	2.50	1.50
37	1949 - Sox Miss Out Again	5.00	2.50	1.50
38	1949 - Power Rampage	5.00	2.50	1.50
39	1950 - Great Start	4.50	2.25	1.25
40	July 11, 1950 - Ted Crashes Into Wall			
		5.00	2.50	1.50
41	1950 - Ted Recovers	5.00	2.50	1.50
42	1951 - Williams Slowed By Injury	5.00	2.50	1.50
43	1951 - Leads Outfielders In Double Plays			
		5.00	2.50	1.50
44	1952 - Back To The Marines	5.00	2.50	1.50
45	1952 - Farewell To Baseball?	5.00	2.50	1.50
46	1952 - Ready For Combat	5.00	2.50	1.50
47	1953 - Ted Crash Lands Jet	5.00	2.50	1.50
48	July 14, 1953 - Ted Returns	5.00	2.50	1.50
49	1953 - Smash Return	5.00	2.50	1.50
50	March 1954 - Spring Injury	5.00	2.50	1.50
51	May 16, 1954 - Ted Is Patched Up	5.00	2.50	1.50
52	1954 - Ted's Comeback	5.00	2.50	1.50
53	1954 - Ted's Comeback Is A Sucess			
		5.00	2.50	1.50
54	Dec. 1954, Fisherman Ted Hooks a Big One			
		5.00	2.50	1.50
55	1955 - Ted Decides Retirement Is "No Go"			
		5.00	2.50	1.50
56	1956 - Ted Reaches 400th Homer,			
		5.00	2.50	1.50
58	1957 - Williams Hits .388	5.00	2.50	1.50
59	1957 - Hot September For Ted	5.00	2.50	1.50
60	1957 - More Records For Ted	5.00	2.50	1.50
61	1957 - Outfielder Ted	5.00	2.50	1.50
62	1958 - 6th Batting Title For Ted	5.00	2.50	1.50
63	Ted's All-Star Record	5.00	2.50	1.50
64	1958 - Daughter And Famous Daddy			
		5.00	2.50	1.50
65	August 30, 1958	5.00	2.50	1.50

		NR MT	EX	VG
66	1958 - Powerhouse	5.00	2.50	1.50
67	Two Famous Fisherman	4.50	2.25	1.25
68	Jan. 23, 1959 - Ted Signs For 1959			
		525.00	262.00	157.00
69	A Future Ted Williams?	5.00	2.50	1.50
70	Ted Williams & Jim Thorpe	4.50	2.25	1.25
71	Ted's Hitting Fundamentals #1	5.00	2.50	1.50
72	Ted's Hitting Fundamentals #2	5.00	2.50	1.50
73	Ted's Hitting Fundamentals #3	5.00	2.50	1.50
74	Here's How!	5.00	2.50	1.50
75	Williams' Value To Red Sox	12.00	6.00	3.50
76	Ted's Remarkable "On Base" Record			
		5.00	2.50	1.50
77	Ted Relaxes	5.00	2.50	1.50
78	Honors For Williams	5.00	2.50	1.50
79	Where Ted Stands	5.00	2.50	1.50
80	Ted's Goals For 1959	12.00	6.00	3.50

1960 Fleer

The 1960 Fleer Baseball Greats set consists of 79 cards of the game's top players from the past. (The set does include a card of Ted Williams, who was in his final major league season). The cards are standard size (2-1/2" by 3-1/2") and feature color photos inside blue, green, red or yellow borders. The card backs carry a short player biography plus career hitting or pitching statistics. Cards with a Pepper Martin back (#80), but with another player pictured on the front are in existence.

		NR MT	EX	VG
Complete Set:		400.00	200.00	120.00
Common Player:		2.00	1.00	.60
1	Nap Lajoie	8.00	4.00	2.50
2	Christy Mathewson	8.00	4.00	2.50
3	Babe Ruth	70.00	35.00	21.00
4	Carl Hubbell	2.50	1.25	.70
5	Grover Cleveland Alexander	4.00	2.00	1.25
6	Walter Johnson	8.00	4.00	2.50
7	Chief Bender	2.00	1.00	.60
8	Roger Bresnahan	2.00	1.00	.60
9	Mordecai Brown	2.00	1.00	.60
10	Tris Speaker	2.50	1.25	.70
11	Arky Vaughan	2.00	1.00	.60
12	Zack Wheat	2.00	1.00	.60
13	George Sisler	2.50	1.25	.70
14	Connie Mack	4.00	2.00	1.25
15	Clark Griffith	2.00	1.00	.60
16	Lou Boudreau	2.00	1.00	.60
17	Ernie Lombardi	2.00	1.00	.60
18	Heinie Manush	2.00	1.00	.60
19	Marty Marion	2.00	1.00	.60
20	Eddie Collins	2.50	1.25	.70
21	Rabbit Maranville	2.00	1.00	.60
22	Joe Medwick	2.00	1.00	.60
23	Ed Barrow	2.00	1.00	.60
24	Mickey Cochrane	2.50	1.25	.70
25	Jimmy Collins	2.00	1.00	.60
26	Bob Feller	7.00	3.50	2.00
27	Luke Appling	2.00	1.00	.60
28	Lou Gehrig	35.00	17.50	10.50
29	Gabby Hartnett	2.00	1.00	.60
30	Chuck Klein	2.00	1.00	.60
31	Tony Lazzeri	2.00	1.00	.60
32	Al Simmons	2.00	1.00	.60
33	Wilbert Robinson	2.00	1.00	.60
34	Sam Rice	2.00	1.00	.60
35	Herb Pennock	2.00	1.00	.60

		NR MT	EX	VG
36	Mel Ott	2.50	1.25	.70
37	Lefty O'Doul	2.00	1.00	.60
38	Johnny Mize	2.50	1.25	.70
39	Bing Miller	2.00	1.00	.60
40	Joe Tinker	2.00	1.00	.60
41	Frank Baker	2.00	1.00	.60
42	Ty Cobb	35.00	17.50	10.50
43	Paul Derringer	2.00	1.00	.60
44	Cap Anson	2.50	1.25	.70
45	Jim Bottomley	2.00	1.00	.60
46	Eddie Plank	2.00	1.00	.60
47	Cy Young	5.00	2.50	1.50
48	Hack Wilson	2.00	1.00	.60
49	Ed Walsh	2.00	1.00	.60
50	Frank Chance	2.00	1.00	.60
51	Dazzy Vance	2.00	1.00	.60
52	Bill Terry	2.50	1.25	.70
53	Jimmy Foxx	4.00	2.00	1.25
54	Lefty Gomez	2.50	1.25	.70
55	Branch Rickey	2.00	1.00	.60
56	Ray Schalk	2.00	1.00	.60
57	Johnny Evers	2.00	1.00	.60
58	Charlie Gehringer	2.50	1.25	.70
59	Burleigh Grimes	2.00	1.00	.60
60	Lefty Grove	2.50	1.25	.70
61	Rube Waddell	2.00	1.00	.60
62	Honus Wagner	8.00	4.00	2.50
63	Red Ruffing	2.00	1.00	.60
64	Judge Landis	2.00	1.00	.60
65	Harry Heilmann	2.00	1.00	.60
66	John McGraw	2.50	1.25	.70
67	Hughie Jennings	2.00	1.00	.60
68	Hal Newhouser	2.00	1.00	.60
69	Waite Hoyt	2.00	1.00	.60
70	Bobo Newsom	2.00	1.00	.60
71	Earl Averill	2.00	1.00	.60
72	Ted Williams	55.00	27.00	16.50
73	Warren Giles	2.00	1.00	.60
74	Ford Frick	2.00	1.00	.60
75	Ki Ki Cuyler	2.00	1.00	.60
76	Paul Waner	2.00	1.00	.60
77	Pie Traynor	2.00	1.00	.60
78	Lloyd Waner	2.00	1.00	.60
79	Ralph Kiner	8.00	4.00	2.50

1887 Four Base Hits

Although the exact origin of this set is still in doubt, the Four Base Hits cards are among the rarest and most sought after of all 19th century tobacco issues. There is some speculation that the cards, measuring 2-1/4" by 3-7/8", were produced by Charles Gross & Co. because of their similarity to the Kalamazoo Bats issues, but there is also some evidence to support the theory that they were issued by August Beck & Co., producer of the Yum Yum set. The Four Base Hits cards feature sepia-toned photos with the player's name and position below the picture, and the words "Smoke Four Base Hits. Four For 10 Cents." along the bottom. THe card labeled "Daily" is a double error. The name should have been spelled "Daly," but the card actually pictures Billy Sunday.

	NR MT	EX	VG
Complete Set:	30000.00	15000.00	9000.

	NR MT	EX	VG
Common Player:	2000.00	1000.00	600.00
(1) Tido Daily (Daly)	2000.00	1000.00	600.00
(2) Buck Ewing	3500.00	1750.00	1050.
(3) Pete Gillespie	2000.00	1000.00	600.00
(4) Frank Hankinson	2000.00	1000.00	600.00
(5) King Kelly	4000.00	2000.00	1200.
(6) Al Mays	2000.00	1000.00	600.00
(7) Jim Mutrie	2000.00	1000.00	600.00
(8) Chief Roseman	2000.00	1000.00	600.00
(9) Marty Sullivan	2000.00	1000.00	600.00
(10) Rip Van Haltren	2000.00	1000.00	600.00
(11) Mickey Welch	3500.00	1750.00	1050.

1928 Fro-joy

Boys—Girls:

Make a "home run" to health and strength by eating Fro-joy Ice Cream every day. Its "Youth Units" build strong bones, sound teeth, and healthy bodies.

Chock-full of "YOUTH UNITS"

PICTURE NO. 4

George Herman ("Babe") Ruth

Capitalizing on the extreme popularity of Babe Ruth, this six-card set was given away with Fro-joy Cones during the August 6-11, 1928 Fro-joy Cone Week. The cards, which measure 2-1/16" by 4" in size, contain black and white photos designed on either a horizontal or vertical format. The card fronts also contain a caption with a few sentences explaining the photo. The card backs contain advertising for Fro-joy Ice Cream and Cones.

	NR MT	EX	VG
Complete Set:	750.00	375.00	225.00
Common Player:	100.00	50.00	30.00
1 George Herman ("Babe") Ruth	125.00	62.00	37.00
2 Look Out, Mr. Pitcher!	125.00	62.00	37.00
3 "Babe" Ruth's Grip!	100.00	50.00	30.00
4 Ruth is a Crack Fielder	125.00	62.00	37.00
5 Bang! The Babe Lines Out!	125.00	62.00	37.00
6 When The "Babe" Comes Home	125.00	62.00	37.00

G

1933 George C. Miller

Charles Ruffing, Pitcher

The George C. Miller & Co. of Boston, Mass. issued a 32-card set in 1933. The set, which received limited distribution, consists of 16 National League and 16 American League players. The cards are color art reproductions of actual photographs and measure 2-3/8" by 2-7/8" in size. Two distinct variations can be found for each card in the set. Two different typefaces were used, one being much smaller than the other. The most substantial difference is "R" and "L" being used for the "Bats/Throws" information on one version, while the other spells out "Right" and "Left." Collectors were advised on the card backs to collect all 32 cards and return them for prizes. The cards, with a cancellation at the bottom, were returned to the collector with the prize. Two forms of cancellation were used; one involved the complete trimming of the bottom one-quarter of the card, the other a series of diamond-shaped punch holes. Cancelled cards have a significantly decreased value.

	NR MT	EX	VG
Complete Set:	14000.00	7000.00	4200.
Common Player:	250.00	125.00	75.00
(1) Dale Alexander	250.00	125.00	75.00
(2) "Ivy" Paul Andrews	2000.00	1000.00	600.00
(3) Earl Averill	400.00	200.00	120.00
(4) Dick Bartell	250.00	125.00	75.00
(5) Walter Berger	250.00	125.00	75.00
(6) Jim Bottomley	400.00	200.00	120.00
(7) Joe Cronin	500.00	250.00	150.00
(8) Jerome "Dizzy" Dean	800.00	400.00	240.00
(9) William Dickey	600.00	300.00	180.00
(10) Jimmy Dykes	250.00	125.00	75.00
(11) Wesley Ferrell	250.00	125.00	75.00
(12) Jimmy Foxx	600.00	300.00	180.00
(13) Frank Frisch	450.00	225.00	135.00
(14) Charlie Gehringer	450.00	225.00	135.00
(15) Leon "Goose" Goslin	400.00	200.00	120.00
(16) Charlie Grimm	250.00	125.00	75.00
(17) Bob "Lefty" Grove	500.00	250.00	150.00
(18) Charles "Chick" Hafey	400.00	200.00	120.00
(19) Ray Hayworth	250.00	125.00	75.00
(20) Charles "Chuck" Klein	400.00	200.00	120.00
(21) Walter "Rabbit" Maranville	400.00	200.00	120.00
(22) Oscar Melillo	250.00	125.00	75.00
(23) Frank "Lefty" O'Doul	250.00	125.00	75.00
(24) Melvin Ott	500.00	250.00	150.00
(25) Carl Reynolds	250.00	125.00	75.00
(26) Charles Ruffing	400.00	200.00	120.00
(27) Al Simmons	400.00	200.00	120.00
(28) Joe Stripp	250.00	125.00	75.00
(29) Bill Terry	450.00	225.00	135.00
(30) Lloyd Waner	400.00	200.00	120.00
(31) Paul Waner	400.00	200.00	120.00
(32) Lonnie Warneke	250.00	125.00	75.00

1928 George Ruth Candy Co.

(2) "BABE" RUTH

Knocked out 60 Home Runs in 1927. His Candy Helped Him.

When you have a complete set of 6 (six) Pictures Nos. 1, 2, 3, 4, 5 and 6, send them to The Geo. H. Ruth Candy Co., Cleveland, Ohio, and you will receive a Baseball with Babe Ruth's genuine signature on it FREE OF CHARGE.

This obscure six-card set, issued circa 1928, features sepia-toned photos of Babe Ruth, and, according to the back of the cards, was actually issued by the Geo. H. Ruth Candy Co. The cards measure 1-7/8" by 4" and picture Ruth during a

1924 promotional West Coast tour and in scenes from the movie "Babe Comes Home." The cards are numbered and include photo captions at the bottom. the backs of the card contain an offer to exchange the six cards for an autographed baseball, which may explain their scarcity today.

		NR MT	EX	VG
Complete Set:		5000.00	2500.00	1500.
Common Player:		800.00	400.00	240.00

		NR MT	EX	VG
1	"Babe" Ruth (King of them all. Home Run Candy Bar. His Candy Helped Him.)	800.00	400.00	240.00
2	"Babe" Ruth (Knocked out 60 Home Runs in 1927. His Candy Helped Him.)	800.00	400.00	240.00
3	"Babe" Ruth (The only player who broke his own record. His Candy Helped Him.)	800.00	400.00	240.00
4	"Babe" Ruth (The Popular Bambino eating his Home Run Candy. His Candy Helped Him.)	800.00	400.00	240.00
5	"Babe" Ruth (A favorite with the Kiddies. Babe Ruth's Own Candy.)	800.00	400.00	240.00
6	"Babe" Ruth (The King of Swat. Babe Ruth's Own Candy.)	800.00	400.00	240.00

1953 Glendale Hot Dogs Tigers

Glendale Meats issued these unnumbered, full-color cards (2-5/8" by 3-3/4") in packages of hot dogs. Featuring Detroit Tigers players, the card fronts contain a player picture plus the player's name, a facsimile autograph, and the Tigers logo. The card reverses carry player statistical and biographical information plus an offer for a trip for two to the World Series. Collectors were advised to mail all the cards they had saved to Glendale Meats. The World Series trip plus 150 other prizes were to be given to the individuals sending in the most cards. As with most cards issued with food products, quality-condition cards are tough to find because of the cards' susceptibilty to stains. The Houtteman card is extremely scarce.

		NR MT	EX	VG
Complete Set:		6000.00	3000.00	1800.
Common Player:		125.00	62.00	37.00
(1)	Matt Batts	125.00	62.00	37.00
(2)	Johnny Bucha	125.00	62.00	37.00
(3)	Frank Carswell	125.00	62.00	37.00
(4)	Jim Delsing	125.00	62.00	37.00
(5)	Walt Dropo	125.00	62.00	37.00
(6)	Hal Erickson	125.00	62.00	37.00
(7)	Paul Foytack	125.00	62.00	37.00
(8)	Owen Friend	150.00	75.00	45.00
(9)	Ned Garver	125.00	62.00	37.00
(10)	Joe Ginsberg	350.00	175.00	105.00
(11)	Ted Gray	125.00	62.00	37.00
(12)	Fred Hatfield	125.00	62.00	37.00
(13)	Ray Herbert	150.00	75.00	45.00
(14)	Bill Hitchcock	125.00	62.00	37.00
(15)	Bill Hoeft	275.00	137.00	82.00
(16)	Art Houtteman	2200.00	1100.00	660.00
(17)	Milt Jordan	200.00	100.00	60.00

		NR MT	EX	VG
(18)	Harvey Kuenn	325.00	162.00	97.00
(19)	Don Lund	125.00	62.00	37.00
(20)	Dave Madison	125.00	62.00	37.00
(21)	Dick Marlowe	125.00	62.00	37.00
(22)	Pat Mullin	125.00	62.00	37.00
(23)	Bob Neiman	125.00	62.00	37.00
(24)	Johnny Pesky	150.00	75.00	45.00
(25)	Jerry Priddy	125.00	62.00	37.00
(26)	Steve Souchock	125.00	62.00	37.00
(27)	Russ Sullivan	125.00	62.00	37.00
(28)	Bill Wight	200.00	100.00	60.00

1952 Globe Printing

		NR MT	EX	VG
Complete Set:		400.00	200.00	125.00

(1)	Al Benton
(2)	Dain Clay
(3)	John Davis
(4)	Dick Faber
(5)	Ben Flowers
(6)	Murray Franklin
(7)	Herb Gorman
(8)	Jack Graham
(9)	Memo Luna
(10)	Lefty O'Doul (PORTRAIT TO WAIST)
(11)	Lefty O'Doul (2ND POSE UNKNOWN)
(12)	Al Olsen
(13)	Jimmie Reese
(14)	Al Richter
(15)	Jack Salveson
(16)	Lou Stringer
(17)	Lonnie Summers
(18)	Jack Tobin

1934 Gold Medal Flour

This set of 12 unnumbered, blank-backed cards was issued by Gold Medal Flour to commemorate the 1934 World Series. The cards, which measure 3-1/4" by 5-3/8", feature members of the Detroit Tigers and the St. Louis Cardinals, who were participants in the '34 World Series.

	NR MT	EX	VG
Complete Set:	450.00	225.00	135.00
Common Player:	22.00	11.00	6.50
(1) Tommy Bridges	22.00	11.00	6.50
(2) Mickey Cochrane	40.00	20.00	12.00
(3) Dizzy Dean	75.00	37.00	22.00
(4) Paul Dean	30.00	15.00	9.00
(5) Frank Frisch	40.00	20.00	12.00
(6) "Goose" Goslin	40.00	20.00	12.00
(7) William Hallahan	22.00	11.00	6.50
(8) Fred Marberry	22.00	11.00	6.50
(9) John "Pepper" Martin	30.00	15.00	9.00
(10) Joe Medwick	40.00	20.00	12.00
(11) William Rogell	22.00	11.00	6.50
(12) "Jo Jo" White	22.00	11.00	6.50

1933 Goudey

Goudey Gum Co.'s first baseball card issue was their 240-card effort in 1933. The cards are color art reproductions of either portrait or action photos. The numbered cards measure 2-3/8" by 2-7/8" in size and carry a short player biography on the reverses. Card #106 (Napoleon Lajoie) is listed in the set though it was not actually issued until 1934. The card is very scarce and is unique in that it carries a 1934 design obverse and a 1933 reverse. The ACC designation for the set is R319.

	NR MT	EX	VG
Complete Set:	85000.00	40000.00	25000.
Common Player: 1-40	150.00	75.00	45.00
Common Player: 41-44	75.00	37.00	22.00
Common Player: 45-52	150.00	75.00	45.00
Common Player: 53-240	75.00	37.00	22.00
1 Benny Bengough	12000.00	2000.00	1050.
2 Arthur (Dazzy) Vance	500.00	200.00	75.00
3 Hugh Critz	150.00	75.00	45.00
4 Henry "Heinie" Schuble	150.00	75.00	45.00
5 Floyd (Babe) Herman	200.00	80.00	35.00
6a Jimmy Dykes (age is 26 in bio)	200.00	80.00	35.00
6b Jimmy Dykes (age is 36 in bio)	200.00	80.00	35.00
7 Ted Lyons	275.00	125.00	50.00
8 Roy Johnson	150.00	75.00	45.00
9 Dave Harris	150.00	75.00	45.00
10 Glenn Myatt	150.00	75.00	45.00
11 Billy Rogell	150.00	75.00	45.00
12 George Pipgras	150.00	75.00	45.00
13 Lafayette Thompson	150.00	75.00	25.00
14 Henry Johnson	150.00	75.00	45.00
15 Victor Sorrell	150.00	75.00	45.00
16 George Blaeholder	150.00	75.00	45.00
17 Watson Clark	150.00	75.00	45.00
18 Herold (Muddy) Ruel	150.00	75.00	45.00
19 Bill Dickey	550.00	275.00	100.00
20 Bill Terry	425.00	200.00	75.00
21 Phil Collins	150.00	75.00	45.00
22 Harold (Pie) Traynor	400.00	200.00	90.00
23 Hazen (Ki-Ki) Cuyler	350.00	175.00	105.00
24 Horace Ford	150.00	75.00	45.00
25 Paul Waner	350.00	175.00	105.00
26 Chalmer Cissell	150.00	75.00	45.00
27 George Connally	150.00	75.00	45.00
28 Dick Bartell	150.00	75.00	45.00
29 Jimmy Foxx	700.00	350.00	150.00
30 Frank Hogan	150.00	75.00	45.00
31 Tony Lazzeri	400.00	200.00	80.00

	NR MT	EX	VG
32 John (Bud) Clancy	150.00	75.00	45.00
33 Ralph Kress	150.00	75.00	45.00
34 Bob O'Farrell	150.00	75.00	45.00
35 Al Simmons	500.00	225.00	90.00
36 Tommy Thevenow	150.00	75.00	45.00
37 Jimmy Wilson	150.00	75.00	45.00
38 Fred Brickell	150.00	75.00	45.00
39 Mark Koenig	150.00	75.00	45.00
40 Taylor Douthit	150.00	75.00	45.00
41 Gus Mancuso	75.00	37.00	22.00
42 Eddie Collins	225.00	100.00	50.00
43 Lew Fonseca	85.00	40.00	20.00
44 Jim Bottomley	225.00	100.00	50.00
45 Larry Benton	150.00	75.00	45.00
46 Ethan Allen	150.00	75.00	45.00
47 Henry "Heinie" Manush	350.00	150.00	50.00
48 Marty McManus	150.00	75.00	45.00
49 Frank Frisch	400.00	200.00	90.00
50 Ed Brandt	150.00	75.00	45.00
51 Charlie Grimm	200.00	100.00	30.00
52 Andy Cohen	150.00	75.00	45.00
53 George Herman (Babe) Ruth	6000.00	3000.00	1800.
54 Ray Kremer	75.00	37.00	22.00
55 Perce (Pat) Malone	75.00	37.00	22.00
56 Charlie Ruffing	250.00	100.00	45.00
57 Earl Clark	75.00	37.00	22.00
58 Frank (Lefty) O'Doul	100.00	50.00	22.00
59 Edmund (Bing) Miller	75.00	37.00	22.00
60 Waite Hoyt	200.00	100.00	45.00
61 Max Bishop	75.00	37.00	22.00
62 "Pepper" Martin	125.00	60.00	22.00
63 Joe Cronin	275.00	125.00	50.00
64 Burleigh Grimes	225.00	100.00	50.00
65 Milton Gaston	75.00	37.00	22.00
66 George Grantham	75.00	37.00	22.00
67 Guy Bush	75.00	37.00	22.00
68 Horace Lisenbee	75.00	37.00	22.00
69 Randy Moore	75.00	37.00	22.00
70 Floyd (Pete) Scott	75.00	37.00	22.00
71 Robert J. Burke	75.00	37.00	22.00
72 Owen Carroll	75.00	37.00	22.00
73 Jesse Haines	200.00	100.00	45.00
74 Eppa Rixey	200.00	100.00	45.00
75 Willie Kamm	75.00	37.00	22.00
76 Gordon (Mickey) Cochrane	250.00	100.00	50.00
77 Adam Comorosky	75.00	37.00	22.00
78 Jack Quinn	75.00	37.00	22.00
79 Urban (Red) Faber	200.00	100.00	45.00
80 Clyde Manion	75.00	37.00	22.00
81 Sam Jones	85.00	40.00	25.00
82 Dibrell Williams	75.00	37.00	22.00
83 Pete Jablonowski	150.00	75.00	45.00
84 Glenn Spencer	75.00	37.00	22.00
85 John Henry "Heinie" Sand	75.00	37.00	22.00
86 Phil Todt	75.00	37.00	22.00
87 Frank O'Rourke	75.00	37.00	22.00
88 Russell Rollings	75.00	37.00	22.00
89 Tris Speaker	450.00	200.00	70.00
90 Jess Petty	75.00	37.00	22.00
91 Tom Zachary	75.00	37.00	22.00
92 Lou Gehrig	4000.00	2000.00	1200.
93 John Welch	75.00	37.00	22.00
94 Bill Walker	75.00	37.00	22.00
95 Alvin Crowder	75.00	37.00	22.00
96 Willis Hudlin	75.00	37.00	22.00
97 Joe Morrissey	75.00	37.00	22.00
98 Walter Berger	75.00	37.00	22.00
99 Tony Cuccinello	75.00	37.00	22.00
100 George Uhle	90.00	45.00	22.00
101 Richard Coffman	75.00	37.00	22.00
102 Travis C. Jackson	200.00	100.00	45.00
103 Earl Combs (Earle)	200.00	100.00	45.00
104 Fred Marberry	75.00	37.00	22.00
105 Bernie Friberg	75.00	37.00	22.00
106 Napoleon (Larry) Lajoie	30000.00	13500.00	7500.
107 Henry (Heinie) Manush	200.00	100.00	45.00
108 Joe Kuhel	75.00	37.00	22.00
109 Joe Cronin	200.00	100.00	45.00
110 Leon "Goose" Goslin	200.00	100.00	45.00
111 Monte Weaver	75.00	37.00	22.00
112 Fred Schulte	75.00	37.00	22.00
113 Oswald Bluege	75.00	37.00	22.00
114 Luke Sewell	75.00	37.00	22.00
115 Cliff Heathcote	75.00	37.00	22.00
116 Eddie Morgan	75.00	37.00	22.00
117 Walter (Rabbit) Maranville	200.00	100.00	45.00
118 Valentine J. (Val) Picinich	75.00	37.00	22.00
119 Rogers Hornsby	500.00	250.00	100.00
120 Carl Reynolds	75.00	37.00	22.00
121 Walter Stewart	75.00	37.00	22.00
122 Alvin Crowder	75.00	37.00	22.00
123 Jack Russell	75.00	37.00	22.00

		NR MT	EX	VG
124	Earl Whitehill	75.00	37.00	22.00
125	Bill Terry	300.00	135.00	60.00
126	Joe Moore	75.00	37.00	22.00
127	Melvin Ott	350.00	150.00	60.00
128	Charles (Chuck) Klein	225.00	100.00	50.00
129	Harold Schumacher	90.00	40.00	20.00
130	Fred Fitzsimmons	75.00	37.00	22.00
131	Fred Frankhouse	75.00	37.00	22.00
132	Jim Elliott	75.00	37.00	22.00
133	Fred Lindstrom	200.00	100.00	45.00
134	Edgar (Sam) Rice	200.00	100.00	45.00
135	Elwood (Woody) English	75.00	37.00	22.00
136	Flint Rhem	75.00	37.00	22.00
137	Fred (Red) Lucas	75.00	37.00	22.00
138	Herb Pennock	200.00	100.00	45.00
139	Ben Cantwell	75.00	37.00	22.00
140	Irving (Bump) Hadley	75.00	37.00	22.00
141	Ray Benge	75.00	37.00	22.00
142	Paul Richards	125.00	60.00	25.00
143	Glenn Wright	85.00	40.00	22.00
144	George Herman (Babe) Ruth	4500.00	1750.00	1050.
145	George Walberg	75.00	37.00	22.00
146	Walter Stewart	75.00	37.00	22.00
147	Leo Durocher	225.00	100.00	45.00
148	Eddie Farrell	75.00	37.00	22.00
149	George Herman (Babe) Ruth	5500.00	2750.00	1650.
150	Ray Kolp	75.00	37.00	22.00
151	D'Arcy (Jake) Flowers	75.00	37.00	22.00
152	James (Zack) Taylor	75.00	37.00	22.00
153	Charles (Buddy) Myer	75.00	37.00	22.00
154	Jimmy Foxx	450.00	225.00	75.00
155	Joe Judge	75.00	37.00	22.00
156	Danny Macfayden (MacFayden)	100.00	50.00	27.00
157	Sam Byrd	100.00	50.00	27.00
158	Morris (Moe) Berg	150.00	70.00	30.00
159	Oswald Bluege	75.00	37.00	22.00
160	Lou Gehrig	4000.00	2000.00	1200.
161	Al Spohrer	75.00	37.00	22.00
162	Leo Mangum	75.00	37.00	22.00
163	Luke Sewell	75.00	37.00	22.00
164	Lloyd Waner	200.00	100.00	45.00
165	Joe Sewell	200.00	100.00	45.00
166	Sam West	75.00	37.00	22.00
167	Jack Russell	75.00	37.00	22.00
168	Leon (Goose) Goslin	200.00	100.00	45.00
169	Al Thomas	75.00	37.00	22.00
170	Harry McCurdy	75.00	37.00	22.00
171	Charley Jamieson	75.00	37.00	22.00
172	Billy Hargrave	75.00	37.00	22.00
173	Roscoe Holm	75.00	37.00	22.00
174	Warren (Curley) Ogden	75.00	37.00	22.00
175	Dan Howley	75.00	37.00	22.00
176	John Ogden	75.00	37.00	22.00
177	Walter French	75.00	37.00	22.00
178	Jackie Warner	75.00	37.00	22.00
179	Fred Leach	75.00	37.00	22.00
180	Eddie Moore	75.00	37.00	22.00
181	George Herman (Babe) Ruth	5500.00	2750.00	1650.
182	Andy High	75.00	37.00	22.00
183	George Walberg	75.00	37.00	22.00
184	Charley Berry	75.00	37.00	22.00
185	Bob Smith	75.00	37.00	22.00
186	John Schulte	75.00	37.00	22.00
187	Henry (Heinie) Manush	200.00	100.00	45.00
188	Rogers Hornsby	500.00	200.00	105.00
189	Joe Cronin	200.00	100.00	45.00
190	Fred Schulte	75.00	37.00	22.00
191	Ben Chapman	125.00	60.00	27.00
192	Walter Brown	125.00	60.00	27.00
193	Lynford Lary	100.00	50.00	27.00
194	Earl Averill	200.00	100.00	45.00
195	Evar Swanson	75.00	37.00	22.00
196	Leroy Mahaffey	75.00	37.00	22.00
197	Richard (Rick) Ferrell	200.00	100.00	45.00
198	Irving (Jack) Burns	75.00	37.00	22.00
199	Tom Bridges	80.00	40.00	22.00
200	Bill Hallahan	75.00	37.00	22.00
201	Ernie Orsatti	75.00	37.00	22.00
202	Charles Leo (Gabby) Hartnett	200.00	100.00	45.00
203	Lonnie Warneke	75.00	37.00	22.00
204	Jackson Riggs Stephenson	125.00	60.00	27.00
205	Henry (Heinie) Meine	75.00	37.00	22.00
206	Gus Suhr	75.00	37.00	22.00
207	Melvin Ott	400.00	200.00	45.00
208	Byrne (Bernie) James	75.00	37.00	22.00
209	Adolfo Luque	75.00	37.00	22.00
210	Virgil Davis	75.00	37.00	22.00
211	Lewis (Hack) Wilson	350.00	175.00	45.00
212	Billy Urbanski	75.00	37.00	22.00
213	Earl Adams	75.00	37.00	22.00

		NR MT	EX	VG
214	John Kerr	75.00	37.00	22.00
215	Russell Van Atta	90.00	45.00	27.00
216	Vernon Gomez	400.00	175.00	45.00
217	Frank Crosetti	200.00	100.00	45.00
218	Wesley Ferrell	100.00	50.00	27.00
219	George (Mule) Haas	75.00	37.00	22.00
220	Robert (Lefty) Grove	500.00	250.00	100.00
221	Dale Alexander	75.00	37.00	22.00
222	Charley Gehringer	350.00	175.00	67.00
223	Jerome (Dizzy) Dean	800.00	400.00	200.00
224	Frank Demaree	75.00	37.00	22.00
225	Bill Jurges	75.00	37.00	22.00
226	Charley Root	90.00	45.00	22.00
227	Bill Herman	200.00	100.00	45.00
228	Tony Piet	75.00	37.00	22.00
229	Floyd Vaughan	200.00	100.00	45.00
230	Carl Hubbell	300.00	150.00	60.00
231	Joe Moore	75.00	37.00	22.00
232	Frank (Lefty) O'Doul	90.00	45.00	22.00
233	Johnny Vergez	75.00	37.00	22.00
234	Carl Hubbell	300.00	150.00	60.00
235	Fred Fitzsimmons	75.00	37.00	22.00
236	George Davis	75.00	37.00	22.00
237	Gus Mancuso	75.00	37.00	22.00
238	Hugh Critz	75.00	37.00	22.00
239	Leroy Parmelee	100.00	50.00	27.00
240	Harold Schumacher	350.00	125.00	15.00

1934 Goudey

The 1934 Goudey set contains 96 cards (2-3/8" by 2-7/8") that feature color art reproductions of actual photographs. The card fronts have two different designs; one featuring a small head-shot photo of Lou Gehrig with the words "Lou Gehrig says..." inside a blue band, while the other design carries a "Chuck Klein says..." and also has his photo. The card backs contain a short player biography that appears to have been written by Gehrig or Klein. The ACC designation for the set is R320.

		NR MT	EX	VG
Complete Set:		25000.00	12500.00	7500.
Common Player:		75.00	37.00	22.00
Common Player: 49-72		90.00	45.00	27.00
Common Player: 73-96		275.00	137.00	82.00
1	Jimmy Foxx	1000.00	250.00	125.00
2	Gordon (Mickey) Cochrane	250.00	125.00	75.00
3	Charlie Grimm	70.00	35.00	21.00
4	Elwood (Woody) English	75.00	37.00	22.00
5	Ed Brandt	75.00	37.00	22.00
6	Jerome (Dizzy) Dean	600.00	300.00	185.00
7	Leo Durocher	200.00	100.00	60.00
8	Tony Piet	75.00	37.00	22.00
9	Ben Chapman	90.00	45.00	27.00
10	Charles (Chuck) Klein	200.00	100.00	60.00
11	Paul Waner	200.00	100.00	60.00
12	Carl Hubbell	250.00	125.00	75.00
13	Frank Frisch	200.00	100.00	60.00
14	Willie Kamm	75.00	37.00	22.00
15	Alvin Crowder	75.00	37.00	22.00
16	Joe Kuhel	75.00	37.00	22.00
17	Hugh Critz	75.00	37.00	22.00
18	Henry (Heinie) Manush	200.00	100.00	60.00
19	Robert (Lefty) Grove	350.00	175.00	105.00
20	Frank Hogan	75.00	37.00	22.00

		NR MT	EX	VG
21	Bill Terry	250.00	125.00	75.00
22	Floyd Vaughan	200.00	100.00	60.00
23	Charley Gehringer	110.00	55.00	33.00
24	Ray Benge	75.00	37.00	22.00
25	Roger Cramer	75.00	37.00	22.00
26	Gerald Walker	75.00	37.00	22.00
27	Luke Appling	200.00	100.00	60.00
28	Ed. Coleman	75.00	37.00	22.00
29	Larry French	75.00	37.00	22.00
30	Julius Solters	75.00	37.00	22.00
31	Baxter Jordan	75.00	37.00	22.00
32	John (Blondy) Ryan	75.00	37.00	22.00
33	Frank (Don) Hurst	75.00	37.00	22.00
34	Charles (Chick) Hafey	200.00	100.00	60.00
35	Ernie Lombardi	200.00	100.00	60.00
36	Walter (Huck) Betts	75.00	37.00	22.00
37	Lou Gehrig	3500.00	1750.00	1050.
38	Oral Hildebrand	75.00	37.00	22.00
39	Fred Walker	75.00	37.00	22.00
40	John Stone	75.00	37.00	22.00
41	George Earnshaw	75.00	37.00	22.00
42	John Allen	90.00	45.00	27.00
43	Dick Porter	75.00	37.00	22.00
44	Tom Bridges	55.00	27.00	16.50
45	Oscar Melillo	75.00	37.00	22.00
46	Joe Stripp	75.00	37.00	22.00
47	John Frederick	75.00	37.00	22.00
48	James (Tex) Carleton	75.00	37.00	22.00
49	Sam Leslie	90.00	45.00	27.00
50	Walter Beck	90.00	45.00	27.00
51	Jim (Rip) Collins	90.00	45.00	27.00
52	Herman Bell	90.00	45.00	27.00
53	George Watkins	90.00	45.00	27.00
54	Wesley Schulmerich	90.00	45.00	27.00
55	Ed Holley	90.00	45.00	27.00
56	Mark Koenig	90.00	45.00	27.00
57	Bill Swift	90.00	45.00	27.00
58	Earl Grace	90.00	45.00	27.00
59	Joe Mowry	90.00	45.00	27.00
60	Lynn Nelson	90.00	45.00	27.00
61	Lou Gehrig	3700.00	1850.00	1150.
62	Henry Greenberg	350.00	175.00	105.00
63	Minter Hayes	90.00	45.00	27.00
64	Frank Grube	90.00	45.00	27.00
65	Cliff Bolton	90.00	45.00	27.00
66	Mel Harder	90.00	45.00	27.00
67	Bob Weiland	90.00	45.00	27.00
68	Bob Johnson	90.00	45.00	27.00
69	John Marcum	90.00	45.00	27.00
70	Ervin (Pete) Fox	90.00	45.00	27.00
71	Lyle Tinning	90.00	45.00	27.00
72	Arndt Jorgens	45.00	22.00	13.50
73	Ed Wells	275.00	137.00	82.00
74	Bob Boken	275.00	137.00	82.00
75	Bill Werber	275.00	137.00	82.00
76	Hal Trosky	275.00	137.00	82.00
77	Joe Vosmik	275.00	137.00	82.00
78	Frank (Pinkey) Higgins	275.00	137.00	82.00
79	Eddie Durham	275.00	137.00	82.00
80	Marty McManus	275.00	137.00	82.00
81	Bob Brown	275.00	137.00	82.00
82	Bill Hallahan	275.00	137.00	82.00
83	Jim Mooney	275.00	137.00	82.00
84	Paul Derringer	300.00	150.00	90.00
85	Adam Comorosky	275.00	137.00	82.00
86	Lloyd Johnson	275.00	137.00	82.00
87	George Darrow	275.00	137.00	82.00
88	Homer Peel	275.00	137.00	82.00
89	Linus Frey	275.00	137.00	82.00
90	Hazen (Ki-Ki) Cuyler	500.00	250.00	150.00
91	Dolph Camilli	275.00	137.00	82.00
92	Steve Larkin	275.00	137.00	82.00
93	Fred Ostermueller	275.00	137.00	82.00
94	Robert A. (Red) Rolfe	350.00	175.00	105.00
95	Myril Hoag	300.00	150.00	90.00
96	Jim DeShong	400.00	100.00	60.00

1935 Goudey

The 1935 Goudey set features four players from the same team on one card. Thirty-six card fronts make up the set with numerous front/back combinations existing. The card backs form nine different puzzles: 1) Tigers Team, 2) Chuck Klein, 3) Frankie Frisch, 4) Mickey Cochrane, 5) Joe Cronin, 6) Jimmy Foxx, 7) Al Simmons, 8) Indians Team, and 9) Senators Team. The cards, which measure 2-3/8" by 2-7/8", have an ACC designation of R321.

	NR MT	EX	VG
Complete Set:	7500.00	3750.00	2250.
Common Player:	70.00	35.00	21.00

		NR MT	EX	VG
(1)	Sparky Adams, Jim Bottomley, Adam Comorosky, Tony Piet	100.00	50.00	30.00
(2)	Ethan Allen, Fred Brickell, Bubber Jonnard, Hack Wilson	100.00	50.00	30.00
(3)	Johnny Allen, Jimmie Deshong (DeShong), Red Rolfe, Dixie Walker	70.00	35.00	21.00
(4)	Luke Appling, Jimmie Dykes, George Earnshaw, Luke Sewell	100.00	50.00	30.00
(5)	Earl Averill, Oral Hildebrand, Willie Kamm, Hal Trosky	100.00	50.00	30.00
(6)	Dick Bartell, Hughie Critz, Gus Mancuso, Mel Ott	70.00	35.00	21.00
(7)	Ray Benge, Fred Fitzsimmons, Mark Koenig, Tom Zachary	70.00	35.00	21.00
(8)	Larry Benton, Ben Cantwell, Flint Rhem, Al Spohrer	70.00	35.00	21.00
(9)	Charlie Berry, Bobby Burke, Red Kress, Dazzy Vance	100.00	50.00	30.00
(10)	Max Bishop, Bill Cissell, Joe Cronin, Carl Reynolds	125.00	62.00	37.00
(11)	George Blaeholder, Dick Coffman, Oscar Melillo, Sammy West	70.00	35.00	21.00
(12)	Cy Blanton, Babe Herman, Tom Padden, Gus Suhr	70.00	35.00	21.00
(13)	Zeke Bonura, Mule Haas, Jackie Hayes, Ted Lyons	100.00	50.00	30.00
(14)	Jim Bottomley, Adam Comorosky, Willis Hudlin, Glenn Myatt	100.00	50.00	30.00
(15)	Ed Brandt, Fred Frankhouse, Shanty Hogan, Gene Moore	70.00	35.00	21.00
(16)	Ed Brandt, Rabbit Maranville, Marty McManus, Babe Ruth	1800.00	900.00	540.00
(17)	Tommy Bridges, Mickey Cochrane, Charlie Gehringer, Billy Rogell	175.00	87.00	52.00
(18)	Jack Burns, Frank Grube, Rollie Hemsley, Bob Weiland	70.00	35.00	21.00
(19)	Guy Bush, Waite Hoyt, Lloyd Waner, Paul Waner	150.00	75.00	45.00
(20)	Sammy Byrd, Danny MacFayden, Pepper Martin, Bob O'Farrell	70.00	35.00	21.00
(21)	Gilly Campbell, Ival Goodman, Alex Kampouris, Billy Meyers (Myers)	70.00	35.00	21.00
(22)	Tex Carleton, Dizzy Dean, Frankie Frisch, Ernie Orsatti	350.00	175.00	105.00
(23)	Watty Clark, Lonny Frey, Sam Leslie, Joe Stripp	70.00	35.00	21.00
(24)	Mickey Cochrane, Willie Kamm, Muddy Ruel, Al Simmons	150.00	75.00	45.00
(25)	Ed Coleman, Doc Cramer, Bob Johnson, Johnny Marcum	70.00	35.00	21.00
(26)	General Crowder, Goose Goslin, Firpo Marberry, Heinie Schuble	100.00	50.00	30.00
(27)	Kiki Cuyler, Woody English, Burleigh Grimes, Chuck Klein	70.00	35.00	21.00
(28)	Bill Dickey, Tony Lazzeri, Pat Malone, Red Ruffing	250.00	125.00	75.00
(29)	Rick Ferrell, Wes Ferrell, Fritz Ostermueller, Bill Werber	100.00	50.00	30.00
(30)	Pete Fox, Hank Greenberg, Schoolboy Rowe, Gee Walker	150.00	75.00	45.00
(31)	Jimmie Foxx, Pinky Higgins, Roy Mahaffey, Dib Williams	250.00	125.00	75.00
(32)	Bump Hadley, Lyn Lary, Heinie Manush, Monte Weaver	100.00	50.00	30.00
(33)	Mel Harder, Bill Knickerbocker, Lefty Stewart, Joe Vosmik	70.00	35.00	21.00

		NR MT	EX	VG
(34)	Travis Jackson, Gus Mancuso, Hal Schumacher, Bill Terry	175.00	87.00	52.00
(35)	Joe Kuhel, Buddy Meyer (Myer), John Stone, Earl Whitehill	70.00	35.00	21.00
(36)	Red Lucas, Tommy Thevenow, Pie Traynor, Glenn Wright	100.00	50.00	30.00

1936 Goudey

FOUL

Over the press boxes.

Walter (Wally) Berger — National League home run king in 1935 with 34 to his credit. He also lead the league for most runs batted in, 130. One of the game's top ranking stars since 1930.

Too high and wide.

BALL

The 1936 Goudey set consists of 25 black and white cards, each measuring 2-3/8" by 2-7/8". A facsimile autograph is positioned on the card fronts. The card backs contain a brief player biography and were to be used by collectors to play a baseball game. Different game situations (out, single, double, etc.) are given on each card. Numerous front/back exist in the set. The ACC designation for the set is R322.

		NR MT	EX	VG
Complete Set:		2000.00	1000.00	600.00
Common Player:		45.00	22.00	13.50
(1)	Walter Berger	55.00	28.00	16.50
(2)	Henry Bonura	45.00	22.00	13.50
(3)	Stan Bordagaray	45.00	22.00	13.50
(4)	Bill Brubaker	45.00	22.00	13.50
(5)	Dolph Camilli	55.00	27.00	16.50
(6)	Clydell Castleman	45.00	22.00	13.50
(7)	"Mickey" Cochrane	175.00	87.00	52.00
(8)	Joe Coscarart	45.00	22.00	13.50
(9)	Frank Crosetti	100.00	50.00	30.00
(10)	"Kiki" Cuyler	125.00	62.00	37.00
(11)	Paul Derringer	55.00	27.00	16.50
(12)	Jimmy Dykes	55.00	27.00	16.50
(13)	"Rick" Ferrell	125.00	62.00	37.00
(14)	"Lefty" Gomez	250.00	125.00	75.00
(15)	Hank Greenberg	250.00	125.00	75.00
(16)	"Bucky" Harris	125.00	62.00	37.00
(17)	"Rolly" Hemsley	45.00	22.00	13.50
(18)	Frank Higgins	45.00	22.00	13.50
(19)	Oral Hildebrand	45.00	22.00	13.50
(20)	"Chuck" Klein	150.00	75.00	45.00
(21)	"Pepper" Martin	55.00	27.00	16.50
(22)	"Buck" Newsom	55.00	27.00	16.50
(23)	Joe Vosmik	45.00	22.00	13.50
(24)	Paul Waner	150.00	75.00	45.00
(25)	Bill Werber	45.00	22.00	13.50

1938 Goudey

Sometimes referred to as the Goudey Heads-Up set, this issue begins numbering (#241) where the 1933 Goudey set left off. On the card fronts, a photo is used for the player's head with the body being a cartoon drawing. Twenty-four different players are pictured twice in the set. Card #'s 241-264 feature plain backgrounds on the card fronts. Card #'s 265-288 contain the same basic design and photo but include small drawings and comments within the background. The card backs contain player statistical and biographical information. The ACC designation for the issue is R323.

— No. 274 —
JOSEPH "JOE" DI MAGGIO

JOE DI MAGGIO, Yankee

BIG LEAGUE
CHEWING GUM
GOUDEY GUM CO.   BOSTON
Made by the originators of
INDIAN GUM

		NR MT	EX	VG
Complete Set:		20000.00	9000.00	5500.
Common Player: 241-264		125.00	62.00	37.00
Common Player: 265-288		150.00	75.00	45.00
241	Charlie Gehringer	500.00	200.00	100.00
242	Ervin Fox	125.00	62.00	37.00
243	Joe Kuhel	125.00	62.00	37.00
244	Frank DeMaree	125.00	62.00	37.00
245	Frank Pytlak	125.00	62.00	37.00
246	Ernie Lombardi	225.00	110.00	60.00
247	Joe Vosmik	125.00	62.00	37.00
248	Dick Bartell	125.00	62.00	37.00
249	Jimmy Foxx	550.00	250.00	150.00
250	Joe DiMaggio	4000.00	1800.00	1000.
251	Bump Hadley	150.00	75.00	45.00
252	Zeke Bonura	125.00	62.00	37.00
253	Hank Greenberg	450.00	200.00	100.00
254	Van Lingle Mungo	150.00	75.00	45.00
255	Julius Solters	125.00	62.00	37.00
256	Vernon Kennedy	125.00	62.00	37.00
257	Al Lopez	200.00	100.00	50.00
258	Bobby Doerr	350.00	175.00	90.00
259	Bill Werber	125.00	62.00	37.00
260	Rudy York	150.00	75.00	45.00
261	Rip Radcliff	125.00	62.00	37.00
262	Joe Ducky Medwick	350.00	175.00	90.00
263	Marvin Owen	125.00	62.00	37.00
264	Bob Feller	750.00	350.00	200.00
265	Charlie Gehringer	450.00	225.00	125.00
266	Ervin Fox	150.00	75.00	45.00
267	Joe Kuhel	150.00	75.00	45.00
268	Frank DeMaree	150.00	75.00	45.00
269	Frank Pytlak	150.00	75.00	45.00
270	Ernie Lombardi	275.00	125.00	67.00
271	Joe Vosmik	150.00	75.00	45.00
272	Dick Bartell	150.00	75.00	45.00
273	Jimmy Foxx	600.00	300.00	165.00
274	Joe DiMaggio	4500.00	2000.00	900.00
275	Bump Hadley	150.00	75.00	45.00
276	Zeke Bonura	150.00	75.00	45.00
277	Hank Greenberg	500.00	250.00	125.00
278	Van Lingle Mungo	150.00	75.00	45.00
279	Julius Solters	150.00	75.00	45.00
280	Vernon Kennedy	150.00	75.00	45.00
281	Al Lopez	250.00	125.00	70.00
282	Bobby Doerr	400.00	200.00	100.00
283	Bill Werber	150.00	75.00	45.00
284	Rudy York	150.00	75.00	45.00
285	Rip Radcliff	150.00	75.00	45.00
286	Joe Ducky Medwick	400.00	200.00	100.00
287	Marvin Owen	150.00	75.00	45.00
288	Bob Feller	900.00	400.00	150.00

1941 Goudey

Goudey Gum Co.'s last set was issued in 1941. The cards, which measure 2-3/8" by 2-7/8" in size, contain black and white photos set against blue, green, red or yellow backgrounds. The player's name, team and position plus the card number are situated in a box at the bottom of the card. The card reverses are blank. The ACC designation for the set is R324.

	NR MT	EX	VG
Complete Set:	3000.00	1500.00	900.00
Common Player:	50.00	25.00	15.00

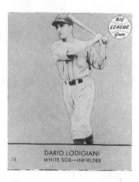

DARIO LODIGIANI
WHITE SOX—INFIELDER

1	Hugh Mulcahy	100.00	50.00	30.00
2	Harlond Clift	50.00	25.00	15.00
3	Louis Chiozza	50.00	25.00	15.00
4	Warren (Buddy) Rosar	50.00	25.00	15.00
5	George McQuinn	50.00	25.00	15.00
6	Emerson Dickman	50.00	25.00	15.00
7	Wayne Ambler	50.00	25.00	15.00
8	Bob Muncrief	50.00	25.00	15.00
9	Bill Dietrich	50.00	25.00	15.00
10	Taft Wright	50.00	25.00	15.00
11	Don Heffner	50.00	25.00	15.00
12	Fritz Ostermueller	50.00	25.00	15.00
13	Frank Hayes	50.00	25.00	15.00
14	John (Jack) Kramer	50.00	25.00	15.00
15	Dario Lodigiani	50.00	25.00	15.00
16	George Case	50.00	25.00	15.00
17	Vito Tamulis	50.00	25.00	15.00
18	Whitlow Wyatt	50.00	25.00	15.00
19	Bill Posedel	50.00	25.00	15.00
20	Carl Hubbell	175.00	90.00	50.00
21	Harold Warstler	175.00	90.00	50.00
22	Joe Sullivan	250.00	125.00	70.00
23	Norman (Babe) Young	175.00	90.00	50.00
24	Stanley Andrews	250.00	125.00	70.00
25	Morris Arnovich	175.00	90.00	50.00
26	Elburt Fletcher	50.00	25.00	15.00
27	Bill Crouch	60.00	30.00	18.00
28	Al Todd	50.00	25.00	15.00
29	Debs Garms	50.00	25.00	15.00
30	Jim Tobin	50.00	25.00	15.00
31	Chester Ross	50.00	25.00	15.00
32	George Coffman	60.00	30.00	18.00
33	Mel Ott	275.00	150.00	80.00

1887 Gypsy Queens

The 1887 Gypsy Queen set is very closely related to the N172 Old Judge set and employs the same poses. The Gypsy Queens are easily identified by the words "Gypsy Queen" along the top of the cards. A line near the bottom lists the player's name, position and team, followed by an 1887 copyright line and words "Cigarettes" and "Goodwin & Co. N.Y." Although the checklist is still considered incomplete, 133 different poses have been discovered so far. Collectors should be aware that the Gypsy Queens were issued in two distinct sizes, the more common version measuring 1-1/2" by 2-1/2" (same as Old

Judge) and a larger size measuring 2" by 3-1/2" which are considered extremely rare. The large Gypsy Queens are identical in format to the smaller size.

		NR MT	EX	VG
	Complete Set:	99000.00	50000.00	20000.
	Common Player:	350.00	150.00	50.00
(1)	Tug Arundel	350.00	150.00	50.00
(2)	Fido Baldwin	350.00	150.00	50.00
(3)	Samuel Barkley (fielding)	350.00	150.00	50.00
(4)	Samuel Barkley (tagging player)	350.00	150.00	50.00
(5)	Handsome Boyle	350.00	150.00	50.00
(6)	Dan Brouthers (looking at ball)	1000.00	500.00	190.00
(7)	Dan Brouthers (looking to right)	1000.00	500.00	190.00
(8a)	California Brown (New York, throwing, large size)	4500.00	2000.00	900.00
(8b)	California Brown (New York, throwing, small size)	350.00	150.00	50.00
(9)	California Brown (New York, wearing mask)	350.00	150.00	50.00
(10)	Thomas Brown (Pittsburg, catching)	350.00	150.00	50.00
(11)	Thomas Brown (Pittsburg, with bat)	350.00	150.00	50.00
(12)	Black Jack Burdock	350.00	150.00	50.00
(13)	Watch Burnham	350.00	150.00	50.00
(14)	Doc Bushong	350.00	150.00	50.00
(15)	Patsy Cahill	350.00	150.00	50.00
(16)	Frederick Carroll	350.00	150.00	50.00
(17)	Parisian Bob Caruthers	350.00	150.00	50.00
(18)	Jack Clements (hands on knees)	350.00	150.00	50.00
(19)	Jack Clements (with bat)	350.00	150.00	50.00
(20)	John Coleman	350.00	150.00	50.00
(21)	Commy Comiskey	1000.00	500.00	190.00
(22a)	Roger Connor (large size)	7000.00	3000.00	1250.
(22b)	Roger Connor (small size)	1000.00	500.00	190.
(23)	Dick Conway	350.00	150.00	50.00
(24)	Larry Corcoran	350.00	150.00	50.00
(25)	Samuel Crane (fielding)	350.00	150.00	50.00
(26)	Samuel Crane (with bat)	350.00	150.00	50.00
(27)	Edward Dailey	350.00	150.00	50.00
(28)	Abner Dalrymple	350.00	150.00	50.00
(29)	Dell Darling	350.00	150.00	50.00
(30)	Pat Dealey (bat at side)	350.00	150.00	50.00
(31)	Pat Dealey (bat on right shoulder)	350.00	150.00	50.00
(32)	Jerry Denny (catching)	350.00	150.00	50.00
(33)	Jerry Denny (with bat)	350.00	150.00	50.00
(34)	Jim Donnelly	350.00	150.00	50.00
(35)	Mike Dorgan	350.00	150.00	50.00
(36)	Buck Ewing (large size)	7000.00	3000.00	1250.
(37)	Buck Ewing (small size)	1000.00	500.00	190.00
(38)	Jack Farrell (bat at side)	350.00	150.00	50.00
(39)	Jack Farrell (bat in air)	350.00	150.00	50.00
(40)	Jack Farrell (fielding)	350.00	150.00	50.00
(41)	Jack Farrell (hands on thighs)	350.00	150.00	50.00
(42)	Charlie Ferguson (hands at chest)	350.00	150.00	50.00
(43)	Charlie Ferguson (tagging player)	350.00	150.00	50.00
(44)	Charlie Ferguson (with bat)	350.00	150.00	50.00
(45)	Jocko Fields (catching)	350.00	150.00	50.00
(46)	Jocko Fields (throwing)	350.00	150.00	50.00
(47)	Dave Foutz	350.00	150.00	50.00
(48)	Honest John Gaffney	350.00	150.00	50.00
(49)	Pud Galvin (with bat)	1000.00	500.00	190.00
(50)	Pud Galvin (without bat)	1000.00	500.00	190.00
(51)	Emil Geiss (hands above waist)	350.00	150.00	50.00
(52)	Emil Geiss (right hand extended)	350.00	150.00	50.00
(53)	Barney Gilligan	350.00	150.00	50.00
(54)	Pebbly Jack Glasscock (hands on knees)	350.00	150.00	50.00
(55)	Pebbly Jack Glasscock (throwing)	350.00	150.00	50.00
(56)	Pebbly Jack Glasscock (with bat)	350.00	150.00	50.00
(57)	Will Gleason	350.00	150.00	50.00
(58)	Piano Legs Gore (fielding)	350.00	150.00	50.00
(59)	Piano Legs Gore (hand at head level)	350.00	150.00	50.00
(60)	Ed Greer	350.00	150.00	50.00
(61)	Tom Gunning (stooping to catch low ball on left)	350.00	150.00	50.00
(62)	Tom Gunning (bending, hands by right knee)	350.00	150.00	50.00

		NR MT	EX	VG
(63)	Ned Hanlon (catching)	350.00	150.00	50.00
(64)	Ned Hanlon (with bat)	350.00	150.00	50.00
(65)	Pa Harkins (hands above waist)			
		350.00	150.00	50.00
(66)	Pa Harkins (throwing)	350.00	150.00	50.00
(67)	Egyptian Healey	350.00	150.00	50.00
(68)	Paul Hines	350.00	150.00	50.00
(69)	Joe Hornung	350.00	150.00	50.00
(70)	Nat Hudson	350.00	150.00	50.00
(71)	Cutrate Irwin	350.00	150.00	50.00
(72)	Dick Johnston (catching)	350.00	150.00	50.00
(73)	Dick Johnston (with bat)	350.00	150.00	50.00
(74a)	Tim Keefe (pitching, hands at chest, large			
	size)	7000.00	3000.00	1250.
(74b)	Tim Keefe (pitching, hands at chest, small			
	size)	1000.00	500.00	190.00
(75)	Tim Keefe (pitching, hands above waist,			
	facing front)	1000.00	500.00	190.00
(76)	Tim Keefe (right hand extended at head			
	level)	1000.00	500.00	190.00
(77)	Tim Keefe (with bat)	1000.00	500.00	190.00
(78)	King Kelly (catching)	1200.00	550.00	200.00
(79)	King Kelly (portrait)	1200.00	550.00	200.00
(80a)	King Kelly (with bat, lg. size)	7000.00	3000.00	1250.
(80b)	King Kelly (with bat, sm. size)	1200.00	550.00	200.00
(81)	Rudy Kemmler	350.00	150.00	50.00
(82)	Bill Krieg (catching)	350.00	150.00	50.00
(83)	Bill Krieg (with bat)	350.00	150.00	50.00
(84)	Arlie Latham	350.00	150.00	50.00
(85)	Mike Mattimore (hands above head)			
		350.00	150.00	50.00
(86)	Mike Mattimore (hands at neck)			
		350.00	150.00	50.00
(87)	Tommy McCarthy (catching)	1000.00	500.00	190.00
(88)	Tommy McCarthy (with bat)	1000.00	500.00	190.00
(89)	Bill McClellan	350.00	150.00	50.00
(90)	Jim McCormick	350.00	150.00	50.00
(91)	Jack McGeachy	350.00	150.00	50.00
(92)	Deacon McGuire	350.00	150.00	50.00
(93)	George Myers (Indianapolis, stooping)			
		350.00	150.00	50.00
(94)	George Myers (Indianapolis, with bat)			
		350.00	150.00	50.00
(95)	Al Myers (Washington)	350.00	150.00	50.00
(96)	Little Nick Nicol	350.00	150.00	50.00
(97)	Hank O'Day (ball in hand)	350.00	150.00	50.00
(98)	Hank O'Day (with bat)	350.00	150.00	50.00
(99)	Tip O'Neill	350.00	150.00	50.00
(100)	George Pinkney	350.00	150.00	50.00
(101)	Hardy Richardson (Detroit)	350.00	150.00	50.00
(102)	Danny Richardson (New York, large size)			
		4500.00	2000.00	900.00
(103)	Danny Richardson (New York, small size)			
		350.00	150.00	50.00
(104)	Yank Robinson	350.00	150.00	50.00
(105)	Jack Rowe	350.00	150.00	50.00
(106)	Emmett Seery (arms folded)	350.00	150.00	50.00
(107)	Emmett Seery (ball in hands)	350.00	150.00	50.00
(108)	Emmett Seery (catching)	350.00	150.00	50.00
(109)	George Shoch	350.00	150.00	50.00
(110)	Otto Shomberg (Schomberg)	350.00	150.00	50.00
(111)	Pap Smith	350.00	150.00	50.00
(112)	Cannonball Stemmyer (Stemmeyer)			
	(pitching)	350.00	150.00	50.00
(113)	Cannonball Stemmyer (Stemmeyer) (with			
	bat)	350.00	150.00	50.00
(114)	Ezra Sutton (with bat)	350.00	150.00	50.00
(115)	Big Sam Thompson (arms folded)			
		1000.00	500.00	190.00
(116)	Big Sam Thompson (bat at side)			
		1000.00	500.00	190.00
(117)	Big Sam Thompson (swinging at ball)			
		1000.00	500.00	190.00
(118)	Silent Mike Tiernan (lg. size)	4500.00	2000.00	900.00
(119)	Stephen Toole	350.00	150.00	50.00
(120)	Larry Twitchell (hands by chest)			
		350.00	150.00	50.00
(121)	Larry Twitchell (right hand extended)			
		350.00	150.00	50.00
(122)	Chris Von Der Ahe	350.00	150.00	50.00
(123)	Monte Ward (large size)	7000.00	3000.00	1250.
(124)	Curt Welch	350.00	150.00	50.00
(125)	Art Whitney (Pittsburg, bending)			
		350.00	150.00	50.00
(126)	Art Whitney (Pittsburg, with bat)			
		350.00	150.00	50.00
(127)	Grasshopper Whitney (Washington)			
		350.00	150.00	50.00
(128)	Medoc Wise	350.00	150.00	50.00
(129)	George "Dandy" Wood	350.00	150.00	50.00

H

1910 H801-7 Old Mill Cabinets

Similar in size and style to the more popular T3 Turkey Red cabinet cards of the same period, the Old Mill cabinets are much scarcer and picture fewer players. Issued in 1910 as a premium by Old Mill Cigarettes, these minor league cards measure approximately 5-3/8" by 7-5/8". Unlike the Turkey Reds, which feature full-color lithographs, the Old Mill cabinet cards picture the players in black and white photos surrounded by a wide tan border. The player's last name is printed in black in the lower left corner, while his team designation appears in the lower right corner. The backs of the cards carry an advertisement for Old Mill cigarettes. There are 29 known subjects in the set, all players from the old Virginia League. Only two of them (Enos Kirkpatrick and Clarence Munson) ever reached the major leagues. Twenty-five of the 29 players were also featured in the second series of the T-210 set, a massive 640-card set also issued by Old Mill Cigarettes the same year. The Old Mill cabinet cards carry the ACC designation H801-7.

		NR MT	EX	VG
Complete Set:		8000.00	4000.00	2400.
Common Player:		275.00	137.00	82.00
(1)	Bentley	275.00	137.00	82.00
(2)	Bowen	275.00	137.00	82.00
(3)	Brazile (Brazell)	275.00	137.00	82.00
(4)	Bush (Busch)	275.00	137.00	82.00
(5)	Bussey	275.00	137.00	82.00
(6)	Cross	275.00	137.00	82.00
(7)	Derrick	275.00	137.00	82.00
(8)	Doane	275.00	137.00	82.00
(9)	Doyle	275.00	137.00	82.00
(10)	Fox	275.00	137.00	82.00
(11)	Griffin	275.00	137.00	82.00
(12)	Hearn	275.00	137.00	82.00
(13)	Hooker	275.00	137.00	82.00
(14)	Kirkpatrick	275.00	137.00	82.00
(15)	Laughlin	275.00	137.00	82.00
(16)	McKevitt	275.00	137.00	82.00
(17)	Munson	275.00	137.00	82.00
(18)	Noojin (Noojin)	275.00	137.00	82.00
(19)	O'Halloran	275.00	137.00	82.00
(20)	Pressly	275.00	137.00	82.00
(21)	Revelle	275.00	137.00	82.00
(22)	A. Smith	275.00	137.00	82.00
(23)	Spratt	275.00	137.00	82.00
(24)	Simmons	275.00	137.00	82.00
(25)	Titman	275.00	137.00	82.00
(26)	Walters	275.00	137.00	82.00
(27)	Wallace	275.00	137.00	82.00
(28)	Weherell (Wehrell)	275.00	137.00	82.00
(29)	Woolums	275.00	137.00	82.00

A player's name in *italic* indicates a rookie card. An **(FC)** indicates a player's first card for that particular card company.

1886 H812 New York Baseball Club

This extremely rare 19th Century baseball card issue can be classified under the general category of "trade" cards, a popular advertising vehicle of the period. The cards measure 3" by 4-3/4" and feature blue line drawings of members of the "New York Base Ball Club," which is printed along the top. As was common with this type of trade card, the bottom was left blank to accomodate various messages. The known examples of this set carry ads for local tobacco merchants, and the player potraits are all based on the photographs used in the N167 Goodwin set. The cards, which have been assigned an ACC designation of H812, are printed on thin paper rather than cardboard.

		NR MT	EX	VG
Complete Set:		34000.00	17000.00	10200.
Common Player:		3000.00	1500.00	900.00
(1)	T. Dealsey	3000.00	1500.00	900.00
(2)	M. Dorgan	3000.00	1500.00	900.00
(3)	T. Esterbrook	3000.00	1500.00	900.00
(4)	W. Ewing	5000.00	2500.00	1500.
(5)	J. Gerhardt	3000.00	1500.00	900.00
(6)	J. O'Rourke	5000.00	2500.00	1500.
(7)	D. Richardson	3000.00	1500.00	900.00
(8)	M. Welch	5000.00	2500.00	1500.

1887 H891 Tobin Lithographs

The Tobin lithographs, measuring 3" by 4-1/2", were typical of the various "trade" cards that were popular advertising vehicles cin the late 19th Century. Found in both black and white and color, the Tobin "lithos" include 10 cards depicting caricature action drawings of popular baseball players of the 1887-1888 era. Each cartoon-like drawing is accompanied by a colorful caption along with the player's name in parenthesis below. The team affiliation is printed in the upper left corner, while a large space in the upper right corner was left blank to

accomodate advertising messages. As a result, Tobin cards have been found with this space displaying ads for various cigarettes and other products or left blank. Similarly the backs of te cards are also found either blank or with advertising. The set takes its name from the manufacturer, whose name ("Tobin N.Y." appears in the lower right corner of each card.

		NR MT	EX	VG
Complete Set:		2800.00	1400.00	850.00
Common Player:		200.00	100.00	60.00
(1)	"Go It Old Boy" (Ed Andrews)	200.00	100.00	60.00
(2)	"Oh, Come Off!" (Cap Anson)	600.00	300.00	175.00
(3)	"Watch Me Soak it" (Dan Brouthers)	300.00	150.00	90.00
(4)	"Not Onto It" (Charlie Ferguson)	200.00	100.00	60.00
(5)	"Struck By A Cyclone" (Pebbly Jack Glasscock)	200.00	100.00	60.00
(6)	"An Anxious Moment" (Paul Hines)	200.00	100.00	60.00
(7)	"Where'l You Have It?" (Tim Keefe)	300.00	150.00	90.00
(8)	"The Flower Of The Flock" (Our Own Kelly)	300.00	150.00	90.00
(9)	"A Slide For Home" (Jim M'Cormick) (McCormick)	200.00	100.00	60.00
(10)	"Ain't It A Daisy?" (Smiling Mickey Welch)	300.00	150.00	90.00

1949 Hage's Dairy

Hage's Dairy of California began a three-year run of regional baseball cards featuring Pacific Coast League players in 1949. Despite being produced by the local dairy, the cards were actually distributed inside popcorn boxes at the concession stand in Lane Field Park, home of the P.C.L. San Diego Padres. The 1949 set, like the following two years, was printed on a thin stock measuring 2-5/8" by 3-1/8". The checklist consists of 105 different cards, including several different poses for some of the players. Cards were continually being added or withdrawn to reflect roster changes on the minor league clubs. The Hage's sets were dominated by San Diego players, but also included representatives from the seven other P.C.L. teams. The 1949 cards can be found in four different tints - sepia, green, blue, and black and white. The unnumbered cards have blank backs. The player's name and team appear inside a box in the front of the card, and the 1949 cards can be dated by the large (quarter-inch) type used for the team names, which are sometimes referred to by city and other times by nickname.

		NR MT	EX	VG
Complete Set:		2800.00	1400.00	840.00
Common Player:		25.00	12.50	7.50
(1)	"Buster" Adams	25.00	12.50	7.50
(2)	"Red" Adams	25.00	12.50	7.50
(3)	Lee Anthony	25.00	12.50	7.50
(4)	Rinaldo Ardizoia	25.00	12.50	7.50
(5)	Del Baker	25.00	12.50	7.50

		NR MT	EX	VG
(6)	Ed Basinski	25.00	12.50	7.50
(7)	Jim Baxes	25.00	12.50	7.50
(8)	Heinz Becker	25.00	12.50	7.50
(9)	Herman Besse	25.00	12.50	7.50
(10)	Tom Bridges	30.00	15.00	9.00
(11)	Gene Brocker	25.00	12.50	7.50
(12)	Ralph Bucton	25.00	12.50	7.50
(13)	Mickey Burnett	25.00	12.50	7.50
(14)	Dain Clay (pose)	25.00	12.50	7.50
(15)	Dain Clay (batting)	25.00	12.50	7.50
(16)	Dain Corriden, Jim Reese	25.00	12.50	7.50
(17)	Pete Coscarart	25.00	12.50	7.50
(18)	Dom Dallessandro	25.00	12.50	7.50
(19)	Con Dempsey	25.00	12.50	7.50
(20)	Vince DiBiasi	25.00	12.50	7.50
(21)	Luke Easter (batting stance)	30.00	15.00	9.00
(22)	Luke Easter (batting follow thru)	30.00	15.00	9.00
(23)	Ed Fernandez	25.00	12.50	7.50
(24)	Les Fleming	25.00	12.50	7.50
(25)	Jess Flores	25.00	12.50	7.50
(26)	Cecil Garriott	25.00	12.50	7.50
(27)	Charles Gassaway	25.00	12.50	7.50
(28)	Mickey Grasso	25.00	12.50	7.50
(29)	Will Hafey (pitching)	25.00	12.50	7.50
(30)	Will Hafey (pose)	25.00	12.50	7.50
(31)	"Jeep" Handley	25.00	12.50	7.50
(32)	"Bucky" Harris (pose)	40.00	20.00	12.00
(33)	"Bucky" Harris (shouting)	40.00	20.00	12.00
(34)	Roy Helser	25.00	12.50	7.50
(35)	Lloyd Hittle	25.00	12.50	7.50
(36)	Ralph Hodgin	25.00	12.50	7.50
(37)	Leroy Jarvis	25.00	12.50	7.50
(38)	John Jensen	25.00	12.50	7.50
(39)	Al Jurisich	25.00	12.50	7.50
(40)	Herb Karpel	25.00	12.50	7.50
(41)	Frank Kelleher	25.00	12.50	7.50
(42)	Bill Kelly	25.00	12.50	7.50
(43)	Bob Kelly	25.00	12.50	7.50
(44)	Frank Kerr	25.00	12.50	7.50
(45)	Thomas Kipp	25.00	12.50	7.50
(46)	Al Lien	25.00	12.50	7.50
(47)	Lyman Linde (pose)	25.00	12.50	7.50
(48)	Lyman Linde (pitching)	25.00	12.50	7.50
(49)	Dennis Luby	25.00	12.50	7.50
(50)	"Red" Lynn	25.00	12.50	7.50
(51)	Pat Malone	25.00	12.50	7.50
(52)	Billy Martin	100.00	50.00	30.00
(53)	Joe Marty	25.00	12.50	7.50
(54)	Cliff Melton	25.00	12.50	7.50
(55)	Steve Mesner	25.00	12.50	7.50
(56)	Leon Mohr	25.00	12.50	7.50
(57)	"Butch" Moran	25.00	12.50	7.50
(58)	Glen Moulder	25.00	12.50	7.50
(59)	Steve Nagy	25.00	12.50	7.50
(60)	Roy Nicely	25.00	12.50	7.50
(61)	Walt Nothe	25.00	12.50	7.50
(62)	John O'Neill	25.00	12.50	7.50
(63)	"Pluto" Oliver	25.00	12.50	7.50
(64)	Al Olsen (pose)	25.00	12.50	7.50
(65)	Al Olsen (throwing)	25.00	12.50	7.50
(66)	Johnny Ostrowski	25.00	12.50	7.50
(67)	Ray Partee	25.00	12.50	7.50
(68)	Bill Raimondi	25.00	12.50	7.50
(69)	Bill Ramsey	25.00	12.50	7.50
(70)	Len Ratto	25.00	12.50	7.50
(71)	Xavier Rescigno	25.00	12.50	7.50
(72)	John Ritchey (batting)	25.00	12.50	7.50
(73)	John Ritchey (catching)	25.00	12.50	7.50
(74)	Mickey Rocco	25.00	12.50	7.50
(75)	John Rucker	25.00	12.50	7.50
(76)	Clarence Russell	25.00	12.50	7.50
(77)	Jack Salverson	25.00	12.50	7.50
(78)	Bill Schuster	25.00	12.50	7.50
(79)	Tom Seats	25.00	12.50	7.50
(80)	Neil Sheridan	25.00	12.50	7.50
(81)	Vince Shupe	25.00	12.50	7.50
(82)	Joe Sprinz	25.00	12.50	7.50
(83)	Chuck Stevens	25.00	12.50	7.50
(84)	Harvey Storey	25.00	12.50	7.50
(85)	Jim Tabor (Sacramento)	25.00	12.50	7.50
(86)	Jim Tabor (Seattle)	25.00	12.50	7.50
(87)	"Junior" Thompson	25.00	12.50	7.50
(88)	Arky Vaughn	45.00	22.00	13.50
(89)	Jackie Warner	25.00	12.50	7.50
(90)	Jim Warner	25.00	12.50	7.50
(91)	Dick Wenner	25.00	12.50	7.50
(92)	Max West (pose)	25.00	12.50	7.50
(93)	Max West (batting swing)	25.00	12.50	7.50
(94)	Max West (batting follow-thru)	25.00	12.50	7.50
(95)	Hank Weyse	25.00	12.50	7.50
(96)	"Fuzzy" White	25.00	12.50	7.50
(97)	Jo Jo White	25.00	12.50	7.50

		NR MT	EX	VG
(98)	Artie Wilson	25.00	12.50	7.50
(99)	Bill Wilson	25.00	12.50	7.50
(100)	Bobbie Wilson (pose)	25.00	12.50	7.50
(101)	Bobbie Wilson (pitching)	25.00	12.50	7.50
(102)	"Pinky" Woods	25.00	12.50	7.50
(103)	Tony York	25.00	12.50	7.50
(104)	Del Young	25.00	12.50	7.50
(105)	Frank Zak	25.00	12.50	7.50

1950 Hage's Dairy

Perfect team for every taste

GEORGE ZUVERINK : Playing his first season of Triple A baseball, Zuverink already is one of the mainstays of the San Diego Padre mound staff. Is with the Padres on option from Cleveland and is expected to be in the major leagues before long.

The 1950 P.C.L. set from Hage's Dairy was similar in design and size (2-5/8" by 3-1/8") to the previous year and was again distributed in popcorn boxes at the San Diego stadium. The 1950 set is found with either a blank back or a back containing an advertisement for Hage's Ice Cream, "Your Favorite Brand". The advertising backs also contain the player's name and brief 1949 statistics at the bottom. There are 126 different cards in the 1950 set, including different poses of the players. Again, Padres dominate the unnumbered set with lesser representation from the other P.C.L. clubs. For the 1950 edition all team names are referred to by city (no nicknames) and the typeface is smaller.

		NR MT	EX	VG
Complete Set:		2000.00	1000.00	600.00
Common Player:		15.00	7.50	4.50
(1)	"Buster" Adams (kneeling)	15.00	7.50	4.50
(2a)	"Buster" Adams (batting follow-thru, with inscription)	15.00	7.50	4.50
(2b)	"Buster" Adams (batting follow-thru, no inscription)	15.00	7.50	4.50
(2c)	"Buster" Adams (batting follow-thru, body to left)	15.00	7.50	4.50
3a	"Buster" Adams (batting stance, caption box touching waist)	15.00	7.50	4.50
(3b)	"Buster" Adams (batting stance, caption box not touching waist)	15.00	7.50	4.50
(4)	"Red" Adams	15.00	7.50	4.50
(5)	Dewey Adkins (photo actually Albie Glossop)	15.00	7.50	4.50
(6)	Rinaldo Ardizoia	15.00	7.50	4.50
(7)	Jose Bache	15.00	7.50	4.50
(8a)	Del Baker, Jim Reese (bat visible at lower right)	15.00	7.50	4.50
(8b)	Del Baker, Jim Reese (no bat visible)	15.00	7.50	4.50
(9)	George Bamberger	15.00	7.50	4.50
(10)	Richard Barrett	15.00	7.50	4.50
(11)	Frank Baumholtz	25.00	12.50	7.50
(12)	Henry Behrman	15.00	7.50	4.50
(13)	Bill Bevens	25.00	12.50	7.50
(14)	Ernie Bickhaus	15.00	7.50	4.50
(15)	Bill Burgher (pose)	15.00	7.50	4.50
(16)	Bill Burgher (catching)	15.00	7.50	4.50
(17)	Mark Christman	15.00	7.50	4.50
(18)	Clint Conaster	15.00	7.50	4.50
(19)	Herb Conyers (fielding)	15.00	7.50	4.50
(20)	Herb Conyers (batting)	15.00	7.50	4.50
(21)	Jim Davis	15.00	7.50	4.50
(22)	Ted Del Guercio	15.00	7.50	4.50
(23)	Vince DiBiasi	15.00	7.50	4.50
(24)	Jess Dobernic	15.00	7.50	4.50

		NR MT	EX	VG
(25)	"Red" Embree (pose)	15.00	7.50	4.50
(26)	"Red" Embree (pitching)	15.00	7.50	4.50
(27)	Elbie Fletcher	15.00	7.50	4.50
(28)	Guy Fletcher	15.00	7.50	4.50
(29)	Tony Freitas	15.00	7.50	4.50
(30)	Denny Galehouse	15.00	7.50	4.50
(31)	Jack Graham (pose, looking to left) 15.00		7.50	4.50
(32)	Jack Graham (pose, looking straight ahead)	15.00	7.50	4.50
(33)	Jack Graham (batting swing)	15.00	7.50	4.50
(34)	Jack Graham (batting stance)	15.00	7.50	4.50
(35)	Orval Grove	15.00	7.50	4.50
(36)	Lee Handley	15.00	7.50	4.50
(37)	Ralph Hodgin	15.00	7.50	4.50
(38)	Don Johnson	15.00	7.50	4.50
(39)	Al Jurisich (pose)	15.00	7.50	4.50
(40)	Al Jurisich (pitching wind-up)	15.00	7.50	4.50
(41)	Al Jurisich (pitching follow-thru)	15.00	7.50	4.50
(42)	Bill Kelly	15.00	7.50	4.50
(43)	Frank Kerr	15.00	7.50	4.50
(44)	Tom Kipp (pose)	15.00	7.50	4.50
(45)	Tom Kipp (pitching)	15.00	7.50	4.50
(46)	Mel Knezovich	15.00	7.50	4.50
(47)	Red Kress	15.00	7.50	4.50
(48)	Dario Lodigiani	15.00	7.50	4.50
(49)	Dennis Luby (pose)	15.00	7.50	4.50
(50)	Dennis Luby (throwing)	15.00	7.50	4.50
(51)	Al Lyons	15.00	7.50	4.50
(52)	Clarence Maddern	15.00	7.50	4.50
(53)	Joe Marty	15.00	7.50	4.50
(54)	Bob McCall	15.00	7.50	4.50
(55)	Cal McIrvin	15.00	7.50	4.50
(56)	Orestes Minoso (batting follow-thru)	40.00	20.00	12.00
(57)	Orestes Minoso (bunting)	40.00	20.00	12.00
(58)	Leon Mohr	15.00	7.50	4.50
(59)	Dee Moore (batting)	15.00	7.50	4.50
(60)	Dee Moore (catching)	15.00	7.50	4.50
(61)	Jim Moran	15.00	7.50	4.50
(62)	Glen Moulder	15.00	7.50	4.50
(63)	Milt Neilsen (pose)	15.00	7.50	4.50
(64)	Milt Neilsen (batting)	15.00	7.50	4.50
(65)	Milt Neilsen (throwing)	15.00	7.50	4.50
(66)	Rube Novotney	15.00	7.50	4.50
(67)	Al Olsen	15.00	7.50	4.50
(68)	Manny Perez	15.00	7.50	4.50
(69)	Bill Raemondi (Raimondi)	15.00	7.50	4.50
(70)	Len Ratto	15.00	7.50	4.50
(71)	Mickey Rocco	15.00	7.50	4.50
(72)	Marv Rotblatt	15.00	7.50	4.50
(73)	Lynwood Rowe (pose)	25.00	12.50	7.50
(74)	Lynwood Rowe (pitching)	25.00	12.50	7.50
(75)	Clarence Russell	15.00	7.50	4.50
(76)	Hal Saltzman (pitching follow-thru)	15.00	7.50	4.50
(77)	Hal Saltzman (pitching wind-up)	15.00	7.50	4.50
(78)	Hal Saltzman (pitching, leg in air)	15.00	7.50	4.50
(79)	Bob Savage (pose)	15.00	7.50	4.50
(80)	Bob Savage (pitching)	15.00	7.50	4.50
(81)	Charlie Schanz	15.00	7.50	4.50
(82)	Bill Schuster	15.00	7.50	4.50
(83)	Neil Sheridan	15.00	7.50	4.50
(84)	Harry Simpson (batting swing)	15.00	7.50	4.50
(85)	Harry Simpson (batting stance)	15.00	7.50	4.50
(86)	Harry Simpson (batting stance, close up)	15.00	7.50	4.50
(87)	Harry Simpson (batting follow-thru)	15.00	7.50	4.50
(88)	Elmer Singleton	15.00	7.50	4.50
(89)	Al Smith (pose)	15.00	7.50	4.50
(90)	Al Smith (batting stance)	15.00	7.50	4.50
(91)	Al Smith (fielding)	15.00	7.50	4.50
(92)	Alphonse Smith (glove above knee)	15.00	7.50	4.50
(93)	Alphonse Smith (glove below knee)	15.00	7.50	4.50
(94)	Steve Souchock	15.00	7.50	4.50
(95)	Jim Steiner	15.00	7.50	4.50
(96)	Harvey Storey (batting stance)	15.00	7.50	4.50
(97)	Harvey Storey (swinging bat)	15.00	7.50	4.50
(98)	Harvey Storey (throwing)	15.00	7.50	4.50
(99)	Harvey Storey (fielding, ball in glove)	15.00	7.50	4.50
(100)	Max Surkont	15.00	7.50	4.50
(101)	Jim Tabor	15.00	7.50	4.50
(102)	Forrest Thompson	15.00	7.50	4.50
(103)	Mike Tresh (pose)	15.00	7.50	4.50
(104)	Mike Tresh (catching)	15.00	7.50	4.50
(105)	Kenny Washington	15.00	7.50	4.50
(106)	Bill Waters (pose)	15.00	7.50	4.50

		NR MT	EX	VG
(107)	Bill Waters (pitching)	15.00	7.50	4.50
(108)	Roy Welmaker (pose)	15.00	7.50	4.50
(109)	Roy Welmaker (pitching)	15.00	7.50	4.50
(110)	Max West (pose)	15.00	7.50	4.50
(111)	Max West (batting stance)	15.00	7.50	4.50
(112)	Max West (kneeling)	15.00	7.50	4.50
(113)	Max West (batting follow-thru)	15.00	7.50	4.50
(114)	Al White	15.00	7.50	4.50
(115)	"Whitey" Wietelmann (pose)	15.00	7.50	4.50
(116)	"Whitey" Wietelmann (bunting)	15.00	7.50	4.50
(117)	"Whitey" Wietelmann (batting stance)	15.00	7.50	4.50
(118)	"Whitey" Wietelmann (throwing)	15.00	7.50	4.50
(119)	Bobbie Wilson	15.00	7.50	4.50
(120)	Bobby Wilson	15.00	7.50	4.50
(121)	Roy Zimmerman	15.00	7.50	4.50
(122)	George Zuverink	15.00	7.50	4.50

1951 Hage's Dairy

The final year of the Hage's P.C.L. issues saw the set reduced to 52 different unnumbered cards, all but 12 of them Padres. The set also includes six cards of Cleveland Indians players, which were issued during an exhibition series with the major league club, and six cards picturing members of the Hollywood Stars. No other P.C.L. teams are represented. The cards maintained the same size and style of the previous two years but were printed in more color tints, including blue, green, burgundy, gold, gray and sepia (but not black and white). The 1951 cards have blank backs and were again distributed in popcorn boxes at the San Diego stadium. The 1951 cards are the most common of the three sets issued by Hage's Dairy. The Indians and Stars players were issued in lesser quantities than the Padres, however, and command a higher value.

		NR MT	EX	VG
Complete Set:		1000.00	500.00	300.00
Common Player:		15.00	7.50	4.50
(1)	"Buster" Adams	15.00	7.50	4.50
(2)	Del Baker	15.00	7.50	4.50
(3)	Ray Boone	25.00	12.50	7.50
(4)	Russ Christopher	15.00	7.50	4.50
(5)	Allie Clark	25.00	12.50	7.50
(6)	Herb Conyers	15.00	7.50	4.50
(7)	"Red" Embree (pitching, foot in air)	15.00	7.50	4.50
(8)	"Red" Embree (pitching, hands up)	15.00	7.50	4.50
(9)	Jess Flores	25.00	12.50	7.50
(10)	Murray Franklin	25.00	12.50	7.50
(11)	Jack Graham (portrait)	15.00	7.50	4.50
(12)	Jack Graham (batting)	15.00	7.50	4.50
(13)	Gene Handley	25.00	12.50	7.50
(14)	Charles Harris	15.00	7.50	4.50
(15)	Sam Jones (pitching, hands back)	15.00	7.50	4.50
(16)	Sam Jones (pitching, hands up)	15.00	7.50	4.50
(17)	Sam Jones (pitching, leg in air)	15.00	7.50	4.50
(18)	Al Jurisich	15.00	7.50	4.50
(19)	Frank Kerr (batting)	15.00	7.50	4.50
(20)	Frank Kerr (catching)	15.00	7.50	4.50
(21)	Dick Kinaman	15.00	7.50	4.50

		NR MT	EX	VG
(22)	Clarence Maddern (batting)	15.00	7.50	4.50
(23)	Clarence Maddern (fielding)	15.00	7.50	4.50
(24)	Harry Malmberg (bunting)	15.00	7.50	4.50
(25)	Harry Malmberg (batting follow-thru)	15.00	7.50	4.50
(26)	Harry Malmberg (fielding)	15.00	7.50	4.50
(27)	Gordon Maltzberger	25.00	12.50	7.50
(28)	Al Olsen (Cleveland)	25.00	12.50	7.50
(29)	Al Olsen (San Diego)	15.00	7.50	4.50
(30)	Jimmy Reese (clapping)	20.00	10.00	6.00
(31)	Jimmy Reese (hands on knees)	20.00	10.00	6.00
(32)	Al Rosen	45.00	22.00	13.50
(33)	Joe Rowell	15.00	7.50	4.50
(34)	Mike Sandlock	25.00	12.50	7.50
(35)	George Schmees	25.00	12.50	7.50
(36)	Charlie Sipple	15.00	7.50	4.50
(37)	Harvey Storey (batting follow-thru)	15.00	7.50	4.50
(38)	Harvey Storey (batting stance)	15.00	7.50	4.50
(39)	Harvey Storey (fielding)	15.00	7.50	4.50
(40)	Jack Tobin	15.00	7.50	4.50
(41)	Frank Tornay	15.00	7.50	4.50
(42)	Thurman Tucker	15.00	7.50	4.50
(43)	Ben Wade	25.00	12.50	7.50
(44)	Roy Welmaker	15.00	7.50	4.50
(45)	Leroy Wheat	15.00	7.50	4.50
(46)	Don White	15.00	7.50	4.50
(47)	"Whitey" Wietelman (batting)	15.00	7.50	4.50
(48)	"Whitey" Wietelman (fielding)	15.00	7.50	4.50
(49)	Bobby Wilson (batting)	15.00	7.50	4.50
(50)	Bobby Wilson (fielding)	15.00	7.50	4.50
(51)	Tony York	15.00	7.50	4.50
(52)	George Zuverink	25.00	12.50	7.50

1958 Hires Root Beer Test Set

PITCHER—SAN FRANCISCO GIANTS

Among the scarcest of the regional issues of the late 1950s is the eight-card test issue which preceded the Hires Root Beer set of 66 cards. Probably issued in a very limited area in the Northeast, the test cards differ from the regular issue in that they have sepia-toned, rather than color pictures, which are set against plain yellow or orange backgrounds (much like the 1958 Topps), instead of viewed through a knothole. Like the regular Hires cards, the 2-5/16" by 3-1/2" cards were issued with an attached wedge-shaped tab of like size. The tab offered membership in Hires baseball fan club, and served to hold the card into the carton of bottled root beer with which it was given away. Values quoted here are for cards with tabs. Cards without tabs would be valued approximately 50 per cent lower.

		NR MT	EX	VG
	Complete Set:	1550.00	775.00	465.00
	Common Player:	130.00	65.00	39.00
(1)	Johnny Antonelli	150.00	75.00	45.00
(2)	Jim Busby	130.00	65.00	39.00
(3)	Chico Fernandez	130.00	65.00	39.00
(4)	Bob Friend	150.00	75.00	45.00
(5)	Vern Law	150.00	75.00	45.00
(6)	Stan Lopata	130.00	65.00	39.00
(7)	Willie Mays	550.00	280.00	165.00
(8)	Al Pilarcik	130.00	65.00	39.00

1958 Hires Root Beer

TED KLUSZEWSKI
INFIELD—PITTSBURGH PIRATES

Like most baseball cards issued with a tab in the 1950s, the Hires cards are extremely scarce today in their original form. The Hires cards were attached to a wedge-shaped tab that served the dual purpose of offering a fan club membership and of holding the card into the cardboard carton of soda bottles with which it was distributed. The card itself measures 2-5/16" by 3-1/2". The tab extends for another 3-1/2". Numbering of the Hires set begins at 10 and goes through 76, with card #69 never issued, making a set complete at 66 cards. Values given below are for cards with tabs. Cards without tabs would be valued approximately 50 per cent lower.

		NR MT	EX	VG
	Complete Set:	2400.00	1200.00	720.00
	Common Player:	25.00	12.50	7.50
10	Richie Ashburn	100.00	50.00	30.00
11	Chico Carrasquel	25.00	12.50	7.50
12	Dave Philley	25.00	12.50	7.50
13	Don Newcombe	28.00	14.00	8.50
14	Wally Post	25.00	12.50	7.50
15	Rip Repulski	25.00	12.50	7.50
16	Chico Fernandez	25.00	12.50	7.50
17	Larry Doby	28.00	14.00	8.50
18	Hector Brown	25.00	12.50	7.50
19	Danny O'Connell	25.00	12.50	7.50
20	Granny Hamner	25.00	12.50	7.50
21	Dick Groat	30.00	15.00	9.00
22	Ray Narleski	25.00	12.50	7.50
23	Pee Wee Reese	100.00	50.00	30.00
24	Bob Friend	30.00	15.00	9.00
25	Willie Mays	275.00	150.00	80.00
26	Bob Nieman	25.00	12.50	7.50
27	Frank Thomas	25.00	12.50	7.50
28	Curt Simmons	30.00	15.00	9.00
29	Stan Lopata	25.00	12.50	7.50
30	Bob Skinner	25.00	12.50	7.50
31	Ron Kline	25.00	12.50	7.50
32	Willie Miranda	25.00	12.50	7.50
33	Bob Avila	25.00	12.50	7.50
34	Clem Labine	30.00	15.00	9.00
35	Ray Jablonski	25.00	12.50	7.50
36	Bill Mazeroski	28.00	14.00	8.50
37	Billy Gardner	25.00	12.50	7.50
38	Pete Runnels	30.00	15.00	9.00
39	Jack Sanford	25.00	12.50	7.50
40	Dave Sisler	25.00	12.50	7.50
41	Don Zimmer	30.00	15.00	9.00
42	Johnny Podres	28.00	14.00	8.50
43	Dick Farrell	25.00	12.50	7.50
44	Hank Aaron	275.00	150.00	80.00
45	Bill Virdon	30.00	15.00	9.00
46	Bobby Thomson	30.00	15.00	9.00
47	Willard Nixon	25.00	12.50	7.50
48	Billy Loes	25.00	12.50	7.50
49	Hank Sauer	25.00	12.50	7.50
50	Johnny Antonelli	30.00	15.00	9.00
51	Daryl Spencer	25.00	12.50	7.50
52	Ken Lehman	25.00	12.50	7.50
53	Sammy White	25.00	12.50	7.50
54	Charley Neal	25.00	12.50	7.50
55	Don Drysdale	80.00	40.00	24.00
56	Jack Jensen	28.00	14.00	8.50
57	Ray Katt	25.00	12.50	7.50
58	Franklin Sullivan	25.00	12.50	7.50

		NR MT	EX	VG
59	Roy Face	30.00	15.00	9.00
60	Willie Jones	25.00	12.50	7.50
61	Duke Snider	125.00	62.00	37.00
62	Whitey Lockman	25.00	12.50	7.50
63	Gino Cimoli	30.00	15.00	9.00
64	Marv Grissom	25.00	12.50	7.50
65	Gene Baker	25.00	12.50	7.50
66	George Zuverink	25.00	12.50	7.50
67	Ted Kluszewski	28.00	14.00	8.50
68	Jim Busby	25.00	12.50	7.50
69	Not Issued			
70	Curt Barclay	25.00	12.50	7.50
71	Hank Foiles	25.00	12.50	7.50
72	Gene Stephens	25.00	12.50	7.50
73	Al Worthington	25.00	12.50	7.50
74	Al Walker	25.00	12.50	7.50
75	Bob Boyd	25.00	12.50	7.50
76	Al Pilarcik	30.00	9.00	5.50

1959 Home Run Derby

HANK AARON
MILWAUKEE BRAVES

This 20-card unnumbered set was produced by American Motors to publicize the Home Run Derby television program. The cards measure approximately 3-1/4" by 5-1/4" and feature black and white player photos on black-backed white stock. The player name and team are printed beneath the photo. This set was reprinted (and marked as such) in 1988 by Card Collectors' Company of New York.

		NR MT	EX	VG
Complete Set:		4000.00	2000.00	1200.
Common Player:		100.00	50.00	30.00
(1)	Hank Aaron	450.00	225.00	135.00
(2)	Bob Allison	100.00	50.00	30.00
(3)	Ernie Banks	300.00	150.00	90.00
(4)	Ken Boyer	175.00	87.00	52.00
(5)	Bob Cerv	100.00	50.00	30.00
(6)	Rocky Colavito	175.00	87.00	52.00
(7)	Gil Hodges	225.00	112.00	67.00
(8)	Jackie Jensen	175.00	87.00	52.00
(9)	Al Kaline	300.00	150.00	90.00
(10)	Harmon Killebrew	225.00	112.00	67.00
(11)	Jim Lemon	100.00	50.00	30.00
(12)	Mickey Mantle	1200.00	600.00	400.00
(13)	Ed Mathews	275.00	137.00	82.00
(14)	Willie Mays	450.00	225.00	135.00
(15)	Wally Post	100.00	50.00	30.00
(16)	Frank Robinson	275.00	137.00	82.00
(17)	Mark Scott (host)	175.00	87.00	52.00
(18)	Duke Snider	450.00	225.00	135.00
(19)	Dick Stuart	100.00	50.00	30.00
(20)	Gus Triandos	100.00	50.00	30.00

1947 Homogenized
Bond Bread

Issued by Homogenized Bond Bread in 1947, this set consists of 48 unnumbered black and white cards, each measuring 2-1/4" by 3-1/2". Of the 48 cards, 44 are baseball players. The remaining four cards picture boxers. The cards are usually found with

Tommy Holmes

rounded corners, although cards with square corners are also known to exist. The set contains both portrait and action photos, and features the player's facsimile autograph on the front.

		NR MT	EX	VG
Complete Set:		750.00	375.00	225.00
Common Player:		4.00	2.00	1.25
(1)	Rex Barney	4.00	2.00	1.25
(2)	Larry Berra	55.00	27.00	16.50
(3)	Ewell Blackwell	4.00	2.00	1.25
(4)	Lou Boudreau	8.00	4.00	2.50
(5)	Ralph Branca	8.00	4.00	2.50
(6)	Harry Brecheen	4.00	2.00	1.25
(7)	Dom DiMaggio	8.00	4.00	2.50
(8)	Joe DiMaggio	150.00	75.00	45.00
(9)	Bobbie Doerr (Bobby)	8.00	4.00	2.50
(10)	Bruce Edwards	4.00	2.00	1.25
(11)	Bob Elliott	4.00	2.00	1.25
(12)	Del Ennis	4.00	2.00	1.25
(13)	Bob Feller	15.00	7.50	4.50
(14)	Carl Furillo	8.00	4.00	2.50
(15)	Cid Gordon (Sid)	4.00	2.00	1.25
(16)	Joe Gordon	4.00	2.00	1.25
(17)	Joe Hatten	4.00	2.00	1.25
(18)	Gil Hodges	35.00	17.50	10.50
(19)	Tommy Holmes	4.00	2.00	1.25
(20)	Larry Janson (Jansen)	4.00	2.00	1.25
(21)	Sheldon Jones	4.00	2.00	1.25
(22)	Edwin Joost	4.00	2.00	1.25
(23)	Charlie Keller	8.00	4.00	2.50
(24)	Ken Keltner	4.00	2.00	1.25
(25)	Buddy Kerr	4.00	2.00	1.25
(26)	Ralph Kiner	8.00	4.00	2.50
(27)	John Lindell	4.00	2.00	1.25
(28)	Whitey Lockman	4.00	2.00	1.25
(29)	Willard Marshall	4.00	2.00	1.25
(30)	Johnny Mize	8.00	4.00	2.50
(31)	Stan Musial	55.00	27.00	16.50
(32)	Andy Pafko	4.00	2.00	1.25
(33)	Johnny Pesky	4.00	2.00	1.25
(34)	Pee Wee Reese	55.00	27.00	16.50
(35)	Phil Rizzuto	15.00	7.50	4.50
(36)	Aaron Robinson	4.00	2.00	1.25
(37)	Jackie Robinson	60.00	30.00	18.00
(38)	John Sain	5.00	2.50	1.50
(39)	Enos Slaughter	8.00	4.00	2.50
(40)	Vern Stephens	4.00	2.00	1.25
(41)	George Tebbetts	4.00	2.00	1.25
(42)	Bob Thomson	8.00	4.00	2.50
(43)	Johnny Vandermeer (VanderMeer)	8.00	4.00	2.50
(44)	Ted Williams	55.00	27.00	16.50

1953 Hunter
Wieners Cardinals

From the great era of the regionally issued hot dog cards in the mid-1950s, the 1953 Hunter wieners set of St. Louis Cardinals is certainly among the rarest today. Originally issued in two-card panels, the cards are most often found as 2-1/4" by 3-1/4" singles today when they can be found at all. The cards feature a light blue facsimile autograph printed over

ST. LOUIS CARDINALS TRADING CARDS

ALBERT SCHOENDIENST, Infielder
JOHN CRIMIAN, Pitcher

KIDS! Cut Out and Save These Cards! Collect them. Trade them. Enter the big Hunter Baseball Contest. 110 VALUABLE PRIZES! Get contest rules and list of prizes from your Hunter meat dealer.

the stat box at the bottom. They are blank-backed.

		NR MT	EX	VG
Complete Set:		2500.00	1250.00	750.00
Common Player:		60.00	30.00	18.00
(1)	Steve Bilko	60.00	30.00	18.00
(2)	Alpha Brazle	60.00	30.00	18.00
(3)	Cloyd Boyer	60.00	30.00	18.00
(4)	Cliff Chambers	60.00	30.00	18.00
(5)	Michael Clark	60.00	30.00	18.00
(6)	Jack Crimian	60.00	30.00	18.00
(7)	Lester Fusselman	60.00	30.00	18.00
(8)	Harvey Haddix	65.00	33.00	20.00
(9)	Solly Hemus	60.00	30.00	18.00
(10)	Ray Jablonski	60.00	30.00	18.00
(11)	William Johnson	60.00	30.00	18.00
(12)	Harry Lowrey	60.00	30.00	18.00
(13)	Lawrence Miggins	60.00	30.00	18.00
(14)	Stuart Miller	60.00	30.00	18.00
(15)	Wilmer Mizell	60.00	30.00	18.00
(16)	Stanley Musial	600.00	300.00	175.00
(17)	Joseph Presko	60.00	30.00	18.00
(18)	Delbert Rice	60.00	30.00	18.00
(19)	Harold Rice	60.00	30.00	18.00
(20)	Willard Schmidt	60.00	30.00	18.00
(21)	Albert Schoendienst	100.00	50.00	30.00
(22)	Richard Sisler	60.00	30.00	18.00
(23)	Enos Slaughter	150.00	75.00	45.00
(24)	Gerald Staley	60.00	30.00	18.00
(25)	Edward Stanky	70.00	35.00	21.00
(26)	John Yuhas	60.00	30.00	18.00

1954 Hunter
Wieners Cardinals

ST. LOUIS CARDINALS TRADING CARDS

WHAT'S MY NAME?
WHAT'S MY RECORD?

BOYS! GIRLS! Cut out and save these cards. Match up player picture with correct player record and add the correct autograph from Hunter Franks Smokies packages. Enter the big Hunter Baseball Contest. 200 prizes. Get rules and prize list from your Hunter dealer.

A nearly impossible set to complete today by virtue of the method of its issue, the 1954 Hunter hot dog set essentially features what would traditionally be the front and back of a normal baseball card on two different cards. The "front," containing a color photo of one of 30 St. Louis Cardinals has a box at bottom challenging the collector to name him and quote his stats. The "back" features cartoon Cardinals in action, and contains the answers. However, because both parts were printed on a single panel, and because most of the back (non-picture) panels were

thrown away years ago, it is an impossible challenge to complete a '54 Hunter set today. There is no back printing on the 2-1/4" by 3-1/2" cards.

		NR MT	EX	VG
Complete Set:		4000.00	2000.00	1200.
Common Player:		60.00	30.00	18.00
(1)	Tom Alston	60.00	30.00	18.00
(2)	Steve Bilko	60.00	30.00	18.00
(3)	Al Brazle	60.00	30.00	18.00
(4)	Tom Burgess	60.00	30.00	18.00
(5)	Cot Deal	60.00	30.00	18.00
(6)	Alex Grammas	60.00	30.00	18.00
(7)	Harvey Haddix	60.00	30.00	18.00
(8)	Solly Hemus	60.00	30.00	18.00
(9)	Ray Jablonski	60.00	30.00	18.00
(10)	Royce Lint	60.00	30.00	18.00
(11)	Peanuts Lowrey	60.00	30.00	18.00
(12)	Memo Luna	60.00	30.00	18.00
(13)	Stu Miller	60.00	30.00	18.00
(14)	Stan Musial	600.00	300.00	180.00
(15)	Tom Poholsky	60.00	30.00	18.00
(16)	Bill Posedel	60.00	30.00	18.00
(17)	Joe Presko	60.00	30.00	18.00
(18)	Vic Raschi	60.00	30.00	18.00
(19)	Dick Rand	60.00	30.00	18.00
(20)	Rip Repulski	60.00	30.00	18.00
(21)	Del Rice	60.00	30.00	18.00
(22)	John Riddle	60.00	30.00	18.00
(23)	Mike Ryba	60.00	30.00	18.00
(24)	Red Schoendienst	100.00	50.00	30.00
(25)	Dick Schofield	100.00	50.00	30.00
(26)	Eddie Stanky	110.00	55.00	33.00
(27)	Enos Slaughter	150.00	75.00	45.00
(28)	Gerry Staley	60.00	30.00	18.00
(29)	Ed Yuhas	60.00	30.00	18.00
(30)	Sal Yvars	60.00	30.00	18.00

1955 Hunter
Wieners Cardinals

TRADING CARDS
Cut out, Trade and Save

The 1955 team set of St. Louis Cardinals, included with packages of Hunter hot dogs, features the third format change in three years of issue. For 1955, the cards were printed in a tall, narrow 2" by 4-3/4" format, two to a panel. The cards featured both a posed action photo and a portrait photo, along with a facsimile autograph and brief biographical data on the front. There is no back printing, as the cards were part of the wrapping for packages of hot dogs.

		NR MT	EX	VG
Complete Set:		3500.00	1750.00	1050.
Common Player:		75.00	37.00	22.00
(1)	Thomas Edison Alston	75.00	37.00	22.00
(2)	Kenton Lloyd Boyer	225.00	112.00	67.00
(3)	Harry Lewis Elliott	75.00	37.00	22.00
(4)	John Edward Faszholz	75.00	37.00	22.00
(5)	Joseph Filmore Frazier	75.00	37.00	22.00
(6)	Alexander Pete Grammas	75.00	37.00	22.00
(7)	Harvey Haddix	125.00	62.00	37.00
(8)	Solly Joseph Hemus	75.00	37.00	22.00
(9)	Lawrence Curtis Jackson	75.00	37.00	22.00
(10)	Tony R. Jacobs	75.00	37.00	22.00

		NR MT	EX	VG
(11)	Gordon Bassett Jones	75.00	37.00	22.00
(12)	Paul Edmore LaPalme	75.00	37.00	22.00
(13)	Brooks Ulysses Lawrence	75.00	37.00	22.00
(14)	Wallace Wade Moon	125.00	62.00	37.00
(15)	Stanley Frank Musial	1000.00	500.00	300.00
(16)	Thomas George Poholsky	75.00	37.00	22.00
(17)	William John Posedel	75.00	37.00	22.00
(18)	Victor Angelo John Raschi	75.00	37.00	22.00
(19)	Eldon John Repulski	75.00	37.00	22.00
(20)	Delbert Rice	75.00	37.00	22.00
(21)	John Ludy Riddle	75.00	37.00	22.00
(22)	William F. Sarni	75.00	37.00	22.00
(23)	Albert Fred Schoendienst	175.00	87.00	52.00
(24)	Richard John Schofield (actually John Richard)	75.00	37.00	22.00
(25)	Frank Thomas Smith	75.00	37.00	22.00
(26)	Edward R. Stanky	125.00	62.00	37.00
(27)	Bobby Gene Tiefenauer	75.00	37.00	22.00
(28)	William Charles Virdon	175.00	87.00	52.00
(29)	Frederick E. Walker	75.00	37.00	22.00
(30)	Floyd Lewis Woolridge	75.00	37.00	22.00

		NR MT	EX	VG
22	Bill Bruton	10.00	5.00	3.00
23	Sid Gordon	8.00	4.00	2.50
24	Andy Pafko	10.00	5.00	3.00
25	Jim Pendleton	8.00	4.00	2.50

1954 Johnston Cookies Braves

HENRY AARON

In its second of three annual issues, Johnston's increased the number of cards in its 1954 Braves issue to 35, and switched to an unusual size, a narrow format, 2" by 3-7/8". Besides the players and managers, the '54 set also includes unnumbered cards of the team trainer and equipment manager. Other cards are numbered by uniform number. After his early-season injury (which gave Hank Aaron a chance to play regularly), Bobby Thomson's card was withdrawn, accounting for its scarcity and high value. A cardboard wall-hanging display into which cards could be inserted was available as a premium offer.

		NR MT	EX	VG
Complete Set:		1250.00	625.00	375.00
Common Player:		10.00	5.00	3.00
1	Del Crandall	15.00	7.50	4.50
3	Jim Pendleton	10.00	5.00	3.00
4	Danny O'Connell	10.00	5.00	3.00
5	Henry Aaron	500.00	250.00	150.00
6	Jack Dittmer	10.00	5.00	3.00
9	Joe Adcock	15.00	7.50	4.50
10	Robert Buhl	15.00	7.50	4.50
11	Phillip Paine (Phillips)	10.00	5.00	3.00
12	Ben Johnson	10.00	5.00	3.00
13	Sibby Sisti	10.00	5.00	3.00
15	Charles Gorin	10.00	5.00	3.00
16	Chet Nichols	10.00	5.00	3.00
17	Dave Jolly	10.00	5.00	3.00
19	Jim Wilson	10.00	5.00	3.00
20	Ray Crone	10.00	5.00	3.00
21	Warren Spahn	65.00	32.00	19.50
22	Gene Conley	10.00	5.00	3.00
23	Johnny Logan	12.00	6.00	3.50
24	Charlie White	10.00	5.00	3.00
27	George Metkovich	10.00	5.00	3.00
28	John Cooney	10.00	5.00	3.00
29	Paul Burris	10.00	5.00	3.00
31	Wm. Walters	10.00	5.00	3.00
32	Ernest T. Johnson	10.00	5.00	3.00
33	Lew Burdette	20.00	10.00	6.00
34	Bob Thomson	200.00	100.00	60.00
35	Robert Keely	10.00	5.00	3.00
38	Billy Bruton	10.00	5.00	3.00
40	Charles Grimm	10.00	5.00	3.00
41	Ed Mathews	65.00	32.00	19.50
42	Sam Calderone	10.00	5.00	3.00
47	Joey Jay	10.00	5.00	3.00
48	Andy Pafko	12.00	6.00	3.50
----	Dr. Charles Lacks (trainer)	10.00	5.00	3.00
----	Joseph F. Taylor (asst. trainer)	10.00	5.00	3.00

A player's name in *italic* type indicates a rookie card. An (FC) indicates a player's first card for that particular card company.

1953 Johnston Cookies Braves

JOE ADCOCK

The first and most common of three annual issues, the '53 Johnston's were inserted into boxes of cookies on a regional basis. Complete sets were also available from the company, whose factory sits in the shadow of Milwaukee County Stadium. While at first glance appearing to be color photos, the pictures on the 25 cards in the set are actually well-done colorizations of black and white photos. Cards measure 2-9/16" by 3-5/8". Write-ups on the backs were "borrowed" from the Braves' 1953 yearbook.

		NR MT	EX	VG
Complete Set:		325.00	175.00	100.00
Common Player:		8.00	4.00	2.50
1	Charlie Grimm	10.00	5.00	3.00
2	John Antonelli	10.00	5.00	3.00
3	Vern Bickford	8.00	4.00	2.50
4	Bob Buhl	10.00	5.00	3.00
5	Lew Burdette	15.00	7.50	4.50
6	Dave Cole	8.00	4.00	2.50
7	Ernie Johnson	8.00	4.00	2.50
8	Dave Jolly	8.00	4.00	2.50
9	Don Liddle	8.00	4.00	2.50
10	Warren Spahn	55.00	27.00	16.50
11	Max Surkont	8.00	4.00	2.50
12	Jim Wilson	8.00	4.00	2.50
13	Sibby Sisti	8.00	4.00	2.50
14	Walker Cooper	8.00	4.00	2.50
15	Del Crandall	15.00	7.50	4.50
16	Ebba St. Claire	8.00	4.00	2.50
17	Joe Adcock	15.00	7.50	4.50
18	George Crowe	8.00	4.00	2.50
19	Jack Dittmer	8.00	4.00	2.50
20	Johnny Logan	10.00	5.00	3.00
21	Ed Mathews	55.00	27.00	16.50

1955 Johnston Cookies Braves

A third change in size and format was undertaken in the third and final year of Braves sets produced by Johnston's. The 35 cards in the 1955 set were issued in six fold-out panels of six cards each (Andy Pafko was double-printed). As in 1954, cards are numbered by uniform number, except those of the team equipment manager, trainer and road secretary (former Boston star Duffy Lewis). Single cards measure 2-7/8" by 4". Besides including panels in boxes of cookies, the '55 Johnston's could be ordered for 5¢ per panel by mail. The scarcest of the Johnston's issues, the 1955 set can be found today still in complete panels, or as single cards.

		NR MT	EX	VG
Complete Folder Set:		1500.00	750.00	450.00
Complete Singles Set:		1000.00	500.00	300.00
Common Player:		15.00	7.50	4.50
Common Folder:		125.00	62.00	37.00
1	Del Crandall	25.00	12.50	7.50
3	Jim Pendleton	15.00	7.50	4.50
4	Danny O'Connell	15.00	7.50	4.50
6	Jack Dittmer	15.00	7.50	4.50
9	Joe Adcock	25.00	12.50	7.50
10	Bob Buhl	20.00	10.00	6.00
11	Phil Paine	15.00	7.50	4.50
12	Ray Crone	15.00	7.50	4.50
15	Charlie Gorin	15.00	7.50	4.50
16	Dave Jolly	15.00	7.50	4.50
17	Chet Nichols	15.00	7.50	4.50
18	Chuck Tanner	25.00	12.50	7.50
19	Jim Wilson	15.00	7.50	4.50
20	Dave Koslo	15.00	7.50	4.50
21	Warren Spahn	80.00	40.00	24.00
22	Gene Conley	20.00	10.00	6.00
23	John Logan	20.00	10.00	6.00
24	Charlie White	15.00	7.50	4.50
28	Johnny Cooney	15.00	7.50	4.50
30	Roy Smalley	15.00	7.50	4.50
31	Bucky Walters	15.00	7.50	4.50
32	Ernie Johnson	15.00	7.50	4.50
33	Lew Burdette	25.00	12.50	7.50
34	Bobby Thomson	25.00	12.50	7.50
35	Bob Keely	15.00	7.50	4.50
38	Billy Bruton	20.00	10.00	6.00
39	George Crowe	15.00	7.50	4.50
40	Charlie Grimm	20.00	10.00	6.00
41	Eddie Mathews	80.00	40.00	24.00
44	Hank Aaron	400.00	200.00	120.00
47	Joe Jay	15.00	7.50	4.50
48	Andy Pafko	20.00	10.00	6.00
----	Dr. Charles K. Lacks	15.00	7.50	4.50
----	Duffy Lewis	15.00	7.50	4.50
----	Joe Taylor	15.00	7.50	4.50
----	Series 1 Folder (Hank Aaron, Lew Burdette, Del Crandall, Charlie Gorin, Bob Keely, Danny O'Connell)	400.00	200.00	120.00
----	Series 2 Folder (Joe Adcock, Joe Jay, Dr. Charles K. Lacks, Chet Nichols, Andy Pafko, Charlie White)	125.00	62.00	37.00
----	Series 3 Folder (Gene Conley, George Crowe, Jim Pendleton, Roy Smalley, Warren Spahn, Joe Taylor)	175.00	87.00	52.00
----	Series 4 Folder (Billy Bruton, John Cooney, Dave Jolly, Dave Koslo, Johnny Logan, Andy Pafko)	125.00	62.00	37.00
----	Series 5 Folder (Ray Crone, Ernie Johnson, Duffy Lewis, Eddie Mathews, Phil Paine, Chuck Tanner)	200.00	100.00	60.00
----	Series 6 Folder (Bob Buhl, Jack Dittmer, Charlie Grimm, Bobby Thomson, Bucky Walters, Jim Wilson)	125.00	62.00	37.00

1888 Joseph Hall Cabinets

These fourteen cabinet-size (6-1/2" by 4-1/2") cards feature team photos taken by Joseph Hall, a well-known photographer of the day. The cards, which are extremely rare, all have Hall's name beneath the photo and some include his Brooklyn address. The team is identified in large capital letters with the individual players identified in smaller type on both sides. Fourteen teams are known to date, but others may also exist, and Hall may have produced similar team cabinets in other years as well.

	NR MT	EX	VG
Complete Set:	22000.00	11000.00	65000.
Common Team:	6500.00	3250.00	2000.
(1) Athletic Ball Club, 1888	7500.00	3750.00	2300.
(2) Boston Ball Club, 1888	18000.00	9000.00	550.00
(3) Brooklyn Ball Club, 1888	6500.00	3250.00	2000.
(4) Chicago Ball Club, 1888	10000.00	5000.00	3000.
(5) Cincinnati Ball Club, 1888	6500.00	3250.00	2000.
(6) Cleveland Ball Club, 1888	6500.00	3250.00	2000.
(7) Detroit Ball Club, 1888	8000.00	4000.00	2500.
(8) Indianapolis Ball Club, 1888	6500.00	3250.00	2000.
(9) Kansas City Ball Club, 1888	6500.00	3250.00	2000.
(10) Louisville Ball Club, 1888	6500.00	3250.00	2000.
(11) New York Ball Club, 1888 (wearing baseball uniforms)	10000.00	5000.00	3000.
(12) New York Ball Club, 1888 (wearing tuxedos)	10000.00	5000.00	3000.
(13) St. Louis Baseball Club, 1888	7500.00	3750.00	2300.
(14) Washington Baseball Club, 1888	12500.00	6250.00	4000.

1893 Just So Tobacco

This set, issued by the Just So tobacco brand in 1893, is so rare that only seven examples are known, although more undoubtedly exist. The set apparently features only members of the Cleveland club, known then as the "Spiders". Measuring 2-1/2" by 3-7/8", these sepia-colored cards were printed on heavy paper. The player appears in a portrait photo with his name beneath and an ad for Just So Tobacco along the bottom. The existence of this set wasn't even established until the 1960s, and for 15 years only two subjects were known. In 1981, several more cards were discovered. To date only one copy of each of the known cards has turned up in collectors' hands, making it among the rarest of all baseball card issues.

		NR MT	EX	VG
Complete Set:		12000.00	6000.00	3500.
Common Player:		1200.00	600.00	350.00
(1)	F.W. Boyd	1200.00	600.00	350.00
(2)	Burkette	2500.00	2500.00	750.00
(3)	C.L. Childs	1200.00	600.00	350.00
(4)	John Clarkson	3000.00	1500.00	900.00
(5)	C.M. Hastings	1200.00	600.00	350.00
(6)	E.J. McKean	1200.00	600.00	350.00
(7)	J.K. Virtue	1200.00	600.00	350.00
(8)	T.C. Williams	1200.00	600.00	350.00
(9)	Young	4000.00	2000.00	1250.

1955 Kahn's Wieners Reds

Compliments of Kahn's Wieners
"THE WIENER THE WORLD AWAITED"

The first of what would become 15 successive years of baseball card issues by the Kahn's meat company of Cincinnati is also the rarest. The set consists of six Cincinnati Redlegs player cards, 3-1/4" by 4". Printed in black and white, with blank backs, the '55 Kahn's cards were distributed at a one-day promotional event at a Cincinnati amusement park, where the featured players were on hand to sign autographs. Like the other Kahn's issues through 1963, the '55 cards have a 1/2" white panel containing an advertising message below the player photo. These cards are sometimes found with this portion cut off, greatly reducing the value of the card.

		NR MT	EX	VG
Complete Set:		3100.00	1550.00	930.00
Common Player:		450.00	225.00	135.00
(1)	Gus Bell	800.00	400.00	240.00
(2)	Ted Kluszewski	750.00	375.00	225.00
(3)	Roy McMillan	450.00	225.00	135.00
(4)	Joe Nuxhall	450.00	225.00	135.00
(5)	Wally Post	450.00	225.00	135.00
(6)	Johnny Temple	450.00	225.00	135.00

1956 Kahn's Wieners Reds

Compliments of Kahn's Wieners
"THE WIENER THE WORLD AWAITED"

In 1956, Kahn's expanded its baseball card program to include 15 Redlegs players, and began issuing the cards one per pack in packages of hot dogs. Because the cards were packaged in direct contact with the meat, they are often found today in stained condition. In 3-1/4" by 4" format, black and white with blank backs, the '56 Kahn's cards can be distinguished from later issues by the presence of full stadium photographic backgrounds behind the player photos. Like all Kahn's issues, the 1956 set is unnumbered; the checklists are arranged alphabetically for convenience. The set features the first-ever baseball card of Hall of Famer Frank Robinson.

		NR MT	EX	VG
Complete Set:		1600.00	800.00	480.00
Common Player:		75.00	37.00	22.00
(1)	Ed Bailey	75.00	37.00	22.00
(2)	Gus Bell	100.00	50.00	30.00
(3)	Joe Black	100.00	50.00	30.00
(4)	"Smokey" Burgess	100.00	50.00	30.00
(5)	Art Fowler	75.00	37.00	22.00
(6)	Hershell Freeman	75.00	37.00	22.00
(7)	Ray Jablonski	75.00	37.00	22.00
(8)	John Klippstein	75.00	37.00	22.00
(9)	Ted Kluszewski	150.00	75.00	45.00
(10)	Brooks Lawrence	75.00	37.00	22.00
(11)	Roy McMillan	75.00	37.00	22.00
(12)	Joe Nuxhall	100.00	50.00	30.00
(13)	Wally Post	75.00	37.00	22.00
(14)	Frank Robinson	350.00	175.00	105.00
(15)	Johnny Temple	100.00	50.00	30.00

1957 Kahn's Wieners

Compliments of Kahn's Wieners
"THE WIENER THE WORLD AWAITED"

In its third season of baseball card issue, Kahn's kept the basic 3-1/4" by 4" format, with black and white photos and blank backs. The issue was expanded to 28 players, all Pirates or Reds. The last of the blank-backed Kahn's sets, the 1957 Reds players can be distinguished from the 1956 issue by the general lack of background photo detail, in favor of a neutral light gray background. The Dick Groat card appears with two name variations, a facsimile autograph, "Richard Groat," and a printed "Dick Groat." Both Groat varieties are included in the complete set price.

		NR MT	EX	VG
	Complete Set	2600.00	1300.00	780.00
	Common Player	50.00	25.00	15.00
(1)	Tom Acker	50.00	25.00	15.00
(2)	Ed Bailey	50.00	25.00	15.00
(3)	Gus Bell	70.00	35.00	21.00
(4)	Smokey Burgess	70.00	35.00	21.00
(5)	Roberto Clemente	650.00	325.00	195.00
(6)	George Crowe	50.00	25.00	15.00
(7)	Elroy Face	70.00	35.00	21.00
(8)	Hershell Freeman	50.00	25.00	15.00
(9)	Robert Friend	50.00	25.00	15.00
(10)	Don Gross	50.00	25.00	15.00
(11a)	Dick Groat	70.00	35.00	21.00
(11b)	Richard Groat	175.00	87.00	52.00
(12)	Warren Hacker	50.00	25.00	15.00
(13)	Don Hoak	70.00	35.00	21.00
(14)	Hal Jeffcoat	50.00	25.00	15.00
(15)	Ron Kline	50.00	25.00	15.00
(16)	John Klippstein	50.00	25.00	15.00
(17)	Ted Kluszewski	100.00	50.00	30.00
(18)	Brooks Lawrence	50.00	25.00	15.00
(19)	Dale Long	50.00	25.00	15.00
(20)	Wm. Mazeroski	100.00	50.00	30.00
(21)	Roy McMillan	50.00	25.00	15.00
(22)	Joe Nuxhall	50.00	25.00	15.00
(23)	Wally Post	50.00	25.00	15.00
(24)	Frank Robinson	250.00	125.00	75.00
(25)	Johnny Temple	50.00	25.00	15.00
(26)	Frank Thomas	50.00	25.00	15.00
(27)	Bob Thurman	50.00	25.00	15.00
(28)	Lee Walls	50.00	25.00	15.00

1958 Kahn's Wieners

Compliments of Kahn's Wieners
"THE WIENER THE WORLD AWAITED"

MY GREATEST THRILL IN BASEBALL
By GEORGE CROWE

I've had lots of big and little thrills in my baseball career, both in the minors and when I was playing with Milwaukee. Looking back, I think my biggest moment was really a whole season long. It was the 1957 season when I was playing first base for the Cincinnati Redlegs.

I played in 133 games that year. I managed to hit 31 home runs and drive in 92 runs, leading the Redlegs in both departments that year. No doubt about it—1957 was my top thrill in baseball.

Long-time Cincinnati favorite Wally Post became the only Philadelphia Phillies ballplayer to appear in the 15-year run of Kahn's issues when he was traded in 1958, but included as part of the otherwise exclusively Pirates-Reds set. Like previous years, the '58 Kahn's were 3-1/4" by 4", with black and white player photos. Unlike previous years, however, the cards had printing on the back, a story by the pictured player, titled "My Greatest Thrill in Baseball." Quite similar to the 1959 issue, the '58 Kahn's can be distinguished by the fact that the top line of the advertising panel at bottom has the word "Wieners" in 1958, but not in 1959.

		NR MT	EX	VG
	Complete Set:	2600.00	1300.00	780.00
	Common Player:	50.00	25.00	15.00
(1)	Ed Bailey	50.00	25.00	15.00
(2)	Gene Baker	50.00	25.00	15.00
(3)	Gus Bell	60.00	30.00	18.00
(4)	Smokey Burgess	60.00	30.00	18.00
(5)	Roberto Clemente	500.00	250.00	150.00
(6)	George Crowe	50.00	25.00	15.00
(7)	Elroy Face	60.00	30.00	18.00

		NR MT	EX	VG
(8)	Henry Foiles	50.00	25.00	15.00
(9)	Dee Fondy	50.00	25.00	15.00
(10)	Robert Friend	60.00	30.00	18.00
(11)	Richard Groat	100.00	50.00	30.00
(12)	Harvey Haddix	60.00	30.00	18.00
(13)	Don Hoak	60.00	30.00	18.00
(14)	Hal Jeffcoat	60.00	30.00	18.00
(15)	Ronald L. Kline	60.00	30.00	18.00
(16)	Ted Kluszewski	100.00	50.00	30.00
(17)	Vernon Law	60.00	30.00	18.00
(18)	Brooks Lawrence	50.00	25.00	15.00
(19)	William Mazeroski	100.00	50.00	30.00
(20)	Roy McMillan	50.00	25.00	15.00
(21)	Joe Nuxhall	60.00	30.00	18.00
(22)	Wally Post	275.00	137.00	80.00
(23)	John Powers	50.00	25.00	15.00
(24)	Robert T. Purkey	50.00	25.00	15.00
(25)	Charles Rabe	275.00	137.00	80.00
(26)	Frank Robinson	275.00	137.00	80.00
(27)	Robert Skinner	50.00	25.00	15.00
(28)	Johnny Temple	50.00	25.00	15.00
(29)	Frank Thomas	275.00	137.00	80.00

1959 Kahn's Wieners

Compliments of Kahn's
"THE WIENER THE WORLD AWAITED"

THE MOST DIFFICULT PLAY I HAVE TO MAKE
by GARY BELL

"I think the most difficult play for me to make as a pitcher is a bunt down the third base line. It is difficult because you must charge off the mound toward the line, field the ball, turn completely around and throw the ball hard to first base to get the hitter. I try to make this play by going over and fielding the ball with both feet planted firmly so I stay well balanced. That way, I don't have to throw off balance."

A third team was added to the Kahn's lineup in 1959, the Cleveland Indians joining the Pirates and Reds, bringing the number of cards in the set to 38. Again printed in black and white in the 3-1/4" by 4" size, the 1959 Kahn's cards can be differentiated from the previous issue by the lack of the word "Wieners" on the top line of the advertising panel at bottom. Backs again featured a story written by the pictured player, titled "The Toughest Play I Had to Make," "My Most Difficult Moment in Baseball," or "The Toughest Batters I Have to Face."

		NR MT	EX	VG
	Complete Set:	4250.00	2125.00	1275.
	Common Player:	45.00	22.00	13.50
(1)	Ed Bailey	45.00	22.00	13.50
(2)	Gary Bell	45.00	22.00	13.50
(3)	Gus Bell	50.00	25.00	15.00
(4)	Richard Brodowski	500.00	250.00	150.00
(5)	Forrest Burgess	50.00	25.00	15.00
(6)	Roberto Clemente	450.00	225.00	135.00
(7)	Rocky Colavito	75.00	37.00	22.00
(8)	ElRoy Face	50.00	25.00	15.00
(9)	Robert Friend	50.00	25.00	15.00
(10)	Joe Gordon	50.00	25.00	15.00
(11)	Jim Grant	45.00	22.00	13.50
(12)	Richard M. Groat	60.00	30.00	18.00
(13)	Harvey Haddix	350.00	175.00	105.00
(14)	Woodie Held	350.00	175.00	105.00
(15)	Don Hoak	50.00	25.00	15.00
(16)	Ronald Kline	45.00	22.00	13.50
(17)	Ted Kluszewski	75.00	37.00	22.00
(18)	Vernon Law	50.00	25.00	15.00
(19)	Jerry Lynch	45.00	22.00	13.50
(20)	Billy Martin	75.00	37.00	22.00
(21)	William Mazeroski	50.00	25.00	15.00
(22)	Cal McLish	350.00	175.00	105.00
(23)	Roy McMillan	45.00	22.00	13.50
(24)	Minnie Minoso	60.00	30.00	18.00
(25)	Russell Nixon	45.00	22.00	13.50
(26)	Joe Nuxhall	50.00	25.00	15.00
(27)	Jim Perry	50.00	25.00	15.00

		NR MT	EX	VG
(28)	Vada Pinson	60.00	30.00	18.00
(29)	Vic Power	45.00	22.00	13.50
(30)	Robert Purkey	45.00	22.00	13.50
(31)	Frank Robinson	175.00	87.00	52.00
(32)	Herb Score	50.00	25.00	15.00
(33)	Robert Skinner	45.00	22.00	13.50
(34)	George Strickland	45.00	22.00	13.50
(35)	Richard L. Stuart	50.00	25.00	15.00
(36)	John Temple	45.00	22.00	13.50
(37)	Frank Thomas	50.00	25.00	15.00
(38)	George A. Witt	45.00	22.00	13.50

1960 Kahn's Wieners

Compliments of Kahn's
"THE WIENER THE WORLD AWAITED"

Three more teams joined the Kahn's roster in 1960, the Chicago Cubs, Chicago White Sox and St. Louis Cardinals. A total of 42 different players are represented in the set. Again 3-1/4" by 4" with black and white photos, the 1960 Kahn's cards featured for the first time player stats and personal data on the back, except Harvey Kuenn, which was issued with blank back, probably because of the lateness of his trade to the Indians.

		NR MT	EX	VG
Complete Set:		2000.00	1000.00	600.00
Common Player:		30.00	15.00	9.00
(1)	Ed Bailey	30.00	15.00	9.00
(2)	Gary Bell	30.00	15.00	9.00
(3)	Gus Bell	35.00	17.50	10.50
(4)	Forrest Burgess	35.00	17.50	10.50
(5)	Gino N. Cimoli	30.00	15.00	9.00
(6)	Roberto Clemente	300.00	150.00	90.00
(7)	ElRoy Face	35.00	17.50	10.50
(8)	Tito Francona	35.00	17.50	10.50
(9)	Robert Friend	35.00	17.50	10.50
(10)	Jim Grant	30.00	15.00	9.00
(11)	Richard Groat	40.00	20.00	12.00
(12)	Harvey Haddix	35.00	17.50	10.50
(13)	Woodie Held	30.00	15.00	9.00
(14)	Bill Henry	30.00	15.00	9.00
(15)	Don Hoak	35.00	17.50	10.50
(16)	Jay Hook	30.00	15.00	9.00
(17)	Eddie Kasko	30.00	15.00	9.00
(18)	Ronnie Kline	40.00	20.00	12.00
(19)	Ted Kluszewski	50.00	25.00	15.00
(20)	Harvey Kuenn	300.00	150.00	90.00
(21)	Vernon S. Law	35.00	17.50	10.50
(22)	Brooks Lawrence	30.00	15.00	9.00
(23)	Jerry Lynch	30.00	15.00	9.00
(24)	Billy Martin	60.00	30.00	18.00
(25)	William Mazeroski	40.00	20.00	12.00
(26)	Cal McLish	30.00	15.00	9.00
(27)	Roy McMillan	30.00	15.00	9.00
(28)	Don Newcombe	35.00	17.50	10.50
(29)	Russ Nixon	30.00	15.00	9.00
(30)	Joe Nuxhall	35.00	17.50	10.50
(31)	James J. O'Toole	30.00	15.00	9.00
(32)	Jim Perry	35.00	17.50	10.50
(33)	Vada Pinson	40.00	20.00	12.00
(34)	Vic Power	30.00	15.00	9.00
(35)	Robert T. Purkey	30.00	15.00	9.00
(36)	Frank Robinson	150.00	75.00	45.00
(37)	Herb Score	35.00	17.50	10.50
(38)	Robert R. Skinner	30.00	15.00	9.00
(39)	Richard L. Stuart	35.00	17.50	10.50
(40)	John Temple	30.00	15.00	9.00

		NR MT	EX	VG
(41)	Frank Thomas	40.00	20.00	12.00
(42)	Lee Walls	35.00	17.50	10.50

L

1912 L1 Leathers

One of the more unusual baseball collectibles of the tobacco era, the L1 "Leathers" were issued by Helmar Tobacco Co. in 1912 as a premium with its "Turkish Trophies" brand of cigarettes. The set featured 25 of the top baseball players and shared a checklist with the closely-related S81 "Silks," which were another part of the same promotion. The "Leathers," advertised as being 10" by 12", featured drawings of baseball players on horsehide-shaped pieces of leather. The drawings were based on the pictures used for the popular T-3 Turkey Red series issued a year earlier. Twenty of the 25 players in the "Leathers" set are from the T3 set. Five pitchers (Rube Marquard, Rube Benton, Marty O'Toole, Grover Alexander and Russ Ford) not pictured in T3 were added to the "Leathers" set, and the Frank Baker error was corrected. According to the promotion, each "Leather" was available in exchange for 50 Helmar coupons. In addition to the 25 baseball stars, the "Leathers" set also included more than one hundred other subjects, including female athletes and bathing beauties, famous generals, Indian chiefs, actresses, national flags, college mascots and others.

		NR MT	EX	VG
Complete Set:		95000.00	47500.00	28500.
Common Player:		2250.00	1125.00	675.00
86	Rube Marquard	5000.00	2000.00	800.00
87	Marty O'Toole	2250.00	1125.00	675.00
88	Rube Benton	2250.00	1125.00	675.00
89	Grover Alexander	6000.00	3000.00	1750.
90	Russ Ford	2250.00	1125.00	675.00
91	John McGraw	5250.00	2100.00	825.00
92	Nap Rucker	2250.00	1125.00	675.00
93	Mike Mitchell	2250.00	1125.00	675.00
94	Chief Bender	4500.00	1800.00	700.00
95	Home Run Baker	4500.00	1800.00	700.00
96	Nap Lajoie	8000.00	4000.00	2400.
97	Joe Tinker	4750.00	1900.00	775.00
98	Sherry Magee	2250.00	1125.00	675.00
99	Howie Camnitz	2250.00	1125.00	675.00
100	Eddie Collins	4900.00	2000.00	800.00
101	Red Dooin	2250.00	1125.00	675.00
102	Ty Cobb	15000.00	6000.00	2400.
103	Hugh Jennings	4500.00	1800.00	700.00
104	Roger Bresnahan	4500.00	1800.00	700.00
105	Jake Stahl	2250.00	1125.00	675.00
106	Tris Speaker	8000.00	4000.00	2400.
107	Ed Walsh	5500.00	2100.00	800.00
108	Christy Mathewson	9000.00	4000.00	1800.
109	Johnny Evers	5000.00	2000.00	800.00

	NR MT	EX	VG
110 Walter Johnson	10000.00	4000.00	1800.

1960 Lake To Lake Dairy Braves

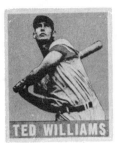

buyers of the day, the set is skip-numbered between 1-168. Card backs contain offers of felt pennants, an album for the cards or 5-1/2" by 7-1/2" premium photos of Hall of Famers.

This 28-card set of unnumbered 2-1/2" by 3-1/4" cards offers a special challenge for the condition-conscious collector. Originally issued by being stapled to milk cartons, the cards were redeemable for prizes ranging from pen and pencil sets to Braves tickets. When sent in for redemption, the cards had a hole punched in the corner. Naturally, collectors most desire cards without the staple or punch holes. Cards are printed in blue ink on front, red ink on back. Because he was traded in May, and his card withdrawn, the Ray Boone card is scarce; the Billy Bruton card is unaccountably scarcer still.

		NR MT	EX	VG
Complete Set:		1200.00	600.00	360.00
Common Player:		13.00	6.50	4.00
(1)	Henry Aaron	275.00	137.00	82.00
(2)	Joe Adcock	17.50	8.75	5.25
(3)	Ray Boone	125.00	62.00	37.00
(4)	Bill Bruton	275.00	137.00	82.00
(5)	Bob Buhl	17.50	8.75	5.25
(6)	Lou Burdette	20.00	10.00	6.00
(7)	Chuck Cottier	13.00	6.50	4.00
(8)	Wes Covington	15.00	7.50	4.50
(9)	Del Crandall	17.50	8.75	5.25
(10)	Charlie Dressen	15.00	7.50	4.50
(11)	Bob Giggie	13.00	6.50	4.00
(12)	Joey Jay	13.00	6.50	4.00
(13)	Johnny Logan	15.00	7.50	4.50
(14)	Felix Mantilla	13.00	6.50	4.00
(15)	Lee Maye	13.00	6.50	4.00
(16)	Don McMahon	13.00	6.50	4.00
(17)	George Myatt	13.00	6.50	4.00
(18)	Andy Pafko	15.00	7.50	4.50
(19)	Juan Pizarro	13.00	6.50	4.00
(20)	Mel Roach	13.00	6.50	4.00
(21)	Bob Rush	13.00	6.50	4.00
(22)	Bob Scheffing	13.00	6.50	4.00
(23)	Red Schoendienst	20.00	10.00	6.00
(24)	Warren Spahn	75.00	37.00	22.00
(25)	Al Spangler	13.00	6.50	4.00
(26)	Frank Torre	13.00	6.50	4.00
(27)	Carl Willey	13.00	6.50	4.00
(28)	Whitlow Wyatt	13.00	6.50	4.00

1948 Leaf

The first color baseball cards of the post-World War II era were the 98-card, 2-3/8" by 2-7/8", set produced by Chicago's Leaf Gum Company in 1948-1949. The color was crude, probably helping to make the set less popular than the Bowman issues of the same era. One of the toughest post-war sets to complete, exactly half of the Leaf issue - 49 of the cards - are significantly harder to find than the other 49. Probably intended to confound bubble gum

		NR MT	EX	VG
Complete Set:		30000.00	15000.00	9000.
Common Player:		25.00	12.50	7.50
Common Scarce Player:		300.00	150.00	90.00
1	Joe DiMaggio	2000.00	1000.00	600.00
3	Babe Ruth	2200.00	1100.00	650.00
4	Stan Musial	700.00	350.00	200.00
5	Virgil Trucks	400.00	200.00	125.00
8	Leroy Paige	2000.00	1000.00	600.00
10	Paul Trout	25.00	12.50	7.50
11	Phil Rizzuto	150.00	75.00	45.00
13	Casimer Michaels	300.00	150.00	90.00
14	Billy Johnson	30.00	15.00	9.00
17	Frank Overmire	25.00	12.50	7.50
19	John Wyrostek	300.00	150.00	90.00
20	Hank Sauer	400.00	200.00	125.00
22	Al Evans	25.00	12.50	7.50
26	Sam Chapman	25.00	12.50	7.50
27	Mickey Harris	25.00	12.50	7.50
28	Jim Hegan	25.00	12.50	7.50
29	Elmer Valo	25.00	12.50	7.50
30	Bill Goodman	300.00	150.00	90.00
31	Lou Brissie	25.00	12.50	7.50
32	Warren Spahn	200.00	100.00	60.00
33	Harry Lowrey	300.00	150.00	90.00
36	Al Zarilla	300.00	150.00	90.00
38	Ted Kluszewski	80.00	40.00	25.00
39	Ewell Blackwell	50.00	25.00	15.00
42	Kent Peterson	25.00	12.50	7.50
43	Eddie Stevens	300.00	150.00	90.00
45	Ken Keltner	300.00	150.00	90.00
46	Johnny Mize	90.00	45.00	27.00
47	George Vico	25.00	12.50	7.50
48	Johnny Schmitz	300.00	150.00	90.00
49	Del Ennis	40.00	20.00	12.00
50	Dick Wakefield	25.00	12.50	7.50
51	Alvin Dark	400.00	200.00	125.00
53	John Vandermeer (Vander Meer)	40.00	20.00	12.00
54	Bobby Adams	300.00	150.00	90.00
55	Tommy Henrich	400.00	200.00	125.00
56	Larry Jensen (Jansen)	25.00	12.50	7.50
57	Bob McCall	25.00	12.50	7.50
59	Lucius Appling	80.00	40.00	25.00
61	Jake Early	25.00	12.50	7.50
62	Eddie Joost	300.00	150.00	90.00
63	Barney McCosky	300.00	150.00	90.00
65	Bob Elliot (Elliott)	25.00	12.50	7.50
66	Orval Grove	300.00	150.00	90.00
68	Ed Miller	300.00	150.00	90.00
70	John Wagner	250.00	125.00	75.00
72	Hank Edwards	25.00	12.50	7.50
73	Pat Seerey	25.00	12.50	7.50
75	Dom DiMaggio	500.00	250.00	150.00
76	Ted Williams	900.00	450.00	275.00
77	Roy Smalley	25.00	12.50	7.50
78	Walter Evers	300.00	150.00	90.00
79	Jackie Robinson	700.00	350.00	210.00
81	George Kurowski	300.00	150.00	90.00
82	Johnny Lindell	25.00	12.50	7.50
83	Bobby Doerr	100.00	50.00	30.00
84	Sid Hudson	25.00	12.50	7.50
85	Dave Philley	300.00	150.00	90.00
86	Ralph Weigel	25.00	12.50	7.50
88	Frank Gustine	300.00	150.00	90.00

		NR MT	EX	VG
91	Ralph Kiner	150.00	75.00	45.00
93	Bob Feller	1200.00	600.00	350.00
95	George Stirnweiss	25.00	12.50	7.50
97	Martin Marion	40.00	20.00	12.00
98	Hal Newhouser	500.00	250.00	150.00
102a	Gene Hermansk (incorrect spelling)	300.00	150.00	90.00
102b	Gene Hermanski (correct spelling)	25.00	12.50	7.50
104	Edward Stewart	300.00	150.00	90.00
106	Lou Boudreau	100.00	50.00	30.00
108	Matthew Batts	300.00	150.00	90.00
111	Gerald Priddy	25.00	12.50	7.50
113	Emil Leonard	300.00	150.00	90.00
117	Joe Gordon	25.00	12.50	7.50
120	George Kell	550.00	275.00	165.00
121	John Pesky	400.00	200.00	120.00
123	Clifford Fannin	300.00	150.00	90.00
125	Andy Pafko	25.00	12.50	7.50
127	Enos Slaughter	600.00	300.00	180.00
128	Warren Rosar	25.00	12.50	7.50
129	Kirby Higbe	300.00	150.00	90.00
131	Sid Gordon	300.00	150.00	90.00
133	Tommy Holmes	400.00	200.00	120.00
136a	Cliff Aberson (full sleeve)	25.00	12.50	7.50
136b	Cliff Aberson (short sleeve)	175.00	87.00	52.00
137	Harry Walker	300.00	150.00	90.00
138	Larry Doby	500.00	250.00	150.00
139	Johnny Hopp	25.00	12.50	7.50
142	Danny Murtaugh	300.00	150.00	90.00
143	Dick Sisler	300.00	150.00	90.00
144	Bob Dillinger	300.00	150.00	90.00
146	Harold Reiser	400.00	200.00	120.00
149	Henry Majeski	300.00	150.00	90.00
153	Floyd Baker	300.00	150.00	90.00
158	Harry Brecheen	400.00	200.00	120.00
159	Mizell Platt	25.00	12.50	7.50
160	Bob Scheffing	400.00	200.00	120.00
161	Vernon Stephens	400.00	200.00	120.00
163	Freddy Hutchinson	400.00	200.00	120.00
165	Dale Mitchell	400.00	200.00	120.00
168	Phil Cavaretta (Cavarretta)	400.00	200.00	120.00

1960 Leaf

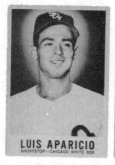

LUIS APARICIO
SHORTSTOP • CHICAGO WHITE SOX

While known to the hobby as "Leaf" cards, this set of 144 cards carries the copyright of Sports Novelties Inc., Chicago. The 2-1/2" by 3-1/2" cards feature black and white player portrait photos, with background airbrushed away. Cards were sold in 5¢ wax packs with a marble, rather than a piece of bubble gum. The second half of the set, cards #73-144, are very scarce and make the set a real challenge for the collector. Card #25, Jim Grant, is found in two versions, with his own picture (black cap) and with a photo of Brooks Lawrence (white cap). Eight cards (#'s 1, 12, 17, 23, 35, 58, 61 and 72) exist with close-up photos that are much rarer than the normal cap to chest photos. It is believed the scarce "face only" cards are proof cards prepared by Leaf as only a handful are known to exist.

		NR MT	EX	VG
Complete Set:		1800.00	900.00	550.00
Common Player: 1-72		4.00	2.00	1.25
Common Player: 73-144		15.00	7.50	4.50

		NR MT	EX	VG
1	Luis Aparicio	25.00	12.50	7.50
2	Woody Held	4.00	2.00	1.25
3	Frank Lary	3.00	1.50	.90
4	Camilo Pascual	3.00	1.50	.90
5	Frank Herrera	4.00	2.00	1.25
6	Felipe Alou	3.00	1.50	.90
7	Bennie Daniels	4.00	2.00	1.25
8	Roger Craig	3.00	1.50	.90
9	Eddie Kasko	4.00	2.00	1.25
10	Bob Grim	4.00	2.00	1.25
11	Jim Busby	4.00	2.00	1.25
12	Ken Boyer	4.00	2.00	1.25
13	Bob Boyd	4.00	2.00	1.25
14	Sam Jones	4.00	2.00	1.25
15	Larry Jackson	4.00	2.00	1.25
16	Roy Face	4.00	2.00	1.25
17	Walt Moryn	4.00	2.00	1.25
18	Jim Gilliam	4.00	2.00	1.25
19	Don Newcombe	3.00	1.50	.90
20	Glen Hobbie	4.00	2.00	1.25
21	Pedro Ramos	4.00	2.00	1.25
22	Ryne Duren	4.00	2.00	1.25
23	Joe Jay	4.00	2.00	1.25
24	Lou Berberet	4.00	2.00	1.25
25a	Jim Grant (white cap, photo actually Brooks Lawrence)	25.00	12.50	7.50
25b	Jim Grant (dark cap, correct photo)	50.00	25.00	15.00
26	Tom Borland	4.00	2.00	1.25
27	Brooks Robinson	50.00	25.00	15.00
28	Jerry Adair	3.00	1.50	.90
29	Ron Jackson	4.00	2.00	1.25
30	George Strickland	4.00	2.00	1.25
31	Rocky Bridges	4.00	2.00	1.25
32	Bill Tuttle	4.00	2.00	1.25
33	Ken Hunt	3.00	1.50	.90
34	Hal Griggs	4.00	2.00	1.25
35	Jim Coates	3.00	1.50	.90
36	Brooks Lawrence	4.00	2.00	1.25
37	Duke Snider	50.00	25.00	15.00
38	Al Spangler	4.00	2.00	1.25
39	Jim Owens	4.00	2.00	1.25
40	Bill Virdon	4.00	2.00	1.25
41	Ernie Broglio	4.00	2.00	1.25
42	Andre Rodgers	4.00	2.00	1.25
43	Julio Becquer	4.00	2.00	1.25
44	Tony Taylor	4.00	2.00	1.25
45	Jerry Lynch	3.00	1.50	.90
46	Cletis Boyer	4.00	2.00	1.25
47	Jerry Lumpe	3.00	1.50	.90
48	Charlie Maxwell	4.00	2.00	1.25
49	Jim Perry	3.00	1.50	.90
50	Danny McDevitt	4.00	2.00	1.25
51	Juan Pizarro	4.00	2.00	1.25
52	Dallas Green	4.00	2.00	1.25
53	Bob Friend	3.00	1.50	.90
54	Jack Sanford	3.00	1.50	.90
55	Jim Rivera	4.00	2.00	1.25
56	Ted Wills	4.00	2.00	1.25
57	Milt Pappas	3.00	1.50	.90
58a	Hal Smith (team & position on back)	4.00	2.00	1.25
58b	Hal Smith (team blackened out on back)	50.00	25.00	15.00
58c	Hal Smith (team missing on back)	50.00	25.00	15.00
59	Bob Avila	4.00	2.00	1.25
60	Clem Labine	3.00	1.50	.90
61	Vic Rehm	3.00	1.50	.90
62	John Gabler	3.00	1.50	.90
63	John Tsitouris	4.00	2.00	1.25
64	Dave Sisler	4.00	2.00	1.25
65	Vic Power	3.00	1.50	.90
66	Earl Battey	3.00	1.50	.90
67	Bob Purkey	3.00	1.50	.90
68	Moe Drabowsky	4.00	2.00	1.25
69	Hoyt Wilhelm	6.00	3.00	1.75
70	Humberto Robinson	4.00	2.00	1.25
71	Whitey Herzog	4.00	2.00	1.25
72	Dick Donovan	3.00	1.50	.90
73	Gordon Jones	15.00	7.50	4.50
74	Joe Hicks	15.00	7.50	4.50
75	Ray Culp	18.00	9.00	5.50
76	Dick Drott	15.00	7.50	4.50
77	Bob Duliba	15.00	7.50	4.50
78	Art Ditmar	18.00	9.00	5.50
79	Steve Korcheck	15.00	7.50	4.50
80	Henry Mason	15.00	7.50	4.50
81	Harry Simpson	15.00	7.50	4.50
82	Gene Green	15.00	7.50	4.50
83	Bob Shaw	15.00	7.50	4.50
84	Howard Reed	15.00	7.50	4.50

		NR MT	EX	VG
85	Dick Stigman	15.00	7.50	4.50
86	Rip Repulski	15.00	7.50	4.50
87	Seth Morehead	15.00	7.50	4.50
88	Camilo Carreon	15.00	7.50	4.50
89	John Blanchard	18.00	9.00	5.50
90	Billy Hoeft	15.00	7.50	4.50
91	Fred Hopke	18.00	9.00	5.50
92	Joe Martin	15.00	7.50	4.50
93	Wally Shannon	18.00	9.00	5.50
94	Baseball's Two Hal Smiths (Harold Raymond Smith, Harold Wayne Smith)	20.00	10.00	6.00
95	Al Schroll	15.00	7.50	4.50
96	John Kucks	15.00	7.50	4.50
97	Tom Morgan	15.00	7.50	4.50
98	Willie Jones	15.00	7.50	4.50
99	Marshall Renfroe	18.00	9.00	5.50
100	Willie Tasby	15.00	7.50	4.50
101	Irv Noren	15.00	7.50	4.50
102	Russ Snyder	15.00	7.50	4.50
103	Bob Turley	30.00	15.00	9.00
104	Jim Woods	15.00	7.50	4.50
105	Ronnie Kline	15.00	7.50	4.50
106	Steve Bilko	15.00	7.50	4.50
107	Elmer Valo	18.00	9.00	5.50
108	Tom McAvoy	18.00	9.00	5.50
109	Stan Williams	15.00	7.50	4.50
110	Earl Averill	15.00	7.50	4.50
111	Lee Walls	15.00	7.50	4.50
112	Paul Richards	18.00	9.00	5.50
113	Ed Sadowski	15.00	7.50	4.50
114	Stover McIlwain	18.00	9.00	5.50
115	Chuck Tanner (photo actually Ken Kuhn)	20.00	10.00	6.00
116	Lou Klimchock	15.00	7.50	4.50
117	Neil Chrisley	15.00	7.50	4.50
118	John Callison	20.00	10.00	6.00
119	Hal Smith	15.00	7.50	4.50
120	Carl Sawatski	15.00	7.50	4.50
121	Frank Leja	18.00	9.00	5.50
122	Earl Torgeson	15.00	7.50	4.50
123	Art Schult	15.00	7.50	4.50
124	Jim Brosnan	18.00	9.00	5.50
125	George Anderson	40.00	20.00	12.00
126	Joe Pignatano	15.00	7.50	4.50
127	Rocky Nelson	15.00	7.50	4.50
128	Orlando Cepeda	50.00	25.00	15.00
129	Daryl Spencer	15.00	7.50	4.50
130	Ralph Lumenti	15.00	7.50	4.50
131	Sam Taylor	15.00	7.50	4.50
132	Harry Brecheen	18.00	9.00	5.50
133	Johnny Groth	15.00	7.50	4.50
134	Wayne Terwilliger	15.00	7.50	4.50
135	Kent Hadley	18.00	9.00	5.50
136	Faye Throneberry	15.00	7.50	4.50
137	Jack Meyer	15.00	7.50	4.50
138	Chuck Cottier	15.00	7.50	4.50
139	Joe DeMaestri	18.00	9.00	5.50
140	Gene Freese	15.00	7.50	4.50
141	Curt Flood	40.00	20.00	12.00
142	Gino Cimoli	15.00	7.50	4.50
143	Clay Dalrymple	15.00	7.50	4.50
144	Jim Bunning	75.00	38.00	23.00

1886 Lorillard Team Card

Issued in 1886 by Lorillard Tobacco Co., these 4" by 5-1/2" cards were issued for the Chicago, Detroit and New York baseball clubs. Each card carries the team's schedule (starting with June) on one side and features 11 player portraits enclosed in circles on the other. Both sides have advertising for Lorillard's Climax Plug tobacco.

		NR MT	EX	VG
Complete Set:		30000.00	15000.00	9000.
Common Team:		5000.00	2500.00	1500.
(1)	Chicago League Base Ball Club	6500.00	3250.00	2000.
(2)	Detroit League Base Ball Club	5500.00	2750.00	1650.
(3)	New York League Base Ball Club	9000.00	4500.00	2750.
(4)	Philadelphia League Base Ball Club	5000.00	2500.00	1500.

1949 Lummis Peanut Butter Phillies

This 12-card regional set featuring the Phillies was issued in the Philadelphia area by Lummis Peanut Butter in 1949. The cards measure 3-1/4" by 4-1/4" and are unnumbered. The fronts feature an action photo with a facsimile autograph, while the backs advertise a game ticket promotion by Lummis Peanut Butter. The same photos and checklist were also used for a regional sticker card set issued by Sealtest Dairy the same year.

		NR MT	EX	VG
Complete Set:		850.00	425.00	255.00
Common Player:		60.00	30.00	18.00
(1)	Rich Ashburn	150.00	75.00	45.00
(2)	Hank Borowy	60.00	30.00	18.00
(3)	Del Ennis	100.00	50.00	30.00
(4)	Granny Hamner	60.00	30.00	18.00
(5)	Puddinhead Jones	60.00	30.00	18.00
(6)	Russ Meyer	60.00	30.00	18.00
(7)	Bill Nicholson	60.00	30.00	18.00
(8)	Robin Roberts	200.00	100.00	60.00
(9)	"Schoolboy" Rowe	60.00	30.00	18.00
(10)	Andy Seminick	60.00	30.00	18.00
(11)	Curt Simmons	100.00	50.00	30.00
(12)	Eddie Waitkus	60.00	30.00	18.00

M

1916 M101-4 The Sporting News

This 200-card set was issued as a premium by The Sporting News and was also used by Weil Baking, the Globe Stores, and several other regional advertisers. The 1-5/8" by 3" cards contain bordered black and

RAY MORGAN
2nd B.—Washington Am.
224

white photos on the fronts, with the player name, position and team, as well as a card number. Card backs are in a horizontal format and show an advertisement for the sponsoring sports weekly. Most of the day's top players and many Hall of Famers are included in the set, with the Babe Ruth card carrying the highest value. The complete set price includes all variations.

		NR MT	EX	VG
Complete Set:		15000.00	7500.00	4500.
Common Player:		35.00	17.50	10.50
1	Babe Adams	50.00	25.00	15.00
2	Sam Agnew	40.00	20.00	12.00
3	Eddie Ainsmith	35.00	17.50	10.50
4	Grover Alexander	100.00	50.00	30.00
5	Leon Ames	35.00	17.50	10.50
6	Jimmy Archer	35.00	17.50	10.50
7	Jimmy Austin	35.00	17.50	10.50
8	H.D. Baird	50.00	25.00	15.00
9	J. Franklin Baker	70.00	35.00	21.00
10	Dave Bancroft	70.00	35.00	21.00
11	Jack Barry	35.00	17.50	10.50
12	Zinn Beck	35.00	17.50	10.50
13	"Chief" Bender	70.00	35.00	21.00
14	Joe Benz	35.00	17.50	10.50
15	Bob Bescher	35.00	17.50	10.50
16	Al Betzel	35.00	17.50	10.50
17	Mordecai Brown	70.00	35.00	21.00
18	Eddie Burns	35.00	17.50	10.50
19	George Burns	50.00	25.00	15.00
20	Geo. J. Burns	35.00	17.50	10.50
21	Joe Bush	40.00	20.00	12.00
22	"Donie" Bush	45.00	22.00	13.50
23	Art Butler	35.00	17.50	10.50
24	Bobbie Byrne	35.00	17.50	10.50
25	Forrest Cady	50.00	25.00	15.00
26	Jimmy Callahan	35.00	17.50	10.50
27	Ray Caldwell	35.00	17.50	10.50
28	Max Carey	70.00	35.00	21.00
29	George Chalmers	35.00	17.50	10.50
30	Ray Chapman	40.00	20.00	12.00
31	Larry Cheney	35.00	17.50	10.50
32	Eddie Cicotte	45.00	22.00	13.50
33	Tom Clarke	35.00	17.50	10.50
34	Eddie Collins	90.00	45.00	27.00
35	"Shauno" Collins	35.00	17.50	10.50
36	Charles Comiskey	60.00	30.00	18.00
37	Joe Connolly	35.00	17.50	10.50
38	Ty Cobb	1500.00	750.00	450.00
39	Harry Coveleskie (Coveleski)	35.00	17.50	10.50
40	Gavvy Cravath	40.00	20.00	12.00
41	Sam Crawford	70.00	35.00	21.00
42	Jean Dale	35.00	17.50	10.50
43	Jake Daubert	40.00	20.00	12.00
44	Charles Deal	35.00	17.50	10.50
45	Al Demaree	35.00	17.50	10.50
46	Josh Devore	50.00	25.00	15.00
47	William Doak	35.00	17.50	10.50
48	Bill Donovan	35.00	17.50	10.50
49	Charles Dooin	35.00	17.50	10.50
50	Mike Doolan	35.00	17.50	10.50
51	Larry Doyle	40.00	20.00	12.00
52	Jean Dubuc	35.00	17.50	10.50
53	Oscar Dugey	35.00	17.50	10.50
54	Johnny Evers	70.00	35.00	21.00
55	Urban Faber	70.00	35.00	21.00
56	"Hap" Felsch	45.00	22.00	13.50
57	Bill Fischer	35.00	17.50	10.50

		NR MT	EX	VG
58	Ray Fisher	35.00	17.50	10.50
59	Max Flack	35.00	17.50	10.50
60	Art Fletcher	35.00	17.50	10.50
61	Eddie Foster	35.00	17.50	10.50
62	Jacques Fournier	35.00	17.50	10.50
63	Del Gainer (Gainor)	35.00	17.50	10.50
64	"Chic" Gandil	65.00	32.00	19.50
65	Larry Gardner	35.00	17.50	10.50
66	Joe Gedeon	35.00	17.50	10.50
67	Gus Getz	35.00	17.50	10.50
68	Geo. Gibson	35.00	17.50	10.50
69	Wilbur Good	35.00	17.50	10.50
70	Hank Gowdy	35.00	17.50	10.50
71	John Graney	35.00	17.50	10.50
72	Clark Griffith	90.00	45.00	27.00
73	Tom Griffith	35.00	17.50	10.50
74	Heinie Groh	40.00	20.00	12.00
75	Earl Hamilton	35.00	17.50	10.50
76	Bob Harmon	35.00	17.50	10.50
77	Roy Hartzell	35.00	17.50	10.50
78	Claude Hendrix	35.00	17.50	10.50
79	Olaf Henriksen	35.00	17.50	10.50
80	John Henry	35.00	17.50	10.50
81	"Buck" Herzog	35.00	17.50	10.50
82	Hugh High	35.00	17.50	10.50
83	Dick Hoblitzell	35.00	17.50	10.50
84	Harry Hooper	70.00	35.00	21.00
85	Ivan Howard	35.00	17.50	10.50
86	Miller Huggins	70.00	35.00	21.00
87	Joe Jackson	2000.00	1000.00	600.00
88	William James	35.00	17.50	10.50
89	Harold Janvrin	35.00	17.50	10.50
90	Hugh Jennings	70.00	35.00	21.00
91	Walter Johnson	450.00	225.00	135.00
92	Fielder Jones	35.00	17.50	10.50
93	Joe Judge	50.00	25.00	15.00
94	Bennie Kauff	35.00	17.50	10.50
95	Wm. Killefer Jr.	35.00	17.50	10.50
96	Ed. Konetchy	35.00	17.50	10.50
97	Napoleon Lajoie	150.00	75.00	45.00
98	Jack Lapp	35.00	17.50	10.50
99	John Lavan	35.00	17.50	10.50
100	Jimmy Lavender	35.00	17.50	10.50
101	"Nemo" Leibold	35.00	17.50	10.50
102	H.B. Leonard	35.00	17.50	10.50
103	Duffy Lewis	40.00	20.00	12.00
104	Hans Lobert	35.00	17.50	10.50
105	Tom Long	35.00	17.50	10.50
106	Fred Luderus	35.00	17.50	10.50
107	Connie Mack	125.00	62.00	37.00
108	Lee Magee	35.00	17.50	10.50
109	Sherwood Magee	55.00	27.00	16.50
110	Al. Mamaux	35.00	17.50	10.50
111	Leslie Mann	35.00	17.50	10.50
112	"Rabbit" Maranville	70.00	35.00	21.00
113	Rube Marquard	70.00	35.00	21.00
114	J. Erskine Mayer	35.00	17.50	10.50
115	George McBride	35.00	17.50	10.50
116	John J. McGraw	70.00	35.00	21.00
117	Jack McInnis	35.00	17.50	10.50
118	Fred Merkle	40.00	20.00	12.00
119	Chief Meyers	35.00	17.50	10.50
120	Clyde Milan	35.00	17.50	10.50
121	John Miller	50.00	25.00	15.00
122	Otto Miller	35.00	17.50	10.50
123	Willie Mitchell	35.00	17.50	10.50
124	Fred Mollwitz	35.00	17.50	10.50
125	Pat Moran	35.00	17.50	10.50
126	Ray Morgan	35.00	17.50	10.50
127	Geo. Moriarty	35.00	17.50	10.50
128	Guy Morton	35.00	17.50	10.50
129	Mike Mowrey	50.00	25.00	15.00
130	Ed. Murphy	50.00	25.00	15.00
131	"Hy" Myers	35.00	17.50	10.50
132	J.A. Niehoff	35.00	17.50	10.50
133	Rube Oldring	35.00	17.50	10.50
134	Oliver O'Mara	35.00	17.50	10.50
135	Steve O'Neill	35.00	17.50	10.50
136	"Dode" Paskert	35.00	17.50	10.50
137	Roger Peckinpaugh	50.00	25.00	15.00
138	Walter Pipp	45.00	22.00	13.50
139	Derril Pratt (Derrill)	35.00	17.50	10.50
140	Pat Ragan	50.00	25.00	15.00
141	Bill Rariden	35.00	17.50	10.50
142	Eppa Rixey	70.00	35.00	21.00
143	Davey Robertson	35.00	17.50	10.50
144	Wilbert Robinson	70.00	35.00	21.00
145	Bob Roth	35.00	17.50	10.50
146	Ed. Roush	70.00	35.00	21.00
147	Clarence Rowland	35.00	17.50	10.50
148	"Nap" Rucker	35.00	17.50	10.50

		NR MT	EX	VG
149	Dick Rudolph	35.00	17.50	10.50
150	Reb Russell	35.00	17.50	10.50
151	Babe Ruth	3750.00	1875.00	1125.
152	Vic Saier	35.00	17.50	10.50
153	"Slim" Sallee	35.00	17.50	10.50
154	Ray Schalk	70.00	35.00	21.00
155	Walter Schang	35.00	17.50	10.50
156	Frank Schulte	35.00	17.50	10.50
157	Everett Scott	35.00	17.50	10.50
158	Jim Scott	35.00	17.50	10.50
159	Tom Seaton	35.00	17.50	10.50
160	Howard Shanks	35.00	17.50	10.50
161	Bob Shawkey	50.00	25.00	15.00
162	Ernie Shore	20.00	10.00	6.00
163	Burt Shotton	20.00	10.00	6.00
164	Geo. Sisler	90.00	45.00	27.00
165	J. Carlisle Smith	35.00	17.50	10.50
166	Fred Snodgrass	35.00	17.50	10.50
167	Geo. Stallings	35.00	17.50	10.50
168a	Oscar Stanage (catching)	50.00	25.00	15.00
168b	Oscar Stanage (portrait to waist)			
		50.00	25.00	15.00
169	Charles Stengel	225.00	112.00	67.00
170	Milton Stock	35.00	17.50	10.50
171	Amos Strunk	50.00	25.00	15.00
172	Billy Sullivan	35.00	17.50	10.50
173	"Jeff" Tesreau	35.00	17.50	10.50
174	Joe Tinker	70.00	35.00	21.00
175	Fred Toney	35.00	17.50	10.50
176	Terry Turner	35.00	17.50	10.50
177	George Tyler	50.00	25.00	15.00
178	Jim Vaughn	35.00	17.50	10.50
179	Bob Veach	35.00	17.50	10.50
180	James Viox	35.00	17.50	10.50
181	Oscar Vitt	35.00	17.50	10.50
182	Hans Wagner	450.00	225.00	135.00
183	Clarence Walker	50.00	25.00	15.00
184	Ed. Walsh	70.00	35.00	21.00
185	W. Wambsganss (photo actually Fritz Coumbe)			
		50.00	25.00	15.00
186	Buck Weaver	45.00	22.00	13.50
187	Carl Weilman	35.00	17.50	10.50
188	Zach Wheat	70.00	35.00	21.00
189	Geo. Whitted	35.00	17.50	10.50
190	Fred Williams	40.00	20.00	12.00
191	Art Wilson	35.00	17.50	10.50
192	J. Owen Wilson	35.00	17.50	10.50
193	Ivy Wingo	35.00	17.50	10.50
194	"Mel" Wolfgang	35.00	17.50	10.50
195	Joe Wood	45.00	22.00	13.50
196	Steve Yerkes	35.00	17.50	10.50
197	"Pep" Young	50.00	25.00	15.00
198	Rollie Zeider	35.00	17.50	10.50
199	Heiny Zimmerman	40.00	20.00	12.00
200	Ed. Zwilling	50.00	25.00	15.00

1915 M101-5
The Sporting News

This set, which is quite similar to the M101-5 The Sporting News issue, was also issued as a promotional premium by The Sporting News. The 200 black and white cards once again are printed with player photo, name, position, team and card number on the and advertising on the backs. The set checklist is the same as for sets issued by Morehouse Baking and Standard Baking. Most of the players

included in the 1-5/8" by 3" set also appear in the prior The Sporting News edition. The complete set price includes all variations.

		NR MT	EX	VG
Complete Set:		18000.00	9000.00	5400.
Common Player:		35.00	17.50	10.50
1	Babe Adams	50.00	25.00	15.00
2	Sam Agnew	40.00	20.00	12.00
3	Eddie Ainsmith	35.00	17.50	10.50
4	Grover Alexander	110.00	55.00	33.00
5	Leon Ames	35.00	17.50	10.50
6	Jimmy Archer	35.00	17.50	10.50
7	Jimmy Austin	35.00	17.50	10.50
8	J. Franklin Baker	75.00	37.00	22.00
9	Dave Bancroft	75.00	37.00	22.00
10	Jack Barry	35.00	17.50	10.50
11	Zinn Beck	35.00	17.50	10.50
12	Lute Boone	50.00	25.00	15.00
13	Joe Benz	35.00	17.50	10.50
14	Bob Bescher	35.00	17.50	10.50
15	Al Betzel	35.00	17.50	10.50
16	Roger Bresnahan	90.00	45.00	27.00
17	Eddie Burns	35.00	17.50	10.50
18	Geo. J. Burns	35.00	17.50	10.50
19	Joe Bush	40.00	20.00	12.00
20	Owen Bush	45.00	22.00	13.50
21	Art Butler	35.00	17.50	10.50
22	Bobbie Byrne	35.00	17.50	10.50
23a	Forrest Cady	110.00	55.00	33.00
23b	Mordecai Brown	90.00	45.00	27.00
24	Jimmy Callahan	35.00	17.50	10.50
25	Ray Caldwell	35.00	17.50	10.50
26	Max Carey	75.00	37.00	22.00
27	George Chalmers	35.00	17.50	10.50
28	Frank Chance	110.00	55.00	33.00
29	Ray Chapman	40.00	20.00	12.00
30	Larry Cheney	35.00	17.50	10.50
31	Eddie Cicotte	45.00	22.00	13.50
32	Tom Clarke	35.00	17.50	10.50
33	Eddie Collins	90.00	45.00	27.00
34	"Shauno" Collins	35.00	17.50	10.50
35	Charles Comisky (Comiskey)	80.00	40.00	24.00
36	Joe Connolly	35.00	17.50	10.50
37	Luther Cook	50.00	25.00	15.00
38	Jack Coombs	50.00	25.00	15.00
39	Dan Costello	50.00	25.00	15.00
40	Harry Coveleskie (Coveleski)	35.00	17.50	10.50
41	Gavvy Cravath	40.00	20.00	12.00
42	Sam Crawford	75.00	37.00	22.00
43	Jean Dale	35.00	17.50	10.50
44	Jake Daubert	40.00	20.00	12.00
45	Geo. A. Davis Jr.	50.00	25.00	15.00
46	Charles Deal	35.00	17.50	10.50
47	Al Demaree	35.00	17.50	10.50
48	William Doak	35.00	17.50	10.50
49	Bill Donovan	35.00	17.50	10.50
50	Charles Dooin	35.00	17.50	10.50
51	Mike Doolan	35.00	17.50	10.50
52	Larry Doyle	40.00	20.00	12.00
53	Jean Dubuc	35.00	17.50	10.50
54	Oscar Dugey	35.00	17.50	10.50
55	Johnny Evers	75.00	37.00	22.00
56	Urban Faber	75.00	37.00	22.00
57	"Hap" Felsch	45.00	22.00	13.50
58	Bill Fischer	35.00	17.50	10.50
59	Ray Fisher	35.00	17.50	10.50
60	Max Flack	35.00	17.50	10.50
61	Art Fletcher	35.00	17.50	10.50
62	Eddie Foster	35.00	17.50	10.50
63	Jacques Fournier	35.00	17.50	10.50
64	Del Gainer (Gainor)	35.00	17.50	10.50
65	Larry Gardner	35.00	17.50	10.50
66	Joe Gedeon	35.00	17.50	10.50
67	Gus Getz	35.00	17.50	10.50
68	Geo. Gibson	35.00	17.50	10.50
69	Wilbur Good	35.00	17.50	10.50
70	Hank Gowdy	35.00	17.50	10.50
71	John Graney	35.00	17.50	10.50
72	Tom Griffith	35.00	17.50	10.50
73	Heinie Groh	40.00	20.00	12.00
74	Earl Hamilton	35.00	17.50	10.50
75	Bob Harmon	35.00	17.50	10.50
76	Roy Hartzell	35.00	17.50	10.50
77	Claude Hendrix	35.00	17.50	10.50
78	Olaf Henriksen	35.00	17.50	10.50
79	John Henry	35.00	17.50	10.50
80	"Buck" Herzog	35.00	17.50	10.50
81	Hugh High	35.00	17.50	10.50
82	Dick Hoblitzell	35.00	17.50	10.50

		NR MT	EX	VG
83	Harry Hooper	75.00	37.00	22.00
84	Ivan Howard	35.00	17.50	10.50
85	Miller Huggins	75.00	37.00	22.00
86	Joe Jackson	2500.00	1250.00	750.00
87	William James	35.00	17.50	10.50
88	Harold Janvrin	35.00	17.50	10.50
89	Hugh Jennings	75.00	37.00	22.00
90	Walter Johnson	500.00	250.00	150.00
91	Fielder Jones	35.00	17.50	10.50
92	Bennie Kauff	35.00	17.50	10.50
93	Wm. Killefer Jr.	35.00	17.50	10.50
94	Ed. Konetchy	35.00	17.50	10.50
95	Napoleon Lajoie	475.00	237.00	142.00
96	Jack Lapp	35.00	17.50	10.50
97a	John Lavan (correct spelling)	50.00	25.00	15.00
97b	John Lavin (incorrect spelling)	50.00	25.00	15.00
98	Jimmy Lavender	35.00	17.50	10.50
99	"Nemo" Leibold	35.00	17.50	10.50
100	H.B. Leonard	35.00	17.50	10.50
101	Duffy Lewis	40.00	20.00	12.00
102	Hans Lobert	35.00	17.50	10.50
103	Tom Long	35.00	17.50	10.50
104	Fred Luderus	35.00	17.50	10.50
105	Connie Mack	200.00	100.00	60.00
106	Lee Magee	35.00	17.50	10.50
107	Al. Mamaux	35.00	17.50	10.50
108	Leslie Mann	35.00	17.50	10.50
109	"Rabbit" Maranville	75.00	37.00	22.00
110	Rube Marquard	75.00	37.00	22.00
111	Armando Marsans	50.00	25.00	15.00
112	J. Erskine Mayer	35.00	17.50	10.50
113	George McBride	35.00	17.50	10.50
114	John J. McGraw	100.00	50.00	30.00
115	Jack McInnis	35.00	17.50	10.50
116	Fred Merkle	40.00	20.00	12.00
117	Chief Meyers	35.00	17.50	10.50
118	Clyde Milan	35.00	17.50	10.50
119	Otto Miller	35.00	17.50	10.50
120	Willie Mitchel (Mitchell)	35.00	17.50	10.50
121	Fred Mollwitz	35.00	17.50	10.50
122	J. Herbert Moran	50.00	25.00	15.00
123	Pat Moran	35.00	17.50	10.50
124	Ray Morgan	35.00	17.50	10.50
125	Geo. Moriarty	35.00	17.50	10.50
126	Guy Morton	35.00	17.50	10.50
127	Ed. Murphy (photo actually Danny Murphy)	50.00	25.00	15.00
128	John Murray	50.00	25.00	15.00
129	"Hy" Myers	35.00	17.50	10.50
130	J.A. Niehoff	35.00	17.50	10.50
131	Leslie Nunamaker	50.00	25.00	15.00
132	Rube Oldring	35.00	17.50	10.50
133	Oliver O'Mara	35.00	17.50	10.50
134	Steve O'Neill	35.00	17.50	10.50
135	"Dode" Paskert	35.00	17.50	10.50
136	Roger Peckinpaugh (photo actually Gavvy Cravath)	50.00	25.00	15.00
137	E.J. Pfeffer (photo actually Jeff Pfeffer)	50.00	25.00	15.00
138	Geo. Pierce (Pearce)	50.00	25.00	15.00
139	Walter Pipp	45.00	22.00	13.50
140	Derril Pratt (Derrill)	35.00	17.50	10.50
141	Bill Rariden	35.00	17.50	10.50
142	Eppa Rixey	75.00	37.00	22.00
143	Davey Robertson	35.00	17.50	10.50
144	Wilbert Robertson	75.00	37.00	22.00
145	Bob Roth	35.00	17.50	10.50
146	Ed. Roush	75.00	37.00	22.00
147	Clarence Rowland	35.00	17.50	10.50
148	"Nap" Rucker	35.00	17.50	10.50
149	Dick Rudolph	35.00	17.50	10.50
150	Reb Russell	35.00	17.50	10.50
151	Babe Ruth	5000.00	2500.00	1500.
152	Vic Saier	35.00	17.50	10.50
153	"Slim" Sallee	35.00	17.50	10.50
154	"Germany" Schaefer	50.00	25.00	15.00
155	Ray Schalk	75.00	37.00	22.00
156	Walter Schang	35.00	17.50	10.50
157	Chas. Schmidt	50.00	25.00	15.00
158	Frank Schulte	35.00	17.50	10.50
159	Jim Scott	35.00	17.50	10.50
160	Everett Scott	35.00	17.50	10.50
161	Tom Seaton	35.00	17.50	10.50
162	Howard Shanks	35.00	17.50	10.50
163	Bob Shawkey (photo actually Jack McInnis)	50.00	25.00	15.00
164	Ernie Shore	35.00	17.50	10.50
165	Burt Shotton	35.00	17.50	10.50
166	George Sisler	90.00	45.00	27.00
167	J. Carlisle Smith	35.00	17.50	10.50
168	Fred Snodgrass	35.00	17.50	10.50

		NR MT	EX	VG
169	Geo. Stallings	35.00	17.50	10.50
170	Oscar Stanage (photo actually Chas. Schmidt)	45.00	22.00	13.50
171	Charles Stengel	475.00	237.00	142.00
172	Milton Stock	35.00	17.50	10.50
173	Amos Strunk (photo actually Olaf Henriksen)	50.00	25.00	15.00
174	Billy Sullivan	35.00	17.50	10.50
175	Chas. Tesreau	50.00	25.00	15.00
176	Jim Thorpe	5000.00	2500.00	1500.
177	Joe Tinker	75.00	37.00	22.00
178	Fred Toney	35.00	17.50	10.50
179	Terry Turner	35.00	17.50	10.50
180	Jim Vaughn	35.00	17.50	10.50
181	Bob Veach	35.00	17.50	10.50
182	James Voix	35.00	17.50	10.50
183	Oscar Vitt	35.00	17.50	10.50
184	Hans Wagner	500.00	250.00	150.00
185	Clarence Walker (photo not Walker)	50.00	25.00	15.00
186	Zach Wheat	75.00	37.00	22.00
187	Ed. Walsh	75.00	37.00	22.00
188	Buck Weaver	45.00	22.00	13.50
189	Carl Weilman	35.00	17.50	10.50
190	Geo. Whitted	35.00	17.50	10.50
191	Fred Williams	40.00	20.00	12.00
192	Art Wilson	35.00	17.50	10.50
193	J. Owen Wilson	35.00	17.50	10.50
194	Ivy Wingo	35.00	17.50	10.50
195	"Mel" Wolfgang	35.00	17.50	10.50
196	Joe Wood	45.00	22.00	13.50
197	Steve Yerkes	35.00	17.50	10.50
198	Rollie Zeider	35.00	17.50	10.50
199	Heiny Zimmerman	40.00	20.00	12.00
200	Ed. Zwilling	50.00	25.00	15.00

1919 M101-6 Sporting News

This set of glossy black and white player photos was issued in 1919 by The Sporting News. The cards measure 4-1/2" by 6-1/2" and included action photos with the player's name and team listed at the bottom of the borderless cards. The unnumbered cards had blank backs. There are two cards of Babe Ruth in the set, one identifying him as a member of the Red Sox, the other as a Yankee. The card of Hugh High actually pictures Bob Shawkey.

		NR MT	EX	VG
Complete Set:		20000.00	10000.00	6000.
Common Player:		45.00	22.00	13.50
(1)	Grover C. Alexander (Philadelphia)	90.00	45.00	27.00
(2)	Grover C. Alexander (Chicago)	90.00	45.00	27.00
(3)	Jim Bagby	45.00	22.00	13.50
(4)	Franklin Baker	75.00	37.00	22.00
(5)	Dave Bancroft	45.00	22.00	13.50
(6)	Jack Barry	45.00	22.00	13.50
(7)	Johnny Bates	45.00	22.00	13.50
(8)	Carson Bigbee	45.00	22.00	13.50
(9)	Geo. Burns	45.00	22.00	13.50
(10)	Owen Bush	45.00	22.00	13.50
(11)	Max Carey	75.00	37.00	22.00
(12)	Ray Chapman	50.00	25.00	15.00
(13)	Hal Chase	55.00	27.00	16.50
(14)	Eddie Cicotte	50.00	25.00	15.00
(15)	Ty Cobb	3000.00	1500.00	900.00

		NR MT	EX	VG
(16)	Eddie Collins	75.00	37.00	22.00
(17)	"Gavvy" Cravath	50.00	25.00	15.00
(18)	Walton Cruise	45.00	22.00	13.50
(19)	George Cutshaw	45.00	22.00	13.50
(20)	George Dauss	45.00	22.00	13.50
(21)	Dave Davenport	45.00	22.00	13.50
(22)	Bill Doak	45.00	22.00	13.50
(23)	Larry Doyle	45.00	22.00	13.50
(24)	Howard Ehmke	45.00	22.00	13.50
(25)	Urban Faber	75.00	37.00	22.00
(26)	Happy Felsch	65.00	32.00	19.50
(27)	Del Gainer (Gainor)	45.00	22.00	13.50
(28)	Chick Gandil	55.00	27.00	16.50
(29)	Larry Gardner	45.00	22.00	13.50
(30)	Mike Gonzales	45.00	22.00	13.50
(31)	Jack Graney	45.00	22.00	13.50
(32)	Heinie Groh	45.00	22.00	13.50
(33)	Earl Hamilton	45.00	22.00	13.50
(34)	Harry Heilmann	75.00	37.00	22.00
(35)	Hugh High (New York, photo actually Bob			
	Shawkey)	45.00	22.00	13.50
(36)	Hugh High (Detroit)	45.00	22.00	13.50
(37)	Bill Hinchman	45.00	22.00	13.50
(38)	Walter Holke (New York)	45.00	22.00	13.50
(39)	Walter Holke (Boston)	45.00	22.00	13.50
(40)	Harry Hooper	75.00	37.00	22.00
(41)	Rogers Hornsby	500.00	250.00	150.00
(42)	Joe Jackson	1000.00	500.00	300.00
(43)	Bill Jacobson	45.00	22.00	13.50
(44)	Walter Johnson	600.00	300.00	180.00
(45)	Sam Jones	45.00	22.00	13.50
(46)	Joe Judge	45.00	22.00	13.50
(47)	Benny Kauff	45.00	22.00	13.50
(48)	Ed Konetchy (Boston)	45.00	22.00	13.50
(49)	Ed Konetchy (Brooklyn)	45.00	22.00	13.50
(50)	Nemo Leibold	45.00	22.00	13.50
(51)	Duffy Lewis	45.00	22.00	13.50
(52)	Fred Luderas (Luderus)	45.00	22.00	13.50
(53)	Les Mann	45.00	22.00	13.50
(54)	"Rabbit" Maranville	75.00	37.00	22.00
(55)	John McGraw	90.00	45.00	27.00
(56)	Fred Merkle	50.00	25.00	15.00
(57)	Clyde Milan	45.00	22.00	13.50
(58)	Otto Miller	45.00	22.00	13.50
(59)	Guy Morton	45.00	22.00	13.50
(60)	Hy Myers	45.00	22.00	13.50
(61)	Greasy Neale	55.00	27.00	16.50
(62)	Dode Paskert	45.00	22.00	13.50
(63)	Roger Peckinpaugh	50.00	25.00	15.00
(64)	Jeff Pfeffer	45.00	22.00	13.50
(65)	Walter Pipp	65.00	32.00	19.50
(66)	Johnny Rawlings	45.00	22.00	13.50
(67)	Sam Rice	75.00	37.00	22.00
(68)	Ed Roush	75.00	37.00	22.00
(69)	Dick Rudolph	45.00	22.00	13.50
(70)	Babe Ruth (Red Sox)	3000.00	1500.00	900.00
(71)	"Babe" Ruth (New York)	3000.00	1500.00	900.00
(72)	Ray Schalk	75.00	37.00	22.00
(73)	Hank Severeid	45.00	22.00	13.50
(74)	Burt Shotton	45.00	22.00	13.50
(75)	Geo. Sisler	75.00	37.00	22.00
(76)	Jack Smith	45.00	22.00	13.50
(77)	Frank Snyder	45.00	22.00	13.50
(78)	Tris Speaker	90.00	45.00	27.00
(79)	Oscar Stanage	45.00	22.00	13.50
(80)	Casey Stengel	600.00	300.00	180.00
(81)	Amos Strunk	45.00	22.00	13.50
(82)	Fred Toney	45.00	22.00	13.50
(83)	Jim Vaughn	45.00	22.00	13.50
(84)	Bobby Veach	45.00	22.00	13.50
(85)	Oscar Vitt	45.00	22.00	13.50
(86)	"Honus" Wagner	700.00	350.00	175.00
(87)	Tilly Walker	45.00	22.00	13.50
(88)	Bill Wambsganss	50.00	25.00	15.00
(89)	"Buck" Weaver	65.00	32.00	19.50
(90)	Zack Wheat	75.00	37.00	22.00
(91)	George Whitted	45.00	22.00	13.50
(92)	Cy Williams	50.00	25.00	15.00
(93)	Ivy Wingo	45.00	22.00	13.50
(94)	Pep ("Pep" Young)	45.00	22.00	13.50
(95)	Heinie Zimmerman	45.00	22.00	13.50

NOTE: A card number in parentheses ( ) indicates the set is unnumbered.

1926 M101-7 Sporting News Supplements

This set of 11 player photos was issued as a supplement by The Sporting News in 1926. The sepia-toned portrait photos were enclosed inside an oval on the 7" x 10" supplements. The player's name and team are printed at the bottom, while a line indentifying The Sporting News and the date appear in the upper left corner. The unnumbered set includes a half-dozen Hall of Famers.

		NR MT	EX	VG
Complete Set:		1500.00	750.00	450.00
Common Player:		40.00	20.00	12.00
(1)	Hazen "Kiki" Cuyler	125.00	62.00	37.00
(2)	Rogers Hornsby	150.00	75.00	45.00
(3)	Tony Lazzeri	75.00	37.00	22.00
(4)	Harry E. Manush	110.00	55.00	33.00
(5)	John Mostil	40.00	20.00	12.00
(6)	Harry Rice	40.00	20.00	12.00
(7)	George Herman Ruth	600.00	300.00	175.00
(8)	Al Simmons	110.00	55.00	33.00
(9)	Harold "Pie" Traynor	110.00	55.00	33.00
(10)	George Uhle	40.00	20.00	12.00
(11)	Glenn Wright	40.00	20.00	12.00

1900 M116

This set of 1-1/2" by 2-3/4" cards was offered to subscribers of Sporting Life, a major competitor of The Sporting News in the early part of the century. The cards were issued in 24 series of 12 cards each. Specialists consider the set complete at 310 different cards, including variations on which the background is in blue, rather than pastel colors. Each of the 16 major league teams are represented by 13 to 21 players, with nine minor leaguers also included. The card fronts are black and white photos that have been hand colored and carry the player's name and team. The card backs show various ads for the magazine. The last 72 cards issued are scarcer than the earlier series.

		NR MT	EX	VG
	Complete Set:	25000.00	12500.00	7500.
	Common Player:	150.00	75.00	45.00
(1)	Ed Abbaticchio	150.00	75.00	45.00
(2)	Babe Adams	400.00	175.00	75.00
(3)	Red Ames	400.00	175.00	75.00
(4)	Jimmy Archer	400.00	175.00	75.00
(5)	Frank Arrelanes (Arellanes)	150.00	75.00	45.00
(6)	Tommy Atkins	400.00	175.00	75.00
(7)	Jimmy Austin	400.00	175.00	75.00
(8)	Les Bachman (Backman)	150.00	75.00	45.00
(9)	Bill Bailey	150.00	75.00	45.00
(10)	Home Run Baker	500.00	250.00	100.00
(11)	Cy Barger	150.00	75.00	45.00
(12)	Jack Barry	150.00	75.00	45.00
(13)	Johnny Bates	150.00	75.00	45.00
(14)	Ginger Beaumont	150.00	75.00	45.00
(15)	Fred Beck	150.00	75.00	45.00
(16)	Heinie Beckendorf	150.00	75.00	45.00
(17)	Fred Beebe	150.00	75.00	45.00
(18)	George Bell	150.00	75.00	45.00
(19)	Harry Bemis	150.00	75.00	45.00
(20a)	Chief Bender (blue background)			
		900.00	450.00	200.00
(20b)	Chief Bender (pastel background)			
		500.00	250.00	100.00
(21)	Bill Bergen	150.00	75.00	45.00
(22)	Heinie Berger	150.00	75.00	45.00
(23)	Bob Bescher	150.00	75.00	45.00
(24)	Joe Birmingham	150.00	75.00	45.00
(25)	Lena Blackburn (Blackburne)	150.00	75.00	45.00
(26)	John Bliss	400.00	175.00	75.00
(27)	Bruno Block	400.00	175.00	75.00
(28)	Bill Bradley	150.00	75.00	45.00
(29)	Kitty Bransfield	150.00	75.00	45.00
(30)	Roger Bresnahan	700.00	350.00	200.00
(31)	Al Bridwell	150.00	75.00	45.00
(32)	Buster Brown (Boston N.L.)	150.00	75.00	45.00
(33a)	Mordecai Brown (blue background, Chicago N.L.)	900.00	450.00	200.00
(33b)	Mordecai Brown (pastel background, Chicago N.L.)	500.00	250.00	100.00
(34)	Al Burch	150.00	75.00	45.00
(35)	Donie Bush	150.00	75.00	45.00
(36)	Bobby Byrne	150.00	75.00	45.00
(37)	Howie Camnitz	150.00	75.00	45.00
(38)	Vin Campbell	400.00	175.00	75.00
(39)	Bill Carrigan	150.00	75.00	45.00
(40a)	Frank Chance (blue background)			
		900.00	450.00	200.00
(40b)	Frank Chance (pastel background)			
		500.00	250.00	100.00
(41)	Chappy Charles	150.00	75.00	45.00
(42a)	Hal Chase (blue)	700.00	350.00	200.00
(42b)	Hal Chase (pastel)	350.00	175.00	75.00
(43)	Ed Cicotte	200.00	90.00	40.00
(44)	Fred Clarke (Pittsburgh)	550.00	275.00	125.00
(45)	Nig Clarke (Cleveland)	150.00	75.00	45.00
(46)	Tommy Clarke (Cincinnati)	400.00	175.00	75.00
(47a)	Ty Cobb (blue background)	4500.00	2000.00	950.00
(47b)	Ty Cobb (pastel background)	2500.00	1000.00	475.00
(48a)	Eddie Collins (blue background)			
		1000.00	500.00	225.00
(48b)	Eddie Collins (pastel background)			
		600.00	300.00	140.00
(49)	Ray Collins	400.00	175.00	75.00
(50)	Wid Conroy	150.00	75.00	45.00
(51)	Jack Coombs	175.00	65.00	25.00
(52)	Frank Corridon	150.00	75.00	45.00
(53)	Harry Coveleskie (Coveleski)	500.00	250.00	100.00
(54)	Doc Crandall	150.00	75.00	45.00
(55a)	Sam Crawford (blue background)			
		900.00	450.00	200.00
(55b)	Sam Crawford (pastel background)			
		500.00	250.00	100.00
(56)	Birdie Cree	150.00	75.00	45.00
(57)	Lou Criger	150.00	75.00	45.00
(58)	Dode Criss	400.00	175.00	75.00
(59)	Cliff Curtis	400.00	175.00	75.00
(60)	Bill Dahlen	150.00	75.00	45.00
(61)	Bill Davidson	400.00	175.00	75.00
(62a)	Harry Davis (blue)	400.00	175.00	75.00
(62b)	Harry Davis (pastel background)			
		150.00	75.00	45.00
(63)	Jim Delehanty (Delahanty)	150.00	75.00	45.00
(64)	Ray Demmitt	400.00	175.00	75.00
(65)	Rube Dessau	400.00	175.00	75.00
(66)	Art Devlin	150.00	75.00	45.00
(67)	Josh Devore	400.00	175.00	75.00

		NR MT	EX	VG
(68)	Pat Donahue	150.00	75.00	45.00
(69)	Patsy Donovan	400.00	175.00	75.00
(70)	Wild Bill Donovan	150.00	75.00	45.00
(71a)	Red Dooin (blue)	400.00	175.00	75.00
(71b)	Red Dooin (pastel)	150.00	75.00	45.00
(72)	Mickey Doolan	150.00	75.00	45.00
(73)	Patsy Dougherty	150.00	75.00	45.00
(74)	Tom Downey	150.00	75.00	45.00
(75)	Jim Doyle	150.00	75.00	45.00
(76a)	Larry Doyle (blue)	400.00	175.00	75.00
(76b)	Larry Doyle (pastel)	30.00	15.00	9.00
(77)	Hugh Duffy	600.00	300.00	125.00
(78)	Jimmy Dygert	150.00	75.00	45.00
(79)	Dick Eagan (Egan)	150.00	75.00	45.00
(80)	Kid Elberfeld	150.00	75.00	45.00
(81)	Rube Ellis	150.00	75.00	45.00
(82)	Clyde Engle	150.00	75.00	45.00
(83)	Tex Erwin	400.00	175.00	75.00
(84)	Steve Evans	400.00	175.00	75.00
(85)	Johnny Evers	500.00	250.00	100.00
(86)	Bob Ewing	150.00	75.00	45.00
(87)	Cy Falkenberg	150.00	75.00	45.00
(88)	George Ferguson	150.00	75.00	45.00
(89)	Art Fletcher	400.00	175.00	75.00
(90)	Elmer Flick	500.00	250.00	100.00
(91)	John Flynn	400.00	175.00	75.00
(92)	Russ Ford	400.00	175.00	75.00
(93)	Eddie Foster	500.00	250.00	100.00
(94)	Bill Foxen	150.00	75.00	45.00
(95)	John Frill	500.00	250.00	100.00
(96)	Sam Frock	400.00	175.00	75.00
(97)	Art Fromme	150.00	75.00	45.00
(98)	Earl Gardner (New York A.L.)	400.00	175.00	75.00
(99)	Larry Gardner (Boston A.L.)	400.00	175.00	75.00
(100)	Harry Gaspar	400.00	175.00	75.00
(101)	Doc Gessler	150.00	75.00	45.00
(102a)	George Gibson (blue background)			
		400.00	175.00	75.00
(102b)	George Gibson (pastel background)			
		150.00	75.00	45.00
(103)	Bill Graham (St. Louis A.L.)	150.00	75.00	45.00
(104)	Peaches Graham (Boston)	150.00	75.00	45.00
(105)	Eddie Grant	150.00	75.00	45.00
(106)	Clark Griffith	500.00	250.00	100.00
(107)	Ed Hahn	150.00	75.00	45.00
(108)	Charley Hall	150.00	75.00	45.00
(109)	Bob Harmon	400.00	175.00	75.00
(110)	Topsy Hartsel	150.00	75.00	45.00
(111)	Roy Hartzell	150.00	75.00	45.00
(112)	Heinie Heitmuller	150.00	75.00	45.00
(113)	Buck Herzog	150.00	75.00	45.00
(114)	Dick Hoblitzel (Hoblitzell)	150.00	75.00	45.00
(115)	Danny Hoffman	150.00	75.00	45.00
(116)	Solly Hofman	150.00	75.00	45.00
(117)	Harry Hooper	700.00	350.00	150.00
(118)	Harry Howell	150.00	75.00	45.00
(119)	Miller Huggins	600.00	300.00	125.00
(120)	Long Tom Hughes	500.00	200.00	90.00
(121)	Rudy Hulswitt	150.00	75.00	45.00
(122)	John Hummel	150.00	75.00	45.00
(123)	George Hunter	150.00	75.00	45.00
(124)	Ham Hyatt	150.00	75.00	45.00
(125)	Fred Jacklitsch	150.00	75.00	45.00
(126a)	Hughie Jennings (blue background)			
		1000.00	500.00	225.00
(126b)	Hughie Jennings (pastel background)			
		600.00	300.00	125.00
(127)	Walter Johnson	1500.00	750.00	300.00
(128)	Davy Jones	150.00	75.00	45.00
(129)	Tom Jones	150.00	75.00	45.00
(130a)	Tim Jordan (blue background)	400.00	200.00	90.00
(130b)	Tim Jordan (pastel background)			
		150.00	75.00	45.00
(131)	Addie Joss	650.00	300.00	125.00
(132)	Johnny Kane	150.00	75.00	45.00
(133)	Ed Karger	150.00	75.00	45.00
(134)	Red Killifer (Killefer)	400.00	175.00	75.00
(135)	Johnny Kling	150.00	75.00	45.00
(136)	Otto Knabe	150.00	75.00	45.00
(137)	John Knight	400.00	175.00	75.00
(138)	Ed Konetchy	150.00	75.00	45.00
(139)	Harry Krause	150.00	75.00	45.00
(140)	Rube Kroh	150.00	75.00	45.00
(141)	Art Krueger	400.00	200.00	90.00
(142a)	Nap Lajoie (blue background)	1400.00	700.00	315.00
(142b)	Nap Lajoie (pastel)	850.00	400.00	190.00
(143)	Fred Lake (Boston N.L.)	150.00	75.00	45.00
(144)	Joe Lake (St. Louis A.L.)	400.00	175.00	75.00
(145)	Frank LaPorte	150.00	75.00	45.00
(146)	Jack Lapp	400.00	175.00	75.00
(147)	Chick Lathers	400.00	175.00	75.00

		NR MT	EX	VG
(148a)	Tommy Leach (blue background)			
		400.00	175.00	75.00
(148b)	Tommy Leach (pastel background)			
		150.00	75.00	45.00
(149)	Sam Leever	150.00	75.00	45.00
(150)	Lefty Leifield	150.00	75.00	45.00
(151)	Ed Lennox	150.00	75.00	45.00
(152)	Fred Linke (Link)	400.00	175.00	75.00
(153)	Paddy Livingstone (ston)	150.00	75.00	45.00
(154)	Hans Lobert	150.00	75.00	45.00
(155)	Bris Lord (Cleveland)	150.00	75.00	45.00
(156a)	Harry Lord (blue background, Boston A.L.)			
		400.00	200.00	90.00
(156b)	Harry Lord (pastel background, Boston A.L.)			
		150.00	75.00	45.00
(157)	Johnny Lush	150.00	75.00	45.00
(158)	Connie Mack	900.00	450.00	200.00
(159)	Tom Madden	400.00	175.00	75.00
(160)	Nick Maddox	150.00	75.00	45.00
(161)	Sherry Magee	175.00	65.00	25.00
(162a)	Christy Mathewson (Blue Background)			
		2500.00	1000.00	475.00
162b	Christy Mathewson (pastel background)			
		1500.00	700.00	350.00
(163)	Al Mattern	150.00	75.00	45.00
(164)	Jimmy McAleer	150.00	75.00	45.00
(165)	George McBride	400.00	175.00	75.00
(166a)	Amby McConnell (Boston)	150.00	75.00	45.00
(166b)	Amby McConnell (Chicago A.L.)			
		4500.00	2000.00	800.00
(167)	Pryor McElveen	150.00	75.00	45.00
(168)	John McGraw	700.00	350.00	150.00
(169)	Deacon McGuire	150.00	75.00	45.00
(170)	Stuffy McInnes (McInnis)	400.00	175.00	75.00
(171)	Harry McIntire (McIntyre)	150.00	75.00	45.00
(172)	Matty McIntyre	150.00	75.00	45.00
(173)	Larry McLean	150.00	75.00	45.00
(174)	Tommy McMillan	150.00	75.00	45.00
(175a)	George McQuillan (blue background, Philadelphia N.L.)			
		400.00	200.00	90.00
(175b)	George McQuillan (pastel background, Philadelphia N.L.)			
		150.00	75.00	45.00
(175c)	George McQuillan (Cincinnati)	4500.00	2000.00	800.00
(176)	Paul Meloan	400.00	175.00	75.00
(177)	Fred Merkle	150.00	75.00	45.00
(178)	Clyde Milan	150.00	75.00	45.00
(179)	Dots Miller (Pittsburgh)	150.00	75.00	45.00
(180)	Warren Miller (Washington)	400.00	175.00	75.00
(181)	Fred Mitchell	500.00	200.00	90.00
(182)	Mike Mitchell	150.00	75.00	45.00
(183)	Earl Moore	150.00	75.00	45.00
(184)	Pat Moran	150.00	75.00	45.00
(185)	Lew Moren	150.00	75.00	45.00
(186)	Cy Morgan	150.00	75.00	45.00
(187)	George Moriarty	150.00	75.00	45.00
(188)	Mike Mowrey	400.00	175.00	75.00
(189)	George Mullin	150.00	75.00	45.00
(190)	Danny Murphy	150.00	75.00	45.00
(191)	Red Murray	150.00	75.00	45.00
(192)	Chief Myers (Meyers)	400.00	175.00	75.00
(193)	Tom Needham	150.00	75.00	45.00
(194)	Harry Niles	150.00	75.00	45.00
(195)	Rebel Oakes	400.00	175.00	75.00
(196)	Jack O'Connor	150.00	75.00	45.00
(197)	Paddy O'Connor	150.00	75.00	45.00
(198)	Bill O'Hara	500.00	200.00	90.00
(199)	Rube Oldring	150.00	75.00	45.00
(200)	Charley O'Leary	150.00	75.00	45.00
(201)	Orval Overall	150.00	75.00	45.00
(202)	Freddy Parent	150.00	75.00	45.00
(203)	Dode Paskert	400.00	175.00	75.00
(204)	Fred Payne	400.00	175.00	75.00
(205)	Barney Pelty	150.00	75.00	45.00
(206)	Hub Pernoll	400.00	175.00	75.00
(207)	George Perring	500.00	200.00	90.00
(208)	Big Jeff Pfeffer	400.00	175.00	75.00
(209)	Jack Pfiester	150.00	75.00	45.00
(210)	Art Phelan	400.00	175.00	75.00
(211)	Ed Phelps	150.00	75.00	45.00
(212)	Deacon Phillippe	150.00	75.00	45.00
(213)	Eddie Plank	900.00	450.00	200.00
(214)	Jack Powell	150.00	75.00	45.00
(215)	Billy Purtell	150.00	75.00	45.00
(216)	Farmer Ray	500.00	200.00	90.00
(217)	Bugs Raymond	150.00	75.00	45.00
(218)	Doc Reisling	150.00	75.00	45.00
(219)	Ed Reulbach	150.00	75.00	45.00
(220)	Lew Richie	150.00	75.00	45.00
(221)	Jack Rowan	150.00	75.00	45.00
(222)	Nap Rucker	150.00	75.00	45.00
(223)	Slim Sallee	150.00	75.00	45.00
(224)	Doc Scanlon	150.00	75.00	45.00
(225)	Germany Schaefer	150.00	75.00	45.00
(226)	Lou Schettler	400.00	175.00	75.00
(227)	Admiral Schlei	150.00	75.00	45.00
(228)	Boss Schmidt	150.00	75.00	45.00
(229)	Wildfire Schulte	150.00	75.00	45.00
(230)	Al Schweitzer	150.00	75.00	45.00
(231)	Jim Scott	400.00	175.00	75.00
(232)	Cy Seymour	150.00	75.00	45.00
(233)	Tillie Shafer	150.00	75.00	45.00
(234)	Bud Sharpe	400.00	175.00	75.00
(235)	Dave Shean	400.00	175.00	75.00
(236)	Jimmy Sheckard	150.00	75.00	45.00
(237)	Mike Simon	400.00	175.00	75.00
(238)	Charlie Smith (Boston N.L.)	400.00	175.00	75.00
(239)	Frank Smith (Chicago A.L.)	150.00	75.00	45.00
(240)	Harry Smith (Boston N.L.)	150.00	75.00	45.00
(241)	Fred Snodgrass	150.00	75.00	45.00
(242)	Bob Spade	150.00	75.00	45.00
(243)	Tully Sparks	150.00	75.00	45.00
(244)	Tris Speaker	1500.00	750.00	300.00
(245)	Jake Stahl	150.00	75.00	45.00
(246)	George Stallings	150.00	75.00	45.00
(247)	Oscar Stanage	150.00	75.00	45.00
(248)	Harry Steinfeldt	175.00	75.00	30.00
(249)	Jim Stephens	150.00	75.00	45.00
(250)	George Stone	150.00	75.00	45.00
(251)	George Stovall	150.00	75.00	45.00
(252)	Gabby Street	150.00	75.00	45.00
(253)	Sailor Stroud	400.00	175.00	75.00
(254)	Amos Strunk	400.00	175.00	75.00
(255)	George Suggs	150.00	75.00	45.00
(256)	Billy Sullivan	150.00	75.00	45.00
(257)	Ed Summers	150.00	75.00	45.00
(258)	Bill Sweeney (Boston N.L.)	150.00	75.00	45.00
(259)	Jeff Sweeney (New York)	400.00	175.00	75.00
(260)	Lee Tannehill	150.00	75.00	45.00
(261a)	Fred Tenney (blue background)			
		400.00	175.00	75.00
(261b)	Fred Tenney (pastel background)			
		150.00	75.00	45.00
(262a)	Ira Thomas (blue)	400.00	175.00	75.00
(262b)	Ira Thomas (pastel background)			
		150.00	75.00	45.00
(263)	Jack Thoney	150.00	75.00	45.00
(264)	Joe Tinker	500.00	250.00	100.00
(265)	John Titus	400.00	175.00	75.00
(266)	Terry Turner	150.00	75.00	45.00
(267)	Bob Unglaub	150.00	75.00	45.00
(268)	Rube Waddell	650.00	300.00	125.00
(269a)	Hans Wagner (blue background, Pittsburgh)			
		3000.00	1500.00	650.00
(269b)	Hans Wagner (pastel background, Pittsburgh)			
		25000.00	12500.00	7500.
(270)	Heinie Wagner (Boston A.L.)	150.00	75.00	45.00
(271)	Bobby Wallace	550.00	250.00	100.00
(272)	Ed Walsh (Chicago A.L.)	700.00	350.00	150.00
(273a)	Jimmy Walsh (grey background)			
		600.00	250.00	100.00
(273b)	Jimmy Walsh (white background)			
		600.00	250.00	100.00
(274)	Doc White	150.00	75.00	45.00
(275)	Kaiser Wilhelm	150.00	75.00	45.00
(276)	Ed Willett	150.00	75.00	45.00
(277)	Vic Willis	150.00	75.00	45.00
(278)	Art Wilson (New York N.L.)	150.00	75.00	45.00
(279)	Owen Wilson (Pittsburgh)	150.00	75.00	45.00
(280)	Hooks Wiltse	150.00	75.00	45.00
(281)	Harry Wolter	150.00	75.00	45.00
(282)	Smoky Joe Wood	400.00	175.00	75.00
(283)	Ralph Works	150.00	75.00	45.00
(284)	Cy Young (Cleveland)	950.00	425.00	200.00
(285)	Irv Young (Chicago A.L.)	150.00	75.00	45.00
(286)	Heinie Zimmerman	400.00	175.00	75.00
(287)	Dutch Zwilling	400.00	175.00	75.00

NOTE: A card number in parentheses ( ) indicates the set is unnumbered.

1888 M117 Sporting Times

A player's name in *italic* indicates a rookie card. An (FC) indicates a player's first card for that particular card company.

Examples of these cards, issued in 1888 and 1889 by the Sporting Times weekly newspaper, are very rare. The complete set price includes all variations. The cabinet-size cards (7-1/4" by 4-1/2") feature line drawings of players in action poses on soft cardboard stock. The cards came in a variety of pastel colors surrounded by a 1/4" white border. The player's last name is printed on each drawing, as are the words "Courtesy Sporting Times New York." A pair of crossed bats and a baseball appear along the bottom of the card. Twenty-seven different players are known to exist. The drawing of Cap Anson is the same one used in the N28 Allen & Ginter series, and some of the other drawings are based on photos used in the popular Old Judge series. The Sporting Times set has an American Card Catalog number of M117.

		NR MT	EX	VG
Complete Set:		20000.00	10000.00	6000.00
Common Player:		500.00	250.00	150.00
(1)	Cap Anson	2500.00	1250.00	750.00
(2)	Jersey Bakely	500.00	250.00	150.00
(3)	Dan Brouthers	1000.00	500.00	300.00
(4)	Doc Bushong	500.00	250.00	150.00
(5)	Jack Clements	500.00	250.00	150.00
(6)	Commy Comiskey	1000.00	500.00	300.00
(7)	Jerry Denny	500.00	250.00	150.00
(8)	Buck Ewing	1000.00	500.00	300.00
(9)	Dude Esterbrook	500.00	250.00	150.00
(10)	Jay Faatz	500.00	250.00	150.00
(11)	Pud Galvin	1000.00	500.00	300.00
(12)	Pebbly Jack Glasscock	500.00	250.00	150.00
(13)	Tim Keefe	1000.00	500.00	300.00
(14)	King Kelly	1000.00	500.00	300.00
(15)	Matt Kilroy	500.00	250.00	150.00
(16)	Arlie Latham	500.00	250.00	150.00
(17)	Doggie Miller	500.00	250.00	150.00
(18)	Hank O'Day	500.00	250.00	150.00
(19)	Fred Pfeffer	500.00	250.00	150.00
(20)	Henry Porter	500.00	250.00	150.00
(21)	Toad Ramsey	500.00	250.00	150.00
(22)	Long John Reilly	500.00	250.00	150.00
(23)	Mike Smith	500.00	250.00	150.00
(24)	Harry Stovey	500.00	250.00	150.00
(25)	Big Sam Thompson	1000.00	500.00	300.00
(26)	Monte Ward	1000.00	500.00	300.00
(27)	Mickey Welch	1000.00	500.00	300.00

1927 Middy Bread

		NR MT	EX	VG
Complete Set:		600.00	300.00	180.00

1   Spencer Adams, Grover Alexander, Babe Ruth
2   Win. Ballou, Herman Bell, Lou Gehrig
3   Walter Beck, Lester Bell, Ross Young
4   Herschel Bennett, Ray Blades, Emil Muesel
5   Stewart Bolen, Jim Bottomley, Earle Combs
6   Danny Clark, Leo Dixon, Bob Meusel
7   Taylor Douhit, Chester Falk, Miller Huggins
8   Pat Collins, Frank Frisch, Milton Gaston
9   Walter Gerber, Chic Hafey, Herb Pennock
10   Jess Haines, Sam Jones
11   Vic Keen, Carlise Littlejohn
12   Bob Mc Graw, Oscar Melillo
13   Bing Miller, A Reinhardt
14   Otis Miller, Jimmy Ring
15   Billie Mullen, Walter Roetger
16   Ernie Nevers, Robert Shang
17   Steve O'Neil, Willie Sherdel
18   Harry Rice, Billy Southworth
19   George Sisler, Tommy Thevenow
20   Walter Stewart, George Toporcer
21   Elom Van Gilder
22   Ken Williams
23   Ernie Wingard

1933 Minneapolis Star Worch Tobacco

This set of unnumbered postcard-size cards, apparently produced by the Minneapolis Star newspaper, was used as a promotion by Worch Cigar Co. of St. Paul, Minn. Although there is no advertising for Worch Cigars on the cards themselves, the cards were mailed in envelopes bearing the Worch name. The borderless cards featured action photos with the player's name and team appearing in hand-lettered type near the bottom.

		NR MT	EX	VG
	Complete Set:	7500.00	3750.00	2250.00
	Common Player:	18.00	9.00	5.50
(1)	Adams	18.00	9.00	5.50
(2)	Dale Alexander	18.00	9.00	5.50
(3)	Ivy Paul Andrews	18.00	9.00	5.50
(4a)	Earl Averill (Cleveland)	40.00	20.00	12.00
(4b)	Earl Averill (no team designation)	40.00	20.00	12.00
(5)	Richard Bartell	18.00	9.00	5.50
(6)	Herman Bell	18.00	9.00	5.50
(7)	Walter Berger	18.00	9.00	5.50
(8)	Huck Betts	18.00	9.00	5.50
(9)	Max Bishop	18.00	9.00	5.50
(10)	Jim Bottomley	40.00	20.00	12.00
(11a)	Tom Bridges (name and team in box)	18.00	9.00	5.50
(11b)	Tom Bridges (no box)	18.00	9.00	5.50
(12)	Clint Brown	18.00	9.00	5.50
(13)	May Carey	40.00	20.00	12.00
(14)	Tex Carlton	18.00	9.00	5.50
(15)	Chalmer Cissell	18.00	9.00	5.50
(16)	Cochrane	40.00	20.00	12.00
(17)	Collins	40.00	20.00	12.00
(18)	Earle Combs	40.00	20.00	12.00
(19)	Comorosky	18.00	9.00	5.50
(20)	Crabtree	18.00	9.00	5.50
(21)	Rodger Cramer (Roger)	18.00	9.00	5.50
(22)	Pat Crawford	18.00	9.00	5.50
(23)	Hugh Critz	18.00	9.00	5.50
(24)	Frank Crosetti	25.00	12.50	7.50
(25a)	Joe Cronin (name and team in box)	40.00	20.00	12.00
(25b)	Joe Cronin (no box)	40.00	20.00	12.00
(26)	Alvin Crowder	18.00	9.00	5.50
(27)	Cuccinello	18.00	9.00	5.50
(28)	Cuyler	40.00	20.00	12.00
(29)	Geo. Davis	18.00	9.00	5.50
(30)	Dizzy Dean	100.00	50.00	30.00
(31)	Wm. Dickey	100.00	50.00	30.00
(32)	Leo Durocher	60.00	30.00	18.00
(33)	James Dykes	25.00	12.50	7.50
(34)	George Earnshaw	18.00	9.00	5.50
(35)	English	18.00	9.00	5.50
(36a)	Richard Ferrell (name and team in box)	40.00	20.00	12.00
(36b)	Richard Ferrell (no box)	40.00	20.00	12.00
(37a)	Wesley Ferrell (name and team in box)	18.00	9.00	5.50
(37b)	Wesley Ferrell (no box)	18.00	9.00	5.50
(38)	Fred Fitzsimmons	18.00	9.00	5.50
(39)	Lew Fonseca	25.00	12.50	7.50
(40)	James Foxx	100.00	50.00	30.00
(41)	Fred Frankhouse	18.00	9.00	5.50
(42)	Frank Frisch	40.00	20.00	12.00
(43a)	Leon Gaslin (name incorrect)	40.00	20.00	12.00
(43b)	Leon Goslin (name correct)	40.00	20.00	12.00
(44)	Lou Gehrig	350.00	175.00	105.00
(45)	Charles Gehringer	40.00	20.00	12.00
(46)	Vernon Gomez	40.00	20.00	12.00
(47)	George Grantham	18.00	9.00	5.50
(48)	Grimes The Lord Of Burleigh (Burleigh Grimes)	40.00	20.00	12.00
(49)	Grimm	25.00	12.50	7.50
(50)	Robert Grove	60.00	30.00	18.00
(51)	Chic Hafey (Chick)	40.00	20.00	12.00
(52)	Jess Haines	40.00	20.00	12.00
(53)	Bill Hallahan	18.00	9.00	5.50
(54)	Mel Harder	18.00	9.00	5.50
(55)	Dave Harris	18.00	9.00	5.50
(56)	Hartnett	40.00	20.00	12.00
(57)	George Hass	18.00	9.00	5.50
(58)	Ray Hayworth	18.00	9.00	5.50
(59)	Hendrick	18.00	9.00	5.50
(60)	Dutch Henry	18.00	9.00	5.50
(61)	"Babe" Herman	25.00	12.50	7.50
(62)	Bill Herman	40.00	20.00	12.00
(63)	Frank Higgins	18.00	9.00	5.50
(64)	O. Hildebrand	18.00	9.00	5.50
(65)	Roger Hornsby (Rogers)	150.00	75.00	45.00
(66)	Carl Hubbell	55.00	27.00	16.50
(67)	Travis Jackson	40.00	20.00	12.00
(68)	Smead Jolley	18.00	9.00	5.50
(69)	Wm. Kamm	18.00	9.00	5.50
(70)	Charles Klein	40.00	20.00	12.00
(71)	Jos. Kuhel	18.00	9.00	5.50
(72)	Tony Lazzeri	25.00	12.50	7.50

		NR MT	EX	VG
(73)	Sam Leslie	18.00	9.00	5.50
(74)	Al Lopez	40.00	20.00	12.00
(75)	Red Lucas	18.00	9.00	5.50
(76)	Adolfo Luque	18.00	9.00	5.50
(77)	Connie Mack	100.00	50.00	30.00
(78)	Gus Mancuso	18.00	9.00	5.50
(79)	Henry Manush	40.00	20.00	12.00
(80)	Fred Marberry	18.00	9.00	5.50
(81)	Pepper Martin	25.00	12.50	7.50
(82)	Wm. McKechnie	40.00	20.00	12.00
(83)	Joe Medwick	40.00	20.00	12.00
(84)	Jim Mooney	18.00	9.00	5.50
(85)	Joe Moore	18.00	9.00	5.50
(86)	Joe Mowry	18.00	9.00	5.50
(87)	Van Mungo	18.00	9.00	5.50
(88)	Buddy Myer	18.00	9.00	5.50
(89)	"Lefty" O'Doul	25.00	12.50	7.50
(90)	O'Farrell	18.00	9.00	5.50
(91)	Orsatti	18.00	9.00	5.50
(92)	Melvin Ott	65.00	32.00	19.50
(93)	Parmelee	18.00	9.00	5.50
(94)	Homer Peel	18.00	9.00	5.50
(95)	George Pipgras	18.00	9.00	5.50
(96)	Harry Rice	18.00	9.00	5.50
(97)	Paul Richards	25.00	12.50	7.50
(98)	Eppa Rixey	40.00	20.00	12.00
(99)	Charles Ruffing	40.00	20.00	12.00
(100)	Jack Russell	18.00	9.00	5.50
(101)	Babe Ruth	900.00	450.00	270.00
(102)	"Blondy" Ryan	18.00	9.00	5.50
(103)	Wilfred Ryan	18.00	9.00	5.50
(104)	Fred Schulte	18.00	9.00	5.50
(105)	Schumacher	18.00	9.00	5.50
(106)	Luke Sewel (Sewell)	18.00	9.00	5.50
(107)	Al Simmons	40.00	20.00	12.00
(108)	Ray Spencer	18.00	9.00	5.50
(109)	Casey Stengel	300.00	150.00	90.00
(110)	Stephenson	25.00	12.50	7.50
(111)	Walter Stewart	18.00	9.00	5.50
(112)	John T. Stone	18.00	9.00	5.50
(113)	Suhr	18.00	9.00	5.50
(114)	Dan Taylor	18.00	9.00	5.50
(115)	Bill Terry	65.00	32.00	19.50
(116)	Traynor	40.00	20.00	12.00
(117)	William Urbanski	18.00	9.00	5.50
(118)	Lloyd Vaughan	40.00	20.00	12.00
(119)	Johnny Vergez	18.00	9.00	5.50
(120)	George Walberg	18.00	9.00	5.50
(121)	Bill Walker	18.00	9.00	5.50
(122)	Gerald Walker	18.00	9.00	5.50
(123a)	Lloyd Waner (background blanked out)	40.00	20.00	12.00
(123b)	Lloyd Waner (with background)	40.00	20.00	12.00
(124a)	Paul Waner (background blanked out)	40.00	20.00	12.00
(124b)	Paul Waner (with background)	40.00	20.00	12.00
(125)	Lon Warneke	18.00	9.00	5.50
(126)	George Watkins	18.00	9.00	5.50
(127)	Monte Weaver	18.00	9.00	5.50
(128)	Sam West	18.00	9.00	5.50
(129)	Earl Whitehill	18.00	9.00	5.50
(130)	Hack Wilson	40.00	20.00	12.00
(131)	Jimmy Wilson	18.00	9.00	5.50

1952 Mother's Cookies

This is one of the most popular regional minor league sets ever issued. Cards of Pacific Coast League players were included in packages of cookies.

Distribution was limited to the West Coast. The 64 cards feature full color photos on a colored background, with player name and team. The cards measure 2-13/16" by 3-1/2", though the cards' rounded corners cause some variation in listed size. Card backs feature a very brief player statistic, card numbers and an offer for purchasing postage stamps. Five cards (11, 16, 29, 37 and 43) are considered scarce, while card #4 (Chuck Connors) is the most popular.

		NR MT	EX	VG
Complete Set:		1500.00	750.00	450.00
Common Player:		12.00	6.00	3.50
1	Johnny Lindell	18.00	9.00	5.50
2	Jim Davis	12.00	6.00	3.50
3	Al Gettle (Gettel)	12.00	6.00	3.50
4	Chuck Connors	200.00	100.00	60.00
5	Joe Grace	12.00	6.00	3.50
6	Eddie Basinski	12.00	6.00	3.50
7	Gene Handley	12.00	6.00	3.50
8	Walt Judnich	12.00	6.00	3.50
9	Jim Marshall	12.00	6.00	3.50
10	Max West	12.00	6.00	3.50
11	Bill MacCawley	50.00	25.00	15.00
12	Moreno Peiretti	12.00	6.00	3.50
13	Fred Haney	18.00	9.00	5.50
14	Earl Johnson	12.00	6.00	3.50
15	Dave Dahle	12.00	6.00	3.50
16	Bob Talbot	50.00	25.00	15.00
17	Smokey Singleton	12.00	6.00	3.50
18	Frank Austin	12.00	6.00	3.50
19	Joe Gordon	18.00	9.00	5.50
20	Joe Marty	12.00	6.00	3.50
21	Bob Gillespie	12.00	6.00	3.50
22	Red Embree	12.00	6.00	3.50
23	Lefty Olsen	12.00	6.00	3.50
24	Whitey Wietelmann	12.00	6.00	3.50
25	Frank O'Doul	18.00	9.00	5.50
26	Memo Luna	12.00	6.00	3.50
27	John Davis	12.00	6.00	3.50
28	Dick Faber	12.00	6.00	3.50
29	Buddy Peterson	125.00	62.00	37.00
30	Hank Schenz	12.00	6.00	3.50
31	Tookie Gilbert	12.00	6.00	3.50
32	Mel Ott	60.00	30.00	18.00
33	Sam Chapman	12.00	6.00	3.50
34	Dick Cole	12.00	6.00	3.50
35	John Ragni	12.00	6.00	3.50
36	Tom Saffell	12.00	6.00	3.50
37	Roy Welmaker	50.00	25.00	15.00
38	Lou Stringer	12.00	6.00	3.50
39	Artie Wilson	12.00	6.00	3.50
40	Chuck Stevens	12.00	6.00	3.50
41	Charlie Schanz	12.00	6.00	3.50
42	Al Lyons	12.00	6.00	3.50
43	Joe Erautt	125.00	62.00	37.00
44	Clarence Maddern	12.00	6.00	3.50
45	Gene Baker	12.00	6.00	3.50
46	Tom Heath	12.00	6.00	3.50
47	Al Lien	12.00	6.00	3.50
48	Bill Reeder	12.00	6.00	3.50
49	Bob Thurman	12.00	6.00	3.50
50	Ray Orteig	12.00	6.00	3.50
51	Joe Brovia	12.00	6.00	3.50
52	Jim Russell	12.00	6.00	3.50
53	Fred Sanford	12.00	6.00	3.50
54	Jim Gladd	12.00	6.00	3.50
55	Clay Hopper	12.00	6.00	3.50
56	Bill Glynn	12.00	6.00	3.50
57	Mike McCormick	12.00	6.00	3.50
58	Richie Myers	12.00	6.00	3.50
59	Vinnie Smith	12.00	6.00	3.50
60	Stan Hack	18.00	9.00	5.50
61	Bob Spicer	12.00	6.00	3.50
62	Jack Hollis	12.00	6.00	3.50
63	Ed Chandler	12.00	6.00	3.50
64	Bill Moisan	18.00	9.00	5.50

1953 Mother's Cookies

The 1953 Mother's Cookies cards are again 2-3/16" by 3-1/2", with rounded corners. There are 63 players from Pacific Coast League teams included. The full-color fronts have facsimile autographs rather than printed player names, and card backs offer a trading card album. Cards are generally more plentiful than in the 1952 set, with 11 of the cards apparently double printed.

		NR MT	EX	VG
Complete Set:		425.00	213.00	128.00
Common Player:		6.00	3.00	1.75
1	Lee Winter	9.00	4.50	2.75
2	Joe Ostrowski	6.00	3.00	1.75
3	Will Ramsdell	6.00	3.00	1.75
4	Bobby Bragan	9.00	4.50	2.75
5	Fletcher Robbe	6.00	3.00	1.75
6	Aaron Robinson	6.00	3.00	1.75
7	Augie Galan	6.00	3.00	1.75
8	Buddy Peterson	6.00	3.00	1.75
9	Frank Lefty O'Doul	18.00	9.00	5.50
10	Walt Pocekay	6.00	3.00	1.75
11	Nini Tornay	6.00	3.00	1.75
12	Jim Moran	6.00	3.00	1.75
13	George Schmees	6.00	3.00	1.75
14	Al Widmar	6.00	3.00	1.75
15	Ritchie Myers	6.00	3.00	1.75
16	Bill Howerton	6.00	3.00	1.75
17	Chuck Stevens	6.00	3.00	1.75
18	Joe Brovia	6.00	3.00	1.75
19	Max West	6.00	3.00	1.75
20	Eddie Malone	6.00	3.00	1.75
21	Gene Handley	6.00	3.00	1.75
22	William D. McCawley	6.00	3.00	1.75
23	Bill Sweeney	6.00	3.00	1.75
24	Tom Alston	6.00	3.00	1.75
25	George Vico	6.00	3.00	1.75
26	Hank Arft	6.00	3.00	1.75
27	Al Benton	6.00	3.00	1.75
28	"Pete" Milne	6.00	3.00	1.75
29	Jim Gladd	6.00	3.00	1.75
30	Earl Rapp	6.00	3.00	1.75
31	Ray Orteig	6.00	3.00	1.75
32	Eddie Basinski	6.00	3.00	1.75
33	Reno Cheso	6.00	3.00	1.75
34	Clarence Maddern	6.00	3.00	1.75
35	Marino Pieretti	6.00	3.00	1.75
36	Bill Raimondi	6.00	3.00	1.75
37	Frank Kelleher	6.00	3.00	1.75
38	George Bamberger	18.00	9.00	5.50
39	Dick Smith	6.00	3.00	1.75
40	Charley Schanz	6.00	3.00	1.75
41	John Van Cuyk	6.00	3.00	1.75
42	Lloyd Hittle	6.00	3.00	1.75
43	Tommy Heath	6.00	3.00	1.75
44	Frank Kalin	6.00	3.00	1.75
45	Jack Tobin	6.00	3.00	1.75
46	Jim Davis	6.00	3.00	1.75
47	Claude Christie	6.00	3.00	1.75
48	Elvin Tappe	6.00	3.00	1.75
49	Stan Hack	9.00	4.50	2.75
50	Fred Richards	6.00	3.00	1.75
51	Clay Hopper	6.00	3.00	1.75
52	Roy Welmaker	6.00	3.00	1.75
53	Red Adams	6.00	3.00	1.75
54	Piper Davis	6.00	3.00	1.75
55	Spider Jorgensen	6.00	3.00	1.75
56	Lee Walls	6.00	3.00	1.75
57	Jack Phillips	6.00	3.00	1.75
58	Red Lynn	6.00	3.00	1.75

		NR MT	EX	VG
59	Eddie Beckman	6.00	3.00	1.75
60	Gene Desautels	6.00	3.00	1.75
61	Bob Dillinger	6.00	3.00	1.75
62	Al Federoff	6.00	3.00	1.75
63	Bill Boemler	6.00	3.00	1.75

N

1888 N173
Old Judge Cabinets

OLD JUDGE CIGARETTES

These large cabinet cards were issued by Goodwin & Co. in 1888 and 1889. They were a popular premium available by exchanging coupons found in Old Judge or Dogs Head brand cigarettes. The cabinet cards consist of 3-3/4" by 5-3/4" photographs affixed to a cardboard backing that measures approximately 4-1/4" by 6-1/2". The mounting is usually a yellow color, but backins have also been found in pink, blue or black. An ad for Olf Judge Cigarettes appears along the bottom of the cabinet. (Cabinets obtained by exchanging coupons from Dogs Head cigarettes include an ad for both Old Judge and Dogs Head, and are considered scarcer.) According to an advertising sheet, cabinets were available of "every prominent player in the National League, Western League and American Association." There are additions to the following checklist that will be included in subsequent editions of this catalog. The poses used for the cabinet photos are enlarged versions of the popular N172 Old Judge cards.

		NR MT	EX	VG
Common Player:		350.00	175.00	105.00
(1)	Bob Allen	350.00	175.00	105.00
(2)	Ed Andrews (both hands at shoulder level)			
		350.00	175.00	105.00
(3)	Ed Andrews (one hand above head)			
		350.00	175.00	105.00
(4)	Ed Andrews, Buster Hoover	700.00	350.00	210.00
(5)	Cap Anson (Dogs Head)	5000.00	2500.00	1500.
(6)	Fido Baldwin (Chicago, pitching)			
		350.00	175.00	105.00
(7)	Fido Baldwin (Chicago, with bat)			
		350.00	175.00	105.00
(8)	Kid Baldwin (Detroit)	350.00	175.00	105.00
(9)	John Barnes	350.00	175.00	105.00
(10)	Bald Billy Barnie	350.00	175.00	105.00
(11)	Charles Bassett	350.00	175.00	105.00
(12)	Charles Bastian (Chicago)	350.00	175.00	105.00
(13)	Charles Bastian (Philly)	350.00	175.00	105.00
(14)	Bastian, Pop Schriver	350.00	175.00	105.00
(15)	Ed Beatin	350.00	175.00	105.00
(16)	Charles Bennett (Dogs H)	350.00	175.00	105.00
(17)	Louis Bierbauer	350.00	175.00	105.00
(18)	Ned Bligh	350.00	175.00	105.00
(19)	Bogart	350.00	175.00	105.00
(20)	Handsome Boyle (Indy)	350.00	175.00	105.00
(21)	Honest John Boyle (St. Louis, bat at side)			
		350.00	175.00	105.00
(22)	Honest John Boyle (St. Louis, bat in air)			
		350.00	175.00	105.00

		NR MT	EX	VG
(23)	Grin Bradley	350.00	175.00	105.00
(24)	Dan Brouthers (catching)	1600.00	800.00	475.00
(25)	Dan Brouthers (with bat, Dogs Head)			
		1500.00	750.00	450.00
(26)	California Brown (Boston, catching)			
		350.00	175.00	105.00
(27)	California Brown (Boston, with bat)			
		350.00	175.00	105.00
(28)	Thomas Brown (New York, throwing)			
		350.00	175.00	105.00
(29)	Thomas Brown (New York, with bat)			
		350.00	175.00	105.00
(30)	Charles Brynan (Chicago)	350.00	175.00	105.00
(31)	Charles Brynan (Des Moines)	350.00	175.00	105.00
(32)	Al Buckenberger	350.00	175.00	105.00
(33)	Dick Buckley	350.00	175.00	105.00
(34)	Charles Buffinton (hands chest high)			
		350.00	175.00	105.00
(35)	Charles Buffinton (right hand above head, Dogs Head)			
		350.00	175.00	105.00
(36)	Black Jack Burdock	350.00	175.00	105.00
(37)	James Burns (Kansas City)	350.00	175.00	105.00
(38)	Oyster Burns (Brooklyn)	350.00	175.00	105.00
(39)	Thomas Burns (Chicago, bat at side)			
		350.00	175.00	105.00
(40)	Thomas Burns (Chicago, bat in air)			
		350.00	175.00	105.00
(41)	Thomas Burns (catching)	350.00	175.00	105.00
(42)	Doc Bushong	350.00	175.00	105.00
(43)	Hick Carpenter	350.00	175.00	105.00
(44)	Jumbo Cartwright	350.00	175.00	105.00
(45)	Parisian Bob Caruthers (holding ball)			
		350.00	175.00	105.00
(46)	Parisian Bob Caruthers (with bat)			
		350.00	175.00	105.00
(47)	Daniel Casey	350.00	175.00	105.00
(48)	Icebox Chamberlain (boths hands at chest level)			
		350.00	175.00	105.00
(49)	Icebox Chamberlain (right hand extended)			
		350.00	175.00	105.00
(50)	Chamberlain (with bat)	350.00	175.00	105.00
(51)	Cupid Childs	350.00	175.00	105.00
(52)	Clark (Brooklyn, catching)	350.00	175.00	105.00
(53)	Bob Clark (Brooklyn, right hand shoulder high)			
		350.00	175.00	105.00
(54)	Bob Clark, Mickey Hughes (Dogs Head)			
		350.00	175.00	105.00
(55)	Dad Clark (Clarke) (Chicago)	350.00	175.00	105.00
(56)	John Clarkson (Dogs Head)	2250.00	1125.00	700.00
(57)	John Clarkson (right arm extended)			
		1600.00	800.00	475.00
(58)	John Clarkson (with bat)	1600.00	800.00	475.00
(59)	Jack Clements (hands on knees)			
		350.00	175.00	105.00
(60)	Jack Clements (hands outstreched at neck level)			
		350.00	175.00	105.00
(61)	Jack Clements (with bat)	350.00	175.00	105.00
(62)	Monk Cline	350.00	175.00	105.00
(63)	John Coleman (holding ball)	350.00	175.00	105.00
(64)	John Coleman (with bat)	350.00	175.00	105.00
(65)	Hub Collins	350.00	175.00	105.00
(66)	Commy Comiskey (arms folded)			
		1600.00	800.00	475.00
(67)	Commy Comiskey (Dogs Head)	1500.00	750.00	450.00
(68)	Roger Connor (catching)	1600.00	800.00	475.00
(69)	Roger Connor (hands on knees)			
		1600.00	800.00	475.00
(70)	Roger Connor (with bat)	1600.00	800.00	475.00
(71)	Jim Conway (Kansas City)	350.00	175.00	105.00
(72)	Pete Conway (Detroit)	350.00	175.00	105.00
(73)	Paul Cook (fielding)	350.00	175.00	105.00
(74)	Paul Cook (wearing mask)	350.00	175.00	105.00
(75)	Pop Corkhill	350.00	175.00	105.00
(76)	Samuel Crane	350.00	175.00	105.00
(77)	Lave Cross	350.00	175.00	105.00
(78)	Edward Daily	350.00	175.00	105.00
(79)	Bill Daley (Boston)	350.00	175.00	105.00
(80)	Con Daley (Daily) (Indianapolis)			
		350.00	175.00	105.00
(81)	Abner Dalrymple	350.00	175.00	105.00
(82)	Sun Daly (Minneapolis)	350.00	175.00	105.00
(83)	Tido Daly (Washington)	350.00	175.00	105.00
(84)	Tido Daly (Chicago)	350.00	175.00	105.00
(85)	Dell Darling	350.00	175.00	105.00
(86)	William Darnbrough	350.00	175.00	105.00
(87)	Big Ed Delehanty (bat held at right shoulder)			
		1850.00	925.00	575.00
(88)	Big Ed Delehanty (bat held at horizontal level)			
		1850.00	925.00	575.00
(89)	Jerry Denny	350.00	175.00	105.00
(90)	Jim Devlin (pitching)	350.00	175.00	105.00
(91)	Jim Devlin (sliding)	350.00	175.00	105.00

	NR MT	EX	VG
(92) Jim Donnelly	350.00	175.00	105.00
(93) Home Run Duffe (Duffee) (bending)	350.00	175.00	105.00
(94) Home Run Duffe (Duffee) (catching, standing upright)	350.00	175.00	105.00
(95) Home Run Duffe (Duffee) (with bat)	350.00	175.00	105.00
(96) Hugh Duffy (catching)	1600.00	800.00	475.00
(97) Hugh Duffy (fielding)	1600.00	800.00	475.00
(98) Hugh Duffy (with bat)	1600.00	800.00	475.00
(99) Duck Duke	350.00	175.00	105.00
(100) Sure Shot Dunlap (arms at side)	350.00	175.00	105.00
(101) Sure Shot Dunlap (Dogs H)	350.00	175.00	105.00
(102) Jesse Duryea	350.00	175.00	105.00
(103) Frank Dwyer (bat at side)	350.00	175.00	105.00
(104) Frank Dwyer (bat in air)	350.00	175.00	105.00
(105) Frank Dwyer (ball in hands)	350.00	175.00	105.00
(106) Frank Dwyer (hands cupped at chest)	350.00	175.00	105.00
(107) Billy Earle	350.00	175.00	105.00
(108) Red Ehret	350.00	175.00	105.00
(109) Dude Esterbrook	350.00	175.00	105.00
(110) Buck Ewing (New York, bat at side)	1600.00	800.00	475.00
(111) Buck Ewing (New York, bat in air)	1600.00	800.00	475.00
(112) Buck Ewing (New York, hands at head level)	1600.00	800.00	475.00
(113) Buck Ewing (New York, hands on knees)	1600.00	800.00	475.00
(114) Willie Breslin-mascot, Buck Ewing	350.00	175.00	105.00
(115) Long John Ewing (Louisville)	350.00	175.00	105.00
(116) Jay Faatz	350.00	175.00	105.00
(117) Bill Farmer	350.00	175.00	105.00
(118) Sid Farrar (hands outstreched at head level)	350.00	175.00	105.00
(119) Sid Farrar (stooping)	350.00	175.00	105.00
(120) Duke Farrell (fielding)	350.00	175.00	105.00
(121) Duke Farrell (hands on knees)	350.00	175.00	105.00
(122) Frank Fennelly	350.00	175.00	105.00
(123) Charlie Ferguson	350.00	175.00	105.00
(124) Alex Ferson	350.00	175.00	105.00
(125) Jocko Fields	350.00	175.00	105.00
(126) Silver Flint (with bat)	350.00	175.00	105.00
(127) Silver Flint (with mask)	350.00	175.00	105.00
(128) Jim Fogarty (catching, hands at neck level)	350.00	175.00	105.00
(129) Jim Fogarty (running to left, hands at head level)	350.00	175.00	105.00
(130) Jim Fogarty (sliding)	350.00	175.00	105.00
(131) Jim Fogarty (with bat)	350.00	175.00	105.00
(132) Elmer Foster (Minneapolis)	350.00	175.00	105.00
(133) Elmer Foster (New York)	350.00	175.00	105.00
(134) Dave Foutz	350.00	175.00	105.00
(135) Shorty Fuller (catching)	350.00	175.00	105.00
(136) Shorty Fuller (hands on knees)	350.00	175.00	105.00
(137) Shorty Fuller (swinging bat)	350.00	175.00	105.00
(138) Chris Fulmer, Foghorn Tucker (Dogs Head)	1000.00	500.00	300.00
(139) Pud Galvin	350.00	175.00	105.00
(140) Charlie Ganzel (catching, hands at shoulder level)	350.00	175.00	105.00
(141) Charlie Ganzel (catching, hands at thigh level)	350.00	175.00	105.00
(142) Charlie Ganzel (with bat)	350.00	175.00	105.00
(143) Gid Gardner	350.00	175.00	105.00
(144) Hank Gastreich	350.00	175.00	105.00
(145) Frenchy Genins (bat in air, looking at camera)	350.00	175.00	105.00
(146) Frenchy Genins (swinging at ball)	350.00	175.00	105.00
(147) Bill George	350.00	175.00	105.00
(148) Charlie Getzein	350.00	175.00	105.00
(149) Bobby Gilks	350.00	175.00	105.00
(150) Barney Gilligan	350.00	175.00	105.00
(151) Frank Gilmore	350.00	175.00	105.00
(152) Pebbly Jack Glasscock (Dogs Head)	350.00	175.00	105.00
(153) Pebbly Jack Glasscock (hands on knees)	350.00	175.00	105.00
(154) Pebbly Jack Glasscock (throwing)	350.00	175.00	105.00
(155) Kid Gleason (Philadelphia, fielding)	350.00	175.00	105.00
(156) Kid Gleason (Philadelphia, pitching)	350.00	175.00	105.00
(157) Will Gleason (Louisville)	350.00	175.00	105.00
(158) Mouse Glenn	350.00	175.00	105.00
(159) Piano Legs Gore (fielding)	350.00	175.00	105.00
(160) Piano Legs Gore (with bat)	350.00	175.00	105.00
(161) Henry Gruber	350.00	175.00	105.00
(162) Ad Gumbert (right hand at eye level)	350.00	175.00	105.00
(163) Ad Gumbert (right hand at waist level)	350.00	175.00	105.00
(164) Tom Gunning	350.00	175.00	105.00
(165) Joe Gunson	350.00	175.00	105.00
(166) Bill Hallman	350.00	175.00	105.00
(167) Billy Hamilton (fielding)	1600.00	800.00	475.00
(168) Billy Hamilton (with bat)	1600.00	800.00	475.00
(169) Ned Hanlon	350.00	175.00	105.00
(170) William Hanrahan	350.00	175.00	105.00
(171) Gill Hatfield (bat at waist)	350.00	175.00	105.00
(172) Hatfield (bat over shoulder)	350.00	175.00	105.00
(173) Gill Hatfield (catching)	350.00	175.00	105.00
(174) Egyptian Healey	350.00	175.00	105.00
(175) Hardie Henderson	350.00	175.00	105.00
(176) Moxie Hengle	350.00	175.00	105.00
(177) John Henry	350.00	175.00	105.00
(178) Paul Hines	350.00	175.00	105.00
(179) Texas Wonder Hoffman	350.00	175.00	105.00
(180) Bug Holliday	350.00	175.00	105.00
(181) Buster Hoover (Philadelphia)	350.00	175.00	105.00
(182) Charles Hoover (Chicago or Kansas City)	350.00	175.00	105.00
(183) Joe Hornung	350.00	175.00	105.00
(184) Dummy Hoy	350.00	175.00	105.00
(185) Nat Hudson	350.00	175.00	105.00
(186) Mickey Hughes (holding ball at chest)	350.00	175.00	105.00
(187) Mickey Hughes (holding ball at side)	350.00	175.00	105.00
(188) Mickey Hughes (right hand extended)	350.00	175.00	105.00
(189) Wild Bill Hutchinson (ball in hand, right heel hidden)	350.00	175.00	105.00
(190) Wild Bill Hutchinson (ball in hand, right heel visible)	350.00	175.00	105.00
(191) Bill Hutchinson (with bat)	350.00	175.00	105.00
(192) Cutrate Irwin (Philadelphia, catching)	350.00	175.00	105.00
(193) Cutrate Irwin (Philadelphia, throwing)	350.00	175.00	105.00
(194) John Irwin (Washington)	350.00	175.00	105.00
(195) A.C. Jantzen	350.00	175.00	105.00
(196) Spud Johnson	350.00	175.00	105.00
(197) Johnston (hands on hip)	350.00	175.00	105.00
(198) Dick Johnston (with bat)	350.00	175.00	105.00
(199) Tim Keefe (Dogs Head)	2000.00	1000.00	600.00
(200) Tim Keefe (hands at chest)	1600.00	800.00	475.00
(201) Tim Keefe (pitching, right hand at head level)	1600.00	800.00	475.00
(202) Tim Keefe (pitching, right hand at waist level)	1600.00	800.00	475.00
(203) Charles Kelly (Philadelphia)	350.00	175.00	105.00
(204) King Kelly (Boston, Dogs H)	1750.00	875.00	525.00
(205) John Kerins	350.00	175.00	105.00
(206) Silver King (hands at chest level)	350.00	175.00	105.00
(207) Silver King (hands at chin)	350.00	175.00	105.00
(208) William Klusman	350.00	175.00	105.00
(209) Gus Krock (right hand extended)	350.00	175.00	105.00
(210) Gus Krock (with bat)	350.00	175.00	105.00
(211) Willie Kuehne	350.00	175.00	105.00
(212) Ted Larkin	350.00	175.00	105.00
(213) Arlie Latham (throwing)	350.00	175.00	105.00
(214) Arlie Latham (with bat)	350.00	175.00	105.00
(215) Germany Long	350.00	175.00	105.00
(216) Tom Lovett (right hand extended)	350.00	175.00	105.00
(217) Tom Lovett (with bat)	350.00	175.00	105.00
(218) Denny Lyons (left hand above head)	350.00	175.00	105.00
(219) Denny Lyons (with bat)	350.00	175.00	105.00
(220) Connie Mack	5000.00	2500.00	1500.
(221) Little Mac Macullar	350.00	175.00	105.00
(222) Kid Madden (ball in left hand at eye level)	350.00	175.00	105.00
(223) Kid Madden (ball in hand above head)	350.00	175.00	105.00
(224) Kid Madden (ball in hands at neck level)	350.00	175.00	105.00
(225) Jimmy Manning (fielding)	350.00	175.00	105.00
(226) Jimmy Manning (with bat)	350.00	175.00	105.00
(227) Lefty Marr	350.00	175.00	105.00
(228) Leech Maskrey	350.00	175.00	105.00
(229) Mike Mattimore	350.00	175.00	105.00
(230) Smiling Al Maul	350.00	175.00	105.00
(231) Al Mays	350.00	175.00	105.00

	NR MT	EX	VG
(232) Jimmy McAleer	350.00	175.00	105.00
(233) Tommy McCarthy (right hand at head level)	1500.00	750.00	450.00
(234) Tommy McCarthy (with bat)	1500.00	750.00	450.00
(235) Deacon McGuire	350.00	175.00	105.00
(236) Bill McGunnigle	350.00	175.00	105.00
(237) Ed McKean (hands above head)	350.00	175.00	105.00
(238) Ed McKean (with bat)	350.00	175.00	105.00
(239) James McQuaid	350.00	175.00	105.00
(240) Doggie Miller (Pittsburgh, ball in hands)	350.00	175.00	105.00
(241) Doggie Miller (Pittsburgh, Dogs Head)	350.00	175.00	105.00
(242) Joseph Miller (Minneapolis, hands outstretched)	350.00	175.00	105.00
(243) Joseph Miller (Minneapolis, with bat)	350.00	175.00	105.00
(244) Jocko Milligan (bat at side)	350.00	175.00	105.00
(245) Jocko Milligan (bat in air)	350.00	175.00	105.00
(246) Jocko Milligan (stooping)	350.00	175.00	105.00
(247) Daniel Minnehan (Minahan)	350.00	175.00	105.00
(248) Sam Moffet	350.00	175.00	105.00
(249) Honest John Morrill	350.00	175.00	105.00
(250) Joseph Mulvey (catching)	350.00	175.00	105.00
(251) Joseph Mulvey (with bat)	350.00	175.00	105.00
(252) Pat Murphy	350.00	175.00	105.00
(253) Miah Murray	350.00	175.00	105.00
(254) Truthful Jim Mutrie	350.00	175.00	105.00
(255) Al Myers (Washington)	350.00	175.00	105.00
(256) George Myers (Indianapolis)	350.00	175.00	105.00
(257) Tom Nagle	350.00	175.00	105.00
(258) Billy Nash (hands on knees)	350.00	175.00	105.00
(259) Billy Nash (throwing)	350.00	175.00	105.00
(260) Kid Nichols	1800.00	900.00	550.00
(261) Little Nick Nicol, Big John Reilly	350.00	175.00	105.00
(262) Darby O'Brien (Brooklyn)	350.00	175.00	105.00
(263) John O'Brien (Cleveland)	350.00	175.00	105.00
(264) Rowdy Jack O'Connor	350.00	175.00	105.00
(265) Hank O'Day	350.00	175.00	105.00
(266) Tip O'Neill (bat held horizontally)	350.00	175.00	105.00
(267) O'Neill (bat over shoulder)	350.00	175.00	105.00
(268) Tip O'Neill (fielding)	350.00	175.00	105.00
(269) Tip O'Neill (throwing)	350.00	175.00	105.00
(270) Orator Jim O'Rourke (New York, right hand in air)	1600.00	800.00	475.00
(271) Orator Jim O'Rourke (New York, with bat)	1600.00	800.00	475.00
(272) Tom O'Rourke (Boston)	350.00	175.00	105.00
(273) Dave Orr	350.00	175.00	105.00
(274) Fred Pfeffer (right hand at neck level)	350.00	175.00	105.00
(275) Fred Pfeffer (with bat)	350.00	175.00	105.00
(276) Dick Phelan	350.00	175.00	105.00
(277) Jack Pickett (right hand at head level)	350.00	175.00	105.00
(278) Jack Pickett (stooping)	350.00	175.00	105.00
(279) Jack Pickett (with bat)	350.00	175.00	105.00
(280) George Pinkney (bat in air, nearly vertical)	350.00	175.00	105.00
(281) George Pinkney (bat over right shoulder)	350.00	175.00	105.00
(282) Jim Powell	350.00	175.00	105.00
(283) Blondie Purcell	350.00	175.00	105.00
(284) Joe Quinn (ball in hands)	350.00	175.00	105.00
(285) Joe Quinn (ready to run)	350.00	175.00	105.00
(286) Old Hoss Radbourn (Dogs Head)	2000.00	1000.00	600.00
(287) Old Hoss Radbourn (hands on hips with bat)	1600.00	800.00	475.00
(288) Toad Ramsey	350.00	175.00	105.00
(289) Princeton Charlie Reilly (St. Paul)	350.00	175.00	105.00
(290) Long John Reilly (Cincinnati)	350.00	175.00	105.00
(291) Danny Richardson (New York, arms at side)	350.00	175.00	105.00
(292) Danny Richardson (New York, right hand at head level)	350.00	175.00	105.00
(293) Hardy Richardson (Boston, hands at head level)	350.00	175.00	105.00
(294) Hardy Richardson (Boston or Detroit, with bat)	350.00	175.00	105.00
(295) Uncle Robbie Robinson (Athletics, catching)	1700.00	850.00	475.00
(296) Uncle Robbie Robinson (Athletics, with bat)	1700.00	850.00	475.00
(297) Yank Robinson (St. Louis, fielding)	350.00	175.00	105.00
(298) Yank Robinson (St. Louis, with bat)	350.00	175.00	105.00

	NR MT	EX	VG
(299) Dave Rowe (Kansas City, Dogs Head)	350.00	175.00	105.00
(300) Jack Rowe (Detroit)	350.00	175.00	105.00
(301) Jimmy Ryan (fielding)	350.00	175.00	105.00
(302) Jimmy Ryan (with bat)	350.00	175.00	105.00
(303) Ben Sanders (hands at neck level)	350.00	175.00	105.00
(304) Ben Sanders (right hand at head level)	350.00	175.00	105.00
(305) Frank Scheibeck	350.00	175.00	105.00
(306) Gus Schmelz	350.00	175.00	105.00
(307) Jumbo Schoeneck	350.00	175.00	105.00
(308) Pop Schriver (hands at ankle level)	350.00	175.00	105.00
(309) Pop Schriver (hands cupped at chest level)	350.00	175.00	105.00
(310) Emmett Seery	350.00	175.00	105.00
(311) Ed Seward	350.00	175.00	105.00
(312) Daniel Shannon	350.00	175.00	105.00
(313) William Sharsig	350.00	175.00	105.00
(314) George Shoch	350.00	175.00	105.00
(315) Otto Shomberg (Schomberg)	350.00	175.00	105.00
(316) Lev Shreve	350.00	175.00	105.00
(317) Mike Slattery	350.00	175.00	105.00
(318) Germany Smith (Brooklyn, hands on knees)	350.00	175.00	105.00
(319) Germany Smith (Brooklyn, right hand at head level)	350.00	175.00	105.00
(320) Germany Smith (Brooklyn, with bat)	350.00	175.00	105.00
(321) Pap Smith (Pittsburg, hands on knees)	350.00	175.00	105.00
(322) Pap Smith (Pittsburg or Boston, with bat)	350.00	175.00	105.00
(323) Little Bill Sowders	350.00	175.00	105.00
(324) Charlie Sprague	350.00	175.00	105.00
(325) Harry Staley	350.00	175.00	105.00
(326) Dan Stearns	350.00	175.00	105.00
(327) Stovey (hands on knees)	350.00	175.00	105.00
(328) Harry Stovey (with bat)	350.00	175.00	105.00
(329) Joe Straus (Strauss)	350.00	175.00	105.00
(330) Cub Stricker	350.00	175.00	105.00
(331) Marty Sullivan (Indianapolis)	350.00	175.00	105.00
(332) Marty Sullivan (Chicago)	350.00	175.00	105.00
(333) Billy Sunday (bending to left)	1000.00	500.00	300.00
(334) Billy Sunday (with bat)	1000.00	500.00	300.00
(335) Ezra Sutton (hands at shoulder level)	350.00	175.00	105.00
(336) Ezra Sutton (with bat)	350.00	175.00	105.00
(337) Park Swartzel	350.00	175.00	105.00
(338) Pop Tate	350.00	175.00	105.00
(339) Patsy Tebeau	350.00	175.00	105.00
(340) John Tener	350.00	175.00	105.00
(341) Adonis Terry (arms extended)	350.00	175.00	105.00
(342) Adonis Terry (with bat)	350.00	175.00	105.00
(343) Big Sam Thompson (Detroit)	1600.00	800.00	475.00
(344) Big Sam Thompson (Philadelphia)	1600.00	800.00	475.00
(345) Silent Mike Tiernan	350.00	175.00	105.00
(346) Cannonball Titcomb	350.00	175.00	105.00
(347) Buster Tomney	350.00	175.00	105.00
(348) Sleepy Townsend (hands at head level)	350.00	175.00	105.00
(349) Sleepy Townsend (with bat)	350.00	175.00	105.00
(350) Bill Traffley	350.00	175.00	105.00
(351) Foghorn Tucker	350.00	175.00	105.00
(352) George Turner	350.00	175.00	105.00
(353) Larry Twitchell	350.00	175.00	105.00
(354) Jim Tyng	350.00	175.00	105.00
(355) Rip Van Haltren (hands above waist)	350.00	175.00	105.00
(356) Rip Van Haltren (right hand at right thigh)	350.00	175.00	105.00
(357) Rip Van Haltren (with bat)	350.00	175.00	105.00
(358) Farmer Vaughn	350.00	175.00	105.00
(359) Joe Visner (arms at side)	350.00	175.00	105.00
(360) Joe Visner (with bat)	350.00	175.00	105.00
(361) Monte Ward (Dogs Head)	2000.00	1000.00	600.00
(362) Monte Ward (hands on hips)	1600.00	800.00	475.00
(363) Monte Ward (throwing)	1600.00	800.00	475.00
(364) Bill Watkins	350.00	175.00	105.00
(365) Farmer Weaver	350.00	175.00	105.00
(366) Stump Weidman	350.00	175.00	105.00
(367) Wild Bill Weidner	350.00	175.00	105.00
(368) Curt Welch (Athletics)	350.00	175.00	105.00
(369) Will Gleason, Curt Welch	1000.00	500.00	300.00
(370) Mickey Welch (New York)	350.00	175.00	105.00
(371) A.C. "Cannonball" Weyhing	350.00	175.00	105.00
(372) John Weyhing	350.00	175.00	105.00
(373) Deacon White (hands above head)	350.00	175.00	105.00

	NR MT	EX	VG
(374) Deacon White (looking down at ball)			
	350.00	175.00	105.00
(375) Art Whitney (Pittsburg)	350.00	175.00	105.00
(376) Grasshopper Whitney (Washington)			
	350.00	175.00	105.00
(377) Ned Williamson (arm folded)	350.00	175.00	105.00
(378) Ned Williamson (with bat)	350.00	175.00	105.00
(379) Watt Wilmot	350.00	175.00	105.00
(380) Medoc Wise	350.00	175.00	105.00
(381) Chicken Wolf	350.00	175.00	105.00
(382) George "Dandy" Wood (L.F., both hands at neck level)			
	350.00	175.00	105.00
(383) George "Dandy" Wood (L.F., right hand at head level)			
	350.00	175.00	105.00
(384) Pete Wood (P., with bat)	350.00	175.00	105.00
(385) Harry Wright	4000.00	2000.00	1200.

1887 N184
Kimball Champions

Similar to sets issued by Allen & Ginter and Goodwin, the Kimaball tobacco company of Rochester, N.Y., issued its own 50-card set of "Champions of Games nad Sport" in 1888, and included four baseball players among the "billiardists, girl riders, tight-rope walkers" and other popular celebrities featured in the series. Measuring 1-1/2" by 2-3/4", the color lithographs were inserted in packages of Kimball Cigarettes. The artwork on the card features a posed portrait, which occupies the top three-fourths, and a drawing of the player in action at the bottom. The back of the card contains an ad for Kimball Cigarettes along with a list of the various sports and activities depicted in the set. James O'Neill, whose name is misspelled on the card, is the best known of the four baseball players. His .435 batting average in 1887 is the highest ever recorded. The Kimball promotion also included an album to house the card set.

	NR MT	EX	VG
Complete Set:	2500.00	1250.00	750.00
Common Player:	600.00	300.00	175.00
(1) E.A. Burch	600.00	300.00	175.00
(2) Dell Darling	600.00	300.00	175.00
(3) Hardie Henderson	600.00	300.00	175.00
(4) James O'Neil (O'Neill)	750.00	375.00	225.00

1887 N284 Buchner Gold Coin

Issued circa 1887, the N284 issue was produced by D. Buchner & Company for its Gold Coin brand of chewing tobacco. Actually, the series was not comprised only of baseball players - actors, jockeys, firemen and policemen were also included. The cards, which measure 1-3/4" by 3", are color drawings. The set is not a popular one among collectors as the drawings do not represent the players designated on the cards. In most instances,

players at a given position share the same drawing depicted on the card front. Three different card backs are found, all advising collectors to save the valuable chewing tobacco wrappers. Wrappers could be redeemed for various prizes.

	NR MT	EX	VG
Complete Set:	20000.00	10000.00	6000.
Common Player:	90.00	45.00	27.00
(1) Ed Andrews (hands at neck)	90.00	45.00	27.00
(2) Andrews (hands waist high)	110.00	55.00	33.00
(3) Cap Anson (hands outstretched)			
	500.00	250.00	150.00
(4) Cap Anson (left hand on hip)	550.00	275.00	165.00
(5) Tug Arundel	90.00	45.00	27.00
(6) Sam Barkley (Pittsburgh)	90.00	45.00	27.00
(7) Sam Barkley (St. Louis)	125.00	62.00	37.00
(8) Charley Bassett	90.00	45.00	27.00
(9) Charlie Bastian	90.00	45.00	27.00
(10) Ed Beecher	90.00	45.00	27.00
(11) Charlie Bennett	90.00	45.00	27.00
(12) Handsome Henry Boyle	110.00	55.00	33.00
(13) Dan Brouthers (hands outstretched)			
	225.00	112.00	67.00
(14) Dan Brouthers (with bat)	250.00	125.00	75.00
(15) Tom Brown	90.00	45.00	27.00
(16) Jack Burdock	90.00	45.00	27.00
(17) Oyster Burns (Baltimore)	110.00	55.00	33.00
(18) Tom Burns (Chicago)	90.00	45.00	27.00
(19) Doc Bushong	125.00	62.00	37.00
(20) John Cahill	110.00	55.00	33.00
(21) Cliff Carroll (Washington)	90.00	45.00	27.00
(22) Fred Carroll (Pittsburgh)	90.00	45.00	27.00
(23) Parisian Bob Carruthers (Caruthers)			
	150.00	75.00	45.00
(24) Dan Casey	125.00	62.00	37.00
(25) John Clarkson (ball at chest)	225.00	112.00	67.00
(26) John Clarkson (arm outstretched)			
	250.00	125.00	75.00
(27) Jack Clements	90.00	45.00	27.00
(28) John Coleman	90.00	45.00	27.00
(29) Charles Comiskey	500.00	250.00	150.00
(30) Roger Connor (hands outstretched)			
	225.00	112.00	67.00
(31) Roger Connor (hands oustretched, face level)			
	250.00	125.00	75.00
(32) Corbett	110.00	55.00	33.00
(33) Sam Craig (Crane)	110.00	55.00	33.00
(34) Sam Crane	110.00	55.00	33.00
(35) Crowley	110.00	55.00	33.00
(36) Ed Cushmann (Cushman)	110.00	55.00	33.00
(37) Ed Dailey (Daily)	90.00	45.00	27.00
(38) Con Daley (Daily)	90.00	45.00	27.00
(39) Pat Deasley	110.00	55.00	33.00
(40) Jerry Denny (hands on knees)	90.00	45.00	27.00
(41) Jerry Denny (hands on thighs)	110.00	55.00	33.00
(42) Jim Donnelly	90.00	45.00	27.00
(43) Jim Donohue (Donahue)	110.00	55.00	33.00
(44) Mike Dorgan (right field)	90.00	45.00	27.00
(45) Mike Dorgan (batter)	110.00	55.00	33.00
(46) Sure Shot Dunlap	90.00	45.00	27.00
(47) Dude Esterbrook	110.00	55.00	33.00
(48) Buck Ewing (ready to tag)	225.00	112.00	67.00
(49) Buck Ewing (hands at neck)	250.00	125.00	75.00
(50) Sid Farrar	90.00	45.00	27.00
(51) Jack Farrell (ready to tag)	90.00	45.00	27.00
(52) Jack Farrell (hands at knees)	110.00	55.00	33.00
(53) Charlie Ferguson	90.00	45.00	27.00
(54) Silver Flint	90.00	45.00	27.00

		NR MT	EX	VG
(55)	Jim Fogerty (Fogarty)	90.00	45.00	27.00
(56)	Tom Forster	110.00	55.00	33.00
(57)	Dave Foutz	150.00	75.00	45.00
(58)	Chris Fulmer	110.00	55.00	33.00
(59)	Joe Gerhardt	110.00	55.00	33.00
(60)	Charlie Getzein	90.00	45.00	27.00
(61)	Pete Gillespie (left field)	90.00	45.00	27.00
(62)	Pete Gillespie (batter)	110.00	55.00	33.00
(63)	Barney Gilligan	90.00	45.00	27.00
(64)	Pebbly Jack Glasscock (fielding grounder)			
		110.00	55.00	33.00
(65)	Pebbly Jack Glasscock (hands on knees)			
		125.00	62.00	37.00
(66)	Will Gleason	125.00	62.00	37.00
(67)	Piano Legs Gore	90.00	45.00	27.00
(68)	Frank Hankinson	110.00	55.00	33.00
(69)	Ned Hanlon	90.00	45.00	27.00
(70)	Hart	110.00	55.00	33.00
(71)	Egyptian Healy	90.00	45.00	27.00
(72)	Paul Hines (centre field)	90.00	45.00	27.00
(73)	Paul Hines (batter)	110.00	55.00	33.00
(74)	Joe Hornung	90.00	45.00	27.00
(75)	Cutrate Irwin	90.00	45.00	27.00
(76)	Dick Johnston	90.00	45.00	27.00
(77)	Tim Keefe (right arm outstretched)			
		225.00	112.00	67.00
(78)	Keefe (arm outstretched)	250.00	125.00	75.00
(79)	King Kelly (right field)	250.00	125.00	75.00
(80)	King Kelly (catcher)	275.00	137.00	82.00
(81)	Kennedy	110.00	55.00	33.00
(82)	Matt Kilroy	110.00	55.00	33.00
(83)	Arlie Latham	150.00	75.00	45.00
(84)	Jimmy Manning	90.00	45.00	27.00
(85)	Bill McClellan (existence not confirmed)			
(86)	Jim McCormick	110.00	55.00	33.00
(87)	Jack McGeachy	90.00	45.00	27.00
(88)	Jumbo McGinnis	125.00	62.00	37.00
(89)	George Meyers (Myers)	110.00	55.00	33.00
(90)	Doggie Miller	90.00	45.00	27.00
(91)	Honest John Morrill (hands outstretched)			
		90.00	45.00	27.00
(92)	Honest John Morrill (hands at neck)			
		110.00	55.00	33.00
(93)	Tom Morrissy (Morrissey)	110.00	55.00	33.00
(94)	Joe Mulvey (hands on knees)	90.00	45.00	27.00
(95)	Joe Mulvey (hands above head)			
		110.00	55.00	33.00
(96)	Al Myers	90.00	45.00	27.00
(97)	Candy Nelson	110.00	55.00	33.00
(98)	Little Nick Nichol	125.00	62.00	37.00
(99)	Billy O'Brien	90.00	45.00	27.00
(100)	Tip O'Neil (O'Neill)	150.00	75.00	45.00
(101)	Orator Jim O'Rourke (hands cupped)			
		225.00	112.00	67.00
(102)	Orator Jim O'Rourke (hands on thighs)			
		250.00	125.00	75.00
(103)	Dave Orr	110.00	55.00	33.00
(104)	Jimmy Peoples	90.00	45.00	27.00
(105)	Fred Pfeffer	90.00	45.00	27.00
(106)	Bill Phillips	90.00	45.00	27.00
(107)	Mark Polhemus	90.00	45.00	27.00
(108)	Henry Porter	90.00	45.00	27.00
(109)	Blondie Purcell	110.00	55.00	33.00
(110)	Old Hoss Radbourn (hands at chest)			
		225.00	112.00	67.00
(111)	Old Hoss Radbourn (hands above waist)			
		250.00	125.00	75.00
(112)	Danny Richardson (New York, hands at knees)	90.00	45.00	27.00
(113)	Danny Richardson (New York, foot on base)	110.00	55.00	33.00
(114)	Hardy Richardson (Detroit, hands at right shoulder)	90.00	45.00	27.00
(115)	Hardy Richardson (Detroit, hands above head)	110.00	55.00	33.00
(116)	Yank Robinson	125.00	62.00	37.00
(117)	George Rooks	110.00	55.00	33.00
(118)	Chief Rosemann (Roseman)	110.00	55.00	33.00
(119)	Jimmy Ryan	110.00	55.00	33.00
(120)	Emmett Seery (hands at right shoulder)			
		90.00	45.00	27.00
(121)	Emmett Seery (hands outstretched)			
		110.00	55.00	33.00
(122)	Otto Shomberg (Schomberg)	90.00	45.00	27.00
(123)	Pap Smith	90.00	45.00	27.00
(124)	Joe Strauss	110.00	55.00	33.00
(125)	Danny Sullivan	125.00	62.00	37.00
(126)	Marty Sullivan	90.00	45.00	27.00
(127)	Billy Sunday	125.00	62.00	37.00
(128)	Ezra Sutton	90.00	45.00	27.00

		NR MT	EX	VG
(129)	Big Sam Thompson (hand at belt)			
		225.00	112.00	67.00
(130)	Big Sam Thompson (hands chest high)			
		250.00	125.00	75.00
(131)	Chris Von Der Ahe	500.00	250.00	150.00
(132)	Ward (fielding grounder)	225.00	112.00	67.00
(133)	Monte Ward (hands by knee)	250.00	125.00	75.00
(134)	Ward (hands on knees)	250.00	125.00	75.00
(135)	Curt Welch	125.00	62.00	37.00
(136)	Deacon White	110.00	55.00	33.00
(137)	Art Whitney (Pittsburgh)	90.00	45.00	27.00
(138)	Grasshopper Whitney (Washington)			
		90.00	45.00	27.00
(139)	Ned Williamson (fielding grounder)			
		125.00	62.00	37.00
(140)	Ned Williamson (hands at chest)			
		150.00	75.00	45.00
(141)	Medoc Wise	90.00	45.00	27.00
(142)	Dandy Wood (hands at right shoulder)			
		90.00	45.00	27.00
(143)	Dandy Wood (stealing base)	110.00	55.00	33.00

1895 N300 Mayo's Cut Plug

These 1-5/8" by 2-7/8" cards were issued by the Mayo Tobacco Works of Richmond, Virginia. There are 48 cards in the set, with 40 different players pictured. Twenty-eight of the players are pictured in uniform and 12 are shown in street clothes. Eight players appear both ways. Eight of the uniformed players also appear in two variations, creating the 48-card total. Card fronts are black and white or sepia portraits on black cardboard, with a Mayo's Cut Pug ad at the bottom of each card. Cards are unnumbered.

		NR MT	EX	VG
Complete Set:		22500.00	11250.00	6750.
Common Player:		300.00	150.00	90.00
(1)	Charlie Abbey	300.00	150.00	90.00
(2)	Cap Anson	2000.00	1000.00	600.00
(3)	Jimmy Bannon	300.00	150.00	90.00
(4a)	Dan Brouthers (Baltimore on shirt)			
		800.00	400.00	250.00
(4b)	Dan Brouthers (Louisville on shirt)			
		900.00	450.00	275.00
(5)	Ed Cartwright	300.00	150.00	90.00
(6)	John Clarkson	800.00	400.00	250.00
(7)	Tommy Corcoran	300.00	150.00	90.00
(8)	Lave Cross	300.00	150.00	90.00
(9)	Bill Dahlen	300.00	150.00	90.00
(10)	Tom Daly	300.00	150.00	90.00
(11)	Ed Delehanty (Delahanty)	900.00	450.00	275.00
(12)	Hugh Duffy	800.00	400.00	250.00
(13a)	Buck Ewing (Cleveland on shirt)			
		800.00	400.00	250.00
(13b)	Buck Ewing (Cincinnati on shirt)			
		900.00	450.00	275.00
(14)	Dave Foutz	300.00	150.00	90.00
(15)	Charlie Ganzel	300.00	150.00	90.00
(16a)	Jack Glasscock (Pittsburg on shirt)			
		325.00	162.00	100.00
(16b)	Jack Glasscock (Louisville on shirt)			
		350.00	175.00	105.00
(17)	Mike Griffin	300.00	150.00	90.00
(18a)	George Haddock (no team on shirt)			
		350.00	175.00	105.00

		NR MT	EX	VG
(18b)	George Haddock (Philadelphia on shirt)			
		300.00	150.00	90.00
(19)	Bill Hallman	300.00	150.00	90.00
(20)	Billy Hamilton	800.00	400.00	250.00
(21)	Bill Joyce	300.00	150.00	90.00
(22)	Brickyard Kennedy	300.00	150.00	90.00
(23a)	Tom Kinslow (no team on shirt)			
		350.00	175.00	105.00
(23b)	Tom Kinslow (Pittsburg on shirt)			
		300.00	150.00	90.00
(24)	Arlie Latham	325.00	162.00	100.00
(25)	Herman Long	325.00	162.00	100.00
(26)	Tom Lovett	300.00	150.00	90.00
(27)	Bobby Lowe	350.00	175.00	105.00
(28)	Tommy McCarthy	700.00	350.00	210.00
(29)	Yale Murphy	300.00	150.00	90.00
(30)	Billy Nash	325.00	162.00	100.00
(31)	Kid Nichols	850.00	425.00	260.00
(32a)	Fred Pfeffer (2nd Base)	300.00	150.00	90.00
(32b)	Fred Pfeffer (Retired)	350.00	175.00	105.00
(33)	Wilbert Robinson	875.00	437.00	265.00
(34a)	Amos Russie (incorrect spelling)			
		875.00	437.00	265.00
(34b)	Amos Rusie (correct spell)	800.00	400.00	250.00
(35)	Jimmy Ryan	325.00	162.00	100.00
(36)	Bill Shindle	300.00	150.00	90.00
(37)	Germany Smith	300.00	150.00	90.00
(38)	Otis Stocksdale (Stockdale)	300.00	150.00	90.00
(39)	Tommy Tucker	300.00	150.00	90.00
(40a)	Monte Ward (2nd Base)	800.00	400.00	250.00
(40b)	Monte Ward (Retired)	900.00	450.00	275.00

A player's name in *italic* indicates a rookie card. An (FC) indicates a player's first card for that particular card company.

1896 N301
Mayo Die-Cut Game Cards

Mayo Tobacco Works of Richmond, Va., issued an innovative, if not very popular, series of die-cut baseball player figures in 1896. These tiny (1-1/2" long by just 3/16" wide) cardboard figures were inserted in packages of Mayo's Cut Plug Tobacco and were designed to be used as part of a baseball board game. A "grandstand, base and teetotum" were available free by mail to complete the game pieces. Twenty-eight different die-cut figures were available, representing 26 unspecified New York and Boston players along with two umpires. The players are shown in various action poses--either running, batting, pitching or fielding. The backs carry an ad for Mayo's Tobacco. The players shown do not relate to any actual members of the New York or Boston clubs, diminishing the popularity of this issue, which has an American Card Catalog designation of N301.

		NR MT	EX	VG
Complete Set:		1000.00	500.00	300.00
Common Player:		35.00	17.50	10.50
(1a)	Pitcher (Boston)	35.00	17.50	10.50
(1b)	Pitcher (New York)	35.00	17.50	10.50
(2a)	1st Baseman (Boston)	35.00	17.50	10.50
(2b)	1st Baseman (New York)	35.00	17.50	10.50
(3a)	2nd Baseman (Boston)	35.00	17.50	10.50
(3b)	2nd Baseman (New York)	35.00	17.50	10.50
(4a)	3rd Baseman (Boston)	35.00	17.50	10.50
(4b)	3rd Baseman (New York)	35.00	17.50	10.50

		NR MT	EX	VG
(5a)	Right Fielder (Boston)	35.00	17.50	10.50
(5b)	Right Fielder (New York)	35.00	17.50	10.50
(6a)	Center Fielder (Boston)	35.00	17.50	10.50
(6b)	Center Fielder (New York)	35.00	17.50	10.50
(7a)	Left Fielder (Boston)	35.00	17.50	10.50
(7b)	Left Fielder (New York)	35.00	17.50	10.50
(8a)	Short Stop (Boston)	35.00	17.50	10.50
(8b)	Short Stop (New York)	35.00	17.50	10.50
(9a)	Catcher (Boston)	35.00	17.50	10.50
(9b)	Catcher (New York)	35.00	17.50	10.50
(10a)	Batman (Boston)	35.00	17.50	10.50
(10b)	Batman (New York)	35.00	17.50	10.50
(11a)	Runner (Boston, standing upright)			
		35.00	17.50	10.50
(11b)	Runner (New York, standing upright)			
		35.00	17.50	10.50
(12a)	Runner (Boston, bent slightly forward)			
		35.00	17.50	10.50
(12b)	Runner (New York, bent slightly forward)			
		35.00	17.50	10.50
(13a)	Runner (Boston, bent well forward)			
		35.00	17.50	10.50
(13b)	Runner (New York, bent well forward)			
		35.00	17.50	10.50
(14)	Umpire (facing front)	35.00	17.50	10.50
(15)	Field Umpire (rear view)	35.00	17.50	10.50

1888 N321 S.F. Hess

One of several tobacco card sets produced by S.F. Hess & Co. of Rochester, the N321 set is a rare 40-card issue featuring players from the California League. The cards measure 2-7/8" by 1-1/2" and feature color drawings of players. The player's name and team are printed along the top margin of the card, while the words "S.F. Hess and Co.'s/Creole Cigarettes" appear at the bottom. "California League" is also printed in large capital letters above the player drawing, while the 1888 copyright date appears below. There are 35 players (including one umpire) in the set, and five players are pictured on two cards each, resulting in 40 different cards.

		NR MT	EX	VG
Complete Set:		20000.00	10000.00	6000.
Common Player:		500.00	250.00	150.00
(1)	Bennett	500.00	250.00	150.00
(2)	Borchers	500.00	250.00	150.00
(3)	Buckley	500.00	250.00	150.00
(4)	Burke (batting)	500.00	250.00	150.00
(5)	Burke (ready to pitch)	500.00	250.00	150.00
(6)	Burnett	500.00	250.00	150.00
(7)	Carroll	500.00	250.00	150.00
(8)	Donohue	500.00	250.00	150.00
(9)	Donovan	500.00	250.00	150.00
(10)	Finn	500.00	250.00	150.00
(11)	Gagus	500.00	250.00	150.00
(12)	Hanley	500.00	250.00	150.00
(13)	Hardie (C., wearing mask)	500.00	250.00	150.00
(14)	Hardie (C.F., with bat)	500.00	250.00	150.00
(15)	Hayes	500.00	250.00	150.00
(16)	Lawton	500.00	250.00	150.00
(17)	Levy	500.00	250.00	150.00
(18)	Long	500.00	250.00	150.00
(19)	McCord	500.00	250.00	150.00
(20)	Meegan	500.00	250.00	150.00

		NR MT	EX	VG
(21)	Moore	500.00	250.00	150.00
(22)	Mullee	500.00	250.00	150.00
(23)	Newhert	500.00	250.00	150.00
(24)	Noonan	500.00	250.00	150.00
(25)	O'Day	500.00	250.00	150.00
(26)	Perrier	500.00	250.00	150.00
(27)	Powers (1st B., catching)	500.00	250.00	150.00
(28)	Powers (1st B. & Capt., with bat)			
		500.00	250.00	150.00
(29)	Ryan	500.00	250.00	150.00
(30)	Selna	500.00	250.00	150.00
(31)	Shea	500.00	250.00	150.00
(32)	J. Sheridan (umpire)	500.00	250.00	150.00
(33)	"Big" Smith	500.00	250.00	150.00
(34)	H. Smith	500.00	250.00	150.00
(35)	J. Smith	500.00	250.00	150.00
(36)	Smett	500.00	250.00	150.00
(37)	Stockwell (throwing)	500.00	250.00	150.00
(38)	Stockwell (with bat)	500.00	250.00	150.00
(39)	Sweeney	500.00	250.00	150.00
(40)	Whitehead	500.00	250.00	150.00

1888 N333 S.F. Hess
Newsboys League

Although not picturing actual baseball players, this 44-card set issued S.F. Hess and Co. has a baseball theme. The cards measured 2-7/8" by 1-1/2" and featured pictures of newspaper boys from eight different papers in eight different cities (Rochester, Cleveland, Philadelphia, Boston, Albany, Detroit, New York and Syracuse). The boys are pictured in a portrait photo wearing a baseball-style shirt bearing the name of their newspaper. The boy's name, position and newspaper are printed below, while the words "Newsboys League" appears in capital letters at the top of the card. No identification is provided for the four Philadelphia newsboys, so a photo description is provided in the checklist that follows.

		NR MT	EX	VG
Complete Set:		3000.00	1500.00	900.00
Common Player:		70.00	35.00	21.00
(1)	R.J. Bell	70.00	35.00	21.00
(2)	Binden	70.00	35.00	21.00
(3)	Bowen	70.00	35.00	21.00
(4)	Boyle	70.00	35.00	21.00
(5)	Britcher	70.00	35.00	21.00
(6)	Caine	70.00	35.00	21.00
(7)	I. Cohen	70.00	35.00	21.00
(8)	R. Cohen	70.00	35.00	21.00
(9)	Cross	70.00	35.00	21.00
(10)	F. Cuddy	70.00	35.00	21.00
(11)	E. Daisey	70.00	35.00	21.00
(12)	Davis	70.00	35.00	21.00
(13)	B. Dinsmore	70.00	35.00	21.00
(14)	Donovan	70.00	35.00	21.00
(15)	A. Downer	70.00	35.00	21.00
(16)	Fanelly	70.00	35.00	21.00
(17)	J. Flood	70.00	35.00	21.00
(18)	C. Gallagher	70.00	35.00	21.00
(19)	M.H. Gallagher	70.00	35.00	21.00
(20)	D. Galligher	70.00	35.00	21.00

		NR MT	EX	VG
(21)	J. Galligher	70.00	35.00	21.00
(22)	Haskins	70.00	35.00	21.00
(23)	Herze	70.00	35.00	21.00
(24)	F. Horan	70.00	35.00	21.00
(25)	Hosler	70.00	35.00	21.00
(26)	Hyde	70.00	35.00	21.00
(27)	Keilty	70.00	35.00	21.00
(28)	C. Kellogg	70.00	35.00	21.00
(29)	Mahoney	70.00	35.00	21.00
(30)	Mayer	70.00	35.00	21.00
(31)	I. McDonald	70.00	35.00	21.00
(32)	McGrady	70.00	35.00	21.00
(33)	O'Brien	70.00	35.00	21.00
(34)	E.C. Murphy	70.00	35.00	21.00
(35)	Sabin	70.00	35.00	21.00
(36)	Shedd	70.00	35.00	21.00
(37)	R. Sheehan	70.00	35.00	21.00
(38)	Smith	70.00	35.00	21.00
(39)	Talbot	70.00	35.00	21.00
(40)	Walsh	70.00	35.00	21.00
(41)	Philadelphia newsboy (hair parted on right side)	70.00	35.00	21.00
(42)	Philadelphia newsboy (hair parted on left side)	70.00	35.00	21.00
(43)	Philadelphia newsboy (no part in hair)	70.00	35.00	21.00
(44)	Philadelphia newsboy (head shaved)	70.00	35.00	21.00

1888 N338-1 S.F. Hess
California League

This tobacco card set picturing players from the California League is one of the rarest of all 19th century issues. Issued in the late 1880s by S.F. Hess & Co. of Rochester, these 2-7/8" by 1-1/2" cards are so rare that only several examples are known to exist. Some of the photos in the N338-1 set are identical to the drawings in teh N321 set, issued by S.F. Hess in 1888. The N338-1 cards are found with the words "California League" printed in an arc either above or below the player photo. The player's name appears below the photo. At the bottom of the card the words "S.F. Hess & Co.'s Creole Cigarettes" are printed in a rolling style.

		NR MT	EX	VG
Complete Set:		16000.00	8000.00	4800.
Common Player:		1000.00	500.00	300.00
(1)	Borsher	1000.00	500.00	300.00
(2)	Carroll	1000.00	500.00	300.00
(3)	C. Ebright	1000.00	500.00	300.00
(4)	P. Incell	1000.00	500.00	300.00
(5)	C.F. Lawton	1000.00	500.00	300.00
(6)	C.F. Levy (throwing)	1000.00	500.00	300.00
(7)	C.F. Levy (with bat)	1000.00	500.00	300.00
(8)	C. McDonald	1000.00	500.00	300.00
(9)	P Meegan	1000.00	500.00	300.00
(10)	S.S. Newhert	1000.00	500.00	300.00
(11)	P. Noonan	1000.00	500.00	300.00
(12)	R.F. Perrier	1000.00	500.00	300.00
(13)	Perrier, H. Smith	1000.00	500.00	300.00
(14)	Ryan	1000.00	500.00	300.00
(15)	J. Smith, N. Smith	1000.00	500.00	300.00
(16)	P. Sweeney	1000.00	500.00	300.00

1889 N338-2S.F Hess

The most popular of the S.F. Hess & Co. issues, this 21-card set was issued in 1889 and pictures 16 players from the New York Giants, two New York Mets players, two from St. Louis and one from Detroit. The cards measure 2-3/4" by 1-1/2" and feature sepia-toned photographs, most of which are enclosed in ovals with a dark background. The player's name is printed in capital letters just beneath the photo, and the S.F. Hess & Co. logo appears at the bottom (without using the Creole Cigarette brand name).

		NR MT	EX	VG
Complete Set:		21000.00	10500.00	6300.
Common Player:		750.00	375.00	225.00
(1)	Bill Brown	750.00	375.00	225.00
(2)	Roger Conner (Connor)	1800.00	900.00	550.00
(3)	Ed Crane	750.00	375.00	225.00
(4)	Buck Ewing	1800.00	900.00	550.00
(5)	Elmer Foster	750.00	375.00	225.00
(6)	Wm. George	750.00	375.00	225.00
(7)	Joe Gerhardt	750.00	375.00	225.00
(8)	Chas. Getzein	750.00	375.00	225.00
(9)	Geo. Gore	750.00	375.00	225.00
(10)	Gil Hatfield	750.00	375.00	225.00
(11)	Tim Keefe	1800.00	900.00	550.00
(12)	Arlie Latham	750.00	375.00	225.00
(13)	Pat Murphy	750.00	375.00	225.00
(14)	Jim Mutrie	750.00	375.00	225.00
(15)	Dave Orr	750.00	375.00	225.00
(16)	Danny Richardson	750.00	375.00	225.00
(17)	Mike Slattery	750.00	375.00	225.00
(18)	Silent Mike Tiernan	750.00	375.00	225.00
(19)	Lidell Titcomb	750.00	375.00	225.00
(20)	Johnny Ward	1800.00	900.00	550.00
(21)	Curt Welch	750.00	375.00	225.00
(22)	Mickey Welch	1800.00	900.00	550.00
(23)	Arthur Whitney	750.00	375.00	225.00

1886 N370 Lone Jack

The 1886 Lone Jack set is among the rarest of all 19th Century tobacco issues. Issued by the Lone

Jack Cigarette Co. of Lynchburg, Va., the set consists of 13 subjects, all members of the champion St. Louis Browns. Photos for the set are enlarged versions of those used in the more popular N172 Old Judge series. Cards in the set measure 2-1/2" by 1-1/2" and carry an ad for Lond Jack Cigarettes along the bottom of the front. The set features the Browns' starting lineup for 1886 along with their two top pitchers, backup catcher and owner, Chris Von Der Ahe.

		NR MT	EX	VG
Complete Set:		12000.00	6000.00	3300.
Common Player:		750.00	375.00	225.00
(1)	Doc Bushong	750.00	375.00	225.00
(2)	Parisian Bob Caruthers	750.00	375.00	225.00
(3)	Commy Commiskey (Comiskey)			
		2500.00	1250.00	750.00
(4)	Dave Foutz	750.00	375.00	225.00
(5)	Will Gleason	750.00	375.00	225.00
(6)	Nat Hudson	750.00	375.00	225.00
(7)	Rudy Kimler (Kemmler)	750.00	375.00	225.00
(8)	Arlie Latham	750.00	375.00	225.00
(9)	Little Nick Nicol	750.00	375.00	225.00
(10)	Tip O'Neil (O'Neill)	750.00	375.00	225.00
(11)	Yank Robinson	750.00	375.00	225.00
(12)	Chris Von Der Ahe	1250.00	625.00	400.00
(13)	Curt Welsh (Welch)	750.00	375.00	225.00

1888 N403 Yum Yum Tobacco

An extremely rare series of tobacco cards, this set was issued in 1888 by August Beck & Co. of Chicago. The cards, which vary slightly in size but average 1-3/8" by 2-3/4", were distributed in packages of the company's Yum Yum smoking and chewing tobacco. Yum Yum cards carry the American Card Catalog designation N403 and are found in two distinct types: photographic portraits and full-length action drawings that appear to be copied from photos used in the Old Judge sets of the same period. In both types, the player's name and position appear in capital letters below the photo, while the very bottom of the card states: "Smoke and Chew "Yum Yum" Tobacco. A. Beck & Co. Chicago, Ill." Players from all eight National League clubs, plus Brooklyn of the American Association, are included in the set.

		NR MT	MT	VG
Complete Set:		40000.00	20000.00	12500.
Common Line Drawing:		600.00	300.00	175.00
Common Portrait:		750.00	375.00	230.00
(1)	Cap Anson	10000.00	5000.00	3000.
(2)	Lady Baldwin	600.00	300.00	175.00
(3)	Dan Brouthers	1000.00	500.00	300.00
(4)	Bill "California" Brown	600.00	300.00	175.00
(5)	Buffington (Buffinton)	600.00	300.00	180.00
(6)	Thomas Burns (portrait)	750.00	375.00	230.00
(7)	Thomas Burns (with bat)	600.00	300.00	175.00
(8)	John Clarkson (portrait)	1800.00	900.00	550.00
(9)	John Clarkson (throwing)	1000.00	500.00	300.00
(10)	John Coleman	750.00	375.00	230.00

		NR MT	EX	VG
(11)	Larry Corcoran	750.00	375.00	230.00
(12)	Tido Daily (Daly) (photo actually Billy			
	Sunday)	750.00	375.00	230.00
(13)	Tom Deasley	750.00	375.00	230.00
(14)	Mike Dorgan	750.00	375.00	230.00
(15)	Buck Ewing (portrait)	1800.00	900.00	550.00
(16)	Buck Ewing (with bat)	1000.00	500.00	300.00
(17)	Silver Flint	750.00	375.00	230.00
(18)	Pud Galvin	1000.00	500.00	300.00
(19)	Joe Gerhardt	750.00	375.00	230.00
(20)	Pete Gillespie	750.00	375.00	230.00
(21)	Pebbly Jack Glasscock	600.00	300.00	175.00
(22)	Ed Greer	750.00	375.00	230.00
(23)	Tim Keefe (pitching)	1000.00	500.00	300.00
(24)	Tim Keefe (portrait)	1800.00	900.00	550.00
(25)	King Kelly	1200.00	600.00	350.00
26	King Kelly (photo)	5000.00	2500.00	1500.
(27)	Gus Krock	750.00	375.00	230.00
(28)	Connie Mack	1400.00	700.00	425.00
(29)	Kid Madden	600.00	300.00	175.00
(30)	Doggie Miller	600.00	300.00	175.00
(31)	Billy Nash	600.00	300.00	175.00
(32)	O'Rourke (portrait)	1800.00	900.00	550.00
(33)	O'Rourke (with bat)	1000.00	500.00	300.00
(34)	Danny Richardson	750.00	375.00	230.00
(35)	Chief Roseman	750.00	375.00	230.00
(36)	Jimmy Ryan (portrait)	750.00	375.00	230.00
(37)	Jimmy Ryan (throwing)	600.00	300.00	175.00
(38)	Little Bill Sowders	600.00	300.00	175.00
(39)	Marty Sullivan	750.00	375.00	230.00
(40)	Billy Sunday (line drawing)	900.00	450.00	275.00
(41)	Billy Sunday (portrait)	1500.00	750.00	450.00
(42)	Ezra Sutton	600.00	300.00	175.00
(43)	Tiernan (portrait)	750.00	375.00	230.00
(44)	Tiernan (with bat)	600.00	300.00	175.00
(45)	Rip Van Haltren (photo not Van Haltren)			
		750.00	375.00	230.00
(46)	Mickey Welch (hands clasped at chest)			
		1000.00	500.00	300.00
(47)	Mickey Welch (portrait)	1800.00	900.00	550.00
(48)	Mickey Welch (right arm extended)			
		1000.00	500.00	300.00
(49)	Grasshopper Whitney	600.00	300.00	175.00
(50)	George "Dandy" Wood	600.00	300.00	175.00

1889 N526 No. 7 Diamond S Cigars

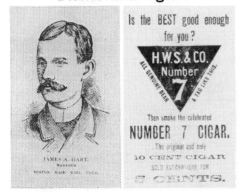

Is the BEST good enough for you?

H.W.S. & CO. Number 7

Then smoke the celebrated

NUMBER 7 CIGAR.

The original and only

10 CENT CIGAR

SOLD EVERYWHERE FOR

5 CENTS.

Two versions of this set picturing Boston players were issued in 1889 by Number 7 Cigars and Diamond S Cigars. The cards measure approximately 3-1/8" by 4-1/2" and feature black and white line portrait drawings of the players with their name printed below in capital letters along with the team name ("Boston Base Ball Club"). The backs carry an ad for either Number 7 Cigars, a product of H.W.S. & Co., or Diamond S Cigars, advertised as the "Best 10 cent Cigar in America." Except for the backs, the two sets are identical.

		NR MT	EX	VG
Complete Set:		10000.00	5000.00	3000.
Common Player:		500.00	250.00	150.00
(1)	C.W. Bennett	500.00	250.00	150.00
(2)	Dennis Brouthers	1000.00	500.00	300.00

		NR MT	EX	VG
(3)	T.T. Brown	500.00	250.00	150.00
(4)	John G. Clarkson	1000.00	500.00	300.00
(5)	C.W. Ganzel	500.00	250.00	150.00
(6)	James A. Hart	500.00	250.00	150.00
(7)	R.F. Johnston	500.00	250.00	150.00
(8)	M.J. Kelly	1200.00	600.00	350.00
(9)	M.J. Madden	500.00	250.00	150.00
(10)	Wm. Nash	500.00	250.00	150.00
(11)	Jos. Quinn	500.00	250.00	150.00
(12)	Chas. Radbourn	1000.00	500.00	300.00
(13)	J.B. Ray (should be I.B.)	500.00	250.00	150.00
(14)	Hardie Richardson	500.00	250.00	150.00
(15)	Wm. Sowders	500.00	250.00	150.00

1895 N566 Newsboy

Issued in the 1890s by the National Tobacco Works, this massive cabinet card set was distributed as a premium with the Newsboy tobacco brand. Although the set contained over 500 popular actresses, athletes, politicians and other celebrities of the day, only a dozen cards of baseball players have been found. The cards measure 4-1/4" by 6-1/2" and feature sepia-toned photographs mounted on a backing that has "Newsboy" written in script in the lower left corner. Each photograph is numbered. The baseball players included in the set are all members of the 1894 New York Giants, except Dave Foutz, who was Brooklyn's playing manager. There are two known poses of John Ward.

		NR MT	EX	VG
Complete Set:		15500.00	7750.00	5000.
Common Player:		750.00	375.00	225.00
174	W.H. Murphy	750.00	375.00	225.00
175	Amos Rusie	3500.00	1750.00	1050.
176	Michael Tiernan	750.00	375.00	225.00
177	E.D. Burke	750.00	375.00	225.00
178	J.J. Doyle	750.00	375.00	225.00
179	W.B. Fuller	750.00	375.00	225.00
180	Geo. Van Haltren	850.00	425.00	255.00
181	Dave Foutz	750.00	375.00	225.00
182	Jouett Meekin	850.00	425.00	255.00
201	W.H. Clark (Clarke)	750.00	375.00	225.00
202	Parke Wilson	750.00	375.00	225.00
586	John M. Ward (portrait, arms folded)			
		2500.00	1250.00	750.00
587	John M. Ward (standing, with bat)			
		1800.00	900.00	550.00

1887 N690 Kalamazoo Bats

This set, issued circa 1887 by Charles Gross & Co. of Philadelphia, is one of the most popular and most difficult of all 19th century tobacco issues. The cards measure a rather large 2-1/4" by 4" and feature a sepia-toned photograph on heavy cardboard. The player's name and team appear inside a white rectangle at the bottom of the photo, while a small ad for Kalamazoo Bats cigarettes is included at the very bottom of the card. Some cards carry an 1887

copyright line, but there are indications that some of the cards date from 1886 or even 1888. The unnumbered set pictures players from four teams - two from New York (Giants and Mets) and two from Philadelphia (Athletics and Phillies). A few of the cards picture more than one player, and some cards have been found with an ad on the back offering various prizes in exchange for saving the cards. The set has been assigned the American Card Catalog number N690. Because of the rareness of the N690 Kalamazoo Bats issue, no complete set is given.

		NR MT	EX	VG
Complete Set:				
Common Player:		650.00	325.00	200.00
(1)	Ed Andrews	650.00	325.00	200.00
(2)	Charles Bastian, Lyons	800.00	400.00	250.00
(3)	Louis Bierbauer	650.00	325.00	200.00
(4)	Louis Bierbauer, Gallagher	800.00	400.00	250.00
(5)	Buffington (Buffinton)	650.00	325.00	200.00
(6)	Daniel Casey	650.00	325.00	195.00
(7)	Jack Clements	650.00	325.00	200.00
(8)	Roger Connor	3000.00	1500.00	900.00
(9)	Larry Corcoran	1200.00	600.00	350.00
(10)	Ed Cushman	1200.00	600.00	350.00
(11)	Pat Deasley	1200.00	600.00	350.00
(12)	Jim Devlin	650.00	325.00	200.00
(13)	Jim Donahue	1200.00	600.00	350.00
(14)	Mike Dorgan	1200.00	600.00	350.00
(15)	Dude Esterbrooke (Esterbrook)	1200.00	600.00	350.00
(16)	Buck Ewing	3000.00	1500.00	900.00
(17)	Sid Farrar	650.00	325.00	200.00
(18)	Charlie Ferguson	650.00	325.00	200.00
(19)	Jim Fogarty	650.00	325.00	200.00
(20)	Fogarty, Deacon McGuire	800.00	400.00	250.00
(21)	Elmer Foster	1200.00	600.00	350.00
(22)	Whitey Gibson	650.00	325.00	200.00
(23)	Pete Gillespie	600.00	300.00	180.00
(24)	Tom Gunning	650.00	325.00	200.00
(25)	Cutrate Irwin	650.00	325.00	200.00
(26)	Irwin, Smiling Al Maul	800.00	400.00	250.00
(27)	Tim Keefe	1800.00	900.00	540.00
(28)	Ted Larkin	650.00	325.00	200.00
(29)	Ted Larkins, Jocko Milligan	800.00	400.00	250.00
(30)	Jack Lynch	1200.00	600.00	350.00
(31)	Denny Lyons	650.00	325.00	200.00
(32)	Denny Lyons, Taylor	650.00	325.00	200.00
(33)	Fred Mann	600.00	300.00	180.00
(34)	Fred Mann, Uncle Robbie Robinson	1800.00	900.00	550.00
(35)	Charlie Mason	650.00	325.00	200.00
(36)	Bobby Mathews	650.00	325.00	200.00
(37)	Smiling Al Maul	650.00	325.00	200.00
(38)	Al Mays	1200.00	600.00	350.00
(39)	Jim McGan (McGarr)	650.00	325.00	200.00
(40)	Deacon McGuire (catching)	650.00	325.00	200.00
(41)	Deacon McGuire (throwing)	650.00	325.00	200.00
(42)	Jocko Milligan, Harry Stowe (Stovey)	800.00	400.00	250.00
(43)	Joseph Mulvey	650.00	325.00	200.00
(44)	Candy Nelson	1200.00	600.00	350.00

		NR MT	EX	VG
(45)	Orator Jim O'Rourke	3000.00	1500.00	900.00
(46)	Dave Orr	1200.00	600.00	350.00
(47)	Tom Poorman	650.00	325.00	200.00
(48)	Danny Richardson	1200.00	600.00	350.00
(49)	Uncle Robbie Robinson	2000.00	1000.00	600.00
(50)	Chief Roseman	1200.00	600.00	350.00
(51)	Harry Stowe (Stovey) (hands on hips)	750.00	375.00	230.00
(52)	Harry Stowe (Stovey) (hands outstretched)	750.00	375.00	230.00
(53)	Sleepy Townsend	650.00	325.00	200.00
(54)	Jocko Milligan, Sleepy Townsend	800.00	400.00	250.00
(55)	Monte Ward	3000.00	1500.00	900.00
(56)	Gus Weyhing	650.00	325.00	200.00
(57)	George "Dandy" Wood	650.00	325.00	200.00
(58)	Harry Wright	2500.00	1250.00	750.00

1887 N690
Kalamazoo Bats Cabinets

Another extremely rare issue, this series of cabinet cards was issued either as a proof or a premium by Charles Gross & Co. of Philadelphia, makers of the Kalamazoo Bats brand of cigarettes. Two distinct types have been found, both measuring 4-1/4" by 6-1/2". One variety displays the photo on a black mount with the words "Smoke Kalamazoo Bats" embossed in gold to the left. The other contains no advertising, although there is an oval embossment on the card, along with the words "Chas. Gross & Co." and an 1887 copyright line. These cards also have a distinctive pink color on the back of the cardboard mount. Because of the rareness of the N690 Kalamazoo Bats Cabinets, no complete set price is given.

		NR MT	EX	VG
Complete Set:				
Common Player:		1200.00	600.00	350.00
Common Team:		10000.00	5000.00	3000.
(1)	Ed Andrews	1200.00	600.00	350.00
(2)	Charles Bastian, Daniel Casey, Taylor	1200.00	600.00	350.00
(3)	Charles Bastian, Denny Lyons	1200.00	600.00	350.00
(4)	Louis Bierbauer, Gallagher	1200.00	600.00	350.00
(5)	Charles Buffington (Buffinton)	1200.00	600.00	350.00
(6)	Daniel Casey	1200.00	600.00	350.00
(7)	Jack Clements	1200.00	600.00	350.00
(8)	Jim Devlin	1200.00	600.00	350.00
(9)	Sid Farrar	1200.00	600.00	350.00
(10)	Charlie Ferguson	1200.00	600.00	350.00
(11)	Jim Fogarty	1200.00	600.00	350.00
(12)	Whitey Gibson	1200.00	600.00	350.00
(13)	Tom Gunning	1200.00	600.00	350.00
(14)	Cutrate Irwin	1200.00	600.00	350.00
(15)	Cutrate Irwin, Smiling Al Maul	1200.00	600.00	350.00
(16)	Ted Larkins (Larkin), Jocko Milligan	1200.00	600.00	350.00
(17)	Denny Lyons	1200.00	600.00	350.00
(18)	Denny Lyons, Taylor	1200.00	600.00	350.00
(19)	Fred Mann	1200.00	600.00	350.00
(20)	Bobby Mathews	1200.00	600.00	350.00
(21)	Smiling Al Maul	1200.00	600.00	350.00
(22)	Chippy McCan (McGarr)	1200.00	600.00	350.00
(23)	Deacon McGuire	1200.00	600.00	350.00
(24)	Jocko Milligan, Harry Stowe (Stovey)	1200.00	600.00	350.00
(25)	Joseph Mulvey	1200.00	600.00	350.00
(26)	Tim Poorman	1200.00	600.00	350.00

		NR MT	EX	VG
(27)	Ed Seward	1200.00	600.00	350.00
(28)	Harry Stowe (Stovey)	1200.00	600.00	350.00
(29)	Sleepy Townsend	1200.00	600.00	350.00
(30)	George "Dandy" Wood	1200.00	600.00	350.00
(31)	Athletic Club	10000.00	5000.00	3000.
(32)	Boston B.B.C.	20000.00	10000.00	6000.
(33)	Philadelphia B.B.C.	10000.00	5000.00	3000.
(34)	Pittsburg B.B.C.	10000.00	5000.00	3000.

1887 N690-1 Kalamazoo Bats Team Cards

The six team photos in this set were issued by Charles Gross & Co. of Philadelphia as a promotion for its Kalamazoo Bats brand of cigarettes. The cards, which are similar in design to the related N690 series, are extremely rare. They feature a team photo with the caption in a white box at the bottom of the photo and an ad for Kalamazoo Bats to the left.

		NR MT	EX	VG
Complete Set:		20000.00	10000.00	6000.
Common Team:		3500.00	1750.00	1050.
(1)	Athletic Club	3500.00	1750.00	1050.
(2)	Baltimore B.B.C.	3500.00	1750.00	1050.
(3)	Boston B.B.C.	5000.00	2500.00	1500.
(4)	Detroit B.B.C.	3500.00	1750.00	1050.
(5)	Philadelphia B.B.C.	3500.00	1750.00	1050.
(6)	Pittsburg B.B.C.	3500.00	1750.00	1050.

A player's name in italic indicates a rookie card. An (FC) indicates a player's first card for that particular card company.

1952 National Tea Labels

Another set of bread end-labels, this issue consists of 42 players, although there is speculation that six more labels may exist. The unnumbered lables measure approximately 2-3/4" by 2-11/16" and are sometimes referred to as "Red Borders" because of their wide, red borders. The player's name and team are printed alongside his photo, and the slogan "Eat More Bread for Health" also appears.

		NR MT	EX	VG
Complete Set:		2250.00	1125.00	675.00
Common Player:		110.00	55.00	33.00
(1)	Gene Bearden	110.00	55.00	33.00
(2)	Yogi Berra	300.00	150.00	90.00
(3)	Lou Brissie	110.00	55.00	33.00
(4)	Sam Chapman	110.00	55.00	33.00
(5)	Chuck Diering	110.00	55.00	33.00
(6)	Dom DiMaggio	125.00	62.00	37.00
(7)	Bruce Edwards	110.00	55.00	33.00
(8)	Del Ennis	110.00	55.00	33.00
(9)	Ferris Fain	110.00	55.00	33.00
(10)	Howie Fox	110.00	55.00	33.00
(11)	Sid Gordon	110.00	55.00	33.00
(12)	John Groth	110.00	55.00	33.00
(13)	Granny Hamner	110.00	55.00	33.00
(14)	Sheldon Jones	110.00	55.00	33.00
(15)	Howie Judson	110.00	55.00	33.00
(16)	Sherman Lollar	110.00	55.00	33.00
(17)	Clarence Marshall	110.00	55.00	33.00
(18)	Don Mueller	110.00	55.00	33.00
(19)	Danny Murtaugh	110.00	55.00	33.00
(20)	Dave Philley	110.00	55.00	33.00
(21)	Jerry Priddy	110.00	55.00	33.00
(22)	Robin Roberts	175.00	87.00	52.00
(23)	Eddie Robinson	110.00	55.00	33.00
(24)	Preacher Roe	125.00	62.00	37.00
(25)	Stan Rojek	110.00	55.00	33.00
(26)	Al Rosen	125.00	62.00	37.00
(27)	Bob Rush	110.00	55.00	33.00
(28)	Hank Sauer	110.00	55.00	33.00
(29)	Enos Slaughter	175.00	87.00	52.00
(30)	Duke Snider	300.00	150.00	90.00
(31)	Warren Spahn	200.00	100.00	60.00
(32)	Gerry Staley	110.00	55.00	33.00
(33)	Virgil Stallcup	110.00	55.00	33.00
(34)	George Stirnweiss	110.00	55.00	33.00
(35)	Earl Torgeson	110.00	55.00	33.00
(36)	Dizzy Trout	110.00	55.00	33.00
(37)	Mickey Vernon	110.00	55.00	33.00
(38)	Wally Westlake	110.00	55.00	33.00
(39)	Johnny Wyrostek	110.00	55.00	33.00
(40)	Eddie Yost	110.00	55.00	33.00

1954 N.Y. Journal-American

Issued during the Golden Age of baseball in New York City, this 59-card set features only players from the three New York teams of the day - the Giants, Yankees and Dodgers. The 2" by 4" cards were issued at newsstands with the purchase of the now-extinct newspaper. Card fronts have promotional copy and a contest serial number in addition to the player's name and photo. Cards are black and white and unnumbered. Many of the game's top stars are included, such as Mickey Mantle, Willie Mays, Gil Hodges, Duke Snider, Jackie Robinson and Yogi Berra. Card backs featured team schedules. It has been theorized that a 60th Dodgers card should exist. Don Hoak and Bob Milliken have been suggested as the missing card, but the existence of either card has never been confirmed.

	NR MT	EX	VG
Complete Set:	2250.00	1125.00	675.00
Common Player:	10.00	5.00	3.00

		NR MT	EX	VG
(1)	Johnny Antonelli	12.00	6.00	3.50
(2)	Hank Bauer	20.00	10.00	6.00
(3)	Yogi Berra	100.00	50.00	30.00
(4)	Joe Black	12.00	6.00	3.50
(5)	Harry Byrd	10.00	5.00	3.00
(6)	Roy Campanella	100.00	50.00	30.00
(7)	Andy Carey	10.00	5.00	3.00
(8)	Jerry Coleman	10.00	5.00	3.00
(9)	Joe Collins	10.00	5.00	3.00
(10)	Billy Cox	10.00	5.00	3.00
(11)	Al Dark	12.00	6.00	3.50
(12)	Carl Erskine	20.00	10.00	6.00
(13)	Whitey Ford	40.00	20.00	12.00
(14)	Carl Furillo	20.00	10.00	6.00
(15)	Junior Gilliam	20.00	10.00	6.00
(16)	Ruben Gomez	10.00	5.00	3.00
(17)	Marv Grissom	10.00	5.00	3.00
(18)	Jim Hearn	10.00	5.00	3.00
(19)	Gil Hodges	35.00	17.50	10.50
(20)	Bobby Hofman	10.00	5.00	3.00
(21)	Jim Hughes	10.00	5.00	3.00
(22)	Monte Irvin	25.00	12.50	7.50
(23)	Larry Jansen	10.00	5.00	3.00
(24)	Ray Katt	10.00	5.00	3.00
(25)	Steve Kraly	10.00	5.00	3.00
(26)	Bob Kuzava	10.00	5.00	3.00
(27)	Clem Labine	12.00	6.00	3.50
(28)	Frank Leja	10.00	5.00	3.00
(29)	Don Liddle	10.00	5.00	3.00
(30)	Whitey Lockman	10.00	5.00	3.00
(31)	Billy Loes	10.00	5.00	3.00
(32)	Eddie Lopat	20.00	10.00	6.00
(33)	Gil McDougald	20.00	10.00	6.00
(34)	Sal Maglie	12.00	6.00	3.50
(35)	Mickey Mantle	450.00	225.00	135.00
(36)	Willie Mays	200.00	100.00	60.00
(37)	Russ Meyer	10.00	5.00	3.00
(38)	Bill Miller	10.00	5.00	3.00
(39)	Tom Morgan	10.00	5.00	3.00
(40)	Don Mueller	10.00	5.00	3.00
(41)	Don Newcombe	20.00	10.00	6.00
(42)	Irv Noren	10.00	5.00	3.00
(43)	Erv Palica	10.00	5.00	3.00
(44)	PeeWee Reese	55.00	27.00	16.50
(45)	Allie Reynolds	20.00	10.00	6.00
(46)	Dusty Rhodes	10.00	5.00	3.00
(47)	Phil Rizzuto	35.00	17.50	10.50
(48)	Ed Robinson	10.00	5.00	3.00
(49)	Jackie Robinson	225.00	112.00	67.00
(50)	Preacher Roe	20.00	10.00	6.00
(51)	George Shuba	10.00	5.00	3.00
(52)	Duke Snider	150.00	75.00	45.00
(53)	Hank Thompson	10.00	5.00	3.00
(54)	Wes Westrum	10.00	5.00	3.00
(55)	Hoyt Wilhelm	30.00	15.00	9.00
(56)	Davey Williams	10.00	5.00	3.00
(57)	Dick Williams	12.00	6.00	3.50
(58)	Gene Woodling	12.00	6.00	3.50
(59)	Al Worthington	10.00	5.00	3.00

O

1910 Orange Borders

Known in the hobby as "Orange Borders", these

1-5/8" by 2-5/8" cards were issued in 1910 and were printed on candy boxes that displayed the words "American Sports and Candy and Jewelry." The end flaps indicate the producers as the "Geo. Davis Co., Inc." and the "P.R. Warren Co., Warrenville Lowell, Mass." According to the box, the complete set includes "144 leading ballplayers," but to date only 25 different subjects are known. When found today, these black and white photos are usually surrounded by orange borders which, in reality, were part of the candy box.

		NR MT	EX	VG
Complete Set:		4000.00	2000.00	1200.
Common Player:		75.00	37.00	22.00
(1)	Bill Bergen	75.00	37.00	22.00
(2)	Bill Carrigan	75.00	37.00	22.00
(3)	Hal Chase	90.00	45.00	27.00
(4)	Fred Clark (Clarke)	125.00	62.00	37.00
(5)	Ty Cobb	600.00	300.00	180.00
(6)	Sam Crawford	125.00	62.00	37.00
(7)	Lou Criger	75.00	37.00	22.00
(8)	Art Devlin	75.00	37.00	22.00
(9)	Mickey Doolan	75.00	37.00	22.00
(10)	George Gibson	75.00	37.00	22.00
(11)	Nap Lajoie	250.00	125.00	75.00
(12)	Frank LaPorte	75.00	37.00	22.00
(13)	Harry Lord	75.00	37.00	22.00
(14)	Christy Mathewson	250.00	125.00	75.00
(15)	John McGraw	150.00	75.00	45.00
(16)	Dots Miller	75.00	37.00	22.00
(17)	George Mullin	75.00	37.00	22.00
(18)	Eddie Plank	125.00	62.00	37.00
(19)	Tris Speaker	75.00	37.00	22.00
(20)	Jake Stahl	75.00	37.00	22.00
(21)	Honus Wagner (batting)	375.00	187.00	112.00
(22)	Honus Wagner (portrait)	375.00	187.00	112.00
(23)	Jack Warhop	75.00	37.00	22.00
(24)	American League Champions, 1909			
		75.00	37.00	22.00
(25)	National League Champions, 1909			
		75.00	37.00	22.00

P

1910 P2 Sweet Caporal Pins

Expanding their premiums to include more than just trading cards, the American Tobacco Company issued a series of baseball pins between 1910 and 1912. The sepia-colored pins, each measuring 7/8" in diameter, were distributed under the Sweet Caporal brand name. The set includes 152 different major league players, but because of numerous "large letter" variations, collectors generally consider the set complete at 204 different pins. Fifty of the players are pictured on a second pin that usually displays the same photo but has the player's name and team designation printed in larger letters. Two players (Roger Bresnahan and Bobby Wallace) have three pins each. It is now generally accepted that there are 153 pins with "small letters" and another 51 "large letter" variations in a complete set. Research among advanced collectors has shown that 19 of the pins, including six of the "large letter" variations, are considered more difficult to find. The back of each pin has either a black or a red paper insert advertising Sweet Caporal Cigarettes. The red backings, issued only with the "large letter" pins are generally less common. The Sweet Caporal pins are closely related to the popular T205 Gold Border tobacco cards, also issued by the American Tobacco Company about the same time. All but nine of the players featured in the pin set were also pictured on T205 cards, and in nearly all cases the photos are identical. The Sweet Caporal pins are designated as P2 in the American Card Catalog. The complete set price includes all variations.

		NR MT	EX	VG
	Complete Set:	5250.00	2625.00	1575.
	Common Player:	12.00	6.00	3.50
(1)	Ed Abbaticchio	12.00	6.00	3.50
(2)	Red Ames	12.00	6.00	3.50
(3a)	Jimmy Archer (small letters)	12.00	6.00	3.50
(3b)	Jimmy Archer (large letters)	20.00	10.00	6.00
(4a)	Jimmy Austin (small letters)	12.00	6.00	3.50
(4b)	Jimmy Austin (large letters)	20.00	10.00	6.00
(5)	Home Run Baker	30.00	15.00	9.00
(6)	Neal Ball	12.00	6.00	3.50
(7)	Cy Barger	12.00	6.00	3.50
(8)	Jack Barry	12.00	6.00	3.50
(9)	Johnny Bates	12.00	6.00	3.50
(10)	Beals Becker	12.00	6.00	3.50
(11)	Fred Beebe	12.00	6.00	3.50
(12a)	George Bell (small letters)	12.00	6.00	3.50
(12b)	George Bell (large letters)	20.00	10.00	6.00
(13a)	Chief Bender (small letters)	30.00	15.00	9.00
(13b)	Chief Bender (large letters)	50.00	25.00	15.00
(14)	Bill Bergen	12.00	6.00	3.50
(15)	Bob Bescher	12.00	6.00	3.50
(16)	Joe Birmingham	12.00	6.00	3.50
(17)	Kitty Bransfield	35.00	17.50	10.50
(18a)	Roger Bresnahan (mouth closed, small letters)	30.00	15.00	9.00
(18b)	Roger Bresnahan (mouth closed, large letters)	90.00	45.00	27.00
(19)	Roger Bresnahan (mouth open)	30.00	15.00	9.00
(20)	Al Bridwell	12.00	6.00	3.50
(21a)	Mordecai Brown (small letters)	30.00	15.00	9.00
(21b)	Mordecai Brown (large letters)	50.00	25.00	15.00
(22)	Bobby Byrne	12.00	6.00	3.50
(23)	Nixey Callahan	12.00	6.00	3.50
(24a)	Howie Camnitz (small letters)	12.00	6.00	3.50
(24b)	Howie Camnitz (large letters)	20.00	10.00	6.00
(25a)	Bill Carrigan (small letters)	12.00	6.00	3.50
(25b)	Bill Carrigan (large letters)	20.00	10.00	6.00
(26a)	Frank Chance (small letters)	35.00	17.50	10.50
(26b)	Frank Chance (large letters)	50.00	25.00	15.00
(27)	Hal Chase (different photo, small letters)	15.00	7.50	4.50
(28)	Hal Chase (different photo, large letters)	25.00	12.50	7.50
(29)	Ed Cicotte	15.00	7.50	4.50
(30a)	Fred Clarke (small letters)	30.00	15.00	9.00
(30b)	Fred Clarke (large letters)	50.00	25.00	15.00
(31a)	Ty Cobb (small letters)	250.00	125.00	75.00
(31b)	Ty Cobb (large letters)	375.00	187.00	112.00
(32a)	Eddie Collins (small letters)	30.00	15.00	9.00
(32b)	Eddie Collins (large letters)	70.00	35.00	21.00
(33)	Doc Crandall	12.00	6.00	3.50
(34)	Birdie Cree	35.00	17.50	10.50
(35)	Bill Dahlen	12.00	6.00	3.50
(36)	Jim Delahanty	12.00	6.00	3.50
(37)	Art Devlin	12.00	6.00	3.50
(38)	Josh Devore	12.00	6.00	3.50
(39)	Wild Bill Donovan	35.00	17.50	10.50
(40a)	Red Dooin (small letters)	12.00	6.00	3.50
(40b)	Red Dooin (large letters)	20.00	10.00	6.00
(41a)	Mickey Doolan (small letters)	12.00	6.00	3.50
(41b)	Mickey Doolan (large letters)	20.00	10.00	6.00
(42)	Patsy Dougherty	12.00	6.00	3.50
(43a)	Tom Downey (small letters)	12.00	6.00	3.50
(43b)	Tom Downey (large letters)	20.00	10.00	6.00
(44a)	Larry Doyle (small letters)	12.00	6.00	3.50
(44b)	Larry Doyle (large letters)	20.00	10.00	6.00
(45)	Louis Drucke	12.00	6.00	3.50
(46a)	Hugh Duffy (small letters)	30.00	15.00	9.00

		NR MT	EX	VG
(46b)	Hugh Duffy (large letters)	50.00	25.00	15.00
(47)	Jimmy Dygert	12.00	6.00	3.50
(48a)	Kid Elberfeld (small letters)	12.00	6.00	3.50
(48b)	Kid Elberfeld (large letters)	20.00	10.00	6.00
(49a)	Clyde Engle (small letters)	12.00	6.00	3.50
(49b)	Clyde Engle (large letters)	20.00	10.00	6.00
(50)	Tex Erwin	12.00	6.00	3.50
(51)	Steve Evans	12.00	6.00	3.50
(52)	Johnny Evers	30.00	15.00	9.00
(53)	Cecil Ferguson	12.00	6.00	3.50
(54)	John Flynn	12.00	6.00	3.50
(55a)	Russ Ford (small letters)	12.00	6.00	3.50
(55b)	Russ Ford (large letters)	20.00	10.00	6.00
(56)	Art Fromme	12.00	6.00	3.50
(57)	Harry Gaspar	12.00	6.00	3.50
(58a)	George Gibson (small letters)	12.00	6.00	3.50
(58b)	George Gibson (large letters)	20.00	10.00	6.00
(59)	Eddie Grant	35.00	17.50	10.50
(60)	Dolly Gray	12.00	6.00	3.50
(61a)	Clark Griffith (small letters)	30.00	15.00	9.00
(61b)	Clark Griffith (large letters)	50.00	25.00	15.00
(62)	Bob Groom	12.00	6.00	3.50
(63)	Bob Harmon	12.00	6.00	3.50
(64)	Topsy Hartsel	12.00	6.00	3.50
(65)	Arnold Hauser	35.00	17.50	10.50
(66)	Ira Hemphill	12.00	6.00	3.50
(67a)	Buck Herzog (small letters)	12.00	6.00	3.50
(67b)	Buck Herzog (large letters)	20.00	10.00	6.00
(68)	Dick Hoblitzell	12.00	6.00	3.50
(69)	Danny Hoffman	12.00	6.00	3.50
(70)	Harry Hooper	12.00	6.00	3.50
(71a)	Miller Huggins (small letters)	30.00	15.00	9.00
(71b)	Miller Huggins (large letters)	50.00	25.00	15.00
(72)	John Hummel	12.00	6.00	3.50
(73)	Hugh Jennings (different photo, small letters)	30.00	15.00	9.00
(74)	Hugh Jennings (different photo, large letters)	50.00	25.00	15.00
(75a)	Walter Johnson (small letters)	90.00	45.00	27.00
(75b)	Walter Johnson (large letters)	125.00	62.00	37.00
(76)	Tom Jones	35.00	17.50	10.50
(77)	Ed Karger	12.00	6.00	3.50
(78)	Ed Killian	35.00	17.50	10.50
(79a)	Jack Knight (small letters)	12.00	6.00	3.50
(79b)	Jack Knight (large letters)	20.00	10.00	6.00
(80)	Ed Konetchy	12.00	6.00	3.50
(81)	Harry Krause	12.00	6.00	3.50
(82)	Rube Kroh	12.00	6.00	3.50
(83)	Nap Lajoie	60.00	30.00	18.00
(84a)	Frank LaPorte (small letters)	12.00	6.00	3.50
(84b)	Frank LaPorte (large letters)	20.00	10.00	6.00
(85)	Arlie Latham	12.00	6.00	3.50
(86a)	Tommy Leach (small letters)	12.00	6.00	3.50
(86b)	Tommy Leach (large letters)	20.00	10.00	6.00
(87)	Sam Leever	12.00	6.00	3.50
(88)	Lefty Leifield	12.00	6.00	3.50
(89)	Hans Lobert	12.00	6.00	3.50
(90a)	Harry Lord (small letters)	12.00	6.00	3.50
(90b)	Harry Lord (large letters)	20.00	10.00	6.00
(91)	Paddy Livingston	12.00	6.00	3.50
(92)	Nick Maddox	12.00	6.00	3.50
(93)	Sherry Magee	12.00	6.00	3.50
(94)	Rube Marquard	30.00	15.00	9.00
(95a)	Christy Mathewson (small letters)	90.00	45.00	27.00
(95b)	Christy Mathewson (large letters)	110.00	55.00	33.00
(96a)	Al Mattern (small letters)	12.00	6.00	3.50
(96b)	Al Mattern (large letters)	20.00	10.00	6.00
(97)	George McBride	12.00	6.00	3.50
(98a)	John McGraw (small letters)	40.00	20.00	12.00
(98b)	John McGraw (large letters)	60.00	30.00	18.00
(99a)	Larry McLean (small letters)	12.00	6.00	3.50
(99b)	Larry McLean (large letters)	20.00	10.00	6.00
(100)	Harry McIntyre (Cubs)	12.00	6.00	3.50
(101a)	Matty McIntyre (White Sox, small letters)	12.00	6.00	3.50
(101b)	Matty McIntyre (White Sox, large letters)	20.00	10.00	6.00
(102)	Fred Merkle	12.00	6.00	3.50
(103)	Chief Meyers	12.00	6.00	3.50
(104)	Clyde Milan	12.00	6.00	3.50
(105)	Dots Miller	12.00	6.00	3.50
(106)	Mike Mitchell	12.00	6.00	3.50
(107)	Pat Moran	12.00	6.00	3.50
(108a)	George Mullen (Mullin) (small letters)	12.00	6.00	3.50
(108b)	George Mullen (Mullin) (large letters)	20.00	10.00	6.00
(109)	Danny Murphy	12.00	6.00	3.50
(110a)	Red Murray (small letters)	20.00	10.00	6.00

		NR MT	EX	VG
(110b)	Red Murray (large letters)	12.00	6.00	3.50
(111)	Tom Needham	35.00	17.50	10.50
(112a)	Rebel Oakes (small letters)	12.00	6.00	3.50
(112b)	Rebel Oakes (large letters)	20.00	10.00	6.00
(113)	Rube Oldring	12.00	6.00	3.50
(114)	Charley O'Leary	12.00	6.00	3.50
(115)	Orval Overall	35.00	17.50	10.50
(116)	Fred Parent	12.00	6.00	3.50
(117a)	Dode Paskert (small letters)	12.00	6.00	3.50
(117b)	Dode Paskert (large letters)	20.00	10.00	6.00
(118)	Barney Pelty	12.00	6.00	3.50
(119)	Jake Pfeister	12.00	6.00	3.50
(120)	Eddie Phelps	12.00	6.00	3.50
(121)	Deacon Phillippe	12.00	6.00	3.50
(122)	Jack Quinn	12.00	6.00	3.50
(123)	Ed Reulbach	12.00	6.00	3.50
124	Lew Richie	12.00	6.00	3.50
(125)	Jack Rowan	12.00	6.00	3.50
(126a)	Nap Rucker (small letters)	12.00	6.00	3.50
(126b)	Nap Rucker (large letters)	20.00	10.00	6.00
(127)	Doc Scanlon (Scanlan)	35.00	17.50	10.50
(128)	Germany Schaefer	12.00	6.00	3.50
(129)	Jimmy Scheckard (Sheckard)	12.00	6.00	3.50
(130a)	Boss Schmidt (small letters)	12.00	6.00	3.50
(130b)	Boss Schmidt (large letters)	20.00	10.00	6.00
(131)	Wildfire Schulte	12.00	6.00	3.50
(132)	Hap Smith	12.00	6.00	3.50
(133a)	Tris Speaker (small letters)	50.00	25.00	15.00
(133b)	Tris Speaker (large letters)	70.00	35.00	21.00
(134)	Oscar Stanage	12.00	6.00	3.50
(135)	Harry Steinfeldt	15.00	7.50	4.50
(136)	George Stone	12.00	6.00	3.50
(137a)	George Stoval (Stovall) (small letters)			
		12.00	6.00	3.50
(137b)	George Stoval (Stovall) (large letters)			
		20.00	10.00	6.00
(138a)	Gabby Street (small letters)	12.00	6.00	3.50
(138b)	Gabby Street (large letters)	20.00	10.00	6.00
(139)	George Suggs	12.00	6.00	3.50
(140a)	Ira Thomas (small letters)	12.00	6.00	3.50
(140b)	Ira Thomas (large letters)	20.00	10.00	6.00
(141a)	Joe Tinker (small letters)	30.00	15.00	9.00
(141b)	Joe Tinker (large letters)	50.00	25.00	15.00
(142a)	John Titus (small letters)	12.00	6.00	3.50
(142b)	John Titus (large letters)	20.00	10.00	6.00
(143)	Terry Turner	20.00	10.00	6.00
(144)	Heinie Wagner	12.00	6.00	3.50
(145a)	Bobby Wallace (with cap, small letters)			
		30.00	15.00	9.00
(145b)	Bobby Wallace (with cap, large letters)			
		50.00	25.00	15.00
(146)	Bobby Wallace (without cap)	30.00	15.00	9.00
(147)	Ed Walsh	30.00	15.00	9.00
(148)	Jack Warhop	35.00	17.50	10.50
(149a)	Zach Wheat (small letters)	30.00	15.00	9.00
(149b)	Zach Wheat (large letters)	50.00	25.00	15.00
(150)	Doc White	12.00	6.00	3.50
(151)	Art Wilson (Giants)	35.00	17.50	10.50
(152)	Owen Wilson (Pirates)	12.00	6.00	3.50
(153)	Hooks Wiltse	12.00	6.00	3.50
(154)	Harry Wolter	12.00	6.00	3.50
(155a)	Cy Young (small letters)	55.00	27.00	16.50
(155b)	Cy Young (large letters)	75.00	37.00	22.00

1930 Pm8
Our National Game Pins

This unnumbered 30-pin set issued in the 1930s

carries the American Card Catalog designation of PM8 and is known as "Our National Game." The pins, which measure 7/8" in diameter, have a "tab" rather than a pin back. The black and white player photo is tinted blue, and the player's name and team are printed in a band near the bottom.

		NR MT	EX	VG
Complete Set:		525.00	262.00	157.00
Common Player:		6.00	3.00	1.75
(1)	Wally Berger	6.00	3.00	1.75
(2)	Lou Chiozza	6.00	3.00	1.75
(3)	Joe Cronin	15.00	7.50	4.50
(4)	Frank Crosetti	8.00	4.00	2.50
(5)	Jerome (Dizzy) Dean	25.00	12.50	7.50
(6)	Frank DeMaree	6.00	3.00	1.75
(7)	Joe DiMaggio	90.00	45.00	27.00
(8)	Bob Feller	20.00	10.00	6.00
(9)	Jimmy Foxx	20.00	10.00	6.00
(10)	Charles Gehringer	15.00	7.50	4.50
(11)	Lou Gehrig	90.00	45.00	27.00
(12)	Lefty Gomez	15.00	7.50	4.50
(13)	Hank Greenberg	15.00	7.50	4.50
(14)	Irving (Bump) Hadley	6.00	3.00	1.75
(15)	Leo Hartnett	15.00	7.50	4.50
(16)	Carl Hubbell	15.00	7.50	4.50
(17)	John (Buddy) Lewis	6.00	3.00	1.75
(18)	Gus Mancuso	6.00	3.00	1.75
(19)	Joe McCarthy	15.00	7.50	4.50
(20)	Joe Medwick	15.00	7.50	4.50
(21)	Joe Moore	6.00	3.00	1.75
(22)	Mel Ott	15.00	7.50	4.50
(23)	Jake Powell	6.00	3.00	1.75
(24)	Jimmy Ripple	6.00	3.00	1.75
(25)	Red Ruffing	15.00	7.50	4.50
(26)	Hal Schumacher	6.00	3.00	1.75
(27)	George Selkirk	6.00	3.00	1.75
(28)	"Al" Simmons	15.00	7.50	4.50
(29)	Bill Terry	15.00	7.50	4.50
(30)	Harold Trosky	6.00	3.00	1.75

1956 Pm15
Yellow Basepath Pins

Issued circa 1956, the sponsor of this 32-pin set is not indicated. The set, which has been assigned the American Card Catalog designation PM15, is commonly called "Yellow Basepaths" because of the design of the pin, which features a black and white player photo set inside a green infield with yellow basepaths. The unnumbered pins measure 7/8" in diameter. The names of Kluszewski and Mathews are misspelled.

		NR MT	EX	VG
Complete Set:		2000.00	1000.00	600.00
Common Player:		25.00	12.50	7.50
(1)	Hank Aaron	150.00	75.00	45.00
(2)	Joe Adcock	30.00	15.00	9.00
(3)	Luis Aparicio	50.00	25.00	15.00
(4)	Richie Ashburn	40.00	20.00	12.00
(5)	Gene Baker	25.00	12.50	7.50
(6)	Ernie Banks	70.00	35.00	21.00

		NR MT	EX	VG
(7)	Yogi Berra	70.00	35.00	21.00
(8)	Bill Bruton	25.00	12.50	7.50
(9)	Larry Doby	30.00	15.00	9.00
(10)	Bob Friend	25.00	12.50	7.50
(11)	Nellie Fox	40.00	20.00	12.00
(12)	Jim Greengrass	25.00	12.50	7.50
(13)	Steve Gromek	25.00	12.50	7.50
(14)	Johnny Groth	25.00	12.50	7.50
(15)	Gil Hodges	70.00	35.00	21.00
(16)	Al Kaline	70.00	35.00	21.00
(17)	Ted Kluzewski (Kluszewski)	35.00	17.50	10.50
(18)	Johnny Logan	25.00	12.50	7.50
(19)	Dale Long	25.00	12.50	7.50
(20)	Mickey Mantle	400.00	200.00	120.00
(21)	Ed Mathews	70.00	35.00	21.00
(22)	Orestes Minoso	30.00	15.00	9.00
(23)	Stan Musial	150.00	75.00	45.00
(24)	Don Newcombe	30.00	15.00	9.00
(25)	Bob Porterfield	25.00	12.50	7.50
(26)	Pee Wee Reese	70.00	35.00	21.00
(27)	Robin Roberts	50.00	25.00	15.00
(28)	Red Schoendienst	35.00	17.50	10.50
(29)	Duke Snider	70.00	35.00	21.00
(30)	Vern Stephens	25.00	12.50	7.50
(31)	Gene Woodling	25.00	12.50	7.50
(32)	Gus Zernial	25.00	12.50	7.50

		NR MT	EX	VG
26	Burleigh Grimes	27.00	13.50	8.00
27	Dale Alexander	12.00	6.00	3.50
28	Mickey Cochrane	30.00	15.00	9.00
29	Mel Harder	12.00	6.00	3.50
30	Mark Koenig	12.00	6.00	3.50
31a	"Lefty" O'Doul (Dodgers)	45.00	22.00	13.50
31b	"Lefty" O'Doul (Giants)	20.00	10.00	6.00
32a	Woody English (with bat)	12.00	6.00	3.50
32b	Woody English (without bat)	45.00	22.00	13.50
33a	Billy Jurges (with bat)	12.00	6.00	3.50
33b	Billy Jurges (without bat)	45.00	22.00	13.50
34	Bruce Campbell	12.00	6.00	3.50
35	Joe Vosmik	12.00	6.00	3.50
36	Dick Porter	12.00	6.00	3.50
37	Charlie Grimm	18.00	9.00	5.50
38	Geo. Earnshaw	12.00	6.00	3.50
39	Al Simmons	27.00	13.50	8.00
40	"Red" Lucas	12.00	6.00	3.50
51	Wally Berger	12.00	6.00	3.50
52	Jim Levey	12.00	6.00	3.50
58	Ernie Lombardi	27.00	13.50	8.00
64	Jack Burns	12.00	6.00	3.50
67	Billy Herman	27.00	13.50	8.00
72	Bill Hallahan	12.00	6.00	3.50
92	Don Brennan	12.00	6.00	3.50
96	Sam Byrd	12.00	6.00	3.50
99	Ben Chapman	12.00	6.00	3.50
103	John Allen	12.00	6.00	3.50
107	Tony Lazzeri	24.00	12.00	7.25
111	Earl Combs (Earle)	27.00	13.50	8.00
116	Joe Sewell	27.00	13.50	8.00
120	Vernon Gomez	30.00	15.00	9.00

1933 Pr2 Orbit Gum Pins Numbered

Issued circa 1933, this skip-numbered set of small (13/16" in diameter) pins was produced by Orbit Gum and carries the Amerian Card Catalog designation of PR2. A player lithograph is set against a green background with the player's name and team printed on a strip of yellow below. The pin number is at the very bottom.

		NR MT	EX	VG
Complete Set:		1000.00	500.00	300.00
Common Player:		12.00	6.00	3.50
1	Ivy Andrews	12.00	6.00	3.50
2	Carl Reynolds	12.00	6.00	3.50
3	Riggs Stephenson	18.00	9.00	5.50
4	Lon Warneke	12.00	6.00	3.50
5	Frank Grube	12.00	6.00	3.50
6	"Kiki" Cuyler	27.00	13.50	8.00
7	Marty McManus	12.00	6.00	3.50
8	"Lefty" Clark	12.00	6.00	3.50
9	George Blaeholder	12.00	6.00	3.50
10	Willie Kamm	12.00	6.00	3.50
11	Jimmy "Dykes"	18.00	9.00	5.50
12	Earl Averill	27.00	13.50	8.00
13	Pat Malone	12.00	6.00	3.50
14	"Dizzy" Dean	60.00	30.00	18.00
15	Dick Bartell	12.00	6.00	3.50
16	Guy Bush	12.00	6.00	3.50
17	Bud Tinning	12.00	6.00	3.50
18	Jimmy Foxx	45.00	22.00	13.50
19	"Mule" Haas	12.00	6.00	3.50
20	Lew Fonseca	12.00	6.00	3.50
21	"Pepper" Martin	20.00	10.00	6.00
22	Phil Collins	12.00	6.00	3.50
23	Bill Cissell	12.00	6.00	3.50
24	Bump Hadley	12.00	6.00	3.50
25	Smead Jolley	12.00	6.00	3.50

1934 Pr3 Orbit Gum Pins Unnumbered

This set, issued by Orbit Gum circa 1934, has the American Card Catalog designation PR3. The pins are identical to the PR2 set, except they are unnumbered.

		NR MT	EX	VG
Complete Set:		1800.00	900.00	540.00
Common Player:		20.00	10.00	6.00
(1)	Dale Alexander	20.00	10.00	6.00
(2)	Ivy Andrews	20.00	10.00	6.00
(3)	Earl Averill	40.00	20.00	12.00
(4)	Dick Bartell	20.00	10.00	6.00
(5)	Wally Berger	20.00	10.00	6.00
(6)	George Blaeholder	20.00	10.00	6.00
(7)	Jack Burns	20.00	10.00	6.00
(8)	Guy Bush	20.00	10.00	6.00
(9)	Bruce Campbell	20.00	10.00	6.00
(10)	Bill Cissell	20.00	10.00	6.00
(11)	"Lefty" Clark	20.00	10.00	6.00
(12)	Mickey Cochrane	45.00	22.00	13.50
(13)	Phil Collins	20.00	10.00	6.00
(14)	"Kiki" Cuyler	40.00	20.00	12.00
(15)	"Dizzy" Dean	75.00	37.00	22.00
(16)	Jimmy "Dykes"	27.00	13.50	8.00
(17)	Geo. Earnshaw	20.00	10.00	6.00
(18)	Woody English	20.00	10.00	6.00
(19)	Lew Fonseca	20.00	10.00	6.00
(20)	Jimmy Foxx	60.00	30.00	18.00
(21)	Burleigh Grimes	40.00	20.00	12.00
(22)	Charlie Grimm	27.00	13.50	8.00

		NR MT	EX	VG
(23)	"Lefty" Grove	65.00	32.00	19.50
(24)	Frank Grube	20.00	10.00	6.00
(25)	"Mule" Haas	20.00	10.00	6.00
(26)	Bump Hadley	20.00	10.00	6.00
(27)	"Chick" Hafey	50.00	25.00	15.00
(28)	Jesse Haines	50.00	25.00	15.00
(29)	Bill Hallahan	20.00	10.00	6.00
(30)	Mel Harder	20.00	10.00	6.00
(31)	"Gabby" Hartnett	50.00	25.00	15.00
(32)	"Babe" Herman	35.00	17.50	10.50
(33)	Billy Herman	40.00	20.00	12.00
(34)	Rogers Hornsby	75.00	37.00	22.00
(35)	Roy Johnson	30.00	15.00	9.00
(36)	Smead Jolley	20.00	10.00	6.00
(37)	Billy Jurges	20.00	10.00	6.00
(38)	Willie Kamm	20.00	10.00	6.00
(39)	Mark Koenig	20.00	10.00	6.00
(40)	Jim Levey	20.00	10.00	6.00
(41)	Ernie Lombardi	40.00	20.00	12.00
(42)	Red Lucas	20.00	10.00	6.00
(43)	Ted Lyons	50.00	25.00	15.00
(44)	Connie Mack	70.00	35.00	21.00
(45)	Pat Malone	20.00	10.00	6.00
(46)	"Pepper" Martin	27.00	13.50	8.00
(47)	Marty McManus	20.00	10.00	6.00
(48)	"Lefty" O'Doul	20.00	10.00	6.00
(49)	Dick Porter	20.00	10.00	6.00
(50)	Carl Reynolds	20.00	10.00	6.00
(51)	Charlie Root	30.00	15.00	9.00
(52)	Bob Seeds	30.00	15.00	9.00
(53)	Al Simmons	40.00	20.00	12.00
(54)	Riggs Stephenson	27.00	13.50	8.00
(55)	Bud Tinning	20.00	10.00	6.00
(56)	Joe Vosmik	20.00	10.00	6.00
(57)	Rube Walberg	30.00	15.00	9.00
(58)	Paul Waner	50.00	25.00	15.00
(59)	Lon Warneke	20.00	10.00	6.00
(60)	Pinky Whitney	30.00	15.00	9.00

1930 Pr4 Cracker Jack Pins

Although no manufacturer is indicated on the pins themselves, this 25-player set was apparently issued by Cracker Jack in the early 1930's. Each pin measures 13/16" in diameter and features a line drawing of a player portrait. The unnumbered pins are printed in blue and gray with a background of yellow. The player's name appears below.

		NR MT	EX	VG
Complete Set:		700.00	350.00	210.00
Common Player:		15.00	7.50	4.50
(1)	Charles Berry	15.00	7.50	4.50
(2)	Bill Cissell	15.00	7.50	4.50
(3)	KiKi Cuyler	25.00	12.50	7.50
(4)	Dizzy Dean	40.00	20.00	12.00
(5)	Wesley Ferrell	15.00	7.50	4.50
(6)	Frank Frisch	25.00	12.50	7.50
(7)	Lou Gehrig	100.00	50.00	30.00
(8)	Vernon Gomez	25.00	12.50	7.50
(9)	Goose Goslin	25.00	12.50	7.50
(10)	George Grantham	15.00	7.50	4.50
(11)	Charley Grimm	15.00	7.50	4.50
(12)	Lefty Grove	30.00	15.00	9.00
(13)	Gabby Hartnett	25.00	12.50	7.50
(14)	Travis Jackson	25.00	12.50	7.50
(15)	Tony Lazzeri	20.00	10.00	6.00

		NR MT	EX	VG
(16)	Ted Lyons	25.00	12.50	7.50
(17)	Rabbit Maranville	25.00	12.50	7.50
(18)	Carl Reynolds	15.00	7.50	4.50
(19)	Charles Ruffing	25.00	12.50	7.50
(20)	Al Simmons	25.00	12.50	7.50
(21)	Gus Suhr	15.00	7.50	4.50
(22)	Bill Terry	25.00	12.50	7.50
(23)	Dazzy Vance	25.00	12.50	7.50
(24)	Paul Waner	25.00	12.50	7.50
(25)	Lon Warneke	15.00	7.50	4.50

1933 Px3 Double Header Pins

Issued by Gum, Inc. circa 1933, this unnumbered set consists of 43 metal discs approximately 1-1/4" in diameter. The front of the pin lists the player's name and team beneath his picture. The numbers "1" or "2" also appear inside a small circle at the bottom of the disc, and the wrapper advised collectors to "Put 1 and 2 together and make a double header." The set is designated as PX3 in the American Card Catalog.

		NR MT	EX	VG
Complete Set:		900.00	450.00	270.00
Common Player:		15.00	7.50	4.50
(1)	"Sparky" Adams	15.00	7.50	4.50
(2)	Dale Alexander	15.00	7.50	4.50
(3)	Earl Averill	30.00	15.00	9.00
(4)	Dick Bartell	15.00	7.50	4.50
(5)	Walter Berger	15.00	7.50	4.50
(6)	"Sunny" Jim Bottomley	30.00	15.00	9.00
(7)	"Lefty" Brandt	15.00	7.50	4.50
(8)	Owen T. Carroll	15.00	7.50	4.50
(9)	"Lefty" Clark	15.00	7.50	4.50
(10)	Mickey Cochrane	30.00	15.00	9.00
(11)	Joe Cronin	30.00	15.00	9.00
(12)	Jimmy Dykes	18.00	9.00	5.50
(13)	George Earnshaw	15.00	7.50	4.50
(14)	Wes Ferrell	15.00	7.50	4.50
(15)	Neal Finn	15.00	7.50	4.50
(16)	Lew Fonseca	15.00	7.50	4.50
(17)	Jimmy Foxx	45.00	22.00	13.50
(18)	Frankie Frisch	30.00	15.00	9.00
(19)	"Chick" Fullis	15.00	7.50	4.50
(20)	Charley Gehringer	30.00	15.00	9.00
(21)	"Goose" Goslin	30.00	15.00	9.00
(22)	Johnny Hodapp	15.00	7.50	4.50
(23)	Frank Hogan	15.00	7.50	4.50
(24)	Si Johnson	15.00	7.50	4.50
(25)	Joe Judge	15.00	7.50	4.50
(26)	"Chuck" Klein	30.00	15.00	9.00
(27)	Al Lopez	30.00	15.00	9.00
(28)	Ray Lucas	15.00	7.50	4.50
(29)	Red Lucas	15.00	7.50	4.50
(30)	Ted Lyons	30.00	15.00	9.00
(31)	"Firpo" Marberry	15.00	7.50	4.50
(32)	Oscar Melillo	15.00	7.50	4.50
(33)	Lefty O'Doul	18.00	9.00	5.50
(34)	George Pipgras	15.00	7.50	4.50
(35)	Flint Rhem	15.00	7.50	4.50
(36)	Sam Rice	30.00	15.00	9.00
(37)	"Muddy" Ruel	15.00	7.50	4.50
(38)	Harry Seibold	15.00	7.50	4.50
(39)	Al Simmons	30.00	15.00	9.00
(40)	Joe Vosmik	15.00	7.50	4.50
(41)	Gerald Walker	15.00	7.50	4.50

		NR MT	EX	VG
(42)	"Pinky" Whitney	15.00	7.50	4.50
(43)	Hack Wilson	30.00	15.00	9.00

1909 Px7 Domino Discs

Domino Discs, distributed by Sweet Caporal Cigarettes from 1909 to 1912, are among the more obscure 20th Century tobacco issues. Although the disc set contains many of the same players - some even pictured in the same poses - as the Sweet Caporal P2 pin set, the discs have always lagged behind the pins in collector appeal. The Domino Discs, so called because each disc has a large, white domino printed on the back, measure approximately 1-1/8" in diameter and are made of thin card cardboard surrounded by a metal rim. The fronts of the discs contain a player portrait set against a background of either red, green or blue. The words "Sweet Caporal Cigarettes" appear on the front along with the player's last name and team. There are 135 different major leaguers featured in the set, each pictured in two different poses for a total of 270 different subjects. Also known to exist as part of the set is a "game disc" which pictures a "generic" player and contains the words "Home Team" against a red background on one side and "Visiting Team" with a green background on the reverse. Because each of the 135 players in the set can theoretically be found with three different background colors and with varying numbers of dots on the dominoes, there is almost an impossible number of variations available. Collectos, however, generally collect the discs without regard to background color or domino arrangement. The Domino Disc set was assigned the designation PX7 in the American Card Catalog.

	NR MT	EX	VG
Complete Set:	4400.00	2200.00	1320.
Complete Set: (Including variations)	8500.00	4250.00	2650.
Common Player:	15.00	7.50	4.50

		NR MT	EX	VG
(1)	Red Ames	15.00	7.50	4.50
(2)	Jimmy Archer	15.00	7.50	4.50
(3)	Jimmy Austin	15.00	7.50	4.50
(4)	Home Run Baker	40.00	20.00	12.00
(5)	Neal Ball	15.00	7.50	4.50
(6)	Cy Barger	15.00	7.50	4.50
(7)	Jack Barry	15.00	7.50	4.50
(8)	Johnny Bates	15.00	7.50	4.50
(9)	Beals Becker	15.00	7.50	4.50
(10)	George Bell	15.00	7.50	4.50
(11)	Chief Bender	40.00	20.00	12.00
(12)	Bill Bergen	15.00	7.50	4.50
(13)	Bob Bescher	15.00	7.50	4.50
(14)	Joe Birmingham	15.00	7.50	4.50
(15)	Roger Bresnahan	40.00	20.00	12.00
(16)	Al Bridwell	15.00	7.50	4.50
(17)	Mordecai Brown	40.00	20.00	12.00
(18)	Bobby Byrne	15.00	7.50	4.50
(19)	Nixey Callahan	15.00	7.50	4.50
(20)	Howie Camnitz	15.00	7.50	4.50
(21)	Bill Carrigan	15.00	7.50	4.50
(22)	Frank Chance	35.00	17.50	10.50

		NR MT	EX	VG
(23)	Hal Chase	20.00	10.00	6.00
(24)	Ed Cicotte	20.00	10.00	6.00
(25)	Fred Clarke	35.00	17.50	10.50
(26)	Ty Cobb	500.00	250.00	150.00
(27)	Eddie Collins	40.00	20.00	12.00
(28)	Doc Crandall	15.00	7.50	4.50
(29)	Birdie Cree	15.00	7.50	4.50
(30)	Bill Dahlen	15.00	7.50	4.50
(31)	Jim Delahanty	15.00	7.50	4.50
(32)	Art Devlin	15.00	7.50	4.50
(33)	Josh Devore	15.00	7.50	4.50
(34)	Red Dooin	15.00	7.50	4.50
(35)	Mickey Doolan	15.00	7.50	4.50
(36)	Patsy Dougherty	15.00	7.50	4.50
(37)	Tom Downey	15.00	7.50	4.50
(38)	Larry Doyle	15.00	7.50	4.50
(39)	Louis Drucke	15.00	7.50	4.50
(40)	Clyde Engle	15.00	7.50	4.50
(41)	Tex Erwin	15.00	7.50	4.50
(42)	Steve Evans	15.00	7.50	4.50
(43)	Johnny Evers	40.00	20.00	12.00
(44)	Cecil Ferguson	15.00	7.50	4.50
(45)	Russ Ford	15.00	7.50	4.50
(46)	Art Fromme	15.00	7.50	4.50
(47)	Harry Gaspar	15.00	7.50	4.50
(48)	George Gibson	15.00	7.50	4.50
(49)	Eddie Grant	15.00	7.50	4.50
(50)	Clark Griffith	40.00	20.00	12.00
(51)	Bob Groom	15.00	7.50	4.50
(52)	Bob Harmon	15.00	7.50	4.50
(53)	Topsy Hartsel	15.00	7.50	4.50
(54)	Arnold Hauser	15.00	7.50	4.50
(55)	Dick Hoblitzell	15.00	7.50	4.50
(56)	Danny Hoffman	15.00	7.50	4.50
(57)	Miller Huggins	40.00	20.00	12.00
(58)	John Hummel	15.00	7.50	4.50
(59)	Hugh Jennings	40.00	20.00	12.00
(60)	Walter Johnson	225.00	112.00	67.00
(61)	Ed Karger	15.00	7.50	4.50
(62a)	Jack Knight (Yankees)	15.00	7.50	4.50
(62b)	Jack Knight (Senators)	15.00	7.50	4.50
(63)	Ed Konetchy	15.00	7.50	4.50
(64)	Harry Krause	15.00	7.50	4.50
(65)	Frank LaPorte	15.00	7.50	4.50
(66)	Nap Lajoie	150.00	75.00	45.00
(67)	Tommy Leach	15.00	7.50	4.50
(68)	Sam Leever	15.00	7.50	4.50
(69)	Lefty Leifield	15.00	7.50	4.50
(70)	Paddy Livingston	15.00	7.50	4.50
(71)	Hans Lobert	15.00	7.50	4.50
(72)	Harry Lord	15.00	7.50	4.50
(73)	Nick Maddox	15.00	7.50	4.50
(74)	Sherry Magee	15.00	7.50	4.50
(75)	Rube Marquard	40.00	20.00	12.00
(76)	Christy Mathewson	225.00	112.00	67.00
(77)	Al Mattern	15.00	7.50	4.50
(78)	George McBride	15.00	7.50	4.50
(79)	John McGraw	100.00	50.00	30.00
(80)	Harry McIntire (McIntyre)	15.00	7.50	4.50
(81)	Matty McIntyre	15.00	7.50	4.50
(82)	Larry McLean	15.00	7.50	4.50
(83)	Fred Merkle	15.00	7.50	4.50
(84)	Chief Meyers	15.00	7.50	4.50
(85)	Clyde Milan	15.00	7.50	4.50
(86)	Dots Miller	15.00	7.50	4.50
(87)	Mike Mitchell	15.00	7.50	4.50
(88a)	Pat Moran (Cubs)	15.00	7.50	4.50
(88b)	Pat Moran (Phillies)	15.00	7.50	4.50
(89)	George Mullen (Mullin)	15.00	7.50	4.50
(90)	Danny Murphy	15.00	7.50	4.50
(91)	Red Murray	15.00	7.50	4.50
(92)	Tom Needham	15.00	7.50	4.50
(93)	Rebel Oakes	15.00	7.50	4.50
(94)	Rube Oldring	15.00	7.50	4.50
(95)	Fred Parent	15.00	7.50	4.50
(96)	Dode Paskert	15.00	7.50	4.50
(97)	Barney Pelty	15.00	7.50	4.50
(98)	Eddie Phelps	15.00	7.50	4.50
(99)	Deacon Phillippe	15.00	7.50	4.50
(100)	Jack Quinn	15.00	7.50	4.50
(101)	Ed Reulbach	15.00	7.50	4.50
(102)	Lew Richie	15.00	7.50	4.50
(103)	Jack Rowan	15.00	7.50	4.50
(104)	Nap Rucker	15.00	7.50	4.50
(105a)	Doc Scanlon (Scanlan) (Superbas)		7.50	4.50
(105b)	Doc Scanlon (Scanlan) (Phillies)	15.00	7.50	4.50
(106)	Germany Schaefer	15.00	7.50	4.50
(107)	Boss Schmidt	15.00	7.50	4.50
(108)	Wildfire Schulte	15.00	7.50	4.50
(109)	Jimmy Sheckard	15.00	7.50	4.50

		NR MT	EX	VG
(110)	Hap Smith	15.00	7.50	4.50
(111)	Tris Speaker	150.00	75.00	45.00
(112)	Harry Stovall	15.00	7.50	4.50
(113a)	Gabby Street (Senators)	15.00	7.50	4.50
(113b)	Gabby Street (Yankees)	15.00	7.50	4.50
(114)	George Suggs	15.00	7.50	4.50
(115)	Ira Thomas	15.00	7.50	4.50
(116)	Joe Tinker	40.00	20.00	12.00
(117)	John Titus	15.00	7.50	4.50
(118)	Terry Turner	15.00	7.50	4.50
(119)	Heinie Wagner	15.00	7.50	4.50
(120)	Bobby Wallace	35.00	17.50	10.50
(121)	Ed Walsh	40.00	20.00	12.00
(122)	Jack Warhop	15.00	7.50	4.50
(123)	Zach Wheat	40.00	20.00	12.00
(124)	Doc White	15.00	7.50	4.50
(125a)	Art Wilson (dark cap, Pirates)	15.00	7.50	4.50
(125b)	Art Wilson (dark cap, Giants)	15.00	7.50	4.50
(126a)	Owen Wilson (white cap, Giants)	15.00	7.50	4.50
(126b)	Owen Wilson (white cap, Pirates)	15.00	7.50	4.50
(127)	Hooks Wiltse	15.00	7.50	4.50
(128)	Harry Wolter	15.00	7.50	4.50
(129)	Cy Young	175.00	87.00	52.00

1958 Packard-Bell

Issued in 1958 by Packard-Bell, the "world's largest seller of TVs, radios and hi-fis", this seven-card set was distributed in California and features members of the Los Angeles Dodgers and San Francisco Giants. The large (3-1/2" by 5-1/2") cards are unnumbered and carry an American Card Catalog designation of H801-5.

		NR MT	EX	VG
Complete Set:		275.00	137.00	82.00
Common Player:		12.00	6.00	3.50
(1)	Walter Alston	35.00	17.50	10.50
(2)	John A. Antonelli	12.00	6.00	3.50
(3)	Jim Gilliam	25.00	12.50	7.50
(4)	Gil Hodges	50.00	25.00	15.00
(5)	Willie Mays	125.00	62.00	37.00
(6)	Bill Rigney	12.00	6.00	3.50
(7)	Hank Sauer	12.00	6.00	3.50

1939 Play Ball

With the issuance of this card set by Gum Incorporated, a new era of baseball cards was born. Although the cards are black and white, the full-frame, actual photos on the card fronts are of better quality than previously seen, and the 2-1/2" by 3-1/4" size was larger and more popular than the smaller tobacco and caramel cards of the early 20th Century. Card backs featured player names and extensive biographies. There are 162 cards in the set, including superstars Joe DiMaggio and Ted Williams. Card number 126 was never issued. The complete set price does not include all back variations found in the low-numbered series.

		NR MT	EX	VG
Complete Set:		13500.00	6750.00	4250.
Common Player: 1-115		20.00	10.00	6.00
Common Player: 116-162		125.00	62.00	37.00
1	Alvin Jacob Powell	150.00	40.00	25.00
2a	Lee Theo Grissom (name in upper case letters)	25.00	9.00	5.50
2b	Lee Theo Grissom (name in upper and lower case)	35.00	12.50	7.50
3a	Charles Herbert Ruffing (name in upper case letters)	125.00	62.00	37.00
3b	Charles Herbert Ruffing (name in upper and lower case)	135.00	67.00	40.00
4a	Eldon LeRoy Auker (name in upper case letters)	20.00	10.00	6.00
4b	Eldon LeRoy Auker (name in upper and lower case)	22.00	11.00	6.50
5a	James Luther Sewell (name in upper case letters)	22.00	11.00	6.50
5b	James Luther Sewell (name in upper and lower case)	24.00	12.00	7.25
6a	Leo Ernest Durocher (name in upper case letters)	100.00	50.00	30.00
6b	Leo Ernest Durocher (name in upper and lower case)	125.00	62.00	37.00
7a	Robert Pershing Doerr (name in upper case letters)	100.00	50.00	30.00
7b	Robert Pershing Doerr (name in upper and lower case)	100.00	50.00	30.00
8	Henry Pippen	20.00	10.00	6.00
9a	James Tobin (name in upper case letters)	20.00	10.00	6.00
9b	James Tobin (name in upper and lower case)	22.00	11.00	6.50
10	James Brooklyn DeShong	20.00	10.00	6.00
11	John Costa Rizzo	20.00	10.00	6.00
12	Hershel Ray Martin (Herschel)	20.00	10.00	6.00
13a	Luke Daniel Hamlin (name in upper case letters)	20.00	10.00	6.00
13b	Luke Daniel Hamlin (name in upper and lower case)	22.00	11.00	6.50
14a	James R. Tabor ("...Tabor batted .295,...")	20.00	10.00	6.00
14b	James R. Tabor ("...Tabor batted 295,...")	22.00	11.00	6.50
15a	Paul Derringer (name in upper case letters)	22.00	11.00	6.50
15b	Paul Derringer (name in upper and lower case)	24.00	12.00	7.25
16	John Peacock	20.00	10.00	6.00
17	Emerson Dickman	20.00	10.00	6.00
18a	Harry Danning (name in upper case letters)	20.00	10.00	6.00
18b	Harry Danning (name in upper and lower case)	22.00	11.00	6.50
19	Paul Dean	35.00	17.50	10.50
20	Joseph Heving	20.00	10.00	6.00
21a	Emil Leonard (name in upper case letters)	20.00	10.00	6.00
21b	Emil Leonard (name in upper and lower case)	22.00	11.00	6.50
22a	William Henry Walters (name in upper case letters)	22.00	11.00	6.50
22b	William Henry Walters (name in upper and lower case)	24.00	12.00	7.25
23	Burgess U. Whitehead	20.00	10.00	6.00
24a	Richard S. Coffman (S. Richard) ("...Senators the same year.")	20.00	10.00	6.00
24b	Richard S. Coffman (S. Richard) ("...Browns the same year.")	35.00	17.50	10.50
25a	George Alexander Selkirk (name in upper case letters)	35.00	17.50	10.50
25b	George Alexander Selkirk (name in upper and lower case)	40.00	20.00	12.00

	NR MT	EX	VG
26a Joseph Paul DiMaggio ("...206 hits in 1938 games...")	2000.00	1000.00	600.00
26b Joseph Paul DiMaggio ("...206 hits in 138 games...")	2000.00	1000.00	600.00
27a Fred Ray Ostermueller (name in upper case letters)	20.00	10.00	6.00
27b Fred Ray Ostermueller (name in upper and lower case)	22.00	11.00	6.50
28 Sylvester Johnson	20.00	10.00	6.00
29a John Francis Wilson (name in upper case letters)	20.00	10.00	6.00
29b John Francis Wilson (name in upper and lower case)	22.00	11.00	6.50
30a William Malcolm Dickey (name in upper case letters)	200.00	100.00	60.00
30b William Malcolm Dickey (name in upper and lower case)	225.00	125.00	70.00
31a Samuel West (name in upper case letters)	20.00	10.00	6.00
31b Samuel West (name in upper and lower case)	22.00	11.00	6.50
32 Robert I. Seeds	20.00	10.00	6.00
33 Del Howard Young (name actually Del Edward)	20.00	10.00	6.00
34a Frank Joseph Demaree (Joseph Franklin) (name in upper case letters)	20.00	10.00	6.00
34b Frank Joseph Demaree (Joseph Franklin) (name in upper and lower case)	22.00	11.00	6.50
35a William Frederick Jurges (name in upper case letters)	22.00	11.00	6.50
35b William Frederick Jurges (name in upper and lower case)	24.00	12.00	7.25
36a Frank Andrew McCormick (name in upper case letters)	20.00	10.00	6.00
36b Frank Andrew McCormick (name in upper and lower case)	22.00	11.00	6.50
37 Virgil Lawrence Davis	20.00	10.00	6.00
38a William Harrison Myers (name in upper case letters)	20.00	10.00	6.00
38b William Harrison Myers (name in upper and lower case)	22.00	11.00	6.50
39a Richard Benjamin Ferrell (name in upper case letters)	100.00	50.00	30.00
39b Richard Benjamin Ferrell (name in upper and lower case)	125.00	62.00	37.00
40 James Charles Bagby Jr.	20.00	10.00	6.00
41a Lonnie Warneke ("...the earned run department...")	20.00	10.00	6.00
41b Lonnie Warneke ("...the earned-run department...")	22.00	11.00	6.50
42 Arndt Jorgens	24.00	12.00	7.25
43 Melo Almada	20.00	10.00	6.00
44 Donald Henry Heffner	20.00	10.00	6.00
45a Merrill May (name in upper case letters)	20.00	10.00	6.00
45b Merrill May (name in upper and lower case)	22.00	11.00	6.50
46a Morris Arnovich (name in upper case letters)	20.00	10.00	6.00
46b Morris Arnovich (name in upper and lower case)	22.00	11.00	6.50
47a John Kelly Lewis, Jr. (name in upper case letters)	20.00	10.00	6.00
47b John Kelly Lewis, Jr. (name in upper and lower case)	22.00	11.00	6.50
48a Vernon Gomez (name in upper case letters)	200.00	100.00	60.00
48b Vernon Gomez (name in upper and lower case)	225.00	125.00	70.00
49 Edward Miller	20.00	10.00	6.00
50a Charles Len Gehringer (name actually Charles Leonard) (name in upper case letters)	200.00	100.00	60.00
50b Charles Len Gehringer (name actually Charles Leonard) (name in upper & lower case)	225.00	125.00	70.00
51a Melvin Thomas Ott (name in upper case letters)	200.00	100.00	60.00
51b Melvin Thomas Ott (name in upper and lower case)	225.00	125.00	70.00
52a Thomas D. Henrich (name in upper case letters)	40.00	20.00	12.00
52b Thomas D. Henrich (name in upper and lower case)	45.00	22.00	13.50
53a Carl Owen Hubbell (name in upper case letters)	200.00	100.00	60.00
53b Carl Owen Hubbell (name in upper and lower case)	225.00	125.00	70.00
54a Harry Edward Gumbert (name in upper case letters)	20.00	10.00	6.00
54b Harry Edward Gumbert (name in upper and lower case)	22.00	11.00	6.50
55a Floyd E. Vaughan (Joseph Floyd) (name in upper case letters)	125.00	62.00	37.00
55b Floyd E. Vaughan (Joseph Floyd) (name in upper and lower case)	125.00	62.00	37.00
56a Henry Greenberg (name in upper case letters)	150.00	75.00	45.00
56b Henry Greenberg (name in upper and lower case)	160.00	80.00	48.00
57a John A. Hassett (name in upper case letters)	20.00	10.00	6.00
57b John A. Hassett (name in upper and lower case)	22.00	11.00	6.50
58 Louis Peo Chiozza	20.00	10.00	6.00
59 Kendall Chase	20.00	10.00	6.00
60a Lynwood Thomas Rowe (name in upper case letters)	22.00	11.00	6.50
60b Lynwood Thomas Rowe (name in upper and lower case)	24.00	12.00	7.25
61a Anthony F. Cuccinello (name in upper case letters)	20.00	10.00	6.00
61b Anthony F. Cuccinello (name in upper and lower case)	22.00	11.00	6.50
62 Thomas Carey	20.00	10.00	6.00
63 Emmett Mueller	20.00	10.00	6.00
64a Wallace Moses, Jr. (name in upper case letters)	20.00	10.00	6.00
64b Wallace Moses, Jr. (name in upper and lower case)	22.00	11.00	6.50
65a Harry Francis Craft (name in upper case letters)	20.00	10.00	6.00
65b Harry Francis Craft (name in upper and lower case)	22.00	11.00	6.50
66 James A. Ripple	20.00	10.00	6.00
67 Edwin Joost	20.00	10.00	6.00
68 Fred Singleton	20.00	10.00	6.00
69 Elbert Preston Fletcher (Elburt)	20.00	10.00	6.00
70 Fred Maloy Frankhouse (Meloy)	20.00	10.00	6.00
71a Marcellus Monte Pearson (name actually Montgomery Marcellus) (name in upper case)	24.00	12.00	7.25
71b Marcellus Monte Pearson (name actually Montgomery Marcellus) (name in upper & lower)	35.00	17.50	10.50
72a Debs Garms (Born: Bango, Tex.)	20.00	10.00	6.00
72b Debs Garms (Born: Bangs, Tex.)	25.00	12.50	7.50
73a Harold H. Schumacher (Born: Dolgville, N.Y.)	22.00	11.00	6.50
73b Harold H. Schumacher (Born: Dolgeville, N.Y.)	40.00	20.00	12.00
74a Harry A. Lavagetto (name in upper case letters)	24.00	12.00	7.25
74b Harry A. Lavagetto (name in upper and lower case)	15.00	7.50	4.50
75a Stanley Bordagaray (name in upper case letters)	20.00	10.00	6.00
75b Stanley Bordagaray (name in upper and lower case)	22.00	11.00	6.50
76 Goodwin George Rosen	20.00	10.00	6.00
77 Lewis Sidney Riggs	20.00	10.00	6.00
78a Julius Joseph Solters (name in upper case letters)	20.00	10.00	6.00
78b Julius Joseph Solters (name in upper and lower case)	22.00	11.00	6.50
79a Joseph Gregg Moore (given name is Joe) (Weight: 157 lbs.)	20.00	10.00	6.00
79b Joseph Gregg Moore (given name is Joe) (Weight: 175 lbs.)	25.00	12.50	7.50
80a Irwin Fox (Ervin) (Weight: 165 lbs.)	20.00	10.00	6.00
80b Irwin Fox (Ervin) (Weight: 157 lbs.)	25.00	12.50	7.50
81a Ellsworth Dahlgren (name in upper case letters)	24.00	12.00	7.25
81b Ellsworth Dahlgren (name in upper and lower case)	35.00	17.50	10.50
82a Charles Herbert Klein (name in upper case letters)	165.00	82.00	49.00
82b Charles Herbert Klein (name in upper and lower case)	175.00	87.00	52.00
83a August Richard Suhr (name in upper case letters)	20.00	10.00	6.00
83b August Richard Suhr (name in upper and lower case)	22.00	11.00	6.50
84 Lamar Newsome	20.00	10.00	6.00
85 John Walter Cooney	20.00	10.00	6.00
86a Adolph Camilli (Adolf) ("...start of the 1928 season,...")	22.00	11.00	6.50
86b Adolph Camilli (Adolf) ("...start of the 1938 season,...")	35.00	17.50	10.50
87 Milburn G. Shoffner (middle initial actually J.)	20.00	10.00	6.00

		NR MT	EX	VG
88	Charles Keller	50.00	25.00	15.00
89a	Lloyd James Waner (name in upper case letters)	125.00	62.00	37.00
89b	Lloyd James Waner (name in upper and lower case)	135.00	67.00	40.00
90a	Robert H. Klinger (name in upper case letters)	20.00	10.00	6.00
90b	Robert H. Klinger (name in upper and lower case)	22.00	11.00	6.50
91a	John H. Knott (name in upper case letters)	20.00	10.00	6.00
91b	John H. Knott (name in upper and lower case)	22.00	11.00	6.50
92a	Ted Williams (name in upper case letters)	1800.00	900.00	540.00
92b	Ted Williams (name in upper and lower case)	2000.00	1000.00	600.00
93	Charles M. Gelbert	20.00	10.00	6.00
94	Henry E. Manush	125.00	62.00	37.00
95a	Whitlow Wyatt (name in upper case letters)	22.00	11.00	6.50
95b	Whitlow Wyatt (name in upper and lower case)	24.00	12.00	7.25
96a	Ernest Gordon Phelps (name in upper case letters)	22.00	11.00	6.50
96b	Ernest Gordon Phelps (name in upper and lower case)	24.00	12.00	7.25
97a	Robert Lee Johnson (name in upper case letters)	20.00	10.00	6.00
97b	Robert Lee Johnson (name in upper and lower case)	22.00	11.00	6.50
98	Arthur Carter Whitney	20.00	10.00	6.00
99a	Walter Anton Berger (name in upper case letters)	22.00	11.00	6.50
99b	Walter Anton Berger (name in upper and lower case)	24.00	12.00	7.25
100a	Charles Solomon Myer (name in upper case letters)	20.00	10.00	6.00
100b	Charles Solomon Myer (name in upper and lower case)	22.00	11.00	6.50
101a	Roger M. Cramer ("...the Martinburg Club...")	20.00	10.00	6.00
101b	Roger M. Cramer ("...the Martinsburg Club...")	25.00	12.50	7.50
102a	Lemuel Floyd Young (name in upper case letters)	20.00	10.00	6.00
102b	Lemuel Floyd Young (name in upper and lower case)	22.00	11.00	6.50
103	Morris Berg	22.00	11.00	6.50
104a	Thomas Davis Bridges ("...280 games, winning 283,...")	22.00	11.00	6.50
104b	Thomas Davis Bridges ("...280 games, winning 133,...")	35.00	17.50	10.50
105a	Donald Eric McNair (name in upper case letters)	20.00	10.00	6.00
105b	Donald Eric McNair (name in upper and lower case)	22.00	11.00	6.50
106	Albert Stark	20.00	10.00	6.00
107	Joseph Franklin Vosmik	20.00	10.00	6.00
108a	Frank Witman Hayes (name in upper case letters)	20.00	10.00	6.00
108b	Frank Witman Hayes (name in upper and lower case)	22.00	11.00	6.50
109a	Myril Hoag (name in upper case letters)	20.00	10.00	6.00
109b	Myril Hoag (name in upper and lower case)	22.00	11.00	6.50
110	Fred L. Fitzsimmons	22.00	11.00	6.50
111a	Van Lingle Mungo (name in upper case letters)	35.00	17.50	10.50
111b	Van Lingle Mungo (name in upper and lower case)	40.00	20.00	12.00
112a	Paul Glee Waner ("...Waner, the older...")	125.00	62.00	37.00
112b	Paul Glee Waner ("...Waner, the elder...")	150.00	75.00	45.00
113	Al Schacht	25.00	12.50	7.50
114a	Cecil Travis (name in upper case letters)	20.00	10.00	6.00
114b	Cecil Travis (name in upper and lower case)	22.00	11.00	6.50
115a	Ralph Kress (name in upper case letters)	20.00	10.00	6.00
115b	Ralph Kress (name in upper and lower case)	22.00	11.00	6.50
116	Eugene A. Desautels	125.00	62.00	37.00
117	Wayne Ambler	125.00	62.00	37.00
118	Lynn Nelson	125.00	62.00	37.00
119	Willard McKee Hershberger	125.00	62.00	37.00
120	Harold Benton Warstler (middle name actually Burton)	125.00	62.00	37.00

		NR MT	EX	VG
121	William J. Posedel	125.00	62.00	37.00
122	George Hartley McQuinn	125.00	62.00	37.00
123	Ray T. Davis	125.00	62.00	37.00
124	Walter George Brown	125.00	62.00	37.00
125	Clifford George Melton	125.00	62.00	37.00
126	Not Issued			
127	Gilbert Herman Brack	125.00	62.00	37.00
128	Joseph Emil Bowman	125.00	62.00	37.00
129	William Swift	125.00	62.00	37.00
130	Wilbur Lee Brubaker	125.00	62.00	37.00
131	Morton Cecil Cooper	125.00	62.00	37.00
132	James Roberson Brown	125.00	62.00	37.00
133	Lynn Myers	125.00	62.00	37.00
134	Forrest Pressnell	125.00	62.00	37.00
135	Arnold Malcolm Owen	125.00	62.00	37.00
136	Roy Chester Bell	125.00	62.00	37.00
137	Peter William Appleton	125.00	62.00	37.00
138	George Washington Case Jr.	125.00	62.00	37.00
139	Vitautas C. Tamulis	125.00	62.00	37.00
140	Raymond Hall Hayworth	125.00	62.00	37.00
141	Peter Coscarart	125.00	62.00	37.00
142	Ira Kendall Hutchinson	125.00	62.00	37.00
143	Howard Earl Averill	275.00	140.00	85.00
144	Henry J. Bonura	125.00	62.00	37.00
145	Hugh Noyes Mulcahy	125.00	62.00	37.00
146	Thomas Sunkel	125.00	62.00	37.00
147	George D. Coffman	125.00	62.00	37.00
148	William Trotter	125.00	62.00	37.00
149	Max Edward West	125.00	62.00	37.00
150	James Elton Walkup	125.00	62.00	37.00
151	Hugh Thomas Casey	125.00	62.00	37.00
152	Roy Weatherly	125.00	62.00	37.00
153	Paul H. Trout	150.00	75.00	45.00
154	John W. Hudson	125.00	62.00	37.00
155	James Paul Outlaw (middle name actually Paulus)	125.00	62.00	37.00
156	Raymond Berres	125.00	62.00	37.00
157	Donald Willard Padgett (middle name actually Wilson)	125.00	62.00	37.00
158	Luther Baxter Thomas	125.00	62.00	37.00
159	Russell E. Evans	125.00	62.00	37.00
160	Eugene Moore Jr.	125.00	62.00	37.00
161	Linus Reinhard Frey	135.00	67.00	40.00
162	Lloyd Albert Moore	250.00	90.00	55.00

1940 Play Ball

Following the success of their initial effort in 1939, Gum Incorporated issued a bigger and better set in 1940. The 240 black and white cards are once again in the 2-1/2" by 3-1/8" size, but the photos on the card fronts are enclosed by a frame which listed the player's name. Card backs again offer extensive biographies. Backs are also dated. A number of old-timers were issued along with the current day's players, and many Hall of Famers are included. The final 60 cards of the set are more difficult to obtain.

	NR MT	EX	VG
Complete Set:	20000.00	10000.00	6000.
Common Player: 1-120	22.00	11.00	6.50
Common Player: 121-180	25.00	12.50	7.50
Common Player: 181-240	80.00	40.00	24.00

		NR MT	EX	VG
1	Joe DiMaggio	2500.00	1250.00	750.00
2	"Art" Jorgens	25.00	12.50	7.50
3	"Babe" Dahlgren	25.00	12.50	7.50

		NR MT	EX	VG			NR MT	EX	VG
4	"Tommy" Henrich	35.00	17.50	10.50	95	"Mul" Mulcahy	22.00	11.00	6.50
5	"Monte" Pearson	25.00	12.50	7.50	96	"Heinie" Mueller	22.00	11.00	6.50
6	"Lefty" Gomez	200.00	100.00	60.00	97	"Morry" Arnovich	22.00	11.00	6.50
7	"Bill" Dickey	200.00	100.00	60.00	98	"Pinky" May	22.00	11.00	6.50
8	"Twinkletoes" Selkirk	25.00	12.50	7.50	99	"Syl" Johnson	22.00	11.00	6.50
9	"Charley" Keller	35.00	17.50	10.50	100	"Hersh" Martin	22.00	11.00	6.50
10	"Red" Ruffing	75.00	37.00	22.00	101	"Del" Young	22.00	11.00	6.50
11	"Jake" Powell	25.00	12.50	7.50	102	"Chuck" Klein	150.00	75.00	45.00
12	"Johnny" Schulte	25.00	12.50	7.50	103	"Elbie" Fletcher	22.00	11.00	6.50
13	"Jack" Knott	22.00	11.00	6.50	104	"Big Poison" Waner	150.00	75.00	45.00
14	"Rabbit" McNair	22.00	11.00	6.50	105	"Little Poison" Waner	150.00	75.00	45.00
15	George Case	22.00	11.00	6.50	106	"Pep" Young	22.00	11.00	6.50
16	Cecil Travis	22.00	11.00	6.50	107	"Arky" Vaughan	100.00	50.00	30.00
17	"Buddy" Myer	22.00	11.00	6.50	108	"Johnny" Rizzo	22.00	11.00	6.50
18	"Charley" Gelbert	22.00	11.00	6.50	109	"Don" Padgett	22.00	11.00	6.50
19	"Ken" Chase	22.00	11.00	6.50	110	"Tom" Sunkel	22.00	11.00	6.50
20	"Buddy" Lewis	22.00	11.00	6.50	111	"Mickey" Owen	22.00	11.00	6.50
21	"Rick" Ferrell	65.00	32.00	19.50	112	"Jimmy" Brown	22.00	11.00	6.50
22	"Sammy" West	22.00	11.00	6.50	113	"Mort" Cooper	22.00	11.00	6.50
23	"Dutch" Leonard	22.00	11.00	6.50	114	"Lon" Warneke	22.00	11.00	6.50
24	Frank "Blimp" Hayes	22.00	11.00	6.50	115	"Mike" Gonzales (Gonzalez)	22.00	11.00	6.50
25	"Cherokee" Bob Johnson	22.00	11.00	6.50	116	"Al" Schacht	25.00	12.50	7.50
26	"Wally" Moses	22.00	11.00	6.50	117	"Dolly" Stark	22.00	11.00	6.50
27	"Ted" Williams	1800.00	900.00	550.00	118	"Schoolboy" Hoyt	100.00	50.00	30.00
28	"Gene" Desautels	22.00	11.00	6.50	119	"Ol Pete" Alexander	180.00	90.00	54.00
29	"Doc" Cramer	22.00	11.00	6.50	120	Walter "Big Train" Johnson	275.00	137.00	82.00
30	"Moe" Berg	25.00	12.50	7.50	121	Atley Donald	25.00	12.50	7.50
31	"Jack" Wilson	22.00	11.00	6.50	122	"Sandy" Sundra	25.00	12.50	7.50
32	"Jim" Bagby	22.00	11.00	6.50	123	"Hildy" Hildebrand	25.00	12.50	7.50
33	"Fritz" Ostermueller	22.00	11.00	6.50	124	"Colonel" Combs	135.00	67.00	40.00
34	John Peacock	22.00	11.00	6.50	125	"Art" Fletcher	25.00	12.50	7.50
35	"Joe" Heving	22.00	11.00	6.50	126	"Jake" Solters	25.00	12.50	7.50
36	"Jim" Tabor	22.00	11.00	6.50	127	"Muddy" Ruel	25.00	12.50	7.50
37	Emerson Dickman	22.00	11.00	6.50	128	"Pete" Appleton	25.00	12.50	7.50
38	"Bobby" Doerr	100.00	50.00	30.00	129	"Bucky" Harris	100.00	50.00	30.00
39	"Tom" Carey	22.00	11.00	6.50	130	"Deerfoot" Milan	25.00	12.50	7.50
40	"Hank" Greenberg	250.00	125.00	75.00	131	"Zeke" Bonura	25.00	12.50	7.50
41	"Charley" Gehringer	150.00	75.00	45.00	132	Connie Mack	225.00	112.00	67.00
42	"Bud" Thomas	22.00	11.00	6.50	133	"Jimmie" Foxx	275.00	137.00	82.00
43	Pete Fox	22.00	11.00	6.50	134	"Joe" Cronin	150.00	75.00	45.00
44	"Dizzy" Trout	25.00	12.50	7.50	135	"Line Drive" Nelson	25.00	12.50	7.50
45	"Red" Kress	22.00	11.00	6.50	136	"Cotton" Pippen	25.00	12.50	7.50
46	Earl Averill	100.00	50.00	30.00	137	"Bing" Miller	25.00	12.50	7.50
47	"Old Os" Vitt	22.00	11.00	6.50	138	"Beau" Bell	25.00	12.50	7.50
48	"Luke" Sewell	25.00	12.50	7.50	139	Elden Auker (Eldon)	25.00	12.50	7.50
49	"Stormy Weather" Weatherly	22.00	11.00	6.50	140	"Dick" Coffman	25.00	12.50	7.50
50	"Hal" Trosky	22.00	11.00	6.50	141	"Casey" Stengel	200.00	100.00	60.00
51	"Don" Heffner	22.00	11.00	6.50	142	"Highpockets" Kelly	100.00	50.00	30.00
52	Myril Hoag	22.00	11.00	6.50	143	"Gene" Moore	25.00	12.50	7.50
53	"Mac" McQuinn	22.00	11.00	6.50	144	"Joe" Vosmik	25.00	12.50	7.50
54	"Bill" Trotter	22.00	11.00	6.50	145	"Vito" Tamulis	25.00	12.50	7.50
55	"Slick" Coffman	22.00	11.00	6.50	146	"Tot" Pressnell	25.00	12.50	7.50
56	"Eddie" Miller	22.00	11.00	6.50	147	"Johnny" Hudson	25.00	12.50	7.50
57	Max West	22.00	11.00	6.50	148	"Hugh" Casey	25.00	12.50	7.50
58	"Bill" Posedel	22.00	11.00	6.50	149	"Pinky" Shoffner	25.00	12.50	7.50
59	"Rabbit" Warstler	22.00	11.00	6.50	150	"Whitey" Moore	25.00	12.50	7.50
60	John Cooney	22.00	11.00	6.50	151	Edwin Joost	25.00	12.50	7.50
61	"Tony" Cuccinello	22.00	11.00	6.50	152	"Jimmy" Wilson	25.00	12.50	7.50
62	"Buddy" Hassett	22.00	11.00	6.50	153	"Bill" McKechnie	100.00	50.00	30.00
63	"Pete" Cascarart	22.00	11.00	6.50	154	"Jumbo" Brown	25.00	12.50	7.50
64	"Van" Mungo	30.00	15.00	9.00	155	"Ray" Hayworth	25.00	12.50	7.50
65	"Fitz" Fitzsimmons	25.00	12.50	7.50	156	"Daffy" Dean	30.00	15.00	9.00
66	"Babe" Phelps	25.00	12.50	7.50	157	"Lou" Chiozza	25.00	12.50	7.50
67	"Whit" Wyatt	25.00	12.50	7.50	158	"Stonewall" Jackson	100.00	50.00	30.00
68	"Dolph" Camilli	25.00	12.50	7.50	159	"Pancho" Snyder	25.00	12.50	7.50
69	"Cookie" Lavagetto	25.00	12.50	7.50	160	"Hans" Lobert	25.00	12.50	7.50
70	"Hot Potato" Hamlin	22.00	11.00	6.50	161	"Debs" Garms	25.00	12.50	7.50
71	"Mel" Almada	22.00	11.00	6.50	162	"Joe" Bowman	25.00	12.50	7.50
72	"Chuck" Dressen	25.00	12.50	7.50	163	"Spud" Davis	25.00	12.50	7.50
73	"Bucky" Walters	25.00	12.50	7.50	164	"Ray" Berres	25.00	12.50	7.50
74	"Duke" Derringer	25.00	12.50	7.50	165	"Bob" Klinger	25.00	12.50	7.50
75	"Buck" McCormick	22.00	11.00	6.50	166	"Bill" Brubaker	25.00	12.50	7.50
76	"Lonny" Frey	22.00	11.00	6.50	167	"Frankie" Frisch	150.00	75.00	45.00
77	"Bill" Hershberger	22.00	11.00	6.50	168	"Honus" Wagner	275.00	137.00	82.00
78	"Lew" Riggs	22.00	11.00	6.50	169	"Gabby" Street	25.00	12.50	7.50
79	"Wildfire" Craft	22.00	11.00	6.50	170	"Tris" Speaker	250.00	125.00	75.00
80	"Bill" Myers	22.00	11.00	6.50	171	Harry Heilmann	150.00	75.00	45.00
81	"Wally" Berger	25.00	12.50	7.50	172	"Chief" Bender	150.00	75.00	45.00
82	"Hank" Gowdy	22.00	11.00	6.50	173	"Larry" Lajoie	275.00	137.00	82.00
83	"Clif" Melton (Cliff)	22.00	11.00	6.50	174	"Johnny" Evers	150.00	75.00	45.00
84	"Jo-Jo" Moore	22.00	11.00	6.50	175	"Christy" Mathewson	275.00	137.00	82.00
85	"Hal" Schumacher	25.00	12.50	7.50	176	"Heinie" Manush	150.00	75.00	45.00
86	Harry Gumbert	22.00	11.00	6.50	177	Frank "Homerun" Baker	150.00	75.00	45.00
87	Carl Hubbell	200.00	100.00	60.00	178	Max Carey	150.00	75.00	45.00
88	"Mel" Ott	200.00	100.00	60.00	179	George Sisler	135.00	67.00	40.00
89	"Bill" Jurges	25.00	12.50	7.50	180	"Mickey" Cochrane	150.00	75.00	45.00
90	Frank Demaree	22.00	11.00	6.50	181	"Spud" Chandler	80.00	40.00	25.00
91	Bob "Suitcase" Seeds	22.00	11.00	6.50	182	"Knick" Knickerbocker	80.00	40.00	25.00
92	"Whitey" Whitehead	22.00	11.00	6.50	183	Marvin Breuer	80.00	40.00	25.00
93	Harry "The Horse" Danning	22.00	11.00	6.50	184	"Mule" Haas	80.00	40.00	24.00
94	"Gus" Suhr	22.00	11.00	6.50	185	"Joe" Kuhel	80.00	40.00	24.00

		NR MT	EX	VG
186	Taft Wright	80.00	40.00	24.00
187	"Jimmy" Dykes	60.00	30.00	18.00
188	"Joe" Krakauskas	80.00	40.00	24.00
189	"Jim" Bloodworth	80.00	40.00	24.00
190	"Charley" Berry	80.00	40.00	24.00
191	John Babich	80.00	40.00	24.00
192	"Dick" Siebert	80.00	40.00	24.00
193	"Chubby" Dean	80.00	40.00	24.00
194	"Sam" Chapman	80.00	40.00	24.00
195	"Dee" Miles	80.00	40.00	24.00
196	"Nonny" Nonnenkamp	80.00	40.00	24.00
197	"Lou" Finney	80.00	40.00	24.00
198	"Denny" Galehouse	80.00	40.00	24.00
199	"Pinky" Higgins	80.00	40.00	24.00
200	"Soupy" Campbell	80.00	40.00	24.00
201	Barney McCosky	80.00	40.00	24.00
202	"Al" Milnar	80.00	40.00	24.00
203	"Bad News" Hale	80.00	40.00	24.00
204	Harry Eisenstat	80.00	40.00	24.00
205	"Rollie" Hemsley	80.00	40.00	24.00
206	"Chet" Laabs	80.00	40.00	24.00
207	"Gus" Mancuso	80.00	40.00	24.00
208	Lee Gamble	80.00	40.00	24.00
209	"Hy" Vandenberg	80.00	40.00	24.00
210	"Bill" Lohrman	80.00	40.00	24.00
211	"Pop" Joiner	80.00	40.00	24.00
212	"Babe" Young	80.00	40.00	24.00
213	John Rucker	80.00	40.00	24.00
214	"Ken" O'Dea	80.00	40.00	24.00
215	"Johnnie" McCarthy	80.00	40.00	24.00
216	"Joe" Marty	80.00	40.00	24.00
217	Walter Beck	80.00	40.00	24.00
218	"Wally" Millies	80.00	40.00	24.00
219	"Russ" Bauers	80.00	40.00	24.00
220	Mace Brown	80.00	40.00	24.00
221	Lee Handley	80.00	40.00	24.00
222	"Max" Butcher	80.00	40.00	24.00
223	Hugh "Ee-Yah" Jennings	150.00	75.00	45.00
224	"Pie" Traynor	250.00	125.00	75.00
225	"Shoeless Joe" Jackson	2500.00	1250.00	750.00
226	Harry Hooper	150.00	75.00	45.00
227	"Pop" Haines	150.00	75.00	45.00
228	"Charley" Grimm	80.00	40.00	25.00
229	"Buck" Herzog	80.00	40.00	24.00
230	"Red" Faber	150.00	75.00	45.00
231	"Dolf" Luque	80.00	40.00	24.00
232	"Goose" Goslin	150.00	75.00	45.00
233	"Moose" Earnshaw	80.00	40.00	24.00
234	Frank "Husk" Chance	200.00	100.00	60.00
235	John J. McGraw	250.00	125.00	75.00
236	"Sunny Jim" Bottomley	150.00	75.00	45.00
237	"Wee Willie" Keeler	225.00	112.00	67.00
238	"Poosh 'Em Up Tony" Lazzeri	100.00	50.00	30.00
239	George Uhle	80.00	40.00	25.00
240	"Bill" Atwood	200.00	60.00	35.00

1941 Play Ball

While the card backs are quite similar to the black and white cards Gum Incorporated issued in 1940, the card fronts in the 1941 set are printed in color. Many of the card photos, however, are just color versions of the player's 1940 card. The cards are still in the 2-1/2" by 3-1/8" size, but only 72 cards are included in the set. Joe DiMaggio and Ted Williams continue to be the key players in the set, while card numbers 49-72 are rarer than the lower-numbered cards. The cards were printed in sheets, and can still

be found that way, or in paper strips, lacking the cardboard backing.

		NR MT	EX	VG
Complete Set:		14500.00	6500.00	4000.
Common Player: 1-48		55.00	27.00	16.50
Common Player: 49-72		75.00	37.00	22.00
1	"Eddie" Miller	200.00	100.00	60.00
2	Max West	55.00	27.00	16.50
3	"Bucky" Walters	55.00	27.00	16.50
4	"Duke" Derringer	75.00	37.00	22.00
5	"Buck" McCormick	55.00	27.00	16.50
6	Carl Hubbell	250.00	125.00	75.00
7	"The Horse" Danning	55.00	27.00	16.50
8	"Mel" Ott	300.00	150.00	90.00
9	"Pinky" May	55.00	27.00	16.50
10	"Arky" Vaughan	75.00	37.00	22.00
11	Debs Garms	55.00	27.00	16.50
12	"Jimmy" Brown	55.00	27.00	16.50
13	"Jimmie" Foxx	375.00	187.00	110.00
14	"Ted" Williams	2000.00	1000.00	600.00
15	"Joe" Cronin	175.00	87.00	50.00
16	"Hal" Trosky	55.00	27.00	16.50
17	"Stormy" Weatherly	55.00	27.00	16.50
18	"Hank" Greenberg	350.00	175.00	105.00
19	"Charley" Gehringer	250.00	125.00	75.00
20	"Red" Ruffing	175.00	87.00	50.00
21	"Charlie" Keller	75.00	37.00	22.00
22	"Indian Bob" Johnson	55.00	27.00	16.50
23	"Mac" McQuinn	55.00	27.00	16.50
24	"Dutch" Leonard	55.00	27.00	16.50
25	"Gene" Moore	55.00	27.00	16.50
26	Harry "Gunboat" Gumbert	55.00	27.00	16.50
27	"Babe" Young	55.00	27.00	16.50
28	"Joe" Marty	55.00	27.00	16.50
29	"Jack" Wilson	55.00	27.00	16.50
30	"Lou" Finney	55.00	27.00	16.50
31	"Joe" Kuhel	55.00	27.00	16.50
32	Taft Wright	55.00	27.00	16.50
33	"Happy" Milnar	55.00	27.00	16.50
34	"Rollie" Hemsley	55.00	27.00	16.50
35	"Pinky" Higgins	55.00	27.00	16.50
36	Barney McCosky	55.00	27.00	16.50
37	"Soupy" Campbell	55.00	27.00	16.50
38	Atley Donald	75.00	37.00	22.00
39	"Tommy" Henrich	75.00	37.00	22.00
40	"Johnny" Babich	55.00	27.00	16.50
41	Frank "Blimp" Hayes	55.00	27.00	16.50
42	"Wally" Moses	55.00	27.00	16.50
43	Albert "Bronk" Brancato	55.00	27.00	16.50
44	"Sam" Chapman	55.00	27.00	16.50
45	Elden Auker (Eldon)	55.00	27.00	16.50
46	"Sid" Hudson	55.00	27.00	16.50
47	"Buddy" Lewis	55.00	27.00	16.50
48	Cecil Travis	55.00	27.00	16.50
49	"Babe" Dahlgren	75.00	37.00	22.00
50	"Johnny" Cooney	75.00	37.00	22.00
51	"Dolph" Camilli	55.00	27.00	16.50
52	Kirby Higbe	75.00	37.00	22.00
53	Luke "Hot Potato" Hamlin	75.00	37.00	22.00
54	"Pee Wee" Reese	750.00	375.00	225.00
55	"Whit" Wyatt	75.00	37.00	22.00
56	"Vandy" Vander Meer	75.00	37.00	22.00
57	"Moe" Arnovich	75.00	37.00	22.00
58	"Frank" Demaree	75.00	37.00	22.00
59	"Bill" Jurges	75.00	37.00	22.00
60	"Chuck" Klein	250.00	125.00	75.00
61	"Vince" DiMaggio	200.00	100.00	60.00
62	"Elbie" Fletcher	75.00	37.00	22.00
63	"Dom" DiMaggio	200.00	100.00	60.00
64	"Bobby" Doerr	225.00	112.00	70.00
65	"Tommy" Bridges	75.00	37.00	22.00
66	Harland Clift (Harlond)	75.00	37.00	22.00
67	"Walt" Judnich	75.00	37.00	22.00
68	"Jack" Knott	75.00	37.00	22.00
69	George Case	75.00	37.00	22.00
70	"Bill" Dickey	650.00	325.00	200.00
71	"Joe" DiMaggio	2500.00	1250.00	750.00
72	"Lefty" Gomez	600.00	300.00	180.00

1910 Plow Boy Tobacco

Plowboy Tobacco, a product of the Spaulding & Merrick Company, issued a set of bainet-size cards in the Chicago area featuring members of the Cubs and the White Sox. From the checklist of the 50

		NR MT	EX	VG
(47)	Irv Young	200.00	100.00	60.00
(48)	Rollie Zeider	200.00	100.00	60.00
(49)	Heinie Zimmerman	200.00	100.00	60.00

1889 Police Gazette Cabinets

Issued in the late 1880s as a premium by Police Gazette, a popular newspaper of the day, these cabinet cards were only recently discovered and are very rare. The 4-1/2" by 6-1/2" cards consist of oval, sepia-toned photographs mounted on cardboard of various colors. Only eight players are known and, except for Keefe, their photographs correspond to those used in the better-known S.F. Hess card series. All of the cards display the name of the player next to his portrait, along with the signature of "Richard K. Fox" and a line identifying him as "Editor and Proprietor/Police Gazette/Franklin Sqaure, New York."

known cards, it appears that the bulk of the set was originally issued in 1910 with a few additional cards appearing over the next several years. The set appears to be complete at 25 Cubs and 25 White Sox players, although there is some speculation that other cards may still be discovered. Measuring approximately 5-3/4" by 8", the Plowboys are one of the largest tobacco cards of the 20th Century. They feature very nice sepia-toned player photos in poses not found on other tobacco issues. The player's name appears in the lower left corner, while the team name appears in the lower right. Two different backs are known to exist. One consists of a simple advertisement for Plowboy Tobacco, while a second more difficult variety includes a list of premiums available in exchange for coupons. The set is among the rarest of all 20th Century tobacco issues.

		NR MT	EX	VG
Complete Set:		9000.00	4500.00	2750.
Common Player:		200.00	100.00	60.00
(1)	Jimmy Archer	200.00	100.00	60.00
(2)	Ginger Beaumont	200.00	100.00	60.00
(3)	Lena Blackburne	200.00	100.00	60.00
(4)	Bruno Block	200.00	100.00	60.00
(5)	Ping Bodie	200.00	100.00	60.00
(6)	Mordecai Brown	500.00	250.00	150.00
(7)	Al Carson	200.00	100.00	60.00
(8)	Frank Chance	550.00	275.00	165.00
(9)	Ed Cicotte	275.00	137.00	80.00
(10)	King Cole	200.00	100.00	60.00
(11)	Eddie Collins	500.00	250.00	150.00
(12)	George Davis	200.00	100.00	60.00
(13)	Patsy Dougherty	200.00	100.00	60.00
(14)	Johnny Evers	500.00	250.00	150.00
(15)	Chick Gandel (Gandil)	275.00	137.00	80.00
(16)	Ed Hahn	200.00	100.00	60.00
(17)	Solly Hoffman (Hofman)	200.00	100.00	60.00
(18)	Del Howard	200.00	100.00	60.00
(19)	Bill Jones	200.00	100.00	60.00
(20)	Johnny Kling	200.00	100.00	60.00
(21)	Rube Kroh	200.00	100.00	60.00
(22)	Frank Lange	200.00	100.00	60.00
(23)	Fred Luderus	200.00	100.00	60.00
(24)	Harry McIntyre	200.00	100.00	60.00
(25)	Ward Miller	200.00	100.00	60.00
(26)	Charlie Mullen	200.00	100.00	60.00
(27)	Tom Needham	200.00	100.00	60.00
(28)	Fred Olmstead	200.00	100.00	60.00
(29)	Orval Overall	200.00	100.00	60.00
(30)	Fred Parent	200.00	100.00	60.00
(31)	Fred Payne	200.00	100.00	60.00
(32)	Francis "Big Jeff" Pfeffer	200.00	100.00	60.00
(33)	Jake Pfeister	200.00	100.00	60.00
(34)	Billy Purtell	200.00	100.00	60.00
(35)	Ed Reulbach	200.00	100.00	60.00
(36)	Lew Richie	200.00	100.00	60.00
(37)	Jimmy Scheckard (Sheckard)	200.00	100.00	60.00
(38)	Wildfire Schulte	200.00	100.00	60.00
(39a)	Jim Scot (name incorrect)	200.00	100.00	60.00
(39b)	Jim Scott (name correct)	200.00	100.00	60.00
(40)	Frank Smith	200.00	100.00	60.00
(41)	Harry Steinfeldt	275.00	137.00	80.00
(42)	Billy Sullivan	200.00	100.00	60.00
(43)	Lee Tannehill	200.00	100.00	60.00
(44)	Joe Tinker	500.00	250.00	150.00
(45)	Ed Walsh	500.00	250.00	150.00
(46)	Doc White	200.00	100.00	60.00

		NR MT	EX	VG
Complete Set:		12000.00	6000.00	3500.
Common Player:		1200.00	600.00	350.00
(1)	Roger Conner (Connor)	2000.00	1000.00	600.00
(2)	Jerry Denny	1200.00	600.00	350.00
(3)	Buck Ewing	2000.00	1000.00	600.00
(4)	Elmer Foster	1200.00	600.00	350.00
(5)	Pebbly Jack Glasscock	1200.00	600.00	350.00
(6)	Tim Keefe	2000.00	1000.00	600.00
(7)	Tip O'Neil	1500.00	750.00	450.00
(8)	Curt Welch	1200.00	600.00	350.00

R

1943 R302-1 M.P. & Co.

One of the few baseball card sets issued during the war years, this set of unnumbered cards, each measuring approximately 2-11/16" by 2-1/4", feature rather crude drawings that have little resemblance to the player named. The cards were originally produced in strips and sold inexpensively in candy stores. The backs contain brief player write-ups.

		NR MT	EX	VG
Complete Set:		450.00	225.00	135.00
Common Player:		8.00	4.00	2.50
(1)	Ernie Bonham	8.00	4.00	2.50
(2)	Lou Boudreau	12.00	6.00	3.50
(3)	Dolph Camilli	8.00	4.00	2.50
(4)	Mort Cooper	8.00	4.00	2.50
(5)	Walker Cooper	8.00	4.00	2.50
(6)	Joe Cronin	12.00	6.00	3.50
(7)	Hank Danning	8.00	4.00	2.50
(8)	Bill Dickey	18.00	9.00	5.50
(9)	Joe DiMaggio	90.00	45.00	27.00
(10)	Bobby Feller	25.00	12.50	7.50
(11)	Jimmy Foxx	25.00	12.50	7.50
(12)	Hank Greenberg	15.00	7.50	4.50
(13)	Stan Hack	8.00	4.00	2.50
(14)	Tom Henrich	9.00	4.50	2.75
(15)	Carl Hubbell	12.00	6.00	3.50
(16)	Joe Medwick	12.00	6.00	3.50
(17)	John Mize	12.00	6.00	3.50
(18)	Lou Novikoff	8.00	4.00	2.50
(19)	Mel Ott	15.00	7.50	4.50
(20)	Pee Wee Reese	25.00	12.50	7.50
(21)	Pete Reiser	8.00	4.00	2.50
(22)	Charlie Ruffing	12.00	6.00	3.50
(23)	Johnny Vander Meer	9.00	4.50	2.75
(24)	Ted Williams	60.00	30.00	18.00

1949 R302-2 M.P. & Co.

This set appears to be a re-issue of M.P. & Company's 1943 card set with different players and numbers added to the back. The cards, which measure 2-11/16" by 2-1/4", feature crude drawings of generic baseball players which have little resemblance to the player named. The backs include the card number and player information. The numbering sequence begins with card 100, and numbers 104, 118, and 120 are unknown, while two of the cards (Henrich and Kozar) are unnumbered. The set is assigned the American Card Catalog number R302-2.

		NR MT	EX	VG
Complete Set:		425.00	212.00	127.00
Common Player:		8.00	4.00	2.50
100	Lou Boudreau	12.00	6.00	3.50
101	Ted Williams	60.00	30.00	18.00
102	Buddy Kerr	8.00	4.00	2.50
103	Bobby Feller	25.00	12.50	7.50
104	Unknown			
105	Joe DiMaggio	90.00	45.00	27.00
106	Pee Wee Reese	25.00	12.50	7.50
107	Ferris Fain	8.00	4.00	2.50
108	Andy Pafko	8.00	4.00	2.50
109	Del Ennis	8.00	4.00	2.50
110	Ralph Kiner	12.00	6.00	3.50
111	Nippy Jones	8.00	4.00	2.50
112	Del Rice	8.00	4.00	2.50
113	Hank Sauer	8.00	4.00	2.50

		NR MT	EX	VG
114	Gil Coan	8.00	4.00	2.50
115	Eddie Joost	8.00	4.00	2.50
116	Alvin Dark	9.00	4.50	2.75
117	Larry Berra	25.00	12.50	7.50
118	Unknown			
119	Bob Lemon	12.00	6.00	3.50
120	Unknown			
121	Johnny Pesky	8.00	4.00	2.50
122	Johnny Sain	9.00	4.50	2.75
123	Hoot Evers	8.00	4.00	2.50
124	Larry Doby	9.00	4.50	2.75
----	Tom Henrich	9.00	4.50	2.75
----	Al Kozar	8.00	4.00	2.50

1939 R303-A
Goudey Premiums

Although this unnumbered set of paper premiums has the name "Diamond Stars Gum" on the back, it is not related to National Chicle's Diamond Stars card sets. Rather, this 48-player set was a premium issued by the Goudey Gum Company. Each premium photo measures 6-3/16" by 4" and is printed in a brown-toned sepia. The front of the photo includes a facsimile autograph, while the back contains drawings that illustrate various baseball tips.

		NR MT	EX	VG
Complete Set:		2300.00	1150.00	690.00
Common Player:		25.00	12.50	7.50
(1)	Luke Appling	45.00	22.00	13.50
(2)	Earl Averill	45.00	22.00	13.50
(3)	Wally Berger	25.00	12.50	7.50
(4)	Darrell Blanton	25.00	12.50	7.50
(5)	Zeke Bonura	25.00	12.50	7.50
(6)	Mace Brown	25.00	12.50	7.50
(7)	George Case	25.00	12.50	7.50
(8)	Ben Chapman	25.00	12.50	7.50
(9)	Joe Cronin	45.00	22.00	13.50
(10)	Frank Crosetti	25.00	12.50	7.50
(11)	Paul Derringer	25.00	12.50	7.50
(12)	Bill Dickey	75.00	37.00	22.00
(13)	Joe DiMaggio	275.00	137.00	82.00
(14)	Bob Feller	80.00	40.00	24.00
(15)	Jimmy Foxx	80.00	40.00	24.00
(16)	Charles Gehringer	45.00	22.00	13.50
(17)	Lefty Gomez	45.00	22.00	13.50
(18)	Ival Goodman	25.00	12.50	7.50
(19)	Joe Gordon	25.00	12.50	7.50
(20)	Hank Greenberg	45.00	22.00	13.50
(21)	Buddy Hassett	25.00	12.50	7.50
(22)	Jeff Heath	25.00	12.50	7.50
(23)	Tom Henrich	25.00	12.50	7.50
(24)	Billy Herman	40.00	20.00	12.00
(25)	Frank Higgins	25.00	12.50	7.50
(26)	Fred Hutchinson	25.00	12.50	7.50
(27)	Bob Johnson	25.00	12.50	7.50
(28)	Ken Keltner	25.00	12.50	7.50
(29)	Mike Kreevich	25.00	12.50	7.50
(30)	Ernie Lombardi	45.00	22.00	13.50
(31)	Gus Mancuso	25.00	12.50	7.50
(32)	Eric McNair	25.00	12.50	7.50
(33)	Van Mungo	25.00	12.50	7.50
(34)	Buck Newsom	25.00	12.50	7.50
(35)	Mel Ott	35.00	17.50	10.50
(36)	Marvin Owen	25.00	12.50	7.50

		NR MT	EX	VG
(37)	Frank Pytlak	25.00	12.50	7.50
(38)	Woodrow Rich	25.00	12.50	7.50
(39)	Charley Root	25.00	12.50	7.50
(40)	Al Simmons	45.00	22.00	13.50
(41)	James Tabor	25.00	12.50	7.50
(42)	Cecil Travis	25.00	12.50	7.50
(43)	Hal Trosky	25.00	12.50	7.50
(44)	Arky Vaughan	45.00	22.00	13.50
(45)	Joe Vosmik	25.00	12.50	7.50
(46)	Lon Warneke	25.00	12.50	7.50
(47)	Ted Williams	350.00	175.00	105.00
(48)	Rudy York	25.00	12.50	7.50

1939 R303-B
Goudey Premiums

HOW TO SIGNAL

Although larger (7-5/16" by 4-3/4"), the photos in this 24-player set are identical to those in the R303-A set of the same year, and the format of the set is unchanges. The set, designated as R303-B, can be found in both black and white sepia.

		NR MT	EX	VG
Complete Set:		1200.00	600.00	360.00
Common Player:		20.00	10.00	6.00
(1)	Luke Appling	40.00	20.00	12.00
(2)	George Case	20.00	10.00	6.00
(3)	Ben Chapman	20.00	10.00	6.00
(4)	Joe Cronin	40.00	20.00	12.00
(5)	Bill Dickey	50.00	25.00	15.00
(6)	Joe DiMaggio	300.00	150.00	90.00
(7)	Bob Feller	60.00	30.00	18.00
(8)	Jimmy Foxx	60.00	30.00	18.00
(9)	Lefty Gomez	40.00	20.00	12.00
(10)	Ival Goodman	20.00	10.00	6.00
(11)	Joe Gordon	22.00	11.00	6.50
(12)	Hank Greenberg	40.00	20.00	12.00
(13)	Jeff Heath	20.00	10.00	6.00
(14)	Billy Herman	35.00	17.50	10.50
(15)	Frank Higgins	20.00	10.00	6.00
(16)	Ken Keltner	22.00	11.00	6.50
(17)	Mike Kreevich	20.00	10.00	6.00
(18)	Ernie Lombardi	35.00	17.50	10.50
(19)	Gus Mancuso	20.00	10.00	6.00
(20)	Mel Ott	40.00	20.00	12.00
(21)	Al Simmons	40.00	20.00	12.00
(22)	Arky Vaughan	40.00	20.00	12.00
(23)	Joe Vosmik	20.00	10.00	6.00
(24)	Rudy York	20.00	10.00	6.00

1933 R308 Tatoo Orbit

This obscure set of cards, issued by Tatoo Orbit, is numbered from 151 through 207, with a few of the numbers still unknown. The tiny cards measure just 1-7/8" by 1-1/4" and were considered more of a novelty item because the crude player drawings on the cards actually "developed" when moistened and exposed to light.

		NR MT	EX	VG
Complete Set:		1800.00	900.00	540.00
Common Player:		20.00	10.00	6.00
151	Vernon Gomez	50.00	25.00	15.00
152	Kiki Cuyler	50.00	25.00	15.00
153	Jimmy Foxx	75.00	38.00	23.00
154	Al Simmons	50.00	25.00	15.00
155	Chas. J. Grimm	22.00	11.00	6.50
156	William Jurges	20.00	10.00	6.00
157	Chuck Klein	50.00	25.00	15.00
158	Richard Bartell	20.00	10.00	6.00
159	Pepper Martin	30.00	15.00	9.00
160	Earl Averill	50.00	25.00	15.00
161	William Dickey	60.00	30.00	18.00
162	Wesley Ferrell	20.00	10.00	6.00
163	Oral Hildebrand	20.00	10.00	6.00
164	Wm. Kamm	20.00	10.00	6.00
165	Earl Whitehill	20.00	10.00	6.00
166	Charles Fullis	20.00	10.00	6.00
167	Jimmy Dykes	22.00	11.00	6.50
168	Ben Cantwell	20.00	10.00	6.00
169	George Earnshaw	20.00	10.00	6.00
170	Jackson Stephenson	22.00	11.00	6.50
171	Randolph Moore	20.00	10.00	6.00
172	Ted Lyons	50.00	25.00	15.00
173	Goose Goslin	50.00	25.00	15.00
174	E. Swanson	20.00	10.00	6.00
175	Lee Roy Mahaffey	20.00	10.00	6.00
176	Joe Cronin	50.00	25.00	15.00
177	Tom Bridges	20.00	10.00	6.00
178	Henry Manush	50.00	25.00	15.00
179	Walter Stewart	20.00	10.00	6.00
180	Frank Pytlak	20.00	10.00	6.00
181	Dale Alexander	20.00	10.00	6.00
182	Robert Grove	60.00	30.00	18.00
183	Charles Gehringer	50.00	25.00	15.00
184	Lewis Fonseca	20.00	10.00	6.00
185	Alvin Crowder	20.00	10.00	6.00
186	Mickey Cochrane	50.00	25.00	15.00
187	Max Bishop	20.00	10.00	6.00
188	Connie Mack	60.00	30.00	18.00
189	Guy Bush	20.00	10.00	6.00
190	Charlie Root	20.00	10.00	6.00
191a	Burleigh Grimes	50.00	25.00	15.00
191b	Gabby Hartnett	50.00	25.00	15.00
192	Pat Malone	20.00	10.00	6.00
193	Woody English	20.00	10.00	6.00
194	Lonnie Warneke	20.00	10.00	6.00
195	Babe Herman	22.00	11.00	6.50
196	Unknown			
197	Unknown			
198	Unknown			
199	Unknown			
200	Gabby Hartnett	50.00	25.00	15.00
201	Paul Waner	50.00	25.00	15.00
202	Dizzy Dean	100.00	50.00	30.00
203	Unknown			
204	Unknown			
205	Jim Bottomley	50.00	25.00	15.00
206	Unknown			
207	Charles Hafey	50.00	25.00	15.00
208	Unknown			
209	Unknown			
210	Unknown			

NOTE: A card number in parentheses ( ) indicates the set is unnumbered.

1934 R309-1
Goudey Premiums

Consisting of just four unnumbered cards, this set of black and white photos was printed on heavy cardboard and issued as a premium by the Goudey Gum Co. in 1934. The cards measure 5-1/2" by 8-5/16" and were accented with a gold, picture-frame border and an easel on the back.

	NR MT	EX	VG
Complete Set:	4500.00	2250.00	1350.
Common Player:	800.00	400.00	240.00
(1) American League All-Stars of 1933	800.00	400.00	240.00
(2) National League All-Stars of 1933	800.00	400.00	240.00
(3) "Worlds Champions 1933" (New York Giants)	1000.00	500.00	300.00
(4) George Herman (Babe) Ruth	1800.00	900.00	540.00

A player's name in italic indicates a rookie card. An (FC) indicates a player's first card for that particular card company.

1935 R309-2
Goudey Premiums

The 18 glossy, black-and-white photos in this set, issued as a premium by Goudey in 1935, measure 5-1/2" by 9", and were printed on thin paper. The unnumbered set includes three team photos and 15 players, whose names are written in script in the "wide pen" style by Goudey in other issues.

		NR MT	EX	VG
Complete Set:		2600.00	1300.00	780.00
Common Player:		110.00	55.00	33.00
(1)	Elden Auker	110.00	55.00	33.00
(2)	Johnny Babich	110.00	55.00	33.00
(3)	Dick Bartell	110.00	55.00	33.00
(4)	Lester R. Bell	110.00	55.00	33.00
(5)	Wally Berger	110.00	55.00	33.00
(6)	Mickey Cochrane	200.00	100.00	60.00
(7)	Ervin Fox	110.00	55.00	33.00
(8)	Vernon Gomez	110.00	55.00	33.00
(9)	Leon "Goose" Goslin	200.00	100.00	60.00
(10)	Hank Greenberg	200.00	100.00	60.00
(11)	Oscar Melillo	110.00	55.00	33.00
(12)	Mel Ott	200.00	100.00	60.00
(13)	Schoolboy Rowe	110.00	55.00	33.00
(14)	Vito Tamulis	110.00	55.00	33.00
(15)	Gerald Walker	110.00	55.00	33.00
(16)	Boston Red Sox	150.00	75.00	45.00
(17)	Cleveland Indians	150.00	75.00	45.00
(18)	Washington Senators	150.00	75.00	45.00

1934 R310 Butterfinger

Cards in this 65-card set were available as a premium from Butterfinger and other candy products. The unnumbered cards measure approximately 7-3/4" by 9-3/4" and the heavy cardboard variety carry advertising for Butterfinger. The cards feature a player photo with facsimile autograph surrounded by an off-white border. The cards are found on either paper or heavy cardboard stock, with the cardboard versions commanding a price about triple that listed here. The Foxx card is found spelled both "Fox" and "Foxx."

		NR MT	EX	VG
Complete Set:		2000.00	1000.00	600.00
Common Player:		15.00	7.50	4.50
1	Earl Averill	30.00	15.00	9.00
2	Richard Bartell	15.00	7.50	4.50
3	Larry Benton	15.00	7.50	4.50
4	Walter Berger	15.00	7.50	4.50
5	Jim Bottomley	30.00	15.00	9.00
6	Ralph Boyle	15.00	7.50	4.50
7	Tex Carleton	15.00	7.50	4.50
8	Owen T. Carroll	15.00	7.50	4.50
9	Ben Chapman	15.00	7.50	4.50
10	Gordon "Mickey" Cochrane	30.00	15.00	9.00
11	James Collins	15.00	7.50	4.50
12	Joe Cronin	30.00	15.00	9.00
13	Alvin Crowder	15.00	7.50	4.50
14	Dizzy Dean	60.00	30.00	18.00
15	Paul Derringer	15.00	7.50	4.50
16	William Dickey	45.00	22.00	13.50
17	Leo Durocher	30.00	15.00	9.00
18	George Earnshaw	15.00	7.50	4.50
19	Richard Farrell	30.00	15.00	9.00
20	Lew Fonseca	15.00	7.50	4.50
21a	Jimmy Fox (name incorrect)	50.00	25.00	15.00
21b	Jimmy Foxx (name correct)	50.00	25.00	15.00
22	Benny Frey	15.00	7.50	4.50
23	Frankie Frisch	30.00	15.00	9.00
24	Lou Gehrig	200.00	100.00	60.00
25	Charles Gehringer	30.00	15.00	9.00
26	Vernon Gomez	30.00	15.00	9.00
27	Ray Grabowski	15.00	7.50	4.50
28	Robert Grove	45.00	22.00	13.50
29	George "Mule" Haas	15.00	7.50	4.50
30	"Chick" Hafey	30.00	15.00	9.00
31	Stanley Harris	30.00	15.00	9.00
32	J. Francis Hogan	15.00	7.50	4.50
33	Ed Holley	15.00	7.50	4.50
34	Rogers Hornsby	50.00	25.00	15.00
35	Waite Hoyt	30.00	15.00	9.00
36	Walter Johnson	55.00	27.00	16.50
37	Jim Jordan	15.00	7.50	4.50
38	Joe Kuhel	15.00	7.50	4.50

		NR MT	EX	VG
39	Hal Lee	15.00	7.50	4.50
40	Gus Mancuso	15.00	7.50	4.50
41	Henry Manush	30.00	15.00	9.00
42	Fred Marberry	15.00	7.50	4.50
43	Pepper Martin	20.00	10.00	6.00
44	Oscar Melillo	15.00	7.50	4.50
45	Johnny Moore	15.00	7.50	4.50
46	Joe Morrissey	15.00	7.50	4.50
47	Joe Mowrey	15.00	7.50	4.50
48	Bob O'Farrell	15.00	7.50	4.50
49	Melvin Ott	40.00	20.00	12.00
50	Monte Pearson	15.00	7.50	4.50
51	Carl Reynolds	15.00	7.50	4.50
52	Charles Ruffing	30.00	15.00	9.00
53	Babe Ruth	250.00	125.00	75.00
54	John "Blondy" Ryan	15.00	7.50	4.50
55	Al Simmons	30.00	15.00	9.00
56	Al Spohrer	15.00	7.50	4.50
57	Gus Suhr	15.00	7.50	4.50
58	Steve Swetonic	15.00	7.50	4.50
59	Dazzy Vance	30.00	15.00	9.00
60	Joe Vosmik	15.00	7.50	4.50
61	Lloyd Waner	30.00	15.00	9.00
62	Paul Waner	30.00	15.00	9.00
63	Sam West	15.00	7.50	4.50
64	Earl Whitehill	15.00	7.50	4.50
65	Jimmy Wilson	15.00	7.50	4.50

1936 R311 Glossy Finish

The cards in this 28-card set, which was available as a premium in 1936, measure 6" by 8" and were printed on a glossy cardboard. The photos are either black and white or sepia-toned and include a facsimile autograph. The unnumbered set includes individual players and team photos. The Boston Red Sox team card can be found in two varieties; one shows the sky above the building on the card's right side, while the other does not. Some of the cards are scarcer than others in the set and command a premium. Babe Ruth is featured on the Boston Braves team card.

		NR MT	EX	VG
	Complete Set:	1200.00	600.00	360.00
	Common Player:	18.00	9.00	5.50
(1)	Earl Averill	30.00	15.00	9.00
(2)	James L. "Jim" Bottomley	30.00	15.00	9.00
(3)	Gordon S. "Mickey" Cochrane	30.00	15.00	9.00
(4)	Joe Cronin	30.00	15.00	9.00
(5)	Jerome "Dizzy" Dean	50.00	25.00	15.00
(6)	Jimmy Dykes	20.00	10.00	6.00
(7)	Jimmy Foxx	45.00	22.00	13.50
(8)	Frankie Frisch	30.00	15.00	9.00
(9)	Henry "Hank" Greenberg	30.00	15.00	9.00
(10)	Mel Harder	18.00	9.00	5.50
(11)	Ken Keltner	18.00	9.00	5.50
(12)	Pepper Martin	50.00	25.00	15.00
(13)	Lynwood "Schoolboy" Rowe	18.00	9.00	5.50
(14)	William "Bill" Terry	35.00	17.50	10.50
(15)	Harold "Pie" Traynor	30.00	15.00	9.00
(16)	American League All-Stars - 1935	50.00	25.00	15.00
(17)	American League Pennant Winners - 1934 (Detroit Tigers)	30.00	15.00	9.00
(18)	Boston Braves - 1935	200.00	100.00	60.00

		NR MT	EX	VG
(19)	Boston Red Sox	30.00	15.00	9.00
(20)	Brooklyn Dodgers - 1935	100.00	50.00	30.00
(21)	Chicago White Sox - 1935	30.00	15.00	9.00
(22)	Columbus Red Birds (1934 Pennant Winners of American Association)	20.00	10.00	6.00
(23)	National League All-Stars - 1934	50.00	25.00	15.00
(24)	National League Champions - 1935 (Chicago Cubs)	30.00	15.00	9.00
(25)	New York Yankees - 1935	150.00	75.00	45.00
(26)	Pittsburgh Pirates - 1935	30.00	15.00	9.00
(27)	St. Louis Browns - 1935	30.00	15.00	9.00
(28)	The World Champions, 1934 (St. Louis Cardinals)	30.00	15.00	9.00

A player's name in *italic* indicates a rookie card. An (FC) indicates a player's first card for that particular card company.

1936 R311 Leather Finish

This set of 15 unnumbered cards, issued as a premium in 1936, is distinctive because of its uneven, leather-like surface. The cards measure 6" by 8" and display a facsimilie autograph on the black and white photo surrounded by a plain border. The cards are unnumbered and include individual player photos, multi-player photos and team photos of the 1935 pennant winners.

		NR MT	EX	VG
	Complete Set:	1000.00	500.00	300.00
	Common Player:	20.00	10.00	6.00
(1)	Frank Crosetti, Joe DiMaggio, Tony Lazzeri	225.00	112.00	67.00
(2)	Paul Derringer	20.00	10.00	6.00
(3)	Wes Ferrell	20.00	10.00	6.00
(4)	Jimmy Foxx	80.00	40.00	24.00
(5)	Charlie Gehringer	40.00	20.00	12.00
(6)	Mel Harder	20.00	10.00	6.00
(7)	Gabby Hartnett	40.00	20.00	12.00
(8)	Rogers Hornsby	80.00	40.00	24.00
(9)	Connie Mack	55.00	27.00	16.50
(10)	Van Mungo	20.00	10.00	6.00
(11)	Steve O'Neill	20.00	10.00	6.00
(12)	Charles Ruffing	40.00	20.00	12.00
(13)	Arky Vaughan, Honus Wagner	80.00	40.00	24.00
(14)	American League Pennant Winners - 1935 (Detroit Tigers)	30.00	15.00	9.00
(15)	National League Pennant Winners - 1935 (Chicago Cubs)	30.00	15.00	9.00

1936 R312

The 50 cards in this set are black and white photos that have been tinted in soft pastel colors. The set includes 25 individual player portraits, 14 multi-player cards and 11 action photos. Six of the action photos include facsimilie autographs, while the other five have printed legends. The Allen card is more scarce than the others in the set.

		NR MT	EX	VG
	Complete Set:	2200.00	1100.00	660.00
	Common Player:	20.00	10.00	6.00
(1)	John Thomas Allen	30.00	15.00	9.00

		NR MT	EX	VG
(2)	Nick Altrock, Al Schact	20.00	10.00	6.00
(3)	Ollie Bejma, Rolly Hemsley	20.00	10.00	6.00
(4)	Les Bell, Zeke Bonura	20.00	10.00	6.00
(5)	Cy Blanton	20.00	10.00	6.00
(6)	Cliff Bolton, Earl Whitehill	20.00	10.00	6.00
(7)	Frenchy Bordagaray, George Earnshaw	20.00	10.00	6.00
(8)	Mace Brown	20.00	10.00	6.00
(9)	Dolph Camilli	20.00	10.00	6.00
(10)	Phil Cavaretta (Cavarretta), Frank Demaree, Augie Galan, Stan Hack, Gabby Hartnett, Billy Herman, Billy Jurges, Chuck Klein, Fred Lindstrom	40.00	20.00	12.00
(11)	Phil Cavaretta (Cavarretta), Stan Hack, Billy Herman, Billy Jurges	25.00	12.50	7.50
(12)	Gordon Cochrane	40.00	20.00	12.00
(13)	Jim Collins, Stan Hack	20.00	10.00	6.00
(14)	Rip Collins	20.00	10.00	6.00
(15)	Joe Cronin, Buckey Harris (Bucky)	40.00	20.00	12.00
(16)	Alvin Crowder	20.00	10.00	6.00
(17)	Kiki Cuyler	40.00	20.00	12.00
(18)	Kiki Cuyler, Tris Speaker, Danny Taylor	40.00	20.00	12.00
(19)	"Bill" Dickey	20.00	10.00	6.00
(20)	Joe DiMagio (DiMaggio)	350.00	175.00	105.00
(21)	"Chas." Dressen	20.00	10.00	6.00
(22)	Rick Ferrell, Russ Van Atta	20.00	10.00	6.00
(23)	Pete Fox, Goose Goslin, "Jo Jo" White	35.00	17.50	10.50
(24)	Jimmey Foxx (Jimmie), Luke Sewell	60.00	30.00	18.00
(25)	Benny Frey	20.00	10.00	6.00
(26)	Augie Galan, "Pie" Traynor	35.00	17.50	10.50
(27)	Lefty Gomez, Myril Hoag	35.00	17.50	10.50
(28)	"Hank" Greenberg	40.00	20.00	12.00
(29)	Lefty Grove, Connie Mack	80.00	40.00	24.00
(30)	Muel Haas (Mule), Mike Kreevich, Dixie Walker	20.00	10.00	6.00
(31)	Mel Harder	20.00	10.00	6.00
(32)	Gabby Hartnett (Mickey Cochrane, Frank Demaree, Ernie Quigley (ump) in photo)	35.00	17.50	10.50
(33)	Gabby Hartnett, Lonnie Warnecke (Warneke)	30.00	15.00	9.00
(34)	Roger Hornsby (Rogers)	80.00	40.00	24.00
(35)	Rogers Hornsby, Allen Sothoren	40.00	20.00	12.00
(36)	Ernie Lombardi	40.00	20.00	12.00
(37)	Al Lopez	40.00	20.00	12.00
(38)	Pepper Martin	25.00	12.50	7.50
(39)	"Johnny" Mize	40.00	20.00	12.00
(40)	Van L. Mungo	20.00	10.00	6.00
(41)	Bud Parmelee	20.00	10.00	6.00
(42)	Schoolboy Rowe	20.00	10.00	6.00
(43)	Chas. Ruffing	40.00	20.00	12.00
(44)	Eugene Schott	20.00	10.00	6.00
(45)	Casey Stengel	150.00	75.00	45.00
(46)	Bill Sullivan	20.00	10.00	6.00
(47)	Bill Swift	20.00	10.00	6.00
(48)	Floyd Vaughan, Hans Wagner	60.00	30.00	18.00
(49)	L. Waner, P. Waner, Big Jim Weaver	45.00	23.00	13.50
(50)	Ralph Winegarner	20.00	10.00	6.00

NOTE: A card number in parentheses ( ) indicates the set is unnumbered.

1936 R313

Issued in 1936 by the National Chicle Company, this set consists of 120 cards, each measuring 3-1/4" by 5-3/8". The black and white cards are blank-backed and unnumbered. Although issued by National Chicle, the name of the company does not appear on the cards. The set includes individual player portraits with facsimilie autographs, multi-player cards and action photos. The cards, known in the hobby as "Fine Pen" because of the thin style of writing used for the facsimilie autographs, were originally available as an in-store premium.

		NR MT	EX	VG
Complete Set:		2000.00	1000.00	600.00
Common Player:		10.00	5.00	3.00
(1)	Melo Almada	10.00	5.00	3.00
(2)	Nick Altrock, Al Schacht	10.00	5.00	3.00
(3)	Paul Andrews	10.00	5.00	3.00
(4)	Elden Auker (Eldon)	10.00	5.00	3.00
(5)	Earl Averill	16.00	8.00	4.75
(6)	John Babich, James Bucher	10.00	5.00	3.00
(7)	Jim Becher (Bucher)	10.00	5.00	3.00
(8)	Moe Berg	12.00	6.00	3.50
(9)	Walter Berger	10.00	5.00	3.00
(10)	Charles Berry	10.00	5.00	3.00
(11)	Ralph Birkhofer (Birkofer)	10.00	5.00	3.00
(12)	"Cy" Blanton	10.00	5.00	3.00
(13)	O. Bluege	10.00	5.00	3.00
(14)	Cliff Bolton	10.00	5.00	3.00
(15)	Zeke Bonura	10.00	5.00	3.00
(16)	Stan Bordagaray, George Earnshaw	10.00	5.00	3.00
(17)	Jim Bottomley, Charley Gelbert	14.00	7.00	4.25
(18)	Thos. Bridges	10.00	5.00	3.00
(19)	Sam Byrd	10.00	5.00	3.00
(20)	Dolph Camilli	10.00	5.00	3.00
(21)	Dolph Camilli, Billy Jurges	10.00	5.00	3.00
(22)	Bruce Campbell	10.00	5.00	3.00
(23)	Walter "Kit" Carson	10.00	5.00	3.00
(24)	Ben Chapman	10.00	5.00	3.00
(25)	Harland Clift, Luke Sewell	10.00	5.00	3.00
(26)	Mickey Cochrane, Jimmy Fox (Foxx), Al Simmons	20.00	10.00	6.00
(27)	"Rip" Collins	10.00	5.00	3.00
(28)	Joe Cronin	16.00	8.00	4.75
(29)	Frank Crossetti (Crosetti)	12.00	6.00	3.50
(30)	Frank Crosetti, Jimmy Dykes	12.00	6.00	3.50
(31)	Kiki Cuyler, Gabby Hartnett	20.00	10.00	6.00
(32)	Paul Derringer	10.00	5.00	3.00
(33)	Bill Dickey, Hank Greenberg	25.00	12.50	7.50
(34)	Bill Dietrich	10.00	5.00	3.00
(35)	Joe DiMaggio, Hank Erickson	175.00	87.00	52.00
(36)	Carl Doyle	10.00	5.00	3.00
(37)	Charles Dressen, Bill Myers	10.00	5.00	3.00
(38)	Jimmie Dykes	12.00	6.00	3.50
(39)	Rick Ferrell, Wess Ferrell (Wes)	10.00	5.00	3.00
(40)	Pete Fox	10.00	5.00	3.00
(41)	Frankie Frisch	20.00	10.00	6.00
(42)	Milton Galatzer	10.00	5.00	3.00
(43)	Chas. Gehringer	20.00	10.00	6.00
(44)	Charley Gelbert	10.00	5.00	3.00
(45)	Joe Glenn	10.00	5.00	3.00
(46)	Jose Gomez	10.00	5.00	3.00
(47)	Lefty Gomez, Red Ruffing	20.00	10.00	6.00
(48)	Vernon Gomez	20.00	10.00	6.00
(49)	Leon Goslin	20.00	10.00	6.00

		NR MT	EX	VG
(50)	Hank Gowdy	10.00	5.00	3.00
(51)	"Hank" Greenberg	20.00	10.00	6.00
(52)	"Lefty" Grove	20.00	10.00	6.00
(53)	Stan Hack	10.00	5.00	3.00
(54)	Odell Hale	10.00	5.00	3.00
(55)	Wild Bill Hallahan	10.00	5.00	3.00
(56)	Mel Harder	10.00	5.00	3.00
(57)	Stanley Bucky Harriss (Harris)	16.00	8.00	4.75
(58)	Gabby Hartnett, Rip Radcliff	14.00	7.00	4.25
(59)	Gabby Hartnett, L. Waner	20.00	10.00	6.00
(60)	Gabby Hartnett, Lon Warnecke (Warneke)			
		14.00	7.00	4.25
(61)	Buddy Hassett	10.00	5.00	3.00
(62)	Babe Herman	12.00	6.00	3.50
(63)	Frank Higgins	10.00	5.00	3.00
(64)	Oral C. Hildebrand	10.00	5.00	3.00
(65)	Myril Hoag	10.00	5.00	3.00
(66)	Rogers Hornsby	25.00	12.50	7.50
(67)	Waite Hoyt	16.00	8.00	4.75
(68)	Willis G. Hudlin	10.00	5.00	3.00
(69)	"Woody" Jensen	10.00	5.00	3.00
(70)	Woody Jenson (Jensen)	10.00	5.00	3.00
(71)	William Knickerbocker	10.00	5.00	3.00
(72)	Joseph Kuhel	10.00	5.00	3.00
(73)	Cookie Lavagetto	12.00	6.00	3.50
(74)	Thornton Lee	10.00	5.00	3.00
(75)	Ernie Lombardi	16.00	8.00	4.75
(76)	Red Lucas	10.00	5.00	3.00
(77)	Connie Mack, John McGraw	40.00	20.00	12.00
(78)	Pepper Martin	12.00	6.00	3.50
(79)	George McQuinn	10.00	5.00	3.00
(80)	George McQuinn, Lee Stine	10.00	5.00	3.00
(81)	Joe Medwick	16.00	8.00	4.75
(82)	Oscar Melillo	10.00	5.00	3.00
(83)	"Buddy" Meyer	10.00	5.00	3.00
(84)	Randy Moore	10.00	5.00	3.00
(85)	T. Moore, Jimmie Wilson	10.00	5.00	3.00
(86)	Wallace Moses	10.00	5.00	3.00
(87)	V. Mungo	10.00	5.00	3.00
(88)	Lamar Newsom	10.00	5.00	3.00
(89)	Lewis "Buck" Newsom (Louis)	10.00	5.00	3.00
(90)	Steve O'Neill	10.00	5.00	3.00
(91)	Tommie Padden	10.00	5.00	3.00
(92)	E. Babe Philips (Phelps)	10.00	5.00	3.00
(93)	Bill Rogel (Rogell)	10.00	5.00	3.00
(94)	Lynn "Schoolboy" Rowe	10.00	5.00	3.00
(95)	Luke Sewell	10.00	5.00	3.00
(96)	Al Simmons	20.00	10.00	6.00
(97)	Casey Stengel	40.00	20.00	12.00
(98)	Bill Swift	10.00	5.00	3.00
(99)	Cecil Travis	10.00	5.00	3.00
(100)	"Pie" Traynor	20.00	10.00	6.00
(101)	William Urbansky (Urbanski)	10.00	5.00	3.00
(102)	Arky Vaughn (Vaughan)	20.00	10.00	6.00
(103)	Joe Vosmik	10.00	5.00	3.00
(104)	Honus Wagner	40.00	20.00	12.00
(105)	Rube Walberg	10.00	5.00	3.00
(106)	Bill Walker	10.00	5.00	3.00
(107)	Gerald Walker	10.00	5.00	3.00
(108)	L. Waner, P. Waner, Big Jim Weaver			
		20.00	10.00	6.00
(109)	George Washington	10.00	5.00	3.00
(110)	Bill Werber	10.00	5.00	3.00
(111)	Sam West	10.00	5.00	3.00
(112)	Pinkey Whitney	10.00	5.00	3.00
(113)	Vernon Wiltshere (Wilshere)	10.00	5.00	3.00
(114)	"Pep" Young	10.00	5.00	3.00
(115)	Chicago White Sox 1936	10.00	5.00	3.00
(116)	Fence Busters	10.00	5.00	3.00
(117)	Talking It Over (Leo Durocher)	12.00	6.00	3.50
(118)	There She Goes! Chicago City Series			
		10.00	5.00	3.00
(119)	Ump Says No - Cleveland vs. Detroit			
		10.00	5.00	3.00
(120)	World Series 1935 (Phil Cavarretta, Goose Goslin, Lon Warneke)	12.00	6.00	3.50

1936 R314

Issued in 1936 by the Goudey Gum Company, these cards are known in the hobby as "Wide Pens" because of the distinctive, thick style of writing used for the facsimilie autographs. The black and white, unnumbered cards measure 3-1/4" by 5-1/2" and are found in several different types. Some cards have borders, while others do not, and cards are found both with and without a "Litho USA" line along the

bottom. Some cards in the set are found on a creamy paper stock. The set includes both major leaguers and players from the Canadian minor league teams in Montreal and Toronto. The cards were originally available as an in-store premium.

		NR MT	EX	VG
Complete Set:		1750.00	875.00	525.00
Common Player:		10.00	5.00	3.00
(1)	Ethan Allen	10.00	5.00	3.00
(2)	Earl Averill	16.00	8.00	4.75
(3)	Dick Bartell (portrait)	10.00	5.00	3.00
(4)	Dick Bartell (sliding)	10.00	5.00	3.00
(5)	Walter Berger	10.00	5.00	3.00
(6)	Geo. Blaeholder	10.00	5.00	3.00
(7)	"Cy" Blanton	10.00	5.00	3.00
(8)	"Cliff" Bolton	10.00	5.00	3.00
(9)	Stan Bordagaray	10.00	5.00	3.00
(10)	Tommy Bridges	10.00	5.00	3.00
(11)	Bill Brubaker	10.00	5.00	3.00
(12)	Sam Byrd	10.00	5.00	3.00
(13)	Dolph Camilli	10.00	5.00	3.00
(14)	Clydell Castleman (pitching)	10.00	5.00	3.00
(15)	Clydell Castleman (portrait)	10.00	5.00	3.00
(16)	"Phil" Cavaretta (Cavarretta)	10.00	5.00	3.00
(17)	Ben Chapman, Bill Werber	10.00	5.00	3.00
(18)	Mickey Cochrane	20.00	10.00	6.00
(19)	Earl Coombs (Earle Combs)	16.00	8.00	4.75
(20)	Joe Coscarart	10.00	5.00	3.00
(21)	Joe Cronin	16.00	8.00	4.75
(22)	Frank Crosetti	12.00	6.00	3.50
(23)	Tony Cuccinello	10.00	5.00	3.00
(24)	"Kiki" Cuyler	16.00	8.00	4.75
(25)	Curt Davis	10.00	5.00	3.00
(26)	Virgil Davis	10.00	5.00	3.00
(27)	Paul Derringer	10.00	5.00	3.00
(28)	Bill Dickey	20.00	10.00	6.00
(29)	Joe DiMaggio, Joe McCarthy	90.00	45.00	27.00
(30)	Jimmy Dykes	12.00	6.00	3.50
(31)	Rick Ferrell	16.00	8.00	4.75
(32)	Wes Ferrell	10.00	5.00	3.00
(33)	Rick Ferrell, Wes Ferrell	14.00	7.00	4.25
(34)	Lou Finney	10.00	5.00	3.00
(35)	Erwin "Pete" Fox	10.00	5.00	3.00
(36)	Tony Freitas	10.00	5.00	3.00
(37)	Lonnie Frey	10.00	5.00	3.00
(38)	Frankie Frisch	20.00	10.00	6.00
(39)	"Augie" Galan	10.00	5.00	3.00
(40)	Charles Gehringer	20.00	10.00	6.00
(41)	Charlie Gelbert	10.00	5.00	3.00
(42)	"Lefty" Gomez	20.00	10.00	6.00
(43)	"Goose" Goslin	20.00	10.00	6.00
(44)	Earl Grace	10.00	5.00	3.00
(45)	Hank Greenberg	20.00	10.00	6.00
(46)	"Mule" Haas	10.00	5.00	3.00
(47)	Odell Hale	10.00	5.00	3.00
(48)	Bill Hallahan	10.00	5.00	3.00
(49)	"Mel" Harder	10.00	5.00	3.00
(50)	"Bucky" Harris	16.00	8.00	4.75
(51)	"Gabby" Hartnett	20.00	10.00	6.00
(52)	Ray Hayworth	10.00	5.00	3.00
(53)	"Rollie" Hemsley	10.00	5.00	3.00
(54)	Babe Herman	12.00	6.00	3.50
(55)	Frank Higgins	10.00	5.00	3.00
(56)	Oral Hildebrand	10.00	5.00	3.00
(57)	Myril Hoag	10.00	5.00	3.00
(58)	Waite Hoyt	16.00	8.00	4.75
(59)	Woody Jensen	10.00	5.00	3.00
(60)	Bob Johnson	10.00	5.00	3.00

		NR MT	EX	VG
(61)	"Buck" Jordan	10.00	5.00	3.00
(62)	Alex Kampouris	10.00	5.00	3.00
(63)	"Chuck" Klein	20.00	10.00	6.00
(64)	Joe Kuhel	10.00	5.00	3.00
(65)	Lyn Lary	10.00	5.00	3.00
(66)	Harry Lavagetto	12.00	6.00	3.50
(67)	Sam Leslie	10.00	5.00	3.00
(68)	Freddie Lindstrom	16.00	8.00	4.75
(69)	Lombardi	16.00	8.00	4.75
(70)	"Al" Lopez	16.00	8.00	4.75
(71)	Dan MacFayden	10.00	5.00	3.00
(72)	John Marcum	10.00	5.00	3.00
(73)	"Pepper" Martin	14.00	7.00	4.25
(74)	Eric McNair	10.00	5.00	3.00
(75)	"Ducky" Medwick	16.00	8.00	4.75
(76)	Gene Moore	10.00	5.00	3.00
(77)	Randy Moore	10.00	5.00	3.00
(78)	Terry Moore	10.00	5.00	3.00
(79)	Edward Moriarty	10.00	5.00	3.00
(80)	"Wally" Moses	10.00	5.00	3.00
(81)	"Buddy" Myer	10.00	5.00	3.00
(82)	"Buck" Newsom	10.00	5.00	3.00
(83)	Steve O'Neill, Frank Pytlak	10.00	5.00	3.00
(84)	Fred Ostermueller	10.00	5.00	3.00
(85)	Marvin Owen	10.00	5.00	3.00
(86)	Tommy Padden	10.00	5.00	3.00
(87)	Ray Pepper	10.00	5.00	3.00
(88)	Tony Piet	10.00	5.00	3.00
(89)	"Rabbit" Pytlak	10.00	5.00	3.00
(90)	"Rip" Radcliff	10.00	5.00	3.00
(91)	Bobby Reis	10.00	5.00	3.00
(92)	"Lew" Riggs	10.00	5.00	3.00
(93)	Bill Rogell	10.00	5.00	3.00
(94)	"Red" Rolfe	12.00	6.00	3.50
(95)	"Schoolboy" Rowe	10.00	5.00	3.00
(96)	Al Schacht	10.00	5.00	3.00
(97)	"Luke" Sewell	10.00	5.00	3.00
(98)	Al Simmons	10.00	5.00	3.00
(99)	John Stone	10.00	5.00	3.00
(100)	Gus Suhr	10.00	5.00	3.00
(101)	Joe Sullivan	10.00	5.00	3.00
(102)	Bill Swift	10.00	5.00	3.00
(103)	Vito Tamulis	10.00	5.00	3.00
(104)	Dan Taylor	10.00	5.00	3.00
(105)	Cecil Travis	10.00	5.00	3.00
(106)	Hal Trosky	10.00	5.00	3.00
(107)	"Bill" Urbanski	10.00	5.00	3.00
(108)	Russ Van Atta	10.00	5.00	3.00
(109)	"Arky" Vaughan	20.00	10.00	6.00
(110)	Gerald Walker	10.00	5.00	3.00
(111)	"Buck" Walter (Bucky)	10.00	5.00	3.00
(112)	Lloyd Waner	20.00	10.00	6.00
(113)	Paul Waner	20.00	10.00	6.00
(114)	"Lon" Warneke	10.00	5.00	3.00
(115)	Warstler	10.00	5.00	3.00
(116)	Bill Werber	10.00	5.00	3.00
(117)	"Jo Jo" White	10.00	5.00	3.00
(118)	Burgess Whitehead	10.00	5.00	3.00
(119)	John Whitehead	10.00	5.00	3.00
(120)	Whitlow Wyatt	10.00	5.00	3.00

be found with the player's name and team inside a white box in a lower corner; other cards add the position and team in small type in the bottom border; a third type has the player's name in hand lettering near the bottom; and the final type includes the position and team printed in small type along the bottom border.

		NR MT	EX	VG
Complete Set:		750.00	375.00	225.00
Common Player:		10.00	5.00	3.00
(1)	Earl Averill	20.00	10.00	6.00
(2)	"Benny" Bengough	10.00	5.00	3.00
(3)	Laurence Benton (Lawrence)	10.00	5.00	3.00
(4)	"Max" Bishop	10.00	5.00	3.00
(5)	"Sunny Jim" Bottomley	20.00	10.00	6.00
(6)	Bill Cissell	10.00	5.00	3.00
(7)	Bud Clancey (Clancy)	10.00	5.00	3.00
(8)	"Freddy" Fitzsimmons	10.00	5.00	3.00
(9)	"Jimmy" Foxx	30.00	15.00	9.00
(10)	"Johnny" Fredericks (Frederick)	10.00	5.00	3.00
(11)	Frank Frisch	25.00	12.50	7.50
(12)	"Lou" Gehrig	200.00	100.00	60.00
(13)	"Goose" Goslin	20.00	10.00	6.00
(14)	Burleigh Grimes	20.00	10.00	6.00
(15)	"Lefty" Grove	25.00	12.50	7.50
(16)	"Mule" Haas	10.00	5.00	3.00
(17)	Harvey Hendricks (Hendrick)	10.00	5.00	3.00
(18)	"Babe" Herman	12.00	6.00	3.50
(19)	"Roger" Hornsby (Rogers)	30.00	15.00	9.00
(20)	Karl Hubbell (Carl)	20.00	10.00	6.00
(21)	"Stonewall" Jackson	20.00	10.00	6.00
(22)	Smead Jolley	10.00	5.00	3.00
(23)	"Chuck" Klein	20.00	10.00	6.00
(24)	Mark Koenig	10.00	5.00	3.00
(25)	"Tony" Lazerri (Lazzeri)	15.00	7.50	4.50
(26)	Fred Leach	10.00	5.00	3.00
(27)	"Freddy" Lindstrom	20.00	10.00	6.00
(28)	Fred Marberry	10.00	5.00	3.00
(29)	"Bing" Miller	10.00	5.00	3.00
(30)	"Bob" O'Farrell	10.00	5.00	3.00
(31)	Frank O'Doul	12.00	6.00	3.50
(32)	"Herbie" Pennock	20.00	10.00	6.00
(33)	George Pipgras	10.00	5.00	3.00
(34)	Andrew Reese	10.00	5.00	3.00
(35)	Carl Reynolds	10.00	5.00	3.00
(36)	"Babe" Ruth	200.00	100.00	60.00
(37)	"Bob" Shawkey	12.00	6.00	3.50
(38)	Art Shires	10.00	5.00	3.00
(39)	"Al" Simmons	20.00	10.00	6.00
(40)	"Riggs" Stephenson	12.00	6.00	3.50
(41)	"Bill" Terry	25.00	12.50	7.50
(42)	"Pie" Traynor	20.00	10.00	6.00
(43)	"Dazzy" Vance	20.00	10.00	6.00
(44)	Paul Waner	20.00	10.00	6.00
(45)	"Hack" Wilson	20.00	10.00	6.00
(46)	"Tom" Zachary	10.00	5.00	3.00

1929 R316

This set of 101 unnumbered cards was issued in 1929 and measures 3-1/2" by 4-1/2". The cards feature black-and-white photos with the player's name printed in script near the bottom of the photo. The backs of the cards are blank. Four of the cards (Hadley, Haines, Siebold and Todt) are considered to be scarcer than the rest of the set.

1930 R315

Issued in 1928, the 58 cards in this set can be found in either black and white or yellow and black. The unnumbered, blank-backed cards measure 3-1/4" by 5-1/4" and feature both portraits and action photos. THe set includes several different types of cards, depending in the caption. Cards can

		NR MT	EX	VG
Complete Set:		2750.00	1375.00	825.00
Common Player:		15.00	7.50	4.50
(1)	Dale Alexander	15.00	7.50	4.50
(2)	Ethan N. Allen	15.00	7.50	4.50
(3)	Larry Benton	15.00	7.50	4.50
(4)	Moe Berg	20.00	10.00	6.00
(5)	Max Bishop	15.00	7.50	4.50
(6)	Del Bissonette	15.00	7.50	4.50
(7)	Lucerne A. Blue	15.00	7.50	4.50
(8)	James Bottomley	30.00	15.00	9.00
(9)	Guy T. Bush	15.00	7.50	4.50
(10)	Harold G. Carlson	15.00	7.50	4.50
(11)	Owen Carroll	15.00	7.50	4.50
(12)	Chalmers W. Cissell (Chalmer)	15.00	7.50	4.50
(13)	Earl Combs	30.00	15.00	9.00
(14)	Hugh M. Critz	15.00	7.50	4.50
(15)	H.J. DeBerry	15.00	7.50	4.50
(16)	Pete Donohue	15.00	7.50	4.50
(17)	Taylor Douthit	15.00	7.50	4.50
(18)	Chas. W. Dressen	18.00	9.00	5.50
(19)	Jimmy Dykes	18.00	9.00	5.50
(20)	Howard Ehmke	15.00	7.50	4.50
(21)	Elwood English	15.00	7.50	4.50
(22)	Urban Faber	30.00	15.00	9.00
(23)	Fred Fitzsimmons	15.00	7.50	4.50
(24)	Lewis A. Fonseca	15.00	7.50	4.50
(25)	Horace H. Ford	15.00	7.50	4.50
(26)	Jimmy Foxx	40.00	20.00	12.00
(27)	Frank Frisch	30.00	15.00	9.00
(28)	Lou Gehrig	225.00	112.00	67.00
(29)	Charles Gehringer	30.00	15.00	9.00
(30)	Leon Goslin	30.00	15.00	9.00
(31)	George Grantham	15.00	7.50	4.50
(32)	Burleigh Grimes	30.00	15.00	9.00
(33)	Robert Grove	35.00	17.50	10.50
(34)	Bump Hadley	100.00	50.00	30.00
(35)	Charlie Hafey	30.00	15.00	9.00
(36)	Jesse J. Haines	100.00	50.00	30.00
(37)	Harvey Hendrick	15.00	7.50	4.50
(38)	Floyd C. Herman	18.00	9.00	5.50
(39)	Andy High	15.00	7.50	4.50
(40)	Urban J. Hodapp	15.00	7.50	4.50
(41)	Frank Hogan	15.00	7.50	4.50
(42)	Rogers Hornsby	40.00	20.00	12.00
(43)	Waite Hoyt	30.00	15.00	9.00
(44)	Willis Hudlin	15.00	7.50	4.50
(45)	Frank O. Hurst	15.00	7.50	4.50
(46)	Charlie Jamieson	15.00	7.50	4.50
(47)	Roy C. Johnson	15.00	7.50	4.50
(48)	Percy Jones	15.00	7.50	4.50
(49)	Sam Jones	15.00	7.50	4.50
(50)	Joseph Judge	15.00	7.50	4.50
(51)	Willie Kamm	15.00	7.50	4.50
(52)	Charles Klein	30.00	15.00	9.00
(53)	Mark Koenig	15.00	7.50	4.50
(54)	Ralph Kress	15.00	7.50	4.50
(55)	Fred M. Leach	15.00	7.50	4.50
(56)	Fred Lindstrom	30.00	15.00	9.00
(57)	Ad Liska	15.00	7.50	4.50
(58)	Fred Lucas (Red)	15.00	7.50	4.50
(59)	Fred Maguire	15.00	7.50	4.50
(60)	Perce L. Malone	15.00	7.50	4.50
(61)	Harry Manush (Henry)	30.00	15.00	9.00
(62)	Walter Maranville	30.00	15.00	9.00
(63)	Douglas McWeeney (McWeeny)	15.00	7.50	4.50
(64)	Oscar Melillo	15.00	7.50	4.50
(65)	Ed "Bing" Miller	15.00	7.50	4.50
(66)	Frank O'Doul	18.00	9.00	5.50
(67)	Melvin Ott	35.00	17.50	10.50
(68)	Herbert Pennock	30.00	15.00	9.00
(69)	William W. Regan	15.00	7.50	4.50
(70)	Harry F. Rice	15.00	7.50	4.50
(71)	Sam Rice	30.00	15.00	9.00
(72)	Lance Richbourgh (Richbourg)	15.00	7.50	4.50
(73)	Eddie Rommel	15.00	7.50	4.50
(74)	Chas. H. Root	15.00	7.50	4.50
(75)	Ed Roush	30.00	15.00	9.00
(76)	Harold Ruel (Herold)	15.00	7.50	4.50
(77)	Charles Ruffing	30.00	15.00	9.00
(78)	Jack Russell	15.00	7.50	4.50
(79)	Babe Ruth	225.00	112.00	67.00
(80)	Fred Schulte	15.00	7.50	4.50
(81)	Harry Seibold	100.00	50.00	30.00
(82)	Joe Sewell	30.00	15.00	9.00
(83)	Luke Sewell	15.00	7.50	4.50
(84)	Art Shires	15.00	7.50	4.50
(85)	Al Simmons	30.00	15.00	9.00
(86)	Bob Smith	15.00	7.50	4.50

		NR MT	EX	VG
(87)	Riggs Stephenson	18.00	9.00	5.50
(88)	Wm. H. Terry	35.00	17.50	10.50
(89)	Alphonse Thomas	15.00	7.50	4.50
(90)	Lafayette F. Thompson	15.00	7.50	4.50
(91)	Phil Todt	100.00	50.00	30.00
(92)	Harold J. Traynor	30.00	15.00	9.00
(93)	Dazzy Vance	30.00	15.00	9.00
(94)	Lloyd Waner	30.00	15.00	9.00
(95)	Paul Waner	30.00	15.00	9.00
(96)	Jimmy Welsh	15.00	7.50	4.50
(97)	Earl Whitehill	15.00	7.50	4.50
(98)	A.C. Whitney	15.00	7.50	4.50
(99)	Claude Willoughby	15.00	7.50	4.50
(100)	Hack Wilson	30.00	15.00	9.00
(101)	Tom Zachary	15.00	7.50	4.50

1937 R326 Goudey Baseball Movies

Issued circa 1937, this set of "flip movies" was comprised of small (2" by 3") booklets whose pages produced a movie effect when flipped rapidly, similar to a penny arcade novelty popular at the time. There are 13 players in the set, each movie having two cleary labeled parts. The cover of the booklets identify the set as "Big League Baseball Movies." Issued by Goudey, they carry the American Card Catalog designation R326.

		NR MT	EX	VG
Complete Set:		1750.00	875.00	525.00
Common Player:		25.00	12.50	7.50
1a	John Irving Burns (Part 1)	25.00	12.50	7.50
1b	John Irving Burns (Part 2)	25.00	12.50	7.50
2a	Joe Vosmik (Part 1)	25.00	12.50	7.50
2b	Joe Vosmik (Part 2)	25.00	12.50	7.50
3a	Mel Ott (Part 1)	60.00	30.00	18.00
3b	Mel Ott (Part 2)	60.00	30.00	18.00
4a	Joe DiMaggio (Part 1)	350.00	175.00	105.00
4b	Joe DiMaggio (Part 2)	350.00	175.00	105.00
5a	Wally Moses (Part 1)	25.00	12.50	7.50
5b	Wally Moses (Part 2)	25.00	12.50	7.50
6a	Van Lingle Mungo (Part 1)	25.00	12.50	7.50
6b	Van Lingle Mungo (Part 2)	25.00	12.50	7.50
7a	Luke Appling (Part 1)	40.00	20.00	12.00
7b	Luke Appling (Part 2)	40.00	20.00	12.00
8a	Bob Feller (Part 1)	90.00	45.00	27.00
8b	Bob Feller (Part 2)	90.00	45.00	27.00
9a	Paul Derringer (Part 1)	25.00	12.50	7.50
9b	Paul Derringer (Part 2)	25.00	12.50	7.50
10a	Paul Waner (Part 1)	40.00	20.00	12.00
10b	Paul Waner (Part 2)	40.00	20.00	12.00
11a	Joe Medwick (Part 1)	40.00	20.00	12.00
11b	Joe Medwick (Part 2)	40.00	20.00	12.00
12a	James Emory Foxx (Part 1)	90.00	45.00	27.00
12b	James Emory Foxx (Part 2)	90.00	45.00	27.00
13a	Wally Berger (Part 1)	25.00	12.50	7.50
13b	Wally Berger (Part 2)	25.00	12.50	7.50

A player's name in italic type indicates a rookie card. An (FC) indicates a player's first card for that particular card company.

1935 R332 Schutter-Johnson

This 50-card set was issued by the Schutter-Johnson Candy Corp. of Chicago and Brooklyn circa 1930 and features drawings of major league players offering baseball playing tips. The cards measure 2-1/4" by 2-7/8". The drawings on the front are set against a red background while the backs are titled "Major League Secrets" and give the player's advice on some aspect of the game. The Scutter-Johnson name appears at the bottom.

		NR MT	EX	VG
	Complete Set:	3500.00	1750.00	1050.
	Common Player:	35.00	17.50	10.50
1	Al Simmons	50.00	25.00	15.00
2	Lloyd Waner	50.00	25.00	15.00
3	Kiki Cuyler	50.00	25.00	15.00
4	Frank Frisch	60.00	30.00	18.00
5	Chick Hafey	50.00	25.00	15.00
6	Bill Klem (umpire)	50.00	25.00	15.00
7	Rogers Hornsby	90.00	45.00	27.00
8	Carl Mays	35.00	17.50	10.50
9	Chas. Wrigley (umpire)	35.00	17.50	10.50
10	Christy Mathewson	90.00	45.00	27.00
11	Bill Dickey	70.00	35.00	21.00
12	Walter Berger	35.00	17.50	10.50
13	George Earnshaw	35.00	17.50	10.50
14	"Hack" Wilson	50.00	25.00	15.00
15	Charley Grimm	35.00	17.50	10.50
16	Lloyd Waner, Paul Waner	50.00	25.00	15.00
17	Chuck Klein	50.00	25.00	15.00
18	Woody English	35.00	17.50	10.50
19	Grover Alexander	70.00	35.00	21.00
20	Lou Gehrig	300.00	150.00	90.00
21	Wes Ferrell	35.00	17.50	10.50
22	Carl Hubbell	60.00	30.00	18.00
23	Pie Traynor	50.00	25.00	15.00
24	Gus Mancuso	35.00	17.50	10.50
25	Ben Cantwell	35.00	17.50	10.50
26	Babe Ruth	450.00	225.00	135.00
27	"Goose" Goslin	50.00	25.00	15.00
28	Earle Combs	50.00	25.00	15.00
29	"Kiki" Cuyler	50.00	25.00	15.00
30	Jimmy Wilson	35.00	17.50	10.50
31	Dizzy Dean	100.00	50.00	30.00
32	Mickey Cochrane	60.00	30.00	18.00
33	Ted Lyons	50.00	25.00	15.00
34	Si Johnson	35.00	17.50	10.50
35	Dizzy Dean	100.00	50.00	30.00
36	Pepper Martin	40.00	20.00	12.00
37	Joe Cronin	50.00	25.00	15.00
38	Gabby Hartnett	50.00	25.00	15.00
39	Oscar Melillo	35.00	17.50	10.50
40	Ben Chapman	35.00	17.50	10.50
41	John McGraw	70.00	35.00	21.00
42	Babe Ruth	250.00	125.00	75.00
43	"Red" Lucas	35.00	17.50	10.50
44	Charley Root	35.00	17.50	10.50
45	Dazzy Vance	50.00	25.00	15.00
46	Hugh Critz	35.00	17.50	10.50
47	"Firpo" Marberry	35.00	17.50	10.50
48	Grover Alexander	70.00	35.00	21.00
49	Lefty Grove	70.00	35.00	21.00
50	Heinie Meine	35.00	17.50	10.50

1932 R337

Issued circa 1932, little is known about the origin of this 24-card set, which is numbered from 401 through 424. The cards measure 2-5/16" by 2-13/16", and the design is similar to the M.P. & Co. sets with a crude drawing of the player on the front. The back of the card displays the card number at the top followed by the player's name, team and a brief write-up. Card numbers 403, 413, and 414 are missing and probably correspond to the three unnumbered cards in the set (Foxx, Johnson and Traynor).

		NR MT	EX	VG
	Complete Set:	1500.00	750.00	450.00
	Common Player:	35.00	17.50	10.50
401	Johnny Vergez	35.00	17.50	10.50
402	Babe Ruth	450.00	225.00	135.00
403	Not Issued			
404	George Pipgras	35.00	17.50	10.50
405	Bill Terry	60.00	30.00	18.00
406	George Connally	35.00	17.50	10.50
407	Watson Clark	35.00	17.50	10.50
408	"Lefty" Grove	70.00	35.00	21.00
409	Henry Johnson	35.00	17.50	10.50
410	Jimmy Dykes	35.00	17.50	10.50
411	Henry Hine Schuble	35.00	17.50	10.50
412	Bucky Harris	50.00	25.00	15.00
413	Not Issued			
414	Not Issued			
415	Al Simmons	50.00	25.00	15.00
416	Henry "Heinie" Manush	50.00	25.00	15.00
417	Glen Myatt	35.00	17.50	10.50
418	Babe Herman	40.00	20.00	12.00
419	Frank Frisch	60.00	30.00	18.00
420	Tony Lazzeri	40.00	20.00	12.00
421	Paul Waner	50.00	25.00	15.00
422	Jimmy Wilson	35.00	17.50	10.50
423	Charles Grimm	35.00	17.50	10.50
424	Dick Bartell	35.00	17.50	10.50
-----	Jimmy Fox (Foxx)	100.00	50.00	30.00
-----	Roy Johnson	35.00	17.50	10.50
-----	Pie Traynor	50.00	25.00	15.00

1934 R342 Goudey
Thum Movies

Assigned the American Card Catalog number R342, these 2" by 3" booklets are similar to the "Big League Baseball Movies" (R326) issued by Goudey circa 1937. The "Thum Movies" set consists of 13 players. The booklets are numbered on the top of the back page.

		NR MT	EX	VG
	Complete Set:	900.00	450.00	275.00
	Common Player:	35.00	17.50	10.50
1	John Irving Burns	35.00	17.50	10.50
2	Joe Vosmik	35.00	17.50	10.50
3	Mel Ott	80.00	40.00	24.00
4	Joe DiMaggio	300.00	150.00	90.00
5	Wally Moses	35.00	17.50	10.50
6	Van Lingle Mungo	35.00	17.50	10.50
7	Luke Appling	50.00	25.00	15.00
8	Bob Feller	80.00	40.00	24.00
9	Paul Derringer	35.00	17.50	10.50
10	Paul Waner	50.00	25.00	15.00
11	Joe Medwick	50.00	25.00	15.00
12	James Emory Foxx	80.00	40.00	24.00
13	Wally Berger	35.00	17.50	10.50

1936 R344 National Chicle

Issued by National Chicle in 1936, this 20-card set was a paper issue distributed with Batter-Up Gum. Unfolded, each paper measured 3-5/8" by 6". The numbered set featured a series of baseball tips from Rabbit Maranville and are illustrated with line drawings.

		NR MT	EX	VG
	Complete Set:	450.00	225.00	135.00
	Common Card:	22.00	11.00	6.50
1	How to Pitch the Out Shoot	22.00	11.00	6.50
2	How to Throw the In Shoot	22.00	11.00	6.50
3	How to Pitch the Drop	22.00	11.00	6.50
4	How to Pitch the Floater	22.00	11.00	6.50
5	How to Run Bases	22.00	11.00	6.50
6	How to Slide	22.00	11.00	6.50
7	How to Catch Flies	22.00	11.00	6.50
8	How to Field Grounders	22.00	11.00	6.50
9	How to Tag A Man Out	22.00	11.00	6.50
10	How to Cover A Base	22.00	11.00	6.50
11	How to Bat	22.00	11.00	6.50
12	How to Steal Bases	22.00	11.00	6.50
13	How to Bunt	22.00	11.00	6.50
14	How to Coach Base Runner	22.00	11.00	6.50
15	How to Catch Behind the Bat	22.00	11.00	6.50
16	How to Throw to Bases	22.00	11.00	6.50
17	How to Signal	22.00	11.00	6.50
18	How to Umpire Balls and Strikes	22.00	11.00	6.50
19	How to Umpire Bases	22.00	11.00	6.50
20	How to Lay Out a Ball Field	22.00	11.00	6.50

A player's name in italic type indicates a rookie card. An (FC) indicates a player's first card for that particular card company.

1948-49 R 346 Blue Tint

JOHNNY MIZE
N. Y. GIANTS

Issued during 1948-49, the cards in this 48-card set derive their name from the distinctive blue coloring used to tint the black and white photos. The cards have blank backs and measure 2" by 2-5/8". The set, which has a high percentage of New York players, was originally issued in strips of six or eight cards each and therefore would be more appropriately cataloged as a "W" strip card set, although collectors still commonly refer to it by the R346 designation. The set includes two major variations: Leo Durocher can be found as both a Dodger and a Giant; and Mel Ott can be found as a Giant or with no team designation. The complete set price does not include the variations.

		NR MT	EX	VG
	Complete Set:	1400.00	700.00	420.00
	Common Player:	12.00	6.00	3.50
1	Bill Johnson	12.00	6.00	3.50
2a	Leo Durocher (Brooklyn)	25.00	12.50	7.50
2b	Leo Durocher (New York)	25.00	12.50	7.50
3	Marty Marion	15.00	7.50	4.50
4	Ewell Blackwell	15.00	7.50	4.50
5	John Lindell	12.00	6.00	3.50
6	Larry Jansen	12.00	6.00	3.50
7	Ralph Kiner	25.00	12.50	7.50
8	Chuck Dressen	12.00	6.00	3.50
9	Bobby Brown	15.00	7.50	4.50
10	Luke Appling	25.00	12.50	7.50
11	Bill Nicholson	12.00	6.00	3.50
12	Phil Masi	12.00	6.00	3.50
13	Frank Shea	12.00	6.00	3.50
14	Bob Dillinger	12.00	6.00	3.50
15	Pete Suder	12.00	6.00	3.50
16	Joe DiMaggio	225.00	112.00	67.00
17	John Corriden	12.00	6.00	3.50
18a	Mel Ott (New York)	30.00	15.00	9.00
18b	Mel Ott (no team designation)	30.00	15.00	9.00
19	Warren Rosar	12.00	6.00	3.50
20	Warren Spahn	30.00	15.00	9.00
21	Allie Reynolds	18.00	9.00	5.50
22	Lou Boudreau	25.00	12.50	7.50
23	Harry Majeski	12.00	6.00	3.50
24	Frank Crosetti	15.00	7.50	4.50
25	Gus Niarhos	12.00	6.00	3.50
26	Bruce Edwards	12.00	6.00	3.50
27	Rudy York	12.00	6.00	3.50
28	Don Black	12.00	6.00	3.50
29	Lou Gehrig	225.00	112.00	67.00
30	Johnny Mize	25.00	12.50	7.50
31	Ed Stanky	15.00	7.50	4.50
32	Vic Raschi	15.00	7.50	4.50
33	Cliff Mapes	12.00	6.00	3.50
34	Enos Slaughter	25.00	12.50	7.50
35	Hank Greenberg	25.00	12.50	7.50
36	Jackie Robinson	125.00	62.00	37.00
37	Frank Hiller	12.00	6.00	3.50
38	Bob Elliot (Elliott)	12.00	6.00	3.50
39	Harry Walker	12.00	6.00	3.50
40	Ed Lopat	15.00	7.50	4.50
41	Bobby Thomson	15.00	7.50	4.50
42	Tommy Henrich	18.00	9.00	5.50
43	Bobby Feller	40.00	20.00	12.00
44	Ted Williams	125.00	62.00	37.00
45	Dixie Walker	12.00	6.00	3.50
46	Johnnie Vander Meer	15.00	7.50	4.50

		NR MT	EX	VG
47	Clint Hartung	12.00	6.00	3.50
48	Charlie Keller	18.00	9.00	5.50

1950 R423

109. DAZZY VANCE

These tiny (3/4" by 5/8") cards are numbered from 1 through 120, although many numbers are still unknown or were never issued. The cards were available in long perforated strips from vending machines in the 1950s. The cards are printed on thin stock and include the player's name beneath his photo. The backs display a rough drawing of a baseball infield with tiny figures at the various positions. It appears the cards were intended to be used to play a game of baseball.

		NR MT	EX	VG
Complete Set:		150.00	75.00	45.00
Common Player:		.40	.20	.12
(1)	Richie Ashburn	.90	.45	.25
(2)	Unknown			
(3)	Frank Baumholtz	.40	.20	.12
(4)	Ralph Branca	.50	.25	.15
(5)	Unknown			
(6)	Unknown			
(7)	Unknown			
(8)	Harry Brecheen	.40	.20	.12
(9)	Chico Carrasquel	.40	.20	.12
(10)	Jerry Coleman	.40	.20	.12
(11)	Walker Cooper	.40	.20	.12
(12)	Unknown			
(13)	Phil Cavaretta (Cavarretta)	.40	.20	.12
(14)	Ty Cobb	10.00	5.00	3.00
(15)	Unknown			
(16)	Unknown			
(17)	Frank Crosetti	.50	.25	.15
(18)	Larry Doby	.90	.45	.25
(19)	Walter Dropo	.40	.20	.12
(20)	Unknown			
(21)	Dizzy Dean	4.00	2.00	1.25
(22)	Bill Dickey	1.75	.90	.50
(23)	Murray Dickson (Murry)	.40	.20	.12
(24)	Dom DiMaggio	.90	.45	.25
(25)	Joe DiMaggio	10.00	5.00	3.00
(26)	Unknown			
(27)	Unknown			
(28)	Bob Elliott	.40	.20	.12
(29)	Unknown			
(30)	Unknown			
(31)	Bob Feller	2.50	1.25	.70
(32)	Frank Frisch	1.00	.50	.30
(33)	Unknown			
(34)	Unknown			
(35)	Lou Gehrig	10.00	5.00	3.00
(36)	Joe Gordon	.50	.25	.15
(37)	Unknown			
(38)	Hank Greenberg	1.25	.60	.40
(39)	Lefty Grove	1.25	.60	.40
(40)	Unknown			
(41)	Unknown			
(42)	Ken Heintzelman	.40	.20	.12
(43)	Unknown			
(44)	Jim Hearn	.40	.20	.12
(45)	Unknown			
(46)	Harry Heilman (Heilmann)	.90	.45	.25
(47)	Tommy Henrich	.50	.25	.15
(48)	Roger Hornsby (Rogers)	2.00	1.00	.60

		NR MT	EX	VG
(49)	Unknown			
(50)	Edwin Joost	.40	.20	.12
(51)	Unknown			
(52)	Unknown			
(53)	Nippy Jones	.40	.20	.12
(54)	Walter Johnson	4.00	2.00	1.25
(55)	Ellis Kinder	.40	.20	.12
(56)	Jim Konstanty	.40	.20	.12
(57)	Unknown			
(58)	Ralph Kiner	1.00	.50	.30
(59)	Bob Lemon	.90	.45	.25
(60)	Unknown			
(61)	Unknown			
(62)	Unknown			
(63)	Cass Michaels	.40	.20	.12
(64)	Unknown			
(65)	Unknown			
(66)	Clyde McCullough	.40	.20	.12
(67)	Connie Mack	1.00	.50	.30
(68)	Christy Mathewson	2.50	1.25	.70
(69)	Joe Medwick	.90	.45	.25
(70)	Johnny Mize	1.00	.50	.30
(71)	Terry Moore	.40	.20	.12
(72)	Stan Musial	5.00	2.50	1.50
(73)	Hal Newhouser	.50	.25	.15
(74)	Don Newcombe	.50	.25	.15
(75)	Lefty O'Doul	.50	.25	.15
(76)	Unknown			
(77)	Mel Parnell	.40	.20	.12
(78)	Unknown			
(79)	Gerald Priddy	.40	.20	.12
(80)	Dave Philley	.40	.20	.12
(81)	Bob Porterfield	.40	.20	.12
(82)	Andy Pafko	.50	.25	.15
(83)	Howie Pollet	.40	.20	.12
(84)	Herb Pennock	.40	.20	.12
(85)	Al Rosen	.90	.45	.25
(86)	Peewee Reese	1.75	.90	.50
(87)	Del Rice	.40	.20	.12
(88)	Unknown			
(89)	Unknown			
(90)	Unknown			
(91)	Unknown			
(92)	Babe Ruth	18.00	9.00	5.50
(93)	Casey Stengel	2.25	1.25	.70
(94)	Vern Stephens	.40	.20	.12
(95)	Duke Snider	2.25	1.25	.70
(96)	Enos Slaughter	.90	.45	.25
(97)	Al Schoendienst	.50	.25	.15
(98)	Gerald Staley	.40	.20	.12
(99)	Clyde Shoun	.40	.20	.12
(100)	Unknown			
(101)	Unknown			
(102)	Al Simmons	.90	.45	.25
(103)	George Sisler	.90	.45	.25
(104)	Tris Speaker	1.25	.60	.40
(105)	Ed Stanky	.50	.25	.15
(106)	Virgil Trucks	.40	.20	.12
(107)	Henry Thompson	.40	.20	.12
(108)	Unknown			
(109)	Dazzy Vance	.90	.45	.25
(110)	Lloyd Waner	.90	.45	.25
(111)	Paul Waner	.90	.45	.25
(112)	Gene Woodling	.40	.20	.12
(113)	Ted Williams	8.00	4.00	2.50
(114)	Unknown			
(115)	Wes Westrum	.40	.20	.12
(116)	Johnny Wyrostek	.40	.20	.12
(117)	Eddie Yost	.40	.20	.12
(118)	Allen Zarilla	.40	.20	.12
(119)	Gus Zernial	.40	.20	.12
(120)	Sam Zoldack (Zoldak)	.40	.20	.12

1952 Red Man Tobacco

WES WESTRUM
CATCHER
NEW YORK GIANTS

1952 RED MAN ALL-STAR TEAM
NATIONAL LEAGUE SERIES—PLAYER 17A

RED MAN'S DOUBLE-HEADER
FOR BASEBALL FANS!

(1) 52 Full-Color Picture Cards of Red Man's All-Star Major League Baseball Players

(2) FREE OF EXTRA COST—Big League Style Baseball Cap! (See details below)

RED MAN CHEWING TOBACCO

These Baseball Cards are for Red Man "Chewers" and Their Boys

This was the first national set of tobacco cards produced since the golden days of tobacco sets in the early part of the century. There are 52 cards in the set, with 25 top players and one manager from each league. Player selection was made by editor J.G. Taylor Spink of The Sporting News. Cards measure 3-1/2"by 4", including a 1/2" tab at the bottom of each card. These tabs were redeemable for a free baseball cap from Red Man. Cards are harder to find with tabs intact, and thus more valuable in that form. Values quoted here are for cards with tabs. Cards with the tabs removed would be valued about 35-40 percent of the quoted figures. Card fronts are full color paintings of each player with biographical information inset in the portrait area. Card backs contain company advertising. Cards are numbered and dated only on the tabs.

		NR MT	EX	VG
Complete Set:		2000.00	1000.00	600.00
Common Player:		20.00	10.00	6.00
1A	Casey Stengel	55.00	27.00	16.50
1N	Leo Durocher	40.00	20.00	12.00
2A	Roberto Avila	20.00	10.00	6.00
2N	Richie Ashburn	35.00	17.50	10.50
3A	Larry "Yogi" Berra	80.00	40.00	24.00
3N	Ewell Blackwell	25.00	12.50	7.50
4A	Gil Coan	20.00	10.00	6.00
4N	Cliff Chambers	20.00	10.00	6.00
5A	Dom DiMaggio	30.00	15.00	9.00
5N	Murry Dickson	20.00	10.00	6.00
6A	Larry Doby	30.00	15.00	9.00
6N	Sid Gordon	20.00	10.00	6.00
7A	Ferris Fain	25.00	12.50	7.50
7N	Granny Hamner	20.00	10.00	6.00
8A	Bob Feller	80.00	40.00	24.00
8N	Jim Hearn	20.00	10.00	6.00
9A	Nelson Fox	35.00	17.50	10.50
9N	Monte Irvin	50.00	25.00	15.00
10A	Johnny Groth	20.00	10.00	6.00
10N	Larry Jansen	20.00	10.00	6.00
11A	Jim Hegan	20.00	10.00	6.00
11N	Willie Jones	20.00	10.00	6.00
12A	Eddie Joost	20.00	10.00	6.00
12N	Ralph Kiner	50.00	25.00	15.00
13A	George Kell	50.00	25.00	15.00
13N	Whitey Lockman	20.00	10.00	6.00
14A	Gil McDougald	30.00	15.00	9.00
14N	Sal Maglie	25.00	12.50	7.50
15A	Orestes Minoso	25.00	12.50	7.50
15N	Willie Mays	150.00	75.00	45.00
16A	Bill Pierce	25.00	12.50	7.50
16N	Stan Musial	150.00	75.00	45.00
17A	Bob Porterfield	20.00	10.00	6.00
17N	Pee Wee Reese	75.00	37.00	22.00
18A	Eddie Robinson	20.00	10.00	6.00
18N	Robin Roberts	50.00	25.00	15.00
19A	Saul Rogovin	20.00	10.00	6.00
19N	Al Schoendienst	30.00	15.00	9.00
20A	Bobby Shantz	25.00	12.50	7.50
20N	Enos Slaughter	50.00	25.00	15.00
21A	Vern Stephens	20.00	10.00	6.00
21N	Duke Snider	100.00	50.00	30.00
22A	Vic Wertz	20.00	10.00	6.00
22N	Warren Spahn	60.00	30.00	18.00
23A	Ted Williams	175.00	87.00	52.00
23N	Eddie Stanky	25.00	12.50	7.50
24A	Early Wynn	50.00	25.00	15.00
24N	Bobby Thomson	30.00	15.00	9.00
25A	Eddie Yost	20.00	10.00	6.00
25N	Earl Torgeson	20.00	10.00	6.00
26A	Gus Zernial	20.00	10.00	6.00
26N	Wes Westrum	20.00	10.00	6.00

1953 Red Man Tobacco

This was the chewing tobacco company's second annual set of 3-1/2" by 4" cards, including the tabs at the bottom of the cards. Formats for both the fronts and backs are similar to the '52 edition. The 1953 Red Man cards, however, include card numbers within the player biographical section, and the card backs are headlined "New for '53." Once again, cards with intact tabs (which were redeemable for a free cap) are more valuable. Prices below are for cards with tabs. Cards with tabs removed are worth about 35-40 percent of the stated values. Each league is represented by 25 players and a manager on the full-color cards, a total of 52.

		NR MT	EX	VG
Complete Set:		1800.00	900.00	540.00
Common Player:		20.00	10.00	6.00
1A	Casey Stengel	55.00	27.00	16.50
1N	Charlie Dressen	25.00	12.50	7.50
2A	Hank Bauer	25.00	12.50	7.50
2N	Bobby Adams	20.00	10.00	6.00
3A	Larry "Yogi" Berra	80.00	40.00	24.00
3N	Richie Ashburn	35.00	17.50	10.50
4A	Walt Dropo	20.00	10.00	6.00
4N	Joe Black	25.00	12.50	7.50
5A	Nelson Fox	35.00	17.50	10.50
5N	Roy Campanella	80.00	40.00	24.00
6A	Jackie Jensen	25.00	12.50	7.50
6N	Ted Kluszewski	30.00	15.00	9.00
7A	Eddie Joost	20.00	10.00	6.00
7N	Whitey Lockman	20.00	10.00	6.00
8A	George Kell	50.00	25.00	15.00
8N	Sal Maglie	25.00	12.50	7.50
9A	Dale Mitchell	20.00	10.00	6.00
9N	Andy Pafko	25.00	12.50	7.50
10A	Phil Rizzuto	60.00	30.00	18.00
10N	Pee Wee Reese	75.00	37.00	22.00
11A	Eddie Robinson	20.00	10.00	6.00
11N	Robin Roberts	50.00	25.00	15.00
12A	Gene Woodling	25.00	12.50	7.50
12N	Al Schoendienst	30.00	15.00	9.00
13A	Gus Zernial	20.00	10.00	6.00
13N	Enos Slaughter	50.00	25.00	15.00
14A	Early Wynn	50.00	25.00	15.00
14N	Edwin "Duke" Snider	100.00	50.00	30.00
15A	Joe Dobson	20.00	10.00	6.00
15N	Ralph Kiner	50.00	25.00	15.00
16A	Billy Pierce	25.00	12.50	7.50
16N	Hank Sauer	20.00	10.00	6.00
17A	Bob Lemon	50.00	25.00	15.00
17N	Del Ennis	20.00	10.00	6.00
18A	Johnny Mize	50.00	25.00	15.00
18N	Granny Hamner	20.00	10.00	6.00
19A	Bob Porterfield	20.00	10.00	6.00
19N	Warren Spahn	60.00	30.00	18.00
20A	Bobby Shantz	25.00	12.50	7.50
20N	Wes Westrum	20.00	10.00	6.00
21A	"Mickey" Vernon	25.00	12.50	7.50
21N	Hoyt Wilhelm	50.00	25.00	15.00
22A	Dom DiMaggio	30.00	15.00	9.00
22N	Murry Dickson	20.00	10.00	6.00
23A	Gil McDougald	30.00	15.00	9.00
23N	Warren Hacker	20.00	10.00	6.00
24A	Al Rosen	30.00	15.00	9.00
24N	Gerry Staley	20.00	10.00	6.00
25A	Mel Parnell	20.00	10.00	6.00
25N	Bobby Thomson	25.00	12.50	7.50
26A	Roberto Avila	20.00	10.00	6.00
26N	Stan Musial	150.00	75.00	45.00

A player's name in italic type indicates a rookie card. An (FC) indicates a player's first card for that particular card company.

1954 Red Man Tobacco

		NR MT	EX	VG
23A	Hank Bauer	25.00	12.50	7.50
23N	Eddie Mathews	55.00	27.00	16.50
24A	Jim Delsing	20.00	10.00	6.00
24N	Lew Burdette	30.00	15.00	9.00
25A	Gil McDougald	30.00	15.00	9.00
25N	Willie Mays	150.00	75.00	45.00

1955 Red Man Tobacco

In 1954, the Red Man set eliminated managers from the set, and issued only 25 player cards for each league. There are, however, four variations which bring the total set size to 54 full-color cards. Two cards exist for Gus Bell and Enos Slaughter, while American Leaguers George Kell, Sam Mele and Dave Philley are each shown with two different teams. Complete set prices quoted below do not include the scarcer of the variation pairs. Cards still measure 3-1/2" by 4" with tabs intact. Cards without tabs are worth about 35-40 per cent of the values quoted below. Formats for the cards remain virtually unchanged, with card numbers included within the player information boxes as well as on the tabs.

		NR MT	EX	VG
Complete Set:		1600.00	800.00	480.00
Common Player:		20.00	10.00	6.00
1A	Bobby Avila	20.00	10.00	6.00
1N	Richie Ashburn	35.00	17.50	10.50
2A	Jim Busby	20.00	10.00	6.00
2N	Billy Cox	25.00	12.50	7.50
3A	Nelson Fox	35.00	17.50	10.50
3N	Del Crandall	25.00	12.50	7.50
4Aa	George Kell (Boston)	65.00	32.00	19.50
4Ab	George Kell (Chicago)	75.00	37.00	22.00
4N	Carl Erskine	30.00	15.00	9.00
5A	Sherman Lollar	20.00	10.00	6.00
5N	Monte Irvin	50.00	25.00	15.00
6Aa	Sam Mele (Baltimore)	50.00	25.00	15.00
6Ab	Sam Mele (Chicago)	75.00	37.00	22.00
6N	Ted Kluszewski	30.00	15.00	9.00
7A	Orestes Minoso	25.00	12.50	7.50
7N	Don Mueller	20.00	10.00	6.00
8A	Mel Parnell	20.00	10.00	6.00
8N	Andy Pafko	25.00	12.50	7.50
9Aa	Dave Philley (Cleveland)	50.00	25.00	15.00
9Ab	Dave Philley (Philadelphia)	75.00	37.00	22.00
9N	Del Rice	20.00	10.00	6.00
10A	Billy Pierce	25.00	12.50	7.50
10N	Al Schoendienst	30.00	15.00	9.00
11A	Jim Piersall	25.00	12.50	7.50
11N	Warren Spahn	60.00	30.00	18.00
12A	Al Rosen	30.00	15.00	9.00
12N	Curt Simmons	25.00	12.50	7.50
13A	"Mickey" Vernon	25.00	12.50	7.50
13N	Roy Campanella	80.00	40.00	24.00
14A	Sammy White	20.00	10.00	6.00
14N	Jim Gilliam	30.00	15.00	9.00
15A	Gene Woodling	25.00	12.50	7.50
15N	"Pee Wee" Reese	75.00	37.00	22.00
16A	Ed "Whitey" Ford	65.00	32.00	19.50
16N	Edwin "Duke" Snider	100.00	50.00	30.00
17A	Phil Rizzuto	60.00	30.00	18.00
17N	Rip Repulski	20.00	10.00	6.00
18A	Bob Porterfield	20.00	10.00	6.00
18N	Robin Roberts	50.00	25.00	15.00
19A	Al "Chico" Carrasquel	20.00	10.00	6.00
19Na	Enos Slaughter	90.00	45.00	27.00
19Nb	Gus Bell	90.00	45.00	27.00
20A	Larry "Yogi" Berra	80.00	40.00	24.00
20N	Johnny Logan	20.00	10.00	6.00
21A	Bob Lemon	50.00	25.00	15.00
21N	Johnny Antonelli	25.00	12.50	7.50
22A	Ferris Fain	25.00	12.50	7.50
22N	Gil Hodges	55.00	27.00	16.50

These 50 cards are quite similar to the 1954 edition, with card fronts virtually unchanged except for the data in the biographical box on the color picture area. This set of the 3-1/2" by 4" cards includes 25 players from each league, with no known variations. As with all Red Man sets, those cards complete with the redeemable tabs are more valuable. Values quoted below are for cards with tabs. Cards with the tabs removed are worth about 35-40 percent of those figures.

		NR MT	EX	VG
Complete Set:		1500.00	750.00	450.00
Common Player:		20.00	10.00	6.00
1A	Ray Boone	20.00	10.00	6.00
1N	Richie Ashburn	35.00	17.50	10.50
2A	Jim Busby	20.00	10.00	6.00
2N	Del Crandall	25.00	12.50	7.50
3A	Ed "Whitey" Ford	55.00	27.00	16.50
3N	Gil Hodges	65.00	32.00	19.50
4A	Nelson Fox	35.00	17.50	10.50
4N	Brooks Lawrence	20.00	10.00	6.00
5A	Bob Grim	20.00	10.00	6.00
5N	Johnny Logan	20.00	10.00	6.00
6A	Jack Harshman	20.00	10.00	6.00
6N	Sal Maglie	25.00	12.50	7.50
7A	Jim Hegan	20.00	10.00	6.00
7N	Willie Mays	150.00	75.00	45.00
8A	Bob Lemon	50.00	25.00	15.00
8N	Don Mueller	20.00	10.00	6.00
9A	Irv Noren	20.00	10.00	6.00
9N	Bill Sarni	20.00	10.00	6.00
10A	Bob Porterfield	20.00	10.00	6.00
10N	Warren Spahn	60.00	30.00	18.00
11A	Al Rosen	30.00	15.00	9.00
11N	Henry Thompson	20.00	10.00	6.00
12A	"Mickey" Vernon	25.00	12.50	7.50
12N	Hoyt Wilhelm	50.00	25.00	15.00
13A	Vic Wertz	20.00	10.00	6.00
13N	Johnny Antonelli	25.00	12.50	7.50
14A	Early Wynn	50.00	25.00	15.00
14N	Carl Erskine	30.00	15.00	9.00
15A	Bobby Avila	20.00	10.00	6.00
15N	Granny Hamner	20.00	10.00	6.00
16A	Larry "Yogi" Berra	80.00	40.00	24.00
16N	Ted Kluszewski	30.00	15.00	9.00
17A	Joe Coleman	20.00	10.00	6.00
17N	Pee Wee Reese	75.00	37.00	22.00
18A	Larry Doby	30.00	15.00	9.00
18N	Al Schoendienst	30.00	15.00	9.00
19A	Jackie Jensen	25.00	12.50	7.50
19N	Duke Snider	100.00	50.00	30.00
20A	Pete Runnels	20.00	10.00	6.00
20N	Frank Thomas	20.00	10.00	6.00
21A	Jim Piersall	25.00	12.50	7.50
21N	Ray Jablonski	20.00	10.00	6.00
22A	Hank Bauer	25.00	12.50	7.50
22N	James "Dusty" Rhodes	20.00	10.00	6.00

		NR MT	EX	VG
23A	"Chico" Carrasquel	20.00	10.00	6.00
23N	Gus Bell	20.00	10.00	6.00
24A	Orestes Minoso	25.00	12.50	7.50
24N	Curt Simmons	25.00	12.50	7.50
25A	Sandy Consuegra	20.00	10.00	6.00
25N	Marvin Grissom	20.00	10.00	6.00

1886 Red Stocking Cigars

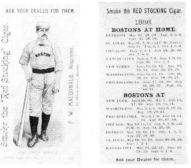

This set of Boston Red Stockings schedule cards was issued in 1886, and the three known cards measure 6-1/2" by 3-3/4". The cards were printed in black and red. One side carries the 1886 Boston schedule, while the other side features a full-length player drawing. Both sides include advertising for "Red Stocking" cigars. Only three different players are known.

		NR MT	EX	VG
Complete Set:		12000.00	6000.00	3250.
Common Player:		3500.00	1750.00	1050.
(1)	C.G. Buffington	3500.00	1750.00	1050.
(2)	Capt. John F. Morrill	3500.00	1750.00	1050.
(3)	Charles Radbourn	5000.00	2500.00	1500.

1946 Remar Bread Oakland Oaks

AMBROSE (Bo) PALICA
Oaks Pitcher   22

Remar Baking Company issued several baseball card sets in the northern California area from 1946-1950, all picturing members of the Oakland Oaks of the Pacific Coast League. The 1946 set consists of 23 cards (five unnumbered, 18 numbered). Measuring 2" by 3", the cards were printed on heavy paper and feature black and white photos with the player's name, team and postition at the bottom. The backs contain a brief write-up plus an ad for Remar Bread printed in red. The cards were distributed one per week. The first five cards were unnumbered. The rest of the set is numbered on the front, but begins with number "5", rather than "6".

		NR MT	EX	VG
Complete Set:		375.00	187.00	112.00
Common Player:		12.00	6.00	3.50
5	Hershell Martin (Herschel)	12.00	6.00	3.50
6	Bill Hart	12.00	6.00	3.50
7	Charlie Gassaway	12.00	6.00	3.50
8	Wally Westlake	12.00	6.00	3.50
9	Mickey Burnett	12.00	6.00	3.50
10	Charles (Casey) Stengel	80.00	40.00	24.00
11	Charlie Metro	12.00	6.00	3.50
12	Tom Hafey	12.00	6.00	3.50
13	Tony Sabol	12.00	6.00	3.50
14	Ed Kearse	12.00	6.00	3.50
15	Bud Foster (announcer)	12.00	6.00	3.50
16	Johnny Price	12.00	6.00	3.50
17	Gene Bearden	12.00	6.00	3.50
18	Floyd Speer	12.00	6.00	3.50
19	Bryan Stephens	12.00	6.00	3.50
20	Rinaldo (Rugger) Ardizoia	12.00	6.00	3.50
21	Ralph Buxton	12.00	6.00	3.50
22	Ambrose (Bo) Palica	12.00	6.00	3.50
----	Brooks Holder	15.00	7.50	4.50
----	Henry (Cotton) Pippen	15.00	7.50	4.50
----	Billy Raimondi	60.00	30.00	18.00
----	Les Scarsella	15.00	7.50	4.50
----	Glen (Gabby) Stewart	15.00	7.50	4.50

1947 Remar Bread Oakland Oaks

CHARLES (Casey) STENGEL
Oaks Manager   8

REMAR BAKING CO.

Remar's second set consisted of 25 numbered cards, again measuring 2" by 3". The cards are nearly identical to the previous year's set, except the loaf of bread on the back is printed in blue, rather than red.

		NR MT	EX	VG
Complete Set:		350.00	175.00	105.00
Common Player:		12.00	6.00	3.50
1	Billy Raimondi	12.00	6.00	3.50
2	Les Scarsella	12.00	6.00	3.50
3	Brooks Holder	12.00	6.00	3.50
4	Charlie Gassaway	12.00	6.00	3.50
5	Mickey Burnett	12.00	6.00	3.50
6	Ralph Buxton	12.00	6.00	3.50
7	Ed Kearse	12.00	6.00	3.50
8	Charles (Casey) Stengel	70.00	35.00	21.00
9	Bud Foster (announcer)	12.00	6.00	3.50
10	Ambrose (Bo) Palica	12.00	6.00	3.50
11	Tom Hafey	12.00	6.00	3.50
12	Hershel Martin (Herschel)	12.00	6.00	3.50
13	Henry (Cotton) Pippen	12.00	6.00	3.50
14	Floyd Speer	12.00	6.00	3.50
15	Tony Sabol	12.00	6.00	3.50
16	Will Hafey	12.00	6.00	3.50
17	Ray Hamrick	12.00	6.00	3.50
18	Maurice Van Robays	12.00	6.00	3.50
19	Dario Lodigiani	12.00	6.00	3.50
20	Mel (Dizz) Duezabou	12.00	6.00	3.50
21	Damon Hayes	12.00	6.00	3.50
22	Gene Lillard	12.00	6.00	3.50
23	Aldon Wilkie	12.00	6.00	3.50
24	Dewey Soriano	12.00	6.00	3.50

		NR MT	EX	VG
25	Glen Crawford	12.00	6.00	3.50

1949 Remar Bread
Oakland Oaks

DON PADGETT
Oaks Catcher

The 1949 Remar Bread issue was increased to 32 cards, again measuring 2" by 3". Unlike the two earlier sets, photos in the 1949 Remar set are surrounded by a thin, white border and are unnumbered. The player's name, team and position appear below the black and white photo. The backs are printed in blue and include the player's 1948 statistics and the distinctive loaf of bread.

		NR MT	EX	VG
Complete Set:		350.00	175.00	105.00
Common Player:		7.00	3.50	2.00
(1)	Ralph Buxton	7.00	3.50	2.00
(2)	Milo Candini	15.00	7.50	4.50
(3)	Rex Cecil	15.00	7.50	4.50
(4)	Loyd Christopher (Lloyd)	7.00	3.50	2.00
(5)	Charles Dressen	12.00	6.00	3.50
(6)	Mel Duezabou	7.00	3.50	2.00
(7)	Bud Foster (sportscaster)	7.00	3.50	2.00
(8)	Charlie Gassaway	7.00	3.50	2.00
(9)	Ray Hamrick	7.00	3.50	2.00
(10)	Jack Jensen	15.00	7.50	4.50
(11)	Earl Jones	7.00	3.50	2.00
(12)	George Kelly	18.00	9.00	5.50
(13)	Frank Kerr	15.00	7.50	4.50
(14)	Richard Kryhoski	7.00	3.50	2.00
(15)	Harry Lavagetto	12.00	6.00	3.50
(16)	Dario Lodigiani	7.00	3.50	2.00
(17)	Billy Martin	60.00	30.00	18.00
(18)	George Metkovich	7.00	3.50	2.00
(19)	Frank Nelson	7.00	3.50	2.00
(20)	Don Padgett	7.00	3.50	2.00
(21)	Alonzo Perry	15.00	7.50	4.50
(22)	Bill Raimondi	7.00	3.50	2.00
(23)	Earl Rapp	7.00	3.50	2.00
(24)	Eddie Samcoff	7.00	3.50	2.00
(25)	Les Scarsella	7.00	3.50	2.00
(26)	Forest Thompson (Forrest)	15.00	7.50	4.50
(27)	Earl Toolson	7.00	3.50	2.00
(28)	Lou Tost	15.00	7.50	4.50
(29)	Maurice Van Robays	7.00	3.50	2.00
(30)	Jim Wallace	7.00	3.50	2.00
(31)	Arthur Lee Wilson	7.00	3.50	2.00
(32)	Parnell Woods	15.00	7.50	4.50

1950 Remar Bread
Oakland Oaks

The most common of the Remar Bread issues, the 1950 set contains 27 unnumbered cards, again measuring 2" by 3" and featuring members of the Oakland Oaks. The cards are nearly identical to the previous year's set but can be differentiated by the 1949 statistics on the back.

ALLEN GETTEL
Oaks Pitcher

		NR MT	EX	VG
Complete Set:		200.00	100.00	60.00
Common Player:		7.00	3.50	2.00
(1)	George Bamberger	12.00	6.00	3.50
(2)	Hank Behrman	7.00	3.50	2.00
(3)	Loyd Christopher (Lloyd)	7.00	3.50	2.00
(4)	Chuck Dressen	12.00	6.00	3.50
(5)	Mel Duezabou	7.00	3.50	2.00
(6)	Augie Galan	7.00	3.50	2.00
(7)	Charlie Gassaway	7.00	3.50	2.00
(8)	Allen Gettel	7.00	3.50	2.00
(9)	Ernie W. Groth	7.00	3.50	2.00
(10)	Ray Hamrick	7.00	3.50	2.00
(11)	Earl Harrist	7.00	3.50	2.00
(12)	Billy Herman	18.00	9.00	5.50
(13)	Bob Hofman	7.00	3.50	2.00
(14)	George Kelly	18.00	9.00	5.50
(15)	Harry Lavagetto	12.00	6.00	3.50
(16)	Eddie Malone	7.00	3.50	2.00
(17)	George Metkovich	7.00	3.50	2.00
(18)	Frank Nelson	7.00	3.50	2.00
(19)	Rafael (Ray) Noble	7.00	3.50	2.00
(20)	Don Padgett	7.00	3.50	2.00
(21)	Earl Rapp	7.00	3.50	2.00
(22)	Clyde Shoun	7.00	3.50	2.00
(23)	Forrest Thompson	7.00	3.50	2.00
(24)	Louis Tost	7.00	3.50	2.00
(25)	Dick Wakefield	12.00	6.00	3.50
(26)	Artie Wilson	7.00	3.50	2.00
(27)	Roy Zimmerman	7.00	3.50	2.00

1955 Rodeo Meats Athletics

Cloyd Boyer

This set of 2-1/2" by 3-1/2" color cards was issued by a local meat company to commemorate the first year of the Athletics in Kansas City. There are 38 different players included in the set, with nine players known to apppear in two different variations for a total of 47 cards in the set. Most variations are in background colors, although Bobby Shantz is also listed incorrectly as "Schantz" on one variation. The cards are unnumbered, with the Rodeo logo and player name on the fronts, and an ad for a scrapbook album listed on the backs.

	NR MT	EX	VG
Complete Set:	4250.00	2125.00	1275.

		NR MT	EX	VG
Common Player:		70.00	35.00	21.00
(1)	Joe Astroth	70.00	35.00	21.00
(2)	Harold Bevan	100.00	50.00	30.00
(3)	Charles Bishop	100.00	50.00	30.00
(4)	Don Bollweg	100.00	50.00	30.00
(5)	Lou Boudreau	250.00	125.00	75.00
(6)	Cloyd Boyer (blue background)	100.00	50.00	30.00
(7)	Cloyd Boyer (pink background)	70.00	35.00	21.00
(8)	Ed Burtschy	100.00	50.00	30.00
(9)	Art Ceccarelli	70.00	35.00	21.00
(10)	Joe DeMaestri (pea green background)			
		100.00	50.00	30.00
(11)	Joe DeMaestri (light green background)			
		70.00	35.00	21.00
(12)	Art Ditmar	70.00	35.00	21.00
(13)	John Dixon	100.00	50.00	30.00
(14)	Jim Finigan	70.00	35.00	21.00
(15)	Marion Fricano	100.00	50.00	30.00
(16)	John Gray	100.00	50.00	30.00
(17)	Tom Gorman	70.00	35.00	21.00
(18)	Ray Herbert	70.00	35.00	21.00
(19)	Forest "Spook" Jacobs (Forrest)			
		100.00	50.00	30.00
(20)	Alex Kellner	100.00	50.00	30.00
(21)	Harry Kraft (Craft)	70.00	35.00	21.00
(22)	Jack Littrell	70.00	35.00	21.00
(23)	Hector Lopez	80.00	40.00	24.00
(24)	Oscar Melillo	70.00	35.00	21.00
(25)	Arnold Portocarrero (purple background)			
		100.00	50.00	30.00
(26)	Arnold Portocarrero (grey background)			
		70.00	35.00	21.00
(27)	Vic Power (pink background)	125.00	62.00	37.00
(28)	Vic Power (yellow background)	80.00	40.00	24.00
(29)	Vic Raschi	100.00	50.00	30.00
(30)	Bill Renna (dark pink background)			
		100.00	50.00	30.00
(31)	Bill Renna (light pink background)			
		70.00	35.00	21.00
(32)	Al Robertson	100.00	50.00	30.00
(33)	Johnny Sain	125.00	62.00	37.00
(34a)	Bobby Schantz (incorrect spelling)			
		250.00	125.00	75.00
(34b)	Bobby Shantz (correct spelling)			
		125.00	62.00	37.00
(35)	Wilmer Shantz (orange background)			
		100.00	50.00	30.00
(36)	Wilmer Shantz (purple background)			
		70.00	35.00	21.00
(37)	Harry Simpson	70.00	35.00	21.00
(38)	Enos Slaughter	300.00	150.00	90.00
(39)	Lou Sleater	70.00	35.00	21.00
(40)	George Susce	70.00	35.00	21.00
(41)	Bob Trice	100.00	50.00	30.00
(42)	Elmer Valo (yellow background)			
		100.00	50.00	30.00
(43)	Elmer Valo (green background)	70.00	35.00	21.00
(44)	Bill Wilson (yellow background)	100.00	50.00	30.00
(45)	Bill Wilson (purple background)	70.00	35.00	21.00
(46)	Gus Zernial	80.00	40.00	24.00

1956 Rodeo Meats Athletics

Gus Zernial

Rodeo Meats issued another Kansas City Athletics set in 1956, but this one was a much smaller 13-card set. The 2-1/2" by 3-1/2" cards are again unnumbered, with the player name and Rodeo logo on the fronts. Card backs feature some of the same

graphics and copy as the 1955 cards, but the album offer is omitted. The full-color cards were only available in packages of Rodeo hot dogs.

		NR MT	EX	VG
Complete Set:		1250.00	625.00	375.00
Common Player:		70.00	35.00	21.00
(1)	Joe Astroth	70.00	35.00	21.00
(2)	Lou Boudreau	250.00	125.00	75.00
(3)	Joe DeMaestri	70.00	35.00	21.00
(4)	Art Ditmar	70.00	35.00	21.00
(5)	Jim Finigan	70.00	35.00	21.00
(6)	Hector Lopez	80.00	40.00	24.00
(7)	Vic Power	80.00	40.00	24.00
(8)	Bobby Shantz	125.00	62.00	37.00
(9)	Harry Simpson	70.00	35.00	21.00
(10)	Enos Slaughter	250.00	125.00	75.00
(11)	Elmer Valo	70.00	35.00	21.00
(12)	Gus Zernial	80.00	40.00	24.00

1950 Royal Desserts

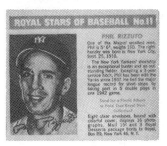

This set of 24 cards was issued one per box on the backs of various Royal Dessert products over a period of three years. The basic set contains 24 players, however a number of variations create the much higher total for the set. In 1950, Royal issued cards with two different tints - black and white with red, or blue and white with red. Over the next two years, various sentences of the cards' biographies were updated up to three times in some cases. Some players from the set left the majors after 1950 and others were apparently never updated, but the 23 biography updates that do exist, added to the original 24 cards issued in 1950, give the set a total of 47 cards. The 2-1/2" by 3-1/2" cards are blank-backed with personal and playing biographies alongside the card front photos.

	NR MT	EX	VG
Complete Set:	1200.00	600.00	360.00
Common Player:	20.00	10.00	6.00
1a Stan Musial (2nd paragraph begins "Musial's 207...")	125.00	62.00	37.00
1b Stan Musial (2nd paragraph begins "Musial batted...")	125.00	62.00	37.00
2a Pee Wee Reese (2nd paragraph begins "Pee Wee's...")	70.00	35.00	21.00
2b Pee Wee Reese (2nd paragraph begins "Captain...")	70.00	35.00	21.00
3a George Kell (2nd paragraph ends "...in 1945, '46.")	35.00	17.50	10.50
3b George Kell (2nd paragraph ends "...two base hits, 56.")	35.00	17.50	10.50
4a Dom DiMaggio (2nd paragraph ends "...during 1947.")	30.00	15.00	9.00
4b Dom DiMaggio (2nd paragraph ends "...with 11.")	30.00	15.00	9.00
5a Warren Spahn (2nd paragraph ends "...shutouts 7.")	50.00	25.00	15.00
5b Warren Spahn (2nd paragraph ends "...with 191.")	50.00	25.00	15.00
6a Andy Pafko (2nd paragraph ends "...7 games.")	25.00	12.50	7.50

		NR MT	EX	VG
6b	Andy Pafko (2nd paragraph ends "...National League.")	25.00	12.50	7.50
6c	Andy Pafko (2nd paragraph ends "...weighs 190.")	25.00	12.50	7.50
7a	Andy Seminick (2nd paragraph ends "...as outfield.")	20.00	10.00	6.00
7b	Andy Seminick (2nd paragraph ends "...since 1916.")	20.00	10.00	6.00
7c	Andy Seminick (2nd paragraph ends "...in the outfield.")	20.00	10.00	6.00
7d	Andy Seminick (2nd paragraph ends "...right handed.")	20.00	10.00	6.00
8a	Lou Brissie (2nd paragraph ends "...when pitching.")	20.00	10.00	6.00
8b	Lou Brissie (2nd paragraph ends "...weighs 215.")	20.00	10.00	6.00
9a	Ewell Blackwell (2nd paragraph begins "Despite recent illness...")	25.00	12.50	7.50
9b	Ewell Blackwell (2nd paragraph begins "Blackwell's...")	25.00	12.50	7.50
10a	Bobby Thomson (2nd paragraph begins "In 1949...")	25.00	12.50	7.50
10b	Bobby Thomson (2nd paragraph begins "Thomson is...")	25.00	12.50	7.50
11a	Phil Rizzuto (2nd paragraph ends "...one 1942 game.")	60.00	30.00	18.00
11b	Phil Rizzuto (2nd paragraph ends "...Most Valuable Player.")	60.00	30.00	18.00
12	Tommy Henrich	30.00	15.00	9.00
13	Joe Gordon	25.00	12.50	7.50
14a	Ray Scarborough (Senators)	20.00	10.00	6.00
14b	Ray Scarborough (White Sox, 2nd paragraph ends "...military service.")	20.00	10.00	6.00
14c	Ray Scarborough (White Sox, 2nd paragraph ends "...the season.")	20.00	10.00	6.00
14d	Ray Scarborough (Red Sox)	20.00	10.00	6.00
15a	Stan Rojek (Pirates)	20.00	10.00	6.00
15b	Stan Rojek (Browns)	20.00	10.00	6.00
16	Luke Appling	30.00	15.00	9.00
17	Willard Marshall	20.00	10.00	6.00
18	Alvin Dark	30.00	15.00	9.00
19a	Dick Sisler (2nd paragraph ends "...service record.")	20.00	10.00	6.00
19b	Dick Sisler (2nd paragraph ends "...National League flag.")	20.00	10.00	6.00
19c	Dick Sisler (2nd paragraph ends "...Nov. 2, 1920.")	20.00	10.00	6.00
19d	Dick Sisler (2nd paragraph ends "...from '46 to '48.")	20.00	10.00	6.00
20	Johnny Ostrowski	20.00	10.00	6.00
21a	Virgil Trucks (2nd paragraph ends "...in military service.")	25.00	12.50	7.50
21b	Virgil Trucks (2nd paragraph ends "...that year.")	25.00	12.50	7.50
21c	Virgil Trucks (2nd paragraph ends "...for military service.")	25.00	12.50	7.50
22	Eddie Robinson	20.00	10.00	6.00
23	Nanny Fernandez	20.00	10.00	6.00
24	Ferris Fain	25.00	12.50	7.50

1952 Royal Desserts

This set, issued as a premium by Royal Desserts in 1952, consists of 16 unnumbered black and white cards, each measuring 5" by 7". The cards include the inscription "To A Royal Fan" along with the player's facsimile autograph.

		NR MT	EX	VG
	Complete Set:	450.00	225.00	135.00
	Common Player:	15.00	7.50	4.50
(1)	Ewell Blackwell	18.00	9.00	5.50
(2)	Leland V. Brissie Jr.	15.00	7.50	4.50
(3)	Alvin Dark	18.00	9.00	5.50
(4)	Dom DiMaggio	25.00	12.50	7.50
(5)	Ferris Fain	15.00	7.50	4.50
(6)	George Kell	28.00	14.00	8.50
(7)	Stan Musial	75.00	37.00	22.00
(8)	Andy Pafko	18.00	9.00	5.50
(9)	Pee Wee Reese	40.00	20.00	12.00
(10)	Phil Rizzuto	40.00	20.00	12.00
(11)	Eddie Robinson	15.00	7.50	4.50
(12)	Ray Scarborough	15.00	7.50	4.50
(13)	Andy Seminick	15.00	7.50	4.50
(14)	Dick Sisler	15.00	7.50	4.50
(15)	Warren Spahn	40.00	20.00	12.00
(16)	Bobby Thomson	25.00	12.50	7.50

1909 S74 Silks - White

Designated as S74 in Jefferson Burdick's American Card Catalog, these small, delicate fabric collectibles are growing in popularity among advanced collectors. Another tobacco issue from the 1910-1911 period, the silks were issued as premiums with three different brands of cigarettes: Turkey Red, Old Mill and Helmar. The satin-like silks can be found in two different styles, either "white" or "colored." The white silks measure 1-7/8" by 3" and were originally issued with a brown paper backing that carried an advertisement for one of the three cigarette brands mentioned above. The backing also advised that the silks were "useful in making pillow covers and other fancy articles for home decoration." Many undoubtedly were used for such purposes, making silks with the paper backing still intact more difficult to find. White silks must, however, have the backing intact to command top value. Although similar, the S74 "colored" silks, as their name indicates were issued in a variety of colors. They are also slightly larger, measuring 1-7/8" by 3-1/2", and were issued without a paper backing. The colored silks, therefore, contained the cigarette brand name on the lower front of the fabric, either "Old Mill Cigarettes" or "Turkey Red Cigarettes." (No colored silks advertising the Helmar brand are known to exist.) There are 121 different players reported: six have been found in two poses, resulting in 127 different subjects. Ninety-two subjects are known in the "white" silk, while 120 have been found in the "colored." The silks feature the same players pictured in the popular T205 Gold Border tobacco card set.

	NR MT	EX	VG
Complete Set:	30000.00	15000.00	9000.
Common Player:	175.00	87.00	52.00

		NR MT	EX	VG
(1)	Home Run Baker	400.00	200.00	120.00
(2)	Cy Barger	175.00	87.00	52.00
(3)	Jack Barry	175.00	87.00	52.00
(4)	Johnny Bates	175.00	87.00	52.00
(5)	Fred Beck	175.00	87.00	52.00
(6)	Beals Becker	175.00	87.00	52.00
(7)	George Bell	175.00	87.00	52.00
(8)	Chief Bender	400.00	200.00	120.00
(9)	Roger Bresnahan	400.00	200.00	120.00
(10)	Al Bridwell	175.00	87.00	52.00
(11)	Mordecai Brown	400.00	200.00	120.00
(12)	Bobby Byrne	175.00	87.00	52.00
(13)	Howie Camnitz	175.00	87.00	52.00
(14)	Bill Carrigan	175.00	87.00	52.00
(15)	Frank Chance	500.00	250.00	150.00
(16)	Hal Chase	250.00	125.00	50.00
(17)	Fred Clarke	400.00	200.00	120.00
(18)	Ty Cobb	3000.00	1500.00	600.00
(19)	Eddie Collins	400.00	200.00	120.00
(20)	Doc Crandall	175.00	87.00	52.00
(21)	Lou Criger	175.00	87.00	52.00
(22)	Jim Delahanty	175.00	87.00	52.00
(23)	Art Devlin	175.00	87.00	52.00
(24)	Red Dooin	175.00	87.00	52.00
(25)	Mickey Doolan	175.00	87.00	52.00
(26)	Larry Doyle	175.00	87.00	52.00
(27)	Jimmy Dygert	175.00	87.00	52.00
(28)	Kid Elberfield (Elberfeld)	175.00	87.00	52.00
(29)	Steve Evans	175.00	87.00	52.00
(30)	Johnny Evers	400.00	200.00	120.00
(31)	Bob Ewing	175.00	87.00	52.00
(32)	Art Fletcher	175.00	87.00	52.00
(33)	John Flynn	175.00	87.00	52.00
(34)	Bill Foxen	175.00	87.00	52.00
(35)	George Gibson	175.00	87.00	52.00
(36)	Peaches Graham (Cubs)	175.00	87.00	52.00
(37)	Peaches Graham (Rustlers)	175.00	87.00	52.00
(38)	Clark Griffith	400.00	200.00	120.00
(39)	Topsy Hartsel	175.00	87.00	52.00
(40)	Arnold Hauser	175.00	87.00	52.00
(41)	Charlie Hemphill	175.00	87.00	52.00
(42)	Tom Jones	175.00	87.00	52.00
(43)	Jack Knight	175.00	87.00	52.00
(44)	Ed Konetchy	175.00	87.00	52.00
(45)	Harry Krause	175.00	87.00	52.00
(46)	Tommy Leach	175.00	87.00	52.00
(47)	Rube Marquard	400.00	200.00	120.00
(48)	Christy Mathewson	900.00	400.00	190.00
(49)	Al Mattern	175.00	87.00	52.00
(50)	Amby McConnell	175.00	87.00	52.00
(51)	John McGraw	500.00	250.00	150.00
(52)	Harry McIntire (McIntyre)	175.00	87.00	52.00
(53)	Fred Merkle	200.00	100.00	60.00
(54)	Chief Meyers	175.00	87.00	52.00
(55)	Dots Miller	175.00	87.00	52.00
(56)	Danny Murphy	175.00	87.00	52.00
(57)	Red Murray	175.00	87.00	52.00
(58)	Tom Needham	175.00	87.00	52.00
(59)	Rebel Oakes	175.00	87.00	52.00
(60)	Rube Oldring	175.00	87.00	52.00
(61)	Orval Overall	175.00	87.00	52.00
(62)	Fred Parent	175.00	87.00	52.00
(63)	Fred Payne	175.00	87.00	52.00
(64)	Barney Pelty	175.00	87.00	52.00
(65)	Deacon Phillippe	175.00	87.00	52.00
(66)	Jack Quinn	175.00	87.00	52.00
(67)	Bugs Raymond	175.00	87.00	52.00
(68)	Ed Reulbach	175.00	87.00	52.00
(69)	Doc Scanlon (Scanlan)	175.00	87.00	52.00
(70)	Germany Schaefer	175.00	87.00	52.00
(71)	Admiral Schlei	175.00	87.00	52.00
(72)	Wildfire Schulte	175.00	87.00	52.00
(73)	Dave Shean	175.00	87.00	52.00
(74)	Jimmy Sheckard	175.00	87.00	52.00
(75)	Hap Smith (Superbas)	175.00	87.00	52.00
(76)	Harry Smith (Rustlers)	700.00	350.00	190.00
(77)	Fred Snodgrass	175.00	87.00	52.00
(78)	Tris Speaker	600.00	300.00	100.00
(79)	Harry Steinfeldt (Cubs)	200.00	100.00	60.00
(80)	Harry Steinfeldt (Rustlers)	200.00	100.00	60.00
(81)	George Stone	175.00	87.00	52.00
(82)	Gabby Street	175.00	87.00	52.00
(83)	Ed Summers	175.00	87.00	52.00
(84)	Lee Tannehill	175.00	87.00	52.00
(85)	Joe Tinker	400.00	200.00	120.00
(86)	John Titus	175.00	87.00	52.00
(87)	Terry Turner	175.00	87.00	52.00
(88)	Bobby Wallace	400.00	200.00	120.00
(89)	Doc White	175.00	87.00	52.00
(90)	Ed Willett	175.00	87.00	52.00
(91)	Art Wilson	175.00	87.00	52.00
(92)	Harry Wolter	175.00	87.00	52.00

1910 S74 Silks - Colored

	NR MT	EX	VG
Complete Set:	27000.00	13500.00	8100.
Common Player:	150.00	75.00	45.00

		NR MT	EX	VG
(1)	Red Ames	150.00	75.00	45.00
(2)	Jimmy Archer	150.00	75.00	45.00
(3)	Home Run Baker	300.00	150.00	90.00
(4)	Cy Barger	150.00	75.00	45.00
(5)	Jack Barry	150.00	75.00	45.00
(6)	Johnny Bates	150.00	75.00	45.00
(7)	Beals Becker	150.00	75.00	45.00
(8)	George Bell	150.00	75.00	45.00
(9)	Chief Bender	300.00	150.00	90.00
(10)	Bill Bergen	150.00	75.00	45.00
(11)	Bob Bescher	150.00	75.00	45.00
(12)	Roger Bresnahan (mouth closed)	400.00	190.00	90.00
(13)	Roger Bresnahan (mouth open)	400.00	190.00	90.00
(14)	Al Bridwell	150.00	75.00	45.00
(15)	Mordecai Brown	300.00	150.00	90.00
(16)	Bobby Byrne	150.00	75.00	45.00
(17)	Howie Camnitz	150.00	75.00	45.00
(18)	Bill Carrigan	150.00	75.00	45.00
(19)	Frank Chance	400.00	200.00	120.00
(20)	Hal Chase	250.00	125.00	75.00
(21)	Ed Cicotte	200.00	100.00	60.00
(22)	Fred Clarke	300.00	150.00	90.00
(23)	Ty Cobb	2500.00	1250.00	750.00
(24)	Eddie Collins	300.00	150.00	90.00
(25)	Doc Crandall	150.00	75.00	45.00
(26)	Bill Dahlen	150.00	75.00	45.00
(27)	Jake Daubert	200.00	100.00	60.00
(28)	Jim Delahanty	150.00	75.00	45.00
(29)	Art Devlin	150.00	75.00	45.00
(30)	Josh Devore	150.00	75.00	45.00
(31)	Red Dooin	150.00	75.00	45.00
(32)	Mickey Doolan	150.00	75.00	45.00
(33)	Tom Downey	150.00	75.00	45.00
(34)	Larry Doyle	150.00	75.00	45.00
(35)	Hugh Duffy	300.00	150.00	90.00
(36)	Jimmy Dygert	150.00	75.00	45.00
(37)	Kid Elberfield (Elberfeld)	150.00	75.00	45.00
(38)	Steve Evans	150.00	75.00	45.00
(39)	Johnny Evers	300.00	150.00	90.00
(40)	Bob Ewing	150.00	75.00	45.00
(41)	Art Fletcher	150.00	75.00	45.00
(42)	John Flynn	150.00	75.00	45.00
(43)	Russ Ford	150.00	75.00	45.00
(44)	Bill Foxen	150.00	75.00	45.00
(45)	Art Fromme	150.00	75.00	45.00
(46)	George Gibson	150.00	75.00	45.00
(47)	Peaches Graham	150.00	75.00	45.00
(48)	Eddie Grant	150.00	75.00	45.00
(49)	Clark Griffith	300.00	150.00	90.00
(50)	Topsy Hartsel	150.00	75.00	45.00
(51)	Arnold Hauser	150.00	75.00	45.00
(52)	Charlie Hemphill	150.00	75.00	45.00
(53)	Dick Hoblitzell	150.00	75.00	45.00
(54)	Miller Huggins	300.00	150.00	90.00
(55)	John Hummel	150.00	75.00	45.00
(56)	Walter Johnson	800.00	400.00	240.00
(57)	Davy Jones	150.00	75.00	45.00
(58)	Johnny Kling	150.00	75.00	45.00

		NR MT	EX	VG
(59)	Jack Knight	150.00	75.00	45.00
(60)	Ed Konetchy	150.00	75.00	45.00
(61)	Harry Krause	150.00	75.00	45.00
(62)	Tommy Leach	150.00	75.00	45.00
(63)	Lefty Leifield	150.00	75.00	45.00
(64)	Hans Lobert	150.00	75.00	45.00
(65)	Rube Marquard	300.00	150.00	90.00
(66)	Christy Mathewson	800.00	400.00	240.00
(67)	Al Mattern	150.00	75.00	45.00
(68)	Amby McConnell	150.00	75.00	45.00
(69)	John McGraw	400.00	200.00	120.00
(70)	Harry McIntire (McIntyre)	150.00	75.00	45.00
(71)	Fred Merkle	200.00	100.00	60.00
(72)	Chief Meyers	150.00	75.00	45.00
(73)	Dots Miller	150.00	75.00	45.00
(74)	Mike Mitchell	150.00	75.00	45.00
(75)	Pat Moran	150.00	75.00	45.00
(76)	George Moriarty	150.00	75.00	45.00
(77)	George Mullin	150.00	75.00	45.00
(78)	Danny Murphy	150.00	75.00	45.00
(79)	Red Murray	150.00	75.00	45.00
(80)	Tom Needham	150.00	75.00	45.00
(81)	Rebel Oakes	150.00	75.00	45.00
(82)	Rube Oldring	150.00	75.00	45.00
(83)	Orval Overall	150.00	75.00	45.00
(84)	Fred Parent	150.00	75.00	45.00
(85)	Dode Paskert	150.00	75.00	45.00
(86)	Billy Payne	150.00	75.00	45.00
(87)	Barney Pelty	150.00	75.00	45.00
(88)	Deacon Phillippe	150.00	75.00	45.00
(89)	Jack Quinn	150.00	75.00	45.00
(90)	Bugs Raymond	150.00	75.00	45.00
(91)	Ed Reulbach	150.00	75.00	45.00
(92)	Jack Rowan	150.00	75.00	45.00
(93)	Nap Rucker	150.00	75.00	45.00
(94)	Doc Scanlon (Scanlan)	150.00	75.00	45.00
(95)	Germany Schaefer	150.00	75.00	45.00
(96)	Admiral Schlei	150.00	75.00	45.00
(97)	Wildfire Schulte	150.00	75.00	45.00
(98)	Dave Shean	150.00	75.00	45.00
(99)	Jimmy Sheckard	150.00	75.00	45.00
(100)	Happy Smith	150.00	75.00	45.00
(101)	Fred Snodgrass	150.00	75.00	45.00
(102)	Tris Speaker	600.00	300.00	180.00
(103)	Jake Stahl	150.00	75.00	45.00
(104)	Harry Steinfeldt	200.00	100.00	60.00
(105)	George Stone	150.00	75.00	45.00
(106)	Gabby Street	150.00	75.00	45.00
(107)	Ed Summers	150.00	75.00	45.00
(108)	Lee Tannehill	150.00	75.00	45.00
(109)	Joe Tinker	300.00	150.00	90.00
(110)	John Titus	150.00	75.00	45.00
(111)	Terry Turner	150.00	75.00	45.00
(112)	Bobby Wallace	300.00	150.00	90.00
(113)	Zack Wheat	300.00	150.00	90.00
(114)	Doc White (White Sox)	150.00	75.00	45.00
(115)	Kirby White (Pirates)	150.00	75.00	45.00
(116)	Ed Willett	150.00	75.00	45.00
(117)	Owen Wilson	150.00	75.00	45.00
(118)	Hooks Wiltse	150.00	75.00	45.00
(119)	Harry Wolter	150.00	75.00	45.00
(120)	Cy Young	800.00	400.00	240.00

1912 S81 Silks

The 1912 S81 "Silks," so-called because they featured pictures of baseball players on a satin-like fabric rather than paper or cardboard, are closely related to the better-known T3 Turkey Red cabinet

cards of the same era. The silks, which featured 25 of the day's top baseball players among its other various subjects, were available as a premium with Helmar "Turkish Trophies" cigarettes. According to an advertising sheet, one silk could be obtained for 25 Helmar coupons. The silks measure 7" by 9" and, with a few exceptions, used the same pictures featured on the popular Turkey Red cards. Five players (Pitchers Rube Marquard, Rube Benton, Marty O'Toole, Grover Alexander and Russ Ford) appear in the "Silks" set that were not included in the T3 set. In addition, an error involving the Frank Baker card was corrected for the "Silks" set. (In the T3 set, Baker's card actually pictured Jack Barry.) Several years ago a pair of New England collectors found a small stack of Christy Mathewson "Silks," making his, by far, the most common. Otherwise, the "Silks" are generally so rare that it is difficult to determine the relative scarcity of the others. Baseball enthusiasts are usually only attached to the 25 baseball players in the "Silks" premium set, but it is interesting to note that the promotion also offered dozens of other subjects, including "beautiful women in bathing and athletic costumes, charming dancers in gorgeous attire, natiional flags and generals on horseback."

		NR MT	EX	VG
Complete Set:		92000.00	46000.00	27600.
Common Player:		1500.00	750.00	450.00
111	Rube Marquard	4000.00	2000.00	1200.
112	Marty O'Toole	1500.00	750.00	450.00
113	Rube Benton	1500.00	750.00	450.00
114	Grover Alexander	4250.00	2125.00	1275.
115	Russ Ford	1700.00	850.00	500.00
116	John McGraw	5000.00	2500.00	1500.
117	Nap Rucker	1500.00	750.00	450.00
118	Mike Mitchell	1500.00	750.00	450.00
119	Chief Bender	4000.00	2000.00	1200.
120	Home Run Baker	4000.00	2000.00	1200.
121	Nap Lajoie	5500.00	2250.00	1650.
122	Joe Tinker	4000.00	2000.00	1200.
123	Sherry Magee	1500.00	750.00	450.00
124	Howie Camnitz	1500.00	750.00	450.00
125	Eddie Collins	4000.00	2000.00	1200.
126	Red Dooin	1500.00	750.00	450.00
127	Ty Cobb	12000.00	6000.00	3600.
128	Hugh Jennings	4000.00	2000.00	1200.
129	Roger Bresnahan	4000.00	2000.00	1200.
130	Jake Stahl	1700.00	850.00	500.00
131	Tris Speaker	6500.00	3250.00	2000.
132	Ed Walsh	4000.00	2000.00	1200.
133	Christy Mathewson	2800.00	1400.00	800.00
134	Johnny Evers	4250.00	2125.00	1275.
135	Walter Johnson	7000.00	3500.00	2200.

1958 San Francisco Call-Bulletin Giants

These unnumbered cards, picturing members of the San Francisco Giants, were inserted in copies of the San Francisco Call-Bulletin newspaper as part of a promotional contest. The 25 cards in the set measure 2" by 4" and were printed on orange paper.

The top of the card contains a black and white player photo, while the bottom contains a perforated stub with a serial number used to win prizes. (Cards without the stub intact are approximately 50 percent of the prices listed.) The contest name, "Giant Payoff", appears prominently on both sides of the stub. The back of the card contains a 1958 Giants schedule.

		NR MT	EX	VG
Complete Set:		1200.00	600.00	360.00
Common Player:		10.00	5.00	3.00
(1)	Johnny Antonelli	15.00	7.50	4.50
(2)	Curt Barclay	10.00	5.00	3.00
(3)	Tom Bowers	500.00	250.00	150.00
(4)	Ed Bressoud	90.00	45.00	27.00
(5)	Orlando Cepeda	90.00	45.00	27.00
(6)	Ray Crone	10.00	5.00	3.00
(7)	Jim Davenport	15.00	7.50	4.50
(8)	Paul Giel	10.00	5.00	3.00
(9)	Ruben Gomez	10.00	5.00	3.00
(10)	Marv Grissom	10.00	5.00	3.00
(11)	Ray Jablonski	90.00	45.00	27.00
(12)	Willie Kirkland	100.00	50.00	30.00
(13)	Whitey Lockman	15.00	7.50	4.50
(14)	Willie Mays	300.00	150.00	90.00
(15)	Mike McCormick	15.00	7.50	4.50
(16)	Stu Miller	15.00	7.50	4.50
(17)	Ramon Monzant	10.00	5.00	3.00
(18)	Danny O'Connell	10.00	5.00	3.00
(19)	Bill Rigney	15.00	7.50	4.50
(20)	Hank Sauer	15.00	7.50	4.50
(21)	Bob Schmidt	10.00	5.00	3.00
(22)	Daryl Spencer	10.00	5.00	3.00
(23)	Valmy Thomas	10.00	5.00	3.00
(24)	Bobby Thomson	30.00	15.00	9.00
(25)	Allan Worthington	10.00	5.00	3.00

1888 Scrapps

The origin of these die-cut, embossed player busts is not known, but they were apparently part of a book of "punch-outs" issued in the late 1880s. When out of their original album, they apparently resembled scraps of paper, presumably leading to their unusual name. An earlier theory that they were issued by "Scrapps Tobacco" has since been disocunted after research indicated there never was such a company. The die-cuts include 18 different players - nine members of the American Association St. Louis Browns and nine from the National League Detroit Wolverines. Although they vary slightly in size, the player busts are generally about 2" wide and 3" high. The drawings for the St. Louis player busts were taken from the Old Judge "Brown's Champions" set. The player's name appears along the bottom.

		NR MT	EX	VG
Complete Set:		6500.00	3250.00	1900.
Common Player:		250.00	125.00	75.00
(1)	C.W. Bennett	250.00	125.00	75.00
(2)	D. Brouthers	500.00	250.00	150.00
(3)	A.J. Bushong	250.00	125.00	75.00
(4)	Robert L. Caruthers	250.00	125.00	75.00

		NR MT	EX	VG
(5)	Charles Comiskey	600.00	300.00	175.00
(6)	F. Dunlap	300.00	150.00	90.00
(7)	David L. Foutz	250.00	125.00	75.00
(8)	C.H. Getzen (Geitzen)	300.00	150.00	90.00
(9)	Wm. Gleason	250.00	125.00	75.00
(10)	E. Hanlon	300.00	150.00	90.00
(11)	Walter A. Latham	250.00	125.00	75.00
(12)	James O'Neill	250.00	125.00	75.00
(13)	H. Richardson	300.00	150.00	90.00
(14)	Wm. Robinson	500.00	250.00	150.00
(15)	J.C. Rowe	300.00	150.00	90.00
(16)	S. Thompson	500.00	250.00	150.00
(17)	Curtis Welch	250.00	125.00	75.00
(18)	J.L. White	300.00	150.00	90.00

1949 Sealtest Phillies

This regional Phillies set was issued in the Philadelphia area in 1949 by Sealtest Dairy. It consisted of 12 large (3-1/2" by 4-1/4") sticker cards with peel-off backs. The front of the unnumbered cards featured an action photo with facsimilie autograph, while the back was an advertisement for Sealtest products. The same photos and checklist were also used for the Lummis Peanut Butter card set issued in Philadelphia the same year.

		NR MT	EX	VG
Complete Set:		650.00	325.00	195.00
Common Player:		35.00	17.50	10.50
(1)	Rich Ashburn	110.00	55.00	35.00
(2)	Hank Borowy	35.00	17.50	10.50
(3)	Del Ennis	60.00	30.00	17.50
(4)	Granny Hamner	35.00	17.50	10.50
(5)	Puddinhead Jones	35.00	17.50	10.50
(6)	Russ Meyer	35.00	17.50	10.50
(7)	Bill Nicholson	35.00	17.50	10.50
(8)	Robin Roberts	150.00	75.00	45.00
(9)	"Schoolboy" Rowe	35.00	17.50	10.50
(10)	Andy Seminick	35.00	17.50	10.50
(11)	Curt Simmons	60.00	30.00	18.00
(12)	Eddie Waitkus	35.00	17.50	10.50

1947 Signal Gasoline

	NR MT	EX	VG
Complete Set:	2250.00	1125.00	675.00
Common Player:	8.00	4.00	2.50

(1) "Vic" Buccola
(2) "Mickey" Burnett
(3) Ralph Buxton
(4) Vince DiMaggio
(5) "Dizz" Duezabou
(6) "Bud" Foster (announcer)
(7) "Sherriff" Gassaway
(8) Tom Hafey
(9) Brooks Holder
(10) "Gene" Lillard
(11) Dario Lodigiani
(12) Hershel Martin (Herschel)
(13) Henry "Cotton" Pippen
(14) Billy Raimondi
(15) Tony Sabol
(16) Les Scarsella
(17) Floyd Speer
(18) Casey Stengel
(19) Maurice Van Robays

1948 Signal Gasoline Oakland Oaks

Issued by Signal Oil in the Oakland area in 1948, this 24-card set features members of the Oakland Oaks of the Pacific Coast League. The unnumbered cards, measuring 2-3/8" by 3-1/2", were given away at gas stations. The front consists of a color photo, while the backs (printed in either blue or black) conatin a breif player write-up along with a Signal Oil ad and logo.

	NR MT	EX	VG
Complete Set:	475.00	237.00	142.00
Common Player:	15.00	7.50	4.50

		NR MT	EX	VG
(1)	John C. Babich	15.00	7.50	4.50
(2)	Ralph Buxton	15.00	7.50	4.50
(3)	Loyd E. Christopher (Lloyd)	15.00	7.50	4.50
(4)	Merrill Russell Combs	15.00	7.50	4.50
(5)	Melvin E. Deuzabou	15.00	7.50	4.50
(6)	Nicholas ("Nick") Etten	20.00	10.00	6.00
(7)	Bud Foster (announcer)	15.00	7.50	4.50
(8)	Charles Gassaway	15.00	7.50	4.50
(9)	Will Hafey	15.00	7.50	4.50
(10)	Ray Hamrick	15.00	7.50	4.50
(11)	Brooks Richard Holder	20.00	10.00	6.00
(12)	Earl Jones	15.00	7.50	4.50
(13)	Harry "Cookie" Lavagetto	18.00	9.00	5.50
(14)	Robert E. Lillard	15.00	7.50	4.50
(15)	Dario Lodigiani	15.00	7.50	4.50
(16)	Ernie Lombardi	30.00	15.00	9.00
(17)	Alfred Manuel Martin	90.00	45.00	27.00
(18)	George Michael Metkovich	15.00	7.50	4.50
(19)	William L. Raimondi	15.00	7.50	4.50
(20)	Les George Scarsella	15.00	7.50	4.50
(21)	Floyd Vernie Speer	15.00	7.50	4.50
(22)	Charles "Casey" Stengel	90.00	45.00	27.00
(23)	Maurice Van Robays	15.00	7.50	4.50
(24)	Aldon Jay Wilkie	15.00	7.50	4.50

1947 Smith's Oakland Oaks

A veteran of several seasons with Pittsburgh Pirates of the National League, horsehide-mauler MAURICE VAN RO-BAYS figures to give the '47 Acorns right-hand sock power. Maurice banged out 31 safeties in 57 tilts with the '46 Pirates. He usually covers right field.

Smiths
12th and Washington, Oakland
Largest men's and boys' store west of Chicago

MAURICE VAN ROBAYS
Oaks Outfielder 7

This regional set of Oakland Oaks (Pacific Coast League) cards was issued in 1947 by Smith's Clothing stores and is numbered in the lower right corner. The card fronts include a black and white photo with the player's name, team and position below. The backs carry a breif player write-up and an advertisement for Smith's Clothing. The cards measure 2" by 3". The Max Marshall card was apparently short- printed and is much scarcer than the rest of the set.

	NR MT	EX	VG
Complete Set:	575.00	287.00	172.00
Common Player:	15.00	7.50	4.50

		NR MT	EX	VG
1	Charles (Casey) Stengel	90.00	45.00	27.00
2	Billy Raimondi	15.00	7.50	4.50
3	Les Scarsella	15.00	7.50	4.50
4	Brooks Holder	15.00	7.50	4.50
5	Ray Hamrick	15.00	7.50	4.50
6	Gene Lillard	15.00	7.50	4.50
7	Maurice Van Robays	15.00	7.50	4.50
8	Charlie (Sheriff) Gassaway	15.00	7.50	4.50
9	Henry (Cotton) Pippen	15.00	7.50	4.50
10	James Arnold	15.00	7.50	4.50
11	Ralph (Buck) Buxton	15.00	7.50	4.50
12	Ambrose (Bo) Palica	15.00	7.50	4.50
13	Tony Sabol	15.00	7.50	4.50
14	Ed Kearse	15.00	7.50	4.50
15	Bill Hart	15.00	7.50	4.50
16	Donald (Snuffy) Smith	15.00	7.50	4.50
17	Oral (Mickey) Burnett	15.00	7.50	4.50
18	Tom Hafey	15.00	7.50	4.50
19	Will Hafey	15.00	7.50	4.50
20	Paul Gillespie	25.00	6.00	3.50
21	Damon Hayes	25.00	6.00	3.50
22	Max Marshall	125.00	6.00	3.50
23	Mel (Dizz) Duezabou	15.00	7.50	4.50
24	Mel Reeves	15.00	7.50	4.50
25	Joe Faria	25.00	6.00	3.50

1948 Smith's Oakland Oaks

Slugging LES SCARSELLA, 34, played in only half the games last year but hit 13 homers. Played in majors with Reds, Braves. Came to Oaks in '42 from Seattle. Bats and throws left. Hit .255 last year. Lives in Oakland.

Smith
12th and Washington, Oakland
Largest men's and boys' store west of Chicago

LES SCARSELLA
Oaks Outfielder 6

The 1948 Smith's Clothing issue was another 25-card regional set featuring members of the Oakland Oaks of the Pacific Coast featuring members of the Oakland Oaks of the Pacific Coast black and white cards again measure 2" by 3" but were printed on heavier, glossy stock. The player's name, team and position appear below the photo with the card number in the lower right corner. The back has a brief player write-up and an ad for Smith's Clothing.

		NR MT	EX	VG
	Complete Set:	500.00	250.00	150.00
	Common Player:	15.00	7.50	4.50
1	Billy Raimondi	15.00	7.50	4.50
2	Brooks Holder	15.00	7.50	4.50
3	Will Hafey	20.00	6.00	3.50
4	Nick Etten	15.00	7.50	4.50
5	Lloyd Christopher	15.00	7.50	4.50
6	Les Scarsella	15.00	7.50	4.50
7	Ray Hamrick	15.00	7.50	4.50
8	Gene Lillard	15.00	7.50	4.50
9	Maurice Van Robays	15.00	7.50	4.50
10	Charlie Gassaway	15.00	7.50	4.50
11	Ralph (Buck) Buxton	15.00	7.50	4.50
12	Tom Hafey	15.00	7.50	4.50
13	Damon Hayes	15.00	7.50	4.50
14	Mel (Dizz) Duezabou	15.00	7.50	4.50
15	Dario Lodigiani	15.00	7.50	4.50
16	Vic Buccola	15.00	7.50	4.50
17	Billy Martin	90.00	45.00	27.00
18	Floyd Speer	15.00	7.50	4.50
19	Eddie Samcoff	15.00	7.50	4.50
20	Charles (Casey) Stengel	90.00	45.00	27.00
21	Lloyd Hittle	15.00	7.50	4.50
22	Johnny Babich	15.00	7.50	4.50
23	Merrill Combs	15.00	7.50	4.50
24	Eddie Murphy	15.00	7.50	4.50
25	Bob Klinger	15.00	7.50	4.50

1953 Spic and Span Braves

The first of several regional issues from a Milwaukee dry cleaner, the 1953-54 Spic and Span Braves set consists of 27 cards, each measuring 3-1/4" by 5-1/2". The fronts of the card have a facsimilie autograph beneath the player photo. Cards are found with blank backs or with a Spic and Span advertising message on the back.

		NR MT	EX	VG
	Complete Set:	800.00	400.00	240.00
	Common Player:	25.00	12.50	7.50
(1)	Joe Adcock	35.00	17.50	10.50
(2)	John Antonelli	30.00	15.00	9.00
(3)	Vern Bickford	25.00	12.50	7.50
(4)	Bill Bruton	30.00	15.00	9.00
(5)	Bob Buhl	30.00	15.00	9.00
(6)	Lew Burdette	35.00	17.50	10.50
(7)	Dick Cole	25.00	12.50	7.50
(8)	Walker Cooper	25.00	12.50	7.50
(9)	Del Crandall	35.00	17.50	10.50
(10)	George Crowe	25.00	12.50	7.50
(11)	Jack Dittmer	25.00	12.50	7.50
(12)	Sid Gordon	25.00	12.50	7.50
(13)	Ernie Johnson	25.00	12.50	7.50
(14)	Dave Jolly	25.00	12.50	7.50
(15)	Don Liddle	25.00	12.50	7.50
(16)	John Logan	30.00	15.00	9.00
(17)	Ed Mathews	100.00	50.00	30.00
(18)	Dan O'Connell	25.00	12.50	7.50
(19)	Andy Pafko	30.00	15.00	9.00
(20)	Jim Pendleton	25.00	12.50	7.50
(21)	Ebba St. Claire	25.00	12.50	7.50
(22)	Warren Spahn	100.00	50.00	30.00
(23)	Max Surkont	25.00	12.50	7.50
(24)	Bob Thomson	30.00	15.00	9.00
(25)	Bob Thorpe	25.00	12.50	7.50
(26)	Roberto Vargas	25.00	12.50	7.50
(27)	Jim Wilson	25.00	12.50	7.50

1953 Spic and Span Braves 7x10 Photos

This regional set was issued by Spic and Span Dry Cleaners of Milwaukee over a four-year period and consists of 13 large (7" by 10") photos of Braves players. Of all the various Spic and Span sets, this one seems to be the easiest to find. The fronts feature a player photo with a facsimilie autograph below. The Spic and Span logo also appears on the fronts, while the backs are blank. A photo of Milwaukee County Stadium also exists but is not generally considered to be part of the set.

		NR MT	EX	VG
	Complete Set:	250.00	125.00	75.00
	Common Player:	10.00	5.00	3.00
(1)	Joe Adcock	18.00	9.00	5.50
(2)	Bill Bruton	12.00	6.00	3.50
(3)	Bob Buhl	12.00	6.00	3.50
(4)	Lew Burdette	18.00	9.00	5.50
(5)	Del Crandall	18.00	9.00	5.50
(6)	Jack Dittmer	10.00	5.00	3.00
(7)	John Logan	12.00	6.00	3.50
(8)	Ed Mathews	50.00	25.00	15.00
(9)	Chet Nichols	10.00	5.00	3.00
(10)	Dan O'Connell	10.00	5.00	3.00
(11)	Andy Pafko	12.00	6.00	3.50
(12)	Warren Spahn	50.00	25.00	15.00
(13)	Bob Thomson	12.00	6.00	3.50

1954 Spic and Span Braves

Issued during the three-year period from 1954-1956, this Spic and Span set consists of 18

postcard-size (4" by 6") cards. The front of the cards include a facsimilie autograph printed in white and the Spic and Span logo.

		NR MT	EX	VG
Complete Set:		500.00	250.00	150.00
Common Player:		12.00	6.00	3.50
(1)	Hank Aaron	180.00	90.00	54.00
(2)	Joe Adcock	25.00	12.50	7.50
(3)	Bill Bruton	18.00	9.00	5.50
(4)	Bob Buhl	18.00	9.00	5.50
(5)	Lew Burdette	25.00	12.50	7.50
(6)	Gene Conley	18.00	9.00	5.50
(7)	Del Crandall	25.00	12.50	7.50
(8)	Ray Crone	12.00	6.00	3.50
(9)	Jack Dittmer	12.00	6.00	3.50
(10)	Ernie Johnson	12.00	6.00	3.50
(11)	Dave Jolly	12.00	6.00	3.50
(12)	John Logan	18.00	9.00	5.50
(13)	Ed Mathews	80.00	40.00	24.00
(14)	Chet Nichols	12.00	6.00	3.50
(15)	Dan O'Connell	12.00	6.00	3.50
(16)	Andy Pafko	18.00	9.00	5.50
(17)	Warren Spahn	80.00	40.00	24.00
(18)	Bob Thomson	18.00	9.00	5.50

1955 Spic and Span Braves Die-cuts

This 17-card, die-cut set is the rarest of all the Spic and Span issues. The stand-ups, which measure approximately 7-1/2" by 7", picture the players in action poses and were designed to be punched out, allowing them to stand up. Most cards were used in this fashion, making better-condition cards very rare today. The front of the card includes a facsimilie autograph and the Spic and Span logo.

		NR MT	EX	VG
Complete Set:		3750.00	1875.00	1125.
Common Player:		125.00	62.00	37.00
(1)	Hank Aaron	800.00	400.00	240.00
(2)	Joe Adcock	175.00	87.00	52.00
(3)	Bill Bruton	150.00	75.00	45.00
(4)	Bob Buhl	150.00	75.00	45.00
(5)	Lew Burdette	175.00	87.00	52.00
(6)	Gene Conley	150.00	75.00	45.00
(7)	Del Crandall	175.00	87.00	52.00
(8)	Jack Dittmer	125.00	62.00	37.00
(9)	Ernie Johnson	125.00	62.00	37.00
(10)	Dave Jolly	125.00	62.00	37.00
(11)	John Logan	150.00	75.00	45.00
(12)	Ed Mathews	350.00	175.00	105.00
(13)	Chet Nichols	125.00	62.00	37.00
(14)	Dan O'Connell	125.00	62.00	37.00
(15)	Andy Pafko	150.00	75.00	45.00
(16)	Warren Spahn	350.00	175.00	105.00
(17)	Bob Thomson	150.00	75.00	45.00
(18)	Jim Wilson	125.00	62.00	37.00

1957 Spic and Span Braves

This 20-card set was issued in 1957, the year the Braves were World Champions and is a highly desirable set. The cards measure 4" by 5" and have a wide, white border surrounding the player photo. A blue Spic and Span logo appears in the extreme lower right corner, and the card includes a salutation and facsimilie autograph, also in blue.

		NR MT	EX	VG
Complete Set:		425.00	212.00	127.00
Common Player:		12.00	6.00	3.50
(1)	Hank Aaron	125.00	62.00	37.00
(2)	Joe Adcock	25.00	12.50	7.50
(3)	Bill Bruton	18.00	9.00	5.50
(4)	Bob Buhl	18.00	9.00	5.50
(5)	Lew Burdette	25.00	12.50	7.50
(6)	Gene Conley	18.00	9.00	5.50
(7)	Wes Covington	18.00	9.00	5.50
(8)	Del Crandall	25.00	12.50	7.50
(9)	Ray Crone	12.00	6.00	3.50
(10)	Fred Haney	18.00	9.00	5.50
(11)	Ernie Johnson	12.00	6.00	3.50
(12)	Felix Mantilla	25.00	12.50	7.50
(13)	Ed Mathews	60.00	30.00	18.00
(14)	John Logan	18.00	9.00	5.50
(15)	Dan O'Connell	12.00	6.00	3.50
(16)	Andy Pafko	18.00	9.00	5.50
(17)	Red Schoendienst	40.00	20.00	12.00
(18)	Warren Spahn	60.00	30.00	18.00
(19)	Bob Thomson	18.00	9.00	5.50
(20)	Bob Trowbridge	25.00	12.50	7.50

1960 Spic and Span Braves

Spic and Span's final Milwaukee Braves issue consisted of 26 cards, each measuring 2-3/4" by 3-1/8". The fronts contain a white-bordered photo with no printing, while the backs include a facsimilie autograph and the words "Photographed and Autographed Exclusively for Spic and Span." The 1960 set includes the only known variation in the Spic and Span sets. A "flopped" negative error showing catcher Del Crandell batting left-handed was later corrected.

		NR MT	EX	VG
Complete Set:		600.00	300.00	180.00
Common Player:		12.00	6.00	3.50
(1)	Hank Aaron	125.00	62.00	37.00
(2)	Joe Adcock	25.00	12.50	7.50
(3)	Bill Bruton	18.00	9.00	5.50
(4)	Bob Buhl	18.00	9.00	5.50
(5)	Lew Burdette	25.00	12.50	7.50
(6)	Chuck Cottier	12.00	6.00	3.50
(7a)	Del Crandall (photo reversed)	35.00	17.50	10.50
(7b)	Del Crandall (correct photo)	35.00	17.50	10.50
(8)	Chuck Dressen	12.00	6.00	3.50
(9)	Joey Jay	12.00	6.00	3.50
(10)	John Logan	18.00	9.00	5.50
(11)	Felix Mantilla	12.00	6.00	3.50
(12)	Ed Mathews	60.00	30.00	18.00
(13)	Lee Maye	12.00	6.00	3.50
(14)	Don McMahon	12.00	6.00	3.50
(15)	George Myatt	12.00	6.00	3.50
(16)	Andy Pafko	18.00	9.00	5.50
(17)	Juan Pizarro	12.00	6.00	3.50
(18)	Mel Roach	12.00	6.00	3.50
(19)	Bob Rush	12.00	6.00	3.50
(20)	Bob Scheffing	12.00	6.00	3.50
(21)	Red Schoendienst	35.00	17.50	10.50
(22)	Warren Spahn	60.00	30.00	18.00
(23)	Al Spangler	12.00	6.00	3.50
(24)	Frank Torre	12.00	6.00	3.50
(25)	Carl Willey	12.00	6.00	3.50
(26)	Whit Wyatt	12.00	6.00	3.50

		NR MT	EX	VG
18	Gene Tunney	200.00	100.00	60.00
19	Eddie Shore	125.00	67.00	37.00
20	Duke Kahanamoku	30.00	15.00	9.00
21	Johnny Weissmuller	175.00	87.00	52.00
22	Gene Sarazen	50.00	25.00	15.00
23	Vincent Richards	50.00	25.00	15.00
24	Howie Morenz	175.00	87.00	52.00
25	Ralph Snoddy	60.00	30.00	18.00
26	James Wedell	80.00	40.00	25.00
27	Roscoe Turner	90.00	45.00	27.00
28	James Doolittle	175.00	87.00	52.00
29	Ace Bailey	250.00	125.00	75.00
30	Irvin Johnson	250.00	125.00	75.00
31	Bobby Walthour, Jr.	60.00	30.00	18.00
32	Joe Lopchick	125.00	62.50	37.50
33	Eddie Burke	75.00	37.50	22.50
34	Irving Jaffee	60.00	30.00	18.00
35	Knute Rockne	950.00	475.00	300.00
36	Willie Hoppe	60.00	30.00	18.00
37	Helene Madison	60.00	30.00	18.00
38	Bobby Jones	100.00	50.00	30.00
39	Jack Westrope	60.00	30.00	18.00
40	Don George	60.00	30.00	18.00
41	Jim Browning	60.00	30.00	18.00
42	Carl Hubbell	400.00	200.00	125.00
43	Primo Carnera	75.00	38.00	23.00
44	Max Baer	100.00	50.00	30.00
45	Babe Didrickson	700.00	350.00	200.00
46	Ellsworth Vines	60.00	30.00	18.00
47	J.H. Stevens	60.00	30.00	18.00
48	Leonard Seppala	90.00	45.00	27.00

1933 Sport Kings

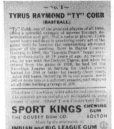

This 48-card set was issued by the Goudey Gum Company. Participants in 18 different sports are included in the set, which honors the top sports figures of the era. Three baseball players are pictured on the 2-3/8" by 2-7/8" cards. The card fronts are color portraits and include the player's name and silhouette representations of the respective sport. The card backs are numbered and list biographical information and a company ad.

		NR MT	EX	VG
Complete Set:		12000.00	6000.00	3500.
Common Player: 1-24		30.00	15.00	9.00
Common Player: 25-48		60.00	30.00	18.00
1	Ty Cobb	2000.00	1000.00	600.00
2	Babe Ruth	4200.00	2100.00	1300.
3	Nat Holman	125.00	67.00	37.00
4	Red Grange	600.00	300.00	180.00
5	Ed Wachter	125.00	67.00	37.00
6	Jim Thorpe	950.00	475.00	300.00
7	Bobby Walthour, Sr.	30.00	15.00	9.00
8	Walter Hagen	50.00	25.00	15.00
9	Ed Blood	30.00	15.00	9.00
10	Anston Lekang	30.00	15.00	9.00
11	Charles Jewtraw	30.00	15.00	9.00
12	Bobby McLean	30.00	15.00	9.00
13	Laverne Fator	30.00	15.00	9.00
14	Jim Londos	30.00	15.00	9.00
15	Reggie McNamara	30.00	15.00	9.00
16	Bill Tilden	50.00	25.00	15.00
17	Jack Dempsey	225.00	112.00	70.00

1928 Star Player Candy

L. A. BLUE

This somewhat confusing issue can be dated to 1928, although little is known about its origin. The producer of the set is not identified, but experienced collectors generally refer to it as the Star Player Candy set, apparently because it was distributed with a product of that name. The cards measure 1-7/8" by 2-7/8", are sepia-toned and blank-backed. The player's name (but no team designation) appears in the border below the photo in brown capital letters. To date the checklist of baseball players numbers 72, but more may exist, and cards of football players have also been found.

		NR MT	EX	VG
Complete Set:		9500.00	4750.00	2850.
Common Player:		60.00	30.00	18.00
(1)	Dave Bancroft	125.00	62.00	37.00
(2)	Emile Barnes	60.00	30.00	18.00
(3)	L.A. Blue	60.00	30.00	18.00
(4)	Garland Buckeye	60.00	30.00	18.00
(5)	George Burns	60.00	30.00	18.00
(6)	Guy T. Bush	60.00	30.00	18.00
(7)	Owen T. Carroll	60.00	30.00	18.00
(8)	Chalmer Cissell	60.00	30.00	18.00
(9)	Ty Cobb	1500.00	750.00	450.00
(10)	Gordon Cochrane	125.00	62.00	37.00
(11)	Richard Coffman	60.00	30.00	18.00
(12)	Eddie Collins	125.00	62.00	37.00
(13)	Stanley Coveleskie (Coveleski)	125.00	62.00	37.00
(14)	Hugh Critz	60.00	30.00	18.00
(15)	Hazen Cuyler	125.00	62.00	37.00
(16)	Charles Dressen	80.00	40.00	24.00
(17)	Joe Dugan	80.00	40.00	24.00

		NR MT	EX	VG
(18)	Elwood English	60.00	30.00	18.00
(19)	Bib Falk (Bibb)	60.00	30.00	18.00
(20)	Ira Flagstead	60.00	30.00	18.00
(21)	Bob Fothergill	60.00	30.00	18.00
(22)	Frank T. Frisch	125.00	62.00	37.00
(23)	Foster Ganzel	60.00	30.00	18.00
(24)	Lou Gehrig	1500.00	750.00	450.00
(25)	Chas. Gihringer (Gehringer)	125.00	62.00	37.00
(26)	George Gerken	60.00	30.00	18.00
(27)	Grant Gillis	60.00	30.00	18.00
(28)	Miguel Gonzales	60.00	30.00	18.00
(29)	Sam Gray	60.00	30.00	18.00
(30)	Chas. J. Grimm	80.00	40.00	24.00
(31)	Robert M. Grove	200.00	100.00	60.00
(32)	Chas. J. Hafey	125.00	62.00	37.00
(33)	Jesse Haines	125.00	62.00	37.00
(34)	Chas. L. Hartnett	125.00	62.00	37.00
(35)	Clifton HHeathcote	60.00	30.00	18.00
(36)	Harry Heilmann	125.00	62.00	37.00
(37)	John Heving	60.00	30.00	18.00
(38)	Waite Hoyt	125.00	62.00	37.00
(39)	Chas. Jamieson	60.00	30.00	18.00
(40)	Joe Judge	60.00	30.00	18.00
(41)	Willie Kamm	60.00	30.00	18.00
(42)	George Kelly	125.00	62.00	37.00
(43)	Tony Lazzeri	100.00	50.00	30.00
(44)	Adolfo Luque	60.00	30.00	18.00
(45)	Ted Lyons	125.00	62.00	37.00
(46)	Hugh McMullen	60.00	30.00	18.00
(47)	Bob Meusel	80.00	40.00	24.00
(48)	Wilcey Moore (Wilcy)	60.00	30.00	18.00
(49)	Ed C. Morgan	60.00	30.00	18.00
(50)	Herb Pennock	125.00	62.00	37.00
(51)	Everett Purdy	60.00	30.00	18.00
(52)	William Regan	60.00	30.00	18.00
(53)	Eppa Rixey	125.00	62.00	37.00
(54)	Charles Root	80.00	40.00	24.00
(55)	Jack Rothrock	60.00	30.00	18.00
(56)	Harold Ruel (Herold)	60.00	30.00	18.00
(57)	Babe Ruth	1500.00	750.00	450.00
(58)	Wally Schang	60.00	30.00	18.00
(59)	Joe Sewell	125.00	62.00	37.00
(60)	Luke Sewell	60.00	30.00	18.00
(61)	Joe Shaute	60.00	30.00	18.00
(62)	George Sisler	125.00	62.00	37.00
(63)	Tris Speaker	200.00	100.00	60.00
(64)	Riggs Stephenson	80.00	40.00	24.00
(65)	Jack Tavener	60.00	30.00	18.00
(66)	Al Thomas	60.00	30.00	18.00
(67)	Harold J. Traynor	125.00	62.00	37.00
(68)	George Uhle	60.00	30.00	18.00
(69)	Dazzy Vance	125.00	62.00	37.00
(70)	Cy Williams	80.00	40.00	24.00
(71)	Ken Williams	80.00	40.00	24.00
(72)	Lewis R. Wilson	125.00	62.00	37.00

T

1911 T3 Turkey Reds

Turkey Reds are the only cabinet cards the average collector can have a realistic chance to complete. Obtained by mailing in coupons found in Turkey Red, Fez and Old Mill brand cigarettes, the Turkey Reds measure 5 3/4" by 8", a size known to collectors as "cabinet cards." Turkey Reds feature full color lithograph fronts with wide gray frames. Backs carried either a numbered ordering list or an ad for Turkey Red cigarettes. The Turkey Red series consists of 25 boxers and 100 baseball players. Despite their cost, Turkey Reds remain very popular today as the most attractive of the cabinet sets.

		NR MT	EX	VG
Complete Set:		70000.00	35000.00	21000.
Common Player: 1-50		300.00	150.00	90.00
Common Player: 77-126		325.00	162.00	97.00
1	Mordecai Brown	1000.00	500.00	300.00
2	Bill Bergen	300.00	150.00	90.00
3	Tommy Leach	300.00	150.00	90.00
4	Roger Bresnahan	1200.00	600.00	360.00
5	Sam Crawford	1200.00	600.00	360.00
6	Hal Chase	400.00	200.00	125.00
7	Howie Camnitz	300.00	150.00	90.00
8	Fred Clarke	1000.00	500.00	300.00
9	Ty Cobb	8500.00	4250.00	2550.
10	Art Devlin	300.00	150.00	90.00
11	Bill Dahlen	300.00	150.00	90.00
12	Wil Bill Donovan	300.00	150.00	90.00
13	Larry Doyle	300.00	150.00	90.00
14	Red Dooin	300.00	150.00	90.00
15	Kid Elberfeld	300.00	150.00	90.00
16	Johnny Evers	1200.00	600.00	360.00
17	Clark Griffith	1200.00	600.00	360.00
18	Hughie Jennings	1200.00	600.00	360.00
19	Addie Joss	1200.00	600.00	360.00
20	Tim Jordan	300.00	150.00	90.00
21	Red Kleinow	300.00	150.00	90.00
22	Harry Krause	300.00	150.00	90.00
23	Nap Lajoie	2800.00	1400.00	840.00
24	Mike Mitchell	300.00	150.00	90.00
25	Matty McIntyre	300.00	150.00	90.00
26	John McGraw	1350.00	775.00	375.00
27	Christy Mathewson	3750.00	1875.00	1125.
28a	Harry McIntyre (Brooklyn)	300.00	150.00	90.00
28b	Harry McIntyre (Brooklyn and Chicago)	350.00	175.00	105.00
29	Amby McConnell	300.00	150.00	90.00
30	George Mullin	300.00	150.00	90.00
31	Sherry Magee	300.00	150.00	90.00
32	Orval Overall	300.00	150.00	90.00
33	Jake Pfeister	300.00	150.00	90.00
34	Nap Rucker	300.00	150.00	90.00
35	Joe Tinker	1200.00	600.00	360.00
36	Tris Speaker	2800.00	1400.00	840.00
37	Slim Sallee	300.00	150.00	90.00
38	Jake Stahl	300.00	150.00	90.00
39	Rube Waddell	1200.00	600.00	360.00
40a	Vic Willis (Pittsburg)	300.00	150.00	90.00
40b	Vic Willis (Pittsburg and St. Louis)	350.00	175.00	105.00
41	Hooks Wiltse	300.00	150.00	90.00
42	Cy Young	3500.00	1750.00	1050.
43	Out At Third	200.00	100.00	60.00
44	Trying To Catch Him Napping	200.00	100.00	60.00
45	Jordan & Herzog At First	300.00	150.00	90.00
46	Safe At Third	200.00	100.00	60.00
47	Frank Chance At Bat	1000.00	500.00	300.00
48	Jack Murray At Bat	300.00	150.00	90.00
49	A Close Play At Second	300.00	150.00	90.00
50	Chief Myers At Bat	300.00	150.00	90.00
77	Red Ames	325.00	162.00	97.00
78	Home Run Baker	1200.00	600.00	360.00
79	George Bell	325.00	162.00	97.00
80	Chief Bender	1000.00	500.00	300.00
81	Bob Bescher	325.00	162.00	97.00
82	Kitty Bransfield	325.00	162.00	97.00
83	Al Bridwell	325.00	162.00	97.00
84	George Browne	325.00	162.00	97.00
85	Bill Burns	325.00	162.00	97.00
86	Bill Carrigan	325.00	162.00	97.00
87	Eddie Collins	1000.00	500.00	300.00
88	Harry Coveleski	325.00	162.00	97.00
89	Lou Criger	325.00	162.00	97.00
90a	Mickey Doolin (name incorrect)	375.00	187.00	112.00
90b	Mickey Doolan (name correct)	325.00	162.00	97.00
91	Tom Downey	325.00	162.00	97.00
92	Jimmy Dygert	325.00	162.00	97.00
93	Art Fromme	325.00	162.00	97.00
94	George Gibson	325.00	162.00	97.00
95	Peaches Graham	325.00	162.00	97.00
96	Bob Groom	325.00	162.00	97.00

		NR MT	EX	VG
97	Dick Hoblitzell	325.00	162.00	97.00
98	Solly Hofman	325.00	162.00	97.00
99	Walter Johnson	4000.00	2000.00	1200.
100	Davy Jones	325.00	162.00	97.00
101	Wee Willie Keeler	450.00	225.00	135.00
102	Johnny Kling	325.00	162.00	97.00
103	Ed Konetchy	325.00	162.00	97.00
104	Ed Lennox	325.00	162.00	97.00
105	Hans Lobert	325.00	162.00	97.00
106	Harry Lord	325.00	162.00	97.00
107	Rube Manning	325.00	162.00	97.00
108	Fred Merkle	325.00	162.00	97.00
109	Pat Moran	325.00	162.00	97.00
110	George McBride	325.00	162.00	97.00
111	Harry Niles	325.00	162.00	97.00
112a	Dode Paskert (Cincinnati)	350.00	175.00	105.00
112b	Dode Paskert (Cincinnati and Philadelphia)	325.00	162.00	97.00
113	Bugs Raymond	325.00	162.00	97.00
114	Bob Rhoades (Rhoads)	350.00	175.00	105.00
115	Admiral Schlei	325.00	162.00	97.00
116	Boss Schmidt	325.00	162.00	97.00
117	Wildfire Schulte	325.00	162.00	97.00
118	Frank Smith	325.00	162.00	97.00
119	George Stone	325.00	162.00	97.00
120	Gabby Street	325.00	162.00	97.00
121	Billy Sullivan	325.00	162.00	97.00
122a	Fred Tenney (New York)	350.00	175.00	105.00
122b	Fred Tenney (New York and Boston)	325.00	162.00	97.00
123	Ira Thomas	325.00	162.00	97.00
124	Bobby Wallace	1000.00	500.00	300.00
125	Ed Walsh	1200.00	600.00	360.00
126	Owen Wilson	325.00	162.00	97.00

		NR MT	EX	VG
Complete Set:		9500.00	4750.00	2850.
Common Player:		300.00	150.00	90.00
3	Howard	300.00	150.00	90.00
22	Christian	300.00	150.00	90.00
24	Maggert	300.00	150.00	90.00
33	Flater	300.00	150.00	90.00
34	Zacher	300.00	150.00	90.00
37	Ryan	300.00	150.00	90.00
49	Kuhn	300.00	150.00	90.00
59	Baum	300.00	150.00	90.00
71	Melchoir	300.00	150.00	90.00
72	Vitt	300.00	150.00	90.00
74	Berry	300.00	150.00	90.00
75	Miller	300.00	150.00	90.00
76	Tennant	300.00	150.00	90.00
77	Mohler	300.00	150.00	90.00
79	Sutor	300.00	150.00	90.00
80	Browning	300.00	150.00	90.00
81	Ryan	300.00	150.00	90.00
82	Powell	300.00	150.00	90.00
83	Schmidt	300.00	150.00	90.00
84	Meikle	300.00	150.00	90.00
85	Madden	300.00	150.00	90.00
87	Moskiman	300.00	150.00	90.00
88	Zamlock	300.00	150.00	90.00
92	Carlisle	300.00	150.00	90.00
97	Stewart	300.00	150.00	90.00
111	Mundorff	300.00	150.00	90.00
140	Annis	300.00	150.00	90.00
159	Dashwood	300.00	150.00	90.00
167	Spencer	300.00	150.00	90.00

1911 T4 Obak Premiums

Among the scarcest of all the 20th Century tobacco issues, the T4 Obak Premiums were cabinet-sized cards distributed in conjunction with the more popular and better-known Obak T212 card set. Both sets were issued in 1911 by Obak "mouthpiece" cigarettes and featured players from the Pacific Coast League. The Obak Premiums measured a large 5" by 7" and were printed on a cardboard-like paper. The attractive cards featured a greyish monochrome player photo inside a 3-1/2" by 5" oval. There was no printing on the front of the card to identify the player or indicate the Manufacturer, and the backs of the cards were blank. In most cases the photos used for the premiums were identical to the T212 photos, except for some cropping differences. Under the Obak mail-in promotion, 50 coupons from cigarette packages were required to obtain just one premium card, which may explain their extreme scarcity today. According to the coupon, all 175 players pictured in the regular T212 set were available as premium cards, but to date 30 differnt players have been found in the larger cabinet size. Most of the Obak premiums that exist in original condition contain a number, written in pencil on the back of the card, that corresponds to the checklist printed on the coupon. Because of their extreme scarcity, these cards are quite expensive and generally appeal only to the very advanced Pacific Coast League collectors.

1911 T5 Pinkerton

Because they were photographs affixed to a cardboard backing, the cards in the 1911 T5 Pinkerton set are considered by today's advanced collectors to be "true" cabinet cards. The Pinkerton cabinets are a rather obscure issue, and because of their original method of distribution, it would be virtually impossible to assemble a complete set today. It has never actually been determined how many subjects in the set even exist. Pinkerton, the parent of Red Man and other tobacco products, offered the cabinets in exchange for coupons found in cigarette packages. According to an original advertising sheet, some 376 different photos were available. A consumer could exchange ten coupons for the cabinet card of his choice. The photos available included players from the 16 major league teams plus five teams from the American Association (Indianapolis, Columbus, Toledo, Kansas City and Minneapolis.) Pinkerton cabinet cards have been found to vary in both size and type of mount. The most desirable combination is a 3-3/8" by 5-1/2" photograph affixed to a thick, cardboard mount measuring approximately 4-3/4" by 7-3/4". But original Pinkerton cabinets have also been found in slightly different sizes with less substantial backings. The most attractive mounts are embossed around the picture, but some Pinkertons have been found with a white border surrounding the photograph.

Prices listed are for cards with cardboard mounts. Cards with paper mounts are worth about 75" of listed prices. Collectors should be aware that some of the Pinkerton photos were reproduced in postcard size issues in later years. Because of the rareness of the T5s, no complete set price is given.

	NR MT	EX	VG
Common Player:	150.00	75.00	45.00
101 Jim Stephens	150.00	75.00	45.00
102 Bobby Wallace	500.00	250.00	150.00
103 Joe Lake	150.00	75.00	45.00
104 George Stone	150.00	75.00	45.00
105 Jack O'Connor	150.00	75.00	45.00
106 Bill Abstein	150.00	75.00	45.00
107 Rube Waddell	500.00	250.00	150.00
108 Roy Hartzell	150.00	75.00	45.00
109 Danny Hoffman	150.00	75.00	45.00
110 Dode Cris	150.00	75.00	45.00
111 Al Schweitzer	150.00	75.00	45.00
112 Art Griggs	150.00	75.00	45.00
113 Bill Bailey	150.00	75.00	45.00
114 Pat Newman	150.00	75.00	45.00
115 Harry Howell	150.00	75.00	45.00
117 Hobe Ferris	150.00	75.00	45.00
118 John McAleese	150.00	75.00	45.00
119 Ray Demmitt	150.00	75.00	45.00
120 Red Fisher	150.00	75.00	45.00
121 Frank Truesdale	150.00	75.00	45.00
122 Barney Pelty	150.00	75.00	45.00
123 Ed Killifer (Killefer)	150.00	75.00	45.00
151 Matty McIntyre	150.00	75.00	45.00
152 Jim Delahanty	150.00	75.00	45.00
153 Hughey Jennings	500.00	250.00	150.00
154 Ralph Works	150.00	75.00	45.00
155 George Moriarity (Moriarty)	150.00	75.00	45.00
156 Sam Crawford	500.00	250.00	150.00
157 Boss Schmidt	150.00	75.00	45.00
158 Owen Bush	150.00	75.00	45.00
159 Ty Cobb	5000.00	2500.00	1500.
160 Bill Donovan	150.00	75.00	45.00
161 Oscar Stanage	150.00	75.00	45.00
162 George Mullin	150.00	75.00	45.00
163 Davy Jones	150.00	75.00	45.00
164 Charley O'Leary	150.00	75.00	45.00
165 Tom Jones	150.00	75.00	45.00
166 Joe Casey	150.00	75.00	45.00
167 Ed Willetts (Willett)	150.00	75.00	45.00
168 Ed Lafeite (Lafitte)	150.00	75.00	45.00
169 Ty Cobb	5000.00	2500.00	1500.
170 Ty Cobb	5000.00	2500.00	1500.
201 John Evers	500.00	250.00	150.00
202 Mordecai Brown	500.00	250.00	150.00
203 King Cole	150.00	75.00	45.00
204 Johnny Cane	150.00	75.00	45.00
205 Heinie Zimmerman	150.00	75.00	45.00
206 Wildfire Schulte	150.00	75.00	45.00
207 Frank Chance	500.00	250.00	150.00
208 Joe Tinker	500.00	250.00	150.00
209 Orvall Overall	150.00	75.00	45.00
210 Jimmy Archer	150.00	75.00	45.00
211 Johnny Kling	150.00	75.00	45.00
212 Jimmy Sheckard	150.00	75.00	45.00
213 Harry McIntyre	150.00	75.00	45.00
214 Lew Richie	150.00	75.00	45.00
215 Ed Ruelbach	150.00	75.00	45.00
216 Artie Hoffman (Hofman)	150.00	75.00	45.00
217 Jake Pfeister	150.00	75.00	45.00
218 Harry Steinfeldt	150.00	75.00	45.00
219 Tom Needham	150.00	75.00	45.00
220 Ginger Beaumont	150.00	75.00	45.00
251 Christy Mathewson	2000.00	1000.00	600.00
252 Fred Merkle	150.00	75.00	45.00
253 Hooks Wiltsie	150.00	75.00	45.00
254 Art Devlin	150.00	75.00	45.00
255 Fred Snodgrass	150.00	75.00	45.00
256 Josh Devore	150.00	75.00	45.00
257 Red Murray	150.00	75.00	45.00
258 Cy Seymour	150.00	75.00	45.00
259 Al Bridwell	150.00	75.00	45.00
260 Larry Doyle	150.00	75.00	45.00
261 Bugs Raymond	150.00	75.00	45.00
262 Doc Crandall	150.00	75.00	45.00
263 Admiral Schlei	150.00	75.00	45.00
264 Chief Myers (Meyers)	150.00	75.00	45.00
265 Bill Dahlen	150.00	75.00	45.00
266 Beals Becker	150.00	75.00	45.00
267 Louis Drucke	150.00	75.00	45.00
301 Fred Luderus	150.00	75.00	45.00
302 John Titus	150.00	75.00	45.00
303 Red Dooin	150.00	75.00	45.00
304 Eddie Stack	150.00	75.00	45.00
305 Kitty Bransfield	150.00	75.00	45.00
306 Sherry Magee	150.00	75.00	45.00
307 Otto Knabe	150.00	75.00	45.00
308 Jimmy "Runt" Walsh	150.00	75.00	45.00
309 Earl Moore	150.00	75.00	45.00
310 Mickey Doolan	150.00	75.00	45.00
311 Ad Brennan	150.00	75.00	45.00
312 Bob Ewing	150.00	75.00	45.00
313 Lou Schettler	150.00	75.00	45.00
351 Joe Willis	150.00	75.00	45.00
352 Rube Ellis	150.00	75.00	45.00
353 Steve Evans	150.00	75.00	45.00
354 Miller Huggins	500.00	250.00	150.00
355 Arnold Hauser	150.00	75.00	45.00
356 Frank Corridon	150.00	75.00	45.00
357 Roger Bresnahan	500.00	250.00	150.00
358 Slim Sallee	150.00	75.00	45.00
359 Mike Mowrey	150.00	75.00	45.00
360 Ed Konetchy	150.00	75.00	45.00
361 Beckman	150.00	75.00	45.00
362 Rebel Oakes	150.00	75.00	45.00
363 Johnny Lush	150.00	75.00	45.00
364 Eddie Phelps	150.00	75.00	45.00
365 Robert Harmon	150.00	75.00	45.00
401 Lew Moren	150.00	75.00	45.00
402 George McQuillian (McQuallan)	150.00	75.00	45.00
403 Johnny Bates	150.00	75.00	45.00
404 Eddie Grant	150.00	75.00	45.00
405 Tommy McMillan	150.00	75.00	45.00
406 Tommy Clark (Clarke)	150.00	75.00	45.00
407 Jack Rowan	150.00	75.00	45.00
408 Bob Bescher	150.00	75.00	45.00
409 Fred Beebe	150.00	75.00	45.00
410 Tom Downey	150.00	75.00	45.00
411 George Suggs	150.00	75.00	45.00
412 Hans Lobert	150.00	75.00	45.00
413 Jimmy Phelan	150.00	75.00	45.00
414 Dode Paskert	150.00	75.00	45.00
415 Ward Miller	150.00	75.00	45.00
416 Dick Egan	150.00	75.00	45.00
417 Art Fromme	150.00	75.00	45.00
418 Bill Burns	150.00	75.00	45.00
419 Clark Griffith	500.00	250.00	150.00
420 Dick Hoblitzell	150.00	75.00	45.00
421 Harry Gasper	150.00	75.00	45.00
422 Dave Altizer	150.00	75.00	45.00
423 Larry McLean	150.00	75.00	45.00
424 Mike Mitchell	150.00	75.00	45.00
451 John Hummel	150.00	75.00	45.00
452 Tony Smith	150.00	75.00	45.00
453 Bill Davidson	150.00	75.00	45.00
454 Ed Lennox	150.00	75.00	45.00
455 Zach Wheat	500.00	250.00	150.00
457 Elmer Knetzer	150.00	75.00	45.00
458 Rube Dessau	150.00	75.00	45.00
459 George Bell	150.00	75.00	45.00
460 Jake Daubert	150.00	75.00	45.00
461 Doc Scanlan	150.00	75.00	45.00
462 Nap Rucker	150.00	75.00	45.00
463 Cy Barger	150.00	75.00	45.00
464 Kaiser Wilhelm	150.00	75.00	45.00
465 Bill Bergen	150.00	75.00	45.00
466 Tex Erwin	150.00	75.00	45.00
501 Chief Bender	500.00	250.00	150.00
502 John Coombs	150.00	75.00	45.00
503 Eddie Plank	500.00	250.00	150.00
504 Amos Strunk	150.00	75.00	45.00
505 Connie Mack	1000.00	500.00	300.00
506 Ira Thomas	150.00	75.00	45.00
507 Biscoe Lord (Briscoe)	150.00	75.00	45.00
508 Stuffy McInnis	150.00	75.00	45.00
509 Jimmy Dygert	150.00	75.00	45.00
510 Rube Oldring	150.00	75.00	45.00
511 Eddie Collins	500.00	250.00	150.00
512 Home Run Baker	500.00	250.00	150.00
513 Harry Krause	150.00	75.00	45.00
514 Harry Davis	150.00	75.00	45.00
515 Jack Barry	150.00	75.00	45.00
516 Jack Lapp	150.00	75.00	45.00
517 Cy Morgan	150.00	75.00	45.00
518 Danny Murphy	150.00	75.00	45.00
519 Topsy Hartsell	150.00	75.00	45.00
520 Paddy Livingston	150.00	75.00	45.00
521 P. Adkins	150.00	75.00	45.00
522 Eddie Collins	500.00	250.00	150.00
523 Paddy Livingston	150.00	75.00	45.00
551 Doc Gessler	150.00	75.00	45.00
552 Bill Cunningham	150.00	75.00	45.00
554 John Henry	150.00	75.00	45.00

		NR MT	EX	VG				NR MT	EX	VG
555	Jack Lelivelt	150.00	75.00	45.00		763	Doc White	150.00	75.00	45.00
556	Bobby Groome	150.00	75.00	45.00		764	Rollie Zeider	150.00	75.00	45.00
557	Doc Ralston	150.00	75.00	45.00		765	Fred Payne	150.00	75.00	45.00
558	Kid Elberfelt (Elberfeld)	150.00	75.00	45.00		766	Lee Tannehill	150.00	75.00	45.00
559	Doc Reisling	150.00	75.00	45.00		767	Eddie Hahn	150.00	75.00	45.00
560	Herman Schaefer	150.00	75.00	45.00		768	Hugh Duffy	500.00	250.00	150.00
561	Walter Johnson	2000.00	1000.00	600.00		769	Fred Olmstead	150.00	75.00	45.00
562	Dolly Gray	150.00	75.00	45.00		770	Lena Blackbourne (Blackburne)			
563	Wid Conroy	150.00	75.00	45.00				150.00	75.00	45.00
564	Charley Street	150.00	75.00	45.00		771	Young "Cy" Young	150.00	75.00	45.00
565	Bob Unglaub	150.00	75.00	45.00		801	Lew Brockett	150.00	75.00	45.00
566	Clyde Milan	150.00	75.00	45.00		802	Frank Laporte (LaPorte)	150.00	75.00	45.00
567	George Browne	150.00	75.00	45.00		803	Bert Daniels	150.00	75.00	45.00
568	George McBride	150.00	75.00	45.00		804	Walter Blair	150.00	75.00	45.00
569	Red Killifer (Killefer)	150.00	75.00	45.00		805	Jack Knight	150.00	75.00	45.00
601	Addie Joss	500.00	250.00	150.00		806	Jimmy Austin	150.00	75.00	45.00
602	Addie Joss	500.00	250.00	150.00		807	Hal Chase	175.00	87.00	52.00
603	Napoleon Lajoie	800.00	400.00	240.00		808	Birdie Cree	150.00	75.00	45.00
604	Nig Clark (Clarke)	150.00	75.00	45.00		809	Jack Quinn	150.00	75.00	45.00
605	Cy Falkenberg	150.00	75.00	45.00		810	Walter Manning	150.00	75.00	45.00
606	Harry Bemis	150.00	75.00	45.00		811	Jack Warhop	150.00	75.00	45.00
607	George Stovall	150.00	75.00	45.00		812	Jeff Sweeney	150.00	75.00	45.00
608	Fred Blanding	150.00	75.00	45.00		813	Charley Hemphill	150.00	75.00	45.00
609	Elmer Koestner	150.00	75.00	45.00		814	Harry Wolters	150.00	75.00	45.00
610	Ted Easterly	150.00	75.00	45.00		815	Tom Hughes	150.00	75.00	45.00
611	Willie Mitchell	150.00	75.00	45.00		816	Earl Gardiner (Gardner)	150.00	75.00	45.00
612	Hornhorst	150.00	75.00	45.00		851	John Flynn	150.00	75.00	45.00
613	Elmer Flick	500.00	250.00	150.00		852	Bill Powell	150.00	75.00	45.00
614	Speck Harkness	150.00	75.00	45.00		853	Honus Wagner	2500.00	1250.00	750.00
615	Tuck Turner	150.00	75.00	45.00		854	Bill Powell	150.00	75.00	45.00
616	Joe Jackson	7500.00	3750.00	2100.		855	Fred Clarke	500.00	250.00	150.00
617	Grover Land	150.00	75.00	45.00		856	Owen Wilson	150.00	75.00	45.00
618	Gladstone Graney	150.00	75.00	45.00		857	George Gibson	150.00	75.00	45.00
619	Dave Callahan	150.00	75.00	45.00		858	Mike Simon	150.00	75.00	45.00
620	Ben DeMott	150.00	75.00	45.00		859	Tommy Leach	150.00	75.00	45.00
621	Neill Ball (Neal)	150.00	75.00	45.00		860	Lefty Leifeld (Leifield)	150.00	75.00	45.00
622	Dode Birmingham	150.00	75.00	45.00		861	Nick Maddox	150.00	75.00	45.00
623	George Kaler (Kahler)	150.00	75.00	45.00		862	Dots Miller	150.00	75.00	45.00
624	Sid Smith	150.00	75.00	45.00		863	Howard Camnitz	150.00	75.00	45.00
625	Bert Adams	150.00	75.00	45.00		864	Deacon Phillippi (Phillippe)	150.00	75.00	45.00
626	Bill Bradley	150.00	75.00	45.00		865	Babe Adams	150.00	75.00	45.00
627	Napoleon Lajoie	1000.00	500.00	300.00		866	Ed Abbaticchio	150.00	75.00	45.00
651	Bill Corrigan (Carrigan)	150.00	75.00	45.00		867	Paddy O'Connor	150.00	75.00	45.00
652	Joe Wood	150.00	75.00	45.00		868	Bobby Byrne	150.00	75.00	45.00
653	Heinie Wagner	150.00	75.00	45.00		869	Vin Campbell	150.00	75.00	45.00
654	Billy Purtell	150.00	75.00	45.00		870	Ham Hyatt	150.00	75.00	45.00
655	Frank Smith	150.00	75.00	45.00		871	Sam Leever	150.00	75.00	45.00
656	Harry Lord	150.00	75.00	45.00		872	Hans Wagner	2500.00	1250.00	750.00
657	Patsy Donovan	150.00	75.00	45.00		873	Hans Wagner	2500.00	1250.00	750.00
658	Duffy Lewis	150.00	75.00	45.00		874	Bill McKecknie (McKechnie)	500.00	250.00	150.00
659	Jack Kleinow	150.00	75.00	45.00		875	Kirby White	150.00	75.00	45.00
660	Ed Karger	150.00	75.00	45.00		901	Jimmie Burke	150.00	75.00	45.00
661	Clyde Engle	150.00	75.00	45.00		902	Charlie Carr	150.00	75.00	45.00
662	Ben Hunt	150.00	75.00	45.00		903	Larry Cheney	150.00	75.00	45.00
663	Charlie Smith	150.00	75.00	45.00		904	Chet Chadbourne	150.00	75.00	45.00
664	Tris Speaker	900.00	450.00	270.00		905	Dan Howley	150.00	75.00	45.00
665	Tom Madden	150.00	75.00	45.00		906	Jimmie Burke	150.00	75.00	45.00
666	Larry Gardner	150.00	75.00	45.00		907	Ray Mowe	150.00	75.00	45.00
667	Harry Hooper	500.00	250.00	150.00		908	Billy Milligan	150.00	75.00	45.00
668	Marty McHale	150.00	75.00	45.00		909	Frank Oberlin	150.00	75.00	45.00
669	Ray Collins	150.00	75.00	45.00		910	Ralph Glaze	150.00	75.00	45.00
670	Jake Stahl	150.00	75.00	45.00		911	O'Day	150.00	75.00	45.00
701	Dave Shean	150.00	75.00	45.00		912	Kerns	150.00	75.00	45.00
702	Roy Miller	150.00	75.00	45.00		913	Jim Duggan	150.00	75.00	45.00
703	Fred Beck	150.00	75.00	45.00		914	Simmy Murch	150.00	75.00	45.00
704	Bill Collings (Collins)	150.00	75.00	45.00		915	Frank Delehanty	150.00	75.00	45.00
705	Bill Sweeney	150.00	75.00	45.00		916	Craig	150.00	75.00	45.00
706	Buck Herzog	150.00	75.00	45.00		917	Jack Coffee (Coffey)	150.00	75.00	45.00
707	Bud Sharp (Sharpe)	150.00	75.00	45.00		918	Lefty George	150.00	75.00	45.00
708	Cliff Curtis	150.00	75.00	45.00		919	Otto Williams	150.00	75.00	45.00
709	Al Mattern	150.00	75.00	45.00		920	M. Hayden	150.00	75.00	45.00
710	Buster Brown	150.00	75.00	45.00		951	Joe Cantillion	150.00	75.00	45.00
711	Bill Rariden	150.00	75.00	45.00		952	Smith	150.00	75.00	45.00
712	Grant	150.00	75.00	45.00		953	Claud Rossman (Claude)	150.00	75.00	45.00
713	Ed Abbaticchio	150.00	75.00	45.00		1001	Tony James	150.00	75.00	45.00
714	Cecil Ferguson	150.00	75.00	45.00		1002	Jack Powell	150.00	75.00	45.00
715	Billy Burke	150.00	75.00	45.00		1003	Wm. J. Harbeau	150.00	75.00	45.00
716	Sam Frock	150.00	75.00	45.00		1004	Homer Smoot	150.00	75.00	45.00
717	Wilbur Goode (Good)	150.00	75.00	45.00		1051	Bill Friel	150.00	75.00	45.00
751	Charlie French	150.00	75.00	45.00		1052	Bill Friel	150.00	75.00	45.00
752	Patsy Dougherty	150.00	75.00	45.00		1053	Fred Odwell	150.00	75.00	45.00
753	Shano Collins	150.00	75.00	45.00		1054	Alex Reilley	150.00	75.00	45.00
754	Fred Parent	150.00	75.00	45.00		1055	Eugene Packard	150.00	75.00	45.00
755	Willis Cole	150.00	75.00	45.00		1056	Irve Wrattan	150.00	75.00	45.00
756	Billy Sullivan	150.00	75.00	45.00		1057	"Red" Nelson	150.00	75.00	45.00
757	Rube Sutor (Suter)	150.00	75.00	45.00		1058	George Perring	150.00	75.00	45.00
758	Chick Gandil	150.00	75.00	45.00		1059	Glen Liebhardt	150.00	75.00	45.00
759	Jim Scott	150.00	75.00	45.00		1060	Jimmie O'Rourke	150.00	75.00	45.00
760	Ed Walsh	500.00	250.00	150.00		1061	Fred Cook	150.00	75.00	45.00
761	Gavvy Cravath	150.00	75.00	45.00		1062	Charles Arbogast	150.00	75.00	45.00
762	Bobby Messenger	150.00	75.00	45.00		1063	Jerry Downs	150.00	75.00	45.00

		NR MT	EX	VG
1064	"Bunk" Congalton	150.00	75.00	45.00
1065	Fred Carisch	150.00	75.00	45.00
1066	"Red" Sitton	150.00	75.00	45.00
1067	George Kaler (Kahler)	150.00	75.00	45.00
1068	Arthur Kruger	150.00	75.00	45.00
1102	Earl Yingling	150.00	75.00	45.00
1103	Jerry Freeman	150.00	75.00	45.00
1104	Harry Hinchman	150.00	75.00	45.00
1105	Jim Baskette	150.00	75.00	45.00
1106	Denny Sullivan	150.00	75.00	45.00
1107	Carl Robinson	150.00	75.00	45.00
1108	Bill Rodgers	150.00	75.00	45.00
1109	Hi West	150.00	75.00	45.00
1110	Billy Hallman	150.00	75.00	45.00
1111	Wm. Elwert	150.00	75.00	45.00
1112	Piano Legs Hickman	150.00	75.00	45.00
1113	Joe McCarthy	350.00	175.00	105.00
1114	Fred Abbott	150.00	75.00	45.00
1115	Jack Gilligan	150.00	75.00	45.00
	Complete Set:			

1913 T200 Fatima Team Cards

Issued by the Ligget & Myers Tobacco Co. in 1913 with Fatima brand cigarettes, the T200 set consists of eight National and eight American League team cards. The cards measure 2-5/8" by 4-3/4" and are glossy photographs on paper stock. Although it is unknown why, several of the cards are more difficult to obtain than others. The team cards feature 369 different players, managers and mascots. The card backs contain an offer for an enlarged copy (13" by 21") of a team card, minus the advertising on front, in exchange for 40 Fatima cigarette coupons. These large T200 premiums are very rare and have a value of 12-15 times greater than a common T200 card.

		NR MT	EX	VG
	Complete Set:	8000.00	4000.00	2400.
	Common Team:	300.00	150.00	90.00
(1)	Boston Nationals	475.00	237.00	142.00
(2)	Brooklyn Nationals	300.00	150.00	90.00
(3)	Chicago Nationals	300.00	150.00	90.00
(4)	Cincinnati Nationals	300.00	150.00	90.00
(5)	New York Nationals	350.00	175.00	105.00
(6)	Philadelphia Nationals	300.00	150.00	90.00
(7)	Pittsburgh Nationals	300.00	150.00	90.00
(8)	St. Louis Nationals	475.00	237.00	142.00
(9)	Boston Americans	275.00	137.00	83.00
(10)	Chicago Americans	375.00	187.00	112.00
(11)	Cleveland Americans	500.00	250.00	150.00
(12)	Detroit Americans	700.00	350.00	150.00
(13)	New York Americans	1200.00	600.00	350.00
(14)	Philadelphia Americans	300.00	150.00	90.00
(15)	St. Louis Americans	1000.00	500.00	300.00
(16)	Washington Americans	400.00	200.00	80.00

A player's name in italic type indicates a rookie card. An (FC) indicates a player's first card for that particular card company.

1911 T201
Mecca Double Folders

These cards found in packages of Mecca cigarettes feature one player when the card is open, and another when the card is folded; two players sharing the same pair of legs. Mecca Double Folders measure 2-1/4" by 4-11/16." The fronts are color lithographs with the player's name appearing in black script in the upper left. The backs are printed in red and contain an innovation in the form of player statistics. The 50-card set contains 100 different players including a number of Hall of Famers. The Mecca Double Folders, with two players (Topps "borrowed" the idea in 1955) and statistics, were one of the most innovative of the tobacco card era.

		NR MT	EX	VG
	Complete Set:	10000.00	5000.00	3000.
	Common Player:	75.00	37.00	22.00
(1)	Abstein, Butler	75.00	37.00	22.00
(2)	Baker, Collins	400.00	200.00	125.00
(3)	Baker, Downie (Downey)	75.00	37.00	22.00
(4)	Barrett, McGlynn	75.00	37.00	22.00
(5)	Barry, Lapp	75.00	37.00	22.00
(6)	Bender, Oldring	250.00	125.00	75.00
(7)	Bergen, Wheat	250.00	125.00	75.00
(8)	Blair, Hartzell	75.00	37.00	22.00
(9)	Bresnahan, Huggins	500.00	250.00	150.00
(10)	Bridwell, Matthewson (Mathewson)	750.00	375.00	230.00
(11)	Brown, Hofman	250.00	125.00	75.00
(12)	Byrne, Clarke	200.00	100.00	60.00
(13)	Chance, Evers	450.00	225.00	135.00
(14)	Chase, Sweeney	125.00	62.00	37.00
(15)	Cicotte, Thoney	100.00	50.00	30.00
(16)	Clarke, Gaspar	75.00	37.00	22.00
(17)	Cobb, Crawford	2500.00	1250.00	750.00
(18)	Cole, Kling	75.00	37.00	22.00
(19)	Coombs, Thomas	75.00	37.00	22.00
(20)	Daubert, Rucker	100.00	50.00	30.00
(21)	Donovan, Stroud	75.00	37.00	22.00
(22)	Dooin, Titus	75.00	37.00	22.00
(23)	Dougherty, Lord	400.00	200.00	125.00
(24)	Downs, Odwell	75.00	37.00	22.00
(25)	Doyle, Meyers	75.00	37.00	22.00
(26)	Dygert, Seymour	75.00	37.00	22.00
(27)	Elberfeld, McBride	75.00	37.00	22.00
(28)	Falkenberg, Lajoie	500.00	250.00	150.00
(29)	Fitzpatrick, Killian	75.00	37.00	22.00
(30)	Ford, Johnson	75.00	37.00	22.00
(31)	Foster, Ward	75.00	37.00	22.00
(32)	Gardner, Speaker	150.00	75.00	45.00
(33)	Gibson, Leach	75.00	37.00	22.00
(34)	Graham, Mattern	75.00	37.00	22.00
(35)	Grant, McLean	75.00	37.00	22.00
(36)	Hauser, Lush	75.00	37.00	22.00
(37)	Herzog, Miller	75.00	37.00	22.00
(38)	Hickman, Hinchman	75.00	37.00	22.00
(39)	Jennings, Summers	250.00	125.00	75.00
(40)	Johnson, Street	750.00	375.00	230.00
(41)	LaPorte, Stephens	75.00	37.00	22.00
(42)	Lake, Wallace	200.00	100.00	60.00
(43)	Leifield, Simon	75.00	37.00	22.00
(44)	Lobert, Moore	75.00	37.00	22.00
(45)	McCabe, Starr	75.00	37.00	22.00
(46)	McCarty, McGinnity	200.00	100.00	60.00

		NR MT	EX	VG
(47)	Merkle, Wiltse	100.00	50.00	30.00
(48)	Payne, Walsh	250.00	125.00	75.00
(49)	Stovall, Turner	75.00	37.00	22.00
(50)	Williams, Woodruff	75.00	37.00	22.00

1911 T202 Hassan Triple Folders

Measuring 5-1/2" by 2-1/4", Hassan cigarette cards carried the concept of multiple-player cards even further than the innovative Mecca set of the previous year. Scored so that the two end cards - which are full-color and very close to exact duplicates of T205 "Gold Borders" - can fold over the black and white center panel, the Hassan Triple Folder appears like a booklet when closed. The two end cards are individual player cards, while the larger center panel contains an action scene. Usually the two player cards are not related to the action scene. The unique Hassan Triple Folders feature player biographies on the back of the two individual cards with a description of the action on the back of the center panel. Values depend on the player featured in the center panel, as well as the players featured on the end cards.

		NR MT	EX	VG
	Complete Set of 132:	75000.00	37500.00	22500.
	Common Player:	225.00	112.00	67.00
(1a)	A Close Play At The Home Plate (LaPorte, Wallace)	250.00	125.00	75.00
(1b)	A Close Play At The Home Plate (Pelty, Wallace)	250.00	125.00	75.00
(2)	A Desperate Slide For Third (Ty Cobb, O'Leary)	2500.00	1250.00	750.00
(3a)	A Great Batsman (Barger, Bergen)	225.00	112.00	67.00
(3b)	A Great Batsman (Bergen, Rucker)	225.00	112.00	67.00
(4)	Ambrose McConnell At Bat (Blair, Quinn)	225.00	112.00	67.00
(5)	A Wide Throw Saves Crawford (Mullin, Stanage)	225.00	112.00	67.00
(6)	Baker Gets His Man (Baker, Collins)	500.00	250.00	150.00
(7)	Birmingham Gets To Third (Johnson, Street)	750.00	375.00	225.00
(8)	Birmingham's Home Run (Birmingham, Turner)	800.00	400.00	250.00
(9)	Bush Just Misses Austin (Magee, Moran)	225.00	112.00	67.00
(10a)	Carrigan Blocks His Man (Gaspar, McLean)	225.00	112.00	67.00
(10b)	Carrigan Blocks His Man (Carrigan, Wagner)	225.00	112.00	67.00
(11)	Catching Him Napping (Bresnahan, Oakes)	400.00	200.00	120.00
(12)	Caught Asleep Off First (Bresnahan, Harmon)	400.00	200.00	120.00
(13a)	Chance Beats Out A Hit (Chance, Foxen)	400.00	200.00	120.00
(13b)	Chance Beats Out A Hit (Archer, McIntyre)	225.00	112.00	67.00
(13c)	Chance Beats Out A Hit (Archer, Overall)	225.00	112.00	67.00

		NR MT	EX	VG
(13d)	Chance Beats Out A Hit (Archer, Rowan)-	225.00	112.00	67.00
(13e)	Chance Beats Out A Hit (Chance, Shean)	400.00	200.00	120.00
(14a)	Chase Dives Into Third (Chase, Wolter)	225.00	112.00	67.00
(14b)	Chase Dives Into Third (Clarke, Gibson)	250.00	125.00	75.00
(14c)	Chase Dives Into Third (Gibson, Phillippe)	225.00	112.00	67.00
(15a)	Chase Gets Ball Too Late (Egan, Mitchell)	225.00	112.00	67.00
(15b)	Chase Gets Ball Too Late (Chase, Wolter)	225.00	112.00	67.00
(16a)	Chase Guarding First (Chase, Wolter)	225.00	112.00	67.00
(16b)	Chase Guarding First (Clarke, Gibson)	250.00	125.00	75.00
(16c)	Chase Guarding First (Gibson, Leifield)	225.00	112.00	67.00
(17)	Chase Ready For The Squeeze Play (Magee, Paskert)	225.00	112.00	67.00
(18)	Chase Safe At Third (Baker, Barry)	400.00	200.00	120.00
(19)	Chief Bender Waiting For A Good One (Bender, Thomas)	400.00	200.00	120.00
(20)	Clarke Hikes For Home (Bridwell, Kling)	225.00	112.00	67.00
(21)	Close At First (Ball, Stovall)	225.00	112.00	67.00
(22a)	Close At The Plate (Payne, Walsh)	400.00	200.00	120.00
(22b)	Close At The Plate (Payne, White)	225.00	112.00	67.00
(23)	Close At Third - Speaker (Speaker, Wood)	500.00	250.00	150.00
(24)	Close At Third - Wagner (Carrigan, Wagner)	225.00	112.00	67.00
(25a)	Collins Easily Safe (Byrne, Clarke)	300.00	150.00	90.00
(25b)	Collins Easily Safe (Baker, Collins)	500.00	250.00	150.00
(25c)	Collins Easily Safe (Collins, Murphy)	400.00	200.00	120.00
(26)	Crawford About To Smash One (Stanage, Summers)	225.00	112.00	67.00
(27)	Cree Rolls Home (Daubert, Hummel)	225.00	112.00	67.00
(28)	Davy Jones' Great Slide (Delahanty, Jones)	225.00	112.00	67.00
(29a)	Devlin Gets His Man (Devlin (Giants), Mathewson)	1000.00	500.00	300.00
(29b)	Devlin Gets His Man (Devlin (Rustlers), Mathewson)	650.00	325.00	200.00
(29c)	Devlin Gets His Man (Fletcher, Mathewson)	650.00	325.00	200.00
(29d)	Devlin Gets His Man (Mathewson, Meyers)	650.00	325.00	200.00
(30a)	Donlin Out At First (Camnitz, Gibson)	225.00	112.00	67.00
(30b)	Donlin Out At First (Doyle, Merlke)	225.00	112.00	67.00
(30c)	Donlin Out At First (Leach, Wilson)	225.00	112.00	67.00
(30d)	Donlin Out At First (Dooin, Magee)	225.00	112.00	67.00
(30e)	Donlin Out At First (Gibson, Phillippe)	225.00	112.00	67.00
(31a)	Dooin Gets His Man (Dooin, Doolan)	225.00	112.00	67.00
(31b)	Dooin Gets His Man (Dooin, Lobert)	225.00	112.00	67.00
(31c)	Dooin Gets His Man (Dooin, Titus)	225.00	112.00	67.00
(32)	Easy For Larry (Doyle, Merlke)	225.00	112.00	67.00
(33)	Elberfeld Beats The Throw (Elberfeld, Milan)	225.00	112.00	67.00
(34)	Elberfeld Gets His Man (Elberfeld, Milan)	225.00	112.00	67.00
(35)	Engle In A Close Play (Engle, Speaker)	450.00	225.00	135.00
(36a)	Evers Makes A Safe Slide (Archer, Evers)	400.00	200.00	120.00
(36b)	Evers Makes A Safe Slide (Chance, Evers)	500.00	250.00	150.00
(36c)	Evers Makes A Safe Slide (Archer, Overall)	225.00	112.00	67.00
(36d)	Evers Makes A Safe Slide (Archer, Reulbach)	225.00	112.00	67.00
(36e)	Evers Makes A Safe Slide (Chance, Tinker)	550.00	275.00	165.00

		NR MT	EX	VG
(37)	Fast Work At Third (Cobb, O'Leary)	2500.00	1250.00	750.00
(38a)	Ford Putting Over A Spitter (Ford, Vaughn)	225.00	112.00	67.00
(38b)	Ford Putting Over A Spitter (Sweeney, Ford)	225.00	112.00	67.00
(39)	Good Play At Third (Cobb, Moriarity)	2500.00	1250.00	750.00
(40)	Grant Gets His Man (Grant, Hoblitzell)	225.00	112.00	67.00
(41a)	Hal Chase Too Late (McConnell, McIntyre)	225.00	112.00	67.00
(41b)	Hal Chase Too Late (McLean, Suggs)	225.00	112.00	67.00
(42)	Harry Lord At Third (Lennox, Tinker)	150.00	75.00	45.00
(43)	Hartzell Covering Third (Dahlen, Scanlan)	225.00	112.00	67.00
(44)	Hartsel Strikes Out (Gray, Groom)	225.00	112.00	67.00
(45)	Held At Third (Lord, Tannehill)	225.00	112.00	67.00
(46)	Jake Stahl Guarding First (Cicotte, Stahl)	225.00	112.00	67.00
(47)	Jim Delahanty At Bat (Delahanty, Jones)	225.00	112.00	67.00
(48a)	Just Before The Battle (Ames, Meyers)	225.00	112.00	67.00
(48b)	Just Before The Battle (Bresnahan, McGraw)	500.00	250.00	150.00
(48c)	Just Before The Battle (Crandall, Meyers)	225.00	112.00	67.00
(48d)	Just Before The Battle (Becker, Devore)	225.00	112.00	67.00
(48e)	Just Before The Battle (Fletcher, Mathewson)	650.00	325.00	200.00
(48f)	Just Before The Battle (Marquard, Meyers)	400.00	200.00	120.00
(48g)	Just Before The Battle (Jennings, McGraw)	550.00	275.00	165.00
(48h)	Just Before The Battle (Mathewson, Meyers)	650.00	325.00	200.00
(48i)	Just Before The Battle (Murray, Snodgrass)	225.00	112.00	67.00
(48j)	Just Before The Battle (Meyers, Wiltse)	225.00	112.00	67.00
(49)	Knight Catches A Runner (Johnson, Knight)	750.00	375.00	225.00
(50a)	Lobert Almost Caught (Bridwell, Kling)	225.00	112.00	67.00
(50b)	Lobert Almost Caught (Kling, Young)	550.00	275.00	165.00
(50c)	Lobert Almost Caught (Kling, Mattern)	225.00	112.00	67.00
(50d)	Lobert Almost Caught (Kling, Steinfeldt)	225.00	112.00	67.00
(51)	Lobert Gets Tenney (Dooin, Lobert)	225.00	112.00	67.00
(52)	Lord Catches His Man (Lord, Tannehil)	225.00	112.00	67.00
(53)	McConnell Caught (Needham, Richie)	225.00	112.00	67.00
(54)	McIntyre At Bat (McConnell, McIntyre)	225.00	112.00	67.00
(55)	Moriarty Spiked (Stanage, Willett)	225.00	112.00	67.00
(56)	Nearly Caught (Bates, Bescher)	225.00	112.00	67.00
(57)	Oldring Almost Home (Lord, Oldring)	225.00	112.00	67.00
(58)	Schaefer On First (McBride, Milan)	225.00	112.00	67.00
(59)	Schaefer Steals Second (Clark Griffith, McBride)	400.00	200.00	120.00
(60)	Scoring From Second (Lord, Oldring)	225.00	112.00	67.00
(61a)	Scrambling Back To First (Barger, Bergen)	225.00	112.00	67.00
(61b)	Scrambling Back To First (Chase, Wolter)	225.00	112.00	67.00
(62)	Speaker Almost Caught (Clarke, Miller)	300.00	150.00	90.00
(63)	Speaker Rounding Third (Speaker, Wood)	500.00	250.00	150.00
(64)	Speaker Scores (Engle, Speaker)	500.00	250.00	150.00
(65)	Stahl Safe (Austin, Stovall)	225.00	112.00	67.00
(66)	Stone About To Swing (Schulte, Sheckard)	225.00	112.00	67.00
(67a)	Sullivan Puts Up A High One (Evans, Huggins)	400.00	200.00	125.00
(67b)	Sullivan Puts Up A High One (Gray, Groom)	225.00	112.00	67.00

		NR MT	EX	VG
(68a)	Sweeney Gets Stahl (Ford, Vaughn)	225.00	112.00	67.00
(68b)	Sweeney Gets Stahl (Ford, Sweeney)	225.00	112.00	67.00
(69)	Tenney Lands Safely (Latham, Raymond)	225.00	112.00	67.00
(70a)	The Athletic Infield (Baker, Barry)	400.00	200.00	125.00
(70b)	The Athletic Infield (Brown, Graham)	400.00	200.00	125.00
(70c)	The Athletic Infield (Hauser, Konetchy)	150.00	75.00	45.00
(70d)	The Athletic Infield (Krause, Thomas)	225.00	112.00	67.00
(71)	The Pinch Hitter (Egan, Hoblitzell)	225.00	112.00	67.00
(72)	The Scissors Slide (Birmingham, Turner)	225.00	112.00	67.00
(73a)	Tom Jones At Bat (Fromme, McLean)	225.00	112.00	67.00
(73b)	Tom Jones At Bat (Gaspar, McLean)	225.00	112.00	67.00
(74a)	Too Late For Devlin (Ames, Meyers)	225.00	112.00	67.00
(74b)	Too Late For Devlin (Crandall, Meyers)	225.00	112.00	67.00
(74c)	Too Late For Devlin (Devlin (Giants), Mathewson)	850.00	425.00	265.00
(74d)	Too Late For Devlin (Devlin (Rustlers), Mathewson)	650.00	325.00	200.00
(74e)	Too Late For Devlin (Marquard, Meyers)	400.00	200.00	120.00
(74f)	Too Late For Devlin (Meyers, Wiltse)	225.00	112.00	67.00
(75a)	Ty Cobb Steals Third (Cobb, Jennings)	3000.00	1500.00	900.00
(75b)	Ty Cobb Steals Third (Cobb, Moriarty)	2500.00	1250.00	750.00
(75c)	Ty Cobb Steals Third (Austin, Stovall)	1200.00	600.00	350.00
(76)	Wheat Strikes Out (Dahlen, Wheat)	450.00	225.00	135.00

T203 Baseball Comics

As their name implies, the T203 Baseball Comics feature cartoon-like drawings that illustrate various baseball phrases and terminology. Issued with Winner Cut Plug and Mayo Cut Plug tobacco products, the complete set consists of 25 different comics, each measuring approximately 2-1/16" by 3-1.8". Because they do not picture individual players, these cards have never attracted much of a following among serious baseball card collectors. They do, however, hold some interest as a novelty item of the period.

		NR MT	EX	VG
Complete Set:		900.00	450.00	270.00
Common Player:		25.00	12.50	7.50
(1)	"A Crack Outfielder"	25.00	12.50	7.50
(2)	"A Fancy Twirler"	25.00	12.50	7.50
(3)	"A Fine Slide"	25.00	12.50	7.50
(4)	"A Fowl Bawl"	25.00	12.50	7.50
(5)	"A Great Game"	25.00	12.50	7.50
(6)	"A Home Run"	25.00	12.50	7.50

		NR MT	EX	VG
(7)	"An All Star Battery"	25.00	12.50	7.50
(8)	"A Short Stop"	25.00	12.50	7.50
(9)	"A Star Catcher"	25.00	12.50	7.50
(10)	"A White Wash"	25.00	12.50	7.50
(11)	"A Tie Game"	25.00	12.50	7.50
(12)	"A Two Bagger"	25.00	12.50	7.50
(13)	"A Wild Pitch"	25.00	12.50	7.50
(14)	"Caught Napping"	25.00	12.50	7.50
(15)	"On To The Curves"	25.00	12.50	7.50
(16)	"Out"	25.00	12.50	7.50
(17)	"Put Out On 1st"	25.00	12.50	7.50
(18)	"Right Over The Plate"	25.00	12.50	7.50
(19)	"Rooting For The Home Team"	25.00	12.50	7.50
(20)	"Stealing A Base"	25.00	12.50	7.50
(21)	"Stealing Home"	25.00	12.50	7.50
(22)	"Strike One"	25.00	12.50	7.50
(23)	"The Bleacher"	25.00	12.50	7.50
(24)	"The Naps"	25.00	12.50	7.50
(25)	"The Red Sox"	25.00	12.50	7.50

1909 T204 Ramly

While issued with both Ramly and T.T.T. brand Turkish tobacco cigarettes, the 121 cards in this set take their name from the more common of the two brands. By any name, the set is one of the more interesting and attractive of the early 20th Century. The 2-1/2" by 2-1/2" cards carry black and white oval photographic portraits with impressive gold embossed frames and borders on the front. Toward the bottom appears the player's last name, position, team and league. The backs carry only the most basic information on the cigarette company. Due to their scarcity, the Ramly set is not widely collected. The complete set price does not include the scarce variations.

		NR MT	EX	VG
Complete Set:		70000.00	35000.00	21000.
Common Player:		350.00	175.00	105.00
(1)	Whitey Alperman	350.00	175.00	105.00
(2)	John Anderson	350.00	175.00	105.00
(3)	Jimmy Archer	350.00	175.00	105.00
(4)	Frank Arrelanes (Arellanes)	350.00	175.00	105.00
(5)	Jim Ball	350.00	175.00	105.00
(6)	Neal Ball	350.00	175.00	105.00
(7a)	Frank C. Bancroft (photo inside oval frame)	350.00	175.00	105.00
(7b)	Frank C. Bancroft (photo inside square frame)	1500.00	750.00	450.00
(8)	Johnny Bates	350.00	175.00	105.00
(9)	Fred Beebe	350.00	175.00	105.00
(10)	George Bell	350.00	175.00	105.00
(11)	Chief Bender	1700.00	850.00	510.00
(12)	Walter Blair	350.00	175.00	105.00
(13)	Cliff Blankenship	350.00	175.00	105.00
(14)	Frank Bowerman	350.00	175.00	105.00
(15a)	Wm. Bransfield (photo inside oval frame)	350.00	175.00	105.00
(15b)	Wm. Bransfield (photo inside square frame)	1750.00	875.00	525.00
(16)	Roger Bresnahan	600.00	300.00	180.00
(17)	Al Bridwell	350.00	175.00	105.00
(18)	Mordecai Brown	1700.00	850.00	510.00
(19)	Fred Burchell	350.00	175.00	105.00
(20a)	Jesse C. Burkett (photo inside oval frame)	1500.00	750.00	450.00

		NR MT	EX	VG
(20b)	Jesse C. Burkett (photo inside square frame)	2200.00	1100.00	660.00
(21)	Bobby Byrnes (Byrne)	350.00	175.00	105.00
(22)	Bill Carrigan	350.00	175.00	105.00
(23)	Frank Chance	1500.00	750.00	450.00
(24)	Charlie Chech	350.00	175.00	105.00
(25)	Ed Cicolte (Cicotte)	400.00	200.00	125.00
(26)	Bill Clymer	350.00	175.00	105.00
(27)	Andy Coakley	350.00	175.00	105.00
(28)	Jimmy Collins	1500.00	750.00	450.00
(29)	Ed. Collins	2200.00	1100.00	660.00
(30)	Wid Conroy	350.00	175.00	105.00
(31)	Jack Coombs	350.00	175.00	105.00
(32)	Doc Crandall	350.00	175.00	105.00
(33)	Lou Criger	350.00	175.00	105.00
(34)	Harry Davis	350.00	175.00	105.00
(35)	Art Devlin	350.00	175.00	105.00
(36a)	Wm. H. Dineen (Dinneen) (photo inside oval frame)	350.00	175.00	105.00
(36b)	Wm. H. Dineen (Dinneen) (photo inside square frame)	1000.00	500.00	300.00
(37)	Jiggs Donahue	350.00	175.00	105.00
(38)	Mike Donlin	350.00	175.00	105.00
(39)	Wild Bill Donovan	350.00	175.00	105.00
(40)	Gus Dorner	350.00	175.00	105.00
(41)	Joe Dunn	350.00	175.00	105.00
(42)	Kid Elberfield (Elberfeld)	350.00	175.00	105.00
(43)	Johnny Evers	1700.00	850.00	510.00
(44)	Bob Ewing	350.00	175.00	105.00
(45)	Cecil Ferguson	350.00	175.00	105.00
(46)	Hobe Ferris	350.00	175.00	105.00
(47)	Jerry Freeman	350.00	175.00	105.00
(48)	Art Fromme	350.00	175.00	105.00
(49)	Bob Ganley	350.00	175.00	105.00
(50)	Doc Gessler	350.00	175.00	105.00
(51)	Peaches Graham	350.00	175.00	105.00
(52)	Clark Griffith	1500.00	750.00	450.00
(53)	Roy Hartzell	350.00	175.00	105.00
(54)	Charlie Hemphill	350.00	175.00	105.00
(55)	Dick Hoblitzel (Hoblitzell)	350.00	175.00	105.00
(56)	Geo. Howard	350.00	175.00	105.00
(57)	Harry Howell	350.00	175.00	105.00
(58)	Miller Huggins	1700.00	850.00	510.00
(59)	John Hummell (Hummel)	350.00	175.00	105.00
(60)	Walter Johnson	8500.00	4250.00	2550.
(61)	Thos. Jones	350.00	175.00	105.00
(62)	Mike Kahoe	350.00	175.00	105.00
(63)	Ed Kargar	350.00	175.00	105.00
(64)	Wee Willie Keeler	2200.00	1100.00	660.00
(65)	Red Kleinon (Kleinow)	350.00	175.00	105.00
(66)	Jack Knight	350.00	175.00	105.00
(67)	Ed Konetchey (Konetchy)	350.00	175.00	105.00
(68)	Vive Lindaman	350.00	175.00	105.00
(69)	Hans Loebert (Lobert)	350.00	175.00	105.00
(70)	Harry Lord	350.00	175.00	105.00
(71)	Harry Lumley	350.00	175.00	105.00
(72)	Johnny Lush	350.00	175.00	105.00
(73)	Rube Manning	350.00	175.00	105.00
(74)	Jimmy McAleer	350.00	175.00	105.00
(75)	Amby McConnell	350.00	175.00	105.00
(76)	Moose McCormick	350.00	175.00	105.00
(77)	Harry McIntyre	350.00	175.00	105.00
(78)	Larry McLean	350.00	175.00	105.00
(79)	Fred Merkle	350.00	175.00	105.00
(80)	Clyde Milan	350.00	175.00	105.00
(81)	Mike Mitchell	350.00	175.00	105.00
(82a)	Pat Moran (photo inside oval frame)	350.00	175.00	105.00
(82b)	Pat Moran (photo inside square frame)	500.00	250.00	150.00
(83)	Cy Morgan	350.00	175.00	105.00
(84)	Tim Murname (Murnane)	350.00	175.00	105.00
(85)	Danny Murphy	350.00	175.00	105.00
(86)	Red Murray	350.00	175.00	105.00
(87)	Doc Newton	350.00	175.00	105.00
(88)	Simon Nichols (Nicholls)	350.00	175.00	105.00
(89)	Harry Niles	350.00	175.00	105.00
(90)	Bill O'Hare (O'Hara)	350.00	175.00	105.00
(91)	Charley O'Leary	350.00	175.00	105.00
(92)	Dode Paskert	350.00	175.00	105.00
(93)	Barney Pelty	350.00	175.00	105.00
(94)	Jake Pfeister	350.00	175.00	105.00
(95)	Ed Plank	3000.00	1500.00	900.00
(96)	Jack Powell	350.00	175.00	105.00
(97)	Bugs Raymond	350.00	175.00	105.00
(98)	Tom Reilly	350.00	175.00	105.00
(99)	Claude Ritchey	350.00	175.00	105.00
(100)	Nap Rucker	350.00	175.00	105.00
(101)	Ed Ruelbach (Reulbach)	350.00	175.00	105.00
(102)	Slim Sallee	350.00	175.00	105.00
(103)	Germany Schaefer	350.00	175.00	105.00
(104)	Jimmy Schekard (Sheckard)	350.00	175.00	105.00

		NR MT	EX	VG
(105)	Admiral Schlei	350.00	175.00	105.00
(106)	Wildfire Schulte	350.00	175.00	105.00
(107)	Jimmy Sebring	350.00	175.00	105.00
(108)	Bill Shipke	350.00	175.00	105.00
(109)	Charlie Smith	350.00	175.00	105.00
(110)	Tubby Spencer	350.00	175.00	105.00
(111)	Jake Stahl	350.00	175.00	105.00
(112)	Jim Stephens	350.00	175.00	105.00
(113)	Harry Stienfeldt (Steinfeldt)	350.00	175.00	105.00
(114)	Gabby Street	350.00	175.00	105.00
(115)	Bill Sweeney	350.00	175.00	105.00
(116)	Fred Tenney	350.00	175.00	105.00
(117)	Ira Thomas	350.00	175.00	105.00
(118)	Joe Tinker	1500.00	750.00	450.00
(119)	Bob Unclane (Unglaub)	350.00	175.00	105.00
(120)	Heinie Wagner	350.00	175.00	105.00
(121)	Bobby Wallace	1500.00	750.00	450.00

1911 T205 Gold Border

Taking their hobby nickname from their border color, these cards were issued in a number of different cigarette brands. The cards measure 1-1/2" by 2-5/8". American League cards feature a color lithograph of the player inside a stylized baseball diamond. National League cards have head-and-shoulders portraits and a plain background, plus the first ever use of a facsimile autograph in a major card set. The 12 minor league players in the set feature three-quarter length portraits or action pictures in an elaborate frame of columns and other devices. Card backs of the major leaguers carry the player's full name (a first) and statistics. Card backs of the minor leaguers lack the statistics. The complete set price does not include the scarcer variations.

		NR MT	EX	VG
Complete Set:		85000.00	42500.00	25500.
Common Player:		120.00	60.00	36.00
(1)	Edward J. Abbaticchio	120.00	60.00	36.00
(2)	Doc Adkins	375.00	150.00	90.00
(3)	Leon K. Ames	120.00	60.00	36.00
(4)	Jas. P. Archer	120.00	60.00	36.00
(5)	Jimmy Austin	120.00	60.00	36.00
(6)	Bill Bailey	120.00	60.00	36.00
(7)	Home Run Baker	600.00	300.00	180.00
(8)	Neal Ball	800.00	400.00	240.00
(9)	E.B. Barger (full "B" on cap)	120.00	60.00	36.00
(10)	E.B. Barger (partial "B" on cap)	600.00	300.00	180.00
(11)	Jack Barry	120.00	60.00	36.00
(12)	Emil Batch	375.00	150.00	90.00
(13)	John W. Bates	120.00	60.00	36.00
(14)	Fred Beck	120.00	60.00	36.00
(15)	B. Becker	120.00	60.00	36.00
(16)	George G. Bell	120.00	60.00	36.00
(17)	Chas. Bender	800.00	400.00	240.00
(18)	William Bergen	120.00	60.00	36.00
(19)	Bob Bescher	120.00	60.00	36.00
(20)	Joe Birmingham	120.00	60.00	36.00
(21)	Lena Blackburne	120.00	60.00	36.00
(22)	William E. Bransfield	120.00	60.00	36.00
(23)	Roger P. Bresnahan (mouth closed)			
		800.00	400.00	240.00
(24)	Roger P. Bresnahan (mouth open)			
		750.00	300.00	180.00

		NR MT	EX	VG
(25)	A.H. Bridwell	120.00	60.00	36.00
(26)	Mordecai Brown	800.00	400.00	240.00
(27)	Robert Byrne	120.00	60.00	36.00
(28)	Hick Cady	375.00	150.00	90.00
(29)	H. Camnitz	120.00	60.00	36.00
(30)	Bill Carrigan	120.00	60.00	36.00
(31)	Frank J. Chance	800.00	400.00	240.00
(32a)	Hal Chase (both ears show, gold diamond frame extends below shoulders)	200.00	100.00	60.00
(32b)	Hal Chase (both ears show, gold diamond frame ends at shoulders)	200.00	100.00	60.00
(33)	Hal Chase (only left ear shows)	650.00	275.00	165.00
(34)	Ed Cicotte	150.00	75.00	45.00
(35)	Fred C. Clarke	350.00	137.00	82.00
(36)	Ty Cobb	7500.00	3750.00	2250.
(37)	Eddie Collins (mouth closed)	800.00	400.00	240.00
(38)	Eddie Collins (mouth open)	750.00	250.00	150.00
(39)	Jimmy Collins	800.00	400.00	240.00
(40)	Frank J. Corridon	120.00	60.00	36.00
(41a)	Otis Crandall ("t" not crossed in name)	120.00	60.00	36.00
(41b)	Otis Crandall ("t" crossed in name)	120.00	60.00	36.00
(42)	Lou Criger	120.00	60.00	36.00
(43)	W.F. Dahlen	325.00	137.00	82.00
(44)	Jake Daubert	125.00	55.00	33.00
(45)	Jim Delahanty	120.00	60.00	36.00
(46)	Arthur Devlin	120.00	60.00	36.00
(47)	Josh Devore	120.00	60.00	36.00
(48)	W.R. Dickson	120.00	60.00	36.00
(49)	Jiggs Donohue (Donahue)	600.00	300.00	180.00
(50)	Chas. S. Dooin	120.00	60.00	36.00
(51)	Michael J. Doolan	120.00	60.00	36.00
(52a)	Patsy Dougherty (red sock for team emblem)	120.00	60.00	36.00
(52b)	Patsy Dougherty (white sock for team emblem)	350.00	175.00	105.00
(53)	Thomas Downey	120.00	60.00	36.00
(54)	Larry Doyle	120.00	60.00	36.00
(55)	Hugh Duffy	800.00	400.00	240.00
(56)	Jack Dunn	375.00	150.00	90.00
(57)	Jimmy Dygert	120.00	60.00	36.00
(58)	R. Egan	120.00	60.00	36.00
(59)	Kid Elberfeld	120.00	60.00	36.00
(60)	Clyde Engle	120.00	60.00	36.00
(61)	Louis Evans	120.00	60.00	36.00
(62)	John J. Evers	600.00	300.00	180.00
(63)	Robert Ewing	120.00	60.00	36.00
(64)	G.C. Ferguson	120.00	60.00	36.00
(65)	Ray Fisher	450.00	175.00	105.00
(66)	Arthur Fletcher	120.00	60.00	36.00
(67)	John A. Flynn	120.00	60.00	36.00
(68)	Russ Ford (black cap)	120.00	60.00	36.00
(69)	Russ Ford (white cap)	450.00	175.00	105.00
(70)	Wm. A. Foxen	120.00	60.00	36.00
(71)	Jimmy Frick	375.00	150.00	90.00
(72)	Arthur Fromme	120.00	60.00	36.00
(73)	Earl Gardner	120.00	60.00	36.00
(74)	H.L. Gaspar	120.00	60.00	36.00
(75)	George Gibson	120.00	60.00	36.00
(76)	Wilbur Goode	120.00	60.00	36.00
(77)	George F. Graham (Rustlers)	120.00	60.00	36.00
(78)	George F. Graham (Cubs)	600.00	300.00	180.00
(79)	Edward L. Grant	450.00	200.00	120.00
(80a)	Dolly Gray (no stats on back)	120.00	60.00	36.00
(80b)	Dolly Gray (stats on back)	275.00	137.00	82.00
(81)	Clark Griffith	600.00	300.00	180.00
(82)	Bob Groom	120.00	60.00	36.00
(83)	Charlie Hanford	375.00	150.00	90.00
(84)	Bob Harmon (both ears show)	120.00	60.00	36.00
(85)	Bob Harmon (only left ear shows)	600.00	300.00	180.00
(86)	Topsy Hartsel	120.00	60.00	36.00
(87)	Arnold J. Hauser	120.00	60.00	36.00
(88)	Charlie Hemphill	120.00	60.00	36.00
(89)	C.L. Herzog	120.00	60.00	36.00
(90a)	R. Hoblitzel (no stats on back)	800.00	400.00	240.00
(90b)	R. Hoblitzel ("Cin." after 2nd 1908 in stats)	300.00	150.00	90.00
(90c)	R. Hoblitzel (name incorrect, no "Cin." after 1908 in stats)	120.00	60.00	36.00
(90d)	R. Hoblitzell (name correct, no "Cin." after 1908 in stats)	300.00	150.00	90.00
(91)	Danny Hoffman	120.00	60.00	36.00
(92)	Miller J. Huggins	450.00	225.00	135.00
(93)	John E. Hummel	120.00	60.00	36.00
(94)	Fred Jacklitsch	120.00	60.00	36.00
(95)	Hughie Jennings	800.00	400.00	240.00
(96)	Walter Johnson	2500.00	1250.00	750.00
(97)	D. Jones	120.00	60.00	36.00
(98)	Tom Jones	120.00	60.00	36.00
(99)	Addie Joss	800.00	300.00	180.00

		NR MT	EX	VG
(100)	Ed Karger	375.00	137.00	82.00
(101)	Ed Killian	120.00	60.00	36.00
(102)	Red Kleinow	375.00	137.00	82.00
(103)	John G. Kling	120.00	60.00	36.00
(104)	Jack Knight	120.00	60.00	36.00
(105)	Ed Konetchy	120.00	60.00	36.00
(106)	Harry Krause	120.00	60.00	36.00
(107)	Floyd M. Kroh	120.00	60.00	36.00
(108)	Frank LaPorte	120.00	60.00	36.00
(109)	Frank Lang (Lange)	120.00	60.00	36.00
(110a)	A. Latham (A. Latham on back)	120.00	60.00	36.00
(110b)	A. Latham (W.A. Latham on back)	120.00	60.00	36.00
(111)	Thomas W. Leach	120.00	60.00	36.00
(112)	Watty Lee	375.00	150.00	90.00
(113)	Sam Leever	120.00	60.00	36.00
(114a)	A. Leifield (initial "A." on front)	120.00	60.00	36.00
(114b)	A.P. Leifield (initials "A.P." on front)	120.00	60.00	36.00
(115)	Edgar Lennox	120.00	60.00	36.00
(116)	Paddy Livingston	120.00	60.00	36.00
(117)	John B. Lobert	120.00	60.00	36.00
(118)	Bris Lord (Athletics)	120.00	60.00	36.00
(119)	Harry Lord (White Sox)	120.00	60.00	36.00
(120)	Jno. C. Lush	120.00	60.00	36.00
(121)	Nick Maddox	120.00	60.00	36.00
(122)	Sherwood R. Magee	110.00	55.00	33.00
(123)	R.W. Marquard	550.00	200.00	120.00
(124)	C. Mathewson	1500.00	750.00	450.00
(125)	A.A. Mattern	120.00	60.00	36.00
(126)	Sport McAllister	375.00	150.00	90.00
(127)	George McBride	120.00	60.00	36.00
(128)	Amby McConnell	120.00	60.00	36.00
(129)	P.M. McElveen	120.00	60.00	36.00
(130)	J.J. McGraw	800.00	400.00	240.00
(131)	Harry McIntyre (Cubs)	120.00	60.00	36.00
(132)	Matty McIntyre (White Sox)	120.00	60.00	36.00
(133)	M.A. McLean (initials actually J.B.)	120.00	60.00	36.00
(134)	Fred Merkle	125.00	55.00	33.00
(135)	George Merritt	375.00	150.00	90.00
(136)	J.T. Meyers	120.00	60.00	36.00
(137)	Clyde Milan	120.00	60.00	36.00
(138)	J.D. Miller	120.00	60.00	36.00
(139)	M.F. Mitchell	120.00	60.00	36.00
(140a)	P.J. Moran (stray line of type below stats)	120.00	60.00	36.00
(140b)	P.J. Moran (no stray line)	120.00	60.00	36.00
(141)	George Moriarty	120.00	60.00	36.00
(142)	George Mullin	120.00	60.00	36.00
(143)	Danny Murphy	120.00	60.00	36.00
(144)	Jack Murray	120.00	60.00	36.00
(145)	John Nee	375.00	150.00	90.00
(146)	Thomas J. Needham	120.00	60.00	36.00
(147)	Rebel Oakes	120.00	60.00	36.00
(148)	Rube Oldring	120.00	60.00	36.00
(149)	Charley O'Leary	120.00	60.00	36.00
(150)	Fred Olmstead	120.00	60.00	36.00
(151)	Orval Overall	120.00	60.00	36.00
(152)	Freddy Parent	120.00	60.00	36.00
(153)	George Paskert	120.00	60.00	36.00
(154)	Billy Payne	120.00	60.00	36.00
(155)	Barney Pelty	120.00	60.00	36.00
(156)	John Pfeister	120.00	60.00	36.00
(157)	Jimmy Phelan	375.00	150.00	90.00
(158)	E.J. Phelps	120.00	60.00	36.00
(159)	C. Phillippe	120.00	60.00	36.00
(160)	Jack Quinn	120.00	60.00	36.00
(161)	A.L. Raymond	600.00	300.00	180.00
(162)	E.M. Reulbach	120.00	60.00	36.00
(163)	Lewis Richie	120.00	60.00	36.00
(164)	John A. Rowan	400.00	200.00	120.00
(165)	George N. Rucker	120.00	60.00	36.00
(166)	W.D. Scanlan	375.00	175.00	105.00
(167)	Germany Schaefer	120.00	60.00	36.00
(168)	George Schlei	120.00	60.00	36.00
(169)	Boss Schmidt	120.00	60.00	36.00
(170)	F.M. Schulte	120.00	60.00	36.00
(171)	Jim Scott	120.00	60.00	36.00
(172)	B.H. Sharpe	120.00	60.00	36.00
(173)	David Shean (Rustlers)	120.00	60.00	36.00
(174)	David Shean (Cubs)	600.00	300.00	180.00
(175)	Jas. T. Sheckard	120.00	60.00	36.00
(176)	Hack Simmons	120.00	60.00	36.00
(177)	Tony Smith	120.00	60.00	36.00
(178)	Fred C. Snodgrass	120.00	60.00	36.00
(179)	Tris Speaker	725.00	300.00	180.00
(180)	Jake Stahl	120.00	60.00	36.00
(181)	Oscar Stanage	120.00	60.00	36.00
(182)	Harry Steinfeldt	125.00	55.00	33.00
(183)	George Stone	120.00	60.00	36.00

		NR MT	EX	VG
(184)	George Stovall	120.00	60.00	36.00
(185)	Gabby Street	120.00	60.00	36.00
(186)	George F. Suggs	600.00	300.00	180.00
(187)	Ed Summers	120.00	60.00	36.00
(188)	Jeff Sweeney	400.00	175.00	105.00
(189)	Lee Tannehill	120.00	60.00	36.00
(190)	Ira Thomas	120.00	60.00	36.00
(191)	Joe Tinker	800.00	400.00	240.00
(192)	John Titus	120.00	60.00	36.00
(193)	Terry Turner	600.00	300.00	180.00
(194)	James Vaughn	120.00	60.00	36.00
(195)	Heinie Wagner	400.00	175.00	105.00
(196)	Bobby Wallace (with cap)	375.00	175.00	105.00
(197a)	Bobby Wallace (no cap, one line of 1910 stats)	800.00	400.00	240.00
(197b)	Bobby Wallace (no cap, two lines of 1910 stats)	625.00	275.00	165.00
(198)	Ed Walsh	650.00	250.00	150.00
(199)	Z.D. Wheat	600.00	300.00	180.00
(200)	Doc White (White Sox)	120.00	60.00	36.00
(201)	Kirb. White (Pirates)	400.00	200.00	120.00
(202)	Irvin K. Wilhelm	600.00	300.00	180.00
(203)	Ed Willett	120.00	60.00	36.00
(204)	J. Owen Wilson	120.00	60.00	36.00
(205)	George R. Wiltse (both ears show)	120.00	60.00	36.00
(206)	George R. Wiltse (only right ear shows)	600.00	300.00	180.00
(207)	Harry Wolter	120.00	60.00	36.00
(208)	Cy Young	1500.00	750.00	450.00

1909-11 T206 White Border

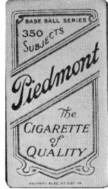

The nearly 525 cards which make up the T206 set are the most popular of the early tobacco card issues. Players are depicted in a color lithograph against a variety of colorful backgrounds, surrounded by a white border. The player names on the 1-1/2" by 2-5/8" cards appear at the bottom with the city and league, when a city has more than one team. Backs contain an ad for one of 16 brands of cigarettes. There are 389 major leaguer cards and 134 minor leaguer cards in the set, but with front/back varieties the number of potentially different cards runs into the thousands. The set features many expensive cards including a number of pose and/or team variations, along with the very scarce Eddie Plank card and the "King of Baseball Cards," the T206 Honus Wagner, the most avidly sought of all baseball cards. The complete set price does not include the Doyle (N.Y. Natl.), Magie, Plank and Wagner cards.

		NR MT	EX	VG
Complete Set:		1500.00	7500.00	2250.
Common Player:		100.00	50.00	30.00
Common Minor Leaguer:		105.00	52.00	31.00
Common Southern Leaguer:		225.00	112.00	67.00
(1)	Ed Abbaticchio (blue sleeves)	150.00	75.00	45.00
(2)	Ed Abbaticchio (brown sleeves)	100.00	50.00	30.00
(3)	Fred Abbott	105.00	52.00	31.00
(4)	Bill Abstein	100.00	50.00	30.00
(5)	Doc Adkins	105.00	52.00	31.00
(6)	Whitey Alperman	125.00	62.00	37.00
(7)	Red Ames (hands at chest)	125.00	62.00	37.00

		NR MT	EX	VG
(8)	Red Ames (hands above head)	125.00	62.00	37.00
(9)	Red Ames (portrait)	100.00	50.00	30.00
(10)	John Anderson	105.00	52.00	31.00
(11)	Frank Arellanes	100.00	50.00	30.00
(12)	Herman Armbruster	105.00	52.00	31.00
(13)	Harry Arndt	105.00	52.00	31.00
(14)	Jake Atz	100.00	50.00	30.00
(15)	Home Run Baker	450.00	225.00	135.00
(16)	Neal Ball (New York)	125.00	62.00	37.00
(17)	Neal Ball (Cleveland)	100.00	50.00	30.00
(18)	Jap Barbeau	125.00	62.00	37.00
(19)	Cy Barger	105.00	52.00	31.00
(20)	Jack Barry (Philadelphia)	100.00	50.00	30.00
(21)	Shad Barry (Milwaukee)	105.00	52.00	31.00
(22)	Jack Bastian	225.00	112.00	67.00
(23)	Emil Batch	105.00	52.00	31.00
(24)	Johnny Bates	125.00	62.00	37.00
(25)	Harry Bay	300.00	150.00	90.00
(26)	Ginger Beaumont	125.00	62.00	37.00
(27)	Fred Beck	100.00	50.00	30.00
(28)	Beals Becker	100.00	50.00	30.00
(29)	Jake Beckley	300.00	150.00	90.00
(30)	George Bell (hands above head)	125.00	62.00	37.00
(31)	George Bell (pitching follow thru)	100.00	50.00	30.00
(32)	Chief Bender (pitching, no trees in background)	400.00	200.00	120.00
(33)	Chief Bender (pitching, trees in background)	400.00	200.00	120.00
(34)	Chief Bender (portrait)	500.00	250.00	150.00
(35)	Bill Bergen (batting)	125.00	62.00	37.00
(36)	Bill Bergen (catching)	105.00	52.00	31.00
(37)	Heinie Berger	100.00	50.00	30.00
(38)	Bill Bernhard	225.00	112.00	67.00
(39)	Bob Bescher (hands in air)	100.00	50.00	30.00
(40)	Bob Bescher (portrait)	100.00	50.00	30.00
(41)	Joe Birmingham	135.00	67.00	40.00
(42)	Lena Blackburne	105.00	52.00	31.00
(43)	Jack Bliss	100.00	50.00	30.00
(44)	Frank Bowerman	125.00	62.00	37.00
(45)	Bill Bradley (portrait)	125.00	62.00	37.00
(46)	Bill Bradley (with bat)	100.00	50.00	30.00
(47)	Dave Brain	105.00	52.00	31.00
(48)	Kitty Bransfield	125.00	62.00	37.00
(49)	Roy Brashear	105.00	52.00	31.00
(50)	Ted Breitenstein	225.00	112.00	67.00
(51)	Roger Bresnahan (portrait)	550.00	275.00	165.00
(52)	Roger Bresnahan (with bat)	400.00	200.00	120.00
(53)	Al Bridwell (portrait, no cap)	100.00	50.00	30.00
(54)	Al Bridwell (portrait, with cap)	125.00	62.00	37.00
(55a)	George Brown (Browne) (Chicago)	125.00	62.00	37.00
(55b)	George Brown (Browne) (Washington)	1000.00	500.00	300.00
(56)	Mordecai Brown (Chicago on shirt)	400.00	200.00	120.00
(57)	Mordecai Brown (Cubs on shirt)	550.00	275.00	165.00
(58)	Mordecai Brown (portrait)	450.00	225.00	135.00
(59)	Al Burch (batting)	275.00	137.00	80.00
(60)	Al Burch (fielding)	100.00	50.00	30.00
(61)	Fred Burchell	105.00	52.00	31.00
(62)	Jimmy Burke	105.00	52.00	31.00
(63)	Bill Burns	100.00	50.00	30.00
(64)	Donie Bush	100.00	50.00	30.00
(65)	John Butler	105.00	52.00	31.00
(66)	Bobby Byrne	100.00	50.00	30.00
(67)	Howie Camnitz (arm at side)	100.00	50.00	30.00
(68)	Howie Camnitz (arms folded)	125.00	62.00	37.00
(69)	Howie Camnitz (hands above head)	100.00	50.00	30.00
(70)	Billy Campbell	100.00	50.00	30.00
(71)	Scoops Carey	225.00	112.00	67.00
(72)	Charley Carr	105.00	52.00	31.00
(73)	Bill Carrigan	100.00	50.00	30.00
(74)	Doc Casey	105.00	52.00	31.00
(75)	Peter Cassidy	105.00	52.00	31.00
(76)	Frank Chance (batting)	400.00	200.00	120.00
(77)	Frank Chance (portrait, red background)	550.00	275.00	165.00
(78)	Frank Chance (portrait, yellow background)	450.00	225.00	135.00
(79)	Bill Chappelle	105.00	52.00	31.00
(80)	Chappie Charles	100.00	50.00	30.00
(81)	Hal Chase (holding trophy)	225.00	112.00	67.00
(82)	Hal Chase (portrait, blue background)	250.00	125.00	75.00
(83)	Hal Chase (portrait, pink background)	350.00	175.00	105.00
(84)	Hal Chase (throwing, dark cap)	200.00	100.00	60.00
(85)	Hal Chase (throwing, white cap)	475.00	237.00	145.00
(86)	Jack Chesbro	600.00	300.00	180.00
(87)	Ed Cicotte	175.00	87.00	52.00
(88)	Bill Clancy (Clancey)	105.00	52.00	31.00
(89)	Josh Clark (Clarke) (Columbus)	105.00	52.00	31.00
(90)	Fred Clarke (Pittsburg, holding bat)	400.00	200.00	120.00
(91)	Fred Clarke (Pittsburg, portrait)	450.00	225.00	135.00
(92)	Nig Clarke (Cleveland)	125.00	62.00	37.00
(93)	Bill Clymer	105.00	52.00	31.00
(94)	Ty Cobb (portrait, green background)	3250.00	1625.00	975.00
(95)	Ty Cobb (portrait, red background)	2500.00	1250.00	750.00
(96)	Ty Cobb (bat off shoulder)	2500.00	1250.00	750.00
(97)	Ty Cobb (bat on shoulder)	2500.00	1250.00	750.00
(98)	Cad Coles	225.00	112.00	67.00
(99)	Eddie Collins (Philadelphia)	500.00	250.00	150.00
(100)	Jimmy Collins (Minneapolis)	375.00	187.00	110.00
(101)	Bunk Congalton	105.00	52.00	31.00
(102)	Wid Conroy (fielding)	125.00	62.00	37.00
(103)	Wid Conroy (with bat)	100.00	50.00	30.00
(104)	Harry Covaleski (Coveleski)	125.00	62.00	37.00
(105)	Doc Crandall (portrait, no cap)	125.00	62.00	37.00
(106)	Doc Crandall (portrait, with cap)	100.00	50.00	30.00
(107)	Bill Cranston	250.00	125.00	75.00
(108)	Gavvy Cravath	175.00	87.00	52.00
(109)	Sam Crawford (throwing)	500.00	250.00	150.00
(110)	Sam Crawford (with bat)	450.00	225.00	135.00
(111)	Birdie Cree	100.00	50.00	30.00
(112)	Lou Criger	125.00	62.00	37.00
(113)	Dode Criss	125.00	62.00	37.00
(114)	Monte Cross	105.00	52.00	31.00
(115a)	Bill Dahlen (Boston)	150.00	75.00	45.00
(115b)	Bill Dahlen (Brooklyn)	600.00	300.00	175.00
(116)	Paul Davidson	105.00	52.00	31.00
(117)	George Davis (Chicago)	125.00	62.00	37.00
(118)	Harry Davis (Philadelphia, Davis on front)	100.00	50.00	30.00
(119)	Harry Davis (Philadelphia, H. Davis on front)	125.00	62.00	37.00
(120)	Frank Delehanty (Delahanty) (Louisville)	105.00	52.00	31.00
(121)	Jim Delehanty (Delahanty) (Washington)	125.00	62.00	37.00
(122a)	Ray Demmitt (New York)	100.00	50.00	30.00
(122b)	Ray Demmitt (St. Louis)	7500.00	3750.00	2300.
(123)	Rube Dessau	105.00	52.00	31.00
(124)	Art Devlin	125.00	62.00	37.00
(125)	Josh Devore	100.00	50.00	30.00
(126)	Bill Dineen (Dinneen)	100.00	50.00	30.00
(127)	Mike Donlin (fielding)	350.00	175.00	105.00
(128)	Mike Donlin (seated)	125.00	62.00	37.00
(129)	Mike Donlin (with bat)	100.00	50.00	30.00
(130)	Jiggs Donohue (Donahue)	125.00	62.00	37.00
(131)	Wild Bill Donovan (portrait)	125.00	62.00	37.00
(132)	Wild Bill Donovan (throwing)	100.00	50.00	30.00
(133)	Red Dooin	125.00	62.00	37.00
(134)	Mickey Doolan (batting)	100.00	50.00	30.00
(135)	Mickey Doolan (fielding)	100.00	50.00	30.00
(136)	Mickey Doolin (Doolan)	125.00	62.00	37.00
(137)	Gus Dorner	105.00	52.00	31.00
(138)	Patsy Dougherty (arm in air)	100.00	50.00	30.00
(139)	Patsy Dougherty (portrait)	125.00	62.00	37.00
(140)	Tom Downey (batting)	100.00	50.00	30.00
(141)	Tom Downey (fielding)	100.00	50.00	30.00
(142)	Jerry Downs	105.00	52.00	31.00
(143a)	Joe Doyle (N.Y. Natl., hands above head)	30000.00	15000.00	9000.
(143b)	Joe Doyle (N.Y., hands above head)	100.00	50.00	30.00
(144)	Larry Doyle (N.Y. Nat'l., portrait)	125.00	62.00	37.00
(145)	Larry Doyle (N.Y. Nat'l., throwing)	175.00	87.00	52.00
(146)	Larry Doyle (N.Y. Nat'l., with bat)	125.00	62.00	37.00
(147)	Jean Dubuc	100.00	50.00	30.00
(148)	Hugh Duffy	400.00	200.00	120.00
(149)	Jack Dunn (Baltimore)	105.00	52.00	31.00
(150)	Joe Dunn (Brooklyn)	100.00	50.00	30.00
(151)	Bull Durham	135.00	67.00	40.00
(152)	Jimmy Dygert	100.00	50.00	30.00
(153)	Ted Easterly	100.00	50.00	30.00
(154)	Dick Egan	100.00	50.00	30.00
(155a)	Kid Elberfeld (New York)	125.00	62.00	37.00
(155b)	Kid Elberfeld (Washington, portrait)	2500.00	1250.00	750.00

	NR MT	EX	VG
(156) Kid Elberfeld (Washington, fielding)			
	100.00	50.00	30.00
(157) Roy Ellam	250.00	125.00	75.00
(158) Clyde Engle	100.00	50.00	30.00
(159) Steve Evans	100.00	50.00	30.00
(160) Johnny Evers (portrait)	650.00	325.00	200.00
(161) Johnny Evers (with bat, Chicago on shirt)			
	400.00	200.00	120.00
(162) Johnny Evers (with bat, Cubs on shirt)			
	500.00	250.00	150.00
(163) Bob Ewing	125.00	62.00	37.00
(164) Cecil Ferguson	100.00	50.00	30.00
(165) Hobe Ferris	125.00	62.00	37.00
(166) Lou Fiene (portrait)	100.00	50.00	30.00
(167) Lou Fiene (throwing)	100.00	50.00	30.00
(168) Steamer Flanagan	105.00	52.00	31.00
(169) Art Fletcher	100.00	50.00	30.00
(170) Elmer Flick	450.00	225.00	135.00
(171) Russ Ford	100.00	50.00	30.00
(172) Ed Foster	225.00	112.00	67.00
(173) Jerry Freeman	105.00	52.00	31.00
(174) John Frill	100.00	50.00	30.00
(175) Charlie Fritz	225.00	112.00	67.00
(176) Art Fromme	100.00	50.00	30.00
(177) Chick Gandil	125.00	62.00	37.00
(178) Bob Ganley	125.00	62.00	37.00
(179) John Ganzel	105.00	52.00	31.00
(180) Harry Gasper	100.00	50.00	30.00
(181) Rube Geyer	100.00	50.00	30.00
(182) George Gibson	125.00	62.00	37.00
(183) Billy Gilbert	125.00	62.00	37.00
(184) Wilbur Goode (Good)	125.00	62.00	37.00
(185) Bill Graham (St. Louis)	100.00	50.00	30.00
(186) Peaches Graham (Boston)	100.00	50.00	30.00
(187) Dolly Gray	100.00	50.00	30.00
(188) Ed Greminger	225.00	112.00	67.00
(189) Clark Griffith (batting)	450.00	225.00	135.00
(190) Clark Griffith (portrait)	500.00	250.00	150.00
(191) Moose Grimshaw	105.00	52.00	31.00
(192) Bob Groom	100.00	50.00	30.00
(193) Guiheen	250.00	125.00	75.00
(194) Ed Hahn	125.00	62.00	37.00
(195) Bob Hall	105.00	52.00	31.00
(196) Bill Hallman	105.00	52.00	31.00
(197) Jack Hannifan (Hannifin)	105.00	52.00	31.00
(198) Bill Hart (Little Rock)	300.00	150.00	90.00
(199) Jimmy Hart (Montgomery)	250.00	125.00	75.00
(200) Topsy Hartsel	100.00	50.00	30.00
(201) Jack Hayden	105.00	52.00	31.00
(202) J. Ross Helm	225.00	112.00	67.00
(203) Charlie Hemphill	125.00	62.00	37.00
(204) Buck Herzog (Boston)	100.00	50.00	30.00
(205) Buck Herzog (New York)	125.00	62.00	37.00
(206) Gordon Hickman	225.00	112.00	67.00
(207) Bill Hinchman (Cleveland)	125.00	62.00	37.00
(208) Harry Hinchman (Toledo)	105.00	52.00	31.00
(209) Dick Hoblitzell	100.00	50.00	30.00
(210) Danny Hoffman (St. Louis)	100.00	50.00	30.00
(211) Izzy Hoffman (Providence)	105.00	52.00	31.00
(212) Solly Hofman	100.00	50.00	30.00
(213) Bock Hooker	225.00	112.00	67.00
(214) Del Howard (Chicago)	100.00	50.00	30.00
(215) Ernie Howard (Savannah)	225.00	112.00	67.00
(216) Harry Howell (hand at waist)	100.00	50.00	30.00
(217) Harry Howell (portrait)	100.00	50.00	30.00
(218) Miller Huggins (hands at mouth)			
	400.00	200.00	120.00
(219) Miller Huggins (portrait)	450.00	225.00	135.00
(220) Rudy Hulswitt	100.00	50.00	30.00
(221) John Hummel	100.00	50.00	30.00
(222) George Hunter	100.00	50.00	30.00
(223) Frank Isbell	135.00	67.00	40.00
(224) Fred Jacklitsch	135.00	67.00	40.00
(225) Jimmy Jackson	105.00	52.00	31.00
(226) Hughie Jennings (one hand showing)			
	400.00	200.00	120.00
(227) Hughie Jennings (both hands showing)			
	400.00	200.00	120.00
(228) Hughie Jennings (portrait)	450.00	225.00	135.00
(229) Walter Johnson (hands at chest)			
	1250.00	625.00	375.00
(230) Walter Johnson (portrait)	1400.00	700.00	400.00
(231) Fielder Jones (Chicago, hands at hips)			
	125.00	62.00	37.00
(232) Fielder Jones (Chicago, portrait)			
	125.00	62.00	37.00
(233) Davy Jones (Detroit)	100.00	50.00	30.00
(234) Tom Jones (St. Louis)	125.00	62.00	37.00
(235) Dutch Jordan (Atlanta)	225.00	112.00	67.00
(236) Tim Jordan (Brooklyn, batting)	100.00	50.00	30.00
(237) Tim Jordan (Brooklyn, portrait)			
	125.00	62.00	37.00

	NR MT	EX	VG
(238) Addie Joss (hands at chest)	450.00	225.00	135.00
(239) Addie Joss (portrait)	550.00	275.00	165.00
(240) Ed Karger	125.00	62.00	37.00
(241) Willie Keeler (portrait)	750.00	375.00	225.00
(242) Willie Keeler (with bat)	700.00	350.00	210.00
(243) Joe Kelley	300.00	150.00	90.00
(244) J.F. Kiernan	225.00	112.00	67.00
(245) Ed Killian (hands at chest)	100.00	50.00	30.00
(246) Ed Killian (portrait)	125.00	62.00	37.00
(247) Frank King	225.00	112.00	67.00
(248) Rube Kisinger (Kissinger)	105.00	52.00	31.00
(249a) Red Kleinow (Boston)	1250.00	625.00	375.00
(249b) Red Kleinow (New York, catching)			
	100.00	50.00	30.00
(250) Red Kleinow (New York, with bat)			
	125.00	62.00	37.00
(251) Johnny Kling	125.00	62.00	37.00
(252) Otto Knabe	100.00	50.00	30.00
(253) Jack Knight (portrait)	100.00	50.00	30.00
(254) Jack Knight (with bat)	100.00	50.00	30.00
(255) Ed Konetchy (glove above head)			
	125.00	62.00	37.00
(256) Ed Konetchy (glove near ground)			
	100.00	50.00	30.00
(257) Harry Krause (pitching)	100.00	50.00	30.00
(258) Harry Krause (portrait)	100.00	50.00	30.00
(259) Rube Kroh	100.00	50.00	30.00
(260) Otto Kruger (Krueger)	105.00	52.00	31.00
(261) James Lafitte	225.00	112.00	67.00
(262) Nap Lajoie (portrait)	1250.00	625.00	375.00
(263) Nap Lajoie (throwing)	700.00	350.00	200.00
(264) Nap Lajoie (with bat)	700.00	350.00	200.00
(265) Joe Lake (New York)	125.00	62.00	37.00
(266) Joe Lake (St. Louis, ball in hand)			
	100.00	50.00	30.00
(267) Joe Lake (St. Louis, no ball in hand)			
	100.00	50.00	30.00
(268) Frank LaPorte	100.00	50.00	30.00
(269) Arlie Latham	100.00	50.00	30.00
(270) Bill Lattimore	105.00	52.00	31.00
(271) Jimmy Lavender	105.00	52.00	31.00
(272) Tommy Leach (bending over)	100.00	50.00	30.00
(273) Tommy Leach (portrait)	125.00	62.00	37.00
(274) Lefty Leifield (batting)	100.00	50.00	30.00
(275) Lefty Leifield (pitching)	125.00	62.00	37.00
(276) Ed Lennox	100.00	50.00	30.00
(277) Harry Lentz (Sentz)	225.00	112.00	67.00
(278) Glenn Liebhardt	125.00	62.00	37.00
(279) Vive Lindaman	125.00	62.00	37.00
(280) Perry Lipe	225.00	112.00	67.00
(281) Paddy Livingstone (Livingston)	100.00	50.00	30.00
(282) Hans Lobert	125.00	62.00	37.00
(283) Harry Lord	100.00	50.00	30.00
(284) Harry Lumley	125.00	62.00	37.00
(285a) Carl Lundgren (Chicago)	700.00	350.00	200.00
(285b) Carl Lundgren (Kansas City)	105.00	52.00	31.00
(286) Nick Maddox	100.00	50.00	30.00
(287a) Sherry Magie (Magee)	30000.00	15000.00	9000.
(287b) Sherry Magee (portrait)	175.00	87.00	52.00
(288) Sherry Magee (with bat)	125.00	62.00	37.00
(289) Bill Malarkey	105.00	52.00	31.00
(290) Billy Maloney	105.00	52.00	31.00
(291) George Manion	225.00	112.00	67.00
(292) Rube Manning (batting)	125.00	62.00	37.00
(293) Rube Manning (pitching)	100.00	50.00	30.00
(294) Rube Marquard (hands at thighs)			
	500.00	250.00	150.00
(295) Rube Marquard (pitching follow thru)			
	450.00	225.00	135.00
(296) Rube Marquard (portrait)	475.00	237.00	140.00
(297) Doc Marshall	100.00	50.00	30.00
(298) Christy Mathewson (dark cap)	800.00	400.00	250.00
(299) Christy Mathewson (portrait)	1400.00	700.00	400.00
(300) Christy Mathewson (white cap)	1200.00	600.00	350.00
(301) Al Mattern	100.00	50.00	30.00
(302) John McAleese	100.00	50.00	30.00
(303) George McBride	100.00	50.00	30.00
(304) Pat McCauley	225.00	112.00	67.00
(305) Moose McCormick	100.00	50.00	30.00
(306) Pryor McElveen	100.00	50.00	30.00
(307) Dan McGann	105.00	52.00	31.00
(308) Jim McGinley	105.00	52.00	31.00
(309) Iron Man McGinnity	350.00	175.00	105.00
(310) Stoney McGlynn	105.00	52.00	31.00
(311) John McGraw (finger in air)	500.00	250.00	150.00
(312) John McGraw (glove at hip)	475.00	237.00	140.00
(313) John McGraw (portrait, no cap)			
	600.00	300.00	175.00
(314) John McGraw (portrait, with cap)			
	400.00	200.00	120.00
(315) Harry McIntyre (Brooklyn)	125.00	62.00	37.00

	NR MT	EX	VG
(316) Harry McIntyre (Brooklyn & Chicago)			
	100.00	50.00	30.00
(317) Matty McIntyre (Detroit)	100.00	50.00	30.00
(318) Larry McLean	100.00	50.00	30.00
(319) George McQuillan (ball in hand)	125.00	62.00	37.00
(320) George McQuillan (with bat)	100.00	50.00	30.00
(321) Fred Merkle (portrait)	150.00	75.00	45.00
(322) Fred Merkle (throwing)	125.00	62.00	37.00
(323) George Merritt	105.00	52.00	31.00
(324) Chief Meyers	100.00	50.00	30.00
(325) Clyde Milan	100.00	50.00	30.00
(326) Dots Miller (Pittsburg)	100.00	50.00	30.00
(327) Molly Miller (Dallas)	225.00	112.00	67.00
(328) Bill Milligan	105.00	52.00	31.00
(329) Fred Mitchell (Toronto)	105.00	52.00	31.00
(330) Mike Mitchell (Cincinnati)	100.00	50.00	30.00
(331) Dan Moeller	105.00	52.00	31.00
(332) Carlton Molesworth	225.00	112.00	67.00
(333) Herbie Moran (Providence)	105.00	52.00	31.00
(334) Pat Moran (Chicago)	100.00	50.00	30.00
(335) George Moriarty	100.00	50.00	30.00
(336) Mike Mowrey	100.00	50.00	30.00
(337) Dom Mullaney	225.00	112.00	67.00
(338) George Mullen (Mullin)	100.00	50.00	30.00
(339) George Mullin (throwing)	125.00	62.00	37.00
(340) George Mullin (with bat)	100.00	50.00	30.00
(341) Danny Murphy (batting)	100.00	50.00	30.00
(342) Danny Murphy (throwing)	125.00	62.00	37.00
(343) Red Murray (batting)	100.00	50.00	30.00
(344) Red Murray (portrait)	100.00	50.00	30.00
(345) Chief Myers (Meyers) (batting)	100.00	50.00	30.00
(346) Chief Myers (Meyers) (fielding)	100.00	50.00	30.00
(347) Billy Nattress	105.00	52.00	31.00
(348) Tom Needham	100.00	50.00	30.00
(349) Simon Nicholls (hands on knees)			
	125.00	62.00	37.00
(350) Simon Nichols (Nicholls) (batting)			
	100.00	50.00	30.00
(351) Harry Niles	125.00	62.00	37.00
(352) Rebel Oakes	100.00	50.00	30.00
(353) Frank Oberlin	105.00	52.00	31.00
(354) Peter O'Brien	105.00	52.00	31.00
(355a)Bill O'Hara (New York)	100.00	50.00	30.00
(355b)Bill O'Hara (St. Louis)	7500.00	3750.00	2250.
(356) Rube Oldring (batting)	100.00	50.00	30.00
(357) Rube Oldring (fielding)	125.00	62.00	37.00
(358) Charley O'Leary (hands on knees)			
	100.00	50.00	30.00
(359) Charley O'Leary (portrait)	125.00	62.00	37.00
(360) William J. O'Neil	105.00	52.00	31.00
(361) Al Orth	225.00	112.00	67.00
(362) William Otey	225.00	112.00	67.00
(363) Orval Overall (hand face level)	100.00	50.00	30.00
(364) Orval Overall (hands waist level)			
	100.00	50.00	30.00
(365) Orval Overall (portrait)	125.00	62.00	37.00
(366) Frank Owen	125.00	62.00	37.00
(367) George Paige	225.00	112.00	67.00
(368) Fred Parent	125.00	62.00	37.00
(369) Dode Paskert	100.00	50.00	30.00
(370) Jim Pastorius	125.00	62.00	37.00
(371) Harry Pattee	550.00	275.00	165.00
(372) Billy Payne	100.00	50.00	30.00
(373) Barney Pelty (horizontal photo)			
	350.00	175.00	105.00
(374) Barney Pelty (vertical photo)	100.00	50.00	30.00
(375) Hub Perdue	225.00	112.00	67.00
(376) George Perring	100.00	50.00	30.00
(377) Arch Persons	225.00	112.00	67.00
(378) Francis (Big Jeff) Pfeffer	100.00	50.00	30.00
(379) Jake Pfeister (Pfiester) (seated)			
	100.00	50.00	30.00
(380) Jake Pfeister (Pfiester) (throwing)			
	100.00	50.00	30.00
(381) Jimmy Phelan	105.00	52.00	31.00
(382) Eddie Phelps	100.00	50.00	30.00
(383) Deacon Phillippe	100.00	50.00	30.00
(384) Ollie Pickering	105.00	52.00	31.00
(385) Eddie Plank	25000.00	12500.00	7500.
(386) Phil Poland	105.00	52.00	31.00
(387) Jack Powell	125.00	62.00	37.00
(388) Mike Powers	350.00	175.00	105.00
(389) Billy Purtell	100.00	50.00	30.00
(390) Ambrose Puttman (Puttmann)	105.00	52.00	31.00
(391) Lee Quillen (Quillin)	105.00	52.00	31.00
(392) Jack Quinn	100.00	50.00	30.00
(393) Newt Randall	105.00	52.00	31.00
(394) Bugs Raymond	100.00	50.00	30.00
(395) Ed Reagan	225.00	112.00	67.00
(396) Ed Reulbach (glove showing)	275.00	137.00	80.00
(397) Ed Reulbach (no glove showing)			
	100.00	50.00	30.00
(398) Dutch Revelle	225.00	112.00	67.00
(399) Bob Rhoades (Rhoads) (hands at chest)			
	100.00	50.00	30.00
(400) Bob Rhoades (Rhoads) (right arm extended)			
	100.00	50.00	30.00
(401) Charlie Rhodes	100.00	50.00	30.00
(402) Claude Ritchey	125.00	62.00	37.00
(403) Lou Ritter	105.00	52.00	31.00
(404) Ike Rockenfeld	225.00	112.00	67.00
(405) Claude Rossman	100.00	50.00	30.00
(406) Nap Rucker (portrait)	125.00	62.00	37.00
(407) Nap Rucker (throwing)	100.00	50.00	30.00
(408) Dick Rudolph	105.00	52.00	31.00
(409) Ray Ryan	225.00	112.00	67.00
(410) Germany Schaefer (Detroit)	125.00	62.00	37.00
(411) Germany Schaefer (Washington)			
	100.00	50.00	30.00
(412) George Schirm	105.00	52.00	31.00
(413) Larry Schlafly	105.00	52.00	31.00
(414) Admiral Schlei (batting)	100.00	50.00	30.00
(415) Admiral Schlei (catching)	125.00	62.00	37.00
(416) Admiral Schlei (portrait)	100.00	50.00	30.00
(417) Boss Schmidt (portrait)	100.00	50.00	30.00
(418) Boss Schmidt (throwing)	125.00	62.00	37.00
(419) Ossee Schreck (Schreckengost)			
	105.00	52.00	31.00
(420) Wildfire Schulte (front view)	125.00	62.00	37.00
(421) Wildfire Schulte (back view)	100.00	50.00	30.00
(422) Jim Scott	100.00	50.00	30.00
(423) Charles Seitz	225.00	112.00	67.00
(424) Cy Seymour (batting)	125.00	62.00	37.00
(425) Cy Seymour (portrait)	100.00	50.00	30.00
(426) Cy Seymour (throwing)	100.00	50.00	30.00
(427) Spike Shannon	105.00	52.00	31.00
(428) Bud Sharpe	105.00	52.00	31.00
(429) Shag Shaughnessy	225.00	112.00	67.00
(430) Al Shaw (St. Louis)	125.00	62.00	37.00
(431) Hunky Shaw (Providence)	105.00	52.00	31.00
(432) Jimmy Sheckard (glove showing)			
	100.00	50.00	30.00
(433) Jimmy Sheckard (no glove showing)			
	125.00	62.00	37.00
(434) Bill Shipke	125.00	62.00	37.00
(435) Jimmy Slagle	105.00	52.00	31.00
(436) Carlos Smith (Shreveport)	225.00	112.00	67.00
(437) Frank Smith (Chicago, F. Smith on front)			
	250.00	125.00	75.00
(438a)Frank Smith (Chicago, white cap)			
	100.00	50.00	30.00
(438b)Frank Smith (Chicago & Boston)			
	1250.00	625.00	375.00
(439) "Happy" Smith (Brooklyn)	100.00	50.00	30.00
(440) Heinie Smith (Buffalo)	105.00	52.00	31.00
(441) Sid Smith (Atlanta)	225.00	112.00	67.00
(442) Fred Snodgrass (batting)	125.00	62.00	37.00
(443) Fred Snodgrass (catching)	125.00	62.00	37.00
(444) Bob Spade	100.00	50.00	30.00
(445) Tris Speaker	1250.00	625.00	375.00
(446) Tubby Spencer	125.00	62.00	37.00
(447) Jake Stahl (glove shows)	100.00	50.00	30.00
(448) Jake Stahl (no glove shows)	125.00	62.00	37.00
(449) Oscar Stanage	100.00	50.00	30.00
(450) Dolly Stark	225.00	112.00	67.00
(451) Charlie Starr	100.00	50.00	30.00
(452) Harry Steinfeldt (portrait)	150.00	75.00	45.00
(453) Harry Steinfeldt (with bat)	125.00	62.00	37.00
(454) Jim Stephens	100.00	50.00	30.00
(455) George Stone	125.00	62.00	37.00
(456) George Stovall (batting)	100.00	50.00	30.00
(457) George Stovall (portrait)	125.00	62.00	37.00
(458) Sam Strang	105.00	52.00	31.00
(459) Gabby Street (catching)	100.00	50.00	30.00
(460) Gabby Street (portrait)	100.00	50.00	30.00
(461) Billy Sullivan	125.00	62.00	37.00
(462) Ed Summers	100.00	50.00	30.00
(463) Bill Sweeney (Boston)	100.00	50.00	30.00
(464) Jeff Sweeney (New York)	100.00	50.00	30.00
(465) Jesse Tannehill (Washington)	100.00	50.00	30.00
(466) Lee Tannehill (Chicago, L. Tannehill on front)			
	125.00	62.00	37.00
(467) Lee Tannehill (Chicago, Tannehill on front)			
	100.00	50.00	30.00
(468) Dummy Taylor	105.00	52.00	31.00
(469) Fred Tenney	125.00	62.00	37.00
(470) Tony Thebo	225.00	112.00	67.00
(471) Jake Thielman	105.00	52.00	31.00
(472) Ira Thomas	100.00	50.00	30.00
(473) Woodie Thornton	225.00	112.00	67.00
(474) Joe Tinker (bat off shoulder)	450.00	225.00	135.00
(475) Joe Tinker (bat on shoulder)	450.00	225.00	135.00
(476) Joe Tinker (hands on knees)	500.00	250.00	150.00

		NR MT	EX	VG
(477)	Joe Tinker (portrait)	550.00	275.00	165.00
(478)	John Titus	100.00	50.00	30.00
(479)	Terry Turner	125.00	62.00	37.00
(480)	Bob Unglaub	100.00	50.00	30.00
(481)	Juan Violat (Viola)	225.00	112.00	67.00
(482)	Rube Waddell (portrait)	500.00	250.00	150.00
(483)	Rube Waddell (throwing)	500.00	250.00	150.00
(484)	Heinie Wagner (bat on left shoulder)			
		125.00	67.00	40.00
(485)	Heinie Wagner (bat on right shoulder)			
		100.00	50.00	30.00
(486)	Honus Wagner	300000	150000	105000
(487)	Bobby Wallace	400.00	200.00	120.00
(488)	Ed Walsh	550.00	275.00	165.00
(489)	Jack Warhop	100.00	50.00	30.00
(490)	Jake Weimer	125.00	62.00	37.00
(491)	James Westlake	225.00	112.00	67.00
(492)	Zack Wheat	550.00	275.00	165.00
(493)	Doc White (Chicago, pitching)	100.00	50.00	30.00
(494)	Doc White (Chicago, portrait)	125.00	62.00	37.00
(495)	Foley White (Houston)	225.00	112.00	67.00
(496)	Jack White (Buffalo)	105.00	52.00	31.00
(497)	Kaiser Wilhelm (hands at chest)			
		125.00	62.00	37.00
(498)	Kaiser Wilhelm (with bat)	100.00	50.00	30.00
(499)	Ed Willett	100.00	50.00	30.00
(500)	Ed Willetts (Willett)	100.00	50.00	30.00
(501)	Jimmy Williams	125.00	62.00	37.00
(502)	Vic Willis (Pittsburg)	100.00	50.00	30.00
(503)	Vic Willis (St. Louis, throwing)	100.00	50.00	30.00
(504)	Vic Willis (St. Louis, with bat)	100.00	50.00	30.00
(505)	Owen Wilson	100.00	50.00	30.00
(506)	Hooks Wiltse (pitching)	105.00	52.00	31.00
(507)	Hooks Wiltse (portrait, no cap)	125.00	62.00	37.00
(508)	Hooks Wiltse (portrait, with cap)			
		100.00	50.00	30.00
(509)	Lucky Wright	105.00	52.00	31.00
(510)	Cy Young (Cleveland, glove shows)			
		750.00	375.00	225.00
(511)	Cy Young (Cleveland, bare hand shows)			
		750.00	375.00	225.00
(512)	Cy Young (Cleveland, portrait)	1400.00	700.00	400.00
(513)	Irv Young (Minneapolis)	105.00	52.00	31.00
(514)	Heinie Zimmerman	100.00	50.00	30.00

1912 T207 Brown Background

RECRUIT
LITTLE CIGARS

These 1-1/2" by 2-5/8" cards take their name from the background color which frames the rather drab sepia and white player drawings. They have tan borders making them less colorful than the more popular issues of their era. Player pictures are also on the dull side, with a white strip containing the player's last name, team and league. The card backs have the player's full name, a baseball biography and an ad for one of several brands of cigarettes. The set features 200 players including stars and three classic rarities: Irving Lewis (Boston-Nat.), Ward Miller (Chicago-Nat.) and Louis Lowdermilk (St. Louis-Nat.). There are a number of other scarce cards in the set, including a higher than usual number of obscure players.

		NR MT	EX	VG
Complete Set:		40000.00	20000.00	12000.
Common Player:		90.00	45.00	27.00

		NR MT	EX	VG
(1)	John B. Adams	250.00	125.00	75.00
(2)	Edward Ainsmith	90.00	45.00	27.00
(3)	Rafael Almeida	250.00	125.00	75.00
(4a)	James Austin (insignia on shirt)	175.00	87.00	52.00
(4b)	James Austin (no insignia on shirt)			
		250.00	125.00	75.00
(5)	Neal Ball	90.00	45.00	27.00
(6)	Eros Barger	90.00	45.00	27.00
(7)	Jack Barry	90.00	45.00	27.00
(8)	Charles Bauman	250.00	125.00	75.00
(9)	Beals Becker	90.00	45.00	27.00
(10)	Chief (Albert) Bender	550.00	275.00	165.00
(11)	Joseph Benz	250.00	125.00	75.00
(12)	Robert Bescher	90.00	45.00	27.00
(13)	Joe Birmingham	250.00	125.00	75.00
(14)	Russell Blackburne	250.00	125.00	75.00
(15)	Fred Blanding	250.00	125.00	75.00
(16)	Jimmy Block	90.00	45.00	27.00
(17)	Ping Bodie	90.00	45.00	27.00
(18)	Hugh Bradley	90.00	45.00	27.00
(19)	Roger Bresnahan	550.00	275.00	165.00
(20)	J.F. Bushelman	250.00	125.00	75.00
(21)	Henry (Hank) Butcher	250.00	125.00	75.00
(22)	Robert M. Byrne	90.00	45.00	27.00
(23)	John James Callahan	90.00	45.00	27.00
(24)	Howard Camnitz	90.00	45.00	27.00
(25)	Max Carey	375.00	187.00	112.00
(26)	William Carrigan	90.00	45.00	27.00
(27)	George Chalmers	90.00	45.00	27.00
(28)	Frank Leroy Chance	550.00	275.00	165.00
(29)	Edward Cicotte	150.00	75.00	45.00
(30)	Tom Clarke	90.00	45.00	27.00
(31)	Leonard Cole	90.00	45.00	27.00
(32)	John Collins	200.00	100.00	60.00
(33)	Robert Coulson	90.00	45.00	27.00
(34)	Tex Covington	90.00	45.00	27.00
(35)	Otis Crandall	90.00	45.00	27.00
(36)	William Cunningham	250.00	125.00	75.00
(37)	Dave Danforth	90.00	45.00	27.00
(38)	Bert Daniels	90.00	45.00	27.00
(39)	John Daubert	150.00	75.00	45.00
(40a)	Harry Davis (brown "C" on cap)			
		175.00	87.00	52.00
(40b)	Harry Davis (blue "C" on cap)	175.00	87.00	52.00
(41)	Jim Delehanty	90.00	45.00	27.00
(42)	Claude Derrick	90.00	45.00	27.00
(43)	Arthur Devlin	90.00	45.00	27.00
(44)	Joshua Devore	90.00	45.00	27.00
(45)	Mike Donlin	250.00	125.00	75.00
(46)	Edward Donnelly	250.00	125.00	75.00
(47)	Charles Dooin	90.00	45.00	27.00
(48)	Tom Downey	250.00	125.00	75.00
(49)	Lawrence Doyle	90.00	45.00	27.00
(50)	Del Drake	90.00	45.00	27.00
(51)	Ted Easterly	90.00	45.00	27.00
(52)	George Ellis	90.00	45.00	27.00
(53)	Clyde Engle	90.00	45.00	27.00
(54)	R.E. Erwin	90.00	45.00	27.00
(55)	Louis Evans	90.00	45.00	27.00
(56)	John Ferry	90.00	45.00	27.00
(57a)	Ray Fisher (blue cap)	175.00	87.00	52.00
(57b)	Ray Fisher (white cap)	175.00	87.00	52.00
(58)	Arthur Fletcher	90.00	45.00	27.00
(59)	Jacques Fournier	250.00	125.00	75.00
(60)	Arthur Fromme	90.00	45.00	27.00
(61)	Del Gainor	90.00	45.00	27.00
(62)	William Lawrence Gardner	90.00	45.00	27.00
(63)	Lefty George	90.00	45.00	27.00
(64)	Roy Golden	90.00	45.00	27.00
(65)	Harry Gowdy	90.00	45.00	27.00
(66)	George Graham	200.00	100.00	60.00
(67)	J.G. Graney	90.00	45.00	27.00
(68)	Vean Gregg	250.00	125.00	75.00
(69)	Casey Hageman	90.00	45.00	27.00
(70)	Charlie Hall	90.00	45.00	27.00
(71)	E.S. Hallinan	90.00	45.00	27.00
(72)	Earl Hamilton	90.00	45.00	27.00
(73)	Robert Harmon	90.00	45.00	27.00
(74)	Grover Hartley	250.00	125.00	75.00
(75)	Olaf Henriksen	90.00	45.00	27.00
(76)	John Henry	200.00	100.00	60.00
(77)	Charles Herzog	250.00	125.00	75.00
(78)	Robert Higgins	90.00	45.00	27.00
(79)	Chester Hoff	250.00	125.00	75.00
(80)	William Hogan	90.00	45.00	27.00
(81)	Harry Hooper	650.00	325.00	200.00
(82)	Ben Houser	250.00	125.00	75.00
(83)	Hamilton Hyatt	250.00	125.00	75.00
(84)	Walter Johnson	1500.00	750.00	450.00
(85)	George Kaler	90.00	45.00	27.00
(86)	William Kelly	250.00	125.00	75.00
(87)	Jay Kirke	250.00	125.00	75.00

		NR MT	EX	VG
(88)	John Kling	90.00	45.00	27.00
(89)	Otto Knabe	90.00	45.00	27.00
(90)	Elmer Knetzer	90.00	45.00	27.00
(91)	Edward Konetchy	90.00	45.00	27.00
(92)	Harry Krause	90.00	45.00	27.00
(93)	"Red" Kuhn	250.00	125.00	75.00
(94)	Joseph Kutina	250.00	125.00	75.00
(95)	F.H. (Bill) Lange	250.00	125.00	75.00
(96)	Jack Lapp	90.00	45.00	27.00
(97)	W. Arlington Latham	90.00	45.00	27.00
(98)	Thomas W. Leach	90.00	45.00	27.00
(99)	Albert Leifield	90.00	45.00	27.00
(100)	Edgar Lennox	90.00	45.00	27.00
(101)	Duffy Lewis	90.00	45.00	27.00
(102a)	Irving Lewis (no emblem on sleeve)	2000.00	1000.00	600.00
(102b)	Irving Lewis (emblem on sleeve)	1800.00	900.00	540.00
(103)	Jack Lively	90.00	45.00	27.00
(104a)	Paddy Livingston ("A" on shirt)	550.00	275.00	165.00
(104b)	Paddy Livingston (big "C" on shirt)	550.00	275.00	165.00
(104c)	Paddy Livingston (little "C" on shirt)	175.00	87.00	52.00
(105)	Briscoe Lord (Philadelphia)	90.00	45.00	27.00
(106)	Harry Lord (Chicago)	90.00	45.00	27.00
(107)	Louis Lowdermilk	4000.00	2000.00	1200.
(108)	Richard Marquard	550.00	275.00	165.00
(109)	Armando Marsans	90.00	45.00	27.00
(110)	George McBride	90.00	45.00	27.00
(111)	Alexander McCarthy	175.00	87.00	52.00
(112)	Edward McDonald	90.00	45.00	27.00
(113)	John J. McGraw	750.00	375.00	225.00
(114)	Harry McIntire (McIntyre)	90.00	45.00	27.00
(115)	Matthew McIntyre	90.00	45.00	27.00
(116)	William McKechnie	400.00	200.00	120.00
(117)	Larry McLean	90.00	45.00	27.00
(118)	Clyde Milan	90.00	45.00	27.00
(119)	John B. Miller (Pittsburg)	90.00	45.00	27.00
(120)	Otto Miller (Brooklyn)	250.00	125.00	75.00
(121)	Roy Miller (Boston)	250.00	125.00	75.00
(122)	Ward Miller (Chicago)	200.00	100.00	60.00
(123)	Mike Mitchell (Cleveland, front depicts Willie Mitchell)	200.00	100.00	60.00
(124)	Mike Mitchell (Cincinnati)	90.00	45.00	27.00
(125)	Geo. Mogridge	250.00	125.00	75.00
(126)	Earl Moore	250.00	125.00	75.00
(127)	Patrick J. Moran	90.00	45.00	27.00
(128)	Cy Morgan (Philadelphia)	90.00	45.00	27.00
(129)	Ray Morgan (Washington)	90.00	45.00	27.00
(130)	George Moriarty	250.00	125.00	75.00
(131a)	George Mullin ("D" on cap)	175.00	87.00	52.00
(131b)	George Mullin (no "D" on cap)	175.00	87.00	52.00
(132)	Thomas Needham	90.00	45.00	27.00
(133)	Red Nelson	250.00	125.00	75.00
(134)	Herbert Northen	90.00	45.00	27.00
(135)	Leslie Nunamaker	90.00	45.00	27.00
(136)	Rebel Oakes	90.00	45.00	27.00
(137)	Buck O'Brien	90.00	45.00	27.00
(138)	Rube Oldring	90.00	45.00	27.00
(139)	Ivan Olson	90.00	45.00	27.00
(140)	Martin J. O'Toole	90.00	45.00	27.00
(141)	George Paskart (Paskert)	90.00	45.00	27.00
(142)	Barney Pelty	250.00	125.00	75.00
(143)	Herbert Perdue	90.00	45.00	27.00
(144)	O.C. Peters	250.00	125.00	75.00
(145)	Arthur Phelan	250.00	125.00	75.00
(146)	Jack Quinn	90.00	45.00	27.00
(147)	Don Carlos Ragan	225.00	112.00	67.00
(148)	Arthur Rasmussen	250.00	125.00	75.00
(149)	Morris Rath	250.00	125.00	75.00
(150)	Edward Reulbach	90.00	45.00	27.00
(151)	Napoleon Rucker	90.00	45.00	27.00
(152)	J.B. Ryan	250.00	125.00	75.00
(153)	Victor Saier	1500.00	750.00	450.00
(154)	William Scanlon	90.00	45.00	27.00
(155)	Germany Schaefer	90.00	45.00	27.00
(156)	Wilbur Schardt	90.00	45.00	27.00
(157)	Frank Schulte	90.00	45.00	27.00
(158)	Jim Scott	90.00	45.00	27.00
(159)	Henry Severoid (Severeid)	90.00	45.00	27.00
(160)	Mike Simon	90.00	45.00	27.00
(161)	Frank E. Smith (Cincinnati)	90.00	45.00	27.00
(162)	Wallace Smith (St. Louis)	90.00	45.00	27.00
(163)	Fred Snodgrass	90.00	45.00	27.00
(164)	Tristam Speaker	2000.00	1000.00	600.00
(165)	Harry Lee Spratt	90.00	45.00	27.00
(166)	Edward Stack	90.00	45.00	27.00
(167)	Oscar Stanage	90.00	45.00	27.00
(168)	William Steele	90.00	45.00	27.00
(169)	Harry Steinfeldt	90.00	45.00	27.00

		NR MT	EX	VG
(170)	George Stovall	90.00	45.00	27.00
(171)	Charles (Gabby) Street	90.00	45.00	27.00
(172)	Amos Strunk	90.00	45.00	27.00
(173)	William Sullivan	90.00	45.00	27.00
(174)	William J. Sweeney	250.00	125.00	75.00
(175)	Leeford Tannehill	90.00	45.00	27.00
(176)	C.D. Thomas	90.00	45.00	27.00
(177)	Joseph Tinker	550.00	275.00	165.00
(178)	Bert Tooley	90.00	45.00	27.00
(179)	Terence Turner (Terrence)	90.00	45.00	27.00
(180)	George Tyler	300.00	150.00	90.00
(181)	Jim Vaughn	90.00	45.00	27.00
(182)	Chas. (Heinie) Wagner	90.00	45.00	27.00
(183)	Ed (Dixie) Walker	90.00	45.00	27.00
(184)	Robert Wallace	375.00	187.00	112.00
(185)	John Warhop	90.00	45.00	27.00
(186)	George Weaver	250.00	125.00	75.00
(187)	Zach Wheat	450.00	225.00	135.00
(188)	G. Harris White	250.00	125.00	75.00
(189)	Ernest Wilie	250.00	125.00	75.00
(190)	Bob Williams	90.00	45.00	27.00
(191)	Arthur Wilson (New York)	250.00	125.00	75.00
(192)	Owen Wilson (Pittsburg)	90.00	45.00	27.00
(193)	George Wiltse	90.00	45.00	27.00
(194)	Ivey Wingo	90.00	45.00	27.00
(195)	Harry Wolverton	90.00	45.00	27.00
(196)	Joe Wood	200.00	100.00	60.00
(197)	Eugene Woodburn	250.00	125.00	75.00
(198)	Ralph Works	200.00	100.00	60.00
(199)	Stanley Yerkes	90.00	45.00	27.00
(200)	Rollie Zeider	200.00	100.00	60.00

1911 T208 Fireside

The 1911 T208 Fireside set, an 18-card Philadelphia Althletics set issued by the Thomas Cullivan Tobacco Company of Syracuse, N.Y., is among the rarest and most valuable of all 20th Century tobacco issues. Cullivan issued the set to commemorate the Athletics' 1910 Championship season, and, except for pitcher Jack Coombs, the checklist includes nearly all key members of the club, including manager Connie Mack. The cards are the standard size for tobacco issues, 1-1/2" by 2-5/8". The front of each card features a player portrait set against a colored background. The player's name and the word "Athletics" appear at the bottom, while "World's Champions 1910" is printed along the top. The backs of the cards advertise the set as the "Athletics Series" and advise that one card is included in each package of "Cullivan's Fireside Plain Scrap" tobacco. Collectors should be aware that the same checklist was used for a similar Athletics set issued by Rochester Baking/Williams Baking (D359) and also that blank-backed versions are also known to exist, but these are classified as E104 cards in the American Card Catalog.

		NR MT	EX	VG
Complete Set:		13000.00	6500.00	3900.
Common Player:		500.00	250.00	150.00
(1)	Home Run Baker	1500.00	750.00	450.00
(2)	Jack Barry	500.00	250.00	150.00
(3)	Chief Bender	1500.00	750.00	450.00

		NR MT	EX	VG
(4)	Eddie Collins	1500.00	750.00	450.00
(5)	Harry Davis	500.00	250.00	150.00
(6)	Jimmy Dygert	500.00	250.00	150.00
(7)	Topsy Hartsel	500.00	250.00	150.00
(8)	Harry Krause	500.00	250.00	150.00
(9)	Jack Lapp	500.00	250.00	150.00
(10)	Paddy Livingstone (Livingston)	500.00	250.00	150.00
(11)	Bris Lord	500.00	250.00	150.00
(12)	Connie Mack	2000.00	1000.00	600.00
(13)	Cy Morgan	500.00	250.00	150.00
(14)	Danny Murphy	500.00	250.00	150.00
(15)	Rube Oldring	500.00	250.00	150.00
(16)	Eddie Plank	2000.00	1000.00	600.00
(17)	Amos Strunk	500.00	250.00	150.00
(18)	Ira Thomas	500.00	250.00	150.00

1910 T209 Contentnea
1st Series

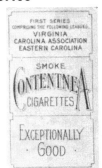

The 1910 Contentnea minor league set actually consists of two distinctively different series, both featuring players from the Virginia League, Carolina Association and Eastern Carolina League. The cards were distributed in packages of Contentnea Cigarettes. The first series, featuring color photographs, consists of just 16 cards, each measuring 1-9/16" by 2-11/16". The front of the card has the player's last name and team printed at the bottom, while the back identifies the card as "First Series" and carries an advertisement for Contentnea Cigarettes. The second series, believed to be issued later in 1910, is a massive 221-card set consisting of black and white player photos. The cards in this series are slightly larger, measuring 1-5/8" by 2-3/4". THey carry the words "Photo Series" on the back, along with the cigarette advertisement. Only a handful of players in the Contentnea set ever advanced to the major leagues and the set contains no major stars. Subsequently, it generally holds interest only to collectors who specialize in the old Southern minor leagues.

		NR MT	EX	VG
Complete Set:		2000.00	1000.00	600.00
Common Player:		125.00	62.00	37.00
(1)	Armstrong	125.00	62.00	37.00
(2)	Booles	125.00	62.00	37.00
(3)	Bourquise (Bourquoise)	125.00	62.00	37.00
(4)	Cooper	125.00	62.00	37.00
(5)	Cowell	125.00	62.00	37.00
(6)	Crockett	125.00	62.00	37.00
(7)	Fullenwider	125.00	62.00	37.00
(8)	Gilmore	125.00	62.00	37.00
(9)	Hoffman	125.00	62.00	37.00
(10)	Lane	125.00	62.00	37.00
(11)	Martin	125.00	62.00	37.00
(12)	McGeehan	125.00	62.00	37.00
(13)	Pope	125.00	62.00	37.00
(14)	Sisson	125.00	62.00	37.00
(15)	Stubbe	125.00	62.00	37.00
(16)	Walsh	125.00	62.00	37.00

1910 T209 Contentnea
2nd Series

		NR MT	EX	VG
Complete Set:		6000.00	3000.00	1800.
Common Player:		30.00	15.00	9.00
(1)	Abercrombie	30.00	15.00	9.00
(2)	Andrada	30.00	15.00	9.00
(3)	Armstrong	30.00	15.00	9.00
(4)	Averett	30.00	15.00	9.00
(5)	Baker	30.00	15.00	9.00
(6)	Banner (Bonner)	30.00	15.00	9.00
(7)	Bausewein (Bansewein)	30.00	15.00	9.00
(8)	Beatty	30.00	15.00	9.00
(9)	Bentley	30.00	15.00	9.00
(10)	Beusse	30.00	15.00	9.00
(11)	Biel	30.00	15.00	9.00
(12)	Bigbie (Raleigh)	30.00	15.00	9.00
(13)	Bigbie (Richmond)	30.00	15.00	9.00
(14)	Blackstone	30.00	15.00	9.00
(15)	Bonner	30.00	15.00	9.00
(16)	Bourquin	30.00	15.00	9.00
(17)	Bowen	30.00	15.00	9.00
(18)	Boyle	30.00	15.00	9.00
(19)	Brandon	30.00	15.00	9.00
(20)	Brazelle (Brazell)	30.00	15.00	9.00
(21)	Brent	30.00	15.00	9.00
(22)	Brown	30.00	15.00	9.00
(23)	Busch	30.00	15.00	9.00
(24)	Bussey	30.00	15.00	9.00
(25)	Byrd	30.00	15.00	9.00
(26)	Cafalu (Cefalu)	30.00	15.00	9.00
(27)	Callahan	30.00	15.00	9.00
(28)	Chandler	30.00	15.00	9.00
(29)	Clapp	30.00	15.00	9.00
(30)	Clark (Clarke)	30.00	15.00	9.00
(31)	Clemens	30.00	15.00	9.00
(32)	Clunk	30.00	15.00	9.00
(33)	Cooper	30.00	15.00	9.00
(34)	Corbett	30.00	15.00	9.00
(35)	Cote	30.00	15.00	9.00
(36)	Coutts	30.00	15.00	9.00
(37)	Cowan (Cowen)	30.00	15.00	9.00
(38)	Cowells (Cowell)	30.00	15.00	9.00
(39)	Creagan (Cregan)	30.00	15.00	9.00
(40)	Crockett	30.00	15.00	9.00
(41)	Cross	30.00	15.00	9.00
(42)	Dailey	30.00	15.00	9.00
(43)	C. Derrck (Derrick)	30.00	15.00	9.00
(44)	F. Derrick	30.00	15.00	9.00
(45)	Doak (Greensboro)	30.00	15.00	9.00
(46)	Doak (Wilmington)	30.00	15.00	9.00
(47)	Dobard	30.00	15.00	9.00
(48)	Dobson	30.00	15.00	9.00
(49)	Doyle	30.00	15.00	9.00
(50)	Drumm	30.00	15.00	9.00
(51)	Duvie	30.00	15.00	9.00
(52)	Ebinger	30.00	15.00	9.00
(53)	Eldridge	30.00	15.00	9.00
(54)	Evvans	30.00	15.00	9.00
(55)	Fairbanks	30.00	15.00	9.00
(56)	Farmer	30.00	15.00	9.00
(57)	Ferrell	30.00	15.00	9.00
(58)	Fisher	30.00	15.00	9.00
(59)	Flowers	30.00	15.00	9.00
(60)	Fogarty	30.00	15.00	9.00
(61)	Foltz	30.00	15.00	9.00
(62)	Foreman	30.00	15.00	9.00

		NR MT	EX	VG			NR MT	EX	VG
(63)	Forque	30.00	15.00	9.00	(154)	Painter	30.00	15.00	9.00
(64)	Francis	30.00	15.00	9.00	(155)	Peloguin	30.00	15.00	9.00
(65)	Fulton	30.00	15.00	9.00	(156)	Phealean (Phelan)	30.00	15.00	9.00
(66)	Galvin	30.00	15.00	9.00	(157)	Phoenix	30.00	15.00	9.00
(67)	Gardin	30.00	15.00	9.00	(158)	Powell	30.00	15.00	9.00
(68)	Garman	30.00	15.00	9.00	(159)	Presley (Pressley), Pritchard	30.00	15.00	9.00
(69)	Gastmeyer	30.00	15.00	9.00	(160)	Priest	30.00	15.00	9.00
(70)	Gaston	30.00	15.00	9.00	(161)	Prim	30.00	15.00	9.00
(71)	Gates	30.00	15.00	9.00	(162)	Pritchard	30.00	15.00	9.00
(72)	Gehring	30.00	15.00	9.00	(163)	Rawe (Rowe)	30.00	15.00	9.00
(73)	Gillespie	30.00	15.00	9.00	(164)	Redfern (Redfearn)	30.00	15.00	9.00
(74)	Gorham	30.00	15.00	9.00	(165)	Reggy	30.00	15.00	9.00
(75)	Griffin (Danville)	30.00	15.00	9.00	(166)	Richardson	30.00	15.00	9.00
(76)	Griffin (Lynchburg)	30.00	15.00	9.00	(167)	Rickard	30.00	15.00	9.00
(77)	Guiheen	30.00	15.00	9.00	(168)	Rickert	30.00	15.00	9.00
(78)	Gunderson	30.00	15.00	9.00	(169)	Ridgeway (Ridgway)	30.00	15.00	9.00
(79)	Hale	30.00	15.00	9.00	(170)	Roth	30.00	15.00	9.00
(80)	Halland (Holland)	30.00	15.00	9.00	(171)	Salve	30.00	15.00	9.00
(81)	Hamilton	30.00	15.00	9.00	(172)	Schmidt	30.00	15.00	9.00
(82)	Hammersley	30.00	15.00	9.00	(173)	Schrader	30.00	15.00	9.00
(83)	Handiboe	30.00	15.00	9.00	(174)	Schumaker	30.00	15.00	9.00
(84)	Hannifen (Hannifan)	30.00	15.00	9.00	(175)	Sexton	30.00	15.00	9.00
(85)	Hargrave	30.00	15.00	9.00	(176)	Shanghnessy (Shaughnessy)	30.00	15.00	9.00
(86)	Harrington	30.00	15.00	9.00	(177)	Sharp	30.00	15.00	9.00
(87)	Harris	30.00	15.00	9.00	(178)	Shaw	30.00	15.00	9.00
(88)	Hart	30.00	15.00	9.00	(179)	Simmons	30.00	15.00	9.00
(89)	Hartley	30.00	15.00	9.00	(180)	A. Smith	30.00	15.00	9.00
(90)	Hawkins	30.00	15.00	9.00	(181)	D. Smith	30.00	15.00	9.00
(91)	Hearne (Hearn)	30.00	15.00	9.00	(182)	Spratt	30.00	15.00	9.00
(92)	Hicks	30.00	15.00	9.00	(183)	Springs	30.00	15.00	9.00
(93)	Hobbs	30.00	15.00	9.00	(184)	Stewart	30.00	15.00	9.00
(94)	Hoffman	30.00	15.00	9.00	(185)	Stoehr	30.00	15.00	9.00
(95)	Hooker	30.00	15.00	9.00	(186)	Stouch	30.00	15.00	9.00
(96)	Howard	30.00	15.00	9.00	(187)	Sullivan	30.00	15.00	9.00
(97)	Howedel (Howedell)	30.00	15.00	9.00	(188)	Swindell	30.00	15.00	9.00
(98)	Hudson	30.00	15.00	9.00	(189)	Taxis	30.00	15.00	9.00
(99)	Humphrey	30.00	15.00	9.00	(190)	Templin	30.00	15.00	9.00
(100)	Hyames	30.00	15.00	9.00	(191)	Thompson	30.00	15.00	9.00
(101)	Irvine	30.00	15.00	9.00	(192)	B.E. Thompson	30.00	15.00	9.00
(102)	Irving	30.00	15.00	9.00	(193)	Tiedeman	30.00	15.00	9.00
(103)	Jackson (Greensboro)	30.00	15.00	9.00	(194)	Titman	30.00	15.00	9.00
(104)	Jackson (Spartanburg)	30.00	15.00	9.00	(195)	Toner	30.00	15.00	9.00
(105)	Jenkins (Greenville)	30.00	15.00	9.00	(196)	Turner	30.00	15.00	9.00
(106)	Jenkins (Roanoke)	30.00	15.00	9.00	(197)	Tydeman	30.00	15.00	9.00
(107)	Jobson	30.00	15.00	9.00	(198)	Vail	30.00	15.00	9.00
(108)	Johnson	30.00	15.00	9.00	(199)	Verbout	30.00	15.00	9.00
(109)	Keating	30.00	15.00	9.00	(200)	Vickery	30.00	15.00	9.00
(110)	Kelley	30.00	15.00	9.00	(201)	Walker (Norfolk)	30.00	15.00	9.00
(111)	Kelly (Anderson)	30.00	15.00	9.00	(202)	Walker (Spartanburg)	30.00	15.00	9.00
(112)	Kelly (Goldsboro)	30.00	15.00	9.00	(203)	Wallace	30.00	15.00	9.00
(113)	"King" Kelly	30.00	15.00	9.00	(204)	Walsh	30.00	15.00	9.00
(114)	King	30.00	15.00	9.00	(205)	Walters	30.00	15.00	9.00
(115)	Kite	30.00	15.00	9.00	(206)	Watters	30.00	15.00	9.00
(116)	Kunkle	30.00	15.00	9.00	(207)	Waymack	30.00	15.00	9.00
(117)	Landgraff	30.00	15.00	9.00	(208)	Webb	30.00	15.00	9.00
(118)	Lane	30.00	15.00	9.00	(209)	Wehrell	30.00	15.00	9.00
(119)	Lathrop	30.00	15.00	9.00	(210)	Weldon	30.00	15.00	9.00
(120)	Lavoia	30.00	15.00	9.00	(211)	Welsher	30.00	15.00	9.00
(121)	Levy	30.00	15.00	9.00	(212)	Westlake	30.00	15.00	9.00
(122)	Lloyd	30.00	15.00	9.00	(213)	Williams	30.00	15.00	9.00
(123)	Loval	30.00	15.00	9.00	(214)	Willis	30.00	15.00	9.00
(124)	Lucia	30.00	15.00	9.00	(215)	Wingo	30.00	15.00	9.00
(125)	Luyster	30.00	15.00	9.00	(216)	Wolf	30.00	15.00	9.00
(126)	MacConachie	30.00	15.00	9.00	(217)	Wood	30.00	15.00	9.00
(127)	Malcolm	30.00	15.00	9.00	(218)	Woolums	30.00	15.00	9.00
(128)	Martin	30.00	15.00	9.00	(219)	Workman	30.00	15.00	9.00
(129)	Mayberry	30.00	15.00	9.00	(220)	Wright	30.00	15.00	9.00
(130)	A. McCarthy	30.00	15.00	9.00	(221)	Wynne	30.00	15.00	9.00
(131)	J. McCarthy	30.00	15.00	9.00					
(132)	McCormick	30.00	15.00	9.00					
(133)	McFarland	30.00	15.00	9.00					
(134)	McFarlin	30.00	15.00	9.00					
(135)	C. McGeehan	30.00	15.00	9.00					
(136)	Dan McGeehan	30.00	15.00	9.00					
(137)	McHugh	30.00	15.00	9.00					
(138)	McKeavitt (McKevitt)	30.00	15.00	9.00					
(139)	Merchant	30.00	15.00	9.00					
(140)	Midkiff	30.00	15.00	9.00					
(141)	Miller	30.00	15.00	9.00					
(142)	Missitt	30.00	15.00	9.00					
(143)	Morgan	30.00	15.00	9.00					
(144)	Morrissey (Morrisey)	30.00	15.00	9.00					
(145)	Mullany (Mullaney)	30.00	15.00	9.00					
(146)	Mullinix	30.00	15.00	9.00					
(147)	Mundell	30.00	15.00	9.00					
(148)	Munsen (Munson)	30.00	15.00	9.00					
(149)	Murdock (Murdoch)	30.00	15.00	9.00					
(150)	Newton	30.00	15.00	9.00					
(151)	Noojin	30.00	15.00	9.00					
(152)	Novak	30.00	15.00	9.00					
(153)	Ochs	30.00	15.00	9.00					

1910 T210 Old Mill
Series No. 1

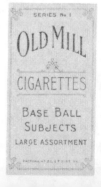

Because of their distinctive red borders, this 1910 minor league tobacco issue is often called the Red Border set by collectors. A massive set, it consists of eight different series and totals some 640 cards, each measuring 1-1/2" by 2-5/8". The fronts of the cards feature a glossy black and white photo, while the backs carry an ad for Old Mill Cigarettes. Each of the eight series is devoted to a different minor league. Series 1 features players from the South Atlantic League; Series 2 pictures players from the Virginia League; Series 3 is devoted to the Texas League; Series 4 features the Virginia Valley League; Series 5 pictures players from the Carolina Associations; Series 6 spotlights the Blue Grass League; Series 7 is devoted to the Eastern Carolina League; and Series 8 show players from the Southern Association. The various series are identified by number along the top on the back of the cards. Collectors generally agree that Series 7 cards (Eastern Carolina League players) are the most difficult to find, while Series 2 cards (Virginia League) are the most common. The relative scarcity of the various series is reflected in the prices listed. Collectors should be aware that some Series 3 cards (Texas League) can be found with orange, rather than red, borders - apparently because not enough red ink was used during part of the print run.

		NR MT	EX	VG
Complete Set:		900.00	450.00	270.00
Common Player:		15.00	7.50	4.50
(1)	Bagwell	15.00	7.50	4.50
(2)	Balenti	15.00	7.50	4.50
(3)	Becker	15.00	7.50	4.50
(4)	Bensen	15.00	7.50	4.50
(5)	Benton	15.00	7.50	4.50
(6)	Bierkortte	15.00	7.50	4.50
(7)	Bierman	15.00	7.50	4.50
(8)	Breitenstein	15.00	7.50	4.50
(9)	Bremmerhof	15.00	7.50	4.50
(10)	Carter	15.00	7.50	4.50
(11)	Cavender	15.00	7.50	4.50
(12)	Collins	15.00	7.50	4.50
(13)	DeFraites	15.00	7.50	4.50
(14)	Dudley	15.00	7.50	4.50
(15)	Dwyer	15.00	7.50	4.50
(16)	Edwards	15.00	7.50	4.50
(17)	Enbanks	15.00	7.50	4.50
(18)	Eubank	15.00	7.50	4.50
(19)	Fox	15.00	7.50	4.50
(20)	Hannifan	15.00	7.50	4.50
(21)	Hartley	15.00	7.50	4.50
(22)	Hauser	15.00	7.50	4.50
(23)	Hille	15.00	7.50	4.50
(24)	Howard	15.00	7.50	4.50
(25)	Hoyt	15.00	7.50	4.50
(27)	Ison	15.00	7.50	4.50
(28)	Jones	15.00	7.50	4.50
(29)	Kalkhoff	15.00	7.50	4.50
(30)	Krebs	15.00	7.50	4.50
(31)	Lawrence	15.00	7.50	4.50
(32)	Lee (Jacksonville)	15.00	7.50	4.50
(33)	Lee (Macon)	15.00	7.50	4.50
(34)	Lewis (Columbia)	15.00	7.50	4.50
(35)	Lewis (Columbus)	15.00	7.50	4.50
(36)	Lipe (batting)	15.00	7.50	4.50
(37)	Lipe (portrait)	15.00	7.50	4.50
(38)	Long	15.00	7.50	4.50
(39)	Magoon	15.00	7.50	4.50
(40)	Manion	15.00	7.50	4.50
(41)	Marshall	15.00	7.50	4.50
(42)	Martin	15.00	7.50	4.50
(43)	Martina	15.00	7.50	4.50
(44)	Massing	15.00	7.50	4.50
(45)	McLeod	15.00	7.50	4.50
(46)	McMahon	15.00	7.50	4.50
(47)	Morse	15.00	7.50	4.50
(48)	Mullane	15.00	7.50	4.50
(49)	Mulldowney	15.00	7.50	4.50
(50)	Murch	15.00	7.50	4.50
(51)	Norcum	15.00	7.50	4.50
(52)	Pelkey	15.00	7.50	4.50
(53)	Petit	15.00	7.50	4.50
(54)	Pierce	15.00	7.50	4.50
(55)	Pope	15.00	7.50	4.50
(56)	Radebaugh	15.00	7.50	4.50
(57)	Raynolds	15.00	7.50	4.50
(58)	Reagan	15.00	7.50	4.50

		NR MT	EX	VG
(59)	Redfern (Redfearn)	15.00	7.50	4.50
(60)	Reynolds	15.00	7.50	4.50
(61)	Schulz	15.00	7.50	4.50
(62)	Schulze	15.00	7.50	4.50
(63)	Schwietzka	15.00	7.50	4.50
(64)	Shields	15.00	7.50	4.50
(65)	Sisson	15.00	7.50	4.50
(66)	Smith	15.00	7.50	4.50
(67)	Sweeney	15.00	7.50	4.50
(68)	Taffee	15.00	7.50	4.50
(69)	Toren	15.00	7.50	4.50
(70)	Viola	15.00	7.50	4.50
(71)	Wagner	15.00	7.50	4.50
(72)	Wahl	15.00	7.50	4.50
(73)	Weems	15.00	7.50	4.50
(74)	Wells	15.00	7.50	4.50
(75)	Wohlleben	15.00	7.50	4.50

1910 T210 Old Mill
Series No. 2

		NR MT	EX	VG
Complete Set:		900.00	450.00	270.00
Common Player:		12.00	6.00	3.50
(1)	Andrada	12.00	6.00	3.50
(2)	Archer	12.00	6.00	3.50
(3)	Baker	12.00	6.00	3.50
(4)	Beham	12.00	6.00	3.50
(5)	Bonner	12.00	6.00	3.50
(6)	Bowen	12.00	6.00	3.50
(7)	Brandon	12.00	6.00	3.50
(8)	Breivogel	12.00	6.00	3.50
(9)	Brooks	12.00	6.00	3.50
(10)	Brown	12.00	6.00	3.50
(11)	Busch	12.00	6.00	3.50
(12)	Bussey	12.00	6.00	3.50
(13)	Cefalu	12.00	6.00	3.50
(14)	Chandler	12.00	6.00	3.50
(15)	Clarke	12.00	6.00	3.50
(16)	Clunk	12.00	6.00	3.50
(17)	Cote	12.00	6.00	3.50
(18)	Cowan	12.00	6.00	3.50
(19)	Decker	12.00	6.00	3.50
(20)	Doyle	12.00	6.00	3.50
(21)	Eddowes	12.00	6.00	3.50
(22)	Fisher	12.00	6.00	3.50
(23)	Fox	12.00	6.00	3.50
(24)	Foxen	12.00	6.00	3.50
(25)	Gaston	12.00	6.00	3.50
(26)	Gehring	12.00	6.00	3.50
(27)	Griffin (Danville)	12.00	6.00	3.50
(28)	Griffin (Lynchburg)	12.00	6.00	3.50
(29)	Hale	12.00	6.00	3.50
(30)	Hamilton	12.00	6.00	3.50
(31)	Hanks	12.00	6.00	3.50
(32)	Hannafin	12.00	6.00	3.50
(33)	Hoffman	12.00	6.00	3.50
(34)	Holland	12.00	6.00	3.50
(35)	Hooker	12.00	6.00	3.50
(36)	Irving	12.00	6.00	3.50
(37)	Jackson (Lynchburg)	12.00	6.00	3.50
(38)	Jackson (Norfolk)	12.00	6.00	3.50
(39)	Jackson (Portsmouth)	12.00	6.00	3.50
(40)	Jackson (Richmond)	12.00	6.00	3.50
(41)	Jenkins	12.00	6.00	3.50
(42)	Keifel	12.00	6.00	3.50
(43)	Kirkpatrick	12.00	6.00	3.50
(44)	Kunkel	12.00	6.00	3.50
(45)	Landgraff	12.00	6.00	3.50
(46)	Larkins	12.00	6.00	3.50
(47)	Laughlin	12.00	6.00	3.50
(48)	Lawlor	12.00	6.00	3.50
(49)	Levy	12.00	6.00	3.50
(50)	Lloyd	12.00	6.00	3.50
(51)	Loos	12.00	6.00	3.50
(52)	Lovell	12.00	6.00	3.50
(53)	Lucia	12.00	6.00	3.50
(54)	MacConachie	12.00	6.00	3.50
(55)	Mayberry	12.00	6.00	3.50
(56)	McFarland	12.00	6.00	3.50
(57)	Messitt	12.00	6.00	3.50
(58)	Michel	12.00	6.00	3.50
(59)	Mullaney	12.00	6.00	3.50
(60)	Munson	12.00	6.00	3.50
(61)	Neuton	12.00	6.00	3.50

		NR MT	EX	VG
(62)	Nimmo	12.00	6.00	3.50
(63)	Norris	12.00	6.00	3.50
(64)	Peterson	12.00	6.00	3.50
(65)	Powell	12.00	6.00	3.50
(66)	Pressly (Pressley)	12.00	6.00	3.50
(67)	Pritchard	12.00	6.00	3.50
(68)	Revelle	12.00	6.00	3.50
(69)	Rowe	12.00	6.00	3.50
(70)	Schmidt	12.00	6.00	3.50
(71)	Schrader	12.00	6.00	3.50
(72)	Sharp	12.00	6.00	3.50
(73)	Shaw	12.00	6.00	3.50
(74)	Smith (Lynchburg, batting)	12.00	6.00	3.50
(75)	Smith (Lynchburg, catching)	12.00	6.00	3.50
(76)	Smith (Portsmouth)	12.00	6.00	3.50
(77)	Spicer	12.00	6.00	3.50
(78)	Titman	12.00	6.00	3.50
(79)	Toner	12.00	6.00	3.50
(80)	Tydeman	12.00	6.00	3.50
(81)	Vail	12.00	6.00	3.50
(82)	Verbout	12.00	6.00	3.50
(83)	Walker	12.00	6.00	3.50
(84)	Wallace	12.00	6.00	3.50
(85)	Waymack	12.00	6.00	3.50
(86)	Woolums	12.00	6.00	3.50
(87)	Zimmerman	12.00	6.00	3.50

1910 T210 Old Mill
Series No. 3

		NR MT	EX	VG
Complete Set:		1100.00	550.00	330.00
Common Player:		15.00	7.50	4.50
(1)	Alexander	15.00	7.50	4.50
(2)	Ash	15.00	7.50	4.50
(3)	Bandy	15.00	7.50	4.50
(4)	Barenkemp	15.00	7.50	4.50
(5)	Belew	15.00	7.50	4.50
(6)	Bell	15.00	7.50	4.50
(7)	Bennett	15.00	7.50	4.50
(8)	Berlck	15.00	7.50	4.50
(9)	Billiard	15.00	7.50	4.50
(10)	Blanding	15.00	7.50	4.50
(11)	Blue	15.00	7.50	4.50
(12)	Burch	15.00	7.50	4.50
(13)	Burk	15.00	7.50	4.50
(14)	Carlin	15.00	7.50	4.50
(15)	Conaway	15.00	7.50	4.50
(16)	Corkhill	15.00	7.50	4.50
(17)	Cowan	15.00	7.50	4.50
(18)	Coyle	15.00	7.50	4.50
(19)	Crable	15.00	7.50	4.50
(20)	Curry	15.00	7.50	4.50
(21)	Dale	15.00	7.50	4.50
(22)	Davis	15.00	7.50	4.50
(23)	Deardorff	15.00	7.50	4.50
(24)	Donnelley	15.00	7.50	4.50
(25)	Doyle	15.00	7.50	4.50
(26)	Druke	15.00	7.50	4.50
(27)	Dugey	15.00	7.50	4.50
(28)	Ens	15.00	7.50	4.50
(29)	Evans	15.00	7.50	4.50
(30)	Fillman	15.00	7.50	4.50
(31)	Firestine	15.00	7.50	4.50
(32)	Francis	15.00	7.50	4.50
(33)	Galloway	15.00	7.50	4.50
(34)	Gardner	15.00	7.50	4.50
(35)	Gear	15.00	7.50	4.50
(36)	Glawe	15.00	7.50	4.50
(37)	Gordon	15.00	7.50	4.50
(38)	Gowdy	15.00	7.50	4.50
(39)	Harbison	15.00	7.50	4.50
(40)	Harper	15.00	7.50	4.50
(41)	Hicks	15.00	7.50	4.50
(42)	Hill	15.00	7.50	4.50
(43)	Hinninger	15.00	7.50	4.50
(44)	Hirsch	15.00	7.50	4.50
(45)	Hise	15.00	7.50	4.50
(46)	Hooks	15.00	7.50	4.50
(47)	Hornsby	15.00	7.50	4.50
(48)	Howell	15.00	7.50	4.50
(49)	Johnston	15.00	7.50	4.50
(50)	Jolley	15.00	7.50	4.50
(51)	Jones	15.00	7.50	4.50
(52)	Kaphan	15.00	7.50	4.50

		NR MT	EX	VG
(53)	Kipp	15.00	7.50	4.50
(54)	Leidy	15.00	7.50	4.50
(55)	Malloy	15.00	7.50	4.50
(56)	Maloney	15.00	7.50	4.50
(57)	Meagher	15.00	7.50	4.50
(58)	Merritt	15.00	7.50	4.50
(59)	McKay	15.00	7.50	4.50
(60)	Mills	15.00	7.50	4.50
(61)	Morris	15.00	7.50	4.50
(63)	Munsell	15.00	7.50	4.50
(64)	Nagel	15.00	7.50	4.50
(65)	Northen	15.00	7.50	4.50
(66)	Ogle	15.00	7.50	4.50
(67)	Onslow	15.00	7.50	4.50
(68)	Pendleton	15.00	7.50	4.50
(69)	Powell	15.00	7.50	4.50
(70)	Riley	15.00	7.50	4.50
(71)	Robertson	15.00	7.50	4.50
(72)	Rose	15.00	7.50	4.50
(73)	Salazor	15.00	7.50	4.50
(74)	Shindel	15.00	7.50	4.50
(75)	Shontz	15.00	7.50	4.50
(76)	Slaven	15.00	7.50	4.50
(77)	Smith (bat over shoulder)	15.00	7.50	4.50
(78)	Smith (bat at hip level)	15.00	7.50	4.50
(79)	Spangler	15.00	7.50	4.50
(80)	Stadeli	15.00	7.50	4.50
(81)	Stinson	15.00	7.50	4.50
(82)	Storch	15.00	7.50	4.50
(83)	Stringer	15.00	7.50	4.50
(84)	Tesreau	15.00	7.50	4.50
(85)	Thebo	15.00	7.50	4.50
(86)	Tullas	15.00	7.50	4.50
(87)	Walsh	15.00	7.50	4.50
(88)	Watson	15.00	7.50	4.50
(89)	Weber	15.00	7.50	4.50
(90)	Weeks	15.00	7.50	4.50
(91)	Wertherford	15.00	7.50	4.50
(92)	Wickenhofer	15.00	7.50	4.50
(93)	Williams	15.00	7.50	4.50
(94)	Woodburn	15.00	7.50	4.50
(95)	Yantz	15.00	7.50	4.50

1910 T210 Old Mill
Series No. 4

		NR MT	EX	VG
Complete Set:		625.00	312.00	187.00
Common Player:		15.00	7.50	4.50
(1)	Aylor	15.00	7.50	4.50
(2)	Benney	15.00	7.50	4.50
(3)	Best	15.00	7.50	4.50
(4)	Bonno	15.00	7.50	4.50
(5)	Brown	15.00	7.50	4.50
(6)	Brumfield	15.00	7.50	4.50
(7)	Campbell	15.00	7.50	4.50
(8)	Canepa	15.00	7.50	4.50
(9)	Carney	15.00	7.50	4.50
(10)	Carter	15.00	7.50	4.50
(11)	Cochrane	15.00	7.50	4.50
(12)	Coller	15.00	7.50	4.50
(13)	Connolly	15.00	7.50	4.50
(14)	Davis	15.00	7.50	4.50
(15)	Connell	15.00	7.50	4.50
(16)	Doshmer	15.00	7.50	4.50
(17)	Dougherty	15.00	7.50	4.50
(18)	Erlewein	15.00	7.50	4.50
(19)	Farrell	15.00	7.50	4.50
(20)	Geary	15.00	7.50	4.50
(21)	Halterman	15.00	7.50	4.50
(22)	Headly	15.00	7.50	4.50
(23)	Hollis	15.00	7.50	4.50
(24)	Hunter	15.00	7.50	4.50
(25)	Johnson	15.00	7.50	4.50
(26)	Kane	15.00	7.50	4.50
(27)	Kuehn	15.00	7.50	4.50
(28)	Leonard	15.00	7.50	4.50
(29)	Lux	15.00	7.50	4.50
(30)	McClain	15.00	7.50	4.50
(31)	Mollenkamp	15.00	7.50	4.50
(32)	Moore	15.00	7.50	4.50
(33)	Moye	15.00	7.50	4.50
(34)	O'Connor	15.00	7.50	4.50
(36)	Pick	15.00	7.50	4.50

		NR MT	EX	VG
(37)	Pickels	15.00	7.50	4.50
(38)	Schafer	15.00	7.50	4.50
(39)	Seaman	15.00	7.50	4.50
(40)	Spicer	15.00	7.50	4.50
(41)	Stanley	15.00	7.50	4.50
(42)	Stockum	15.00	7.50	4.50
(43)	Titlow	15.00	7.50	4.50
(44)	Waldron	15.00	7.50	4.50
(45)	Wills	15.00	7.50	4.50
(46)	Witter	15.00	7.50	4.50
(47)	Womach	15.00	7.50	4.50
(48)	Young	15.00	7.50	4.50
(49)	Zurlage	15.00	7.50	4.50

1910 T210 Old Mill
Series No. 5

		NR MT	EX	VG
Complete Set:		1100.00	550.00	330.00
Common Player:		15.00	7.50	4.50
(1)	Abercrombie	15.00	7.50	4.50
(2)	Averett	15.00	7.50	4.50
(3)	Bansewein	15.00	7.50	4.50
(4)	Bentley	15.00	7.50	4.50
(5)	C.G. Beusse	15.00	7.50	4.50
(6)	Fred Beusse	15.00	7.50	4.50
(7)	Bigbie	15.00	7.50	4.50
(8)	Eivens	15.00	7.50	4.50
(9)	Blackstone	15.00	7.50	4.50
(10)	Brannon	15.00	7.50	4.50
(11)	Brazell	15.00	7.50	4.50
(12)	Brent	15.00	7.50	4.50
(13)	Bullock	15.00	7.50	4.50
(14)	Cashion	15.00	7.50	4.50
(15)	Corbett	15.00	7.50	4.50
(16)	Corbett	15.00	7.50	4.50
(17)	Coutts	15.00	7.50	4.50
(18)	Lave Cross	15.00	7.50	4.50
(19)	Crouch	15.00	7.50	4.50
(20)	C.L. Derrick	15.00	7.50	4.50
(21)	F.B. Derrick	15.00	7.50	4.50
(22)	Dobard	15.00	7.50	4.50
(23)	Drumm	15.00	7.50	4.50
(24)	Duvie	15.00	7.50	4.50
(25)	Ehrhardt	15.00	7.50	4.50
(26)	Eldridge	15.00	7.50	4.50
(27)	Fairbanks	15.00	7.50	4.50
(28)	Farmer	15.00	7.50	4.50
(29)	Ferrell	15.00	7.50	4.50
(30)	Finn	15.00	7.50	4.50
(31)	Flowers	15.00	7.50	4.50
(32)	Fogarty	15.00	7.50	4.50
(33)	Francisco	15.00	7.50	4.50
(34)	Gardin	15.00	7.50	4.50
(35)	Gilmore	15.00	7.50	4.50
(36)	Gorham	15.00	7.50	4.50
(37)	Gorman	15.00	7.50	4.50
(38)	Guss	15.00	7.50	4.50
(39)	Hammersley	15.00	7.50	4.50
(40)	Hargrave	15.00	7.50	4.50
(41)	Harrington	15.00	7.50	4.50
(42)	Harris	15.00	7.50	4.50
(43)	Hartley	15.00	7.50	4.50
(44)	Hayes	15.00	7.50	4.50
(45)	Hicks	15.00	7.50	4.50
(46)	Humphrey	15.00	7.50	4.50
(47)	Jackson	15.00	7.50	4.50
(48)	James	15.00	7.50	4.50
(49)	Jenkins	15.00	7.50	4.50
(50)	Johnston	15.00	7.50	4.50
(51)	Kelly	15.00	7.50	4.50
(52)	Laval	15.00	7.50	4.50
(53)	Lothrop	15.00	7.50	4.50
(54)	MacConachie	15.00	7.50	4.50
(55)	Mangum	15.00	7.50	4.50
(56)	A. McCarthy	15.00	7.50	4.50
(57)	J. McCarthy	15.00	7.50	4.50
(58)	McEnroe	15.00	7.50	4.50
(59)	McFarlin	15.00	7.50	4.50
(60)	McHugh	15.00	7.50	4.50
(61)	McKevitt	15.00	7.50	4.50
(62)	Midkiff	15.00	7.50	4.50
(63)	Moore	15.00	7.50	4.50
(64)	Noojin	15.00	7.50	4.50

		NR MT	EX	VG
(65)	Ochs	15.00	7.50	4.50
(66)	Painter	15.00	7.50	4.50
(67)	Redfern (Redfearn)	15.00	7.50	4.50
(68)	Reis	15.00	7.50	4.50
(69)	Rickard	15.00	7.50	4.50
(70)	Roth (batting)	15.00	7.50	4.50
(71)	Roth (fielding)	15.00	7.50	4.50
(72)	Smith	15.00	7.50	4.50
(73)	Springs	15.00	7.50	4.50
(74)	Stouch	15.00	7.50	4.50
(75)	Taxis	15.00	7.50	4.50
(76)	Templin	15.00	7.50	4.50
(77)	Thrasher	15.00	7.50	4.50
(78)	Trammell	15.00	7.50	4.50
(79)	Walker	15.00	7.50	4.50
(80)	Walters	15.00	7.50	4.50
(81)	Wehrell	15.00	7.50	4.50
(82)	Weldon	15.00	7.50	4.50
(83)	Williams	15.00	7.50	4.50
(84)	Wingo	15.00	7.50	4.50
(85)	Workman	15.00	7.50	4.50
(86)	Wynne	15.00	7.50	4.50
(87)	Wysong	15.00	7.50	4.50

1910 T210 Old Mill
Series No. 6

		NR MT	EX	VG
Complete Set:		2800.00	1400.00	840.00
Common Player:		16.00	8.00	4.75
(1)	Angermeier (fielding)	16.00	8.00	4.75
(2)	Angermeir (portrait)	16.00	8.00	4.75
(3)	Atwell	16.00	8.00	4.75
(4)	Badger	16.00	8.00	4.75
(5)	Barnett	16.00	8.00	4.75
(6)	Barney	16.00	8.00	4.75
(7)	Beard	16.00	8.00	4.75
(8)	Bohannon	16.00	8.00	4.75
(9)	Callahan	16.00	8.00	4.75
(10)	Chapman	16.00	8.00	4.75
(11)	Chase	16.00	8.00	4.75
(12)	Coleman	16.00	8.00	4.75
(13)	Cornell (Frankfort)	16.00	8.00	4.75
(14)	Cornell (Winchester)	16.00	8.00	4.75
(15)	Creager	16.00	8.00	4.75
(16)	Dailey	16.00	8.00	4.75
(17)	Edington	16.00	8.00	4.75
(18)	Elgin	16.00	8.00	4.75
(19)	Ellis	16.00	8.00	4.75
(20)	Everden	16.00	8.00	4.75
(21)	Gisler	16.00	8.00	4.75
(22)	Goodman	16.00	8.00	4.75
(23)	Goostree (hands behind back)	16.00	8.00	4.75
(24)	Goostree (leaning on bat)	16.00	8.00	4.75
(25)	Haines	16.00	8.00	4.75
(26)	Harold	16.00	8.00	4.75
(27)	Heveron	16.00	8.00	4.75
(28)	Hicks	16.00	8.00	4.75
(29)	Hoffmann	16.00	8.00	4.75
(30)	Horn	16.00	8.00	4.75
(31)	Kaiser	16.00	8.00	4.75
(32)	Keifel	16.00	8.00	4.75
(33)	Kimbrough	16.00	8.00	4.75
(34)	Kirchen	16.00	8.00	4.75
(35)	Kircher	16.00	8.00	4.75
(36)	Kuhlman	16.00	8.00	4.75
(37)	Kuhlmann	16.00	8.00	4.75
(38)	L'Heureux	16.00	8.00	4.75
(39)	Mulvain	16.00	8.00	4.75
(40)	McKernan	16.00	8.00	4.75
(41)	Meyers	16.00	8.00	4.75
(42)	Moloney	16.00	8.00	4.75
(43)	Mullin	16.00	8.00	4.75
(44)	Olson	16.00	8.00	4.75
(45)	Oyler	16.00	8.00	4.75
(46)	Reed	16.00	8.00	4.75
(47)	Ross	16.00	8.00	4.75
(48)	Scheneberg (fielding)	16.00	8.00	4.75
(49)	Scheneberg (portrait)	16.00	8.00	4.75
(50)	Schultz	16.00	8.00	4.75
(51)	Scott	16.00	8.00	4.75
(52)	Sinex	16.00	8.00	4.75
(53)	Stengel	2500.00	1250.00	750.00
(54)	Thoss	16.00	8.00	4.75

		NR MT	EX	VG
(55)	Tilford	16.00	8.00	4.75
(56)	Toney	16.00	8.00	4.75
(57)	Van Landingham (Valladingham) (Lexington)	16.00	8.00	4.75
(58)	Van Landingham (Valladingham) (Shelbyville)	16.00	8.00	4.75
(59)	Viox	16.00	8.00	4.75
(60)	Walden	16.00	8.00	4.75
(61)	Whitaker	16.00	8.00	4.75
(62)	Wills	16.00	8.00	4.75
(63)	Womble	16.00	8.00	4.75
(64)	Wright	16.00	8.00	4.75
(65)	Yaeger	16.00	8.00	4.75
(66)	Yancey	16.00	8.00	4.75

1910 T210 Old Mill
Series No. 7

		NR MT	EX	VG
Complete Set:		1300.00	650.00	390.00
Common Player:		18.00	9.00	5.50
(1)	Armstrong	18.00	9.00	5.50
(2)	Beatty	18.00	9.00	5.50
(3)	Biel	18.00	9.00	5.50
(4)	Bonner	18.00	9.00	5.50
(5)	Brandt	18.00	9.00	5.50
(6)	Brown	18.00	9.00	5.50
(7)	Cantwell	18.00	9.00	5.50
(8)	Carrol	18.00	9.00	5.50
(9)	Cooney	18.00	9.00	5.50
(10)	Cooper	18.00	9.00	5.50
(11)	Cowell	18.00	9.00	5.50
(12)	Creager (Cregan)	18.00	9.00	5.50
(13)	Crockett	18.00	9.00	5.50
(14)	Dailey	18.00	9.00	5.50
(15)	Dobbs	18.00	9.00	5.50
(16)	Dussault	18.00	9.00	5.50
(17)	Dwyer	18.00	9.00	5.50
(18)	Evans	18.00	9.00	5.50
(19)	Forgue	18.00	9.00	5.50
(20)	Fulton	18.00	9.00	5.50
(21)	Galvin	18.00	9.00	5.50
(22)	Gastmeyer (batting)	18.00	9.00	5.50
(23)	Gastmeyer (fielding)	18.00	9.00	5.50
(24)	Gates	18.00	9.00	5.50
(25)	Gillespie	18.00	9.00	5.50
(26)	Griffin	18.00	9.00	5.50
(27)	Gunderson	18.00	9.00	5.50
(28)	Ham	18.00	9.00	5.50
(29)	Handibe (Handiboe)	18.00	9.00	5.50
(30)	Hart	18.00	9.00	5.50
(31)	Hartley	18.00	9.00	5.50
(32)	Hobbs	18.00	9.00	5.50
(33)	Hyames	18.00	9.00	5.50
(34)	Irving	18.00	9.00	5.50
(35)	Kaiser	18.00	9.00	5.50
(36)	Kelley	18.00	9.00	5.50
(37)	Kelly	18.00	9.00	5.50
(38)	Kelly (mascot)	18.00	9.00	5.50
(39)	Luyster	18.00	9.00	5.50
(40)	MacDonald	18.00	9.00	5.50
(41)	Malcolm	18.00	9.00	5.50
(42)	Mayer	18.00	9.00	5.50
(43)	McCormac (McCormick)	18.00	9.00	5.50
(44)	McGeeham (McGeehan)	18.00	9.00	5.50
(45)	Merchant	18.00	9.00	5.50
(46)	Mills	18.00	9.00	5.50
(47)	Morgan	18.00	9.00	5.50
(48)	Morris	18.00	9.00	5.50
(49)	Munson	18.00	9.00	5.50
(50)	Newman	18.00	9.00	5.50
(51)	Noval (Novak)	18.00	9.00	5.50
(52)	O'Halloran	18.00	9.00	5.50
(53)	Phelan	18.00	9.00	5.50
(54)	Prim	18.00	9.00	5.50
(55)	Reeves	18.00	9.00	5.50
(56)	Richardson	18.00	9.00	5.50
(57)	Schumaker	18.00	9.00	5.50
(58)	Sharp	18.00	9.00	5.50
(59)	Sherrill	18.00	9.00	5.50
(60)	Simmons	18.00	9.00	5.50
(61)	Steinbach	18.00	9.00	5.50
(62)	Stohr	18.00	9.00	5.50
(63)	Taylor	18.00	9.00	5.50
(64)	Webb	18.00	9.00	5.50

		NR MT	EX	VG
(65)	Whelan	18.00	9.00	5.50
(66)	Wolf	18.00	9.00	5.50
(67)	Wright	18.00	9.00	5.50

1910 T210 Old Mill
Series No. 8

		NR MT	EX	VG
Complete Set:		5000.00	2500.00	1500.
Common Player:		16.00	8.00	4.75
(1)	Allen (Memphis)	16.00	8.00	4.75
(2)	Allen (Mobile)	16.00	8.00	4.75
(3)	Anderson	16.00	8.00	4.75
(4)	Babb	16.00	8.00	4.75
(5)	Bartley	16.00	8.00	4.75
(6)	Bauer	16.00	8.00	4.75
(7)	Bay	16.00	8.00	4.75
(8)	Bayliss	16.00	8.00	4.75
(9)	Berger	16.00	8.00	4.75
(10)	Bernhard	16.00	8.00	4.75
(11)	Bitroff	16.00	8.00	4.75
(12)	Breitenstein	16.00	8.00	4.75
(13)	Bronkie	16.00	8.00	4.75
(14)	Brooks	16.00	8.00	4.75
(15)	Burnett	16.00	8.00	4.75
(16)	Cafalu	16.00	8.00	4.75
(17)	Carson	16.00	8.00	4.75
(18)	Case	16.00	8.00	4.75
(19)	Chappelle	16.00	8.00	4.75
(20)	Cohen	16.00	8.00	4.75
(21)	Collins	16.00	8.00	4.75
(22)	Crandall	16.00	8.00	4.75
(23)	Cross	16.00	8.00	4.75
(24)	Jud. Daly	16.00	8.00	4.75
(25)	Davis	16.00	8.00	4.75
(26)	Demaree	16.00	8.00	4.75
(27)	DeMontreville	16.00	8.00	4.75
(28)	E. DeMontreville	16.00	8.00	4.75
(29)	Dick	16.00	8.00	4.75
(30)	Dobbs	16.00	8.00	4.75
(31)	Dudley	16.00	8.00	4.75
(32)	Dunn	16.00	8.00	4.75
(33)	Elliot	16.00	8.00	4.75
(34)	Emery	16.00	8.00	4.75
(35)	Erloff	16.00	8.00	4.75
(36)	Farrell	16.00	8.00	4.75
(37)	Fisher	16.00	8.00	4.75
(38)	Fleharty	16.00	8.00	4.75
(39)	Flood	16.00	8.00	4.75
(40)	Foster	16.00	8.00	4.75
(41)	Fritz	16.00	8.00	4.75
(42)	Greminger	16.00	8.00	4.75
(43)	Gribbon	16.00	8.00	4.75
(44)	Griffin	16.00	8.00	4.75
(45)	Gygli	16.00	8.00	4.75
(46)	Hanks	16.00	8.00	4.75
(47)	Hart	16.00	8.00	4.75
(48)	Hess	16.00	8.00	4.75
(49)	Hickman	16.00	8.00	4.75
(50)	Hohnhorst	16.00	8.00	4.75
(51)	Huelsman	16.00	8.00	4.75
(52)	Jackson	3500.00	1750.00	1050.
(53)	Jordan	16.00	8.00	4.75
(54)	Kane	16.00	8.00	4.75
(55)	Kelly	16.00	8.00	4.75
(56)	Kerwin	16.00	8.00	4.75
(57)	Keupper	16.00	8.00	4.75
(58)	LaFitte	16.00	8.00	4.75
(59)	Larsen	16.00	8.00	4.75
(60)	Lindsay	16.00	8.00	4.75
(61)	Lynch	16.00	8.00	4.75
(62)	Manuel	16.00	8.00	4.75
(63)	Manush	16.00	8.00	4.75
(64)	Marcan	16.00	8.00	4.75
(65)	Maxwell	16.00	8.00	4.75
(66)	McBride	16.00	8.00	4.75
(67)	McCreery	16.00	8.00	4.75
(68)	McGilvray	16.00	8.00	4.75
(69)	McLaurin	16.00	8.00	4.75
(70)	McTigue	16.00	8.00	4.75
(71)	Miller (Chattanooga)	16.00	8.00	4.75
(72)	Miller (Montgomery)	16.00	8.00	4.75
(73)	Molesworth	16.00	8.00	4.75
(74)	Moran	16.00	8.00	4.75

		NR MT	EX	VG			NR MT	EX	VG
(75)	Newton	16.00	8.00	4.75	(95)	Schopp	16.00	8.00	4.75
(76)	Nolley	16.00	8.00	4.75	(96)	Siegle	16.00	8.00	4.75
(77)	Osteen	16.00	8.00	4.75	(97)	Smith	16.00	8.00	4.75
(78)	Owen	16.00	8.00	4.75	(98)	Sid. Smith	16.00	8.00	4.75
(79)	Paige	16.00	8.00	4.75	(99)	Steele	16.00	8.00	4.75
(80)	Patterson	16.00	8.00	4.75	(100)	Swacina	16.00	8.00	4.75
(81)	Pepe	16.00	8.00	4.75	(101)	Sweeney	16.00	8.00	4.75
(82)	Perdue	16.00	8.00	4.75	(102)	Thomas (fielding)	16.00	8.00	4.75
(83)	Peters	16.00	8.00	4.75	(103)	Thomas (portrait)	16.00	8.00	4.75
(84)	Phillips	16.00	8.00	4.75	(104)	Vinson	16.00	8.00	4.75
(85)	Pratt	16.00	8.00	4.75	(105)	Wagner (Birmingham)	16.00	8.00	4.75
(86)	Rementer	16.00	8.00	4.75	(106)	Wagner (Mobile)	16.00	8.00	4.75
(87)	Rhodes	16.00	8.00	4.75	(107)	Walker	16.00	8.00	4.75
(88)	Rhoton	16.00	8.00	4.75	(108)	Wanner	16.00	8.00	4.75
(89)	Robertson	16.00	8.00	4.75	(109)	Welf	16.00	8.00	4.75
(90)	Rogers	16.00	8.00	4.75	(110)	Whiteman	16.00	8.00	4.75
(91)	Rohe	16.00	8.00	4.75	(111)	Whitney	16.00	8.00	4.75
(92)	Seabough (Seabaugh)	16.00	8.00	4.75	(112)	Wilder	16.00	8.00	4.75
(93)	Seitz	16.00	8.00	4.75	(113)	Wiseman	16.00	8.00	4.75
(94)	Schlitzer	16.00	8.00	4.75	(114)	Yerkes	16.00	8.00	4.75

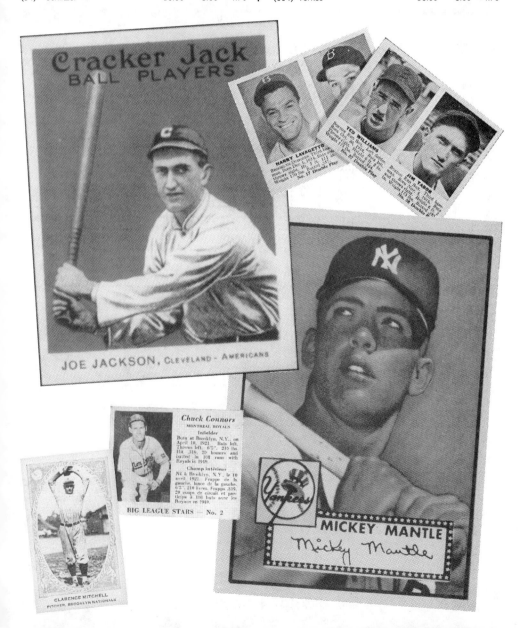

1910 T211 Red Sun

		NR MT	EX	VG
Complete Set:		2700.00	1350.00	810.00
Common Player:		35.00	17.50	10.50
(1)	Allen	35.00	17.50	10.50
(2)	Anderson	35.00	17.50	10.50
(3)	Babb	35.00	17.50	10.50
(4)	Bartley	35.00	17.50	10.50
(5)	Bay	35.00	17.50	10.50
(6)	Bayliss	35.00	17.50	10.50
(7)	Berger	35.00	17.50	10.50
(8)	Bernard	35.00	17.50	10.50
(9)	Bitroff	35.00	17.50	10.50
(10)	Breitenstein	35.00	17.50	10.50
(11)	Bronkie	35.00	17.50	10.50
(12)	Brooks	35.00	17.50	10.50
(13)	Cafalu	35.00	17.50	10.50
(14)	Case	35.00	17.50	10.50
(15)	Chappelle	35.00	17.50	10.50
(16)	Cohen	35.00	17.50	10.50
(17)	Cross	35.00	17.50	10.50
(18)	Jud. Daly	35.00	17.50	10.50
(19)	Davis	35.00	17.50	10.50
(20)	DeMontreville	35.00	17.50	10.50
(21)	E. DeMontreville	35.00	17.50	10.50
(22)	Dick	35.00	17.50	10.50
(23)	Dunn	35.00	17.50	10.50
(24)	Erloff	35.00	17.50	10.50
(25)	Fisher	35.00	17.50	10.50
(26)	Flood	35.00	17.50	10.50
(27)	Foster	35.00	17.50	10.50
(28)	Fritz	35.00	17.50	10.50
(29)	Greminger	35.00	17.50	10.50
(30)	Gribbon	35.00	17.50	10.50
(31)	Griffin	35.00	17.50	10.50
(32)	Gygli	35.00	17.50	10.50
(33)	Hanks	35.00	17.50	10.50
(34)	Hart	35.00	17.50	10.50
(35)	Hess	35.00	17.50	10.50
(36)	Hickman	35.00	17.50	10.50
(37)	Hohnhorst	35.00	17.50	10.50
(38)	Huelsman	35.00	17.50	10.50
(39)	Jordan	35.00	17.50	10.50
(40)	Kane	35.00	17.50	10.50
(41)	Kelly	35.00	17.50	10.50
(42)	Kerwin	35.00	17.50	10.50
(43)	Keupper	35.00	17.50	10.50
(44)	LaFitte	35.00	17.50	10.50
(45)	Lindsay	35.00	17.50	10.50
(46)	Lynch	35.00	17.50	10.50
(47)	Manush	35.00	17.50	10.50
(48)	McCreery	35.00	17.50	10.50
(49)	Miller	35.00	17.50	10.50
(50)	Molesworth	35.00	17.50	10.50
(51)	Moran	35.00	17.50	10.50
(52)	Nolley	35.00	17.50	10.50
(53)	Paige	35.00	17.50	10.50
(54)	Pepe	35.00	17.50	10.50
(55)	Perdue	35.00	17.50	10.50
(56)	Pratt	35.00	17.50	10.50
(57)	Rhoton	35.00	17.50	10.50
(58)	Robertson	35.00	17.50	10.50
(59)	Rogers	35.00	17.50	10.50
(60)	Rohe	35.00	17.50	10.50
(61)	Seabaugh	35.00	17.50	10.50
(62)	Seitz	35.00	17.50	10.50
(63)	Siegle	35.00	17.50	10.50
(64)	Smith	35.00	17.50	10.50

		NR MT	EX	VG
(65)	Sid. Smith	35.00	17.50	10.50
(66)	Steele	35.00	17.50	10.50
(67)	Swacina	35.00	17.50	10.50
(68)	Sweeney	35.00	17.50	10.50
(69)	Thomas	35.00	17.50	10.50
(70)	Vinson	35.00	17.50	10.50
(71)	Wagner	35.00	17.50	10.50
(72)	Walker	35.00	17.50	10.50
(73)	Welf	35.00	17.50	10.50
(74)	Wilder	35.00	17.50	10.50
(75)	Wiseman	35.00	17.50	10.50

1909 T212 Obak

Collectors of early Pacific Coast League memorabilia consider the Obak Cigarette cards to be among the most significant of all the 20th Century minor league tobacco issues. Produced annually from 1909 to 1911, the Obak cards were actually three separate and distinct sets, but because they were all grouped together under a single T212 designation in the American Card Catalog, they are generally collected that way today. The Obak sets are closely related in style to the more popular T206 "White Border" set issued over the same three-year period, and, in fact, were producedby the California branch of the same American Tobacco Company conglomerate. The Obaks are the standard tobacco card size, 1-1/2" by 2-5/8" and feature a colored lithograph, along with the player's name and team, on the front of the card. The year of the issue can easily be determined by examining the back. The 1909 issue has blue printing with the name "Obak" appearing in an "Old English" type style; for 1910 the type face was changed to straight block letters; and in 1911 the backs were printed in red and included a brief biography and player statistics. There are 269 different players in the three issues, but, because of the subjects appeared in more than one year, Obak collectors generally consider the set complete at 426 different cards. The 1909 edition featured only teams from the Pacific Coast League, while the 1910 and 1911 sets were expanded to also include players from the Northwestern League. The Obak sets offer advanced collectors a challenging number of variations, and they have additional appeal beacause about 40 percent of the checklisted players had minor league experience.

		NR MT	EX	VG
Complete Set:		2300.00	1150.00	690.00
Common Player:		30.00	15.00	9.00
(1)	Baum	30.00	15.00	9.00
(2)	Bernard	30.00	15.00	9.00
(3)	Berry	30.00	15.00	9.00
(4)	Bodie	30.00	15.00	9.00
(5)	Boyce	30.00	15.00	9.00
(6)	Brackenridge	30.00	15.00	9.00
(7)	N. Brashear	30.00	15.00	9.00
(8)	Breen	30.00	15.00	9.00
(9)	Brown	30.00	15.00	9.00
(10)	D. Brown	30.00	15.00	9.00
(11)	Browning	30.00	15.00	9.00
(12)	Byrnes	30.00	15.00	9.00

		NR MT	EX	VG
(13)	Cameron	30.00	15.00	9.00
(14)	Carroll	30.00	15.00	9.00
(15)	Carson	30.00	15.00	9.00
(16)	Christian	30.00	15.00	9.00
(17)	Coy	30.00	15.00	9.00
(18)	Delmas	30.00	15.00	9.00
(19)	Dillon	30.00	15.00	9.00
(20)	Eagan	30.00	15.00	9.00
(21)	Easterly (Eastley)	30.00	15.00	9.00
(22)	Flannagan	30.00	15.00	9.00
(23)	Fisher	30.00	15.00	9.00
(24)	Fitzgerald	30.00	15.00	9.00
(25)	Gandil	45.00	22.00	13.50
(26)	Garrett	30.00	15.00	9.00
(27)	Graham	30.00	15.00	9.00
(28)	Graney	30.00	15.00	9.00
(29)	Griffin	30.00	15.00	9.00
(30)	Guyn	30.00	15.00	9.00
(31)	Haley	30.00	15.00	9.00
(32)	Harkins	30.00	15.00	9.00
(33)	Henley	30.00	15.00	9.00
(34)	Hitt	30.00	15.00	9.00
(35)	Hogan	30.00	15.00	9.00
(36)	W. Hogan	30.00	15.00	9.00
(37)	Howard	30.00	15.00	9.00
(38)	Howse	30.00	15.00	9.00
(39)	Jansing	30.00	15.00	9.00
(40)	LaLonge	30.00	15.00	9.00
(41)	C. Lewis	30.00	15.00	9.00
(42)	D. Lewis	35.00	17.50	10.50
(43)	J. Lewis	30.00	15.00	9.00
(44)	Martinez	30.00	15.00	9.00
(45)	McArdle	30.00	15.00	9.00
(46)	McCredie	30.00	15.00	9.00
(47)	McKune	30.00	15.00	9.00
(48)	Melchoir	30.00	15.00	9.00
(49)	Mohler	30.00	15.00	9.00
(50)	Mott	30.00	15.00	9.00
(51)	Mundorff	30.00	15.00	9.00
(52)	Murphy	30.00	15.00	9.00
(53)	Nagle	30.00	15.00	9.00
(54)	Nelson	30.00	15.00	9.00
(55)	Olson	30.00	15.00	9.00
(56)	Ornsdorff	30.00	15.00	9.00
(57)	Ort	30.00	15.00	9.00
(58)	Ragan	30.00	15.00	9.00
(59)	Raymer	30.00	15.00	9.00
(60)	Raymond	30.00	15.00	9.00
(61)	Reidy	30.00	15.00	9.00
(62)	Ryan	30.00	15.00	9.00
(63)	Shinn	30.00	15.00	9.00
(64)	Smith	30.00	15.00	9.00
(65)	Speas	30.00	15.00	9.00
(66)	Stoval (Stovall)	30.00	15.00	9.00
(67)	Tennant	30.00	15.00	9.00
(68)	Whalen	30.00	15.00	9.00
(69)	Wheeler	30.00	15.00	9.00
(70)	Wiggs	30.00	15.00	9.00
(71)	Willett	30.00	15.00	9.00
(72)	J. Williams	30.00	15.00	9.00
(73)	R. Williams	30.00	15.00	9.00
(74)	Willis	30.00	15.00	9.00
(75)	Zeider	30.00	15.00	9.00

1910 T212 Obak

	NR MT	EX	VG
Complete Set:	3200.00	1600.00	960.00
Common Player:	15.00	7.50	4.50

		NR MT	EX	VG
(1)	Agnew	15.00	7.50	4.50
(2)	Akin	15.00	7.50	4.50
(3)	Ames	15.00	7.50	4.50
(4)	Annis	15.00	7.50	4.50
(5a)	Armbuster (Armbruster) ("150 subjects" back)	15.00	7.50	4.50
(5b)	Armbuster (Armbruster) ("175 subjects" back)	15.00	7.50	4.50
(6)	Baker	15.00	7.50	4.50
(7)	Bassey	15.00	7.50	4.50
(8)	Baum	15.00	7.50	4.50
(9)	Beall	15.00	7.50	4.50
(10)	Bennett	15.00	7.50	4.50
(11)	Bernard	15.00	7.50	4.50
(12a)	Berry ("150 subjects" back)	15.00	7.50	4.50
(12b)	Berry ("175 subjects" back)	15.00	7.50	4.50
(13)	Blankenship	15.00	7.50	4.50
(14)	Boardman	15.00	7.50	4.50
(15)	Bodie	15.00	7.50	4.50
(16)	Bonner	15.00	7.50	4.50
(17a)	Brackenridge ("150 subjects" back)	15.00	7.50	4.50
(17b)	Brackenridge ("175 subjects" back)	15.00	7.50	4.50
(18a)	N. Brashear ("150 subjects" back)	15.00	7.50	4.50
(18b)	N. Brashear ("175 subjects" back)	15.00	7.50	4.50
(19)	R. Brashear	15.00	7.50	4.50
(20)	Breen	15.00	7.50	4.50
(21a)	Briggs ("150 subjects" back)	15.00	7.50	4.50
(21b)	Briggs ("175 subjects" back)	15.00	7.50	4.50
(22)	Brinker	15.00	7.50	4.50
(23)	Briswalter	15.00	7.50	4.50
(24)	Brooks	15.00	7.50	4.50
(25)	Brown (Sacramento)	15.00	7.50	4.50
(26)	Brown (Vancouver)	15.00	7.50	4.50
(27)	D. Brown	15.00	7.50	4.50
(28)	Browning	15.00	7.50	4.50
(29)	Burrell, Byrd	5.00	3.00	
(30)	Byrnes	15.00	7.50	4.50
(31a)	Cameron ("150 subjects" back)	15.00	7.50	4.50
(31b)	Cameron ("175 subjects" back)	15.00	7.50	4.50
(32)	Capren (Capron)	15.00	7.50	4.50
(33)	Carlisle	15.00	7.50	4.50
(34)	Carroll	15.00	7.50	4.50
(35)	Cartwright	15.00	7.50	4.50
(36)	Casey	15.00	7.50	4.50
(37)	Caslleton (Castleton)	15.00	7.50	4.50
(38)	Chenault	15.00	7.50	4.50
(39)	Christian	15.00	7.50	4.50
(40)	Coleman	15.00	7.50	4.50
(41)	Cooney	15.00	7.50	4.50
(42a)	Coy ("150 subjects" back)	15.00	7.50	4.50
(42b)	Coy ("175 subjects" back)	15.00	7.50	4.50
(43a)	Criger ("150 subjects" back)	15.00	7.50	4.50
(43b)	Criger ("175 subjects" back)	15.00	7.50	4.50
(44)	Custer	15.00	7.50	4.50
(45)	Cutshaw	15.00	7.50	4.50
(46)	Daley	15.00	7.50	4.50
(47a)	Danzig ("150 subjects" back)	15.00	7.50	4.50
(47b)	Danzig ("175 subjects" back)	15.00	7.50	4.50
(48)	Daringer	15.00	7.50	4.50
(49)	Davis	15.00	7.50	4.50
(50)	Delhi	15.00	7.50	4.50
(51)	Delmas	15.00	7.50	4.50
(52a)	Dillon ("150 subjects" back)	15.00	7.50	4.50
(52b)	Dillon ("175 subjects" back)	15.00	7.50	4.50
(53)	Dretchko	15.00	7.50	4.50
(54)	Eastley	15.00	7.50	4.50
(55)	Erickson	15.00	7.50	4.50
(56)	Flannagan	15.00	7.50	4.50
(57)	Fisher (Portland)	15.00	7.50	4.50
(58a)	Fisher (Vernon, "150 subjects" back)	15.00	7.50	4.50
(58b)	Fisher (Vernon, "175 subjects" back)	15.00	7.50	4.50
(59)	Fitzgerald	15.00	7.50	4.50
(60)	Flood	15.00	7.50	4.50
(61)	Fournier	15.00	7.50	4.50
(62)	Frisk	15.00	7.50	4.50
(63)	Gaddy	15.00	7.50	4.50
(64)	Gardner	15.00	7.50	4.50
(65)	Garrett	15.00	7.50	4.50
(66)	Greggs (Gregg)	15.00	7.50	4.50
(67a)	Griffin ("150 subjects" back)	15.00	7.50	4.50
(67b)	Griffin ("175 subjects" back)	15.00	7.50	4.50
(68)	Gurney	15.00	7.50	4.50
(69)	Hall (Seattle)	15.00	7.50	4.50
(70)	Hall (Tacoma)	15.00	7.50	4.50
(71)	Harkins	15.00	7.50	4.50

		NR MT	EX	VG
(72)	Hartman	15.00	7.50	4.50
(73)	Hendrix	15.00	7.50	4.50
(74a)	Henley ("150 subjects" back)	15.00	7.50	4.50
(74b)	Henley ("175 subjects" back)	15.00	7.50	4.50
(75)	Hensling	15.00	7.50	4.50
(76)	Hetling	15.00	7.50	4.50
(77)	Hickey	15.00	7.50	4.50
(78a)	Hiester ("150 subjects" back)	15.00	7.50	4.50
(78b)	Hiester ("175 subjects" back)	15.00	7.50	4.50
(79)	Hitt	15.00	7.50	4.50
(80)	Hogan (Oakland)	15.00	7.50	4.50
(81a)	Hogan (Vernon, "150 subjects" back)			
		15.00	7.50	4.50
(81b)	Hogan (Vernon, "175 subjects" back)			
		15.00	7.50	4.50
(82)	Hollis	15.00	7.50	4.50
(83)	Holm	15.00	7.50	4.50
(84a)	Howard ("150 subjects" back)	15.00	7.50	4.50
(84b)	Howard ("175 subjects" back)	15.00	7.50	4.50
(85)	Hunt	15.00	7.50	4.50
(86)	James	15.00	7.50	4.50
(87)	Jansing	15.00	7.50	4.50
(88)	Jensen	15.00	7.50	4.50
(89)	Johnston	15.00	7.50	4.50
(90)	Keener	15.00	7.50	4.50
(91)	Killilay	15.00	7.50	4.50
(92)	Kippert	15.00	7.50	4.50
(93)	Klein	15.00	7.50	4.50
(94a)	Krapp ("150 subjects" back)	15.00	7.50	4.50
(94b)	Krapp ("175 subjects" back)	15.00	7.50	4.50
(95)	Kusel	15.00	7.50	4.50
(96a)	LaLonge ("150 subjects" back)	15.00	7.50	4.50
(96b)	LaLonge ("175 subjects" back)	15.00	7.50	4.50
(97)	Lewis	15.00	7.50	4.50
(98)	J. Lewis	15.00	7.50	4.50
(99)	Lindsay	15.00	7.50	4.50
(100)	Lively	15.00	7.50	4.50
(101)	Lynch	15.00	7.50	4.50
(102a)	Manush ("150 subjects" back)	15.00	7.50	4.50
(102b)	Manush ("175 subjects" back)	15.00	7.50	4.50
(103)	Martinke	15.00	7.50	4.50
(104a)	McArdle ("150 subjects" back)	15.00	7.50	4.50
(104b)	McArdle ("175 subjects" back)	15.00	7.50	4.50
(105a)	McCredie ("150 subjects" back)	15.00	7.50	4.50
(105b)	McCredie ("175 subjects" back)	15.00	7.50	4.50
(106a)	Melchoir ("150 subjects" back)	15.00	7.50	4.50
(106b)	Melchoir ("175 subjects" back)	15.00	7.50	4.50
(107)	Miller (San Francisco)	15.00	7.50	4.50
(108)	Miller (Seattle)	15.00	7.50	4.50
(109)	Mitze	15.00	7.50	4.50
(110a)	Mohler ("150 subjects" back)	15.00	7.50	4.50
(110b)	Mohler ("175 subjects" back)	15.00	7.50	4.50
(111a)	Moser ("150 subjects" back)	15.00	7.50	4.50
(111b)	Moser ("175 subjects" back)	15.00	7.50	4.50
(112)	Mott	15.00	7.50	4.50
(113a)	Mundorf (name incorrect, "150 subjects" back)	50.00	25.00	15.00
(113b)	Mundorff (name correct, "175 subjects" back)	15.00	7.50	4.50
(114a)	Murphy ("150 subjects" back)	15.00	7.50	4.50
(114b)	Murphy ("175 subjects" back)	15.00	7.50	4.50
(115)	Nagle	15.00	7.50	4.50
(116)	Nelson	15.00	7.50	4.50
(117)	Netzel	15.00	7.50	4.50
(118)	Nourse	15.00	7.50	4.50
(119)	Nordyke	15.00	7.50	4.50
(120)	Olson	15.00	7.50	4.50
(121)	Orendorff (Orsnsdorff)	15.00	7.50	4.50
(122a)	Ort ("150 subjects" back)	15.00	7.50	4.50
(122b)	Ort ("175 subjects" back)	15.00	7.50	4.50
(123)	Ostdiek	15.00	7.50	4.50
(124)	Pennington	15.00	7.50	4.50
(125)	Perrine	15.00	7.50	4.50
(126a)	Perry ("150 subjects" back)	15.00	7.50	4.50
(126b)	Perry ("175 subjects" back)	15.00	7.50	4.50
(127)	Persons	15.00	7.50	4.50
(128a)	Rapps ("150 subjects" back)	15.00	7.50	4.50
(128b)	Rapps ("175 subjects" back)	15.00	7.50	4.50
(129)	Raymer	15.00	7.50	4.50
(130)	Raymond	15.00	7.50	4.50
(131)	Rockenfield	15.00	7.50	4.50
(132)	Roth	15.00	7.50	4.50
(133)	D. Ryan	15.00	7.50	4.50
(134)	J. Ryan	15.00	7.50	4.50
(135)	Scharnweber	15.00	7.50	4.50
(136)	Schmutz	15.00	7.50	4.50
(137)	Seaton (Portland)	15.00	7.50	4.50
(138)	Seaton (Seattle)	15.00	7.50	4.50
(139)	Shafer	15.00	7.50	4.50
(140)	Shaw	15.00	7.50	4.50
(141)	Shea	15.00	7.50	4.50

		NR MT	EX	VG
(142)	Shinn	15.00	7.50	4.50
(143)	Smith	15.00	7.50	4.50
(144a)	H. Smith ("150 subjects" back)	15.00	7.50	4.50
(144b)	H. Smith ("175 subjects" back)	15.00	7.50	4.50
(145a)	J. Smith ("150 subjects" back)	15.00	7.50	4.50
(145b)	J. Smith ("175 subjects" back)	15.00	7.50	4.50
(146)	Speas	15.00	7.50	4.50
(147)	Spiesman	15.00	7.50	4.50
(148)	Starkell	15.00	7.50	4.50
(149a)	Steen ("150 subjects" back)	15.00	7.50	4.50
(149b)	Steen ("175 subjects" back)	15.00	7.50	4.50
(150)	Stevens	15.00	7.50	4.50
(151a)	Stewart ("150 subjects" back)	15.00	7.50	4.50
(151b)	Stewart ("175 subjects" back)	15.00	7.50	4.50
(152)	Stovell (Stovall)	15.00	7.50	4.50
(153)	Streib	15.00	7.50	4.50
(154)	Sugden	15.00	7.50	4.50
(155)	Sutor	15.00	7.50	4.50
(156)	Swain	15.00	7.50	4.50
(157a)	Swander ("150 subjects" back)	15.00	7.50	4.50
(157b)	Swander ("175 subjects" back)	15.00	7.50	4.50
(158)	Tennant	15.00	7.50	4.50
(159)	Thomas	15.00	7.50	4.50
(160)	Thompson	15.00	7.50	4.50
(161)	Thorsen	15.00	7.50	4.50
(162a)	Tonnesen ("150 subjects" back)	15.00	7.50	4.50
(162b)	Tonnesen ("175 subjects" back)	15.00	7.50	4.50
(163)	Tozer	15.00	7.50	4.50
(164)	Van Buren	15.00	7.50	4.50
(165)	Vitt	15.00	7.50	4.50
(166)	Wares	15.00	7.50	4.50
(167)	Waring	15.00	7.50	4.50
(168)	Warren	15.00	7.50	4.50
(169)	Weed	15.00	7.50	4.50
(170a)	Whalen ("150 subjects" back)	15.00	7.50	4.50
(170b)	Whalen ("175 subjects" back)	15.00	7.50	4.50
(171a)	Willett ("150 subjects" back)	15.00	7.50	4.50
(171b)	Willett ("175 subjects" back)	15.00	7.50	4.50
(172a)	Williams ("150 subjects" back)	15.00	7.50	4.50
(172b)	Williams ("175 subjects" back)	15.00	7.50	4.50
(173a)	Willis ("150 subjects" back)	15.00	7.50	4.50
(173b)	Willis ("175 subjects" back)	15.00	7.50	4.50
(174a)	Wolverton ("150 subjects" back)			
		15.00	7.50	4.50
(174b)	Wolverton ("175 subjects" back)			
		15.00	7.50	4.50
(175)	Zackert	15.00	7.50	4.50

1911 T212 Obak

		NR MT	EX	VG
Complete Set:		2500.00	1250.00	750.00
Common Player:		15.00	7.50	4.50
(1)	Abbott	15.00	7.50	4.50
(2)	Ables	15.00	7.50	4.50
(3)	Adams	15.00	7.50	4.50
(4)	Agnew	15.00	7.50	4.50
(5)	Akin	15.00	7.50	4.50
(6)	Annis	15.00	7.50	4.50
(7)	Arrelanes (Arellanes)	15.00	7.50	4.50
(8)	Barry	15.00	7.50	4.50
(9)	Bassey	15.00	7.50	4.50
(10)	Baum	15.00	7.50	4.50
(11)	Bennett	15.00	7.50	4.50
(12)	Bernard	15.00	7.50	4.50
(13)	Berry	15.00	7.50	4.50
(14)	Bloomfield	15.00	7.50	4.50

		NR MT	EX	VG
(15)	Bonner	15.00	7.50	4.50
(16)	Brackenridge	15.00	7.50	4.50
(17)	Brashear	15.00	7.50	4.50
(18)	R. Brashear	15.00	7.50	4.50
(19)	Brinker	15.00	7.50	4.50
(20)	Brown	15.00	7.50	4.50
(21)	Browning	15.00	7.50	4.50
(22)	Bues	15.00	7.50	4.50
(23)	Burrell	15.00	7.50	4.50
(24)	Burns	15.00	7.50	4.50
(25)	Butler	15.00	7.50	4.50
(26)	Byram	15.00	7.50	4.50
(27)	Carlisle	15.00	7.50	4.50
(28)	Carson	15.00	7.50	4.50
(29)	Cartwright	15.00	7.50	4.50
(30)	Casey	15.00	7.50	4.50
(31)	Castleton	15.00	7.50	4.50
(32)	Chadbourne	15.00	7.50	4.50
(33)	Christian	15.00	7.50	4.50
(34)	Coleman	15.00	7.50	4.50
(35)	Cooney	15.00	7.50	4.50
(36)	Coy	15.00	7.50	4.50
(37)	Criger	15.00	7.50	4.50
(38)	Crukshank	15.00	7.50	4.50
(39)	Cutshaw	15.00	7.50	4.50
(40)	Daley	15.00	7.50	4.50
(41)	Danzig	15.00	7.50	4.50
(42)	Dashwood	15.00	7.50	4.50
(43)	Davis	15.00	7.50	4.50
(44)	Delhi	15.00	7.50	4.50
(45)	Delmas	15.00	7.50	4.50
(46)	Dillon	15.00	7.50	4.50
(47)	Engel	15.00	7.50	4.50
(48)	Erickson	15.00	7.50	4.50
(49)	Fitzgerald	15.00	7.50	4.50
(50)	Flater	15.00	7.50	4.50
(51)	Frisk	15.00	7.50	4.50
(52)	Fullerton	15.00	7.50	4.50
(53)	Garrett	15.00	7.50	4.50
(54)	Goodman	15.00	7.50	4.50
(55)	Gordon	15.00	7.50	4.50
(56)	Grindle	15.00	7.50	4.50
(57)	Hall	15.00	7.50	4.50
(58)	Harris	15.00	7.50	4.50
(59)	Hasty	15.00	7.50	4.50
(60)	Henderson	15.00	7.50	4.50
(61)	Henley	15.00	7.50	4.50
(62)	Hetling	15.00	7.50	4.50
(63)	Hiester	15.00	7.50	4.50
(64)	Higgins	15.00	7.50	4.50
(65)	Hitt	15.00	7.50	4.50
(66)	Hoffman	15.00	7.50	4.50
(67)	Hogan	15.00	7.50	4.50
(68)	Holm	15.00	7.50	4.50
(69)	Householder	15.00	7.50	4.50
(70)	Hosp	15.00	7.50	4.50
(71)	Howard	15.00	7.50	4.50
(72)	Hunt	15.00	7.50	4.50
(73)	James	15.00	7.50	4.50
(74)	Jensen	15.00	7.50	4.50
(75)	Kading	15.00	7.50	4.50
(76)	Kane	15.00	7.50	4.50
(77)	Kippert	15.00	7.50	4.50
(78)	Knight	15.00	7.50	4.50
(79)	Koestner	15.00	7.50	4.50
(80)	Krueger	15.00	7.50	4.50
(81)	Kuhn	15.00	7.50	4.50
(82)	LaLonge	15.00	7.50	4.50
(83)	Lamline	15.00	7.50	4.50
(84)	Leard	15.00	7.50	4.50
(85)	Lerchen	15.00	7.50	4.50
(86)	Lewis	15.00	7.50	4.50
(87)	Madden	15.00	7.50	4.50
(88)	Maggert	15.00	7.50	4.50
(89)	Mahoney	15.00	7.50	4.50
(90)	McArdle	15.00	7.50	4.50
(91)	McCredie	15.00	7.50	4.50
(92)	McDonnell	15.00	7.50	4.50
(93)	Meikle	15.00	7.50	4.50
(94)	Melchoir	15.00	7.50	4.50
(95)	Mensor	15.00	7.50	4.50
(96)	Metzger	15.00	7.50	4.50
(97)	Miller (Oakland)	15.00	7.50	4.50
(98)	Miller (San Francisco)	15.00	7.50	4.50
(99)	Ten Million	15.00	7.50	4.50
(100)	Mitze	15.00	7.50	4.50
(101)	Mohler	15.00	7.50	4.50
(102)	Moore	15.00	7.50	4.50
(103)	Morse	15.00	7.50	4.50
(104)	Moskiman	15.00	7.50	4.50
(105)	Mundorff	15.00	7.50	4.50

		NR MT	EX	VG
(106)	Murray	15.00	7.50	4.50
(107)	Netzel	15.00	7.50	4.50
(108)	Nordyke	15.00	7.50	4.50
(109)	Nourse	15.00	7.50	4.50
(110)	O'Rourke	15.00	7.50	4.50
(111)	Ostdiek	15.00	7.50	4.50
(112)	Patterson	15.00	7.50	4.50
(113)	Pearce	15.00	7.50	4.50
(114)	Peckinpaugh	15.00	7.50	4.50
(115)	Pernoll	15.00	7.50	4.50
(116)	Pfyl	15.00	7.50	4.50
(117)	Powell	15.00	7.50	4.50
(118)	Raleigh	15.00	7.50	4.50
(119)	Rapps	15.00	7.50	4.50
(120)	Raymer	15.00	7.50	4.50
(121)	Raymond	15.00	7.50	4.50
(122)	Reddick	15.00	7.50	4.50
(123)	Roche	15.00	7.50	4.50
(124)	Rockenfield	15.00	7.50	4.50
(125)	Rogers	15.00	7.50	4.50
(126)	Ross	15.00	7.50	4.50
(127)	Ryan	15.00	7.50	4.50
(128)	J. Ryan	15.00	7.50	4.50
(129)	Scharnweber	15.00	7.50	4.50
(130)	Schmidt	15.00	7.50	4.50
(131)	Schmutz	15.00	7.50	4.50
(132)	Seaton (Portland)	15.00	7.50	4.50
(133)	Seaton (Seattle)	15.00	7.50	4.50
(134)	Shaw	15.00	7.50	4.50
(135)	Shea	15.00	7.50	4.50
(136)	Sheehan (Portland)	15.00	7.50	4.50
(137)	Sheehan (Vernon)	15.00	7.50	4.50
(138)	Shinn	15.00	7.50	4.50
(139)	Skeels	15.00	7.50	4.50
(140)	H. Smith	15.00	7.50	4.50
(141)	Speas	15.00	7.50	4.50
(142)	Spencer	15.00	7.50	4.50
(143)	Spiesman	15.00	7.50	4.50
(144)	Starkel	15.00	7.50	4.50
(145)	Steen	15.00	7.50	4.50
(146)	Stewart	15.00	7.50	4.50
(147)	Stinson	15.00	7.50	4.50
(148)	Stovall	15.00	7.50	4.50
(149)	Strand	15.00	7.50	4.50
(150)	Sutor	15.00	7.50	4.50
(151)	Swain	15.00	7.50	4.50
(152)	Tennant	15.00	7.50	4.50
(153)	Thomas (Sacramento)	15.00	7.50	4.50
(154)	Thomas (Victoria)	15.00	7.50	4.50
(155)	Thompson	15.00	7.50	4.50
(156)	Thornton	15.00	7.50	4.50
(157)	Thorsen	15.00	7.50	4.50
(158)	Tiedeman	15.00	7.50	4.50
(159)	Tozer	15.00	7.50	4.50
(160)	Van Buren	15.00	7.50	4.50
(161)	Vitt	15.00	7.50	4.50
(162)	Ward	15.00	7.50	4.50
(163)	Wares	15.00	7.50	4.50
(164)	Warren	15.00	7.50	4.50
(165)	Weaver	20.00	10.00	6.00
(166)	Weed	15.00	7.50	4.50
(167)	Wheeler	15.00	7.50	4.50
(168)	Wiggs	15.00	7.50	4.50
(169)	Willett	15.00	7.50	4.50
(170)	Williams	15.00	7.50	4.50
(171)	Wolverton	15.00	7.50	4.50
(172)	Zacher	15.00	7.50	4.50
(173)	Zackert	15.00	7.50	4.50
(174)	Zamlock	15.00	7.50	4.50
(175)	Zimmerman	15.00	7.50	4.50

1910 T213 Coupon - Type 1

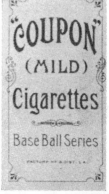

Because they feature the same photos used in the classic T206 tobacco set, some collectors fail to recognize the T213 Coupon set as a separate issue. Actually, the Coupon Cigarette cards make up three separate issues, produced from 1910 to 1919 and featuring a mix of players from the major leagues, the Federal League and the Southern League. While the fronts of the Coupon cards appear to be identical to the more popular T206 series, the backs clearly identify the cards as being a product of Coupon Cigarettes and allow the collector to easily differentiate between the three types. The Type I cards, produced in 1910, carry a general advertisement for Coupon "Mild" Cigarettes, while the Type II cards, issued from 1914 to 1916, contain the words "20 for 5 cents," and the Type III cards, issued in 1919, advertise "16 for 10 cts." Distribution of the Coupon cards was limited to the Louisiana area, making the set very obscure and difficult to checklist. Numerous variations further complicate the situation. To date, 68 different Type I cards have been found, 188 different Type II, and 69 Type III. Advanced collectors, however, speculate that more may exist. Type I cards are considered the rarest of the Coupon issues, and, because they were printed on a thinner stock, they are especially difficult to find in top condition. Although Type II cards are the most common, they were printed with a "glossy" coating, making them susceptible to cracking and creasing.

	NR MT	EX	VG
Complete Set:	10000.00	5000.00	3000.
Common Player:	75.00	37.00	22.00

		NR MT	EX	VG
(1)	Harry Bay	75.00	37.00	22.00
(2)	Beals Becker	75.00	37.00	22.00
(3)	Chief Bender	250.00	125.00	75.00
(4)	Bernhard	75.00	37.00	22.00
(5)	Ted Breitenstein	75.00	37.00	22.00
(6)	Bobby Byrne	75.00	37.00	22.00
(7)	Billy Campbell	75.00	37.00	22.00
(8)	Scoops Carey	250.00	125.00	75.00
(9)	Frank Chance	250.00	125.00	75.00
(10)	Chappy Charles	75.00	37.00	22.00
(11)	Hal Chase (portrait)	125.00	62.00	37.00
(12)	Hal Chase (throwing)	125.00	62.00	37.00
(13)	Ty Cobb	2000.00	1000.00	600.00
(14)	Bill Cranston	75.00	37.00	22.00
(15)	Birdie Cree	75.00	37.00	22.00
(16)	Wild Bill Donovan	75.00	37.00	22.00
(17)	Mickey Doolan	75.00	37.00	22.00
(18)	Jean Dubuc	75.00	37.00	22.00
(19)	Joe Dunn	75.00	37.00	22.00
(20)	Roy Ellam	75.00	37.00	22.00
(21)	Clyde Engle	75.00	37.00	22.00
(22)	Johnny Evers	250.00	125.00	75.00
(23)	Art Fletcher	75.00	37.00	22.00
(24)	Charlie Fritz	75.00	37.00	22.00
(25)	Ed Greminger	75.00	37.00	22.00
(26)	Bill Hart (Little Rock)	75.00	37.00	22.00
(27)	Jimmy Hart (Montgomery)	75.00	37.00	22.00
(28)	Topsy Hartsel	75.00	37.00	22.00
(29)	Gordon Hickman	75.00	37.00	22.00
(30)	Danny Hoffman	75.00	37.00	22.00
(31)	Harry Howell	75.00	37.00	22.00
(32)	Miller Huggins (hands at mouth)			
		250.00	125.00	75.00
(33)	Miller Huggins (portrait)	250.00	125.00	75.00
(34)	George Hunter	75.00	37.00	22.00
(35)	A.O. "Dutch" Jordan	75.00	37.00	22.00
(36)	Ed Killian	75.00	37.00	22.00
(37)	Otto Knabe	75.00	37.00	22.00
(38)	Frank LaPorte	75.00	37.00	22.00
(39)	Ed Lennox	75.00	37.00	22.00
(40)	Harry Lentz (Sentz)	75.00	37.00	22.00
(41)	Rube Marquard	250.00	125.00	75.00
(42)	Doc Marshall	75.00	37.00	22.00
(43)	Christy Mathewson	750.00	375.00	225.00
(44)	George McBride	75.00	37.00	22.00
(45)	Pryor McElveen	75.00	37.00	22.00
(46)	Matty McIntyre	75.00	37.00	22.00
(47)	Mike Mitchell	75.00	37.00	22.00
(48)	Carlton Molesworth	75.00	37.00	22.00
(49)	Mike Mowrey	75.00	37.00	22.00
(50)	Chief Myers (Meyers) (batting)	75.00	37.00	22.00
(51)	Chief Myers (Meyers) (fielding)	75.00	37.00	22.00
(52)	Dode Paskert	75.00	37.00	22.00
(53)	Hub Perdue	75.00	37.00	22.00

		NR MT	EX	VG
(54)	Arch Persons	75.00	37.00	22.00
(55)	Ed Reagan	75.00	37.00	22.00
(56)	Bob Rhoades (Rhoads)	75.00	37.00	22.00
(57)	Ike Rockenfeld	75.00	37.00	22.00
(58)	Claude Rossman	75.00	37.00	22.00
(59)	Boss Schmidt	75.00	37.00	22.00
(60)	Sid Smith	75.00	37.00	22.00
(61)	Charlie Starr	75.00	37.00	22.00
(62)	Gabby Street	75.00	37.00	22.00
(63)	Ed Summers	75.00	37.00	22.00
(64)	Jeff Sweeney	75.00	37.00	22.00
(65)	Ira Thomas	75.00	37.00	22.00
(66)	Woodie Thornton	75.00	37.00	22.00
(67)	Ed Willett	75.00	37.00	22.00
(68)	Owen Wilson	75.00	37.00	22.00

1914 T213 Coupon - Type 2

		NR MT	EX	VG
Complete Set:		14000.00	7000.00	4200.
Common Player:		65.00	32.00	19.50
(1a)	Red Ames (Cincinnati)	65.00	32.00	19.50
(1b)	Red Ames (St. Louis)	65.00	32.00	19.50
(2a)	Home Run Baker (Phila. Amer.)			
		150.00	75.00	45.00
(2b)	Home Run Baker (Philadelphia Amer.)			
		150.00	75.00	45.00
(2c)	Home Run Baker (New York)	150.00	75.00	45.00
(3)	Cy Barger	65.00	32.00	19.50
(4a)	Chief Bender (trees in background, Philadelphia Amer.)			
		150.00	75.00	45.00
(4b)	Chief Bender (trees in background, Baltimore)			
		150.00	75.00	45.00
(4c)	Chief Bender (trees in background, Philadelphia Nat.)			
		150.00	75.00	45.00
(5a)	Chief Bender (no trees in background, Philadelphia Amer.)			
		150.00	75.00	45.00
(5b)	Chief Bender (no trees in background, Baltimore)			
		150.00	75.00	45.00
(5c)	Chief Bender (no trees in background, Philadelphia Nat.)			
		150.00	75.00	45.00
(6)	Bill Bradley	65.00	32.00	19.50
(7a)	Roger Bresnahan (Chicago)	150.00	75.00	45.00
(7b)	Roger Bresnahan (Toledo)	150.00	75.00	45.00
(8a)	Al Bridwell (St. Louis)	65.00	32.00	19.50
(8b)	Al Bridwell (Nashville)	65.00	32.00	19.50
(9a)	Mordecai Brown (Chicago)	150.00	75.00	45.00
(9b)	Mordecai Brown (St. Louis)	150.00	75.00	45.00
(10)	Bobby Byrne	65.00	32.00	19.50
(11)	Howie Camnitz (arm at side)	65.00	32.00	19.50
(12a)	Howie Camnitz (Pittsburgh, hands above head)			
		65.00	32.00	19.50
(12b)	Howie Camnitz (Savannah, hands above head)			
		65.00	32.00	19.50
(13)	Billy Campbell	65.00	32.00	19.50
(14a)	Frank Chance (batting, New York)			
		85.00	42.00	25.00
(14b)	Frank Chance (Los Angeles, batting)			
		85.00	42.00	25.00
(15a)	Frank Chance (New York, portrait)			
		85.00	42.00	25.00
(15b)	Frank Chance (Los Angeles, portrait)			
		85.00	42.00	25.00
(16a)	Bill Chapelle (Brooklyn, "R" on shirt)			
		65.00	32.00	19.50
(16b)	Larry Chapelle (Chappel) (Cleveland, no "R" on shirt, photo actually Bill Chapelle)			
		65.00	32.00	19.50

	NR MT	EX	VG
(17a) Hal Chase (Chicago, holding trophy)			
	90.00	45.00	27.00
(17b) Hal Chase (Buffalo, holding trophy)			
	90.00	45.00	27.00
(18a) Hal Chase (Chicago, portrait, blue background)			
	90.00	45.00	27.00
(18b) Hal Chase (Buffalo, portrait, blue background)			
	90.00	45.00	27.00
(19a) Hal Chase (Chicago, throwing)	90.00	45.00	27.00
(19b) Hal Chase (Buffalo, throwing)	90.00	45.00	27.00
(20) Ty Cobb (portrait)	900.00	450.00	270.00
(21) Ty Cobb (with bat off shoulder)	900.00	450.00	270.00
(22a) Eddie Collins (Philadelphia, "A" on shirt)			
	150.00	75.00	45.00
(22b) Eddie Collins (Chicago, "A" on shirt)			
	150.00	75.00	45.00
(22c) Eddie Collins (Chicago, no "A" on shirt)			
	150.00	75.00	45.00
(23a) Doc Crandall (St. Louis Nat.)	65.00	32.00	19.50
(23b) Doc Crandall (St. Louis Fed.)	65.00	32.00	19.50
(24) Sam Crawford	150.00	75.00	45.00
(25) Birdie Cree	65.00	32.00	19.50
(26a) Harry Davis (Phila. Amer.)	65.00	32.00	19.50
(26b) Harry Davis (Philadelphia Amer.)			
	65.00	32.00	19.50
(27a) Ray Demmitt (New York)	65.00	32.00	19.50
27b Ray Demmitt (Chicago)	65.00	32.00	19.50
(28a) Josh Devore (Philadelphia)	65.00	32.00	19.50
(28b) Josh Devore (Chillicothe)	65.00	32.00	19.50
(29a) Mike Donlin (New York)	65.00	32.00	19.50
(29b) Mike Donlin (.300 batter 7 years)			
	65.00	32.00	19.50
(30) Wild Bill Donovan	65.00	32.00	19.50
(31a) Mickey Doolan (Baltimore, batting)			
	65.00	32.00	19.50
(31b) Mickey Doolan (Chicago, batting)			
	65.00	32.00	19.50
(32a) Mickey Doolan (Baltimore, fielding)			
	65.00	32.00	19.50
(32b) Mickey Doolan (Chicago, fielding)			
	65.00	32.00	19.50
(33) Tom Downey	65.00	32.00	19.50
(34) Larry Doyle (batting)	65.00	32.00	19.50
(35) Larry Doyle (portrait)	65.00	32.00	19.50
(36) Jean Dubuc	65.00	32.00	19.50
(37) Jack Dunn	65.00	32.00	19.50
(38a) Kid Elberfield (Elberfeld) (Brooklyn)			
	65.00	32.00	19.50
(38b) Kid Elberfield (Elberfeld) (Chatanooga)			
	65.00	32.00	19.50
(39) Steve Evans	65.00	32.00	19.50
(40) Johnny Evers	150.00	75.00	45.00
(41) Russ Ford	65.00	32.00	19.50
(42) Art Fromme	65.00	32.00	19.50
(43a) Chick Gandil (Washington)	80.00	40.00	24.00
(43b) Chick Gandil (Cleveland)	80.00	40.00	24.00
(44) Rube Geyer	65.00	32.00	19.50
(45) Clark Griffith	65.00	32.00	19.50
(46) Bob Groom	65.00	32.00	19.50
(47a) Buck Herzog ("B" on shirt)	65.00	32.00	19.50
(47b) Buck Herzog (no "B" on shirt)	65.00	32.00	19.50
(48a) Dick Hoblitzell (Cincinnati)	65.00	32.00	19.50
(48b) Dick Hoblitzell (Boston Nat.)	65.00	32.00	19.50
(48c) Dick Hoblitzell (Boston Amer.)	65.00	32.00	19.50
(49a) Solly Hofman (Chicago)	65.00	32.00	19.50
(49b) Solly Hofmann (Hofman)	65.00	32.00	19.50
(50) Miller Huggins (hands at mouth)			
	150.00	75.00	45.00
(51) Miller Huggins (portrait)	150.00	75.00	45.00
(52a) John Hummel (Brooklyn Nat.)	65.00	32.00	19.50
(52b) John Hummel (Brooklyn)	65.00	32.00	19.50
(53) Hughie Jennings (both hands showing)			
	150.00	75.00	45.00
(54) Hughie Jennings (one hand showing)			
	150.00	75.00	45.00
(55) Walter Johnson	900.00	450.00	270.00
(56a) Tim Jordan (Toronto)	65.00	32.00	19.50
(56b) Tim Jordan (Ft. Worth)	65.00	32.00	19.50
(57a) Joe Kelley (New York)	150.00	75.00	45.00
(57b) Joe Kelley (Toronto)	150.00	75.00	45.00
(58) Otto Knabe	65.00	32.00	19.50
(59a) Ed Konetchy (Pittsburgh Nat.)	65.00	32.00	19.50
(59b) Ed Konetchy (Pittsburgh Fed.)	65.00	32.00	19.50
(59c) Ed Konetchy (Boston)	65.00	32.00	19.50
(60) Harry Krause	65.00	32.00	19.50
(61a) Nap Lajoie (Phila. Amer.)	250.00	125.00	75.00
(61b) Nap Lajoie (Philadelphia Amer.)			
	250.00	125.00	75.00
(61c) Nap Lajoie (Cleveland)	250.00	125.00	75.00
(62a) Tommy Leach (Chicago)	65.00	32.00	19.50
(62b) Tommy Leach (Cincinnati)	65.00	32.00	19.50

	NR MT	EX	VG
(62c) Tommy Leach (Rochester)	65.00	32.00	19.50
(63) Ed Lennox	65.00	32.00	19.50
(64a) Sherry Magee (Phila. Nat.)	80.00	40.00	24.00
(64b) Sherry Magee (Philadelphia Nat.)			
	80.00	40.00	24.00
(64c) Sherry Magee (Boston)	80.00	40.00	24.00
(65a) Rube Marquard (New York, pitching, "NY" on shirt)			
	150.00	75.00	45.00
(65b) Rube Marquard (Brooklyn, pitching, no "NY" on shirt)			
	150.00	75.00	45.00
(66a) Rube Marquard (New York, portrait, "NY" on shirt)			
	150.00	75.00	45.00
(66b) Rube Marquard (Brooklyn, portrait, no "NY" on shirt)			
	150.00	75.00	45.00
(67) Christy Mathewson	900.00	450.00	270.00
(68) John McGraw (glove at side)	90.00	45.00	27.00
(69) John McGraw (portrait)	90.00	45.00	27.00
(70) Larry McLean	65.00	32.00	19.50
(71a) George McQuillan (Pittsburgh)	65.00	32.00	19.50
(71b) George McQuillan (Phila. Nat.)	65.00	32.00	19.50
(72c) George McQuillan (Philadelphia Nat.)			
	65.00	32.00	19.50
(73) Fred Merkle	80.00	40.00	24.00
(74a) Chief Meyers (New York, fielding)			
	65.00	32.00	19.50
(74b) Chief Meyers (Brooklyn, fielding)			
	65.00	32.00	19.50
(75a) Chief Meyers (New York, portrait)			
	65.00	32.00	19.50
(75b) Chief Meyers (Brooklyn, portrait)			
	65.00	32.00	19.50
(76) Dots Miller	65.00	32.00	19.50
(77) Mike Mitchell	65.00	32.00	19.50
(78a) Mike Mowrey (Pittsburgh Nat.)	65.00	32.00	19.50
(78b) Mike Mowrey (Pittsburgh Fed.)	65.00	32.00	19.50
(78c) Mike Mowrey (Brooklyn)	65.00	32.00	19.50
(79a) George Mullin (Indianapolis)	65.00	32.00	19.50
(79b) George Mullin (Newark)	65.00	32.00	19.50
(80) Danny Murphy	65.00	32.00	19.50
(81a) Red Murray (New York)	65.00	32.00	19.50
(81b) Red Murray (Chicago)	65.00	32.00	19.50
(81c) Red Murray (Kansas City)	65.00	32.00	19.50
(82) Tom Needham	65.00	32.00	19.50
(83) Rebel Oakes	65.00	32.00	19.50
(84a) Rube Oldring (Phila. Amer.)	65.00	32.00	19.50
(84b) Rube Oldring (Philadelphia Amer.)			
	65.00	32.00	19.50
(85a) Dode Paskert (Phila. Nat.)	65.00	32.00	19.50
(85b) Dode Paskert (Philadelphia Nat.)			
	65.00	32.00	19.50
(86) Billy Purtell	65.00	32.00	19.50
(87a) Jack Quinn (Baltimore)	65.00	32.00	19.50
(87b) Jack Quinn (Vernon)	65.00	32.00	19.50
(88a) Ed Reulbach (Brooklyn Nat.)	65.00	32.00	19.50
(88b) Ed Reulbach (Brooklyn Fed.)	65.00	32.00	19.50
(88c) Ed Reulbach (Pittsburgh)	65.00	32.00	19.50
(89a) Nap Rucker (Brooklyn)	65.00	32.00	19.50
(89b) Nap Rucker (Brooklyn Nat.)	65.00	32.00	19.50
(90) Dick Rudolph	65.00	32.00	19.50
(91a) Germany Schaefer (Washington, "W" on shirt)			
	65.00	32.00	19.50
(91b) Germany Schaefer (K.C. Fed., "W" on shirt)			
	65.00	32.00	19.50
(91c) Germany Schaefer (New York, no "W" on shirt)			
	65.00	32.00	19.50
(92) Admiral Schlei (batting)	65.00	32.00	19.50
(93) Admiral Schlei (portrait)	65.00	32.00	19.50
(94) Boss Schmidt	65.00	32.00	19.50
(95) Wildfire Schulte	65.00	32.00	19.50
(96) Frank Smith	65.00	32.00	19.50
(97) Tris Speaker	350.00	175.00	105.00
(98) George Stovall	65.00	32.00	19.50
(99) Gabby Street (catching)	65.00	32.00	19.50
(100) Gabby Street (portrait)	65.00	32.00	19.50
(101) Ed Summers	65.00	32.00	19.50
(102a) Bill Sweeney (Boston)	65.00	32.00	19.50
(102b) Bill Sweeney (Chicago)	65.00	32.00	19.50
(103a) Jeff Sweeney (New York)	65.00	32.00	19.50
(103b) Jeff Sweeney (Richmond)	65.00	32.00	19.50
(104a) Ira Thomas (Phila. Amer.)	65.00	32.00	19.50
(104b) Ira Thomas (Philadelphia Amer.)	65.00	32.00	19.50
(105a) Joe Tinker (Chicago Fed., bat off shoulder)			
	150.00	75.00	45.00
(105b) Joe Tinker (Chicago Nat., bat on shoulder)			
	150.00	75.00	45.00
(106a) Joe Tinker (Chicago Fed., bat off shoulder)			
	150.00	75.00	45.00
(106b) Joe Tinker (Chicago Nat., bat off shoulder)			
	150.00	75.00	45.00
(107) Heinie Wagner	65.00	32.00	19.50
(108a) Jack Warhop (New York, "NY" on shirt)			
	65.00	32.00	19.50

	NR MT	EX	VG
(108b)Jack Warhop (St. Louis, no "NY" om shirt)			
	65.00	32.00	19.50
(109a)Zach Wheat (Brooklyn)	150.00	75.00	45.00
(109b)Zach Wheat (Brooklyn Nat.)	150.00	75.00	45.00
(110) Kaiser Wilhelm	65.00	32.00	19.50
(111a)Ed Willett (St. Louis)	65.00	32.00	19.50
(111b)Ed Willett (Memphis)	65.00	32.00	19.50
(112) Owen Wilson	65.00	32.00	19.50
(113a)Hooks Wiltse (New York, pitching)			
	65.00	32.00	19.50
(113b)Hooks Wiltse (Brooklyn, pitching)			
	65.00	32.00	19.50
(113c)Hooks Wiltse (Jersey City, pitching)			
	65.00	32.00	19.50
(114a)Hooks Wiltse (New York, portrait)			
	65.00	32.00	19.50
(114b)Hooks Wiltse (Brooklyn, portrait)			
	65.00	32.00	19.50
(114c)Hooks Wiltse (Jersey City, portrait)			
	65.00	32.00	19.50
(115) Heinie Zimmerman	65.00	32.00	19.50

1919 T213 Coupon - Type 3

	NR MT	EX	VG
Complete Set:	13500.00	6750.00	4050.
Common Player:	100.00	50.00	30.00
(1) Red Ames	100.00	50.00	30.00
(2) Home Run Baker	225.00	112.00	67.00
(3) Chief Bender (no trees in background)			
	225.00	112.00	67.00
(4) Chief Bender (trees in background)			
	225.00	112.00	67.00
(5) Roger Bresnahan	225.00	112.00	67.00
(6) Al Bridwell	100.00	50.00	30.00
(7) Miner Brown	100.00	50.00	30.00
(8) Bobby Byrne	100.00	50.00	30.00
(9) Frank Chance (batting)	110.00	55.00	33.00
(10) Frank Chance (portrait)	110.00	55.00	33.00
(11) Hal Chase (holding trophy)	65.00	32.00	19.50
(12) Hal Chase (portrait)	65.00	32.00	19.50
(13) Hal Chase (throwing)	65.00	32.00	19.50
(14) Ty Cobb (batting)	2000.00	1000.00	600.00
(15) Ty Cobb (portrait)	2000.00	1000.00	600.00
(16) Eddie Collins	225.00	112.00	67.00
(17) Sam Crawford	225.00	112.00	67.00
(18) Harry Davis	100.00	50.00	30.00
(19) Mike Donlin	100.00	50.00	30.00
(20) Wild Bill Donovan	100.00	50.00	30.00
(21) Mickey Doolan (batting)	100.00	50.00	30.00
(22) Mickey Doolan (fielding)	100.00	50.00	30.00
(23) Larry Doyle (batting)	100.00	50.00	30.00
(24) Larry Doyle (portrait)	100.00	50.00	30.00
(25) Jean Dubuc	100.00	50.00	30.00
(26) Jack Dunn	100.00	50.00	30.00
(27) Kid Elberfeld	100.00	50.00	30.00
(28) Johnny Evers	225.00	112.00	67.00
(29) Chick Gandil	55.00	27.00	16.50
(30) Clark Griffith	100.00	50.00	30.00
(31) Buck Herzog	100.00	50.00	30.00
(32) Dick Hoblitzell	100.00	50.00	30.00
(33) Miller Huggins (hands at mouth)			
	225.00	112.00	67.00
(34) Miller Huggins (portrait)	225.00	112.00	67.00
(35) John Hummel	100.00	50.00	30.00
(36) Hughie Jennings (both hands showing)			
	225.00	112.00	67.00

	NR MT	EX	VG
(37) Hughie Jennings (one hand showing)			
	225.00	112.00	67.00
(38) Walter Johnson	800.00	400.00	240.00
(39) Tim Jordan	100.00	50.00	30.00
(40) Joe Kelley	225.00	112.00	67.00
(41) Ed Konetchy	100.00	50.00	30.00
(42) Larry Lajoie	225.00	112.00	67.00
(43) Sherry Magee	55.00	27.00	16.50
(44) Rube Marquard	225.00	112.00	67.00
(45) Christy Mathewson	800.00	400.00	240.00
(47) John McGraw (glove at side)	250.00	125.00	75.00
(48) John McGraw (portrait)	250.00	125.00	75.00
(49) George McQuillan	100.00	50.00	30.00
(50) Fred Merkle	55.00	27.00	16.50
(51) Dots Miller	100.00	50.00	30.00
(52) Mike Mowrey	100.00	50.00	30.00
(53) Chief Myers (Meyers) (Brooklyn)			
	100.00	50.00	30.00
(54) Chief Myers (Meyers) (New Haven)			
	100.00	50.00	30.00
(55) Dode Paskert	100.00	50.00	30.00
(56) Jack Quinn	100.00	50.00	30.00
(57) Ed Reulbach	100.00	50.00	30.00
(58) Nap Rucker	100.00	50.00	30.00
(59) Dick Rudolph	100.00	50.00	30.00
(60) Herman Schaeffer (Schaefer)	100.00	50.00	30.00
(61) Wildfire Schulte	100.00	50.00	30.00
(62) Tris Speaker	450.00	225.00	135.00
(63) Gabby Street (catching)	100.00	50.00	30.00
(64) Gabby Street (portrait)	100.00	50.00	30.00
(65) Jeff Sweeney	100.00	50.00	30.00
(66) Ira Thomas	100.00	50.00	30.00
(67) Joe Tinker	225.00	112.00	67.00
(68) Zach Wheat	225.00	112.00	67.00
(69) Geo. Wiltse	100.00	50.00	30.00
(70) Heinie Zimmerman	100.00	50.00	30.00

1915 T214 Victory

The T214 Victory set of 1915 is another obscure series of tobacco cards that is sometimes mistaken for the better-known T206 "White Border" set. The confusion is understandable because identical player poses were used for both sets. The Victory Tobacco set can be easily identified, however, by the advertising for the Victory brand on the back of the cards. The set features players from both the Federal League and the major leagues, and although the card backs advertise "90 Designs," only 30 different subjects have surfaced to date. The set had such limited distribution - apparently restricted to just the Louisiana area - and the cards are so rare that it may be virtually impossible to ever checklist the set completely. Except for the advertising on the backs, the Victory cards are almost identical to the "Type II" Coupon cards (T213), another obscure Louisiana tobacco set issued during the same period. Of the several tobacco sets issued in Louisiana in the early part of the 20th Century, the T214 Victory cards are considered the most difficult to find.

	NR MT	EX	VG
Complete Set:	12000.00	6000.00	3600.
Common Player:	325.00	162.00	97.00

		NR MT	EX	VG
(1)	Chief Bender	700.00	350.00	210.00
(2)	Roger Bresnahan	700.00	350.00	210.00
(3)	Howie Camnitz	325.00	162.00	97.00
(4)	Ty Cobb	3000.00	1500.00	900.00
(5)	Birdie Cree	325.00	162.00	97.00
(6)	Ray Demmitt	325.00	162.00	97.00
(7)	Mickey Doolan	325.00	162.00	97.00
(8)	Tom Downey	325.00	162.00	97.00
(9)	Kid Elberfeld	325.00	162.00	97.00
(10)	Russ Ford	325.00	162.00	97.00
(11)	Art Fromme	325.00	162.00	97.00
(12)	Rube Geyer	325.00	162.00	97.00
(13)	Clark Griffith	700.00	350.00	210.00
(14)	Bob Groom	325.00	162.00	97.00
(15)	Walter Johnson	1500.00	750.00	450.00
(16)	Ed Konetchy	325.00	162.00	97.00
(17)	Nap Lajoie	1000.00	500.00	300.00
(18)	Ed Lennox	325.00	162.00	97.00
(19)	Sherry Magee	325.00	162.00	97.00
(20)	Chief Meyers	325.00	162.00	97.00
(21)	George Mullin	325.00	162.00	97.00
(22)	Tom Needham	325.00	162.00	97.00
(23)	Rebel Oakes	325.00	162.00	97.00
(24)	Jack Quinn	325.00	162.00	97.00
(25)	Wildfire Schulte	325.00	162.00	97.00
(26)	Jeff Sweeney	325.00	162.00	97.00
(27)	Joe Tinker	700.00	350.00	210.00
(28)	Heinie Wagner	325.00	162.00	97.00
(29)	Zack Wheat	700.00	350.00	210.00
(30)	Hooks Wiltse	325.00	162.00	97.00

1910 T215 Red Cross - Type 1

The T215 set issued by Red Cross Tobacco is another of the Louisana area sets closely related to the popular T206 "White Border" tobacco cards. Very similar to the T213 Coupon cards, the Red Cross Tobacco cards are found in two distinct types, both featuring color player lithographs and measuring approximately 1-1/2" by 2-5/8", the standard tobacco card size. Type I Red Cross cards, issued from 1910 to 1912, have brown captions; while Type II cards, most of which appear to be from 1912, have blue printing. The backs of both types are identical, displaying the Red Cross name and emblem which can be used to positively identify the set and differentiate it from the other Louisana sets of the same period. Numerous variations have been found, most of them involving caption changes.

		NR MT	EX	VG
Complete Set:		10000.00	5000.00	3000.
Common Player:		125.00	62.00	37.00
(1)	Red Ames	125.00	62.00	37.00
(2)	Home Run Baker	700.00	350.00	210.00
(3)	Neal Ball	125.00	62.00	37.00
(4)	Chief Bender (no trees in background)			
		700.00	350.00	210.00
(5)	Chief Bender (trees in background)			
		700.00	350.00	210.00
(6)	Al Bridwell	125.00	62.00	37.00
(7)	Bobby Byrne	125.00	62.00	37.00
(8)	Howie Camnitz	125.00	62.00	37.00
(9)	Frank Chance	700.00	350.00	210.00
(10)	Hal Chase	125.00	62.00	37.00
(11)	Ty Cobb	2000.00	1000.00	600.00
(12)	Eddie Collins	700.00	350.00	210.00

		NR MT	EX	VG
(13)	Wid Conroy	125.00	62.00	37.00
(14)	Doc Crandall	125.00	62.00	37.00
(15)	Sam Crawford	700.00	350.00	210.00
(16)	Birdie Cree	125.00	62.00	37.00
(17)	Harry Davis	125.00	62.00	37.00
(18)	Josh Devore	125.00	62.00	37.00
(19)	Mike Donlin	125.00	62.00	37.00
(20)	Mickey Doolan	125.00	62.00	37.00
(21)	Patsy Dougherty	125.00	62.00	37.00
(22)	Larry Doyle (batting)	125.00	62.00	37.00
(23)	Larry Doyle (portrait)	125.00	62.00	37.00
(24)	Kid Elberfeld	125.00	62.00	37.00
(25)	Russ Ford	125.00	62.00	37.00
(26)	Art Fromme	125.00	62.00	37.00
(27)	Clark Griffith	700.00	350.00	210.00
(28)	Topsy Hartsel	125.00	62.00	37.00
(29)	Dick Hoblitzell	125.00	62.00	37.00
(30)	Solly Hofman	125.00	62.00	37.00
(31)	Del Howard	125.00	62.00	37.00
(32)	Miller Huggins	700.00	350.00	210.00
(33)	John Hummel	125.00	62.00	37.00
(34)	Hughie Jennings (both hands showing)			
		700.00	350.00	210.00
(35)	Hughie Jennings (one hand showing)			
		700.00	350.00	210.00
(36)	Walter Johnson	800.00	400.00	240.00
(37)	Ed Konetchy	125.00	62.00	37.00
(38)	Harry Krause	125.00	62.00	37.00
(39)	Nap Lajoie	700.00	350.00	210.00
(40)	Arlie Latham	125.00	62.00	37.00
(41)	Tommy Leach	125.00	62.00	37.00
(42)	Lefty Leifield	125.00	62.00	37.00
(43)	Harry Lord	125.00	62.00	37.00
(44)	Sherry Magee	125.00	62.00	37.00
(45)	Rube Marquard (pitching)	700.00	350.00	210.00
(46)	Rube Marquard (portrait)	700.00	350.00	210.00
(47)	Christy Mathewson (dark cap)	800.00	400.00	240.00
(48)	Christy Mathewson (white cap)	800.00	400.00	240.00
(49)	Joe McGinnity	700.00	350.00	210.00
(50)	John McGraw (glove at hip)	500.00	250.00	150.00
(51)	John McGraw (portrait)	500.00	250.00	150.00
(52)	Harry McIntyre	125.00	62.00	37.00
(53)	Fred Merkle	125.00	62.00	37.00
(54)	Chief Meyers	125.00	62.00	37.00
(55)	Dots Miller	125.00	62.00	37.00
(56)	Danny Murphy	125.00	62.00	37.00
(57)	Red Murray	125.00	62.00	37.00
(58)	Rebel Oakes	125.00	62.00	37.00
(59)	Charley O'Leary	125.00	62.00	37.00
(60)	Dode Paskert	125.00	62.00	37.00
(61)	Barney Pelty	125.00	62.00	37.00
(62)	Jack Quinn	125.00	62.00	37.00
(63)	Ed Reulbach	125.00	62.00	37.00
(64)	Nap Rucker	125.00	62.00	37.00
(65)	Germany Schaefer	125.00	62.00	37.00
(66)	Wildfire Schulte	125.00	62.00	37.00
(67)	Jimmy Sheckard	125.00	62.00	37.00
(68a)	Frank Smith	125.00	62.00	37.00
(68b)	Frank Smither (Smith)	125.00	62.00	37.00
(69)	Tris Speaker	650.00	325.00	195.00
(70)	Jake Stahl	125.00	62.00	37.00
(71)	Harry Steinfeldt	125.00	62.00	37.00
(72)	Gabby Street (catching)	125.00	62.00	37.00
(73)	Gabby Street (portrait)	125.00	62.00	37.00
(74)	Jeff Sweeney	125.00	62.00	37.00
(75)	Lee Tannehill	125.00	62.00	37.00
(76)	Joe Tinker (bat off shoulder)	700.00	350.00	210.00
(77)	Joe Tinker (bat on shoulder)	700.00	350.00	210.00
(78)	Heinie Wagner	125.00	62.00	37.00
(79)	Jack Warhop	125.00	62.00	37.00
(80)	Zach Wheat	700.00	350.00	210.00
(81)	Doc White	125.00	62.00	37.00
(82)	Ed Willetts (Willett)	125.00	62.00	37.00
(83)	Owen Wilson	125.00	62.00	37.00
(84)	Hooks Wiltse (pitching)	125.00	62.00	37.00
(85)	Hooks Wiltse (portrait)	125.00	62.00	37.00
(86)	Cy Young	700.00	350.00	210.00

1912 T215 Red Cross - Type 2

		NR MT	EX	VG
Complete Set:		15000.00	7500.00	4500.
Common Player:		125.00	62.00	37.00
(1)	Red Ames	125.00	62.00	37.00
(2)	Chief Bender (no trees in background)			
		400.00	200.00	120.00

		NR MT	EX	VG
(70)	Ed Summers	125.00	62.00	37.00
(71)	Jeff Sweeney	125.00	62.00	37.00
(72)	Joe Tinker	325.00	162.00	97.00
(73)	Heinie Wagner	125.00	62.00	37.00
(74)	Jack Warhop	125.00	62.00	37.00
(75)	Doc White	125.00	62.00	37.00
(76)	Hooks Wiltse (pitching)	125.00	62.00	37.00
(77)	Hooks Wiltse (portrait)	125.00	62.00	37.00

1912 T215 Pirate

This set can be considerd a British version of the Red Cross set. Distributed by Pirate brand cigarettes of Bristol and London, England, the fronts of the cards are identical to the Type I Red Cross cards, but the green backs carry advertising for Pirate Cigarettes. It is believed that the Pirate cards were printed for distribution to U.S. servicemen in the South Seas. They are very rare in both England and the United States.

		NR MT	EX	VG
Complete Set:		14000.00	7000.00	4200.
Common Player:		100.00	50.00	30.00
(1)	Red Ames	100.00	50.00	30.00
(2)	Home Run Baker	300.00	150.00	90.00
(3)	Neal Ball	100.00	50.00	30.00
(4)	Chief Bender	300.00	150.00	90.00
(5)	Al Bridwell	100.00	50.00	30.00
(6)	Bobby Byrne	100.00	50.00	30.00
(7)	Howie Camnitz	100.00	50.00	30.00
(8)	Frank Chance	325.00	162.00	97.00
(9)	Hal Chase	100.00	50.00	30.00
(10)	Eddie Collins	325.00	162.00	97.00
(11)	Doc Crandall	100.00	50.00	30.00
(12)	Sam Crawford	300.00	150.00	90.00
(13)	Birdie Cree	100.00	50.00	30.00
(14)	Harry Davis	100.00	50.00	30.00
(15)	Josh Devore	100.00	50.00	30.00
(16)	Mike Donlin	100.00	50.00	30.00
(17)	Mickey Doolan (batting)	100.00	50.00	30.00
(18)	Mickey Doolan (fielding)	100.00	50.00	30.00
(19)	Patsy Dougherty	100.00	50.00	30.00
(20)	Larry Doyle (batting)	100.00	50.00	30.00
(21)	Larry Doyle (portrait)	100.00	50.00	30.00
(22)	Jean Dubuc	100.00	50.00	30.00
(23)	Kid Elberfeld	100.00	50.00	30.00
(24)	Steve Evans	100.00	50.00	30.00
(25)	Johnny Evers	300.00	150.00	90.00
(26)	Russ Ford	100.00	50.00	30.00
(27)	Art Fromme	100.00	50.00	30.00
(28)	Clark Griffith	300.00	150.00	90.00
(29)	Bob Groom	100.00	50.00	30.00
(30)	Topsy Hartsel	100.00	50.00	30.00
(31)	Buck Herzog	100.00	50.00	30.00
(32)	Dick Hoblitzell	100.00	50.00	30.00
(33)	Solly Hofman	100.00	50.00	30.00
(34)	Del Howard	100.00	50.00	30.00
(35)	Miller Huggins (hands at mouth)			
		300.00	150.00	90.00
(36)	Miller Huggins (portrait)	300.00	150.00	90.00
(37)	John Hummel	100.00	50.00	30.00
(38)	Hughie Jennings (both hands showing)			
		300.00	150.00	90.00
(39)	Hughie Jennings (one hand showing)			
		300.00	150.00	90.00
(40)	Walter Johnson	500.00	250.00	150.00

		NR MT	EX	VG
(3)	Chief Bender (trees in background)			
		400.00	200.00	120.00
(4)	Roger Bresnahan	325.00	162.00	97.00
(5)	Mordecai Brown	325.00	162.00	97.00
(6)	Bobby Byrne	125.00	62.00	37.00
(7)	Howie Camnitz	125.00	62.00	37.00
(8)	Frank Chance	325.00	162.00	97.00
(9)	Ty Cobb	2000.00	1000.00	600.00
(10)	Eddie Collins	325.00	162.00	97.00
(11)	Doc Crandall	125.00	62.00	37.00
(12)	Birdie Cree	125.00	62.00	37.00
(13)	Harry Davis	125.00	62.00	37.00
(14)	Josh Devore	125.00	62.00	37.00
(15)	Mike Donlin	125.00	62.00	37.00
(16)	Mickey Doolan (batting)	125.00	62.00	37.00
(17)	Mickey Doolan (fielding)	125.00	62.00	37.00
(18)	Patsy Dougherty	125.00	62.00	37.00
(19)	Larry Doyle (batting)	125.00	62.00	37.00
(20)	Larry Doyle (portrait)	125.00	62.00	37.00
(21)	Jean Dubuc	125.00	62.00	37.00
(22)	Kid Elberfeld	125.00	62.00	37.00
(23)	Johnny Evers	325.00	162.00	97.00
(24)	Russ Ford	125.00	62.00	37.00
(25)	Art Fromme	125.00	62.00	37.00
(26)	Clark Griffith	325.00	162.00	97.00
(27)	Bob Groom	125.00	62.00	37.00
(28)	Topsy Hartsel	125.00	62.00	37.00
(29)	Buck Herzog	125.00	62.00	37.00
(30)	Dick Hoblitzell	125.00	62.00	37.00
(31)	Solly Hofman	125.00	62.00	37.00
(32)	Miller Huggins (hands at mouth)			
		325.00	162.00	97.00
(33)	Miller Huggins (portrait)	325.00	162.00	97.00
(34)	John Hummel	125.00	62.00	37.00
(35)	Hughie Jennings	325.00	162.00	97.00
(36)	Walter Johnson	800.00	400.00	240.00
(37)	Joe Kelley	325.00	162.00	97.00
(38)	Ed Konetchy	125.00	62.00	37.00
(39)	Harry Krause	125.00	62.00	37.00
(40)	Nap Lajoie	225.00	112.00	67.00
(41)	Joe Lake	125.00	62.00	37.00
(42)	Tommy Leach	125.00	62.00	37.00
(43)	Lefty Leifield	125.00	62.00	37.00
(44)	Harry Lord	125.00	62.00	37.00
(45)	Rube Marquard	325.00	162.00	97.00
(46)	Christy Mathewson	800.00	400.00	240.00
(47)	John McGraw (glove at side)	350.00	175.00	105.00
(48)	John McGraw (portrait)	350.00	175.00	105.00
(49)	Larry McLean	125.00	62.00	37.00
(50)	Dots Miller	125.00	62.00	37.00
(51)	Mike Mitchell	125.00	62.00	37.00
(52)	Mike Mowrey	125.00	62.00	37.00
(53)	George Mullin	125.00	62.00	37.00
(54)	Danny Murphy	125.00	62.00	37.00
(55)	Red Murray	125.00	62.00	37.00
(56)	Rebel Oakes	125.00	62.00	37.00
(57)	Rube Oldring	125.00	62.00	37.00
(58)	Charley O'Leary	125.00	62.00	37.00
(59)	Dode Paskert	125.00	62.00	37.00
(60)	Barney Pelty	125.00	62.00	37.00
(61)	Billy Purtell	125.00	62.00	37.00
(62)	Ed Reulbach	125.00	62.00	37.00
(63)	Nap Rucker	125.00	62.00	37.00
(64a)	Germany Schaefer (Chicago)	125.00	62.00	37.00
(64b)	Germany Schaefer (Washington)			
		125.00	62.00	37.00
(65)	Wildfire Schulte	125.00	62.00	37.00
(66a)	Frank Smith	125.00	62.00	37.00
(66b)	Frank Smither (Smith)	125.00	62.00	37.00
(67)	Tris Speaker	600.00	300.00	175.00
(68)	Jake Stahl	125.00	62.00	37.00
(69)	Harry Steinfeldt	150.00	75.00	45.00

		NR MT	EX	VG
(41)	Joe Kelley	300.00	150.00	90.00
(42)	Ed Konetchy	100.00	50.00	30.00
(43)	Harry Krause	100.00	50.00	30.00
(44)	Nap Lajoie	400.00	200.00	120.00
(45)	Joe Lake	100.00	50.00	30.00
(46)	Lefty Leifield	100.00	50.00	30.00
(47)	Harry Lord	100.00	50.00	30.00
(48)	Sherry Magee	100.00	50.00	30.00
(49)	Rube Marquard (pitching)	300.00	150.00	90.00
(50)	Rube Marquard (portrait)	300.00	150.00	90.00
(51)	Joe McGinnity	300.00	150.00	90.00
(52)	John McGraw (glove at side)	300.00	150.00	90.00
(53)	John McGraw (portrait)	300.00	150.00	90.00
(54)	Harry McIntyre (Chicago)	100.00	50.00	30.00
(55)	Harry McIntyre (Brooklyn & Chicago)	100.00	50.00	30.00
(56)	Larry McLean	100.00	50.00	30.00
(57)	Fred Merkle	100.00	50.00	30.00
(58)	Chief Meyers	100.00	50.00	30.00
(59)	Mike Mitchell	100.00	50.00	30.00
(60)	Mike Mowrey	100.00	50.00	30.00
(61)	George Mullin	100.00	50.00	30.00
(62)	Danny Murphy	100.00	50.00	30.00
(63)	Red Murray	100.00	50.00	30.00
(64)	Rebel Oakes	100.00	50.00	30.00
(65)	Rube Oldring	100.00	50.00	30.00
(66)	Charley O'Leary	100.00	50.00	30.00
(67)	Dode Paskert	100.00	50.00	30.00
(68)	Barney Pelty	100.00	50.00	30.00
(69)	Billy Purtell	100.00	50.00	30.00
(70)	Jack Quinn	100.00	50.00	30.00
(71)	Ed Reulbach	100.00	50.00	30.00
(72)	Nap Rucker	100.00	50.00	30.00
(73)	Germany Schaefer	100.00	50.00	30.00
(74)	Wildfire Schulte	100.00	50.00	30.00
(75)	Jimmy Sheckard	100.00	50.00	30.00
(76)	Frank Smith	100.00	50.00	30.00
(77)	Tris Speaker	375.00	187.00	112.00
(78)	Jake Stahl	100.00	50.00	30.00
(79)	Harry Steinfeldt	100.00	50.00	30.00
(80)	Gabby Street	100.00	50.00	30.00
(81)	Ed Summers	100.00	50.00	30.00
(82)	Jeff Sweeney	100.00	50.00	30.00
(83)	Lee Tannehill	100.00	50.00	30.00
(84)	Ira Thomas	100.00	50.00	30.00
(85)	Joe Tinker	300.00	150.00	90.00
(86)	Heinie Wagner	100.00	50.00	30.00
(87)	Jack Warhop	100.00	50.00	30.00
(88)	Zack Wheat (Brooklyn)	300.00	150.00	90.00
(89)	Ed Willetts (Willett)	100.00	50.00	30.00
(90)	Owen Wilson	100.00	50.00	30.00
(91)	Hooks Wiltse (pitching)	100.00	50.00	30.00
(92)	Hooks Wiltse (portrait)	100.00	50.00	30.00

1914 T216 Kotton

Booth, c. Phila. Nat.

KOTTON
CIGARETTES

NEVER GO OUT.

EXTRA MILD

NOT IN A TRUST

PEOPLES TOBACCO CO. Ltd.
Factory No. 4. District of La
NEW ORLEANS, LA

The T216 baseball card set, issued by several brands of the Peoples Tobacco Co., is the last of the Louisana area tobacco sets and the most confusing. Apparently issued over a period of several years between 1911 and 1916, the set emplys the same pictures in the E90-1 and E92 caramel card sets and is also closely related to the E106 American Caramal and D303 General Baking sets. Exact identification of cards from this era is often complicated by the fact that it was common for the same picture to be used in several different sets. Positive identification can usually be determined by the backs of the cards. The

Peoples Tobacco cards carry advertising for one of three brands of cigarettes: Kotton, Mino or Virginia Extra. The Kotton brand are the most common, while the Virginia Extra and Mino backs command a 50-100" premium. T216 cards are found in two types; one has a glossy card stock, while a second scarcer type is printed on a thin paper. The thin paper cards command an additional 15" premium. There are 73 poses known to exist plus 29 variations, mostly involving caption changes. The cards represent players from both major leagues and the Federal League. Of the 73 poses identified, 23 were taken from the E90-1 set, 38 originated in the E92 set and a dozen appeared in both of the earlier caramel sets.

		NR MT	EX	VG
Complete Set:		18000.00	9000.00	5400.
Common Player:		100.00	50.00	30.00
(1)	Jack Barry (batting)	100.00	50.00	30.00
(2)	Jack Barry (fielding)	100.00	50.00	30.00
(3)	Harry Bemis	100.00	50.00	30.00
(4a)	Chief Bender (Philadelphia, striped cap)	250.00	125.00	75.00
(4b)	Chief Bender (Baltimore, striped cap)	250.00	125.00	75.00
(5a)	Chief Bender (Philadelphia, white cap)	250.00	125.00	75.00
(5b)	Chief Bender (Baltimore, white cap)	250.00	125.00	75.00
(6)	Bill Bergen	100.00	50.00	30.00
(7a)	Bob Bescher (Cincinnati)	100.00	50.00	30.00
(7b)	Bob Bescher (St. Louis)	100.00	50.00	30.00
(8)	Roger Bresnahan	250.00	125.00	75.00
(9)	Al Bridwell (batting)	100.00	50.00	30.00
(10a)	Al Bridwell (New York, sliding)	100.00	50.00	30.00
(10b)	Al Bridwell (St. Louis, sliding)	100.00	50.00	30.00
(11)	Donie Bush	100.00	50.00	30.00
(12)	Doc Casey	100.00	50.00	30.00
(13)	Frank Chance	250.00	125.00	75.00
(14a)	Hal Chase (New York, fielding)	65.00	32.00	19.50
(14b)	Hal Chase (Buffalo, fielding)	65.00	32.00	19.50
(15)	Hal Chase (portrait)	65.00	32.00	19.50
(16a)	Ty Cobb (Detroit Am., standing)	2000.00	1000.00	600.00
(16b)	Ty Cobb (Detroit Americans, standing)	2000.00	1000.00	600.00
(17)	"Ty" Cobb (batting)	2000.00	1000.00	600.00
(18a)	Eddie Collins (Phila. Am.)	250.00	125.00	75.00
(18b)	Eddie Collins (Phila. Amer.)	250.00	125.00	75.00
(19)	Eddie Collins (Chicago)	250.00	125.00	75.00
(20)	Sam Crawford	250.00	125.00	75.00
(21)	Harry Davis	100.00	50.00	30.00
(22)	Ray Demmitt	100.00	50.00	30.00
(23a)	Wild Bill Donovan (Detroit)	100.00	50.00	30.00
(23b)	Wild Bill Donovan (New York)	100.00	50.00	30.00
(24a)	Red Dooin (Philadelphia)	100.00	50.00	30.00
(24b)	Red Dooin (Cincinnati)	100.00	50.00	30.00
(25a)	Mickey Doolan (Philadelphia)	100.00	50.00	30.00
(25b)	Mickey Doolan (Baltimore)	100.00	50.00	30.00
(26)	Patsy Dougherty	100.00	50.00	30.00
(27a)	Larry Doyle, Larry Doyle (New York Nat'l, batting)	100.00	50.00	30.00
(28)	Larry Doyle (throwing)	100.00	50.00	30.00
(29)	Clyde Engle	100.00	50.00	30.00
(30a)	Johnny Evers (Chicago)	250.00	125.00	75.00
(30b)	Johnny Evers (Boston)	250.00	125.00	75.00
(31)	Art Fromme	100.00	50.00	30.00
(32a)	George Gibson (Pittsburg Nat'l, back view)	100.00	50.00	30.00
(32b)	George Gibson (Pittsburgh Nat'l., back view)	100.00	50.00	30.00
(33a)	George Gibson (Pittsburg Nat'l, front view)	100.00	50.00	30.00
(33b)	George Gibson (Pittsburgh Nat'l., front view)	100.00	50.00	30.00
(34a)	Topsy Hartsel (Phila. Am.)	100.00	50.00	30.00
(34b)	Topsy Hartsel (Phila. Amer.)	100.00	50.00	30.00
(35)	Roy Hartzell (batting)	100.00	50.00	30.00
(36)	Roy Hartzell (catching)	100.00	50.00	30.00
(37a)	Fred Jacklitsch (Philadelphia)	100.00	50.00	30.00
(37b)	Fred Jacklitsch (Baltimore)	100.00	50.00	30.00
(38a)	Hughie Jennings (orange background)	250.00	125.00	75.00
(38b)	Hughie Jennings (red background)	250.00	125.00	75.00
(39)	Red Kleinow	100.00	50.00	30.00
(40a)	Otto Knabe (Philadelphia)	100.00	50.00	30.00

		NR MT	EX	VG
(40b)	Otto Knabe (Baltimore)	100.00	50.00	30.00
(41)	Jack Knight	100.00	50.00	30.00
(42a)	Nap Lajoie (Philadelphia, fielding)			
		400.00	200.00	120.00
(42b)	Nap Lajoie (Cleveland, fielding)	400.00	200.00	120.00
(43)	Nap Lajoie (portrait)	400.00	200.00	120.00
(44a)	Hans Lobert (Cincinnati)	100.00	50.00	30.00
(44b)	Hans Lobert (New York)	100.00	50.00	30.00
(45)	Sherry Magee	55.00	27.00	16.50
(46)	Rube Marquard	250.00	125.00	75.00
(47a)	Christy Matthewson (Mathewson) (large print)			
		600.00	300.00	180.00
(47b)	Christy Matthewson (Mathewson) (small print)			
		600.00	300.00	180.00
(48a)	John McGraw (large print)	90.00	45.00	27.00
(48b)	John McGraw (small print)	90.00	45.00	27.00
(49)	Larry McLean	100.00	50.00	30.00
(50)	George McQuillan	100.00	50.00	30.00
(51)	Dots Miller (batting)	100.00	50.00	30.00
(52a)	Dots Miller (Pittsburg, fielding)	100.00	50.00	30.00
(52b)	Dots Miller (St. Louis, fielding)	100.00	50.00	30.00
(53a)	Danny Murphy (Philadelphia)	100.00	50.00	30.00
(53b)	Danny Murphy (Brooklyn)	100.00	50.00	30.00
(54)	Rebel Oakes	100.00	50.00	30.00
(55)	Bill O'Hara	100.00	50.00	30.00
(56)	Eddie Plank	250.00	125.00	75.00
(57a)	Germany Schaefer (Washington)			
		100.00	50.00	30.00
(57b)	Germany Schaefer (Newark)	100.00	50.00	30.00
(58)	Admiral Schlei	100.00	50.00	30.00
(59)	Boss Schmidt	100.00	50.00	30.00
(60)	Johnny Seigle	100.00	50.00	30.00
(61)	Dave Shean	100.00	50.00	30.00
(62)	Boss Smith (Schmidt)	100.00	50.00	30.00
(63)	Tris Speaker	500.00	250.00	150.00
(64)	Oscar Stanage	100.00	50.00	30.00
(65)	George Stovall	100.00	50.00	30.00
(66)	Jeff Sweeney	100.00	50.00	30.00
(67a)	Joe Tinker (Chicago Nat'l, batting)			
		250.00	125.00	75.00
(67b)	Joe Tinker (Chicago Feds, batting)			
		250.00	125.00	75.00
(68)	Joe Tinker (portrait)	250.00	125.00	75.00
(69a)	Honus Wagner (batting, S.S.)	1000.00	500.00	300.00
(69b)	Honus Wagner (batting, 2b.)	1000.00	500.00	300.00
(70a)	Honus Wagner (throwing, S.S.)	1000.00	500.00	300.00
(70b)	Honus Wagner (throwing, 2b.)	1000.00	500.00	300.00
(71)	Hooks Wiltse	100.00	50.00	30.00
(72)	Cy Young	225.00	112.00	67.00
(73a)	Heinie Zimmerman (2b.)	100.00	50.00	30.00
(73b)	Heinie Zimmerman (3b.)	100.00	50.00	30.00

1911 T217 Mono

W. Delhi, L. A.

As was common with many tobacco issues of the period, the T217 set - distributed on the West Coast by Mono Cigarettes - feature both baseball players and "Leading Actresses." The 23 baseball players in the Mono set are all from the Pacific Coast League. Two of the players (Delhi and Hughie Smith) are shown in two poses, resulting in a total of 25 different cards. The players are pictured in black and white photos on a card that measures approximately 1-1/2" by 2-5/8"m the standard size of a tobacco card. The player's name and team appear at the bottom, while the back of the card carries an advertisement for Mono Cigarettes. The Mono set, which can be dated to the 1909-1911 period, is among the rarest of all tobacco cards.

		NR MT	EX	VG
Complete Set:		6250.00	3125.00	1875.
Common Player:		225.00	112.00	67.00
(1)	Aiken	225.00	112.00	67.00
(2)	Curtis Bernard	225.00	112.00	67.00
(3)	L. Burrell	225.00	112.00	67.00
(4)	Chadbourn	225.00	112.00	67.00
(5)	R. Couchman	225.00	112.00	67.00
(6)	Elmer Criger	225.00	112.00	67.00
(7)	Pete Daley	225.00	112.00	67.00
(8)	W. Delhi (glove at chest level)	225.00	112.00	67.00
(9)	W. Delhi (glove at shoulder level)			
		225.00	112.00	67.00
(10)	Bert Delmas	225.00	112.00	67.00
(11)	Ivan Howard	225.00	112.00	67.00
(12)	Kitty Knight	225.00	112.00	67.00
(13)	Gene Knapp (Krapp)	225.00	112.00	67.00
(14)	Metzger	225.00	112.00	67.00
(15)	Carl Mitze	225.00	112.00	67.00
(16)	J. O'Rourke	225.00	112.00	67.00
(17)	R. Peckinpaugh	250.00	125.00	75.00
(18)	Walter Schmidt	225.00	112.00	67.00
(19)	Hughie Smith (batting)	225.00	112.00	67.00
(20)	Hughie Smith (fielding)	225.00	112.00	67.00
(21)	Wm. Stein	225.00	112.00	67.00
(22)	Elmer Thorsen	225.00	112.00	67.00
(23)	Oscar Vitt	225.00	112.00	67.00
(24)	Clyde Wares	225.00	112.00	67.00
(25)	Geo. Wheeler	225.00	112.00	67.00

1914 T222 Fatima

Unlike the typical 20th Century tobacco card issues, the T222 Fatima cards were glossy photographs on a thin paper stock and measure a larger 2-1/2" by 4-1/2". According to the back of the card, the set includes "100 photographs of famous Baseball Players, American Athletic Champions and Photoplay stars," but apparently not all were issued. The baseball portion of the set appears to be complete at 52, while only four other athletes and four "photoplay" stars have been found. The set, issued in 1913, includes players from 13 of the 16 major league teams (all except the Red Sox, White Sox and Pirates.) The set features a mix of star and lesser-known players.

		NR MT	EX	VG
Complete Set:		15000.00	7500.00	4500.
Common Player:		150.00	75.00	45.00
(1)	Grover Alexander	600.00	300.00	175.00
(2)	Jimmy Archer	150.00	75.00	45.00
(3)	Jimmy Austin	200.00	100.00	60.00
(4)	Jack Barry	150.00	75.00	45.00
(5)	George Baumgardner	150.00	75.00	45.00
(6)	Rube Benton	150.00	75.00	45.00
(7)	Roger Bresnahan	400.00	200.00	120.00
(8)	Boardwalk Brown	150.00	75.00	45.00
(9)	George Burns	150.00	75.00	45.00
(10)	Bullet Joe Bush	160.00	80.00	48.00
(11)	George Chalmers	150.00	75.00	45.00
(12)	Frank Chance	450.00	225.00	135.00
(13)	Al Demaree	150.00	75.00	45.00

		NR MT	EX	VG
(14)	Art Fletcher	150.00	75.00	45.00
(15)	Earl Hamilton	150.00	75.00	45.00
(16)	John Henry	150.00	75.00	45.00
(17)	Byron Houck	150.00	75.00	45.00
(18)	Miller Huggins	400.00	200.00	120.00
(19)	Hughie Jennings	400.00	200.00	120.00
(20)	Walter Johnson	1500.00	750.00	450.00
(21)	Ray Keating	150.00	75.00	45.00
(22)	Jack Lapp	150.00	75.00	45.00
(23)	Tommy Leach	150.00	75.00	45.00
(24)	Nemo Leibold	150.00	75.00	45.00
(25)	Jack Lelivelt	200.00	100.00	60.00
(26)	Hans Lobert	150.00	75.00	45.00
(27)	Lee Magee	150.00	75.00	45.00
(28)	Sherry Magee	160.00	80.00	48.00
(29)	Fritz Maisel	150.00	75.00	45.00
(30)	Rube Marquard	400.00	200.00	120.00
(31)	George McBride	150.00	75.00	45.00
(32)	Larry McLean	150.00	75.00	45.00
(33)	Stuffy McInnis	150.00	75.00	45.00
(34)	Ray Morgan	150.00	75.00	45.00
(35)	Eddie Murphy	150.00	75.00	45.00
(36)	Red Murray	150.00	75.00	45.00
(37)	Rube Oldring	150.00	75.00	45.00
(38)	Bill Orr	150.00	75.00	45.00
(39)	Hub Perdue	150.00	75.00	45.00
(40)	Art Phelan	150.00	75.00	45.00
(41)	Ed Reulbach	150.00	75.00	45.00
(42)	Vic Saier	150.00	75.00	45.00
(43)	Slim Sallee	150.00	75.00	45.00
(44)	Wally Schang	150.00	75.00	45.00
(45)	Wildfire Schulte	150.00	75.00	45.00
(46)	J.C. "Red" Smith	150.00	75.00	45.00
(47)	Amos Strunk	150.00	75.00	45.00
(48)	Bill Sweeney	150.00	75.00	45.00
(49)	Lefty Tyler	150.00	75.00	45.00
(50)	Ossie Vitt	150.00	75.00	45.00
(51)	Ivy Wingo	150.00	75.00	45.00
(52)	Heinie Zimmerman	150.00	75.00	45.00

1912 T227
Series Of Champions

The 1912 "Series of Champions" card set issued by the "Honest Long Cut" and "Miners Extra" tobacco brands features several baseball stars among its 25 famous athletes of the day. Larger than a standard-size tobacco issue, each card in the "Champions" series measures 3-3/8" by 2-5/16". The back includes a relatively lengthy player biography, while the front features a lithograph of the player in action. Although the set includes only four baseball players, these attractive cards are popular among collectors because of the stature of the four players selected. The "Champions" series holds additional significance because it includes the only known baseball cards issued under the "Miners Extra" brand name. The set carries the American Card Catalog designation of T227.

		NR MT	EX	VG
Complete Set:		9000.00	4500.00	2700.
Common Player:		1250.00	625.00	375.00
(1)	"Home Run" Baker	1250.00	625.00	375.00
(2)	"Chief" Bender	1250.00	625.00	375.00

		NR MT	EX	VG
(3)	Ty Cobb	5000.00	2500.00	1500.
(4)	R. Marquard	1250.00	625.00	375.00

1922 T231 Fans

More mystery surrounds this obscure set, issued in 1922 by Fans Cigarettes, than any other tobacco issue. In fact, the only evidence of its existence until 1992 was a photocopy of a single card of Pittsburgh Pirates outfielder Carson Bigbee. Even the owner of teh card is unknown. Assuming the photocopy is actual size, the card measures approximately 2-1/2" by 1-1/2" and is believed to be sepia-toned. Adding to the mystery is the number "85" which appears in the lower right corner on the front of the card. apparently indicating there were at least that many cards in the set. In 1992 card "61" was reported. The back of teh card displays Bigbee's batting averages for each season from 1918 through 1921 and includes the line: "I select C. Bigbee leading batter of all center fielders, packed with FANS cigarettes." The statement is followed by blanks for a person to fill in his name and address, as if the card were some sort of "ballot." Although it has not received much publicity, this card - of ir even exists - may be the rarest baseball card in the hobby. As such, no value will be placed on the card in this catalog until it is proven the card exists. The Frank Baker card cannot be priced at this time. American Card Catalog designation is T231.

Complete Set:

61   Frank Baker
85   Carson Bigbee

1914 T330-2
Piedmont Art Stamps

The 1914 series of "Piedmont Art Stamps" look like a fragile "stamp" version of the more popular T205 Gold Border tobacco cards. Issued by employed the same basic design as the T205 set produced three years earlier. The stamps in the Piedmont series measure 1-1/2" by 205/8". Even though the backs of the stamps advertise "100 designs," at leat 102 different players are known. And, because four of the players (Hal Chase, Eddie Collins, Russ Ford and Bobby Wallace) are pictured in two separate poses, there are sctually 106 different stamps in a complete set. All but three of the subjects in the Piedmont set were taken from the T205 set, with the exceptions being Joe Wood, Walt Blair and Bill Killifer. Because of their fragile composition, and since they are "stamps" that were frequently stuck to album pages, examples of Piedmont Art Stamps in Mint or Near Mint condition are very scarce. The back of the stamps offered a "handsome" album in exchange for 25 Piedmont coupons. The set has an American Card Catalog designation of T330-2.

	NR MT	EX	VG
Complete Set:	9500.00	4750.00	2850.
Common Player:	85.00	42.00	25.00

		NR MT	EX	VG
(1)	Jimmy Archer	85.00	42.00	25.00
(2)	Jimmy Austin	85.00	42.00	25.00
(3)	Home Run Baker	150.00	75.00	45.00
(4)	Cy Barger	85.00	42.00	25.00
(5)	Jack Barry	85.00	42.00	25.00
(6)	Johnny Bates	85.00	42.00	25.00
(7)	Beals Becker	85.00	42.00	25.00
(8)	Chief Bender	150.00	75.00	45.00
(9)	Bob Bescher	85.00	42.00	25.00
(10)	Joe Birmingham	85.00	42.00	25.00
(11)	Walt Blair	85.00	42.00	25.00
(12)	Roger Bresnahan	150.00	75.00	45.00
(13)	Al Bridwell	85.00	42.00	25.00
(14)	Mordecai Brown	150.00	75.00	45.00
(15)	Bobby Byrne	85.00	42.00	25.00
(16)	Howie Camnitz	85.00	42.00	25.00
(17)	Bill Carrigan	85.00	42.00	25.00
(18)	Frank Chance	110.00	55.00	33.00
(19)	Hal Chase ("Chase" on front)	65.00	32.00	19.50
(20)	Hal Chase ("Hal Chase" on front)	65.00	32.00	19.50
(21)	Ed Cicotte	65.00	32.00	19.50
(22)	Fred Clarke	150.00	75.00	45.00
(23)	Ty Cobb	1500.00	750.00	450.00
(24)	Eddie Collins (mouth closed)	150.00	75.00	45.00
(25)	Eddie Collins (mouth open)	150.00	75.00	45.00
(26)	Otis "Doc" Crandall	85.00	42.00	25.00
(27)	Bill Dahlen	85.00	42.00	25.00
(28)	Jake Daubert	90.00	45.00	27.00
(29)	Jim Delanhanty	85.00	42.00	25.00
(30)	Josh Devore	85.00	42.00	25.00
(31)	Red Dooin	85.00	42.00	25.00
(32)	Mickey Doolan	85.00	42.00	25.00
(33)	Tom Downey	85.00	42.00	25.00
(34)	Larry Doyle	85.00	42.00	25.00
(35)	Dick Egan	85.00	42.00	25.00
(36)	Kid Elberfield (Elberfeld)	85.00	42.00	25.00
(37)	Clyde Engle	85.00	42.00	25.00
(38)	Johnny Evers	150.00	75.00	45.00
(39)	Art Fletcher	85.00	42.00	25.00
(40)	Russ Ford (dark cap)	85.00	42.00	25.00
(41)	Russ Ford (white cap)	85.00	42.00	25.00
(42)	Art Fromme	85.00	42.00	25.00
(43)	George Gibson	85.00	42.00	25.00
(44)	William Goode (Wilbur Good)	85.00	42.00	25.00
(45)	Clark Griiifith	150.00	75.00	45.00
(46)	Bob Groom	85.00	42.00	25.00
(47)	Bob Harmon	85.00	42.00	25.00
(48)	Arnold Hauser	85.00	42.00	25.00
(49)	Buck Herzog	85.00	42.00	25.00
(50)	Dick Hoblitzell	85.00	42.00	25.00
(51)	Miller Huggins	150.00	75.00	45.00
(52)	John Hummel	85.00	42.00	25.00
(53)	Hughie Jennings	150.00	75.00	45.00
(54)	Walter Johnson	500.00	250.00	150.00
(55)	Davy Jones	85.00	42.00	25.00
(56)	Bill Killifer (Killefer)	75.00	37.00	22.00
(57)	Ed Konetchy	85.00	42.00	25.00

		NR MT	EX	VG
(58)	Frank LaPorte	85.00	42.00	25.00
(59)	Hans Lobert	85.00	42.00	25.00
(60)	Harry Lord	85.00	42.00	25.00
(61)	Sherry Magee	90.00	45.00	27.00
(62)	Rube Marquard	150.00	75.00	45.00
(63)	Christy Mathewson	500.00	250.00	150.00
(64)	George McBride	85.00	42.00	25.00
(65)	Larry McLean	85.00	42.00	25.00
(66)	Fred Merkle	90.00	45.00	27.00
(67)	Chief Meyers	85.00	42.00	25.00
(68)	Clyde Milan	85.00	42.00	25.00
(69)	Dots Miller	85.00	42.00	25.00
(70)	Mike Mitchell	85.00	42.00	25.00
(71)	Pat Moran	85.00	42.00	25.00
(72)	George Moriarity (Moriarty)	85.00	42.00	25.00
(73)	George Mullin	85.00	42.00	25.00
(74)	Danny Murphy	85.00	42.00	25.00
(75)	Jack "Red" Murray	85.00	42.00	25.00
(76)	Tom Needham	85.00	42.00	25.00
(77)	Rebel Oakes	85.00	42.00	25.00
(78)	Rube Oldring	85.00	42.00	25.00
(79)	Fred Parent	85.00	42.00	25.00
(80)	Dode Paskert	85.00	42.00	25.00
(81)	Jack Quinn	85.00	42.00	25.00
(82)	Ed Reulbach	85.00	42.00	25.00
(83)	Lewis Ritchie	85.00	42.00	25.00
(84)	Jack Rowan	85.00	42.00	25.00
(85)	Nap Rucker	85.00	42.00	25.00
(86)	Germany Schaefer	85.00	42.00	25.00
(87)	Wildfire Schulte	85.00	42.00	25.00
(88)	Jim Scott	85.00	42.00	25.00
(89)	Fred Snodgrass	85.00	42.00	25.00
(90)	Tris Speaker	450.00	225.00	135.00
(91)	Oscar Stamage (Stanage)	85.00	42.00	25.00
(92)	Jeff Sweeney	85.00	42.00	25.00
(93)	Ira Thomas	85.00	42.00	25.00
(94)	Joe Tinker	150.00	75.00	45.00
(95)	Terry Turner	85.00	42.00	25.00
(96)	Hippo Vaughn	85.00	42.00	25.00
(97)	Heinie Wagner	85.00	42.00	25.00
(98)	Bobby Wallace (no cap)	150.00	75.00	45.00
(99)	Bobby Wallace (with cap)	150.00	75.00	45.00
(100)	Ed Walsh	110.00	55.00	33.00
(101)	Zach Wheat	150.00	75.00	45.00
(102)	Irwin "Kaiser" Wilhelm	85.00	42.00	25.00
(103)	Ed Willett	85.00	42.00	25.00
(104)	Owen Wilson	85.00	42.00	25.00
(105)	Hooks Wiltse	85.00	42.00	25.00
(106)	Joe Wood	65.00	32.00	19.50

1911 T332 Helmar Stamps

In an interesting departure from the traditional tobacco cards of the period, Helmar Cigarettes in 1911 issued a series of small major league baseball player "stamps." The stamps, each measuring approximately 1-1/8" by 1-3/8", feature a black and white player portrait surrounded by a colorful, ornate frame. The stamps were originally issued in a 2" by 2-1/2" glassine envelope which advertised the Helmar brand and promoted "Philately - the Popular European Rage." To date, 181 different player stamps have been found. The set includes as many as 50 different frame designs are also known to exist. The Helmar stamp set has been assigned a T332 designation by the American Card Catalog.

		NR MT	EX	VG
Complete Set:		8500.00	4250.00	2550.
Common Player:		30.00	15.00	9.00
(1)	Babe Adams	30.00	15.00	9.00
(2)	Red Ames	30.00	15.00	9.00
(3)	Jimmy Archer	30.00	15.00	9.00
(4)	Jimmy Austin	30.00	15.00	9.00
(5)	Home Run Baker	75.00	37.00	22.00
(6)	Neal Ball	30.00	15.00	9.00
(7)	Cy Barger	30.00	15.00	9.00
(8)	Jack Barry	30.00	15.00	9.00
(9)	Johnny Bates	30.00	15.00	9.00
(10)	Fred Beck	30.00	15.00	9.00
(11)	Beals Becker	30.00	15.00	9.00
(12)	George Bell	30.00	15.00	9.00
(13)	Chief Bender	75.00	37.00	22.00
(14)	Bob Bescher	30.00	15.00	9.00
(15)	Joe Birmingham	30.00	15.00	9.00
(16)	John Bliss	30.00	15.00	9.00
(17)	Bruno Block	30.00	15.00	9.00
(18)	Ping Bodie	30.00	15.00	9.00
(19)	Roger Bresnahan	75.00	37.00	22.00
(20)	Al Bridwell	30.00	15.00	9.00
(21)	Lew Brockett	30.00	15.00	9.00
(22)	Mordecai Brown	75.00	37.00	22.00
(23)	Bill Burns	30.00	15.00	9.00
(24)	Donie Bush	30.00	15.00	9.00
(25)	Bobby Byrne	30.00	15.00	9.00
(26)	Nixey Callahan	30.00	15.00	9.00
(27)	Howie Camnitz	30.00	15.00	9.00
(28)	Max Carey	75.00	37.00	22.00
(29)	Bill Carrigan	30.00	15.00	9.00
(30)	Frank Chance	35.00	17.50	10.50
(31)	Hal Chase	20.00	10.00	6.00
(32)	Ed Cicotte	20.00	10.00	6.00
(33)	Fred Clarke	75.00	37.00	22.00
(34)	Tommy Clarke	30.00	15.00	9.00
(35)	Ty Cobb	1000.00	500.00	300.00
(36)	King Cole	30.00	15.00	9.00
(37)	Eddie Collins (Philadelphia)	75.00	37.00	22.00
(38)	Shano Collins (Chicago)	75.00	37.00	22.00
(39)	Wid Conroy	30.00	15.00	9.00
(40)	Doc Crandall	30.00	15.00	9.00
(41)	Sam Crawford	75.00	37.00	22.00
(42)	Birdie Cree	30.00	15.00	9.00
(43)	Bill Dahlen	30.00	15.00	9.00
(44)	Jake Daubert	35.00	17.50	10.50
(45)	Harry Davis	30.00	15.00	9.00
(46)	Jim Delahanty	30.00	15.00	9.00
(47)	Art Devlin	30.00	15.00	9.00
(48)	Josh Devore	30.00	15.00	9.00
(49)	Mike Donlin	30.00	15.00	9.00
(50)	Wild Bill Donovan	30.00	15.00	9.00
(51)	Red Dooin	30.00	15.00	9.00
(52)	Mickey Doolan	30.00	15.00	9.00
(53)	Patsy Dougherty	30.00	15.00	9.00
(54)	Tom Downey	30.00	15.00	9.00
(55)	Larry Doyle	30.00	15.00	9.00
(56)	Louis Drucke	30.00	15.00	9.00
(57)	Clyde Engle	30.00	15.00	9.00
(58)	Tex Erwin	30.00	15.00	9.00
(59)	Steve Evans	30.00	15.00	9.00
(60)	Johnny Evers	75.00	37.00	22.00
(61)	Jack Ferry	30.00	15.00	9.00
(62)	Ray Fisher	30.00	15.00	9.00
(63)	Art Fletcher	30.00	15.00	9.00
(64)	Russ Ford	30.00	15.00	9.00
(65)	Art Fromme	30.00	15.00	9.00
(66)	Earl Gardner	30.00	15.00	9.00
(67)	Harry Gaspar	30.00	15.00	9.00
(68)	George Gibson	30.00	15.00	9.00
(69)	Roy Golden	30.00	15.00	9.00
(70)	Hank Gowdy	30.00	15.00	9.00
(71)	Peaches Graham	30.00	15.00	9.00
(72)	Eddie Grant	30.00	15.00	9.00
(73)	Dolly Gray	30.00	15.00	9.00
(74)	Clark Griffith	75.00	37.00	22.00
(75)	Bob Groom	30.00	15.00	9.00
(76)	Bob Harmon	30.00	15.00	9.00
(77)	Grover Hartley	30.00	15.00	9.00
(78)	Arnold Hauser	30.00	15.00	9.00
(79)	Buck Herzog	30.00	15.00	9.00
(80)	Dick Hoblitzell	30.00	15.00	9.00
(81)	Solly Hoffman (Hofman)	30.00	15.00	9.00
(82)	Miller Huggins	75.00	37.00	22.00
(83)	Long Tom Hughes	30.00	15.00	9.00
(84)	John Hummel	30.00	15.00	9.00
(85)	Hughie Jennings	75.00	37.00	22.00
(86)	Walter Johnson	400.00	200.00	120.00
(87)	Davy Jones	30.00	15.00	9.00
(88)	Johnny Kling	30.00	15.00	9.00
(89)	Otto Knabe	30.00	15.00	9.00
(90)	Jack Knight	30.00	15.00	9.00
(91)	Ed Konetchy	30.00	15.00	9.00
(92)	Harry Krause	30.00	15.00	9.00
(93)	Nap Lajoie	250.00	125.00	75.00
(94)	Joe Lake	30.00	15.00	9.00
(95)	Frank LaPorte	30.00	15.00	9.00
(96)	Tommy Leach	30.00	15.00	9.00
(97)	Lefty Leifield	30.00	15.00	9.00
(98)	Ed Lennox	30.00	15.00	9.00
(99)	Paddy Livingston	30.00	15.00	9.00
(100)	Hans Lobert	30.00	15.00	9.00
(101)	Harry Lord	30.00	15.00	9.00
(102)	Fred Luderas (Luderus)	30.00	15.00	9.00
(103)	Sherry Magee	35.00	17.50	10.50
(104)	Rube Marquard	75.00	37.00	22.00
(105)	Christy Mathewson	400.00	200.00	120.00
(106)	Al Mattern	30.00	15.00	9.00
(107)	George McBride	30.00	15.00	9.00
(108)	Amby McConnell	30.00	15.00	9.00
(109)	John McGraw	200.00	100.00	60.00
(110)	Harry McIntire (McIntyre)	30.00	15.00	9.00
(111)	Matty McIntyre	30.00	15.00	9.00
(112)	Larry McLean	30.00	15.00	9.00
(113)	Fred Merkle	35.00	17.50	10.50
(114)	Chief Meyers	30.00	15.00	9.00
(115)	Clyde Milan	30.00	15.00	9.00
(116)	Dots Miller	30.00	15.00	9.00
(117)	Mike Mitchell	30.00	15.00	9.00
(118)	Earl Moore	30.00	15.00	9.00
(119)	Pat Moran	30.00	15.00	9.00
(120)	George Moriarty	30.00	15.00	9.00
(121)	Mike Mowrey	30.00	15.00	9.00
(122)	George Mullin	30.00	15.00	9.00
(123)	Danny Murphy	30.00	15.00	9.00
(124)	Red Murray	30.00	15.00	9.00
(125)	Tom Needham	30.00	15.00	9.00
(126)	Rebel Oakes	30.00	15.00	9.00
(127)	Rube Oldring	30.00	15.00	9.00
(128)	Marty O'Toole	30.00	15.00	9.00
(129)	Fred Parent	30.00	15.00	9.00
(130)	Dode Paskert	30.00	15.00	9.00
(131)	Barney Pelty	30.00	15.00	9.00
(132)	Eddie Phelps	30.00	15.00	9.00
(133)	Jack Powell	30.00	15.00	9.00
(134)	Jack Quinn	30.00	15.00	9.00
(135)	Ed Reulbach	30.00	15.00	9.00
(136)	Lew Richie	30.00	15.00	9.00
(137)	Reggie Richter	30.00	15.00	9.00
(138)	Jack Rowan	30.00	15.00	9.00
(139)	Nap Rucker	30.00	15.00	9.00
(140)	Slim Sallee	30.00	15.00	9.00
(141)	Doc Scanlan	30.00	15.00	9.00
(142)	Germany Schaefer	30.00	15.00	9.00
(143)	Boss Schmidt	30.00	15.00	9.00
(144)	Wildfire Schulte	30.00	15.00	9.00
(145)	Jim Scott	30.00	15.00	9.00
(146)	Tillie Shafer	30.00	15.00	9.00
(147)	Dave Shean	30.00	15.00	9.00
(148)	Jimmy Sheckard	30.00	15.00	9.00
(149)	Mike Simon	30.00	15.00	9.00
(150)	Fred Snodgrass	30.00	15.00	9.00
(151)	Tris Speaker	250.00	125.00	75.00
(152)	Oscar Stanage	30.00	15.00	9.00
(153)	Bill Steele	30.00	15.00	9.00
(154)	Harry Stovall	30.00	15.00	9.00
(155)	Gabby Street	30.00	15.00	9.00
(156)	George Suggs	30.00	15.00	9.00
(157)	Billy Sullivan	30.00	15.00	9.00
(158)	Bill Sweeney	30.00	15.00	9.00
(159)	Jeff Sweeney	30.00	15.00	9.00
(160)	Lee Tannehill	30.00	15.00	9.00
(161)	Ira Thomas	30.00	15.00	9.00
(162)	Joe Tinker	75.00	37.00	22.00
(163)	John Titus	30.00	15.00	9.00
(164)	Fred Toney	30.00	15.00	9.00
(165)	Terry Turner	30.00	15.00	9.00
(166)	Hippo Vaughn	30.00	15.00	9.00
(167)	Heinie Wagner	30.00	15.00	9.00
(168)	Bobby Wallace	75.00	37.00	22.00
(169)	Ed Walsh	200.00	100.00	60.00
(170)	Jack Warhop	30.00	15.00	9.00
(171)	Zach Wheat	75.00	37.00	22.00
(172)	Doc White	30.00	15.00	9.00
(173)	Ed Willett	30.00	15.00	9.00
(174)	Art Wilson (New York)	30.00	15.00	9.00
(175)	Owen Wilson (Pittsburgh)	30.00	15.00	9.00
(176)	Hooks Wiltse	30.00	15.00	9.00
(177)	Harry Wolter	30.00	15.00	9.00
(178)	Harry Wolverton	30.00	15.00	9.00
(179)	Cy Young	500.00	250.00	150.00

		NR MT	EX	VG
(180)	Irv Young	30.00	15.00	9.00

1933 Tattoo Orbit

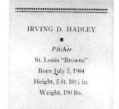

Found in 1¢ packages of Tattoo gum, these 2" by 2-1/4" cards were produced by the Orbit Gum Company of Chicago, Illinois. The fronts feature a photograph which is tinted to give skin some color. Stylized baseball park backgrounds are separated from the photograph by a black line. The rest of the background is printed in vivid red, yellow and green. Card backs have the player's name, team, position, birth date, height and weight. The 60-card set is not common, but their interesting format does not seem to have struck a responsive chord in today's collectors. Cards of Bump Hadley and George Blaeholder are the most elusive, followed by those of Ivy Andrews and Rogers Hornsby.

		NR MT	EX	VG
Complete Set:		3500.00	1750.00	1050.
Common Player:		35.00	17.50	10.50
(1)	Dale Alexander	70.00	35.00	21.00
(2)	Ivy Paul Andrews	150.00	75.00	45.00
(3)	Earl Averill	70.00	35.00	21.00
(4)	Richard Bartell	35.00	17.50	10.50
(5)	Walter Berger	35.00	17.50	10.50
(6)	George F. Blaeholder	100.00	50.00	30.00
(7)	Irving J. Burns	35.00	17.50	10.50
(8)	Guy T. Bush	35.00	17.50	10.50
(9)	Bruce D. Campbell	35.00	17.50	10.50
(10)	William Cissell	35.00	17.50	10.50
(11)	Lefty Clark	35.00	17.50	10.50
(12)	Mickey Cochrane	65.00	32.00	19.50
(13)	Phil Collins	35.00	17.50	10.50
(14)	Hazen Kiki Cuyler	70.00	35.00	21.00
(15)	Dizzy Dean	150.00	75.00	45.00
(16)	Jimmy Dykes	40.00	20.00	12.00
(17)	George L. Earnshaw	35.00	17.50	10.50
(18)	Woody English	35.00	17.50	10.50
(19)	Lewis A. Fonseca	40.00	20.00	12.00
(20)	Jimmy Foxx	125.00	62.00	37.00
(21)	Burleigh A. Grimes	70.00	35.00	21.00
(22)	Charles John Grimm	40.00	20.00	12.00
(23)	Robert M. Grove	65.00	32.00	19.50
(24)	Frank Grube	35.00	17.50	10.50
(25)	George W. Haas	35.00	17.50	10.50
(26)	Irving D. Hadley	100.00	50.00	30.00
(27)	Chick Hafey	70.00	35.00	21.00
(28)	Jesse Joseph Haines	70.00	35.00	21.00
(29)	William Hallahan	35.00	17.50	10.50
(30)	Melvin Harder	35.00	17.50	10.50
(31)	Gabby Hartnett	70.00	35.00	21.00
(32)	Babe Herman	40.00	20.00	12.00
(33)	William Herman	70.00	35.00	21.00
(34)	Rogers Hornsby	200.00	100.00	60.00
(35)	Roy C. Johnson	35.00	17.50	10.50
(36)	J. Smead Jolley	35.00	17.50	10.50
(37)	William Jurges	35.00	17.50	10.50
(38)	William Kamm	35.00	17.50	10.50
(39)	Mark A. Koenig	35.00	17.50	10.50
(40)	James J. Levey	35.00	17.50	10.50
(41)	Ernie Lombardi	70.00	35.00	21.00
(42)	Red Lucas	35.00	17.50	10.50
(43)	Ted Lyons	70.00	35.00	21.00
(44)	Connie Mack	125.00	62.00	37.00

		NR MT	EX	VG
(45)	Pat Malone	35.00	17.50	10.50
(46)	Pepper Martin	40.00	20.00	12.00
(47)	Marty McManus	35.00	17.50	10.50
(48)	Frank J. O'Doul	40.00	20.00	12.00
(49)	Richard Porter	35.00	17.50	10.50
(50)	Carl N. Reynolds	35.00	17.50	10.50
(51)	Charles Henry Root	35.00	17.50	10.50
(52)	Robert Seeds	35.00	17.50	10.50
(53)	Al H. Simmons	70.00	35.00	21.00
(54)	Jackson Riggs Stepheson	40.00	20.00	12.00
(55)	Bud Tinning	35.00	17.50	10.50
(56)	Joe Vosmik	35.00	17.50	10.50
(57)	Rube Walberg	35.00	17.50	10.50
(58)	Paul Waner	70.00	35.00	21.00
(59)	Lonnie Warneke	35.00	17.50	10.50
(60)	Arthur C. Whitney	35.00	17.50	10.50

1947 Tip Top Bread

This 163-card set actually consists of a group of regional issues, some of which are more scarce then others. The 2-1/4" by 3" cards are borderless with a black and white player photo below which is a white strip containing the player's name, position, city name and league. Backs carry an advertisement. The set is known for a quantity of obscure players, many of whom played during the talent-lean World War II seasons. Overall it is a scarce set, with a number of interesting cards including first-issues of Yogi Berra and Joe Garagiola.

		NR MT	EX	VG
Complete Set:		12000.00	6000.00	3500.
Common Player:		35.00	17.50	10.50
(1)	Bill Ayers	35.00	17.50	10.50
(2)	Floyd Baker	50.00	25.00	15.00
(3)	Charles Barrett	50.00	25.00	15.00
(4)	Eddie Basinski	35.00	17.50	10.50
(5)	John Berardino	50.00	25.00	15.00
(6)	Larry Berra	400.00	200.00	120.00
(7)	Bill Bevens	50.00	25.00	15.00
(8)	Robert Blattner	35.00	17.50	10.50
(9)	Ernie Bonham	35.00	17.50	10.50
(10)	Bob Bragan	45.00	22.00	13.50
(11)	Ralph Branca	70.00	35.00	21.00
(12)	Alpha Brazle	35.00	17.50	10.50
(13)	Bobbie Brown	60.00	30.00	18.00
(14)	Mike Budnick	35.00	17.50	10.50
(15)	Ken Burkhart	35.00	17.50	10.50
(16)	Thomas Byrne	50.00	25.00	15.00
(17)	Earl Caldwell	50.00	25.00	15.00
(18)	"Hank" Camelli	50.00	25.00	15.00
(19)	Hugh Casey	45.00	22.00	13.50
(20)	Phil Cavarretta	65.00	32.00	19.50
(21)	Bob Chipman	50.00	25.00	15.00
(22)	Lloyd Christopher	50.00	25.00	15.00
(23)	Bill Cox	35.00	17.50	10.50
(24)	Bernard Creger	35.00	17.50	10.50
(25)	Frank Crosetti	65.00	32.00	19.50
(26)	Joffre Cross	35.00	17.50	10.50
(27)	Leon Culberson	50.00	25.00	15.00
(28)	Dick Culler	50.00	25.00	15.00
(29)	Dom DiMaggio	200.00	100.00	60.00
(30)	George Dickey	60.00	30.00	18.00
(31)	Chas. E. Diering	35.00	17.50	10.50
(32)	Joseph Dobson	50.00	25.00	15.00

		NR MT	EX	VG
(33)	Bob Doerr	275.00	137.00	82.00
(34)	Ervin Dusak	35.00	17.50	10.50
(35)	Bruce Edwards	40.00	20.00	12.00
(36)	Walter "Hoot" Evers	50.00	25.00	15.00
(37)	Clifford Fannin	35.00	17.50	10.50
(38)	"Nanny" Fernandez	50.00	25.00	15.00
(39)	Dave "Boo" Ferriss	50.00	25.00	15.00
(40)	Elbie Fletcher	35.00	17.50	10.50
(41)	Dennis Galehouse	35.00	17.50	10.50
(42)	Joe Garagiola	200.00	100.00	60.00
(43)	Sid Gordon	35.00	17.50	10.50
(44)	John Gorsica	50.00	25.00	15.00
(45)	Hal Gregg	40.00	20.00	12.00
(46)	Frank Gustine	35.00	17.50	10.50
(47)	Stanley Hack	65.00	32.00	19.50
(48)	Mickey Harris	50.00	25.00	15.00
(49)	Clinton Hartung	35.00	17.50	10.50
(50)	Joe Hatten	40.00	20.00	12.00
(51)	Frank Hayes	50.00	25.00	15.00
(52)	"Jeff" Heath	35.00	17.50	10.50
(53)	Tom Henrich	70.00	35.00	21.00
(54)	Gene Hermanski	40.00	20.00	12.00
(55)	Kirby Higbe	35.00	17.50	10.50
(56)	Ralph Hodgin	50.00	25.00	15.00
(57)	Tex Hughson	50.00	25.00	15.00
(58)	Fred Hutchinson	70.00	35.00	21.00
(59)	LeRoy Jarvis	35.00	17.50	10.50
(60)	"Si" Johnson	50.00	25.00	15.00
(61)	Don Johnson	50.00	25.00	15.00
(62)	Earl Johnson	50.00	25.00	15.00
(63)	John Jorgensen	40.00	20.00	12.00
(64)	Walter Judnick (Judnich)	35.00	17.50	10.50
(65)	Tony Kaufmann	35.00	17.50	10.50
(66)	George Kell	400.00	200.00	120.00
(67)	Charlie Keller	65.00	32.00	19.50
(68)	Bob Kennedy	50.00	25.00	15.00
(69)	Montia Kennedy	35.00	17.50	10.50
(70)	Ralph Kiner	80.00	40.00	24.00
(71)	Dave Koslo	35.00	17.50	10.50
(72)	Jack Kramer	35.00	17.50	10.50
(73)	Joe Kuhel	50.00	25.00	15.00
(74)	George Kurowski	35.00	17.50	10.50
(75)	Emil Kush	50.00	25.00	15.00
(76)	"Eddie" Lake	50.00	25.00	15.00
(77)	Harry Lavagetto	45.00	22.00	13.50
(78)	Bill Lee	50.00	25.00	15.00
(79)	Thornton Lee	50.00	25.00	15.00
(80)	Paul Lehner	35.00	17.50	10.50
(81)	John Lindell	50.00	25.00	15.00
(82)	Danny Litwhiler	50.00	25.00	15.00
(83)	"Mickey" Livingston	50.00	25.00	15.00
(84)	Carroll Lockman	35.00	17.50	10.50
(85)	Jack Lohrke	35.00	17.50	10.50
(86)	Ernie Lombardi	80.00	40.00	24.00
(87)	Vic Lombardi	40.00	20.00	12.00
(88)	Edmund Lopat	65.00	32.00	19.50
(89)	Harry Lowrey	50.00	25.00	15.00
(90)	Marty Marion	50.00	25.00	15.00
(91)	Willard Marshall	35.00	17.50	10.50
(92)	Phil Masi	50.00	25.00	15.00
(93)	Edward J. Mayo	50.00	25.00	15.00
(94)	Clyde McCullough	50.00	25.00	15.00
(95)	Frank Melton	40.00	20.00	12.00
(96)	Cass Michaels	50.00	25.00	15.00
(97)	Ed Miksis	40.00	20.00	12.00
(98)	Arthur Mills	50.00	25.00	15.00
(99)	Johnny Mize	80.00	40.00	24.00
(100)	Lester Moss	35.00	17.50	10.50
(101)	"Pat" Mullin	50.00	25.00	15.00
(102)	"Bob" Muncrief	35.00	17.50	10.50
(103)	George Munger	35.00	17.50	10.50
(104)	Fritz Ostermueller	35.00	17.50	10.50
(105)	James P. Outlaw	50.00	25.00	15.00
(106)	Frank "Stub" Overmire	50.00	25.00	15.00
(107)	Andy Pafko	60.00	30.00	18.00
(108)	Joe Page	50.00	25.00	15.00
(109)	Roy Partee	50.00	25.00	15.00
(110)	Johnny Pesky	60.00	30.00	18.00
(111)	Nelson Potter	35.00	17.50	10.50
(112)	Mel Queen	50.00	25.00	15.00
(113)	Marion Rackley	40.00	20.00	12.00
(114)	Al Reynolds	70.00	35.00	21.00
(115)	Del Rice	35.00	17.50	10.50
(116)	Marv Rickert	50.00	25.00	15.00
(117)	John Rigney	50.00	25.00	15.00
(118)	Aaron Robinson	50.00	25.00	15.00
(119)	"Preacher" Roe	45.00	22.00	13.50
(120)	Carvel Rowell	50.00	25.00	15.00
(121)	Jim Russell	35.00	17.50	10.50
(122)	Rip Russell	50.00	25.00	15.00
(123)	Phil Rizzuto	200.00	100.00	60.00

		NR MT	EX	VG
(124)	Connie Ryan	50.00	25.00	15.00
(125)	John Sain	90.00	45.00	27.00
(126)	Ray Sanders	50.00	25.00	15.00
(127)	Fred Sanford	35.00	17.50	10.50
(128)	Johnny Schmitz	50.00	25.00	15.00
(129)	Joe Schultz	35.00	17.50	10.50
(130)	"Rip" Sewell	35.00	17.50	10.50
(131)	Dick Sisler	35.00	17.50	10.50
(132)	"Sibby" Sisti	50.00	25.00	15.00
(133)	Enos Slaughter	80.00	40.00	24.00
(134)	"Billy" Southworth	50.00	25.00	15.00
(135)	Warren Spahn	400.00	200.00	120.00
(136)	Verne Stephens (Vern)	35.00	17.50	10.50
(137)	George Sternweiss (Stirnweiss)	50.00	25.00	15.00
(138)	Ed Stevens	40.00	20.00	12.00
(139)	Nick Strincevich	35.00	17.50	10.50
(140)	"Bobby" Sturgeon	50.00	25.00	15.00
(141)	Robt. "Bob" Swift	50.00	25.00	15.00
(142)	Geo. "Birdie" Tibbetts (Tebbetts)	55.00	27.00	16.50
(143)	"Mike" Tresh	55.00	27.00	16.50
(144)	Ken Trinkle	35.00	17.50	10.50
(145)	Paul "Diz" Trout	55.00	27.00	16.50
(146)	Virgil "Fire" Trucks	55.00	27.00	16.50
(147)	Thurman Tucker	50.00	25.00	15.00
(148)	Bill Voiselle	35.00	17.50	10.50
(149)	Hal Wagner	50.00	25.00	15.00
(150)	Honus Wagner	200.00	100.00	60.00
(151)	Eddy Waitkus	50.00	25.00	15.00
(152)	Richard "Dick" Wakefield	50.00	25.00	15.00
(153)	Jack Wallaesa	50.00	25.00	15.00
(154)	Charles Wensloff	50.00	25.00	15.00
(155)	Ted Wilks	35.00	17.50	10.50
(156)	Mickey Witek	35.00	17.50	10.50
(157)	"Jerry" Witte	35.00	17.50	10.50
(158)	Ed Wright	50.00	25.00	15.00
(159)	Taft Wright	50.00	25.00	15.00
(160)	Henry Wyse	50.00	25.00	15.00
(161)	"Rudy" York	55.00	27.00	16.50
(162)	Al Zarilla	35.00	17.50	10.50
(163)	Bill Zuber	50.00	25.00	15.00

A player's name in italic indicates a rookie card. An (FC) indicates a player's first card for that particular card company.

1952 Tip Top Bread Labels

This unnumbered set of bread end-labels consists of 48 different labels, including two of Phil Rizzuto. The player's photo, name and team appear inside a star, with the words "Tip Top" printed above. The labels measure approximately 2-1/2" by 2-3/4".

		NR MT	EX	VG
Complete Set:		5500.00	2750.00	1650.
Common Player:		65.00	32.00	19.50
(1)	Hank Bauer	80.00	40.00	24.00
(2)	Yogi Berra	200.00	100.00	60.00
(3)	Ralph Branca	55.00	27.00	16.50
(4)	Lou Brissie	65.00	32.00	19.50
(5)	Roy Campanella	250.00	125.00	75.00
(6)	Phil Cavarreta (Cavarretta)	65.00	32.00	19.50
(7)	Murray Dickson (Murry)	65.00	32.00	19.50
(8)	Ferris Fain	65.00	32.00	19.50
(9)	Carl Furillo	80.00	40.00	24.00
(10)	Ned Garver	65.00	32.00	19.50
(11)	Sid Gordon	65.00	32.00	19.50
(12)	John Groth	65.00	32.00	19.50
(13)	Gran Hamner	65.00	32.00	19.50
(14)	Jim Hearn	65.00	32.00	19.50

		NR MT	EX	VG
(15)	Gene Hermanski	65.00	32.00	19.50
(16)	Gil Hodges	110.00	55.00	33.00
(17)	Larry Jansen	65.00	32.00	19.50
(18)	Eddie Joost	65.00	32.00	19.50
(19)	George Kell	100.00	50.00	30.00
(20)	Dutch Leonard	65.00	32.00	19.50
(21)	Whitey Lockman	65.00	32.00	19.50
(22)	Ed Lopat	80.00	40.00	24.00
(23)	Sal Maglie	55.00	27.00	16.50
(24)	Mickey Mantle	1500.00	750.00	450.00
(25)	Gil McDougald	80.00	40.00	24.00
(26)	Dale Mitchell	65.00	32.00	19.50
(27)	Don Mueller	65.00	32.00	19.50
(28)	Andy Pafko	55.00	27.00	16.50
(29)	Bob Porterfield	65.00	32.00	19.50
(30)	Ken Raffensberger	65.00	32.00	19.50
(31)	Allie Reynolds	80.00	40.00	24.00
(32a)	Phil Rizzutto (Rizzuto) ("NY" shows on shirt)	110.00	55.00	33.00
(32b)	Phil Rizzutto (Rizzuto) (no "NY" visible on shirt)	110.00	55.00	33.00
(33)	Robin Roberts	100.00	50.00	30.00
(34)	Saul Rogovin	65.00	32.00	19.50
(35)	Ray Scarborough	65.00	32.00	19.50
(36)	Red Schoendienst	80.00	40.00	24.00
(37)	Dick Sisler	65.00	32.00	19.50
(38)	Enos Slaughter	100.00	50.00	30.00
(39)	Duke Snider	200.00	100.00	60.00
(40)	Warren Spahn	110.00	55.00	33.00
(41)	Vern Stephens	65.00	32.00	19.50
(42)	Earl Torgeson	65.00	32.00	19.50
(43)	Mickey Vernon	65.00	32.00	19.50
(44)	Ed Waitkus	65.00	32.00	19.50
(45)	Wes Westrum	65.00	32.00	19.50
(46)	Eddie Yost	65.00	32.00	19.50
(47)	Al Zarilla	65.00	32.00	19.50

1948 Topps Magic Photos

The first Topps baseball cards appeared as a subset of 19 cards from an issue of 252 "Magic Photos." The set takes its name from the self-developing nature of the cards. The cards were blank on the front when first taken from the wrapper. By spitting on the wrapper and holding it to the card while exposing it to light the black and white photo appeared. Measuring 7/8" by 1-1/2," the cards are very similar to Topps 1956 "Hocus Focus" issue.

		NR MT	EX	VG
Complete Set:		750.00	375.00	225.00
Common Player:		10.00	5.00	3.00
1	Lou Boudreau	20.00	10.00	6.00
2	Cleveland Indians	10.00	5.00	3.00
3	Bob Eliott	15.00	7.50	4.50
4	Cleveland Indians 4-3	10.00	5.00	3.00
5	Cleveland Indians 4-1 (Lou Boudreau Scoring)	20.00	10.00	6.00
6	"Babe" Ruth 714	200.00	100.00	60.00
7	Tris Speaker 793	25.00	12.50	7.50
8	Rogers Hornsby	50.00	25.00	15.00
9	Connie Mack	40.00	20.00	12.00
10	Christy Mathewson	50.00	25.00	15.00
11	Hans Wagner	50.00	25.00	15.00
12	Grover Alexander	30.00	15.00	9.00
13	Ty Cobb	100.00	50.00	30.00
14	Lou Gehrig	100.00	50.00	30.00

		NR MT	EX	VG
15	Walter Johnson	50.00	25.00	15.00
16	Cy Young	30.00	15.00	9.00
17	George Sisler 257	20.00	10.00	6.00
18	Tinker and Evers	20.00	10.00	6.00
19	Third Base Cleveland Indians	10.00	5.00	3.00

1951 Topps Blue Backs

Sold two cards in a package with a piece of candy for 1¢, the Topps Blue Backs are more scarce then their Red Back counterparts. The 2" by 2-5/8" cards carry a black and white player photograph on a red, white, yellow and green background along with the player's name and other information including their 1950 record on the front. The back is printed in blue on a white background. The 52-card set has varied baseball situations on them, making the playing of a rather elementary game of baseball possible. Although scarce, Blue Backs were printed on thick cardboard and have survived quite well over the years. There are, however, few stars (Johnny Mize and Enos Slaughter are two) in the set. Despite being a Topps product, Blue Backs do not currently enjoy great popularity.

		NR MT	EX	VG
Complete Set:		2100.00	1050.00	630.00
Common Player:		30.00	15.00	9.00
1	Eddie Yost	30.00	15.00	9.00
2	Henry (Hank) Majeski	30.00	15.00	9.00
3	Richie Ashburn	50.00	25.00	15.00
4	Del Ennis	30.00	15.00	9.00
5	Johnny Pesky	25.00	12.50	7.50
6	Albert (Red) Schoendienst	35.00	17.50	10.50
7	Gerald Staley	30.00	15.00	9.00
8	Dick Sisler	30.00	15.00	9.00
9	Johnny Sain	35.00	17.50	10.50
10	Joe Page	30.00	15.00	9.00
11	Johnny Groth	30.00	15.00	9.00
12	Sam Jethroe	30.00	15.00	9.00
13	James (Mickey) Vernon	25.00	12.50	7.50
14	George Munger	30.00	15.00	9.00
15	Eddie Joost	30.00	15.00	9.00
16	Murry Dickson	30.00	15.00	9.00
17	Roy Smalley	30.00	15.00	9.00
18	Ned Garver	30.00	15.00	9.00
19	Phil Masi	30.00	15.00	9.00
20	Ralph Branca	30.00	15.00	9.00
21	Billy Johnson	30.00	15.00	9.00
22	Bob Kuzava	30.00	15.00	9.00
23	Paul (Dizzy) Trout	30.00	15.00	9.00
24	Sherman Lollar	30.00	15.00	9.00
25	Sam Mele	30.00	15.00	9.00
26	Chico Carresquel (Carrasquel)	30.00	15.00	9.00
27	Andy Pafko	25.00	12.50	7.50
28	Harry (The Cat) Brecheen	30.00	15.00	9.00
29	Granville Hamner	30.00	15.00	9.00
30	Enos (Country) Slaughter	60.00	30.00	18.00
31	Lou Brissie	30.00	15.00	9.00
32	Bob Elliott	30.00	15.00	9.00
33	Don Lenhardt	30.00	15.00	9.00
34	Earl Torgeson	30.00	15.00	9.00
35	Tommy Byrne	30.00	15.00	9.00
36	Cliff Fannin	30.00	15.00	9.00
37	Bobby Doerr	55.00	27.00	16.50
38	Irv Noren	30.00	15.00	9.00

		NR MT	EX	VG
39	Ed Lopat	30.00	15.00	9.00
40	Vic Wertz	25.00	12.50	7.50
41	Johnny Schmitz	30.00	15.00	9.00
42	Bruce Edwards	30.00	15.00	9.00
43	Willie (Puddin' Head) Jones	30.00	15.00	9.00
44	Johnny Wyrostek	30.00	15.00	9.00
45	Bill Pierce	25.00	12.50	7.50
46	Gerry Priddy	30.00	15.00	9.00
47	Herman Wehmeier	30.00	15.00	9.00
48	Billy Cox	30.00	15.00	9.00
49	Henry (Hank) Sauer	30.00	15.00	9.00
50	Johnny Mize	60.00	30.00	18.00
51	Eddie Waitkus	30.00	15.00	9.00
52	Sam Chapman	30.00	15.00	9.00

		NR MT	EX	VG
36a	Gus Zernial (Chicago in bio)	20.00	10.00	6.00
36b	Gus Zernial (Philadelphia in bio)	12.00	6.00	3.50
37	Wes Westrum	9.00	4.50	2.75
38	Ed (Duke) Snider	60.00	30.00	17.50
39	Ted Kluszewski	10.00	5.00	3.00
40	Mike Garcia	9.00	4.50	2.75
41	Whitey Lockman	5.00	2.50	1.50
42	Ray Scarborough	5.00	2.50	1.50
43	Maurice McDermott	5.00	2.50	1.50
44	Sid Hudson	5.00	2.50	1.50
45	Andy Seminick	5.00	2.50	1.50
46	Billy Goodman	5.00	2.50	1.50
47	Tommy Glaviano	5.00	2.50	1.50
48	Eddie Stanky	9.00	4.50	2.75
49	Al Zarilla	5.00	2.50	1.50
50	Monte Irvin	25.00	12.50	7.50
51	Eddie Robinson	5.00	2.50	1.50
52a	Tommy Holmes (Boston in bio)	20.00	10.00	6.00
52b	Tommy Holmes (Hartford in bio)	20.00	10.00	6.00

1951 Topps Red Backs

Like the Blue Backs, the Topps Red Backs which were sold at the same time, came two to a package for 1¢. Their black and white photographs appear on a red, white, blue and yellow background. The back printing is red on white. Their 2" by 2-5/8" size is the same as Blue Backs. Also identical is the set size (52 cards) and the game situations to be found on the fronts of the cards, for use in playing a card game of baseball. Red Backs are more common than the Blue Backs by virtue of a recent discovery of a large hoard of unopened boxes.

		NR MT	EX	VG
Complete Set:		750.00	375.00	230.00
Common Player:		9.00	4.50	2.75
1	Larry (Yogi) Berra	75.00	38.00	23.50
2	Sid Gordon	5.00	2.50	1.50
3	Ferris Fain	9.00	4.50	2.75
4	Verne Stephens (Vern)	9.00	4.50	2.75
5	Phil Rizzuto	25.00	12.50	7.50
6	Allie Reynolds	10.00	5.00	3.00
7	Howie Pollet	5.00	2.50	1.50
8	Early Wynn	25.00	12.50	7.50
9	Roy Sievers	9.00	4.50	2.75
10	Mel Parnell	9.00	4.50	2.75
11	Gene Hermanski	5.00	2.50	1.50
12	Jim Hegan	5.00	2.50	1.50
13	Dale Mitchell	5.00	2.50	1.50
14	Wayne Terwilliger	5.00	2.50	1.50
15	Ralph Kiner	25.00	12.50	7.50
16	Preacher Roe	8.00	4.00	2.50
17	Dave Bell	8.00	4.00	2.50
18	Gerry Coleman	8.00	4.00	2.50
19	Dick Kokos	5.00	2.50	1.50
20	Dominick DiMaggio (Dominic)	10.00	5.00	3.00
21	Larry Jansen	5.00	2.50	1.50
22	Bob Feller	25.00	12.50	7.50
23	Ray Boone	9.00	4.50	2.75
24	Hank Bauer	10.00	5.00	3.00
25	Cliff Chambers	5.00	2.50	1.50
26	Luke Easter	9.00	4.50	2.75
27	Wally Westlake	5.00	2.50	1.50
28	Elmer Valo	5.00	2.50	1.50
29	Bob Kennedy	5.00	2.50	1.50
30	Warren Spahn	25.00	12.50	7.50
31	Gil Hodges	25.00	12.50	7.50
32	Henry Thompson	5.00	2.50	1.50
33	William Werle	5.00	2.50	1.50
34	Grady Hatton	5.00	2.50	1.50
35	Al Rosen	10.00	5.00	3.00

1951 Topps Connie Mack's All-Stars

A set of die-cut, 2-1/16" by 5-1/4" cards, all eleven players are Hall of Famers. The cards feature a black and white photograph of the player printed on a red background with a red, white, blue, yellow and black plaque underneath. Like the "Current All-Stars," with which they were issued, the background could be removed making it possible for the card to stand up. This practice, however, resulted in the card's mutilation and lowers its condition in the eyes of today's collectors. Connie Mack All-Stars are scarce today and, despite being relatively expensive, retain a certain popularity as one of Topps first issues.

		NR MT	EX	VG
Complete Set:		9500.00	4500.00	1950.
Common Player:		350.00	150.00	60.00
(1)	Grover Cleveland Alexander	550.00	275.00	100.00
(2)	Gordon Stanley Cochrane	400.00	175.00	75.00
(3)	Edward Trowbridge Collins	350.00	150.00	60.00
(4)	James J. Collins	350.00	150.00	60.00
(5)	Henry Louis Gehrig	2000.00	1000.00	350.00
(6)	Walter Johnson	750.00	325.00	150.00
(7)	Connie Mack	400.00	175.00	75.00
(8)	Christopher Mathewson	750.00	325.00	135.00
(9)	George Herman Ruth	2250.00	1150.00	450.00
(10)	Tristram Speaker	575.00	275.00	100.00
(11)	John Peter Wagner	500.00	225.00	100.00

1951 Topps Current All-Stars

The Topps Current All-Stars are very similar to the Connie Mack All-Stars of the same year. The 2-1/16 by 5-1/4" cards have a black and white photograph on a red die-cut background. Most of the background could be folded over or removed so that the card would stand up. A plaque at the base carries brief biographical information. The set was to contain 11 cards, but only eight were actually issued in gum

packs. Those of Jim Konstanty, Robin Roberts and Eddie Stanky were not released and are very rare. A big problem with the set is that if the card was used as it was intended it was folded and, thus, damaged from a collector's viewpoint. That makes top quality examples of any players difficult to find and quite expensive.

	NR MT	EX	VG
Complete Set:	40000.00	20000.00	8500.
Common Player:	500.00	250.00	100.00
(1) Lawrence (Yogi) Berra	1500.00	750.00	450.00
(2) Lawrence Eugene Doby	750.00	375.00	150.00
(3) Walter Dropo	750.00	375.00	150.00
(4) Walter (Hoot) Evers	500.00	250.00	100.00
(5) George Clyde Kell	1000.00	500.00	200.00
(6) Ralph McPherran Kiner	1075.00	525.00	200.00
(7) James Casimir Konstanty	8500.00	4250.00	2000.
(8) Robert G. Lemon	1075.00	525.00	200.00
(9) Phillip Rizzuto	1200.00	600.00	225.00
(10) Robin Evan Roberts	9500.00	4750.00	2250.
(11) Edward Raymond Stanky	8500.00	4250.00	2000.

1951 Topps Teams

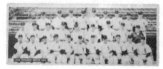

An innovative issue for 1951, the Topps team cards were a nine-card set, 5-1/4" by 2-1/16," which carried a black and white picture of a major league team surrounded by a yellow border on the front. The back identifies team members with red printing on white cardboard. There are two versions of each card, with and without the date "1950" in the banner that carries the team name. Undated versions are valued slightly higher than the cards with dates. Strangely only nine teams were issued. Scarcity varies, with the Cardinals and Red Sox being the most difficult to obtain. The complete set price does not include the scarcer variations.

	NR MT	EX	VG
Complete Set:	4500.00	2200.00	975.00
Common Team:	150.00	70.00	30.00
(1a) Boston Red Sox (1950)	250.00	100.00	50.00
(1b) Boston Red Sox (without 1950)			

		NR MT	EX	VG
		300.00	125.00	60.00
(2a)	Brooklyn Dodgers (1950)	300.00	125.00	60.00
(2b)	Brooklyn Dodgers (without 1950)			
		350.00	150.00	70.00
(3a)	Chicago White Sox (1950)	150.00	75.00	45.00
(3b)	Chicago White Sox (without 1950)			
		200.00	85.00	40.00
(4a)	Cincinnati Reds (1950)	150.00	70.00	30.00
(4b)	Cincinnati Reds (without 1950)	200.00	85.00	40.00
(5a)	New York Giants (1950)	250.00	100.00	50.00
(5b)	New York Giants (without 1950)			
		300.00	125.00	60.00
(6a)	Philadelphia Athletics (1950)	150.00	70.00	30.00
(6b)	Philadelphia Athletics (without 1950)			
		200.00	85.00	40.00
(7a)	Philadelphia Phillies (1950)	150.00	70.00	30.00
(7b)	Philadelphia Phillies (without 1950)			
		200.00	85.00	40.00
(8a)	St. Louis Cardinals (1950)	150.00	70.00	30.00
(8b)	St. Louis Cardinals (without 1950)			
		200.00	85.00	40.00
(9a)	Washington Senators (1950)	150.00	70.00	30.00
(9b)	Washington Senators (without 1950)			
		200.00	85.00	40.00

1952 Topps

At 407 cards, the 1952 Topps set was the largest set of its day, both in number of cards and physical dimensions of the cards. Cards are 2-5/8" by 3-3/4" with a hand-colored black and white photo on front. Major baseball card innovations presented in the set include the first-ever use of color team logos as part of the design, and the inclusion of stats for the previous season and overall career on the backs. A major variety in the set is that first 80 cards can be found with backs printed entirely in black or black and red. Backs entirely in black command a $10-15 premium. Card numbers 311-407 were printed in limited supplies and are extremely rare.

	NR MT	EX	VG
Complete Set:	70000.00	35000.00	20000.
Common Player: 1-80	50.00	25.00	15.00
Common Player: 81-250	25.00	12.50	7.50
Common Player: 251-280	40.00	20.00	12.00
Common Player: 281-300	50.00	25.00	15.00
Common Player: 301-310	40.00	20.00	12.00
Common Player: 311-407	175.00	87.00	52.00
1 Andy Pafko	1200.00	150.00	25.00
2 *James E. Runnels*	80.00	20.00	6.00
3 Hank Thompson	55.00	15.00	5.50
4 Don Lenhardt	55.00	15.00	5.50
5 Larry Jansen	55.00	15.00	5.50
6 Grady Hatton	60.00	15.00	5.50
7 Wayne Terwilliger	60.00	16.00	6.00
8 Fred Marsh	55.00	15.00	5.50
9 Bobby Hogue	65.00	18.00	6.50
10 Al Rosen	80.00	24.00	8.00
11 Phil Rizzuto	175.00	87.00	52.00
12 Monty Basgall	55.00	15.00	5.50
13 Johnny Wyrostek	55.00	15.00	5.50
14 Bob Elliott	55.00	15.00	5.50
15 Johnny Pesky	60.00	16.00	6.00
16 Gene Hermanski	55.00	15.00	5.50
17 Jim Hegan	55.00	15.00	5.50

		NR MT	EX	VG			NR MT	EX	VG
18	Merrill Combs	55.00	15.00	5.50	107	Connie Ryan	25.00	12.50	7.50
19	Johnny Bucha	55.00	15.00	5.50	108	Jim Konstanty	25.00	11.00	6.25
20	*Billy Loes*	110.00	55.00	32.00	109	Ted Wilks	25.00	12.50	7.50
21	Ferris Fain	60.00	16.00	6.00	110	Dutch Leonard	25.00	12.50	7.50
22	Dom DiMaggio	100.00	50.00	30.00	111	Harry Lowrey	25.00	12.50	7.50
23	Billy Goodman	55.00	15.00	5.50	112	Henry Majeski	25.00	12.50	7.50
24	Luke Easter	60.00	16.00	6.00	113	Dick Sisler	25.00	12.50	7.50
25	Johnny Groth	55.00	15.00	5.50	114	Willard Ramsdell	25.00	12.50	7.50
26	Monty Irvin	100.00	50.00	30.00	115	George Munger	25.00	12.50	7.50
27	Sam Jethroe	55.00	15.00	5.50	116	Carl Scheib	25.00	12.50	7.50
28	Jerry Priddy	55.00	15.00	5.50	117	Sherman Lollar	25.00	11.00	6.25
29	Ted Kluszewski	100.00	50.00	30.00	118	Ken Raffensberger	25.00	12.50	7.50
30	Mel Parnell	60.00	16.00	6.00	119	Maurice McDermott	25.00	12.50	7.50
31	Gus Zernial	60.00	16.00	6.00	120	Bob Chakales	25.00	12.50	7.50
32	Eddie Robinson	55.00	15.00	5.50	121	Gus Niarhos	25.00	12.50	7.50
33	Warren Spahn	250.00	125.00	75.00	122	Jack Jensen	70.00	35.00	21.00
34	Elmer Valo	55.00	15.00	5.50	123	Eddie Yost	25.00	11.00	6.25
35	Hank Sauer	60.00	16.00	6.00	124	Monte Kennedy	25.00	12.50	7.50
36	Gil Hodges	150.00	75.00	45.00	125	Bill Rigney	25.00	11.00	6.25
37	Duke Snider	300.00	150.00	90.00	126	Fred Hutchinson	25.00	11.00	6.25
38	Wally Westlake	55.00	15.00	5.50	127	Paul Minner	25.00	12.50	7.50
39	"Dizzy" Trout	60.00	16.00	6.00	128	Don Bollweg	50.00	25.00	15.00
40	Irv Noren	55.00	15.00	5.50	129	Johnny Mize	70.00	35.00	21.00
41	Bob Wellman	55.00	15.00	5.50	130	Sheldon Jones	25.00	12.50	7.50
42	Lou Kretlow	55.00	15.00	5.50	131	Morrie Martin	25.00	12.50	7.50
43	Ray Scarborough	55.00	15.00	5.50	132	Clyde Kluttz	25.00	12.50	7.50
44	Con Dempsey	55.00	15.00	5.50	133	Al Widmar	25.00	12.50	7.50
45	Eddie Joost	55.00	15.00	5.50	134	Joe Tipton	25.00	12.50	7.50
46	Gordon Goldsberry	55.00	15.00	5.50	135	Dixie Howell	25.00	12.50	7.50
47	Willie Jones	55.00	15.00	5.50	136	Johnny Schmitz	25.00	11.00	6.25
48a	Joe Page (Johnny Sain bio)	225.00	68.00	23.00	137	*Roy McMillan*	25.00	11.00	6.25
48b	Joe Page (correct bio)	80.00	24.00	8.00	138	Bill MacDonald	25.00	12.50	7.50
49a	Johnny Sain (Joe Page bio)	250.00	100.00	40.00	139	Ken Wood	25.00	12.50	7.50
49b	Johnny Sain (correct bio)	80.00	24.00	8.00	140	John Antonelli	25.00	11.00	6.25
50	Marv Rickert	55.00	15.00	5.50	141	Clint Hartung	25.00	12.50	7.50
51	Jim Russell	60.00	16.00	6.00	142	Harry Perkowski	25.00	12.50	7.50
52	Don Mueller	55.00	15.00	5.50	143	Les Moss	25.00	12.50	7.50
53	Chris Van Cuyk	60.00	16.00	6.00	144	Ed Blake	25.00	12.50	7.50
54	Leo Kiely	55.00	15.00	5.50	145	Joe Haynes	25.00	12.50	7.50
55	Ray Boone	60.00	16.00	6.00	146	Frank House	25.00	12.50	7.50
56	Tommy Glaviano	55.00	15.00	5.50	147	Bob Young	25.00	12.50	7.50
57	Ed Lopat	80.00	40.00	25.00	148	Johnny Klippstein	25.00	12.50	7.50
58	Bob Mahoney	55.00	15.00	5.50	149	Dick Kryhoski	25.00	12.50	7.50
59	Robin Roberts	125.00	62.00	37.00	150	Ted Beard	25.00	12.50	7.50
60	Sid Hudson	55.00	15.00	5.50	151	Wally Post	25.00	12.50	7.50
61	"Tookie" Gilbert	55.00	15.00	5.50	152	Al Evans	25.00	12.50	7.50
62	Chuck Stobbs	55.00	15.00	5.50	153	Bob Rush	25.00	12.50	7.50
63	Howie Pollet	55.00	15.00	5.50	154	Joe Muir	25.00	12.50	7.50
64	Roy Sievers	65.00	18.00	6.50	155	Frank Overmire	50.00	25.00	15.00
65	Enos Slaughter	100.00	50.00	30.00	156	Frank Hiller	25.00	12.50	7.50
66	"Preacher" Roe	100.00	50.00	30.00	157	Bob Usher	25.00	12.50	7.50
67	Allie Reynolds	90.00	45.00	27.00	158	Eddie Waitkus	25.00	12.50	7.50
68	Cliff Chambers	55.00	15.00	5.50	159	Saul Rogovin	25.00	12.50	7.50
69	Virgil Stallcup	55.00	15.00	5.50	160	Owen Friend	25.00	12.50	7.50
70	Al Zarilla	55.00	15.00	5.50	161	Bud Byerly	25.00	12.50	7.50
71	Tom Upton	55.00	15.00	5.50	162	Del Crandall	25.00	11.00	6.25
72	Karl Olson	55.00	15.00	5.50	163	Stan Rojek	25.00	12.50	7.50
73	William Werle	55.00	15.00	5.50	164	Walt Dubiel	25.00	12.50	7.50
74	Andy Hansen	55.00	15.00	5.50	165	Eddie Kazak	25.00	12.50	7.50
75	Wes Westrum	60.00	16.00	6.00	166	Paul LaPalme	25.00	12.50	7.50
76	Eddie Stanky	65.00	18.00	6.50	167	Bill Howerton	25.00	12.50	7.50
77	Bob Kennedy	55.00	15.00	5.50	168	Charlie Silvera	50.00	25.00	15.00
78	Ellis Kinder	55.00	15.00	5.50	169	Howie Judson	25.00	12.50	7.50
79	Gerald Staley	55.00	15.00	5.50	170	Gus Bell	25.00	11.00	6.25
80	Herman Wehmeier	55.00	15.00	5.50	171	Ed Erautt	25.00	12.50	7.50
81	Vernon Law	25.00	11.00	6.25	172	Eddie Miksis	25.00	12.50	7.50
82	Duane Pillette	25.00	12.50	7.50	173	Roy Smalley	25.00	12.50	7.50
83	Billy Johnson	25.00	12.50	7.50	174	Clarence Marshall	25.00	12.50	7.50
84	Vern Stephens	25.00	12.50	7.50	175	*Billy Martin*	350.00	175.00	105.00
85	Bob Kuzava	50.00	25.00	15.00	176	Hank Edwards	25.00	12.50	7.50
86	Ted Gray	25.00	12.50	7.50	177	Bill Wight	25.00	12.50	7.50
87	Dale Coogan	25.00	12.50	7.50	178	Cass Michaels	25.00	12.50	7.50
88	Bob Feller	175.00	87.00	52.00	179	Frank Smith	25.00	12.50	7.50
89	Johnny Lipon	25.00	12.50	7.50	180	*Charley Maxwell*	25.00	11.00	6.25
90	Mickey Grasso	25.00	12.50	7.50	181	Bob Swift	25.00	12.50	7.50
91	Al Schoendienst	80.00	20.00	6.00	182	Billy Hitchcock	25.00	12.50	7.50
92	Dale Mitchell	25.00	12.50	7.50	183	Erv Dusak	25.00	12.50	7.50
93	Al Sima	25.00	12.50	7.50	184	Bob Ramazzotti	25.00	12.50	7.50
94	Sam Mele	25.00	12.50	7.50	185	Bill Nicholson	25.00	12.50	7.50
95	Ken Holcombe	25.00	12.50	7.50	186	Walt Masterson	25.00	12.50	7.50
96	Willard Marshall	25.00	12.50	7.50	187	Bob Miller	25.00	12.50	7.50
97	Earl Torgeson	25.00	12.50	7.50	188	Clarence Podbielan	25.00	11.00	6.25
98	Bill Pierce	25.00	11.00	6.25	189	Pete Reiser	25.00	11.00	6.25
99	Gene Woodling	50.00	25.00	15.00	190	Don Johnson	25.00	12.50	7.50
100	Del Rice	25.00	12.50	7.50	191	Yogi Berra	350.00	175.00	100.00
101	Max Lanier	25.00	12.50	7.50	192	Myron Ginsberg	25.00	12.50	7.50
102	Bill Kennedy	25.00	12.50	7.50	193	Harry Simpson	25.00	12.50	7.50
103	Cliff Mapes	25.00	12.50	7.50	194	Joe Hatten	25.00	12.50	7.50
104	Don Kolloway	25.00	12.50	7.50	195	*Orestes Minoso*	150.00	75.00	52.00
105	John Pramesa	25.00	12.50	7.50	196	Solly Hemus	25.00	12.50	7.50
106	Mickey Vernon	25.00	11.00	6.25	197	George Strickland	25.00	12.50	7.50

		NR MT	EX	VG
198	Phil Haugstad	25.00	11.00	6.25
199	George Zuverink	25.00	12.50	7.50
200	Ralph Houk	60.00	30.00	18.00
201	Alex Kellner	25.00	12.50	7.50
202	Joe Collins	50.00	25.00	15.00
203	Curt Simmons	25.00	11.00	6.25
204	Ron Northey	25.00	12.50	7.50
205	Clyde King	25.00	11.00	6.25
206	Joe Ostrowski	50.00	25.00	15.00
207	Mickey Harris	25.00	12.50	7.50
208	Marlin Stuart	25.00	12.50	7.50
209	Howie Fox	25.00	12.50	7.50
210	Dick Fowler	25.00	12.50	7.50
211	Ray Coleman	25.00	12.50	7.50
212	Ned Garver	25.00	12.50	7.50
213	Nippy Jones	25.00	12.50	7.50
214	Johnny Hopp	50.00	25.00	15.00
215	Hank Bauer	40.00	18.00	11.00
216	Richie Ashburn	80.00	40.00	25.00
217	George Stirnweiss	25.00	12.50	7.50
218	Clyde McCullough	25.00	12.50	7.50
219	Bobby Shantz	25.00	11.00	6.25
220	Joe Presko	25.00	12.50	7.50
221	Granny Hamner	25.00	12.50	7.50
222	"Hoot" Evers	25.00	12.50	7.50
223	Del Ennis	25.00	11.00	6.25
224	Bruce Edwards	25.00	12.50	7.50
225	Frank Baumholtz	25.00	12.50	7.50
226	Dave Philley	25.00	11.00	6.25
227	Joe Garagiola	100.00	50.00	30.00
228	Al Brazle	25.00	12.50	7.50
229	Gene Bearden	25.00	12.50	7.50
230	Matt Batts	25.00	12.50	7.50
231	Sam Zoldak	25.00	12.50	7.50
232	Billy Cox	50.00	25.00	15.00
233	Bob Friend	25.00	11.00	6.25
234	Steve Souchock	25.00	12.50	7.50
235	Walt Dropo	25.00	11.00	6.25
236	Ed Fitz Gerald	25.00	12.50	7.50
237	Jerry Coleman	50.00	25.00	15.00
238	Art Houtteman	25.00	12.50	7.50
239	Rocky Bridges	25.00	11.00	6.25
240	Jack Phillips	25.00	12.50	7.50
241	Tommy Byrne	25.00	12.50	7.50
242	Tom Poholsky	25.00	12.50	7.50
243	Larry Doby	40.00	18.00	11.00
244	Vic Wertz	25.00	11.00	6.25
245	Sherry Robertson	25.00	12.50	7.50
246	George Kell	60.00	30.00	18.00
247	Randy Gumpert	25.00	12.50	7.50
248	Frank Shea	25.00	12.50	7.50
249	Bobby Adams	25.00	12.50	7.50
250	Carl Erskine	60.00	30.00	18.00
251	Chico Carrasquel	40.00	20.00	12.00
252	Vern Bickford	40.00	20.00	12.00
253	Johnny Berardino	50.00	25.00	15.00
254	Joe Dobson	40.00	20.00	12.00
255	Clyde Vollmer	40.00	20.00	12.00
256	Pete Suder	40.00	20.00	12.00
257	Bobby Avila	40.00	20.00	12.00
258	Steve Gromek	40.00	20.00	12.00
259	Bob Addis	40.00	20.00	12.00
260	Pete Castiglione	40.00	20.00	12.00
261	Willie Mays	2800.00	1400.00	825.00
262	Virgil Trucks	50.00	25.00	15.00
263	Harry Brecheen	50.00	25.00	15.00
264	Roy Hartsfield	40.00	20.00	12.00
265	Chuck Diering	40.00	20.00	12.00
266	Murry Dickson	40.00	20.00	12.00
267	Sid Gordon	40.00	20.00	12.00
268	Bob Lemon	200.00	100.00	60.00
269	Willard Nixon	40.00	20.00	12.00
270	Lou Brissie	40.00	20.00	12.00
271	Jim Delsing	40.00	20.00	12.00
272	Mike Garcia	50.00	25.00	15.00
273	Erv Palica	50.00	25.00	15.00
274	Ralph Branca	70.00	35.00	21.00
275	Pat Mullin	40.00	20.00	12.00
276	Jim Wilson	40.00	20.00	12.00
277	Early Wynn	175.00	87.00	52.00
278	Al Clark	40.00	20.00	12.00
279	Ed Stewart	40.00	20.00	12.00
280	Cloyd Boyer	40.00	20.00	12.00
281	Tommy Brown	50.00	25.00	15.00
282	Birdie Tebbetts	50.00	25.00	15.00
283	Phil Masi	50.00	25.00	15.00
284	Hank Arft	50.00	25.00	15.00
285	Cliff Fannin	50.00	25.00	15.00
286	Joe DeMaestri	50.00	25.00	15.00
287	Steve Bilko	50.00	25.00	15.00
288	Chet Nichols	50.00	25.00	15.00

		NR MT	EX	VG
289	Tommy Holmes	55.00	25.00	8.25
290	Joe Astroth	50.00	25.00	15.00
291	Gil Coan	50.00	25.00	15.00
292	Floyd Baker	50.00	25.00	15.00
293	Sibby Sisti	50.00	25.00	15.00
294	Walker Cooper	50.00	25.00	15.00
295	Phil Cavarretta	55.00	22.00	8.25
296	"Red" Rolfe	50.00	25.00	15.00
297	Andy Seminick	50.00	25.00	15.00
298	Bob Ross	50.00	25.00	15.00
299	Ray Murray	50.00	25.00	15.00
300	Barney McCosky	50.00	25.00	15.00
301	Bob Porterfield	40.00	20.00	12.00
302	Max Surkont	40.00	20.00	12.00
303	Harry Dorish	40.00	20.00	12.00
304	Sam Dente	40.00	20.00	12.00
305	Paul Richards	50.00	25.00	15.00
306	Lou Sleator	40.00	20.00	12.00
307	Frank Campos	40.00	20.00	12.00
308	Luis Aloma	40.00	20.00	12.00
309	Jim Busby	40.00	20.00	12.00
310	George Metkovich	40.00	20.00	12.00
311	Mickey Mantle	30000.00	15000.00	8000.
312	Jackie Robinson	1300.00	650.00	375.00
313	Bobby Thomson	200.00	100.00	60.00
314	Roy Campanella	1800.00	900.00	550.00
315	Leo Durocher	350.00	175.00	87.00
316	Davey Williams	175.00	87.00	52.00
317	Connie Marrero	175.00	87.00	52.00
318	Hal Gregg	175.00	87.00	52.00
319	Al Walker	175.00	87.00	52.00
320	John Rutherford	175.00	87.00	52.00
321	*Joe Black*	225.00	90.00	56.00
322	Randy Jackson	175.00	87.00	52.00
323	Bubba Church	175.00	87.00	52.00
324	Warren Hacker	175.00	87.00	52.00
325	Bill Serena	175.00	87.00	52.00
326	George Shuba	175.00	87.00	52.00
327	Archie Wilson	175.00	87.00	52.00
328	Bob Borkowski	175.00	87.00	52.00
329	Ivan Delock	175.00	87.00	52.00
330	Turk Lown	175.00	87.00	52.00
331	Tom Morgan	160.00	80.00	48.00
332	Tony Bartirome	175.00	87.00	52.00
333	Pee Wee Reese	1200.00	600.00	350.00
334	Wilmer Mizell	175.00	87.00	52.00
335	Ted Lepcio	175.00	87.00	52.00
336	Dave Koslo	175.00	87.00	52.00
337	Jim Hearn	175.00	87.00	52.00
338	Sal Yvars	175.00	87.00	52.00
339	Russ Meyer	175.00	87.00	52.00
340	Bob Hooper	175.00	87.00	52.00
341	Hal Jeffcoat	175.00	87.00	52.00
342	*Clem Labine*	200.00	90.00	52.00
343	Dick Gernert	175.00	87.00	52.00
344	Ewell Blackwell	160.00	80.00	48.00
345	Sam White	175.00	87.00	52.00
346	George Spencer	175.00	87.00	52.00
347	Joe Adcock	200.00	100.00	60.00
348	Bob Kelly	175.00	87.00	52.00
349	Bob Cain	175.00	87.00	52.00
350	Cal Abrams	175.00	87.00	52.00
351	Al Dark	175.00	87.00	52.00
352	Karl Drews	175.00	87.00	52.00
353	Bob Del Greco	175.00	87.00	52.00
354	Fred Hatfield	175.00	87.00	52.00
355	Bobby Morgan	175.00	87.00	52.00
356	Toby Atwell	175.00	87.00	52.00
357	Smoky Burgess	250.00	125.00	75.00
358	John Kucab	175.00	87.00	52.00
359	Dee Fondy	175.00	87.00	52.00
360	George Crowe	175.00	87.00	52.00
361	Bill Posedel	175.00	87.00	52.00
362	Ken Heintzelman	175.00	87.00	52.00
363	Dick Rozek	175.00	87.00	52.00
364	Clyde Sukeforth	175.00	87.00	52.00
365	"Cookie" Lavagetto	175.00	87.00	52.00
366	Dave Madison	175.00	87.00	52.00
367	Bob Thorpe	175.00	87.00	52.00
368	Ed Wright	175.00	87.00	52.00
369	*Dick Groat*	350.00	175.00	105.00
370	Billy Hoeft	175.00	87.00	52.00
371	Bob Hofman	175.00	87.00	52.00
372	*Gil McDougald*	350.00	175.00	105.00
373	Jim Turner	160.00	80.00	48.00
374	Al Benton	175.00	87.00	52.00
375	Jack Merson	175.00	87.00	52.00
376	Faye Throneberry	175.00	87.00	52.00
377	Chuck Dressen	175.00	90.00	52.00
378	Les Fusselman	175.00	87.00	52.00
379	Joe Rossi	175.00	87.00	52.00

		NR MT	EX	VG
380	Clem Koshorek	175.00	87.00	52.00
381	Milton Stock	175.00	87.00	52.00
382	Sam Jones	175.00	87.00	52.00
383	Del Wilber	175.00	87.00	52.00
384	Frank Crosetti	250.00	125.00	67.00
385	Herman Franks	175.00	87.00	52.00
386	Eddie Yuhas	175.00	87.00	52.00
387	Billy Meyer	175.00	87.00	52.00
388	Bob Chipman	175.00	87.00	52.00
389	Ben Wade	175.00	87.00	52.00
390	Glenn Nelson	175.00	87.00	52.00
391	Ben Chapman (photo actually Sam Chapman)	175.00	87.00	52.00
392	*Hoyt Wilhelm*	700.00	350.00	200.00
393	Ebba St. Claire	175.00	87.00	52.00
394	Billy Herman	250.00	125.00	75.00
395	Jake Pitler	175.00	87.00	52.00
396	*Dick Williams*	250.00	125.00	75.00
397	Forrest Main	175.00	87.00	52.00
398	Hal Rice	175.00	87.00	52.00
399	Jim Fridley	175.00	87.00	52.00
400	Bill Dickey	650.00	325.00	200.00
401	Bob Schultz	175.00	87.00	52.00
402	Earl Harrist	175.00	87.00	52.00
403	Bill Miller	160.00	80.00	48.00
404	Dick Brodowski	175.00	87.00	52.00
405	Eddie Pellagrini	175.00	87.00	52.00
406	*Joe Nuxhall*	200.00	100.00	60.00
407	*Ed Mathews*	3000.00	1500.00	900.00

1953 Topps

The 1953 Topps set reflects the company's continuing legal battles with Bowman. The set, originally intended to consist of 280 cards, is lacking six numbers (#'s 253, 261, 267, 268, 271 and 275) which probably represent players whose contracts were lost to the competition. The 2-5/8" by 3-3/4" cards feature painted player pictures. A color team logo appears at the bottom panel (red for American League and black for National.) Card backs contain the first baseball trivia questions along with brief statistics and player biographies. In the red panel at the top which lists the player's personal data, cards from the 2nd Series (#'s 86-165 plus 10, 44, 61, 72 and 81) can be found with that data printed in either black or white, black being the scarcer variety. Card numbers 221-280 are the scarce high numbers.

	NR MT	EX	VG
Complete Set:	14000.00	7000.00	4000.
Common Player Singleprint: 1-165	25.00	12.50	7.50
Common Player: 1-165	16.00	8.00	4.75
Common Player: 166-220	16.00	8.00	4.75
Common Player Singleprint: 221-280	90.00	45.00	27.00
Common Player: 221-280	50.00	25.00	15.00

		NR MT	EX	VG
1	Jackie Robinson	650.00	275.00	175.00
2	Luke Easter	25.00	12.50	7.50
3	George Crowe	25.00	12.50	7.50
4	Ben Wade	25.00	12.50	7.50
5	Joe Dobson	25.00	12.50	7.50
6	Sam Jones	25.00	12.50	7.50
7	Bob Borkowski	16.00	8.00	4.75
8	Clem Koshorek	16.00	8.00	4.75
9	Joe Collins	30.00	15.00	9.00
10	Smoky Burgess	40.00	20.00	12.00

		NR MT	EX	VG
11	Sal Yvars	25.00	12.50	7.50
12	Howie Judson	16.00	8.00	4.75
13	Connie Marrero	16.00	8.00	4.75
14	Clem Labine	25.00	12.50	7.50
15	Bobo Newsom	25.00	12.50	7.50
16	Harry Lowrey	16.00	8.00	4.75
17	Billy Hitchcock	25.00	12.50	7.50
18	Ted Lepcio	16.00	8.00	4.75
19	Mel Parnell	16.00	8.00	4.75
20	Hank Thompson	25.00	12.50	7.50
21	Billy Johnson	25.00	12.50	7.50
22	Howie Fox	25.00	12.50	7.50
23	Toby Atwell	16.00	8.00	4.75
24	Ferris Fain	25.00	12.50	7.50
25	Ray Boone	25.00	12.50	7.50
26	Dale Mitchell	16.00	8.00	4.75
27	Roy Campanella	225.00	112.00	67.00
28	Eddie Pellagrini	25.00	12.50	7.50
29	Hal Jeffcoat	25.00	12.50	7.50
30	Willard Nixon	25.00	12.50	7.50
31	Ewell Blackwell	40.00	20.00	12.00
32	Clyde Vollmer	25.00	12.50	7.50
33	Bob Kennedy	16.00	8.00	4.75
34	George Shuba	25.00	12.50	7.50
35	Irv Noren	25.00	12.50	7.50
36	Johnny Groth	16.00	8.00	4.75
37	Ed Mathews	115.00	57.50	34.50
38	Jim Hearn	16.00	8.00	4.75
39	Eddie Miksis	25.00	12.50	7.50
40	John Lipon	25.00	12.50	7.50
41	Enos Slaughter	90.00	45.00	27.00
42	Gus Zernial	16.00	8.00	4.75
43	Gil McDougald	50.00	25.00	15.00
44	Ellis Kinder	30.00	15.00	9.00
45	Grady Hatton	16.00	8.00	4.75
46	Johnny Klippstein	16.00	8.00	4.75
47	Bubba Church	16.00	8.00	4.75
48	Bob Del Greco	16.00	8.00	4.75
49	Faye Throneberry	16.00	8.00	4.75
50	Chuck Dressen	25.00	12.50	7.50
51	Frank Campos	16.00	8.00	4.75
52	Ted Gray	16.00	8.00	4.75
53	Sherman Lollar	16.00	8.00	4.75
54	Bob Feller	125.00	67.00	37.00
55	Maurice McDermott	16.00	8.00	4.75
56	Gerald Staley	16.00	8.00	4.75
57	Carl Scheib	25.00	12.50	7.50
58	George Metkovich	25.00	12.50	7.50
59	Karl Drews	16.00	8.00	4.75
60	Cloyd Boyer	16.00	8.00	4.75
61	Early Wynn	80.00	40.00	25.00
62	Monte Irvin	45.00	23.00	13.50
63	Gus Niarhos	16.00	8.00	4.75
64	Dave Philley	25.00	12.50	7.50
65	Earl Harrist	25.00	12.50	7.50
66	Orestes Minoso	30.00	15.00	9.00
67	Roy Sievers	25.00	12.50	7.50
68	Del Rice	25.00	12.50	7.50
69	Dick Brodowski	25.00	12.50	7.50
70	Ed Yuhas	25.00	12.50	7.50
71	Tony Bartirome	25.00	12.50	7.50
72	Fred Hutchinson	25.00	12.50	7.50
73	Eddie Robinson	25.00	12.50	7.50
74	Joe Rossi	25.00	12.50	7.50
75	Mike Garcia	25.00	12.50	7.50
76	Pee Wee Reese	175.00	87.00	52.00
77	John Mize	60.00	30.00	18.00
78	Al Schoendienst	65.00	33.00	20.00
79	Johnny Wyrostek	25.00	12.50	7.50
80	Jim Hegan	25.00	12.50	7.50
82	Mickey Mantle	3500.00	1750.00	1050.
83	Howie Pollet	25.00	12.50	7.50
84	Bob Hooper	16.00	8.00	4.75
85	Bobby Morgan	25.00	12.50	7.50
86	Billy Martin	125.00	67.00	37.00
87	Ed Lopat	35.00	17.50	10.50
88	Willie Jones	16.00	8.00	4.75
89	Chuck Stobbs	16.00	8.00	4.75
90	Hank Edwards	16.00	8.00	4.75
91	Ebba St. Claire	16.00	8.00	4.75
92	Paul Minner	16.00	8.00	4.75
93	Hal Rice	16.00	8.00	4.75
94	William Kennedy	16.00	8.00	4.75
95	Willard Marshall	16.00	8.00	4.75
96	Virgil Trucks	25.00	12.50	7.50
97	Don Kolloway	16.00	8.00	4.75
98	Cal Abrams	16.00	8.00	4.75
99	Dave Madison	16.00	8.00	4.75
100	Bill Miller	25.00	12.50	7.50
101	Ted Wilks	16.00	8.00	4.75
102	Connie Ryan	16.00	8.00	4.75
103	Joe Astroth	16.00	8.00	4.75

	NR MT	EX	VG
104 Yogi Berra	250.00	125.00	75.00
105 Joe Nuxhall	25.00	12.50	7.50
106 Johnny Antonelli	25.00	12.50	7.50
107 Danny O'Connell	16.00	8.00	4.75
108 Bob Porterfield	16.00	8.00	4.75
109 Alvin Dark	30.00	15.00	9.00
110 Herman Wehmeier	16.00	8.00	4.75
111 Hank Sauer	16.00	8.00	4.75
112 Ned Garver	16.00	8.00	4.75
113 Jerry Priddy	16.00	8.00	4.75
114 Phil Rizzuto	125.00	62.00	37.00
115 George Spencer	16.00	8.00	4.75
116 Frank Smith	16.00	8.00	4.75
117 Sid Gordon	16.00	8.00	4.75
118 Gus Bell	16.00	8.00	4.75
119 John Sain	40.00	20.00	12.00
120 Davey Williams	16.00	8.00	4.75
121 Walt Dropo	16.00	8.00	4.75
122 Elmer Valo	16.00	8.00	4.75
123 Tommy Byrne	16.00	8.00	4.75
124 Sibby Sisti	16.00	8.00	4.75
125 Dick Williams	25.00	12.50	7.50
126 Bill Connelly	16.00	8.00	4.75
127 Clint Courtney	16.00	8.00	4.75
128 Wilmer Mizell	16.00	8.00	4.75
129 Keith Thomas	16.00	8.00	4.75
130 Turk Lown	16.00	8.00	4.75
131 Harry Byrd	16.00	8.00	4.75
132 Tom Morgan	25.00	12.50	7.50
133 Gil Coan	16.00	8.00	4.75
134 Rube Walker	25.00	12.50	7.50
135 Al Rosen	35.00	17.50	10.50
136 Ken Heintzelman	16.00	8.00	4.75
137 John Rutherford	25.00	12.50	7.50
138 George Kell	65.00	32.50	19.50
139 Sammy White	16.00	8.00	4.75
140 Tommy Glaviano	16.00	8.00	4.75
141 Allie Reynolds	35.00	17.50	10.50
142 Vic Wertz	25.00	12.50	7.50
143 Billy Pierce	25.00	12.50	7.50
144 Bob Schultz	16.00	8.00	4.75
145 Harry Dorish	16.00	8.00	4.75
146 Granville Hamner	16.00	8.00	4.75
147 Warren Spahn	150.00	75.00	45.00
148 Mickey Grasso	16.00	8.00	4.75
149 Dom DiMaggio	30.00	15.00	9.00
150 Harry Simpson	16.00	8.00	4.75
151 Hoyt Wilhelm	70.00	35.00	20.00
152 Bob Adams	16.00	8.00	4.75
153 Andy Seminick	16.00	8.00	4.75
154 Dick Groat	25.00	12.50	7.50
155 Dutch Leonard	16.00	8.00	4.75
156 Jim Rivera	16.00	8.00	4.75
157 Bob Addis	16.00	8.00	4.75
158 John Logan	25.00	12.50	7.50
159 Wayne Terwilliger	16.00	8.00	4.75
160 Bob Young	16.00	8.00	4.75
161 Vern Bickford	16.00	8.00	4.75
162 Ted Kluszewski	50.00	25.00	15.00
163 Fred Hatfield	16.00	8.00	4.75
164 Frank Shea	16.00	8.00	4.75
165 Billy Hoeft	16.00	8.00	4.75
166 Bill Hunter	16.00	8.00	4.75
167 Art Schult	16.00	8.00	4.75
168 Willard Schmidt	16.00	8.00	4.75
169 Dizzy Trout	16.00	8.00	4.75
170 Bill Werle	16.00	8.00	4.75
171 Bill Glynn	16.00	8.00	4.75
172 Rip Repulski	16.00	8.00	4.75
173 Preston Ward	16.00	8.00	4.75
174 Billy Loes	16.00	8.00	4.75
175 Ron Kline	16.00	8.00	4.75
176 Don Hoak	16.00	8.00	4.75
177 Jim Dyck	16.00	8.00	4.75
178 Jim Waugh	16.00	8.00	4.75
179 Gene Hermanski	16.00	8.00	4.75
180 Virgil Stallcup	16.00	8.00	4.75
181 Al Zarilla	16.00	8.00	4.75
182 Bob Hofman	16.00	8.00	4.75
183 Stu Miller	16.00	8.00	4.75
184 Hal Brown	16.00	8.00	4.75
185 Jim Pendleton	16.00	8.00	4.75
186 Charlie Bishop	16.00	8.00	4.75
187 Jim Fridley	16.00	8.00	4.75
188 Andy Carey	16.00	8.00	4.75
189 Ray Jablonski	16.00	8.00	4.75
190 Dixie Walker	16.00	8.00	4.75
191 Ralph Kiner	70.00	35.00	21.00
192 Wally Westlake	16.00	8.00	4.75
193 Mike Clark	16.00	8.00	4.75
194 Eddie Kazak	16.00	8.00	4.75

	NR MT	EX	VG
195 Ed McGhee	16.00	8.00	4.75
196 Bob Keegan	16.00	8.00	4.75
197 Del Crandall	16.00	8.00	4.75
198 Forrest Main	16.00	8.00	4.75
199 Marion Fricano	16.00	8.00	4.75
200 Gordon Goldsberry	16.00	8.00	4.75
201 Paul LaPalme	16.00	8.00	4.75
202 Carl Sawatski	16.00	8.00	4.75
203 Cliff Fannin	16.00	8.00	4.75
204 Dick Bokelmann	16.00	8.00	4.75
205 Vern Benson	16.00	8.00	4.75
206 Ed Bailey	16.00	8.00	4.75
207 Whitey Ford	150.00	75.00	45.00
208 Jim Wilson	16.00	8.00	4.75
209 Jim Greengrass	16.00	8.00	4.75
210 Bob Cerv	16.00	8.00	4.75
211 J.W. Porter	16.00	8.00	4.75
212 Jack Dittmer	16.00	8.00	4.75
213 Ray Scarborough	16.00	8.00	4.75
214 Bill Bruton	16.00	8.00	4.75
215 Gene Conley	16.00	8.00	4.75
216 Jim Hughes	16.00	8.00	4.75
217 Murray Wall	16.00	8.00	4.75
218 Les Fusselman	16.00	8.00	4.75
219 Pete Runnels (photo actually Don Johnson)	16.00	8.00	4.75
220 Satchell Paige	450.00	225.00	135.00
221 Bob Milliken	90.00	45.00	27.00
222 Vic Janowicz	50.00	25.00	15.00
223 John O'Brien	50.00	25.00	15.00
224 Lou Sleater	50.00	25.00	15.00
225 Bobby Shantz	100.00	50.00	30.00
226 Ed Erautt	90.00	45.00	27.00
227 Morris Martin	50.00	25.00	15.00
228 Hal Newhouser	125.00	67.00	37.00
229 Rocky Krsnich	90.00	45.00	27.00
230 Johnny Lindell	50.00	25.00	15.00
231 Solly Hemus	50.00	25.00	15.00
232 Dick Kokos	90.00	45.00	27.00
233 Al Aber	90.00	45.00	27.00
234 Ray Murray	50.00	25.00	15.00
235 John Hetki	50.00	25.00	15.00
236 Harry Perkowski	90.00	45.00	27.00
237 Clarence Podbielan	50.00	25.00	15.00
238 Cal Hogue	50.00	25.00	15.00
239 Jim Delsing	90.00	45.00	27.00
240 Freddie Marsh	50.00	25.00	15.00
241 Al Sima	50.00	25.00	15.00
242 Charlie Silvera	90.00	45.00	27.00
243 Carlos Bernier	50.00	25.00	15.00
244 Willie Mays	2600.00	1300.00	800.00
245 Bill Norman	90.00	45.00	27.00
246 Roy Face	80.00	40.00	25.00
247 Mike Sandlock	50.00	25.00	15.00
248 Gene Stephens	50.00	25.00	15.00
249 Ed O'Brien	50.00	25.00	15.00
250 Bob Wilson	90.00	45.00	27.00
251 Sid Hudson	90.00	45.00	27.00
252 Henry Foiles	90.00	45.00	27.00
253 Not Issued			
254 Preacher Roe	80.00	40.00	24.00
255 Dixie Howell	90.00	45.00	27.00
256 Les Peden	90.00	45.00	27.00
257 Bob Boyd	90.00	45.00	27.00
258 Jim Gilliam	300.00	150.00	90.00
259 Roy McMillan	90.00	45.00	27.00
260 Sam Calderone	90.00	45.00	27.00
261 Not Issued			
262 Bob Oldis	90.00	45.00	27.00
263 John Podres	250.00	125.00	70.00
264 Gene Woodling	70.00	35.00	20.00
265 Jackie Jensen	125.00	67.00	37.00
266 Bob Cain	90.00	45.00	27.00
267 Not Issued			
268 Not Issued			
269 Duane Pillette	90.00	45.00	27.00
270 Vern Stephens	90.00	45.00	27.00
271 Not Issued			
272 Bill Antonello	90.00	45.00	27.00
273 Harvey Haddix	150.00	75.00	40.00
274 John Riddle	90.00	45.00	27.00
275 Not Issued			
276 Ken Raffensberger	50.00	25.00	15.00
277 Don Lund	90.00	45.00	27.00
278 Willie Miranda	90.00	45.00	27.00
279 Joe Coleman	50.00	25.00	15.00
280 Milt Bolling	300.00	150.00	60.00

1954 Topps

The first issue to use two player pictures on the front, the 1954 Topps set is very popular today. Solid color backgrounds frame both color head- and-shoulders and black and white action pictures of the player. The player's name, position, team and team logo appear at the top. Backs include an "Inside Baseball" cartoon regarding the player as well as statistics and biography. The 250-card, 2-5/8" by 3-3/4", set includes manager and coaches cards, and the first use of two players together on a modern card; the players were, appropriately, the O'Brien twins.

	NR MT	EX	VG
Complete Set:	8200.00	4100.00	2550.
Common Player: 1-50	13.00	6.50	4.00
Common Player: 51-75	30.00	15.00	9.00
Common Player: 76-250	13.00	6.50	4.00

		NR MT	EX	VG
1	Ted Williams	650.00	200.00	125.00
2	Gus Zernial	13.00	6.50	4.00
3	Monte Irvin	35.00	17.50	10.50
4	Hank Sauer	15.00	7.50	4.50
5	Ed Lopat	20.00	10.00	6.00
6	Pete Runnels	13.00	6.50	4.00
7	Ted Kluszewski	30.00	15.00	9.00
8	Bobby Young	13.00	6.50	4.00
9	Harvey Haddix	13.00	6.50	4.00
10	Jackie Robinson	300.00	150.00	90.00
11	Paul Smith	13.00	6.50	4.00
12	Del Crandall	13.00	6.50	4.00
13	Billy Martin	85.00	42.00	26.00
14	Preacher Roe	40.00	20.00	12.00
15	Al Rosen	20.00	10.00	6.00
16	Vic Janowicz	13.00	6.50	4.00
17	Phil Rizzuto	70.00	35.00	20.00
18	Walt Dropo	13.00	6.50	4.00
19	Johnny Lipon	13.00	6.50	4.00
20	Warren Spahn	110.00	55.00	33.00
21	Bobby Shantz	13.00	6.50	4.00
22	Jim Greengrass	13.00	6.50	4.00
23	Luke Easter	13.00	6.50	4.00
24	Granny Hamner	13.00	6.50	4.00
25	*Harvey Kuenn*	50.00	25.00	15.00
26	Ray Jablonski	13.00	6.50	4.00
27	Ferris Fain	13.00	6.50	4.00
28	Paul Minner	13.00	6.50	4.00
29	Jim Hegan	13.00	6.50	4.00
30	Ed Mathews	100.00	50.00	30.00
31	Johnny Klippstein	13.00	6.50	4.00
32	Duke Snider	150.00	75.00	45.00
33	Johnny Schmitz	13.00	6.50	4.00
34	Jim Rivera	13.00	6.50	4.00
35	Junior Gilliam	30.00	15.00	9.00
36	Hoyt Wilhelm	50.00	25.00	15.00
37	Whitey Ford	110.00	55.00	33.00
38	Eddie Stanky	13.00	6.50	4.00
39	Sherm Lollar	13.00	6.50	4.00
40	Mel Parnell	13.00	6.50	4.00
41	Willie Jones	13.00	6.50	4.00
42	Don Mueller	13.00	6.50	4.00
43	Dick Groat	13.00	6.50	4.00
44	Ned Garver	13.00	6.50	4.00
45	Richie Ashburn	40.00	20.00	12.00
46	Ken Raffensberger	13.00	6.50	4.00
47	Ellis Kinder	13.00	6.50	4.00
48	Billy Hunter	13.00	6.50	4.00

		NR MT	EX	VG
49	Ray Murray	13.00	6.50	4.00
50	Yogi Berra	260.00	130.00	78.00
51	Johnny Lindell	30.00	15.00	9.00
52	Vic Power	30.00	15.00	9.00
53	Jack Dittmer	30.00	15.00	9.00
54	Vern Stephens	30.00	15.00	9.00
55	Phil Cavarretta	30.00	15.00	9.00
56	Willie Miranda	30.00	15.00	9.00
57	Luis Aloma	30.00	15.00	9.00
58	Bob Wilson	30.00	15.00	9.00
59	Gene Conley	30.00	15.00	9.00
60	Frank Baumholtz	30.00	15.00	9.00
61	Bob Cain	30.00	15.00	9.00
62	Eddie Robinson	30.00	15.00	9.00
63	Johnny Pesky	30.00	15.00	9.00
64	Hank Thompson	30.00	15.00	9.00
65	Bob Swift	30.00	15.00	9.00
66	Ted Lepcio	30.00	15.00	9.00
67	Jim Willis	30.00	15.00	9.00
68	Sammy Calderone	30.00	15.00	9.00
69	Bud Podbielan	30.00	15.00	9.00
70	Larry Doby	70.00	35.00	21.00
71	Frank Smith	30.00	15.00	9.00
72	Preston Ward	30.00	15.00	9.00
73	Wayne Terwilliger	30.00	15.00	9.00
74	Bill Taylor	30.00	15.00	9.00
75	Fred Haney	30.00	15.00	9.00
76	Bob Scheffing	13.00	6.50	4.00
77	Ray Boone	13.00	6.50	4.00
78	Ted Kazanski	13.00	6.50	4.00
79	Andy Pafko	13.00	6.50	4.00
80	Jackie Jensen	13.00	6.50	4.00
81	Dave Hoskins	13.00	6.50	4.00
82	Milt Bolling	13.00	6.50	4.00
83	Joe Collins	13.00	6.50	4.00
84	Dick Cole	13.00	6.50	4.00
85	*Bob Turley*	13.00	6.50	4.00
86	Billy Herman	30.00	15.00	9.00
87	Roy Face	13.00	6.50	4.00
88	Matt Batts	13.00	6.50	4.00
89	Howie Pollet	13.00	6.50	4.00
90	Willie Mays	600.00	300.00	175.00
91	Bob Oldis	13.00	6.50	4.00
92	Wally Westlake	13.00	6.50	4.00
93	Sid Hudson	13.00	6.50	4.00
94	*Ernie Banks*	800.00	400.00	250.00
95	Hal Rice	13.00	6.50	4.00
96	Charlie Silvera	13.00	6.50	4.00
97	Jerry Lane	13.00	6.50	4.00
98	Joe Black	13.00	6.50	4.00
99	Bob Hofman	13.00	6.50	4.00
100	Bob Keegan	13.00	6.50	4.00
101	Gene Woodling	20.00	10.00	6.00
102	Gil Hodges	75.00	38.00	23.00
103	*Jim Lemon*	13.00	6.50	4.00
104	Mike Sandlock	13.00	6.50	4.00
105	Andy Carey	13.00	6.50	4.00
106	Dick Kokos	13.00	6.50	4.00
107	Duane Pillette	13.00	6.50	4.00
108	Thornton Kipper	13.00	6.50	4.00
109	Bill Bruton	13.00	6.50	4.00
110	Harry Dorish	13.00	6.50	4.00
111	Jim Delsing	13.00	6.50	4.00
112	Bill Renna	13.00	6.50	4.00
113	Bob Boyd	13.00	6.50	4.00
114	Dean Stone	13.00	6.50	4.00
115	"Rip" Repulski	13.00	6.50	4.00
116	Steve Bilko	13.00	6.50	4.00
117	Solly Hemus	13.00	6.50	4.00
118	Carl Scheib	13.00	6.50	4.00
119	Johnny Antonelli	13.00	6.50	4.00
120	Roy McMillan	13.00	6.50	4.00
121	Clem Labine	13.00	6.50	4.00
122	Johnny Logan	13.00	6.50	4.00
123	Bobby Adams	13.00	6.50	4.00
124	Marion Fricano	13.00	6.50	4.00
125	Harry Perkowski	13.00	6.50	4.00
126	Ben Wade	13.00	6.50	4.00
127	Steve O'Neill	13.00	6.50	4.00
128	Henry Aaron	2000.00	1000.00	600.00
129	Forrest Jacobs	13.00	6.50	4.00
130	Hank Bauer	30.00	15.00	9.00
131	Reno Bertoia	13.00	6.50	4.00
132	*Tom Lasorda*	175.00	87.00	52.00
133	Del Baker	13.00	6.50	4.00
134	Cal Hogue	13.00	6.50	4.00
135	Joe Presko	13.00	6.50	4.00
136	Connie Ryan	13.00	6.50	4.00
137	*Wally Moon*	13.00	6.50	4.00
138	Bob Borkowski	13.00	6.50	4.00
139	Ed & Johnny O'Brien	30.00	15.00	9.00

		NR MT	EX	VG
140	Tom Wright	13.00	6.50	4.00
141	*Joe Jay*	13.00	6.50	4.00
142	Tom Poholsky	13.00	6.50	4.00
143	Rollie Hemsley	13.00	6.50	4.00
144	Bill Werle	13.00	6.50	4.00
145	Elmer Valo	13.00	6.50	4.00
146	Don Johnson	13.00	6.50	4.00
147	John Riddle	13.00	6.50	4.00
148	Bob Trice	13.00	6.50	4.00
149	Jim Robertson	13.00	6.50	4.00
150	Dick Kryhoski	13.00	6.50	4.00
151	Alex Grammas	13.00	6.50	4.00
152	Mike Blyzka	13.00	6.50	4.00
153	"Rube" Walker	13.00	6.50	4.00
154	Mike Fornieles	13.00	6.50	4.00
155	Bob Kennedy	13.00	6.50	4.00
156	Joe Coleman	13.00	6.50	4.00
157	Don Lenhardt	13.00	6.50	4.00
158	"Peanuts" Lowrey	13.00	6.50	4.00
159	Dave Philley	13.00	6.50	4.00
160	"Red" Kress	13.00	6.50	4.00
161	John Hetki	13.00	6.50	4.00
162	Herman Wehmeier	13.00	6.50	4.00
163	Frank House	13.00	6.50	4.00
164	Stu Miller	13.00	6.50	4.00
165	Jim Pendleton	13.00	6.50	4.00
166	Johnny Podres	30.00	15.00	9.00
167	Don Lund	13.00	6.50	4.00
168	Morrie Martin	13.00	6.50	4.00
169	Jim Hughes	13.00	6.50	4.00
170	*Jim Rhodes*	13.00	6.50	4.00
171	Leo Kiely	13.00	6.50	4.00
172	Hal Brown	13.00	6.50	4.00
173	Jack Harshman	13.00	6.50	4.00
174	Tom Qualters	13.00	6.50	4.00
175	Frank Leja	13.00	6.50	4.00
176	Bob Keely	13.00	6.50	4.00
177	Bob Milliken	13.00	6.50	4.00
178	Bill Gylnn (Glynn)	13.00	6.50	4.00
179	Gair Allie	13.00	6.50	4.00
180	Wes Westrum	13.00	6.50	4.00
181	Mel Roach	13.00	6.50	4.00
182	Chuck Harmon	13.00	6.50	4.00
183	Earle Combs	35.00	17.50	10.50
184	Ed Bailey	13.00	6.50	4.00
185	Chuck Stobbs	13.00	6.50	4.00
186	Karl Olson	13.00	6.50	4.00
187	"Heinie" Manush	35.00	17.50	10.50
188	Dave Jolly	13.00	6.50	4.00
189	Bob Ross	13.00	6.50	4.00
190	Ray Herbert	13.00	6.50	4.00
191	*Dick Schofield*	13.00	6.50	4.00
192	"Cot" Deal	13.00	6.50	4.00
193	Johnny Hopp	13.00	6.50	4.00
194	Bill Sarni	13.00	6.50	4.00
195	Bill Consolo	13.00	6.50	4.00
196	Stan Jok	13.00	6.50	4.00
197	"Schoolboy" Rowe	13.00	6.50	4.00
198	Carl Sawatski	13.00	6.50	4.00
199	"Rocky" Nelson	13.00	6.50	4.00
200	Larry Jansen	13.00	6.50	4.00
201	*Al Kaline*	900.00	450.00	275.00
202	*Bob Purkey*	13.00	6.50	4.00
203	Harry Brecheen	13.00	6.50	4.00
204	Angel Scull	13.00	6.50	4.00
205	Johnny Sain	35.00	17.50	10.50
206	Ray Crone	13.00	6.50	4.00
207	Tom Oliver	13.00	6.50	4.00
208	Grady Hatton	13.00	6.50	4.00
209	Charlie Thompson	13.00	6.50	4.00
210	*Bob Buhl*	13.00	6.50	4.00
211	Don Hoak	13.00	6.50	4.00
212	Mickey Micelotta	13.00	6.50	4.00
213	John Fitzpatrick	13.00	6.50	4.00
214	Arnold Portocarrero	13.00	6.50	4.00
215	Ed McGhee	13.00	6.50	4.00
216	Al Sima	13.00	6.50	4.00
217	Paul Schreiber	13.00	6.50	4.00
218	Fred Marsh	13.00	6.50	4.00
219	Charlie Kress	13.00	6.50	4.00
220	Ruben Gomez	13.00	6.50	4.00
221	Dick Brodowski	13.00	6.50	4.00
222	Bill Wilson	13.00	6.50	4.00
223	Joe Haynes	13.00	6.50	4.00
224	Dick Weik	13.00	6.50	4.00
225	Don Liddle	13.00	6.50	4.00
226	Jehosie Heard	13.00	6.50	4.00
227	Buster Mills	13.00	6.50	4.00
228	Gene Hermanski	13.00	6.50	4.00
229	Bob Talbot	13.00	6.50	4.00
230	Bob Kuzava	13.00	6.50	4.00

		NR MT	EX	VG
231	Roy Smalley	13.00	6.50	4.00
232	Lou Limmer	13.00	6.50	4.00
233	Augie Galan	13.00	6.50	4.00
234	*Jerry Lynch*	13.00	6.50	4.00
235	Vern Law	13.00	6.50	4.00
236	Paul Penson	13.00	6.50	4.00
237	Mike Ryba	13.00	6.50	4.00
238	Al Aber	13.00	6.50	4.00
239	*Bill Skowron*	90.00	45.00	27.00
240	Sam Mele	13.00	6.50	4.00
241	Bob Miller	13.00	6.50	4.00
242	Curt Roberts	13.00	6.50	4.00
243	Ray Blades	13.00	6.50	4.00
244	Leroy Wheat	13.00	6.50	4.00
245	Roy Sievers	13.00	6.50	4.00
246	Howie Fox	13.00	6.50	4.00
247	Eddie Mayo	13.00	6.50	4.00
248	*Al Smith*	13.00	6.50	4.00
249	*Wilmer Mizell*	13.00	6.50	4.00
250	Ted Williams	700.00	225.00	110.00

1955 Topps

MONTE IRVIN   outfield NEW YORK GIANTS

The 1955 Topps set is numerically the smallest of the regular issue Topps sets. The 3-3/4" by 2-5/8" cards mark the first time that Topps used a horizontal format. While that format was new, the design was not; they are very similar to the 1954 cards to the point many pictures appeared in both years. Although it was slated for a 210-card set, the 1955 Topps set turned out to be only 206 cards with numbers 175, 186, 203 and 209 never being released. The scarce high numbers in this set begin with #161.

		NR MT	EX	VG
Complete Set:		7750.00	3825.00	2300.
Common Player: 1-150		8.00	4.00	2.50
Common Player: 151-160		17.00	8.50	5.00
Common Player: 161-210		25.00	12.50	7.50
1	"Dusty" Rhodes	50.00	15.00	9.00
2	Ted Williams	400.00	200.00	125.00
3	Art Fowler	8.00	4.00	2.50
4	Al Kaline	250.00	125.00	75.00
5	Jim Gilliam	10.00	5.00	3.00
6	Stan Hack	8.00	4.00	2.50
7	Jim Hegan	8.00	4.00	2.50
8	Hal Smith	8.00	4.00	2.50
9	Bob Miller	8.00	4.00	2.50
10	Bob Keegan	8.00	4.00	2.50
11	Ferris Fain	8.00	4.00	2.50
12	"Jake" Thies	8.00	4.00	2.50
13	Fred Marsh	8.00	4.00	2.50
14	Jim Finigan	8.00	4.00	2.50
15	Jim Pendleton	8.00	4.00	2.50
16	Roy Sievers	15.00	7.50	4.50
17	Bobby Hofman	8.00	4.00	2.50
18	Russ Kemmerer	8.00	4.00	2.50
19	Billy Herman	12.00	6.00	3.50
20	Andy Carey	9.00	4.50	2.75
21	Alex Grammas	8.00	4.00	2.50
22	Bill Skowron	20.00	10.00	6.00
23	Jack Parks	8.00	4.00	2.50
24	Hal Newhouser	8.00	4.00	2.50
25	Johnny Podres	20.00	10.00	6.00
26	Dick Groat	15.00	7.50	4.50
27	Billy Gardner	8.00	4.00	2.50

		NR MT	EX	VG			NR MT	EX	VG
28	Ernie Banks	250.00	125.00	75.00	119	Bob Lennon	8.00	4.00	2.50
29	Herman Wehmeier	8.00	4.00	2.50	120	Ted Kluszewski	25.00	12.50	7.50
30	Vic Power	8.00	4.00	2.50	121	Bill Renna	8.00	4.00	2.50
31	Warren Spahn	90.00	45.00	27.00	122	Carl Sawatski	8.00	4.00	2.50
32	Ed McGhee	8.00	4.00	2.50	123	Sandy Koufax	1400.00	700.00	375.00
33	Tom Qualters	8.00	4.00	2.50	124	Harmon Killebrew	400.00	200.00	125.00
34	Wayne Terwilliger	8.00	4.00	2.50	125	Ken Boyer	75.00	38.00	23.00
35	Dave Jolly	8.00	4.00	2.50	126	Dick Hall	8.00	4.00	2.50
36	Leo Kiely	8.00	4.00	2.50	127	Dale Long	8.00	4.00	2.50
37	Joe Cunningham	10.00	5.00	3.00	128	Ted Lepcio	8.00	4.00	2.50
38	Bob Turley	17.00	8.50	5.00	129	Elvin Tappe	8.00	4.00	2.50
39	Bill Glynn	8.00	4.00	2.50	130	Mayo Smith	8.00	4.00	2.50
40	Don Hoak	10.00	5.00	3.00	131	Grady Hatton	8.00	4.00	2.50
41	Chuck Stobbs	8.00	4.00	2.50	132	Bob Trice	8.00	4.00	2.50
42	"Windy" McCall	8.00	4.00	2.50	133	Dave Hoskins	8.00	4.00	2.50
43	Harvey Haddix	8.00	4.00	2.50	134	Joe Jay	8.00	4.00	2.50
44	"Corky" Valentine	8.00	4.00	2.50	135	Johnny O'Brien	8.00	4.00	2.50
45	Hank Sauer	8.00	4.00	2.50	136	"Bunky" Stewart	8.00	4.00	2.50
46	Ted Kazanski	8.00	4.00	2.50	137	Harry Elliott	8.00	4.00	2.50
47	Hank Aaron	400.00	200.00	125.00	138	Ray Herbert	8.00	4.00	2.50
48	Bob Kennedy	8.00	4.00	2.50	139	Steve Kraly	9.00	4.50	2.75
49	J.W. Porter	8.00	4.00	2.50	140	Mel Parnell	8.00	4.00	2.50
50	Jackie Robinson	250.00	125.00	75.00	141	Tom Wright	8.00	4.00	2.50
51	Jim Hughes	8.00	4.00	2.50	142	Jerry Lynch	8.00	4.00	2.50
52	Bill Tremel	8.00	4.00	2.50	143	Dick Schofield	8.00	4.00	2.50
53	Bill Taylor	8.00	4.00	2.50	144	Joe Amalfitano	8.00	4.00	2.50
54	Lou Limmer	8.00	4.00	2.50	145	Elmer Valo	8.00	4.00	2.50
55	"Rip" Repulski	8.00	4.00	2.50	146	Dick Donovan	8.00	4.00	2.50
56	Ray Jablonski	8.00	4.00	2.50	147	Laurin Pepper	8.00	4.00	2.50
57	Billy O'Dell	8.00	4.00	2.50	148	Hal Brown	8.00	4.00	2.50
58	Jim Rivera	8.00	4.00	2.50	149	Ray Crone	8.00	4.00	2.50
59	Gair Allie	8.00	4.00	2.50	150	Mike Higgins	8.00	4.00	2.50
60	Dean Stone	8.00	4.00	2.50	151	"Red" Kress	17.00	8.50	5.00
61	"Spook" Jacobs	8.00	4.00	2.50	152	Harry Agganis	80.00	40.00	25.00
62	Thornton Kipper	8.00	4.00	2.50	153	"Bud" Podbielan	17.00	8.50	5.00
63	Joe Collins	9.00	4.50	2.75	154	Willie Miranda	17.00	8.50	5.00
64	Gus Triandos	10.00	5.00	3.00	155	Ed Mathews	125.00	67.00	37.00
65	Ray Boone	8.00	4.00	2.50	156	Joe Black	20.00	10.00	6.00
66	Ron Jackson	8.00	4.00	2.50	157	Bob Miller	17.00	8.50	5.00
67	Wally Moon	8.00	4.00	2.50	158	Tom Carroll	20.00	10.00	6.00
68	Jim Davis	8.00	4.00	2.50	159	Johnny Schmitz	17.00	8.50	5.00
69	Ed Bailey	8.00	4.00	2.50	160	Ray Narleski	17.00	8.50	5.00
70	Al Rosen	17.00	8.50	5.00	161	Chuck Tanner	30.00	15.00	9.00
71	Ruben Gomez	8.00	4.00	2.50	162	Joe Coleman	25.00	12.50	7.50
72	Karl Olson	8.00	4.00	2.50	163	Faye Throneberry	25.00	12.50	7.50
73	Jack Shepard	8.00	4.00	2.50	164	Roberto Clemente	2000.00	1000.00	600.00
74	Bob Borkowski	8.00	4.00	2.50	165	Don Johnson	25.00	12.50	7.50
75	Sandy Amoros	8.00	4.00	2.50	166	Hank Bauer	40.00	20.00	12.00
76	Howie Pollet	8.00	4.00	2.50	167	Tom Casagrande	25.00	12.50	7.50
77	Arnold Portocarrero	8.00	4.00	2.50	168	Duane Pillette	25.00	12.50	7.50
78	Gordon Jones	8.00	4.00	2.50	169	Bob Oldis	25.00	12.50	7.50
79	Danny Schell	8.00	4.00	2.50	170	Jim Pearce	25.00	12.50	7.50
80	Bob Grim	9.00	4.50	2.75	171	Dick Brodowski	25.00	12.50	7.50
81	Gene Conley	8.00	4.00	2.50	172	Frank Baumholtz	25.00	12.50	7.50
82	Chuck Harmon	8.00	4.00	2.50	173	Bob Kline	25.00	12.50	7.50
83	Tom Brewer	8.00	4.00	2.50	174	Rudy Minarcin	25.00	12.50	7.50
84	Camilo Pascual	8.00	4.00	2.50	175	Not Issued			
85	Don Mossi	8.00	4.00	2.50	176	Norm Zauchin	25.00	12.50	7.50
86	Bill Wilson	8.00	4.00	2.50	177	Jim Robertson	25.00	12.50	7.50
87	Frank House	8.00	4.00	2.50	178	Bobby Adams	25.00	12.50	7.50
88	Bob Skinner	8.00	4.00	2.50	179	Jim Bolger	25.00	12.50	7.50
89	Joe Frazier	8.00	4.00	2.50	180	Clem Labine	25.00	12.50	7.50
90	Karl Spooner	9.00	4.50	2.75	181	Roy McMillan	25.00	12.50	7.50
91	Milt Bolling	8.00	4.00	2.50	182	Humberto Robinson	25.00	12.50	7.50
92	Don Zimmer	40.00	20.00	12.00	183	Tony Jacobs	25.00	12.50	7.50
93	Steve Bilko	8.00	4.00	2.50	184	Harry Perkowski	25.00	12.50	7.50
94	Reno Bertoia	8.00	4.00	2.50	185	Don Ferrarese	25.00	12.50	7.50
95	Preston Ward	8.00	4.00	2.50	186	Not Issued			
96	Charlie Bishop	8.00	4.00	2.50	187	Gil Hodges	150.00	75.00	45.00
97	Carlos Paula	8.00	4.00	2.50	188	Charlie Silvera	25.00	12.50	7.50
98	Johnny Riddle	8.00	4.00	2.50	189	Phil Rizzuto	150.00	75.00	45.00
99	Frank Leja	9.00	4.50	2.75	190	Gene Woodling	25.00	12.50	7.50
100	Monte Irvin	30.00	15.00	9.00	191	Ed Stanky	25.00	12.50	7.50
101	Johnny Gray	8.00	4.00	2.50	192	Jim Delsing	25.00	12.50	7.50
102	Wally Westlake	8.00	4.00	2.50	193	Johnny Sain	40.00	20.00	12.00
103	Charlie White	8.00	4.00	2.50	194	Willie Mays	550.00	275.00	165.00
104	Jack Harshman	8.00	4.00	2.50	195	Ed Roebuck	25.00	12.50	7.50
105	Chuck Diering	8.00	4.00	2.50	196	Gale Wade	25.00	12.50	7.50
106	Frank Sullivan	8.00	4.00	2.50	197	Al Smith	25.00	12.50	7.50
107	Curt Roberts	8.00	4.00	2.50	198	Yogi Berra	250.00	125.00	75.00
108	"Rube" Walker	8.00	4.00	2.50	199	Bert Hamric	25.00	12.50	7.50
109	Ed Lopat	10.00	5.00	3.00	200	Jack Jensen	50.00	25.00	15.00
110	Gus Zernial	8.00	4.00	2.50	201	Sherm Lollar	25.00	12.50	7.50
111	Bob Milliken	8.00	4.00	2.50	202	Jim Owens	25.00	12.50	7.50
112	Nelson King	8.00	4.00	2.50	203	Not Issued			
113	Harry Brecheen	8.00	4.00	2.50	204	Frank Smith	25.00	12.50	7.50
114	Lou Ortiz	8.00	4.00	2.50	205	Gene Freese	25.00	12.50	7.50
115	Ellis Kinder	8.00	4.00	2.50	206	Pete Daley	25.00	12.50	7.50
116	Tom Hurd	8.00	4.00	2.50	207	Bill Consolo	25.00	12.50	7.50
117	Mel Roach	8.00	4.00	2.50	208	Ray Moore	25.00	12.50	7.50
118	Bob Purkey	8.00	4.00	2.50	209	Not Issued			

		NR MT	EX	VG
210	Duke Snider	500.00	200.00	110.00

1955 Topps Doubleheaders

This set is a throwback to the 1911 T201 Mecca Double Folders. The cards were perforated allowing them to be folded. Open, there is a color painting of a player set against a ballpark background. When folded , a different stadium and player appears, although both share the same lower legs and feet. Back gives abbreviated career histories. Placed side by side in reverse numerical order, the backgrounds form a continuous stadium scene. When open, the cards measure 2-1/16" by 4-7/8." The 66 cards in the set mean 132 total players, all of whom also appeared in the lower number regular 1955 Topps set.

		NR MT	EX	VG
Complete Set:		3750.00	1875.00	1125.
Common Player:		30.00	15.00	9.00
1	Al Rosen			
2	Chuck Diering	30.00	15.00	9.00
3	Monte Irvin			
4	Russ Kemmerer	30.00	15.00	9.00
5	Ted Kazanski			
6	Gordon Jones	30.00	15.00	9.00
7	Bill Taylor			
8	Billy O'Dell	30.00	15.00	9.00
9	J.W. Porter			
10	Thornton Kipper	30.00	15.00	9.00
11	Curt Roberts			
12	Arnie Portocarrero	30.00	15.00	9.00
13	Wally Westlake			
14	Frank House	30.00	15.00	9.00
15	"Rube" Walker			
16	Lou Limmer	30.00	15.00	9.00
17	Dean Stone			
18	Charlie White	30.00	15.00	9.00
19	Karl Spooner			
20	Jim Hughes	30.00	15.00	9.00
21	Bill Skowron			
22	Frank Sullivan	30.00	15.00	9.00
23	Jack Shepard			
24	Stan Hack	30.00	15.00	9.00
25	Jackie Robinson			
26	Don Hoak	275.00	137.00	80.00
27	"Dusty" Rhodes			
28	Jim Davis	30.00	15.00	9.00
29	Vic Power			
30	Ed Bailey	30.00	15.00	9.00
31	Howie Pollet			
32	Ernie Banks	150.00	75.00	45.00
33	Jim Pendleton			
34	Gene Conley	30.00	15.00	9.00
35	Karl Olson	30.00	15.00	9.00
36	Andy Carey	30.00	15.00	9.00
37	Wally Moon	30.00	15.00	9.00
38	Joe Cunningham	30.00	15.00	9.00
39	Fred Marsh			
40	"Jake" Thies	30.00	15.00	9.00
41	Ed Lopat			
42	Harvey Haddix	30.00	15.00	9.00
43	Leo Kiely			
44	Chuck Stobbs	30.00	15.00	9.00
45	Al Kaline			

		NR MT	EX	VG
46	"Corky" Valentine	300.00	150.00	90.00
47	"Spook" Jacobs			
48	Johnny Gray	30.00	15.00	9.00
49	Ron Jackson			
50	Jim Finigan	30.00	15.00	9.00
51	Ray Jablonski			
52	Bob Keegan	30.00	15.00	9.00
53	Billy Herman			
54	Sandy Amoros	30.00	15.00	9.00
55	Chuck Harmon			
56	Bob Skinner	30.00	15.00	9.00
57	Dick Hall			
58	Bob Grim	30.00	15.00	9.00
59	Billy Glynn			
60	Bob Miller	30.00	15.00	9.00
61	Billy Gardner			
62	John Hetki	30.00	15.00	9.00
63	Bob Borkowski			
64	Bob Turley	30.00	15.00	9.00
65	Joe Collins			
66	Jack Harshman	30.00	15.00	9.00
67	Jim Hegan			
68	Jack Parks	30.00	15.00	9.00
69	Ted Williams			
70	Hal Smith	300.00	150.00	90.00
71	Gair Allie			
72	Grady Hatton	30.00	15.00	9.00
73	Jerry Lynch			
74	Harry Brecheen	30.00	15.00	9.00
75	Tom Wright			
76	"Bunky" Stewart	30.00	15.00	9.00
77	Dave Hoskins			
78	Ed McGhee	30.00	15.00	9.00
79	Roy Sievers			
80	Art Fowler	30.00	15.00	9.00
81	Danny Schell			
82	Gus Triandos	30.00	15.00	9.00
83	Joe Frazier			
84	Don Mossi	30.00	15.00	9.00
85	Elmer Valo			
86	Hal Brown	30.00	15.00	9.00
87	Bob Kennedy			
88	"Windy" McCall	30.00	15.00	9.00
89	Ruben Gomez			
90	Jim Rivera	30.00	15.00	9.00
91	Lou Ortiz			
92	Milt Bolling	30.00	15.00	9.00
93	Carl Sawatski			
94	Elvin Tappe	30.00	15.00	9.00
95	Dave Jolly			
96	Bobby Hofman	30.00	15.00	9.00
97	Preston Ward			
98	Don Zimmer	30.00	15.00	9.00
99	Bill Renna			
100	Dick Groat	30.00	15.00	9.00
101	Bill Wilson			
102	Bill Tremel	30.00	15.00	9.00
103	Hank Sauer			
104	Camilo Pascual	30.00	15.00	9.00
105	Hank Aaron			
106	Ray Herbert	450.00	225.00	135.00
107	Alex Grammas			
108	Tom Qualters	30.00	15.00	9.00
109	Hal Newhouser			
110	Charlie Bishop	30.00	15.00	9.00
111	Harmon Killebrew			
112	John Podres	250.00	125.00	75.00
113	Ray Boone			
114	Bob Purkey	30.00	15.00	9.00
115	Dale Long			
116	Ferris Fain	30.00	15.00	9.00
117	Steve Bilko			
118	Bob Milliken	30.00	15.00	9.00
119	Mel Parnell			
120	Tom Hurd	30.00	15.00	9.00
121	Ted Kluszewski			
122	Jim Owens	30.00	15.00	9.00
123	Gus Zernial			
124	Bob Trice	30.00	15.00	9.00
125	"Rip" Repulski			
126	Ted Lepcio	30.00	15.00	9.00
127	Warren Spahn			
128	Tom Brewer	200.00	100.00	60.00
129	Jim Gilliam			
130	Ellis Kinder	30.00	15.00	9.00
131	Herm Wehmeier			
132	Wayne Terwilliger	30.00	15.00	9.00

U

1932 U.S. Caramel

Produced by the U.S. Caramel Company, Boston, this set is not limited to baseball. Rather, it is a set of 31 "Famous Athletes" of which some 27 are baseball players. The 2-1/2" by 3" cards have a black and white picture on the front with a red background and white border. The player's name appears in white above the picture. The backs feature the player's name, position, team and league as well as a redemption ad and card number. The cards were among the last of the caramel card sets and are very scarce today. The cards could be redeemed for a baseball and baseball glove. Card #16 was recently discovered and is not included in the complete set price.

		NR MT	EX	VG
Complete Set:		22000.00	11000.00	6600.
Common Player.		450.00	225.00	135.00
1	Edward T. (Eddie) Collins	650.00	325.00	200.00
2	Paul (Big Poison) Waner	500.00	250.00	150.00
4	William (Bill) Terry	500.00	250.00	150.00
5	Earl B. Combs (Earle)	500.00	250.00	150.00
6	William (Bill) Dickey	650.00	325.00	200.00
7	Joseph (Joe) Cronin	675.00	337.00	202.00
8	Charles (Chick) Hafey	500.00	250.00	150.00
10	Walter (Rabbit) Maranville	500.00	250.00	150.00
11	Rogers (Rajah) Hornsby	900.00	450.00	275.00
12	Gordon (Mickey) Cochrane	500.00	250.00	150.00
13	Lloyd (Little Poison) Waner	500.00	250.00	150.00
14	Tyrus (Ty) Cobb	2500.00	1250.00	750.00
16	Charles (Lindy) Lindstrom	25000.00	12500.00	7500.
17	Al. Simmons	500.00	250.00	150.00
18	Anthony (Tony) Lazzeri	500.00	250.00	150.00
19	Walter (Wally) Berger	450.00	225.00	135.00
20	Charles (Large Charlie) Ruffing	500.00	250.00	150.00
21	Charles (Chuck) Klein	500.00	250.00	150.00
23	James (Jimmy) Foxx	650.00	325.00	195.00
24	Frank J. (Lefty) O'Doul	450.00	225.00	135.00
26	Henry (Lou) Gehrig	2500.00	1250.00	750.00
27	Robert (Lefty) Grove	750.00	375.00	225.00
28	Edward Brant (Brandt)	450.00	225.00	135.00
29	George Earnshaw	450.00	225.00	135.00
30	Frank (Frankie) Frisch	675.00	337.00	202.00
31	Vernon (Lefty) Gomez	675.00	337.00	202.00
32	George (Babe) Ruth	3500.00	1750.00	1050.

V

1921 V61

Another set closely related to the popular 1922 American Caramel set (E120), this 120-card set was issued by Neilson's Chocolate Bars and carries the American Card Catalog designation V61. The front of the black and white cards are very similar to the E120 set, while the backs contain an ad for Neilson's Chocolates. Backs exist with the Neilson's name printed in Old English type or in regular printing.

		NR MT	EX	VG
Complete Set:		10250.00	5125.00	3075.
Common Player:		55.00	27.00	16.50
1	George Burns	55.00	27.00	16.50
2	John Tobin	55.00	27.00	16.50
3	J.T. Zachary	55.00	27.00	16.50
4	"Bullet" Joe Bush	75.00	37.00	22.00
5	Lu Blue	55.00	27.00	16.50
6	Clarence (Tillie) Walker	55.00	27.00	16.50
7	Carl Mays	75.00	37.00	22.00
8	Leon Goslin	125.00	62.00	37.00
9	Ed Rommel	55.00	27.00	16.50
10	Charles Robertson	55.00	27.00	16.50
11	Ralph (Cy) Perkins	55.00	27.00	16.50
12	Joe Sewell	125.00	62.00	37.00
13	Harry Hooper	125.00	62.00	37.00
14	Urban (Red) Faber	125.00	62.00	37.00
15	Bib Falk ((Bibb))	55.00	27.00	16.50
16	George Uhle	55.00	27.00	16.50
17	Emory Rigney	55.00	27.00	16.50
18	George Dauss	55.00	27.00	16.50
19	Herman Pillette	55.00	27.00	16.50
20	Wallie Schang	55.00	27.00	16.50
21	Lawrence Woodall	55.00	27.00	16.50
22	Steve O'Neill	55.00	27.00	16.50
23	Edmund (Bing) Miller	55.00	27.00	16.50
24	Sylvester Johnson	55.00	27.00	16.50
25	Henry Severeid	55.00	27.00	16.50
26	Dave Danforth	55.00	27.00	16.50
27	Harry Heilmann	125.00	62.00	37.00
28	Bert Cole	55.00	27.00	16.50
29	Eddie Collins	125.00	62.00	37.00
30	Ty Cob (Cobb)	1500.00	750.00	450.00
31	Bill Wambsganss	75.00	37.00	22.00
32	George Sisler	125.00	62.00	37.00
33	Bob Veach	55.00	27.00	16.50
34	Earl Sheely	55.00	27.00	16.50
35	T.P. (Pat) Collins	55.00	27.00	16.50
36	Frank (Dixie) Davis	55.00	27.00	16.50
37	Babe Ruth	1750.00	875.00	525.00
38	Bryan Harris	55.00	27.00	16.50
39	Bob Shawkey	75.00	37.00	22.00
40	Urban Shocker	55.00	27.00	16.50
41	Martin McManus	55.00	27.00	16.50
42	Clark Pittenger	55.00	27.00	16.50
43	"Deacon" Sam Jones	55.00	27.00	16.50
44	Waite Hoyt	125.00	62.00	37.00
45	Johnny Mostil	55.00	27.00	16.50
46	Mike Menosky	55.00	27.00	16.50
47	Walter Johnson	750.00	375.00	225.00
48	Wallie Pipp	80.00	40.00	24.00
49	Walter Gerber	55.00	27.00	16.50
50	Ed Gharrity	55.00	27.00	16.50
51	Frank Ellerbe	55.00	27.00	16.50
52	Kenneth Williams	75.00	37.00	22.00
53	Joe Hauser	55.00	27.00	16.50
54	Carson Bigbee	55.00	27.00	16.50
55	Emil (Irish) Meusel	55.00	27.00	16.50

		NR MT	EX	VG
56	Milton Stock	55.00	27.00	16.50
57	Wilbur Cooper	55.00	27.00	16.50
58	Tom Griffith	55.00	27.00	16.50
59	Clarence (Shovel) Hodge	55.00	27.00	16.50
60	Gene (Bubbles) Hargrave	55.00	27.00	16.50
61	Russell Wrightstone	55.00	27.00	16.50
62	Frank Frisch	125.00	62.00	37.00
63	Jack Peters	55.00	27.00	16.50
64	Walter (Dutch) Reuther	55.00	27.00	16.50
65	Bill Doak	55.00	27.00	16.50
66	Marty Callaghan	55.00	27.00	16.50
67	Sammy Bohne	55.00	27.00	16.50
68	Earl Hamilton	55.00	27.00	16.50
69	Grover C. Alexander	250.00	125.00	75.00
70	George Burns	55.00	27.00	16.50
71	Max Carey	125.00	62.00	37.00
72	Adolfo Luque	55.00	27.00	16.50
73	Walt Barbare	55.00	27.00	16.50
74	Vic Aldridge	55.00	27.00	16.50
75	Jack Smith	55.00	27.00	16.50
76	Bob O'Farrell	55.00	27.00	16.50
77	Pete Donohue	55.00	27.00	16.50
78	Ralph Pinelli	75.00	37.00	22.00
79	Eddie Roush	125.00	62.00	37.00
80	Norman Boeckel	55.00	27.00	16.50
81	Rogers Hornsby	500.00	250.00	150.00
82	George Toporcer	55.00	27.00	16.50
83	Ivy Wingo	55.00	27.00	16.50
84	Virgil Cheeves	55.00	27.00	16.50
85	Vern Clemons	55.00	27.00	16.50
86	Lawrence (Hack) Miller	55.00	27.00	16.50
87	Johnny Kelleher	55.00	27.00	16.50
88	Heinie Groh	55.00	27.00	16.50
89	Burleigh Grimes	125.00	62.00	37.00
90	"Rabbit" Maranville	125.00	62.00	37.00
91	Charles (Babe) Adams	55.00	27.00	16.50
92	Lee King	55.00	27.00	16.50
93	Art Nehf	55.00	27.00	16.50
94	Frank Snyder	55.00	27.00	16.50
95	Raymond Powell	55.00	27.00	16.50
96	Wilbur Hubbell	55.00	27.00	16.50
97	Leon Cadore	55.00	27.00	16.50
98	Joe Oeschger	55.00	27.00	16.50
99	Jake Daubert	75.00	37.00	22.00
100	Will Sherdel	55.00	27.00	16.50
101	Hank DeBerry	55.00	27.00	16.50
102	Johnny Lavan	55.00	27.00	16.50
103	Jesse Haines	125.00	62.00	37.00
104	Joe (Goldie) Rapp	55.00	27.00	16.50
105	Oscar Ray Grimes	55.00	27.00	16.50
106	Ross Young (Youngs)	125.00	62.00	37.00
107	Art Fletcher	55.00	27.00	16.50
108	Clyde Barnhart	55.00	27.00	16.50
109	Louis (Pat) Duncan	55.00	27.00	16.50
110	Charlie Hollocher	55.00	27.00	16.50
111	Horace Ford	55.00	27.00	16.50
112	Bill Cunningham	55.00	27.00	16.50
113	Walter Schmidt	55.00	27.00	16.50
114	Joe Schultz	55.00	27.00	16.50
115	John Morrison	55.00	27.00	16.50
116	Jimmy Caveney	55.00	27.00	16.50
117	Zach Wheat	125.00	62.00	37.00
118	Fred (Cy) Williams	75.00	37.00	22.00
119	George Kelly	125.00	62.00	37.00
120	Jimmy Ring	55.00	27.00	16.50

1923 V100

Issued circa 1923, this set was produced by the Willard Chocolate Company of Canada and features sepia-toned photographs on cards measuring 3-1/4" by 2-1/16". The cards are blank-backed and feature the player's name in script on the front. The set is complete at 180 cards and nearly one-fourth of the photos used in the set are identical to the better known E120 American Caramel setr. The Willard set is identified as V100 in the American Card Catalog.

		NR MT	EX	VG
Complete Set:		11500.00	5750.00	3450.
Common Player:		50.00	25.00	15.00
(1)	Chas. B. Adams	50.00	25.00	15.00
(2)	Grover C. Alexander	65.00	32.00	19.50
(3)	J.P. Austin	50.00	25.00	15.00
(4)	J.C. Bagby	50.00	25.00	15.00
(5)	J. Franklin Baker	225.00	112.00	67.00
(6)	David J. Bancroft	225.00	112.00	67.00
(7)	Turner Barber	50.00	25.00	15.00
(8)	Jesse L. Barnes	50.00	25.00	15.00
(9)	J.C. Bassler	50.00	25.00	15.00
(10)	L.A. Blue	50.00	25.00	15.00
(11)	Norman D. Boeckel	50.00	25.00	15.00
(12)	F.L. Brazil (Brazill)	50.00	25.00	15.00
(13)	G.H. Burns	50.00	25.00	15.00
(14)	Geo. J. Burns	50.00	25.00	15.00
(15)	Leon Cadore	50.00	25.00	15.00
(16)	Max G. Carey	225.00	112.00	67.00
(17)	Harold G. Carlson	50.00	25.00	15.00
(18)	Lloyd R Christenberry (Christenbury)	50.00	25.00	15.00
(19)	Vernon J. Clemons	50.00	25.00	15.00
(20)	T.R. Cobb	1200.00	600.00	360.00
(21)	Bert Cole	50.00	25.00	15.00
(22)	John F. Collins	50.00	25.00	15.00
(23)	S. Coveleskie (Coveleski)	225.00	112.00	67.00
(24)	Walton E. Cruise	50.00	25.00	15.00
(25)	G.W. Cutshaw	50.00	25.00	15.00
(26)	Jacob E. Daubert	75.00	37.00	22.00
(27)	Geo. Dauss	50.00	25.00	15.00
(28)	F.T. Davis	50.00	25.00	15.00
(29)	Chas. A. Deal	50.00	25.00	15.00
(30)	William L. Doak	50.00	25.00	15.00
(31)	William E. Donovan	50.00	25.00	15.00
(32)	Hugh Duffy	225.00	112.00	67.00
(33)	J.A. Dugan	75.00	37.00	22.00
(34)	Louis B. Duncan	50.00	25.00	15.00
(35)	James Dykes	75.00	37.00	22.00
(36)	H.J. Ehmke	50.00	25.00	15.00
(37)	F.R. Ellerbe	50.00	25.00	15.00
(38)	E.G. Erickson	50.00	25.00	15.00
(39)	John J. Evers	225.00	112.00	67.00
(40)	U.C. Faber	225.00	112.00	67.00
(41)	B.A. Falk	50.00	25.00	15.00
(42)	Max Flack	50.00	25.00	15.00
(43)	Lee Fohl	50.00	25.00	15.00
(44)	Jacques F. Fournier	50.00	25.00	15.00
(45)	Frank F. Frisch	225.00	112.00	67.00
(46)	C.E. Galloway	50.00	25.00	15.00
(47)	W.C. Gardner	50.00	25.00	15.00
(48)	E.P. Gharrity	50.00	25.00	15.00
(49)	Geo. Gibson	50.00	25.00	15.00
(50)	Wm. Gleason	50.00	25.00	15.00
(51)	William Gleason	50.00	25.00	15.00
(52)	Henry M. Gowdy	50.00	25.00	15.00
(53)	I.M. Griffin	50.00	25.00	15.00
(54)	Griffith	225.00	112.00	67.00
(55)	Burleigh A. Grimes	225.00	112.00	67.00
(56)	Charles J. Grimm	75.00	37.00	22.00
(57)	Jesse J. Haines	75.00	37.00	22.00
(58)	S.R. Harris	225.00	112.00	67.00
(59)	W.B. Harris	50.00	25.00	15.00
(60)	R.K. Hasty	50.00	25.00	15.00
(61)	H.E. Heilman (Heilmann)	225.00	112.00	67.00
(62)	Walter J. Henline	50.00	25.00	15.00
(63)	Walter L. Holke	50.00	25.00	15.00
(64)	Charles J. Hollocher	50.00	25.00	15.00
(65)	H.B. Hooper	225.00	112.00	67.00
(66)	Rogers Hornsby	400.00	200.00	120.00
(67)	W.C. Hoyt	225.00	112.00	67.00
(68)	Miller Huggins	225.00	112.00	67.00
(69)	W.C. Jacobsen (Jacobson)	50.00	25.00	15.00
(70)	C.D. Jamieson	50.00	25.00	15.00
(71)	Ernest Johnson	50.00	25.00	15.00
(72)	W.P. Johnson	600.00	300.00	180.00
(73)	James H. Johnston	50.00	25.00	15.00
(74)	R.W. Jones	50.00	25.00	15.00
(75)	Samuel Pond Jones	50.00	25.00	15.00
(76)	J.I. Judge	50.00	25.00	15.00
(77)	James W. Keenan	50.00	25.00	15.00

		NR MT	EX	VG
(78)	Geo. L. Kelly	225.00	112.00	67.00
(79)	Peter J. Kilduff	50.00	25.00	15.00
(80)	William Killefer	50.00	25.00	15.00
(81)	Lee King	50.00	25.00	15.00
(82)	Ray Kolp	50.00	25.00	15.00
(83)	John Lavan	50.00	25.00	15.00
(84)	H.L. Leibold	50.00	25.00	15.00
(85)	Connie Mack	300.00	150.00	90.00
(86)	J.W. Mails	50.00	25.00	15.00
(87)	Walter J. Maranville	225.00	112.00	67.00
(88)	Richard W. Marquard	225.00	112.00	67.00
(89)	C.W. Mays	75.00	37.00	22.00
(90)	Geo. F. McBride	50.00	25.00	15.00
(91)	H.M. McClellan	50.00	25.00	15.00
(92)	John J. McGraw	250.00	125.00	75.00
(93)	Austin B. McHenry	50.00	25.00	15.00
(94)	J. McInnis	50.00	25.00	15.00
(95)	Douglas McWeeney (McWeeny)	50.00	25.00	15.00
(96)	M. Menosky	50.00	25.00	15.00
(97)	Emil F. Meusel	50.00	25.00	15.00
(98)	R. Meusel	75.00	37.00	22.00
(99)	Henry W. Meyers	50.00	25.00	15.00
(100)	J.C. Milan	50.00	25.00	15.00
(101)	John K. Miljus	50.00	25.00	15.00
(102)	Edmund J. Miller	50.00	25.00	15.00
(103)	Elmer Miller	50.00	25.00	15.00
(104)	Otto L. Miller	50.00	25.00	15.00
(105)	Fred Mitchell	50.00	25.00	15.00
(106)	Geo. Mogridge	50.00	25.00	15.00
(107)	Patrick J. Moran	50.00	25.00	15.00
(108)	John D. Morrison	50.00	25.00	15.00
(109)	J.A. Mostil	50.00	25.00	15.00
(110)	Clarence F. Mueller	50.00	25.00	15.00
(111)	A. Earle Neale	175.00	87.00	52.00
(112)	Joseph Oeschger	50.00	25.00	15.00
(113)	Robert J. O'Farrell	50.00	25.00	15.00
(114)	J.C. Oldham	50.00	25.00	15.00
(115)	I.M. Olson	50.00	25.00	15.00
(116)	Geo. M. O'Neil	50.00	25.00	15.00
(117)	S.F. O'Neill	50.00	25.00	15.00
(118)	Frank J. Parkinson	50.00	25.00	15.00
(119)	Geo. H. Paskert	50.00	25.00	15.00
(120)	R.T. Peckinpaugh	50.00	25.00	15.00
(121)	H.J. Pennock	225.00	112.00	67.00
(122)	Ralph Perkins	50.00	25.00	15.00
(123)	Edw. J. Pfeffer	50.00	25.00	15.00
(124)	W.C. Pipp	175.00	87.00	52.00
(125)	Charles Elmer Ponder	50.00	25.00	15.00
(126)	Raymond R. Powell	50.00	25.00	15.00
(127)	D.B. Pratt	50.00	25.00	15.00
(128)	Joseph Rapp	50.00	25.00	15.00
(129)	John H. Rawlings	50.00	25.00	15.00
(130)	E.S. Rice (should be E.C.)	225.00	112.00	67.00
(131)	Rickey	300.00	150.00	90.00
(132)	James J. Ring	50.00	25.00	15.00
(133)	Eppa J. Rixey	225.00	112.00	67.00
(134)	Davis A. Robertson	50.00	25.00	15.00
(135)	Edwin Rommel	50.00	25.00	15.00
(136)	Edd J. Roush	225.00	112.00	67.00
(137)	Harold Ruel (Herold)	50.00	25.00	15.00
(138)	Allen Russell	50.00	25.00	15.00
(139)	G.H. Ruth	1500.00	750.00	450.00
(140)	Wilfred D. Ryan	50.00	25.00	15.00
(141)	Henry F. Sallee	50.00	25.00	15.00
(142)	W.H. Schang	50.00	25.00	15.00
(143)	Raymond H. Schmandt	50.00	25.00	15.00
(144)	Everett Scott	50.00	25.00	15.00
(145)	Henry Severeid	50.00	25.00	15.00
(146)	Jos. W. Sewell	225.00	112.00	67.00
(147)	Howard S. Shanks	50.00	25.00	15.00
(148)	E.H. Sheely	50.00	25.00	15.00
(149)	Ralph Shinners	50.00	25.00	15.00
(150)	U.J. Shocker	50.00	25.00	15.00
(151)	G.H. Sisler	225.00	112.00	67.00
(152)	Earl L. Smith	50.00	25.00	15.00
(153)	Earl S. Smith	50.00	25.00	15.00
(154)	Geo. A. Smith	50.00	25.00	15.00
(155)	J.W. Smith	50.00	25.00	15.00
(156)	Tris E. Speaker	250.00	125.00	75.00
(157)	Arnold Staatz	50.00	25.00	15.00
(158)	J.R. Stephenson	75.00	37.00	22.00
(159)	Milton J. Stock	50.00	25.00	15.00
(160)	John L. Sullivan	50.00	25.00	15.00
(161)	H.F. Tormahlen	50.00	25.00	15.00
(162)	Jas. A. Tierney	50.00	25.00	15.00
(163)	J.T. Tobin	50.00	25.00	15.00
(164)	Jas. L. Vaughn	50.00	25.00	15.00
(165)	R.H. Veach	50.00	25.00	15.00
(166)	C.W. Walker	50.00	25.00	15.00
(167)	A.L. Ward	50.00	25.00	15.00
(168)	Zack D. Wheat	225.00	112.00	67.00

		NR MT	EX	VG
(169)	George B. Whitted	50.00	25.00	15.00
(170)	Irvin K. Wilhelm	50.00	25.00	15.00
(171)	Roy H. Wilkinson	50.00	25.00	15.00
(172)	Fred C. Williams	75.00	37.00	22.00
(173)	K.R. Williams	75.00	37.00	22.00
(174)	Sam'l W. Wilson	50.00	25.00	15.00
(175)	Ivy B. Wingo	50.00	25.00	15.00
(176)	L.W. Witt	50.00	25.00	15.00
(177)	Joseph Wood	75.00	37.00	22.00
(178)	E. Yaryan	50.00	25.00	15.00
(179)	R.S. Young	50.00	25.00	15.00
(180)	Ross Young (Youngs)	225.00	112.00	67.00

1936 V355 World Wide Gum

This black and white Canadian set was issued by World Wide Gum in 1936. The cards measure approximately 2-1/2" by 2-7/8", and the set includes both portrait and action photos. The card number and player's name (appearing in all capital letters) are printed inside a white box below the photo.

		NR MT	EX	VG
Complete Set:		20500.00	10250.00	6150.
Common Player:		110.00	55.00	33.00
1	Jimmy Dykes	125.00	62.00	37.00
2	Paul Waner	250.00	125.00	75.00
3	Cy Blanton	110.00	55.00	33.00
4	Sam Leslie	110.00	55.00	33.00
5	Johnny Louis Vergez	110.00	55.00	33.00
6	Arky Vaughan	250.00	125.00	75.00
7	Bill Terry	300.00	150.00	90.00
8	Joe Moore	110.00	55.00	33.00
9	Gus Mancuso	110.00	55.00	33.00
10	Fred Marberry	110.00	55.00	33.00
11	George Selkirk	110.00	55.00	33.00
12	Spud Davis	110.00	55.00	33.00
13	Chuck Klein	250.00	125.00	75.00
14	Fred Fitzsimmons	110.00	55.00	33.00
15	Bill Delancey	110.00	55.00	33.00
17	George Davis	110.00	55.00	33.00
20	Roy Parmelee	110.00	55.00	33.00
21	Vic Sorrell	110.00	55.00	33.00
22	Harry Danning	110.00	55.00	33.00
23	Hal Schumacher	110.00	55.00	33.00
24	Cy Perkins	110.00	55.00	33.00
25	Speedy Durocher	300.00	150.00	90.00
26	Glenn Myatt	110.00	55.00	33.00
27	Bob Seeds	110.00	55.00	33.00
28	Jimmy Ripple	110.00	55.00	33.00
29	Al Schacht	110.00	55.00	33.00
31	Del Baker	110.00	55.00	33.00
32	Flea Clifton	110.00	55.00	33.00
33	Tommy Bridges	110.00	55.00	33.00
34	Bill Dickey	400.00	200.00	120.00
35	Wally Berger	110.00	55.00	33.00
36	Slick Castleman	110.00	55.00	33.00
37	Dick Bartell	110.00	55.00	33.00
38	Red Rolfe	110.00	55.00	33.00
39	Waite Hoyt	250.00	125.00	75.00
40	Wes Ferrell	110.00	55.00	33.00
41	Hank Greenberg	400.00	200.00	120.00
42	Charlie Gehringer	250.00	125.00	75.00
43	Goose Goslin	250.00	125.00	75.00
44	Schoolboy Rowe	110.00	55.00	33.00
45	Mickey Cochrane	300.00	150.00	90.00
46	Joe Cronin	300.00	150.00	90.00

		NR MT	EX	VG
48	Jerry Walker	110.00	55.00	33.00
49	Charlie Gelbert	110.00	55.00	33.00
50	Roy Hayworth (Ray)	110.00	55.00	33.00
51	Joe DiMaggio	1800.00	900.00	540.00
52	Billy Rogell	110.00	55.00	33.00
53	Joe McCarthy	300.00	150.00	90.00
54	Phil Cavaretta (Cavarretta)	110.00	55.00	33.00
55	Kiki Cuyler	250.00	125.00	75.00
56	Lefty Gomez	300.00	150.00	90.00
57	Gabby Hartnett	250.00	125.00	75.00
59	Burgess Whitehead	110.00	55.00	33.00
60	Whitey Whitehill	110.00	55.00	33.00
61	Buckey Walters	110.00	55.00	33.00
62	Luke Sewell	110.00	55.00	33.00
63	Joey Kuhel	110.00	55.00	33.00
64	Lou Finney	110.00	55.00	33.00
65	Fred Lindstrom	250.00	125.00	75.00
66	Paul Derringer	110.00	55.00	33.00
67	Steve O'Neil (O'Neill)	110.00	55.00	33.00
68	Mule Haas	110.00	55.00	33.00
69	Freck Owen	110.00	55.00	33.00
70	Wild Bill Hallahan	110.00	55.00	33.00
72	Dan Taylor	110.00	55.00	33.00
74	Jo-Jo White	110.00	55.00	33.00
75	Mickey Medwick (Ducky)	250.00	125.00	75.00
76	Joe Vosmik	110.00	55.00	33.00
77	Al Simmons	250.00	125.00	75.00
78	Shag Shaughnessy	110.00	55.00	33.00
79	Harry Smythe	110.00	55.00	33.00
80	Benny Tate	110.00	55.00	33.00
81	Billy Rhiel	110.00	55.00	33.00
82	Lauri Myllykangas	110.00	55.00	33.00
83	Ben Sankey	110.00	55.00	33.00
85	Jim Bottomley	250.00	125.00	75.00
87	Ossie Bluege	110.00	55.00	33.00
88	Lefty Grove	300.00	150.00	90.00
89	Charlie Grimm	110.00	55.00	33.00
90	Ben Chapman	110.00	55.00	33.00
91	Frank Crosetti	200.00	100.00	60.00
92	John Pomorski	110.00	55.00	33.00
93	Jesse Haines	250.00	125.00	75.00
94	Chick Hafey	250.00	125.00	75.00
95	Tony Piet	110.00	55.00	33.00
96	Lou Gehrig	2000.00	1000.00	600.00
97	Bill Jurges	110.00	55.00	33.00
98	Smead Jolley	110.00	55.00	33.00
99	Jimmy Wilson	110.00	55.00	33.00
100	Lonnie Warneke	110.00	55.00	33.00
101	Lefty Tamulis	110.00	55.00	33.00
103	Earl Grace	110.00	55.00	33.00
104	Rox Lawson	110.00	55.00	33.00
105	Stan Hack	110.00	55.00	33.00
106	August Galan	110.00	55.00	33.00
107	Frank Frisch	250.00	125.00	75.00
108	Bill McKechnie	250.00	125.00	75.00
109	Bill Lee	110.00	55.00	33.00
110	Connie Mack	300.00	150.00	90.00
111	Frank Reiber	110.00	55.00	33.00
112	Zeke Bonura	110.00	55.00	33.00
113	Luke Appling	250.00	125.00	75.00
114	Monte Pearson	110.00	55.00	33.00
115	Bob O'Farrell	110.00	55.00	33.00
116	Marvin Duke	110.00	55.00	33.00
117	Paul Florence	110.00	55.00	33.00
118	John Berley	110.00	55.00	33.00
119	Tom Oliver	110.00	55.00	33.00
120	Norman Kies	110.00	55.00	33.00
121	Hal King	110.00	55.00	33.00
122	Tom Abernathy	110.00	55.00	33.00
123	Phil Hensick	110.00	55.00	33.00
124	Roy Schalk (Ray)	250.00	125.00	75.00
125	Paul Dunlap	110.00	55.00	33.00
126	Benny Bates	110.00	55.00	33.00
127	George Puccinelli	110.00	55.00	33.00
128	Stevie Stevenson	110.00	55.00	33.00
129	Rabbit Maranville	250.00	125.00	75.00
130	Bucky Harris	250.00	125.00	75.00
132	Buddy Myer	110.00	55.00	33.00
133	Cliff Bolton	110.00	55.00	33.00
134	Estel Crabtree	110.00	55.00	33.00

1922 W501

W. WAMBSGANSS
2B.—Cleveland Americans

This "strip card" set, known as W501 in the American Card Catalog, is closely connected to the more popular E121 American Caramel set of 1921 and 1922. Measuring the same 2" by 3-1/2", the cards are actually reproductions of the E121 120-card series distributed as strip cards. The W501 cards are numbered in the upper left corner and have the notation "G-4-22" in the upper right corner, apparrently indicating the cards were issued in April of 1922.

		NR MT	EX	VG
Complete Set:		6000.00	3000.00	1800.
Common Player:		25.00	12.50	7.50
1	Ed Rounnel (Rommel)	25.00	12.50	7.50
2	Urban Shocker	25.00	12.50	7.50
3	Dixie Davis	25.00	12.50	7.50
4	George Sisler	40.00	20.00	12.00
5	Bob Veach	25.00	12.50	7.50
6	Harry Heilman (Heilmann)	40.00	20.00	12.00
7a	Ira Falgstead (name incorrect)	25.00	12.50	7.50
7b	Ira Flagstead (name correct)	25.00	12.50	7.50
8	Ty Cobb	700.00	350.00	210.00
9	Oscar Vitt	25.00	12.50	7.50
10	Muddy Ruel	25.00	12.50	7.50
11	Derrill Pratt	25.00	12.50	7.50
12	Ed Gharrity	25.00	12.50	7.50
13	Joe Judge	25.00	12.50	7.50
14	Sam Rice	40.00	20.00	12.00
15	Clyde Milan	25.00	12.50	7.50
16	Joe Sewell	40.00	20.00	12.00
17	Walter Johnson	200.00	100.00	60.00
18	Jack McInnis	25.00	12.50	7.50
19	Tris Speaker	60.00	30.00	18.00
20	Jim Bagby	25.00	12.50	7.50
21	Stanley Coveleskie (Coveleski)	40.00	20.00	12.00
22	Bill Wambsganss	30.00	15.00	9.00
23	Walter Mails	25.00	12.50	7.50
24	Larry Gardner	25.00	12.50	7.50
25	Aaron Ward	25.00	12.50	7.50
26	Miller Huggins	40.00	20.00	12.00
27	Wally Schang	25.00	12.50	7.50
28	Tom Rogers	25.00	12.50	7.50
29	Carl Mays	30.00	15.00	9.00
30	Everett Scott	25.00	12.50	7.50
31	Robert Shawkey	30.00	15.00	9.00
32	Waite Hoyt	40.00	20.00	12.00
33	Mike McNally	25.00	12.50	7.50
34	Joe Bush	30.00	15.00	9.00
35	Bob Meusel	30.00	15.00	9.00
36	Elmer Miller	25.00	12.50	7.50
37	Dick Kerr	25.00	12.50	7.50
38	Eddie Collins	40.00	20.00	12.00
39	Kid Gleason	25.00	12.50	7.50
40	Johnny Mostil	25.00	12.50	7.50
41	Bib Falk (Bibb)	25.00	12.50	7.50
42	Clarence Hodge	25.00	12.50	7.50
43	Ray Schalk	40.00	20.00	12.00
44	Amos Strunk	25.00	12.50	7.50
45	Eddie Mulligan	25.00	12.50	7.50
46	Earl Sheely	25.00	12.50	7.50
47	Harry Hooper	40.00	20.00	12.00
48	Urban Faber	40.00	20.00	12.00
49	Babe Ruth	1000.00	500.00	300.00
50	Ivy B. Wingo	25.00	12.50	7.50
51	Earle Neale	30.00	15.00	9.00

W

		NR MT	EX	VG
52	Jake Daubert	30.00	15.00	9.00
53	Ed Roush	40.00	20.00	12.00
54	Eppa J. Rixey	40.00	20.00	12.00
55	Elwood Martin	25.00	12.50	7.50
56	Bill Killifer (Killefer)	25.00	12.50	7.50
57	Charles Hollocher	25.00	12.50	7.50
58	Zeb Terry	25.00	12.50	7.50
59	Grover Alexander	60.00	30.00	18.00
60	Turner Barber	25.00	12.50	7.50
61	John Rawlings	25.00	12.50	7.50
62	Frank Frisch	40.00	20.00	12.00
63	Pat Shea	25.00	12.50	7.50
64	Dave Bancroft	40.00	20.00	12.00
65	Cecil Causey	25.00	12.50	7.50
66	Frank Snyder	25.00	12.50	7.50
67	Heinie Groh	25.00	12.50	7.50
68	Ross Young (Youngs)	40.00	20.00	12.00
69	Fred Toney	25.00	12.50	7.50
70	Arthur Nehf	25.00	12.50	7.50
71	Earl Smith	25.00	12.50	7.50
72	George Kelly	40.00	20.00	12.00
73	John J. McGraw	50.00	25.00	15.00
74	Phil Douglas	25.00	12.50	7.50
75	Bill Ryan	25.00	12.50	7.50
76	Jess Haines	40.00	20.00	12.00
77	Milt Stock	25.00	12.50	7.50
78	William Doak	25.00	12.50	7.50
79	George Toporcer	25.00	12.50	7.50
80	Wilbur Cooper	25.00	12.50	7.50
81	George Whitted	25.00	12.50	7.50
82	Chas. Grimm	30.00	15.00	9.00
83	Rabbit Maranville	40.00	20.00	12.00
84	Babe Adams	25.00	12.50	7.50
85	Carson Bigbee	25.00	12.50	7.50
86	Max Carey	40.00	20.00	12.00
87	Whitey Glazner	25.00	12.50	7.50
88	George Gibson	25.00	12.50	7.50
89	Bill Southworth	25.00	12.50	7.50
90	Hank Gowdy	25.00	12.50	7.50
91	Walter Holke	25.00	12.50	7.50
92	Joe Oeschger	25.00	12.50	7.50
93	Pete Kilduff	25.00	12.50	7.50
94	Hy Myers	25.00	12.50	7.50
95	Otto Miller	25.00	12.50	7.50
96	Wilbert Robinson	40.00	20.00	12.00
97	Zach Wheat	40.00	20.00	12.00
98	Walter Ruether	25.00	12.50	7.50
99	Curtis Walker	25.00	12.50	7.50
100	Fred Williams	30.00	15.00	9.00
101	Dave Danforth	25.00	12.50	7.50
102	Ed Rounnel (Rommel)	25.00	12.50	7.50
103	Carl Mays	30.00	15.00	9.00
104	Frank Frisch	40.00	20.00	12.00
105	Lou DeVormer	25.00	12.50	7.50
106	Tom Griffith	25.00	12.50	7.50
107	Harry Harper	25.00	12.50	7.50
108a	John Lavan	25.00	12.50	7.50
108b	John J. McGraw	60.00	30.00	18.00
109	Elmer Smith	25.00	12.50	7.50
110	George Dauss	25.00	12.50	7.50
111	Alexander Gaston	25.00	12.50	7.50
112	John Graney	25.00	12.50	7.50
113	Emil Muesel	25.00	12.50	7.50
114	Rogers Hornsby	100.00	50.00	30.00
115	Leslie Nunamaker	25.00	12.50	7.50
116	Steve O'Neill	25.00	12.50	7.50
117	Max Flack	25.00	12.50	7.50
118	Bill Southworth	25.00	12.50	7.50
119	Arthur Nehf	25.00	12.50	7.50
120	Chick Fewster	25.00	12.50	7.50

1927 W502

(15) CLARENCE MITCHELL

Issued in 1927, this 63-card set is closely related to the York Caramel set (E210) of the same year. The black and white cards measure 1-3/8" by 2-1/2" and display the player's name at the bottom in capital letters preceded by a number in parenthesis. The backs of the cards read either "One Bagger," "Three Bagger" or "Home Run", and were apparently designed to be used as part of a baseball game. There are tow cards known to exist for cards numbers 26, 38, 40, 55 and 59. The set carries the American Card Catalog designation W502.

		NR MT	EX	VG
	Complete Set:	3600.00	1800.00	1080.
	Common Player:	20.00	10.00	6.00
1	Burleigh Grimes	45.00	22.00	13.50
2	Walter Reuther	20.00	10.00	6.00
3	Joe Dugan	25.00	12.50	7.50
4	Red Faber	45.00	22.00	13.50
5	Gabby Hartnett	45.00	22.00	13.50
6	Babe Ruth	750.00	375.00	225.00
7	Bob Meusel	25.00	12.50	7.50
8	Herb Pennock	45.00	22.00	13.50
9	George Burns (photo is George J., not			
	George H. Burns)	20.00	10.00	6.00
10	Joe Sewell	45.00	22.00	13.50
11	George Uhle	20.00	10.00	6.00
12	Bob O'Farrell	20.00	10.00	6.00
13	Rogers Hornsby	125.00	62.00	37.00
14	Pie Traynor	45.00	22.00	13.50
15	Clarence Mitchell	20.00	10.00	6.00
16	Eppa Rixey	45.00	22.00	13.50
17	Carl Mays	25.00	12.50	7.50
18	Adolfo Luque	20.00	10.00	6.00
19	Dave Bancroft	45.00	22.00	13.50
20	George Kelly	45.00	22.00	13.50
21	Earl Combs (Earle)	45.00	22.00	13.50
22	Harry Heilmann	45.00	22.00	13.50
23	Ray W. Schalk	45.00	22.00	13.50
24	Johnny Mostil	20.00	10.00	6.00
25	Hack Wilson (photo actually Art Wilson)			
		45.00	22.00	13.50
26a	Lou Gehrig	700.00	350.00	210.00
26b	Stanley Harris	20.00	10.00	6.00
27	Ty Cobb	700.00	350.00	210.00
28	Tris Speaker	90.00	45.00	27.00
29	Tony Lazzeri	35.00	17.50	10.50
30	Waite Hoyt	45.00	22.00	13.50
31	Sherwood Smith	20.00	10.00	6.00
32	Max Carey	45.00	22.00	13.50
33	Eugene Hargrave	20.00	10.00	6.00
34	Miguel L. Gonzales	20.00	10.00	6.00
35	Joe Judge	20.00	10.00	6.00
36	E.C. (Sam) Rice	45.00	22.00	13.50
37	Earl Sheely	20.00	10.00	6.00
38a	Sam Jones	20.00	10.00	6.00
38b	Emory E. Rigney	20.00	10.00	6.00
39	Bib A. Falk (Bibb)	20.00	10.00	6.00
40a	Nick Altrock	20.00	10.00	6.00
40b	Willie Kamm	20.00	10.00	6.00
42	John J. McGraw	90.00	45.00	27.00
43	Artie Nehf	20.00	10.00	6.00
44	Grover Alexander	90.00	45.00	27.00
45	Paul Waner	45.00	22.00	13.50
46	William H. Terry	70.00	35.00	21.00
47	Glenn Wright	20.00	10.00	6.00
48	Earl Smith	20.00	10.00	6.00
49	Leon (Goose) Goslin	45.00	22.00	13.50
50	Frank Frisch	45.00	22.00	13.50
51	Joe Harris	20.00	10.00	6.00
52	Fred (Cy) Williams	25.00	12.50	7.50
53	Eddie Roush	45.00	22.00	13.50
54	George Sisler	45.00	22.00	13.50
55a	Ed Rommel	20.00	10.00	6.00
55b	L. Waner (photo actually Paul Waner)			
		45.00	22.00	13.50
56	Roger Peckinpaugh	20.00	10.00	6.00
57	Stanley Coveleskie (Coveleski)	45.00	22.00	13.50
58	Lester Bell	20.00	10.00	6.00
59a	Dave Bancroft	45.00	22.00	13.50
59b	L. Waner	45.00	22.00	13.50
60	John P. McInnis	20.00	10.00	6.00

NOTE: A card number in parentheses ( ) indicates the set is unnumbered.

1922 W503

Issued circa 1923, this 64-card set of blank-backed cards, measuring 1-3/4" by 2-3/4", feature black and white player photos surrounded by a white border. The player's name and team appear on the card, along with a card number in either the left or right bottom corner. There is no indication of the set's producer, although it is believed the cards were issued with candy or gum. The set carries a W503 American Card Catalog designation.

		NR MT	EX	VG
Complete Set:		3700.00	1850.00	1110.
Common Player:		35.00	17.50	10.50
1	Joe Bush	25.00	12.50	7.50
2	Wally Schang	35.00	17.50	10.50
3	Dave Robertson	35.00	17.50	10.50
4	Wally Pipp	35.00	17.50	10.50
5	Bill Ryan	35.00	17.50	10.50
6	George Kelly	90.00	45.00	27.00
7	Frank Snyder	35.00	17.50	10.50
8	Jimmy O'Connell	35.00	17.50	10.50
9	Bill Cunningham	35.00	17.50	10.50
10	Norman McMillan	35.00	17.50	10.50
11	Waite Hoyt	90.00	45.00	27.00
12	Art Nehf	35.00	17.50	10.50
13	George Sisler	90.00	45.00	27.00
14	Al DeVormer	35.00	17.50	10.50
15	Casey Stengel	200.00	100.00	60.00
16	Ken Williams	35.00	17.50	10.50
17	Joe Dugan	35.00	17.50	10.50
18	"Irish" Meusel	35.00	17.50	10.50
19	Bob Meusel	35.00	17.50	10.50
20	Carl Mays	35.00	17.50	10.50
22	Jess Barnes	35.00	17.50	10.50
23	Walter Johnson	90.00	45.00	27.00
24	Claude Jonnard	35.00	17.50	10.50
25	Dave Bancroft	90.00	45.00	27.00
26	Johnny Rawlings	35.00	17.50	10.50
27	"Pep" Young	35.00	17.50	10.50
28	Earl Smith	35.00	17.50	10.50
29	Willie Kamm	35.00	17.50	10.50
30	Art Fletcher	35.00	17.50	10.50
31	"Kid" Gleason	35.00	17.50	10.50
32	"Babe" Ruth	900.00	450.00	270.00
33	Guy Morton	35.00	17.50	10.50
34	Heinie Groh	35.00	17.50	10.50
35	Leon Cadore	35.00	17.50	10.50
36	Joe Tobin	35.00	17.50	10.50
37	"Rube" Marquard	90.00	45.00	27.00
38	Grover Alexander	125.00	62.00	37.00
39	George Burns	35.00	17.50	10.50
40	Joe Oeschger	35.00	17.50	10.50
41	"Chick" Shorten	35.00	17.50	10.50
42	Roger Hornsby (Rogers)	200.00	100.00	60.00
43	Adolfo Luque	35.00	17.50	10.50
44	Zack Wheat	125.00	62.00	37.00
45	Herb Pruett (Hub)	35.00	17.50	10.50
46	Rabbit Maranville	125.00	62.00	37.00
47	Jimmy Ring	35.00	17.50	10.50
48	Sherrod Smith	35.00	17.50	10.50
49	Lea Meadows (Lee)	35.00	17.50	10.50
50	Aaron Ward	35.00	17.50	10.50
51	Herb Pennock	125.00	62.00	37.00
52	Carlson Bigbee (Carson)	35.00	17.50	10.50
53	Max Carey	125.00	62.00	37.00
54	Charles Robertson	35.00	17.50	10.50

		NR MT	EX	VG
55	Urban Shocker	35.00	17.50	10.50
56	Dutch Ruether	35.00	17.50	10.50
57	Jake Daubert	35.00	17.50	10.50
58	Louis Guisto	35.00	17.50	10.50
59	Ivy Wingo	35.00	17.50	10.50
60	Bill Pertica	35.00	17.50	10.50
61	Luke Sewell	35.00	17.50	10.50
62	Hank Gowdy	35.00	17.50	10.50
63	Jack Scott	35.00	17.50	10.50
64	Stan Coveleskie (Coveleski)	125.00	62.00	37.00

1926 W512

One of the many "strip card" sets of the period (so-called because the cards were sold in strips), the W512 set was issued in 1926 and includes 20 baseball players among its 60 cards. Also featured are boxers, golfers, tennis players, aviators, movie stars and other celebrities. The tiny (1-3/8" by 2-1/4") cards feature rather crude color drawings of the subjects with their names below. The card number appears in the lower left corner. Baseball players lead off the set and are numbered from 1 to 20. Eight of the players are Hall of Famers. Like most strip cards, they have blank backs.

		NR MT	EX	VG
Complete Set:		500.00	250.00	150.00
Common Player:		15.00	7.50	4.50
1	Dave Bancroft	40.00	20.00	12.00
2	Grover Alexander	65.00	32.00	19.50
3	"Ty" Cobb	175.00	87.00	52.00
4	Tris Speaker	65.00	32.00	19.50
5	Glen Wright (Glenn)	15.00	7.50	4.50
6	"Babe" Ruth	200.00	100.00	60.00
7	Everett Scott	15.00	7.50	4.50
8	Frank Frisch	40.00	20.00	12.00
9	Rogers Hornsby	80.00	40.00	24.00
10	Dazzy Vance	40.00	20.00	12.00

1926 W513

This "strip card" set, issued in 1928 was actually a continuation of the W512 set issued two years earlier and is numbered starting with number 61 where the W512 set ended. The blank-backed cards measure 1-3/8" by 2-1/4" and display color drawings of the various celebrities featured in the set, which includes the 26 baseball palyers listed here. (Ten are Hall of Famers.) The cards are numbered in the lower left corner.

		NR MT	EX	VG
	Complete Set:	550.00	275.00	165.00
	Common Player:	15.00	7.50	4.50
61	Eddie Roush	30.00	15.00	9.00
62	Waite Hoyt	30.00	15.00	9.00
63	"Gink" Hendrick	15.00	7.50	4.50
64	"Jumbo" Elliott	15.00	7.50	4.50
65	John Miljus	15.00	7.50	4.50
66	Jumping Joe Dugan	18.00	9.00	5.50
67	Smiling Bill Terry	40.00	20.00	12.00
68	Herb Pennock	30.00	15.00	9.00
69	Rube Benton	15.00	7.50	4.50
70	Paul Waner	30.00	15.00	9.00
71	Adolfo Luque	15.00	7.50	4.50
72	Burleigh Grimes	30.00	15.00	9.00
73	Lloyd Waner	30.00	15.00	9.00
74	Hack Wilson	30.00	15.00	9.00
75	Hal Carlson	15.00	7.50	4.50
76	L. Grantham	15.00	7.50	4.50
77	Wilcey Moore (Wilcy)	15.00	7.50	4.50
78	Jess Haines	30.00	15.00	9.00
79	Tony Lazzeri	18.00	9.00	5.50
80	Al DeVormer	15.00	7.50	4.50
81	Joe Harris	15.00	7.50	4.50
82	Pie Traynor	30.00	15.00	9.00
83	Mark Koenig	15.00	7.50	4.50
84	Babe Herman	18.00	9.00	5.50
85	George Harper	15.00	7.50	4.50
86	Earl Coombs (Earle Combs)	30.00	15.00	9.00

1919 W514

BOB VEACH
LEFT FIELD
DETROIT "TIGERS" A. L.

Consisting of 120 cards, the W514 set is the largest of the various "strip card" issues, so called because the cards were sold in strips. Dating to 1919, it is also one of the earliest and most widely-collected. The color drawings measure 1-3/8" by 2-1/2" and display the card number in the lower corner inside the frame that surrounds the picture. The player's name, position and team appear in the bottom border of the blank-backed cards. The set contains two dozen Hall of Famers and holds an additional interest for baseball historians because it includes seven of the eight Chicago "Black Sox" who were banned from baseball for their alleged role in throwing the 1919 World Series. The most famous of them, "Shoeless" Joe Jackson, makes his only strip card appearance in this set.

		NR MT	EX	VG
	Complete Set:	2900.00	1450.00	870.00
	Common Player:	15.00	7.50	4.50
1	Ira Flagstead	15.00	7.50	4.50
2	Babe Ruth	350.00	175.00	105.00
3	Happy Felsch	18.00	9.00	5.50
4	Doc Lavan	15.00	7.50	4.50

		NR MT	EX	VG
5	Phil Douglas	15.00	7.50	4.50
6	Earle Neale	18.00	9.00	5.50
7	Leslie Nunamaker	15.00	7.50	4.50
8	Sam Jones	15.00	7.50	4.50
9	Claude Hendrix	15.00	7.50	4.50
10	Frank Schulte	15.00	7.50	4.50
11	Cactus Cravath	18.00	9.00	5.50
12	Pat Moran	15.00	7.50	4.50
13	Dick Rudolph	15.00	7.50	4.50
14	Arthur Fletcher	15.00	7.50	4.50
15	Joe Jackson	500.00	250.00	150.00
16	Bill Southworth	15.00	7.50	4.50
17	Ad Luque	15.00	7.50	4.50
18	Charlie Deal	15.00	7.50	4.50
19	Al Mamaux	15.00	7.50	4.50
20	Stuffy McInness (McInnis)	15.00	7.50	4.50
21	Rabbit Maranville	30.00	15.00	9.00
22	Max Carey	30.00	15.00	9.00
23	Dick Kerr	15.00	7.50	4.50
24	George Burns	15.00	7.50	4.50
25	Eddie Collins	30.00	15.00	9.00
26	Steve O'Neil (O'Neill)	15.00	7.50	4.50
27	Bill Fisher	15.00	7.50	4.50
28	Rube Bressler	15.00	7.50	4.50
29	Bob Shawkey	18.00	9.00	5.50
30	Donie Bush	15.00	7.50	4.50
31	Chick Gandil	18.00	9.00	5.50
32	Ollie Zeider	15.00	7.50	4.50
33	Vean Gregg	15.00	7.50	4.50
34	Miller Huggins	30.00	15.00	9.00
35	Lefty Williams	18.00	9.00	5.50
36	Tub Spencer	15.00	7.50	4.50
37	Lew McCarty	15.00	7.50	4.50
38	Hod Eller	15.00	7.50	4.50
39	Joe Gedeon	15.00	7.50	4.50
40	Dave Bancroft	30.00	15.00	9.00
41	Clark Griffith	30.00	15.00	9.00
42	Wilbur Cooper	15.00	7.50	4.50
43	Ty Cobb	300.00	150.00	90.00
44	Roger Peckinpaugh	15.00	7.50	4.50
45	Nic Carter (Nick)	15.00	7.50	4.50
46	Bob Roth	15.00	7.50	4.50
47	Heinie Groh	15.00	7.50	4.50
48	Frank Davis	15.00	7.50	4.50
49	Leslie Mann	15.00	7.50	4.50
50	Fielder Jones	15.00	7.50	4.50
51	Bill Doak	15.00	7.50	4.50
52	John J. McGraw	20.00	10.00	6.00
53	Charles Hollocher	15.00	7.50	4.50
54	Babe Adams	15.00	7.50	4.50
55	Dode Paskert	15.00	7.50	4.50
56	Roger Hornsby (Rogers)	15.00	7.50	4.50
57	Max Rath	60.00	30.00	18.00
58	Jeff Pfeffer	15.00	7.50	4.50
59	Nick Cullop	15.00	7.50	4.50
60	Ray Schalk	30.00	15.00	9.00
61	Bill Jacobson	15.00	7.50	4.50
62	Nap Lajoie	25.00	12.50	7.50
63	George Gibson	15.00	7.50	4.50
64	Harry Hooper	30.00	15.00	9.00
65	Grover Alexander	20.00	10.00	6.00
66	Ping Bodie	15.00	7.50	4.50
67	Hank Gowdy	15.00	7.50	4.50
68	Jake Daubert	18.00	9.00	5.50
69	Red Faber	30.00	15.00	9.00
70	Ivan Olson	15.00	7.50	4.50
71	Pickles Dilhoefer	15.00	7.50	4.50
72	Christy Mathewson	60.00	30.00	18.00
73	Ira Wingo (Ivy)	15.00	7.50	4.50
74	Fred Merkle	18.00	9.00	5.50
75	Frank Baker	30.00	15.00	9.00
76	Bert Gallia	15.00	7.50	4.50
77	Milton Watson	15.00	7.50	4.50
78	Bert Shotten (Shotton)	15.00	7.50	4.50
79	Sam Rice	30.00	15.00	9.00
80	Dan Greiner	15.00	7.50	4.50
81	Larry Doyle	15.00	7.50	4.50
82	Eddie Cicotte	18.00	9.00	5.50
83	Hugo Bezdek	15.00	7.50	4.50
84	Wally Pipp	12.00	6.00	3.50
85	Eddie Rousch (Roush)	30.00	15.00	9.00
86	Slim Sallee	15.00	7.50	4.50
87	Bill Killifer (Killefer)	15.00	7.50	4.50
88	Bob Veach	15.00	7.50	4.50
89	Jim Burke	15.00	7.50	4.50
90	Everett Scott	15.00	7.50	4.50
91	Buck Weaver	18.00	9.00	5.50
92	George Whitted	15.00	7.50	4.50
93	Ed Konetchy	15.00	7.50	4.50
94	Walter Johnson	60.00	30.00	18.00
95	Sam Crawford	30.00	15.00	9.00
96	Fred Mitchell	15.00	7.50	4.50

		NR MT	EX	VG
97	Ira Thomas	15.00	7.50	4.50
98	Jimmy Ring	15.00	7.50	4.50
99	Wally Shange (Schang)	15.00	7.50	4.50
100	Benny Kauff	15.00	7.50	4.50
101	George Sisler	30.00	15.00	9.00
102	Tris Speaker	20.00	10.00	6.00
103	Carl Mays	18.00	9.00	5.50
104	Buck Herzog	15.00	7.50	4.50
105	Swede Risberg	18.00	9.00	5.50
106	Hugh Jennings	30.00	15.00	9.00
107	Pep Young	15.00	7.50	4.50
108	Walter Reuther	15.00	7.50	4.50
109	Joe Gharrity	15.00	7.50	4.50
110	Zach Wheat	30.00	15.00	9.00
111	Jim Vaughn	15.00	7.50	4.50
112	Kid Gleason	15.00	7.50	4.50
113	Casey Stengel	60.00	30.00	18.00
114	Hal Chase	18.00	9.00	5.50
115	Oscar Stange (Stanage)	15.00	7.50	4.50
116	Larry Shean	15.00	7.50	4.50
117	Steve Pendergast	15.00	7.50	4.50
118	Larry Kopf	15.00	7.50	4.50
119	Charles Whiteman	15.00	7.50	4.50
120	Jess Barnes	15.00	7.50	4.50

1923 W515

Cards in the 60-card "strip set" measure 1-5/8" by 2-3/8" and feature color drawings. The card number along with the player's name, position and team appear in the bottom border. Most cards also display a "U&U" copyright line, indicating that the drawings for the blank-backed set were provided by Underwood & Underwood, a major news photo service of the day. The set has a heavy emphasis on New York players with 39 of the 60 cards depicting members of the Yankees, Dodgers or Giants. Babe Ruth appears on two cards and two other cards picture two players each. The set includes 23 Hall of Famers.

		NR MT	EX	VG
Complete Set:		1750.00	875.00	525.00
Common Player:		15.00	7.50	4.50
1	Bill Cunningham	15.00	7.50	4.50
2	Al Mamaux	15.00	7.50	4.50
3	"Babe" Ruth	350.00	175.00	105.00
4	Dave Bancroft	25.00	12.50	7.50
5	Ed Rommel	15.00	7.50	4.50
6	"Babe" Adams	15.00	7.50	4.50
7	Clarence Walker	15.00	7.50	4.50
8	Waite Hoyt	25.00	12.50	7.50
9	Bob Shawkey	18.00	9.00	5.50
10	"Ty" Cobb	300.00	150.00	90.00
11	George Sisler	25.00	12.50	7.50
12	Jack Bentley	15.00	7.50	4.50
13	Jim O'Connell	15.00	7.50	4.50
14	Frank Frisch	25.00	12.50	7.50
15	Frank Baker	25.00	12.50	7.50
16	Burleigh Grimes	25.00	12.50	7.50
17	Wally Schang	15.00	7.50	4.50
18	Harry Heilman (Heilmann)	25.00	12.50	7.50
19	Aaron Ward	15.00	7.50	4.50
20	Carl Mays	18.00	9.00	5.50
21	The Meusel Bros (Bob Meusel, Irish Meusel)	15.00	7.50	4.50

		NR MT	EX	VG
22	Arthur Nehf	15.00	7.50	4.50
23	Lee Meadows	15.00	7.50	4.50
24	"Casey" Stengel	55.00	27.00	16.50
25	Jack Scott	15.00	7.50	4.50
26	Kenneth Williams	18.00	9.00	5.50
27	Joe Bush	18.00	9.00	5.50
28	Tris Speaker	45.00	22.00	13.50
29	Ross Young (Youngs)	15.00	7.50	4.50
30	Joe Dugan	18.00	9.00	5.50
31	The Barnes Bros. (Jesse Barnes, Virgil Barnes)	18.00	9.00	5.50
32	George Kelly	25.00	12.50	7.50
33	Hugh McQuillen (McQuillan)	15.00	7.50	4.50
34	Hugh Jennings	25.00	12.50	7.50
35	Tom Griffith	15.00	7.50	4.50
36	Miller Huggins	25.00	12.50	7.50
37	"Whitey" Witt	15.00	7.50	4.50
38	Walter Johnson	55.00	27.00	16.50
39	"Wally" Pipp	15.00	7.50	4.50
40	"Dutch" Reuther	15.00	7.50	4.50
41	Jim Johnston	15.00	7.50	4.50
42	Willie Kamm	15.00	7.50	4.50
43	Sam Jones	15.00	7.50	4.50
44	Frank Snyder	15.00	7.50	4.50
45	John McGraw	45.00	22.00	13.50
46	Everett Scott	15.00	7.50	4.50
47	"Babe" Ruth	350.00	175.00	105.00
48	Urban Shocker	15.00	7.50	4.50
49	Grover Alexander	45.00	22.00	13.50
50	"Rabbit" Maranville	25.00	12.50	7.50
51	Ray Schalk	25.00	12.50	7.50
52	"Heinie" Groh	15.00	7.50	4.50
53	Wilbert Robinson	25.00	12.50	7.50
54	George Burns	15.00	7.50	4.50
55	Rogers Hornsby	50.00	25.00	15.00
56	Zack Wheat	25.00	12.50	7.50
57	Eddie Roush	25.00	12.50	7.50
58	Eddie Collins	25.00	12.50	7.50
59	Charlie Hollocher	15.00	7.50	4.50
60	Red Faber	25.00	12.50	7.50

1920 W516

This "strip card" set consists of 30 cards featuring featuring drawings - either portraits or full-length action poses. The blank-backed cards measure 1-1/2" by 2-1/2". The player's name, position and team appear beneath the photo, along with the card number. The set can be identified by an "IFS" copyright symbol. representing International Feature Service. The set includes a dozen Hall of Famers.

		NR MT	EX	VG
Complete Set:		1050.00	525.00	315.00
Common Player:		18.00	9.00	5.50
1	Babe Ruth	350.00	175.00	105.00
2	Heinie Groh	18.00	9.00	5.50
3	Ping Bodie	18.00	9.00	5.50
4	Ray Shalk (Schalk)	30.00	15.00	9.00
5	Tris Speaker	45.00	22.00	13.50
6	Ty Cobb	300.00	150.00	90.00
7	Roger Hornsby (Rogers)	55.00	27.00	16.50
8	Walter Johnson	55.00	27.00	16.50
9	Grover Alexander	45.00	22.00	13.50
10	George Burns	18.00	9.00	5.50
11	Jimmy Ring	18.00	9.00	5.50
12	Jess Barnes	18.00	9.00	5.50

		NR MT	EX	VG
13	Larry Doyle	18.00	9.00	5.50
14	Arty Fletcher	18.00	9.00	5.50
15	Dick Rudolph	18.00	9.00	5.50
16	Benny Kauf (Kauff)	18.00	9.00	5.50
17	Art Nehf	18.00	9.00	5.50
18	Babe Adams	18.00	9.00	5.50
19	Will Cooper	18.00	9.00	5.50
20	R. Peckinpaugh	18.00	9.00	5.50
21	Eddie Cicotte	20.00	10.00	6.00
22	Hank Gowdy	18.00	9.00	5.50
23	Eddie Collins	30.00	15.00	9.00
24	Christy Mathewson	55.00	27.00	16.50
25	Clyde Milan	18.00	9.00	5.50
26	M. Kelley (should be G. Kelly)	15.00	7.50	4.50
27	Ed Hooper (Harry)	15.00	7.50	4.50
28	Pep. Young	18.00	9.00	5.50
29	Eddie Rousch (Roush)	30.00	15.00	9.00
30	Geo. Bancroft (Dave)	55.00	27.00	16.50

1921 W516-2

This set is essentially a re-issue of the W516-1 set of the previous year with one major change. The cards are identical to the W516-1 set, except the numbers have been changed and the pictures have all been reversed. The blank-backed cards measure 1-1/2" by 2-1/2" and feature color drawings with the player's name, position and team beneath the picture, along with the card number. The cards display an "IFS" copyright symbol.

		NR MT	EX	VG
Complete Set:		1200.00	600.00	360.00
Common Player:		18.00	9.00	5.50
1	George Burns	18.00	9.00	5.50
2	Grover Alexander	90.00	45.00	27.00
3	Walter Johnson	150.00	75.00	45.00
4	Roger Hornsby (Rogers)	100.00	50.00	30.00
5	Ty Cobb	325.00	162.00	97.00
6	Tris Speaker	90.00	45.00	27.00
7	Ray Shalk (Schalk)	40.00	20.00	12.00
8	Ping Bodie	18.00	9.00	5.50
9	Heinie Groh	18.00	9.00	5.50
10	Babe Ruth	400.00	200.00	120.00
11	R. Peckinpaugh	18.00	9.00	5.50
12	Will. Cooper	18.00	9.00	5.50
13	Babe Adams	18.00	9.00	5.50
14	Art Nehf	18.00	9.00	5.50
15	Benny Kauf (Kauff)	18.00	9.00	5.50
16	Dick Rudolph	18.00	9.00	5.50
17	Arty. Fletcher	18.00	9.00	5.50
18	Larry Doyle	18.00	9.00	5.50
19	Jess Barnes	18.00	9.00	5.50
20	Jimmy Ring	18.00	9.00	5.50
21	George Bancroft (Dave)	30.00	15.00	9.00
22	Eddie Rousch (Roush)	40.00	20.00	12.00
23	Pep Young	18.00	9.00	5.50
24	Ed Hooper (Harry)	30.00	15.00	9.00
25	M. Kelley (should be G. Kelly)	30.00	15.00	9.00
26	Clyde Milan	18.00	9.00	5.50
27	Christy Mathewson	150.00	75.00	45.00
28	Eddie Collins	40.00	20.00	12.00
29	Hank Gowdy	18.00	9.00	5.50
30	Eddie Cicotte	15.00	7.50	4.50

1931 W517

The 54-card W517 set is a scarce issue of 3" by 4" cards which are generally found in a sepia color. There are, however, other known colors of W517s, and they tend to bring higher prices from specialists. The cards feature a player picture as well as his name and team. The card number appears in a small circle on the front, while the backs are blank. The set is heavy in stars of the period including two Babe Ruths (#'s 4 and 20). Not actively collected by many, the set is a relatively inexpensive way to obtain cards of many contemporary Hall of Famers.

		NR MT	EX	VG
Complete Set:		4500.00	2250.00	1350.
Common Player:		35.00	17.50	10.50
1	Earl Combs (Earle)	75.00	37.00	22.00
2	Pie Traynor	35.00	17.50	10.50
3	Eddie Rausch (Roush)	35.00	17.50	10.50
4	Babe Ruth	850.00	425.00	255.00
5a	Chalmer Cissell (Chicago)	35.00	17.50	10.50
5b	Chalmer Cissell (Cleveland)	35.00	17.50	10.50
6	Bill Sherdel	35.00	17.50	10.50
7	Bill Shore	35.00	17.50	10.50
8	Geo. Earnshaw	35.00	17.50	10.50
9	Bucky Harris	50.00	25.00	15.00
10	Charlie Klein	35.00	17.50	10.50
11a	Geo. Kelly (Reds)	35.00	17.50	10.50
11b	Geo. Kelly (Brooklyn)	35.00	17.50	10.50
12	Travis Jackson	35.00	17.50	10.50
13	Willie Kamm	35.00	17.50	10.50
14	Harry Heilman (Heilmann)	35.00	17.50	10.50
15	Grover Alexander	75.00	37.00	22.00
16	Frank Frisch	35.00	17.50	10.50
17	Jack Quinn	35.00	17.50	10.50
18	Cy Williams	35.00	17.50	10.50
19	Kiki Cuyler	35.00	17.50	10.50
20	Babe Ruth	850.00	425.00	255.00
21	Jimmie Foxx	85.00	42.00	25.00
22	Jimmy Dykes	35.00	17.50	10.50
23	Bill Terry	75.00	37.00	22.00
24	Freddy Lindstrom	35.00	17.50	10.50
25	Hughey Critz	35.00	17.50	10.50
26	Pete Donahue	35.00	17.50	10.50
27	Tony Lazzeri	50.00	25.00	15.00
28	Heine Manush (Heinie)	35.00	17.50	10.50
29a	Chick Hafey (Cardinals)	35.00	17.50	10.50
29b	Chick Hafey (Cincinnati)	35.00	17.50	10.50
30	Melvin Ott	75.00	37.00	22.00
31	Bing Miller	35.00	17.50	10.50
32	Geo. Haas	35.00	17.50	10.50
33a	Lefty O'Doul (Phillies)	35.00	17.50	10.50
33b	Lefty O'Doul (Brooklyn)	35.00	17.50	10.50
34	Paul Waner	35.00	17.50	10.50
35	Lou Gehrig	700.00	350.00	210.00
36	Dazzy Vance	35.00	17.50	10.50
37	Mickey Cochrane	35.00	17.50	10.50
38	Rogers Hornsby	90.00	45.00	27.00
39	Lefty Grove	75.00	37.00	22.00
40	Al Simmons	35.00	17.50	10.50
41	Rube Walberg	35.00	17.50	10.50
42	Hack Wilson	35.00	17.50	10.50
43	Art Shires	35.00	17.50	10.50
44	Sammy Hale	35.00	17.50	10.50
45	Ted Lyons	35.00	17.50	10.50
46	Joe Sewell	35.00	17.50	10.50
47	Goose Goslin	35.00	17.50	10.50

		NR MT	EX	VG
48	Lou Fonseca (Lew)	35.00	17.50	10.50
49	Bob Muesel (Meusel)	35.00	17.50	10.50
50	Lu Blue	35.00	17.50	10.50
52	Eddy Collins (Eddie)	75.00	37.00	22.00
53	Joe Judge	35.00	17.50	10.50
54	Mickey Cochrane	125.00	62.00	37.00

A player's name in italic type indicates a rookie card. An (FC) indicates a player's first card for that particular card company.

1920 W519 - Numbered

◀ERNIE KREUGER

Cards in this 20-card "strip set" measure 1-1/2" by 2-1/2" and feature player drawings set against a background of either red, blue, orange, yellow, violet or green. The card number appears in the lower left corner followed by the player's name, which is printed in all capital letters. The player drawings are all posed portraits, except fot Joe Murphy and Ernie Kreuger, who are shown catching. Like all strip cards, the cards were sold in strips and have blank backs. The W519 set was issued circa 1920.

		NR MT	EX	VG
	Complete Set:	575.00	287.00	172.00
	Common Player:	15.00	7.50	4.50
1	Guy Morton	15.00	7.50	4.50
2	Rube Marquard	50.00	25.00	15.00
3	Gabby Cravath (Gavvy)	18.00	9.00	5.50
4	Ernie Krueger	15.00	7.50	4.50
5	Babe Ruth	350.00	175.00	105.00
6	George Sisler	50.00	25.00	15.00
7	Rube Benton	15.00	7.50	4.50
8	Jimmie Johnston	15.00	7.50	4.50
9	Wilbur Robinson (Wilbert)	50.00	25.00	15.00
10	Johnny Griffith	15.00	7.50	4.50
11	Frank Baker	50.00	25.00	15.00
12	Bob Veach	15.00	7.50	4.50
13	Jesse Barnes	15.00	7.50	4.50
14	Leon Cadore	15.00	7.50	4.50
15	Ray Schalk	50.00	25.00	15.00
16	Kid Gleason (Gleason)	15.00	7.50	4.50
17	Joe Murphy	15.00	7.50	4.50
18	Frank Frisch	50.00	25.00	15.00
19	Eddie Collins	50.00	25.00	15.00
20	Wallie Schang	15.00	7.50	4.50

1920 W519 - Unnumbered

Cards in this 10-card set are identical in design and size (1-1/2" by 2-1/2") to the W519 Numbered set, except the player drawings are all set against a blue background and the cards are not numbered. With the lone exception of Eddie Ciotte, all of the subjects in the unnumbered set also appear in the numbered set.

		NR MT	EX	VG
	Complete Set:	175.00	87.00	52.00
	Common Player:	15.00	7.50	4.50
(1)	Eddie Cicotte	18.00	9.00	5.50
(2)	Eddie Collins	50.00	25.00	15.00
(3)	Gabby Cravath (Gavvy)	18.00	9.00	5.50
(4)	Frank Frisch	50.00	25.00	15.00
(5)	Kid Gleason (Gleason)	15.00	7.50	4.50
(6)	Ernie Kreuger	15.00	7.50	4.50
(7)	Rube Marquard	50.00	25.00	15.00
(8)	Guy Morton	15.00	7.50	4.50
(9)	Joe Murphy	15.00	7.50	4.50
(10)	Babe Ruth	350.00	175.00	105.00

1920 W520

FLETCHER

Another "strip card" set issued circa 1920, cards in this set measure 1-3/8" by 2-1/4" and are numbered in the lower right corner from 1 to 20. The first nine cards in the set display portrait poses, while the rest are full-length action poses. Some of the poses in this set are the same as those in the W516 issue with the pictures reversed. The player's last name appears in the border beneath the picture. The cards are blank-backed.

		NR MT	EX	VG
	Complete Set:	1400.00	700.00	420.00
	Common Player:	30.00	15.00	9.00
1	Dave Bancroft	90.00	45.00	27.00
2	Christy Mathewson	225.00	112.00	67.00
3	Larry Doyle	30.00	15.00	9.00
4	Jess Barnes	30.00	15.00	9.00
5	Art Fletcher	30.00	15.00	9.00
6	Wilbur Cooper	30.00	15.00	9.00
7	Mike Gonzales	30.00	15.00	9.00
8	Zach Wheat	90.00	45.00	27.00
9	Tris Speaker	150.00	75.00	45.00
10	Benny Kauff	30.00	15.00	9.00
11	Zach Wheat	90.00	45.00	27.00
12	Phil Douglas	30.00	15.00	9.00
13	Babe Ruth	500.00	250.00	150.00
14	Stan Koveleski (Coveleski)	90.00	45.00	27.00
15	Goldie Rapp	30.00	15.00	9.00
16	Pol Perritt	30.00	15.00	9.00
17	Otto Miller	30.00	15.00	9.00
18	George Kelly	90.00	45.00	27.00
19	Mike Gonzales	30.00	15.00	9.00
20	Les Nunamaker	30.00	15.00	9.00

1921 W521

10 JOHNNY GRIFFITH

		NR MT	EX	VG
31	Benny Kauf (Kauff)	30.00	15.00	9.00
32	Tris Speaker	100.00	50.00	30.00
33	Zach Wheat	30.00	15.00	9.00
34	Mike Gonzales	30.00	15.00	9.00
35	Wilbur Cooper	30.00	15.00	9.00
36	Art Fletcher	30.00	15.00	9.00
37	Jess Barnes	30.00	15.00	9.00
38	Larry Doyle	30.00	15.00	9.00
39	Christy Mathewson	225.00	112.00	67.00
40	Dave Bancroft	75.00	37.00	22.00
41	Les Nunamaker	30.00	15.00	9.00
42	Mike Gonzales	30.00	15.00	9.00
43	George Kelly	75.00	37.00	22.00
44	Otto Miller	30.00	15.00	9.00
45	Pol Perritt	30.00	15.00	9.00
46	Goldie Rapp	30.00	15.00	9.00
47	Stan Koveleski (Coveleski)	75.00	37.00	22.00
48	Babe Ruth	500.00	250.00	150.00
49	Phil Douglas	30.00	15.00	9.00
50	Zach Wheat	75.00	37.00	22.00

This issue is closely related to the W519 Numbered set. In fact, it uses the same color drawings as that set with the pictures, reversed, resulting in a mirror-image of the W519 cards. The player poses and the numbering system are identical, as are the various background colors. The W521 cards are blank-backed and were sold in strips.

		NR MT	EX	VG
Complete Set:		500.00	250.00	150.00
Common Player:		15.00	7.50	4.50
1	Guy Morton	15.00	7.50	4.50
2	Rube Marquard	40.00	20.00	12.00
3	Gabby Cravath (Gavvy)	10.00	5.00	3.00
4	Ernie Krueger	15.00	7.50	4.50
5	Babe Ruth	300.00	150.00	90.00
6	George Sisler	40.00	20.00	12.00
7	Rube Benton	15.00	7.50	4.50
8	Jimmie Johnston	15.00	7.50	4.50
9	Wilbur Robinson (Wilbert)	40.00	20.00	12.00
10	Johnny Griffith	15.00	7.50	4.50
11	Frank Baker	40.00	20.00	12.00
12	Bob Veach	15.00	7.50	4.50
13	Jesse Barnes	15.00	7.50	4.50
14	Leon Cadore	15.00	7.50	4.50
15	Ray Schalk	40.00	20.00	12.00
16	Kid Gleasen (Gleason)	15.00	7.50	4.50
17	Joe Murphy	15.00	7.50	4.50
18	Frank Frisch	40.00	20.00	12.00
19	Eddie Collins	40.00	20.00	12.00
20	Wallie Schang	15.00	7.50	4.50

1918 W522

42 MIKE GONZALES

The 20 cards in this "strip card" set, issued circa 1920, are numbered from 31-50 and use the same players and drawings as the W520 set, issued about the same time. The cards measure 1-3/8" by 2-1/4" and are numbered int he lower left corner followed by the player's name. The cards have blank backs.

	NR MT	EX	VG
Complete Set:	1200.00	600.00	360.00
Common Player:	30.00	15.00	9.00

1922 W551

JESS BARNES
"GIANTS" N. L.

Another "strip set" issued circa 1920, these ten cards measure 1-3/8" by 2-1/4" and feature color drawings. The cards are unnumbered and blank-backed.

		NR MT	EX	VG
Complete Set:		1250.00	625.00	375.00
Common Player:		45.00	22.00	13.50
(1)	Frank Baker	100.00	50.00	30.00
(2)	Dave Bancroft	100.00	50.00	30.00
(3)	Jess Barnes	45.00	22.00	13.50
(4)	Ty Cobb	400.00	200.00	120.00
(5)	Walter Johnson	200.00	100.00	60.00
(6)	Wally Pipp	45.00	22.00	13.50
(7)	Babe Ruth	425.00	212.00	127.00
(8)	George Sisler	100.00	50.00	30.00
(9)	Tris Speaker	150.00	75.00	45.00
(10)	Casey Stengel	200.00	100.00	60.00

1907 W555

COLLINS, PHILA. AMER.

Designated as W555 in the American Card Catalog, very little is known about this obscure set. The nearly sqaure cards measure a tiny 1-1/8" by 1-3-16" and feature a sepia-colored player photo. Sixty-six different cards have been discovered to date, but more are very likely to exist. The manufacturer of the set is unknown, but the sets appear to be related to a series of four early candy cards that carry the ACC designations of E93, E94, E97 and E98, because, with only two exceptions, the players and poses are the same. It is not known how the cards were issued. There is speculation that they may have been issued as "strip" cards or as part of a candy box.

		NR MT	EX	VG
Complete Set:		4300.00	2150.00	1290.
Common Player:		45.00	22.00	13.50
(1)	Red Ames	45.00	22.00	13.50
(2)	Jimmy Austin	45.00	22.00	13.50
(3)	Johnny Bates	45.00	22.00	13.50
(4)	Chief Bender	125.00	62.00	37.00
(5)	Bob Bescher	45.00	22.00	13.50
(6)	Joe Birmingham	45.00	22.00	13.50
(7)	Bill Bradley	45.00	22.00	13.50
(8)	Kitty Bransfield	45.00	22.00	13.50
(9)	Mordecai Brown	125.00	62.00	37.00
(10)	Bobby Byrne	45.00	22.00	13.50
(11)	Frank Chance	60.00	30.00	18.00
(12)	Hal Chase	70.00	35.00	21.00
(13)	Ed Cicotte	55.00	27.00	16.50
(14)	Fred Clarke	125.00	62.00	37.00
(15)	Ty Cobb	600.00	300.00	180.00
(16)	Eddie Collins (dark uniform)	125.00	62.00	37.00
(17)	Eddie Collins (light uniform)	125.00	62.00	37.00
(18)	Harry Coveleskie (Coveleski)	45.00	22.00	13.50
(19)	Sam Crawford	125.00	62.00	37.00
(20)	Harry Davis	45.00	22.00	13.50
(21)	Jim Delehanty	45.00	22.00	13.50
(22)	Art Devlin	45.00	22.00	13.50
(23)	Josh Devore	45.00	22.00	13.50
(24)	Wild Bill Donovan	45.00	22.00	13.50
(25)	Red Dooin	45.00	22.00	13.50
(26)	Mickey Doolan	45.00	22.00	13.50
(27)	Bull Durham	45.00	22.00	13.50
(28)	Jimmy Dygert	45.00	22.00	13.50
(29)	Johnny Evers	125.00	62.00	37.00
(30)	Russ Ford	45.00	22.00	13.50
(31)	George Gibson	45.00	22.00	13.50
(32)	Clark Griffith	125.00	62.00	37.00
(33)	Topsy Hartsell (Hartsel)	45.00	22.00	13.50
(34)	Bill Heinchman (Hinchman)	45.00	22.00	13.50
(35)	Ira Hemphill	45.00	22.00	13.50
(36)	Hughie Jennings	125.00	62.00	37.00
(37)	Davy Jones	45.00	22.00	13.50
(38)	Addie Joss	125.00	62.00	37.00
(39)	Wee Willie Keeler	45.00	22.00	13.50
(40)	Red Kleinow	45.00	22.00	13.50
(41)	Nap Lajoie	200.00	100.00	60.00
(42)	Joe Lake	45.00	22.00	13.50
(43)	Tommy Leach	45.00	22.00	13.50
(44)	Sherry Magee	55.00	27.00	16.50
(45)	Christy Mathewson	225.00	112.00	67.00
(46)	Amby McConnell	45.00	22.00	13.50
(47)	John McGraw	175.00	87.00	52.00
(48)	Chief Meyers	45.00	22.00	13.50
(49)	Earl Moore	45.00	22.00	13.50
(50)	Mike Mowery	45.00	22.00	13.50
(51)	George Mullin	45.00	22.00	13.50
(52)	Red Murray	45.00	22.00	13.50
(53)	Nichols	45.00	22.00	13.50
(54)	Jim Pastorious (Pastorius)	45.00	22.00	13.50
(55)	Deacon Phillippi (Phillippe)	45.00	22.00	13.50
(56)	Eddie Plank	55.00	27.00	16.50
(57)	Fred Snodgrass	45.00	22.00	13.50
(58)	Harry Steinfeldt	55.00	27.00	16.50
(59)	Joe Tinker	125.00	62.00	37.00
(60)	Hippo Vaughn	45.00	22.00	13.50
(61)	Honus Wagner	600.00	300.00	180.00
(62)	Rube Waddell	125.00	62.00	37.00
(63)	Hooks Wiltse	45.00	22.00	13.50
(64a)	Cy Young (standing, full name on front)			
		175.00	87.00	52.00
(64b)	Cy Young (standing, last name on front)			
		175.00	87.00	52.00
(65)	Cy Young (portrait)	175.00	87.00	52.00

1927 W560

Although assigned a "W" number, this set is not a "strip card" issue in the same sense as the rest of the "W" sets, although W560 cards are frequently found in uncut sheets of three or four across or down. Uncut sheets of 16 cards, in four rows of four cards each, are also known to exist. Cards in the W560 set measure 1-3/4" by 2-3/4" and are designed like a deck of playing cards, with the pictures on the various suits - either hearts, clubs, spades, diamonds or jokers. The set includes movie stars, aviators and other athletes, in addition to baseball players. Because they are designed as a deck of playing cards, the cards are printed in either red or black.

		NR MT	EX	VG
Complete Set:		2000.00	1000.00	600.00
Common Player:		15.00	7.50	4.50
(1)	Vic Aldridge	15.00	7.50	4.50
(2)	Lester Bell	15.00	7.50	4.50
(3)	Larry Benton	15.00	7.50	4.50
(4)	Max Bishop	15.00	7.50	4.50
(5)	Del Bissonette	15.00	7.50	4.50
(6)	Jim Bottomley	35.00	17.50	10.50
(7)	Guy Bush	15.00	7.50	4.50
(8)	W. Clark	15.00	7.50	4.50
(9)	Andy Cohen	15.00	7.50	4.50
(10)	Mickey Cochrane	35.00	17.50	10.50
(11)	Hugh Critz	15.00	7.50	4.50
(12)	Kiki Cuyler	35.00	17.50	10.50
(13)	Taylor Douthit	15.00	7.50	4.50
(14)	Fred Fitzsimmons	15.00	7.50	4.50
(15)	Jim Foxx	225.00	112.00	67.00
(16)	Lou Gehrig	350.00	175.00	105.00
(17)	Goose Goslin	35.00	17.50	10.50
(18)	Sam Gray	15.00	7.50	4.50
(19)	Lefty Grove	100.00	50.00	30.00
(20)	Jesse Haines	35.00	17.50	10.50
(21)	Babe Herman	18.00	9.00	5.50
(22)	Roger Hornsby (Rogers)	125.00	62.00	37.00
(23)	Waite Hoyt	35.00	17.50	10.50
(24)	Henry Johnson	15.00	7.50	4.50
(25)	Walter Johnson	125.00	62.00	37.00
(26)	Willie Kamm	15.00	7.50	4.50
(27)	Fred Lindstrom	35.00	17.50	10.50
(28)	Fred Maguire	15.00	7.50	4.50
(29)	Fred Marberry	15.00	7.50	4.50
(30)	Johnny Mostil	15.00	7.50	4.50
(31)	Buddy Myer	15.00	7.50	4.50
(32)	Herb Pennock	35.00	17.50	10.50
(33)	George Pipgras	15.00	7.50	4.50
(34)	Flint Rhem	15.00	7.50	4.50
(35)	Babe Ruth	500.00	250.00	150.00
(36)	Luke Sewell	15.00	7.50	4.50
(37)	Willie Sherdel	15.00	7.50	4.50
(38)	Al Simmons	35.00	17.50	10.50
(39)	Thomas Thevenow	15.00	7.50	4.50
(40)	Fresco Thompson	15.00	7.50	4.50
(41)	George Uhle	15.00	7.50	4.50
(42)	Dazzy Vance	35.00	17.50	10.50
(43)	Rube Walberg	15.00	7.50	4.50
(44)	Lloyd Waner	35.00	17.50	10.50
(45)	Paul Waner	35.00	17.50	10.50
(46)	Fred "Cy" Williams	18.00	9.00	5.50
(47)	Jim Wilson	15.00	7.50	4.50
(48)	Glen Wright (Glenn)	15.00	7.50	4.50

1923 W572

This set, designated as W572 by the American Card Catalog, measures 1-3/8" by 2-1/2" and are blank-backed. These "strip cards" feature black and white player photos, although some sepia-toned cards have also been found. The set is closely related to the popular E120 American Caramel set issued in 1922 and, with the exception of Ty Cobb, it uses the same photos. The cards were originally issued as strips of ten, with five baseball players and five boxers. They are found on either a white, slick stock or a dark, coarser one. The player's name on the front of the cards appears in script. To date 119 different subjects have been found, although it is likely one more exists.

	NR MT	EX	VG
Complete Set:	4000.00	2000.00	1200.
Common Player:	18.00	9.00	5.50

		NR MT	EX	VG
(1)	Eddie Ainsmith	18.00	9.00	5.50
(2)	Vic Aldridge	18.00	9.00	5.50
(3)	Grover Alexander	65.00	32.00	19.50
(4)	Walt Barbare	18.00	9.00	5.50
(5)	Jess Barnes	18.00	9.00	5.50
(6)	John Bassler	18.00	9.00	5.50
(7)	Lu Blue	18.00	9.00	5.50
(8)	Norman Boeckel	18.00	9.00	5.50
(9)	George Burns	18.00	9.00	5.50
(10)	Joe Bush	20.00	10.00	6.00
(11)	Leon Cadore	18.00	9.00	5.50
(12)	Virgil Cheevers (Cheeves)	18.00	9.00	5.50
(13)	Ty Cobb	700.00	350.00	210.00
(14)	Eddie Collins	50.00	25.00	15.00
(15)	John Collins	18.00	9.00	5.50
(16)	Wilbur Cooper	18.00	9.00	5.50
(17)	Stanley Coveleski	50.00	25.00	15.00
(18)	Walton Cruise	18.00	9.00	5.50
(19)	Dave Danforth	18.00	9.00	5.50
(20)	Jake Daubert	20.00	10.00	6.00
(21)	Hank DeBerry	18.00	9.00	5.50
(22)	Lou DeVormer	18.00	9.00	5.50
(23)	Bill Doak	18.00	9.00	5.50
(24)	Pete Donohue	18.00	9.00	5.50
(25)	Pat Duncan	18.00	9.00	5.50
(26)	Jimmy Dykes	20.00	10.00	6.00
(27)	Urban Faber	50.00	25.00	15.00
(28)	Bib Falk (Bibb)	18.00	9.00	5.50
(29)	Frank Frisch	50.00	25.00	15.00
(30)	C. Galloway	18.00	9.00	5.50
(31)	Ed Gharrity	18.00	9.00	5.50
(32)	Chas. Glazner	18.00	9.00	5.50
(33)	Hank Gowdy	18.00	9.00	5.50
(34)	Tom Griffith	18.00	9.00	5.50
(35)	Burleigh Grimes	50.00	25.00	15.00
(36)	Ray Grimes	18.00	9.00	5.50
(37)	Heinie Groh	18.00	9.00	5.50
(38)	Joe Harris	18.00	9.00	5.50
(39)	Stanley Harris	50.00	25.00	15.00
(40)	Joe Hauser	18.00	9.00	5.50
(41)	Harry Heilmann	50.00	25.00	15.00
(42)	Walter Henline	18.00	9.00	5.50
(43)	Chas. Hollocher	18.00	9.00	5.50
(44)	Harry Hooper	50.00	25.00	15.00
(45)	Rogers Hornsby	150.00	75.00	45.00
(46)	Waite Hoyt	50.00	25.00	15.00
(47)	Wilbur Hubbell	18.00	9.00	5.50
(48)	Wm. Jacobson	18.00	9.00	5.50

		NR MT	EX	VG
(49)	Chas. Jamieson	18.00	9.00	5.50
(50)	S. Johnson	18.00	9.00	5.50
(51)	Walter Johnson	150.00	75.00	45.00
(52)	Jimmy Johnston	18.00	9.00	5.50
(53)	Joe Judge	18.00	9.00	5.50
(54)	Geo. Kelly	50.00	25.00	15.00
(55)	Lee King	18.00	9.00	5.50
(56)	Larry Kopff (Kopf)	18.00	9.00	5.50
(57)	Geo. Leverette	18.00	9.00	5.50
(58)	Al Mamaux	18.00	9.00	5.50
(59)	"Rabbit" Maranville	50.00	25.00	15.00
(60)	"Rube" Marquard	50.00	25.00	15.00
(61)	Martin McManus	18.00	9.00	5.50
(62)	Lee Meadows	18.00	9.00	5.50
(63)	Mike Menosky	18.00	9.00	5.50
(64)	Bob Meusel	30.00	15.00	9.00
(65)	Emil Meusel	18.00	9.00	5.50
(66)	Geo. Mogridge	18.00	9.00	5.50
(67)	John Morrison	18.00	9.00	5.50
(68)	Johnny Mostil	18.00	9.00	5.50
(69)	Roliene Naylor	18.00	9.00	5.50
(70)	Art Nehf	18.00	9.00	5.50
(71)	Joe Oeschger	18.00	9.00	5.50
(72)	Bob O'Farrell	18.00	9.00	5.50
(73)	Steve O'Neill	18.00	9.00	5.50
(74)	Frank Parkinson	18.00	9.00	5.50
(75)	Ralph Perkins	18.00	9.00	5.50
(76)	H. Pillette	18.00	9.00	5.50
(77)	Ralph Pinelli	20.00	10.00	6.00
(78)	Wallie Pipp	35.00	17.50	10.50
(79)	Ray Powell	18.00	9.00	5.50
(80)	Jack Quinn	18.00	9.00	5.50
(81)	Goldie Rapp	18.00	9.00	5.50
(82)	Walter Reuther	18.00	9.00	5.50
(83)	Sam Rice	50.00	25.00	15.00
(84)	Emory Rigney	18.00	9.00	5.50
(85)	Eppa Rixey	50.00	25.00	15.00
(86)	Ed Rommel	18.00	9.00	5.50
(87)	Eddie Roush	50.00	25.00	15.00
(88)	Babe Ruth	900.00	450.00	270.00
(89)	Ray Schalk	18.00	9.00	5.50
(90)	Wallie Schang	18.00	9.00	5.50
(91)	Walter Schmidt	18.00	9.00	5.50
(92)	Joe Schultz	18.00	9.00	5.50
(93)	Hank Severeid	18.00	9.00	5.50
(94)	Joe Sewell	50.00	25.00	15.00
(95)	Bob Shawkey	20.00	10.00	6.00
(96)	Earl Sheely	18.00	9.00	5.50
(97)	Will Sherdel	18.00	9.00	5.50
(98)	Urban Shocker	18.00	9.00	5.50
(99)	George Sisler	50.00	25.00	15.00
(100)	Earl Smith	18.00	9.00	5.50
(101)	Elmer Smith	18.00	9.00	5.50
(102)	Jack Smith	18.00	9.00	5.50
(103)	Bill Southworth	18.00	9.00	5.50
(104)	Tris Speaker	65.00	32.00	19.50
(105)	Milton Stock	18.00	9.00	5.50
(106)	Jim Tierney	18.00	9.00	5.50
(107)	Harold Traynor	18.00	9.00	5.50
(108)	Geo. Uhle	50.00	25.00	15.00
(109)	Bob Veach	18.00	9.00	5.50
(110)	Clarence Walker	18.00	9.00	5.50
(111)	Curtis Walker	18.00	9.00	5.50
(112)	Bill Wambsganss	20.00	10.00	6.00
(113)	Aaron Ward	18.00	9.00	5.50
(114)	Zach Wheat	50.00	25.00	15.00
(115)	Fred Williams	30.00	15.00	9.00
(116)	Ken Williams	30.00	15.00	9.00
(117)	Ivy Wingo	18.00	9.00	5.50
(118)	Joe Wood	30.00	15.00	9.00
(119)	J.T. Zachary	18.00	9.00	5.50

1922 W573

CLARENCE MITCHELL
PITCHER, BROOKLYN NATIONALS

These cards, identified as W573 in the American Card Catalog, appear to be blank-backed versions of the popular E120 American Caramel set. In reality they were "strip cards," produced in 1923 and sold in strips of ten for a penny. The cards feature black and white photos. To date 144 different subjects have been found, but it is likely that all 240 poses from the E120 set actually exist.

		NR MT	EX	VG
	Complete Set:	4500.00	2250.00	1350.
	Common Player:	25.00	12.50	7.50
(1)	Babe Adams	25.00	12.50	7.50
(2)	Eddie Ainsmith	25.00	12.50	7.50
(3)	Vic Aldridge	25.00	12.50	7.50
(4)	Grover Alexander	80.00	40.00	24.00
(5)	Home Run Baker	75.00	37.00	22.00
(6)	Dave Bancroft	75.00	37.00	22.00
(7)	Walt Barbare	25.00	12.50	7.50
(8)	Turner Barber	25.00	12.50	7.50
(9)	Jess Barnes	25.00	12.50	7.50
(10)	John Bassler	25.00	12.50	7.50
(11)	Carson Bigbee	25.00	12.50	7.50
(12)	Lu Blue	25.00	12.50	7.50
(13)	Norman Boeckel	25.00	12.50	7.50
(14)	Geo. Burns (Boston)	25.00	12.50	7.50
(15)	Geo. Burns (Cincinnati)	25.00	12.50	7.50
(16)	Marty Callaghan	25.00	12.50	7.50
(17)	Max Carey	75.00	37.00	22.00
(18)	Jimmy Caveney	25.00	12.50	7.50
(19)	Virgil Cheeves	25.00	12.50	7.50
(20)	Vern Clemons	25.00	12.50	7.50
(21)	Ty Cobb	750.00	375.00	225.00
(22)	Bert Cole	25.00	12.50	7.50
(23)	Eddie Collins	75.00	37.00	22.00
(24)	Pat Collins	25.00	12.50	7.50
(25)	Wilbur Cooper	25.00	12.50	7.50
(26)	Elmer Cox	25.00	12.50	7.50
(27)	Bill Cunningham	25.00	12.50	7.50
(28)	George Cutshaw	25.00	12.50	7.50
(29)	Dave Danforth	25.00	12.50	7.50
(30)	George Dauss	25.00	12.50	7.50
(31)	Dixie Davis	25.00	12.50	7.50
(32)	Hank DeBerry	25.00	12.50	7.50
(33)	Lou DeVormer	25.00	12.50	7.50
(34)	Bill Doak	25.00	12.50	7.50
(35)	Joe Dugan	40.00	20.00	12.00
(36)	Howard Ehmke	25.00	12.50	7.50
(37)	Frank Ellerbe	25.00	12.50	7.50
(38)	Urban Faber	75.00	37.00	22.00
(39)	Bib Falk (Bibb)	25.00	12.50	7.50
(40)	Max Flack	25.00	12.50	7.50
(41)	Ira Flagstead	25.00	12.50	7.50
(42)	Art Fletcher	25.00	12.50	7.50
(43)	Horace Ford	25.00	12.50	7.50
(44)	Jack Fournier	25.00	12.50	7.50
(45)	Frank Frisch	75.00	37.00	22.00
(46)	Ollie Fuhrman	25.00	12.50	7.50
(47)	C. Galloway	25.00	12.50	7.50
(48)	Walter Gerber	25.00	12.50	7.50
(49)	Ed Gharrity	25.00	12.50	7.50
(50)	Chas. Glazner	25.00	12.50	7.50
(51)	Leon Goslin	75.00	37.00	22.00
(52)	Hank Gowdy	25.00	12.50	7.50
(53)	John Graney	25.00	12.50	7.50
(54)	Ray Grimes	25.00	12.50	7.50
(55)	Heinie Groh	25.00	12.50	7.50
(56)	Jesse Haines	75.00	37.00	22.00
(57)	Earl Hamilton	25.00	12.50	7.50
(58)	Bubbles Hargrave	25.00	12.50	7.50
(59)	Bryan Harris	25.00	12.50	7.50
(60)	Cliff Heathcote	25.00	12.50	7.50
(61)	Harry Heilmann	75.00	37.00	22.00
(62)	Clarence Hodge	25.00	12.50	7.50
(63)	Chas. Hollocher	25.00	12.50	7.50
(64)	Harry Hooper	75.00	37.00	22.00
(65)	Rogers Hornsby	150.00	75.00	45.00
(66)	Waite Hoyt	75.00	37.00	22.00
(67)	Ernie Johnson	25.00	12.50	7.50
(68)	S. Johnson	25.00	12.50	7.50
(69)	Walter Johnson	25.00	12.50	7.50
(70)	Doc Johnston	200.00	100.00	60.00
(71)	Sam Jones	25.00	12.50	7.50
(72)	Ben Karr	25.00	12.50	7.50
(73)	Johnny Lavan	25.00	12.50	7.50
(74)	Geo. Leverette	25.00	12.50	7.50
(75)	"Rabbit" Maranville	75.00	37.00	22.00
(76)	Cliff Markle	25.00	12.50	7.50
(77)	Carl Mays	40.00	20.00	12.00

		NR MT	EX	VG
(78)	Hervey McClellan	25.00	12.50	7.50
(79)	Martin McManus	25.00	12.50	7.50
(80)	Lee Meadows	25.00	12.50	7.50
(81)	Mike Menosky	25.00	12.50	7.50
(82)	Emil Meusel	25.00	12.50	7.50
(83)	Clyde Milan	25.00	12.50	7.50
(84)	Bing Miller	25.00	12.50	7.50
(85)	Elmer Miller	25.00	12.50	7.50
(86)	Lawrence Miller	25.00	12.50	7.50
(87)	Clarence Mitchell	25.00	12.50	7.50
(88)	Geo. Mogridge	25.00	12.50	7.50
(89)	John Morrison	25.00	12.50	7.50
(90)	Johnny Mostil	25.00	12.50	7.50
(91)	Elmer Meyers	25.00	12.50	7.50
(92)	Roliene Naylor	25.00	12.50	7.50
(93)	Les Nunamaker	25.00	12.50	7.50
(94)	Bob O'Farrell	25.00	12.50	7.50
(95)	George O'Neil	25.00	12.50	7.50
(96)	Steve O'Neill	25.00	12.50	7.50
(97)	Herb Pennock	75.00	37.00	22.00
(98)	Ralph Perkins	25.00	12.50	7.50
(99)	Tom Phillips	25.00	12.50	7.50
(100)	Val Picinich	25.00	12.50	7.50
(101)	H. Pillette	25.00	12.50	7.50
(102)	Ralph Pinelli	25.00	12.50	7.50
(103)	Wallie Pipp	40.00	20.00	12.00
(104)	Clark Pittenger	25.00	12.50	7.50
(105)	Derrill Pratt	25.00	12.50	7.50
(106)	Goldie Rapp	25.00	12.50	7.50
(107)	John Rawlings	25.00	12.50	7.50
(108)	Walter Reuther	25.00	12.50	7.50
(109)	Emory Rigney	25.00	12.50	7.50
(110)	Charles Robertson	25.00	12.50	7.50
(111)	Ed Rommel	25.00	12.50	7.50
(112)	Muddy Ruel	25.00	12.50	7.50
(113)	Babe Ruth	1000.00	500.00	300.00
(114)	Ray Schalk	75.00	37.00	22.00
(115)	Wallie Schang	25.00	12.50	7.50
(116)	Ray Schmidt	25.00	12.50	7.50
(117)	Walter Schmidt	25.00	12.50	7.50
(118)	Joe Schultz	25.00	12.50	7.50
(119)	Hank Severeid	25.00	12.50	7.50
(120)	Joe Sewell	75.00	37.00	22.00
(121)	Bob Shawkey	40.00	20.00	12.00
(122)	Earl Sheely	25.00	12.50	7.50
(123)	Ralph Shinner	25.00	12.50	7.50
(124)	Urban Shocker	25.00	12.50	7.50
(125)	George Sisler	75.00	37.00	22.00
(126)	Earl Smith (Washington)	25.00	12.50	7.50
(127)	Earl Smith (New York)	25.00	12.50	7.50
(128)	Jack Smith	25.00	12.50	7.50
(129)	Al Sothoron	25.00	12.50	7.50
(130)	Tris Speaker	80.00	40.00	24.00
(131)	Amos Strunk	25.00	12.50	7.50
(132)	Jim Tierney	25.00	12.50	7.50
(133)	John Tobin	25.00	12.50	7.50
(134)	George Toporcer	25.00	12.50	7.50
(135)	Geo. Uhle	25.00	12.50	7.50
(136)	Bob Veach	25.00	12.50	7.50
(137)	John Watson	25.00	12.50	7.50
(138)	Zach Wheat	75.00	37.00	22.00
(139)	Fred Williams	40.00	20.00	12.00
(140)	Ken Williams	25.00	12.50	7.50
(141)	Lawrence Woodall	25.00	12.50	7.50
(142)	Russell Wrightstone	25.00	12.50	7.50
(143)	Ross Young (Youngs)	75.00	37.00	22.00
(144)	J.T. Zachary	25.00	12.50	7.50

1932 W574

WHITE SOX

Issued circa 1932, cards in the W574 set measure 2-1/4" by 2-7/8". They are unnumbered and are listed here in alphabetical order.

	NR MT	EX	VG
Complete Set:	1600.00	800.00	480.00
Common Player:	45.00	22.00	13.50

		NR MT	EX	VG
(1)	Dale Alexander	45.00	22.00	13.50
(2)	Luke Appling	125.00	62.00	37.00
(3)	Earl Averill	125.00	62.00	37.00
(4)	Ivy Paul Andrews	45.00	22.00	13.50
(5)	Geore Blaeholder	45.00	22.00	13.50
(6)	Irving Burns	45.00	22.00	13.50
(7)	Pat Caraway	45.00	22.00	13.50
(8)	Chalmer Cissell	45.00	22.00	13.50
(9)	Harry Davis	45.00	22.00	13.50
(10)	Jimmy Dykes	70.00	35.00	21.00
(11)	George Earnshaw	45.00	22.00	13.50
(12)	Urban Faber	125.00	62.00	37.00
(13)	Lewis Fonseca	45.00	22.00	13.50
(14)	Jimmy Foxx	225.00	112.00	67.00
(15)	Victor Frasier	45.00	22.00	13.50
(16)	Robert Grove	200.00	100.00	60.00
(17)	Frank Grube	45.00	22.00	13.50
(18)	Irving Hadley	45.00	22.00	13.50
(19)	Willie Kamm	45.00	22.00	13.50
(20)	Bill Killefer	45.00	22.00	13.50
(21)	Ralph Kress	45.00	22.00	13.50
(22)	Fred Marberry	45.00	22.00	13.50
(23)	Roger Peckinpaugh	45.00	22.00	13.50
(24)	Frank Reiber	45.00	22.00	13.50
(25)	Carl Reynolds	45.00	22.00	13.50
(26)	Al Simmons	125.00	62.00	37.00
(27)	Joe Vosmik	45.00	22.00	13.50
(28)	Gerald Walker	45.00	22.00	13.50
(29)	Whitlow Wyatt	45.00	22.00	13.50

1922 W575-1

BERNARD (BRUD) KUNGLING
CATCHER, BROOKLYN NATIONALS

Designated as W575 in the American Card Catalog, these "strip cards" are blank-backed. Issued circa 1922, cards in this set measure 2" by 3-1/4". The subjects for the set were taken from the E121 set and include representatives of all 16 major league teams, with heavier emphasis on the New York teams.

	NR MT	EX	VG
Complete Set:	8500.00	4250.00	2550.
Common Player:	30.00	15.00	9.00

		NR MT	EX	VG
(1)	Chas. "Babe" Adams	30.00	15.00	9.00
(2)	G.C. Alexander	100.00	50.00	30.00
(3)	Grover Alexander	100.00	50.00	30.00
(4)	Jim Bagby	30.00	15.00	9.00
(5a)	J. Franklin Baker	85.00	42.00	25.00
(5b)	Frank Baker	85.00	42.00	25.00
(6)	Dave Bancroft (batting)	85.00	42.00	25.00
(7)	Dave Bancroft (fielding)	85.00	42.00	25.00
(8)	Jesse Barnes	30.00	15.00	9.00
(9)	Howard Berry	30.00	15.00	9.00
(10)	L. Bigbee (should be C.)	30.00	15.00	9.00
(11)	Ping Bodie	30.00	15.00	9.00
(13)	"Ed" Brown	30.00	15.00	9.00
(14)	George Burns	30.00	15.00	9.00
(15)	Geo. J. Burns	30.00	15.00	9.00
(16)	"Bullet Joe" Bush	30.00	15.00	9.00
(17)	Owen Bush	30.00	15.00	9.00
(18)	Max Carey (batting)	85.00	42.00	25.00

		NR MT	EX	VG
(19)	Max Carey (hands on hips)	85.00	42.00	25.00
(20)	Ty Cobb	750.00	375.00	225.00
(21)	Eddie Collins	100.00	50.00	30.00
(22)	"Rip" Collins	30.00	15.00	9.00
(23)	Stanley Coveleskie (Coveleski)	85.00	42.00	25.00
(24)	Bill Cunningham	30.00	15.00	9.00
(25)	Jake Daubert	40.00	20.00	12.00
(26)	George Dauss	30.00	15.00	9.00
(27)	"Dixie" Davis	30.00	15.00	9.00
(28)	Charles Deal (dark uniform)	30.00	15.00	9.00
(29)	Charles Deal (light uniform)	30.00	15.00	9.00
(30)	Lou DeVormer	30.00	15.00	9.00
(31)	William Doak	30.00	15.00	9.00
(32)	Bill Donovan	30.00	15.00	9.00
(33)	"Phil" Douglas	30.00	15.00	9.00
(34a)	Johnny Evers (Mgr.)	85.00	42.00	25.00
(34b)	Johnny Evers (Manager)	85.00	42.00	25.00
(35a)	Urban Faber (dark uniform)	85.00	42.00	25.00
(35b)	Urban Faber (white uniform)	85.00	42.00	25.00
(36)	Bib Falk (Bibb)	30.00	15.00	9.00
(37)	Alex Ferguson	30.00	15.00	9.00
(38)	Wm. Fewster	30.00	15.00	9.00
(39)	Eddie Foster	30.00	15.00	9.00
(40)	Frank Frisch	85.00	42.00	25.00
(41)	W.L. Gardner	30.00	15.00	9.00
(42)	Alexander Gaston	30.00	15.00	9.00
(43)	E.P. Gharrity	30.00	15.00	9.00
(44)	Chas. "Whitey" Glazner	30.00	15.00	9.00
(45)	"Kid" Gleason	30.00	15.00	9.00
(46)	"Mike" Gonzalez	30.00	15.00	9.00
(47)	Hank Gowdy	30.00	15.00	9.00
(48a)	John Graney (Util. o.f.)	30.00	15.00	9.00
(49b)	John Graney (O.F.)	30.00	15.00	9.00
(50)	Tom Griffith	30.00	15.00	9.00
(51)	Chas. Grimm	40.00	20.00	12.00
(52a)	Heinie Groh (Cincinnati)	30.00	15.00	9.00
(52b)	Heinie Groh (New York)	30.00	15.00	9.00
(53)	Jess Haines	85.00	42.00	25.00
(54)	Harry Harper	30.00	15.00	9.00
(55)	"Chicken" Hawks	30.00	15.00	9.00
(56)	Harry Heilman (Heilmann) (holding bat)	85.00	42.00	25.00
(57)	Harry Heilman (Heilmann) (running)	85.00	42.00	25.00
(58)	Fred Hoffman	30.00	15.00	9.00
(59a)	Walter Holke (1st B., portrait)	30.00	15.00	9.00
(59b)	Walter Holke (1B, portrait)	30.00	15.00	9.00
(60)	Walter Holke (throwing)	30.00	15.00	9.00
(61a)	Charles Hollacher (name incorrect)	30.00	15.00	9.00
(61b)	Charles Hollocher (name correct)	30.00	15.00	9.00
(62)	Harry Hooper	30.00	15.00	9.00
(63a)	Rogers Hornsby (2nd B.)	150.00	75.00	45.00
(63b)	Rogers Hornsby (O.F.)	150.00	75.00	45.00
(64)	Waite Hoyt	85.00	42.00	25.00
(65)	Miller Huggins	85.00	42.00	25.00
(66)	Wm. C. Jacobson	30.00	15.00	9.00
(67)	Hugh Jennings	30.00	15.00	9.00
(68)	Walter Johnson (arms at chest)	200.00	100.00	60.00
(69)	Walter Johnson (throwing)	200.00	100.00	60.00
(70)	James Johnston	30.00	15.00	9.00
(71)	Joe Judge (batting)	30.00	15.00	9.00
(73a)	George Kelly (1st B.)	85.00	42.00	25.00
(73b)	George Kelly (1B.)	85.00	42.00	25.00
(74)	Dick Kerr	30.00	15.00	9.00
(75)	P.J. Kilduff	30.00	15.00	9.00
(76)	Bill Killefer	30.00	15.00	9.00
(77)	John Lavan	30.00	15.00	9.00
(78)	"Nemo" Leibold	30.00	15.00	9.00
(79)	Duffy Lewis	30.00	15.00	9.00
(80)	Al. Mamaux	30.00	15.00	9.00
(81)	"Rabbit" Maranville	85.00	42.00	25.00
(81b)	Carl Mays (name correct)	40.00	20.00	12.00
(82a)	Carl May (name incorrect)	40.00	20.00	12.00
(83)	John McGraw	110.00	55.00	33.00
(84)	Jack McInnis	30.00	15.00	9.00
(85)	M.J. McNally	30.00	15.00	9.00
(86)	Emil Muesel	30.00	15.00	9.00
(87)	R. Meusel	50.00	25.00	15.00
(88)	Clyde Milan	30.00	15.00	9.00
(89)	Elmer Miller	30.00	15.00	9.00
(90)	Otto Miller	30.00	15.00	9.00
(91a)	John Mitchell (S.S.)	30.00	15.00	9.00
(91b)	John Mitchell (3rd B.)	30.00	15.00	9.00
(92)	Guy Morton	30.00	15.00	9.00
(94)	Eddie Mulligan	30.00	15.00	9.00
(95)	Eddie Murphy	30.00	15.00	9.00
(96a)	"Hy" Myers (C.F./O.F.)	30.00	15.00	9.00
(96b)	Hy Myers (O.F.)	30.00	15.00	9.00

		NR MT	EX	VG
(97)	A.E. Neale	60.00	30.00	18.00
(98)	Arthur Nehf	30.00	15.00	9.00
(99)	Joe Oeschger	30.00	15.00	9.00
(100)	Chas. O'Leary	30.00	15.00	9.00
(101)	Steve O'Neill	30.00	15.00	9.00
(101a)	Jeff Pfeffer (Brooklyn)	30.00	15.00	9.00
(101b)	Jeff Pfeffer (St. Louis)	30.00	15.00	9.00
(102a)	Roger Peckinbaugh (name incorrect)			
		30.00	15.00	9.00
(102b)	Roger Peckinpaugh (name correct)			
		30.00	15.00	9.00
(104)	Walter Pipp	60.00	30.00	18.00
(105)	Jack Quinn	30.00	15.00	9.00
(106a)	John Rawlings (2nd B.)	30.00	15.00	9.00
(106b)	John Rawlings (2B.)	30.00	15.00	9.00
(107a)	E.S. Rice (name incorrect)	85.00	42.00	25.00
(107b)	E.C. Rice (name correct)	85.00	42.00	25.00
(108)	Eppa Rixey, Jr.	85.00	42.00	25.00
(109)	Wilbert Robinson	85.00	42.00	25.00
(110)	Tom Rogers	30.00	15.00	9.00
(111)	Ed Rounnel (Rommel)	30.00	15.00	9.00
112	Robert Roth (Rommel)	30.00	15.00	9.00
(113a)	Ed Roush (O.F.)	85.00	42.00	25.00
(113b)	Ed Roush (C.F.)	85.00	42.00	25.00
(114)	"Muddy" Ruel	30.00	15.00	9.00
(115a)	"Babe" Ruth (R.F.)	900.00	450.00	270.00
(115b)	Babe Ruth (L.F.)	900.00	450.00	270.00
(116)	Bill Ryan	30.00	15.00	9.00
(117)	"Slim" Sallee (ball in hand)	30.00	15.00	9.00
(118)	"Slim" Sallee (no ball in hand)	30.00	15.00	9.00
(119)	Ray Schalk (bunting)	85.00	42.00	25.00
(120)	Ray Schalk (catching)	85.00	42.00	25.00
(121a)	Walter Schang	30.00	15.00	9.00
(121b)	Wally Schang	30.00	15.00	9.00
(122a)	Fred Schupp (name incorrect)	30.00	15.00	9.00
(122b)	Ferd Schupp (name correct)	30.00	15.00	9.00
(123a)	Everett Scott (Boston)	30.00	15.00	9.00
(123b)	Everett Scott (New York)	30.00	15.00	9.00
(124)	Hank Severeid	30.00	15.00	9.00
(125)	Robert Shawkey	40.00	20.00	12.00
(126a)	"Pat" Shea	30.00	15.00	9.00
(126b)	Pat Shea	30.00	15.00	9.00
(127)	Earl Sheely	30.00	15.00	9.00
(128)	Urban Shocker	30.00	15.00	9.00
(129)	George Sisler (batting)	100.00	50.00	30.00
(130)	George Sisler (throwing)	100.00	50.00	30.00
(131)	Earl Smith	30.00	15.00	9.00
(132)	Elmer Smith	30.00	15.00	9.00
(133)	Frank Snyder	30.00	15.00	9.00
(134a)	Tris Speaker (large projection)	110.00	55.00	33.00
(134b)	Tris Speaker (small projection)	110.00	55.00	33.00
(135)	Charles Stengel (batting)	225.00	112.00	67.00
(136)	Charles Stengel (portrait)	225.00	112.00	67.00
(137)	Milton Stock	30.00	15.00	9.00
(138a)	Amos Strunk (C.F.)	30.00	15.00	9.00
(138b)	Amos Strunk (O.F.)	30.00	15.00	9.00
(139)	Zeb Terry	30.00	15.00	9.00
(140)	Chester Thomas	30.00	15.00	9.00
(141)	Fred Toney (both feet on ground)			
		30.00	15.00	9.00
(142)	Fred Toney (one foot in air)	30.00	15.00	9.00
(143)	George Toporcer	30.00	15.00	9.00
(144)	George Tyler	30.00	15.00	9.00
(145)	Jim Vaughn (plain uniform)	30.00	15.00	9.00
(146)	Jim Vaughn (striped uniform)	30.00	15.00	9.00
(147)	Bob Veach (arm raised)	30.00	15.00	9.00
(148)	Bob Veach (arms folded)	30.00	15.00	9.00
(149)	Oscar Vitt	30.00	15.00	9.00
(150)	Curtis Walker	30.00	15.00	9.00
(151)	W. Wambsganss	40.00	20.00	12.00
(152)	Zach Wheat	85.00	42.00	25.00
(153)	George Whitted	30.00	15.00	9.00
(154)	Fred Williams	40.00	20.00	12.00
(155)	Ivy B. Wingo	30.00	15.00	9.00
(156)	Lawton Witt	30.00	15.00	9.00
(157)	Joe Wood	40.00	20.00	12.00
(158)	Pep Young	30.00	15.00	9.00
(159)	Ross Young (Youngs)	85.00	42.00	25.00

		NR MT	EX	VG
Complete Set:		2900.00	1450.00	870.00
Common Player:		35.00	17.50	10.50
(1)	Dave Bancroft	75.00	37.00	22.00
(2)	Johnnie Bassler	35.00	17.50	10.50
(3)	Joe Bush	40.00	20.00	12.00
(4)	Ty Cobb	750.00	375.00	225.00
(5)	Eddie Collins	75.00	37.00	22.00
(6)	Stan Coveleskie (Coveleski)	75.00	37.00	22.00
(7)	Jake Daubert	40.00	20.00	12.00
(8)	Joe Dugan	40.00	20.00	12.00
(9)	Red Faber	75.00	37.00	22.00
(10)	Frank Frisch	75.00	37.00	22.00
(11)	Walter H. Gerber	35.00	17.50	10.50
(12)	Harry Heilmann	75.00	37.00	22.00
(13)	Harry Hooper	75.00	37.00	22.00
(14)	Rogers Hornsby	250.00	125.00	75.00
(15)	Waite Hoyt	75.00	37.00	22.00
(16)	Joe Judge	35.00	17.50	10.50
(17)	Geo. Kelly	75.00	37.00	22.00
(18)	Rabbit Maranville	75.00	37.00	22.00
(19)	Rube Marquard	75.00	37.00	22.00
(20)	Guy Morton	35.00	17.50	10.50
(21)	Art Nehf	35.00	17.50	10.50
(22)	Derrill B. Pratt	35.00	17.50	10.50
(23)	Jimmy Ring	35.00	17.50	10.50
(24)	Eppa Rixey	75.00	37.00	22.00
(25)	Gene Robertson	35.00	17.50	10.50
(26)	Ed Rommell (Rommel)	35.00	17.50	10.50
(27)	Babe Ruth	1000.00	500.00	300.00
(28)	Wally Schang	35.00	17.50	10.50
(29)	Everett Scott	35.00	17.50	10.50
(30)	Henry Severeid	35.00	17.50	10.50
(31)	Joe Sewell	75.00	37.00	22.00
(32)	Geo. Sisler	75.00	37.00	22.00
(33)	Tris Speaker	100.00	50.00	30.00
(34)	Riggs Stephenson	40.00	20.00	12.00
(35)	Zeb Terry	35.00	17.50	10.50
(36)	Bobbie Veach	35.00	17.50	10.50
(37)	Clarence Walker	35.00	17.50	10.50
(38)	Johnnie Walker	35.00	17.50	10.50
(39)	Zach Wheat	75.00	37.00	22.00
(40)	Kenneth Williams	40.00	20.00	12.00

1950 W576
Callahan Hall Of Fame

1922 W575-2

The black and white cards in this set measure 2-1/8" by 3-3/8". Because of the design of the cards the set is sometimes called the "autograph on shoulder" series.

KENESAW MOUNTAIN LANDIS. Elected to the Hall of Fame, 1944. First High Commissioner of Baseball; born at Millville, Ohio, November 20, 1866; died November 25, 1944, age 78.

A lean, dynamic, white-haired Judge Landis brought to baseball one of the greatest and fairest legal minds in America, plus a fanatical love for the game and an uncompromising insistence on all-inclusive fairness and honesty. The Judge knew baseball and knew human nature just as thoroughly. For many years, prior to his appointment as Commissioner he served distinctively and fearlessly on the Federal Bench.

As baseball's High Commissioner, Landis ruled the game impartially and understandingly—but with an iron hand—from 1920 until his death. To him must go the credit for rebuilding a strong and enduring foundation for baseball and restoring public confidence in its integrity after the disturbing "Black Sox" scandal following the 1919 Chicago-Cincinnati World Series. His verdict in that case barred eight White Sox players—including several of the game's brightest stars—from organized ball for life.

Several of his decisions were tough to take, but all were made for the everlasting good of the game. The Judge's constructive work raised high the standard of baseball, set basic ideals which will endure as long as the game endures.

KENESAW M. LANDIS

These cards, which feature drawings of Hall of Famers, were produced from 1950 through 1956 and sold by the Baseball Hall of Fame in Cooperstown. The cards measure 1-3/4" by 2-1/2" and include a detailed player biography on the back. When introduced in 1950 the set included all members of the Hall of Fame up to that time, and then new cards were added each year as more players were elected. Therefore, cards of players appearing in all previous editions are lesser in value than those players who appeared in just one or two years. When the set was discontinued in 1956 it consisted of 82 cards, which is now considered a complete set. The cards are not numbered and are listed here alphabetically.

		NR MT	EX	VG
	Complete Set:	600.00	300.00	180.00
	Common Player:	3.00	1.50	.90
(1)	Grover Alexander	6.00	3.00	1.75
(2)	"Cap" Anson	6.00	3.00	1.75
(3)	J. Franklin "Home Run" Baker	7.00	3.50	2.00
(4)	Edward G. Barrow	7.00	3.50	2.00
(5a)	Charles "Chief" Bender (different biography)	7.00	3.50	2.00
(5b)	Charles "Chief" Bender (different biography)	7.00	3.50	2.00
(6)	Roger Bresnahan	3.00	1.50	.90
(7)	Dan Brouthers	3.00	1.50	.90
(8)	Mordecai Brown	3.00	1.50	.90
(9)	Morgan G. Bulkeley	3.00	1.50	.90
(10)	Jesse Burkett	3.00	1.50	.90
(11)	Alexander Cartwright	3.00	1.50	.90
(12)	Henry Chadwick	3.00	1.50	.90
(13)	Frank Chance	3.00	1.50	.90
(14)	Albert B. Chandler	30.00	15.00	9.00
(15)	Jack Chesbro	3.00	1.50	.90
(16)	Fred Clarke	3.00	1.50	.90
(17)	Ty Cobb	50.00	25.00	15.00
(18a)	Mickey Cochran (name incorrect)	50.00	25.00	15.00
(18b)	Mickey Cochrane (name correct)	6.00	3.00	1.75
(19a)	Eddie Collins (different biography)	6.00	3.00	1.75
(19b)	Eddie Collins (different biography)	6.00	3.00	1.75
(20)	Jimmie Collins	3.00	1.50	.90
(21)	Charles A. Comiskey	3.00	1.50	.90
(22)	Tom Connolly	7.00	3.50	2.00
(23)	"Candy" Cummings	3.00	1.50	.90
(24)	Dizzy Dean	30.00	15.00	9.00
(25)	Ed Delahanty	3.00	1.50	.90
(26a)	Bill Dickey (different biography)	30.00	15.00	9.00
(26b)	Bill Dickey (different biography)	30.00	15.00	9.00
(27)	Joe DiMaggio	100.00	50.00	30.00
(28)	Hugh Duffy	3.00	1.50	.90
(29)	Johnny Evers	3.00	1.50	.90
(30)	Buck Ewing	3.00	1.50	.90
(31)	Jimmie Foxx	7.00	3.50	2.00
(32)	Frank Frisch	3.00	1.50	.90
(33)	Lou Gehrig	50.00	25.00	15.00
(34)	Charles Gehringer	3.00	1.50	.90
(35)	Clark Griffith	3.00	1.50	.90
(36)	Lefty Grove	6.00	3.00	1.75
(37)	Leo "Gabby" Hartnett	7.00	3.50	2.00
(38)	Harry Heilmann	3.00	1.50	.90
(39)	Rogers Hornsby	7.00	3.50	2.00
(40)	Carl Hubbell	6.00	3.00	1.75
(41)	Hughey Jennings	3.00	1.50	.90
(42)	Ban Johnson	3.00	1.50	.90
(43)	Walter Johnson	7.00	3.50	2.00
(44)	Willie Keeler	3.00	1.50	.90
(45)	Mike Kelly	3.00	1.50	.90
(46)	Bill Klem	7.00	3.50	2.00
(47)	Napoleon Lajoie	3.00	1.50	.90
(48)	Kenesaw M. Landis	3.00	1.50	.90
(49)	Ted Lyons	7.00	3.50	2.00
(50)	Connie Mack	7.00	3.50	2.00
(51)	Walter Maranville	7.00	3.50	2.00
(52)	Christy Mathewson	7.00	3.50	2.00
(53)	Tommy McCarthy	3.00	1.50	.90
(54)	Joe McGinnity	3.00	1.50	.90
(55)	John McGraw	6.00	3.00	1.75
(56)	Charles Nichols	3.00	1.50	.90
(57)	Jim O'Rourke	3.00	1.50	.90
(58)	Mel Ott	6.00	3.00	1.75
(59)	Herb Pennock	3.00	1.50	.90
(60)	Eddie Plank	3.00	1.50	.90
(61)	Charles Radbourne	3.00	1.50	.90
(62)	Wilbert Robinson	3.00	1.50	.90
(63)	Babe Ruth	100.00	50.00	30.00
(64)	Ray "Cracker" Schalk	7.00	3.50	2.00

		NR MT	EX	VG
(65)	Al Simmons	7.00	3.50	2.00
(66a)	George Sisler (different biography)	3.00	1.50	.90
(66b)	George Sisler (different biography)	3.00	1.50	.90
(67)	A. G. Spalding	3.00	1.50	.90
(68)	Tris Speaker	3.00	1.50	.90
(69)	Bill Terry	7.00	3.50	2.00
(70)	Joe Tinker	3.00	1.50	.90
(71)	"Pie" Traynor	3.00	1.50	.90
(72)	Clarence A. "Dizzy" Vance	7.00	3.50	2.00
(73)	Rube Waddell	3.00	1.50	.90
(74)	Hans Wagner	30.00	15.00	9.00
(75)	Bobby Wallace	7.00	3.50	2.00
(76)	Ed Walsh	3.00	1.50	.90
(77)	Paul Waner	6.00	3.00	1.75
(78)	George Wright	3.00	1.50	.90
(79)	Harry Wright	7.00	3.50	2.00
(80)	Cy Young	7.00	3.50	2.00
---a)	Museum Exterior View (different biography)	7.00	3.50	2.00
---b)	Museum Exterior View (different biography)	7.00	3.50	2.00
---a)	Museum Interior View (different biography)	7.00	3.50	2.00
---b)	Museum Interior View (different biography)	7.00	3.50	2.00

1938 W711-1 Reds

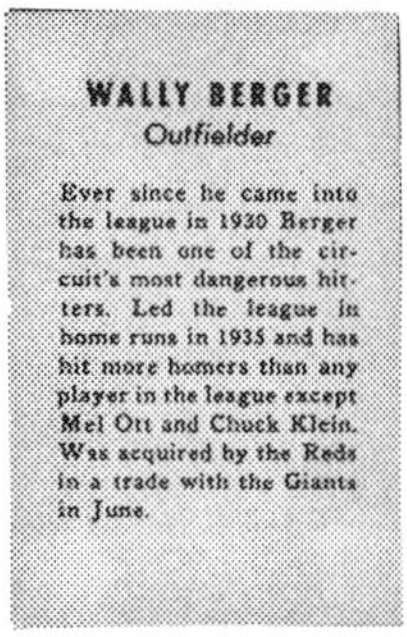

This 32-card set is a challenging one of particular interest to Cincinnati team collectors. The 2" by 3" cards were sold at the ballpark. Fronts feature a picture of the player while backs have the player's name, position and a generally flattering description of the player's talents. The cards are not numbered.

		NR MT	EX	VG
	Complete Set:	300.00	150.00	90.00
	Common Player:	10.00	5.00	3.00
(1)	Wally Berger ("... in a trade with the Giants in June.")	15.00	7.50	4.50
(2)	Joe Cascarella	25.00	12.50	7.50
(3)	Allen "Dusty" Cooke	25.00	12.50	7.50
(4)	Harry Craft	10.00	5.00	3.00
(5)	Ray "Peaches" Davis	10.00	5.00	3.00
(6)	Paul Derringer ("Won 22 games ... this season.")	15.00	7.50	4.50
(7)	Linus Frey ("... only 25 now.")	25.00	12.50	7.50
(8)	Lee Gamble ("... Syracuse last year.")	25.00	12.50	7.50
(9)	Ival Goodman (no mention of 30 homers)	25.00	12.50	7.50
(10)	Harry "Hank" Gowdy	10.00	5.00	3.00
(11)	Lee Grissom (no mention of 1938)	25.00	12.50	7.50
(12)	Willard Hershberger	15.00	7.50	4.50
(13)	Ernie Lombardi (no mention of 1938 MVP)	30.00	15.00	9.00
(14)	Frank McCormick	15.00	7.50	4.50
(15)	Bill McKechnie ("Last year he led ...")	25.00	12.50	7.50
(16)	Lloyd "Whitey" Moore ("... last year with Syracuse.")	25.00	12.50	7.50
(17)	Billy Myers ("... in his fourth year.")	25.00	12.50	7.50
(18)	Lee Riggs ("... in his fourth season ...")	25.00	12.50	7.50

The image caption on the card reads:

WALLY BERGER
Outfielder

Ever since he came into the league in 1930 Berger has been one of the circuit's most dangerous hitters. Led the league in home runs in 1935 and has hit more homers than any player in the league except Mel Ott and Chuck Klein. Was acquired by the Reds in a trade with the Giants in June.

	NR MT	EX	VG
(19) Eddie Roush	25.00	12.50	7.50
(20) Gene Schott	25.00	12.50	7.50
(21) Johnny Vander Meer (pitching pose)			
	20.00	10.00	6.00
(22) Wm. "Bucky" Walter ("... won 14 games			
...")	15.00	7.50	4.50
(23) Jim Weaver	10.00	5.00	3.00

1939 W711-1 Reds

WALLY BERGER
Outfielder

Ever since he came into the league in 1930, Berger has been one of the circuit's most dangerous hitters. Led the league in home runs in 1935 and has hit more homers than any player in the league except Mel Ott and Chuck Klein. Was acquired by the Reds in a trade with the Giants in June, 1938.

An updating by one season of the team-issued 1938 W711-1 issue, most of the players and poses on the 2" by 3" cards remained the same. A close study of the career summary on the card's back is necessary to determine which year of issue is at hand.

	NR MT	EX	VG
Complete Set:	500.00	250.00	150.00
Common Player:	20.00	10.00	6.00
(1) Wally Berger ("... in a trade with the			
Giants in June, 1938.")	30.00	15.00	9.00
(2) Nino Bongiovanni	30.00	15.00	9.00
(3) Stanley 'Frenchy' Bordagaray	30.00	15.00	9.00
(4) Harry Craft	20.00	10.00	6.00
(5) Ray "Peaches" Davis	20.00	10.00	6.00
(6) Paul Derringer ("Won 22 games ... last			
year.")	30.00	15.00	9.00
(7) Linus Frey ("... only 26 now.")	12.00	6.00	3.50
(8) Lee Gamble ("... Syracuse in 1937.")			
	12.00	6.00	3.50
(9) Ival Goodman (mentions hitting 30			
homers)	12.00	6.00	3.50
(10) Harry "Hank" Gowdy	20.00	10.00	6.00
(11) Lee Grissom (mentions 1938)	12.00	6.00	3.50
(12) Willard Hershberger	30.00	15.00	9.00
(13) Eddie Joost	12.00	6.00	3.50
(14) Wes Livengood	80.00	40.00	24.00
(15) Ernie Lombardi (mentions MVP of 1938)			
	30.00	15.00	9.00
(16) Frank McCormick	30.00	15.00	9.00
(17) Bill McKechnie ("In 1937 he led ...")			
	50.00	25.00	15.00
(18) Lloyd "Whitey" Moore ("... in 1937 with			
Syracuse.")	12.00	6.00	3.50
(19) Billy Myers ("... in his fifth year ...")			
	12.00	6.00	3.50
(20) Lee Riggs ("... in his fifth season...")			
	12.00	6.00	3.50
(21) Les Scarsella	30.00	15.00	9.00
(22) Eugene "Junior" Thompson	12.00	6.00	3.50
(23) Johnny Vander Meer (portrait)	20.00	10.00	6.00
(24) Wm. "Bucky" Walters ("Won 15 games			
...")	30.00	15.00	9.00
(25) Jim Weaver	20.00	10.00	6.00
(26) Bill Werber	12.00	6.00	3.50
(27) Jimmy Wilson	12.00	6.00	3.50

A player's name in italic indicates a rookie card. An (FC) indicates a player's first card for that particular card company.

1940 W711-2
Harry Hartman Reds

JOHN HUTCHINGS
Pitcher

Born: April 14, 1916, Sherman, Texas.
Height: 6 feet 3 inches.
Weight: 200 lbs.
Bats: Both right and lefthanded.
Throws: Righthanded.
Professional Start: With Peoria in 1935, winning 12 and losing 17 games for a percentage of .433

FIVE YEAR RECORD

Year	Team	Won	Lost	Pct.
1935	Peoria	13	17	.433
1936	Portsmouth	13	9	.591
1937	Birmingham	6	5	.548
1938	Pensacola	18	6	.750
1939	Pensacola	22	10	.688

Another early set of the Cincinnati Reds, this 32-card set of 2-1/8" by 2-5/8" cards contains a number of interesting items. The black and white cards carry no numbers and feature a picture of the player on the front and name, position and biographical information on the back. As the Reds were World Champions in 1940 after defeating Detroit in four games to three, the set features special cards for the World Series title, making it one of the first to feature events as well as individuals. The set takes it name from Reds' announcer Harry Hartman, who has a card in the issue and supposedly was instrumental in its issue.

	NR MT	EX	VG
Complete Set:	450.00	225.00	135.00
Common Player:	12.00	6.00	3.50
(1) Morris Arnovich	12.00	6.00	3.50
(2) William (Bill) Baker	12.00	6.00	3.50
(3) Joseph Beggs	12.00	6.00	3.50
(4) Harry Craft	12.00	6.00	3.50
(5) Paul Derringer	20.00	10.00	6.00
(6) Linus Frey	12.00	6.00	3.50
(7) Ival Goodman	12.00	6.00	3.50
(8) Harry (Hank) Gowdy	12.00	6.00	3.50
(9) Witt Guise	12.00	6.00	3.50
(10) Harry (Socko) Hartman	12.00	6.00	3.50
(11) Willard Hershberger	15.00	7.50	4.50
(12) John Hutchings	12.00	6.00	3.50
(13) Edwin Joost	12.00	6.00	3.50
(14) Ernie Lombardi	55.00	27.00	16.50
(15) Frank McCormick	20.00	10.00	6.00
(16) Myron McCormick	12.00	6.00	3.50
(17) William Boyd McKechnie	30.00	15.00	9.00
(18) Lloyd (Whitey) Moore	12.00	6.00	3.50
(19) William (Bill) Myers	12.00	6.00	3.50
(20) Lewis Riggs	12.00	6.00	3.50
(21) Elmer Riddle	12.00	6.00	3.50
(22) James A. Ripple	12.00	6.00	3.50
(23) Milburn Shoffner	12.00	6.00	3.50
(24) Eugene Thompson	12.00	6.00	3.50
(25) James Turner	12.00	6.00	3.50
(26) John Vander Meer	30.00	15.00	9.00
(27) Wm. (Bucky) Walters	20.00	10.00	6.00
(28) William (Bill) Werber	12.00	6.00	3.50
(29) James Wilson	15.00	7.50	4.50
(30) The Cincinnati Reds	12.00	6.00	3.50
(31) The Cincinnati Reds World Champions			
	12.00	6.00	3.50
(32) Tell The World About The Cincinnati Reds			
	12.00	6.00	3.50
(33) Tell The World About The Cincinnati Reds			
World (Champions)	12.00	6.00	3.50
(34) Results 1940 World's Series	15.00	7.50	4.50
(35) Debt of Gratitude to Wm. Koehl Co.			
	12.00	6.00	3.50

1941 W753 St. Louis Browns

CLARENCE MITCHELL
PITCHER, BROOKLYN NATIONALS

Measuring 2-1/8" by 2-5/8", this unnumbered set of cards features the St. Louis Browns in black and white portrait photos. There are 29 cards in the set which featured a photo on the front and the player's name, position and personal and statistical information. There are also cards for coaches and one of the the club's two managers that season (Luke Sewell). As the Browns weren't much of a team in 1941 (or in most seasons for that matter) there are no major stars in the set.

		NR MT	EX	VG
Complete Set:		400.00	200.00	120.00
Common Player:		12.00	6.00	3.50
(1)	Johnny Allen	12.00	6.00	3.50
(2)	Elden Auker (Eldon)	12.00	6.00	3.50
(3)	Donald L Barnes	12.00	6.00	3.50
(4)	Johnny Berardino	20.00	10.00	6.00
(5)	George Caster	12.00	6.00	3.50
(6)	Harlond Benton (Darky) Clift	12.00	6.00	3.50
(7)	Roy J. Cullenbine	12.00	6.00	3.50
(8)	William O. DeWitt	12.00	6.00	3.50
(9)	Roberto Estalella	12.00	6.00	3.50
(10)	Richard Benjamin (Rick) Ferrell	60.00	30.00	18.00
(11)	Dennis W. Galehouse	12.00	6.00	3.50
(12)	Joseph L. Grace	12.00	6.00	3.50
(13)	Frank Grube	12.00	6.00	3.50
(14)	Robert A. Harris	12.00	6.00	3.50
(15)	Donald Henry Heffner	12.00	6.00	3.50
(16)	Fred Hofmann	12.00	6.00	3.50
(17)	Walter Franklin Judnich	12.00	6.00	3.50
(18)	John Henry (Jack) Kramer	12.00	6.00	3.50
(19)	Chester (Chet) Laabs	12.00	6.00	3.50
(20)	John Lucadello	12.00	6.00	3.50
(21)	George Hartley McQuinn	12.00	6.00	3.50
(22)	Robert Cleveland Muncrief, Jr.	12.00	6.00	3.50
(23)	John Niggeling	12.00	6.00	3.50
(24)	Fred Raymond (Fritz) Ostermueller	20.00	10.00	6.00
(25)	James Luther (Luke) Sewell	12.00	6.00	3.50
(26)	Alan Cochran Strange (Cochrane)	12.00	6.00	3.50
(27)	Robert Virgil (Bob) Swift	12.00	6.00	3.50
(28)	James W. (Zack) Taylor	12.00	6.00	3.50
(29)	William Felix (Bill) Trotter	12.00	6.00	3.50
(30)	Presentation Card/Order Form	25.00	12.50	7.50

1941 W754 St. Louis Cardinals

A companion set to W753, this time featuring the other team in St. Louis. Cards measure 2-1/8" by 2-5/8" and are unnumbered. Like the Browns set, there are 29 cards featuring black and white photos on the front and the individual's name, position and personal and statistical information on the back. One interesting addition to the set is a card of Branch Rickey which, coupled with cards of Enos Slaughter and Johnny Mize, gives the set a bit more appeal than the Browns set.

WHITE SOX

		NR MT	EX	VG
Complete Set:		500.00	250.00	150.00
Common Player:		12.00	6.00	3.50
(1)	Sam Breadon	12.00	6.00	3.50
(2)	James Brown	12.00	6.00	3.50
(3)	Morton Cooper	12.00	6.00	3.50
(4)	William Walker Cooper	12.00	6.00	3.50
(5)	Estel Crabtree	12.00	6.00	3.50
(6)	Frank Crespi	12.00	6.00	3.50
(7)	William Crouch	12.00	6.00	3.50
(8)	Miguel Mike Gonzalez	12.00	6.00	3.50
(9)	Harry Gumbert	12.00	6.00	3.50
(10)	John Hopp	12.00	6.00	3.50
(11)	Ira Hutchinson	12.00	6.00	3.50
(12)	Howard Krist	12.00	6.00	3.50
(13)	Edward E. Lake	12.00	6.00	3.50
(14)	Hubert Max Lanier	20.00	10.00	6.00
(15)	Gus Mancuso	12.00	6.00	3.50
(16)	Martin Marion	25.00	12.50	7.50
(17)	Steve Mesner	12.00	6.00	3.50
(18)	John Mize	60.00	30.00	18.00
(19)	Capt. Terry Moore	20.00	10.00	6.00
(20)	Sam Nahem	12.00	6.00	3.50
(21)	Don Padgett	12.00	6.00	3.50
(22)	Branch Rickey	60.00	30.00	18.00
(23)	Clyde Shoun	12.00	6.00	3.50
(24)	Enos Slaughter	60.00	30.00	18.00
(25)	William H. (Billy) Southworth	12.00	6.00	3.50
(26)	Herman Coaker Triplett	12.00	6.00	3.50
(27)	Clyde Buzzy Wares	12.00	6.00	3.50
(28)	Lou Warneke	12.00	6.00	3.50
(29)	Ernest White	12.00	6.00	3.50
(30)	Presentation Card/Order Form	25.00	12.50	7.50

A player's name in *italic* indicates a rookie card. An (FC) indicates a player's first card for that particular card company.

W9316

		NR MT	EX	VG
Complete Set:		600.00	500.00	400.00
Common Player:		15.00	10.00	5.00
1	Bob Veach			
2	Frank Baker			
3	Wilbur Robinson			
4	Johnny Griffith			
5	Jimmie Johnston			
6	Wallie Schange (WALLY SCHANG)			
7	Leon Cadore			
8	George Sisler			
9	Ray Schalk			
10	Jedde Barnes			

1888 WG1
Base Ball Playing Cards

This little-known set of playing cards featuring drawings of real baseball players in action poses was issued in 1888 and includes members of the eight National League teams in existence at the time. Each club is represented by nine players - one at each position - making the set complete at 72 cards. The cards measure 2-1/2" by 3-1/2" and have a blue-patterned design on the back. The cards were sold as a complete set packed in their own separate box. They were designed to resemble a deck of regular playing cards, and the various positions were all assigned the same denomination (for example, all of the pitchers were kings, catchers were aces, etc.). There are no cards numbered either two, three, four or five; and rather than the typical hearts, clubs, diamonds and spades, each team represents a different "suit." The actual rules of the game remain open to speculation because no instructions have ever been found. The set has an American Card Catalog designation of WG1.

	NR MT	EX	VG
Complete Set:	40000.00	20000.00	1200.
Common Player:	300.00	150.00	90.00
(1) Ed Andrews	300.00	150.00	90.00
(2) Cap Anson	3000.00	1500.00	900.00
(3) Charles Bassett	300.00	150.00	90.00
(4) Charles Bastian	300.00	150.00	90.00
(5) Charles Bennett	300.00	150.00	90.00
(6) Handsome Boyle	300.00	150.00	90.00
(7) Dan Brouthers	1500.00	750.00	450.00
(8) Thomas Brown	300.00	150.00	90.00
(9) Thomas Burns	300.00	150.00	90.00
(10) Frederick Carroll	300.00	150.00	90.00
(11) Daniel Casey	1000.00	500.00	300.00
(12) John Clarkson	1500.00	750.00	450.00
(13) Jack Clements	300.00	150.00	90.00
(14) John Coleman	300.00	150.00	90.00
(15) Roger Connor	1500.00	750.00	450.00
(16) Abner Dalrymple	300.00	150.00	90.00
(17) Jerry Denny	300.00	150.00	90.00
(18) Jim Donelly	300.00	150.00	90.00
(19) Sure Shot Dunlap	300.00	150.00	90.00
(20) Dude Esterbrook	300.00	150.00	90.00
(21) Buck Ewing	1500.00	750.00	450.00
(22) Sid Farrar	300.00	150.00	90.00
(23) Silver Flint	300.00	150.00	90.00
(24) Jim Fogarty	300.00	150.00	90.00
(25) Elmer Foster	300.00	150.00	90.00
(26) Pud Galvin	1500.00	750.00	450.00
(27) Charlie Getzein	300.00	150.00	90.00
(28) Pebbly Jack Glasscock	1000.00	500.00	300.00
(29) Piano Legs Gore	300.00	150.00	90.00
(30) Ned Hanlon	300.00	150.00	90.00
(31) Paul Hines	300.00	150.00	90.00
(32) Joe Hornung	300.00	150.00	90.00
(33) Dummy Hoy	1000.00	500.00	300.00
(34) Cutrate Irwin (Philadelphia)	300.00	150.00	90.00
(35) John Irwin (Washington)	300.00	150.00	90.00

	NR MT	EX	VG
(36) Dick Johnston	300.00	150.00	90.00
(37) Tim Keefe	1500.00	750.00	450.00
(38) King Kelly	1500.00	750.00	450.00
(39) Willie Kuehne	300.00	150.00	90.00
(40) Connie Mack	2500.00	1250.00	750.00
(41) Smiling Al Maul	300.00	150.00	90.00
(42) Al Meyers (Myers) (Washington)	300.00	150.00	90.00
(43) George Meyers (Myers) (Indianapolis)	300.00	150.00	90.00
(44) Honest John Morrill	300.00	150.00	90.00
(45) Joseph Mulvey	300.00	150.00	90.00
(46) Billy Nash	300.00	150.00	90.00
(47) Billy O'Brien	300.00	150.00	90.00
(48) Orator Jim O'Rourke	1500.00	750.00	450.00
(49) Bob Pettit	300.00	150.00	90.00
(50) Fred Pfeffer	300.00	150.00	90.00
(51) Danny Richardson (New York)	300.00	150.00	90.00
(52) Hardy Richardson (Detroit)	300.00	150.00	90.00
(53) Jack Rowe	300.00	150.00	90.00
(54) Jimmy Ryan	300.00	150.00	90.00
(55) Emmett Seery	300.00	150.00	90.00
(56) George Shoch	300.00	150.00	90.00
(57) Otto Shomberg (Schomberg)	300.00	150.00	90.00
(58) Pap Smith	300.00	150.00	90.00
(59) Marty Sullivan	300.00	150.00	90.00
(60) Billy Sunday	1500.00	750.00	450.00
(61) Ezra Sutton	300.00	150.00	90.00
(62) Big Sam Thompson	1500.00	750.00	450.00
(63) Silent Mike Tiernan	300.00	150.00	90.00
(64) Larry Twitchell	300.00	150.00	90.00
(65) Rip Van Haltren	300.00	150.00	90.00
(66) Monte Ward	1500.00	750.00	450.00
(67) Deacon White	300.00	150.00	90.00
(68) Grasshopper Whitney	300.00	150.00	90.00
(69) Ned Williamson	300.00	150.00	90.00
(70) Watt Wilmot	300.00	150.00	90.00
(71) Medoc Wise	300.00	150.00	90.00
(72) George "Dandy" Wood	300.00	150.00	90.00

1904 WG2 Fan Craze
American League

One of the earliest 20th Century baseball card sets, this 1904 issue from the Fan Craze Company of Cincinnati was designed as a deck of playing cards and was intended to be used as a baseball table game. Separate sets were issued for the National League, which are printed in red, and the American League, which are blue. Both sets feature sepia-toned, black and white player portraits inside an oval with the player's name and team below. The top of the card indicates one of many various baseball plays, such as "Single," "Out at First," "Strike," "Stolen Base," etc. The unnumbered cards measure 2-1/2" by 3-1/2" and are identified as "An Artistic Constellation of Great Stars."

	NR MT	EX	VG
Complete Set:	6000.00	3000.00	1800.
Common Player:	60.00	30.00	18.00
(1) Nick Altrock	60.00	30.00	18.00
(2) Jim Barrett	60.00	30.00	18.00
(3) Harry Bay	60.00	30.00	18.00
(4) Albert Bender	175.00	87.00	52.00

		NR MT	EX	VG
(5)	Bill Bernhardt	60.00	30.00	18.00
(6)	W. Bradley	60.00	30.00	18.00
(7)	Jack Chesbro	375.00	187.00	112.00
(8)	Jimmy Collins	175.00	87.00	52.00
(9)	Sam Crawford	175.00	87.00	52.00
(10)	Lou Criger	60.00	30.00	18.00
(11)	Lave Cross	60.00	30.00	18.00
(12)	Monte Cross	60.00	30.00	18.00
(13)	Harry Davis	60.00	30.00	18.00
(14)	Bill Dinneen	60.00	30.00	18.00
(15)	Pat Donovan	60.00	30.00	18.00
(16)	Pat Dougherty	60.00	30.00	18.00
(17)	Norman Elberfield (Elberfeld)	60.00	30.00	18.00
(18)	Hoke Ferris (Hobe)	60.00	30.00	18.00
(19)	Elmer Flick	175.00	87.00	52.00
(20)	Buck Freeman	60.00	30.00	18.00
(21)	Fred Glade	60.00	30.00	18.00
(22)	Clark Griffith	175.00	87.00	52.00
(23)	Charley Hickman	60.00	30.00	18.00
(24)	Wm. Holmes	60.00	30.00	18.00
(25)	Harry Howell	60.00	30.00	18.00
(26)	Frank Isbel (Isbell)	60.00	30.00	18.00
(27)	Albert Jacobson	60.00	30.00	18.00
(28)	Ban Johnson	200.00	100.00	60.00
(29)	Fielder Jones	60.00	30.00	18.00
(30)	Adrian Joss	175.00	87.00	52.00
(31)	Billy Keeler	250.00	125.00	75.00
(32)	Napolean Lajoie	425.00	212.00	127.00
(33)	Connie Mack	425.00	212.00	127.00
(34)	Jimmy McAleer	60.00	30.00	18.00
(35)	Jim McGuire	60.00	30.00	18.00
(36)	Earl Moore	60.00	30.00	18.00
(37)	George Mullen (Mullin)	60.00	30.00	18.00
(38)	Billy Owen	60.00	30.00	18.00
(39)	Fred Parent	60.00	30.00	18.00
(40)	Case Patten	60.00	30.00	18.00
(41)	Ed Plank	60.00	30.00	18.00
(42)	Ossie Schreckengost	60.00	30.00	18.00
(43)	Jake Stahl	60.00	30.00	18.00
(44)	Fred Stone	60.00	30.00	18.00
(45)	Wm. Sudhoff	60.00	30.00	18.00
(46)	Roy Turner	60.00	30.00	18.00
(47)	G.E. Waddell	175.00	87.00	52.00
(48)	Bob Wallace	175.00	87.00	52.00
(49)	G. Harris White	60.00	30.00	18.00
(50)	Geo. Winters	60.00	30.00	18.00
(51)	Cy Young	550.00	275.00	165.00

1904 WG2 Fan Craze
National League

Identical in size and format to the American League set, this series of unnumbered cards was issued by the Fan Craze Company of Cincinnati in 1904 and was designed like a decl of playing cards. The cards were intended to be used in playing a baseball table game. The National League cards are printed in red.

		NR MT	EX	VG
Complete Set:		6000.00	3000.00	1800.
Common Player:		60.00	30.00	18.00
(1)	Leon Ames	60.00	30.00	18.00
(2)	Clarence Beaumont	60.00	30.00	18.00
(3)	Jake Beckley	200.00	100.00	60.00
(4)	Billy Bergen	60.00	30.00	18.00
(5)	Roger Bresnahan	250.00	125.00	75.00

		NR MT	EX	VG
(6)	George Brown (Browne)	60.00	30.00	18.00
(7)	Mordacai Brown	325.00	162.00	97.00
(8)	Jas. Casey	60.00	30.00	18.00
(9)	Frank Chance	325.00	162.00	97.00
(10)	Fred Clarke	200.00	100.00	60.00
(11)	Thos. Corcoran	60.00	30.00	18.00
(12)	Bill Dahlen	60.00	30.00	18.00
(13)	Mike Donlin	60.00	30.00	18.00
(14)	Charley Dooin	60.00	30.00	18.00
(15)	Mickey Doolin (Doolan)	60.00	30.00	18.00
(16)	Hugh Duffy	200.00	100.00	60.00
(17)	John E. Dunleavy	60.00	30.00	18.00
(18)	Bob Ewing	60.00	30.00	18.00
(19)	"Chick" Fraser	60.00	30.00	18.00
(20)	J. Edward Hanlon	60.00	30.00	18.00
(21)	G.E. Howard	60.00	30.00	18.00
(22)	Miller Huggins	200.00	100.00	60.00
(23)	Joseph Kelley	200.00	100.00	60.00
(24)	John Kling	60.00	30.00	18.00
(25)	Tommy Leach	60.00	30.00	18.00
(26)	Harry Lumley	60.00	30.00	18.00
(27)	Carl Lundgren	60.00	30.00	18.00
(28)	Bill Maloney	60.00	30.00	18.00
(29)	Dan McGann	60.00	30.00	18.00
(30)	Joe McGinnity	125.00	62.00	37.00
(31)	John J. McGraw	450.00	225.00	135.00
(32)	Harry McIntire (McIntyre)	60.00	30.00	18.00
(33)	Charley Nichols	60.00	30.00	18.00
(34)	Mike O'Neil (O'Neill)	60.00	30.00	18.00
(35)	Orville Overall (Orval)	60.00	30.00	18.00
(36)	Frank Pfeffer	60.00	30.00	18.00
(37)	Deacon Phillippe	60.00	30.00	18.00
(38)	Charley Pittinger	60.00	30.00	18.00
(39)	Harry C. Pulliam	60.00	30.00	18.00
(40)	Claude Ritchey	60.00	30.00	18.00
(41)	Ed Ruelbach (Reulbach)	60.00	30.00	18.00
(42)	J. Bentley Seymour	60.00	30.00	18.00
(43)	Jim Sheckard	60.00	30.00	18.00
(44)	Jack Taylor	60.00	30.00	18.00
(45)	Luther H. Taylor	60.00	30.00	18.00
(46)	Fred Tenny (Tenney)	60.00	30.00	18.00
(47)	Harry Theilman	60.00	30.00	18.00
(48)	Roy Thomas	60.00	30.00	18.00
(49)	Hans Wagner	600.00	300.00	180.00
(50)	Jake Weimer	60.00	30.00	18.00
(51)	Bob Wicker	60.00	30.00	18.00
(52)	Victor Willis	60.00	30.00	18.00
(53)	Lew Wiltsie	60.00	30.00	18.00
(54)	Irving Young	60.00	30.00	18.00

1923 WG7 Walter Mails

This set of playing cards features 56 subjects. The back of cards showcase a baseball design. The flip sides feature player photos, name, team, a facsimile signature and game instruction. Both Minor and Major League players are featured in the set. The cards are not numbered.

		NR MT	EX	VG
Complete Set:		3600.00	1800.00	1000.
Common Player:		30.00	15.00	8.00
(1)	Russell "Buzz" Arlett	30.00	15.00	8.00
(2)	J.C. "Jim" Bagby	30.00	15.00	8.00
(3)	Dave "Beauty" Bancroft	125.00	62.00	37.00
(4)	Johnny Basseler	60.00	30.00	18.00

		NR MT	EX	VG
(5)	Jack Bentley	60.00	30.00	18.00
(6)	J.C. "Rube" Benton	60.00	30.00	18.00
(7)	Geo. Burns	60.00	30.00	18.00
(8)	"Bullet Joe" Bush	75.00	38.00	23.00
(9)	Harold P. Chavezo	30.00	15.00	8.00
(10)	Hugh Critz	40.00	20.00	12.00
(11)	"Jake" E. Daubert	75.00	38.00	23.00
(12)	Wheezer Dell	30.00	15.00	8.00
(13)	Joe Dugan	75.00	38.00	23.00
(14)	Pat Duncan	60.00	30.00	18.00
(15)	Howard J. Ehmke	60.00	30.00	18.00
(16)	Lewis Fonseca	60.00	30.00	18.00
(17)	Ray French	60.00	30.00	18.00
(18)	Ed Gharity	60.00	30.00	
(19)	Heinie Groh	75.00	38.00	23.00
(20)	George N. Groves	30.00	15.00	8.00
(21)	E.F. "Red" Hargrave	60.00	30.00	18.00
(22)	Elmer Jacobs	60.00	30.00	18.00
(23)	Walter Johnson	500.00	250.00	150.00
(24)	WM. "Duke" Kenworthy	30.00	15.00	8.00
(25)	Harry Krause	30.00	15.00	8.00
(26)	Ray Kremer	60.00	30.00	18.00
(27)	Walter Mails	50.00	25.00	15.00
(28)	Walter "Rabbitt" Maranville	150.00	75.00	45.00
(29)	John "Stuffy" McInnis	75.00	38.00	23.00
(30)	Marty McManus	60.00	30.00	18.00
(31)	Bob Meusel	75.00	38.00	23.00
(32)	Hack Miller	60.00	30.00	18.00
(33)	Pat J. Moran	60.00	30.00	18.00
(34)	Guy Morton	60.00	30.00	18.00
(35)	Johnny Mostil	60.00	30.00	18.00
(36)	Rod Murphy	30.00	15.00	8.00
(37)	Jimmy O'Connell	60.00	30.00	18.00
(38)	Steve O'Neil	60.00	30.00	18.00
(39)	Joe Oeschger	60.00	30.00	18.00
(40)	Roger Peckinpaugh	75.00	38.00	23.00
(41)	Ralph "Babe" Pinelli	60.00	30.00	18.00
(42)	Wally Pipp	75.00	38.00	23.00
(43)	Elmer Ponder	30.00	15.00	8.00
(44)	Sam Rice	125.00	62.00	37.00
(45)	Edwin Rommell	75.00	38.00	23.00
(46)	Walter Schmidt	60.00	30.00	18.00
(47)	Wilford Shupes	30.00	15.00	8.00
(48)	Joe Sewell	100.00	50.00	30.00
(49)	Pat Shea	30.00	15.00	8.00
(50)	W. "Paddy" Siglin	30.00	15.00	8.00
(51)	Geo. H. Sisler	175.00	87.00	52.00
(52)	William "Bill" Skiff	30.00	15.00	8.00
(53)	J. Smith	60.00	30.00	15.00
(54)	Harry "Suds" Sutherland	30.00	15.00	8.00
(55)	James A. Tierney	60.00	30.00	18.00
(56)	Geo. Uhle	60.00	30.00	18.00

1931 W-unc
Metropolitan Studio

Members of the St. Louis Cardinals are featured in this 30- card set. The cards were printed on heavy paper and feature sepia-toned photos. The player's name appears along the bottom white border below the photo. The cards measure 6 1/4" by 9 1/2" and are not numbered.

	NR MT	EX	VG
Complete Set:	650.00	325.00	200.00
Common Player:	15.00	7.50	4.50

		NR MT	EX	VG
(1)	Earl "Spanky" Adams	15.00	7.50	4.50
(2)	Ray Blades	15.00	7.50	4.50
(3)	James Bottomley	35.00	17.50	10.50
(4)	Sam Breadon	25.00	12.50	7.50
(5)	James "Rip" Collins	20.00	10.00	6.00
(6)	Dizzy Dean	60.00	30.00	18.00
(7)	Paul Derringer	20.00	10.00	6.00
(8)	Jake Flowers	15.00	7.50	4.50
(9)	Frank Frisch	50.00	25.00	15.00
(10)	Charles Gelbert	15.00	7.50	4.50
(11)	Miguel Gonzales	15.00	7.50	4.50
(12)	Burleigh Grimes	35.00	17.50	10.50
(13)	Charles "Chick" Hafey	35.00	17.50	10.50
(14)	William Hallahan	15.00	7.50	4.50
(15)	Jesse Haines	35.00	17.50	10.50
(16)	Andrew High	15.00	7.50	4.50
(17)	Sylvester Johnson	15.00	7.50	4.50
(18)	Tony Kaufmann	15.00	7.50	4.50
(19)	James Lindsey	15.00	7.50	4.50
(20)	Gus Mancuso	15.00	7.50	4.50
(21)	John Leonard "Pepper" Martin	25.00	12.50	7.50
(22)	Ernest Orsatti	15.00	7.50	10.50
(23)	Charles Flint Rhem	15.00	7.50	4.50
(24)	Branch Rickey	40.00	20.00	12.00
25	Walter Roettger	25.00	12.50	7.50
(26)	Allyn Stout	15.00	7.50	4.50
(27)	"Gabby" Street	15.00	7.50	4.50
28	Coach Clyde Wares	15.00	7.50	4.50
(29)	George Watkins	15.00	7.50	4.50
(30)	James Wilson	15.00	7.50	4.50

1935 Wheaties - Series 1

This set of 25 major leaguers was issued on the back of Wheaties cereal boxes in 1935 and , because of its design, is known as "Fancy Frame with Script Signature." The unnumbered cards measure 6" by 6-1/4" with frame, and 5" by 5-1/2" without the frame. The player photo is tinted blue, while the background is blue and orange. A facsimilie autograph appears at the bottom of the photo.

		NR MT	EX	VG
Complete Set:		1600.00	800.00	480.00
Common Player:		25.00	12.50	7.50
(1)	Jack Armstrong (batting)	25.00	12.50	7.50
(2)	Jack Armstrong (throwing)	25.00	12.50	7.50
(3)	Wally Berger	25.00	12.50	7.50
(4)	Tommy Bridges	25.00	12.50	7.50
(5a)	Mickey Cochrane (black hat)	50.00	25.00	15.00
(5b)	Michey Cochrane (white hat)	250.00	125.00	75.00
(6)	James "Rip" Collins	25.00	12.50	7.50
(7)	Dizzy Dean	100.00	50.00	30.00
(8)	Dizzy Dean, Paul Dean	70.00	35.00	21.00
(9)	Paul Dean	30.00	15.00	9.00
(10)	William Delancey	25.00	12.50	7.50
(11)	"Jimmie" Foxx	70.00	35.00	21.00
(12)	Frank Frisch	40.00	20.00	12.00
(13)	Lou Gehrig	350.00	175.00	105.00
(14)	Goose Goslin	40.00	20.00	12.00
(15)	Lefty Grove	60.00	30.00	18.00
(16)	Carl Hubbell	50.00	25.00	15.00
(17)	Travis C. Jackson	40.00	20.00	12.00
(18)	"Chuck" Klein	40.00	20.00	12.00

		NR MT	EX	VG
(19)	Gus Mancuso	25.00	12.50	7.50
(20)	Johnny "Pepper" Martin	30.00	15.00	9.00
(21)	Pepper Martin	30.00	15.00	9.00
(22)	Joe Medwick	40.00	20.00	12.00
(23)	Melvin Ott	60.00	30.00	18.00
(24)	Harold Schumacher	25.00	12.50	7.50
(25)	Al Simmons	40.00	20.00	12.00
(26)	"Jo Jo" White	25.00	12.50	7.50

1936 Wheaties - Series 3

Consisting of 12 unnumbered cards, this set is similar in size (6" by 6-1/4" with frame) and design to the Wheaties of the previous year, but is known as "Fancy Frame with Printed Name and Data" because the cards also include a few printed words describing the player.

		NR MT	EX	VG
Complete Set:		750.00	375.00	225.00
Common Player:		25.00	12.50	7.50
(1)	Earl Averill	40.00	20.00	12.00
(2)	Mickey Cochrane	50.00	25.00	15.00
(3)	Jimmy Foxx	60.00	30.00	18.00
(4)	Lou Gehrig	350.00	175.00	105.00
(5)	Hank Greenberg	50.00	25.00	15.00
(6)	"Gabby" Hartnett	40.00	20.00	12.00
(7)	Carl Hubbell	50.00	25.00	15.00
(8)	"Pepper" Martin	20.00	10.00	6.00
(9)	Van L. Mungo	25.00	12.50	7.50
(10)	"Buck" Newsom	25.00	12.50	7.50
(11)	"Arky" Vaughan	40.00	20.00	12.00
(12)	Jimmy Wilson	25.00	12.50	7.50

1936 Wheaties - Series 4

This larger size (8-1/2" by 6") card also made up the back of a Wheaties box, and because of its

distinctive border which featured drawings of small athletic figures, it is referred to as "Thin Orange Border/Figures in Border." Twelve major leaguers arepictured in the unnumbered set. The photos are enclosed in a 4" by 6-1/2" box. Below the photo is an endorsement for Wheaties, the "Breakfast of Champions," and a facsimilie autograph.

		NR MT	EX	VG
Complete Set:		750.00	375.00	225.00
Common Player:		25.00	12.50	7.50
(1)	Curt Davis	25.00	12.50	7.50
(2)	Lou Gehrig	350.00	175.00	105.00
(3)	Charley Gehringer	50.00	25.00	15.00
(4)	Lefty Grove	60.00	30.00	18.00
(5)	Rollie Hemsley	25.00	12.50	7.50
(6)	Billy Herman	40.00	20.00	12.00
(7)	Joe Medwick	40.00	20.00	12.00
(8)	Mel Ott	60.00	30.00	18.00
(9)	Schoolboy Rowe	25.00	12.50	7.50
(10)	Arky Vaughan	40.00	20.00	12.00
(11)	Joe Vosmik	25.00	12.50	7.50
(12)	Lon Warneke	25.00	12.50	7.50

1936 Wheaties - Series 5

Often referred to as "How to Play Winning Baseball", this 12-card set features a large player photo surrounded by blue and white drawings that illustrate various playing tips. Different major leaguers offer advice on different aspects of the game. The cards again made up the back panel of a Wheaties box and measure 8-1/2" by 6-1/2". The cards are numbered from 1 through 12, and some of the panels are also found with a small number "28" followed by a letter from "A" through "L."

		NR MT	EX	VG
Complete Set:		600.00	300.00	180.00
Common Player:		25.00	12.50	7.50
1	Lefty Gomez	50.00	25.00	15.00
2	Billy Herman	40.00	20.00	12.00
3	Luke Appling	40.00	20.00	12.00
4	Jimmie Foxx	60.00	30.00	18.00
5	Joe Medwick	40.00	20.00	12.00
6	Charles Gehringer	40.00	20.00	12.00
7a	Mel Ott (tips in vertical sequence)			
		60.00	30.00	18.00
7b	Mel Ott (tips in two horizontal rows)			
		60.00	30.00	18.00
8	Odell Hale	25.00	12.50	7.50
9	Bill Dickey	60.00	30.00	18.00
10	"Lefty" Grove	60.00	30.00	18.00
11	Carl Hubbell	50.00	25.00	15.00
12	Earl Averill	40.00	20.00	12.00

1937 Wheaties - Series 6

Similar to the Series 5 set, this numbered, 12-card series is known as "How to Star in Baseball" and again includes a large player photo with small instructional drawins to illustrate playing tips. The cards measure 8-1/4" by 6" and include a facsimilie autograph.

		NR MT	EX	VG
Complete Set:		750.00	375.00	225.00
Common Player:		25.00	12.50	7.50
1	Bill Dickey	60.00	30.00	18.00
2	Red Ruffing	40.00	20.00	12.00
3	Zeke Bonura	25.00	12.50	7.50
4	Charlie Gehringer	50.00	25.00	15.00
5	"Arky" Vaughn (Vaughan)	25.00	12.50	7.50
6	Carl Hubbell	50.00	25.00	15.00
7	John Lewis	25.00	12.50	7.50
8	Heinie Manush	40.00	20.00	12.00
9	"Lefty" Grove	60.00	30.00	18.00
10	Billy Herman	40.00	20.00	12.00
11	Joe DiMaggio	350.00	175.00	105.00
12	Joe Medwick	40.00	20.00	12.00

1937 Wheaties - Series 7

This 15-card set of 6" by 8-1/4" panels contains several different card designs. One style (picturing Lombardi, Travis and Mungo) has a white background with an orange border and a large orange circle behind the player. Another design (showing Bonura, DiMaggio and Bridges) has the player outlined against a bright orange background with a Wheaties endorsement along the bottom. A third format (picturing Moore, Radcliff and Martin) has a distinctive red, white and blue border. And a fourth design (featuring Trosky, Demaree and Vaughan) has a tilted picture against an orange background framed in blue and white. The set also includes three Pacific Coast League Players. The cards are numbered with a small "29" followed by a letter from "A" through "P." Card number "29N," which may be another PCL player, is unknown.

		NR MT	EX	VG
Complete Set:		700.00	350.00	210.00
Common Player:		25.00	12.50	7.50
29A	"Zeke" Bonura	25.00	12.50	7.50
29B	Cecil Travis	25.00	12.50	7.50
29C	Frank Demaree	25.00	12.50	7.50
29D	Joe Moore	25.00	12.50	7.50
29E	Ernie Lombardi	40.00	20.00	12.00
29F	John L. "Pepper" Martin	30.00	15.00	9.00
29G	Harold Trosky	25.00	12.50	7.50
29H	Raymond Radcliff	25.00	12.50	7.50
29I	Joe DiMaggio	350.00	175.00	105.00
29J	Tom Bridges	25.00	12.50	7.50
29K	Van L. Mungo	25.00	12.50	7.50
29L	"Arky" Vaughn (Vaughan)	40.00	20.00	12.00
29M	Arnold Statz	200.00	100.00	60.00
29N	Unknown	25.00	12.50	7.50
29O	Fred Muller (Mueller)	200.00	100.00	60.00
29P	Gene Lillard	200.00	100.00	60.00

1937 Wheaties - Series 8

Another series printed on the back of Wheaties boxes in 1937, the eight cards in this set are unnumbered and measure 8-1/2" by 6". There are several different designs, but in all of them the player photo is surrounded by speckles of color, causing this series to be known as the "Speckled Orange, White and Blue" series. A facsimilie autograph is included, along with brief printed 1936 season statistics.

		NR MT	EX	VG
Complete Set:		700.00	350.00	210.00
Common Player:		40.00	20.00	12.00
(1)	Luke Appling	40.00	20.00	12.00
(2)	Earl Averill	40.00	20.00	12.00
(3)	Joe DiMaggio	350.00	175.00	105.00
(4)	Robert Feller	110.00	55.00	33.00
(5)	Chas. Gehringer	50.00	25.00	15.00
(6)	Lefty Grove	60.00	30.00	18.00
(7)	Carl Hubbell	50.00	25.00	15.00
(8)	Joe Medwick	40.00	20.00	12.00

1937 Wheaties - Series 9

This unnumbered set includes one player from each of the 16 major league teams and is generally referred to as the "Color Series." The cards measure 8-1/2" by 6" and were the back panels of Wheaties boxes. The player photos are shown inside or against large stars, circles, "V" shapes, rectangles and other geometrical designs. A facsimilie autograph and team designation are printed near the photo, while a Wheaties endorsement and a line of player stats appear along the bottom.

		NR MT	EX	VG
Complete Set:		950.00	475.00	285.00
Common Player:		25.00	12.50	7.50
(1)	Zeke Bonura	25.00	12.50	7.50
(2)	Tom Bridges	25.00	12.50	7.50
(3)	Harland Clift (Harlond)	25.00	12.50	7.50
(4)	Kiki Cuyler	40.00	20.00	12.00
(5)	Joe DiMaggio	350.00	175.00	105.00
(6)	Robert Feller	110.00	55.00	33.00
(7)	Lefty Grove	60.00	30.00	18.00
(8)	Billy Herman	40.00	20.00	12.00
(9)	Carl Hubbell	50.00	25.00	15.00
(10)	Buck Jordan	25.00	12.50	7.50
(11)	"Pepper" Martin	20.00	10.00	6.00
(12)	John Moore	25.00	12.50	7.50
(13)	Wally Moses	25.00	12.50	7.50
(14)	Van L. Mungo	25.00	12.50	7.50
(15)	Cecil Travis	25.00	12.50	7.50
(16)	Arky Vaughan	40.00	20.00	12.00

1937 Wheaties - Series 14

Much reduced in size (2-5/8" by 3-7/8"), these unnumbered cards made up the back panels of single-serving size Wheaties boxes. The player photo

(which is sometimes identical to the photos used in the larger series) is set against an orange or white background. The player's name appears in large capital letters with his position and team in smaller capitals. A facsimilie autograph and Wheaties endorsement is also included. Some cards are also found with the number "29" followed by a letter.

		NR MT	EX	VG
Complete Set:		1400.00	700.00	420.00
Common Player:		50.00	25.00	15.00
(1)	"Zeke" Bonura	50.00	25.00	15.00
(2)	Tom Bridges	50.00	25.00	15.00
(3)	Dolph Camilli	50.00	25.00	15.00
(4)	Frank Demaree	50.00	25.00	15.00
(5)	Joe DiMaggio	450.00	225.00	135.00
(6)	Billy Herman	90.00	45.00	27.00
(7)	Carl Hubbell	100.00	50.00	30.00
(8)	Ernie Lombardi	90.00	45.00	27.00
(9)	"Pepper" Martin	60.00	30.00	18.00
(10)	Joe Moore	50.00	25.00	15.00
(11)	Van Mungo	50.00	25.00	15.00
(12)	Mel Ott	125.00	62.00	37.00
(13)	Raymond Radcliff	50.00	25.00	15.00
(14)	Cecil Travis	50.00	25.00	15.00
(15)	Harold Trosky	50.00	25.00	15.00
(16a)	"Arky" Vaughan (29L on card)	90.00	45.00	27.00
(16b)	"Arky" Vaughan (no 29L on card)	90.00	45.00	27.00

1938 Wheaties - Series 10

One player from each major league team is included in this 16-card set, referred to as the "Biggest Thrills in Baseball" series. Measuring 8-1/2" by 6", each numbered card was the back panel of a Wheaties box and pictures a player along with a printed description of his biggest thrill in baseball and facsimilie autograph. All 16 cards in this series have also been found on paper stock.

		NR MT	EX	VG
Complete Set:		600.00	300.00	180.00
Common Player:		25.00	12.50	7.50
1	Bob Feller	110.00	55.00	33.00
2	Cecil Travis	25.00	12.50	7.50
3	Joe Medwick	40.00	20.00	12.00
4	Gerald Walker	25.00	12.50	7.50
5	Carl Hubbell	50.00	25.00	15.00
6	Bob Johnson	25.00	12.50	7.50
7	Beau Bell	25.00	12.50	7.50
8	Ernie Lombardi	40.00	20.00	12.00
9	Lefty Grove	60.00	30.00	18.00
10	Lou Fette	25.00	12.50	7.50
11	Joe DiMaggio	350.00	175.00	105.00
12	Art Whitney	25.00	12.50	7.50
13	Dizzy Dean	110.00	55.00	33.00
14	Charley Gehringer	50.00	25.00	15.00
15	Paul Waner	40.00	20.00	12.00
16	Dolf Camilli	25.00	12.50	7.50

1938 Wheaties - Series 11

Cards in this unnumbered, eight-card series measure 8-1/2" by 6" and show the players in street clothes either eating or getting ready to enjoy a bowl of Wheaties. Sometimes a waitress or other person also appears in the photo. The set is sometimes called the "Dress Clothes" or "Civies" series.

		NR MT	EX	VG
Complete Set:		225.00	112.00	67.00
Common Player:		25.00	12.50	7.50
(1)	Lou Fette	25.00	12.50	7.50
(2)	Jimmie Foxx	75.00	37.00	22.00
(3)	Charlie Gehringer	50.00	25.00	15.00
(4)	Lefty Grove	60.00	30.00	18.00
(5)	Hank Greenberg, Roxie Lawson	50.00	25.00	15.00
(6)	Lee Grissom, Ernie Lombardi	40.00	20.00	12.00
(7)	Joe Medwick	40.00	20.00	12.00
(8)	Lon Warneke	25.00	12.50	7.50

1938 Wheaties - Series 15

Another set of small (2-5/8" by 3-7/8") cards, the photos in this unnumbered series made up the back panels of single-serving size Wheaties boxes. The panels have orange, blue and white backgrounds, and some of the photos are the same as those used in the larger Wheaties panels.

	NR MT	EX	VG
Complete Set:	1500.00	750.00	450.00
Common Player:	50.00	25.00	15.00

		NR MT	EX	VG
(1)	"Zeke" Bonura	50.00	25.00	15.00
(2)	Joe DiMaggio	450.00	225.00	135.00
(3)	Charles Gehringer (batting)	125.00	62.00	37.00
(4)	Chas. Gehringer (leaping)	125.00	62.00	37.00
(5)	Hank Greenberg	125.00	62.00	37.00
(6)	Lefty Grove	150.00	75.00	45.00
(7)	Carl Hubbell	110.00	55.00	33.00
(8)	John (Buddy) Lewis	50.00	25.00	15.00
(9)	Heinie Manush	90.00	45.00	27.00
(10)	Joe Medwick	90.00	45.00	27.00
(11)	Arky Vaughan	90.00	45.00	27.00

1939 Wheaties - Series 12

The nine cards in this numbered series, known as the "Personal Pointers" series, measure 8-1/4" by 6" and feature an instructional format similar to earlier Wheaties issues. The cards feature a player photo along with printed tips on various aspects of hitting and pitching.

		NR MT	EX	VG
Complete Set:		450.00	225.00	135.00
Common Player:		25.00	12.50	7.50
1	Ernie Lombardi	40.00	20.00	12.00
2	Johnny Allen	25.00	12.50	7.50
3	Lefty Gomez	45.00	22.00	13.50
4	Bill Lee	25.00	12.50	7.50
5	Jimmie Foxx	90.00	45.00	27.00
6	Joe Medwick	40.00	20.00	12.00
7	Hank Greenberg	60.00	30.00	18.00
8	Mel Ott	60.00	30.00	18.00
9	Arky Vaughn (Vaughan)	40.00	20.00	12.00

1939 Wheaties - Series 13

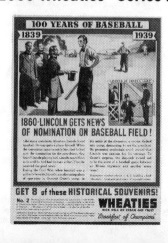

Issued in baseball's centennial year of 1939, this set of eight 6" by 6-3/4" cards commemorates "100 Years of Baseball," each of the numbered panels illustrates a significant event in baseball history.

	NR MT	EX	VG
Complete Set:	200.00	100.00	60.00
Common Panel:	25.00	12.50	7.50

		NR MT	EX	VG
1	Design of First Diamond - 1838 (Abner Doubleday)	25.00	12.50	7.50
2	Gets News of Nomination on Field - 1860 all history. (Abraham Lincoln)	25.00	12.50	7.50
3	Crowd Boos First Baseball Glove - 1869	25.00	12.50	7.50
4	Curve Ball Just an Illusion - 1877	25.00	12.50	7.50
5	Fencer's Mask is Pattern - 1877	25.00	12.50	7.50
6	Baseball Gets "All Dressed Up" - 1895	25.00	12.50	7.50
7	Modern Bludgeon Enters Game - 1895	25.00	12.50	7.50
8	"Casey at the Bat"	25.00	12.50	7.50

1940 Wheaties
Champs of the USA

This numbered set consists of 13 panels, each picturing one baseball player and two other athletes (football stars, golfers, skaters, racers, etc.). The entire panel measures approximately 8-1/4" by 6", while the actual card measures approximately 6" square. Each athlete is pictured in what looks like a postage stamp with a serrated edge. A brief biography appears alongside the "stamp." Some variations are known to exist among the first nine panels. The cards are numbered in the upper right corner.

		NR MT	EX	VG
Complete Set:		900.00	450.00	270.00
Common Panel:		25.00	12.50	7.50

		NR MT	EX	VG
1A	Bob Feller, Lynn Patrick, Charles "Red" Ruffling	75.00	37.00	22.00
1B	Leo Durocher, Lynn Patrick, Charles "Red" Ruffing	50.00	25.00	15.00
2A	Joe DiMaggio, Don Duge, Hank Greenberg	250.00	125.00	75.00
2B	Joe DiMaggio, Mel Ott, Ellsworth Vines	250.00	125.00	75.00
3	Bernie Bierman, Bill Dickey, Jimmie Foxx	75.00	37.00	22.00
4	Morris Arnovich, Capt R.K. Baker, Earl "Dutch" Clark	25.00	12.50	7.50
5	Madison (Matty) Bell, Ab Jenkins, Joe Medwick	25.00	12.50	7.50
6A	Ralph Guldahl, John Mize, Davey O'Brien	25.00	12.50	7.50
6B	Bob Feller, John Mize, Rudy York	50.00	25.00	15.00
6C	Ralph Guldahl, Gabby Hartnett, Davey O'Brien	25.00	12.50	7.50
7A	Joe Cronin, Cecil Isbell, Byron Nelson	25.00	12.50	7.50
7B	Joe Cronin, Hank Greenberg, Byron Nelson	40.00	20.00	12.00

		NR MT	EX	VG
7C	Paul Derringer, Cecil Isbell, Byron Nelson	25.00	12.50	7.50
8A	Ernie Lombardi, Jack Manders, George I. Myers	25.00	12.50	7.50
8B	Paul Derringer, Ernie Lombardi, George I. Myers	25.00	12.50	7.50
9	Bob Bartlett, Captain R.C. Hanson, Terrell Jacobs	25.00	12.50	7.50
10	Lowell "Red" Dawson, Billy Herman, Adele Inge	25.00	12.50	7.50
11	Dolph Camilli, Antoinette Concello, Wallace Wade	25.00	12.50	7.50
12	Luke Appling, Stanley Hack, Hugh McManus	25.00	12.50	7.50
13	Felix Adler, Hal Trosky, Mabel Vinson	25.00	12.50	7.50

1941 Wheaties
Champs of the USA

This eight-card series is actually a continuation of the previous year's Wheaties set, and the format is identical. The set begins with number 14, starting where the 1940 set ended.

		NR MT	EX	VG
Complete Set:		425.00	212.00	127.00
Common Panel:		25.00	12.50	7.50

		NR MT	EX	VG
14	Felix Adler, Jimmie Foxx, Capt. R.G. Hanson	50.00	25.00	15.00
15	Bernie Bierman, Bob Feller, Jessie McLeod	50.00	25.00	15.00
16	Lowell "Red" Dawson, Hank Greenberg, J.W. Stoker	30.00	15.00	9.00
17	Antoinette Concello, Joe DiMaggio, Byron Nelson	250.00	125.00	75.00
18	Capt. R.L. Baker, Frank "Buck" McCormick, Harold "Pee Wee" Reese	50.00	25.00	15.00
19	William W. Robbins, Gene Sarazen, Gerald "Gee" Walker	25.00	12.50	7.50
20	Harry Danning, Barney McCosky, Bucky Walters	25.00	12.50	7.50
21	Joe "Flash" Gordon, Stan Hack, George I. Myers	25.00	12.50	7.50

1951 Wheaties

Printed as the backs of single-serving size of Wheaties, the six-card 1951 set includes three baseball players and one football player, basketball player and golfer. Well-trimmed cards measure 2-1/2" by 3-1/4". The cards feature blue line drawings of the athletes with a facsimile autograph and descriptive title below. There is a wide white border.

		NR MT	EX	VG
Complete Set:		600.00	300.00	180.00
Common Player:		50.00	25.00	15.00
(1)	Bob Feller (baseball)	125.00	62.00	37.00
(2)	John Lujack (football)	75.00	38.00	23.00
(3)	George K. Mikan (basketball)	125.00	62.00	37.00
(4)	Stan Musial (baseball)	175.00	87.00	52.00
(5)	Sam Snead (golfer)	50.00	25.00	15.00
(6)	Ted Williams (baseball)	200.00	100.00	60.00

1952 Wheaties

ELWIN "PREACHER" ROE
PITCHER, BROOKLYN DODGERS

These 2" by 2-3/4" cards appeared on the back of the popular cereal boxes. Actually, sports figures had been appearing on the backs of the boxes for many years, but in 1952, of the 30 athletes depicted, 10 were baseball players. That means there are 20 baseball cards, as each player appears in both a portrait and an action drawing. The cards have a blue line drawing on an orange background with a white border. The player's name, team, and position appear at the bottom. The cards have rounded corners and are not widely collected because they have an outdated look, are mixed with other athletes and are often poorly cut from the boxes.

		NR MT	EX	VG
Complete Set:		800.00	400.00	240.00
Common Player:		15.00	7.50	4.50
(1)	Larry "Yogi" Berra (portrait)	50.00	25.00	15.00
(2)	Larry "Yogi" Berra (action pose)	50.00	25.00	15.00
(3)	Roy Campanella (portrait)	50.00	25.00	15.00
(4)	Roy Campanella (action pose)	50.00	25.00	15.00
(5)	Bob Feller (portrait)	40.00	20.00	12.00
(6)	Bob Feller (action pose)	40.00	20.00	12.00
(7)	George Kell (portrait)	18.00	9.00	5.50
(8)	George Kell (action pose)	18.00	9.00	5.50
(9)	Ralph Kiner (portrait)	25.00	12.50	7.50
(10)	Ralph Kiner (action pose)	25.00	12.50	7.50
(11)	Bob Lemon (portrait)	25.00	12.50	7.50
(12)	Bob Lemon (action pose)	25.00	12.50	7.50
(13)	Stan Musial (portrait)	75.00	37.00	22.00
(14)	Stan Musial (action pose)	75.00	37.00	22.00
(15)	Phil Rizzuto (portrait)	30.00	15.00	9.00
(16)	Phil Rizzuto (action pose)	30.00	15.00	9.00
(17)	Elwin "Preacher" Roe (portrait)	15.00	7.50	4.50
(18)	Elwin "Preacher" Roe (action pose)	15.00	7.50	4.50
(19)	Ted Williams (portrait)	100.00	50.00	30.00
(20)	Ted Williams (action pose)	100.00	50.00	30.00

1954 Wilson Franks

The 2-5/8" by 3-3/4" cards are among the most popular and difficult to find baseball card sets issued with hot dogs during the 1950s. The cards feature color-added photos on the front where the player's name, team and position appear at the top. The front also has a facsimile autograph and a color picture of a package of Wilson's frankfurters. The card backs feature personal information, a short career summary and 1953 and career statistics. The 20-card set includes players from a number of teams and was distributed nationally in the frankfurter packages. The problem with such distribution is that the cards are very tough to find without grease stains from the hot dogs.

		NR MT	EX	VG
Complete Set:		6500.00	3250.00	1950.
Common Player:		175.00	87.00	52.00
(1)	Roy Campanella	750.00	375.00	225.00
(2)	Del Ennis	175.00	87.00	52.00
(3)	Carl Erskine	300.00	150.00	90.00
(4)	Ferris Fain	175.00	87.00	52.00
(5)	Bob Feller	600.00	300.00	180.00
(6)	Nelson Fox	300.00	150.00	90.00
(7)	Johnny Groth	175.00	87.00	52.00
(8)	Stan Hack	175.00	87.00	52.00
(9)	Gil Hodges	500.00	250.00	150.00
(10)	Ray Jablonski	175.00	87.00	52.00
(11)	Harvey Kuenn	300.00	150.00	90.00
(12)	Roy McMillan	175.00	87.00	52.00
(13)	Andy Pafko	175.00	87.00	52.00
(14)	Paul Richards	175.00	87.00	52.00
(15)	Hank Sauer	175.00	87.00	52.00
(16)	Red Schoendienst	300.00	150.00	90.00
(17)	Enos Slaughter	450.00	225.00	135.00
(18)	Vern Stephens	175.00	87.00	52.00
(19)	Sammy White	175.00	87.00	52.00
(20)	Ted Williams	3000.00	1500.00	900.00

1887-1890 N172 Old Judge

Complete checklist with all known variations

One of the most fascinating of all card sets, these cards were issued by the Goodwin & Co. tobacco firm in their Old Judge and, to a lesser extent, Gypsy Queen cigarettes. Players from more than 40 major and minor league teams are pictured on the 1-1/2" by 2-1/2" cards, with some 518 different players known to exist. Up to 17 different pose and team variations exist for some players, and the cards were issued both with and without dates on the card fronts, numbered and unnumbered, and with both handwritten and machine-printed names. Known variations number in the thousands. The cards themselves are blank-backed, sepia-toned photographs pasted onto thick cardboard. The listings are based on the recordings in the The Cartophilic Society's World Index, Part IV, compiled by E.C. Wharton-Tigar with the help of many collectors, especially Donald J. McPherson and Lew Lipset. The list below includes all known variations for each player in the set. Current values for the N172 Old Judge set are found under the regular listings beginning on page 244.

1-1a   Gus Albert (bat at 45 degrees, Clevelands)

1-1b   Gus Albert (bat at 45 degrees, Milwaukees)
1-2a   Gus Albert (bat over shoulder, Clevelands)

1-2b   Gus Albert (bat over shoulder, Milwaukees)
1-3   Gus Albert (fielding grounder)
1-4a   Gus Albert (throwing, Cleveland's)

1-4b   Gus Albert (throwing, Milwaukees)

2-1a   Alcott (hands on hips, St. Louis Whites)

2-1b   Alcott (hands on hips, Mansfields)

2-2   Alcott (ball in hand above head)
2-3a   Alcott (bat at ready position, left arm across belt, 3d B., St. Louis Whites)
2-3b   Alcott (bat at ready position, left arm across belt, 3rd B., St. Louis Whites)

2-3c   Alcott (bat at ready position, left arm across belt, Mansfields)
2-4   Alcott (bat at ready position, left arm clear of belt)
2-5   Alcott (fielding grounder)
3-1   Alexander (ball in hands at chest)

3-2a   Alexander (ball in hand above head, Des Moines)
3-2b   Alexander (ball in hand above head, Des Moine)
3-3   Alexander (ball in hand head-high)

3-4   Alexander (batting)
4-1   Myron Allen (fielding high ball, well clear of glove, Kansas City)
4-2   Myron Allen (fielding high ball, touching glove, Kansas City)
4-3   Myron Allen (stooping, feet apart, looking at ball, Kansas City)
4-4   Myron Allen (stooping, right foot behind left leg, Kansas City)
4-5   Myron Allen (ball in hand head-high, Kansas City)
4-6   Myron Allen (batting, Kansas City)

5-1   Bob Allen (batting, Pittsburghs)

5-2   Bob Allen (hands on thighs, Philadelphia N.L.)
5-3   Bob Allen (hands clasped at waist, Pittsburghs)
5-4a   Bob Allen (fielding, hands at waist, Pittsburghs)
5-4b   Bob Allen (fielding, hands at waist, Philadelphia N.L.)
5-5   Bob Allen (fielding grounder, Pittsburghs)

6-1   Uncle Bill Alvord (fielding grounder)

6-2   Uncle Bill Alvord (batting)
6-3   Uncle Bill Alvord (sliding)
7-1   Varney Anderson (pitching, right hand head-high)
7-2   Varney Anderson (batting)
7-3   Varney Anderson (pitching, hands chest high)
8-1   Wally Andrews (fielding, stretching to right, Omaha)
8-2   Wally Andrews (fielding, hands by right shoulder, Omaha)
8-3   Wally Andrews (batting, Omaha)
9-1a   Ed Andrews (bat in hand at side, Phila)

9-1b   Ed Andrews (bat in hand at side, Phila's)

9-2a   Ed Andrews (striking ball, bat nearly horizontal, Phila)
9-2b   Ed Andrews (striking ball, bat nearly horizontal, Philadelphias)
9-3   Ed Andrews (bat at ready position, no bal visible, Phila's)
9-4   Ed Andrews (right hand above head, left hand behind at side, Phila)
9-5a   Ed Andrews (fielding, hands shoulder high, Phila's)
9-5b   Ed Andrews (fielding, hands shoulder high, Philadelphias)
9-6a   Ed Andrews, Buster Hoover (Andrews being tagged by Hoover, Phila)
9-6b   Ed Andrews, Buster Hoover (Andrews being tagged by Hoover, Phila's)
10-1a   Bill Annis (bat in hand at side, Worcesters)

10-1b   Bill Annis (bat in hand at side, Omaha)

10-2   Bill Annis (striking ball, bat nearly horizontal)
10-3   Bill Annis (lying on ground by base)

11-1a   Cap Anson (portrait, no arms visible, Chicagoes)
11-1b   Cap Anson (portrait, no arms visible, Chicagos)
11-1c   Cap Anson (portrait, no arms visible. Chicagos N.L.)
11-2   Cap Anson (portrait, arms folded)

12-1   Old Hoss Ardner (throwing)
12-2   Old Hoss Ardner (hands on hips)
12-3   Old Hoss Ardner (batting)
13-1   Tug Arundel (fielding, hands head-high)

13-2   Tug Arundel (ball in hands thigh-high)

13-3   Tug Arundel (bat in hand at side)
13-4   Tug Arundel (bat at ready position)

13-5   Tug Arundel (throwing)
14-1a   Jersey Bakley (Bakely) (pitching, hands at chest, Clevelands)
14-1b   Jersey Bakley (Bakely) (pitching, hands at chest, Cleveland's)
14-2a   Jersey Bakley (Bakely) (pitching, left arm half concealing face, Cleveland's)
14-2b   Jersey Bakley (Bakely) (pitching, left arm half concealing face, Clevelands)
14-3a   Jersey Bakley (Bakely) (pitching, right hand head-high, Cleveland's)
14-3b   Jersey Bakley (Bakely) (pitching, right hand head-high, Clevelands)
14-4   Jersey Bakley (Bakely) (batting, feet together)
14-5   Jersey Bakley (Bakely) (batting, feet apart)
15-1a   Fido Baldwin (portrait, P. Chicago)

15-1b   Fido Baldwin (portrait, P., Chicago)

15-1c   Fido Baldwin (portrait, P. (PL))
15-2a   Fido Baldwin (pitching, right hand in back waist-high, Chicago)
15-2b   Fido Baldwin (pitching, right hand in back waist-high, Columbus)
15-3a   Fido Baldwin (pitching, hands neck-high, Chicago)

47-4b Charles Brynan (pitching, right arm stretched forward, Des Moines)
47-5 Charles Brynan (bat at ready position over right shoulder)
48-1 Al Buckenberger (portrait, looking to left)

48-2 Al Buckenberger (portrait, looking to right)
49-1a Dick Buckley (fielding ball ankle-high, no comma after C.)
49-1b Dick Buckley (fielding ball ankle-high, comma after C.)
49-2a Dick Buckley (stooping, hands on knees, Indianapolis)
49-2b Dick Buckley (stooping, hands on knees, New Yorks N.L.)
49-3a Dick Buckley (fielding, hands chest-high, no comma after C.)
49-3b Dick Buckley (fielding, hands chest-high, comma after C.)
49-4a Dick Buckley (bat at ready position, nearly vertical, comma after C., Indianapolis)

49-4b Dick Buckley (bat at ready position, nearly vertical, no comma after C., Indinapolis)

49-4c Dick Buckley (bat at ready position, nearly vertical, New Yorks (N.L.))
49-5 Dick Buckley (about to hit low ball)

50-1a Charles Buffinton (pitching, hands chest high, Phila)
50-1b Charles Buffinton (pitching, hands chest high, Philadelphia)
50-1d Charles Buffington (Buffinton) (pitching, hands chest-high, Philadelphias)
50-1e Charles Buffington (Buffinton) (pitching, hands chest high, Philadelphias (PL))
50-2a Charles Buffinton (Buffinton) (bat at ready position, name incorrect)
50-2b Charles Buffinton (bat at ready position, name correct)
50-3 Charles Buffinton (pitching, right hand above head)
51-1 Ernest Burch (dark uniform, leaning to left, tagging base)
51-2 Ernest Burch (dark uniform, both hands stretching up to left)
51-3 Ernest Burch (dark uniform, fielding, right hand stretching up to left)
51-4 Ernest Burch (dark uniform, throwing, right hand head-high)
51-5 Ernest Burch (dark uniform, bat by left shoulder)
51-6 Ernest Burch (white uniform, bat on left shoulder)
51-7 Ernest Burch (white uniform, leaning left to field)
51-8 Ernest Burch (white uniform, fielding, hands above head on left)
52-1 Bill Burdick (ball in hand above head)

52-2 Bill Burdick (fielding)
52-3a Bill Burdick (bat in hand at side, C.)

52-3b Bill Burdick (bat in hand at side, P.)

53-1a Black Jack Burdock (portrait, 2d B.)

53-1b Black Jack Burdock (portrait, Second Base)
53-2a Black Jack Burdock (throwing, 2d B.)

53-2b Black Jack Burdock (throwing, 2d Base)

53-3a Black Jack Burdock (batting, 2d B.)

53-3b Black Jack Burdock (batting, 2d Base)

53-4a Black Jack Burdock (fielding grounder, 2d B.)
53-4b Black Jack Burdock (fielding grounder, 2d Base)
53-5a Black Jack Burdock (bat in hand at side. 2d B.)
53-5b Black Jack Burdock (bat in hand at side, 2d Base)
54-1 Robert Burks (Burk) (fielding, hands at chest)
54-2 Robert Burks (Burk) (fielding, hands head high)
54-3 Robert Burks (Burk) (batting)
55-1a Watch Burnham (portrait, Man'gr)
55-1b Watch Burnham (portrait, Manager)
56-1 James Burns (fielding grounder by right foot, Kansas Citys)

56-2 James Burns (fielding, hands just above waist, Kansas Citys)
56-3 **James Burns** (fielding, hands shoulder high, Kansas Citys)
56-4 James Burns (bat at ready position over shoulder, Kansas Citys)
56-5 James Burns (bat at 70 degrees, ball nearby, Kansas Citys)
56-6 James Burns (sliding, Kansas Citys)

56-7 James Burns (bat in hand at side, Omaha)

56-8 James Burns (ball in hands above head, Omaha)
58-1a Oyster Burns (bat at ready position vertically, Baltimores)
58-1b Oyster Burns (bat at ready position vertically, Brooklyns)
58-2a Oyster Burns (swinging bat, Brooklyns)

58-2b Oyster Burns (swinging bat, Baltimores)

58-3a Oyster Burns (fielding, Baltimores)

58-3b Oyster Burns (fielding, Brooklyns)

58-4a Oyster Burns (throwing, right hand head high, Brooklyns)
58-4b Oyster Burns (throwing, right hand head high, Baltimores)
58-5 Oyster Burns (throwing, left hand out of picture)
59-1a Thomas Burns (tagging player, Chicago's)

59-1b Thomas Burns (tagging player, Chicagos (NL))
59-1c Thomas Burns (tagging player, Chicagos)

59-2a Thomas Burns (bat in hand at side, Chicago's)
59-2c Thomas Burns (bat in hand at side, Chicago)
59-3a Thomas Burns (fielding, Chicago's)

59-3c Thomas Burns (fielding, Chicagos)

59-3d Thomas E. Burns (fielding, Chicagos (NL))

59-4 Thomas E. Burns (batting)
60-1 Doc Bushong (Brown's Champions)

60-2a Doc Bushong (in mask, hands on knees, no comma after C.)
60-2b Doc Bushong (in mask, hands on knees, comma after C.)
60-3a Doc Bushong (stooping, hands waist-high, no comma after C.)
60-3c Doc Bushong (stooping, hands waist-high. comma after C.)
60-4 Doc Bushong (standing, ball in hands chest-high)
60-5 Doc Bushong (throwing)
60-6a Doc Bushong (batting, no comma after C.)
60-6b Doc Bushong (batting, comma after C.)

61-1a Patsy Cahill (fielding, R.F.)
61-1b Patsy Cahill (fielding, Right Field)

61-2a Patsy Cahill (batting, R.F.)
61-2b Patsy Cahill (batting, Right Field)

62-1 Count Campau (throwing)
62-2 Count Campau (fielding, hands head-high

62-3a Count Campau (fielding, bending to left, Detroits)
62-3b Count Campau (fielding, bending to left, Kansas City)
62-4a Count Campau (fielding, bending to right, Detroits)
62-4b Count Campau (fielding, bending to right, Kansas City)
62-5 Count Campau (bat in hand at side)
63-1 Jimmy Canavan (batting, looking at camera)
63-2a Jimmy Canavan (batting, looking down at ball, Omahas)
63-2b Jimmy Canavan (batting, looking down at ball, Omaha)
63-3 Jimmy Canavan (fielding)
64-1a Bart Cantz (hands on knees, St. Louis Whites)
64-1b Bart Cantz (hands on knees, Baltimores)
64-2 Bart Cantz (fielding, in mask)
64-3a Bart Cantz (fielding, no mask, St. Louis Whites)

64-3b Bart Cantz (fielding, no mask, Baltimores)

64-4a Bart Cantz (batting, St. Louis Whites)

64-4b Bart Cantz (batting, Baltimores)
64-5 Bart Cantz (throwing)
65-1a Handsome Jack Carney (fielding, hands head-high, Washingtons)
65-1b Handsome Jack Carney (fielding, hands head-high, Washington)

65-2a Handsome Jack Carney (throwing, Washingtons)
65-2b Handsome Jack Carney (throwing, Washington)
65-3a Handsome Jack Carney (bat in hand at side, Washingtons)
65-3b Handsome Jack Carney (bat in hand at side, Washington)
65-4 Handsome Jack Carney (batting)

65-5 Handsome Jack Carney (fielding, bending to left)
66-1a Hick Carpenter (tagging player, Cincinnati)
66-1b Hick Carpenter (tagging player, Cincinnati)
66-2a Hick Carpenter (fielding grounder, Cincinnati)
66-2b Hick Carpenter (fielding grounder, Cin.)

66-3a Hick Carpenter (fielding, ball knee-high, Cincinnati)
66-3b Hick Carpenter (fielding, ball knee-high, Cincinnatis)
66-3c Hick Carpenter (fielding, ball knee-high, Cin)
66-4a Hick Carpenter (batting, Cincinnati)

66-4b Hick Carpenter (batting, Cin'ati)
66-4c Hick Carpenter (batting, Cin., N.L.)

66-5a Hick Carpenter (fielding, hands neck-high Cincinnati)
66-5b Hick Carpenter (fielding, hands neck-high, Cin.)
67-1 Cliff Carroll (batting, Washington)

67-2a Cliff Carroll (fielding, L.F., Washington)

67-2b Cliff Carroll (fielding, Left Field, Washington)
68-1a Scrappy Carroll (batting, looking at camera, St. Pauls)
68-1b Scrappy Carroll (batting, looking at camera, St. Paul)
68-2a Scrappy Carroll (batting, looking at ball, St. Pauls)
68-2b Scrappy Carroll (batting, looking at ball, Chicagos (NL))
68-3a Scrappy Carroll (fielding, hands waist high, ball visible, St. Pauls)
68-3b Scrappy Carroll (fielding, hands waist high, no ball visible, St. Paul)
68-4a Scrappy Carroll (fielding, hands chin-high, St. Pauls)
68-4b Scrappy Carroll (fielding, hands chin-high, St. Paul)
68-5a Scrappy Carroll (fielding, hands chest high, St. Pauls)
68-5b Scrappy Carroll (fielding, hands chest high, St. Paul)
68-5c Scrappy Carroll (fielding, hands chest high, Chicagos (NL))
69-1a Fred Carroll (throwing, C., Pittsburg)

69-1b Fred Carroll (throwing, Catcher, Pittsburg)
69-2a Fred Carroll (batting, C., Pittsburg)

69-2b Fred Carroll (batting, Catcher, Pittsburg)

69-3a Fred Carroll (bat in hand at side, C., Pittsburg)
69-3b Fred Carroll (bat in hand at side, Catcher, Pittsburg)
70-1a Jumbo Cartwright (arms folded, St. Josep)
70-1b Jumbo Cartwright (arms folded, St. Joes)

70-1c Jumbo Cartwright (arms folded, Kansas City)
70-2 Jumbo Cartwright (batting)
70-4 Jumbo Cartwright (bat in hand at side)

70-5 Jumbo Cartwright (throwing)
71-1 Parisian Bob Caruthers (Brown's Champions)

71-2 Parisian Bob Caruthers (holding up ball in left hand)
71-3a Parisian Bob Caruthers (ready to pitch, no comma after P.)
71-3b Parisian Bob Caruthers (ready to pitch, comma after P.)
71-4a Parisian Bob Caruthers (end of pitch, no comma after P.)
71-4b Parisian Bob Caruthers (end of pitch, comma after P.)
71-5a Parisian Bob Caruthers (fielding, no comma after P.)
71-5b Parisian Bob Caruthers (fielding, comma after P.)
71-6 Parisian Bob Caruthers (batting, feet together)
71-7a Parisian Bob Caruthers (batting, feet apart, no comma after P.)
71-7b Parisian Bob Caruthers (batting, feet apart, comma after P.)
72-1a Dan Casey (ball in hand at side, P., Phila)

72-1b Dan Casey (ball in hand at side, Pitcher, Philadelphia)
72-1c Dan Casey (ball in hand at side, Casey on front, P., Philadelphias)
72-1d Dan Casey (ball in hand at side, D.M. Casey on front, P., Philadelphias)

72-2a Dan Casey (ready to pitch, Phila)

72-2b Dan Casey (ready to pitch, Philadelphis)

72-3a Dan Casey (start of pitch, Phila)

72-3b Dan Casey (start of pitch, Philadelphia)

72-3c Dan Casey (start of pitch, Philadelphias)

73-1a Icebox Chamberlain (pitching, hands at chest, P.)
73-1c Icebox Chamberlain (pitching, hands at chest, S.)
73-2 Icebox Chamberlain (pitching, hands neck high)
73-3 Icebox Chamberlain (pitching, right hand head-high)
73-4 Icebox Chamberlain (pitching, right hand chest-high)
73-5a Icebox Chamberlain (batting, looking at camera, P., St. Louis)
73-5b Icebox Chamberlain (batting, looking at camera, P., St. Loui)
73-5d Icebox Chamberlain (batting, looking at camera, S.)
73-6 Icebox Chamberlain (batting, looking at ball)
74-1 Cupid Childs (batting, heels together)

74-2 Cupid Childs (batting, heels well apart)

74-3 Cupid Childs (fielding)
74-4a Cupid Childs (throwing, Phila)
74-4b Cupid Childs (throwing, Syracuse)

75-1a Spider Clark (fielding, facing to left, Washingtons)
75-1b Spider Clark (fielding, facing to left, Washington)
75-2a Spider Clark (fielding, facing front, Washingtons)
75-2b Spider Clark (fielding, facing front, Washington)
75-3 Spider Clark (batting)
75-4 Spider Clark (throwing)
76-1 Bob Clark (hands on hips, Brooklyns)

76-2 Bob Clark (stooping, hands on knees, Brooklyns)
76-3 Bob Clark (fielding, hands above waist, Brooklyns)
76-4 Bob Clark (fielding, hands shoulder-high, Brooklyns)
76-5 Bob Clark (throwing, Brooklyns)
76-6 Bob Clark, Mickey Hughes (Clark tagging Hughes)
77-1 Dad Clark (Clarke) (with cap, hands at chest, Omahas)
77-2 Dad Clark (Clarke) (with cap, bat in hand at side, Omahas)
77-3 Dad Clark (Clarke) (with cap, ball in right hand head-high, Omahas)
77-4 Dad Clark (Clarke) (with cap, ball in right hand by right knee, Omahas)
77-5a Dad Clark (Clarke) (no cap, about to hit low ball, name incorrect, Omahas, W.A.)
77-5b Dad Clarke (no cap, about to hit low ball, name correct, Chicago)

90-2   Pete Conway (pitching, feet on ground, Detroits)
90-3a Pete Conway (pitching, hands chest-high, left foot off ground, Detroits)
90-3b Pete Conway (pitching, hands chest-high, left foot off ground, Pittsburgs)
90-3c Pete Conway (pitching, hands chest-high left foot off ground, Pittsburghs)
90-4a Pete Conway (pitching, right hand by head, heels on ground, Detroits)
90-4b Pete Conway (pitching, right hand by head, heels on ground, Pittsburgs)
90-4c Pete Conway (pitching, right hand by head, heels on ground, Pittsburghs)
90-5a Pete Conway (pitching, right hand stretched forward, right heel off ground. Detroits)
90-5c Pete Conway (pitching, right hand stretched forward, right heel off ground, Indianapolis)
91-1   Jim Conway (batting, Kansas City)

91-2   Jim Conway (bat in hand at side, Kansas Citys)
91-3   Jim Conway (ready to pitch, hands chest high, Kansas City)
91-4   Jim Conway (pitching, left ear not visible, Kansas City)
91-5   Jim Conway (pitching, left ear cleary visible, Kansas City)
92-1   Paul Cook (tagging player)
92-2   Paul Cook (fielding grounder)
92-3a Paul Cook (throwing, Louisville)
92-3b Paul Cook (throwing, Louisvilles)
92-4a Paul Cook (in mask, Louisville)
92-4b Paul Cook (in mask, Louisvilles)
93-1   Jimmy Cooney (throwing)
93-2a Jimmy Cooney (batting, Omahas)

93-2b Jimmy Cooney (batting, Chicago)

94-1a Larry Corcoran (pitching, hands above waist, P., Indianapolis)
94-1b Larry Corcoran (pitching, hands above waist, Pitcher)
94-1c Larry Corcoran (pitching, hands above waist, P., London, Ont.)
94-2a Larry Corcoran (pitching, hands near left shoulder, P., Indianapolis)
94-2b Larry Corcoran (Pitching, hands near left shoulder, Pitcher)
94-2c Larry Corcoran (pitching, hands near left shoulder, P., London, Ont.)
95-1   Pop Corkhill (sliding)
95-2a Pop Corkhill (fielding, hands neck-high, Cincinnati)
95-2b Pop Corkhill (fielding, hands neck-high, Brooklyns)
95-3   Pop Corkhill (fielding, hands above head)
95-4a Pop Corkhill (stooping, hands knee-high, Cincinnati)
95-4b Pop Corkhill (stooping, hands knee-high, Brooklyns)
95-5   Pop Corkhill (batting)
96-1a Cannonball Crane (bat at 60 degrees, N.Y.)
96-1b Cannonball Crane (bat at 60 degrees, New Yorks)
96-2a Cannonball Crane (bat nearly horizontal, N.Y.)
96-2b Cannonball Crane (bat nearly horizontal, New Yorks)
96-3a Cannonball Crane (bat in hand at side, N.Y.)
96-3b Cannonball Crane (bat in hand at side, New Yorks)
96-4a Cannonball Crane (ready to pitch, hands above waist, N.Y.)
96-4b Cannonball Crane (ready to pitch, hands above wais, New Yorks)
96-4c Cannonball Crane (ready to pitch, hands above waist, New Yorks (P.L.))
96-5a Cannonball Crane (pitching, hands below waist, N.Y.)
96-5b Cannonball Crane (pitching, hands below waist, New Yorks)
96-6a Cannonball Crane (pitching, right hand head-high, N.Y.)
96-6b Cannonball Crane (pitching, right hand head-high, New Yorks)
97-1a Sam Crane (batting, 2d B., Washington)
97-1b Sam Crane (batting, Second Base, Washington)
97-2a Sam Crane (fielding grounder, 2d B., Washington)
97-2b Sam Crane (fielding grounder, Second Base, Washington)

97-3a Sam Crane (bat in hand at side, 2d B., Washington)
97-3b Sam Crane (bat in hand at side, Second Base, Washington)
98-1   Jack Crogan (Croghan) (fielding grounder)
98-2   Jack Crogan (Croghan) (leaning to right, hands thigh-high)
98-3   Jack Crogan (Croghan) (bat in hand at side)
98-4   Jack Crogan (Croghan) (fielding, hands chest-high)
98-5   Jack Crogan (Croghan) (batting)

99-1a John Crooks (sliding, St. Louis Whites)
99-1b John Crooks (sliding, Omahas)
99-2   John Crooks (bat at ready position behin head)
99-3   John Crooks (bat nearly horizontal)

99-4a John Crooks (ball in hands waist-high, St. Louis Whites)
99-4b John Crooks (ball in hands waist-high, C. Crooks on front, Omahas)
99-4c John Crooks (ball in hands waist-high, Crooks on front, Omahas)
99-5   John Crooks (fielding, hands head-high)

100-1 Lave Cross (batting)
100-2a Lave Cross (hands on thighs, Louisville)

100-2b Lave Cross (hands on thighs, Philadelphias (PL))
100-3 Lave Cross (fielding low throw)
100-4a Lave Cross (throwing, Louisville)

100-4b Lave Cross (throwing, Philadelphias (PL))

101-1a N.C. Crossley (fielding, hands by right knee, Milwaukee)
101-1b N.C. Crossley (fielding, hands hy right knee, Milwaukees)
101-2 N.C. Crossley (fielding, hands waist-high)

101-3a N.C. Crossley (fielding, hands neck-high, Milwaukee)
101-3b N.C. Crossley (fielding, hands neck-high, Milwaukees)
101-4 N.C. Crossley (batting, looking at camera)

101-5 N.C. Crossley (batting, looking at bat)

102-1 Joe Crotty (dotted tie)
102-2a Joe Crotty (fielding ball waist-high, Sioux Citys)
102-2b Joe Crotty (fielding ball waist-high, Sioux City)
102-3a Joe Crotty (fielding, hands shoulder-high, Sioux Citys)
102-3b Joe Crotty (fielding, hands shoulder-high, Sioux City)
102-4 Joe Crotty (batting, looking at camera)

102-5a Joe Crotty (batting, looking at ball, Sioux Citys)
102-5b Joe Crotty (batting, looking at ball, Sioux City)
103-1a Billy Crowell (pitching, facing front, hands above waist, Cleveland's)
103-1b Billy Crowell (pitching, facing front, hands above waist, St. Joes)
103-2 Billy Crowell (pitching, facing half way to left, hands waist-high)
103-3a Billy Crowell (pitching, facing left, hands behind body, Cleveland's)
103-3b Billy Crowell (pitching, facing left, hands behind body, St. Joes)
103-4a Billy Crowell (pitching, right arm extended, Clevelands)
103-4b Billy Crowell (pitching, right arm extended, St. Joes)
103-5a Billy Crowell (batting, Clevelands)
103-5b Billy Crowell (batting, St. Joes)
104-1 Jim Cubworth (fielding low ball)
104-2 Jim Cubworth (fielding, hands head-high)
104-3 Jim Cubworth (throwing)
104-4 Jim Cubworth (batting)
105-1 Bert Cunningham (fielding)
105-2a Bert Cunningham (pitching, hands chest high, Baltimores)
105-2b Bert Cunningham (pitching, hands chest high, Philadelphias)
105-3 Bert Cunningham (pitching, ball in right hand waist-high)
105-4 Bert Cunningham (bat at ready position, held vertically)

105-5 Bert Cunningham (bat at ready position at about 20 degrees)
106-1 Tacks Curtis (fielding, hands ankle-high, feet together)
106-2 Tacks Curtis (fielding, hands ankle-high, feet apart)
106-3 Tacks Curtis (bat at ready position by ground)
106-4 Tacks Curtis (bat at ready position by head)
106-5 Tacks Curtis (fielding, hands head-high)

107-1 Ed Cushman (dotted tie)
107-2 Ed Cushman (pitching, left hand forward, head high)
108-1 Tony Cusick (batting)
108-2 Tony Cusick (throwing)
109-1 Dailey (mask in hand at side, Oakland)

110-1aEdward Dailey (Daily) (pitching, right hand head-high, Phila)
110-1bEdward Daley (Daily) (pitching, right hand head-high, Philadelphia)
110-1cEdward Dailey (Daily) (pitching, right hand head-high, Washington)
110-2aEdward Dailey (Daily) (pitching, hands neck-high, Phila)
110-2bEdward Daley (Daily) (pitching, hands neck-high, Philadelphia)
110-2cEdward Daley (Daily) (pitching, hands neck-high, Washington)
110-3aEdward Dailey (Daily) (bat at ready position at 30 degrees, Phila)
110-3bEdward Daley (Daily) (bat at ready position at 30 degrees, Philadelphia)
110-3cEdward Dailey (Daily) (bat at ready position at 30 degrees, Washington)
110-3dEdward Daley (Daily) (bat at ready position at 30 degrees, Columbus)
111-1aBill Daley (pitching, hands above waist, Bostons)
111-1bBill Daley (pitching, hands above waist, Bostons (PL))
112-1aCon Daley (Daily) (hands on knees, C., Boston)
112-1bCon Daley (Daily) (hands on knees, Catcher, Boston)
112-1cCon Daley (Daily) (hands on knees, no comma after C., Indianapolis)
112-1dCon Daley (Daily) (hands on knees, comma after C., Indianapolis)
112-2aCon Daley (Daily) (right hand on hip, left arm at side, C., Boston)
112-2bCon Daley (Daily) (right hand on hip, left arm at side, Indianapolis)
112-2cCon Daley (Daily) (right hand on hip, left arm at side, Catcher, Boston)
112-3aCon Daley (Daily) (throwing, right hand head-high, Boston)
112-3bCon Daley (Daily) (throwing, right hand head-high, no comma after C., Indianapolis)

112-3cCon Daley (Daily) (throwing, right hand head-high, comma after C., Indianapolis)

112-4aCon Daley (Daily) (batting, bat over left shoulder, C., Boston)
112-4bCon Daley (Daily) (batting, bat over left shoulder, Catcher, Boston)
112-4cCon Daley (Daily) (batting, bat over left shoulder, Indianapolis)
112-5aCon Daley (Daily) (ready to hit, bat vertical, Catcher)
112-5bBobby Wheelock (photo actually Con Daily - caption error) (ready to hit, bat vertical, R.F.)
113-1aAbner Dalrymple (hands on hips, feet apart, L.F., Pittsburg)
113-1bAbner Dalrymple (hands on hips, feet apart, Left Field)
113-1cAbner Dalrymple (hands on hips, feet apart, L.F., Denvers)
113-2aAbner Dalrymple (hands on hips, left foot behind right foot, L.F., Pittsburg)
113-2bAbner Dalrymple (hands on hips, left foot behind right foot, Left Field)
113-2cAbner Dalrymple (hands on hips, left foot behing right foot, L.F., Denvers)
113-4aAbner Dalrymple (throwing, L.F. Pittsburg)
113-4bAbner Dalrymple (throwing, Left Field)

113-4cAbner Dalrymple (throwing, L.F., Denvers)

113-5aAbner Dalrymple (batting, L.F.)
113-5bAbner Dalrymple (batting, Left Field)

114-1aTom Daly (portrait, Chicagos)
114-1bTom Daly (portrait, Chicago)
114-2 Tom Daly (fielding, with cap, Chicagos)

114-3 Tom Daly (fielding, no cap, Washington)

114-4aTom Daly (bat in hand at side, Chicagos)

114-4bTom Daly (bat in hand at side, Chicago)

114-4cTom Daly (bat in hand at side, Clevelands)
114-5aTom Daly (batting, with or without ball visible, Chicagos)
114-5bTom Daly (batting, with or without ball visible, Chicago)
114-5cTom Daly (batting, with or without ball visible, Chicago's)
114-6aTom Daly (hands on knees, Chicagos)

114-6bTom Daly (hands on knees, Chicago's)

115-1 Sun Daly (batting, looking at camera, Minneapolis)
115-2 Sun Daly (batting, looking at ball, Minneapolis)
115-3 Sun Daly (fielding, hands by right thigh, Minneapolis)
115-4 Sun Daly (fielding, hands chest-high, Minneapolis)
115-5 Sun Daly (fielding, hands neck-high, Minneapolis)
116-1 Law Daniels (batting)
116-2 Law Daniels (fielding, head-high)
116-3 Law Daniels (fielding, hands by right thigh)
116-4 Law Daniels (throwing)
117-1 Dell Darling (portrait)
117-2aDell Darling (arms folded, Del. Darling on front, Chicago)
117-2bDell Darling (arms folded, Dell Darling on front, Chicago)
117-2cDell Darling (arms folded, Chicagos)

117-3aDell Darling (fielding, hands chin-high, Del. Darling on front, Chicago)
117-3bDell Darling (fielding, hands chin-high, Dell Darling on front, Chicago)
117-3cDell Darling (fielding, hands chin-high, Chicagos)
117-4aDell Darling (fielding, hands waist-high, Chicago)
117-4bDell Darling (fielding, hands waist-high, Chicagos)
117-4cDell Darling (fielding, hands waist-high, Chicago's)
117-5 Dell Darling (batting)
118-1aWilliam Darnbrough (batting, Denver)

118-1bWilliam Darnbrough (batting, Denvers)

118-2 William Darnbrough (pitching)
118.5 Davin (bat in hand at side)
119-1aJumbo Davis (sliding, 3d B.)
119-1bJumbo Davis (sliding, 3d B.)
119-2 Jumbo Davis (fielding grounder)
119-3aJumbo Davis (fielding, hands shoulder high, Kansas City)
119-3bJumbo Davis (fielding, hands shoulder high, Kansas Citys)
119-4 Jumbo Davis (throwing)
119-5aJumbo Davis (bat in hand at side, no comma after 3d B.)
119-5bJumbo Davis (bat in hand at side, comma after 3d B.)
120-1aPat Dealey (fielding, hands waist-high, standing upright, name correct)
120-1bPat Dealy (fielding, hands waist high, standing upright, name incorrect)
120-2aPat Dealey (fielding, hands waist-high, leaning to left, name correct)
120-2bPat Dealy (Dealey) (fielding, hands waist high, leaning to left, name incorrect)
120-3aPat Dealey (bat in hand at side, name correct)
120-3bPat Dealy (Dealey) (bat in hand at side, name incorrect)
120-4aPat Dealey (hands on thighs, name correct)
120-4bPat Dealy (Dealey) (hands on thighs, name incorrect)
120-5aPat Dealey (bat on right shoulder, name correct)
120-5bPat Dealy (Dealey) (bat on right shoulder, name incorrect)
120-6aPat Dealey (throwing, name correct)

120-6bPat Dealy (Dealey) (throwing, name incorrect)
121-1 Tom Deasley (fielding, hands level with cap)
121-2aTom Deasley (sliding, N.Y's)
121-2bTom Deasley (sliding, Washington)

121-3 Tom Deasley (leaning left, hands touching above waist)
121-4aTom Deasley (leaning left, hands clasped neck-high, N.Y.'s)
121-4bTom Deasley (leaning left, hands clasped neck-high, Washington)
121-5aTom Deasley (bat in hand at side, N.Y's)

121-5bTom Deasley (bat in hand at side, Washington)
121-6 Tom Deasley (leaning left, ball in hands by chin)
121-7aTom Deasley (fielding, hands chest-high, N.Y's)
121-7bTom Deasley (fielding, hands chest-high, Washington)
121-8 Tom Deasley (fielding, hands in front of face)
121-9 Tom Deasley (bat at ready position at about 80 degrees)
121-10Tom Deasley (right hand hip-high, left hand by left knee)
121-11Tom Deasley (throwing, hands to left, chest-high)
121-12aTom Deasley (throwing, right hand neck high, N.Y's)
121-12bTom Deasley (throwing, right hand neck high, Washington)
121-13aTom Deasley (bat at ready position, bat end behind head, N.Y's)
121-13bTom Deasley (bat at ready position, bat end behind head, Washington)
121-14Tom Deasley (fielding grounder)
122-1 Harry Decker (bat at ready position, almost horizontal)
122-2aHarry Decker (bat at ready position, over shoulder, Philadelphias)
122-2bHarry Decker (bat at ready position. over shoulder, Philadelphia (NL))
122-3 Harry Decker (fielding, hands thigh-high)

122-4aHarry Decker (fielding, hands chest-high. Philadelphias)
122-4bHarry Decker (fielding, hands chest-high. Philadelphia)
122-5aHarry Decker (throwing, Philadelphias)

122-5bHarry Decker (throwing, Philadelphia)

122-5cHarry Decker (throwing, Philadelphia (NL))
123-1aEd Delahanty (bat at ready position by shoulder, Phila)
123-1bEd Delahanty (bat at ready position by shoulder, Phila's)
123-2 Ed Delahanty (bat at ready position, nearly horizontal)
123-3aEd Delahanty (fielding, hands at waist, Phila)
123-3bEd Delahanty (fielding, hands at waist. Phila's)
123-4aEd Delahanty (throwing, Phila)
123-4bEd Delahanty (throwing, Phila's)

123-5 Ed Delahanty (fielding grounder)

124-1aJerry Denny (batting, 3d B. Indianapolis)

124-1bJerry Denny (batting, 3d Base, Indianapolis)
124-1cJerry Denny (batting, 3d B., Indianapolis)

124-2aJerry Denny (in jacket, arms at sides, 3d B. Indianapolis)
124-2bJerry Denny (in jacket, arms at sides, 3d Base, Indianapolis)
124-2cJerry Denny (in jacket, arms at sides, 3d B., Indianapolis)
124-2dJerry Denny (in jacket, arms at sides, 3rd B., Indianapolis)
124-2eJerry Denny (in jacket, arms at sides, 3d B., New Yorks (NL))
124-3aJerry Denny (fielding, 3d B.)
124-3bJerry Denny (fielding, 3d Base)
125-1 Jim Devlin (sliding)
125-2aJim Devlin (pitching, left hand at back, shoulder-high, name correct, St. Louis)
125-2bJim Delvin (Devlin) (pitching, left hand at back, shoulder-high, name incorrect, St. Louis)

125-2cJim Devlin (pitching, left hand at back, shoulder-high, Devlin on front, St. Louis Browns)
125-2dJim Devlin (pitching, left hand at back, shoulder-high, J. Devlin on front, St. Louis Browns)
125-3 Jim Devlin (pitching, hands held out, shoulder-high)
125-4aJim Devlin (end of pitch, left hand waist high, St. Louis Browns)
125-4bJim Devlin (end of pitch, left hand waist high, St. Louis)
125-5 Jim Devlin (batting)
126-1aTom Dolan (sliding, Thos. Dolan on front)

126-1bTom Dolan (sliding, Dolan on front)

126-2aTom Dolan (batting, Thos. Dolan on front)

126-2bTom Dolan (batting, Dolan on front)

126-3 Tom Dolan (bat in hand at side)
126-4 Tom Dolan (fielding, hands above waist)

126-5 Tom Dolan (fielding, hands by right knee)

127-1 Jack Donahue (fielding, San Francisco)

128-1 Jim Donohue (Donahue) (dotted tie)

128-2aJim Donahue (throwing, name correct, Kansas City)
128-2bJim Donohue (Donahue) (throwing, name incorrect, Kansas City)
128-3aJim Donohue (Donahue) (batting, no comma after C., Kansas City)
128-3bJim Donohue (Donahue) (batting, no comma after C., Kansas City)
128-4aJim Donahue (fielding grounder by left foot, Kansas City)
128-4bJim Donohue (Donahue) (fielding grounder by left foot, Kansas Citys)
128-5 Jim Donohue (Donahue) (fielding ball knee-high, Kansas City)
128-6 Jim Donahue (ball in hands, head-high, Kansas City)
129-1aJim Donnelly (Donely) (fielding, hands shoulder-high, 3d B.)
129-1bJim Donnelly (Donely) (fielding, hands shoulder-high, Third Base)
129-2aJim Donnelly (Donely) (batting, 3d B.)

129-2bJim Donnelly (Donely) (batting, Third Base)
129-3aJim Donnelly (Donely) (fielding grounder, 3d B.)
129-3bJim Donnelly (Donely) (fielding grounder, Third Base)
130-1 Coley (fielding)
131-1 J. Doran (batting)
131-2 J. Doran (fielding)
132-1 Mike Dorgan (sliding, left hand raised)

132-2 Mike Dorgan (sliding, left hand on ground)

132-3 Mike Dorgan (throwing, right hand eye high, looking front)
132-4 Mike Dorgan (throwing, right hand cap high, looking left)
132-5aMike Dorgan (throwing, right hand chest high, N.Y's)
132-5bMike Dorgan (throwing, right hand chest high, New Yorks)
132-6 Mike Dorgan (fielding, right hand upstretched to left)
132-7aMike Dorgan (fielding, hands above head. N.Y's)
132-7bMike Dorgan (fielding, hands above head, New Yorks)
132-8 Mike Dorgan (fielding, hands chin-high)

132-9aMike Dorgan (fielding, hands ankle-high, N.Y's)
132-9bMike Dorgan (fielding, hands ankle-high, New Yorks)
132-10Mike Dorgan (fielding grounder with both hands)
132-11aMike Dorgan (fielding grounder with right hand by right foot, N.Y's)
132-11bMike Dorgan (fielding grounder with right hand by right foot, New Yorks)
132-12aMike Dorgan (hands on knees, N.Y's)

132-12bMike Dorgan (hands on knees, New Yorks)

132-13 Mike Dorgan (arms folded)
132-14aMike Dorgan (running to left, N.Y's)

132-14b Mike Dorgan (running to left, New Yorks)

132-15a Mike Dorgan (bat in hand at side, N.Y's)

132-15b Mike Dorgan (bat in hand at side, New Yorks)

132-16 Mike Dorgan (bat at ready position over shoulder)

132-17a Mike Dorgan (bat at ready position nearly vertical, N.Y's)

132-17b Mike Dorgan (bat at ready position nearly vertical, New Yorks)

133-1 Doyle (throwing)

134-1 Home Run Duffe (Duffee) (batting)

134-2 Home Run Duffe (Duffee) (fielding grounder)

134-3 Home Run Duffe (Duffee) (fielding, bending to left, hands waist-high)

134-4 Home Run Duffe (Duffee) (fielding, standing upright, hands above waist)

134-5 Home Run Duffe (Duffee) (fielding, leaning forward, hands shoulder-high)

135-1a Hugh Duffy (batting, Chicago)

135-1b Hugh Duffy (batting, Chicago's)

135-1c Hugh Duffy (batting, Chicagos)

135-2a Hugh Duffy (fielding grounder, Chicagos)

135-2b Hugh Duffy (fielding grounder, Chicago)

135-3a Hugh Duffy (throwing, Chicago)

135-3b Hugh Duffy (throwing, Chicagos)

135-4 Hugh Duffy (fielding, hands neck-high, feet apart)

135-5a Hugh Duffy (fielding, hands chin-high, right heel behind left leg, Chicago)

135-5b Hugh Duffy (fielding, hands chin-high, right heel behind left leg, Chicago's)

135-5c Hugh Duffy (fielding, hands chin-high, right heel behind left leg, Chicagos)

136-1 Dan Dugdale (hands on knees, looking at camera)

136-2 Dan Dugdale (hands on knees, left profile)

136-3a Dan Dugdale (bat in hand at side, Chicago Maroons)

136-3b Dan Dugdale (bat in hand at side, Minpls)

136-4 Dan Dugdale (ball in right hand, head high)

137-1 Duck Duke (batting)

137-2 Duck Duke (pitching, right hand by chin, left arm on thigh)

137-3 Duck Duke (pitching, hands waist-high)

137-4 Duck Duke (pitching, hands chest-high)

137-5 Duck Duke (pitching, right arm extended head-high)

138-1a Sure Shot Dunlap (sliding, Pittsburgs)

138-1b Sure Shot Dunlap (sliding, Pittsburghs)

138-2a Sure Shot Dunlap (hands on thighs, Pittsburg)

138-2b Sure Shot Dunlap (hands on thighs, Pittsburgs)

138-3 Sure Shot Dunlap (bat in hand at side)

138-4 Sure Shot Dunlap (batting)

138-5a Sure Shot Dunlap (fielding, hands above waist, Pittsburg)

138-5b Sure Shot Dunlap (fielding, hands above waist, Pittsburgs)

138-6a Sure Shot Dunlap (fielding, hands shoulder-high, Pittsburg)

138-6b Sure Shot Dunlap (fielding, hands shoulder-high, Pittsburgs)

138-7a Sure Shot Dunlap (throwing, right hand waist-high, Pittsburg)

138-7b Sure Shot Dunlap (throwing, right hand waist-high, Pittsburgs)

138-8 Sure Shot Dunlap (throwing, right hand above head)

139-1 Dunn (batting)

139-2 Dunn (pitching, hands chest-high)

139-3 Dunn (ball in right hand head-high, facing front)

139-4 Dunn (ball in right hand chin-high, looking to right)

139-5 Dunn (fielding, hands chest-high)

140-2 Jesse Duryea (bat under left arm, hands together)

140-3a Jesse Duryea (throwing, right hand head high, Cincinnati)

140-3b Jesse Duryea (throwing, right hand head high, Cincinnatis)

140-3c Jesse Duryea (throwing, right hand head high, Cincinnatti)

140-4a Jesse Duryea (throwing, right hand chest high, Cincinnati)

140-4b Jesse Duryea (throwing, right hand chest high, Cincinnati (NL))

140-5 Jesse Duryea (ready to pitch, hands chest high)

141-1a Frank Dwyer (fielding, hands chest-high, Chicagos)

141-1b Frank Dwyer (fielding, hands chest-high, Chicago Maroons)

141-2a Frank Dwyer (throwing, Chicago's)

141-2b Frank Dwyer (throwing, Chicago Maroons)

141-3a Frank Dwyer (bat in hand at side, Chicago's)

141-3b Frank Dwyer (bat in hand at side, Chicagos)

142-1 Billy Earle (fielding, hands above head)

142-2 Billy Earle (fielding, hands thigh-high)

142-3a Billy Earle (bat in hand at side, name correct, Cincinnati)

142-3b Billy Earl (Earle) (bat in hand at side, name incorrect, St. Paul)

143-1a Buck Ebright (hands on knees, Washingtons)

143-1b Buck Ebright (hands on knees, Washington)

143-2 Buck Ebright (throwing)

144-1 Red Ehret (throwing)

144-2 Red Ehret (pitching, hands by left shoulder)

144-3 Red Ehret (pitching, hands head-high)

144-4 Red Ehret (batting)

145-1 R. Emmerke (batting, looking at camera)

145-2 R. Emmerke (batting, looking at ball)

145-3 R. Emmerke (pitching, hands at chest)

145-4 R. Emmerke (pitching, right hand head high)

145-5 R. Emmerke (pitching, left foot off ground)

146-1 Dude Esterbrook (standing upright, right hand on hip)

146-2 Dude Esterbrook (bending, facing to left, hands on knees)

146-3a Dude Esterbrook (bending, facing front, hands on knees, Indianapolis)

146-3b Dude Esterbrook (bending, facing front, hands on knees, N Ys (NL))

146-4 Dude Esterbrook (kneeling to field grounder)

146-5a Dude Esterbrook (batting, Indianapolis)

146-5b Dude Esterbrook (batting, Louisvilles)

146-6 Dude Esterbrook (fielding)

146-7a Dude Esterbrook (right hand over ball in left hand waist-high, Lo'villes)

146-7b Dude Esterbrook (right hand over ball in left hand waist-high, N Ys (NL))

147-1 Henry Esterday (fielding grounder by left foot)

147-2a Henry Esterday (fielding grounder, hands ankle-high, Kansas City)

147-2b Henry Esterday (fielding grounder, hands ankle-high, Columbus)

147-3a Henry Esterday (fielding, hands above head, Kansas City)

147-3b Henry Esterday (fielding, hands above head, Columbus)

147-4 Henry Esterday (throwing)

148-1 Long John Ewing (bat over right shoulder, Louisville)

148-2 Long John Ewing (bat almost vertical, Louisville)

148-3 Long John Ewing (pitching, hands at cap, Louisville)

148-4 Long John Ewing (pitching, hands neck high, Louisville)

149-1a Buck Ewing (sliding, Capt., New York)

149-1b Buck Ewing (sliding, C., New York)

149-2a Buck Ewing (hands on knees, Capt. N.Y's)

149-2b Buck Ewing (hands on knees, Captain, New Yorks)
149-2d Buck Ewing (hands on knees, C. New Yorks)
149-2e Buck Ewing (hands on knees, C. New York (PL))
149-3 Buck Ewing (throwing, right hand waist high at side, New Yorks)
149-4a Buck Ewing (throwing, right arm extended forward, Capt., New Yorks)
149-4b Buck Ewing (throwing, right arm extended forward, C., New Yorks)
149-5a Buck Ewing (fielding, hands head-high, New Yorks)
149-5b Buck Ewing (fielding, hands head-high, N. Y's)
149-6a Buck Ewing (walking to left, hands thigh high, Captain, New Yorks)
149-6b Buck Ewing (walking to left, hands thigh high, C., New Yorks)
149-7 Buck Ewing (fielding grounder, New Yorks)
149-8 Buck Ewing (bat in hand at side, New Yorks)
149-9a Buck Ewing (bat at 45 degrees, looking to front, New Yorks)
149-9b Buck Ewing (bat at 45 degrees, looking to front, N.Y's)
149-10a Buck Ewing (bat nearly horizontal, looking down at ball, Captian, New Yorks)
149-10b Buck Ewing (bat nearly horizontal, looking down at ball, Capt., New Yorks)
149-11a Willie Breslin - mascot, Buck Ewing (New Yorks)
149-11b Willie Breslin - mascot, Buck Ewing (N.Y's)

150-1a Jay Faatz (fielding grounder, Clevelands)

150-1b Jay Faatz (fielding grounder, Cleveland's)

150-2a Jay Faatz (batting, Capt.)
150-2b Jay Faatz (batting, Captain)
150-3a Jay Faatz (throwing, Capt.)
150-3b Jay Faatz (throwing, Captain)
151-1a Bill Fagan (pitching, left hand chin-high, Kansas City)
151-1b Bill Fagan (pitching, left hand chin-high, Denvers)
151-2 Bill Fagan (pitching, hands neck-high)
151-3 Bill Fagan (left profile, left hand forward waist-high)
151-4 Bill Fagan (batting)
152-1 Bill Farmer (tagging player on ground)
152-2a Bill Farmer (hands on knees, Pittsburgh)
152-2b Bill Farmer (hands on knees, Pittsburgh's)
152-2d Bill Farmer (hands on knees, St. Pauls)
152-3a Bill Farmer (fielding, hands thigh-high, Pittsburgh's)
152-3b Bill Farmer (fielding, hands thigh-high, St. Pauls)
152-3c Bill Farmer (fielding, hands thigh-high, St. Paul)
152-4a Bill Farmer (throwing, Pittsburgh)
152-4b Bill Farmer (throwing, St. Pauls)
152-5 Bill Farmer (batting)
153-1a Sid Farrar (fielding, hands head-high, Phila)
153-1b Sid Farrar (fielding, hands head-high, Philadelphia)
153-1c Sid Farrar (fielding, hands head-high, Philadelphias)
153-2a Sid Farrar (fielding grounder, Phila)
153-2b Sid Farrar (fielding grounder, Philadelphia)
153-2c Sid Farrar (fielding grounder, name correct, Philadelphias)
153-2e Sid Faraer (Farrar) (fielding grounder, name incorrect, Philadelphias)
153-3a Sid Farrar (right hand at belt, left arm at side, with cap, Phila)
153-3b Sid Farrar (right hand at belt, left arm at side, with cap, Philadelphia)
153-3c Sid Farrar (right hand at belt, left arm at side, with cap, Phil)
153-3d Sid Farrar (right hand at belt, left arm at side, with cap, name correct, Philadelphias)
153-3e Sid Farrer (Farrar) (right hand at belt, left arm at side, with cap, name incorrect, Philadelphias)

153-4a Sid Farrar (fielding, hands chin-high, Phila)
153-4b Sid Farrar (fielding, hands chin-high, Philadelphia)
153-5a Sid Farrar (fielding, hands ankle-high, Phila)
153-5b Sid Farrar (fielding, hands ankle-high, Philadelphia)
153-5c Sid Farrar (fielding, hands ankle-high, Philadelphias)
153-6a Sid Farrar (arms folded, no cap, Phila)
153-6b Sid Farrar (arms folded, no cap, Philadelphia)
153-6c Sid Farrar (arms folded, no cap, Philadelphias)
153-7 Sid Farrar (hands on thighs, looking at ball head-high)
154-1 Jack Farrell (bat in hand at side, looking at camera, Washington)
154-2a Jack Farrell (batting, looking at ball head high, 2d B., Washington)
154-2b Jack Farrell (batting, looking at ball head high, Second Base, Washington)
154-3a Jack Farrell, Paul Hines (Farrell tagging Hines, 2d B.)
154-3b Jack Farrell, Paul Hines (Farrell tagging Hines, Second Base)
154-4a Jack Farrell (fielding grounder, 2d B., Washington)
154-4b Jack Farrell (fielding grounder, Second Base, Washington)
154-5a Jack Farrell (hands on thighs, 2d B., Washington)
154-5b Jack Farrell (hands on thighs, Second Base, Washington)
154-6a Jack Farrell (bat at ready, looking at camera, wall background, 2d B., Washington)
154-6b Jack Farrell (bat at ready, looking at camera, wall background, Second Base, Washington)
154-7a Jack Farrell (fielding, hands head-high, 2d B., Washington)
154-7b Jack Farrell (fielding, hands head-high, Second Base, Washington)
154-8a Jack Farrell (hands on hips, 2nd B., Baltimores)
154-8b Jack Farrell (hands on hips, S.S., Baltimores)
154-9a Jack Farrell (bat at ready position, looking at camera, field background, 2nd B., Baltimores)
154-9b Jack Farrell (bat at ready position, looking at camera, field background, 2d B., Baltimores)
154-10 Jack Farrell (fielding, hands above head, Baltimores)
154-11a Jack Farrell (throwing, 2nd B., Baltimores)
154-11b Jack Farrell (throwing, no comma after 2d B., Baltimores)
154-11c Jack Farrell (throwing, comma after 2d B., Baltimores)
154-12 Jack Farrell (bat in hand at side, looking to right, Baltimores)
155-1a Duke Farrell (batting, name correct, Chicago)
155-1b Duke Farrel (Farrell) (batting, name incorrect, Chicago's)
155-2a Duke Farrell (fielding, hands above head, name correct, Chicago)
155-2b Duke Farrel (Farrell) (fielding, hands above head, name incorrect, Chicago)
155-3a Duke Farrell (hands on knees, name correct, Chicago's)
155-3b Duke Farrel (Farrell) (hands on knees, name incorrect, Chicago)
155-3c Duke Farrell (hands on knees, name incorrect, Chicago's)
155-4a Duke Farrell (fielding grounder by right foot, name correct, Chicago)
155-4b Duke Farrel (Farrell) (fielding grounder by right foot, name incorrect, Chicagos)
155-5a Duke Farrel (Farrell) (fielding low ball, hands by left ankle, name incorrect, Chicago)
155-5b Duke Farrell (fielding low ball, hands by left ankle, name correct, Chicagos)
156-1 Frank Fennelly (fielding grounder by right foot)
156-2 Frank Fennelly (batting)
156-3a Frank Fennelly (fielding, hands thigh-high, Cincinnati)
156-3b Frank Fennelly (fielding, hands thigh-high, Athletics)

189-2cBarney Gilligan (hands on thighs, C., Detroit)
190-1 Frank Gilmore (batting, feet apart)

190-2 Frank Gilmore (batting, right foot behind left foot)
190-3 Frank Gilmore (ball in hands above head)

190-4 Frank Gilmore (ball touching right hand above head)
190-5 Frank Gilmore (pitching)
191-1aPebbly Jack Glasscock (throwing, S.S., Indianapolis)
191-1bPebbly Jack Glassock (Glasscock) (throwing)
191-1cPebbly Jack Glasscock (throwing, s.s.)

191-1dPebbly Jack Glasscock (throwing, S.S., Indpls)
191-1ePebbly Jack Glasscock (throwing, S.S., New York (NL))
191-2aPebbly Jack Glasscock (hands on knees, S.S., Indianapolis)
191-2bPebbly Jack Glassock (Glasscock) (hands on knees)
191-2cPebbly Jack Glasscock (hands on knees, S.S., Indpls)
191-3aPebbly Jack Glasscock (batting)

191-3bPebbly Jack Glassock (Glasscock) (batting)
191-3cPebbly Jack Glass Cock (Glasscock) (batting)
191-4aPebbly Jack Glasscock (bat in hand at side, s.s.)
191-4bPebbly Jack Glasscock (bat in hand at side, S.S., Indpls)
191-4cPebbly Jack Glassock (Glasscock) (bat in hand at side, name correct, S.S., Indianapolis)
191-4dPebbly Jack Glassock (Glasscock) (bat in hand at side, S.S. Indianapoli)
191-4ePebbly Jack Glasscock (bat in hand at side, name correct, S.S., Indianapolis)

192-1aKid Gleason (fielding grounder, Phila)

192-1bKid Gleason (fielding grounder, Philadelphias)
192-2aKid Gleason (bat at ready position over shoulder, Phila)
192-2bKid Gleason (bat at ready position over shoulder, Philadelphias)
192-3aKid Gleason (bat horizontal, Phila)

192-3bKid Gleason (bat horizontal, Philadelphias)
192-3cKid Gleason (bat horizontal, Phil'a (NL))

192-4 Kid Gleason (pitching, hands at neck, Philadelphias)
192-5 Kid Gleason (pitching, right hand forward head-high, Phila)
193-1 Will Gleason (Brown's Champions)

193-2aWill Gleason (batting, no comma after S.S., Athletics)
193-2bWill Gleason (batting, comma after S.S., Athletics)
193-3aWill Gleason (hands on knees, no comma after S.S., Athletics)
193-3bWill Gleason (hands on knees, comma after S.S., Athletics)
193-4aWill Gleason (leaning to right, hands thigh high, no comma after S.S., Athletics)
193-4bWill Gleason (leaning to right, hands thigh high, comma after S.S., Athletics)
193-5 Will Gleason (stooping, hands clasped hip high, Louisvilles)
194-1 Mouse Glenn (batting, looking at camera)

194-2 Mouse Glenn (batting, looking at ball)

194-3 Mouse Glenn (fielding, hands neck-high, comma after L.F.)
194-4 Mouse Glenn (fielding, hands thigh-high)

194-5 Mouse Glenn (fielding, hands chin-high)

195-1aMike Goodfellow (bat at ready position by head, Cleveland's)
195-1bMike Goodfellow (bat at ready position by head, Detroits)
195-2 Mike Goodfellow (bat at ready position, nearly horizontal)
195-3aMike Goodfellow (fielding, hands chest high, Cleveland's)

195-3bMike Goodfellow (fielding, hands chest high, Detroits)
195-4aMike Goodfellow (fielding, hands waist high, Clevelands)
195-4bMike Goodfellow (fielding, hands waist high, Detroits)
195-5aMike Goodfellow (throwing, Cleveland's)

195-5bMike Goodfellow (throwing, Detroits)

196-1aPiano Legs Gore (fielding gorunder, facing to right, N.Y's)
196-1bGeorge Gore (fielding grounder, facing to right, New York)
196-1cGeorge Gore (fielding grounder, facing to right, New York's)
196-2 George Gore (throwing, right hand head high)
196-3aGeorge Gore (sliding, N.Y's)
196-3bGeorge Gore (sliding, New Yorks)

196-4aGeorge Gore (bat in hand at side, N.Y's)

196-4bGeorge Gore (bat in hand at side, New Yorks)
196-4cGeorge Gore (bat in hand at side, New York)
196-5aGeorge Gore (bat nearly horizontal, N.Y'

196-5bGeorge Gore (bat nearly horizontal, New Yorks)
196-6 George Gore (fielding, hands above head)

196-7 George Gore (bat at ready position over shoulder)
196-8 George Gore (fielding low ball, facing front)
196-9 George Gore (throwing, right hand forward, left hand on hip)
197-1 Frank Graves (in mask, hands on knees)

197-2 Frank Graves (in mask, fielding, hands by right shoulder)
197-3 Frank Graves (fielding grounder)
197-4 Frank Graves (batting)
197-5 Frank Graves (throwing, hands waist high)

197-6 Frank Graves (fielding, hands cap-high)

198-1 Bill Greenwood (sliding)
198-2aBill Greenwood (batting, looking at camera, Baltimores)
198-2bBill Greenwood (batting, looking at camera, Columbus)
198-3aBill Greenwood (batting, looking at ball, Baltimores)
198-3bBill Greenwood (batting, looking at ball, Columbus)
198-4aBill Greenwood (throwing, Baltimores)

198-4bBill Greenwood (throwing, Columbus)

198-5 Bill Greenwood (hands on knees)

199-1 Ed Greer (bat at ready position by head)
199-2 Ed Greer (throwing)
199-3 Ed Greer (bat at ready position, nearly horizontal)
199-4 Ed Greer, Hardie Henderson (Greer catching and Henderson batting) (same card as 222-10)
200-1 Mike Griffin (sliding)
200-2 Mike Griffin (batting)
200-3 Mike Griffin (fielding)
200-4aMike Griffin (throwing, Baltimores)

200-4bMike Griffin (throwing, Philadelphias (PL))

200-5 Mike Griffin (arms folded)
201-1aClark Griffith (batting, looking at camera, Milwaukees)
201-1bClark Griffith (batting, looking at camera, Milwaukeee)
201-2 Clark Griffith (batting, looking at ball)
201-3 Clark Griffith (pitching, hands at chest)

201-4 Clark Griffith (pitching, hands at neck)
201-5 Clark Griffith (pitching, right hand head high)
202-1 Henry Gruber (batting)
202-2aHenry Gruber (pitching, hands at chest, Cleveland)
202-2bHenry Gruber (pitching, hands at chest, Clevelands)
202-3aHenry Gruber (pitching, right hand chin high, left hand just clear of left thigh, Clevelands)

202-3bHenry Gruber (pitching, right hand chin high, left hand just clear of left thigh, Cleveland)
202-4aHenry Gruber (pitching, right hand cap high, left hand on left thigh, Clevelands)

202-4bHenry Gruber (pitching, right hand cap high, left hand on left thigh, Cleveland)

202-5　Henry Gruber (bat in hand at side)

203-1　Ad Gumbert (batting)
203-2　Ad Gumbert (pitching, right hand level with eyes)
203-3　Ad Gumbert (pitching, right hand waist high)
203-4　Ad Gumbert (pitching, right hand level with chin)
204-1aTom Gunning (fielding low ball on left, Phila)
204-1bTom Gunning (fielding low ball on left, Philadelphia)
204-1cTom Gunning (fielding low ball on left, Athletics)
204-2aTom Gunning (bending forward, hands by right knee, Phila)
204-2bTom Gunning (bending forward, hands by right knee, Philadelphia)
204-2cTom Gunning (bending forward, hands by right knee, Athletics)
205-1　Joe Gunson (bat in hand at side)
205-2　Joe Gunson (fielding, hands by left shoulder)
205-3　Joe Gunson (throwing, right hand head high, no cap)
205-4　Joe Gunson (in jacket, gloves in right hand at side)
206-1aGentleman George Haddock (pitching, hands at chest, Washington)
206-1bGentleman George Haddock (pitching, hands at chest, Washingtons)
206-2　Gentleman George Haddock (pitching, hands neck-high)
206-3　Gentleman George Haddock (pitching, hands waist-high)
206-4　Gentleman George Haddock (end of pitch, right hand chin-high)
206-5　Gentleman George Haddock (batting)
207-1　Bill Hafner (Hoffner) (batting)
207-2　Bill Hafner (Hoffner) (pitching, hands by chin)
207-3　Bill Hafner (Hoffner) (pitching, hands above head)
207-4　Bill Hafner (Hoffner) (pitching, right hand neck-high)
207-5　Bill Hafner (Hoffner) (end of pitch, right hand shoulder-high)
208-1　Willie Hahm - mascot, Ned Williamson (card same as 502-7)
209-1　Bill Hallman (bat on shoulder)
209-2aBill Hallman (throwing, right hand head high, Philadelphia)
209-2bBill Hallman (throwing, right hand head high, Philadelphias)
209-3aBill Hallman (fielding, hands chest-high, Philadelphia)
209-3bBill Hallman (fielding, hands chest-high, Philadelphias)
209-4　Bill Hallman (leaning to left, about to catch ball chest-high)
209-5aBill Hallman (bat horizontal, Philadelphias PL)
209-5bBill Hallman (bat horizontal, Phila)
210-1　Sliding Billy Hamilton (batting, looking at camera)
210-2aSliding Billy Hamilton (batting, looking up at ball, Kansas Citys)
210-2cSliding Billy Hamilton (batting, looking up at ball, K.Cs)
210-3　Sliding Billy Hamilton (fielding grounder)
210-4aSliding Billy Hamilton (fielding, hands above waist, Kansas Citys)
210-4bSliding Billy Hamilton (fielding, hands above waist, Philadelphia N.L.)
210-5aSliding Billy Hamilton (fielding, hands neck high, Kansas Citys)
210-5bSliding Billy Hamilton (fielding, hands neck high, Philadelphia N.L.)
211-1　Frank Hankinson (dotted tie)
212-1aNed Hanlon (bat in hand at side, Detroits)

212-1bNed Hanlon (bat in hand at side, Bostons)

212-2aNed Hanlon (batting, Detroits)
212-2bNed Hanlon (batting, Pittsburgs)
212-3aNed Hanlon (fielding, Detroits)
212-3bNed Hanlon (fielding, Pittsburghs)

213-1　William Hanrahan (squatting on bat)

213-2　William Hanrahan (fielding grounder)

213-3aWilliam Hanrahan (hands on knees, Chicago Maroons)
213-3bWilliam Hanrahan (hands on knees, Minneap'l's)
213-4aWilliam Hanrahan (bat in hand at side, Chicago Maroons)
213-4bWilliam Hanrahan (bat in hand at side, Minneap'l's)
213-5aWilliam Hanrahan (fielding, hands head high, Chicago Maroons)
213-5bWilliam Hanrahan (fielding, hands head high, Minneapolis)　　65.00
213-5cWilliam Hanrahan (fielding, hands head high, Minneap'l's)　　65.00
213-6　William Hanrahan (leaning left, right hand thigh-high, left arm at back)
213.5 Hapeman (ball in right hand above waist)
214-1　Pa Harkins (light uniform, bat at ready position)
214-2aPa Harkins (light uniform, fielding, hands above waist, Brooklyn)
214-2bPa Harkens (Harkins) (light uniform, fielding, hands above waist, name incorrect, Baltimore)
214-2cPa Harkins (light uniform, fielding, hands above waist, name correct, Baltimore)

214-3　Pa Harkins (light uniform, throwing, right hand head-high)
214-4　Pa Harkins (dark uniform, bat on shoulder)
214-5　Pa Harkins (dark uniform, bat at ready position at 60 degrees)
214-6　Pa Harkins (dark uniform, hands at chest)

214-7　Pa Harkins (dark uniform, ball in right hand at back)
214-8　Pa Harkins (dark uniform, ball in right hand extended forward chin-high)
215-1　Bill Hart (pitching, hands at chest)

215-2　Bill Hart (pitching, hands above head, on ground)
215-3aBill Hart (pitching, hands above head, left foot off ground, Cincinnati)
215-3bBill Hart (pitching, hands above head, left foot off ground, Des Moines)
215-4　Bill Hart (ready to pitch, right hand by head, left arm at side)
216-1　Bill Hasamdear (Hassamaer) (fielding, hands head-high)
216-2　Bill Hasamdear (Hassamaer) (fielding, hands thigh-high)
216-3　Bill Hasamdear (Hassamaer) (throwing)
217-1aGill Hatfield (bat over right shoulder behind head, New Yorks)
217-1bGill Hatfield (bat over right shoulder behind head, N.Y.)
217-2　Gill Hatfield (bat at ready position, nearly vertical)
217-4aGill Hatfield (fielding, hands chest-high, looking at ball neck-high, New Yorks)
217-4bGill Hatfield (fielding, hands chest-high, looking at ball neck-high, N.Y.)
217-5aGill Hatfield (fielding, hands cupped chest high, looking upwards, New Yorks)
217-5bGill Hatfield (fielding, hands cupped chest high, looking upwards, N.Y.)
217-6aGill Hatfield (fielding, hands by right knee, New Yorks)
217-6bGill Hatfield (fielding, hands by right knee, N.Y.)
217-6cGill Hatfield (fielding, hands by right knee, New York (P.L.))
218-1aEgyptian Healey (Healy) (dark cap, pitching, P., Indianapolis)
218-1bEgyptian Healey (Healy) (dark cap, pitching, Pitcher, Indianapolis)
218-1cEgyptian Healey (Healy) (dark cap, pitching, P., Washingtons)
218-2aEgyptian Healey (Healy) (dark cap, batting, P., Indianapolis)
218-2bEgyptian Healey (Healy) (dark cap, batting, Pitcher, Indianapolis)
218-2cEgyptian Healey (Healy) (dark cap, batting, P., Washingtons)
219-1aHealey (Healy) (ringed cap, pitching, hands above head, Omaha)
219-1bHealy (Healy) (ringed cap, pitching, hands above head, name correct, Washingtons)
219-1cHealy (ringed cap, pitching, hands above head, name correct, Denvers)

219-2a Healey (Healy) (ringed cap, pitching, right hand head-high, name incorrect, Omaha)

219-2b Healy (ringed cap, pitching, right hand head-high, name correct, Washingtons)

219-3 Healy (plain white cap, moustache, pitching, hands neck high, Washingtons)

219-4 Healy (portrait, looking to left, no cap, Washingtons)

220-1a Guy Hecker (batting, Louisvilles)

220-1b Guy Hecker (batting, Louisville)

220-2a Guy Hecker (ball in hands on chest, feet wide apart, Louisvilles)

220-2b Guy Hecker (ball in hands on chest, feet wide apart, Louisville)

220-3 Guy Hecker (right hand extended at side chest-high)

220-4a Guy Hecker (right hand extended forward, Louisvilles)

220-4b Guy Hecker (right hand extended forward, Louisville)

220-5 Guy Hecker (ball in hands on chest, right foot behind left foot)

221-1 Tony Hellman (batting, looking at camera)

221-2 Tony Hellman (batting, looking at ball)

221-3 Tony Hellman (fielding, hands thigh-high, ball by face)

221-4 Tony Hellman (fielding, hands thigh-high, ball by right wrist)

221-5 Tony Hellman (fielding, hands chin-high)

222-1 Hardie Henderson (white cap, bat over shoulder)

222-2 Hardie Henderson (white cap, throwing, right hand head-high)

222-3a Hardie Henderson (white cap, hands at chest, Brooklyn)

222-3b Hardie Henderson (white cap, hands at chest, Pitts)

222-4 Hardie Henderson (white cap, pitching, right hand raised)

222-5 Hardie Henderson (dark cap, bat at ready position at 30 degrees)

222-6 Hardie Henderson (no cap, batting, ball by bat)

222-7 Hardie Henderson (dark cap, throwing, right hand head-high)

222-8 Hardie Henderson (dark cap, hands at waist)

222-9 Hardie Henderson (dark cap, pitching, left arm across neck)

222-10 Ed Greer, Hardie Henderson (Greer catching and Henderson batting) (card same as 199-4)

223-1a Moxie Hengle (sliding, Minneapolis)

223-1b Moxie Hengle (sliding, Chicago Maroons)

223-2a Moxie Hengle (batting, Minneapolis)

223-2b Moxie Hengle (batting, Chicago Maroons)

223-3a Moxie Hengle (hands on knees, Minneapolis)

223-3b Moxie Hengle (hands on knees, Chicago Maroons)

223-4 Moxie Hengle (fielding)

223-5a Moxie Hengle (bat in hand at side Minneapolis)

223-5b Moxie Hengle (bat in hand at side, Chicago Maroons)

223-6 Moxie Hengle (leaning right, right hand pointing at camera, ball in left hand)

224-1 John Henry (bat over shoulder)
224-2 John Henry (batting)
224-3 John Henry (fielding)
224-4 John Henry (throwing)
224-5 John Henry (pitching)

225-1a Ed Herr (bat over shoulder, St. Louis White)

225-1b Ed Herr (bat over shoulder, looking front, J. Herr on front, Milwaukees)

225-1c Ed Herr (bat over shoulder, looking front Herr on front, Milwaukees)

225-2 Ed Herr (batting, looking at ball chin-high)

225-3 Ed Herr (fielding grounder)

225-4a Ed Herr (bat in hand at side, St. Louis Whites)

225-4b Ed Herr (bat in hand at side, Milwaukees)

225-5 Ed Herr (ball in hands by neck)

226-1 Hunkey Hines (fielding, hands knee-high, St. Louis Whites)

226-2 Hunkey Hines (bat on shoulder, St. Louis Whites)

226-3 Hunkey Hines (fielding, hands head-high, St. Louis Whites)

226-4 Hunkey Hines (bat in hand at side, St. Louis Whites)

227-1a Paul Hines (batting, C.F., Washington)

227-1b Paul Hines (batting, Centre Field. Washington)

227-1c Paul Hines (batting, C.F., Indianapolis)

227-2a Paul Hines (arms at sides, C.F., Washington)

227-2b Paul Hines (arms at sides, Centre Field, Washington)

227-3a Paul Hines (arms folded, C.F., Washington)

227-3b Paul Hines (arms folded, Centre Field,)

227-3c Paul Hines (arms folded, L.F., Indianapolis)

227-4a Paul Hines (fielding, C.F., Washington)

227-4b Paul Hines (fielding, Centre Field. Washington)

227-4c Paul Hines (fielding, C.F., Indianapolis)

228-1 Texas Wonder Hoffman (pitching, hands chest-high on left)

228-2 Texas Wonder Hoffman (pitching, hands head-high)

228-3 Texas Wonder Hoffman (pitching, right hand head-high)

228-4 Texas Wonder Hoffman (end of pitch, right hand forward head-high)

229-1 Eddie Hogan (batting, looking at camera)

229-2 Eddie Hogan (batting, looking right)

229-3 Eddie Hogan (fielding grounder)

229-4 Eddie Hogan (fielding, hands head-high)

229-5 Eddie Hogan (throwing)

230-1 Bill Holbert (dotted tie)

230-2a Bill Holbert (batting, Brooklyns)

230-2b Bill Holbert (batting, Mets)

230-3 Bill Holbert (throwing)

230-4 Bill Holbert (fielding, ball by left shoulder)

230-5a Bill Holbert (fielding, hands cupped chin high, Brooklyns)

230-5b Bill Holbert (fielding, hands cupped chin high, Mets)

230-6a Bill Holbert (in mask, no comma after C., Brooklyns)

230-6b Bill Holbert (in mask, comma after C., Brooklyns)

230-6c Bill Holbert (in mask, Mets)

230-6d Bill Holbert (in mask, Jersey Citys)

231-1 Bug Holliday (Halliday) (hands at back)

231-2a Bug Holliday (Halliday) (arms at sides, Des Moines)

231-2b Bug Holliday (Halliday) (arms at sides, Cincinnatis)

231-2c Bug Holliday (arms at sides, Holliday on front)

231-2d Bug Holliday (arms at sides, W. Holliday on front)

231-3a Bug Holliday (hands crossed below waist on bat, name correct)

231-3b Bug Halliday (Holliday) (hands crossed below waist on bat, name incorrect)

231-4a Bug Holliday (Holliday) (batting, name incorrect)

231-4b Bug Holliday (batting, name correct)

231-5 Bug Halliday (Holliday) (ball in hands by left shoulder)

231-6 Bug Halliday (Holliday) (fielding, hands at waist)

232-1a Charles Hoover (hands on thighs, Chicago)

232-1b Charles Hoover (hands on thighs, Kansas City)

232-2a Charles Hoover (kneeling to field low ball, Hoover on front, Chicago)

232-2b Charles Hoover (kneeling to field low ball, C.E. Hoover on front, Chicago)

232-2d Charles Hoover (kneeling to field low ball, C.E. Hoover on front, Kansas Citys)

232-3 Charles Hoover (batting, Chicago)

244-6a Cutrate Irwin (fielding grounder, hands between knees, Phila)
244-6b Cutrate Irwin (fielding grounder, hands between knees, Philadelphia)
244-6c Cutrate Irwin (fielding grounder, hands between knees, Philadelphias)
244-7 Cutrate Irwin (stooping right to field ball by left foot)
244-8 Cutrate Irwin (bat on left shoulder, heels together)
244-9 Cutrate Irwin (bat horizontal, ball not visible)
244-10a Cutrate Irwin (fielding, hands above head, Philadelphias)
244-10b Cutrate Irwin (fielding, hands above head, Bostons (P.L.))
244-11 Cutrate Irwin (doffing cap)
245-1 A.C. Jantzen (batting, looking at camera)

245-2 A.C. Jantzen (batting, looking at ball)

245-3 A.C. Jantzen (fielding, hands at right knee)
245-4 A.C. Jantzen (fielding, hands chest-high)

245-5 A.C. Jantzen (fielding, hands head-high)

246-1 Frederick Jevne (sliding)
246-2 Frederick Jevne (bat in hand at side)

246-3 Frederick Jevne (fielding, hands above head)
246-4 Frederick Jevne (fielding low ball)

246-5 Frederick Jevne (batting)
247-1 Spud Johnson (hands inside tunic above waist)
247-2a Spud Johnson (fielding, hands head-high, Columbus)
247-2b Spud Johnson (fielding, hands head-high, Kansas City)
247-4 Spud Johnson (throwing)
247-5 Spud Johnson (fielding, hands waist-high)

248-1a Dick Johnston (fielding, hands by right thigh, Johnston on front, C.F.)
248-1b Dick Johnston (fielding, hands by right thigh, Johnston on front, Centre Field)

248-1c Dick Johnston (fielding, hands by right thigh, R.F. Johnston on front, C.F.)
248-2a Dick Johnston (batting, looking at ball, Johnston on front, C.F.)
248-2b Dick Johnston (batting, looking at ball, Johnston on front, Centre Field)
248-2c Dick Johnston (batting, looking at ball, R.F. Johnston on front, C.F.)
248-3a Dick Johnston (batting, looking at camera, C.F., Boston)
248-3b Dick Johnston (batting, looking at camera, Centre Field)
248-3c Dick Johnston (batting, looking camera, C.F., Bostons)
248-4a Dick Johnston (hands on hips, C.F., Boston)
248-4b Dick Johnston (hands on hips, Centre Field, Boston)
248-4c Dick Johnston (hands on hips, C.F., Bostons)
248-4d Dick Johnston (hands on hips, C.F., Bostons (PL))
248-5a Dick Johnston (throwing, C.F.)
248-5b Dick Johnston (throwing, Centre Field)

248-5c Dick Johnston (throwing, C.F.)
248-6a Dick Johnston (fielding, hands neck-high, C.F.)
248-6b Dick Johnston (fielding, hands neck-high, Centre Field)
249-1 Jordan (bat over shoulder, ball in hand)
249-2 Jordan (throwing)
249-3 Jordan (fielding, in mask)
249-4 Jordan (fielding, no mask)
249-5 Jordan (batting)
250-1a Heinie Kappell (Kappel) (fielding grounder, Columbus)
250-1b Heinie Kappell (Kappel) (fielding grounder, Cincinnati)
250-2a Heinie Kappell (Kappel) (fielding, hands knee-high, Columbus)
250-2b Heinie Kappell (Kappel) (fielding, hands knee-high, Cincinnati)
250-3a Heinie Kappell (Kappel) (fielding, hands above head, Columbus)
250-3b Heinie Kappell (Kappel) (fielding, hands above head, Cincinnati)
250-4 Heinie Kappell (Kappel) (throwing)

250-5 Heinie Kappell (Kappel) (batting)
251-1a Tim Keefe (pitching, hands at chest, N.Y's)
251-1b Jim Keefe (Tim) (pitching, hands at chest, name incorrect, New Yorks)
251-1c Tim Keefe (pitching, hands at chest, name correct, New Yorks)
251-2a Tim Keefe (pitching, right hand at back waist-high, N.Y's)
251-2b Jim Keefe (Tim) (pitching, right hand at back waist-high, Jim Keefe on front, New Yorks)
251-2c Tim Keefe (pitching, right hand at back waist-high, Keefe on front, New Yorks)
251-2d Tim Keef (Keefe) (pitching, right hand at back waist-high, Keef on front, New Yorks)

251-3a Tim Keefe (pitching, right hand forward head-high, N.Y's)
251-3b Tim Keefep (Keefe) (pitching, right hand forward head-high, New Yorks)
251-4a Tim Keefe (bat nearly horizontal, N.Y's)

251-4b Tim Keefe (bat nearly horizontal, name correct, New Yorks)
251-4c Tim Keef (Keefe) (bat nearly horizontal, name incorrect, New Yorks)
251-5a Tim Keefe (pitching, right hand held out waist-high, N.Y's)
251-5b Tim Keefe (pitching, right hand held out waist-high, New Yorks)
251-6 Tim Keefe (bat at ready position, nearly vertical, N.Y's)
251-7a Tim Keefe (pitching, hands above waist, N.Y's)
251-7b Tim Keefe (pitching, hands above waist, New Yorks)
251-8a Tim Keefe, Danny Richardson (Keefe tagging Richardson, caption reads "Keefe")

251-8b Tim Keefe, Danny Richardson (Keefe tagging Richardson, caption reads "Keefe and Richardson Stealing 2d")
251-8c Tim Keefe, Danny Richardson (Keefe tagging Richardson, caption reads "Keefe & Richardson")
251-9 Tim Keefe, Danny Richardson (Keefe fielding ball, Richardson sliding to base)

252-1 George Keefe (batting, Washington)
252-2a George Keefe (pitching, hands at chest, looking to front, Washington)
252-2b George Keefe (pitching, hands at chest, looking to front, Washingtons)
252-3 George Keefe (pitching, hands at chest, right profile, Washingtons)
252-4 George Keefe (pitching, hands above head, Washington)   65.00
252-5a George Keefe (pitching, left hand forward head-high, Washington)
252-5b George Keefe (pitching, left hand forward head-high, Washingtons)
253-1a Jim Keenan (hands on knees, Cincinnatis)

253-1b Jim Keenan (hands on knees, Cincinnati)

253-2a Jim Keenan (fielding grounder, Cinncinnatti)
253-2b Jim Keenan (fielding grounder, Cincinnati)   65.00
253-3a Jim Keenan (batting, Cincinnatti)

253-3b Jim Keenan (batting, Cincinnati)
253-4 Jim Keenan (fielding, hands chest-high)
253-5a Jim Keenan (fielding, hands above head, Keenan on front)
253-5b Jim Keenan (fielding, hands above head, J.M. Keenan on front)
254-1 King Kelly (portrait, in cap, "Chicago" on shirt)
254-2 King Kelly (portrait, bare head, "Chicago" on shirt)
254-3 King Kelly (portrait, bare head, "Boston" on shirt)
254-4 King Kelly (bat at ready position at 45 degrees, left-handed, $10,000 Kelly on front)
254-5a King Kelly (bat at ready position at 45 degrees, right-handed, $10,000 Kelly on front)
254-5b King Kelly (bat at ready position at 45 degrees, right-handed. Boston)
254-5c King Kelly (bat at ready position at 45 degrees, right-handed, Bostons)
254-5d King Kelly (bat at ready position at 45 degrees, right-handed, no position on front, Boston)

254-5eKing Kelly (bat at ready position at 45 degrees, right-handed, no position on front, Boston (PL))
254-6 King Kelly (bat at ready position, horizontal, right-handed, $10,000 Kelly on front)
254-7 King Kelly (bat in left hand at side, $10,000 Kelly on front)
254-8 King Kelly (bat on right shoulder, $10,000 Kelly on front)
254-9 King Kelly (fielding, hands chest-high, $10,000 Kelly on front)
254-10King Kelly (fielding, hands head-high, $10,000 Kelly on front)
255-1 Honest John Kelly (portrait, looking to left, Louisville)
255-2 Honest John Kelly (full length, coat over left arm. Louisville)
255-3aHonest John Kelly (umpire) (looking at approaching ball, Western Ass')
255-3bHonest John Kelly (umpire) (looking at approaching ball, Western Ass'n)
255-4 Honest John Kelly (umpire), Jim Powell (manager)
256   No World Index Listing
257-1 Charles Kelly (batting, hands close to body, Philadelphia)
257-2 Charles Kelly (batting, hands clear of body, Philadelphia)
257-3 Charles Kelly (fielding, hands head-high, Philadelphia)
257-4 Charles Kelly (fielding, hands thigh-high, Philadelphia)
257-5 Charles Kelly (throwing, Philadelphia)

258-1 Rudy Kemmler (Kemmler) (portrait in striped cap)
258-2 Rudy Kemmler (batting)
259-1 Theodore Kennedy (batting)
259-2aTheodore Kennedy (bat in hand at side. Des Moines)
259-2bTheodore Kennedy (bat in hand at side, Omaha's)
259-3aTheodore Kennedy (fielding, Des Moines)

259-3bTheodore Kennedy (fielding, Omahas)

259-4aTheodore Kennedy (pitching, hands chest high, Des Moines)
259-4bTheodore Kennedy (pitching, hands chest high, Omahas)
259-5aTheodore Kennedy (pitching, right arm extended at side, Des Moines)
259-5bTheodore Kennedy (pitching, right arm extended at side, Omahas)
260-1aJ.J. Kenyon (batting, Des Moines)

260-1bJ.J. Kenyon (batting, St. Louis Whites)

260-2 J.J. Kenyon (bat in hand at side)
260-3aJ.J. Kenyon (fielding, hands chest-high, Des Moines)
260-3bJ.J. Kenyon (fielding, hands chest-high, St. Louis Whites)
260-4 J.J. Kenyon (in mask, hands on knees)

260-5 J.J. Kenyon (right hand in glove head high)
261-1aJohn Kerins (batting, Louisville)
261-1bJohn Kerins (batting, Louisville)
261-2aJohn Kerins (hands on thighs, Louisville)

261-2bJohn Kerins (hands on thighs, Louisvilles)
261-3 John Kerins (in mask, stooping, hands thigh-high)
261-4 John Kerins (fielding, kneeling, hands by left knee)
261-5aJohn Kerins (fielding, hands chest-high. Louisville)
261-5bJohn Kerins (fielding, hands chest-high. Louisvilles)
262-1aMatt Kilroy (batting, Bostons (PL))
262-1bMatt Kilroy (batting, Baltimores)
262-2aMatt Kilroy (pitching, hand chest-high, Bostons)
262-2bMatt Kilroy (pitching, hand chest-high, Bostons (PL))
262-2cMatt Kilroy (pitching, hand chest-high, Baltimores)
262-3 Matt Kilroy (fielding, hands head-high)

262-4 Matt Kilroy (pitching, hands to left waist high)
262-5 Matt Kilroy (pitching, left hand head-high)

263-1 Silver King (pitching, hands chin-high)

263-2aSilver King (pitching, hands chest-high, no comma after P., St. Louis Browns)
263-2bSilver King (pitching, hands chest-high, comma after P., St. Louis Browns)
263-2cSilver King (pitching, hands chest-high, St. Louis)
263-2dSilver King (pitching, hands chest-high, Chicagos (PL))
264-1 August Kloff (Klopf) (pitching, right hand above head, arm bent)
264-2 August Kloff (Klopf) (pitching, ball leaving hand head-high)
264-3 August Kloff (Klopf) (hands at neck)

264-4aAugust Kloff (Klopf) (fielding, leaning to right, hands waist high, Minneapolis)

264-4bAugust Kloff (Klopf) (fielding, leaning to right, hands waist high, St. Joes)
264-5 August Kloff (Klopf) (batting)
264-6 August Kloff (Klopf) (pitching, right hand vertically above head, arm almost straight)

265-1 William Klusman (fielding, hands by right foot)
265-2aWilliam Klusman (batting, looking at camera, Denvers)
265-2bWilliam Klusman (batting, looking at camera, Milwaukee)
265-3aWilliam Klusman (batting, looking at ball, Denvers)
265-3bWilliam Klusman (batting, looking at ball, Milwaukee)
265-4aWilliam Klusman (fielding, hands head high, Denvers)
265-4bWilliam Klusman (fielding, hands head high, Milwaukee)
265-5 William Klusman (fielding, hands waist high)   65.00
266-1aPhilip Knell (pitching, hands at chest, St. Josephs)   65.00
266-1bPhilip Knell (pitching, hands at chest, St. Joes)   65.00
266-2 Philip Knell (pitching, left hand by head, looking at camera)   65.00
266-3aPhilip Knell (pitching, nearly back view, left hand head-high, St. Joes)   65.00
266-3bPhilip Knell (pitching, nearly back view, left hand head-high, St. Josephs)   65.00
266-4 Philip Knell (pitching, left hand forward head-high)
266-5 Philip Knell (batting)
267-1 Fred Knouff (sliding)
267-2 Fred Knouff (batting)
267-3 Fred Knouff (pitching)
267-4 Fred Knouff (ball in right hand waist-high)

267-5 Fred Knouff (ball in right hand head-high)

268-1 Charles Kremmeyer (Krehmeyer) (fielding)
269-1aBill Krieg (ringed cap, fielding, hands chest-high, 1st B., Washington)
269-1bBill Krieg (Krieg) (ringed cap, fielding, hands chest-high, First Base, Washington)

269-1cBill Krieg (ringed cap, fielding, hands chest-high, St. Joes)
269-2aBill Krieg (ringed cap, fielding, hands thigh high, 1st B., Washington)
269-2bBill Kreig (Krieg) (ringed cap, fielding, hands thigh-high, First Base, Washington)

269-2cBill Krieg (ringed cap, fielding, hands thigh high, Minne)
269-2dBill Krieg (ringed cap, fielding, hands thigh high, C., St. Joes)
269-2eBill Krieg (ringed cap, fielding hands thigh high, 1st B., St. Joe)
269-3aBill Kreig (ringed cap, batting, 1st B.)

269-3bBill Kreig (Krieg) (ringed cap, batting, First Base)
269-4 Bill Krieg (dark cap, tagging player)

269-5aBill Krieg (dark cap, batting, C.)
269-5bBill Krieg (dark cap, batting, 1st B.)

269-6aBill Krieg (dark cap, throwing, Minneapolis)
269-6bBill Krieg (Krieg) (dark cap, throwing, St. Joes)
269-7 Bill Krieg (dark cap, fielding, stretching up to left)
269-8 Bill Krieg (dark cap, fielding, hands by left shoulder)
269-9 Bill Krieg (in mask, hands on knees)

287-3 Little Mac Macullar (bat in hand at side)

287-4 Little Mac Macullar (fielding grounder)

287-5 Little Mac Macullar (throwing)
287-6a Leech Maskrey (Little Mac Macullar)
(arms at sides, R.F., Des Moines)
287-6b Little Mac Macollar (arms at sides, S.S.
Des Moins)
288-1a Kid Madden (portrait, Boston's)
288-1b Kid Madden (portrait, Boston)
288-1c Kid Madden (portrait, Bostons)
288-2a Kid Madden (bat in hand at side, P.,
Boston)
288-2b Kid Madden (bat in hand at side, Pitcher)

288-2c Kid Madden (bat in hand at side, Bostons
(PL))
288-3a Kid Madden (ball in hands at neck, P.,
Boston)
288-3b Kid Madden (ball in hands at neck,
Pitcher)
288-3c Kid Madden (ball in hands at neck,
Bostons (P.L.))
288-4a Kid Madden (batting, P., Boston)

288-4b Kid Madden (batting, Pitcher)
288-4c Kid Madden (batting, Bostons (P.L.)

288-5 Kid Madden (ball in left hand just above
head)
288-6 Kid Madden (arms folded, bat against
rock)
289-1 Danny Mahoney (hands on thighs)

290-1 Grasshopper Maines (Mains) (batting,
looking at camera)
290-2a Grasshopper Maines (Mains) (batting,
looking down at ball, St. Pauls)
290-2b Grasshopper Maines (Mains) (batting,
looking down at ball, St. Paul)
290-3 Grasshopper Maines (Mains) (pitching,
hands by neck)
290-4a Grasshopper Maines (Mains) (ball in bent
right hand head-high, St. Pauls)
290-4b Grasshopper Maines (Mains) (ball in bent
right hand head-high, St. Paul)
290-5 Grasshopper Maines (Mains) (ball in
extended right hand head-high)
291-1a Fred Mann (fielding, hands head-high, St.
Louis Browns)
291-1b Fred Mann (fielding, hands head-high, St.
Louis Brown)
291-1c Fred Mann (fielding, hands head-high,
Hartfords)
291-2 Fred Mann (batting)
291-3 Fred Mann (sliding)
291-4a Fred Mann (fielding grounder, St. Louis
Brown)
291-4b Fred Mann (fielding grounder, St. Louis
Browns)
292-1 Jimmy Manning (fielding grounder)

292-2 Jimmy Manning (batting)
292-3a Jimmy Manning (throwing, right hand
above head, Kansas City)
292-3b Jimmy Manning (throwing, right hand
above head, Kansas Citys)
292-4 Jimmy Manning (fielding, hands neck
high)
292-5a Jimmy Manning (bat in hand at side, no
comma after S.S.)
292-5b Jimmy Manning (bat in hand at side,
comma after S.S.)
292-6 Jimmy Manning (hands on thighs)

293-1 Lefty Marr (fielding grounder)
293-2 Lefty Marr (bat over left shoulder)

293-3a Lefty Marr (bat at 45 degree angle,
Cincinnati (NL))
293-3b Lefty Marr (bat at 45 degree angle,
Columbus)
293-4 Lefty Marr (throwing)
293-5a Lefty Marr (fielding, hands neck-high,
Columbus)
293-5b Lefty Marr (fielding, hands neck-high,
Cincinnati (NL))
294-1a Willie Breslin - mascot (caption reads
"Mascot, New York")
294-1b Willie Breslin Mascot (caption reads "New
York Mascot")
295-1a Leech Maskrey (fielding, hands chest
high, R.F.)
295-1b Little Mac Macullar (Leech Maskrey)
(fielding, hands chest-high, S.S.)
295-2 Leech Maskrey (ball in hands chin-high)

295-3a Leech Maskrey (throwing, Des Moines)

295-3b Leech Maskrey (throwing, Milwaukee)

296-1 Bobby Mathews (pitching)
296-2 Bobby Mathews (throwing)
296-3 Bobby Mathews (fielding)
297-1a Mike Mattimore (pitching, hands shoulder
high on left, N.Y's)
297-1b Mike Mattimore (pitching, hands shoulder
high on left, Athletics)
297-11 Mike Mattimore (throwing)
297-2 Mike Mattimore (pitching, hands above
head)
297-3a Mike Mattimore (batting, standing
upright, N.Y's)
297-3b Mike Mattimore (batting, standing
upright, Athletics)
297-4a Mike Mattimore (pitching, hands at neck,
N.Y's)
297-4b Mike Mattimore (pitching, hands at neck,
Athletics)
297-5a Mike Mattimore (batting, left knee bent,
N.Y's)
297-5b Mike Mattimore (batting, left knee bent,
Athletics)
297-6a Mike Mattimore (pitching, hands waist
high on left, N.Y's)
297-6b Mike Mattimore (pitching, hands waist
high on left, Athletics)
297-7 Mike Mattimore (sliding)
297-8a Mike Mattimore (fielding grounder, N.Y's)

297-8b Mike Mattimore (fielding grounder, name
correct, Athletics)
297-8c Mike Mattemore (Mattimore) (fielding
grounder, name incorrect, Athletics)

297-9a Mike Mattimore (sliding, left hand raised,
N.Y's)
297-9b Mike Mattimore (sliding, left hand raised,
Athletics)
297-10a Mike Mattimore (bat in hand at side,
N.Y's)
297-10b Mike Mattimore (bat in hand at side,
Athletics)
298-1a Smiling Al Maul (batting, left foot pointing
at camera, Pittsburghs)
298-1b Smiling Al Maul (batting, left foot pointing
at camera, Pittsburgs)
298-1c Smiling Al Maul (batting, left foot pointing
at camera, Pittsburgh)
298-2 Smiling Al Maul (batting, left foot pointing
diagonally left)
298-3a Smiling Al Maul (pitching, hands at chest,
Pittsburghs)
298-3b Smiling Al Maul (pitching, hands at chest,
Pittsburgh)
298-4 Smiling Al Maul (ball in right hand above
head, both heels on ground)
298-5 Smiling Al Maul (ball in right hand above
head, right heel off ground)
298-6a Smiling Al Maul (fielding, hands head-high,
Pittsburgh's)
298-6b Smiling Al Maul (fielding, hands head-high,
Pittsburgs)
298-7a Smiling Al Maul (fielding, hands thigh-high,
Pittsburgh's)
298-7b Smiling Al Maul (fielding, hands thigh-high,
Pittsburgs)
299-1 Al Mays (portrait, dotted tie)
299-2 Al Mays (pitching, hands waist-high)

299-3 Al Mays (pitching, hands chest-high)
299-4 Al Mays (pitching, right hand head-high)

299-5 Al Mays (batting)
300-1 Jimmy McAleer (batting, looking at
camera)
300-3 Jimmy McAleer (fielding low ball)

300-4 Jimmy McAleer (fielding, hands above
head)
300-5 Jimmy McAleer (fielding, hands above
waist)
301-1a Tommy McCarthy (sliding, indoor
background, Phila)
301-1b Tommy McCarthy (sliding, indoor
background, Philadelphia)
301-1c Tommy McCarthy (sliding, indoor
background, 2d B., St. Louis)
301-1d Tommy McCarthy (sliding, indoor
background, C.F., St. Louis)
301-2a Tommy McCarthy (throwing, indoor
background, Phila)
301-2b Tommy McCarthy (throwing, indoor
background, Philadelphia)

301-2c Tommy McCarthy (throwing, indoor background, St. Louis)
301-3a Tommy McCarthy (tagging player, Phila)

301-3b Tommy McCarthy (tagging player, Philadelphia)
301-3c Tommy McCarthy (tagging player, C.F., St. Louis)
301-3d Tommy McCarthy (tagging player, 2d B., St. Louis)
301-4a Tommy McCarthy (batting, indoor background, Phila)
301-4b Tommy McCarthy (batting, indoor background, Philadelphia)
301-4c Tommy McCarthy (batting, indoor background, St. Louis)
301-5a Tommy McCarthy (fielding, hands chest high, Phila)
301-5b Tommy McCarthy (fielding, hands chest high, Philadelphia)
301-5c Tommy McCarthy (fielding, hands chest high, 2d B. St. Louis)
301-5d Tommy McCarthy (fielding, hands chest high, C.F., St. Louis)
301-6a Tommy McCarthy (sliding, outdoor background, St. Louis Browns)
301-6b Tommy McCarthy (sliding, outdoor background, St. Louis)
301-7a Tommy McCarthy (batting, outdoor background, St. Louis Browns)
301-7b Tommy McCarthy (batting, outdoor background, St. Louis)
301-8a Tommy McCarthy (throwing, outdoor background, T. McCarthy on front, St. Louis Browns)
301-8b Tommy McCarthy (throwing, outdoor background, St. Louis)
301-8c Tommy McCarthy (throwing, outdoor background, McCarthy on front, St. Louis Browns)
301-9a Tommy McCarthy (fielding, hands head high, St. Louis Browns)
301-9b Tommy McCarthy (fielding, hands head high, name correct, St. Louis Brown)

301-9c Tommy Carthy (McCarthy) (fielding, hands head-high, name incorrect, St. Louis Brown)
302-1 John McCarthy (McCarty) (pitching, hands head-high, Kansas Citys)
302-2 John McCarthy (McCarty) (pitching, hands below chin, Kansas City)
302-3 John McCarthy (McCarty) (fielding, Kansas City)
303-1 Jim McCauley (batting)
303-2 Jim McCauley (fielding)
303-3 Jim McCauley (throwing)
304-1a Bill McClellan (stooping, hands knee-high, name correct)
304-1b Bill McClennan (McClellan) (stooping, hands knee-high, name incorrect))
304-2 Bill McClellan (fielding, hands head-high)

304-3a Bill McClellan (batting, name correct)

304-3b Bill McClennan (McClellan) (batting, name incorrect)
305-1 Jerry McCormack (McCormick) (batting)

305-2 Jerry McCormack (McCormick) (fielding hands shoulder-high)
305-3 Jerry McCormack (McCormick) (fielding grounder)
305-4 Jerry McCormack (McCormick) (throwing)
306-1 Jim McCormick (portrait, bare head)

306-2 Jim McCormick (portrait, peaked cap)

306-3 Jim McCormick (portrait, bowler hat)

306-4 Jim McCormick (standing, arms folded)
306-5a Jim McCormick (pitching, hands at chest, looking at camera, P.)
306-5b Jim McCormick (pitching, hands at chest, looking at camera, Pitcher)
306-6 Jim McCormick (batting, left-handed)

306-7a Jim McCormick (fielding, Pitcher)

306-7b Jim McCormick (fielding, P.)

306-8 Jim McCormick (standing, arms at sides)

306-9a Jim McCormick (batting, right-handed, Pitcher)
306-9b Jim McCormick (batting, right-handed, P.)

306-10a Jim McCormick (pitching, hands at chest, right profile, Pitcher)

306-10b Jim McCormick (pitching, hands at chest, right profile, P.)
307-1 McCreachery (photo actually Deacon White) (portrait)
308-1 Thomas McCullum (McCallum) (batting)

308-2 Thomas McCullum (McCallum) (fielding)

308-3 Thomas McCullum (McCallum) (throwing)

308-4 Thomas McCullum (McCallum) (bat in hand at side)
308.5 McDonald (standing, ball in hand)

309-1 Chippy McGarr (stooping, hands thigh high)
309-2 Chippy McGarr (fielding, hands head-high)

309-3 Chippy McGarr (batting, looking at camera)
309-4a Chippy McGarr (batting, umpire behind, St. Louis Browns)
309-4b Chippy McGarr (batting, umpire behind, K.C.)
309-4c Chippy McGarr (batting, umpire behind, Kansas City)
310-1a Jack McGeachy (bat in hand at side, Indianapolis)
310-1b Jack McGeachy (bat in hand at side. Indianap's)
310-2 Jack McGeachy (batting)
310-3a Jack McGeachy (fielding, McGeachy on front, no comma after C.F., Indianapolis)

310-3b Jack McGeachy (fielding, McGeachy on front, comma after C.F., Indianapolis)

310-3c Jack McGeachy (fielding, Indianap's)

310-3d Jack McGeachy (fielding, C. McGeachy on front)
310-4 Jack McGeachy (throwing)
311-1a John McGlone (tagging player, Cleveland's)
311-1b John McGlone (tagging player, Detroits)

311-2 John McGlone (fielding, hands neck-high)

311-3 John McGlone (throwing)
311-4 John McGlone (fielding grounder)

311-5 John McGlone (batting)
312-1a Deacon McGuire (hands on knees, Phila)

312-1b Deacon McGuire (hands on knees. Philadelphia)
312-2a Deacon McGuire (right hand on hip, left arm at side, Phila)
312-2b Deacon McGuire (right hand on hip, left arm at side, Philadelphia)
312-2c Deacon McGuire (right hand on hip, left arm at side, Phil)
312-3a Deacon McGuire (fielding, hands shoulder high, Phila)
312-3b Deacon McGuire (fielding, hands shoulder high, Philadelphia)
312-3d Deacon McGuire (fielding, hands shoulder high, Torontos)
312-4a Deacon McGuire (batting, Phila)
312-4b Deacon McGuire (batting, Philadelphia)

313-1a Bill McGunnigle (three-quarter length, looking to right, Brooklyns)
313-1b Bill McGunnigle (three-quarter length, looking to right, Brookly)
314-1 Ed McKean (batting, looking at camera)
314-2 Ed McKean (batting, looking at ball)

314-3 Ed McKean (fielding, hands thigh-high)

314-4 Ed McKean (fielding, hands chest-high)

314-5 Ed McKean (fielding, hands above head)

315-1a Alex McKinnon (fielding grounder, 1st B.)

315-1b Alex McKinnon (fielding grounder, First Base)
315-2a Alex McKinnon (fielding, hands waist-high, 1st B.)
315-2b Alex McKinnon (fielding, hands waist-high, 1st Base)
315-3a Alex McKinnon (batting, 1st B.)
315-3b Alex McKinnon (batting, 1st Base)

315-4a Alex McKinnon (bat in hand at side, 1st B.)

315-4bAlex McKinnon (bat in hand at side, 1st
Base)
316-1 Tom McLaughlin (portrait, dotted tie)

317-1aBid McPhee (batting, looking at camera,
Cincinnatti)
317-1bBid McPhee (batting, looking at camera,
Cincinnati (NL))
317-1cBid McPhee (batting, looking at camera,
Cincinnati)
317-2aBid McPhee (batting, looking at ball,
McPhee on front)
317-2bBid McPhee (batting, looking at ball, John
McPhee on front)
317-3aBid McPhee (fielding, hands ankle-high,
Cincinnatis)
317-3bBid McPhee (fielding, hands ankle-high,
Cincinnati)
317-3cBid McPhee (fielding, hands ankle-high,
Cincinnatis)
317-4aBid McPhee (fielding, hands head-high,
McPhee on front, Cincinnati)
317-4bBid McPhee (fielding, hands head-high,
Cincinnatis)
317-4cBid McPhee (fielding, hands head-high,
Cincinnatti)
317-4dBid McPhee (fielding, hands head-high,
John McPhee on front, Cincinnati)
317-5aBid McPhee (throwing, Cincinnati)

317-5bBid McPhee (throwing, Cincinnatti)

318-1 James McQuaid (batting, Denver)

318-2 James McQuaid (fielding, hands near
chin, Denver)
318-3 James McQuaid (fielding, hands head
high, Denver)
319-1aJohn McQuaid (umpire) (McQuaid on
front)
319-1bJohn McQuaid (umpire) (Jack McQuaid on
front)
320-1 Jim McTamany (fielding, hands head
high)
320-2aJim McTamany (fielding, right hand above
head, Brooklyn)
320-2bJim McTammany (McTamany) (fielding,
right hand above head, Columbus)
320-2cJim McTammany (McTamany) (fielding,
right hand above head, Kansas City)

320-3aJim McTamany (batting, name correct)

320-3bJim McTammany (McTamany) (batting,
name incorrect)
320-4 Jim McTammany (McTamany) (right hand
extended head-high on left)
321-1aGeorge McVey (bending to left, hands
knee-high, left foot forward, Denvers)

321-1bGeorge McVey (bending to left, hands
knee-high, left foot forward, St. Joe)

321-2aGeorge McVey (bending to left , hands
nearly waist-high, feet level, Denvers)

321-2bGeorge McVey (bending to left, hands
nearly waist-high, feet level, Milwaukees)

321-3aGeorge McVey (standing upright, hands
outstretched shoulder-high, St. Joe)

321-4aGeorge McVey (batting, looking at
camera, Denvers)
321-4bGeorge McVey (batting, looking at
camera, St. Joe)
321-5aGeorge McVey (batting, looking down at
bat, Denvers)
321.5 Steady Pete Meegan (standing, hands
together at waist)
322-1 John Messitt (leaning left, arms at sides)

322-2aJohn Massitt (Messitt) (throwing)

322-2bJohn Wassitt (Messitt) (throwing)

322-3 John Messitt (bat in hand at side)

323-1aDoggie Miller (batting, C., Pittsburg)

323-1bDoggie Miller (batting, Catcher, Pittsburg)

323-1cDoggie Miller (batting, Miller on front,
Pittsburgh)
323-1dDoggie Miller (batting, Geo. F. Miller on
front, Pittsburgh)
323-1eDoggie Miller (batting, Pittsburghs)

323-2aDoggie Miller (bat in hand at side, C.,
Pittsburg)
323-2bDoggie Miller (bat in hand at side,
Catcher, Pittsburg)
323-3aDoggie Miller (fielding, hands chest-high,
C., Pittsburg)
323-3bDoggie Miller (fielding, hands chest-high,
Catcher, Pittsburg)
323-4aDoggie Miller (ball in hands at waist, C.,
Pittsburg)
323-4bDoggie Miller (ball in hands at waist,
Catcher, Pittsburg)
323-5 Doggie Miller (hands on thighs,
Pittsburghs)
324-1 Joseph Miller (batting, Omaha)
324-2 Joseph Miller (fielding, hands at ankles,
Minneapolis)
324-3 Joseph Miller (bat in hand at side, Omaha)

325-1aJocko Milligan (batting, looking at camera,
St. Louis)
325-1bJocko Milligan (batting, looking at camera,
no comma after C., St. Louis Browns)

325-1cJocko Milligan (batting, looking at camera,
comma)
325-1dJocko Milligan (batting, looking at camera,
Philadelphias (PL))
325-2aJocko Milligan (bat in hand at side.
Milligan on front)
325-2bJocko Milligan (bat in hand at side, J.
Milligan on front)
325-3aJocko Milligan (throwing, St. Louis)

325-3bJocko Milligan (throwing, Philadelphias)

325-3cJocko Milligan (throwing, Philadelphias
(PL))
325-4 Jocko Milligan (fielding)
326-1 E.L. Mills (batting)
326-2 E.L. Mills (bat in hand at side)
326-3aE.L. Mills (fielding, hands shoulder-high,
Milwaukees)
326-3bE.L. Mills (fielding, hands shoulder-high,
Milwaukees, W. Ass'n)
326-4 E.L. Mills (ball in left hand above head)

326-5 E.L. Mills (throwing, ball in right hand
head-high)
327-1 Daniel Minnehan (Minahan) (batting,
looking at camera)
327-2 Daniel Minnehan (Minahan) (batting,
looking at ball)
327-3 Daniel Minnehan (Minahan) (fielding,
hands chin-high)
327-4 Daniel Minnehan (Minahan) (fielding,
hands chest-high)
328-1 Sam Moffet (batting)
328-2 Sam Moffet (pitching)
328-3 Sam Moffet (throwing)
329-1aHonest John Morrell (Morrill) (portrait, no
position)
329-1bHonest John Morrill (portrait, First Base,
Manager)
329-1cJohn Morrell (Morrill) (portrait, 1st B.)

329-1dJohn Morrell (Morrill) (portrait, 1st Base
and Manager)
329-2aJohn Morrell (Morrill) (hands on hips,
name incorrect)
329-2bJohn Morrill (hands on hips, name
correct)
329-3 John Morrill (bat in hand at side)
329-4 John Morrill (batting)
330-1aEd Morris (bat at ready position, clear of
head, Pittsburgh)
330-1bEd Morris (bat at ready position, clear of
head, Pittsburgs)
330-2aEd Morris (bat at ready position, partly
behind cap, Pittsburgh)
330-2bEd Morris (bat at ready position, partly
behind cap, Pittsburgh's)
330-3aEd Morris (ball in left hand head-high,
right hand over right thigh, Pittsburgh)
330-3bEd Morris (ball in left hand head-high,
right hand over right thigh, Pittsburgs)

330-4aEd Morris (ball in left hand head-high,
right hand clear of right thigh, Pittsburgh)

330-4bEd Morris (ball in left hand head-high,
right hand clear of right thigh, Pittsburghs)

330-5 Ed Morris (hands at chest, feet together
no space between ankles)
330-6aEd Morris (hands at chest, feet just apart
with background visible between ankles,
Pittsburgh)

330-6b Ed Morris (hands at chest, feet just apart with background visible between ankles, Pittsburgh's)

331-1a Count Mullane (bat at ready position, looking at camera, Tony Mullane on front)

331-1b Count Mullane (bat at ready position, looking at camera, Mullane on front)

331-2a Count Mullane (pitching, hands above head, Tony Mullane on front)
331-2b Count Mullane (pitching, hands above head, Mullane on front)
331-3a Count Mullane (pitching, hands above waist clear of belt, Cincinnati)
331-3b Count Mullane (pitching, hands above waist clear of belt, Cincinnatti)
331-3c Count Mullane (pitching, hands above waist clear of belt, Cincinnatis)
331-4 Count Mullane (pitching, hands at waist left arm across belt)
331-5a Count Mullane (pitching, hands held out on left clear of belt, Cincinnati)
331-5b Count Mullane (pitching, hands held out on left clear of belt, Cincinnatti)
331-5c Count Mullane (pitching, hands held out on left clear of belt, Cincinnatis)
331-6a Count Mullane (pitching, right hand hip high at back, Tony Mullane on front, Cincinnati)
331-6b Count Mullane (pitching, right hand hip high at back, Cincinnatti)
331-6c Count Mullane (pitching, right hand hip high at back, Mullane on front, Cincinnati)
331-6d Count Mullane (pitching, right hand hip high at back, Cincinnatis)
331-7a Count Mullane (pitching, right hand extended forward thigh-high, Cincinnati)

331-7b Count Mullane (pitching, right hand extended forward thigh-high, Cincinnatti)

332-1a Joseph Mulvey (hands on thighs, ball head-high, 3d B.)
332-1b Joseph Mulvey (hands on thighs, ball head-high, Third Base)
332-2a Joseph Mulvey (batting, 3d B.)
332-2b Joseph Mulvey (batting, Third Base)

332-3a Joseph Mulvey (fielding, hands above waist, 3d B., Phila)
332-3b Joseph Mulvey (fielding, hands above waist, Third Base)
332-3d Joseph Mulvey (fielding, hand above waist, 3d B., Philadelphia)
332-3e Joseph Mulvey (fielding, hands above waist, Philadelphia (PL))
333-1 P.L. Murphy (bat in hand at side, St. Pauls)
333-2 P.L. Murphy (batting, St. Pauls)
333-3 P.L. Murphy (standing, hands on thighs, St. Pauls)
333-4a P.L. Murphy (throwing, St. Pauls)

333-4b P.L. Murphy (throwing, St. Paul)
333-5 P.L. Murphy (fielding, St. Paul)
334-1a Pat Murphy (bat in hand at side, New Yorks)

334-1b Pat Murphy (bat in hand at side, N.Y's)

334-2a Pat Murphy (fielding, hands chin-high, New Yorks)
334-2c Pat Murphy (fielding, hands chin-high, N.Y's)
334-2d Pat Murphy (fielding, hands chin-high, New Yorks (N.L.))
334-3 Pat Murphy (ball almost in right hand, neck-high, New Yorks)
335-1 Miah Murray (on right knee, hands by left shoulder)
335-2 Miah Murray (bat over right shoulder)

335-3 Miah Murray (bat held horizontally)

335-4 Miah Murray (fielding, stretching to high right)
335-5 Miah Murray (throwing)
336-1a Truthful Jim Mutrie (portrait, bare head, N.Y.)
336-1b Truthful Jim Mutrie (portrait, bare head, New Yorks)
336-2a Truthful Jim Mutrie (seated, bowler hat in right hand, N.Y.)
336-2b Truthful Jim Mutrie (seated, bowler hat in right hand, New Yorks)
336-3a Truthful Jim Mutrie (standing, bowler hat on head, N.Y.)

336-3b Truthful Jim Mutrie (standing, bowler hat on head, New Yorks)
337-1a George Myers (batting, no comma after C., Indianapolis)
337-1b George Myers (batting, Catcher, Indianapolis)
337-1c George Myers (batting, comma after C., Indianapolis)
337-2a George Myers (stooping, hands waist high, C., Indianapolis)
337-2b George Myers (stooping, hands waist high, Catcher, Indianapolis)
337-3 George Myers (tagging player, Indianapolis)
338-1a Al Myers (portrait, no comma after S.S., Washingtons)
338-1b Al Myers (portrait, Short Stop, Washington)
338-1c Al Myers (portrait, comma after S.S., Washingtons)
338-2a Al Myers (batting, no comma after S.S., Washingtons)
338-2b Al Myers (batting, Short Stop, Washington)
338-2c Al Myers (batting, comma after S.S., Washingtons)
338-2e Al Myers (batting, 2 B, Philadelphia (N.L.)

338-3a Al Myers (hands on knees, no comma after S.S., Washingtons)
338-3b Al Myers (hands on knees, Short Stop, Washington)
338-3c Al Myers (hands on knees, comma after S.S., Washingtons)
338-4 Al Myers (fielding, Washingtons),
338-5 Al Myers (right hand at side, left hand at back, Washington's)
339-1a Tom Nagle (batting, looking at camera, Omahas)
339-1b Tom Nagle (batting, looking at camera, Chicagos (NL))
339-2 Tom Nagle (batting, looking at ball)

339-3 Tom Nagle (stooping, hands by right foot)

339-4 Tom Nagle (hands on knees)
339-5a Tom Nagle (fielding, hands chest-high, Omahas)
339-5b Tom Nagle (fielding, hands chest-high, Chicagos (NL))
340-1a Billy Nash (tagging falling player, 3d B., Boston)
340-1b Billy Nash (tagging falling player, Third Base)
340-1c Billy Nash (tagging falling player, 3d B., Bostons)
340-1d Billy Nash (tagging falling player, 3rd.)

340-2a Billy Nash (portrait, 3d B.,)
340-2b Billy Nash (portrait, Third Base)
340-3a Billy Nash (hands on knees, 3d B.)

340-3b Billy Nash (hands on knees, Third Base)

340-4a Billy Nash (hands on bat between knees, Nash on front)
340-4b Billy Nash (hands on bat between knees, Billie Nash on front)
340-4c Billy Nash (hands on bat between knees, B. Nash on front)
340-5a Billy Nash (batting, 3d B.)
340-5b Billy Nash (batting, Third Base)
340-6a Billy Nash (throwing, Nash on front)

340-6b Billy Nash (throwing, B. Nash on front)

340-6c Billy Nash (throwing, Billie Nash on front)

341-1 Candy Nelson (dotted tie)
342-1a Kid Nichols (batting, looking at camera, Omahas)
342-1b Kid Nichols (batting, looking at camera, Omaha)
342-2 Kid Nichols (batting, looking at ball, Omaha)
342-3 Kid Nichols (pitching, hands at chest, Omaha)
342-4 Kid Nichols (pitching, right hand behind back, Omaha)
342-5a Kid Nichols (pitching, right hand forward, Omahas)
342-5b Kid Nichols (pitching, right hand forward, Omaha)
343-1 Samuel Nichols (Nichol) (bat in hand at side, Pittsburghs)
343-2 Samuel Nichols (Nichol) (fielding, hands above waist, Pittsburghs)

343-3 Samuel Nichols (Nichol) (fielding, hands by neck, Pittsburghs)

343-4 Samuel Nichols (Nichol) (batting, Pittsburghs)

344-1 J.W. Nicholson (leaning to left, hands on knees, Chicago Maroons)

344-2 J.W. Nicholson (bat in hand at side, Chicago Maroons)

344-3 J.W. Nicholson (pitching, hands at chest, Chicago Maroons)

344-4 J.W. Nicholson (pitching, right hand head high, Chicago Maroons)

344-5 J.W. Nicholson (pitching, right hand head high close to cap, Chicago Maroons)

345-1aParson Nicholson (bat in hand at side, St. Louis Whites)

345-1bParson Nicholson (bat in hand at side, Cleveland)

345-2aParson Nicholson (fielding, ball in hands by right knee, St. Louis Whites)

345-2bParson Nicholson (fielding, ball in hands by right knee, Clevelan)

345-2cParson Nicholson (fielding, ball in hands by right knee, C. Nicholson, Cleveland)

345-2dParson Nicholson (fielding, ball in hands by right knee, Nicholson on front, Cleveland)

345-3 Parson Micholson (Nicholson) (fielding, hands by right knee, no ball, St. Louis Whites)

345-4aParson Micholson (Nicholson) (tagging player, name incorrect, St. Louis Whites)

345-4bParson Nicholson (tagging player, name correct, St. Louis Whites)

345-5 Parson Nicholson (batting, St. Louis Whites)

346-1 Little Nick Nicoll (Nicol) (Brown's Champions)

346-2aLittle Nick Nicol (batting, Nicol on front)

346-2bLittle Nick Nicol (batting, H. Nicol on front)

346-3aLittle Nick Nicol (sliding, Nicol on front)

346-3bLittle Nick Nicol (sliding, Little Nick on front)

346-4aLittle Nick Nicol (fielding, stretching up to left, Cincinnatis)

346-4bLittle Nick Nicol (fielding, stretching up to left, Cincinnatti)

346-4cLittle Nick Nicol (fielding, stretching up to left, Cincinnati)

346-4dLittle Nick Nicol (fielding, stretching up to left, Cincinnati (N.L.))

346-5aLittle Nick Nicol (leaning forward, hands outstretched for catch, Hugh Nicol on front, Cincinnatis)

346-5bLittle Nick Nicol (leaning forward, hands outstretched for catch, Nicol on front, Cincinnatis)

346-5cLittle Nick Nicol (leaning forward. hands outstretched for catch, Cincinnatti)

346-5dLittle Nick Nicol (leaning forward, hands outstretched for catch, Cincinnati)

346-6 Little Nick Nicol (leaning forward, right hand at hip, left hand by knee)

346-7aLittle Nick Nicol, Big John Reilly (Nicol and Reilly side by side, Cincinnatti)

346-7bLittle Nick Nicol, Big John Reilly (Nicol and Reilly side by side, caption reads "(Long & Short)")

346-7cLittle Nick Nicol, Big John Reilly (Nicol and Reilly side by side, caption reads "(Long & Short) Cin")

346-8 Little Nick Nicol, Big John Reilly (Nicol and Reilly facing each other)

347-1 Frederick Nyce (batting)

347-2aFrederick Nyce (ball in right hand neck high, St. Louis Whites)

347-2bFrederick Nyce (ball in right hand neck high, Burlingtons (Fc))

347-3 Frederick Nyce (ball in right hand thigh high)

347-4 Frederick Nyce (ball in hands at chest)

348-1aDoc Oberlander (batting, Cleveland's)

348-1bDoc Oberlander (batting, Syracuse)

348-2 Doc Oberlander (pitching, hands above waist)

348-3aDoc Oberlander (pitching, left hand cap high, looking to left, Cleveland's)

348-3bDoc Oberlander (pitching, left hand cap high, looking to left, Syracuse)

348-4aDoc Oberlander (pitching, left hand cap high, looking at camera, hand at back, Clevelands)

348-4bDoc Oberlander (pitching, left hand cap high, looking at camera, hand at back, Syracuse)

348-5 Doc Oberlander (pitching, left hand cap high, looking at camera, hand well forward)

349-1 Jack O'Brien (in mask, hands on knees, Brooklyn)

349-2 Jack O'Brien (mask in left hand, Brooklyn)

349-3 Jack O'Brien (bat over right shoulder, Brooklyn)

349-4 Jack O'Brien (ball in right hand head-high, Brooklyn)

349-5 Jack O'Brien (throwing, right hand neck high, Baltimores)

349-6 Jack O'Brien (fielding, hands at chest, Baltimores)

349-7 Jack O'Brien (batting, feet well apart, Baltimores)

349-8 Jack O'Brien (batting, heels together, Baltimores)

350-1aBilly O'Brien (batting, feet close together, Washington)

350-1bBilly O'Brien (batting, feet close together, Washingtons)

350-2 Billy O'Brien (batting, feet wide apart, Washingtons)

350-3aBilly O'Brien (hands on knees, Washington)

350-3bBilly O'Brien (hands on knees, Washingtons)

350-4aBilly O'Brien (fielding, hands waist-high, Washington)

350-4bBilly O'Brien (fielding, hands waist-high, Washingtons)

350-5 Billy O'Brien (fielding grounder, Washington)

351-1aDarby O'Brien (batting, looking at camera, Brooklyns)

351-1bDarby O'Brien (batting, looking at camera, Bk'ns)

351-2aDarby O'Brien (batting, looking at ball, Brooklyns)

351-2bDarby O'Brien (batting, looking at ball, Bk'ns)

351-3 Darby O'Brien (fielding, right hand high to left, Brooklyns)

351-4 Darby O'Brien (fielding, hands head-high on left, Brooklyns)

351-5aDarby O'Brien (throwing, Brooklyns)

351-5bDarby O'Brien (throwing, Bk'ns)

352-1 John O'Brien (batting, Clevelands)

352-2 John O'Brien (pitching, ball in right hand at chest, Clevelands)

352-3 John O'Brien (pitching, hands shoulder high, feet on ground, Clevelands)

352-4 John O'Brien (pitching, hands shoulder high, left foot off ground, Clevelands)

353-1aP.J. O'Connell (batting, Des Moines)

353-1bP.J. O'Connell (batting, Omaha)

353-2 P.J. O'Connell (fielding grounder)

353-3aP.J. O'Connell (tagging player, Des Moines)

353-3bP.J. O'Connell (tagging player, Omaha)

353-4 P.J. O'Connell (bat in hand at side)

354-1aRowdy Jack O'Connor (batting, Cincinnati)

354-1bRowdy Jack O'Connor (batting, Columbus)

354-2aRowdy Jack O'Connor (fielding grounder, Cincinnati)

354-2bRowdy Jack O'Connor (fielding grounder, Columbus)

354-3aRowdy Jack O'Connor (fielding, hands above waist, Cincinnati)

354-3bRowdy Jack O'Connor (fielding, hands above waist, Columbus)

354-4aJack O'Connor (throwing, Cincinnati)

354-4bJack O'Connor (throwing, Columbus)

355-1aHank O'Day (batting, P.)

355-1bHank O'Day (batting, Pitcher)

355-2aHank O'Day (ball in right hand head-high, P. Washington)

355-2bHank O'Day (ball in right hand head-high, Pitcher, Washington)

355-2c Hank O'Day (ball in right hand head-high, Washingtons)
355-3a Hank O'Day (pitching, hands at chest, O'Day on front, P., Washington)
355-3b Hank O'Day (pitching, hands at chest, Pitcher, Washington)
355-3c Hank O'Day (pitching, hands at chest, Washingtons)
355-3d Hank O'Day (pitching, hands at chest, H. O'Day on front, P. Washington)
356-1 Tip O'Neil (O'Neill) (bat over right shoulder, St. Louis)
356-2 Tip O'Neil (O'Neill) (bat at ready, St. Louis)
356-3 Tip O'Neil (O'Neill) (fielding grounder, St. Louis)
356-4 Tip O'Neil (O'Neill) (fielding, hands head high, St. Louis)
356-5 Tip O'Neil (O'Neill) (throwing, St. Louis)

356-6 Tip O'Neil (O'Neill) (Brown's Champions)

357-1 O'Neill (photo actually Bill White) (batting, St. Louis Browns)
357-2a O'Neill (photo actually Bill White) (fielding grounder, name correct, St. Louis Browns)

357-2b O'Neill (O'Neill) (photo actually Bill White) (fielding grounder, name incorrect, St. Louis Bro.)
357-3 O'Neill (photo actually Bill White) (throwing, St. Louis Browns)
357-4 O'Neill (photo actually Bill White) (fielding, hands above head, St. Louis Browns)

357.1 O'Neill (bat in hand at side, Omaha)

358-1 Orator Jim O'Rourke (fielding, N.Y's)
358-2a Orator Jim O'Rourke (bat in hand at side, 3d B., N.Y's)
358-2b Orator Jim O'Rourke (bat in hand at side, C., New Yorks)
358-2c Orator Jim O'Rourke (bat in hand at side, 3d B., New Yorks)
358-3 Orator Jim O'Rourke (throwing, 3d B., N.Y's)
358-4a Orator Jim O'Rourke (batting, 3d B., N.Y's)
358-4b Orator Jim O'Rourke (batting, 3d B., New Yorks)
359-1a Tom O'Rourke (fielding, hands head-high, C., Boston)
359-1b Tom Rourke (O'Rourke) (known in proof form only) (fielding, hands head-high, Catcher, Boston)
359-2a Tom Rourke (O'Rourke) (fielding, hands thigh-high, Boston)
359-2b Tom Rourke (O'Rourke) (known in proof form only) (fielding, hands thigh-high, Catcher, Boston)
359-2d Tom Rourke (O'Rourke) (fielding, hands thigh-high, Jersey Citys)
359-3a Tom Rourke (O'Rourke) (throwing, right hand head high, Boston)
359-3b Tom Rourke (O'Rourke) (throwing, right hand head-high, Boston)
359-4a Tom Rourke (O'Rourke) (batting, Boston)
359-4b Tom Rourke (O'Rourke) (known in proof form only) (batting, Boston)
359-5a Tom O'Rourke (bat in hand at side, Boston)
359-5b Tom Rourke (O'Rourke) (known in proof form only) (bat in hand at side, Boston)

359-5c Tom O'Rourke (bat in hand at side, Jersey Citys)
359-6a Tom Rourke (O'Rourke) (fielding, hands at neck, C., Boston)
359-6b Tom Rourke (O'Rourke) (fielding, hands at neck, Boston)
359-6c Tom Rourke (O'Rourke) (fielding, hands at neck, Catcher, Boston)
360-1 Dave Orr (portrait, dotted tie)
360-2a Dave Orr (fielding, hands by right knee, no team designation)
360-2b Dave Orr (fielding, hands by right knee, Columbus)
360-3 Dave Orr (fielding, hands head-high on left)
360-4a Dave Orr (fielding, hands head-high on right, Brooklyns)
360-4b Dave Orr (fielding, hands head-high on right, Columbus)
360-5a Dave Orr (bat at ready position, nearly vertical, Brooklyns)
360-5b Dave Orr (bat at ready position, nearly vertical, Columbus)

360-6a Dave Orr (bat at ready position at about 45 degrees, Brooklyns)
360-6b Dave Orr (bat at ready position at about 45 degrees, Columbus)
361-1 Charles Parsons (moving forward, hands waist-high)
361-2 Charles Parsons (bat in hand at side)
361-3 Charles Parsons (pitching, hands chest high)
361-4 Charles Parsons (batting)
362-1 Owen Patton (batting)
362-2 Owen Patton (fielding ball by right foot)

362-3a Owen Patton (fielding, ball in hands by neck, Minneapolis)
362-3b Owen Patton (fielding, ball in hands by neck, Des Moines)
362-4 Owen Patton (fielding, right hand above head)
362-5a Owen Patton (fielding, hands chin-high, Minneapolis)
362-5b Owen Patton (fielding, hands chin-high, Des Moines)
362-6 Owen Patton (throwing)
363-1a Jimmy Peeples (Peoples) (in mask, hands waist-high, Brooklyn)
363-1b Jimmy Peeples (Peoples) (in mask, hands waist-high, Columbus)
363-2a Jimmy Peeples (Peoples) (batting, Brooklyn)
363-2b Jimmy Peeples (Peoples) (batting, Columbus)
363-3a Hardie Henderson, Jimmy Peeples (Peoples) (Henderson tagging Peoples, Columbus)
363-3b Hardie Henderson, Jimmy Peeples (Peoples) (Henderson tagging Peoples, Brooklyn)
364-1 Hip Perrier (batting)
365-1 Patrick Pettee (batting)
365-3 Patrick Pettee (throwing)
365-4 Patrick Pettee (sliding)
365-5 Bobby Lowe, Patrick Pettee (Pettee about to tag Lowe)
366-1 Fred Pfeffer (fielding)
366-2a Fred Pfeffer (throwing, right hand neck high, Pfeffer on front, Chicago)
366-2b Fred Pfeffer (throwing, right hand neck high, Pfeffer on front, Chicago's)
366-2c Fred Pfeffer (throwing, right hand neck high, W.T. Pfeffer on front, Chicago)
366-2d Fred Pfeffer (throwing, right hand neck high, W.T. Pfeffer on front, Chicagos)

366-3 Fred Pfeffer (batting, looking at ball by bat)
366-4a Fred Pfeffer (bat on right shoulder, Pfeffer on front, Chicago)
366-4b Fred Pfeffer (bat on right shoulder, Pfeffer on front, Chicago's)
366-4c Fred Pfeffer (bat on right shoulder, W.T. Pfeffer on front)
366-4d Fred Pfeffer (bat on right shoulder, N.F. Pfeffer on front)
366-5a Fred Pfeffer (tagging player, Pfeffer on front)
366-5b Fred Pfeffer (tagging player, N.T. Pfeffer on front)
366-5c Fred Pfeffer (tagging player, N.F. Pfeffer on front)
367-1 Dick Phelan (batting, looking at camera)

367-2 Dick Phelan (batting, looking at ball)

367-3 Dick Phelan (fielding, hands waist-high)

367-4a Dick Phelan (fielding, hands chest-high, Des Moines)
367-4b Dick Phelan (fielding, hands chest-high, Des Moine)
367-5 Dick Phelan (fielding, hands chin-high)

368-1a Bill Phillips (hands on knees, Brooklyn)

368-1b Bill Phillips (hands on knees, Kansas City)

368-2a Bill Phillips (fielding, hands head-high, Brooklyn)
368-2b Bill Phillips (fielding, hands head-high, Kansas City)
368-3 Bill Phillips (stooping to left)
368-4a Bill Phillips (batting, Brooklyn)
368-4b Bill Phillips (batting, Kansas City)

369-1a Jack Pickett (bat over right shoulder, Kansas Citys)
369-1b Jack Pickett (bat over right shoulder, St. Pauls)

369-1d Jack Pickett (bat over right shoulder, Philadelphias)
369-2 Jack Pickett (bat in hand at side)

369-3a Jack Pickett (fielding, bending to left, hands neck-high, Kansas City)
369-3b Jack Pickett (fielding, bending to left, hands neck-high, St. Pauls)
369-4 Jack Pickett (fielding, bending to left, hands thigh-high)
369-5 Jack Pickett (ball in right hand on ground by left foot)
369-6 Jack Pickett (fielding grounder by feet)

369-7b Jack Pickett (throwing, St. Pauls)

369-7c Jack Pickett (throwing, Philadelphias)

369-8 Jack Pickett (bending to left, side view)

370-1 George Pinkney (fielding, hands chest high)
370-2 George Pinkney (hands on knees)
370-3a George Pinkney (bat at ready position, nearly vertical, Brooklyn)
370-3b George Pinkney (bat at ready position, nearly vertical, Brooklyns)
370-4 George Pinkney (fielding, hands ankle high)
370-5 George Pinkney (bat over right shoulder)

371-1 Tom Poorman (sliding)
371-2a Tom Poorman (fielding, ankle-high, Athletics)
371-2b Tom Poorman (fielding, ankle-high, Milwaukees)
371-3a Tom Poorman (throwing, Athletics)

371-3b Tom Poorman (throwing, Milwaukees)

371-4a Tom Poorman (fielding, hands chest-high, Athletics)
371-4b Tom Porrman (Poorman) (fielding, hands chest-high, Milwaukees)
372-1 Henry Porter (tagging player)
372-2 Henry Porter (pitching, hands chest-high)

372-3 Henry Porter (batting)
372-4a Henry Porter (throwing, right hand neck high, Brooklyn)
372-4b Henry Porter (throwing, right hand neck high, Kansas City)
372-5 Henry Porter (throwing, right hand cap high)
372-6 Henry Porter (fielding, hands head-high)

373-1a Jim Powell (bat at ready position, looking at camera, Mgr.)
373-1b Jim Powell (bat at ready position, looking at camera, 1st B.)
373-2a Jim Powell (swinging bat, looking at camera, Mgr.)
373-2b Jim Powell (swinging bat, looking at camera, 1st B.)
373-3 Jim Powell (fielding, hands on knees, ball approaching)
373-4 Jim Powell (fielding, looking at ball head high)
373-5a Jim Powell (fielding, looking at ball above head, Mgr.)
373-5b Jim Powell (fielding, looking at ball above head, 1st B.)
373.5 Thomas Powers (Power) (batting)

374-1a Blondie Purcell (sliding, Baltimores)

374-1b Blondie Purcell (sliding, Athletics)
374-2a Blondie Purcell (fielding, stretching up to left, Baltimores)
374-2b Blondie Purcell (fielding, stretching up to left, Athletics)
374-3 Blondie Purcell (fielding, stretching up to right)
374-4 Blondie Purcell (throwing)
374-5 Blondie Purcell (batting)
375-1 Tom Quinn (hands on knees, Baltimore)

375-2 Tom Quinn (batting, Baltimore)
375-3 Tom Quinn (arms at sides, Baltimore)
375-4 Tom Quinn (throwing, Baltimore)

375-5 Tom Quinn (fielding, hands at waist, Baltimore)
376-1 Joe Quinn (sliding, Bostons)
376-2a Joe Quinn (ball in hands by chin, Boston)

376-2b Joe Quinn (ball in hands by chin, Bostons)

376-4 Joe Quinn (right hand extended forward head-high, Des Moines)
377-1a Old Hoss Radbourn (hands on hips, bat on left, P., Boston)
377-1b Old Hoss Radbourn (hands on hips. bat on left, Pitcher, Boston)
377-1c Old Hoss Radbourn (hands on hips, bat on left, Boston (PL))
377-2a Old Hoss Radbourn (tagging player, P.)

377-2b Old Hoss Radbourn (tagging player, Pitcher)
377-3a Old Hoss Radbourn (batting, P., Boston)

377-3b Old Hoss Radbourn (batting, Pitcher, Boston)
377-3c Old Hoss Radbourn (batting, Bostons)

377-4a Old Hoss Radbourn (hands clasped at waist, no space visible between hands and belt, P.)
377-4b Old Hoss Radbourn (hands clasped at waist, no space visible between hands and belt, Pitcher)
377-5a Old Hoss Radbourn (hands clasped at waist, white uniform visible between hands and belt, P.)
377-5b Old Hoss Radbourn (hands clasped at waist, white uniform visible between hands and belt, Pitcher)
377-6a Old Hoss Radbourn (portrait, P.)

377-6b Old Hoss Radbourn (portrait, Pitcher)

378-1 Shorty Radford (batting, looking at camera)
378-2a Shorty Radford (batting, looking at ball, Brooklyns)
378-2b Shorty Radford (batting, looking at ball, Clevelands)
378-3a Shorty Radford (leaning to left, ball in right hand by right knee, Brooklyns)
378-3b Shorty Radford (leaning to left, ball in right hand by right knee, Clevelands)
378-4 Shorty Radford (throwing)
378-5a Shorty Radford (fielding, hands above head, Brooklyns)
378-5b Shorty Radford (fielding, hands above head, Clevelands)
379-1a Toad Ramsey (bat over right shoulder, Louisville)
379-1b Toad Ramsey (bat over right shoulder, Louisvills)
379-2a Toad Ramsey (bat nearly vertical, Ramsey on front)
379-2b Toad Ramsey (bat nearly vertical, Thomas Rmasey on front)
379-3a Toad Ramsey (pitching, Louisvills)

379-3b Toad Ramsey (pitching, Louisville)

380-1 Rehse (batting)
380-2 Rehse (bat in hand at side)
380-3 Rehse (fielding, hands head-high)

380-4 Rehse (fielding, hands thigh-high)

380-5 Rehse (pitching)
381-1 Big John Reilly (batting, Cincinnati)

381-2a Big John Reilly (fielding, 1st B., Cincinnati)

381-2b Big John Reilly (fielding, 1 B., Cincinnati)

381-2c Big John Reilly (fielding, Cincinnatti)

381-2d Big John Reilly (fielding, Cincinnatis)

381-3a Big John Reilly (throwing, Cincinnati)

381-3b Big John Reilly (throwing, Cincinnatti)

381-3c Big John Reilly (throwing, Cincinnatis)

382-1a Princeton Charlie Reilly (hands on thighs, St. Pauls)
382-1b Princeton Charlie Riley (Reilly) (hands on thighs, St. Paul)
382-2 Princeton Charlie Reilly (fielding, hands waist-high, St. Pauls)
382-3 Princeton Charlie Reilly (throwing, St. Pauls)
382-4 Princeton Charlie Reilly (batting, St. Pauls)
383 Charlie Reynolds (throwing)
383-1 Charlie Reynolds (hands on thighs)

383-2 Charlie Reynolds (arms at sides)
383-3 Charlie Reynolds (bat in hand at side)

384-1aHardy Richardson (fielding, hands head high, Detroits)
384-1cHardy Richardson (fielding, hands head high, Bostons)
384-2aHardy Richardson (bat over right shoulder, Detroits)
384-2bHardy Richardson (bat over right shoulder, Bostons)
384-3 Hardy Richardson (bat nearly horizontal, Detroits)
385-1aDanny Richardson (bat over right shoulder, Danny Richardson on front, N.Y's)
385-1bDanny Richardson (bat over right shoulder, New Yorks)
385-1cDanny Richardson (bat over right shoulder, Richardson on front, N.Y's)
385-2aDanny Richardson (moving to left, arms at sides, Danny Richardson on front, N.Y's)
385-2bDanny Richardson (moving to left, arms at sides, New Yorks)
385-2dDanny Richardson (moving to left, arms at sides, Richardson on front, N.Y's)
385-3aDanny Richardson (bat at ready position at 45 degrees, N.Y's)
385-3bDanny Richardson (bat at ready position at 45 degrees, New Yorks)
385-4aDanny Richardson (throwing, N.Y's)
385-4bDanny Richardson (throwing, New Yorks)
385-5aDanny Richardson (fielding grounder, N.Y's)
385-5bDanny Richardson (fielding grounder, New Yorks)
386-1 Charles Ripslager (Reipschlager) (dotted tie)
387-1 John Roach (pitching, hands by chin)
387-2 John Roach (bat at ready position, standing upright)
387-3 John Roach (bat in hand at side)
387-4 John Roach (leaning to left, hands on thighs)
387-5 John Roach (pitching, left hand chest high at back)
387-6 John Roach (bat at ready position, leaning forward)
388-1 Uncle Robbie Robinson (batting, Athletics)
388-2aUncle Robbie Robinson (fielding, hands above head, no comma after C., Athletics)
388-2bUncle Robbie Robinson (fielding, hands above head, comma after C., Athletics)
388-3 Uncle Robbie Robinson (fielding, hands neck-high, Athletics)
388-4 Uncle Robbie Robinson (fielding, hands thigh-high, Athletics)
388-5 Uncle Robbie Robinson (throwing, Athletics)
389-1 M.C. Robinson (batting, Minneapolis)
389-2 M.C. Robinson (tagging player, Minneapolis)
389-3 M.C. Robinson (fielding grounder, Minneapolis)
389-4 M.C. Robinson (throwing, right hand head high, Minneapolis)
389-5 M.C. Robinson (fielding, hands chest-high, Minneapolis)
389-6 M.C. Robinson (ball in hands waist-high, Minneapolis)
390-1aYank Robinson (batting, St. Louis Browns)
390-1bYank Robinson (batting, St. Louis)
390-2aYank Robinson (fielding grounder, St. Louis Browns)
390-2bYank Robinson (fielding grounder, St. L. Brow)
390-3 Yank Robinson (throwing, right hand neck high, St. Louis)
390-4 Yank Robinson (sliding, St. Louis)
390-5 Yank Robinson (fielding, hands shoulder high, St. Louis)
390-6 Yank Robinson (Brown's Champions)
391-1aGeorge Rooks (bat in hand at side, Chicago Maroons)

391-1bGeorge Rooks (bat in hand at side, Detroits)
391-2 George Rooks (bat over left shoulder)
391-3 George Rooks (fielding, hands chin-high)
391-4 George Rooks (fielding, hands head-high)
391-5 George Rooks (throwing)
392-1 Chief Roseman (dotted tie)
393-1 Dave Rowe (portrait, Kansas City)
393-2aDave Rowe (throwing, Kansas City)
393-2bDave Rowe (throwing, Mgr. & C.F., Denvers)
393-2cDave Rowe (throwing, Mg'r., Denvers)
393-3 Dave Rowe (fielding, hands shoulder-high, Kansas City)
393-4 Dave Rowe (fielding, hands thigh-high, Kansas City)
393-5 Dave Rowe (fielding grounder, Kansas City)
393-6 Dave Rowe (batting, Kansas City)
394-1aJack Rowe (batting, looking at camera, no comma after S.S., Detroits)
394-1cJack Rowe (batting, looking at camera, comma after S.S., Detroits)
394-2 Jack Rowe (bat in hand at side, Detroits)
394-3 Jack Rowe (batting, looking at approaching ball, Detroits)
395-1aAmos Rusie (pitching, hands at neck, Indianapolis)
395-1bAmos Rusie (pitching, hands at neck, New Yorks (N.L.))
395-2 Amos Rusie (pitching, right hand thigh high)
395-3aAmos Rusie (pitching, right hand head high at side, name correct)
395-3bAmos Russie (Rusie) (pitching, right hand head-high at side, name incorrect)
395-4aAmos Rusie (pitching, right hand forward chin-high, Indianapolis)
395-4bAmos Rusie (pitching, right hand forward chin-high, New Yorks (N.L.))
395-5 Amos Rusie (batting)
396-1aJimmy Ryan (stooping for catch knee high, Chicago)
396-1bJimmy Ryan (stooping for catch knee high, Chicago's)
396-1cJimmy Ryan (stooping for catch knee high, Chicago (PL))
396-2aJimmy Ryan (ball in hands at neck, Ryan on front)
396-2bJimmy Ryan (ball in hands at neck, J. Ryan on front)
396-3 Jimmy Ryan (throwing, left hand head high)
396-4aJimmy Ryan (bat in hand at side, Chicago)
396-4bJimmy Ryan (bat in hand at side, Chicagos (PL))
396-5aJimmy Ryan (fielding, hands head-high, Ryan on front)
396-5bJimmy Ryan (fielding, hands head-high, J. Ryan on front)
396-6 Jimmy Ryan (batting)
397-1 Doc Sage (stooping for low ball)
397-2 Doc Sage (bat on right shoulder, looking at camera)
397-3 Doc Sage (batting, looking at approaching ball)
397-4aDoc Sage, Bill Van Dyke (Toledos)
397-4bDoc Sage, Bill Van Dyke (Des Moines)
398-1 Ben Sanders (pitching)
398-2aBen Sanders (throwing, Phila)
398-2bBen Sanders (throwing, Philadelphias)
398-3aBen Sanders (fielding, Phila)
398-3bBen Sanders (fielding, Philadelphias)
398-3dBen Sanders (fielding, Philadelphias (PL))
398-4 Ben Sanders (batting)
399-1 Frank Scheibeck (fielding, hands waist high)
399-2 Frank Scheibeck (fielding, hands above head)
399-3 Frank Scheibeck (fielding ball at feet)
399-4 Frank Scheibeck (batting)
400-1 Al Schellhase (Schellhasse) (fielding, hands above head)

400-2 Al Schellhase (Schellhasse) (fielding, ball by hands chest-high)
400-3 Al Schellhase (Schellhasse) (fielding, hands thigh-high, left leg straight)
400-4 Al Schellhase (Schellhasse) (fielding, hands thigh-high, left leg bent)
400-5 Al Schellhase (Schellhasse) (batting)

401-1 William Schenkel (batting)
401-2 William Schenkel (ball in hands chest high)
401-3a William Schenkel (fielding, hands cupped chest-high, name correct)
401-3b William Schenkle (Schenkel) (fielding, hands cupped chest-high, name incorrect)

401-4 William Schenkle (Schenkel) (left hand chin-high, right arm at side)
402-1a Schildknecht (batting, Milwa'k's)

402-1b Schildknecht (batting, Milwaukee)

402-1c Schildknecht (batting, Milwaukees)

402-1d Schildknecht (batting, Des Moines)

402-2 Schildknecht (fielding, hands thigh-high)

402-3 Schildknecht (fielding, ball in hands chest high)

403-1 Gus Schmelz (head and shoulder portrait)

403-2a Gus Schmelz (full length, street clothes, G.H. Schmelz on front)
403-2b Gus Schmelz (full length, street clothes, H. Schmelz on front)
403-2c Gus Schmelz (full length, street clothes, Schmelz on front)
403-2d Gus Schmelz (full length, street clothes, Cincinnatis)
404-1a Jumbo Schoeneck (batting, Chicago Maroons)
404-1b Jumbo Schoeneck (batting, Indianapoli)

404-1c Jumbo Schoeneck (batting, Indianapolis)

404-1d Jumbo Schoeneck (batting, Indianap's)

404-2 Jumbo Schoeneck (hands on knees)

404-3a Jumbo Schoeneck (fielding grounder, Chicago Maroons)
404-3b Jumbo Schoeneck (fielding grounder, Indianapoli)
404-3c Jumbo Schoeneck (fielding grounder, Indianapolis)
404-3d Jumbo Schoeneck (fielding grounder, Indianap's)
404-4 Jumbo Schoeneck (fielding, hands chin high)
404-5a Jumbo Schoeneck (ball in left hand head high, Chicago Maroons)
404-5b Jumbo Schoeneck (ball in left hand head high, Indianapolis)
404-5c Jumbo Schoeneck (ball in left hand head high, Indianap's)
405-1a Pop Schriver (bat over right shoulder, Phila)
405-1b Pop Schriver (bat over right shoulder, Philadelphias)
405-2 Pop Schriver (bat held horizontally)

405-3 Pop Schriver (fielding, hands ankle-high)

405-4a Pop Schriver (fielding, hands chest-high, Phila)
405-4b Pop Schriver (fielding, hands chest-high, Philadelphias)
405-5a Pop Schriver (throwing, Phila)

405-5b Pop Schriver (throwing, Philadelphias)

405-5c Pop Schriver (throwing, Phila (N.L.)

406-1a Emmett Seery (fielding, hands above head, L.F.)
406-1b Emmett Seery (fielding, hands above head, Left Field)
406-2a Emmett Seery (ball in hands at neck, no comma after L.F.)
406-2b Emmett Seery (ball in hands at neck. Left Field)
406-2c Emmett Seery (ball in hands at neck comma after L.F.)
406-3a Emmett Seery (arms folded, no comma after L.F.)
406-3b Emmett Seery (arms folded, Left Field)

406-3c Emmett Seery (arms folded, comma after L.F.)
406-4a Emmett Seery (batting, no comma after L.F.)
406-4b Emmett Seery (batting, comma after L.F.)

407-1a Billy Serad (batting, Cincinnati)
407-1b Billy Serad (batting, Toronto)
407-2 Billy Serad (ball in hands chin-high)

407-3a Billy Serad (ball in right hand neck-high, Cincinnati)
407-3b Billy Serad (ball in right hand neck-high Toronto)
408-1a Ed Seward (ball in hands neck-high, no comma after P.)
408-1c Ed Seward (ball in hands neck-high, comma after P.)
408-2a Ed Seward (pitching, right hand head-high at back, no comma after P.)
408-2b Ed Seward (pitching, right hand head-high at back, comma after P.)
408-3a Ed Seward (pitching, right hand forward head-high, no comma after P.)
408-3b Ed Seward (pitching, right hand forward head-high, comma after P.)
409-1 Orator Shafer (Shaffer) (arms folded, Des Moines)
409-2 Orator Shafer (Shaffer) (throwing, right hand head-high, Des Moines)
409-3 Orator Shafer (Shaffer) (bat in left hand at side, Des Moines)
409-4 Orator Shafer (Shaffer) (bat at ready position, looking at camera, Des Moines)

410-1 Taylor Shafer (Shaffer) (bending to right, hands over base, St. Louis)
410-2 Taylor Shafer (Shaffer) (throwing, St. Paul)
410-3 Taylor Shafer (Shaffer) (ball in hands by left shoulder, St. Paul)
411-1a Daniel Shannon (batting, name correct)

411-1b Daniel Hannon (Shannon) (batting, name incorrect)
411-2a Daniel Shannon (ball in hands at chest, leaning towards player sliding, Philadelphias (PL))
411-2b Daniel Shannon (ball in hands at chest, leaning towards player sliding, Louisvilles)

411-3 Daniel Shannon (fielding, hands at chest)

411-4 Daniel Shannon (sliding)
411-5 Daniel Shannon (bat in hand at side)

412-1a William Sharsig (full length, in bowler hat, Mg'r.)
412-1b William Sharsig (full length, in bowler hat, Manager)
413-1a Samuel Shaw (pitching, hands above waist, Baltimores)
413-1b Samuel Shaw (pitching, hands above waist, Newarks)
413-2a Samuel Shaw (pitching, right arm extended forward, Baltimores)
413-2b Samuel Shaw (pitching, right arm extended forward, Newarks)
413-3 Samuel Shaw (batting, Baltimores)

414-1 John Shaw (batting, Minneapolis)
414-2 John Shaw (stooping to left, Minneapolis)

414-3 John Shaw (sliding, Minneapolis)
414-4 John Shaw (fielding hands neck-high, Minneapolis)
414-5 John Shaw (throwing, Minneapolis)

415-1 Bill Shindle (fielding grounder)
415-2 Bill Shindle (fielding, hands above head)

415-3a Bill Shindle (batting, name correct)

415-3b Bill Shindel (batting, name incorrect)

415-4a Bill Shindle (hands on knees, name correct, Baltimores)
415-4b Bill Shindel (Shindle) (hands on knees, name incorrect, Baltimores)
415-4c Bill Shindle (hands on knees, Philadelphias)
415-5a Bill Shindle (throwing, 3rd B.)
415-5b Bill Shindle (throwing, 3d B., Baltimores)

415-5c Bill Shindle (throwing, 3d B., Philadelphias)
416-1a George Schoch (Shoch) (fielding grounder, R.F., Washington)

416-1b George Shoch (fielding grounder, Right Field)

416-1d George Shoch (fielding grounder, R.F., Washingtons)

416-2a George Shoch (fielding, hands head-high, Right Field)

416-2b George Schoch (Shoch) (fielding, hands head-high, G. Schoch on front)

416-2c George Shoch (fielding, hands head-high, Washingtons)

416-2d George Schoch (Shoch) (fielding, hands head-high, Schoch on front)

416-3a George Schoch (Shoch) (batting, Schoch on front)

416-3b George Shoch (batting, Right Field)

416-3c George Shoch (batting, G. Schoch on front)

416-4 Honest John Gaffney, George Shoch (Shoch batting with Gaffney behind him)

417-1a Otto Shomberg (Schomberg) (fielding, hands head-high, 1st B.)

417-1b Otto Shomberg (Schomberg) (fielding, hands head-high, 1st Base)

417-2a Otto Shomberg (Schomberg) (throwing, 1st B.)

417-2b Otto Shomberg (Schomberg) (throwing, 1st Base)

417-3a Otto Shomberg (Schomberg) (fielding, hands waist-high, 1st B.)

417-3b Otto Shomberg (Schomberg) (fielding, hands waist-high, 1st Base)

418-1a Lev Shreve (batting, name correct)

418-1b Lev Chreve (Shreve) (batting, name incorrect)

418-2a Lev Shreve (pitching, ball in hands at chest, comma after P.)

418-2b Lev Shreve (pitching, ball in hands at chest, no comma after P.)

418-3a Lev Shreve (pitching, right hand above head, facing front, name correct)

418-3b Lev Chreve (Shreve) (pitching, right hand above head, facing front, name incorrect)

418-4a Lev Shreve (pitching, right hand level with cap, looking at camera, name correct)

418-4b Lev Shreve (pitching, right hand level with cap, looking at camera, name incorrect)

418-5a Lev Shreve (pitching, right hand level with eyes, looking at camera, comma after P.)

418-5b Lev Shreve (pitching, right hand level with eyes, looking at camera, no comma after P.)

418-6a Lev Shreve (pitching, right hand level with chin, looking to left, comma after P., Indianapolis)

418-6b Lev Shreve (pitching, right hand level with chin, looking to left, no comma after P., Indianapolis)

418-6c Lev Shreve (pitching, right hand level with chin, looking to left, Ind'p'l's)

418-7a Lev Shreve (pitching, right hand at rear level with cap, right profile, name correct)

418-7b Lev Shreve (pitching, right hand at rear level with cap, right profile, name incorrect)

419-1 Ed Silch (batting, looking at camera)

419-2 Ed Silch (batting, looking at ball)

419-3a Ed Silch (fielding, hands head-high, Denvers)

419-3b Ed Silch (fielding, hands head-high, Brooklyns)

419-4a Ed Silch (ball in hands above head, Brooklyns)

419-4b Ed Silch (ball in hands above head, Denvers)

419-5a Ed Silch (throwing, Brooklyns)

419-5b Ed Silch (throwing, Denvers)

420-1a Mike Slattery (batting, N.Y.)

420-1b Mike Slattery (batting, New Yorks)

420-2a Mike Slattery (fielding, hands chest-high, N.Y.)

420-2b Mike Slattery (fielding, hands chest-high, New York)

420-3 Mike Slattery (fielding, left hand extended head-high)

420-4a Mike Slattery (ready to pitch, N.Y.)

420-4b Mike Slattery (ready to pitch, New Yorks)

420-4c Mike Slattery (ready to pitch, New York PL)

420-5a Mike Slattery (right hand across body by left thigh, N.Y.)

420-5b Mike Slattery (right hand across body by left thigh, New Yorks)

421-1 Skyrocket Smith (batting, ball about thigh high, Louisville)

421-2 Skyrocket Smith (ball in hands head-high on left, Louisville)

421-3 Skyrocket Smith (catching, stooping, hands by right knee, Louisville)

421-4 Skyrocket Smith (stooping to field grounder by right foot, Louisville)

422-1 Phenomenal Smith (portrait, no team designation)

422-2a Phenomenal Smith (pitching, hands above waist, Baltimores)

422-2b Phenomenal Smith (pitching, hands above waist, Athletics)

422-3a Phenomenal Smith (pitching, hands by right shoulder, Baltimores)

422-3b Phenomenal Smith (pitching, hands by right shoulder, Athletics)

422-4a Phenomenal Smith (batting, Baltimores)

422-4b Phenomenal Smith (batting, Athleticss)

422-5a Phenomenal Smith (pitching, left hand neck-high, both ears visible, Baltimores)

422-5b Phenomenal Smith (pitching, left hand neck-high, both ears visible, Athletics)

422-6 Phenomenal Smith (pitching, left hand shoulder-high, left ear only visible, Baltimores)

423-1 Mike Smith (batting, looking at approaching ball, Cincinnati)

423-2a Mike Smith (pitching, hands at chest, E. Smith on front, Cincinnati)

423-2b Mike Smith (pitching, hands at chest, Smith on front, Cincinnati)

423-2c Mike Smith (pitching, hands at chest, Cincinnatti)

423-3a Mike Smith (pitching, left hand chest-high at rear, looking to left, Cincinnatis)

423-3b Mike Smith (pitching, left hand chest-high at rear, looking to left, Cincinnati)

423-3c Mike Smith (pitching, left hand chest-high at rear, looking to left, Cincinnatti)

423-4a Mike Smith (pitching, left hand head-high looking at camera, right hand by right thigh, Cincinnatis)

423-4b Mike Smith (pitching, left hand head-high, looking at camera, right hand by right thigh, Cincinnati)

423-5 Mike Smith (pitching, left hand head-high, glancing to left, right arm across waist, Cincinnati)

424-1 Sam Smith (pitching, hands at throat, ball visible between palms, Des Moines)

424-2 Sam Smith (pitching, ball in right hand by face, Des Moines)

424-3a Sam Smith (fielding grounder, no comma after P., Des Moines)

424-3b Sam Smith (fielding grounder, comma after P., Des Moines)

424-4 Sam Smith (pitching, hands at throat, ball not visible, Des Moines)

425-1a Germany Smith (hands on knees, Brooklyn)

425-1c Germany Smith (hands on knees, Brooklyn's)

425-2a Germany Smith (batting, looking at camera, Smith on front, Brooklyns)

425-2b Germany Smith (batting, looking at camera, G. Smith on front, Brooklyns)

425-2c Germany Smith (batting, looking at camera, Geo. Smith on front, Brooklyns)

425-3a Germany Smith (batting, looking at ball, comma after S.S., Brooklyns)

425-3b Germany Smith (batting, looking at ball, no comma after S.S., Brooklyns)

425-4a Germany Smith (fielding grounder, Smith on front, Brooklyn's)

425-4b Germany Smith (fielding grounder, Geo. Smith on front, Brooklyns)

425-5a Germany Smith (throwing, Smith on front, Brooklyns)

425-5b Germany Smith (throwing, G. Smith on front, Brooklyns)

426-1a Pap Smith (fielding grounder with right hand, S.S., Pittsburg)

426-1b Pap Smith (fielding grounder with right hand, Short Stop, Pittsburg)
426-1c Pap Smith (fielding grounder with right hand, Pittsburgs)
426-1d Pap Smith (fielding grounder with right hand, Bostons)
426-2a Pap Smith (batting, S.S., Pittsburg)

426-2b Pap Smith (batting, Short Stop, Pittsburg)

426-2c Pap Smith (batting, S.S., Pittsburgs)

426-3a Pap Smith (hands on knees, S.S., Pittsburg)
426-3b Pap Smith (hands on knees, Short Stop, Pittsburg)
426-3c Pap Smith (hands on knees, Pittsburgh)

426-3d Pap Smith (hands on knees, Pittsburgs)

426-4a Pap Smith (fielding grounder with both hands, S.S., Pittsburg)
426-4b Pap Smith (fielding grounder with both hands, Short Stop, Pittsburg)
426-4c Pap Smith (fielding grounder hands, Pittsburgh)
427-1a Nick Smith (fielding, hands head-high, feet together, St. Josephs)
427-1b Nick Smith (fielding, hands head-high, feet together, St. Joe)
427-2a Nick Smith (fielding, hands head-high, feet apart, St. Josephs)
427-2b Nick Smith (fielding, hands head-high, feet apart, St. Joe)
427-3 Nick Smith (batting, looking at camera, St. Josephs)
427-4a Nick Smith (batting, looking down at bat, St. Josephs)
427-4b Nick Smith (batting, looking down at bat, St. Joe)
427-5 Nick Smith (fielding, hands at right knee, St. Josephs)
428-1 P.T. Somers (batting)
428-2 P.T. Somers (arms folded)
428-3 P.T. Somers (pitching, looking to left)

428-4 P.T. Somers (pitching, looking to right)

429-1a Joe Sommer (sliding, name correct)

429-1b Joe Sommers (Sommer) (sliding, name incorrect, Baltimores)
429-2a Joe Sommer (fielding grounder, name correct)
429-2b Joe Sommers (Sommer) (fielding grounder, name incorrect, Baltimores)

429-3 Joe Sommers (Sommer) (throwing, Baltimores)
429-4 Joe Sommers (Sommer) (fielding, hands above head, Baltimores)
429-5a Joe Sommer (batting, name correct)

429-5b Joe Sommers (Sommer) (batting, incorrect, Baltimores)
430-1 Pete Sommers (batting, Chicago's)

430-2a Pete Sommers (fielding, ball by hands chest-high, Chicago's)
430-2b Pete Sommers (fielding, ball by hands chest-high, New Yorks (NL))
430-3 Pete Sommers (fielding, hands head-high, Chicago's)
430-4 Pete Sommers (fielding, right hand above head, Chicagos)
430-5 Pete Sommers (fielding, arms extended left at waist, Chicago's)
430-6 Pete Sommers (portrait, Chicagos)

431-1a Little Bill Sowders (in light uniform, pitching, hands at throat, Sowders on front, Boston)
431-1b Little Bill Sowders (in light uniform, pitching, hands at throat, Bostons)
431-1c Little Bill Sowders (in light uniform, pitching, hands at throat, W. Sowders on front, Boston)
431-2a Little Bill Sowders (in light uniform, pitching, ball in right hand chin-high, left elbow held up shoulder-high, Bostons)
431-2b Little Bill Sowders (in light uniform, pitching, ball in right hand chin-high, left elbow held up shoulder-high, Boston)
431-3a Little Bill Sowders (in light uniform, pitching, ball in right hand cap-high, left hand waist-high, Bostons)

431-3b Little Bill Sowders (in light uniform, pitching, ball in right hand cap-high, left hand waist-high, Boston)
431-4a Little Bill Sowders (in light uniform, pitching, right hand forward head-high, ball just released, Sowders on front, Boston)

431-4b Little Bill Souders (Sowders) (in light uniform, pitching, right hand forward head high, ball just released, Bostons)
431-4c Little Bill Sowders (in light uniform, pitching, right hand forward head-high, ball just released, W. Sowders on front, Bostons)

431 5a Little Bill Sowders (in light uniform, hands at sides, ball at top right, Bostons)
431-5b Little Bill Sowders (in light uniform, hands at sides, ball at top right, Boston)
431-6a Little Bill Sowders (in light uniform, bat at ready by head, Bostons)
431-6b Little Bill Sowders (in light uniform, bat at ready position by head, Boston)
431-7a Little Bill Sowders (in light uniform, batting, ball cap-high, Bostons)
431-7b Little Bill Sowders (in light uniform, batting, ball cap-high, Boston)
432-1 John Sowders (in dark uniform, pitching, hands at chest, St. Pauls)
432-2a John Sowders (in dark uniform, fielding, ball in right hand thigh-high, St. Paul)
432-2b John Sowders (in dark uniform, fielding, ball in right hand thigh-high, St. Pauls)

432-3 John Sowders (in dark uniform, pitching, ball in left hand chin-high, Kansas Citys)

432-4a John Sowders (in dark uniform, batting, Kansas City)
432-4b John Sowders (in dark uniform, batting, Kansas Citys)
433-1 Charlie Sprague (batting, light cap)

433-2 Charlie Sprague (batting, dark cap)

433-3 Charlie Sprague (bat at side in hand)

433-4 Charlie Sprague (pitching, hands at waist, light cap)
433-5 Charlie Sprague (pitching, hands at waist, dark cap)
433-6 Charlie Sprague (pitching, left hand head high, light cap)
433-7a Charlie Sprague (pitching, left hand head high, no cap, Sprague on front, Chicago)

433-7b Charlie Sprague (pitching, left hand head high, no cap, C.W. Sprague on front, Chicago)

433-7c Charlie Sprague (pitching, left hand head high, no cap, Sprague on front, Clevelands)

433-7d Charlie Sprague (pitching, left hand head high, no cap, C.W.Sprague on front, Clevelands)
433-8 Charlie Sprague (pitching, left hand extended forward, no cap)
434-1 Ed Sproat (bat at ready position on shoulder)
434-2 Ed Sproat (batting, ball thigh-high)

434-3 Ed Sproat (pitching, hands at chin)

434-4 Ed Sproat (pitching, right hand head-high)

434-5 Ed Sproat (pitching, right hand waist-high)

435-1a Harry Staley (pitching, hands at chest. St. Louis Whites)
435-1b Harry Staley (pitching, hands at chest, Pittsburgs)
435-1c Harry Staley (pitching, hands at chest, Pittsburghs)
435-2a Harry Staley (pitching, right hand neck high, right heel off ground, St. Louis Whites)
435-2b Harry Staley (pitching, right hand neck high, right heel off ground, Pittsburgs)

435-2c Harry Staley (pitching, right hand neck high, right heel off ground, St. Louis Whites)

435-3 Harry Staley (pitching, right hand chest high, both heels on ground)
435-4a Harry Staley (bat at ready, looking at camera, name correct)
435-4b Harry Stoley (Staley) (bat at ready, looking at camera, name incorrect)

435-5 Harry Staley (batting, ball by horizontal bat)
436-1a Dan Stearns (fielding, hands neck-high, Kansas City)
436-1b Dan Stearns (fielding, hands neck-high, Kansas Citys)
436-2a Dan Stearns (fielding, hands thigh-high, name correct)
436-2b Dan Tearns (Stearns) (fielding, hands thigh-high, name incorrect)
436-3 Dan Stearns (throwing, right hand thigh high)
436-4 Dan Stearns (batting)
437-1a Cannonball Stemmeyer (pitching, hands at chest, name correct)
437-1b Cannonball Stemmyer (Stemmeyer) (pitching, hands at chest, name incorrect)
437-2a Cannonball Stemmeyer (batting, white uniform, name correct)
437-2b Cannonball Stemmyer (Stemmeyer) (batting, white uniform, name incorrect)
437-3a Cannonball Stemmeyer (pitching, right hand head-high, white uniform, name correct)
437-3b Cannonball Stemmyer (Stemmeyer) (pitching, right hand head-high, white uniform, name incorrect)
437-4a Cannonball Stemmeyer (ball in right hand waist high, name correct)
437-4b Cannonball Stemmyer (Stemmeyer) (ball in right hand waist high, name incorrect)
437-5 Cannonball Stemmyer (Stemmeyer) (batting, dark uniform)
437-6 Cannonball Stemmyer (right hand vertically above head)
438-1 B.F. Stephens (batting)
438-2 B.F. Stephens (catching)
438-3 B.F. Stephens (ready to pitch)
439-1 John Sterling (bat in right hand, looking at camera)
439-2 John Sterling (batting, looking down at ball)
439-3 John Sterling (pitching, hands at chest)
439-4 John Sterling (pitching, right hand thigh high)
439.5 Stockwell (batting)
440-1a Harry Stovey (hands on knees, no comma after L.F.)
440-1b Harry Stovey (hands on knees, comma after L.F.)
440-2 Harry Stovey (bat in hand at side)
440-3a Harry Stovey (bat at ready position by head, no comma after L.F.)
440-3c Harry Stovey (bat at ready position by head, comma after L.F.)
440-4 Harry Stovey (bat at ready position, horizontal)
440-5a Harry Stovey (fielding, hands above head, no comma after L.F., Athletics)
440-5b Harry Stovey (fielding, hands above head, comma after L.F., Athletics)
440-5c Harry Stovey (fielding, hands above head, Bostons (PL))
440-6 Harry Stovey (fielding, hands at chest)
440-7 Harry Stovey (fielding, right hand above head)
440-8 Harry Stovey (throwing)
441-1 Scott Stratton (batting)
441-2a Scott Stratton (pitching, hands at chest Louisville)
441-2b Scott Stratton (pitching, hands at chest, Louisvilles)
441-3a Scott Stratton (pitching, right hand at side head-high, Louisville)
441-3b Scott Stratton (pitching, right hand at side head-high, Louisvilles)
441-4a Scott Stratton (pitching, right hand forward head-high, Louisville)
441-4b Scott Stratton (pitching, right hand forward head-high, Louisvilles)
441-5a Scott Stratton (underhand throw, right hand waist-high, Louisville)
441-5b Scott Stratton (underhand throw, right hand waist-high, Louisvilles)
442-1a Joe Straus (Strauss) (kneeling looking left, Omahas)
442-1b Joe Struck (Strauss) (kneeling looking left, Milwaukee)
442-2 Joe Straus (Strauss) (kneeling, looking to right)
442-3 Joe Straus (Strauss) (throwing)
442-4a Joe Straus (Strauss) (fielding, stooping, hands waist-high, Omahas)

442-4b Joe Strauss (fielding, stooping, hands waist-high, Omahas, W.A.)
442-4c Joe Straus (Strauss) (fielding, stooping, hands waist-high, Milwaukee)
442-5 Joe Straus (Strauss) (fielding, stooping, hands by right ankle)
442-6 Joe Straus (Strauss) (batting)
443-1 Cub Stricker (batting)
443-2 Cub Stricker (fielding ball by left foot)
443-3 Cub Stricker (fielding, hands above head)
444-1a Marty Sullivan (dark uniform, throwing, right hand head-high, Chicago's)
444-1b Marty Sullivan (dark uniform, throwing, right hand head-high, Chicago)
444-2a Marty Sullivan (dark uniform, fielding, hands chest-high, Chicago's)
444-2b Marty Sullivan (dark uniform, fielding, hands chest-high, Chicago)
444-2c Marty Sullivan (dark uniform, fielding, hands chest-high, Indianapolis)
444-3 Marty Sullivan (dark uniform, batting, looking at camera, Chicago's)
444-4 Marty Sullivan (dark uniform, bat in hand at side, Chicago's)
444-5a Marty Sullivan (dark uniform, batting, looking at approaching ball, Chicago's)
444-5c Marty Sullivan (dark uniform, batting, looking at approaching ball, Indianapolis)
445-1 Mike Sullivan (light shirt, bat at ready position on base, Athletics)
445-2 Mike Sullivan (light shirt, hands on knees, Athletics)
445-3 Mike Sullivan (light shirt, sliding, Athletics)
446-1a Billy Sunday (fielding, hands thigh-high, Chicago)
446-1b Billy Sunday (fielding, hands thigh-high, Pittsburgs)
446-2a Billy Sunday (batting, Chicago)
446-2b Billy Sunday (batting, Pittsburghs)
446-3a Billy Sunday (throwing, Chicago)
446-3b Billy Sunday (throwing, Pittsburgs)
446-4a Billy Sunday (fielding, hands chin-high, Chicago)
446-4b Billy Sunday (fielding, hands chin-high, Pittsburgs)
446-5a Billy Sunday (bat in hand at side, Chicago)
446-5b Billy Sunday (bat in hand at side, Pittsburghs)
447-1 Sy Sutcliffe (fielding grounder)
447-2 Sy Sutcliffe (fielding, hands neck-high)
447-3 Sy Sutcliffe (fielding, hands above waist)
447-4 Sy Sutcliffe (batting, looking at camera)
447-5 Sy Sutcliffe (batting, looking at ball)
448-1a Ezra Sutton (fielding, hands shoulder high, 3d B.)
448-1b Ezra Sutton (fielding, hands shoulder high, Third Base)
448-2a Ezra Sutton (throwing, hands chest-high, 3d B.)
448-2b Ezra Sutton (throwing, hands chest-high, Third Base)
448-3a Ezra Sutton (fielding grounder, 3d B.)
448-3b Ezra Sutton (fielding grounder, Third Base)
448-3c Ezra Sutton (fielding grounder, 2d B.)
448-4a Ezra Sutton (batting, ball above bat, 3d B.)
448-4b Ezra Sutton (batting, ball above bat, Third Base)
448-5a Ezra Sutton (bat in hand at side, 3d B.)
448-5b Ezra Sutton (bat in hand at side, Third Base)
448-5c Ezra Sutton (bat in hand at side, 2nd B.)
448-6a Ezra Sutton (throwing, right hand just releasing ball, 3d B.)
448-6b Ezra Sutton (throwing, right hand just releasing ball, Third Base)
448-7a Ezra Sutton (batting, looking down at ball, 3d B., Boston)

448-7bEzra Sutton (batting, looking down at ball, Third Base)
448-7cEzra Sutton (batting, looking down at ball, 3d B., Milwaukees)
448-7dEzra Sutton (batting, looking down at ball, 3d B. Milwaukee)
449-1aEd Swartwood (fielding, hands above head, Brooklyn)
449-1bEd Schwartwood (Swartwood) (fielding, hands above head, Des Moines)
449-2aEd Swartwood (fielding, kneeling, hands ankle-high, Brooklyn)
449-2bEd Schwartwood (Swartwood) (fielding, kneeling, hands ankle-high, Des Moines)
449-3aEd Schwartwood (Swartwood) (on ground, right hand on base)
449-4aEd Schwartwood (Swartwood) (tagging player, Des Moines)
449-4bEd Schwartwood (Swartwood) (tagging player, Hamlts)
450-1aPark Swartzel (batting, no comma after P.)
450-1bPark Swartzel (batting, comma after P.

450-2aPark Swartzel (fielding, stooping, hands cupped, Kansas City)
450-2bPark Swartzel (fielding, stooping, hands cupped, Kansas Citys)
450-3 Park Swartzel (pitching, hands by left shoulder)
450-4 Park Swartzel (pitching, ball in right hand thigh-high)
450-5 Park Swartzel (pitching, right hand by head)
450-6 Park Swartzel (in jacket, arms at sides)

451-1aPete Sweeney (hands on knees, name correct)
451-1bPete Sweeny (Sweeney) (hands on knees, name incorrect, Washington)
451-1cPete Sweeny (Sweeney) (hands on knees, name incorrect, Washingtons)
451-2aPete Sweeny (Sweeney) (batting, Washington)
451-2bPete Sweeny (Sweeney) (batting, Washingtons)
451-3aPete Sweeny (Sweeney) (fielding, hands head-high, Washington)
451-3bPete Sweeny (Sweeney) (fielding, hands head-high, Washingtons)
451-4 Pete Sweeny (Sweeney) (throwing)

451.5 Louis Sylvester (batting)
452-1aPop Tate (hands on knees, C.)
452-1bPop Tate (hands on knees, Catcher)

452-2aPop Tate (batting, C., Boston)
452-2bPop Tate (batting, Catcher)
452-2cPop Tate (batting, C., Baltimores)
452-3aPop Tate (fielding, hands chest-high, Catcher)
452-3bPop Tate (fielding, hands chest-high, E.C. Tate on front, C., Boston)
452-3cPop Tate (fielding, hands chest-high, Baltimores)
452-3ePop Tate (fielding, hands chest-high, Tate on front, C., Boston)
453-1aPatsy Tebeau (bat by head, looking at camera, Chicago)
453-1bPatsy Tebeau (bat by head, looking at camera, Clevelands)
453-2aPatsy Tebeau (batting, ball thigh-high, Chicago)
453-2bPatsy Tebeau (batting, ball thigh-high, Clevelands)
453-3aPatsy Tebeau (fielding, hands by right ankle, Tebeau on front)
453-3bPatsy Tebeau (fielding, hands by right ankle, Oliver Tebeau on front)
453-4aPatsy Tebeau (ball in right hand chest high, Chicago)
453-4bPatsy Tebeau (ball in right hand chest high, Clevelands)
453-5 Patsy Tebeau (ball in left hand knee-high)

454-1 John Tener (ball in right hand cap-high, arm bent)
454-2 John Tener (ball in right hand chin-high, arm straight)
454-3 John Tener (ball in right hand thigh-high)

454-4 John Tener (ball in hands by right shoulder)
454-5 John Tener (batting)
455-1aAdonis Terry (throwing, pivoting on right foot)

455-2aAdonis Terry (pitching, hands chest-high, P., Brooklyn)
455-2bAdonis Terry (pitching, hands chest-high, Brooklyns)
455-2cAdonis Terry (pitching, hands chest-high, Pitcher, Brooklyn)
455-3aAdonis Terry (batting, P.)
455-3cAdonis Terry (batting, Pitcher)
455-4 Adonis Terry (throwing, arms extended horizontally)
455-5 Adonis Terry (fielding, hands chest-high)

456-1 Big Sam Thompson (batting, ball chest high)
456-2 Big Sam Thompson (bat at ready position at 45 degrees)
456-3aBig Sam Thompson (arms folded, Detroits)
456-3bBig Sam Thompson (arms folded, Phil'a (NL))
456-4aBig Sam Thompson (bat in hand at side, Detroits)
456-4bBig Sam Thompson (bat in hand at side, Phila's)
456-4cBig Sam Thompson (bat in hand at side, Philadelphia)
456-4dBig Sam Thompson (bat in hand at side. Philadelphias)
456-5 Big Sam Thompson (batting, ball above head)
457-1aSilent Mike Tiernan (ball in hands above waist, R.F.)
457-1bSilent Mike Tiernan (ball in hands above waist, C.F.)
457-2 Silent Mike Tiernan (fielding, hands chest high)
457-3 Silent Mike Tiernan (fielding grounder)

457-4aSilent Mike Tiernan (throwing, left hand chin-high, R.F.)
457-4bSilent Mike Tiernan (throwing, left hand chin-high, C.F.)
457-5aSilent Mike Tiernan (sliding, R.F.)

457-5bSilent Mike Tiernan (sliding, C.F.)

457-6aSilent Mike Tiernan (batting, N.Y's)

457-6bSilent Mike Tiernan (batting, New Yorks)

458-1 Cannonball Titcomb (batting)
458-2aCannonball Titcomb (bat in hand at side, N.Y.)
458-2bCannonball Titcomb (bat in hand at side, New Yorks)
458-3 Cannonball Titcomb (pitching, looking front)
458-4 Cannonball Titcomb (pitching, right profile)
458-5 Cannonball Titcomb (pitching, right arm across body, hand at thigh)
459-1 Buster Tomney (batting)
459-2 Buster Tomney (fielding, hands by right foot)
459-3 Buster Tomney (fielding, hands above waist)
459-4 Buster Tomney (fielding, hands above head)
460-1 Stephen Toole (pitching, left hand extended chin-high)
460-2 Stephen Toole (pitching, hands shoulder high)
460-3aStephen Toole (pitching, ball in left hand above head, Brooklyn)
460-3bStephen Toole (pitching, ball in left hand above head, Rochesters)
460-4aStephen Toole (batting, Brooklyn)

460-4bStephen Toole (batting, Rochesters)

460-5 Stephen Toole (pitching, hands at chest)

461-1 Sleepy Townsend (bat at ready position behind head)
461-2aSleepy Townsend (bat at ready position, nearly horizontal, no comma after C.)

461-2bSleepy Townsend (bat at ready position, nearly horizontal, comma after C.)
461-3aSleepy Townsend (fielding, hands chest high, no comma after C.)
461-3bSleepy Townsend (fielding, hands chest high, comma after C.)
462-1 Bill Traffley (fielding, hands above head)
462-2 Bill Traffley (fielding, hands chest-high)

462-3 Bill Traffley (hands on thighs)

495-4 Pat Whitaker (pitching, right hand forward neck-high)

496-1 Deacon White (batting, looking at camera, Detroits)

496-2 Deacon White (batting looking down at ball, Detroits)

496-3 Deacon White (fielding, hands waist-high, Detroits)

496-4 Deacon White (fielding, hands neck-high, Detroits)

496-5a Deacon White (fielding, hands above head, Detroits)

496-5b Deacon White (fielding, hands above head, Pittsburghs)

496-6a Deacon White (throwing, Detroits)

496-6b Deacon White (throwing, Pittsburghs)

496-7 Deacon White (fielding grounder, hands together by left foot, Detroits)

496-8 Deacon White (fielding grounder with right hand, Detroits)

497-1 Bill White (batting, Louisville)

497-2 Bill White (stooping, ball in left hand on grass, Louisville)

497-3 Bill White (fielding ground ball, Louisville)

497-4 Bill White (throwing, Louisville)

497-5 Bill White (fielding, hands neck-high, Louisville)

498-1a Grasshopper Whitney (batting, looking at camera, P., Washington)

498-1b Grasshopper Whitney (batting, looking at camera, Pitcher, Washington)

498-2a Grasshopper Whitney (pitching, hands at chest, no comma after P., Washington)

498-2b Grasshopper Whitney (pitching, hands at chest, Pitcher, Washington)

498-2c Grasshopper Whitney (pitching, hands at chest, comma after P., Washington)

498-3a Grasshopper Whitney (pitching, right hand waist-high, P., Washington)

498-3b Grasshopper Whitney (pitching, right hand waist-high, Pitcher, Washington)

498-3c Grasshopper Whitney (pitching, right hand waist-high, Indianapolis)

499-1a Art Whitney (white uniform, stooping, dog with paw on his knee, 3d B., Pittsburg)

499-1b Art Whitney (white uniform, stooping, dog with paw on his knee, 3d Base, Pittsburg)

499-1c Art Whitney (white uniform, stooping, dog with paw on his knee, Whitney on front, New Yorks)

499-1d Art Whitney (white uniform, stooping, dog with paw on his knee, A. Whitney on front, New Yorks)

499-2a Art Whitney (white uniform, bending to left, hands thigh-high, 3d B. Pittsburg)

499-2b Art Whitney (white uniform, bending to left, hands thigh-high, 3d Base, Pittsburg)

499-2c Art Whitney (white uniform, bending to left, hands thigh-high, Whitney on front, New Yorks)

499-2d Art Whitney (white uniform, bending to left, hands thigh-high, A. Whitney on front, New Yorks)

499-2e Art Whitney (white uniform, bending to left, hands thigh-high, New York (PL))

499-3a Art Whitney (white uniform, batting, 3d B., Pittsburg)

499-3b Art Whitney (white uniform, batting, 3d Base, Pittsburg)

499-3c Art Whitney (white uniform, batting, New Yorks)

500-1 G. Whitney (dark uniform, batting, looking at camera, St. Joes)

500-2 G. Whitney (dark uniform, batting, looking down at ball, St. Joes)

500-3 G. Whitney (dark uniform, fielding grounder, St. Joes)

500-4 G. Whitney (dark uniform, throwing, St. Joes)

500-5 G. Whitney (dark uniform, fielding, hands at waist, St. Joes)

501-1 James Williams (hat in right hand)

501-2 James Williams (hat on head)

502-1 Ned Williamson (in top hat, looking to right)

502-2 Ned Williamson (fielding, hands neck-high)

502-3a Ned Williamson (throwing, Chicago's)

502-3b Ned Williamson (throwing, Chicago)

502-3c Ned Williamson (throwing, W. Williamson on front, Chicagos)

502-3d Ned Williamson (throwing, Chicag.)

502-3e Ned Williamson (throwing, C.W. Williamson on front, Chicagos)

502-4a Ned Williamson (fielding, hands above head, Chicago's)

502-4b Ned Williamson (fielding, hands above head, E. Williamson on front, Chicago)

502-4c Ned Williamson (fielding, hands above head, Chica.)

502-4d Ned Williamson (fielding, hands above head, C.W. Williamson on front, Chicago)

502-4e Ned Williamson (fielding, hands above head, Chicagos)

502-4f Ned Williamson (fielding, hands above head, W. Williamson on front, Chicago)

502-5a Ned Williamson (arms folded, no comma after S.S., Chicago's)

502-5b Ned Williamson (arms folded, comma after S.S., Chicago's)

502-5c Ned Williamson (arms folded, Chicago)

502-6a Ned Williamson (batting, looking down at ball, Chicago's)

502-6c Ned Williamson (batting, looking down at ball, E. Williamson on front, Chicago)

502-6d Ned Williamson (batting, looking down at ball, Chicagos)

502-6e Ned Williamson (batting, looking down at ball, W. Williamson on front, Chicago)

502-7 Willie Hahm - mascot, Ned Williamson

503-1 C.H. Willis (pitching, hands in front of cap)

503-2 C.H. Willis (pitching, hands at waist)

503-3 C.H. Willis (pitching, hands out to left chin high)

503-4 C.H. Willis (pitching, right hand forward head-high)

503-5 C.H. Willis (batting)

504-1a Watt Wilmot (batting, looking down at ball, Washington)

504-1b Watt Wilmot (batting, looking down at ball, Chicagos (N L))

504-2a Watt Wilmot (bat in hand at side, Washingtons)

504-2b Watt Wilmot (bat in hand at side, Chicagos (N L))

504-3a Watt Wilmot (catching, hands thigh-high, Washingtons)

504-3b Watt Wilmot (catching, hands thigh-high, Washington)

504-4a Watt Wilmot (catching, hands at chest, Washingtons)

504-4b Watt Wilmot (catching, hands at chest. Washington)

504-4c Watt Wilmot (catching, hands at chest, Chicagos (N.L.))

504-5a Watt Wilmot (throwing, Washingtons)

504-5b Watt Wilmot (throwing, Washington)

505-1 George Winkleman (Winkelman) (throwing, hands out to right shoulder-high)

505-2 George Winkleman (Winkelman) (pitching, hands chest-high)

505-3 George Winkleman (Winkelman) (pitching, right hand above waist, left hand by left hip)

505-4 George Winkleman (Winkelman) (fielding)

506-1a Medoc Wise (stooping, hands on knees, S.S., Boston)

506-1b Medoc Wise (stooping, hands on knees, Short Stop)

506-1c Medoc Wise (stooping, hands on knees, S.S., Washingtons)

506-2a Medoc Wise (batting, Wise on front, S.S.)

506-2b Medoc Wise (batting, Short Stop)

506-2c Medoc Wise (batting, Sam W. Wise on front, S.S.)

506-3a Medoc Wise (bat in hand at side, S.S.)

506-3bMedoc Wise (bat in hand at side, Short
Stop)
506-4aMedoc Wise (portrait, Wise on front, S.S.)

506-4bMedoc Wise (portrait, Short Stop)

506-4cMedoc Wise (portrait, Sam W. Wise on
front, S.S.)
507-1 Chicken Wolf (batting, "Louisville" visible
on shirt)
507-2aChicken Wolf (batting, team name not
visible, Louisville)
507-2bChicken Wolf (batting, team name not
visible, Louisvilles)
507-3aChicken Wolf (lying on grass, feet on base.
Louisville)
507-3bChicken Wolf (lying on grass, feet on base,
Louisvilles)
507-4aChicken Wolf (fielding, hands chin-high.
Louisville)
507-4bChicken Wolf (fielding, hands chin-high.
Louisvilles)
507-5aChicken Wolf (fielding, hands by right
ankle, Louisville)
507-5bChicken Wolf (fielding, hands by right
ankle, Louisvilles)
508-1aGeorge "Dandy" Wood (batting, L.F.,
Phila)
508-1bGeorge "Dandy" Wood (batting, Left Field.
Philadelphia)
508-1cGeorge "Dandy" Wood (batting, L.F.,
Philadelphias)
508-2aGeorge "Dandy" Wood (fielding, hands
neck-high, L.F., Phila)
508-2bGeorge "Dandy" Wood (fielding, hands
neck-high, Left Field, Philadelphia)
508-2cGeorge "Dandy" Wood (fielding, hands
neck-high, L.F., Philadelphias)
508-3aGeorge "Dandy" Wood (fielding grounder,
L.F., Phila)
508-3bGeorge "Dandy" Wood (fielding grounder,
Left Field, Philadelphia)
508-3cGeorge "Dandy" Wood (fielding grounder,
L.F., Philadelphias)
508-4aGeorge "Dandy" Wood (throwing, L.F.,
Phila)
508-4bGeorge "Dandy" Wood (throwing, Left
Field, Philadelphia)
508-4cGeorge "Dandy" Wood (throwing, L.F..
Philadelphias)
509-1 Pete Wood (bat on shoulder, P.,
Philadelphias)
509-2 Pete Wood (bat at ready position, nearly
horizontal, P., Philadelphias)
509-3 Pete Wood (pitching, hands at neck. P
Philadelphia)
509-4 Pete Wood (pitching, right hand forward
neck-high, P., Philadelphias)
509-5 Pete Wood (pitching, right hand extended
at side head-high, P., Philadelphias)

510-1aHarry Wright (portrait, looking to right.
Phila)
510-1bHarry Wright (portrait, looking to right,
Phila's)
510-1dHarry Wright (portrait, looking to right,
Phila (N L))
510-2 Harry Wright (portrait, looking to left,
beard clear of right side of collar)
510-3 Harry Wright (portrait, looking to left,
beard just over right side of collar)
511-1 Chief Zimmer (batting)
511-2 Chief Zimmer (fielding, hands chest-high.
feet together)
511-3 Chief Zimmer (fielding, hands chest-high,
feet well apart)
511-4aChief Zimmer (throwing, Cleveland's)

511-4bChief Zimmer (throwing, Clevelands)

512-1 Frank Zinn (fielding grounder)
512-2 Frank Zinn (fielding, hands thigh-high)

512-3 Frank Zinn (fielding, hands head-high)

**One of the most fascinating of all card
sets, the N172 Old Judge cards were
issued by the Goodwin & Co. tobacco
firm in their Old Judge and, to a lesser
extent, Gypsy Queen cigarettes. Players
from more than 40 major and minor
league teams are pictured, with some
518 different players known to exist. Up
to 17 different pose and team variations
exist for some players, and the cards
were issued both with and without dates
on the card fronts, numbered and
unnumbered, and with both handwritten
and machine-printed names. Known
variations number in the thousands. The
cards themselves are blank-backed,
sepia-toned photographs pasted onto
thick cardboard. The listings are based
on the recordings in the The Cartophilic
Society's World Index, Part IV, compiled
by E.C. Wharton-Tigar with the help of
many collectors, especially Donald J.
McPherson and Lew Lipset. The above
list includes all known variations for each
player in the set.**

1956 Topps

This 340-card set is quite similar in design to the 1955 Topps set, again using both a portrait and an "action" picture. Some portraits are the same as those used in 1955 (and even 1954). Innovations found in the 1956 Topps set of 2-5/8" by 3-3/4" cards include team cards introduced as part of a regular set. Additionally, there are two unnumbered checklist cards (the complete set price quoted below does not include the checklist cards). Finally, there are cards of the two league presidents, William Harridge and Warren Giles. On the backs, a three-panel cartoon depicts big moments from the player's career while biographical information appears above the cartoon and the statistics below. Card backs for numbers 1-180 can be found with either white or grey cardboard. Some dealers charge a premium for grey backs (#'s 1-100) and white backs (#'s 101-180).

		NR MT	EX	VG
	Complete Set:	7500.00	3750.00	2250.00
	Common Player: 1-100	7.00	3.50	2.00
	Common Player: 101-180	9.00	4.50	2.75
	Common Player: 181-260	15.00	7.50	4.50
	Common Player: 261-340	9.00	4.50	2.75
1	William Harridge	110.00	25.00	3.75
2	Warren Giles	15.00	7.50	4.50
3	Elmer Valo	7.00	3.50	2.00
4	Carlos Paula	7.00	3.50	2.00
5	Ted Williams	350.00	175.00	105.00
6	Ray Boone	9.00	4.50	2.75
7	Ron Negray	7.00	3.50	2.00
8	Walter Alston	40.00	20.00	12.00
9	Ruben Gomez	7.00	3.50	2.00
10	Warren Spahn	80.00	40.00	25.00
11a	Cubs Team (with date)	50.00	25.00	15.00
11b	Cubs Team (no date, name centered)			
		15.00	7.50	4.50
11c	Cubs Team (no date, name at left)			
		15.00	7.50	4.50
12	Andy Carey	10.00	5.00	3.00
13	Roy Face	10.00	5.00	3.00
14	Ken Boyer	15.00	7.50	4.50
15	Ernie Banks	125.00	62.00	37.00
16	*Hector Lopez*	10.00	5.00	3.00
17	Gene Conley	9.00	4.50	2.75
18	Dick Donovan	7.00	3.50	2.00
19	Chuck Diering	7.00	3.50	2.00
20	Al Kaline	100.00	50.00	30.00
21	Joe Collins	10.00	5.00	3.00
22	Jim Finigan	7.00	3.50	2.00
23	Freddie Marsh	7.00	3.50	2.00
24	Dick Groat	10.00	5.00	3.00
25	Ted Kluszewski	20.00	10.00	6.00
26	Grady Hatton	7.00	3.50	2.00
27	Nelson Burbrink	7.00	3.50	2.00
28	Bobby Hofman	7.00	3.50	2.00
29	Jack Harshman	7.00	3.50	2.00
30	Jackie Robinson	150.00	60.00	38.00
31	Hank Aaron	200.00	100.00	60.00
32	Frank House	7.00	3.50	2.00
33	Roberto Clemente	450.00	225.00	135.00
34	Tom Brewer	7.00	3.50	2.00
35	Al Rosen	15.00	7.50	4.50
36	Rudy Minarcin	7.00	3.50	2.00

		NR MT	EX	VG
37	Alex Grammas	7.00	3.50	2.00
38	Bob Kennedy	7.00	3.50	2.00
39	Don Mossi	9.00	4.50	2.75
40	Bob Turley	15.00	7.50	4.50
41	Hank Sauer	7.00	3.50	2.00
42	Sandy Amoros	9.00	4.50	2.75
43	Ray Moore	7.00	3.50	2.00
44	"Windy" McCall	7.00	3.50	2.00
45	Gus Zernial	9.00	4.50	2.75
46	Gene Freese	7.00	3.50	2.00
47	Art Fowler	7.00	3.50	2.00
48	Jim Hegan	7.00	3.50	2.00
49	*Pedro Ramos*	9.00	4.50	2.75
50	"Dusty" Rhodes	9.00	4.50	2.75
51	Ernie Oravetz	7.00	3.50	2.00
52	Bob Grim	10.00	5.00	3.00
53	Arnold Portocarrero	7.00	3.50	2.00
54	Bob Keegan	7.00	3.50	2.00
55	Wally Moon	9.00	4.50	2.75
56	Dale Long	9.00	4.50	2.75
57	"Duke" Maas	7.00	3.50	2.00
58	Ed Roebuck	9.00	4.50	2.75
59	Jose Santiago	7.00	3.50	2.00
60	Mayo Smith	7.00	3.50	2.00
61	Bill Skowron	15.00	7.50	4.50
62	Hal Smith	7.00	3.50	2.00
63	*Roger Craig*	30.00	15.00	9.00
64	Luis Arroyo	7.00	3.50	2.00
65	Johnny O'Brien	7.00	3.50	2.00
66	Bob Speake	7.00	3.50	2.00
67	Vic Power	7.00	3.50	2.00
68	Chuck Stobbs	7.00	3.50	2.00
69	Chuck Tanner	10.00	5.00	3.00
70	Jim Rivera	7.00	3.50	2.00
71	Frank Sullivan	7.00	3.50	2.00
72a	Phillies Team (with date)	50.00	25.00	15.00
72b	Phillies Team (no date, name centered)			
		15.00	7.50	4.50
72c	Philadelphia Phillies (no date, name at left)			
		15.00	7.50	4.50
73	Wayne Terwilliger	7.00	3.50	2.00
74	Jim King	7.00	3.50	2.00
75	Roy Sievers	9.00	4.50	2.75
76	Ray Crone	7.00	3.50	2.00
77	Harvey Haddix	9.00	4.50	2.75
78	Herman Wehmeier	7.00	3.50	2.00
79	Sandy Koufax	400.00	200.00	125.00
80	Gus Triandos	9.00	4.50	2.75
81	Wally Westlake	7.00	3.50	2.00
82	Bill Renna	7.00	3.50	2.00
83	Karl Spooner	9.00	4.50	2.75
84	"Babe" Birrer	7.00	3.50	2.00
85a	Indians Team (with date)	50.00	25.00	15.00
85b	Indians Team (no date, name centered)			
		15.00	7.50	4.50
85c	Indians Team (no date, name at left)			
		15.00	7.50	4.50
86	Ray Jablonski	7.00	3.50	2.00
87	Dean Stone	7.00	3.50	2.00
88	Johnny Kucks	10.00	5.00	3.00
89	Norm Zauchin	7.00	3.50	2.00
90a	Redlegs Team (with date)	50.00	25.00	15.00
90b	Redlegs Team (no date, name centered)			
		15.00	7.50	4.50
90c	Redlegs Team (no date, name at left)			
		15.00	7.50	4.50
91	Gail Harris	7.00	3.50	2.00
92	"Red" Wilson	7.00	3.50	2.00
93	George Susce, Jr.	7.00	3.50	2.00
94	Ronnie Kline	7.00	3.50	2.00
95a	Braves Team (with date)	50.00	25.00	15.00
95b	Braves Team (no date, name centered)			
		15.00	7.50	4.50
95c	Braves Team (no date, name at left)			
		15.00	7.50	4.50
96	Bill Tremel	7.00	3.50	2.00
97	Jerry Lynch	7.00	3.50	2.00
98	Camilo Pascual	9.00	4.50	2.75
99	Don Zimmer	15.00	7.50	4.50
100a	Orioles Team (with date)	40.00	20.00	12.00
100b	Orioles Team (no date, name centered)			
		15.00	7.50	4.50
100c	Orioles Team (no date, name at left)			
		15.00	7.50	4.50
101	Roy Campanella	150.00	75.00	45.00
102	Jim Davis	9.00	4.50	2.75
103	Willie Miranda	9.00	4.50	2.75
104	Bob Lennon	9.00	4.50	2.75
105	Al Smith	9.00	4.50	2.75
106	Joe Astroth	9.00	4.50	2.75
107	Ed Mathews	60.00	30.00	18.00

		NR MT	EX	VG			NR MT	EX	VG
108	Laurin Pepper	9.00	4.50	2.75	199	Hank Thompson	15.00	7.50	4.50
109	Enos Slaughter	30.00	15.00	9.00	200	Bob Feller	150.00	75.00	45.00
110	Yogi Berra	150.00	75.00	45.00	201	"Rip" Repulski	15.00	7.50	4.50
111	Red Sox Team	9.00	4.50	2.75	202	Jim Hearn	15.00	7.50	4.50
112	Dee Fondy	9.00	4.50	2.75	203	Bill Tuttle	15.00	7.50	4.50
113	Phil Rizzuto	50.00	25.00	15.00	204	Art Swanson	15.00	7.50	4.50
114	Jim Owens	9.00	4.50	2.75	205	"Whitey" Lockman	15.00	7.50	4.50
115	Jackie Jensen	15.00	7.50	4.50	206	Erv Palica	15.00	7.50	4.50
116	Eddie O'Brien	9.00	4.50	2.75	207	Jim Small	15.00	7.50	4.50
117	Virgil Trucks	9.00	4.50	2.75	208	Elston Howard	30.00	15.00	9.00
118	"Nellie" Fox	30.00	15.00	9.00	209	Max Surkont	15.00	7.50	4.50
119	Larry Jackson	9.00	4.50	2.75	210	Mike Garcia	15.00	7.50	4.50
120	Richie Ashburn	35.00	17.50	10.50	211	Murry Dickson	15.00	7.50	4.50
121	Pirates Team	15.00	7.50	4.50	212	Johnny Temple	15.00	7.50	4.50
122	Willard Nixon	9.00	4.50	2.75	213	Tigers Team	50.00	25.00	15.00
123	Roy McMillan	9.00	4.50	2.75	214	Bob Rush	15.00	7.50	4.50
124	Don Kaiser	9.00	4.50	2.75	215	Tommy Byrne	15.00	7.50	4.50
125	"Minnie" Minoso	20.00	10.00	6.00	216	Jerry Schoonmaker	15.00	7.50	4.50
126	Jim Brady	9.00	4.50	2.75	217	Billy Klaus	15.00	7.50	4.50
127	Willie Jones	9.00	4.50	2.75	218	Joe Nuxall (Nuxhall)	15.00	7.50	4.50
128	Eddie Yost	9.00	4.50	2.75	219	Lew Burdette	15.00	7.50	4.50
129	"Jake" Martin	9.00	4.50	2.75	220	Del Ennis	15.00	7.50	4.50
130	Willie Mays	400.00	200.00	125.00	221	Bob Friend	15.00	7.50	4.50
131	Bob Roselli	9.00	4.50	2.75	222	Dave Philley	15.00	7.50	4.50
132	Bobby Avila	9.00	4.50	2.75	223	Randy Jackson	15.00	7.50	4.50
133	Ray Narleski	9.00	4.50	2.75	224	"Bud" Podbielan	15.00	7.50	4.50
134	Cardinals Team	15.00	7.50	4.50	225	Gil McDougald	25.00	12.50	7.50
135	Mickey Mantle	1000.00	500.00	300.00	226	Giants Team	70.00	35.00	21.00
136	Johnny Logan	9.00	4.50	2.75	227	Russ Meyer	15.00	7.50	4.50
137	Al Silvera	9.00	4.50	2.75	228	"Mickey" Vernon	15.00	7.50	4.50
138	Johnny Antonelli	9.00	4.50	2.75	229	Harry Brecheen	15.00	7.50	4.50
139	Tommy Carroll	9.00	4.50	2.75	230	"Chico" Carrasquel	15.00	7.50	4.50
140	Herb Score	35.00	17.50	10.50	231	Bob Hale	15.00	7.50	4.50
141	Joe Frazier	9.00	4.50	2.75	232	"Toby" Atwell	15.00	7.50	4.50
142	Gene Baker	9.00	4.50	2.75	233	Carl Erskine	20.00	10.00	6.00
143	Jim Piersall	9.00	4.50	2.75	234	"Pete" Runnels	15.00	7.50	4.50
144	Leroy Powell	9.00	4.50	2.75	235	Don Newcombe	50.00	25.00	15.00
145	Gil Hodges	45.00	23.00	13.50	236	Athletics Team	15.00	7.50	4.50
146	Senators Team	15.00	7.50	4.50	237	Jose Valdivielso	15.00	7.50	4.50
147	Earl Torgeson	9.00	4.50	2.75	238	Walt Dropo	15.00	7.50	4.50
148	Alvin Dark	9.00	4.50	2.75	239	Harry Simpson	15.00	7.50	4.50
149	"Dixie" Howell	9.00	4.50	2.75	240	"Whitey" Ford	150.00	75.00	45.00
150	"Duke" Snider	100.00	45.00	27.00	241	Don Mueller	15.00	7.50	4.50
151	"Spook" Jacobs	9.00	4.50	2.75	242	Hershell Freeman	15.00	7.50	4.50
152	Billy Hoeft	9.00	4.50	2.75	243	Sherm Lollar	15.00	7.50	4.50
153	Frank Thomas	9.00	4.50	2.75	244	Bob Buhl	15.00	7.50	4.50
154	Dave Pope	9.00	4.50	2.75	245	Billy Goodman	15.00	7.50	4.50
155	Harvey Kuenn	15.00	7.50	4.50	246	Tom Gorman	15.00	7.50	4.50
156	Wes Westrum	9.00	4.50	2.75	247	Bill Sarni	15.00	7.50	4.50
157	Dick Brodowski	9.00	4.50	2.75	248	Bob Porterfield	15.00	7.50	4.50
158	Wally Post	9.00	4.50	2.75	249	Johnny Klippstein	15.00	7.50	4.50
159	Clint Courtney	9.00	4.50	2.75	250	Larry Doby	20.00	10.00	6.00
160	Billy Pierce	15.00	7.50	4.50	251	Yankees Team	225.00	112.00	67.00
161	Joe DeMaestri	9.00	4.50	2.75	252	Vernon Law	15.00	7.50	4.50
162	"Gus" Bell	9.00	4.50	2.75	253	Irv Noren	15.00	7.50	4.50
163	Gene Woodling	9.00	4.50	2.75	254	George Crowe	15.00	7.50	4.50
164	Harmon Killebrew	110.00	55.00	33.00	255	Bob Lemon	25.00	12.50	7.50
165	"Red" Schoendienst	30.00	15.00	9.00	256	Tom Hurd	15.00	7.50	4.50
166	Dodgers Team	200.00	100.00	60.00	257	Bobby Thomson	15.00	7.50	4.50
167	Harry Dorish	9.00	4.50	2.75	258	Art Ditmar	15.00	7.50	4.50
168	Sammy White	9.00	4.50	2.75	259	Sam Jones	15.00	7.50	4.50
169	Bob Nelson	9.00	4.50	2.75	260	"Pee Wee" Reese	150.00	75.00	45.00
170	Bill Virdon	15.00	7.50	4.50	261	Bobby Shantz	9.00	4.50	2.75
171	Jim Wilson	9.00	4.50	2.75	262	Howie Pollet	9.00	4.50	2.75
172	Frank Torre	9.00	4.50	2.75	263	Bob Miller	9.00	4.50	2.75
173	Johnny Podres	15.00	7.50	4.50	264	Ray Monzant	9.00	4.50	2.75
174	Glen Gorbous	9.00	4.50	2.75	265	Sandy Consuegra	9.00	4.50	2.75
175	Del Crandall	15.00	7.50	4.50	266	Don Ferrarese	9.00	4.50	2.75
176	Alex Kellner	9.00	4.50	2.75	267	Bob Nieman	9.00	4.50	2.75
177	Hank Bauer	15.00	7.50	4.50	268	Dale Mitchell	9.00	4.50	2.75
178	Joe Black	9.00	4.50	2.75	269	Jack Meyer	9.00	4.50	2.75
179	Harry Chiti	9.00	4.50	2.75	270	Billy Loes	9.00	4.50	2.75
180	Robin Roberts	25.00	12.50	7.50	271	Foster Castleman	9.00	4.50	2.75
181	Billy Martin	110.00	55.00	33.00	272	Danny O'Connell	9.00	4.50	2.75
182	Paul Minner	15.00	7.50	4.50	273	Walker Cooper	9.00	4.50	2.75
183	Stan Lopata	15.00	7.50	4.50	274	Frank Baumholtz	9.00	4.50	2.75
184	Don Bessent	15.00	7.50	4.50	275	Jim Greengrass	9.00	4.50	2.75
185	Bill Bruton	15.00	7.50	4.50	276	George Zuverink	9.00	4.50	2.75
186	Ron Jackson	15.00	7.50	4.50	277	Daryl Spencer	9.00	4.50	2.75
187	Early Wynn	30.00	15.00	9.00	278	Chet Nichols	9.00	4.50	2.75
188	White Sox Team	15.00	7.50	4.50	279	Johnny Groth	9.00	4.50	2.75
189	Ned Garver	15.00	7.50	4.50	280	Jim Gilliam	15.00	7.50	4.50
190	Carl Furillo	20.00	10.00	6.00	281	Art Houtteman	9.00	4.50	2.75
191	Frank Lary	15.00	7.50	4.50	282	Warren Hacker	9.00	4.50	2.75
192	"Smoky" Burgess	15.00	7.50	4.50	283	Hal Smith	9.00	4.50	2.75
193	Wilmer Mizell	15.00	7.50	4.50	284	Ike Delock	9.00	4.50	2.75
194	Monte Irvin	30.00	15.00	9.00	285	Eddie Miksis	9.00	4.50	2.75
195	George Kell	30.00	15.00	9.00	286	Bill Wight	9.00	4.50	2.75
196	Tom Poholsky	15.00	7.50	4.50	287	Bobby Adams	9.00	4.50	2.75
197	Granny Hamner	15.00	7.50	4.50	288	Bob Cerv	25.00	12.50	7.50
198	Ed Fitzgerald (Fitz Gerald)	15.00	7.50	4.50	289	Hal Jeffcoat	9.00	4.50	2.75

		NR MT	EX	VG
290	Curt Simmons	9.00	4.50	2.75
291	Frank Kellert	9.00	4.50	2.75
292	*Luis Aparicio*	150.00	75.00	45.00
293	Stu Miller	9.00	4.50	2.75
294	Ernie Johnson	9.00	4.50	2.75
295	Clem Labine	9.00	4.50	2.75
296	Andy Seminick	9.00	4.50	2.75
297	Bob Skinner	9.00	4.50	2.75
298	Johnny Schmitz	9.00	4.50	2.75
299	Charley Neal	25.00	12.50	7.50
300	Vic Wertz	9.00	4.50	2.75
301	Marv Grissom	9.00	4.50	2.75
302	Eddie Robinson	15.00	7.50	4.50
303	Jim Dyck	9.00	4.50	2.75
304	Frank Malzone	9.00	4.50	2.75
305	Brooks Lawrence	9.00	4.50	2.75
306	Curt Roberts	9.00	4.50	2.75
307	Hoyt Wilhelm	35.00	17.50	10.50
308	"Chuck" Harmon	9.00	4.50	2.75
309	*Don Blasingame*	9.00	4.50	2.75
310	Steve Gromek	9.00	4.50	2.75
311	Hal Naragon	9.00	4.50	2.75
312	Andy Pafko	9.00	4.50	2.75
313	Gene Stephens	9.00	4.50	2.75
314	Hobie Landrith	9.00	4.50	2.75
315	Milt Bolling	9.00	4.50	2.75
316	Jerry Coleman	9.00	4.50	2.75
317	Al Aber	9.00	4.50	2.75
318	Fred Hatfield	9.00	4.50	2.75
319	Jack Crimian	9.00	4.50	2.75
320	Joe Adcock	9.00	4.50	2.75
321	Jim Konstanty	15.00	7.50	4.50
322	Karl Olson	9.00	4.50	2.75
323	Willard Schmidt	9.00	4.50	2.75
324	"Rocky" Bridges	9.00	4.50	2.75
325	Don Liddle	9.00	4.50	2.75
326	Connie Johnson	9.00	4.50	2.75
327	Bob Wiesler	9.00	4.50	2.75
328	Preston Ward	9.00	4.50	2.75
329	Lou Berberet	9.00	4.50	2.75
330	Jim Busby	9.00	4.50	2.75
331	Dick Hall	9.00	4.50	2.75
332	Don Larsen	35.00	17.50	10.50
333	Rube Walker	9.00	4.50	2.75
334	Bob Miller	9.00	4.50	2.75
335	Don Hoak	9.00	4.50	2.75
336	Ellis Kinder	9.00	4.50	2.75
337	Bobby Morgan	9.00	4.50	2.75
338	Jim Delsing	9.00	4.50	2.75
339	Rance Pless	9.00	4.50	2.75
340	Mickey McDermott	30.00	15.00	9.00
——	Checklist 1/3	250.00	125.00	65.00
——	Checklist 2/4	250.00	125.00	65.00

the Magic Photos series of 1948 is to remember that the 1956 cards actually have the words "Hocus Focus" on the back. The photos on these cards were developed by wetting the cards surface and exposing to light. Prices below are for cards with well-developed pictures. Cards with poorly developed photos are worth significantly less.

		NR MT	EX	VG
Complete Set:		525.00	262.00	157.00
Common Player:		12.00	6.00	3.50
1	Dick Groat	25.00	12.50	7.50
2	Ed Lopat	25.00	12.50	7.50
3	Hank Sauer	12.00	6.00	3.50
4	"Dusty" Rhodes	12.00	6.00	3.50
5	Ted Williams	125.00	62.00	37.00
6	Harvey Haddix	12.00	6.00	3.50
7	Ray Boone	12.00	6.00	3.50
8	Al Rosen	25.00	12.50	7.50
9	Mayo Smith	12.00	6.00	3.50
10	Warren Spahn	70.00	35.00	21.00
11	Jim Rivera	12.00	6.00	3.50
12	Ted Kluszewski	25.00	12.50	7.50
13	Gus Zernial	12.00	6.00	3.50
14	Jackie Robinson	125.00	62.00	37.00
15	Hal Smith	12.00	6.00	3.50
16	Johnny Schmitz	12.00	6.00	3.50
17	"Spook" Jacobs	12.00	6.00	3.50
18	Mel Parnell	12.00	6.00	3.50

A player's name in *italic* indicates a rookie card. An (FC) indicates a player's first card for that particular card company.

1956 Topps Hocus Focus Large

These sets are a direct descendant of the 1948 Topps Magic Photo" issue. Again, the baseball players were part of a larger overall series covering several topical areas. There are two distinct issues of Hocus Focus cards in 1956. The "large" cards, measuring 1" by 1-5/8," consists of 18 players. The "small" cards, 7/8 by 1-3/8," state on the back that they are a series of 23, though only 13 are known. Besides players on the cards themselves, the easiest way to distinguish Hocus Focus cards of 1956 from

1956 Topps Hocus Focus Small

		NR MT	EX	VG
Complete Set:		575.00	287.00	172.00
Common Player: 1-23		10.00	5.00	3.00
1	Babe Ruth	175.00	87.00	52.00
2	Unknown			
3	Dick Groat	15.00	7.50	4.50
4	Unknown			
5	Unknown			
6	"Dusty" Rhodes	10.00	5.00	3.00
7	Ted Williams	125.00	62.00	37.00
8	Harvey Haddix	10.00	5.00	3.00
9	Ray Boone	10.00	5.00	3.00
10	Unknown			
11	Unknown			
12	Warren Spahn	70.00	35.00	21.00
13	Jim Rivera	10.00	5.00	3.00
14	Ted Kluszewski	25.00	12.50	7.50
15	Gus Zernial	10.00	5.00	3.00
16	Unknown			
17	Unknown			
18	Johnny Schmitz	10.00	5.00	3.00
19	Unknown			
20	Karl Spooner	15.00	7.50	4.50
21	Ed Mathews	70.00	35.00	21.00
22	Unknown			
23	Unknown			

1956 Topps Pins

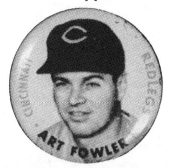

One of Topps first specialty issues, the 60-pin set of ballplayers issued in 1956 contains a high percentage of big-name stars which, combined with the scarcity of the pins, makes collecting a complete set extremely challenging. Compounding the situation is the fact that some pins are seen far less often than others, though the reason is unknown. Chuck Stobbs, Hector Lopez and Chuck Diering are unaccountably scarce. Measuring 1-1/8" in diameter, the pins utilize the same portraits found on 1956 Topps baseball cards. The photos are set against a solid color background.

		NR MT	EX	VG
Complete Set:		2500.00	1250.00	750.00
Common Player:		15.00	7.50	4.50
(1)	Hank Aaron	100.00	50.00	30.00
(2)	Sandy Amoros	15.00	7.50	4.50
(3)	Luis Arroyo	15.00	7.50	4.50
(4)	Ernie Banks	50.00	25.00	15.00
(5)	Yogi Berra	70.00	35.00	21.00
(6)	Joe Black	15.00	7.50	4.50
(7)	Ray Boone	15.00	7.50	4.50
(8)	Ken Boyer	20.00	10.00	6.00
(9)	Joe Collins	15.00	7.50	4.50
(10)	Gene Conley	15.00	7.50	4.50
(11)	Chuck Diering	225.00	112.00	67.00
(12)	Dick Donovan	15.00	7.50	4.50
(13)	Jim Finigan	15.00	7.50	4.50
(14)	Art Fowler	15.00	7.50	4.50
(15)	Ruben Gomez	15.00	7.50	4.50
(16)	Dick Groat	20.00	10.00	6.00
(17)	Harvey Haddix	15.00	7.50	4.50
(18)	Jack Harshman	15.00	7.50	4.50
(19)	Grady Hatton	15.00	7.50	4.50
(20)	Jim Hegan	15.00	7.50	4.50
(21)	Gil Hodges	40.00	20.00	12.00
(22)	Bobby Hofman	15.00	7.50	4.50
(23)	Frank House	15.00	7.50	4.50
(24)	Jackie Jensen	20.00	10.00	6.00
(25)	Al Kaline	60.00	30.00	18.00
(26)	Bob Kennedy	15.00	7.50	4.50
(27)	Ted Kluszewski	25.00	12.50	7.50
(28)	Dale Long	15.00	7.50	4.50
(29)	Hector Lopez	200.00	100.00	60.00
(30)	Ed Mathews	40.00	20.00	12.00
(31)	Willie Mays	100.00	50.00	30.00
(32)	Roy McMillan	15.00	7.50	4.50
(33)	Willie Miranda	15.00	7.50	4.50
(34)	Wally Moon	15.00	7.50	4.50
(35)	Don Mossi	15.00	7.50	4.50
(36)	Ron Negray	15.00	7.50	4.50
(37)	Johnny O'Brien	15.00	7.50	4.50
(38)	Carlos Paula	15.00	7.50	4.50
(39)	Vic Power	15.00	7.50	4.50
(40)	Jim Rivera	15.00	7.50	4.50
(41)	Phil Rizzuto	40.00	20.00	12.00
(42)	Jackie Robinson	100.00	50.00	30.00
(43)	Al Rosen	25.00	12.50	7.50
(44)	Hank Sauer	15.00	7.50	4.50
(45)	Roy Sievers	15.00	7.50	4.50
(46)	Bill Skowron	20.00	10.00	6.00
(47)	Al Smith	15.00	7.50	4.50
(48)	Hal Smith	15.00	7.50	4.50
(49)	Mayo Smith	15.00	7.50	4.50
(50)	Duke Snider	70.00	35.00	21.00
(51)	Warren Spahn	50.00	25.00	15.00
(52)	Karl Spooner	15.00	7.50	4.50
(53)	Chuck Stobbs	175.00	87.00	52.00
(54)	Frank Sullivan	15.00	7.50	4.50
(55)	Bill Tremel	15.00	7.50	4.50
(56)	Gus Triandos	15.00	7.50	4.50
(57)	Bob Turley	20.00	10.00	6.00
(58)	Herman Wehmeier	15.00	7.50	4.50
(59)	Ted Williams	110.00	55.00	33.00
(60)	Gus Zernial	15.00	7.50	4.50

1957 Topps

For 1957, Topps reduced the size of its cards to the now-standard 2-1/2" by 3-1/2." Set size was increased to 407 cards. Another change came in the form of the use of real color photographs as opposed to the hand-colored black and whites of previous years. For the first time since 1954, there were also cards with more than one player. The two, "Dodger Sluggers" and "Yankees' Power Hitters" began a trend toward the increased use of mulitple-player cards. Another first-time innovation, found on the backs, is complete players statistics. The scarce cards in the set are not the highest numbers, but rather numbers 265-352. Four unnumbered checklist cards were issued along with the set. They are quite expensive and are not included in the complete set prices quoted below.

		NR MT	EX	VG
Complete Set:		7500.00	3750.00	2250.
Common Player: 1-264		7.00	3.50	2.00
Common Player: 265-352		18.00	9.00	5.50
Common Player: 353-407		7.00	3.50	2.00
1	Ted Williams	425.00	100.00	38.00
2	Yogi Berra	150.00	70.00	45.00
3	Dale Long	7.00	3.50	2.00
4	Johnny Logan	7.00	3.50	2.00
5	Sal Maglie	8.00	4.00	2.50
6	Hector Lopez	7.00	3.50	2.00
7	Luis Aparicio	30.00	15.00	9.00
8	Don Mossi	7.00	3.50	2.00
9	Johnny Temple	7.00	3.50	2.00
10	Willie Mays	250.00	125.00	75.00
11	George Zuverink	7.00	3.50	2.00
12	Dick Groat	6.00	3.00	1.75
13	Wally Burnette	7.00	3.50	2.00
14	Bob Nieman	7.00	3.50	2.00
15	Robin Roberts	20.00	10.00	6.00
16	Walt Moryn	7.00	3.50	2.00
17	Billy Gardner	7.00	3.50	2.00
18	*Don Drysdale*	250.00	125.00	87.00
19	Bob Wilson	7.00	3.50	2.00
20	Hank Aaron (photo reversed)	225.00	112.00	67.00
21	Frank Sullivan	7.00	3.50	2.00
22	Jerry Snyder (photo actually Ed Fitz Gerald)	7.00	3.50	2.00
23	Sherm Lollar	7.00	3.50	2.00
24	*Bill Mazeroski*	70.00	35.00	21.00
25	Whitey Ford	50.00	25.00	15.00
26	Bob Boyd	7.00	3.50	2.00
27	Ted Kazanski	7.00	3.50	2.00
28	Gene Conley	7.00	3.50	2.00
29	*Whitey Herzog*	30.00	15.00	9.00
30	Pee Wee Reese	60.00	30.00	18.00

#	Player	NR MT	EX	VG
31	Ron Northey	7.00	3.50	2.00
32	Hersh Freeman	7.00	3.50	2.00
33	Jim Small	7.00	3.50	2.00
34	Tom Sturdivant	6.00	3.00	1.75
35	*Frank Robinson*	300.00	150.00	90.00
36	Bob Grim	6.00	3.00	1.75
37	Frank Torre	7.00	3.50	2.00
38	Nellie Fox	20.00	10.00	6.00
39	Al Worthington	7.00	3.50	2.00
40	Early Wynn	20.00	10.00	6.00
41	Hal Smith	7.00	3.50	2.00
42	Dee Fondy	7.00	3.50	2.00
43	Connie Johnson	7.00	3.50	2.00
44	Joe DeMaestri	7.00	3.50	2.00
45	Carl Furillo	9.00	4.50	2.75
46	Bob Miller	7.00	3.50	2.00
47	Don Blasingame	7.00	3.50	2.00
48	Bill Bruton	7.00	3.50	2.00
49	Daryl Spencer	7.00	3.50	2.00
50	Herb Score	6.00	3.00	1.75
51	Clint Courtney	7.00	3.50	2.00
52	Lee Walls	7.00	3.50	2.00
53	Clem Labine	6.00	3.00	1.75
54	Elmer Valo	7.00	3.50	2.00
55	Ernie Banks	125.00	67.00	37.00
56	Dave Sisler	7.00	3.50	2.00
57	Jim Lemon	7.00	3.50	2.00
58	Ruben Gomez	7.00	3.50	2.00
59	Dick Williams	6.00	3.00	1.75
60	Billy Hoeft	7.00	3.50	2.00
61	Dusty Rhodes	7.00	3.50	2.00
62	Billy Martin	50.00	25.00	15.00
63	Ike Delock	7.00	3.50	2.00
64	Pete Runnels	6.00	3.00	1.75
65	Wally Moon	7.00	3.50	2.00
66	Brooks Lawrence	7.00	3.50	2.00
67	Chico Carrasquel	7.00	3.50	2.00
68	Ray Crone	7.00	3.50	2.00
69	Roy McMillan	7.00	3.50	2.00
70	Richie Ashburn	25.00	12.50	7.50
71	Murry Dickson	7.00	3.50	2.00
72	Bill Tuttle	7.00	3.50	2.00
73	George Crowe	7.00	3.50	2.00
74	Vito Valentinetti	7.00	3.50	2.00
75	Jim Piersall	6.00	3.00	1.75
76	Bob Clemente	250.00	125.00	75.00
77	Paul Foytack	7.00	3.50	2.00
78	Vic Wertz	6.00	3.00	1.75
79	*Lindy McDaniel*	6.00	3.00	1.75
80	Gil Hodges	50.00	30.00	15.00
81	Herm Wehmeier	7.00	3.50	2.00
82	Elston Howard	15.00	7.50	4.50
83	Lou Skizas	7.00	3.50	2.00
84	Moe Drabowsky	7.00	3.50	2.00
85	Larry Doby	10.00	5.00	3.00
86	Bill Sarni	7.00	3.50	2.00
87	Tom Gorman	7.00	3.50	2.00
88	Harvey Kuenn	6.00	3.00	1.75
89	Roy Sievers	7.00	3.50	2.00
90	Warren Spahn	75.00	38.00	23.00
91	Mack Burk	7.00	3.50	2.00
92	Mickey Vernon	6.00	3.00	1.75
93	Hal Jeffcoat	7.00	3.50	2.00
94	Bobby Del Greco	7.00	3.50	2.00
95	Mickey Mantle	1000.00	500.00	300.00
96	*Hank Aguirre*	6.00	3.00	1.75
97	Yankees Team	60.00	30.00	18.00
98	Al Dark	8.00	4.00	2.50
99	Bob Keegan	7.00	3.50	2.00
100	League Presidents (Warren Giles, William Harridge)	6.00	3.00	1.75
101	Chuck Stobbs	7.00	3.50	2.00
102	Ray Boone	7.00	3.50	2.00
103	Joe Nuxhall	6.00	3.00	1.75
104	Hank Foiles	7.00	3.50	2.00
105	Johnny Antonelli	7.00	3.50	2.00
106	Ray Moore	7.00	3.50	2.00
107	Jim Rivera	7.00	3.50	2.00
108	Tommy Byrne	6.00	3.00	1.75
109	Hank Thompson	7.00	3.50	2.00
110	Bill Virdon	6.00	3.00	1.75
111	Hal Smith	7.00	3.50	2.00
112	Tom Brewer	7.00	3.50	2.00
113	Wilmer Mizell	7.00	3.50	2.00
114	Braves Team	10.00	5.00	3.00
115	Jim Gilliam	10.00	5.00	3.00
116	Mike Fornieles	7.00	3.50	2.00
117	Joe Adcock	6.00	3.00	1.75
118	Bob Porterfield	7.00	3.50	2.00
119	Stan Lopata	7.00	3.50	2.00
120	Bob Lemon	15.00	7.50	4.50
121	*Cletis Boyer*	15.00	7.50	4.50
122	Ken Boyer	8.00	4.00	2.50
123	Steve Ridzik	7.00	3.50	2.00
124	Dave Philley	7.00	3.50	2.00
125	Al Kaline	100.00	50.00	30.00
126	Bob Wiesler	7.00	3.50	2.00
127	Bob Buhl	7.00	3.50	2.00
128	Ed Bailey	7.00	3.50	2.00
129	Saul Rogovin	7.00	3.50	2.00
130	Don Newcombe	10.00	5.00	3.00
131	Milt Bolling	7.00	3.50	2.00
132	Art Ditmar	6.00	3.00	1.75
133	Del Crandall	6.00	3.00	1.75
134	Don Kaiser	7.00	3.50	2.00
135	Bill Skowron	12.00	6.00	3.50
136	Jim Hegan	7.00	3.50	2.00
137	Bob Rush	7.00	3.50	2.00
138	Minnie Minoso	8.00	4.00	2.50
139	Lou Kretlow	7.00	3.50	2.00
140	Frank Thomas	7.00	3.50	2.00
141	Al Aber	7.00	3.50	2.00
142	Charley Thompson	7.00	3.50	2.00
143	Andy Pafko	6.00	3.00	1.75
144	Ray Narleski	7.00	3.50	2.00
145	Al Smith	7.00	3.50	2.00
146	Don Ferrarese	7.00	3.50	2.00
147	Al Walker	6.00	3.00	1.75
148	Don Mueller	7.00	3.50	2.00
149	Bob Kennedy	7.00	3.50	2.00
150	Bob Friend	6.00	3.00	1.75
151	Willie Miranda	7.00	3.50	2.00
152	Jack Harshman	7.00	3.50	2.00
153	Karl Olson	7.00	3.50	2.00
154	Red Schoendienst	20.00	10.00	6.00
155	Jim Brosnan	7.00	3.50	2.00
156	Gus Triandos	7.00	3.50	2.00
157	Wally Post	7.00	3.50	2.00
158	Curt Simmons	6.00	3.00	1.75
159	Solly Drake	7.00	3.50	2.00
160	Billy Pierce	6.00	3.00	1.75
161	Pirates Team	8.00	4.00	2.50
162	Jack Meyer	7.00	3.50	2.00
163	Sammy White	7.00	3.50	2.00
164	Tommy Carroll	6.00	3.00	1.75
165	Ted Kluszewski	25.00	12.50	7.50
166	Roy Face	6.00	3.00	1.75
167	Vic Power	7.00	3.50	2.00
168	Frank Lary	6.00	3.00	1.75
169	Herb Plews	7.00	3.50	2.00
170	Duke Snider	100.00	50.00	30.00
171	Red Sox Team	9.00	4.50	2.75
172	Gene Woodling	6.00	3.00	1.75
173	Roger Craig	8.00	4.00	2.50
174	Willie Jones	7.00	3.50	2.00
175	Don Larsen	8.00	4.00	2.50
176	Gene Baker	7.00	3.50	2.00
177	Eddie Yost	7.00	3.50	2.00
178	Don Bessent	7.00	3.50	2.00
179	Ernie Oravetz	7.00	3.50	2.00
180	Gus Bell	7.00	3.50	2.00
181	Dick Donovan	7.00	3.50	2.00
182	Hobie Landrith	7.00	3.50	2.00
183	Cubs Team	8.00	4.00	2.50
184	*Tito Francona*	6.00	3.00	1.75
185	Johnny Kucks	6.00	3.00	1.75
186	Jim King	7.00	3.50	2.00
187	Virgil Trucks	7.00	3.50	2.00
188	Felix Mantilla	7.00	3.50	2.00
189	Willard Nixon	7.00	3.50	2.00
190	Randy Jackson	7.00	3.50	2.00
191	Joe Margoneri	7.00	3.50	2.00
192	Jerry Coleman	6.00	3.00	1.75
193	Del Rice	7.00	3.50	2.00
194	Hal Brown	7.00	3.50	2.00
195	Bobby Avila	7.00	3.50	2.00
196	Larry Jackson	7.00	3.50	2.00
197	Hank Sauer	7.00	3.50	2.00
198	Tigers Team	9.00	4.50	2.75
199	Vernon Law	6.00	3.00	1.75
200	Gil McDougald	12.00	6.00	3.50
201	Sandy Amoros	7.00	3.50	2.00
202	Dick Gernert	7.00	3.50	2.00
203	Hoyt Wilhelm	20.00	10.00	6.00
204	Athletics Team	8.00	4.00	2.50
205	Charley Maxwell	7.00	3.50	2.00
206	Willard Schmidt	7.00	3.50	2.00
207	Billy Hunter	7.00	3.50	2.00
208	Lew Burdette	6.00	3.00	1.75
209	Bob Skinner	7.00	3.50	2.00
210	Roy Campanella	125.00	67.00	37.00
211	Camilo Pascual	7.00	3.50	2.00
212	*Rocco Colavito*	135.00	67.00	40.00

#	Name	NR MT	EX	VG
213	Les Moss	7.00	3.50	2.00
214	Phillies Team	8.00	4.00	2.50
215	Enos Slaughter	20.00	10.00	6.00
216	Marv Grissom	7.00	3.50	2.00
217	Gene Stephens	7.00	3.50	2.00
218	Ray Jablonski	7.00	3.50	2.00
219	Tom Acker	7.00	3.50	2.00
220	Jackie Jensen	6.00	3.00	1.75
221	Dixie Howell	7.00	3.50	2.00
222	Alex Grammas	7.00	3.50	2.00
223	Frank House	7.00	3.50	2.00
224	Marv Blaylock	7.00	3.50	2.00
225	Harry Simpson	7.00	3.50	2.00
226	Preston Ward	7.00	3.50	2.00
227	Jerry Staley	7.00	3.50	2.00
228	Smoky Burgess	6.00	3.00	1.75
229	George Susce	7.00	3.50	2.00
230	George Kell	18.00	9.00	5.50
231	Solly Hemus	7.00	3.50	2.00
232	Whitey Lockman	7.00	3.50	2.00
233	Art Fowler	7.00	3.50	2.00
234	Dick Cole	7.00	3.50	2.00
235	Tom Poholsky	7.00	3.50	2.00
236	Joe Ginsberg	7.00	3.50	2.00
237	Foster Castleman	7.00	3.50	2.00
238	Eddie Robinson	7.00	3.50	2.00
239	Tom Morgan	7.00	3.50	2.00
240	Hank Bauer	10.00	5.00	3.00
241	Joe Lonnett	7.00	3.50	2.00
242	Charley Neal	7.00	3.50	2.00
243	Cardinals Team	8.00	4.00	2.50
244	Billy Loes	7.00	3.50	2.00
245	Rip Repulski	7.00	3.50	2.00
246	Jose Valdivielso	7.00	3.50	2.00
247	Turk Lown	7.00	3.50	2.00
248	Jim Finigan	7.00	3.50	2.00
249	Dave Pope	7.00	3.50	2.00
250	Ed Mathews	40.00	20.00	12.00
251	Orioles Team	8.00	4.00	2.50
252	Carl Erskine	10.00	5.00	3.00
253	Gus Zernial	7.00	3.50	2.00
254	Ron Negray	7.00	3.50	2.00
255	Charlie Silvera	7.00	3.50	2.00
256	Ronnie Kline	7.00	3.50	2.00
257	Walt Dropo	7.00	3.50	2.00
258	Steve Gromek	7.00	3.50	2.00
259	Eddie O'Brien	7.00	3.50	2.00
260	Del Ennis	7.00	3.50	2.00
261	Bob Chakales	7.00	3.50	2.00
262	Bobby Thomson	6.00	3.00	1.75
263	George Strickland	7.00	3.50	2.00
264	Bob Turley	8.00	4.00	2.50
265	Harvey Haddix	20.00	10.00	6.00
266	Ken Kuhn	18.00	9.00	5.50
267	Danny Kravitz	18.00	9.00	5.50
268	Jackie Collum	18.00	9.00	5.50
269	Bob Cerv	18.00	9.00	5.50
270	Senators Team	25.00	12.50	7.50
271	Danny O'Connell	18.00	9.00	5.50
272	Bobby Shantz	25.00	12.50	7.50
273	Jim Davis	18.00	9.00	5.50
274	Don Hoak	18.00	9.00	5.50
275	Indians Team	35.00	17.50	10.50
276	Jim Pyburn	18.00	9.00	5.50
277	Johnny Podres	50.00	25.00	15.00
278	Fred Hatfield	18.00	9.00	5.50
279	Bob Thurman	18.00	9.00	5.50
280	Alex Kellner	18.00	9.00	5.50
281	Gail Harris	18.00	9.00	5.50
282	Jack Dittmer	18.00	9.00	5.50
283	*Wes Covington*	18.00	9.00	5.50
284	Don Zimmer	20.00	10.00	6.00
285	Ned Garver	18.00	9.00	5.50
286	*Bobby Richardson*	125.00	67.00	37.00
287	Sam Jones	18.00	9.00	5.50
288	Ted Lepcio	18.00	9.00	5.50
289	Jim Bolger	18.00	9.00	5.50
290	Andy Carey	18.00	9.00	5.50
291	Windy McCall	18.00	9.00	5.50
292	Billy Klaus	18.00	9.00	5.50
293	Ted Abernathy	18.00	9.00	5.50
294	Rocky Bridges	18.00	9.00	5.50
295	Joe Collins	18.00	9.00	5.50
296	Johnny Klippstein	18.00	9.00	5.50
297	Jack Crimian	18.00	9.00	5.50
298	Irv Noren	18.00	9.00	5.50
299	Chuck Harmon	18.00	9.00	5.50
300	Mike Garcia	18.00	9.00	5.50
301	Sam Esposito	18.00	9.00	5.50
302	Sandy Koufax	400.00	200.00	125.00
303	Billy Goodman	18.00	9.00	5.50

#	Name	NR MT	EX	VG
304	Joe Cunningham	18.00	9.00	5.50
305	Chico Fernandez	18.00	9.00	5.50
306	Darrell Johnson	18.00	9.00	5.50
307	Jack Phillips	18.00	9.00	5.50
308	Dick Hall	18.00	9.00	5.50
309	Jim Busby	18.00	9.00	5.50
310	Max Surkont	18.00	9.00	5.50
311	Al Pilarcik	18.00	9.00	5.50
312	*Tony Kubek*	135.00	67.00	40.00
313	Mel Parnell	18.00	9.00	5.50
314	Ed Bouchee	18.00	9.00	5.50
315	Lou Berberet	18.00	9.00	5.50
316	Billy O'Dell	18.00	9.00	5.50
317	Giants Team	50.00	25.00	15.00
318	Mickey McDermott	18.00	9.00	5.50
319	Gino Cimoli	18.00	9.00	5.50
320	Neil Chrisley	18.00	9.00	5.50
321	Red Murff	18.00	9.00	5.50
322	Redlegs Team	50.00	25.00	15.00
323	Wes Westrum	18.00	9.00	5.50
324	Dodgers Team	110.00	55.00	33.00
325	Frank Bolling	18.00	9.00	5.50
326	Pedro Ramos	18.00	9.00	5.50
327	Jim Pendleton	18.00	9.00	5.50
328	*Brooks Robinson*	400.00	200.00	125.00
329	White Sox Team	35.00	17.50	10.50
330	Jim Wilson	18.00	9.00	5.50
331	Ray Katt	18.00	9.00	5.50
332	Bob Bowman	18.00	9.00	5.50
333	Ernie Johnson	18.00	9.00	5.50
334	Jerry Schoonmaker	18.00	9.00	5.50
335	Granny Hamner	18.00	9.00	5.50
336	*Haywood Sullivan*	18.00	9.00	5.50
337	Rene Valdes	18.00	9.00	5.50
338	*Jim Bunning*	125.00	62.00	37.00
339	Bob Speake	18.00	9.00	5.50
340	Bill Wight	18.00	9.00	5.50
341	Don Gross	18.00	9.00	5.50
342	Gene Mauch	18.00	9.00	5.50
343	Taylor Phillips	18.00	9.00	5.50
344	Paul LaPalme	18.00	9.00	5.50
345	Paul Smith	18.00	9.00	5.50
346	Dick Littlefield	18.00	9.00	5.50
347	Hal Naragon	18.00	9.00	5.50
348	Jim Hearn	18.00	9.00	5.50
349	Nelson King	18.00	9.00	5.50
350	Eddie Miksis	18.00	9.00	5.50
351	Dave Hillman	18.00	9.00	5.50
352	Ellis Kinder	18.00	9.00	5.50
353	Cal Neeman	7.00	3.50	2.00
354	Rip Coleman	7.00	3.50	2.00
355	Frank Malzone	7.00	3.50	2.00
356	Faye Throneberry	7.00	3.50	2.00
357	Earl Torgeson	7.00	3.50	2.00
358	Jerry Lynch	7.00	3.50	2.00
359	Tom Cheney	7.00	3.50	2.00
360	Johnny Groth	7.00	3.50	2.00
361	Curt Barclay	7.00	3.50	2.00
362	Roman Mejias	7.00	3.50	2.00
363	Eddie Kasko	7.00	3.50	2.00
364	Cal McLish	7.00	3.50	2.00
365	Ossie Virgil	7.00	3.50	2.00
366	Ken Lehman	7.00	3.50	2.00
367	Ed Fitz Gerald	7.00	3.50	2.00
368	Bob Purkey	7.00	3.50	2.00
369	Milt Graff	7.00	3.50	2.00
370	Warren Hacker	7.00	3.50	2.00
371	Bob Lennon	7.00	3.50	2.00
372	Norm Zauchin	7.00	3.50	2.00
373	Pete Whisenant	7.00	3.50	2.00
374	Don Cardwell	7.00	3.50	2.00
375	*Jim Landis*	6.00	3.00	1.75
376	Don Elston	7.00	3.50	2.00
377	Andre Rodgers	7.00	3.50	2.00
378	Elmer Singleton	7.00	3.50	2.00
379	Don Lee	7.00	3.50	2.00
380	Walker Cooper	7.00	3.50	2.00
381	Dean Stone	7.00	3.50	2.00
382	Jim Brideweser	7.00	3.50	2.00
383	*Juan Pizarro*	6.00	3.00	1.75
384	Bobby Gene Smith	7.00	3.50	2.00
385	Art Houtteman	7.00	3.50	2.00
386	Lyle Luttrell	7.00	3.50	2.00
387	*Jack Sanford*	6.00	3.00	1.75
388	Pete Daley	7.00	3.50	2.00
389	Dave Jolly	7.00	3.50	2.00
390	Reno Bertoia	7.00	3.50	2.00
391	*Ralph Terry*	10.00	5.00	3.00
392	Chuck Tanner	6.00	3.00	1.75
393	Raul Sanchez	7.00	3.50	2.00
394	Luis Arroyo	7.00	3.50	2.00

		NR MT	EX	VG
395	Bubba Phillips	7.00	3.50	2.00
396	Casey Wise	7.00	3.50	2.00
397	Roy Smalley	7.00	3.50	2.00
398	Al Cicotte	6.00	3.00	1.75
399	Billy Consolo	7.00	3.50	2.00
400	Dodgers' Sluggers (Roy Campanella, Carl Furillo, Gil Hodges, Duke Snider)	200.00	100.00	60.00
401	*Earl Battey*	6.00	3.00	1.75
402	Jim Pisoni	7.00	3.50	2.00
403	Dick Hyde	7.00	3.50	2.00
404	Harry Anderson	7.00	3.50	2.00
405	Duke Maas	7.00	3.50	2.00
406	Bob Hale	7.00	3.50	2.00
407	Yankees' Power Hitters (Yogi Berra, Mickey Mantle)	400.00	200.00	125.00
---a	Checklist Series 1-2 (Big Blony ad on back)	175.00	87.00	52.00
---b	Checklist Series 1-2 (Bazooka ad on back)	175.00	87.00	52.00
---a	Checklist Series 2-3 (Big Blony ad on back)	300.00	150.00	90.00
---b	Checklist Series 2-3 (Bazooka ad on back)	300.00	150.00	90.00
---a	Checklist Series 3-4 (Big Blony ad on back)	500.00	250.00	150.00
---b	Checklist Series 3-4 (Bazooka ad on back)	500.00	250.00	150.00
---a	Checklist Series 4-5 (Big Blony ad on back)	750.00	325.00	225.00
---b	Checklist Series 4-5 (Bazooka ad on back)	750.00	325.00	225.00
-----	Contest Card (Saturday, May 4th)	15.00	7.50	4.50
-----	Contest Card (Saturday, May 25th)	15.00	7.50	4.50
-----	Contest Card (Saturday, June 22nd)	15.00	7.50	4.50
-----	Contest Card (Friday, July 19)	15.00	7.50	4.50
-----	Lucky Penny Insert Card	15.00	7.50	4.50

1958 Topps

Topps continued to expand its set size in 1958 with the release of a 494-card set. One card (#145) was not issued after Ed Bouchee was suspended from baseball. Cards retained the 2-1/2" by 3-1/2" size. There are a number of variations, including yellow or white lettering on 33 cards between numbers 2-108 (higher priced yellow letter variations checklisted below are not included in the complete set prices). The number of multiple-player cards was increased. A major innovation is the addition of 20 "All-Star" cards. For the first time, checklists were incorporated into the numbered series, as the backs of team cards.

		NR MT	EX	VG
Complete Set:		5000.00	2500.00	1500.
Common Player: 1-110		7.00	3.50	2.00
Common Player: 111-440		5.00	2.50	1.50
Common Player: 441-495		4.00	2.00	1.25
1	Ted Williams	400.00	125.00	60.00
2a	Bob Lemon (yellow team letters)	35.00	17.50	10.50
2b	Bob Lemon (white team letters)	12.00	6.00	3.50
3	Alex Kellner	7.00	3.50	2.00
4	Hank Foiles	7.00	3.50	2.00

		NR MT	EX	VG
5	Willie Mays	200.00	100.00	60.00
6	George Zuverink	7.00	3.50	2.00
7	Dale Long	7.00	3.50	2.00
8a	Eddie Kasko (yellow name letters)	20.00	10.00	6.00
8b	Eddie Kasko (white name letters)	7.00	3.50	2.00
9	Hank Bauer	12.00	6.00	3.50
10	Lou Burdette	8.00	4.00	2.50
11a	Jim Rivera (yellow team letters)	20.00	10.00	6.00
11b	Jim Rivera (white team letters)	7.00	3.50	2.00
12	George Crowe	7.00	3.50	2.00
13a	Billy Hoeft (yellow name letters)	20.00	10.00	6.00
13b	Billy Hoeft (white name, orange triangle by foot)	7.00	3.50	2.00
13c	Billy Hoeft (white name, red triangle by foot)	7.00	3.50	2.00
14	Rip Repulski	7.00	3.50	2.00
15	Jim Lemon	7.00	3.50	2.00
16	Charley Neal	7.00	3.50	2.00
17	Felix Mantilla	7.00	3.50	2.00
18	Frank Sullivan	7.00	3.50	2.00
19	Giants Team/Checklist 1-88	10.00	5.00	3.00
20a	Gil McDougald (yellow name letters)	25.00	12.50	7.50
20b	Gil McDougald (white name letters)	9.00	4.50	2.75
21	Curt Barclay	7.00	3.50	2.00
22	Hal Naragon	7.00	3.50	2.00
23a	Bill Tuttle (yellow name letters)	20.00	10.00	6.00
23b	Bill Tuttle (white name letters)	7.00	3.50	2.00
24a	Hobie Landrith (yellow name letters)	20.00	10.00	6.00
24b	Hobie Landrith (white name letters)	7.00	3.50	2.00
25	Don Drysdale	60.00	30.00	18.00
26	Ron Jackson	7.00	3.50	2.00
27	Bud Freeman	7.00	3.50	2.00
28	Jim Busby	7.00	3.50	2.00
29	Ted Lepcio	7.00	3.50	2.00
30a	Hank Aaron (yellow name letters)	350.00	140.00	88.00
30b	Hank Aaron (white name letters)	175.00	87.00	52.00
31	Tex Clevenger	7.00	3.50	2.00
32a	J.W. Porter (yellow name letters)	20.00	10.00	6.00
32b	J.W. Porter (white name letters)	7.00	3.50	2.00
33a	Cal Neeman (yellow name letters)	20.00	10.00	6.00
33b	Cal Neeman (white team letters)	7.00	3.50	2.00
34	Bob Thurman	7.00	3.50	2.00
35a	Don Mossi (yellow team letters)	20.00	10.00	6.00
35b	Don Mossi (white team letters)	7.00	3.50	2.00
36	Ted Kazanski	7.00	3.50	2.00
37	*Mike McCormick* (photo actually Ray Monzant)	7.00	3.50	2.00
38	Dick Gernert	7.00	3.50	2.00
39	Bob Martyn	7.00	3.50	2.00
40	George Kell	15.00	7.50	4.50
41	Dave Hillman	7.00	3.50	2.00
42	*John Roseboro*	7.00	3.50	2.00
43	Sal Maglie	10.00	5.00	3.00
44	Senators Team/Checklist 1-88	10.00	5.00	3.00
45	Dick Groat	7.00	3.50	2.00
46a	Lou Sleater (yellow name letters)	20.00	10.00	6.00
46b	Lou Sleater (white name letters)	7.00	3.50	2.00
47	*Roger Maris*	450.00	225.00	135.00
48	Chuck Harmon	7.00	3.50	2.00
49	Smoky Burgess	7.00	3.50	2.00
50a	Billy Pierce (yellow name letters)	20.00	10.00	6.00
50b	Billy Pierce (white name letters)	7.00	3.50	2.00
51	Del Rice	7.00	3.50	2.00
52a	Bob Clemente (yellow name letters)	350.00	175.00	105.00
52b	Bob Clemente (white name letters)	225.00	112.00	67.00
53a	Morrie Martin (yellow name letters)	20.00	10.00	6.00
53b	Morrie Martin (white name letters)	7.00	3.50	2.00
54	*Norm Siebern*	7.00	3.50	2.00
55	Chico Carrasquel	7.00	3.50	2.00
56	Bill Fischer	7.00	3.50	2.00
57a	Tim Thompson (yellow name letters)	20.00	10.00	6.00
57b	Tim Thompson (white name letters)	7.00	3.50	2.00
58a	Art Schult (yellow name letters)	20.00	10.00	6.00
58b	Art Schult (white name letters)	7.00	3.50	2.00
59	Dave Sisler	7.00	3.50	2.00

#	Player	NR MT	EX	VG
60a	Del Ennis (yellow name letters)	20.00	10.00	6.00
60b	Del Ennis (white name letters)	7.00	3.50	2.00
61a	Darrell Johnson (yellow name letters)	20.00	10.00	6.00
61b	Darrell Johnson (white name letters)	7.00	3.50	2.00
62	Joe DeMaestri	7.00	3.50	2.00
63	Joe Nuxhall	7.00	3.50	2.00
64	Joe Lonnett	7.00	3.50	2.00
65a	Von McDaniel (yellow name letters)	20.00	10.00	6.00
65b	Von McDaniel (white name letters)	7.00	3.50	2.00
66	Lee Walls	7.00	3.50	2.00
67	Joe Ginsberg	7.00	3.50	2.00
68	Daryl Spencer	7.00	3.50	2.00
69	Wally Burnette	7.00	3.50	2.00
70a	Al Kaline (yellow name letters)	200.00	100.00	60.00
70b	Al Kaline (white name letters)	75.00	38.00	23.00
71	Dodgers Team/Checklist 1-88	20.00	10.00	6.00
72	Bud Byerly	7.00	3.50	2.00
73	Pete Daley	7.00	3.50	2.00
74	Roy Face	7.00	3.50	2.00
75	Gus Bell	7.00	3.50	2.00
76a	Dick Farrell (yellow team letters)	20.00	10.00	6.00
76b	Dick Farrell (white team letters)	7.00	3.50	2.00
77a	Don Zimmer (yellow team letters)	20.00	10.00	6.00
77b	Don Zimmer (white team letters)	7.00	3.50	2.00
78a	Ernie Johnson (yellow name letters)	20.00	10.00	6.00
78b	Ernie Johnson (white name letters)	7.00	3.50	2.00
79a	Dick Williams (yellow team letters)	20.00	10.00	6.00
79b	Dick Williams (white team letters)	7.00	3.50	2.00
80	Dick Drott	7.00	3.50	2.00
81a	*Steve Boros* (yellow team letters)	20.00	10.00	6.00
81b	*Steve Boros* (white team letters)	7.00	3.50	2.00
82	Ronnie Kline	7.00	3.50	2.00
83	Bob Hazle	7.00	3.50	2.00
84	Billy O'Dell	7.00	3.50	2.00
85a	Luis Aparicio (yellow team letters)	50.00	25.00	15.00
85b	Luis Aparicio (white team letters)	15.00	7.50	4.50
86	Valmy Thomas	7.00	3.50	2.00
87	Johnny Kucks	7.00	3.50	2.00
88	Duke Snider	75.00	38.00	23.00
89	Billy Klaus	7.00	3.50	2.00
90	Robin Roberts	20.00	10.00	6.00
91	Chuck Tanner	7.00	3.50	2.00
92a	Clint Courtney (yellow name letters)	20.00	10.00	6.00
92b	Clint Courtney (white name letters)	7.00	3.50	2.00
93	Sandy Amoros	7.00	3.50	2.00
94	Bob Skinner	7.00	3.50	2.00
95	Frank Bolling	7.00	3.50	2.00
96	Joe Durham	7.00	3.50	2.00
97a	Larry Jackson (yellow name letters)	20.00	10.00	6.00
97b	Larry Jackson (white name letters)	7.00	3.50	2.00
98a	Billy Hunter (yellow name letters)	20.00	10.00	6.00
98b	Billy Hunter (white name letters)	7.00	3.50	2.00
99	Bobby Adams	7.00	3.50	2.00
100a	Early Wynn (yellow team letters)	30.00	15.00	9.00
100b	Early Wynn (white team letters)	15.00	7.50	4.50
101a	Bobby Richardson (yellow name letters)	30.00	15.00	9.00
101b	Bobby Richardson (white name letters)	15.00	7.50	4.50
102	George Strickland	7.00	3.50	2.00
103	Jerry Lynch	7.00	3.50	2.00
104	Jim Pendleton	7.00	3.50	2.00
105	Billy Gardner	7.00	3.50	2.00
106	Dick Schofield	7.00	3.50	2.00
107	Ossie Virgil	7.00	3.50	2.00
108a	Jim Landis (yellow team letters)	20.00	10.00	6.00
108b	Jim Landis (white team letters)	7.00	3.50	2.00
109	Herb Plews	7.00	3.50	2.00
110	Johnny Logan	7.00	3.50	2.00
111	Stu Miller	5.00	2.50	1.50
112	Gus Zernial	5.50	2.75	1.75
113	Jerry Walker	5.00	2.50	1.50
114	Irv Noren	5.00	2.50	1.50
115	Jim Bunning	20.00	10.00	6.00
116	Dave Philley	5.50	2.75	1.75
117	Frank Torre	5.00	2.50	1.50
118	Harvey Haddix	5.00	2.50	1.50
119	Harry Chiti	5.00	2.50	1.50
120	Johnny Podres	7.00	3.50	2.00
121	Eddie Miksis	5.00	2.50	1.50
122	Walt Moryn	5.00	2.50	1.50
123	Dick Tomanek	5.00	2.50	1.50
124	Bobby Usher	5.00	2.50	1.50
125	Al Dark	7.00	3.50	2.00
126	Stan Palys	5.00	2.50	1.50
127	Tom Sturdivant	7.00	3.50	2.00
128	*Willie Kirkland*	5.50	2.75	1.75
129	Jim Derrington	5.00	2.50	1.50
130	Jackie Jensen	7.00	3.50	2.00
131	Bob Henrich	5.00	2.50	1.50
132	Vernon Law	6.00	3.00	1.75
133	Russ Nixon	5.00	2.50	1.50
134	Phillies Team/Checklist 89-176	8.00	4.00	2.50
135	Mike Drabowsky	5.00	2.50	1.50
136	Jim Finingan	5.00	2.50	1.50
137	Russ Kemmerer	5.00	2.50	1.50
138	Earl Torgeson	5.00	2.50	1.50
139	George Brunet	5.00	2.50	1.50
140	Wes Covington	5.50	2.75	1.75
141	Ken Lehman	5.00	2.50	1.50
142	Enos Slaughter	20.00	10.00	6.00
143	Billy Muffett	5.00	2.50	1.50
144	Bobby Morgan	5.00	2.50	1.50
145	Not Issued			
146	Dick Gray	5.00	2.50	1.50
147	*Don McMahon*	6.00	3.00	1.75
148	Billy Consolo	5.00	2.50	1.50
149	Tom Acker	5.00	2.50	1.50
150	Mickey Mantle	650.00	325.00	185.00
151	Buddy Pritchard	5.00	2.50	1.50
152	Johnny Antonelli	6.00	3.00	1.75
153	Les Moss	5.00	2.50	1.50
154	Harry Byrd	5.00	2.50	1.50
155	Hector Lopez	5.00	2.50	1.50
156	Dick Hyde	5.00	2.50	1.50
157	Dee Fondy	5.00	2.50	1.50
158	Indians Team/Checklist 177-264	7.00	3.50	2.00
159	Taylor Phillips	5.00	2.50	1.50
160	Don Hoak	5.50	2.75	1.75
161	Don Larsen	7.00	3.50	2.00
162	Gil Hodges	25.00	12.50	7.50
163	Jim Wilson	5.00	2.50	1.50
164	Bob Taylor	5.00	2.50	1.50
165	Bob Nieman	5.00	2.50	1.50
166	Danny O'Connell	5.00	2.50	1.50
167	Frank Baumann	5.00	2.50	1.50
168	Joe Cunningham	5.50	2.75	1.75
169	Ralph Terry	5.50	2.75	1.75
170	Vic Wertz	6.00	3.00	1.75
171	Harry Anderson	5.00	2.50	1.50
172	Don Gross	5.00	2.50	1.50
173	Eddie Yost	5.50	2.75	1.75
174	A's Team/Checklist 89-176	8.00	4.00	2.50
175	*Marv Throneberry*	12.00	6.00	3.50
176	Bob Buhl	5.50	2.75	1.75
177	Al Smith	5.00	2.50	1.50
178	Ted Kluszewski	5.00	2.50	1.50
179	Willy Miranda	5.00	2.50	1.50
180	Lindy McDaniel	5.00	2.50	1.50
181	Willie Jones	5.00	2.50	1.50
182	Joe Caffie	5.00	2.50	1.50
183	Dave Jolly	5.00	2.50	1.50
184	Elvin Tappe	5.00	2.50	1.50
185	Ray Boone	5.50	2.75	1.75
186	Jack Meyer	5.00	2.50	1.50
187	Sandy Koufax	200.00	100.00	60.00
188	Milt Bolling (photo actually Lou Berberet)	5.00	2.50	1.50
189	George Susce	5.00	2.50	1.50
190	Red Schoendienst	15.00	7.50	4.50
191	Art Ceccarelli	5.00	2.50	1.50
192	Milt Graff	5.00	2.50	1.50
193	*Jerry Lumpe*	5.00	2.50	1.50
194	Roger Craig	6.00	3.00	1.75
195	Whitey Lockman	5.00	2.50	1.50
196	Mike Garcia	5.50	2.75	1.75
197	Haywood Sullivan	5.50	2.75	1.75
198	Bill Virdon	6.00	3.00	1.75
199	Don Blasingame	5.00	2.50	1.50
200	Bob Keegan	5.00	2.50	1.50
201	Jim Bolger	5.00	2.50	1.50
202	*Woody Held*	6.00	3.00	1.75
203	Al Walker	5.00	2.50	1.50
204	Leo Kiely	5.00	2.50	1.50
205	Johnny Temple	5.00	2.50	1.50

		NR MT	EX	VG
206	Bob Shaw	6.00	3.00	1.75
207	Solly Hemus	5.00	2.50	1.50
208	Cal McLish	5.00	2.50	1.50
209	Bob Anderson	5.00	2.50	1.50
210	Wally Moon	5.50	2.75	1.75
211	Pete Burnside	5.00	2.50	1.50
212	Bubba Phillips	5.00	2.50	1.50
213	Red Wilson	5.00	2.50	1.50
214	Willard Schmidt	5.00	2.50	1.50
215	Jim Gilliam	5.00	2.50	1.50
216	Cards Team/Checklist 177-264	7.00	3.50	2.00
217	Jack Harshman	5.00	2.50	1.50
218	Dick Rand	5.00	2.50	1.50
219	Camilo Pascual	5.50	2.75	1.75
220	Tom Brewer	5.00	2.50	1.50
221	Jerry Kindall	5.00	2.50	1.50
222	Bud Daley	5.00	2.50	1.50
223	Andy Pafko	6.00	3.00	1.75
224	Bob Grim	7.00	3.50	2.00
225	Billy Goodman	5.00	2.50	1.50
226	Bob Smith (photo actually Bobby Gene Smith)	5.00	2.50	1.50
227	Gene Stephens	5.00	2.50	1.50
228	Duke Maas	5.00	2.50	1.50
229	Frank Zupo	5.00	2.50	1.50
230	Richie Ashburn	8.00	4.00	2.50
231	Lloyd Merritt	5.00	2.50	1.50
232	Reno Bertoia	5.00	2.50	1.50
233	Mickey Vernon	5.50	2.75	1.75
234	Carl Sawatski	5.00	2.50	1.50
235	Tom Gorman	5.00	2.50	1.50
236	Ed Fitz Gerald	5.00	2.50	1.50
237	Bill Wight	5.00	2.50	1.50
238	Bill Mazeroski	15.00	7.50	4.50
239	Chuck Stobbs	5.00	2.50	1.50
240	Moose Skowron	10.00	5.00	3.00
241	Dick Littlefield	5.00	2.50	1.50
242	Johnny Klippstein	5.00	2.50	1.50
243	Larry Raines	5.00	2.50	1.50
244	*Don Demeter*	5.50	2.75	1.75
245	*Frank Lary*	5.50	2.75	1.75
246	Yankees Team/Checklist 177-264	40.00	20.00	12.00
247	Casey Wise	5.00	2.50	1.50
248	Herm Wehmeier	5.00	2.50	1.50
249	Ray Moore	5.00	2.50	1.50
250	Roy Sievers	6.00	3.00	1.75
251	Warren Hacker	5.00	2.50	1.50
252	Bob Trowbridge	5.00	2.50	1.50
253	Don Mueller	5.00	2.50	1.50
254	Alex Grammas	5.00	2.50	1.50
255	Bob Turley	5.00	2.50	1.50
256	White Sox Team/Checklist 265-352	8.00	4.00	2.50
257	Hal Smith	5.00	2.50	1.50
258	Carl Erskine	5.00	2.50	1.50
259	Al Pilarcik	5.00	2.50	1.50
260	Frank Malzone	5.50	2.75	1.75
261	Turk Lown	5.00	2.50	1.50
262	Johnny Groth	5.00	2.50	1.50
263	Eddie Bressoud	5.50	2.75	1.75
264	Jack Sanford	5.50	2.75	1.75
265	Pete Runnels	5.50	2.75	1.75
266	Connie Johnson	5.00	2.50	1.50
267	Sherm Lollar	5.50	2.75	1.75
268	Granny Hamner	5.00	2.50	1.50
269	Paul Smith	5.00	2.50	1.50
270	Warren Spahn	50.00	25.00	15.00
271	Billy Martin	15.00	7.50	4.50
272	Ray Crone	5.00	2.50	1.50
273	Hal Smith	5.00	2.50	1.50
274	Rocky Bridges	5.00	2.50	1.50
275	Elston Howard	8.00	4.00	2.50
276	Bobby Avila	5.00	2.50	1.50
277	Virgil Trucks	5.50	2.75	1.75
278	Mack Burk	5.00	2.50	1.50
279	Bob Boyd	5.00	2.50	1.50
280	Jim Piersall	6.00	3.00	1.75
281	Sam Taylor	5.00	2.50	1.50
282	Paul Foytack	5.00	2.50	1.50
283	Ray Shearer	5.00	2.50	1.50
284	Ray Katt	5.00	2.50	1.50
285	Frank Robinson	65.00	33.00	20.00
286	Gino Cimoli	5.00	2.50	1.50
287	Sam Jones	5.00	2.50	1.50
288	Harmon Killebrew	50.00	30.00	15.00
289	Series Hurling Rivals (Lou Burdette, Bobby Shantz)	4.00	2.00	1.25
290	Dick Donovan	5.00	2.50	1.50
291	Don Landrum	5.00	2.50	1.50
292	Ned Garver	5.00	2.50	1.50

		NR MT	EX	VG
293	Gene Freese	5.00	2.50	1.50
294	Hal Jeffcoat	5.00	2.50	1.50
295	Minnie Minoso	4.00	2.00	1.25
296	*Ryne Duren*	12.00	6.00	3.50
297	Don Buddin	5.00	2.50	1.50
298	Jim Hearn	5.00	2.50	1.50
299	Harry Simpson	7.00	3.50	2.00
300	League Presidents (Warren Giles, William Harridge)	7.00	3.50	2.00
301	Randy Jackson	5.00	2.50	1.50
302	Mike Baxes	5.00	2.50	1.50
303	Neil Chrisley	5.00	2.50	1.50
304	Tigers' Big Bats (Al Kaline, Harvey Kuenn)	10.00	5.00	3.00
305	Clem Labine	5.50	2.75	1.75
306	Whammy Douglas	5.00	2.50	1.50
307	Brooks Robinson	90.00	45.00	27.00
308	Paul Giel	5.00	2.50	1.50
309	Gail Harris	5.00	2.50	1.50
310	Ernie Banks	90.00	45.00	27.00
311	Bob Purkey	5.00	2.50	1.50
312	Red Sox Team/Checklist 353-440	8.00	4.00	2.50
313	Bob Rush	5.00	2.50	1.50
314	Dodgers' Boss & Power (Walter Alston, Duke Snider)	15.00	7.50	4.50
315	Bob Friend	6.00	3.00	1.75
316	Tito Francona	5.50	2.75	1.75
317	*Albie Pearson*	6.00	3.00	1.75
318	Frank House	5.00	2.50	1.50
319	Lou Skizas	5.00	2.50	1.50
320	Whitey Ford	35.00	17.50	10.50
321	Sluggers Supreme (Ted Kluszewski, Ted Williams)	20.00	10.00	6.00
322	Harding Peterson	5.00	2.50	1.50
323	Elmer Valo	5.00	2.50	1.50
324	Hoyt Wilhelm	15.00	7.50	4.50
325	Joe Adcock	6.00	3.00	1.75
326	Bob Miller	5.00	2.50	1.50
327	Cubs Team/Checklist 265-352	8.00	4.00	2.50
328	Ike Delock	5.00	2.50	1.50
329	Bob Cerv	5.00	2.50	1.50
330	Ed Bailey	5.00	2.50	1.50
331	Pedro Ramos	5.00	2.50	1.50
332	Jim King	5.00	2.50	1.50
333	Andy Carey	7.00	3.50	2.00
334	Mound Aces (Bob Friend, Billy Pierce)	6.00	3.00	1.75
335	Ruben Gomez	5.00	2.50	1.50
336	Bert Hamric	5.00	2.50	1.50
337	Hank Aguirre	5.00	2.50	1.50
338	Walt Dropo	5.50	2.75	1.75
339	Fred Hatfield	5.00	2.50	1.50
340	Don Newcombe	7.00	3.50	2.00
341	Pirates Team/Checklist 265-352	8.00	4.00	2.50
342	Jim Brosnan	5.50	2.75	1.75
343	*Orlando Cepeda*	80.00	40.00	25.00
344	Bob Porterfield	5.00	2.50	1.50
345	Jim Hegan	5.00	2.50	1.50
346	Steve Bilko	5.00	2.50	1.50
347	Don Rudolph	5.00	2.50	1.50
348	Chico Fernandez	5.00	2.50	1.50
349	Murry Dickson	5.00	2.50	1.50
350	Ken Boyer	5.00	2.50	1.50
351	Braves' Fence Busters (Hank Aaron, Joe Adcock, Del Crandall, Ed Mathews)	20.00	10.00	6.00
352	Herb Score	7.00	3.50	2.00
353	Stan Lopata	5.00	2.50	1.50
354	Art Ditmar	7.00	3.50	2.00
355	Bill Bruton	5.50	2.75	1.75
356	Bob Malkmus	5.00	2.50	1.50
357	Danny McDevitt	5.00	2.50	1.50
358	Gene Baker	5.00	2.50	1.50
359	Billy Loes	5.00	2.50	1.50
360	Roy McMillan	5.00	2.50	1.50
361	Mike Fornieles	5.00	2.50	1.50
362	Ray Jablonski	5.00	2.50	1.50
363	Don Elston	5.00	2.50	1.50
364	Earl Battey	5.50	2.75	1.75
365	Tom Morgan	5.00	2.50	1.50
366	Gene Green	5.00	2.50	1.50
367	Jack Urban	5.00	2.50	1.50
368	Rocky Colavito	30.00	15.00	9.00
369	Ralph Lumenti	5.00	2.50	1.50
370	Yogi Berra	100.00	50.00	30.00
371	Marty Keough	5.00	2.50	1.50
372	Don Cardwell	5.00	2.50	1.50
373	Joe Pignatano	5.00	2.50	1.50
374	Brooks Lawrence	5.00	2.50	1.50
375	Pee Wee Reese	50.00	30.00	15.00
376	Charley Rabe	5.00	2.50	1.50

		NR MT	EX	VG
377a	Braves Team (alphabetical checklist on	9.00	4.50	2.75
	back)			
377b	Braves Team (numerical checklist on	60.00	30.00	18.00
	back)			
378	Hank Sauer	5.50	2.75	1.75
379	Ray Herbert	5.00	2.50	1.50
380	Charley Maxwell	5.00	2.50	1.50
381	Hal Brown	5.00	2.50	1.50
382	Al Cicotte	7.00	3.50	2.00
383	Lou Berberet	5.00	2.50	1.50
384	John Goryl	5.00	2.50	1.50
385	Wilmer Mizell	5.00	2.50	1.50
386	Birdie's Young Sluggers (Ed Bailey, Frank			
	Robinson, Birdie Tebbetts)	7.00	3.50	2.00
387	Wally Post	5.00	2.50	1.50
388	Billy Moran	5.00	2.50	1.50
389	Bill Taylor	5.00	2.50	1.50
390	Del Crandall	6.00	3.00	1.75
391	Dave Melton	5.00	2.50	1.50
392	Bennie Daniels	5.00	2.50	1.50
393	Tony Kubek	20.00	10.00	6.00
394	*Jim Grant*	6.00	3.00	1.75
395	Willard Nixon	5.00	2.50	1.50
396	Dutch Dotterer	5.00	2.50	1.50
397a	Tigers Team (alphabetical checklist on			
	back)	9.00	4.50	2.75
397b	Tigers Team (numerical checklist on			
	back)	60.00	30.00	18.00
398	Gene Woodling	5.50	2.75	1.75
399	Marv Grissom	5.00	2.50	1.50
400	Nellie Fox	15.00	7.50	4.50
401	Don Bessent	5.00	2.50	1.50
402	Bobby Gene Smith	5.00	2.50	1.50
403	Steve Korcheck	5.00	2.50	1.50
404	Curt Simmons	6.00	3.00	1.75
405	Ken Aspromonte	5.00	2.50	1.50
406	Vic Power	5.00	2.50	1.50
407	Carlton Willey	5.00	2.50	1.50
408a	Orioles Team (alphabetical checklist on			
	back)	8.00	4.00	2.50
408b	Orioles Team (numerical checklist on			
	back)	60.00	30.00	18.00
409	Frank Thomas	5.00	2.50	1.50
410	Murray Wall	5.00	2.50	1.50
411	*Tony Taylor*	5.50	2.75	1.75
412	Jerry Staley	5.00	2.50	1.50
413	*Jim Davenport*	5.50	2.75	1.75
414	Sammy White	5.00	2.50	1.50
415	Bob Bowman	5.00	2.50	1.50
416	Foster Castleman	5.00	2.50	1.50
417	Carl Furillo	7.00	3.50	2.00
418	World Series Batting Foes (Hank Aaron,			
	Mickey Mantle)	150.00	75.00	45.00
419	Bobby Shantz	7.00	3.50	2.00
420	Vada Pinson	30.00	15.00	9.00
421	Dixie Howell	5.00	2.50	1.50
422	Norm Zauchin	5.00	2.50	1.50
423	Phil Clark	5.00	2.50	1.50
424	Larry Doby	5.00	2.50	1.50
425	Sam Esposito	5.00	2.50	1.50
426	Johnny O'Brien	5.00	2.50	1.50
427	Al Worthington	5.00	2.50	1.50
428a	Redlegs Team (alphabetical checklist on			
	back)	8.00	4.00	2.50
428b	Redlegs Team (numerical checklist on			
	back)	50.00	25.00	15.00
429	Gus Triandos	5.50	2.75	1.75
430	Bobby Thomson	6.00	3.00	1.75
431	Gene Conley	5.50	2.75	1.75
432	John Powers	5.00	2.50	1.50
433	Pancho Herrera	5.00	2.50	1.50
434	Harvey Kuenn	6.00	3.00	1.75
435	Ed Roebuck	5.00	2.50	1.50
436	Rival Fence Busters (Willie Mays, Duke			
	Snider)	55.00	28.00	16.50
437	Bob Speake	5.00	2.50	1.50
438	Whitey Herzog	7.00	3.50	2.00
439	Ray Narleski	5.00	2.50	1.50
440	Ed Mathews	30.00	15.00	9.00
441	Jim Marshall	4.00	2.00	1.25
442	Phil Paine	4.00	2.00	1.25
443	Billy Harrell	7.00	3.50	2.00
444	Danny Kravitz	4.00	2.00	1.25
445	Bob Smith	4.00	2.00	1.25
446	Carroll Hardy	7.00	3.50	2.00
447	Ray Monzant	4.00	2.00	1.25
448	*Charlie Lau*	5.50	2.75	1.75
449	Gene Fodge	4.00	2.00	1.25
450	Preston Ward	7.00	3.50	2.00
451	Joe Taylor	4.00	2.00	1.25
452	Roman Mejias	4.00	2.00	1.25

		NR MT	EX	VG
453	Tom Qualters	4.00	2.00	1.25
454	Harry Hanebrink	4.00	2.00	1.25
455	Hal Griggs	4.00	2.00	1.25
456	Dick Brown	4.00	2.00	1.25
457	*Milt Pappas*	5.50	2.75	1.75
458	Julio Becquer	4.00	2.00	1.25
459	Ron Blackburn	4.00	2.00	1.25
460	Chuck Essegian	4.00	2.00	1.25
461	Ed Mayer	4.00	2.00	1.25
462	Gary Geiger	7.00	3.50	2.00
463	Vito Valentinetti	4.00	2.00	1.25
464	*Curt Flood*	25.00	12.50	7.50
465	Arnie Portocarrero	4.00	2.00	1.25
466	Pete Whisenant	4.00	2.00	1.25
467	Glen Hobbie	4.00	2.00	1.25
468	Bob Schmidt	4.00	2.00	1.25
469	Don Ferrarese	4.00	2.00	1.25
470	R.C. Stevens	4.00	2.00	1.25
471	Lenny Green	4.00	2.00	1.25
472	Joe Jay	4.00	2.00	1.25
473	Bill Renna	4.00	2.00	1.25
474	Roman Semproch	4.00	2.00	1.25
475	All-Star Managers (Fred Haney, Casey			
	Stengel)	18.00	9.00	5.50
476	Stan Musial AS	40.00	20.00	12.00
477	Bill Skowron AS	4.00	2.00	1.25
478	Johnny Temple AS	5.00	2.50	1.50
479	Nellie Fox AS	10.00	5.00	3.00
480	Eddie Mathews AS	10.00	5.00	3.00
481	Frank Malzone AS	5.00	2.50	1.50
482	Ernie Banks AS	25.00	12.50	7.50
483	Luis Aparicio AS	8.00	4.00	2.50
484	Frank Robinson AS	25.00	12.50	7.50
485	Ted Williams AS	65.00	33.00	20.00
486	Willie Mays AS	50.00	25.00	15.00
487	Mickey Mantle AS	110.00	55.00	33.00
488	Hank Aaron AS	50.00	25.00	15.00
489	Jackie Jensen AS	6.00	3.00	1.75
490	Ed Bailey AS	5.00	2.50	1.50
491	Sherm Lollar AS	5.00	2.50	1.50
492	Bob Friend AS	6.00	3.00	1.75
493	Bob Turley AS	7.00	3.50	2.00
494	Warren Spahn AS	15.00	7.50	4.50
495	Herb Score AS	7.00	3.50	2.00
-----	Contest Card (All-Star Game, July 8)			
		15.00	7.50	4.50
-----	Felt Emblems Insert Card	15.00	7.50	4.50

1959 Topps

These 2-1/2" by 3-1/2" cards have a round photograph at the center of the front with a solid-color background and white border. A facsimile autograph is found across the photo. The 572-card set marks the largest set issued to that time. Card numbers below 507 have red and green printing with the card number in white in a green box. On high number cards beginning with #507, the printing is black and red and the card number is in a black box. Specialty cards include multiple-player cards, team cards with checklists, "All-Star" cards, highlights from previous season, and 31 "Rookie Stars." There is also a card of the commissioner, Ford Frick, and one of Roy Campanella in a wheelchair. A handful of cards can be found with and without lines added to the biographies on back indicating trades or demotions; those without the added lines are considerably more rare and valuable and are not included in the complete set price. Card numbers 199-286 can be found with either white or grey backs, with the grey stock being the less common.

		NR MT	EX	VG
	Complete Set:	5000.00	2500.00	1500.
	Common Player: 1-110	5.00	2.50	1.50
	Common Player: 111-506	3.00	1.50	.90
	Common Player: 507-572	15.00	7.50	4.50
1	Ford Frick	70.00	15.00	9.00
2	Eddie Yost	5.00	2.00	1.25
3	Don McMahon	5.00	2.50	1.50
4	Albie Pearson	5.00	2.50	1.50
5	Dick Donovan	5.00	2.50	1.50
6	Alex Grammas	5.00	2.50	1.50
7	Al Pilarcik	5.00	2.50	1.50
8	Phillies Team/Checklist 1-88	20.00	10.00	6.00
9	Paul Giel	5.00	2.50	1.50
10	Mickey Mantle	500.00	250.00	150.00
11	Billy Hunter	5.00	2.50	1.50
12	Vern Law	5.00	2.50	1.50
13	Dick Gernert	5.00	2.50	1.50
14	Pete Whisenant	5.00	2.50	1.50
15	Dick Drott	5.00	2.50	1.50
16	Joe Pignatano	5.00	2.50	1.50
17	Danny's All-Stars (Ted Kluszewski, Danny Murtaugh, Frank Thomas)	5.00	2.50	1.50
18	Jack Urban	5.00	2.50	1.50
19	Ed Bressoud	5.00	2.50	1.50
20	Duke Snider	60.00	30.00	18.00
21	Connie Johnson	5.00	2.50	1.50
22	Al Smith	5.00	2.50	1.50
23	Murry Dickson	5.00	2.50	1.50
24	Red Wilson	5.00	2.50	1.50
25	Don Hoak	6.00	3.00	1.75
26	Chuck Stobbs	5.00	2.50	1.50
27	Andy Pafko	6.00	3.00	1.75
28	Red Worthington	5.00	2.50	1.50
29	Jim Bolger	5.00	2.50	1.50
30	Nellie Fox	20.00	10.00	6.00
31	Ken Lehman	5.00	2.50	1.50
32	Don Buddin	5.00	2.50	1.50
33	Ed Fitz Gerald	5.00	2.50	1.50
34	Pitchers Beware (Al Kaline, Charlie Maxwell)	12.00	6.00	3.25
35	Ted Kluszewski	10.00	5.00	3.00
36	Hank Aguirre	5.00	2.50	1.50
37	Gene Green	5.00	2.50	1.50
38	Morrie Martin	5.00	2.50	1.50
39	Ed Bouchee	5.00	2.50	1.50
40	Warren Spahn	50.00	25.00	15.00
41	Bob Martyn	5.00	2.50	1.50
42	Murray Wall	5.00	2.50	1.50
43	Steve Bilko	5.00	2.50	1.50
44	Vito Valentinetti	5.00	2.50	1.50
45	Andy Carey	5.00	2.50	1.50
46	Bill Henry	5.00	2.50	1.50
47	Jim Finigan	5.00	2.50	1.50
48	Orioles Team/Checklist 1-88	15.00	7.50	4.50
49	Bill Hall	5.00	2.50	1.50
50	Willie Mays	160.00	80.00	50.00
51	Rip Coleman	5.00	2.50	1.50
52	Coot Veal	5.00	2.50	1.50
53	Stan Williams	5.00	2.50	1.50
54	Mel Roach	5.00	2.50	1.50
55	Tom Brewer	5.00	2.50	1.50
56	Carl Sawatski	5.00	2.50	1.50
57	Al Cicotte	5.00	2.50	1.50
58	Eddie Miksis	5.00	2.50	1.50
59	Irv Noren	5.00	2.50	1.50
60	Bob Turley	6.00	3.00	1.75
61	Dick Brown	5.00	2.50	1.50
62	Tony Taylor	5.00	2.50	1.50
63	Jim Hearn	5.00	2.50	1.50
64	Joe DeMaestri	5.00	2.50	1.50
65	Frank Torre	5.00	2.50	1.50
66	Joe Ginsberg	5.00	2.50	1.50
67	Brooks Lawrence	5.00	2.50	1.50
68	Dick Schofield	5.00	2.50	1.50
69	Giants Team/Checklist 89-176	18.00	9.00	5.50
70	Harvey Kuenn	5.00	2.50	1.50
71	Don Bessent	5.00	2.50	1.50
72	Bill Renna	5.00	2.50	1.50
73	Ron Jackson	5.00	2.50	1.50
74	Directing the Power (Cookie Lavagetto, Jim Lemon, Roy Sievers)	6.00	3.00	1.75
75	Sam Jones	5.00	2.50	1.50
76	Bobby Richardson	15.00	7.50	4.50
77	John Goryl	5.00	2.50	1.50

		NR MT	EX	VG
78	Pedro Ramos	5.00	2.50	1.50
79	Harry Chiti	5.00	2.50	1.50
80	Minnie Minoso	5.00	2.50	1.50
81	Hal Jeffcoat	5.00	2.50	1.50
82	Bob Boyd	5.00	2.50	1.50
83	Bob Smith	5.00	2.50	1.50
84	Reno Bertoia	5.00	2.50	1.50
85	Harry Anderson	5.00	2.50	1.50
86	Bob Keegan	5.00	2.50	1.50
87	Danny O'Connell	5.00	2.50	1.50
88	Herb Score	6.00	3.00	1.75
89	Billy Gardner	5.00	2.50	1.50
90	Bill Skowron	15.00	7.50	4.50
91	Herb Moford	5.00	2.50	1.50
92	Dave Philley	5.00	2.50	1.50
93	Julio Becquer	5.00	2.50	1.50
94	W. Sox Team/Checklist 89-176	15.00	7.50	4.50
95	Carl Willey	5.00	2.50	1.50
96	Lou Berberet	5.00	2.50	1.50
97	Jerry Lynch	5.00	2.50	1.50
98	Arnie Portocarrero	5.00	2.50	1.50
99	Ted Kazanski	5.00	2.50	1.50
100	Bob Cerv	5.00	2.50	1.50
101	Alex Kellner	5.00	2.50	1.50
102	*Felipe Alou*	30.00	15.00	9.00
103	Billy Goodman	5.00	2.50	1.50
104	Del Rice	5.00	2.50	1.50
105	Lee Walls	5.00	2.50	1.50
106	Hal Woodeshick	5.00	2.50	1.50
107	Norm Larker	5.00	2.50	1.50
108	Zack Monroe	5.00	2.50	1.50
109	Bob Schmidt	5.00	2.50	1.50
110	George Witt	5.00	2.50	1.50
111	Redlegs Team/Checklist 89-176	8.00	4.00	2.50
112	Billy Consolo	3.00	1.50	.90
113	Taylor Phillips	3.00	1.50	.90
114	Earl Battey	3.25	1.75	1.00
115	Mickey Vernon	3.25	1.75	1.00
116	*Bob Allison*	7.00	3.50	2.00
117	*John Blanchard*	3.25	1.75	1.00
118	John Buzhardt	3.00	1.50	.90
119	*John Callison*	5.00	2.50	1.50
120	Chuck Coles	3.00	1.50	.90
121	Bob Conley	3.00	1.50	.90
122	Bennie Daniels	3.00	1.50	.90
123	Don Dillard	3.00	1.50	.90
124	Dan Dobbek	3.00	1.50	.90
125	*Ron Fairly*	3.50	1.75	1.00
126	Eddie Haas	3.00	1.50	.90
127	Kent Hadley	3.00	1.50	.90
128	Bob Hartman	3.00	1.50	.90
129	Frank Herrera	3.00	1.50	.90
130	Lou Jackson	3.00	1.50	.90
131	*Deron Johnson*	3.25	1.75	1.00
132	Don Lee	3.00	1.50	.90
133	*Bob Lillis*	3.25	1.75	1.00
134	Jim McDaniel	3.00	1.50	.90
135	Gene Oliver	3.00	1.50	.90
136	*Jim O'Toole*	3.25	1.75	1.00
137	Dick Ricketts	3.00	1.50	.90
138	John Romano	3.00	1.50	.90
139	Ed Sadowski	3.00	1.50	.90
140	Charlie Secrest	3.00	1.50	.90
141	Joe Shipley	3.00	1.50	.90
142	Dick Stigman	3.00	1.50	.90
143	Willie Tasby	3.00	1.50	.90
144	Jerry Walker	3.00	1.50	.90
145	Dom Zanni	3.00	1.50	.90
146	Jerry Zimmerman	3.00	1.50	.90
147	Cub's Clubbers (Ernie Banks, Dale Long, Walt Moryn)	10.00	5.00	3.00
148	Mike McCormick	3.25	1.75	1.00
149	Jim Bunning	15.00	7.50	4.50
150	Stan Musial	150.00	75.00	45.00
151	Bob Malkmus	3.00	1.50	.90
152	Johnny Klippstein	3.00	1.50	.90
153	Jim Marshall	3.00	1.50	.90
154	Ray Herbert	3.00	1.50	.90
155	Enos Slaughter	18.00	9.00	5.50
156	Ace Hurlers (Billy Pierce, Robin Roberts)	3.50	1.75	1.00
157	Felix Mantilla	3.00	1.50	.90
158	Walt Dropo	3.25	1.75	1.00
159	Bob Shaw	3.00	1.50	.90
160	Dick Groat	3.00	1.50	.90
161	Frank Baumann	3.00	1.50	.90
162	Bobby G. Smith	3.00	1.50	.90
163	Sandy Koufax	175.00	87.00	52.00
164	Johnny Groth	3.00	1.50	.90
165	Bill Bruton	3.25	1.75	1.00
166	Destruction Crew (Rocky Colavito, Larry Doby, Minnie Minoso)	3.25	1.75	1.00

		NR MT	EX	VG
167	Duke Maas	3.00	1.50	.90
168	Carroll Hardy	3.00	1.50	.90
169	Ted Abernathy	3.00	1.50	.90
170	Gene Woodling	3.25	1.75	1.00
171	Willard Schmidt	3.00	1.50	.90
172	A's Team/Checklist 177-242	7.00	3.50	2.00
173	*Bill Monbouquette*	3.25	1.75	1.00
174	Jim Pendleton	3.00	1.50	.90
175	Dick Farrell	3.00	1.50	.90
176	Preston Ward	3.00	1.50	.90
177	Johnny Briggs	3.00	1.50	.90
178	Ruben Amaro	3.00	1.50	.90
179	Don Rudolph	3.00	1.50	.90
180	Yogi Berra	90.00	45.00	27.00
181	Bob Porterfield	3.00	1.50	.90
182	Milt Graff	3.00	1.50	.90
183	Stu Miller	3.00	1.50	.90
184	Harvey Haddix	3.25	1.75	1.00
185	Jim Busby	3.00	1.50	.90
186	Mudcat Grant	3.25	1.75	1.00
187	Bubba Phillips	3.00	1.50	.90
188	Juan Pizarro	3.00	1.50	.90
189	Neil Chrisley	3.00	1.50	.90
190	Bill Virdon	3.25	1.75	1.00
191	Russ Kemmerer	3.00	1.50	.90
192	Charley Beamon	3.00	1.50	.90
193	Sammy Taylor	3.00	1.50	.90
194	Jim Brosnan	3.25	1.75	1.00
195	Rip Repulski	3.00	1.50	.90
196	Billy Moran	3.00	1.50	.90
197	Ray Semproch	3.00	1.50	.90
198	Jim Davenport	3.00	1.50	.90
199	Leo Kiely	3.00	1.50	.90
200	Warren Giles	3.25	1.75	1.00
201	Tom Acker	3.00	1.50	.90
202	Roger Maris	150.00	75.00	45.00
203	Ozzie Virgil	3.00	1.50	.90
204	Casey Wise	3.00	1.50	.90
205	Don Larsen	7.00	3.50	2.00
206	Carl Furillo	5.00	2.50	1.50
207	George Strickland	3.00	1.50	.90
208	Willie Jones	3.00	1.50	.90
209	Lenny Green	3.00	1.50	.90
210	Ed Bailey	3.00	1.50	.90
211	Bob Blaylock	3.00	1.50	.90
212	Fence Busters (Hank Aaron, Eddie Mathews)	55.00	28.00	16.50
213	Jim Rivera	3.00	1.50	.90
214	Marcelino Solis	3.00	1.50	.90
215	Jim Lemon	3.00	1.50	.90
216	Andre Rodgers	3.00	1.50	.90
217	Carl Erskine	5.00	2.50	1.50
218	Roman Mejias	3.00	1.50	.90
219	George Zuverink	3.00	1.50	.90
220	Frank Malzone	3.25	1.75	1.00
221	Bob Bowman	3.00	1.50	.90
222	Bobby Shantz	3.50	1.75	1.00
223	Cards Team/Checklist 265-352	7.00	3.50	2.00
224	*Claude Osteen*	3.00	1.50	.90
225	Johnny Logan	3.25	1.75	1.00
226	Art Ceccarelli	3.00	1.50	.90
227	Hal Smith	3.00	1.50	.90
228	Don Gross	3.00	1.50	.90
229	Vic Power	3.00	1.50	.90
230	Bill Fischer	3.00	1.50	.90
231	Ellis Burton	3.00	1.50	.90
232	Eddie Kasko	3.00	1.50	.90
233	Paul Foytack	3.00	1.50	.90
234	Chuck Tanner	3.00	1.50	.90
235	Valmy Thomas	3.00	1.50	.90
236	Ted Bowsfield	3.00	1.50	.90
237	Run Preventers (Gil McDougald, Bobby Richardson, Bob Turley)	5.00	2.50	1.50
238	Gene Baker	3.00	1.50	.90
239	Bob Trowbridge	3.00	1.50	.90
240	Hank Bauer	7.00	3.50	2.00
241	Billy Muffett	3.00	1.50	.90
242	Ron Samford	3.00	1.50	.90
243	Marv Grissom	3.00	1.50	.90
244	Dick Gray	3.00	1.50	.90
245	Ned Garver	3.00	1.50	.90
246	J.W. Porter	3.00	1.50	.90
247	Don Ferrarese	3.00	1.50	.90
248	Red Sox Team/Checklist 177-264	8.00	4.00	2.50
249	Bobby Adams	3.00	1.50	.90
250	Billy O'Dell	3.00	1.50	.90
251	Cletis Boyer	6.00	3.00	1.75
252	Ray Boone	3.25	1.75	1.00
253	Seth Morehead	3.00	1.50	.90
254	Zeke Bella	3.00	1.50	.90

		NR MT	EX	VG
255	Del Ennis	3.25	1.75	1.00
256	Jerry Davie	3.00	1.50	.90
257	*Leon Wagner*	3.00	1.50	.90
258	Fred Kipp	3.00	1.50	.90
259	Jim Pisoni	3.00	1.50	.90
260	Early Wynn	15.00	7.50	4.50
261	Gene Stephens	3.00	1.50	.90
262	Hitters' Foes (Don Drysdale, Clem Labine, Johnny Podres)	8.00	4.00	2.50
263	Buddy Daley	3.00	1.50	.90
264	Chico Carrasquel	3.00	1.50	.90
265	Ron Kline	3.00	1.50	.90
266	Woody Held	3.25	1.75	1.00
267	John Romonosky	3.00	1.50	.90
268	Tito Francona	3.25	1.75	1.00
269	Jack Meyer	3.00	1.50	.90
270	Gil Hodges	20.00	10.00	6.00
271	*Orlando Pena*	3.25	1.75	1.00
272	Jerry Lumpe	3.25	1.75	1.00
273	Joe Jay	3.00	1.50	.90
274	Jerry Kindall	3.00	1.50	.90
275	Jack Sanford	3.00	1.50	.90
276	Pete Daley	3.00	1.50	.90
277	Turk Lown	3.00	1.50	.90
278	Chuck Essegian	3.00	1.50	.90
279	Ernie Johnson	3.00	1.50	.90
280	Frank Bolling	3.00	1.50	.90
281	Walt Craddock	3.00	1.50	.90
282	R.C. Stevens	3.00	1.50	.90
283	Russ Heman	3.00	1.50	.90
284	Steve Korcheck	3.00	1.50	.90
285	Joe Cunningham	3.25	1.75	1.00
286	Dean Stone	3.00	1.50	.90
287	Don Zimmer	3.25	1.75	1.00
288	Dutch Dotterer	3.00	1.50	.90
289	Johnny Kucks	3.00	1.50	.90
290	Wes Covington	3.25	1.75	1.00
291	Pitching Partners (Camilo Pascual, Pedro Ramos)	3.25	1.75	1.00
292	Dick Williams	3.25	1.75	1.00
293	Ray Moore	3.00	1.50	.90
294	Hank Foiles	3.00	1.50	.90
295	Billy Martin	15.00	7.50	4.50
296	*Ernie Broglio*	3.25	1.75	1.00
297	*Jackie Brandt*	3.25	1.75	1.00
298	Tex Clevenger	3.00	1.50	.90
299	Billy Klaus	3.00	1.50	.90
300	Richie Ashburn	20.00	10.00	6.00
301	Earl Averill	3.00	1.50	.90
302	Don Mossi	3.25	1.75	1.00
303	Marty Keough	3.00	1.50	.90
304	Cubs Team/Checklist 265-352	7.00	3.50	2.00
305	Curt Raydon	3.00	1.50	.90
306	Jim Gilliam	5.00	2.50	1.50
307	Curt Barclay	3.00	1.50	.90
308	Norm Siebern	3.50	1.75	1.00
309	Sal Maglie	3.00	1.50	.90
310	Luis Aparicio	15.00	7.50	4.50
311	Norm Zauchin	3.00	1.50	.90
312	Don Newcombe	6.00	3.00	1.75
313	Frank House	3.00	1.50	.90
314	Don Cardwell	3.00	1.50	.90
315	Joe Adcock	3.00	1.50	.90
316a	Ralph Lumenti (without option statement)	80.00	40.00	24.00
316b	Ralph Lumenti (with option statement)	3.00	1.50	.90
317	N.L. Hitting Kings (Richie Ashburn, Willie Mays)	25.00	12.50	7.50
318	Rocky Bridges	3.00	1.50	.90
319	Dave Hillman	3.00	1.50	.90
320	Bob Skinner	3.25	1.75	1.00
321a	Bob Giallombardo (without option statement)	80.00	40.00	24.00
321b	Bob Giallombardo (with option statement)	3.00	1.50	.90
322a	Harry Hanebrink (without trade statement)	65.00	33.00	18.00
322b	Harry Hanebrink (with trade statement)	3.00	1.50	.90
323	Frank Sullivan	3.00	1.50	.90
324	Don Demeter	3.00	1.50	.90
325	Ken Boyer	5.00	2.50	1.50
326	Marv Throneberry	5.00	2.50	1.50
327	*Gary Bell*	3.25	1.75	1.00
328	Lou Skizas	3.00	1.50	.90
329	Tigers Team/Checklist 353-429	8.00	4.00	2.50
330	Gus Triandos	3.25	1.75	1.00
331	Steve Boros	3.25	1.75	1.00
332	Ray Monzant	3.00	1.50	.90
333	Harry Simpson	3.00	1.50	.90

#	Player	NR MT	EX	VG
334	Glen Hobbie	3.00	1.50	.90
335	Johnny Temple	3.00	1.50	.90
336a	Billy Loes (without trade statement)	65.00	33.00	18.00
336b	Billy Loes (with trade statement)	3.00	1.50	.90
337	George Crowe	3.00	1.50	.90
338	*George Anderson*	45.00	23.00	13.50
339	Roy Face	3.00	1.50	.90
340	Roy Sievers	3.25	1.75	1.00
341	Tom Qualters	3.00	1.50	.90
342	Ray Jablonski	3.00	1.50	.90
343	Billy Hoeft	3.00	1.50	.90
344	Russ Nixon	3.00	1.50	.90
345	Gil McDougald	8.00	4.00	2.50
346	Batter Bafflers (Tom Brewer, Dave Sisler)	3.25	1.75	1.00
347	Bob Buhl	3.25	1.75	1.00
348	Ted Lepcio	3.00	1.50	.90
349	Hoyt Wilhelm	15.00	7.50	4.50
350	Ernie Banks	75.00	38.00	23.00
351	Earl Torgeson	3.00	1.50	.90
352	Robin Roberts	15.00	7.50	4.50
353	Curt Flood	3.00	1.50	.90
354	Pete Burnside	3.00	1.50	.90
355	Jim Piersall	3.00	1.50	.90
356	Bob Mabe	3.00	1.50	.90
357	*Dick Stuart*	6.00	3.00	1.75
358	Ralph Terry	3.25	1.75	1.00
359	*Bill White*	30.00	15.00	9.00
360	Al Kaline	60.00	30.00	18.00
361	Willard Nixon	3.00	1.50	.90
362a	Dolan Nichols (without option statement)	80.00	40.00	24.00
362b	Dolan Nichols (with option statement)	3.00	1.50	.90
363	Bobby Avila	3.00	1.50	.90
364	Danny McDevitt	3.00	1.50	.90
365	Gus Bell	3.25	1.75	1.00
366	Humberto Robinson	3.00	1.50	.90
367	Cal Neeman	3.00	1.50	.90
368	Don Mueller	3.00	1.50	.90
369	Dick Tomanek	3.00	1.50	.90
370	Pete Runnels	3.25	1.75	1.00
371	Dick Brodowski	3.00	1.50	.90
372	Jim Hegan	3.00	1.50	.90
373	Herb Plews	3.00	1.50	.90
374	Art Ditmar	3.00	1.50	.90
375	Bob Nieman	3.00	1.50	.90
376	Hal Naragon	3.00	1.50	.90
377	Johnny Antonelli	3.25	1.75	1.00
378	Gail Harris	3.00	1.50	.90
379	Bob Miller	3.00	1.50	.90
380	Hank Aaron	125.00	62.00	37.00
381	Mike Baxes	3.00	1.50	.90
382	Curt Simmons	3.25	1.75	1.00
383	Words of Wisdom (Don Larsen, Casey Stengel)	5.00	2.50	1.50
384	Dave Sisler	3.00	1.50	.90
385	Sherm Lollar	3.25	1.75	1.00
386	Jim Delsing	3.00	1.50	.90
387	Don Drysdale	30.00	15.00	9.00
388	Bob Will	3.00	1.50	.90
389	Joe Nuxhall	3.25	1.75	1.00
390	Orlando Cepeda	18.00	9.00	5.50
391	Milt Pappas	3.25	1.75	1.00
392	Whitey Herzog	6.00	3.00	1.75
393	Frank Lary	3.25	1.75	1.00
394	Randy Jackson	3.00	1.50	.90
395	Elston Howard	7.00	3.50	2.00
396	Bob Rush	3.00	1.50	.90
397	Senators Team/Checklist 430-495	7.00	3.50	2.00
398	Wally Post	3.00	1.50	.90
399	Larry Jackson	3.00	1.50	.90
400	Jackie Jensen	5.00	2.50	1.50
401	Ron Blackburn	3.00	1.50	.90
402	Hector Lopez	3.00	1.50	.90
403	Clem Labine	3.25	1.75	1.00
404	Hank Sauer	3.25	1.75	1.00
405	Roy McMillan	3.00	1.50	.90
406	Solly Drake	3.00	1.50	.90
407	Moe Drabowsky	3.00	1.50	.90
408	Keystone Combo (Luis Aparicio, Nellie Fox)	7.00	3.50	2.00
409	Gus Zernial	3.25	1.75	1.00
410	Billy Pierce	3.25	1.75	1.00
411	Whitey Lockman	3.00	1.50	.90
412	Stan Lopata	3.00	1.50	.90
413	Camillo Pascual (Camilo)	3.25	1.75	1.00
414	Dale Long	3.25	1.75	1.00
415	Bill Mazeroski	3.50	1.75	1.00
416	Haywood Sullivan	3.00	1.50	.90
417	Virgil Trucks	3.00	1.50	.90
418	Gino Cimoli	3.00	1.50	.90
419	Braves Team/Checklist 353-429	8.00	4.00	2.50
420	Rocco Colavito	25.00	12.50	7.50
421	Herm Wehmeier	3.00	1.50	.90
422	Hobie Landrith	3.00	1.50	.90
423	Bob Grim	3.00	1.50	.90
424	Ken Aspromonte	3.00	1.50	.90
425	Del Crandall	3.25	1.75	1.00
426	Jerry Staley	3.00	1.50	.90
427	Charlie Neal	3.00	1.50	.90
428	Buc Hill Aces (Roy Face, Bob Friend, Ron Kline, Vern Law)	3.25	1.75	1.00
429	Bobby Thomson	3.25	1.75	1.00
430	Whitey Ford	30.00	15.00	9.00
431	Whammy Douglas	3.00	1.50	.90
432	Smoky Burgess	3.00	1.50	.90
433	Billy Harrell	3.00	1.50	.90
434	Hal Griggs	3.00	1.50	.90
435	Frank Robinson	50.00	25.00	15.00
436	Granny Hamner	3.00	1.50	.90
437	Ike Delock	3.00	1.50	.90
438	Sam Esposito	3.00	1.50	.90
439	Brooks Robinson	50.00	25.00	15.00
440	Lou Burdette	8.00	4.00	2.50
441	John Roseboro	3.25	1.75	1.00
442	Ray Narleski	3.00	1.50	.90
443	Daryl Spencer	3.00	1.50	.90
444	*Ronnie Hansen*	3.25	1.75	1.00
445	Cal McLish	3.00	1.50	.90
446	Rocky Nelson	3.00	1.50	.90
447	Bob Anderson	3.00	1.50	.90
448	Vada Pinson	5.00	2.50	1.50
449	Tom Gorman	3.00	1.50	.90
450	Ed Mathews	30.00	15.00	9.00
451	Jimmy Constable	3.00	1.50	.90
452	Chico Fernandez	3.00	1.50	.90
453	Les Moss	3.00	1.50	.90
454	Phil Clark	3.00	1.50	.90
455	Larry Doby	3.25	1.75	1.00
456	Jerry Casale	3.00	1.50	.90
457	Dodgers Team/Checklist 430-495	20.00	10.00	6.00
458	Gordon Jones	3.00	1.50	.90
459	Bill Tuttle	3.00	1.50	.90
460	Bob Friend	3.25	1.75	1.00
461	Mantle Hits 42nd Homer For Crown	40.00	20.00	12.00
462	Colavito's Great Catch Saves Game	3.00	1.50	.90
463	Kaline Becomes Youngest Bat Champ	8.00	4.00	2.50
464	Mays' Catch Makes Series History	20.00	10.00	6.00
465	Sievers Sets Homer Mark	3.25	1.75	1.00
466	Pierce All Star Starter	3.25	1.75	1.00
467	Aaron Clubs World Series Homer	20.00	10.00	6.00
468	Snider's Play Brings L.A. Victory	9.00	4.50	2.75
469	Hustler Banks Wins M.V.P. Award	8.00	4.00	2.50
470	Musial Raps Out 3,000th Hit	18.00	9.00	5.50
471	Tom Sturdivant	3.00	1.50	.90
472	Gene Freese	3.00	1.50	.90
473	Mike Fornieles	3.00	1.50	.90
474	Moe Thacker	3.00	1.50	.90
475	Jack Harshman	3.00	1.50	.90
476	Indians Team/Checklist 496-572	7.00	3.50	2.00
477	Barry Latman	3.00	1.50	.90
478	Bob Clemente	125.00	67.00	37.00
479	Lindy McDaniel	3.00	1.50	.90
480	Red Schoendienst	18.00	9.00	5.50
481	Charley Maxwell	3.00	1.50	.90
482	Russ Meyer	3.00	1.50	.90
483	Clint Courtney	3.00	1.50	.90
484	Willie Kirkland	3.00	1.50	.90
485	Ryne Duren	3.50	1.75	1.00
486	Sammy White	3.00	1.50	.90
487	Hal Brown	3.00	1.50	.90
488	Walt Moryn	3.00	1.50	.90
489	John C. Powers	3.00	1.50	.90
490	Frank Thomas	3.00	1.50	.90
491	Don Blasingame	3.00	1.50	.90
492	Gene Conley	3.25	1.75	1.00
493	Jim Landis	3.00	1.50	.90
494	Don Pavletich	3.00	1.50	.90
495	Johnny Podres	5.00	2.50	1.50
496	Wayne Terwilliger	3.00	1.50	.90
497	Hal R. Smith	3.00	1.50	.90
498	Dick Hyde	3.00	1.50	.90
499	Johnny O'Brien	3.00	1.50	.90
500	Vic Wertz	3.25	1.75	1.00

		NR MT	EX	VG
501	Bobby Tiefenauer	3.00	1.50	.90
502	Al Dark	3.25	1.75	1.00
503	Jim Owens	3.00	1.50	.90
504	Ossie Alvarez	3.00	1.50	.90
505	Tony Kubek	8.00	4.00	2.50
506	Bob Purkey	3.00	1.50	.90
507	Bob Hale	15.00	7.50	4.50
508	Art Fowler	15.00	7.50	4.50
509	*Norm Cash*	70.00	35.00	21.00
510	Yankees Team/Checklist 496-572			
		70.00	35.00	21.00
511	George Susce	15.00	7.50	4.50
512	George Altman	15.00	7.50	4.50
513	Tom Carroll	15.00	7.50	4.50
514	*Bob Gibson*	420.00	210.00	131.00
515	Harmon Killebrew	150.00	75.00	45.00
516	Mike Garcia	16.00	8.00	4.75
517	Joe Koppe	15.00	7.50	4.50
518	*Mike Cueller (Cuellar)*	15.00	7.50	4.50
519	Infield Power (Dick Gernert, Frank Malzone, Pete Runnels)	18.00	9.00	5.50
520	Don Elston	15.00	7.50	4.50
521	Gary Geiger	15.00	7.50	4.50
522	Gene Snyder	15.00	7.50	4.50
523	Harry Bright	15.00	7.50	4.50
524	Larry Osborne	15.00	7.50	4.50
525	Jim Coates	16.00	8.00	4.75
526	Bob Speake	15.00	7.50	4.50
527	Solly Hemus	15.00	7.50	4.50
528	Pirates Team/Checklist 496-572			
		35.00	17.50	10.50
529	*George Bamberger*	16.00	8.00	4.75
530	Wally Moon	16.00	8.00	4.75
531	Ray Webster	15.00	7.50	4.50
532	Mark Freeman	15.00	7.50	4.50
533	Darrell Johnson	16.00	8.00	4.75
534	Faye Throneberry	15.00	7.50	4.50
535	Ruben Gomez	15.00	7.50	4.50
536	Dan Kravitz	15.00	7.50	4.50
537	Rodolfo Arias	15.00	7.50	4.50
538	Chick King	15.00	7.50	4.50
539	Gary Blaylock	15.00	7.50	4.50
540	Willy Miranda	15.00	7.50	4.50
541	Bob Thurman	15.00	7.50	4.50
542	*Jim Perry*	20.00	10.00	6.00
543	Corsair Outfield Trio (Bob Clemente, Bob Skinner, Bill Virdon)	50.00	25.00	15.00
544	Lee Tate	15.00	7.50	4.50
545	Tom Morgan	15.00	7.50	4.50
546	Al Schroll	15.00	7.50	4.50
547	Jim Baxes	15.00	7.50	4.50
548	Elmer Singleton	15.00	7.50	4.50
549	Howie Nunn	15.00	7.50	4.50
550	Roy Campanella	150.00	75.00	45.00
551	Fred Haney AS	16.00	8.00	4.75
552	Casey Stengel AS	30.00	15.00	9.00
553	Orlando Cepeda AS	18.00	9.00	5.50
554	Bill Skowron AS	18.00	9.00	5.50
555	Bill Mazeroski AS	18.00	9.00	5.50
556	Nellie Fox AS	20.00	10.00	6.00
557	Ken Boyer AS	18.00	9.00	5.50
558	Frank Malzone AS	16.00	8.00	4.75
559	Ernie Banks AS	50.00	25.00	15.00
560	Luis Aparicio AS	20.00	10.00	6.00
561	Hank Aaron AS	125.00	62.00	37.00
562	Al Kaline AS	50.00	25.00	15.00
563	Willie Mays AS	135.00	67.00	40.00
564	Mickey Mantle AS	300.00	150.00	90.00
565	Wes Covington AS	16.00	8.00	4.75
566	Roy Sievers AS	16.00	8.00	4.75
567	Del Crandall AS	16.00	8.00	4.75
568	Gus Triandos AS	16.00	8.00	4.75
569	Bob Friend AS	16.00	8.00	4.75
570	Bob Turley AS	16.00	8.00	4.75
571	Warren Spahn AS	30.00	15.00	9.00
572	Billy Pierce AS	25.00	12.50	7.50
——	Elect Your Favorite Rookie Insert (paper stock, September 29 date on back)	15.00	7.50	4.50
——	Felt Pennants Insert (paper stock)			
		15.00	7.50	4.50

1960 Topps

In 1960, Topps returned to a horizontal format (3-1/2" by 2-1/2") with a color portrait and a black and white "action" photograph on the front. The backs returned to the use of just the previous year and lifetime statistics along with a cartoon and short

career summary or previous season highlights. Specialty cards in the 572-card set are multi-player cards, managers and coaches cards, and highlights of the 1959 World Series. Two groups of rookie cards are included. The first are numbers 117-148, which are the Sport Magazine rookies. The second group is called "Topps All-Star Rookies." Finally, there is a continuation of the All-Star cards to close out the set in the scarcer high numbers. Card #'s 375-440 can be found with backs printed on either white or grey cardboard, with the white stock being the less common.

		NR MT	EX	VG
Complete Set:		4000.00	2000.00	1250.
Common Player: 1-286		3.00	1.50	.90
Common Player: 287-440		3.00	1.50	.90
Common Player: 441-506		4.00	2.00	1.25
Common Player: 507-572		10.00	5.00	3.00
1	Early Wynn	40.00	20.00	12.00
2	Roman Mejias	3.25	1.75	1.00
3	Joe Adcock	3.25	1.75	1.00
4	Bob Purkey	3.00	1.50	.90
5	Wally Moon	3.00	1.50	.90
6	Lou Berberet	3.00	1.50	.90
7	Master & Mentor (Willie Mays, Bill Rigney)	12.00	6.00	3.50
8	Bud Daley	3.00	1.50	.90
9	Faye Throneberry	3.00	1.50	.90
10	Ernie Banks	55.00	28.00	16.50
11	Norm Siebern	3.00	1.50	.90
12	Milt Pappas	3.00	1.50	.90
13	Wally Post	3.00	1.50	.90
14	Jim Grant	3.00	1.50	.90
15	Pete Runnels	3.00	1.50	.90
16	Ernie Broglio	3.00	1.50	.90
17	Johnny Callison	3.00	1.50	.90
18	Dodgers Team/Checklist 1-88	15.00	7.50	4.50
19	Felix Mantilla	3.00	1.50	.90
20	Roy Face	3.00	1.50	.90
21	Dutch Dotterer	3.00	1.50	.90
22	Rocky Bridges	3.00	1.50	.90
23	Eddie Fisher	3.00	1.50	.90
24	Dick Gray	3.00	1.50	.90
25	Roy Sievers	4.00	2.00	1.25
26	Wayne Terwilliger	3.00	1.50	.90
27	Dick Drott	3.00	1.50	.90
28	Brooks Robinson	40.00	20.00	12.00
29	Clem Labine	3.00	1.50	.90
30	Tito Francona	3.00	1.50	.90
31	Sammy Esposito	3.00	1.50	.90
32	Sophomore Stalwarts (Jim O'Toole, Vada Pinson)	4.00	2.00	1.25
33	Tom Morgan	3.00	1.50	.90
34	George Anderson	2.50	1.25	.70
35	Whitey Ford	40.00	20.00	12.00
36	Russ Nixon	3.00	1.50	.90
37	Bill Bruton	3.00	1.50	.90
38	Jerry Casale	3.00	1.50	.90
39	Earl Averill	3.00	1.50	.90
40	Joe Cunningham	3.00	1.50	.90
41	Barry Latman	3.00	1.50	.90
42	Hobie Landrith	3.00	1.50	.90
43	Senators Team/Checklist 1-88	6.00	3.00	1.75
44	Bobby Locke	3.00	1.50	.90
45	Roy McMillan	3.00	1.50	.90
46	Jack Fisher	3.00	1.50	.90
47	Don Zimmer	3.25	1.75	1.00

		NR MT	EX	VG
48	Hal Smith	3.00	1.50	.90
49	Curt Raydon	3.00	1.50	.90
50	Al Kaline	50.00	25.00	15.00
51	Jim Coates	3.00	1.50	.90
52	Dave Philley	3.00	1.50	.90
53	Jackie Brandt	3.00	1.50	.90
54	Mike Fornieles	3.00	1.50	.90
55	Bill Mazeroski	3.00	1.50	.90
56	Steve Korcheck	3.00	1.50	.90
57	Win - Savers (Turk Lown, Gerry Staley)			
		3.00	1.50	.90
58	Gino Cimoli	3.00	1.50	.90
59	Juan Pizarro	3.00	1.50	.90
60	Gus Triandos	3.00	1.50	.90
61	Eddie Kasko	3.00	1.50	.90
62	Roger Craig	3.25	1.75	1.00
63	George Strickland	3.00	1.50	.90
64	Jack Meyer	3.00	1.50	.90
65	Elston Howard	6.00	3.00	1.75
66	Bob Trowbridge	3.00	1.50	.90
67	*Jose Pagan*	3.00	1.50	.90
68	Dave Hillman	3.00	1.50	.90
69	Billy Goodman	3.00	1.50	.90
70	Lou Burdette	3.25	1.75	1.00
71	Marty Keough	3.00	1.50	.90
72	Tigers Team/Checklist 89-176	10.00	5.00	3.00
73	Bob Gibson	60.00	30.00	18.00
74	Walt Moryn	3.00	1.50	.90
75	Vic Power	3.00	1.50	.90
76	Bill Fischer	3.00	1.50	.90
77	Hank Foiles	3.00	1.50	.90
78	Bob Grim	3.00	1.50	.90
79	Walt Dropo	3.00	1.50	.90
80	Johnny Antonelli	3.00	1.50	.90
81	Russ Snyder	3.00	1.50	.90
82	Ruben Gomez	3.00	1.50	.90
83	Tony Kubek	4.50	2.25	1.25
84	Hal Smith	3.00	1.50	.90
85	Frank Lary	3.00	1.50	.90
86	Dick Gernert	3.00	1.50	.90
87	John Romonosky	3.00	1.50	.90
88	John Roseboro	3.00	1.50	.90
89	Hal Brown	3.00	1.50	.90
90	Bobby Avila	3.00	1.50	.90
91	Bennie Daniels	3.00	1.50	.90
92	Whitey Herzog	3.25	1.75	1.00
93	Art Schult	3.00	1.50	.90
94	Leo Kiely	3.00	1.50	.90
95	Frank Thomas	3.00	1.50	.90
96	Ralph Terry	2.50	1.25	.70
97	Ted Lepcio	3.00	1.50	.90
98	Gordon Jones	3.00	1.50	.90
99	Lenny Green	3.00	1.50	.90
100	Nellie Fox	7.00	3.50	2.00
101	Bob Miller	3.00	1.50	.90
102	Kent Hadley	3.00	1.50	.90
103	Dick Farrell	3.00	1.50	.90
104	Dick Schofield	3.00	1.50	.90
105	Larry Sherry	3.00	1.50	.90
106	Billy Gardner	3.00	1.50	.90
107	Carl Willey	3.00	1.50	.90
108	Pete Daley	3.00	1.50	.90
109	Cletis Boyer	3.00	1.50	.90
110	Cal McLish	3.00	1.50	.90
111	Vic Wertz	3.00	1.50	.90
112	Jack Harshman	3.00	1.50	.90
113	Bob Skinner	3.00	1.50	.90
114	Ken Aspromonte	3.00	1.50	.90
115	Fork & Knuckler (Roy Face, Hoyt Wilhelm)			
		4.00	2.00	1.25
116	Jim Rivera	3.00	1.50	.90
117	Tom Borland	3.00	1.50	.90
118	Bob Bruce	3.00	1.50	.90
119	*Chico Cardenas*	3.00	1.50	.90
120	Duke Carmel	3.00	1.50	.90
121	Camilo Carreon	3.00	1.50	.90
122	Don Dillard	3.00	1.50	.90
123	Dan Dobbek	3.00	1.50	.90
124	Jim Donohue	3.00	1.50	.90
125	*Dick Ellsworth*	3.00	1.50	.90
126	*Chuck Estrada*	3.00	1.50	.90
127	Ronnie Hansen	3.00	1.50	.90
128	Bill Harris	3.00	1.50	.90
129	Bob Hartman	3.00	1.50	.90
130	Frank Herrera	3.00	1.50	.90
131	Ed Hobaugh	3.00	1.50	.90
132	*Frank Howard*	18.00	9.00	5.50
133	*Manuel Javier*	3.00	1.50	.90
134	Deron Johnson	3.00	1.50	.90
135	Ken Johnson	3.00	1.50	.90
136	*Jim Kaat*	35.00	17.50	10.50

		NR MT	EX	VG
137	Lou Klimchock	3.00	1.50	.90
138	*Art Mahaffey*	3.00	1.50	.90
139	Carl Mathias	3.00	1.50	.90
140	Julio Navarro	3.00	1.50	.90
141	Jim Proctor	3.00	1.50	.90
142	Bill Short	3.00	1.50	.90
143	Al Spangler	3.00	1.50	.90
144	Al Stieglitz	3.00	1.50	.90
145	Jim Umbricht	3.00	1.50	.90
146	Ted Wieand	3.00	1.50	.90
147	Bob Will	3.00	1.50	.90
148	*Carl Yastrzemski*	250.00	125.00	75.00
149	Bob Nieman	3.00	1.50	.90
150	Billy Pierce	3.25	1.75	1.00
151	Giants Team/Checklist 177-264	6.00	3.00	1.75
152	Gail Harris	3.00	1.50	.90
153	Bobby Thomson	3.00	1.50	.90
154	Jim Davenport	3.00	1.50	.90
155	Charlie Neal	3.00	1.50	.90
156	Art Ceccarelli	3.00	1.50	.90
157	Rocky Nelson	3.00	1.50	.90
158	Wes Covington	3.00	1.50	.90
159	Jim Piersall	3.00	1.50	.90
160	Rival All Stars (Ken Boyer, Mickey Mantle)			
		50.00	25.00	15.00
161	Ray Narleski	3.00	1.50	.90
162	Sammy Taylor	3.00	1.50	.90
163	Hector Lopez	3.00	1.50	.90
164	Reds Team/Checklist 89-176	7.00	3.50	2.00
165	Jack Sanford	3.00	1.50	.90
166	Chuck Essegian	3.00	1.50	.90
167	Valmy Thomas	3.00	1.50	.90
168	Alex Grammas	3.00	1.50	.90
169	Jake Striker	3.00	1.50	.90
170	Del Crandall	3.00	1.50	.90
171	Johnny Groth	3.00	1.50	.90
172	Willie Kirkland	3.00	1.50	.90
173	Billy Martin	10.00	5.00	3.00
174	Indians Team/Checklist 89-176	6.00	3.00	1.75
175	Pedro Ramos	3.00	1.50	.90
176	Vada Pinson	3.25	1.75	1.00
177	Johnny Kucks	3.00	1.50	.90
178	Woody Held	3.00	1.50	.90
179	Rip Coleman	3.00	1.50	.90
180	Harry Simpson	3.00	1.50	.90
181	Billy Loes	3.00	1.50	.90
182	Glen Hobbie	3.00	1.50	.90
183	Eli Grba	3.00	1.50	.90
184	Gary Geiger	3.00	1.50	.90
185	Jim Owens	3.00	1.50	.90
186	Dave Sisler	3.00	1.50	.90
187	Jay Hook	3.00	1.50	.90
188	Dick Williams	3.00	1.50	.90
189	Don McMahon	3.00	1.50	.90
190	Gene Woodling	3.00	1.50	.90
191	Johnny Klippstein	3.00	1.50	.90
192	Danny O'Connell	3.00	1.50	.90
193	Dick Hyde	3.00	1.50	.90
194	Bobby Gene Smith	3.00	1.50	.90
195	Lindy McDaniel	3.00	1.50	.90
196	Andy Carey	3.00	1.50	.90
197	Ron Kline	3.00	1.50	.90
198	Jerry Lynch	3.00	1.50	.90
199	Dick Donovan	3.00	1.50	.90
200	Willie Mays	125.00	67.00	37.00
201	Larry Osborne	3.00	1.50	.90
202	Fred Kipp	3.00	1.50	.90
203	Sammy White	3.00	1.50	.90
204	Ryne Duren	2.50	1.25	.70
205	Johnny Logan	3.00	1.50	.90
206	Claude Osteen	3.00	1.50	.90
207	Bob Boyd	3.00	1.50	.90
208	White Sox Team/Checklist 177-264			
		6.00	3.00	1.75
209	Ron Blackburn	3.00	1.50	.90
210	Harmon Killebrew	25.00	12.50	7.50
211	Taylor Phillips	3.00	1.50	.90
212	Walt Alston	6.00	3.00	1.75
213	Chuck Dressen	3.00	1.50	.90
214	Jimmie Dykes	3.00	1.50	.90
215	Bob Elliott	3.00	1.50	.90
216	Joe Gordon	3.00	1.50	.90
217	Charley Grimm	3.00	1.50	.90
218	Solly Hemus	3.00	1.50	.90
219	Fred Hutchinson	3.00	1.50	.90
220	Billy Jurges	3.00	1.50	.90
221	Cookie Lavagetto	3.00	1.50	.90
222	Al Lopez	5.00	2.50	1.50
223	Danny Murtaugh	3.00	1.50	.90
224	Paul Richards	3.00	1.50	.90
225	Bill Rigney	3.00	1.50	.90

		NR MT	EX	VG
226	Eddie Sawyer	3.00	1.50	.90
227	Casey Stengel	15.00	7.50	4.50
228	Ernie Johnson	3.00	1.50	.90
229	Joe Morgan	3.00	1.50	.90
230	Mound Magicians (Bob Buhl, Lou Burdette, Warren Spahn)	6.00	3.00	1.75
231	Hal Naragon	3.00	1.50	.90
232	Jim Busby	3.00	1.50	.90
233	Don Elston	3.00	1.50	.90
234	Don Demeter	3.00	1.50	.90
235	Gus Bell	3.00	1.50	.90
236	Dick Ricketts	3.00	1.50	.90
237	Elmer Valo	3.00	1.50	.90
238	Danny Kravitz	3.00	1.50	.90
239	Joe Shipley	3.00	1.50	.90
240	Luis Aparicio	10.00	5.00	3.00
241	Albie Pearson	3.00	1.50	.90
242	Cards Team/Checklist 265-352	6.00	3.00	1.75
243	Bubba Phillips	3.00	1.50	.90
244	Hal Griggs	3.00	1.50	.90
245	Eddie Yost	3.00	1.50	.90
246	Lee Maye	3.00	1.50	.90
247	Gil McDougald	4.50	2.25	1.25
248	Del Rice	3.00	1.50	.90
249	*Earl Wilson*	3.00	1.50	.90
250	Stan Musial	110.00	55.00	33.00
251	Bobby Malkmus	3.00	1.50	.90
252	Ray Herbert	3.00	1.50	.90
253	Eddie Bressoud	3.00	1.50	.90
254	Arnie Portocarrero	3.00	1.50	.90
255	Jim Gilliam	3.25	1.75	1.00
256	Dick Brown	3.00	1.50	.90
257	Gordy Coleman	3.00	1.50	.90
258	Dick Groat	4.00	2.00	1.25
259	George Altman	3.00	1.50	.90
260	Power Plus (Rocky Colavito, Tito Francona)	3.00	1.50	.90
261	Pete Burnside	3.00	1.50	.90
262	Hank Bauer	3.00	1.50	.90
263	Darrell Johnson	3.00	1.50	.90
264	Robin Roberts	12.00	6.00	3.50
265	Rip Repulski	3.00	1.50	.90
266	Joe Jay	3.00	1.50	.90
267	Jim Marshall	3.00	1.50	.90
268	Al Worthington	3.00	1.50	.90
269	Gene Green	3.00	1.50	.90
270	Bob Turley	3.25	1.75	1.00
271	Julio Becquer	3.00	1.50	.90
272	Fred Green	3.00	1.50	.90
273	Neil Chrisley	3.00	1.50	.90
274	Tom Acker	3.00	1.50	.90
275	Curt Flood	3.00	1.50	.90
276	Ken McBride	3.00	1.50	.90
277	Harry Bright	3.00	1.50	.90
278	Stan Williams	3.00	1.50	.90
279	Chuck Tanner	2.50	1.25	.70
280	Frank Sullivan	3.00	1.50	.90
281	Ray Boone	3.00	1.50	.90
282	Joe Nuxhall	3.00	1.50	.90
283	John Blanchard	2.75	1.50	.80
284	Don Gross	3.00	1.50	.90
285	Harry Anderson	3.00	1.50	.90
286	Ray Semproch	3.00	1.50	.90
287	Felipe Alou	2.50	1.25	.70
288	Bob Mabe	3.00	1.50	.90
289	Willie Jones	3.00	1.50	.90
290	Jerry Lumpe	3.00	1.50	.90
291	Bob Keegan	3.00	1.50	.90
292	Dodger Backstops (Joe Pignatano, John Roseboro)	3.00	1.50	.90
293	Gene Conley	3.00	1.50	.90
294	Tony Taylor	3.00	1.50	.90
295	Gil Hodges	18.00	9.00	5.50
296	Nelson Chittum	3.00	1.50	.90
297	Reno Bertoia	3.00	1.50	.90
298	George Witt	3.00	1.50	.90
299	Earl Torgeson	3.00	1.50	.90
300	Hank Aaron	125.00	67.00	37.00
301	Jerry Davie	3.00	1.50	.90
302	Phillies Team/Checklist 353-429	7.00	3.50	2.00
303	Billy O'Dell	3.00	1.50	.90
304	Joe Ginsberg	3.00	1.50	.90
305	Richie Ashburn	7.00	3.50	2.00
306	Frank Baumann	3.00	1.50	.90
307	Gene Oliver	3.00	1.50	.90
308	Dick Hall	3.00	1.50	.90
309	Bob Hale	3.00	1.50	.90
310	Frank Malzone	3.00	1.50	.90
311	Raul Sanchez	3.00	1.50	.90
312	Charlie Lau	3.00	1.50	.90
313	Turk Lown	3.00	1.50	.90

		NR MT	EX	VG
314	Chico Fernandez	3.00	1.50	.90
315	Bobby Shantz	3.25	1.75	1.00
316	*Willie McCovey*	200.00	100.00	60.00
317	Pumpsie Green	3.00	1.50	.90
318	Jim Baxes	3.00	1.50	.90
319	Joe Koppe	3.00	1.50	.90
320	Bob Allison	3.25	1.75	1.00
321	Ron Fairly	3.00	1.50	.90
322	Willie Tasby	3.00	1.50	.90
323	Johnny Romano	3.00	1.50	.90
324	Jim Perry	2.50	1.25	.70
325	Jim O'Toole	3.00	1.50	.90
326	Bob Clemente	125.00	87.00	45.00
327	*Ray Sadecki*	3.25	1.75	1.00
328	Earl Battey	3.00	1.50	.90
329	Zack Monroe	3.25	1.75	1.00
330	Harvey Kuenn	3.00	1.50	.90
331	Henry Mason	3.00	1.50	.90
332	Yankees Team/Checklist 265-352	20.00	10.00	6.00
333	Danny McDevitt	3.00	1.50	.90
334	Ted Abernathy	3.00	1.50	.90
335	Red Schoendienst	15.00	7.50	4.50
336	Ike Delock	3.00	1.50	.90
337	Cal Neeman	3.00	1.50	.90
338	Ray Monzant	3.00	1.50	.90
339	Harry Chiti	3.00	1.50	.90
340	Harvey Haddix	3.25	1.75	1.00
341	Carroll Hardy	3.00	1.50	.90
342	Casey Wise	3.00	1.50	.90
343	Sandy Koufax	110.00	55.00	33.00
344	Clint Courtney	3.00	1.50	.90
345	Don Newcombe	2.50	1.25	.70
346	J.C. Martin (photo actually Gary Peters)	3.00	1.50	.90
347	Ed Bouchee	3.00	1.50	.90
348	Barry Shetrone	3.00	1.50	.90
349	Moe Drabowsky	3.00	1.50	.90
350	Mickey Mantle	400.00	200.00	125.00
351	Don Nottebart	3.00	1.50	.90
352	Cincy Clouters (Gus Bell, Jerry Lynch, Frank Robinson)	5.00	2.50	1.50
353	Don Larsen	3.25	1.75	1.00
354	Bob Lillis	3.00	1.50	.90
355	Bill White	3.00	1.50	.90
356	Joe Amalfitano	3.00	1.50	.90
357	Al Schroll	3.00	1.50	.90
358	Joe DeMaestri	3.25	1.75	1.00
359	Buddy Gilbert	3.00	1.50	.90
360	Herb Score	2.50	1.25	.70
361	Bob Oldis	3.00	1.50	.90
362	Russ Kemmerer	3.00	1.50	.90
363	Gene Stephens	3.00	1.50	.90
364	Paul Foytack	3.00	1.50	.90
365	Minnie Minoso	3.00	1.50	.90
366	*Dallas Green*	3.25	1.75	1.00
367	Bill Tuttle	3.00	1.50	.90
368	Daryl Spencer	3.00	1.50	.90
369	Billy Hoeft	3.00	1.50	.90
370	Bill Skowron	6.00	3.00	1.75
371	Bud Byerly	3.00	1.50	.90
372	Frank House	3.00	1.50	.90
373	Don Hoak	3.00	1.50	.90
374	Bob Buhl	3.00	1.50	.90
375	Dale Long	3.00	1.50	.90
376	Johnny Briggs	3.00	1.50	.90
377	Roger Maris	120.00	60.00	36.00
378	Stu Miller	3.00	1.50	.90
379	Red Wilson	3.00	1.50	.90
380	Bob Shaw	3.00	1.50	.90
381	Braves Team/Checklist 353-429	7.00	3.50	2.00
382	Ted Bowsfield	3.00	1.50	.90
383	Leon Wagner	3.00	1.50	.90
384	Don Cardwell	3.00	1.50	.90
385	World Series Game 1 (Neal Steals Second)	4.00	2.00	1.25
386	World Series Game 2 (Neal Belts 2nd Homer)	4.00	2.00	1.25
387	World Series Game 3 (Furillo Breaks Up Game)	4.00	2.00	1.25
388	World Series Game 4 (Hodges' Winning Homer)	4.00	2.00	1.25
389	World Series Game 5 (Luis Swipes Base)	5.00	2.50	1.50
390	World Series Game 6 (Scrambling After Ball)	4.00	2.00	1.25
391	World Series Summary (The Champs Celebrate)	4.00	2.00	1.25
392	Tex Clevenger	3.00	1.50	.90
393	Smoky Burgess	2.50	1.25	.70
394	Norm Larker	3.00	1.50	.90

	NR MT	EX	VG
395 Hoyt Wilhelm	15.00	7.50	4.50
396 Steve Bilko	3.00	1.50	.90
397 Don Blasingame	3.00	1.50	.90
398 Mike Cuellar	3.25	1.75	1.00
399 Young Hill Stars (Jack Fisher, Milt Pappas, Jerry Walker)	3.25	1.75	1.00
400 Rocky Colavito	15.00	7.50	4.50
401 Bob Duliba	3.00	1.50	.90
402 Dick Stuart	3.00	1.50	.90
403 Ed Sadowski	3.00	1.50	.90
404 Bob Rush	3.00	1.50	.90
405 Bobby Richardson	6.00	3.00	1.75
406 Billy Klaus	3.00	1.50	.90
407 *Gary Peters* (photo actually J.C. Martin)	3.25	1.75	1.00
408 Carl Furillo	4.00	2.00	1.25
409 Ron Samford	3.00	1.50	.90
410 Sam Jones	3.00	1.50	.90
411 Ed Bailey	3.00	1.50	.90
412 Bob Anderson	3.00	1.50	.90
413 A's Team/Checklist 430-495	7.00	3.50	2.00
414 Don Williams	3.00	1.50	.90
415 Bob Cerv	3.00	1.50	.90
416 Humberto Robinson	3.00	1.50	.90
417 Chuck Cottier	3.00	1.50	.90
418 Don Mossi	3.00	1.50	.90
419 George Crowe	3.00	1.50	.90
420 Ed Mathews	35.00	17.50	10.50
421 Duke Maas	3.25	1.75	1.00
422 Johnny Powers	3.00	1.50	.90
423 Ed Fitz Gerald	3.00	1.50	.90
424 Pete Whisenant	3.00	1.50	.90
425 Johnny Podres	3.00	1.50	.90
426 Ron Jackson	3.00	1.50	.90
427 Al Grunwald	3.00	1.50	.90
428 Al Smith	3.00	1.50	.90
429 American League Kings (Nellie Fox, Harvey Kuenn)	3.25	1.75	1.00
430 Art Ditmar	3.00	1.50	.90
431 Andre Rodgers	3.00	1.50	.90
432 Chuck Stobbs	3.00	1.50	.90
433 Irv Noren	3.00	1.50	.90
434 Brooks Lawrence	3.00	1.50	.90
435 Gene Freese	3.00	1.50	.90
436 Marv Throneberry	3.25	1.75	1.00
437 Bob Friend	2.50	1.25	.70
438 Jim Coker	3.00	1.50	.90
439 Tom Brewer	3.00	1.50	.90
440 Jim Lemon	3.00	1.50	.90
441 Gary Bell	4.00	2.00	1.25
442 Joe Pignatano	4.00	2.00	1.25
443 Charlie Maxwell	4.00	2.00	1.25
444 Jerry Kindall	4.00	2.00	1.25
445 Warren Spahn	50.00	25.00	15.00
446 Ellis Burton	4.00	2.00	1.25
447 Ray Moore	4.00	2.00	1.25
448 *Jim Gentile*	4.00	2.00	1.25
449 Jim Brosnan	5.00	2.50	1.50
450 Orlando Cepeda	15.00	7.50	4.50
451 Curt Simmons	4.00	2.00	1.25
452 Ray Webster	4.00	2.00	1.25
453 Vern Law	4.50	2.25	1.25
454 Hal Woodeshick	4.00	2.00	1.25
455 Orioles Coaches (Harry Brecheen, Lum Harris, Eddie Robinson)	5.00	2.50	1.50
456 Red Sox Coaches (Del Baker, Billy Herman, Sal Maglie, Rudy York)	4.00	2.00	1.25
457 Cubs Coaches (Lou Klein, Charlie Root, Elvin Tappe)	5.00	2.50	1.50
458 White Sox Coaches (Ray Berres, Johnny Cooney, Tony Cuccinello, Don Gutteridge)	5.00	2.50	1.50
459 Reds Coaches (Cot Deal, Wally Moses, Reggie Otero)	5.00	2.50	1.50
460 Indians Coaches (Mel Harder, Red Kress, Bob Lemon, Jo-Jo White)	4.00	2.00	1.25
461 Tigers Coaches (Luke Appling, Tom Ferrick, Billy Hitchcock)	4.00	2.00	1.25
462 A's Coaches (Walker Cooper, Fred Fitzsimmons, Don Heffner)	5.00	2.50	1.50
463 Dodgers Coaches (Joe Becker, Bobby Bragan, Greg Mulleavy, Pete Reiser)	4.00	2.00	1.25
464 Braves Coaches (George Myatt, Andy Pafko, Bob Scheffing, Whitlow Wyatt)	5.00	2.50	1.50
465 Yankees Coaches (Frank Crosetti, Bill Dickey, Ralph Houk, Ed Lopat)	11.00	5.50	3.25
466 Phillies Coaches (Dick Carter, Andy Cohen, Ken Silvestri)	5.00	2.50	1.50
467 Pirates Coaches (Bill Burwell, Sam Narron, Frank Oceak, Mickey Vernon)	4.00	2.00	1.25
468 Cardinals Coaches (Ray Katt, Johnny Keane, Howie Pollet, Harry Walker)	5.00	2.50	1.50
469 Giants Coaches (Salty Parker, Bill Posedel, Wes Westrum)	5.00	2.50	1.50
470 Senators Coaches (Ellis Clary, Sam Mele, Bob Swift)	5.00	2.50	1.50
471 Ned Garver	4.00	2.00	1.25
472 Al Dark	4.50	2.25	1.25
473 Al Cicotte	4.00	2.00	1.25
474 Haywood Sullivan	5.00	2.50	1.50
475 Don Drysdale	30.00	15.00	9.00
476 Lou Johnson	4.00	2.00	1.25
477 Don Ferrarese	4.00	2.00	1.25
478 Frank Torre	4.00	2.00	1.25
479 Georges Maranda	4.00	2.00	1.25
480 Yogi Berra	80.00	40.00	25.00
481 Wes Stock	4.00	2.00	1.25
482 Frank Bolling	4.00	2.00	1.25
483 Camilo Pascual	5.00	2.50	1.50
484 Pirates Team/Checklist 430-495	15.00	7.50	4.50
485 Ken Boyer	4.50	2.25	1.25
486 Bobby Del Greco	4.00	2.00	1.25
487 Tom Sturdivant	4.00	2.00	1.25
488 Norm Cash	5.00	2.50	1.50
489 Steve Ridzik	4.00	2.00	1.25
490 Frank Robinson	50.00	25.00	15.00
491 Mel Roach	4.00	2.00	1.25
492 Larry Jackson	4.00	2.00	1.25
493 Duke Snider	50.00	25.00	15.00
494 Orioles Team/Checklist 496-572	7.00	3.50	2.00
495 Sherm Lollar	4.00	2.00	1.25
496 Bill Virdon	4.00	2.00	1.25
497 John Tsitouris	4.00	2.00	1.25
498 Al Pilarcik	4.00	2.00	1.25
499 Johnny James	4.00	2.00	1.25
500 Johnny Temple	4.00	2.00	1.25
501 Bob Schmidt	4.00	2.00	1.25
502 Jim Bunning	12.00	6.00	3.50
503 Don Lee	4.00	2.00	1.25
504 Seth Morehead	4.00	2.00	1.25
505 Ted Kluszewski	6.00	3.00	1.75
506 Lee Walls	4.00	2.00	1.25
507 Dick Stigman	10.00	5.00	3.00
508 Billy Consolo	10.00	5.00	3.00
509 *Tommy Davis*	25.00	12.50	7.50
510 Jerry Staley	10.00	5.00	3.00
511 Ken Walters	10.00	5.00	3.00
512 Joe Gibbon	10.00	5.00	3.00
513 Cubs Team/Checklist 496-572	25.00	12.50	7.50
514 *Steve Barber*	11.00	5.50	3.25
515 Stan Lopata	10.00	5.00	3.00
516 Marty Kutyna	10.00	5.00	3.00
517 Charley James	10.00	5.00	3.00
518 *Tony Gonzalez*	11.00	5.50	3.25
519 Ed Roebuck	10.00	5.00	3.00
520 Don Buddin	10.00	5.00	3.00
521 Mike Lee	10.00	5.00	3.00
522 Ken Hunt	11.00	5.50	3.25
523 *Clay Dalrymple*	11.00	5.50	3.25
524 Bill Henry	10.00	5.00	3.00
525 Marv Breeding	10.00	5.00	3.00
526 Paul Giel	10.00	5.00	3.00
527 Jose Valdivielso	10.00	5.00	3.00
528 Ben Johnson	10.00	5.00	3.00
529 Norm Sherry	11.00	5.50	3.25
530 Mike McCormick	10.00	5.00	3.00
531 Sandy Amoros	10.00	5.00	3.00
532 Mike Garcia	10.00	5.00	3.00
533 Lu Clinton	10.00	5.00	3.00
534 Ken MacKenzie	10.00	5.00	3.00
535 Whitey Lockman	10.00	5.00	3.00
536 Wynn Hawkins	10.00	5.00	3.00
537 Red Sox Team/Checklist 496-572	25.00	12.50	7.50
538 Frank Barnes	10.00	5.00	3.00
539 Gene Baker	10.00	5.00	3.00
540 Jerry Walker	10.00	5.00	3.00
541 Tony Curry	10.00	5.00	3.00
542 Ken Hamlin	10.00	5.00	3.00
543 Elio Chacon	10.00	5.00	3.00
544 Bill Monbouquette	11.00	5.50	3.25
545 Carl Sawatski	10.00	5.00	3.00
546 Hank Aguirre	10.00	5.00	3.00
547 *Bob Aspromonte*	11.00	5.50	3.25
548 *Don Mincher*	11.00	5.50	3.25
549 John Buzhardt	10.00	5.00	3.00
550 Jim Landis	10.00	5.00	3.00
551 Ed Rakow	10.00	5.00	3.00
552 Walt Bond	10.00	5.00	3.00
553 Bill Skowron AS	12.00	6.00	3.50

		NR MT	EX	VG
554	Willie McCovey AS	45.00	22.00	13.50
555	Nellie Fox AS	18.00	9.00	5.50
556	Charlie Neal AS	11.00	5.50	3.25
557	Frank Malzone AS	11.00	5.50	3.25
558	Eddie Mathews AS	30.00	15.00	9.00
559	Luis Aparicio AS	20.00	10.00	6.00
560	Ernie Banks AS	40.00	20.00	12.00
561	Al Kaline AS	40.00	20.00	12.00
562	Joe Cunningham AS	11.00	5.50	3.25
563	Mickey Mantle AS	275.00	137.00	82.00
564	Willie Mays AS	100.00	50.00	30.00
565	Roger Maris AS	100.00	50.00	30.00
566	Hank Aaron AS	100.00	50.00	30.00
567	Sherm Lollar AS	11.00	5.50	3.25
568	Del Crandall AS	11.00	5.50	3.25
569	Camilo Pascual AS	11.00	5.50	3.25
570	Don Drysdale AS	20.00	10.00	6.00
571	Billy Pierce AS	11.00	5.50	3.25
572	Johnny Antonelli AS	20.00	7.00	3.00
----	Elect Your Favorite Rookie Insert (paper stock, no date on back)	15.00	7.50	4.50
----	Hot Iron Transfer Insert (paper stock)	15.00	7.50	4.50

1960 Topps Baseball Tattoos

Probably the least popular of all Topps products among parents and teachers, the Topps Tattoos were delightful little items on the reverse of the wrappers of Topps "Tattoo Bubble Gum." The entire wrapper was 1-9/16" by 3-1/2." The happy owner simply moistened his skin and applied the back of the wrapper to the wet spot. Presto, out came a "tattoo" in color (although often blurred by running colors). The set offered 96 tattoo possibilities of which 55 were players, 16 teams, 15 action shots and 10 autographed balls. Surviving specimens are very rare today.

		NR MT	EX	VG
	Complete Set:	675.00	337.00	202.00
	Common Player:	3.00	1.50	.90
(1)	Hank Aaron	25.00	12.50	7.50
(2)	Bob Allison	5.00	2.50	1.50
(3)	John Antonelli	5.00	2.50	1.50
(4)	Richie Ashburn	7.00	3.50	2.00
(5)	Ernie Banks	15.00	7.50	4.50
(6)	Yogi Berra	18.00	9.00	5.50
(7)	Lew Burdette	6.00	3.00	1.75
(8)	Orlando Cepeda	7.00	3.50	2.00
(9)	Rocky Colavito	6.00	3.00	1.75
(10)	Joe Cunningham	3.00	1.50	.90
(11)	Buddy Daley	3.00	1.50	.90
(12)	Don Drysdale	12.00	6.00	3.50
(13)	Ryne Duren	5.00	2.50	1.50
(14)	Roy Face	5.00	2.50	1.50
(15)	Whitey Ford	15.00	7.50	4.50
(16)	Nellie Fox	7.00	3.50	2.00
(17)	Tito Francona	3.00	1.50	.90
(18)	Gene Freese	3.00	1.50	.90
(19)	Jim Gilliam	6.00	3.00	1.75
(20)	Dick Groat	6.00	3.00	1.75
(21)	Ray Herbert	3.00	1.50	.90
(22)	Glen Hobbie	3.00	1.50	.90
(23)	Jackie Jensen	6.00	3.00	1.75
(24)	Sam Jones	3.00	1.50	.90

		NR MT	EX	VG
(25)	Al Kaline	15.00	7.50	4.50
(26)	Harmon Killebrew	12.00	6.00	3.50
(27)	Harvy Kuenn (Harvey)	6.00	3.00	1.75
(28)	Frank Lary	3.00	1.50	.90
(29)	Vernon Law	5.00	2.50	1.50
(30)	Frank Malzone	3.00	1.50	.90
(31)	Mickey Mantle	75.00	37.00	22.00
(32)	Roger Maris	15.00	7.50	4.50
(33)	Ed Mathews	12.00	6.00	3.50
(34)	Willie Mays	25.00	12.50	7.50
(35)	Cal Mclish	3.00	1.50	.90
(36)	Wally Moon	5.00	2.50	1.50
(37)	Walt Moryn	3.00	1.50	.90
(38)	Don Mossi	3.00	1.50	.90
(39)	Stan Musial	25.00	12.50	7.50
(40)	Charlie Neal	3.00	1.50	.90
(41)	Don Newcombe	5.00	2.50	1.50
(42)	Milt Pappas	5.00	2.50	1.50
(43)	Camilo Pascual	5.00	2.50	1.50
(44)	Billie Pierce (Billy)	5.00	2.50	1.50
(45)	Robin Roberts	12.00	6.00	3.50
(46)	Frank Robinson	15.00	7.50	4.50
(47)	Pete Runnels	5.00	2.50	1.50
(48)	Herb Score	5.00	2.50	1.50
(49)	Warren Spahn	12.00	6.00	3.50
(50)	Johnny Temple	3.00	1.50	.90
(51)	Gus Triandos	3.00	1.50	.90
(52)	Jerry Walker	3.00	1.50	.90
(53)	Bill White	5.00	2.50	1.50
(54)	Gene Woodling	5.00	2.50	1.50
(55)	Early Wynn	12.00	6.00	3.50
(56)	Chicago Cubs Logo	3.00	1.50	.90
(57)	Cincinnati Reds Logo	3.00	1.50	.90
(58)	Los Angeles Dodgers Logo	3.00	1.50	.90
(59)	Milwaukee Braves Logo	3.00	1.50	.90
(60)	Philadelphia Phillies Logo	3.00	1.50	.90
(61)	Pittsburgh Pirates Logo	5.00	2.50	1.50
(62)	San Francisco Giants Logo	3.00	1.50	.90
(63)	St. Louis Cardinals Logo	3.00	1.50	.90
(64)	Baltimore Orioles Logo	3.00	1.50	.90
(65)	Boston Red Sox Logo	3.00	1.50	.90
(66)	Chicago White Sox Logo	3.00	1.50	.90
(67)	Cleveland Indians Logo	3.00	1.50	.90
(68)	Detroit Tigers Logo	3.00	1.50	.90
(69)	Kansas City Athletics Logo	3.00	1.50	.90
(70)	New York Yankees Logo	6.00	3.00	1.75
(71)	Washington Senators Logo	3.00	1.50	.90
(72)	Autograph (Richie Ashburn)	3.00	1.50	.90
(73)	Autograph (Rocky Colavito)	3.00	1.50	.90
(74)	Autograph (Roy Face)	3.00	1.50	.90
(75)	Autograph (Jackie Jensen)	3.00	1.50	.90
(76)	Autograph (Harmon Killebrew)	5.00	2.50	1.50
(77)	Autograph (Mickey Mantle)	25.00	12.50	7.50
(78)	Autograph (Willie Mays)	10.00	5.00	3.00
(79)	Autograph (Stan Musial)	10.00	5.00	3.00
(80)	Autograph (Billy Pierce)	3.00	1.50	.90
(81)	Autograph (Jerry Walker)	3.00	1.50	.90
(82)	Run-Down	3.00	1.50	.90
(83)	Out At First	3.00	1.50	.90
(84)	The Final Word	3.00	1.50	.90
(85)	Twisting Foul	3.00	1.50	.90
(86)	Out At Home	3.00	1.50	.90
(87)	Circus Catch	3.00	1.50	.90
(88)	Great Catch	3.00	1.50	.90
(89)	Stolen Base	3.00	1.50	.90
(90)	Grand Slam Homer	3.00	1.50	.90
(91)	Double Play	3.00	1.50	.90
(92)	Right-Handed Follow-Thru (no caption)	3.00	1.50	.90
(93)	Right-Handed High Leg Kick (no caption)	3.00	1.50	.90
(94)	Left-Handed Pitcher (no caption)	3.00	1.50	.90
(95)	Right-Handed Batter (no caption)	3.00	1.50	.90
(96)	Left-Handed Batter (no caption)	3.00	1.50	.90

1961 Topps

Except for some of the specialty cards, Topps returned to a vertical format with their 1961 cards. The set is numbered through 598, however only 587 cards were printed. No numbers 426, 587 and 588 were issued. Two cards numbered 463 exist (one a Braves team card and one a player card of Jack Fisher). Actually, the Braves team card is checklisted as #426. Designs for 1961 are basically large color portraits; the backs return to extensive statistics. A three-panel cartoon highlighting the player's career

appears on the card backs. Innovations include numbered checklists, cards for statistical leaders, and 10 "Baseball Thrills" cards. The scarce high numbers are card numbers 523-589.

		NR MT	EX	VG
Complete Set:		5500.00	2750.00	1650.
Common Player: 1-370		2.00	1.00	.60
Common Player: 371-522		4.00	2.00	1.25
Common Player: 523-589		25.00	12.50	7.50
1	Dick Groat	20.00	5.00	3.00
2	Roger Maris	175.00	87.00	52.00
3	John Buzhardt	2.00	1.00	.60
4	Lenny Green	2.00	1.00	.60
5	Johnny Romano	2.00	1.00	.60
6	Ed Roebuck	2.00	1.00	.60
7	White Sox Team	4.00	2.00	1.25
8	Dick Williams	4.00	2.00	1.25
9	Bob Purkey	2.00	1.00	.60
10	Brooks Robinson	30.00	15.00	9.00
11	Curt Simmons	2.25	1.25	.70
12	Moe Thacker	2.00	1.00	.60
13	Chuck Cottier	2.00	1.00	.60
14	Don Mossi	2.25	1.25	.70
15	Willie Kirkland	2.00	1.00	.60
16	Billy Muffett	2.00	1.00	.60
17	Checklist 1-88	5.00	2.50	1.50
18	Jim Grant	2.00	1.00	.60
19	Cletis Boyer	2.25	1.25	.70
20	Robin Roberts	10.00	5.00	3.00
21	*Zorro Versalles*	4.00	2.00	1.25
22	Clem Labine	2.25	1.25	.70
23	Don Demeter	2.00	1.00	.60
24	Ken Johnson	2.00	1.00	.60
25	Red's Heavy Artillery (Gus Bell, Vada Pinson, Frank Robinson)	6.00	3.00	1.75
26	Wes Stock	2.00	1.00	.60
27	Jerry Kindall	2.00	1.00	.60
28	Hector Lopez	4.00	2.00	1.25
29	Don Nottebart	2.00	1.00	.60
30	Nellie Fox	6.00	3.00	1.75
31	Bob Schmidt	2.00	1.00	.60
32	Ray Sadecki	2.00	1.00	.60
33	Gary Geiger	2.00	1.00	.60
34	Wynn Hawkins	2.00	1.00	.60
35	*Ron Santo*	60.00	30.00	18.00
36	Jack Kralick	2.00	1.00	.60
37	Charlie Maxwell	2.00	1.00	.60
38	Bob Lillis	2.00	1.00	.60
39	Leo Posada	2.00	1.00	.60
40	Bob Turley	4.00	2.00	1.25
41	N.L. Batting Leaders (Bob Clemente, Dick Groat, Norm Larker, Willie Mays)	4.00	2.00	1.25
42	A.L. Batting Leaders (Minnie Minoso, Pete Runnels, Bill Skowron, Al Smith)	4.00	2.00	1.25
43	N.L. Home Run Leaders (Hank Aaron, Ernie Banks, Ken Boyer, Eddie Mathews)	4.00	2.00	1.25
44	A.L. Home Run Leaders (Rocky Colavito, Jim Lemon, Mickey Mantle, Roger Maris)	35.00	17.50	10.50
45	N.L. E.R.A. Leaders (Ernie Broglio, Don Drysdale, Bob Friend, Mike McCormick, Stan Williams)	3.25	1.75	1.00
46	A.L. E.R.A. Leaders (Frank Baumann, Hal Brown, Jim Bunning, Art Ditmar)	4.00	2.00	1.25
47	N.L. Pitching Leaders (Ernie Broglio, Lou Burdette, Vern Law, Warren Spahn)	3.25	1.75	1.00
48	A.L. Pitching Leaders (Bud Daley, Art Ditmar, Chuck Estrada, Frank Lary, Milt Pappas, Jim Perry)	4.00	2.00	1.25

		NR MT	EX	VG
49	N.L. Strikeout Leaders (Ernie Broglio, Don Drysdale, Sam Jones, Sandy Koufax)	4.00	2.00	1.25
50	A.L. Strikeout Leaders (Jim Bunning, Frank Lary, Pedro Ramos, Early Wynn)	5.00	2.50	1.50
51	Tigers Team	5.00	2.50	1.50
52	George Crowe	2.00	1.00	.60
53	Russ Nixon	2.00	1.00	.60
54	Earl Francis	2.00	1.00	.60
55	Jim Davenport	2.00	1.00	.60
56	Russ Kemmerer	2.00	1.00	.60
57	Marv Throneberry	4.00	2.00	1.25
58	Joe Schaffernoth	2.00	1.00	.60
59	Jim Woods	2.00	1.00	.60
60	Woodie Held	2.00	1.00	.60
61	Ron Piche	2.00	1.00	.60
62	Al Pilarcik	2.00	1.00	.60
63	Jim Kaat	9.00	4.50	2.75
64	Alex Grammas	2.00	1.00	.60
65	Ted Kluszewski	4.00	2.00	1.25
66	Bill Henry	2.00	1.00	.60
67	Ossie Virgil	2.00	1.00	.60
68	Deron Johnson	4.00	2.00	1.25
69	Earl Wilson	2.00	1.00	.60
70	Bill Virdon	4.00	2.00	1.25
71	Jerry Adair	2.25	1.25	.70
72	Stu Miller	2.00	1.00	.60
73	Al Spangler	2.00	1.00	.60
74	Joe Pignatano	2.00	1.00	.60
75	Lindy Shows Larry (Larry Jackson, Lindy McDaniel)	4.00	2.00	1.25
76	Harry Anderson	2.00	1.00	.60
77	Dick Stigman	2.00	1.00	.60
78	Lee Walls	2.00	1.00	.60
79	Joe Ginsberg	2.00	1.00	.60
80	Harmon Killebrew	25.00	12.50	7.50
81	Tracy Stallard	2.00	1.00	.60
82	Joe Christopher	2.00	1.00	.60
83	Bob Bruce	2.00	1.00	.60
84	Lee Maye	2.00	1.00	.60
85	Jerry Walker	2.00	1.00	.60
86	Dodgers Team	5.00	2.50	1.50
87	Joe Amalfitano	2.00	1.00	.60
88	Richie Ashburn	6.00	3.00	1.75
89	Billy Martin	8.00	4.00	2.50
90	Jerry Staley	2.00	1.00	.60
91	Walt Moryn	2.00	1.00	.60
92	Hal Naragon	2.00	1.00	.60
93	Tony Gonzalez	2.00	1.00	.60
94	Johnny Kucks	2.00	1.00	.60
95	Norm Cash	5.00	2.50	1.50
96	Billy O'Dell	2.00	1.00	.60
97	Jerry Lynch	2.00	1.00	.60
98a	Checklist 89-176 (word "Checklist" in red on front)	7.00	3.50	2.00
98b	Checklist 89-176 ("Checklist" in yellow, 98 on back in black)	5.00	2.50	1.50
98c	Checklist 89-176 ("Checklist" in yellow, 98 on back in white)	7.00	3.50	2.00
99	Don Buddin	2.00	1.00	.60
100	Harvey Haddix	4.00	2.00	1.25
101	Bubba Phillips	2.00	1.00	.60
102	Gene Stephens	2.00	1.00	.60
103	Ruben Amaro	2.00	1.00	.60
104	John Blanchard	4.00	2.00	1.25
105	Carl Willey	2.00	1.00	.60
106	Whitey Herzog	2.25	1.25	.70
107	Seth Morehead	2.00	1.00	.60
108	Dan Dobbek	2.00	1.00	.60
109	Johnny Podres	2.25	1.25	.70
110	Vada Pinson	5.00	2.50	1.50
111	Jack Meyer	2.00	1.00	.60
112	Chico Fernandez	2.00	1.00	.60
113	Mike Fornieles	2.00	1.00	.60
114	Hobie Landrith	2.00	1.00	.60
115	Johnny Antonelli	2.25	1.25	.70
116	Joe DeMaestri	4.00	2.00	1.25
117	Dale Long	2.25	1.25	.70
118	Chris Cannizzaro	2.00	1.00	.60
119	A's Big Armor (Hank Bauer, Jerry Lumpe, Norm Siebern)	4.00	2.00	1.25
120	Ed Mathews	30.00	15.00	9.00
121	Eli Grba	2.00	1.00	.60
122	Cubs Team	4.00	2.00	1.25
123	Billy Gardner	2.00	1.00	.60
124	J.C. Martin	2.00	1.00	.60
125	Steve Barber	2.00	1.00	.60
126	Dick Stuart	2.25	1.25	.70
127	Ron Kline	2.00	1.00	.60
128	Rip Repulski	2.00	1.00	.60
129	Ed Hobaugh	2.00	1.00	.60
130	Norm Larker	2.00	1.00	.60

#	Player	NR MT	EX	VG
131	Paul Richards	2.25	1.25	.70
132	Al Lopez	5.00	2.50	1.50
133	Ralph Houk	5.00	2.50	1.50
134	Mickey Vernon	2.25	1.25	.70
135	Fred Hutchinson	2.25	1.25	.70
136	Walt Alston	4.00	2.00	1.25
137	Chuck Dressen	2.25	1.25	.70
138	Danny Murtaugh	2.25	1.25	.70
139	Solly Hemus	2.00	1.00	.60
140	Gus Triandos	2.25	1.25	.70
141	*Billy Williams*	125.00	62.00	37.00
142	Luis Arroyo	4.00	2.00	1.25
143	Russ Snyder	2.00	1.00	.60
144	Jim Coker	2.00	1.00	.60
145	Bob Buhl	2.25	1.25	.70
146	Marty Keough	2.00	1.00	.60
147	Ed Rakow	2.00	1.00	.60
148	Julian Javier	2.25	1.25	.70
149	Bob Oldis	2.00	1.00	.60
150	Willie Mays	120.00	60.00	38.00
151	Jim Donohue	2.00	1.00	.60
152	Earl Torgeson	2.00	1.00	.60
153	Don Lee	2.00	1.00	.60
154	Bobby Del Greco	2.00	1.00	.60
155	Johnny Temple	2.00	1.00	.60
156	Ken Hunt	2.00	1.00	.60
157	Cal McLish	2.00	1.00	.60
158	Pete Daley	2.00	1.00	.60
159	Orioles Team	4.00	2.00	1.25
160	Whitey Ford	35.00	17.50	10.50
161	Sherman Jones (photo actually Eddie Fisher)	2.00	1.00	.60
162	Jay Hook	2.00	1.00	.60
163	Ed Sadowski	2.00	1.00	.60
164	Felix Mantilla	2.00	1.00	.60
165	Gino Cimoli	2.00	1.00	.60
166	Danny Kravitz	2.00	1.00	.60
167	Giants Team	4.00	2.00	1.25
168	Tommy Davis	5.00	2.50	1.50
169	Don Elston	2.00	1.00	.60
170	Al Smith	2.00	1.00	.60
171	Paul Foytack	2.00	1.00	.60
172	Don Dillard	2.00	1.00	.60
173	Beantown Bombers (Jackie Jensen, Frank Malzone, Vic Wertz)	4.00	2.00	1.25
174	Ray Semproch	2.00	1.00	.60
175	Gene Freese	2.00	1.00	.60
176	Ken Aspromonte	2.00	1.00	.60
177	Don Larsen	4.00	2.00	1.25
178	Bob Nieman	2.00	1.00	.60
179	Joe Koppe	2.00	1.00	.60
180	Bobby Richardson	6.00	3.00	1.75
181	Fred Green	2.00	1.00	.60
182	Dave Nicholson	2.00	1.00	.60
183	Andre Rodgers	2.00	1.00	.60
184	Steve Bilko	2.00	1.00	.60
185	Herb Score	4.00	2.00	1.25
186	Elmer Valo	2.00	1.00	.60
187	Billy Klaus	2.00	1.00	.60
188	Jim Marshall	2.00	1.00	.60
189	Checklist 177-264	5.00	2.50	1.50
190	Stan Williams	2.00	1.00	.60
191	Mike de la Hoz	2.00	1.00	.60
192	Dick Brown	2.00	1.00	.60
193	Gene Conley	2.25	1.25	.70
194	Gordy Coleman	2.00	1.00	.60
195	Jerry Casale	2.00	1.00	.60
196	Ed Bouchee	2.00	1.00	.60
197	Dick Hall	2.00	1.00	.60
198	Carl Sawatski	2.00	1.00	.60
199	Bob Boyd	2.00	1.00	.60
200	Warren Spahn	30.00	15.00	9.00
201	Pete Whisenant	2.00	1.00	.60
202	Al Neiger	2.00	1.00	.60
203	Eddie Bressoud	2.00	1.00	.60
204	Bob Skinner	2.25	1.25	.70
205	Bill Pierce	4.00	2.00	1.25
206	Gene Green	2.00	1.00	.60
207	Dodger Southpaws (Sandy Koufax, Johnny Podres)	15.00	7.50	4.50
208	Larry Osborne	2.00	1.00	.60
209	Ken McBride	2.00	1.00	.60
210	Pete Runnels	2.25	1.25	.70
211	Bob Gibson	40.00	20.00	12.00
212	Haywood Sullivan	2.25	1.25	.70
213	*Bill Stafford*	4.00	2.00	1.25
214	Danny Murphy	2.00	1.00	.60
215	Gus Bell	2.25	1.25	.70
216	Ted Bowsfield	2.00	1.00	.60
217	Mel Roach	2.00	1.00	.60
218	Hal Brown	2.00	1.00	.60
219	Gene Mauch	4.00	2.00	1.25
220	Al Dark	2.25	1.25	.70
221	Mike Higgins	2.00	1.00	.60
222	Jimmie Dykes	2.00	1.00	.60
223	Bob Scheffing	2.00	1.00	.60
224	Joe Gordon	2.25	1.25	.70
225	Bill Rigney	2.00	1.00	.60
226	Harry Lavagetto	2.00	1.00	.60
227	Juan Pizarro	2.00	1.00	.60
228	Yankees Team	35.00	17.50	10.50
229	Rudy Hernandez	2.00	1.00	.60
230	Don Hoak	2.25	1.25	.70
231	Dick Drott	2.00	1.00	.60
232	Bill White	4.00	2.00	1.25
233	Joe Jay	2.00	1.00	.60
234	Ted Lepcio	2.00	1.00	.60
235	Camilo Pascual	2.25	1.25	.70
236	Don Gile	2.00	1.00	.60
237	Billy Loes	2.00	1.00	.60
238	Jim Gilliam	4.00	2.00	1.25
239	Dave Sisler	2.00	1.00	.60
240	Ron Hansen	2.00	1.00	.60
241	Al Cicotte	2.00	1.00	.60
242	Hal W. Smith	2.00	1.00	.60
243	Frank Lary	2.25	1.25	.70
244	Chico Cardenas	2.25	1.25	.70
245	Joe Adcock	4.00	2.00	1.25
246	Bob Davis	2.00	1.00	.60
247	Billy Goodman	2.00	1.00	.60
248	Ed Keegan	2.00	1.00	.60
249	Reds Team	4.00	2.00	1.25
250	Buc Hill Aces (Roy Face, Vern Law)	4.00	2.00	1.25
251	Bill Bruton	2.00	1.00	.60
252	Bill Short	4.00	2.00	1.25
253	Sammy Taylor	2.00	1.00	.60
254	Ted Sadowski	2.00	1.00	.60
255	Vic Power	2.00	1.00	.60
256	Billy Hoeft	2.00	1.00	.60
257	Carroll Hardy	2.00	1.00	.60
258	Jack Sanford	2.00	1.00	.60
259	John Schaive	2.00	1.00	.60
260	Don Drysdale	25.00	12.50	7.50
261	Charlie Lau	2.25	1.25	.70
262	Tony Curry	2.00	1.00	.60
263	Ken Hamlin	2.00	1.00	.60
264	Glen Hobbie	2.00	1.00	.60
265	Tony Kubek	5.00	2.50	1.50
266	Lindy McDaniel	2.00	1.00	.60
267	Norm Siebern	2.25	1.25	.70
268	Ike DeLock (Delock)	2.00	1.00	.60
269	Harry Chiti	2.00	1.00	.60
270	Bob Friend	4.00	2.00	1.25
271	Jim Landis	2.00	1.00	.60
272	Tom Morgan	2.00	1.00	.60
273	Checklist 265-352	5.00	2.50	1.50
274	Gary Bell	2.00	1.00	.60
275	Gene Woodling	2.25	1.25	.70
276	Ray Rippelmeyer	2.00	1.00	.60
277	Hank Foiles	2.00	1.00	.60
278	Don McMahon	2.00	1.00	.60
279	Jose Pagan	2.00	1.00	.60
280	Frank Howard	4.00	2.00	1.25
281	Frank Sullivan	2.00	1.00	.60
282	Faye Throneberry	2.00	1.00	.60
283	Bob Anderson	2.00	1.00	.60
284	Dick Gernert	2.00	1.00	.60
285	Sherm Lollar	2.25	1.25	.70
286	George Witt	2.00	1.00	.60
287	Carl Yastrzemski	150.00	75.00	45.00
288	Albie Pearson	2.00	1.00	.60
289	Ray Moore	2.00	1.00	.60
290	Stan Musial	100.00	50.00	30.00
291	Tex Clevenger	2.00	1.00	.60
292	Jim Baumer	2.00	1.00	.60
293	Tom Sturdivant	2.00	1.00	.60
294	Don Blasingame	2.00	1.00	.60
295	Milt Pappas	2.25	1.25	.70
296	Wes Covington	2.00	1.00	.60
297	Athletics Team	4.00	2.00	1.25
298	Jim Golden	2.00	1.00	.60
299	Clay Dalrymple	2.00	1.00	.60
300	Mickey Mantle	400.00	200.00	125.00
301	Chet Nichols	2.00	1.00	.60
302	Al Heist	2.00	1.00	.60
303	Gary Peters	2.25	1.25	.70
304	Rocky Nelson	2.00	1.00	.60
305	Mike McCormick	2.25	1.25	.70
306	World Series Game 1 (Virdon Saves Game)	5.00	2.50	1.50
307	World Series Game 2 (Mantle Slams 2 Homers)	30.00	15.00	9.00

		NR MT	EX	VG
308	World Series Game 3 (Richardson Is Hero)	4.00	2.00	1.25
309	World Series Game 4 (Cimoli Is Safe In Crucial Play)	5.00	2.50	1.50
310	World Series Game 5 (Face Saves the Day)	5.00	2.50	1.50
311	World Series Game 6 (Ford Pitches Second Shutout)	5.00	2.50	1.50
312	World Series Game 7 (Mazeroski's Homer Wins It!)	5.00	2.50	1.50
313	World Series Summary (The Winners Celebrate)	5.00	2.50	1.50
314	Bob Miller	2.00	1.00	.60
315	Earl Battey	2.25	1.25	.70
316	Bobby Gene Smith	2.00	1.00	.60
317	*Jim Brewer*	2.25	1.25	.70
318	Danny O'Connell	2.00	1.00	.60
319	Valmy Thomas	2.00	1.00	.60
320	Lou Burdette	4.00	2.00	1.25
321	Marv Breeding	2.00	1.00	.60
322	Bill Kunkel	2.00	1.00	.60
323	Sammy Esposito	2.00	1.00	.60
324	Hank Aguirre	2.00	1.00	.60
325	Wally Moon	2.25	1.25	.70
326	Dave Hillman	2.00	1.00	.60
327	*Matty Alou*	4.00	2.00	1.25
328	Jim O'Toole	2.00	1.00	.60
329	Julio Becquer	2.00	1.00	.60
330	Rocky Colavito	5.00	2.50	1.50
331	Ned Garver	2.00	1.00	.60
332	Dutch Dotterer (photo actually Tommy Dotterer)	2.00	1.00	.60
333	Fritz Brickell	4.00	2.00	1.25
334	Walt Bond	2.00	1.00	.60
335	Frank Bolling	2.00	1.00	.60
336	Don Mincher	2.25	1.25	.70
337	Al's Aces (Al Lopez, Herb Score, Early Wynn)	5.00	2.50	1.50
338	Don Landrum	2.00	1.00	.60
339	Gene Baker	2.00	1.00	.60
340	Vic Wertz	2.25	1.25	.70
341	Jim Owens	2.00	1.00	.60
342	Clint Courtney	2.00	1.00	.60
343	Earl Robinson	2.00	1.00	.60
344	Sandy Koufax	85.00	42.00	26.00
345	Jim Piersall	4.00	2.00	1.25
346	Howie Nunn	2.00	1.00	.60
347	Cardinals Team	4.00	2.00	1.25
348	Steve Boros	2.00	1.00	.60
349	Danny McDevitt	4.00	2.00	1.25
350	Ernie Banks	40.00	20.00	12.00
351	Jim King	2.00	1.00	.60
352	Bob Shaw	2.00	1.00	.60
353	Howie Bedell	2.00	1.00	.60
354	Billy Harrell	2.00	1.00	.60
355	Bob Allison	2.25	1.25	.70
356	Ryne Duren	2.25	1.25	.70
357	Daryl Spencer	2.00	1.00	.60
358	Earl Averill	2.00	1.00	.60
359	Dallas Green	2.25	1.25	.70
360	Frank Robinson	30.00	15.00	9.00
361a	Checklist 353-429 ("Topps Baseball" in black on front)	5.00	2.50	1.50
361b	Checklist 353-429 ("Topps Baseball" in yellow)	6.00	3.00	1.75
362	Frank Funk	2.00	1.00	.60
363	John Roseboro	2.25	1.25	.70
364	Moe Drabowsky	2.00	1.00	.60
365	Jerry Lumpe	2.25	1.25	.70
366	Eddie Fisher	2.00	1.00	.60
367	Jim Rivera	2.00	1.00	.60
368	Bennie Daniels	2.00	1.00	.60
369	Dave Philley	2.25	1.25	.70
370	Roy Face	4.00	2.00	1.25
371	Bill Skowron	5.00	2.50	1.50
372	Bob Hendley	4.00	2.00	1.25
373	Red Sox Team	5.00	2.50	1.50
374	Paul Giel	4.00	2.00	1.25
375	Ken Boyer	4.00	2.00	1.25
376	Mike Roarke	4.00	2.00	1.25
377	Ruben Gomez	4.00	2.00	1.25
378	Wally Post	4.00	2.00	1.25
379	Bobby Shantz	4.00	2.00	1.25
380	Minnie Minoso	5.00	2.50	1.50
381	Dave Wickersham	4.00	2.00	1.25
382	Frank Thomas	4.00	2.00	1.25
383	Frisco First Liners (Mike McCormick, Billy O'Dell, Jack Sanford)	4.00	2.00	1.25
384	Chuck Essegian	4.00	2.00	1.25
385	Jim Perry	4.00	2.00	1.25
386	Joe Hicks	4.00	2.00	1.25

		NR MT	EX	VG
387	Duke Maas	4.00	2.00	1.25
388	Bob Clemente	125.00	67.00	37.00
389	Ralph Terry	5.00	2.50	1.50
390	Del Crandall	4.00	2.00	1.25
391	Winston Brown	4.00	2.00	1.25
392	Reno Bertoia	4.00	2.00	1.25
393	Batter Bafflers (Don Cardwell, Glen Hobbie)	4.00	2.00	1.25
394	Ken Walters	4.00	2.00	1.25
395	Chuck Estrada	4.00	2.00	1.25
396	Bob Aspromonte	4.00	2.00	1.25
397	Hal Woodeshick	4.00	2.00	1.25
398	Hank Bauer	4.00	2.00	1.25
399	Cliff Cook	4.00	2.00	1.25
400	Vern Law	4.00	2.00	1.25
401	Babe Ruth Hits 60th Homer	25.00	12.50	7.50
402	Larsen Pitches Perfect Game	15.00	7.50	4.50
403	Brooklyn-Boston Play 26-Inning Tie	4.00	2.00	1.25
404	Hornsby Tops N.L. With .424 Average	5.00	2.50	1.50
405	Gehrig Benched After 2,130 Games	18.00	9.00	5.50
406	Mantle Blasts 565 ft. Home Run	40.00	20.00	12.00
407	Jack Chesbro Wins 41st Game	4.00	2.00	1.25
408	Mathewson Strikes Out 267 Batters	5.00	2.50	1.50
409	Johnson Hurls 3rd Shutout in 4 Days	4.00	2.00	1.25
410	Haddix Pitches 12 Perfect Innings	4.00	2.00	1.25
411	Tony Taylor	4.00	2.00	1.25
412	Larry Sherry	4.00	2.00	1.25
413	Eddie Yost	4.00	2.00	1.25
414	Dick Donovan	4.00	2.00	1.25
415	Hank Aaron	125.00	67.00	37.00
416	*Dick Howser*	8.00	4.00	2.50
417	*Juan Marichal*	150.00	75.00	50.00
418	Ed Bailey	4.00	2.00	1.25
419	Tom Borland	4.00	2.00	1.25
420	Ernie Broglio	4.00	2.00	1.25
421	Ty Cline	4.00	2.00	1.25
422	Bud Daley	4.00	2.00	1.25
423	Charlie Neal	4.00	2.00	1.25
424	Turk Lown	4.00	2.00	1.25
425	Yogi Berra	60.00	30.00	18.00
426	Not Issued			
427	Dick Ellsworth	4.00	2.00	1.25
428	Ray Barker	4.00	2.00	1.25
429	Al Kaline	40.00	20.00	12.00
430	Bill Mazeroski	10.00	5.00	3.00
431	Chuck Stobbs	4.00	2.00	1.25
432	Coot Veal	4.00	2.00	1.25
433	Art Mahaffey	4.00	2.00	1.25
434	Tom Brewer	4.00	2.00	1.25
435	Orlando Cepeda	10.00	5.00	3.00
436	*Jim Maloney*	4.00	2.00	1.25
437a	Checklist 430-506 (#440 is Louis Aparicio)	6.00	3.00	1.75
437b	Checklist 430-506 (#440 is Luis Aparicio)	6.50	3.25	2.00
438	Curt Flood	4.00	2.00	1.25
439	*Phil Regan*	4.00	2.00	1.25
440	Luis Aparicio	12.00	6.00	3.50
441	Dick Bertell	4.00	2.00	1.25
442	Gordon Jones	4.00	2.00	1.25
443	Duke Snider	40.00	20.00	12.00
444	Joe Nuxhall	4.00	2.00	1.25
445	Frank Malzone	4.00	2.00	1.25
446	Bob "Hawk" Taylor	4.00	2.00	1.25
447	Harry Bright	4.00	2.00	1.25
448	Del Rice	4.00	2.00	1.25
449	*Bobby Bolin*	4.00	2.00	1.25
450	Jim Lemon	4.00	2.00	1.25
451	Power For Ernie (Ernie Broglio, Daryl Spencer, Bill White)	4.00	2.00	1.25
452	Bob Allen	4.00	2.00	1.25
453	Dick Schofield	4.00	2.00	1.25
454	Pumpsie Green	4.00	2.00	1.25
455	Early Wynn	15.00	7.50	4.50
456	Hal Bevan	4.00	2.00	1.25
457	Johnny James	4.00	2.00	1.25
458	Willie Tasby	4.00	2.00	1.25
459	Terry Fox	4.00	2.00	1.25
460	Gil Hodges	18.00	9.00	5.50
461	Smoky Burgess	4.00	2.00	1.25
462	Lou Klimchock	4.00	2.00	1.25
463a	Braves Team (should be card #426)	4.00	2.00	1.25
463b	Jack Fisher	4.00	2.00	1.25
464	*Leroy Thomas*	4.00	2.00	1.25
465	Roy McMillan	4.00	2.00	1.25

		NR MT	EX	VG
466	Ron Moeller	4.00	2.00	1.25
467	Indians Team	5.00	2.50	1.50
468	Johnny Callison	4.00	2.00	1.25
469	Ralph Lumenti	4.00	2.00	1.25
470	Roy Sievers	4.00	2.00	1.25
471	Phil Rizzuto MVP	12.00	6.00	3.50
472	Yogi Berra MVP	40.00	20.00	12.00
473	Bobby Shantz MVP	5.00	2.50	1.50
474	Al Rosen MVP	5.00	2.50	1.50
475	Mickey Mantle MVP	125.00	62.00	37.00
476	Jackie Jensen MVP	5.00	2.50	1.50
477	Nellie Fox MVP	4.00	2.00	1.25
478	Roger Maris MVP	40.00	20.00	12.00
479	Jim Konstanty MVP	4.00	2.00	1.25
480	Roy Campanella MVP	25.00	12.50	7.50
481	Hank Sauer MVP	4.00	2.00	1.25
482	Willie Mays MVP	40.00	20.00	12.00
483	Don Newcombe MVP	5.00	2.50	1.50
484	Hank Aaron MVP	40.00	20.00	12.00
485	Ernie Banks MVP	25.00	12.50	7.50
486	Dick Groat MVP	5.00	2.50	1.50
487	Gene Oliver	4.00	2.00	1.25
488	Joe McClain	4.00	2.00	1.25
489	Walt Dropo	4.00	2.00	1.25
490	Jim Bunning	8.00	4.00	2.50
491	Phillies Team	5.00	2.50	1.50
492	Ron Fairly	4.00	2.00	1.25
493	Don Zimmer	4.00	2.00	1.25
494	Tom Cheney	4.00	2.00	1.25
495	Elston Howard	6.00	3.00	1.75
496	Ken MacKenzie	4.00	2.00	1.25
497	Willie Jones	4.00	2.00	1.25
498	Ray Herbert	4.00	2.00	1.25
499	Chuck Schilling	4.00	2.00	1.25
500	Harvey Kuenn	5.00	2.50	1.50
501	John DeMerit	4.00	2.00	1.25
502	Clarence Coleman	4.00	2.00	1.25
503	Tito Francona	4.00	2.00	1.25
504	Billy Consolo	4.00	2.00	1.25
505	Red Schoendienst	12.00	6.00	3.50
506	*Willie Davis*	10.00	5.00	3.00
507	Pete Burnside	4.00	2.00	1.25
508	Rocky Bridges	4.00	2.00	1.25
509	Camilo Carreon	4.00	2.00	1.25
510	Art Ditmar	4.00	2.00	1.25
511	Joe Morgan	4.00	2.00	1.25
512	Bob Will	4.00	2.00	1.25
513	Jim Brosnan	4.00	2.00	1.25
514	Jake Wood	4.00	2.00	1.25
515	Jackie Brandt	4.00	2.00	1.25
516	Checklist 507-587	10.00	5.00	3.00
517	Willie McCovey	60.00	30.00	18.00
518	Andy Carey	4.00	2.00	1.25
519	Jim Pagliaroni	4.00	2.00	1.25
520	Joe Cunningham	4.00	2.00	1.25
521	Brother Battery (Larry Sherry, Norm Sherry)	4.00	2.00	1.25
522	Dick Farrell	4.00	2.00	1.25
523	Joe Gibbon	25.00	12.50	7.50
524	Johnny Logan	27.00	13.50	8.00
525	*Ron Perranoski*	27.00	13.50	8.00
526	R.C. Stevens	25.00	12.50	7.50
527	Gene Leek	25.00	12.50	7.50
528	Pedro Ramos	25.00	12.50	7.50
529	Bob Roselli	25.00	12.50	7.50
530	Bobby Malkmus	25.00	12.50	7.50
531	Jim Coates	27.00	13.50	8.00
532	Bob Hale	25.00	12.50	7.50
533	Jack Curtis	25.00	12.50	7.50
534	Eddie Kasko	25.00	12.50	7.50
535	Larry Jackson	25.00	12.50	7.50
536	Bill Tuttle	25.00	12.50	7.50
537	Bobby Locke	25.00	12.50	7.50
538	Chuck Hiller	25.00	12.50	7.50
539	Johnny Klippstein	25.00	12.50	7.50
540	Jackie Jensen	35.00	17.50	10.50
541	Roland Sheldon	27.00	13.50	8.00
542	Twins Team	60.00	30.00	18.00
543	Roger Craig	35.00	17.50	10.50
544	George Thomas	25.00	12.50	7.50
545	Hoyt Wilhelm	55.00	28.00	16.50
546	Marty Kutyna	25.00	12.50	7.50
547	Leon Wagner	27.00	13.50	8.00
548	Ted Wills	25.00	12.50	7.50
549	Hal R. Smith	25.00	12.50	7.50
550	Frank Baumann	25.00	12.50	7.50
551	George Altman	25.00	12.50	7.50
552	Jim Archer	25.00	12.50	7.50
553	Bill Fischer	25.00	12.50	7.50
554	Pirates Team	50.00	25.00	15.00
555	Sam Jones	25.00	12.50	7.50

		NR MT	EX	VG
556	Ken R. Hunt	25.00	12.50	7.50
557	Jose Valdivielso	25.00	12.50	7.50
558	Don Ferrarese	25.00	12.50	7.50
559	Jim Gentile	27.00	13.50	8.00
560	Barry Latman	25.00	12.50	7.50
561	Charley James	25.00	12.50	7.50
562	Bill Monbouquette	27.00	13.50	8.00
563	Bob Cerv	27.00	13.50	8.00
564	Don Cardwell	25.00	12.50	7.50
565	Felipe Alou	40.00	20.00	12.00
566	Paul Richards AS	25.00	12.50	7.50
567	Danny Murtaugh AS	25.00	12.50	7.50
568	Bill Skowron AS	35.00	17.50	10.50
569	Frank Herrera AS	25.00	12.50	7.50
570	Nellie Fox AS	40.00	20.00	12.00
571	Bill Mazeroski AS	35.00	17.50	10.50
572	Brooks Robinson AS	75.00	38.00	23.00
573	Ken Boyer AS	35.00	17.50	10.50
574	Luis Aparicio AS	45.00	23.00	13.50
575	Ernie Banks AS	100.00	50.00	30.00
576	Roger Maris AS	100.00	50.00	30.00
577	Hank Aaron AS	150.00	75.00	45.00
578	Mickey Mantle AS	400.00	200.00	120.00
579	Willie Mays AS	150.00	75.00	45.00
580	Al Kaline AS	90.00	45.00	27.00
581	Frank Robinson AS	80.00	40.00	25.00
582	Earl Battey AS	25.00	12.50	7.50
583	Del Crandall AS	30.00	15.00	9.00
584	Jim Perry AS	30.00	15.00	9.00
585	Bob Friend AS	30.00	15.00	9.00
586	Whitey Ford AS	90.00	45.00	27.00
587	Not Issued			
588	Not Issued			
589	Warren Spahn AS	125.00	56.00	35.00

1961 Topps Dice Game

One of the more obscure Topps test issues that may have never actually been issued is the 1961 Topps Dice Game. Eighteen black and white cards, each measuring 2-1/2" by 3-1/2" in size, comprise the set. Interestingly, there are no identifying marks, such as copyrights or trademarks, to indicate the set was produced by Topps. The card backs contain various baseball plays that occur when a certain pitch is called and a specific number of the dice is rolled.

		NR MT	EX	VG
Complete Set:		7500.00	3750.00	2250.
Common Player:		100.00	50.00	30.00
(1)	Earl Battey	100.00	50.00	30.00
(2)	Del Crandall	100.00	50.00	30.00
(3)	Jim Davenport	100.00	50.00	30.00
(4)	Don Drysdale	350.00	175.00	105.00
(5)	Dick Groat	150.00	75.00	45.00
(6)	Al Kaline	600.00	300.00	175.00
(7)	Tony Kubek	150.00	75.00	45.00
(8)	Mickey Mantle	2500.00	1250.00	750.00
(9)	Willie Mays	1000.00	500.00	300.00
(10)	Bill Mazeroski	150.00	75.00	45.00
(11)	Stan Musial	800.00	400.00	240.00
(12)	Camilo Pascual	100.00	50.00	30.00
(13)	Bobby Richardson	150.00	75.00	45.00
(14)	Brooks Robinson	400.00	200.00	120.00
(15)	Frank Robinson	350.00	175.00	105.00
(16)	Norm Siebern	100.00	50.00	30.00
(17)	Leon Wagner	100.00	50.00	30.00

		NR MT	EX	VG
(18)	Bill White	100.00	50.00	30.00

1961 Topps Magic Rub-Offs

Not too different in concept from the tattoos of the previous year, the Topps Magic Rub-Off was designed to leave impressions of team themes or individual players when properly applied. Measuring 2-1/16" by 3-1/16," the Magic Rub-Off was not designed specifically for application to the owner's skin. The set of 36 Rub-Offs seems to almost be a tongue-in-cheek product as the team themes were a far cry from official logos, and the players seem to have been included for their nicknames. Among the players (one representing each team) the best known and most valuable are Yogi Berra and Ernie Banks.

		NR MT	EX	VG
	Complete Set:	85.00	42.00	25.00
	Common Player:	1.00	.50	.30
(1)	Baltimore Orioles Pennant	1.00	.50	.30
(2)	Ernie "Bingo" Banks	12.00	6.00	3.50
(3)	Yogi Berra	20.00	10.00	6.00
(4)	Boston Red Sox Pennant	1.00	.50	.30
(5)	Jackie "Ozark" Brandt	1.25	.60	.40
(6)	Jim "Professor" Brosnan	1.25	.60	.40
(7)	Chicago Cubs Pennant	1.00	.50	.30
(8)	Chicago White Sox Pennant	1.00	.50	.30
(9)	Cincinnati Red Legs Pennant	1.00	.50	.30
(10)	Cleveland Indians Pennant	1.00	.50	.30
(11)	Detroit Tigers Pennant	1.25	.60	.40
(12)	Henry "Dutch" Dotterer	1.25	.60	.40
(13)	Joe "Flash" Gordon	1.50	.70	.45
(14)	Harvey "The Kitten" Haddix	1.50	.70	.45
(15)	Frank "Pancho" Hererra	1.25	.60	.40
(16)	Frank "Tower" Howard	3.50	1.75	1.00
(17)	"Sad" Sam Jones	1.25	.60	.40
(18)	Kansas City Athletics Pennant	1.00	.50	.30
(19)	Los Angeles Angels Pennant	1.00	.50	.30
(20)	Los Angeles Dodgers Pennant	1.25	.60	.40
(21)	Omar "Turk" Lown	1.25	.60	.40
(22)	Billy "The Kid" Martin	8.00	4.00	2.50
(23)	Duane "Duke" Mass (Maas)	1.25	.60	.40
(24)	Charlie "Paw Paw" Maxwell	1.25	.60	.40
(25)	Milwaukee Braves Pennant	1.00	.50	.30
(26)	Minnesota Twins Pennant	1.00	.50	.30
(27)	"Farmer" Ray Moore	1.00	.50	.30
(28)	Walt "Moose" Moryn	1.00	.50	.30
(29)	New York Yankees Pennant	2.50	1.25	.70
(30)	Philadelphia Phillies Pennant	1.00	.50	.30
(31)	Pittsburgh Pirates Pennant	1.00	.50	.30
(32)	John "Honey" Romano	1.25	.60	.40
(33)	"Pistol Pete" Runnels	1.50	.70	.45
(34)	St. Louis Cardinals Pennant	1.00	.50	.30
(35)	San Francisco Giants Pennant	1.00	.50	.30
(36)	Washington Senators Pennant	1.00	.50	.30

1961 Topps Stamps

Issued as an added insert to 1961 Topps wax packs these 1-3/8" by 3/16" stamps were designd to be collected and placed in an album which could be bought for an additional 10¢. Packs of cards

contained two stamps. There are 208 stamps in a complete set which depict 207 different players (Al Kaline appears twice). There are 104 players on brown stamps and 104 on green. While there are many Hall of Famers on the stamps, prices remain low because there is relatively little interest in what is a non-card set.

		NR MT	EX	VG
	Complete Set:	225.00	112.00	70.00
	Stamp Album:	35.00	17.50	10.50
	Common Player:	.40	.20	.12
(1)	Hank Aaron	10.00	5.00	3.00
(2)	Joe Adcock	.50	.25	.15
(3)	Hank Aguirre	.40	.20	.12
(4)	Bob Allison	.50	.25	.15
(5)	George Altman	.40	.20	.12
(6)	Bob Anderson	.40	.20	.12
(7)	Johnny Antonelli	.50	.25	.15
(8)	Luis Aparicio	1.50	.70	.45
(9)	Luis Arroyo	.50	.25	.15
(10)	Richie Ashburn	.80	.40	.25
(11)	Ken Aspromonte	.40	.20	.12
(12)	Ed Bailey	.40	.20	.12
(13)	Ernie Banks	6.00	3.00	1.75
(14)	Steve Barber	.40	.20	.12
(15)	Earl Battey	.50	.25	.15
(16)	Hank Bauer	.50	.25	.15
(17)	Gus Bell	.50	.25	.15
(18)	Yogi Berra	5.00	2.50	1.50
(19)	Reno Bertoia	.40	.20	.12
(20)	John Blanchard	.50	.25	.15
(21)	Don Blasingame	.40	.20	.12
(22)	Frank Bolling	.40	.20	.12
(23)	Steve Boros	.40	.20	.12
(24)	Ed Bouchee	.40	.20	.12
(25)	Bob Boyd	.40	.20	.12
(26)	Cletis Boyer	.50	.25	.15
(27)	Ken Boyer	.50	.25	.15
(28)	Jackie Brandt	.40	.20	.12
(29)	Marv Breeding	.40	.20	.12
(30)	Eddie Bressoud	.40	.20	.12
(31)	Jim Brewer	.40	.20	.12
(32)	Tom Brewer	.40	.20	.12
(33)	Jim Brosnan	.50	.25	.15
(34)	Bill Bruton	.40	.20	.12
(35)	Bob Buhl	.50	.25	.15
(36)	Jim Bunning	1.00	.50	.30
(37)	Smoky Burgess	.50	.25	.15
(38)	John Buzhardt	.40	.20	.12
(39)	Johnny Callison	.50	.25	.15
(40)	Chico Cardenas	.40	.20	.12
(41)	Andy Carey	.40	.20	.12
(42)	Jerry Casale	.40	.20	.12
(43)	Norm Cash	.50	.25	.15
(44)	Orlando Cepeda	1.25	.60	.40
(45)	Bob Cerv	.40	.20	.12
(46)	Harry Chiti	.40	.20	.12
(47)	Gene Conley	.50	.25	.15
(48)	Wes Covington	.40	.20	.12
(49)	Del Crandall	.50	.25	.15
(50)	Tony Curry	.40	.20	.12
(51)	Bud Daley	.40	.20	.12
(52)	Pete Daley	.40	.20	.12
(53)	Clay Dalrymple	.40	.20	.12
(54)	Jim Davenport	.40	.20	.12
(55)	Tommy Davis	.50	.25	.15
(56)	Bobby Del Greco	.40	.20	.12
(57)	Ike Delock	.40	.20	.12

		NR MT	EX	VG
(58)	Art Ditmar	.50	.25	.15
(59)	Dick Donovan	.40	.20	.12
(60)	Don Drysdale	6.00	3.00	1.75
(61)	Dick Ellsworth	.40	.20	.12
(62)	Don Elston	.40	.20	.12
(63)	Chuck Estrada	.40	.20	.12
(64)	Roy Face	.50	.25	.15
(65)	Dick Farrell	.40	.20	.12
(66)	Chico Fernandez	.40	.20	.12
(67)	Curt Flood	.50	.25	.15
(68)	Whitey Ford	4.00	2.00	1.25
(69)	Tito Francona	.40	.20	.12
(70)	Gene Freese	.40	.20	.12
(71)	Bob Friend	.50	.25	.15
(72)	Billy Gardner	.40	.20	.12
(73)	Ned Garver	.40	.20	.12
(74)	Gary Geiger	.40	.20	.12
(75)	Jim Gentile	.40	.20	.12
(76)	Dick Gernert	.40	.20	.12
(77)	Tony Gonzalez	.40	.20	.12
(78)	Alex Grammas	.40	.20	.12
(79)	Jim Grant	.40	.20	.12
(80)	Dick Groat	.50	.25	.15
(81)	Dick Hall	.40	.20	.12
(82)	Ron Hansen	.40	.20	.12
(83)	Bob Hartman	.40	.20	.12
(84)	Woodie Held	.40	.20	.12
(85)	Ray Herbert	.40	.20	.12
(86)	Frank Herrera	.40	.20	.12
(87)	Whitey Herzog	.50	.25	.15
(88)	Don Hoak	.50	.25	.15
(89)	Elston Howard	.80	.40	.25
(90)	Frank Howard	.50	.25	.15
(91)	Ken Hunt	.40	.20	.12
(92)	Larry Jackson	.40	.20	.12
(93)	Julian Javier	.40	.20	.12
(94)	Joe Jay	.40	.20	.12
(95)	Jackie Jensen	.50	.25	.15
(96)	Jim Kaat	1.00	.50	.30
(97a)	Al Kaline (green)	7.00	3.50	2.00
(97b)	Al Kaline (brown)	7.00	3.50	2.00
(98)	Eddie Kasko	.40	.20	.12
(99)	Russ Kemmerer	.40	.20	.12
(100)	Harmon Killebrew	5.00	2.50	1.50
(101)	Billy Klaus	.40	.20	.12
(102)	Ron Kline	.40	.20	.12
(103)	Johnny Klippstein	.40	.20	.12
(104)	Ted Kluszewski	.40	.20	.12
(105)	Tony Kubek	.80	.40	.25
(106)	Harvey Kuenn	.50	.25	.15
(107)	Jim Landis	.40	.20	.12
(108)	Hobie Landrith	.40	.20	.12
(109)	Norm Larker	.40	.20	.12
(110)	Frank Lary	.40	.20	.12
(111)	Barry Latman	.40	.20	.12
(112)	Vern Law	.50	.25	.15
(113)	Jim Lemon	.40	.20	.12
(114)	Sherm Lollar	.50	.25	.15
(115)	Dale Long	.50	.25	.15
(116)	Jerry Lumpe	.40	.20	.12
(117)	Jerry Lynch	.40	.20	.12
(118)	Art Mahaffey	.40	.20	.12
(119)	Frank Malzone	.40	.20	.12
(120)	Felix Mantilla	.40	.20	.12
(121)	Mickey Mantle	50.00	25.00	15.00
(122)	Juan Marichal	5.00	2.50	1.50
(123)	Roger Maris	12.00	6.00	3.50
(124)	Billy Martin	1.00	.50	.30
(125)	J.C. Martin	.40	.20	.12
(126)	Ed Mathews	3.00	1.50	.90
(127)	Charlie Maxwell	.40	.20	.12
(128)	Willie Mays	7.00	3.50	2.00
(129)	Bill Mazeroski	.50	.25	.15
(130)	Mike McCormick	.40	.20	.12
(131)	Willie McCovey	3.00	1.50	.90
(132)	Lindy McDaniel	.40	.20	.12
(133)	Roy McMillan	.40	.20	.12
(134)	Minnie Minoso	.50	.25	.15
(135)	Bill Monbouquette	.40	.20	.12
(136)	Wally Moon	.50	.25	.15
(137)	Stan Musial	7.00	3.50	2.00
(138)	Charlie Neal	.40	.20	.12
(139)	Rocky Nelson	.40	.20	.12
(140)	Russ Nixon	.40	.20	.12
(141)	Billy O'Dell	.40	.20	.12
(142)	Jim O'Toole	.40	.20	.12
(143)	Milt Pappas	.50	.25	.15
(144)	Camilo Pascual	.50	.25	.15
(145)	Jim Perry	.50	.25	.15
(146)	Bubba Phillips	.40	.20	.12
(147)	Bill Pierce	.50	.25	.15

		NR MT	EX	VG
(148)	Jim Piersall	.50	.25	.15
(149)	Vada Pinson	.50	.25	.15
(150)	Johnny Podres	.50	.25	.15
(151)	Wally Post	.40	.20	.12
(152)	Vic Powers (Power)	.40	.20	.12
(153)	Pedro Ramos	.40	.20	.12
(154)	Robin Roberts	1.50	.70	.45
(155)	Brooks Robinson	3.75	2.00	1.25
(156)	Frank Robinson	3.50	1.75	1.00
(157)	Ed Roebuck	.40	.20	.12
(158)	John Romano	.40	.20	.12
(159)	John Roseboro	.50	.25	.15
(160)	Pete Runnels	.50	.25	.15
(161)	Ed Sadowski	.40	.20	.12
(162)	Jack Sanford	.40	.20	.12
(163)	Ron Santo	.50	.25	.15
(164)	Ray Semproch	.40	.20	.12
(165)	Bobby Shantz	.50	.25	.15
(166)	Bob Shaw	.40	.20	.12
(167)	Larry Sherry	.40	.20	.12
(168)	Norm Siebern	.40	.20	.12
(169)	Roy Sievers	.50	.25	.15
(170)	Curt Simmons	.50	.25	.15
(171)	Dave Sisler	.40	.20	.12
(172)	Bob Skinner	.40	.20	.12
(173)	Al Smith	.40	.20	.12
(174)	Hal Smith	.40	.20	.12
(175)	Hal Smith	.40	.20	.12
(176)	Duke Snider	3.75	2.00	1.25
(177)	Warren Spahn	3.00	1.50	.90
(178)	Daryl Spencer	.40	.20	.12
(179)	Bill Stafford	.50	.25	.15
(180)	Jerry Staley	.40	.20	.12
(181)	Gene Stephens	.40	.20	.12
(182)	Chuck Stobbs	.40	.20	.12
(183)	Dick Stuart	.50	.25	.15
(184)	Willie Tasby	.40	.20	.12
(185)	Sammy Taylor	.40	.20	.12
(186)	Tony Taylor	.40	.20	.12
(187)	Johnny Temple	.40	.20	.12
(188)	Marv Throneberry	.50	.25	.15
(189)	Gus Triandos	.50	.25	.15
(190)	Bob Turley	.50	.25	.15
(191)	Bill Tuttle	.40	.20	.12
(192)	Zorro Versalles	.40	.20	.12
(193)	Bill Virdon	.50	.25	.15
(194)	Lee Walls	.40	.20	.12
(195)	Vic Wertz	.50	.25	.15
(196)	Pete Whisenant	.40	.20	.12
(197)	Bill White	.50	.25	.15
(198)	Hoyt Wilhelm	1.50	.70	.45
(199)	Bob Will	.40	.20	.12
(200)	Carl Willey	.40	.20	.12
(201)	Billy Williams	2.50	1.25	.70
(202)	Dick Williams	.50	.25	.15
(203)	Stan Williams	.40	.20	.12
(204)	Gene Woodling	.50	.25	.15
(205)	Early Wynn	2.00	1.00	.60
(206)	Carl Yastrzemski	12.00	6.00	3.50
(207)	Eddie Yost	.40	.20	.12

1962 Topps

The 1962 Topps set established another plateau for set size with 598 cards. The 2-1/2" by 3-1/2" cards feature a photograph set against a woodgrain background. The lower righthand corner has been made to look like it is curling away. Many established specialty cards dot the set including statistical leaders, multi-player cards, team cards, checklists, World Series cards and All-Stars. Of note is that 1962 was the first year of the multi-player rookie card. There is a 9-card "In Action" subset and a 10-card run of special Babe Ruth cards. Photo variations of several cards in the 2nd Series (#'s 110-196) exist. All cards in the 2nd Series can be found with two distinct printing variations, an early printing with the cards containing a very noticeable greenish tint, having been corrected to clear photos in subsequent print runs. The complete set price in the checklist that follows does not include the higher-priced variations.

		NR MT	EX	VG
	Complete Set:	5000.00	2250.00	1350.
	Common Player: 1-370	2.00	1.00	.60
	Common Player: 371-522	4.00	2.00	1.25
	Common Player: 523-598	12.00	5.50	3.00
1	Roger Maris	225.00	45.00	27.00
2	Jim Brosnan	2.25	1.25	.70
3	Pete Runnels	2.00	1.00	.60
4	John DeMerit	2.00	.90	.50
5	Sandy Koufax	110.00	55.00	33.00
6	Marv Breeding	2.00	1.00	.60
7	Frank Thomas	2.00	.90	.50
8	Ray Herbert	2.00	1.00	.60
9	Jim Davenport	2.00	1.00	.60
10	Bob Clemente	125.00	67.00	37.00
11	Tom Morgan	2.00	1.00	.60
12	Harry Craft	2.00	1.00	.60
13	Dick Howser	2.25	1.25	.70
14	Bill White	2.00	1.00	.60
15	Dick Donovan	2.00	1.00	.60
16	Darrell Johnson	2.00	1.00	.60
17	Johnny Callison	2.25	1.25	.70
18	Managers' Dream (Mickey Mantle, Willie Mays)	100.00	50.00	30.00
19	*Ray Washburn*	2.00	1.00	.60
20	Rocky Colavito	8.00	4.00	2.50
21	Jim Kaat	5.00	2.00	1.25
22a	Checklist 1-88 (numbers 121 - 176 on back)	5.00	2.25	1.25
22b	Checklist 1-88 (numbers 33-88 on back)	4.00	1.75	1.00
23	Norm Larker	2.00	1.00	.60
24	Tigers Team	5.00	2.50	1.50
25	Ernie Banks	45.00	23.00	13.50
26	Chris Cannizzaro	2.00	.90	.50
27	Chuck Cottier	2.00	1.00	.60
28	Minnie Minoso	4.00	2.00	1.25
29	Casey Stengel	18.00	9.00	5.50
30	Ed Mathews	20.00	10.00	6.00
31	*Tom Tresh*	10.00	5.00	3.00
32	John Roseboro	2.25	1.25	.70
33	Don Larsen	2.25	1.25	.70
34	Johnny Temple	2.00	1.00	.60
35	*Don Schwall*	2.25	1.25	.70
36	Don Leppert	2.00	1.00	.60
37	Tribe Hill Trio (Barry Latman, Jim Perry, Dick Stigman)	2.25	1.25	.70
38	Gene Stephens	2.00	1.00	.60
39	Joe Koppe	2.00	1.00	.60
40	Orlando Cepeda	5.00	2.25	1.25
41	Cliff Cook	2.00	1.00	.60
42	Jim King	2.00	1.00	.60
43	Dodgers Team	5.00	2.50	1.50
44	Don Taussig	2.00	1.00	.60
45	Brooks Robinson	40.00	15.00	9.00
46	*Jack Baldschun*	2.00	1.00	.60
47	Bob Will	2.00	1.00	.60
48	Ralph Terry	4.00	2.00	1.25
49	Hal Jones	2.00	1.00	.60
50	Stan Musial	110.00	55.00	33.00
51	A.L. Batting Leaders (Norm Cash, Elston Howard, Al Kaline, Jim Piersall)	5.00	2.50	1.50
52	N.L. Batting Leaders (Ken Boyer, Bob Clemente, Wally Moon, Vada Pinson)	5.00	2.50	1.50
53	A.L. Home Run Leaders (Jim Gentile, Harmon Killebrew, Mickey Mantle, Roger Maris)	50.00	25.00	15.00
54	N.L. Home Run Leaders (Orlando Cepeda, Willie Mays, Frank Robinson)	5.00	2.50	1.50
55	A.L. E.R.A. Leaders (Dick Donovan, Don Mossi, Milt Pappas, Bill Stafford)	4.00	2.00	1.25
56	N.L. E.R.A. Leaders (Mike McCormick, Jim O'Toole, Curt Simmons, Warren Spahn)	5.00	2.50	1.50

		NR MT	EX	VG
57	A.L. Win Leaders (Steve Barber, Jim Bunning, Whitey Ford, Frank Lary)	5.00	2.50	1.50
58	N.L. Win Leaders (Joe Jay, Jim O'Toole, Warren Spahn)	5.00	2.50	1.50
59	A.L. Strikeout Leaders (Jim Bunning, Whitey Ford, Camilo Pascual, Juan Pizzaro)	5.00	2.50	1.50
60	N.L. Strikeout Leaders (Don Drysdale, Sandy Koufax, Jim O'Toole, Stan Williams)	5.00	2.50	1.50
61	Cardinals Team	4.00	2.00	1.25
62	Steve Boros	2.00	1.00	.60
63	*Tony Cloninger*	2.00	.90	.50
64	Russ Snyder	2.00	1.00	.60
65	Bobby Richardson	6.00	2.75	1.50
66	Cuno Barragon (Barragan)	2.00	1.00	.60
67	Harvey Haddix	2.25	1.25	.70
68	Ken L. Hunt	2.00	1.00	.60
69	Phil Ortega	2.00	1.00	.60
70	Harmon Killebrew	20.00	10.00	6.00
71	Dick LeMay	2.00	1.00	.60
72	Bob's Pupils (Steve Boros, Bob Scheffing, Jake Wood)	2.25	1.25	.70
73	Nellie Fox	8.00	4.00	2.50
74	Bob Lillis	2.00	1.00	.60
75	Milt Pappas	2.25	1.25	.70
76	Howie Bedell	2.00	1.00	.60
77	Tony Taylor	2.00	1.00	.60
78	Gene Green	2.00	1.00	.60
79	Ed Hobaugh	2.00	1.00	.60
80	Vada Pinson	4.00	2.00	1.25
81	Jim Pagliaroni	2.00	1.00	.60
82	Deron Johnson	2.00	1.00	.60
83	Larry Jackson	2.00	1.00	.60
84	Lenny Green	2.00	1.00	.60
85	Gil Hodges	15.00	7.50	4.50
86	*Donn Clendenon*	2.25	1.25	.70
87	Mike Roarke	2.00	1.00	.60
88	Ralph Houk	4.00	2.00	1.25
89	Barney Schultz	2.00	1.00	.60
90	Jim Piersall	2.00	.90	.50
91	J.C. Martin	2.00	1.00	.60
92	Sam Jones	2.00	1.00	.60
93	John Blanchard	2.00	.90	.50
94	Jay Hook	2.00	.90	.50
95	Don Hoak	2.25	1.25	.70
96	Eli Grba	2.00	1.00	.60
97	Tito Francona	2.00	1.00	.60
98	Checklist 89-176	4.00	1.75	1.00
99	*John Powell*	18.00	9.00	5.50
100	Warren Spahn	30.00	12.50	7.50
101	Carroll Hardy	2.00	1.00	.60
102	Al Schroll	2.00	1.00	.60
103	Don Blasingame	2.00	1.00	.60
104	Ted Savage	2.00	1.00	.60
105	Don Mossi	2.00	1.00	.60
106	Carl Sawatski	2.00	1.00	.60
107	Mike McCormick	2.00	1.00	.60
108	Willie Davis	4.00	2.00	1.25
109	Bob Shaw	2.00	1.00	.60
110	Bill Skowron	5.00	2.25	1.25
111	Dallas Green	2.25	1.25	.70
112	Hank Foiles	2.00	1.00	.60
113	White Sox Team	4.00	2.00	1.25
114	Howie Koplitz	2.00	1.00	.60
115	Bob Skinner	2.00	1.00	.60
116	Herb Score	2.00	.90	.50
117	Gary Geiger	2.00	1.00	.60
118	Julian Javier	2.00	1.00	.60
119	Danny Murphy	2.00	1.00	.60
120	Bob Purkey	2.00	1.00	.60
121	Billy Hitchcock	2.00	1.00	.60
122	Norm Bass	2.00	1.00	.60
123	Mike de la Hoz	2.00	1.00	.60
124	Bill Pleis	2.00	1.00	.60
125	Gene Woodling	2.25	1.25	.70
126	Al Cicotte	2.00	1.00	.60
127	Pride of the A's (Hank Bauer, Jerry Lumpe, Norm Siebern)	2.25	1.25	.70
128	Art Fowler	2.00	1.00	.60
129a	Lee Walls (facing left)	15.00	7.50	4.50
129b	Lee Walls (facing right)	2.00	1.00	.60
130	Frank Bolling	2.00	1.00	.60
131	*Pete Richert*	2.25	1.25	.70
132a	Angels Team (with inset photos)	10.00	4.50	2.50
132b	Angels Team (without inset photos)	5.00	2.50	1.50
133	Felipe Alou	2.25	1.25	.70
134a	Billy Hoeft (green sky in background)	15.00	7.50	4.50
134b	Billy Hoeft (blue sky in background)	2.00	1.00	.60

		NR MT	EX	VG
135	Babe As A Boy	7.00	3.25	1.75
136	Babe Joins Yanks	7.00	3.25	1.75
137	Babe and Mgr. Huggins	7.00	3.25	1.75
138	The Famous Slugger	7.00	3.25	1.75
139a	Hal Reniff (pitching)	40.00	20.00	12.00
139b	Hal Reniff (portrait)	18.00	9.00	5.50
139c	Babe Hits 60	10.00	4.00	2.50
140	Gehrig and Ruth	20.00	10.00	6.00
141	Twilight Years	7.00	3.25	1.75
142	Coaching for the Dodgers	7.00	3.25	1.75
143	Greatest Sports Hero	7.00	3.25	1.75
144	Farewell Speech	7.00	3.25	1.75
145	Barry Latman	2.00	1.00	.60
146	Don Demeter	2.00	1.00	.60
147a	Bill Kunkel (pitching)	15.00	7.50	4.50
147b	Bill Kunkel (portrait)	2.00	1.00	.60
148	Wally Post	2.00	1.00	.60
149	Bob Duliba	2.00	1.00	.60
150	Al Kaline	30.00	15.00	9.00
151	Johnny Klippstein	2.00	1.00	.60
152	Mickey Vernon	2.00	1.00	.60
153	Pumpsie Green	2.00	1.00	.60
154	Lee Thomas	2.00	1.00	.60
155	Stu Miller	2.00	1.00	.60
156	Merritt Ranew	2.00	1.00	.60
157	Wes Covington	2.00	1.00	.60
158	Braves Team	5.00	2.50	1.50
159	Hal Reniff	2.00	.90	.50
160	Dick Stuart	2.00	1.00	.60
161	Frank Baumann	2.00	1.00	.60
162	Sammy Drake	2.00	.90	.50
163	Hot Corner Guardians (Cletis Boyer, Billy Gardner)	5.00	2.50	1.50
164	Hal Naragon	2.00	1.00	.60
165	Jackie Brandt	2.00	1.00	.60
166	Don Lee	2.00	1.00	.60
167	*Tim McCarver*	30.00	12.50	7.50
168	Leo Posada	2.00	1.00	.60
169	Bob Cerv	2.00	.90	.50
170	Ron Santo	5.00	2.50	1.50
171	Dave Sisler	2.00	1.00	.60
172	Fred Hutchinson	2.00	1.00	.60
173	Chico Fernandez	2.00	1.00	.60
174a	Carl Willey (with cap)	15.00	7.50	4.50
174b	Carl Willey (no cap)	2.00	1.00	.60
175	Frank Howard	5.00	2.50	1.50
176a	Eddie Yost (batting)	15.00	7.50	4.50
176b	Eddie Yost (portrait)	2.00	1.00	.60
177	Bobby Shantz	2.25	1.25	.70
178	Camilo Carreon	2.00	1.00	.60
179	Tom Sturdivant	2.00	1.00	.60
180	Bob Allison	2.25	1.25	.70
181	Paul Brown	2.00	1.00	.60
182	Bob Nieman	2.00	1.00	.60
183	Roger Craig	5.00	2.50	1.50
184	Haywood Sullivan	2.00	1.00	.60
185	Roland Sheldon	2.00	.90	.50
186	*Mack Jones*	2.00	1.00	.60
187	Gene Conley	2.00	1.00	.60
188	Chuck Hiller	2.00	1.00	.60
189	Dick Hall	2.00	1.00	.60
190a	Wally Moon (with cap)	9.00	4.00	2.25
190b	Wally Moon (no cap)	2.25	1.25	.70
191	Jim Brewer	2.00	1.00	.60
192a	Checklist 177-264 (192 is Check List, 3)	6.00	2.75	1.50
192b	Checklist 177-264 (192 is Check List 3)	4.00	1.75	1.00
193	Eddie Kasko	2.00	1.00	.60
194	*Dean Chance*	5.00	2.50	1.50
195	Joe Cunningham	2.00	1.00	.60
196	Terry Fox	2.00	1.00	.60
197	Daryl Spencer	2.00	1.00	.60
198	Johnny Keane	2.00	1.00	.60
199	*Gaylord Perry*	150.00	75.00	45.00
200	Mickey Mantle	500.00	250.00	150.00
201	Ike Delock	2.00	1.00	.60
202	Carl Warwick	2.00	1.00	.60
203	Jack Fisher	2.00	1.00	.60
204	Johnny Weekly	2.00	1.00	.60
205	Gene Freese	2.00	1.00	.60
206	Senators Team	4.00	2.00	1.25
207	Pete Burnside	2.00	1.00	.60
208	Billy Martin	6.00	2.75	1.50
209	*Jim Fregosi*	10.00	5.00	3.00
210	Roy Face	2.00	.90	.50
211	Midway Masters (Frank Bolling, Roy McMillan)	2.25	1.25	.70
212	Jim Owens	2.00	1.00	.60
213	Richie Ashburn	6.00	2.75	1.50
214	Dom Zanni	2.00	1.00	.60

		NR MT	EX	VG
215	Woody Held	2.00	1.00	.60
216	Ron Kline	2.00	1.00	.60
217	Walt Alston	4.00	1.75	1.00
218	*Joe Torre*	25.00	12.50	7.50
219	*Al Downing*	4.00	1.75	1.00
220	Roy Sievers	2.25	1.25	.70
221	Bill Short	2.00	1.00	.60
222	Jerry Zimmerman	2.00	1.00	.60
223	Alex Grammas	2.00	1.00	.60
224	Don Rudolph	2.00	1.00	.60
225	Frank Malzone	2.00	1.00	.60
226	Giants Team	4.00	1.75	1.00
227	Bobby Tiefenauer	2.00	1.00	.60
228	Dale Long	2.00	1.00	.60
229	Jesus McFarlane	2.00	1.00	.60
230	Camilo Pascual	2.25	1.25	.70
231	Ernie Bowman	2.00	1.00	.60
232	World Series Game 1 (Yanks Win Opener)	5.00	2.50	1.50
233	World Series Game 2 (Jay Ties It Up)	5.00	2.50	1.50
234	World Series Game 3 (Maris Wins It In The 9th)	8.00	3.50	2.00
235	World Series Game 4 (Ford Sets New Mark)	7.00	3.25	1.75
236	World Series Game 5 (Yanks Crush Reds In Finale)	5.00	2.50	1.50
237	World Series Summary (The Winners Celebrate)	5.00	2.50	1.50
238	Norm Sherry	2.00	1.00	.60
239	Cecil Butler	2.00	1.00	.60
240	George Altman	2.00	1.00	.60
241	Johnny Kucks	2.00	1.00	.60
242	Mel McGaha	2.00	1.00	.60
243	Robin Roberts	12.00	5.50	3.00
244	Don Gile	2.00	1.00	.60
245	Ron Hansen	2.00	1.00	.60
246	Art Ditmar	2.00	1.00	.60
247	Joe Pignatano	2.00	1.00	.60
248	Bob Aspromonte	2.00	1.00	.60
249	Ed Keegan	2.00	1.00	.60
250	Norm Cash	5.00	2.50	1.50
251	Yankees Team	15.00	7.50	4.50
252	Earl Francis	2.00	1.00	.60
253	Harry Chiti	2.00	1.00	.60
254	Gordon Windhorn	2.00	1.00	.60
255	Juan Pizarro	2.00	1.00	.60
256	Elio Chacon	2.00	.90	.50
257	Jack Spring	2.00	1.00	.60
258	Marty Keough	2.00	1.00	.60
259	Lou Klimchock	2.00	1.00	.60
260	Bill Pierce	2.00	.90	.50
261	George Alusik	2.00	1.00	.60
262	Bob Schmidt	2.00	1.00	.60
263	The Right Pitch (Joe Jay, Bob Purkey, Jim Turner)	2.25	1.25	.70
264	Dick Ellsworth	2.00	1.00	.60
265	Joe Adcock	2.00	.90	.50
266	John Anderson	2.00	1.00	.60
267	Dan Dobbek	2.00	1.00	.60
268	Ken McBride	2.00	1.00	.60
269	Bob Oldis	2.00	1.00	.60
270	Dick Groat	2.00	.90	.50
271	Ray Rippelmeyer	2.00	1.00	.60
272	Earl Robinson	2.00	1.00	.60
273	Gary Bell	2.00	1.00	.60
274	Sammy Taylor	2.00	1.00	.60
275	Norm Siebern	2.00	1.00	.60
276	Hal Kostad	2.00	1.00	.60
277	Checklist 265-352	4.00	1.75	1.00
278	Ken Johnson	2.00	1.00	.60
279	Hobie Landrith	2.00	.90	.50
280	Johnny Podres	4.00	2.00	1.25
281	*Jake Gibbs*	2.25	1.00	.60
282	Dave Hillman	2.00	1.00	.60
283	Charlie Smith	2.00	1.00	.60
284	Ruben Amaro	2.00	1.00	.60
285	Curt Simmons	2.00	.90	.50
286	Al Lopez	5.00	2.50	1.50
287	George Witt	2.00	1.00	.60
288	Billy Williams	30.00	15.00	9.00
289	Mike Krsnich	2.00	1.00	.60
290	Jim Gentile	2.00	1.00	.60
291	Hal Stowe	2.00	.90	.50
292	Jerry Kindall	2.00	1.00	.60
293	Bob Miller	2.00	.90	.50
294	Phillies Team	4.00	2.00	1.25
295	Vern Law	2.00	.90	.50
296	Ken Hamlin	2.00	1.00	.60
297	Ron Perranoski	2.00	1.00	.60
298	Bill Tuttle	2.00	1.00	.60

	NR MT	EX	VG
299 Don Wert	2.00	1.00	.60
300 Willie Mays	160.00	75.00	45.00
301 Galen Cisco	2.00	1.00	.60
302 John Edwards	2.00	1.00	.60
303 Frank Torre	2.00	1.00	.60
304 Dick Farrell	2.00	1.00	.60
305 Jerry Lumpe	2.00	1.00	.60
306 Redbird Rippers (Larry Jackson, Lindy McDaniel)	2.25	1.25	.70
307 Jim Grant	2.00	1.00	.60
308 Neil Chrisley	2.00	.90	.50
309 Moe Morhardt	2.00	1.00	.60
310 Whitey Ford	25.00	12.50	7.50
311 Kubek Makes The Double Play	5.00	2.50	1.50
312 Spahn Shows No-Hit Form	7.00	3.50	2.00
313 Maris Blasts 61st	20.00	10.00	6.00
314 Colavito's Power	5.00	2.50	1.50
315 Ford Tosses A Curve	6.00	2.75	1.50
316 Killebrew Sends One Into Orbit	5.00	2.25	1.25
317 Musial Plays 21st Season	18.00	9.00	5.50
318 The Switch Hitter Connects (Mickey Mantle)	50.00	25.00	15.00
319 McCormick Shows His Stuff	2.25	1.25	.70
320 Hank Aaron	125.00	62.00	37.00
321 Lee Stange	2.00	1.00	.60
322 Al Dark	2.25	1.25	.70
323 Don Landrum	2.00	1.00	.60
324 Joe McClain	2.00	1.00	.60
325 Luis Aparicio	15.00	7.50	4.50
326 Tom Parsons	2.00	1.00	.60
327 Ozzie Virgil	2.00	1.00	.60
328 Ken Walters	2.00	1.00	.60
329 Bob Bolin	2.00	1.00	.60
330 Johnny Romano	2.00	1.00	.60
331 Moe Drabowsky	2.00	1.00	.60
332 Don Buddin	2.00	1.00	.60
333 Frank Cipriani	2.00	1.00	.60
334 Red Sox Team	5.00	2.50	1.50
335 Bill Bruton	2.00	1.00	.60
336 Billy Muffett	2.00	1.00	.60
337 Jim Marshall	2.00	.90	.50
338 Billy Gardner	2.25	1.00	.60
339 Jose Valdivielso	2.00	1.00	.60
340 Don Drysdale	30.00	15.00	9.00
341 Mike Hershberger	2.00	1.00	.60
342 Ed Rakow	2.00	1.00	.60
343 Albie Pearson	2.00	1.00	.60
344 Ed Bauta	2.00	1.00	.60
345 Chuck Schilling	2.00	1.00	.60
346 Jack Kralick	2.00	1.00	.60
347 Chuck Hinton	2.00	1.00	.60
348 Larry Burright	2.00	1.00	.60
349 Paul Foytack	2.00	1.00	.60
350 Frank Robinson	50.00	25.00	15.00
351 Braves' Backstops (Del Crandall, Joe Torre)	5.00	2.50	1.50
352 Frank Sullivan	2.00	1.00	.60
353 Bill Mazeroski	5.00	2.50	1.50
354 Roman Mejias	2.00	1.00	.60
355 Steve Barber	2.00	1.00	.60
356 Tom Haller	2.25	1.25	.70
357 Jerry Walker	2.00	1.00	.60
358 Tommy Davis	4.00	2.00	1.25
359 Bobby Locke	2.00	1.00	.60
360 Yogi Berra	70.00	35.00	21.00
361 Bob Hendley	2.00	1.00	.60
362 Ty Cline	2.00	1.00	.60
363 Bob Roselli	2.00	1.00	.60
364 Ken Hunt	2.00	1.00	.60
365 Charley Neal	2.00	.90	.50
366 Phil Regan	2.00	1.00	.60
367 Checklist 353-429	4.00	1.75	1.00
368 Bob Tillman	2.00	1.00	.60
369 Ted Bowsfield	2.00	1.00	.60
370 Ken Boyer	4.00	1.75	1.00
371 Earl Battey	4.00	2.00	1.25
372 Jack Curtis	4.00	2.00	1.25
373 Al Heist	4.00	2.00	1.25
374 Gene Mauch	4.00	2.00	1.25
375 Ron Fairly	4.00	2.00	1.25
376 Bud Daley	5.00	2.50	1.50
377 Johnny Orsino	4.00	2.00	1.25
378 Bennie Daniels	4.00	2.00	1.25
379 Chuck Essegian	4.00	2.00	1.25
380 Lou Burdette	4.00	1.75	1.00
381 Chico Cardenas	4.00	2.00	1.25
382 Dick Williams	5.00	2.50	1.50
383 Ray Sadecki	4.00	2.00	1.25
384 Athletics Team	5.00	2.50	1.50
385 Early Wynn	20.00	10.00	6.00
386 Don Mincher	4.00	2.00	1.25

	NR MT	EX	VG
387 Lou Brock	200.00	100.00	60.00
388 Ryne Duren	4.00	2.00	1.25
389 Smoky Burgess	5.00	2.50	1.50
390 Orlando Cepeda AS	5.00	2.25	1.50
391 Bill Mazeroski AS	5.00	2.50	1.50
392 Ken Boyer AS	5.00	2.50	1.50
393 Roy McMillan AS	4.00	2.00	1.25
394 Hank Aaron AS	30.00	15.00	9.00
395 Willie Mays AS	30.00	15.00	9.00
396 Frank Robinson AS	12.00	5.50	3.00
397 John Roseboro AS	4.00	2.00	1.25
398 Don Drysdale AS	10.00	4.50	2.50
399 Warren Spahn AS	10.00	4.50	2.50
400 Elston Howard	7.00	3.25	1.75
401 AL & NL Homer Kings (Orlando Cepeda, Roger Maris)	35.00	17.50	10.50
402 Gino Cimoli	4.00	2.00	1.25
403 Chet Nichols	4.00	2.00	1.25
404 Tim Harkness	4.00	2.00	1.25
405 Jim Perry	5.00	2.50	1.50
406 Bob Taylor	4.00	2.00	1.25
407 Hank Aguirre	4.00	2.00	1.25
408 Gus Bell	5.00	2.50	1.50
409 Pirates Team	5.00	2.50	1.50
410 Al Smith	4.00	2.00	1.25
411 Danny O'Connell	4.00	2.00	1.25
412 Charlie James	4.00	2.00	1.25
413 Matty Alou	5.00	2.50	1.50
414 Joe Gaines	4.00	2.00	1.25
415 Bill Virdon	5.00	2.50	1.50
416 Bob Scheffing	4.00	2.00	1.25
417 Joe Azcue	4.00	2.00	1.25
418 Andy Carey	4.00	2.00	1.25
419 Bob Bruce	4.00	2.00	1.25
420 Gus Triandos	4.00	2.00	1.25
421 Ken MacKenzie	5.00	2.50	1.50
422 Steve Bilko	4.00	2.00	1.25
423 Rival League Relief Aces (Roy Face, Hoyt Wilhelm)	5.00	2.25	1.25
424 Al McBean	4.00	2.00	1.25
425 Carl Yastrzemski	225.00	100.00	60.00
426 Bob Farley	4.00	2.00	1.25
427 Jake Wood	4.00	2.00	1.25
428 Joe Hicks	4.00	2.00	1.25
429 Bill O'Dell	4.00	2.00	1.25
430 Tony Kubek	7.00	3.25	1.75
431 Bob Rodgers	9.00	4.50	2.75
432 Jim Pendleton	4.00	2.00	1.25
433 Jim Archer	4.00	2.00	1.25
434 Clay Dalrymple	4.00	2.00	1.25
435 Larry Sherry	4.00	2.00	1.25
436 Felix Mantilla	5.00	2.50	1.50
437 Ray Moore	4.00	2.00	1.25
438 Dick Brown	4.00	2.00	1.25
439 Jerry Buchek	4.00	2.00	1.25
440 Joe Jay	4.00	2.00	1.25
441 Checklist 430-506	5.00	2.25	1.25
442 Wes Stock	4.00	2.00	1.25
443 Del Crandall	5.00	2.50	1.50
444 Ted Wills	4.00	2.00	1.25
445 Vic Power	4.00	2.00	1.25
446 Don Elston	4.00	2.00	1.25
447 Willie Kirkland	4.00	2.00	1.25
448 Joe Gibbon	4.00	2.00	1.25
449 Jerry Adair	4.00	2.00	1.25
450 Jim O'Toole	4.00	2.00	1.25
451 Jose Tartabull	4.00	2.00	1.25
452 Earl Averill	4.00	2.00	1.25
453 Cal McLish	4.00	2.00	1.25
454 Floyd Robinson	4.00	2.00	1.25
455 Luis Arroyo	5.00	2.50	1.50
456 Joe Amalfitano	4.00	2.00	1.25
457 Lou Clinton	4.00	2.00	1.25
458a Bob Buhl ("M" on cap)	4.00	2.00	1.25
458b Bob Buhl (plain cap)	60.00	30.00	18.00
459 Ed Bailey	4.00	2.00	1.25
460 Jim Bunning	9.00	4.00	2.50
461 Ken Hubbs	20.00	10.00	6.00
462a Willie Tasby ("W" on cap)	4.00	2.00	1.25
462b Willie Tasby (plain cap)	60.00	30.00	18.00
463 Hank Bauer	5.00	2.50	1.50
464 Al Jackson	5.00	2.50	1.50
465 Reds Team	4.00	1.75	1.00
466 Norm Cash AS	4.00	1.75	1.00
467 Chuck Schilling AS	5.00	2.50	1.50
468 Brooks Robinson AS	12.00	5.50	3.00
469 Luis Aparicio AS	8.00	3.50	2.00
470 Al Kaline AS	18.00	7.50	4.50
471 Mickey Mantle AS	125.00	67.00	37.00
472 Rocky Colavito AS	5.00	2.25	1.25
473 Elston Howard AS	5.00	2.25	1.25

		NR MT	EX	VG
474	Frank Lary AS	5.00	2.50	1.50
475	Whitey Ford AS	10.00	4.50	2.50
476	Orioles Team	5.00	2.50	1.50
477	Andre Rodgers	4.00	2.00	1.25
478	Don Zimmer	5.00	2.50	1.50
479	*Joel Horlen*	4.00	2.00	1.25
480	Harvey Kuenn	5.00	2.50	1.50
481	Vic Wertz	4.00	2.00	1.25
482	Sam Mele	4.00	2.00	1.25
483	Don McMahon	4.00	2.00	1.25
484	Dick Schofield	4.00	2.00	1.25
485	Pedro Ramos	4.00	2.00	1.25
486	Jim Gilliam	4.00	1.75	1.00
487	Jerry Lynch	4.00	2.00	1.25
488	Hal Brown	4.00	2.00	1.25
489	Julio Gotay	4.00	2.00	1.25
490	Clete Boyer	4.00	1.75	1.00
491	Leon Wagner	4.00	2.00	1.25
492	Hal Smith	4.00	2.00	1.25
493	Danny McDevitt	4.00	2.00	1.25
494	Sammy White	4.00	2.00	1.25
495	Don Cardwell	4.00	2.00	1.25
496	Wayne Causey	4.00	2.00	1.25
497	Ed Bouchee	5.00	2.50	1.50
498	Jim Donohue	4.00	2.00	1.25
499	Zoilo Versalles	4.00	2.00	1.25
500	Duke Snider	40.00	20.00	12.00
501	Claude Osteen	4.00	2.00	1.25
502	Hector Lopez	5.00	2.50	1.50
503	Danny Murtaugh	4.00	2.00	1.25
504	Eddie Bressoud	4.00	2.00	1.25
505	Juan Marichal	35.00	17.50	10.50
506	Charley Maxwell	4.00	2.00	1.25
507	Ernie Broglio	4.00	2.00	1.25
508	Gordy Coleman	4.00	2.00	1.25
509	*Dave Giusti*	4.00	2.00	1.25
510	Jim Lemon	4.00	2.00	1.25
511	Bubba Phillips	4.00	2.00	1.25
512	Mike Fornieles	4.00	2.00	1.25
513	Whitey Herzog	4.00	1.75	1.00
514	Sherm Lollar	4.00	2.00	1.25
515	Stan Williams	4.00	2.00	1.25
516	Checklist 507-598	8.00	3.50	2.00
517	Dave Wickersham	4.00	2.00	1.25
518	Lee Maye	4.00	2.00	1.25
519	Bob Johnson	4.00	2.00	1.25
520	Bob Friend	5.00	2.50	1.50
521	Jacke Davis	4.00	2.00	1.25
522	Lindy McDaniel	4.00	2.00	1.25
523	Russ Nixon	12.00	5.50	3.00
524	Howie Nunn	12.00	5.50	3.00
525	George Thomas	12.00	5.50	3.00
526	Hal Woodeshick	12.00	5.50	3.00
527	*Dick McAuliffe*	15.00	5.00	2.75
528	Turk Lown	12.00	5.50	3.00
529	John Schaive	12.00	5.50	3.00
530	Bob Gibson	175.00	87.00	52.00
531	Bobby G. Smith	12.00	5.50	3.00
532	Dick Stigman	12.00	5.50	3.00
533	Charley Lau	13.00	5.75	3.25
534	Tony Gonzalez	12.00	5.50	3.00
535	Ed Roebuck	12.00	5.50	3.00
536	Dick Gernert	12.00	5.50	3.00
537	Indians Team	15.00	6.75	3.75
538	Jack Sanford	12.00	5.50	3.00
539	Billy Moran	12.00	5.50	3.00
540	Jim Landis	12.00	5.50	3.00
541	Don Nottebart	12.00	5.50	3.00
542	Dave Philley	12.00	5.50	3.00
543	Bob Allen	12.00	5.50	3.00
544	Willie McCovey	125.00	62.00	37.00
545	Hoyt Wilhelm	55.00	25.00	14.00
546	Moe Thacker	12.00	5.50	3.00
547	Don Ferrarese	12.00	5.50	3.00
548	Bobby Del Greco	12.00	5.50	3.00
549	Bill Rigney	12.00	5.50	3.00
550	Art Mahaffey	12.00	5.50	3.00
551	Harry Bright	12.00	5.50	3.00
552	Cubs Team	15.00	6.75	3.75
553	Jim Coates	15.00	6.75	3.75
554	Bubba Morton	12.00	5.50	3.00
555	John Buzhardt	12.00	5.50	3.00
556	Al Spangler	12.00	5.50	3.00
557	Bob Anderson	12.00	5.50	3.00
558	John Goryl	12.00	5.50	3.00
559	Mike Higgins	12.00	5.50	3.00
560	Chuck Estrada	12.00	5.50	3.00
561	Gene Oliver	12.00	5.50	3.00
562	Bill Henry	12.00	5.50	3.00
563	Ken Aspromonte	12.00	5.50	3.00
564	Bob Grim	12.00	5.50	3.00

		NR MT	EX	VG
565	Jose Pagan	12.00	5.50	3.00
566	Marty Kutyna	12.00	5.50	3.00
567	Tracy Stallard	12.00	5.50	3.00
568	Jim Golden	12.00	5.50	3.00
569	Ed Sadowski	12.00	5.50	3.00
570	Bill Stafford	15.00	6.75	3.75
571	Billy Klaus	12.00	5.50	3.00
572	Bob Miller	13.00	5.75	3.25
573	Johnny Logan	13.00	5.75	3.25
574	Dean Stone	12.00	5.50	3.00
575	Red Schoendienst	35.00	15.00	9.00
576	Russ Kemmerer	12.00	5.50	3.00
577	Dave Nicholson	12.00	5.50	3.00
578	Jim Duffalo	12.00	5.50	3.00
579	Jim Schaffer	12.00	5.50	3.00
580	Bill Monbouquette	13.00	5.75	3.25
581	Mel Roach	12.00	5.50	3.00
582	Ron Piche	12.00	5.50	3.00
583	Larry Osborne	12.00	5.50	3.00
584	Twins Team	15.00	6.75	3.75
585	Glen Hobbie	12.00	5.50	3.00
586	Sammy Esposito	12.00	5.50	3.00
587	Frank Funk	12.00	5.50	3.00
588	Birdie Tebbetts	12.00	5.50	3.00
589	Bob Turley	18.00	8.00	4.50
590	Curt Flood	18.00	8.00	4.50
591	Rookie Parade Pitchers (*Sam McDowell*, Ron Nischwitz, Art Quirk, *Dick Radatz*, *Ron Taylor*)	60.00	30.00	18.00
592	Rookie Parade Pitchers (*Bo Belinsky*, Joe Bonikowski, *Jim Bouton*, Dan Pfister, Dave Stenhouse)	45.00	20.00	11.25
593	Rookie Parade Pitchers (Craig Anderson, *Jack Hamilton*, Jack Lamabe, Bob Moorhead, *Bob Veale*)	25.00	11.25	6.25
594	Rookie Parade Catchers (Doug Camilli, *Doc Edwards*, Don Pavletich, Ken Retzer, *Bob Uecker*)	100.00	50.00	30.00
595	Rookie Parade Infielders (*Ed Charles*, Marlin Coughtry, Bob Sadowski, Felix Torres)	25.00	11.25	6.25
596	Rookie Parade Infielders (*Bernie Allen*, *Phil Linz*, Joe Pepitone, Rich Rollins)	65.00	33.00	20.00
597	Rookie Parade Infielders (Rod Kanehl, Jim McKnight, *Denis Menke*, Amado Samuel)	25.00	11.25	6.25
598	Rookie Parade Outfielders (Howie Goss, *Jim Hickman*, Manny Jimenez, Al Luplow, Ed Olivares)	65.00	33.00	20.00

1962 Topps Baseball Bucks

Issued in their own 1¢ package, the 1962 Topps "Baseball Bucks" were another in the growing list of specialty Topps items. The 96 Baseball Bucks in the set measure 4-1/8" by 1-3/4," and were designed to look vaguely like dollar bills. The center player portrait has a banner underneath with the player's name. His home park is shown on the right and there is some biographical information on the left. The back features a large denomination, with the player's league and team logo on either side.

	NR MT	EX	VG
Complete Set:	750.00	375.00	225.00
Common Player:	2.00	1.00	.60

		NR MT	EX	VG
(1)	Hank Aaron	30.00	15.00	9.00
(2)	Joe Adcock	3.00	1.50	.90
(3)	George Altman	2.00	1.00	.60
(4)	Jim Archer	2.00	1.00	.60
(5)	Richie Ashburn	5.00	2.50	1.50
(6)	Ernie Banks	20.00	10.00	8.00
(7)	Earl Battey	2.50	1.25	.70
(8)	Gus Bell	2.50	1.25	.70
(9)	Yogi Berra	18.00	9.00	5.50
(10)	Ken Boyer	3.00	1.50	.90
(11)	Jackie Brandt	2.00	1.00	.60
(12)	Jim Bunning	4.00	2.00	1.25
(13)	Lou Burdette	3.00	1.50	.90
(14)	Don Cardwell	2.00	1.00	.60
(15)	Norm Cash	3.00	1.50	.90
(16)	Orlando Cepeda	4.50	2.25	1.25
(17)	Bob Clemente	40.00	20.00	12.50
(18)	Rocky Colavito	3.00	1.50	.90
(19)	Chuck Cottier	2.00	1.00	.60
(20)	Roger Craig	2.50	1.25	.70
(21)	Bennie Daniels	2.00	1.00	.60
(22)	Don Demeter	2.00	1.00	.60
(23)	Don Drysdale	15.00	7.50	4.50
(24)	Chuck Estrada	2.00	1.00	.60
(25)	Dick Farrell	2.00	1.00	.60
(26)	Whitey Ford	12.00	6.00	3.50
(27)	Nellie Fox	4.00	2.00	1.25
(28)	Tito Francona	2.00	1.00	.60
(29)	Bob Friend	2.50	1.25	.70
(30)	Jim Gentile	2.00	1.00	.60
(31)	Dick Gernert	2.00	1.00	.60
(32)	Lenny Green	2.00	1.00	.60
(33)	Dick Groat	3.00	1.50	.90
(34)	Woody Held	2.00	1.00	.60
(35)	Don Hoak	2.50	1.25	.70
(36)	Gil Hodges	10.00	5.00	3.00
(37)	Frank Howard	3.00	1.50	.90
(38)	Elston Howard	4.00	2.00	1.25
(39)	Dick Howser	3.00	1.50	.90
(40)	Ken Hunt	2.00	1.00	.60
(41)	Larry Jackson	2.00	1.00	.60
(42)	Joe Jay	4.00	2.00	1.25
(43)	Al Kaline	12.00	6.00	3.50
(44)	Harmon Killebrew	12.00	6.00	3.50
(45)	Sandy Koufax	35.00	17.50	10.50
(46)	Harvey Kuenn	4.00	2.00	1.25
(47)	Jim Landis	2.00	1.00	.60
(48)	Norm Larker	2.00	1.00	.60
(49)	Frank Lary	2.00	1.00	.60
(50)	Jerry Lumpe	2.00	1.00	.60
(51)	Art Mahaffey	2.00	1.00	.60
(52)	Frank Malzone	2.00	1.00	.60
(53)	Felix Mantilla	2.50	1.25	.70
(54)	Mickey Mantle	125.00	62.00	37.00
(55)	Roger Maris	12.00	6.00	3.50
(56)	Ed Mathews	10.00	5.00	3.00
(57)	Willie Mays	35.00	17.50	10.50
(58)	Ken McBride	2.00	1.00	.60
(59)	Mike McCormick	2.00	1.00	.60
(60)	Minnie Minoso	4.00	2.00	1.25
(61)	Wally Moon	2.50	1.25	.70
(62)	Stu Miller	2.00	1.00	.60
(63)	Stan Musial	30.00	15.00	9.00
(64)	Danny O'Connell	2.00	1.00	.60
(65)	Jim O'Toole	4.00	2.00	1.25
(66)	Camilo Pascual	2.50	1.25	.70
(67)	Jim Perry	3.00	1.50	.90
(68)	Jimmy Piersall	4.00	2.00	1.25
(69)	Vada Pinson	6.00	3.00	1.75
(70)	Juan Pizarro	2.00	1.00	.60
(71)	Johnny Podres	3.00	1.50	.90
(72)	Vic Power	2.00	1.00	.60
(73)	Bob Purkey	12.00	6.00	3.50
(74)	Pedro Ramos	2.00	1.00	.60
(75)	Brooks Robinson	15.00	7.50	4.50
(76)	Floyd Robinson	2.00	1.00	.60
(77)	Frank Robinson	15.00	7.50	4.50
(78)	Johnny Romano	2.00	1.00	.60
(79)	Pete Runnels	2.50	1.25	.70
(80)	Don Schwall	2.00	1.00	.60
(81)	Bobby Shantz	3.00	1.50	.90
(82)	Norm Siebern	2.00	1.00	.60
(83)	Roy Sievers	2.50	1.25	.70
(84)	Hal (W.) Smith	2.00	1.00	.60
(85)	Warren Spahn	10.00	5.00	3.00
(86)	Dick Stuart	2.50	1.25	.70
(87)	Tony Taylor	2.00	1.00	.60
(88)	Lee Thomas	2.00	1.00	.60
(89)	Gus Triandos	2.50	1.25	.70
(90)	Leon Wagner	2.00	1.00	.60
(91)	Jerry Walker	2.00	1.00	.60
(92)	Bill White	2.50	1.25	.70

		NR MT	EX	VG
(93)	Billy Williams	9.00	4.50	2.75
(94)	Gene Woodling	2.50	1.25	.70
(95)	Early Wynn	9.00	4.50	2.75
(96)	Carl Yastrzemski	30.00	15.00	9.00

1962 Topps Stamps

An artistic improvement over the somewhat drab Topps stamps of the previous year, the 1962 stamps, 1-3/8" by 1-7/8," had color player photographs set on red or yellow backgrounds. As in 1961, they were issued in two-stamp panels as insert with Topps baseball cards. A change from 1961 was the inclusion of team emblems in the set. A complete set consists of 201 stamps; Roy Sievers was originally portrayed on the wrong team - Athletics - and was later corrected to the Phillies.

		NR MT	EX	VG
Complete Set:		220.00	110.00	67.00
Stamp Album:		35.00	17.50	10.50
Common Player:		.25	.13	.08
(1)	Hank Aaron	10.00	5.00	3.00
(2)	Jerry Adair	.25	.13	.08
(3)	Joe Adcock	.35	.20	.11
(4)	Bob Allison	.30	.15	.09
(5)	Felipe Alou	.35	.20	.11
(6)	George Altman	.25	.13	.08
(7)	Joe Amalfitano	.25	.13	.08
(8)	Ruben Amaro	.25	.13	.08
(9)	Luis Aparicio	1.50	.70	.45
(10)	Jim Archer	.25	.13	.08
(11)	Bob Aspromonte	.25	.13	.08
(12)	Ed Bailey	.25	.13	.08
(13)	Jack Baldschun	.25	.13	.08
(14)	Ernie Banks	6.00	3.00	1.75
(15)	Earl Battey	.30	.15	.09
(16)	Gus Bell	.35	.20	.11
(17)	Yogi Berra	5.00	2.50	1.50
(18)	Dick Bertell	.25	.13	.08
(19)	Steve Bilko	.25	.13	.08
(20)	Frank Bolling	.25	.13	.08
(21)	Steve Boros	.25	.13	.08
(22)	Ted Bowsfield	.25	.13	.08
(23)	Clete Boyer	.35	.20	.11
(24)	Ken Boyer	.50	.25	.15
(25)	Jackie Brandt	.25	.13	.08
(26)	Bill Bruton	.25	.13	.08
(27)	Jim Bunning	1.00	.50	.30
(28)	Lou Burdette	.35	.20	.11
(29)	Smoky Burgess	.30	.15	.09
(30)	Johnny Callizon (Callison)	.30	.15	.09
(31)	Don Cardwell	.25	.13	.08
(32)	Camilo Carreon	.25	.13	.08
(33)	Norm Cash	.50	.25	.15
(34)	Orlando Cepeda	1.00	.50	.30
(35)	Bob Clemente	15.00	7.50	4.50
(36)	Ty Cline	.25	.13	.08
(37)	Rocky Colavito	.80	.40	.25
(38)	Gordon Coleman	.25	.13	.08
(39)	Chuck Cottier	.25	.13	.08
(40)	Roger Craig	.35	.20	.11
(41)	Del Crandall	.35	.20	.11
(42)	Pete Daley	.25	.13	.08
(43)	Clay Dalrymple	.25	.13	.08
(44)	Bennie Daniels	.25	.13	.08

	NR MT	EX	VG
(45) Jim Davenport	.25	.13	.08
(46) Don Demeter	.25	.13	.08
(47) Dick Donovan	.25	.13	.08
(48) Don Drysdale	7.00	3.50	2.00
(49) John Edwards	.25	.13	.08
(50) Dick Ellsworth	.25	.13	.08
(51) Chuck Estrada	.25	.13	.08
(52) Roy Face	.35	.20	.11
(53) Ron Fairly	.30	.15	.09
(54) Dick Farrell	.25	.13	.08
(55) Whitey Ford	5.00	2.50	1.50
(56) Mike Fornieles	.25	.13	.08
(57) Nellie Fox	.80	.40	.25
(58) Tito Francona	.25	.13	.08
(59) Gene Freese	.25	.13	.08
(60) Bob Friend	.35	.20	.11
(61) Gary Geiger	.25	.13	.08
(62) Jim Gentile	.25	.13	.08
(63) Tony Gonzalez	.25	.13	.08
(64) Lenny Green	.25	.13	.08
(65) Dick Groat	.35	.20	.11
(66) Ron Hansen	.25	.13	.08
(67) Al Heist	.25	.13	.08
(68) Woody Held	.25	.13	.08
(69) Ray Herbert	.25	.13	.08
(70) Chuck Hinton	.25	.13	.08
(71) Don Hoak	.30	.15	.09
(72) Glen Hobbie	.25	.13	.08
(73) Gil Hodges	5.00	2.50	1.50
(74) Jay Hook	.35	.20	.11
(75) Elston Howard	.80	.40	.25
(76) Frank Howard	.50	.25	.15
(77) Dick Howser	.35	.20	.11
(78) Ken Hunt	.25	.13	.08
(79) Larry Jackson	.25	.13	.08
(80) Julian Javier	.25	.13	.08
(81) Joe Jay	.25	.13	.08
(82) Bob Johnson	.25	.13	.08
(83) Sam Jones	.25	.13	.08
(84) Al Kaline	7.00	3.50	2.00
(85) Eddie Kasko	.25	.13	.08
(86) Harmon Killebrew	5.00	2.50	1.50
(87) Sandy Koufax	10.00	5.00	3.00
(88) Jack Kralick	.25	.13	.08
(89) Tony Kubek	.80	.40	.25
(90) Harvey Kuenn	.50	.25	.15
(91) Jim Landis	.25	.13	.08
(92) Hobie Landrith	.35	.20	.11
(93) Frank Lary	.25	.13	.08
(94) Barry Latman	.25	.13	.08
(95) Jerry Lumpe	.25	.13	.08
(96) Art Mahaffey	.25	.13	.08
(97) Frank Malzone	.25	.13	.08
(98) Felix Mantilla	.35	.20	.11
(99) Mickey Mantle	45.00	22.00	13.50
(100) Juan Marichal	2.00	1.00	.60
(101) Roger Maris	5.00	2.50	1.50
(102) J.C. Martin	.25	.13	.08
(103) Ed Mathews	3.00	1.50	.90
(104) Willie Mays	7.00	3.50	2.00
(105) Bill Mazeroski	.50	.25	.15
(106) Ken McBride	.25	.13	.08
(107) Tim McCarver	.50	.25	.15
(108) Joe McClain	.25	.13	.08
(109) Mike McCormick	.25	.13	.08
(110) Lindy McDaniel	.25	.13	.08
(111) Roy McMillan	.25	.13	.08
(112) Bob L. Miller	.35	.20	.11
(113) Stu Miller	.25	.13	.08
(114) Minnie Minoso	.50	.25	.15
(115) Bill Monbouquette	.25	.13	.08
(116) Wally Moon	.30	.15	.09
(117) Don Mossi	.30	.15	.09
(118) Stan Musial	7.00	3.50	2.00
(119) Russ Nixon	.25	.13	.08
(120) Danny O'Connell	.25	.13	.08
(121) Jim O'Toole	.25	.13	.08
(122) Milt Pappas	.30	.15	.09
(123) Camilo Pascual	.30	.15	.09
(124) Albie Pearson	.25	.13	.08
(125) Jim Perry	.35	.20	.11
(126) Bubba Phillips	.25	.13	.08
(127) Jimmy Piersall	.35	.20	.11
(128) Vada Pinson	.50	.25	.15
(129) Juan Pizarro	.25	.13	.08
(130) Johnny Podres	.35	.20	.11
(131) Leo Posada	.25	.13	.08
(132) Vic Power	.25	.13	.08
(133) Bob Purkey	.25	.13	.08
(134) Pedro Ramos	.25	.13	.08
(135) Bobby Richardson	.80	.40	.25

	NR MT	EX	VG
(136) Brooks Robinson	3.75	2.00	1.25
(137) Floyd Robinson	.25	.13	.08
(138) Frank Robinson	3.50	1.75	1.00
(139) Bob Rodgers	.30	.15	.09
(140) Johnny Romano	.25	.13	.08
(141) John Roseboro	.30	.15	.09
(142) Pete Runnels	.30	.15	.09
(143) Ray Sadecki	.25	.13	.08
(144) Ron Santo	.35	.20	.11
(145) Chuck Schilling	.25	.13	.08
(146) Barney Schultz	.25	.13	.08
(147) Don Schwall	.25	.13	.08
(148) Bobby Shantz	.35	.20	.11
(149) Bob Shaw	.25	.13	.08
(150) Norm Siebern	.25	.13	.08
(151a) Roy Sievers (Kansas City)	1.00	.50	.30
(151b) Roy Sievers (Philadelphia)	.30	.15	.09
(152) Bill Skowron	.50	.25	.15
(153) Hal (W.) Smith	.25	.13	.08
(154) Duke Snider	3.75	2.00	1.25
(155) Warren Spahn	3.00	1.50	.90
(156) Al Spangler	.25	.13	.08
(157) Daryl Spencer	.25	.13	.08
(158) Gene Stephens	.25	.13	.08
(159) Dick Stuart	.30	.15	.09
(160) Haywood Sullivan	.25	.13	.08
(161) Tony Taylor	.25	.13	.08
(162) George Thomas	.25	.13	.08
(163) Lee Thomas	.25	.13	.08
(164) Bob Tiefenauer	.25	.13	.08
(165) Joe Torre	.50	.25	.15
(166) Gus Triandos	.30	.15	.09
(167) Bill Tuttle	.25	.13	.08
(168) Zoilo Versalles	.25	.13	.08
(169) Bill Virdon	.35	.20	.11
(170) Leon Wagner	.25	.13	.08
(171) Jerry Walker	.25	.13	.08
(172) Lee Walls	.25	.13	.08
(173) Bill White	.30	.15	.09
(174) Hoyt Wilhelm	1.50	.70	.45
(175) Billy Williams	2.00	1.00	.60
(176) Jake Wood	.25	.13	.08
(177) Gene Woodling	.35	.20	.11
(178) Early Wynn	2.00	1.00	.60
(179) Carl Yastrzemski	12.00	6.00	3.50
(180) Don Zimmer	.35	.20	.11
(181) Baltimore Orioles Logo	.25	.13	.08
(182) Boston Red Sox Logo	.25	.13	.08
(183) Chicago Cubs Logo	.25	.13	.08
(184) Chicago White Sox Logo	.25	.13	.08
(185) Cincinnati Reds Logo	.25	.13	.08
(186) Cleveland Indians Logo	.25	.13	.08
(187) Detroit Tigers Logo	.25	.13	.08
(188) Houston Colts Logo	.25	.13	.08
(189) Kansas City Athletics Logo	.25	.13	.08
(190) Los Angeles Angels Logo	.25	.13	.08
(191) Los Angeles Dodgers Logo	.25	.13	.08
(192) Milwaukee Braves Logo	.25	.13	.08
(193) Minnesota Twins Logo	.25	.13	.08
(194) New York Mets Logo	.35	.20	.11
(195) New York Yankees Logo	.35	.20	.11
(196) Philadelphia Phillies Logo	.25	.13	.08
(197) Pittsburgh Pirates Logo	.25	.13	.08
(198) St. Louis Cardinals Logo	.25	.13	.08
(199) San Francisco Giants Logo	.25	.13	.08
(200) Washington Senators Logo	.25	.13	.08

1963 Topps

Although the number of cards dropped to 576, the

1963 Topps set is among the most popular of the 1960s. A color photo dominates the 2-1/2" by 3-1/2" card, but a colored circle at the bottom carries a black and white portrait as well. A colored band gives the player's name, team and position. The backs again feature career statistics and a cartoon, career summary and brief biographical details. The set is somewhat unlike those immediately preceding it in that there are fewer specialty cards. The major groupings are statistical leaders, World Series highlights and rookies. It is one rookie which makes the set special - Pete Rose. As one of most avidly sought cards in history and a high-numbered card at that, the Rose rookie card accounts for much of the value of a complete set.

	NR MT	EX	VG
Complete Set:	5000.00	2500.00	1500.
Common Player: 1-283	1.50	.70	.45
Common Player: 284-446	3.00	1.50	.90
Common Player: 447-506	10.00	5.00	3.00
Common Player: 507-576	7.00	3.50	2.00

		NR MT	EX	VG
1	N.L. Batting Leaders (Hank Aaron, Tommy Davis, Stan Musial, Frank Robinson, Bill White)	40.00	6.00	3.50
2	A.L. Batting Leaders (Chuck Hinton, Mickey Mantle, Floyd Robinson, Pete Runnels, Norm Siebern)	25.00	12.50	7.50
3	N.L. Home Run Leaders (Hank Aaron, Ernie Banks, Orlando Cepeda, Willie Mays, Frank Robinson)	12.00	6.00	3.50
4	A.L. Home Run Leaders (Norm Cash, Rocky Colavito, Jim Gentile, Harmon Killebrew, Roger Maris, Leon Wagner)	4.00	2.00	1.25
5	N.L. E.R.A. Leaders (Don Drysdale, Bob Gibson, Sandy Koufax, Bob Purkey, Bob Shaw)	4.00	2.00	1.25
6	A.L. E.R.A. Leaders (Hank Aguirre, Dean Chance, Eddie Fisher, Whitey Ford, Robin Roberts)	3.50	1.75	1.00
7	N.L. Pitching Leaders (Don Drysdale, Joe Jay, Art Mahaffey, Billy O'Dell, Bob Purkey, Jack Sanford)	3.50	1.75	1.00
8	A.L. Pitching Leaders (Jim Bunning, Dick Donovan, Ray Herbert, Camilo Pascual, Ralph Terry)	3.00	1.50	.90
9	N.L. Strikeout Leaders (Don Drysdale, Dick Farrell, Bob Gibson, Sandy Koufax, Billy O'Dell)	4.00	2.00	1.25
10	A.L. Strikeout Leaders (Jim Bunning, Jim Kaat, Camilo Pascual, Juan Pizarro, Ralph Terry)	3.00	1.50	.90
11	Lee Walls	1.50	.70	.45
12	Steve Barber	1.50	.70	.45
13	Phillies Team	3.25	1.75	1.00
14	Pedro Ramos	1.50	.70	.45
15	Ken Hubbs	3.00	1.50	.90
16	Al Smith	1.50	.70	.45
17	Ryne Duren	1.75	.90	.50
18	Buc Blasters (Smoky Burgess, Bob Clemente, Bob Skinner, Dick Stuart)	10.00	5.00	3.00
19	Pete Burnside	1.50	.70	.45
20	Tony Kubek	7.00	3.50	2.00
21	Marty Keough	1.50	.70	.45
22	Curt Simmons	1.75	.90	.50
23	Ed Lopat	2.00	1.00	.60
24	Bob Bruce	1.50	.70	.45
25	Al Kaline	40.00	20.00	12.00
26	Ray Moore	1.50	.70	.45
27	Choo Choo Coleman	2.00	1.00	.60
28	Mike Fornieles	1.50	.70	.45
29a	1962 Rookie Stars (John Boozer, *Ray Culp, Sammy Ellis*, Jesse Gonder)	7.00	3.50	2.00
29b	1963 Rookie Stars (John Boozer, *Ray Culp, Sammy Ellis*, Jesse Gonder)	2.00	1.00	.60
30	Harvey Kuenn	1.50	.70	.45
31	Cal Koonce	1.50	.70	.45
32	Tony Gonzalez	1.50	.70	.45
33	Bo Belinsky	3.00	1.50	.90
34	Dick Schofield	1.50	.70	.45
35	John Buzhardt	1.50	.70	.45
36	Jerry Kindall	1.50	.70	.45
37	Jerry Lynch	1.50	.70	.45
38	Bud Daley	2.00	1.00	.60
39	Angels Team	3.25	1.75	1.00
40	Vic Power	1.50	.70	.45

		NR MT	EX	VG
41	Charlie Lau	1.75	.90	.50
42	Stan Williams	2.00	1.00	.60
43	Veteran Masters (Casey Stengel, Gene Woodling)	4.00	2.00	1.25
44	Terry Fox	1.50	.70	.45
45	Bob Aspromonte	1.50	.70	.45
46	*Tommie Aaron*	2.00	1.00	.60
47	Don Lock	1.50	.70	.45
48	Birdie Tebbetts	1.50	.70	.45
49	*Dal Maxvill*	2.00	1.00	.60
50	Bill Pierce	2.00	1.00	.60
51	George Alusik	1.50	.70	.45
52	Chuck Schilling	1.50	.70	.45
53	Joe Moeller	1.50	.70	.45
54a	1962 Rookie Stars (Jack Cullen, *Dave DeBusschere*, Harry Fanok, Nelson Mathews)	15.00	7.50	4.50
54b	1963 Rookie Stars (Jack Cullen, *Dave DeBusschere*, Harry Fanok, Nelson Mathews)	4.00	2.00	1.25
55	Bill Virdon	1.50	.70	.45
56	Dennis Bennett	1.50	.70	.45
57	Billy Moran	1.50	.70	.45
58	Bob Will	1.50	.70	.45
59	Craig Anderson	1.75	.90	.50
60	Elston Howard	8.00	4.00	2.50
61	Ernie Bowman	1.50	.70	.45
62	Bob Hendley	1.50	.70	.45
63	Reds Team	2.50	1.25	.70
64	Dick McAuliffe	1.75	.90	.50
65	Jackie Brandt	1.50	.70	.45
66	Mike Joyce	1.50	.70	.45
67	Ed Charles	1.50	.70	.45
68	Friendly Foes (Gil Hodges, Duke Snider)	8.00	4.00	2.50
69	Bud Zipfel	1.50	.70	.45
70	Jim O'Toole	1.50	.70	.45
71	*Bobby Wine*	1.75	.90	.50
72	Johnny Romano	1.50	.70	.45
73	Bobby Bragan	1.75	.90	.50
74	*Denver Lemaster*	1.75	.90	.50
75	Bob Allison	2.00	1.00	.60
76	Earl Wilson	1.50	.70	.45
77	Al Spangler	1.50	.70	.45
78	Marv Throneberry	3.50	1.75	1.00
79	Checklist 1-88	2.50	1.25	.70
80	Jim Gilliam	3.00	1.50	.90
81	Jimmie Schaffer	1.50	.70	.45
82	Ed Rakow	1.50	.70	.45
83	Charley James	1.50	.70	.45
84	Ron Kline	1.50	.70	.45
85	Tom Haller	1.75	.90	.50
86	Charley Maxwell	1.50	.70	.45
87	Bob Veale	1.75	.90	.50
88	Ron Hansen	1.50	.70	.45
89	Dick Stigman	1.50	.70	.45
90	Gordy Coleman	1.50	.70	.45
91	Dallas Green	1.75	.90	.50
92	Hector Lopez	2.00	1.00	.60
93	Galen Cisco	1.75	.90	.50
94	Bob Schmidt	1.50	.70	.45
95	Larry Jackson	1.50	.70	.45
96	Lou Clinton	1.50	.70	.45
97	Bob Duliba	1.50	.70	.45
98	George Thomas	1.50	.70	.45
99	Jim Umbricht	1.50	.70	.45
100	Joe Cunningham	1.75	.90	.50
101	Joe Gibbon	1.50	.70	.45
102a	Checklist 89-176 ("Checklist" in red on front)	3.00	1.50	.90
102b	Checklist 89-176 ("Checklist" in white)	8.00	4.00	2.50
103	Chuck Essegian	1.50	.70	.45
104	Lew Krausse	1.50	.70	.45
105	Ron Fairly	1.75	.90	.50
106	Bob Bolin	1.50	.70	.45
107	Jim Hickman	1.75	.90	.50
108	Hoyt Wilhelm	11.00	5.50	3.25
109	Lee Maye	1.50	.70	.45
110	Rich Rollins	1.75	.90	.50
111	Al Jackson	1.75	.90	.50
112	Dick Brown	1.50	.70	.45
113	Don Landrum (photo actally Ron Santo)	1.75	.90	.50
114	Dan Osinski	1.50	.70	.45
115	Carl Yastrzemski	70.00	35.00	21.00
116	Jim Brosnan	1.75	.90	.50
117	Jacke Davis	1.50	.70	.45
118	Sherm Lollar	1.75	.90	.50
119	Bob Lillis	1.50	.70	.45
120	Roger Maris	65.00	32.50	19.50

		NR MT	EX	VG
121	Jim Hannan	1.50	.70	.45
122	Julio Gotay	1.50	.70	.45
123	Frank Howard	2.50	1.25	.70
124	Dick Howser	1.50	.70	.45
125	Robin Roberts	8.00	4.00	2.50
126	Bob Uecker	35.00	17.50	10.50
127	Bill Tuttle	1.50	.70	.45
128	Matty Alou	1.75	.90	.50
129	Gary Bell	1.50	.70	.45
130	Dick Groat	1.50	.70	.45
131	Senators Team	3.25	1.75	1.00
132	Jack Hamilton	1.50	.70	.45
133	Gene Freese	1.50	.70	.45
134	Bob Scheffing	1.50	.70	.45
135	Richie Ashburn	8.00	4.00	2.50
136	Ike Delock	1.50	.70	.45
137	Mack Jones	1.50	.70	.45
138	Pride of N.L. (Willie Mays, Stan Musial)	30.00	15.00	9.00
139	Earl Averill	1.50	.70	.45
140	Frank Lary	1.75	.90	.50
141	*Manny Mota*	8.00	4.00	2.50
142	World Series Game 1 (Yanks' Ford Wins Series Opener)	3.50	1.75	1.00
143	World Series Game 2 (Sanford Flashes Shutout Magic)	3.25	1.75	1.00
144	World Series Game 3 (Maris Sparks Yankee Rally)	4.00	2.00	1.25
145	World Series Game 4 (Hiller Blasts Grand Slammer)	3.25	1.75	1.00
146	World Series Game 5 (Tresh's Homer Defeats Giants)	3.00	1.50	.90
147	World Series Game 6 (Pierce Stars In 3 Hit Victory)	3.00	1.50	.90
148	World Series Game 7 (Yanks Celebrate As Terry Wins)	3.00	1.50	.90
149	Marv Breeding	1.50	.70	.45
150	Johnny Podres	3.00	1.50	.90
151	Pirates Team	3.25	1.75	1.00
152	Ron Nischwitz	1.50	.70	.45
153	Hal Smith	1.50	.70	.45
154	Walt Alston	3.00	1.50	.90
155	Bill Stafford	2.00	1.00	.60
156	Roy McMillan	1.50	.70	.45
157	*Diego Segui*	1.75	.90	.50
158	1963 Rookie Stars (Rogelio Alvarez, *Tommy Harper*, Dave Roberts, Bob Saverine)	1.75	.90	.50
159	Jim Pagliaroni	1.50	.70	.45
160	Juan Pizarro	1.50	.70	.45
161	Frank Torre	1.50	.70	.45
162	Twins Team	3.25	1.75	1.00
163	Don Larsen	2.00	1.00	.60
164	Bubba Morton	1.50	.70	.45
165	Jim Kaat	7.00	3.50	2.00
166	Johnny Keane	1.50	.70	.45
167	Jim Fregosi	1.50	.70	.45
168	Russ Nixon	1.50	.70	.45
169	1963 Rookie Stars (Dick Egan, Julio Navarro, Gaylord Perry, Tommie Sisk)	30.00	15.00	9.00
170	Joe Adcock	1.50	.70	.45
171	Steve Hamilton	1.50	.70	.45
172	Gene Oliver	1.50	.70	.45
173	Bomber's Best (Mickey Mantle, Bobby Richardson, Tom Tresh)	65.00	33.00	20.00
174	Larry Burright	1.75	.90	.50
175	Bob Buhl	1.75	.90	.50
176	Jim King	1.50	.70	.45
177	Bubba Phillips	1.50	.70	.45
178	Johnny Edwards	1.50	.70	.45
179	Ron Piche	1.50	.70	.45
180	Bill Skowron	1.50	.70	.45
181	Sammy Esposito	1.50	.70	.45
182	Albie Pearson	1.50	.70	.45
183	Joe Pepitone	4.00	2.00	1.25
184	Vern Law	2.00	1.00	.60
185	Chuck Hiller	1.50	.70	.45
186	Jerry Zimmerman	1.50	.70	.45
187	Willie Kirkland	1.50	.70	.45
188	Eddie Bressoud	1.50	.70	.45
189	Dave Giusti	1.50	.70	.45
190	Minnie Minoso	1.50	.70	.45
191	Checklist 177-264	3.00	1.50	.90
192	Clay Dalrymple	1.50	.70	.45
193	Andre Rodgers	1.50	.70	.45
194	Joe Nuxhall	1.75	.90	.50
195	Manny Jimenez	1.50	.70	.45
196	Doug Camilli	1.50	.70	.45
197	Roger Craig	3.00	1.50	.90
198	Lenny Green	1.50	.70	.45
199	Joe Amalfitano	1.50	.70	.45
200	Mickey Mantle	500.00	250.00	150.00
201	Cecil Butler	1.50	.70	.45
202	Red Sox Team	2.50	1.25	.70
203	Chico Cardenas	1.50	.70	.45
204	Don Nottebart	1.50	.70	.45
205	Luis Aparicio	10.00	5.00	3.00
206	Ray Washburn	1.50	.70	.45
207	Ken Hunt	1.50	.70	.45
208	1963 Rookie Stars (Ron Herbel, John Miller, Ron Taylor, Wally Wolf)	1.50	.70	.45
209	Hobie Landrith	1.50	.70	.45
210	Sandy Koufax	160.00	80.00	50.00
211	Fred Whitfield	1.50	.70	.45
212	Glen Hobbie	1.50	.70	.45
213	Billy Hitchcock	1.50	.70	.45
214	Orlando Pena	1.50	.70	.45
215	Bob Skinner	1.75	.90	.50
216	Gene Conley	1.75	.90	.50
217	Joe Christopher	1.75	.90	.50
218	Tiger Twirlers (Jim Bunning, Frank Lary, Don Mossi)	3.00	1.50	.90
219	Chuck Cottier	1.50	.70	.45
220	Camilo Pascual	1.75	.90	.50
221	*Cookie Rojas*	1.75	.90	.50
222	Cubs Team	3.25	1.75	1.00
223	Eddie Fisher	1.50	.70	.45
224	Mike Roarke	1.50	.70	.45
225	Joe Jay	1.50	.70	.45
226	Julian Javier	1.75	.90	.50
227	Jim Grant	1.50	.70	.45
228	1963 Rookie Stars (*Max Alvis, Bob Bailey, Ed Kranepool, Pedro Oliva*)	50.00	25.00	15.00
229	Willie Davis	1.50	.70	.45
230	Pete Runnels	1.75	.90	.50
231	Eli Grba (photo actually Ryne Duren)	1.75	.90	.50
232	Frank Malzone	1.75	.90	.50
233	Casey Stengel	15.00	7.50	4.50
234	Dave Nicholson	1.50	.70	.45
235	Billy O'Dell	1.50	.70	.45
236	Bill Bryan	1.50	.70	.45
237	Jim Coates	2.00	1.00	.60
238	Lou Johnson	1.50	.70	.45
239	Harvey Haddix	1.75	.90	.50
240	Rocky Colavito	10.00	5.00	3.00
241	Billy Smith	1.50	.70	.45
242	Power Plus (Hank Aaron, Ernie Banks)	35.00	17.50	10.50
243	Don Leppert	1.50	.70	.45
244	John Tsitouris	1.50	.70	.45
245	Gil Hodges	15.00	7.50	4.50
246	Lee Stange	1.50	.70	.45
247	Yankees Team	10.00	5.00	3.00
248	Tito Francona	1.75	.90	.50
249	Leo Burke	1.50	.70	.45
250	Stan Musial	110.00	55.00	33.00
251	Jack Lamabe	1.50	.70	.45
252	Ron Santo	3.00	1.50	.90
253	1963 Rookie Stars (Len Gabrielson, Pete Jernigan, Deacon Jones, John Wojcik)	1.50	.70	.45
254	Mike Hershberger	1.50	.70	.45
255	Bob Shaw	1.50	.70	.45
256	Jerry Lumpe	1.75	.90	.50
257	Hank Aguirre	1.50	.70	.45
258	Alvin Dark	1.75	.90	.50
259	Johnny Logan	1.75	.90	.50
260	Jim Gentile	1.75	.90	.50
261	Bob Miller	1.50	.70	.45
262	Ellis Burton	1.50	.70	.45
263	Dave Stenhouse	1.50	.70	.45
264	Phil Linz	1.50	.70	.45
265	Vada Pinson	2.50	1.25	.70
266	Bob Allen	1.50	.70	.45
267	Carl Sawatski	1.50	.70	.45
268	Don Demeter	1.50	.70	.45
269	Don Mincher	1.75	.90	.50
270	Felipe Alou	1.75	.90	.50
271	Dean Stone	1.50	.70	.45
272	Danny Murphy	1.50	.70	.45
273	Sammy Taylor	1.75	.90	.50
274	Checklist 265-352	3.00	1.50	.90
275	Ed Mathews	20.00	10.00	6.00
276	Barry Shetrone	1.50	.70	.45
277	Dick Farrell	1.50	.70	.45
278	Chico Fernandez	1.50	.70	.45
279	Wally Moon	1.75	.90	.50
280	Bob Rodgers	1.75	.90	.50
281	Tom Sturdivant	1.50	.70	.45
282	Bob Del Greco	1.50	.70	.45

#	Player	NR MT	EX	VG
283	Roy Sievers	1.75	.90	.50
284	Dave Sisler	3.00	1.50	.90
285	Dick Stuart	3.25	1.75	1.00
286	Stu Miller	3.00	1.50	.90
287	Dick Bertell	3.00	1.50	.90
288	White Sox Team	3.50	1.75	1.00
289	Hal Brown	3.50	1.75	1.00
290	Bill White	3.25	1.75	1.00
291	Don Rudolph	3.00	1.50	.90
292	Pumpsie Green	3.25	1.75	1.00
293	Bill Pleis	3.00	1.50	.90
294	Bill Rigney	3.00	1.50	.90
295	Ed Roebuck	3.00	1.50	.90
296	Doc Edwards	3.25	1.75	1.00
297	Jim Golden	3.00	1.50	.90
298	Don Dillard	3.00	1.50	.90
299	1963 Rookie Stars (Tom Butters, Bob Dustal, Dave Morehead, Dan Schneider)	3.00	1.50	.90
300	Willie Mays	160.00	80.00	50.00
301	Bill Fischer	3.00	1.50	.90
302	Whitey Herzog	3.50	1.75	1.00
303	Earl Francis	3.00	1.50	.90
304	Harry Bright	3.00	1.50	.90
305	Don Hoak	3.25	1.75	1.00
306	Star Receivers (Earl Battey, Elston Howard)	3.50	1.75	1.00
307	Chet Nichols	3.00	1.50	.90
308	Camilo Carreon	3.00	1.50	.90
309	Jim Brewer	3.00	1.50	.90
310	Tommy Davis	3.00	1.50	.90
311	Joe McClain	3.00	1.50	.90
312	Colt .45s Team	12.00	6.00	3.50
313	Ernie Broglio	3.00	1.50	.90
314	John Goryl	3.00	1.50	.90
315	Ralph Terry	3.00	1.50	.90
316	Norm Sherry	2.00	1.00	.60
317	Sam McDowell	3.00	1.50	.90
318	Gene Mauch	3.25	1.75	1.00
319	Joe Gaines	3.00	1.50	.90
320	Warren Spahn	25.00	12.50	7.50
321	Gino Cimoli	3.00	1.50	.90
322	Bob Turley	3.25	1.75	1.00
323	Bill Mazeroski	3.50	1.75	1.00
324	1963 Rookie Stars (Vic Davalillo, Phil Roof, Pete Ward, George Williams)	2.50	1.25	.70
325	Jack Sanford	3.00	1.50	.90
326	Hank Foiles	3.00	1.50	.90
327	Paul Foytack	3.00	1.50	.90
328	Dick Williams	3.50	1.75	1.00
329	Lindy McDaniel	3.00	1.50	.90
330	Chuck Hinton	3.00	1.50	.90
331	Series Foes (Bill Pierce, Bill Stafford)	3.00	1.50	.90
332	Joel Horlen	3.00	1.50	.90
333	Carl Warwick	3.00	1.50	.90
334	Wynn Hawkins	3.25	1.75	1.00
335	Leon Wagner	3.25	1.75	1.00
336	Ed Bauta	3.00	1.50	.90
337	Dodgers Team	10.00	5.00	3.00
338	Russ Kemmerer	3.00	1.50	.90
339	Ted Bowsfield	3.00	1.50	.90
340	Yogi Berra	60.00	30.00	18.00
341	Jack Baldschun	3.00	1.50	.90
342	Gene Woodling	2.50	1.25	.70
343	Johnny Pesky	3.25	1.75	1.00
344	Don Schwall	3.00	1.50	.90
345	Brooks Robinson	50.00	25.00	15.00
346	Billy Hoeft	3.00	1.50	.90
347	Joe Torre	6.00	3.00	1.75
348	Vic Wertz	3.25	1.75	1.00
349	Zoilo Versalles	3.25	1.75	1.00
350	Bob Purkey	3.00	1.50	.90
351	Al Luplow	3.00	1.50	.90
352	Ken Johnson	3.00	1.50	.90
353	Billy Williams	25.00	12.50	7.50
354	Dom Zanni	3.00	1.50	.90
355	Dean Chance	3.25	1.75	1.00
356	John Schaive	3.00	1.50	.90
357	George Altman	3.00	1.50	.90
358	Milt Pappas	3.25	1.75	1.00
359	Haywood Sullivan	3.25	1.75	1.00
360	Don Drysdale	30.00	15.00	9.00
361	Clete Boyer	3.50	1.75	1.00
362	Checklist 353-429	4.00	2.00	1.25
363	Dick Radatz	3.25	1.75	1.00
364	Howie Goss	3.00	1.50	.90
365	Jim Bunning	10.00	5.00	3.00
366	Tony Taylor	3.00	1.50	.90
367	Tony Cloninger	3.25	1.75	1.00
368	Ed Bailey	3.00	1.50	.90
369	Jim Lemon	3.00	1.50	.90
370	Dick Donovan	3.00	1.50	.90
371	Rod Kanehl	3.25	1.75	1.00
372	Don Lee	3.00	1.50	.90
373	Jim Campbell	3.00	1.50	.90
374	Claude Osteen	3.25	1.75	1.00
375	Ken Boyer	4.00	2.00	1.25
376	Johnnie Wyatt	3.00	1.50	.90
377	Orioles Team	3.50	1.75	1.00
378	Bill Henry	3.00	1.50	.90
379	Bob Anderson	3.00	1.50	.90
380	Ernie Banks	55.00	28.00	16.50
381	Frank Baumann	3.00	1.50	.90
382	Ralph Houk	3.50	1.75	1.00
383	Pete Richert	3.00	1.50	.90
384	Bob Tillman	3.00	1.50	.90
385	Art Mahaffey	3.00	1.50	.90
386	1963 Rookie Stars (John Bateman, Larry Bearnarth, Ed Kirkpatrick, Garry Roggenburk)	3.25	1.75	1.00
387	Al McBean	3.00	1.50	.90
388	Jim Davenport	3.00	1.50	.90
389	Frank Sullivan	3.00	1.50	.90
390	Hank Aaron	150.00	75.00	45.00
391	Bill Dailey	3.00	1.50	.90
392	Tribe Thumpers (Tito Francona, Johnny Romano)	3.25	1.75	1.00
393	Ken MacKenzie	3.25	1.75	1.00
394	Tim McCarver	4.00	2.00	1.25
395	Don McMahon	3.00	1.50	.90
396	Joe Koppe	3.00	1.50	.90
397	Athletics Team	3.50	1.75	1.00
398	Boog Powell	7.00	3.50	2.00
399	Dick Ellsworth	3.00	1.50	.90
400	Frank Robinson	45.00	23.00	13.50
401	Jim Bouton	10.00	5.00	3.00
402	Mickey Vernon	3.25	1.75	1.00
403	Ron Perranoski	3.25	1.75	1.00
404	Bob Oldis	3.00	1.50	.90
405	Floyd Robinson	3.00	1.50	.90
406	Howie Koplitz	3.00	1.50	.90
407	1963 Rookie Stars (Larry Elliot, Frank Kostro, Chico Ruiz, Dick Simpson)	3.00	1.50	.90
408	Billy Gardner	3.00	1.50	.90
409	Roy Face	3.50	1.75	1.00
410	Earl Battey	3.25	1.75	1.00
411	Jim Constable	3.00	1.50	.90
412	Dodgers' Big Three (Don Drysdale, Sandy Koufax, Johnny Podres)	30.00	15.00	9.00
413	Jerry Walker	3.00	1.50	.90
414	Ty Cline	3.00	1.50	.90
415	Bob Gibson	30.00	15.00	9.00
416	Alex Grammas	3.00	1.50	.90
417	Giants Team	3.50	1.75	1.00
418	Johnny Orsino	3.00	1.50	.90
419	Tracy Stallard	3.25	1.75	1.00
420	Bobby Richardson	10.00	5.00	3.00
421	Tom Morgan	3.00	1.50	.90
422	Fred Hutchinson	3.25	1.75	1.00
423	Ed Hobaugh	3.00	1.50	.90
424	Charley Smith	3.00	1.50	.90
425	Smoky Burgess	2.50	1.25	.70
426	Barry Latman	3.00	1.50	.90
427	Bernie Allen	3.00	1.50	.90
428	Carl Boles	3.00	1.50	.90
429	Lou Burdette	3.00	1.50	.90
430	Norm Siebern	3.25	1.75	1.00
431a	Checklist 430-506 ("Checklist" in black on front)	4.50	2.25	1.25
431b	Checklist 430-506 ("Checklist" in white)	7.00	3.50	2.00
432	Roman Mejias	3.00	1.50	.90
433	Denis Menke	3.25	1.75	1.00
434	Johnny Callison	2.50	1.25	.70
435	Woody Held	3.00	1.50	.90
436	Tim Harkness	3.25	1.75	1.00
437	Bill Bruton	3.00	1.50	.90
438	Wes Stock	3.00	1.50	.90
439	Don Zimmer	3.50	1.75	1.00
440	Juan Marichal	20.00	10.00	6.00
441	Lee Thomas	3.00	1.50	.90
442	J.C. Hartman	3.00	1.50	.90
443	Jim Piersall	3.50	1.75	1.00
444	Jim Maloney	3.25	1.75	1.00
445	Norm Cash	3.00	1.50	.90
446	Whitey Ford	35.00	17.50	10.50
447	Felix Mantilla	10.00	5.00	3.00
448	Jack Kralick	10.00	5.00	3.00
449	Jose Tartabull	10.00	5.00	3.00
450	Bob Friend	11.00	5.50	3.25
451	Indians Team	10.00	5.00	3.00

		NR MT	EX	VG
452	Barney Schultz	10.00	5.00	3.00
453	Jake Wood	10.00	5.00	3.00
454a	Art Fowler (card # on orange background)			
		10.00	5.00	3.00
454b	Art Fowler (card # on white background)			
		10.00	5.00	3.00
455	Ruben Amaro	10.00	5.00	3.00
456	Jim Coker	10.00	5.00	3.00
457	Tex Clevenger	11.00	5.50	3.25
458	Al Lopez	15.00	7.50	4.50
459	Dick LeMay	10.00	5.00	3.00
460	Del Crandall	11.00	5.50	3.25
461	Norm Bass	10.00	5.00	3.00
462	Wally Post	10.00	5.00	3.00
463	Joe Schaffernoth	10.00	5.00	3.00
464	Ken Aspromonte	10.00	5.00	3.00
465	Chuck Estrada	10.00	5.00	3.00
466	1963 Rookie Stars (Bill Freehan, Tony Martinez, Nate Oliver, Jerry Robinson)			
		30.00	15.00	9.00
467	Phil Ortega	10.00	5.00	3.00
468	Carroll Hardy	10.00	5.00	3.00
469	Jay Hook	11.00	5.50	3.25
470	Tom Tresh	20.00	10.00	6.00
471	Ken Retzer	10.00	5.00	3.00
472	Lou Brock	125.00	62.00	37.00
473	Mets Team	100.00	50.00	30.00
474	Jack Fisher	10.00	5.00	3.00
475	Gus Triandos	10.00	5.00	3.00
476	Frank Funk	10.00	5.00	3.00
477	Donn Clendenon	11.00	5.50	3.25
478	Paul Brown	10.00	5.00	3.00
479	Ed Brinkman	11.00	5.50	3.25
480	Bill Monbouquette	11.00	5.50	3.25
481	Bob Taylor	10.00	5.00	3.00
482	Felix Torres	10.00	5.00	3.00
483	Jim Owens	10.00	5.00	3.00
484	Dale Long	11.00	5.50	3.25
485	Jim Landis	10.00	5.00	3.00
486	Ray Sadecki	10.00	5.00	3.00
487	John Roseboro	11.00	5.50	3.25
488	Jerry Adair	10.00	5.00	3.00
489	Paul Toth	10.00	5.00	3.00
490	Willie McCovey	110.00	55.00	33.00
491	Harry Craft	10.00	5.00	3.00
492	Dave Wickersham	10.00	5.00	3.00
493	Walt Bond	10.00	5.00	3.00
494	Phil Regan	10.00	5.00	3.00
495	Frank Thomas	11.00	5.50	3.25
496	1963 Rookie Stars (Carl Bouldin, Steve Dalkowski, Fred Newman, Jack Smith)			
		11.00	5.50	3.25
497	Bennie Daniels	10.00	5.00	3.00
498	Eddie Kasko	10.00	5.00	3.00
499	J.C. Martin	10.00	5.00	3.00
500	Harmon Killebrew	125.00	62.00	37.00
501	Joe Azcue	10.00	5.00	3.00
502	Daryl Spencer	10.00	5.00	3.00
503	Braves Team	10.00	5.00	3.00
504	Bob Johnson	10.00	5.00	3.00
505	Curt Flood	12.00	6.00	3.50
506	Gene Green	11.00	5.50	3.25
507	Roland Sheldon	8.00	4.00	2.50
508	Ted Savage	7.00	3.50	2.00
509a	Checklist 507-576 (copyright centered)			
		15.00	7.50	4.50
509b	Checklist 509-576 (copyright to right)			
		12.00	6.00	3.50
510	Ken McBride	7.00	3.50	2.00
511	Charlie Neal	7.50	3.75	2.25
512	Cal McLish	7.00	3.50	2.00
513	Gary Geiger	7.00	3.50	2.00
514	Larry Osborne	7.00	3.50	2.00
515	Don Elston	7.00	3.50	2.00
516	Purnal Goldy	7.00	3.50	2.00
517	Hal Woodeshick	7.00	3.50	2.00
518	Don Blasingame	7.00	3.50	2.00
519	Claude Raymond	7.00	3.50	2.00
520	Orlando Cepeda	15.00	7.50	4.50
521	Dan Pfister	7.00	3.50	2.00
522	1963 Rookie Stars (Mel Nelson, Gary Peters, Art Quirk, Jim Roland)			
		7.50	3.75	2.25
523	Bill Kunkel	8.00	4.00	2.50
524	Cardinals Team	10.00	5.00	3.00
525	Nellie Fox	12.00	6.00	3.50
526	Dick Hall	7.00	3.50	2.00
527	Ed Sadowski	7.00	3.50	2.00
528	Carl Willey	7.50	3.75	2.25
529	Wes Covington	7.00	3.50	2.00
530	Don Mossi	7.50	3.75	2.25
531	Sam Mele	7.00	3.50	2.00

		NR MT	EX	VG
532	Steve Boros	7.00	3.50	2.00
533	Bobby Shantz	8.00	4.00	2.50
534	Ken Walters	7.00	3.50	2.00
535	Jim Perry	8.00	4.00	2.50
536	Norm Larker	7.00	3.50	2.00
537	1963 Rookie Stars (Pedro Gonzalez, Ken McMullen, Pete Rose, Al Weis)	900.00	450.00	275.00
538	George Brunet	7.00	3.50	2.00
539	Wayne Causey	7.00	3.50	2.00
540	Bob Clemente	250.00	125.00	75.00
541	Ron Moeller	7.00	3.50	2.00
542	Lou Klimchock	7.00	3.50	2.00
543	Russ Snyder	7.00	3.50	2.00
544	1963 Rookie Stars (Duke Carmel, Bill Haas, Dick Phillips, Rusty Staub)	30.00	15.00	9.00
545	Jose Pagan	7.00	3.50	2.00
546	Hal Reniff	8.00	4.00	2.50
547	Gus Bell	7.50	3.75	2.25
548	Tom Satriano	7.00	3.50	2.00
549	1963 Rookie Stars (Marcelino Lopez, Pete Lovrich, Elmo Plaskett, Paul Ratliff)	7.50	3.75	2.25
550	Duke Snider	50.00	25.00	15.00
551	Billy Klaus	7.00	3.50	2.00
552	Tigers Team	20.00	10.00	6.00
553	1963 Rookie Stars (Brock Davis, Jim Gosger, John Herrnstein, Willie Stargell)	250.00	125.00	75.00
554	Hank Fischer	7.00	3.50	2.00
555	John Blanchard	8.00	4.00	2.50
556	Al Worthington	7.00	3.50	2.00
557	Cuno Barragan	7.00	3.50	2.00
558	1963 Rookie Stars (Bill Faul, Ron Hunt, Bob Lipski, Al Moran)	8.00	4.00	2.50
559	Danny Murtaugh	7.50	3.75	2.25
560	Ray Herbert	7.00	3.50	2.00
561	Mike de la Hoz	7.00	3.50	2.00
562	1963 Rookie Stars (Randy Cardinal, Dave McNally, Don Rowe, Ken Rowe)	18.00	9.00	5.50
563	Mike McCormick	7.50	3.75	2.25
564	George Banks	7.00	3.50	2.00
565	Larry Sherry	7.00	3.50	2.00
566	Cliff Cook	7.50	3.75	2.25
567	Jim Duffalo	7.00	3.50	2.00
568	Bob Sadowski	7.00	3.50	2.00
569	Luis Arroyo	8.00	4.00	2.50
570	Frank Bolling	7.00	3.50	2.00
571	Johnny Klippstein	7.00	3.50	2.00
572	Jack Spring	7.00	3.50	2.00
573	Coot Veal	7.00	3.50	2.00
574	Hal Kolstad	7.00	3.50	2.00
575	Don Cardwell	7.50	3.75	2.25
576	Johnny Temple	10.00	5.00	3.00

1963 Topps Peel-Offs

BOB CLEMENTE
PITTS. PIRATES OUTFIELD

Measuring 1-1/4" by 2-3/4," Topps Peel-Offs were an insert with 1963 Topps baseball cards. There are 46 players in the unnumbered set, each pictured in a color photo inside an oval with the player's name, team and position in a band below. The back of the Peel-Off is removable, leaving a sticky surface that made the Peel-Off a popular decorative item among youngsters of the day. Naturally, that makes them quite scarce today, but as a non-card Topps issue, demand is not particularly strong.

	NR MT	EX	VG
Complete Set:	175.00	87.00	52.00

	NR MT	EX	VG
Common Player:	1.00	.50	.30
(1) Hank Aaron	10.00	5.00	3.00
(2) Luis Aparicio	3.00	1.50	.90
(3) Richie Ashburn	2.00	1.00	.60
(4) Bob Aspromonte	1.00	.50	.30
(5) Ernie Banks	5.00	2.50	1.50
(6) Ken Boyer	1.50	.70	.45
(7) Jim Bunning	1.75	.90	.50
(8) Johnny Callison	1.25	.60	.40
(9) Orlando Cepeda	1.75	.90	.50
(10) Bob Clemente	8.00	4.00	2.50
(11) Rocky Colavito	1.75	.90	.50
(12) Tommy Davis	1.50	.70	.45
(13) Dick Donovan	1.00	.50	.30
(14) Don Drysdale	4.00	2.00	1.25
(15) Dick Farrell	1.00	.50	.30
(16) Jim Gentile	1.00	.50	.30
(17) Ray Herbert	1.00	.50	.30
(18) Chuck Hinton	1.00	.50	.30
(19) Ken Hubbs	1.50	.70	.45
(20) Al Jackson	1.00	.50	.30
(21) Al Kaline	5.00	2.50	1.50
(22) Harmon Killebrew	5.00	2.50	1.50
(23) Sandy Koufax	8.00	4.00	2.50
(24) Jerry Lumpe	1.00	.50	.30
(25) Art Mahaffey	1.00	.50	.30
(26) Mickey Mantle	50.00	25.00	15.00
(27) Willie Mays	10.00	5.00	3.00
(28) Bill Mazeroski	1.50	.70	.45
(29) Bill Monbouquette	1.00	.50	.30
(30) Stan Musial	10.00	5.00	3.00
(31) Camilo Pascual	1.25	.60	.40
(32) Bob Purkey	1.00	.50	.30
(33) Bobby Richardson	1.75	.90	.50
(34) Brooks Robinson	6.00	3.00	1.75
(35) Floyd Robinson	1.00	.50	.30
(36) Frank Robinson	5.00	2.50	1.50
(37) Bob Rodgers	1.00	.50	.30
(38) Johnny Romano	1.00	.50	.30
(39) Jack Sanford	1.00	.50	.30
(40) Norm Siebern	1.00	.50	.30
(41) Warren Spahn	5.00	2.50	1.50
(42) Dave Stenhouse	1.00	.50	.30
(43) Ralph Terry	1.25	.60	.40
(44) Lee Thomas	1.00	.50	.30
(45) Bill White	1.25	.60	.40
(46) Carl Yastrzemski	12.00	6.00	3.50

1964 Topps

SMOKY BURGESS catcher

The 1964 Topps set is a 587-card issue of 2-1/2" by 3-1/2" cards which is considered by many as being among the company's best efforts. Card fronts feature a large color photo which blends into a top panel which contains the team name, while a panel below the picture carries the player's name and position. An interesting innovation on the back is a baseball quiz question which required the rubbing of a white panel to reveal the answer. As in 1963, specialty cards remained modest in number with a 12-card set of statistical leaders, a few multi-player cards, rookies and World Series highlights. An interesting card is an "In Memoriam" card for Ken Hubbs who was killed in an airplane crash.

	NR MT	EX	VG
Complete Set:	3000.00	1500.00	900.00
Common Player: 1-370	2.00	1.00	.60
Common Player: 371-522	3.00	1.50	.90
Common Player: 523-587	7.00	3.50	2.00
1 N.L. E.R.A. Leaders (Dick Ellsworth, Bob Friend, Sandy Koufax)	10.00	3.00	1.50
2 A.L. E.R.A. Leaders (Camilo Pascual, Gary Peters, Juan Pizarro)	3.00	1.50	.90
3 N.L. Pitching Leaders (Sandy Koufax, Jim Maloney, Juan Marichal, Warren Spahn)	7.00	3.50	2.00
4a A.L. Pitching Leaders (Jim Bouton, Whitey Ford, Camilo Pascual) (apostrophe after "Pitching" on back)	7.00	3.50	2.00
4b A.L. Pitching Leaders (Jim Bouton, Whitey Ford, Camilo Pascual) (no apostrophe)	3.50	1.75	1.00
5 N.L. Strikeout Leaders (Don Drysdale, Sandy Koufax, Jim Maloney)	7.00	3.50	2.00
6 A.L. Strikeout Leaders (Jim Bunning, Camilo Pascual, Dick Stigman)	3.00	1.50	.90
7 N.L. Batting Leaders (Hank Aaron, Bob Clemente, Tommy Davis, Dick Groat)	7.00	3.50	2.00
8 A.L. Batting Leaders (Al Kaline, Rich Rollins, Carl Yastrzemski)	7.00	3.50	2.00
9 N.L. Home Run Leaders (Hank Aaron, Orlando Cepeda, Willie Mays, Willie McCovey)	7.00	3.50	2.00
10 A.L. Home Run Leaders (Bob Allison, Harmon Killebrew, Dick Stuart)	3.50	1.75	1.00
11 N.L. R.B.I. Leaders (Hank Aaron, Ken Boyer, Bill White)	7.50	3.75	2.25
12 A.L. R.B.I. Leaders (Al Kaline, Harmon Killebrew, Dick Stuart)	7.50	3.75	2.25
13 Hoyt Wilhelm	8.00	4.00	2.50
14 Dodgers Rookies (Dick Nen, Nick Willhite)	2.00	1.00	.60
15 Zoilo Versalles	2.00	1.00	.60
16 John Boozer	2.00	1.00	.60
17 Willie Kirkland	2.00	1.00	.60
18 Billy O'Dell	2.00	1.00	.60
19 Don Wert	2.00	1.00	.60
20 Bob Friend	3.75	2.00	1.25
21 Yogi Berra	40.00	20.00	12.00
22 Jerry Adair	2.00	1.00	.60
23 Chris Zachary	2.00	1.00	.60
24 Carl Sawatski	2.00	1.00	.60
25 Bill Monbouquette	2.00	1.00	.60
26 Gino Cimoli	2.00	1.00	.60
27 Mets Team	3.50	1.75	1.00
28 Claude Osteen	2.00	1.00	.60
29 Lou Brock	35.00	17.50	10.50
30 Ron Perranoski	2.00	1.00	.60
31 Dave Nicholson	2.00	1.00	.60
32 Dean Chance	3.75	2.00	1.25
33 Reds Rookies (Sammy Ellis, Mel Queen)	2.00	1.00	.60
34 Jim Perry	3.75	2.00	1.25
35 Ed Mathews	20.00	10.00	6.00
36 Hal Reniff	3.00	1.50	.90
37 Smoky Burgess	3.75	2.00	1.25
38 *Jim Wynn*	3.25	1.75	1.00
39 Hank Aguirre	2.00	1.00	.60
40 Dick Groat	3.25	1.75	1.00
41 Friendly Foes (Willie McCovey, Leon Wagner)	3.00	1.50	.90
42 Moe Drabowsky	2.00	1.00	.60
43 Roy Sievers	2.25	1.25	.70
44 Duke Carmel	2.00	1.00	.60
45 Milt Pappas	2.25	1.25	.70
46 Ed Brinkman	2.00	1.00	.60
47 Giants Rookies (*Jesus Alou*, Ron Herbel)	3.75	2.00	1.25
48 Bob Perry	2.00	1.00	.60
49 Bill Henry	2.00	1.00	.60
50 Mickey Mantle	300.00	150.00	90.00
51 Pete Richert	2.00	1.00	.60
52 Chuck Hinton	2.00	1.00	.60
53 Denis Menke	2.00	1.00	.60
54 Sam Mele	2.00	1.00	.60
55 Ernie Banks	35.00	17.50	10.50
56 Hal Brown	2.00	1.00	.60
57 Tim Harkness	2.00	1.00	.60
58 Don Demeter	2.00	1.00	.60
59 Ernie Broglio	2.00	1.00	.60
60 Frank Malzone	2.00	1.00	.60
61 Angel Backstops (Bob Rodgers, Ed Sadowski)	2.00	1.00	.60
62 Ted Savage	2.00	1.00	.60
63 Johnny Orsino	2.00	1.00	.60

		NR MT	EX	VG
64	Ted Abernathy	2.00	1.00	.60
65	Felipe Alou	3.75	2.00	1.25
66	Eddie Fisher	2.00	1.00	.60
67	Tigers Team	3.50	1.75	1.00
68	Willie Davis	3.25	1.75	1.00
69	Clete Boyer	3.25	1.75	1.00
70	Joe Torre	2.50	1.25	.70
71	Jack Spring	2.00	1.00	.60
72	Chico Cardenas	2.00	1.00	.60
73	*Jimmie Hall*	2.00	1.00	.60
74	Pirates Rookies (Tom Butters, Bob Priddy)	2.00	1.00	.60
75	Wayne Causey	2.00	1.00	.60
76	Checklist 1-88	3.00	1.50	.90
77	Jerry Walker	2.00	1.00	.60
78	Merritt Ranew	2.00	1.00	.60
79	Bob Heffner	2.00	1.00	.60
80	Vada Pinson	2.50	1.25	.70
81	All-Star Vets (Nellie Fox, Harmon Killebrew)	7.00	3.50	2.00
82	Jim Davenport	2.00	1.00	.60
83	Gus Triandos	2.00	1.00	.60
84	Carl Willey	2.00	1.00	.60
85	Pete Ward	2.00	1.00	.60
86	Al Downing	3.25	1.75	1.00
87	Cardinals Team	7.00	3.50	2.00
88	John Roseboro	2.00	1.00	.60
89	Boog Powell	2.50	1.25	.70
90	Earl Battey	2.00	1.00	.60
91	Bob Bailey	2.00	1.00	.60
92	Steve Ridzik	2.00	1.00	.60
93	Gary Geiger	2.00	1.00	.60
94	Braves Rookies (Jim Britton, Larry Maxie)	2.00	1.00	.60
95	George Altman	2.00	1.00	.60
96	Bob Buhl	2.00	1.00	.60
97	Jim Fregosi	3.75	2.00	1.25
98	Bill Bruton	2.00	1.00	.60
99	Al Stanek	2.00	1.00	.60
100	Elston Howard	7.00	3.50	2.00
101	Walt Alston	3.00	1.50	.90
102	Checklist 89-176	3.00	1.50	.90
103	Curt Flood	3.00	1.50	.90
104	Art Mahaffey	2.00	1.00	.60
105	Woody Held	2.00	1.00	.60
106	Joe Nuxhall	2.00	1.00	.60
107	White Sox Rookies (Bruce Howard, Frank Kreutzer)	2.00	1.00	.60
108	John Wyatt	2.00	1.00	.60
109	Rusty Staub	9.00	4.50	2.75
110	Albie Pearson	2.00	1.00	.60
111	Don Elston	2.00	1.00	.60
112	Bob Tillman	2.00	1.00	.60
113	Grover Powell	2.00	1.00	.60
114	Don Lock	2.00	1.00	.60
115	Frank Bolling	2.00	1.00	.60
116	Twins Rookies (Tony Oliva, Jay Ward)	8.00	4.00	2.50
117	Earl Francis	2.00	1.00	.60
118	John Blanchard	3.00	1.50	.90
119	Gary Kolb	2.00	1.00	.60
120	Don Drysdale	18.00	9.00	5.50
121	Pete Runnels	2.00	1.00	.60
122	Don McMahon	2.00	1.00	.60
123	Jose Pagan	2.00	1.00	.60
124	Orlando Pena	2.00	1.00	.60
125	Pete Rose	175.00	87.00	52.00
126	Russ Snyder	2.00	1.00	.60
127	Angels Rookies (Aubrey Gatewood, Dick Simpson)	2.00	1.00	.60
128	*Mickey Lolich*	12.00	6.00	3.50
129	Amado Samuel	2.00	1.00	.60
130	Gary Peters	2.00	1.00	.60
131	Steve Boros	2.00	1.00	.60
132	Braves Team	3.75	2.00	1.25
133	Jim Grant	2.00	1.00	.60
134	Don Zimmer	3.25	1.75	1.00
135	Johnny Callison	3.25	1.75	1.00
136	World Series Game 1 (Koufax Strikes Out 15)	10.00	5.00	3.00
137	World Series Game 2 (Davis Sparks Rally)	2.50	1.25	.70
138	World Series Game 3 (L.A. Takes 3rd Straight)	2.50	1.25	.70
139	World Series Game 4 (Sealing Yanks' Doom)	2.50	1.25	.70
140	World Series Summary (The Dodgers Celebrate)	2.50	1.25	.70
141	Danny Murtaugh	2.00	1.00	.60
142	John Bateman	2.00	1.00	.60
143	Bubba Phillips	2.00	1.00	.60

		NR MT	EX	VG
144	Al Worthington	2.00	1.00	.60
145	Norm Siebern	2.00	1.00	.60
146	Indians Rookies (Bob Chance, *Tommy John*)	72.00	36.00	20.60
147	Ray Sadecki	2.00	1.00	.60
148	J.C. Martin	2.00	1.00	.60
149	Paul Foytack	2.00	1.00	.60
150	Willie Mays	90.00	45.00	27.00
151	Athletics Team	3.75	2.00	1.25
152	Denver Lemaster	2.00	1.00	.60
153	Dick Williams	3.25	1.75	1.00
154	Dick Tracewski	2.00	1.00	.60
155	Duke Snider	25.00	12.50	7.50
156	Bill Dailey	2.00	1.00	.60
157	Gene Mauch	2.25	1.25	.70
158	Ken Johnson	2.00	1.00	.60
159	Charlie Dees	2.00	1.00	.60
160	Ken Boyer	7.00	3.50	2.00
161	Dave McNally	3.75	2.00	1.25
162	Hitting Area (Vada Pinson, Dick Sisler)	2.00	1.00	.60
163	Donn Clendenon	3.00	1.50	.90
164	Bud Daley	3.00	1.50	.90
165	Jerry Lumpe	2.00	1.00	.60
166	Marty Keough	2.00	1.00	.60
167	Senators Rookies (Mike Brumley, *Lou Piniella*)	30.00	15.00	9.00
168	Al Weis	2.00	1.00	.60
169	Del Crandall	3.75	2.00	1.25
170	Dick Radatz	2.00	1.00	.60
171	Ty Cline	2.00	1.00	.60
172	Indians Team	3.75	2.00	1.25
173	Ryne Duren	2.25	1.25	.70
174	Doc Edwards	2.00	1.00	.60
175	Billy Williams	12.00	6.00	3.50
176	Tracy Stallard	2.00	1.00	.60
177	Harmon Killebrew	20.00	10.00	6.00
178	Hank Bauer	2.25	1.25	.70
179	Carl Warwick	2.00	1.00	.60
180	Tommy Davis	3.25	1.75	1.00
181	Dave Wickersham	2.00	1.00	.60
182	Sox Sockers (Chuck Schilling, Carl Yastrzemski)	10.00	5.00	3.00
183	Ron Taylor	2.00	1.00	.60
184	Al Luplow	2.00	1.00	.60
185	Jim O'Toole	2.00	1.00	.60
186	Roman Mejias	2.00	1.00	.60
187	Ed Roebuck	2.00	1.00	.60
188	Checklist 177-264	3.00	1.50	.90
189	Bob Hendley	2.00	1.00	.60
190	Bobby Richardson	7.50	3.75	2.25
191	Clay Dalrymple	2.00	1.00	.60
192	Cubs Rookies (John Boccabella, Billy Cowan)	2.00	1.00	.60
193	Jerry Lynch	2.00	1.00	.60
194	John Goryl	2.00	1.00	.60
195	Floyd Robinson	2.00	1.00	.60
196	Jim Gentile	2.00	1.00	.60
197	Frank Lary	2.00	1.00	.60
198	Len Gabrielson	2.00	1.00	.60
199	Joe Azcue	2.00	1.00	.60
200	Sandy Koufax	100.00	50.00	30.00
201	Orioles Rookies (Sam Bowens, *Wally Bunker*)	2.00	1.00	.60
202	Galen Cisco	2.00	1.00	.60
203	John Kennedy	2.00	1.00	.60
204	Matty Alou	2.25	1.25	.70
205	Nellie Fox	7.00	3.50	2.00
206	Steve Hamilton	3.00	1.50	.90
207	Fred Hutchinson	2.00	1.00	.60
208	Wes Covington	2.00	1.00	.60
209	Bob Allen	2.00	1.00	.60
210	Carl Yastrzemski	80.00	40.00	25.00
211	Jim Coker	2.00	1.00	.60
212	Pete Lovrich	2.00	1.00	.60
213	Angels Team	3.75	2.00	1.25
214	Ken McMullen	2.00	1.00	.60
215	Ray Herbert	2.00	1.00	.60
216	Mike de la Hoz	2.00	1.00	.60
217	Jim King	2.00	1.00	.60
218	Hank Fischer	2.00	1.00	.60
219	Young Aces (Jim Bouton, Al Downing)	3.00	1.50	.90
220	Dick Ellsworth	2.00	1.00	.60
221	Bob Saverine	2.00	1.00	.60
222	Bill Pierce	2.25	1.25	.70
223	George Banks	2.00	1.00	.60
224	Tommie Sisk	2.00	1.00	.60
225	Roger Maris	60.00	30.00	18.00
226	Colts Rookies (*Gerald Grote*, Larry Yellen)	3.75	2.00	1.25

		NR MT	EX	VG
227	Barry Latman	2.00	1.00	.60
228	Felix Mantilla	2.00	1.00	.60
229	Charley Lau	2.00	1.00	.60
230	Brooks Robinson	30.00	15.00	9.00
231	Dick Calmus	2.00	1.00	.60
232	Al Lopez	3.00	1.50	.90
233	Hal Smith	2.00	1.00	.60
234	Gary Bell	2.00	1.00	.60
235	Ron Hunt	2.00	1.00	.60
236	Bill Faul	2.00	1.00	.60
237	Cubs Team	3.75	2.00	1.25
238	Roy McMillan	2.00	1.00	.60
239	Herm Starrette	2.00	1.00	.60
240	Bill White	3.25	1.75	1.00
241	Jim Owens	2.00	1.00	.60
242	Harvey Kuenn	3.25	1.75	1.00
243	Phillies Rookies (*Richie Allen*, John Herrnstein)	20.00	10.00	6.00
244	*Tony LaRussa*	20.00	10.00	6.00
245	Dick Stigman	2.00	1.00	.60
246	Manny Mota	3.75	2.00	1.25
247	Dave DeBusschere	3.00	1.50	.90
248	Johnny Pesky	2.00	1.00	.60
249	Doug Camilli	2.00	1.00	.60
250	Al Kaline	30.00	15.00	9.00
251	Choo Choo Coleman	2.00	1.00	.60
252	Ken Aspromonte	2.00	1.00	.60
253	Wally Post	2.00	1.00	.60
254	Don Hoak	2.00	1.00	.60
255	Lee Thomas	2.00	1.00	.60
256	Johnny Weekly	2.00	1.00	.60
257	Giants Team	3.75	2.00	1.25
258	Garry Roggenburk	2.00	1.00	.60
259	Harry Bright	3.00	1.50	.90
260	Frank Robinson	25.00	12.50	7.50
261	Jim Hannan	2.00	1.00	.60
262	Cardinals Rookie Stars (Harry Fanok, *Mike Shannon*)	3.25	1.75	1.00
263	Chuck Estrada	2.00	1.00	.60
264	Jim Landis	2.00	1.00	.60
265	Jim Bunning	7.00	3.50	2.00
266	Gene Freese	2.00	1.00	.60
267	*Wilbur Wood*	3.25	1.75	1.00
268	Bill's Got It (Danny Murtaugh, Bill Virdon)	2.25	1.25	.70
269	Ellis Burton	2.00	1.00	.60
270	Rich Rollins	2.00	1.00	.60
271	Bob Sadowski	2.00	1.00	.60
272	Jake Wood	2.00	1.00	.60
273	Mel Nelson	2.00	1.00	.60
274	Checklist 265-352	3.00	1.50	.90
275	John Tsitouris	2.00	1.00	.60
276	Jose Tartabull	2.00	1.00	.60
277	Ken Retzer	2.00	1.00	.60
278	Bobby Shantz	3.25	1.75	1.00
279	Joe Koppe	2.00	1.00	.60
280	Juan Marichal	10.00	5.00	3.00
281	Yankees Rookies (Jake Gibbs, Tom Metcalf)	3.00	1.50	.90
282	Bob Bruce	2.00	1.00	.60
283	*Tommy McCraw*	2.00	1.00	.60
284	Dick Schofield	2.00	1.00	.60
285	Robin Roberts	10.00	5.00	3.00
286	Don Landrum	2.00	1.00	.60
287	Red Sox Rookies (*Tony Conigliaro*, Bill Spanswick)	30.00	15.00	9.00
288	Al Moran	2.00	1.00	.60
289	Frank Funk	2.00	1.00	.60
290	Bob Allison	2.25	1.25	.70
291	Phil Ortega	2.00	1.00	.60
292	Mike Roarke	2.00	1.00	.60
293	Phillies Team	3.75	2.00	1.25
294	Ken Hunt	2.00	1.00	.60
295	Roger Craig	3.25	1.75	1.00
296	Ed Kirkpatrick	2.00	1.00	.60
297	Ken MacKenzie	2.00	1.00	.60
298	Harry Craft	2.00	1.00	.60
299	Bill Stafford	3.00	1.50	.90
300	Hank Aaron	100.00	50.00	30.00
301	Larry Brown	2.00	1.00	.60
302	Dan Pfister	2.00	1.00	.60
303	Jim Campbell	2.00	1.00	.60
304	Bob Johnson	2.00	1.00	.60
305	Jack Lamabe	2.00	1.00	.60
306	Giant Gunners (Orlando Cepeda, Willie Mays)	18.00	9.00	5.50
307	Joe Gibbon	2.00	1.00	.60
308	Gene Stephens	2.00	1.00	.60
309	Paul Toth	2.00	1.00	.60
310	Jim Gilliam	3.00	1.50	.90
311	Tom Brown	2.00	1.00	.60

		NR MT	EX	VG
312	Tigers Rookies (Fritz Fisher, Fred Gladding)	2.00	1.00	.60
313	Chuck Hiller	2.00	1.00	.60
314	Jerry Buchek	2.00	1.00	.60
315	Bo Belinsky	2.25	1.25	.70
316	Gene Oliver	2.00	1.00	.60
317	Al Smith	2.00	1.00	.60
318	Twins Team	3.75	2.00	1.25
319	Paul Brown	2.00	1.00	.60
320	Rocky Colavito	3.00	1.50	.90
321	Bob Lillis	2.00	1.00	.60
322	George Brunet	2.00	1.00	.60
323	John Buzhardt	2.00	1.00	.60
324	Casey Stengel	15.00	7.50	4.50
325	Hector Lopez	3.00	1.50	.90
326	Ron Brand	2.00	1.00	.60
327	Don Blasingame	2.00	1.00	.60
328	Bob Shaw	2.00	1.00	.60
329	Russ Nixon	2.00	1.00	.60
330	Tommy Harper	2.00	1.00	.60
331	A.L. Bombers (Norm Cash, Al Kaline, Mickey Mantle, Roger Maris)	100.00	50.00	30.00
332	Ray Washburn	2.00	1.00	.60
333	Billy Moran	2.00	1.00	.60
334	Lew Krausse	2.00	1.00	.60
335	Don Mossi	2.00	1.00	.60
336	Andre Rodgers	2.00	1.00	.60
337	Dodgers Rookies (*Al Ferrara, Jeff Torborg*)	2.00	1.00	.60
338	Jack Kralick	2.00	1.00	.60
339	Walt Bond	2.00	1.00	.60
340	Joe Cunningham	2.00	1.00	.60
341	Jim Roland	2.00	1.00	.60
342	Willie Stargell	40.00	20.00	12.00
343	Senators Team	3.75	2.00	1.25
344	Phil Linz	3.00	1.50	.90
345	Frank Thomas	2.00	1.00	.60
346	Joe Jay	2.00	1.00	.60
347	Bobby Wine	2.00	1.00	.60
348	Ed Lopat	2.25	1.25	.70
349	Art Fowler	2.00	1.00	.60
350	Willie McCovey	20.00	10.00	6.00
351	Dan Schneider	2.00	1.00	.60
352	Eddie Bressoud	2.00	1.00	.60
353	Wally Moon	2.25	1.25	.70
354	Dave Giusti	2.00	1.00	.60
355	Vic Power	2.00	1.00	.60
356	Reds Rookies (Bill McCool, Chico Ruiz)	2.00	1.00	.60
357	Charley James	2.00	1.00	.60
358	Ron Kline	2.00	1.00	.60
359	Jim Schaffer	2.00	1.00	.60
360	Joe Pepitone	2.50	1.25	.70
361	Jay Hook	2.00	1.00	.60
362	Checklist 353-429	3.00	1.50	.90
363	Dick McAuliffe	2.00	1.00	.60
364	Joe Gaines	2.00	1.00	.60
365	Cal McLish	2.00	1.00	.60
366	Nelson Mathews	2.00	1.00	.60
367	Fred Whitfield	2.00	1.00	.60
368	White Sox Rookies (Fritz Ackley, *Don Buford*)	2.25	1.25	.70
369	Jerry Zimmerman	2.00	1.00	.60
370	Hal Woodeshick	2.00	1.00	.60
371	Frank Howard	3.00	1.50	.90
372	Howie Koplitz	3.00	1.50	.90
373	Pirates Team	3.00	1.50	.90
374	Bobby Bolin	3.00	1.50	.90
375	Ron Santo	2.50	1.25	.70
376	Dave Morehead	3.00	1.50	.90
377	Bob Skinner	3.00	1.50	.90
378	Braves Rookies (Jack Smith, *Woody Woodward*)	3.75	2.00	1.25
379	Tony Gonzalez	3.00	1.50	.90
380	Whitey Ford	30.00	15.00	9.00
381	Bob Taylor	3.75	2.00	1.25
382	Wes Stock	3.00	1.50	.90
383	Bill Rigney	3.00	1.50	.90
384	Ron Hansen	3.00	1.50	.90
385	Curt Simmons	3.75	2.00	1.25
386	Lenny Green	3.00	1.50	.90
387	Terry Fox	3.00	1.50	.90
388	Athletics Rookies (John O'Donoghue, George Williams)	3.00	1.50	.90
389	Jim Umbricht	3.00	1.50	.90
390	Orlando Cepeda	9.00	4.50	2.75
391	Sam McDowell	3.75	2.00	1.25
392	Jim Pagliaroni	3.00	1.50	.90
393	Casey Teaches (Ed Kranepool, Casey Stengel)	7.00	3.50	2.00
394	Bob Miller	3.00	1.50	.90

#	Player	NR MT	EX	VG
395	Tom Tresh	3.00	1.50	.90
396	Dennis Bennett	3.00	1.50	.90
397	Chuck Cottier	3.00	1.50	.90
398	Mets Rookies (Bill Haas, Dick Smith)	3.75	2.00	1.25
399	Jackie Brandt	3.00	1.50	.90
400	Warren Spahn	35.00	17.50	10.50
401	Charlie Maxwell	3.00	1.50	.90
402	Tom Sturdivant	3.00	1.50	.90
403	Reds Team	3.50	1.75	1.00
404	Tony Martinez	3.00	1.50	.90
405	Ken McBride	3.00	1.50	.90
406	Al Spangler	3.00	1.50	.90
407	Bill Freehan	3.00	1.50	.90
408	Cubs Rookies (Fred Burdette, Jim Stewart)	3.00	1.50	.90
409	Bill Fischer	3.00	1.50	.90
410	Dick Stuart	3.75	2.00	1.25
411	Lee Walls	3.00	1.50	.90
412	Ray Culp	3.00	1.50	.90
413	Johnny Keane	3.00	1.50	.90
414	Jack Sanford	3.00	1.50	.90
415	Tony Kubek	7.00	3.50	2.00
416	Lee Maye	3.00	1.50	.90
417	Don Cardwell	3.00	1.50	.90
418	Orioles Rookies (*Darold Knowles*, Les Narum)	3.75	2.00	1.25
419	*Ken Harrelson*	7.00	3.50	2.00
420	Jim Maloney	3.75	2.00	1.25
421	Camilo Carreon	3.00	1.50	.90
422	Jack Fisher	3.75	2.00	1.25
423	Tops In NL (Hank Aaron, Willie Mays)	110.00	55.00	33.00
424	Dick Bertell	3.00	1.50	.90
425	Norm Cash	2.50	1.25	.70
426	Bob Rodgers	3.75	2.00	1.25
427	Don Rudolph	3.00	1.50	.90
428	Red Sox Rookies (Archie Skeen, Pete Smith)	3.00	1.50	.90
429	Tim McCarver	3.00	1.50	.90
430	Juan Pizarro	3.00	1.50	.90
431	George Alusik	3.00	1.50	.90
432	Ruben Amaro	3.00	1.50	.90
433	Yankees Team	10.00	5.00	3.00
434	Don Nottebart	3.00	1.50	.90
435	Vic Davalillo	3.00	1.50	.90
436	Charlie Neal	3.00	1.50	.90
437	Ed Bailey	3.00	1.50	.90
438	Checklist 430-506	7.00	3.50	2.00
439	Harvey Haddix	3.25	1.75	1.00
440	Bob Clemente	125.00	62.00	37.00
441	Bob Duliba	3.00	1.50	.90
442	Pumpsie Green	3.75	2.00	1.25
443	Chuck Dressen	3.75	2.00	1.25
444	Larry Jackson	3.00	1.50	.90
445	Bill Skowron	2.50	1.25	.70
446	Julian Javier	3.75	2.00	1.25
447	Ted Bowsfield	3.00	1.50	.90
448	Cookie Rojas	3.75	2.00	1.25
449	Deron Johnson	3.00	1.50	.90
450	Steve Barber	3.00	1.50	.90
451	Joe Amalfitano	3.00	1.50	.90
452	Giants Rookies (Gil Garrido, *Jim Hart*)	3.75	2.00	1.25
453	Frank Baumann	3.00	1.50	.90
454	Tommie Aaron	3.75	2.00	1.25
455	Bernie Allen	3.00	1.50	.90
456	Dodgers Rookies (*Wes Parker*, John Werhas)	3.00	1.50	.90
457	Jesse Gonder	3.75	2.00	1.25
458	Ralph Terry	3.00	1.50	.90
459	Red Sox Rookies (Pete Charton, Dalton Jones)	3.00	1.50	.90
460	Bob Gibson	25.00	12.50	7.50
461	George Thomas	3.00	1.50	.90
462	Birdie Tebbetts	3.00	1.50	.90
463	Don Leppert	3.00	1.50	.90
464	Dallas Green	3.75	2.00	1.25
465	Mike Hershberger	3.00	1.50	.90
466	Athletics Rookies (*Dick Green*, Aurelio Monteagudo)	3.75	2.00	1.25
467	Bob Aspromonte	3.00	1.50	.90
468	Gaylord Perry	45.00	23.00	13.50
469	Cubs Rookies (Fred Norman, Sterling Slaughter)	3.00	1.50	.90
470	Jim Bouton	3.00	1.50	.90
471	*Gates Brown*	3.75	2.00	1.25
472	Vern Law	3.25	1.75	1.00
473	Orioles Team	3.00	1.50	.90
474	Larry Sherry	3.00	1.50	.90
475	Ed Charles	3.00	1.50	.90
476	Braves Rookies (*Rico Carty*, Dick Kelley)	7.00	3.50	2.00
477	Mike Joyce	2.25	1.25	.70
478	Dick Howser	3.00	1.50	.90
479	Cardinals Rookies (Dave Bakenhaster, Johnny Lewis)	3.00	1.50	.90
480	Bob Purkey	3.00	1.50	.90
481	Chuck Schilling	3.00	1.50	.90
482	Phillies Rookies (*John Briggs, Danny Cater*)	3.75	2.00	1.25
483	Fred Valentine	3.00	1.50	.90
484	Bill Pleis	3.00	1.50	.90
485	Tom Haller	3.75	2.00	1.25
486	Bob Kennedy	3.00	1.50	.90
487	Mike McCormick	3.75	2.00	1.25
488	Yankees Rookies (Bob Meyer, Pete Mikkelsen)	3.25	1.75	1.00
489	Julio Navarro	3.00	1.50	.90
490	Ron Fairly	3.25	1.75	1.00
491	Ed Rakow	3.00	1.50	.90
492	Colts Rookies (Jim Beauchamp, Mike White)	3.00	1.50	.90
493	Don Lee	3.00	1.50	.90
494	Al Jackson	3.75	2.00	1.25
495	Bill Virdon	3.00	1.50	.90
496	White Sox Team	3.00	1.50	.90
497	Jeoff Long	3.00	1.50	.90
498	Dave Stenhouse	3.00	1.50	.90
499	Indians Rookies (Chico Salmon, Gordon Seyfried)	3.00	1.50	.90
500	Camilo Pascual	3.75	2.00	1.25
501	Bob Veale	3.75	2.00	1.25
502	Angels Rookies (*Bobby Knoop*, Bob Lee)	3.75	2.00	1.25
503	Earl Wilson	3.00	1.50	.90
504	Claude Raymond	3.00	1.50	.90
505	Stan Williams	3.25	1.75	1.00
506	Bobby Bragan	3.75	2.00	1.25
507	John Edwards	3.00	1.50	.90
508	Diego Segui	3.00	1.50	.90
509	Pirates Rookies (*Gene Alley*, Orlando McFarlane)	3.75	2.00	1.25
510	Lindy McDaniel	3.00	1.50	.90
511	Lou Jackson	3.00	1.50	.90
512	Tigers Rookies (*Willie Horton, Joe Sparma*)	7.00	3.50	2.00
513	Don Larsen	3.25	1.75	1.00
514	Jim Hickman	3.75	2.00	1.25
515	Johnny Romano	3.00	1.50	.90
516	Twins Rookies (Jerry Arrigo, Dwight Siebler)	3.00	1.50	.90
517a	Checklist 507-587 (wrong numbering on back)	7.00	3.50	2.00
517b	Checklist 507-587 (correct numbering on back)	7.50	3.75	2.25
518	Carl Bouldin	3.00	1.50	.90
519	Charlie Smith	3.75	2.00	1.25
520	Jack Baldschun	3.00	1.50	.90
521	Tom Satriano	3.00	1.50	.90
522	Bobby Tiefenauer	3.00	1.50	.90
523	Lou Burdette	9.00	4.50	2.75
524	Reds Rookies (Jim Dickson, Bobby Klaus)	7.00	3.50	2.00
525	Al McBean	7.00	3.50	2.00
526	Lou Clinton	7.00	3.50	2.00
527	Larry Bearnarth	7.50	3.75	2.25
528	Athletics Rookies (*Dave Duncan, Tom Reynolds*)	7.50	3.75	2.25
529	Al Dark	7.50	3.75	2.25
530	Leon Wagner	7.50	3.75	2.25
531	Dodgers Team	20.00	10.00	6.00
532	Twins Rookies (Bud Bloomfield, Joe Nossek)	7.00	3.50	2.00
533	Johnny Klippstein	7.00	3.50	2.00
534	Gus Bell	7.50	3.75	2.25
535	Phil Regan	7.00	3.50	2.00
536	Mets Rookies (Larry Elliot, John Stephenson)	7.50	3.75	2.25
537	Dan Osinski	7.00	3.50	2.00
538	Minnie Minoso	8.00	4.00	2.50
539	Roy Face	7.00	3.50	2.00
540	Luis Aparicio	15.00	7.50	4.50
541	Braves Rookies (*Phil Niekro*, Phil Roof)	225.00	112.00	65.00
542	Don Mincher	7.50	3.75	2.25
543	Bob Uecker	50.00	25.00	15.00
544	Colts Rookies (Steve Hertz, Joe Hoerner)	7.00	3.50	2.00
545	Max Alvis	7.50	3.75	2.25
546	Joe Christopher	7.50	3.75	2.25
547	Gil Hodges	12.00	6.00	3.50

		NR MT	EX	VG
548	N.L. Rookies (Wayne Schurr, Paul Speckenbach)	7.00	3.50	2.00
549	Joe Moeller	7.00	3.50	2.00
550	Ken Hubbs	20.00	10.00	6.00
551	Billy Hoeft	7.00	3.50	2.00
552	Indians Rookies (Tom Kelley, *Sonny Siebert*)	7.50	3.75	2.25
553	Jim Brewer	7.00	3.50	2.00
554	Hank Foiles	7.00	3.50	2.00
555	Lee Stange	7.00	3.50	2.00
556	Mets Rookies (Steve Dillon, Ron Locke)	7.50	3.75	2.25
557	Leo Burke	7.00	3.50	2.00
558	Don Schwall	7.00	3.50	2.00
559	Dick Phillips	7.00	3.50	2.00
560	Dick Farrell	7.00	3.50	2.00
561	Phillies Rookies (Dave Bennett, *Rick Wise*)	7.50	3.75	2.25
562	Pedro Ramos	7.00	3.50	2.00
563	Dal Maxvill	7.50	3.75	2.25
564	A.L. Rookies (Joe McCabe, Jerry McNertney)	7.00	3.50	2.00
565	Stu Miller	7.00	3.50	2.00
566	Ed Kranepool	7.00	3.50	2.00
567	Jim Kaat	12.00	6.00	3.50
568	N.L. Rookies (Phil Gagliano, Cap Peterson)	7.00	3.50	2.00
569	Fred Newman	7.00	3.50	2.00
570	Bill Mazeroski	8.00	4.00	2.50
571	Gene Conley	3.50	1.75	1.00
572	A.L. Rookies (Dick Egan, Dave Gray)	7.00	3.50	2.00
573	Jim Duffalo	7.00	3.50	2.00
574	Manny Jimenez	7.00	3.50	2.00
575	Tony Cloninger	7.50	3.75	2.25
576	Mets Rookies (Jerry Hinsley, Bill Wakefield)	7.50	3.75	2.25
577	Gordy Coleman	7.00	3.50	2.00
578	Glen Hobbie	7.00	3.50	2.00
579	Red Sox Team	18.00	9.00	5.50
580	Johnny Podres	9.00	4.50	2.75
581	Yankees Rookies (Pedro Gonzalez, Archie Moore)	7.00	3.50	2.00
582	Rod Kanehl	7.50	3.75	2.25
583	Tito Francona	7.50	3.75	2.25
584	Joel Horlen	7.00	3.50	2.00
585	Tony Taylor	7.00	3.50	2.00
586	Jim Piersall	9.00	4.50	2.75
587	Bennie Daniels	8.00	2.50	1.25

1964 Topps Coins

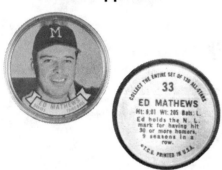

The 164 metal coins in this set were issued by Topps as inserts in the company's baseball card wax packs. The series is divided into two principal types, 120 "regular" coins and 44 All-Star coins. The 1-1/2" diameter coins feature a full-color background for the player photos in the "regular" series, while the players in the All-Star series are featured against plain red or blue backgrounds. There are two variations each of the Mantle, Causey and Hinton coins among the All-Star subset.

	NR MT	EX	VG
Complete Set:	700.00	350.00	210.00
Common Player:	1.00	.50	.30

		NR MT	EX	VG
1	Don Zimmer	1.00	.50	.30
2	Jim Wynn	1.00	.50	.30
3	Johnny Orsino	1.00	.50	.30
4	Jim Bouton	1.25	.60	.40
5	Dick Groat	1.25	.60	.40
6	Leon Wagner	1.00	.50	.30
7	Frank Malzone	1.00	.50	.30
8	Steve Barber	1.00	.50	.30
9	Johnny Romano	1.00	.50	.30
10	Tom Tresh	1.25	.60	.40
11	Felipe Alou	1.00	.50	.30
12	Dick Stuart	1.00	.50	.30
13	Claude Osteen	1.00	.50	.30
14	Juan Pizarro	1.00	.50	.30
15	Donn Clendenon	1.00	.50	.30
16	Jimmie Hall	1.00	.50	.30
17	Larry Jackson	1.00	.50	.30
18	Brooks Robinson	12.00	6.00	3.50
19	Bob Allison	1.00	.50	.30
20	Ed Roebuck	1.00	.50	.30
21	Pete Ward	1.00	.50	.30
22	Willie McCovey	8.00	4.00	2.50
23	Elston Howard	1.50	.70	.45
24	Diego Segui	1.00	.50	.30
25	Ken Boyer	1.50	.70	.45
26	Carl Yastrzemski	20.00	10.00	6.00
27	Bill Mazeroski	1.50	.70	.45
28	Jerry Lumpe	1.00	.50	.30
29	Woody Held	1.00	.50	.30
30	Dick Radatz	1.00	.50	.30
31	Luis Aparicio	5.00	2.50	1.50
32	Dave Nicholson	1.00	.50	.30
33	Ed Mathews	8.00	4.00	2.50
34	Don Drysdale	10.00	5.00	3.00
35	Ray Culp	1.00	.50	.30
36	Juan Marichal	8.00	4.00	2.50
37	Frank Robinson	8.00	4.00	2.50
38	Chuck Hinton	1.00	.50	.30
39	Floyd Robinson	1.00	.50	.30
40	Tommy Harper	1.00	.50	.30
41	Ron Hansen	1.00	.50	.30
42	Ernie Banks	10.00	5.00	3.00
43	Jesse Gonder	1.00	.50	.30
44	Billy Williams	7.00	3.50	2.00
45	Vada Pinson	1.50	.70	.45
46	Rocky Colavito	1.50	.70	.45
47	Bill Monbouquette	1.00	.50	.30
48	Max Alvis	1.00	.50	.30
49	Norm Siebern	1.00	.50	.30
50	John Callison	1.00	.50	.30
51	Rich Rollins	1.00	.50	.30
52	Ken McBride	1.00	.50	.30
53	Don Lock	1.00	.50	.30
54	Ron Fairly	1.00	.50	.30
55	Bob Clemente	20.00	10.00	6.00
56	Dick Ellsworth	1.00	.50	.30
57	Tommy Davis	1.25	.60	.40
58	Tony Gonzalez	1.00	.50	.30
59	Bob Gibson	10.00	5.00	3.00
60	Jim Maloney	1.00	.50	.30
61	Frank Howard	1.50	.70	.45
62	Jim Pagliaroni	1.00	.50	.30
63	Orlando Cepeda	2.00	1.00	.60
64	Ron Perranoski	1.00	.50	.30
65	Curt Flood	1.25	.60	.40
66	Al McBean	1.00	.50	.30
67	Dean Chance	1.00	.50	.30
68	Ron Santo	1.25	.60	.40
69	Jack Baldschun	1.00	.50	.30
70	Milt Pappas	1.00	.50	.30
71	Gary Peters	1.00	.50	.30
72	Bobby Richardson	1.50	.70	.45
73	Lee Thomas	1.00	.50	.30
74	Hank Aguirre	1.00	.50	.30
75	Carl Willey	1.00	.50	.30
76	Camilo Pascual	1.00	.50	.30
77	Bob Friend	1.00	.50	.30
78	Bill White	1.00	.50	.30
79	Norm Cash	1.25	.60	.40
80	Willie Mays	18.00	9.00	5.50
81	Duke Carmel	1.00	.50	.30
82	Pete Rose	25.00	12.50	7.50
83	Hank Aaron	20.00	10.00	6.00
84	Bob Aspromonte	1.00	.50	.30
85	Jim O'Toole	1.00	.50	.30
86	Vic Davalillo	1.00	.50	.30
87	Bill Freehan	1.00	.50	.30
88	Warren Spahn	8.00	4.00	2.50
89	Ron Hunt	1.00	.50	.30
90	Denis Menke	1.00	.50	.30
91	Turk Farrell	1.00	.50	.30

		NR MT	EX	VG
92	Jim Hickman	1.00	.50	.30
93	Jim Bunning	2.00	1.00	.60
94	Bob Hendley	1.00	.50	.30
95	Ernie Broglio	1.00	.50	.30
96	Rusty Staub	1.50	.70	.45
97	Lou Brock	8.00	4.00	2.50
98	Jim Fregosi	1.00	.50	.30
99	Jim Grant	1.00	.50	.30
100	Al Kaline	15.00	7.50	4.50
101	Earl Battey	1.00	.50	.30
102	Wayne Causey	1.00	.50	.30
103	Chuck Schilling	1.00	.50	.30
104	Boog Powell	1.50	.70	.45
105	Dave Wickersham	1.00	.50	.30
106	Sandy Koufax	15.00	7.50	4.50
107	John Bateman	1.00	.50	.30
108	Ed Brinkman	1.00	.50	.30
109	Al Downing	1.00	.50	.30
110	Joe Azcue	1.00	.50	.30
111	Albie Pearson	1.00	.50	.30
112	Harmon Killebrew	10.00	5.00	3.00
113	Tony Taylor	1.00	.50	.30
114	Alvin Jackson	1.00	.50	.30
115	Billy O'Dell	1.00	.50	.30
116	Don Demeter	1.00	.50	.30
117	Ed Charles	1.00	.50	.30
118	Joe Torre	1.50	.70	.45
119	Don Nottebart	1.00	.50	.30
120	Mickey Mantle	40.00	20.00	12.00
121	Joe Pepitone	1.25	.60	.40
122	Dick Stuart	1.00	.50	.30
123	Bobby Richardson	1.50	.70	.45
124	Jerry Lumpe	1.00	.50	.30
125	Brooks Robinson	10.00	5.00	3.00
126	Frank Malzone	1.00	.50	.30
127	Luis Aparicio	5.00	2.50	1.50
128	Jim Fregosi	1.00	.50	.30
129	Al Kaline	15.00	7.50	4.50
130	Leon Wagner	1.00	.50	.30
131a	Mickey Mantle (batting lefthanded)			
		45.00	23.00	13.50
131b	Mickey Mantle (batting righthanded)			
		45.00	23.00	13.50
132	Albie Pearson	1.00	.50	.30
133	Harmon Killebrew	10.00	5.00	3.00
134	Carl Yastrzemski	20.00	10.00	6.00
135	Elston Howard	1.50	.70	.45
136	Earl Battey	1.00	.50	.30
137	Camilo Pascual	1.00	.50	.30
138	Jim Bouton	1.25	.60	.40
139	Whitey Ford	8.00	4.00	2.50
140	Gary Peters	1.00	.50	.30
141	Bill White	1.00	.50	.30
142	Orlando Cepeda	2.00	1.00	.60
143	Bill Mazeroski	1.50	.70	.45
144	Tony Taylor	1.00	.50	.30
145	Ken Boyer	1.50	.70	.45
146	Ron Santo	1.25	.60	.40
147	Dick Groat	1.25	.60	.40
148	Roy McMillan	1.00	.50	.30
149	Hank Aaron	18.00	9.00	4.50
150	Bob Clemente	20.00	10.00	6.00
151	Willie Mays	18.00	9.00	5.50
152	Vada Pinson	1.50	.70	.45
153	Tommy Davis	1.25	.60	.40
154	Frank Robinson	8.00	4.00	2.50
155	Joe Torre	1.50	.70	.45
156	Tim McCarver	1.25	.60	.40
157	Juan Marichal	7.00	3.50	2.00
158	Jim Maloney	1.00	.50	.30
159	Sandy Koufax	15.00	7.50	4.50
160	Warren Spahn	8.00	4.00	2.50
161a	Wayne Causey (N.L. on back)	15.00	7.50	4.50
161b	Wayne Causey (A.L. on back)	1.00	.50	.30
162a	Chuck Hinton (N.L. on back)	15.00	7.50	4.50
162b	Chuck Hinton (A.L. on back)	1.00	.50	.30
163	Bob Aspromonte	1.00	.50	.30
164	Ron Hunt	1.00	.50	.30

1964 Topps Giants

Measuring 3-1/8" by 5-1/4" the Topps Giants were the company's first postcard-size issue. The cards feature large color photographs surrounded by white borders with a white baseball containing the player's name, position and team. Card backs carry another photo of the player surrounded by a newspaper-style

explanation of the depicted career highlight. The 60-card set contains primarily stars which means it's an excellent place to find inexpensive cards of Hall of Famers. The '64 Giants were not printed in equal quantity and seven of the cards, including Sandy Koufax and Willie Mays, are significantly scarcer than the remainder of the set.

		NR MT	EX	VG
Complete Set:		110.00	55.00	33.00
Common Player:		.12	.06	.04
1	Gary Peters	.12	.06	.04
2	Ken Johnson	.12	.06	.04
3	Sandy Koufax	18.00	9.00	5.50
4	Bob Bailey	.12	.06	.04
5	Milt Pappas	.25	.13	.08
6	Ron Hunt	.12	.06	.04
7	Whitey Ford	1.75	.90	.50
8	Roy McMillan	.12	.06	.04
9	Rocky Colavito	.40	.20	.12
10	Jim Bunning	.50	.25	.15
11	Bob Clemente	5.00	2.50	1.50
12	Al Kaline	3.00	1.50	.90
13	Nellie Fox	.60	.30	.20
14	Tony Gonzalez	.12	.06	.04
15	Jim Gentile	.12	.06	.04
16	Dean Chance	.12	.06	.04
17	Dick Ellsworth	.12	.06	.04
18	Jim Fregosi	.25	.13	.08
19	Dick Groat	.40	.20	.12
20	Chuck Hinton	.12	.06	.04
21	Elston Howard	.50	.25	.15
22	Dick Farrell	.12	.06	.04
23	Albie Pearson	.12	.06	.04
24	Frank Howard	.50	.25	.15
25	Mickey Mantle	18.00	9.00	5.50
26	Joe Torre	.40	.20	.12
27	Ed Brinkman	.12	.06	.04
28	Bob Friend	4.00	2.00	1.25
29	Frank Robinson	1.75	.90	.50
30	Bill Freehan	.25	.13	.08
31	Warren Spahn	1.25	.60	.40
32	Camilo Pascual	.12	.06	.04
33	Pete Ward	.12	.06	.04
34	Jim Maloney	.12	.06	.04
35	Dave Wickersham	.12	.06	.04
36	Johnny Callison	.25	.13	.08
37	Juan Marichal	3.00	1.50	.90
38	Harmon Killebrew	3.00	1.50	.90
39	Luis Aparicio	1.25	.60	.40
40	Dick Radatz	.12	.06	.04
41	Bob Gibson	3.00	1.50	.90
42	Dick Stuart	4.00	2.00	1.25
43	Tommy Davis	.40	.20	.12
44	Tony Oliva	.50	.25	.15
45	Wayne Causey	4.00	2.00	1.25
46	Max Alvis	.12	.06	.04
47	Galen Cisco	4.00	2.00	1.25
48	Carl Yastrzemski	3.00	1.50	.90
49	Hank Aaron	5.00	2.50	1.50
50	Brooks Robinson	3.00	1.50	.90
51	Willie Mays	18.00	9.00	5.50
52	Billy Williams	1.25	.60	.40
53	Juan Pizarro	.12	.06	.04
54	Leon Wagner	.12	.06	.04
55	Orlando Cepeda	.70	.35	.20
56	Vada Pinson	.50	.25	.15
57	Ken Boyer	.60	.30	.20
58	Ron Santo	.40	.20	.12

		NR MT	EX	VG
59	John Romano	.12	.06	.04
60	Bill Skowron	4.00	2.00	1.25

1964 Topps Photo Tatoos

Apparently not content to leave the skin of American children without adornment, Topps jumped back into the tattoo field in 1964 with the release of a new series. Measuring 1-9/16" by 3-1/2," there were 75 tattoos in a complete set. The picture side for the 20 team tattoos gives the team logo and name. For the player tattoos, the picture side has the player's face, name and team.

		NR MT	EX	VG
Complete Set:		600.00	300.00	180.00
Common Player:		3.00	1.50	.90
(1)	Hank Aaron	40.00	20.00	12.50
(2)	H. Aguirre	3.00	1.50	.90
(3)	Max Alvis	3.00	1.50	.90
(4)	Ernie Banks	25.00	12.50	7.50
(5)	S. Barber	3.00	1.50	.90
(6)	K. Boyer	5.00	2.50	1.50
(7)	J. Callison	4.00	2.00	1.25
(8)	Norm Cash	5.00	2.50	1.50
(9)	W. Causey	3.00	1.50	.90
(10)	O. Cepeda	7.00	3.50	2.00
(11)	R. Colavito	7.00	3.50	2.00
(12)	Ray Culp	3.00	1.50	.90
(13)	Davalillo	3.00	1.50	.90
(14)	Drabowsky	3.00	1.50	.90
(15)	Ellsworth	3.00	1.50	.90
(16)	Curt Flood	5.00	2.50	1.50
(17)	B. Freehan	4.00	2.00	1.25
(18)	J. Fregosi	4.00	2.00	1.25
(19)	Bob Friend	4.00	2.00	1.25
(20)	D. Groat	4.00	2.00	1.25
(21)	Woody Held	3.00	1.50	.90
(22)	F. Howard	5.00	2.50	1.50
(23)	Al Jackson	3.00	1.50	.90
(24)	L. Jackson	3.00	1.50	.90
(25)	K. Johnson	3.00	1.50	.90
(26)	Al Kaline	25.00	12.50	7.50
(27a)	Killebrew (green background)	25.00	12.50	7.50
(27b)	Killebrew (red background)	25.00	12.50	7.50
(28)	S. Koufax	35.00	17.50	10.50
(29)	Lock	3.00	1.50	.90
(30)	F. Malzone	3.00	1.50	.90
(31)	M. Mantle	100.00	45.00	27.00
(32)	E. Mathews	15.00	7.50	4.50
(33a)	Willie Mays (yellow background encompasses entire head)	40.00	20.00	12.50
(33b)	Willie Mays (yellow background covers one-half of head)	40.00	20.00	12.50
(34)	Mazeroski	5.00	2.50	1.50
(35)	K. McBride	3.00	1.50	.90
(36)	Monbouquette	3.00	1.50	.90
(37)	Nicholson	3.00	1.50	.90
(38)	C. Osteen	4.00	2.00	1.25
(39)	M. Pappas	4.00	2.00	1.25
(40)	C. Pascual	4.00	2.00	1.25
(41)	A. Pearson	3.00	1.50	.90
(42)	Perranoski	3.00	1.50	.90
(43)	G. Peters	3.00	1.50	.90
(44)	B. Powell	5.00	2.50	1.50
(45)	F. Robinson	20.00	10.00	6.00
(46)	J. Romano	3.00	1.50	.90
(47)	N. Siebern	3.00	1.50	.90
(48)	W. Spahn	15.00	7.50	4.50
(49)	D. Stuart	4.00	2.00	1.25
(50)	Lee Thomas	3.00	1.50	.90
(51)	Joe Torre	5.00	2.50	1.50
(52)	Pete Ward	3.00	1.50	.90
(53)	C. Willey	3.00	1.50	.90
(54)	B. Williams	25.00	12.50	7.50
(55)	Yastrzemski	50.00	25.00	15.00
(56)	Baltimore Orioles Logo	3.00	1.50	.90
(57)	Boston Red Sox Logo	3.00	1.50	.90
(58)	Chicago Cubs Logo	3.00	1.50	.90
(59)	Chicago White Sox Logo	3.00	1.50	.90
(60)	Cincinnati Reds Logo	3.00	1.50	.90
(61)	Cleveland Indians Logo	3.00	1.50	.90
(62)	Detroit Tigers Logo	2.50	1.25	.70
(63)	Houston Colts Logo	3.00	1.50	.90
(64)	Kansas City Athletics Logo	3.00	1.50	.90
(65)	Los Angeles Angels Logo	3.00	1.50	.90
(66)	Los Angeles Dodgers Logo	2.50	1.25	.70
(67)	Milwaukee Braves Logo	3.00	1.50	.90
(68)	Minnesota Twins Logo	3.00	1.50	.90
(69)	New York Mets Logo	2.50	1.25	.70
(70)	New York Yankees Logo	4.00	2.00	1.25
(71)	Philadelphia Phillies Logo	3.00	1.50	.90
(72)	Pittsburgh Pirates Logo	3.00	1.50	.90
(73)	St. Louis Cardinals Logo	2.50	1.25	.70
(74)	San Francisco Giants Logo	3.00	1.50	.90
(75)	Washington Senators Logo	3.00	1.50	.90

1964 Topps Stand-Ups

These 2-1/2" by 3-1/2" cards were the first since the All-Star sets of 1951 to be die-cut. This made it possible for a folded card to stand on display. The 77-cards in the set feature color photographs of the player with yellow and green backgrounds. Directions for folding are on the yellow top background, and when folded only the green background remains. Of the 77 cards, 55 were double-printed while 22 were single-printed, making them twice as scarce. Included in the single-printed group are Warren Spahn, Don Drysdale, Juan Marichal, Willie McCovey and Carl Yastrzemski.

		NR MT	EX	VG
Complete Set:		2400.00	1200.00	720.00
Common Player:		3.50	1.75	1.00
(1)	Hank Aaron	110.00	55.00	33.00
(2)	Hank Aguirre	3.50	1.75	1.00
(3)	George Altman	3.50	1.75	1.00
(4)	Max Alvis	3.50	1.75	1.00
(5)	Bob Aspromonte	3.50	1.75	1.00
(6)	Jack Baldschun	20.00	10.00	6.00
(7)	Ernie Banks	40.00	20.00	12.00
(8)	Steve Barber	3.50	1.75	1.00
(9)	Earl Battey	3.50	1.75	1.00
(10)	Ken Boyer	6.00	3.00	1.75
(11)	Ernie Broglio	3.50	1.75	1.00
(12)	Johnny Callison	4.00	2.00	1.25
(13)	Norm Cash	25.00	12.50	7.50
(14)	Wayne Causey	3.50	1.75	1.00
(15)	Orlando Cepeda	8.00	4.00	2.50
(16)	Ed Charles	3.50	1.75	1.00
(17)	Bob Clemente	55.00	27.00	16.50
(18)	Donn Clendenon	20.00	10.00	6.00

		NR MT	EX	VG
(19)	Rocky Colavito	6.00	3.00	1.75
(20)	Ray Culp	20.00	10.00	6.00
(21)	Tommy Davis	6.00	3.00	1.75
(22)	Don Drysdale	125.00	62.00	37.00
(23)	Dick Ellsworth	3.50	1.75	1.00
(24)	Dick Farrell	3.50	1.75	1.00
(25)	Jim Fregosi	4.00	2.00	1.25
(26)	Bob Friend	4.00	2.00	1.25
(27)	Jim Gentile	3.50	1.75	1.00
(28)	Jesse Gonder	20.00	10.00	6.00
(29)	Tony Gonzalez	20.00	10.00	6.00
(30)	Dick Groat	6.00	3.00	1.75
(31)	Woody Held	3.50	1.75	1.00
(32)	Chuck Hinton	3.50	1.75	1.00
(33)	Elston Howard	7.00	3.50	2.00
(34)	Frank Howard	25.00	12.50	7.50
(35)	Ron Hunt	3.50	1.75	1.00
(36)	Al Jackson	3.50	1.75	1.00
(37)	Ken Johnson	3.50	1.75	1.00
(38)	Al Kaline	40.00	20.00	12.00
(39)	Harmon Killebrew	40.00	20.00	12.00
(40)	Sandy Koufax	40.00	20.00	12.00
(41)	Don Lock	20.00	10.00	6.00
(42)	Jerry Lumpe	20.00	10.00	6.00
(43)	Jim Maloney	3.50	1.75	1.00
(44)	Frank Malzone	3.50	1.75	1.00
(45)	Mickey Mantle	400.00	200.00	120.00
(46)	Juan Marichal	125.00	62.00	37.00
(47)	Ed Mathews	125.00	62.00	37.00
(48)	Willie Mays	110.00	55.00	33.00
(49)	Bill Mazeroski	6.00	3.00	1.75
(50)	Ken McBride	3.50	1.75	1.00
(51)	Willie McCovey	125.00	62.00	37.00
(52)	Claude Osteen	3.50	1.75	1.00
(53)	Jim O'Toole	3.50	1.75	1.00
(54)	Camilo Pascual	3.50	1.75	1.00
(55)	Albie Pearson	20.00	10.00	6.00
(56)	Gary Peters	3.50	1.75	1.00
(57)	Vada Pinson	6.00	3.00	1.75
(58)	Juan Pizarro	3.50	1.75	1.00
(59)	Boog Powell	6.00	3.00	1.75
(60)	Bobby Richardson	7.00	3.50	2.00
(61)	Brooks Robinson	50.00	25.00	15.00
(62)	Floyd Robinson	3.50	1.75	1.00
(63)	Frank Robinson	40.00	20.00	12.00
(64)	Ed Roebuck	20.00	10.00	6.00
(65)	Rich Rollins	3.50	1.75	1.00
(66)	Johnny Romano	3.50	1.75	1.00
(67)	Ron Santo	25.00	12.50	7.50
(68)	Norm Siebern	3.50	1.75	1.00
(69)	Warren Spahn	125.00	62.00	37.00
(70)	Dick Stuart	20.00	10.00	6.00
(71)	Lee Thomas	3.50	1.75	1.00
(72)	Joe Torre	7.00	3.50	2.00
(73)	Pete Ward	3.50	1.75	1.00
(74)	Bill White	20.00	10.00	6.00
(75)	Billy Williams	125.00	62.00	37.00
(76)	Hal Woodeshick	20.00	10.00	6.00
(77)	Carl Yastrzemski	400.00	200.00	120.00

1965 Topps

The 1965 Topps set features a large color photograph of the player which was surrounded by a colored, round-cornered frame and a white border. The bottom of the 2-1/2" by 3-1/2" cards include a pennant with a color team logo and name over the left side of a rectangle which features the player's name and position. Backs feature statistics and, if space allowed, a cartoon and headline about the player. There are no multi-player cards in the 1965 set other than the usual team cards and World Series highlights. Rookie cards include team, as well as league groupings from two to four players per card. Also present in the 598-card set are statistical leaders.

		NR MT	EX	VG
Complete Set:		3600.00	1800.00	1150.
Common Player: 1-198		2.00	1.00	.60
Common Player: 199-446		2.00	1.00	.60
Common Player: 447-522		2.00	1.00	.60
Common Player: 523-598		5.00	2.50	1.50
1	A.L. Batting Leaders (Elston Howard, Tony Oliva, Brooks Robinson)	10.00	4.00	2.50
2	N.L. Batting Leaders (Hank Aaron, Rico Carty, Bob Clemente)	5.00	2.50	1.50
3	A.L. Home Run Leaders (Harmon Killebrew, Mickey Mantle, Boog Powell)	20.00	10.00	6.00
4	N.L. Home Run Leaders (Johnny Callison, Orlando Cepeda, Jim Hart, Willie Mays, Billy Williams)	6.00	3.00	1.75
5	A.L. RBI Leaders (Harmon Killebrew, Mickey Mantle, Brooks Robinson, Dick Stuart)	20.00	10.00	6.00
6	N.L. RBI Leaders (Ken Boyer, Willie Mays, Ron Santo)	6.00	3.00	1.75
7	A.L. ERA Leaders (Dean Chance, Joel Horlen)	5.00	2.50	1.50
8	N.L. ERA Leaders (Don Drysdale, Sandy Koufax)	6.00	3.00	1.75
9	A.L. Pitching Leaders (Wally Bunker, Dean Chance, Gary Peters, Juan Pizarro, Dave Wickersham)	5.00	2.50	1.50
10	N.L. Pitching Leaders (Larry Jackson, Juan Marichal, Ray Sadecki)	3.50	1.75	1.00
11	A.L. Strikeout Leaders (Dean Chance, Al Downing, Camilo Pascual)	5.00	2.50	1.50
12	N.L. Strikeout Leaders (Don Drysdale, Bob Gibson, Bob Veale)	3.50	1.75	1.00
13	Pedro Ramos	2.00	1.00	.60
14	Len Gabrielson	2.00	1.00	.60
15	Robin Roberts	10.00	5.00	3.00
16	Astros Rookies (*Sonny Jackson, Joe Morgan*)	175.00	87.00	52.00
17	Johnny Romano	2.00	1.00	.60
18	Bill McCool	2.00	1.00	.60
19	Gates Brown	2.00	1.00	.60
20	Jim Bunning	5.00	2.50	1.50
21	Don Blasingame	2.00	1.00	.60
22	Charlie Smith	2.00	1.00	.60
23	Bob Tiefenauer	2.00	1.00	.60
24	Twins Team	5.00	2.50	1.50
25	Al McBean	2.00	1.00	.60
26	Bobby Knoop	2.00	1.00	.60
27	Dick Bertell	2.00	1.00	.60
28	Barney Schultz	2.00	1.00	.60
29	Felix Mantilla	2.00	1.00	.60
30	Jim Bouton	5.00	2.50	1.50
31	Mike White	2.00	1.00	.60
32	Herman Franks	2.00	1.00	.60
33	Jackie Brandt	2.00	1.00	.60
34	Cal Koonce	2.00	1.00	.60
35	Ed Charles	2.00	1.00	.60
36	Bobby Wine	2.00	1.00	.60
37	Fred Gladding	2.00	1.00	.60
38	Jim King	2.00	1.00	.60
39	Gerry Arrigo	2.00	1.00	.60
40	Frank Howard	5.00	2.50	1.50
41	White Sox Rookies (Bruce Howard, Marv Staehle)	2.00	1.00	.60
42	Earl Wilson	2.00	1.00	.60
43	Mike Shannon	2.00	1.00	.60
44	Wade Blasingame	2.00	1.00	.60
45	Roy McMillan	2.00	1.00	.60
46	Bob Lee	2.00	1.00	.60
47	Tommy Harper	2.00	1.00	.60
48	Claude Raymond	2.00	1.00	.60
49	Orioles Rookies (*Curt Blefary, John Miller*)	2.00	1.00	.60
50	Juan Marichal	10.00	5.00	3.00
51	Billy Bryan	2.00	1.00	.60
52	Ed Roebuck	2.00	1.00	.60
53	Dick McAuliffe	2.00	1.00	.60
54	Joe Gibbon	2.00	1.00	.60
55	Tony Conigliaro	7.00	3.50	2.00
56	Ron Kline	2.00	1.00	.60

		NR MT	EX	VG
57	Cardinals Team	2.25	1.25	.70
58	Fred Talbot	2.00	1.00	.60
59	Nate Oliver	2.00	1.00	.60
60	Jim O'Toole	2.00	1.00	.60
61	Chris Cannizzaro	2.00	1.00	.60
62	Jim Katt (Kaat)	5.00	2.50	1.50
63	Ty Cline	2.00	1.00	.60
64	Lou Burdette	2.00	1.00	.60
65	Tony Kubek	6.00	3.00	1.75
66	Bill Rigney	2.00	1.00	.60
67	Harvey Haddix	2.00	1.00	.60
68	Del Crandall	2.00	1.00	.60
69	Bill Virdon	2.00	1.00	.60
70	Bill Skowron	2.00	1.00	.60
71	John O'Donoghue	2.00	1.00	.60
72	Tony Gonzalez	2.00	1.00	.60
73	Dennis Ribant	2.00	1.00	.60
74	Red Sox Rookies (*Rico Petrocelli*, Jerry Stephenson)	5.00	2.50	1.50
75	Deron Johnson	2.00	1.00	.60
76	Sam McDowell	2.00	1.00	.60
77	Doug Camilli	2.00	1.00	.60
78	Dal Maxvill	2.00	1.00	.60
79a	Checklist 1-88 (61 is C. Cannizzaro)	2.00	1.00	.60
79b	Checklist 1-88 (61 is Cannizzaro)	5.00	2.50	1.50
80	Turk Farrell	2.00	1.00	.60
81	Don Buford	2.00	1.00	.60
82	Braves Rookies (*Santos Alomar*, John Braun)	2.00	1.00	.60
83	George Thomas	2.00	1.00	.60
84	Ron Herbel	2.00	1.00	.60
85	Willie Smith	2.00	1.00	.60
86	Les Narum	2.00	1.00	.60
87	Nelson Mathews	2.00	1.00	.60
88	Jack Lamabe	2.00	1.00	.60
89	Mike Hershberger	2.00	1.00	.60
90	Rich Rollins	2.00	1.00	.60
91	Cubs Team	2.25	1.25	.70
92	Dick Howser	2.00	1.00	.60
93	Jack Fisher	2.00	1.00	.60
94	Charlie Lau	2.00	1.00	.60
95	Bill Mazeroski	5.00	2.50	1.50
96	Sonny Siebert	2.00	1.00	.60
97	Pedro Gonzalez	2.00	1.00	.60
98	Bob Miller	2.00	1.00	.60
99	Gil Hodges	6.00	3.00	1.75
100	Ken Boyer	5.00	2.50	1.50
101	Fred Newman	2.00	1.00	.60
102	Steve Boros	2.00	1.00	.60
103	Harvey Kuenn	2.00	1.00	.60
104	Checklist 89-176	2.00	1.00	.60
105	Chico Salmon	2.00	1.00	.60
106	Gene Oliver	2.00	1.00	.60
107	Phillies Rookies (*Pat Corrales*, Costen Shockley)	2.00	1.00	.60
108	Don Mincher	2.00	1.00	.60
109	Walt Bond	2.00	1.00	.60
110	Ron Santo	2.25	1.25	.70
111	Lee Thomas	2.00	1.00	.60
112	Derrell Griffith	2.00	1.00	.60
113	Steve Barber	2.00	1.00	.60
114	Jim Hickman	2.00	1.00	.60
115	Bobby Richardson	6.00	3.00	1.75
116	Cardinals Rookies (Dave Dowling, *Bob Tolan*)	2.00	1.00	.60
117	Wes Stock	2.00	1.00	.60
118	*Hal Lanier*	2.25	1.25	.70
119	John Kennedy	2.00	1.00	.60
120	Frank Robinson	30.00	15.00	9.00
121	Gene Alley	2.00	1.00	.60
122	Bill Pleis	2.00	1.00	.60
123	Frank Thomas	2.00	1.00	.60
124	Tom Satriano	2.00	1.00	.60
125	Juan Pizarro	2.00	1.00	.60
126	Dodgers Team	5.00	2.50	1.50
127	Frank Lary	2.00	1.00	.60
128	Vic Davalillo	2.00	1.00	.60
129	Bennie Daniels	2.00	1.00	.60
130	Al Kaline	25.00	12.50	7.50
131	Johnny Keane	2.25	1.25	.70
132	World Series Game 1 (Cards Take Opener)	5.00	2.50	1.50
133	World Series Game 2 (Stottlemyre Wins)	2.00	1.00	.60
134	World Series Game 3 (Mantle's Clutch HR)	25.00	12.50	7.50
135	World Series Game 4 (Boyer's Grand Slam)	5.00	2.50	1.50
136	World Series Game 5 (10th Inning Triumph)	5.00	2.50	1.50

		NR MT	EX	VG
137	World Series Game 6 (Bouton Wins Again)	2.00	1.00	.60
138	World Series Game 7 (Gibson Wins Finale)	3.50	1.75	1.00
139	World Series Summary (The Cards Celebrate)	5.00	2.50	1.50
140	Dean Chance	2.00	1.00	.60
141	Charlie James	2.00	1.00	.60
142	Bill Monbouquette	2.00	1.00	.60
143	Pirates Rookies (John Gelnar, Jerry May)	2.00	1.00	.60
144	Ed Kranepool	2.00	1.00	.60
145	*Luis Tiant*	15.00	7.50	4.50
146	Ron Hansen	2.00	1.00	.60
147	Dennis Bennett	2.00	1.00	.60
148	Willie Kirkland	2.00	1.00	.60
149	Wayne Schurr	2.00	1.00	.60
150	Brooks Robinson	25.00	12.50	7.50
151	Athletics Team	2.25	1.25	.70
152	Phil Ortega	2.00	1.00	.60
153	Norm Cash	2.00	1.00	.60
154	Bob Humphreys	2.00	1.00	.60
155	Roger Maris	60.00	30.00	18.00
156	Bob Sadowski	2.00	1.00	.60
157	Zoilo Versalles	2.25	1.25	.70
158	Dick Sisler	2.00	1.00	.60
159	Jim Duffalo	2.00	1.00	.60
160	Bob Clemente	85.00	42.00	26.00
161	Frank Baumann	2.00	1.00	.60
162	Russ Nixon	2.00	1.00	.60
163	John Briggs	2.00	1.00	.60
164	Al Spangler	2.00	1.00	.60
165	Dick Ellsworth	2.00	1.00	.60
166	Indians Rookies (*Tommie Agee*, George Culver)	2.25	1.25	.70
167	Bill Wakefield	2.00	1.00	.60
168	Dick Green	2.00	1.00	.60
169	Dave Vineyard	2.00	1.00	.60
170	Hank Aaron	95.00	47.50	28.50
171	Jim Roland	2.00	1.00	.60
172	Jim Piersall	2.25	1.25	.70
173	Tigers Team	3.25	1.75	1.00
174	Joe Jay	2.00	1.00	.60
175	Bob Aspromonte	2.00	1.00	.60
176	Willie McCovey	20.00	10.00	6.00
177	Pete Mikkelsen	2.00	1.00	.60
178	Dalton Jones	2.00	1.00	.60
179	Hal Woodeshick	2.00	1.00	.60
180	Bob Allison	2.00	1.00	.60
181	Senators Rookies (Don Loun, Joe McCabe)	2.00	1.00	.60
182	Mike de la Hoz	2.00	1.00	.60
183	Dave Nicholson	2.00	1.00	.60
184	John Boozer	2.00	1.00	.60
185	Max Alvis	2.00	1.00	.60
186	Billy Cowan	2.00	1.00	.60
187	Casey Stengel	18.00	9.00	5.00
188	Sam Bowens	2.00	1.00	.60
189	Checklist 177-264	2.00	1.00	.60
190	Bill White	2.00	1.00	.60
191	Phil Regan	2.00	1.00	.60
192	Jim Coker	2.00	1.00	.60
193	Gaylord Perry	20.00	10.00	6.00
194	Angels Rookies (Bill Kelso, *Rick Reichardt*)	2.00	1.00	.60
195	Bob Veale	2.00	1.00	.60
196	Ron Fairly	2.00	1.00	.60
197	Diego Segui	2.00	1.00	.60
198	Smoky Burgess	2.00	1.00	.60
199	Bob Heffner	2.00	1.00	.60
200	Joe Torre	5.00	2.50	1.50
201	Twins Rookies (*Cesar Tovar*, Sandy Valdespino)	2.00	1.00	.60
202	Leo Burke	2.00	1.00	.60
203	Dallas Green	2.00	1.00	.60
204	Russ Snyder	2.00	1.00	.60
205	Warren Spahn	20.00	10.00	6.00
206	Willie Horton	2.00	1.00	.60
207	Pete Rose	150.00	75.00	45.00
208	Tommy John	10.00	5.00	3.00
209	Pirates Team	5.00	2.50	1.50
210	Jim Fregosi	2.25	1.25	.70
211	Steve Ridzik	2.00	1.00	.60
212	Ron Brand	2.00	1.00	.60
213	Jim Davenport	2.00	1.00	.60
214	Bob Purkey	2.00	1.00	.60
215	Pete Ward	2.00	1.00	.60
216	Al Worthington	2.00	1.00	.60
217	Walt Alston	3.50	1.75	1.00
218	Dick Schofield	2.00	1.00	.60
219	Bob Meyer	2.00	1.00	.60

#	Player	NR MT	EX	VG
220	Billy Williams	10.00	5.00	3.00
221	John Tsitouris	2.00	1.00	.60
222	Bob Tillman	2.00	1.00	.60
223	Dan Osinski	2.00	1.00	.60
224	Bob Chance	2.00	1.00	.60
225	Bo Belinsky	2.00	1.00	.60
226	Yankees Rookies (Jake Gibbs, Elvio Jimenez)	2.25	1.25	.70
227	Bobby Klaus	2.00	1.00	.60
228	Jack Sanford	2.00	1.00	.60
229	Lou Clinton	2.00	1.00	.60
230	Ray Sadecki	2.00	1.00	.60
231	Jerry Adair	2.00	1.00	.60
232	Steve Blass	2.00	1.00	.60
233	Don Zimmer	2.25	1.25	.70
234	White Sox Team	5.00	2.50	1.50
235	Chuck Hinton	2.00	1.00	.60
236	Dennis McLain	25.00	12.50	7.50
237	Bernie Allen	2.00	1.00	.60
238	Joe Moeller	2.00	1.00	.60
239	Doc Edwards	2.00	1.00	.60
240	Bob Bruce	2.00	1.00	.60
241	Mack Jones	2.00	1.00	.60
242	George Brunet	2.00	1.00	.60
243	Reds Rookies (Ted Davidson, Tommy Helms)	2.00	1.00	.60
244	Lindy McDaniel	2.00	1.00	.60
245	Joe Pepitone	2.00	1.00	.60
246	Tom Butters	2.00	1.00	.60
247	Wally Moon	2.00	1.00	.60
248	Gus Triandos	2.00	1.00	.60
249	Dave McNally	2.00	1.00	.60
250	Willie Mays	110.00	55.00	33.00
251	Billy Herman	2.00	1.00	.60
252	Pete Richert	2.00	1.00	.60
253	Danny Cater	2.00	1.00	.60
254	Roland Sheldon	2.25	1.25	.70
255	Camilo Pascual	2.00	1.00	.60
256	Tito Francona	2.00	1.00	.60
257	Jim Wynn	2.00	1.00	.60
258	Larry Bearnarth	2.00	1.00	.60
259	Tigers Rookies (Jim Northrup, Ray Oyler)	2.00	1.00	.60
260	Don Drysdale	18.00	9.00	5.50
261	Duke Carmel	2.25	1.25	.70
262	Bud Daley	2.00	1.00	.60
263	Marty Keough	2.00	1.00	.60
264	Bob Buhl	2.00	1.00	.60
265	Jim Pagliaroni	2.00	1.00	.60
266	Bert Campaneris	5.00	2.50	1.50
267	Senators Team	5.00	2.50	1.50
268	Ken McBride	2.00	1.00	.60
269	Frank Bolling	2.00	1.00	.60
270	Milt Pappas	2.00	1.00	.60
271	Don Wert	2.00	1.00	.60
272	Chuck Schilling	2.00	1.00	.60
273	Checklist 265-352	3.25	1.75	1.00
274	Lum Harris	2.00	1.00	.60
275	Dick Groat	3.25	1.75	1.00
276	Hoyt Wilhelm	8.00	4.00	2.50
277	Johnny Lewis	2.00	1.00	.60
278	Ken Retzer	2.00	1.00	.60
279	Dick Tracewski	2.00	1.00	.60
280	Dick Stuart	2.00	1.00	.60
281	Bill Stafford	2.25	1.25	.70
282	Giants Rookies (Dick Estelle, Masanori Murakami)	2.00	1.00	.60
283	Fred Whitfield	2.00	1.00	.60
284	Nick Willhite	2.00	1.00	.60
285	Ron Hunt	2.00	1.00	.60
286	Athletics Rookies (Jim Dickson, Aurelio Monteagudo)	2.00	1.00	.60
287	Gary Kolb	2.00	1.00	.60
288	Jack Hamilton	2.00	1.00	.60
289	Gordy Coleman	2.00	1.00	.60
290	Wally Bunker	2.00	1.00	.60
291	Jerry Lynch	2.00	1.00	.60
292	Larry Yellen	2.00	1.00	.60
293	Angels Team	5.00	2.50	1.50
294	Tim McCarver	2.75	1.50	.80
295	Dick Radatz	2.00	1.00	.60
296	Tony Taylor	2.00	1.00	.60
297	Dave DeBusschere	3.50	1.75	1.00
298	Jim Stewart	2.00	1.00	.60
299	Jerry Zimmerman	2.00	1.00	.60
300	Sandy Koufax	130.00	65.00	37.00
301	Birdie Tebbetts	2.00	1.00	.60
302	Al Stanek	2.00	1.00	.60
303	Johnny Orsino	2.00	1.00	.60
304	Dave Stenhouse	2.00	1.00	.60
305	Rico Carty	2.25	1.25	.70
306	Bubba Phillips	2.00	1.00	.60
307	Barry Latman	2.00	1.00	.60
308	Mets Rookies (Cleon Jones, Tom Parsons)	2.00	1.00	.60
309	Steve Hamilton	2.25	1.25	.70
310	Johnny Callison	2.00	1.00	.60
311	Orlando Pena	2.00	1.00	.60
312	Joe Nuxhall	2.00	1.00	.60
313	Jimmie Schaffer	2.00	1.00	.60
314	Sterling Slaughter	2.00	1.00	.60
315	Frank Malzone	2.00	1.00	.60
316	Reds Team	2.75	1.50	.80
317	Don McMahon	2.00	1.00	.60
318	Matty Alou	2.00	1.00	.60
319	Ken McMullen	2.00	1.00	.60
320	Bob Gibson	30.00	15.00	9.00
321	Rusty Staub	5.00	2.50	1.50
322	Rick Wise	2.00	1.00	.60
323	Hank Bauer	2.00	1.00	.60
324	Bobby Locke	2.00	1.00	.60
325	Donn Clendenon	2.00	1.00	.60
326	Dwight Siebler	2.00	1.00	.60
327	Denis Menke	2.00	1.00	.60
328	Eddie Fisher	2.00	1.00	.60
329	Hawk Taylor	2.00	1.00	.60
330	Whitey Ford	20.00	10.00	6.00
331	Dodgers Rookies (Al Ferrara, John Purdin)	2.00	1.00	.60
332	Ted Abernathy	2.00	1.00	.60
333	Tommie Reynolds	2.00	1.00	.60
334	Vic Roznovsky	2.00	1.00	.60
335	Mickey Lolich	3.50	1.75	1.00
336	Woody Held	2.00	1.00	.60
337	Mike Cuellar	2.25	1.25	.70
338	Phillies Team	5.00	2.50	1.50
339	Ryne Duren	2.00	1.00	.60
340	Tony Oliva	3.50	1.75	1.00
341	Bobby Bolin	2.00	1.00	.60
342	Bob Rodgers	2.00	1.00	.60
343	Mike McCormick	2.00	1.00	.60
344	Wes Parker	2.00	1.00	.60
345	Floyd Robinson	2.00	1.00	.60
346	Bobby Bragan	2.00	1.00	.60
347	Roy Face	2.25	1.25	.70
348	George Banks	2.00	1.00	.60
349	Larry Miller	2.00	1.00	.60
350	Mickey Mantle	450.00	225.00	135.00
351	Jim Perry	2.00	1.00	.60
352	Alex Johnson	2.00	1.00	.60
353	Jerry Lumpe	2.00	1.00	.60
354	Cubs Rookies (Billy Ott, Jack Warner)	2.00	1.00	.60
355	Vada Pinson	5.00	2.50	1.50
356	Bill Spanswick	2.00	1.00	.60
357	Carl Warwick	2.00	1.00	.60
358	Albie Pearson	2.00	1.00	.60
359	Ken Johnson	2.00	1.00	.60
360	Orlando Cepeda	6.00	3.00	1.75
361	Checklist 353-429	3.25	1.75	1.00
362	Don Schwall	2.00	1.00	.60
363	Bob Johnson	2.00	1.00	.60
364	Galen Cisco	2.00	1.00	.60
365	Jim Gentile	2.00	1.00	.60
366	Dan Schneider	2.00	1.00	.60
367	Leon Wagner	2.00	1.00	.60
368	White Sox Rookies (Ken Berry, Joel Gibson)	2.00	1.00	.60
369	Phil Linz	2.25	1.25	.70
370	Tommy Davis	2.25	1.25	.70
371	Frank Kreutzer	2.00	1.00	.60
372	Clay Dalrymple	2.00	1.00	.60
373	Curt Simmons	2.00	1.00	.60
374	Angels Rookies (Jose Cardenal, Dick Simpson)	2.00	1.00	.60
375	Dave Wickersham	2.00	1.00	.60
376	Jim Landis	2.00	1.00	.60
377	Willie Stargell	25.00	12.50	7.50
378	Chuck Estrada	2.00	1.00	.60
379	Giants Team	5.00	2.50	1.50
380	Rocky Colavito	2.00	1.00	.60
381	Al Jackson	2.00	1.00	.60
382	J.C. Martin	2.00	1.00	.60
383	Felipe Alou	2.00	1.00	.60
384	Johnny Klippstein	2.00	1.00	.60
385	Carl Yastrzemski	70.00	35.00	21.00
386	Cubs Rookies (Paul Jaeckel, Fred Norman)	2.00	1.00	.60
387	Johnny Podres	2.00	1.00	.60
388	John Blanchard	2.25	1.25	.70
389	Don Larsen	2.00	1.00	.60
390	Bill Freehan	2.00	1.00	.60

		NR MT	EX	VG
391	Mel McGaha	2.00	1.00	.60
392	Bob Friend	2.25	1.25	.70
393	Ed Kirkpatrick	2.00	1.00	.60
394	Jim Hannan	2.00	1.00	.60
395	Jim Hart	2.00	1.00	.60
396	Frank Bertaina	2.00	1.00	.60
397	Jerry Buchek	2.00	1.00	.60
398	Reds Rookies (Dan Neville, *Art Shamsky*)			
		2.00	1.00	.60
399	Ray Herbert	2.00	1.00	.60
400	Harmon Killebrew	25.00	12.50	7.50
401	Carl Willey	2.00	1.00	.60
402	Joe Amalfitano	2.00	1.00	.60
403	Red Sox Team	2.00	1.00	.60
404	Stan Williams	2.00	1.00	.60
405	John Roseboro	2.00	1.00	.60
406	Ralph Terry	2.00	1.00	.60
407	Lee Maye	2.00	1.00	.60
408	Larry Sherry	2.00	1.00	.60
409	Astros Rookies (Jim Beauchamp, *Larry Dierker*)			
		2.00	1.00	.60
410	Luis Aparicio	9.00	4.50	2.75
411	Roger Craig	2.00	1.00	.60
412	Bob Bailey	2.00	1.00	.60
413	Hal Reniff	2.25	1.25	.70
414	Al Lopez	2.00	1.00	.60
415	Curt Flood	2.25	1.25	.70
416	Jim Brewer	2.00	1.00	.60
417	Ed Brinkman	2.00	1.00	.60
418	Johnny Edwards	2.00	1.00	.60
419	Ruben Amaro	2.00	1.00	.60
420	Larry Jackson	2.00	1.00	.60
421	Twins Rookies (Gary Dotter, Jay Ward)			
		2.00	1.00	.60
422	Aubrey Gatewood	2.00	1.00	.60
423	Jesse Gonder	2.00	1.00	.60
424	Gary Bell	2.00	1.00	.60
425	Wayne Causey	2.00	1.00	.60
426	Braves Team	5.00	2.50	1.50
427	Bob Saverine	2.00	1.00	.60
428	Bob Shaw	2.00	1.00	.60
429	Don Demeter	2.00	1.00	.60
430	Gary Peters	2.00	1.00	.60
431	Cardinals Rookies (*Nelson Briles*, Wayne Spiezio)			
		2.00	1.00	.60
432	Jim Grant	2.00	1.00	.60
433	John Bateman	2.00	1.00	.60
434	Dave Morehead	2.00	1.00	.60
435	Willie Davis	2.25	1.25	.70
436	Don Elston	2.00	1.00	.60
437	Chico Cardenas	2.00	1.00	.60
438	Harry Walker	2.00	1.00	.60
439	Moe Drabowsky	2.00	1.00	.60
440	Tom Tresh	5.00	2.50	1.50
441	Denver Lemaster	2.00	1.00	.60
442	Vic Power	2.00	1.00	.60
443	Checklist 430-506	3.25	1.75	1.00
444	Bob Hendley	2.00	1.00	.60
445	Don Lock	2.00	1.00	.60
446	Art Mahaffey	2.00	1.00	.60
447	Julian Javier	2.00	1.00	.60
448	Lee Stange	2.00	1.00	.60
449	Mets Rookies (Jerry Hinsley, Gary Kroll)			
		2.25	1.25	.70
450	Elston Howard	5.00	2.50	1.50
451	Jim Owens	2.00	1.00	.60
452	Gary Geiger	2.00	1.00	.60
453	Dodgers Rookies (*Willie Crawford*, John Werhas)			
		2.25	1.25	.70
454	Ed Rakow	2.00	1.00	.60
455	Norm Siebern	2.25	1.25	.70
456	Bill Henry	2.00	1.00	.60
457	Bob Kennedy	2.00	1.00	.60
458	John Buzhardt	2.00	1.00	.60
459	Frank Kostro	2.00	1.00	.60
460	Richie Allen	10.00	5.00	3.00
461	Braves Rookies (*Clay Carroll*, Phil Niekro)			
		60.00	30.00	18.00
462	Lew Krausse (photo actually Pete Lovrich)			
		2.00	1.00	.60
463	Manny Mota	2.25	1.25	.70
464	Ron Piche	2.00	1.00	.60
465	Tom Haller	2.00	1.00	.60
466	Senators Rookies (Pete Craig, Dick Nen)			
		2.00	1.00	.60
467	Ray Washburn	2.00	1.00	.60
468	Larry Brown	2.00	1.00	.60
469	Don Nottebart	2.00	1.00	.60
470	Yogi Berra	50.00	30.00	15.00
471	Billy Hoeft	2.00	1.00	.60
472	Don Pavletich	2.00	1.00	.60

		NR MT	EX	VG
473	Orioles Rookies (*Paul Blair, Dave Johnson*)			
		15.00	7.50	4.50
474	Cookie Rojas	2.00	1.00	.60
475	Clete Boyer	2.00	1.00	.60
476	Billy O'Dell	2.00	1.00	.60
477	Cardinals Rookies (Fritz Ackley, *Steve Carlton*)			
		600.00	300.00	175.00
478	Wilbur Wood	2.00	1.00	.60
479	Ken Harrelson	5.00	2.50	1.50
480	Joel Horlen	2.00	1.00	.60
481	Indians Team	2.00	1.00	.60
482	Bob Priddy	2.00	1.00	.60
483	George Smith	2.00	1.00	.60
484	Ron Perranoski	2.25	1.25	.70
485	Nellie Fox	6.00	3.00	1.75
486	Angels Rookies (Tom Egan, Pat Rogan)			
		2.00	1.00	.60
487	Woody Woodward	2.25	1.25	.70
488	Ted Wills	2.00	1.00	.60
489	Gene Mauch	2.25	1.25	.70
490	Earl Battey	2.25	1.25	.70
491	Tracy Stallard	2.00	1.00	.60
492	Gene Freese	2.00	1.00	.60
493	Tigers Rookies (Bruce Brubaker, Bill Roman)			
		2.00	1.00	.60
494	Jay Ritchie	2.00	1.00	.60
495	Joe Christopher	2.25	1.25	.70
496	Joe Cunningham	2.00	1.00	.60
497	Giants Rookies (*Ken Henderson*, Jack Hiatt)			
		2.25	1.25	.70
498	Gene Stephens	2.00	1.00	.60
499	Stu Miller	2.00	1.00	.60
500	Ed Mathews	30.00	15.00	9.00
501	Indians Rookies (Ralph Gagliano, Jim Rittwage)			
		2.00	1.00	.60
502	Don Cardwell	2.00	1.00	.60
503	Phil Gagliano	2.00	1.00	.60
504	Jerry Grote	2.25	1.25	.70
505	Ray Culp	2.00	1.00	.60
506	Sam Mele	2.00	1.00	.60
507	Sammy Ellis	2.00	1.00	.60
508a	Checklist 507-598 (large print on front)			
		6.00	3.00	1.75
508b	Checklist 507-598 (small print on front)			
		5.00	2.50	1.50
509	Red Sox Rookies (Bob Guindon, Gerry Vezendy)			
		2.00	1.00	.60
510	Ernie Banks	75.00	38.00	23.00
511	Ron Locke	2.25	1.25	.70
512	Cap Peterson	2.00	1.00	.60
513	Yankees Team	18.00	9.00	5.50
514	Joe Azcue	2.00	1.00	.60
515	Vern Law	2.00	1.00	.60
516	Al Weis	2.00	1.00	.60
517	Angels Rookies (Paul Schaal, Jack Warner)			
		2.00	1.00	.60
518	Ken Rowe	2.00	1.00	.60
519	Bob Uecker	40.00	20.00	12.00
520	Tony Cloninger	2.25	1.25	.70
521	Phillies Rookies (Dave Bennett, Morrie Stevens)			
		2.00	1.00	.60
522	Hank Aguirre	2.00	1.00	.60
523	Mike Brumley	5.00	2.50	1.50
524	Dave Giusti	5.00	2.50	1.50
525	Eddie Bressoud	5.00	2.50	1.50
526	Athletics Rookies (*Jim Hunter, Rene Lachemann, Skip Lockwood, Johnny Odom*)			
		150.00	75.00	45.00
527	Jeff Torborg	6.00	3.00	1.75
528	George Altman	5.00	2.50	1.50
529	Jerry Fosnow	5.00	2.50	1.50
530	Jim Maloney	6.00	3.00	1.75
531	Chuck Hiller	5.00	2.50	1.50
532	Hector Lopez	5.00	2.50	1.50
533	Mets Rookies (Jim Bethke, *Tug McGraw*, Dan Napolean, *Ron Swoboda*)			
		20.00	10.00	6.00
534	John Herrnstein	5.00	2.50	1.50
535	Jack Kralick	5.00	2.50	1.50
536	Andre Rodgers	5.00	2.50	1.50
537	Angels Rookies (Marcelino Lopez, *Rudy May*, Phil Roof)			
		5.00	2.50	1.50
538	Chuck Dressen	6.00	3.00	1.75
539	Herm Starrette	5.00	2.50	1.50
540	Lou Brock	50.00	25.00	15.00
541	White Sox Rookies (Greg Bollo, Bob Locker)			
		5.00	2.50	1.50
542	Lou Klimchock	5.00	2.50	1.50
543	Ed Connolly	5.00	2.50	1.50
544	Howie Reed	5.00	2.50	1.50
545	Jesus Alou	6.00	3.00	1.75
546	Indians Rookies (Ray Barker, Bill Davis, Mike Hedlund, Floyd Weaver)			
		5.00	2.50	1.50

		NR MT	EX	VG
547	Jake Wood	5.00	2.50	1.50
548	Dick Stigman	5.00	2.50	1.50
549	Cubs Rookies (Glenn Beckert, Roberto Pena)	5.00	2.50	1.50
550	Mel Stottlemyre	25.00	12.50	7.50
551	Mets Team	30.00	15.00	9.00
552	Julio Gotay	5.00	2.50	1.50
553	Astros Rookies (Dan Coombs, Jack McClure, Gene Ratliff)	5.00	2.50	1.50
554	Chico Ruiz	5.00	2.50	1.50
555	Jack Baldschun	5.00	2.50	1.50
556	Red Schoendienst	10.00	5.00	3.00
557	Jose Santiago	5.00	2.50	1.50
558	Tommie Sisk	5.00	2.50	1.50
559	Ed Bailey	5.00	2.50	1.50
560	Boog Powell	12.00	6.00	3.50
561	Dodgers Rookies (Dennis Daboll, Mike Kekich, Jim Lefebvre, Hector Valle)	12.00	6.00	3.50
562	Billy Moran	5.00	2.50	1.50
563	Julio Navarro	5.00	2.50	1.50
564	Mel Nelson	5.00	2.50	1.50
565	Ernie Broglio	5.00	2.50	1.50
566	Yankees Rookies (Gil Blanco, Art Lopez, Ross Moschitto)	5.00	2.50	1.50
567	Tommie Aaron	6.00	3.00	1.75
568	Ron Taylor	5.00	2.50	1.50
569	Gino Cimoli	5.00	2.50	1.50
570	Claude Osteen	6.00	3.00	1.75
571	Ossie Virgil	5.00	2.50	1.50
572	Orioles Team	25.00	12.50	7.50
573	Red Sox Rookies (Jim Lonborg, Gerry Moses, Mike Ryan, Bill Schlesinger)	10.00	5.00	3.00
574	Roy Sievers	6.00	3.00	1.75
575	Jose Pagan	5.00	2.50	1.50
576	Terry Fox	5.00	2.50	1.50
577	A.L. Rookies (Jim Buschhorn, Darold Knowles, Richie Scheinblum)	5.00	2.50	1.50
578	Camilo Carreon	5.00	2.50	1.50
579	Dick Smith	5.00	2.50	1.50
580	Jimmie Hall	5.00	2.50	1.50
581	N.L. Rookies (Kevin Collins, Tony Perez, Dave Ricketts)	175.00	87.00	52.00
582	Bob Schmidt	5.00	2.50	1.50
583	Wes Covington	5.00	2.50	1.50
584	Harry Bright	5.00	2.50	1.50
585	Hank Fischer	5.00	2.50	1.50
586	Tommy McCraw	5.00	2.50	1.50
587	Joe Sparma	5.00	2.50	1.50
588	Lenny Green	5.00	2.50	1.50
589	Giants Rookies (Frank Linzy, Bob Schroder)	5.00	2.50	1.50
590	Johnnie Wyatt	5.00	2.50	1.50
591	Bob Skinner	6.00	3.00	1.75
592	Frank Bork	5.00	2.50	1.50
593	Tigers Rookies (Jackie Moore, John Sullivan)	5.00	2.50	1.50
594	Joe Gaines	5.00	2.50	1.50
595	Don Lee	5.00	2.50	1.50
596	Don Landrum	5.00	2.50	1.50
597	Twins Rookies (Joe Nossek, Dick Reese, John Sevcik)	6.00	3.00	1.75
598	Al Downing	10.00	3.00	1.75

1965 Topps Embossed

Inserted in regular packs, the 2-1/8" by 3-1/2" Topps Embossed cards are one of the more fascinating issues of the company. The fronts feature an embossed profile portrait on gold foil-like

cardboard (some collectors report finding the cards with silver cardboard). The player's name, team and position are below the portrait - which is good, because most of the embossed portraits are otherwise unrecognizable. There is a gold border with American players framed in blue and National Leaguers in red. The set contains 72 cards divided equally bewteen the leagues. The set provides an inexpensive way to add some interesting cards to a collection. Being special cards, many stars appear in the set.

		NR MT	EX	VG
Complete Set:		100.00	50.00	30.00
Common Player:		.50	.25	.15
1	Carl Yastrzemski	5.00	2.50	1.50
2	Ron Fairly	.50	.25	.15
3	Max Alvis	.50	.25	.15
4	Jim Ray Hart	.50	.25	.15
5	Bill Skowron	.60	.30	.20
6	Ed Kranepool	.50	.25	.15
7	Tim McCarver	.60	.30	.20
8	Sandy Koufax	5.00	2.50	1.50
9	Donn Clendenon	.50	.25	.15
10	John Romano	.50	.25	.15
11	Mickey Mantle	15.00	7.50	4.50
12	Joe Torre	.70	.35	.20
13	Al Kaline	5.00	2.50	1.50
14	Al McBean	.50	.25	.15
15	Don Drysdale	1.50	.70	.45
16	Brooks Robinson	2.00	1.00	.60
17	Jim Bunning	1.00	.50	.30
18	Gary Peters	.50	.25	.15
19	Bob Clemente	5.00	2.50	1.50
20	Milt Pappas	.50	.25	.15
21	Wayne Causey	.50	.25	.15
22	Frank Robinson	2.00	1.00	.60
23	Bill Mazeroski	.60	.30	.20
24	Diego Segui	.50	.25	.15
25	Jim Bouton	.60	.30	.20
26	Ed Mathews	1.50	.70	.45
27	Willie Mays	6.00	3.00	1.75
28	Ron Santo	.60	.30	.20
29	Boog Powell	.60	.30	.20
30	Ken McBride	.50	.25	.15
31	Leon Wagner	.50	.25	.15
32	John Callison	.50	.25	.15
33	Zoilo Versalles	.50	.25	.15
34	Jack Baldschun	.50	.25	.15
35	Ron Hunt	.50	.25	.15
36	Richie Allen	.70	.35	.20
37	Frank Malzone	.50	.25	.15
38	Bob Allison	.50	.25	.15
39	Jim Fregosi	.60	.30	.20
40	Billy Williams	1.50	.70	.45
41	Bill Freehan	.50	.25	.15
42	Vada Pinson	.70	.35	.20
43	Bill White	.50	.25	.15
44	Roy McMillan	.50	.25	.15
45	Orlando Cepeda	1.00	.50	.30
46	Rocky Colavito	.70	.35	.20
47	Ken Boyer	.70	.35	.20
48	Dick Radatz	.50	.25	.15
49	Tommy Davis	.60	.30	.20
50	Walt Bond	.50	.25	.15
51	John Orsino	.50	.25	.15
52	Joe Christopher	.50	.25	.15
53	Al Spangler	.50	.25	.15
54	Jim King	.50	.25	.15
55	Mickey Lolich	.70	.35	.20
56	Harmon Killebrew	2.00	1.00	.60
57	Bob Shaw	.50	.25	.15
58	Ernie Banks	4.00	2.00	1.25
59	Hank Aaron	5.00	2.50	1.50
60	Chuck Hinton	.50	.25	.15
61	Bob Aspromonte	.50	.25	.15
62	Lee Maye	.50	.25	.15
63	Joe Cunningham	.50	.25	.15
64	Pete Ward	.50	.25	.15
65	Bobby Richardson	1.00	.50	.30
66	Dean Chance	.50	.25	.15
67	Dick Ellsworth	.50	.25	.15
68	Jim Maloney	.50	.25	.15
69	Bob Gibson	1.50	.70	.45
70	Earl Battey	.50	.25	.15
71	Tony Kubek	1.00	.50	.30
72	Jack Kralick	.50	.25	.15

1965 Topps Transfers

Issued as strips of three players each as inserts in 1965, the Topps Transfers were 2" by 3" portraits of players. The transfers have blue or red bands at the top and bottom with the team name and position in the top band and the player's name in the bottom. As is so often the case, the superstars in the transfer set can be quite expensive, but like many of Topps non-card products, the transfers are neither terribly expensive or popular today.

		NR MT	EX	VG
Complete Set:		225.00	112.00	67.00
Common Player:		.60	.30	.20
(1)	Hank Aaron	15.00	7.50	4.50
(2)	Richie Allen	.80	.40	.25
(3)	Bob Allison	.70	.35	.20
(4)	Max Alvis	.60	.30	.20
(5)	Luis Aparicio	2.50	1.25	.70
(6)	Bob Aspromonte	.60	.30	.20
(7)	Walt Bond	.60	.30	.20
(8)	Jim Bouton	.80	.40	.25
(9)	Ken Boyer	.80	.40	.25
(10)	Jim Bunning	1.00	.50	.30
(11)	John Callison	.70	.35	.20
(12)	Rico Carty	.70	.35	.20
(13)	Wayne Causey	.60	.30	.20
(14)	Orlando Cepeda	1.00	.50	.30
(15)	Bob Chance	.60	.30	.20
(16)	Dean Chance	.60	.30	.20
(17)	Joe Christopher	.60	.30	.20
(18)	Bob Clemente	15.00	7.50	4.50
(19)	Rocky Colavito	.80	.40	.25
(20)	Tony Conigliaro	.70	.35	.20
(21)	Tommy Davis	.80	.40	.25
(22)	Don Drysdale	4.00	2.00	1.25
(23)	Bill Freehan	.70	.35	.20
(24)	Jim Fregosi	.70	.35	.20
(25)	Bob Gibson	4.00	2.00	1.25
(26)	Dick Groat	.70	.35	.20
(27)	Tom Haller	.60	.30	.20
(28)	Chuck Hinton	.60	.30	.20
(29)	Elston Howard	1.00	.50	.30
(30)	Ron Hunt	.60	.30	.20
(31)	Al Jackson	.60	.30	.20
(32)	Al Kaline	5.00	2.50	1.50
(33)	Harmon Killebrew	5.00	2.50	1.50
(34)	Jim King	.60	.30	.20
(35)	Ron Kline	.60	.30	.20
(36)	Bobby Knoop	.60	.30	.20
(37)	Sandy Koufax	10.00	5.00	3.00
(38)	Ed Kranepool	.60	.30	.20
(39)	Jim Maloney	.60	.30	.20
(40)	Mickey Mantle	60.00	30.00	18.00
(41)	Juan Marichal	4.00	2.00	1.25
(42)	Lee Maye	.60	.30	.20
(43)	Willie Mays	15.00	7.50	4.50
(44)	Bill Mazeroski	.80	.40	.25
(45)	Tony Oliva	.80	.40	.25
(46)	Jim O'Toole	.60	.30	.20
(47)	Milt Pappas	.70	.35	.20
(48)	Camilo Pascual	.70	.35	.20
(49)	Gary Peters	.60	.30	.20
(50)	Vada Pinson	.80	.40	.25
(51)	Juan Pizarro	.60	.30	.20
(52)	Boog Powell	.80	.40	.25
(53)	Dick Radatz	.60	.30	.20

		NR MT	EX	VG
(54)	Bobby Richardson	1.00	.50	.30
(55)	Brooks Robinson	6.00	3.00	1.75
(56)	Frank Robinson	5.00	2.50	1.50
(57)	Bob Rodgers	.70	.35	.20
(58)	John Roseboro	.70	.35	.20
(59)	Ron Santo	.80	.40	.25
(60)	Diego Segui	.60	.30	.20
(61)	Bill Skowron	.70	.35	.20
(62)	Al Spangler	.60	.30	.20
(63)	Dick Stuart	.70	.35	.20
(64)	Luis Tiant	.80	.40	.25
(65)	Joe Torre	.80	.40	.25
(66)	Bob Veale	.60	.30	.20
(67)	Leon Wagner	.60	.30	.20
(68)	Pete Ward	.60	.30	.20
(69)	Bill White	.70	.35	.20
(70)	Dave Wickersham	.60	.30	.20
(71)	Billy Williams	3.00	1.50	.90
(72)	Carl Yastrzemski	25.00	12.50	7.50

1966 Topps

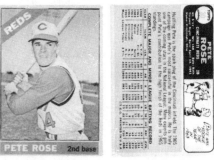

In 1966, Topps produced another 598-card set. The 2-1/2" by 3-1/2" cards feature the almost traditional color photograph with a diagonal strip in the upper left-hand corner carrying the team name. A band at the bottom carries the player's name and position. Multi-player cards returned in 1966 after having had a year's hiatus. The statistical leader cards feature the categorical leader and two runners-up. Most team managers have cards as well. The 1966 set features a handful of cards found with without a notice of the player's sale or trade to another team. Cards without the notice bring higher prices not included in the complete set prices below.

		NR MT	EX	VG
Complete Set:		4500.00	2250.00	1350.
Common Player: 1-110		1.00	.50	.30
Common Player: 111-446		1.25	.60	.40
Common Player: 447-522		5.00	2.50	1.50
Common Player Singleprint: 523-598		20.00	10.00	6.00
Common Player: 523-598		15.00	7.50	4.50
1	Willie Mays	155.00	60.00	30.00
2	Ted Abernathy	1.25	.60	.40
3	Sam Mele	1.00	.50	.30
4	Ray Culp	1.00	.50	.30
5	Jim Fregosi	1.50	.70	.45
6	Chuck Schilling	1.00	.50	.30
7	Tracy Stallard	1.00	.50	.30
8	Floyd Robinson	1.00	.50	.30
9	Clete Boyer	5.00	2.50	1.50
10	Tony Cloninger	1.25	.60	.40
11	Senators Rookies (Brant Alyea, Pete Craig)	1.00	.50	.30
12	John Tsitouris	1.00	.50	.30
13	Lou Johnson	1.00	.50	.30
14	Norm Siebern	1.25	.60	.40
15	Vern Law	1.50	.70	.45
16	Larry Brown	1.25	.60	.40
17	Johnny Stephenson	1.25	.60	.40
18	Roland Sheldon	1.00	.50	.30
19	Giants Team	5.00	2.50	1.50
20	Willie Horton	1.25	.60	.40
21	Don Nottebart	1.00	.50	.30

		NR MT	EX	VG
22	Joe Nossek	1.00	.50	.30
23	Jack Sanford	1.00	.50	.30
24	*Don Kessinger*	1.25	.60	.40
25	Pete Ward	1.00	.50	.30
26	Ray Sadecki	1.00	.50	.30
27	Orioles Rookies (*Andy Etchebarren, Darold Knowles*)	1.25	.60	.40
28	Phil Niekro	20.00	10.00	6.00
29	Mike Brumley	1.00	.50	.30
30	Pete Rose	60.00	30.00	18.00
31	Jack Cullen	1.25	.60	.40
32	Adolfo Phillips	1.00	.50	.30
33	Jim Pagliaroni	1.00	.50	.30
34	Checklist 1-88	5.00	2.50	1.50
35	Ron Swoboda	1.25	.60	.40
36	Jim Hunter	30.00	15.00	9.00
37	Billy Herman	5.00	2.50	1.50
38	Ron Nischwitz	1.00	.50	.30
39	Ken Henderson	1.00	.50	.30
40	Jim Grant	1.00	.50	.30
41	Don LeJohn	1.00	.50	.30
42	Aubrey Gatewood	1.00	.50	.30
43	Don Landrum	1.00	.50	.30
44	Indians Rookies (Bill Davis, Tom Kelley)	1.00	.50	.30
45	Jim Gentile	1.25	.60	.40
46	Howie Koplitz	1.00	.50	.30
47	J.C. Martin	1.00	.50	.30
48	Paul Blair	1.25	.60	.40
49	Woody Woodward	1.25	.60	.40
50	Mickey Mantle	225.00	112.00	70.00
51	Gordon Richardson	1.25	.60	.40
52	Power Plus (Johnny Callison, Wes Covington)	1.50	.70	.45
53	Bob Duliba	1.00	.50	.30
54	Jose Pagan	1.00	.50	.30
55	Ken Harrelson	5.00	2.50	1.50
56	Sandy Valdespino	1.00	.50	.30
57	Jim Lefebvre	1.25	.60	.40
58	Dave Wickersham	1.00	.50	.30
59	Reds Team	2.25	1.25	.70
60	Curt Flood	5.00	2.50	1.50
61	Bob Bolin	1.00	.50	.30
62a	Merritt Ranew (no sold statement)	15.00	7.50	4.50
62b	Merritt Ranew (with sold statement)	1.00	.50	.30
63	Jim Stewart	1.00	.50	.30
64	Bob Bruce	1.00	.50	.30
65	Leon Wagner	1.25	.60	.40
66	Al Weis	1.00	.50	.30
67	Mets Rookies (Cleon Jones, Dick Selma)	1.25	.60	.40
68	Hal Reniff	1.25	.60	.40
69	Ken Hamlin	1.00	.50	.30
70	Carl Yastrzemski	50.00	25.00	15.00
71	Frank Carpin	1.00	.50	.30
72	Tony Perez	35.00	17.50	10.50
73	Jerry Zimmerman	1.00	.50	.30
74	Don Mossi	1.25	.60	.40
75	Tommy Davis	5.00	2.50	1.50
76	Red Schoendienst	4.00	2.00	1.50
77	Johnny Orsino	1.00	.50	.30
78	Frank Linzy	1.00	.50	.30
79	Joe Pepitone	5.00	2.50	1.50
80	Richie Allen	2.50	1.25	.70
81	Ray Oyler	1.00	.50	.30
82	Bob Hendley	1.00	.50	.30
83	Albie Pearson	1.00	.50	.30
84	Braves Rookies (Jim Beauchamp, Dick Kelley)	1.00	.50	.30
85	Eddie Fisher	1.00	.50	.30
86	John Bateman	1.00	.50	.30
87	Dan Napoleon	1.25	.60	.40
88	Fred Whitfield	1.00	.50	.30
89	Ted Davidson	1.00	.50	.30
90	Luis Aparicio	9.00	4.50	2.75
91a	Bob Uecker (no trade statement)	50.00	25.00	15.00
91b	Bob Uecker (with trade statement)	20.00	10.00	6.00
92	Yankees Team	5.00	2.50	1.50
93	Jim Lonborg	1.50	.70	.45
94	Matty Alou	1.50	.70	.45
95	Pete Richert	1.00	.50	.30
96	Felipe Alou	1.50	.70	.45
97	Jim Merritt	1.00	.50	.30
98	Don Demeter	1.00	.50	.30
99	Buc Belters (Donn Clendenon, Willie Stargell)	5.00	2.50	1.50
100	Sandy Koufax	110.00	55.00	33.00
101a	Checklist 89-176 (115 is Spahn)	7.00	3.50	2.00
101b	Checklist 89-176 (115 is Henry)	3.00	1.50	.90
102	Ed Kirkpatrick	1.00	.50	.30
103a	Dick Groat (no trade statement)	20.00	10.00	6.00
103b	Dick Groat (with trade statement)	5.00	2.50	1.50
104a	Alex Johnson (no trade statement)	15.00	7.50	4.50
104b	Alex Johnson (with trade statement)	1.25	.60	.40
105	Milt Pappas	1.25	.60	.40
106	Rusty Staub	2.50	1.25	.70
107	Athletics Rookies (Larry Stahl, Ron Tompkins)	1.00	.50	.30
108	Bobby Klaus	1.25	.60	.40
109	Ralph Terry	1.25	.60	.40
110	Ernie Banks	30.00	15.00	9.00
111	Gary Peters	1.25	.60	.40
112	Manny Mota	1.25	.60	.40
113	Hank Aguirre	1.25	.60	.40
114	Jim Gosger	1.25	.60	.40
115	Bill Henry	1.25	.60	.40
116	Walt Alston	2.50	1.25	.70
117	Jake Gibbs	1.50	.70	.45
118	Mike McCormick	1.25	.60	.40
119	Art Shamsky	1.25	.60	.40
120	Harmon Killebrew	15.00	7.50	4.50
121	Ray Herbert	1.25	.60	.40
122	Joe Gaines	1.25	.60	.40
123	Pirates Rookies (Frank Bork, Jerry May)	1.25	.60	.40
124	Tug McGraw	3.00	1.50	.90
125	Lou Brock	20.00	10.00	6.00
126	*Jim Palmer*	200.00	100.00	60.00
127	Ken Berry	1.25	.60	.40
128	Jim Landis	1.25	.60	.40
129	Jack Kralick	1.25	.60	.40
130	Joe Torre	2.25	1.25	.70
131	Angels Team	2.25	1.25	.70
132	Orlando Cepeda	5.00	2.50	1.50
133	Don McMahon	1.25	.60	.40
134	Wes Parker	1.25	.60	.40
135	Dave Morehead	1.25	.60	.40
136	Woody Held	1.25	.60	.40
137	Pat Corrales	1.50	.70	.45
138	Roger Repoz	1.50	.70	.45
139	Cubs Rookies (Byron Browne, Don Young)	1.25	.60	.40
140	Jim Maloney	1.25	.60	.40
141	Tom McCraw	1.25	.60	.40
142	Don Dennis	1.25	.60	.40
143	Jose Tartabull	1.25	.60	.40
144	Don Schwall	1.25	.60	.40
145	Bill Freehan	1.25	.60	.40
146	George Altman	1.25	.60	.40
147	Lum Harris	1.25	.60	.40
148	Bob Johnson	1.25	.60	.40
149	Dick Nen	1.25	.60	.40
150	Rocky Colavito	2.50	1.25	.70
151	Gary Wagner	1.25	.60	.40
152	Frank Malzone	1.25	.60	.40
153	Rico Carty	5.00	2.50	1.50
154	Chuck Hiller	1.25	.60	.40
155	Marcelino Lopez	1.25	.60	.40
156	DP Combo (Hal Lanier, Dick Schofield)	1.50	.70	.45
157	Rene Lachemann	1.25	.60	.40
158	Jim Brewer	1.25	.60	.40
159	Chico Ruiz	1.25	.60	.40
160	Whitey Ford	25.00	12.50	7.50
161	Jerry Lumpe	1.25	.60	.40
162	Lee Maye	1.25	.60	.40
163	Tito Francona	1.25	.60	.40
164	White Sox Rookies (Tommie Agee, Marv Staehle)	1.25	.60	.40
165	Don Lock	1.25	.60	.40
166	Chris Krug	1.25	.60	.40
167	Boog Powell	2.50	1.25	.70
168	Dan Osinski	1.25	.60	.40
169	Duke Sims	1.25	.60	.40
170	Cookie Rojas	1.25	.60	.40
171	Nick Willhite	1.25	.60	.40
172	Mets Team	3.00	1.50	.90
173	Al Spangler	1.25	.60	.40
174	Ron Taylor	1.25	.60	.40
175	Bert Campaneris	5.00	2.50	1.50
176	Jim Davenport	1.25	.60	.40
177	Hector Lopez	1.50	.70	.45
178	Bob Tillman	1.25	.60	.40
179	Cardinals Rookies (Dennis Aust, Bob Tolan)	1.25	.60	.40
180	Vada Pinson	2.50	1.25	.70

		NR MT	EX	VG
181	Al Worthington	1.25	.60	.40
182	Jerry Lynch	1.25	.60	.40
183a	Checklist 177-264 (large print on front)			
		2.50	1.25	.70
183b	Checklist 177-264 (small print on front)			
		6.00	3.00	1.75
184	Denis Menke	1.25	.60	.40
185	Bob Buhl	1.25	.60	.40
186	Ruben Amaro	1.50	.70	.45
187	Chuck Dressen	1.25	.60	.40
188	Al Luplow	1.25	.60	.40
189	John Roseboro	1.25	.60	.40
190	Jimmie Hall	1.25	.60	.40
191	Darrell Sutherland	1.25	.60	.40
192	Vic Power	1.25	.60	.40
193	Dave McNally	1.50	.70	.45
194	Senators Team	2.25	1.25	.70
195	Joe Morgan	40.00	20.00	12.00
196	Don Pavletich	1.25	.60	.40
197	Sonny Siebert	1.25	.60	.40
198	*Mickey Stanley*	1.50	.70	.45
199	Chisox Clubbers (Floyd Robinson, Johnny			
	Romano, Bill Skowron)	1.50	.70	.45
200	Ed Mathews	15.00	7.50	4.50
201	Jim Dickson	1.25	.60	.40
202	Clay Dalrymple	1.25	.60	.40
203	Jose Santiago	1.25	.60	.40
204	Cubs Team	2.25	1.25	.70
205	Tom Tresh	5.00	2.50	1.50
206	Alvin Jackson	1.25	.60	.40
207	Frank Quilici	1.25	.60	.40
208	Bob Miller	1.25	.60	.40
209	Tigers Rookies (Fritz Fisher, *John Hiller*)			
		1.25	.60	.40
210	Bill Mazeroski	2.50	1.25	.70
211	Frank Kreutzer	1.25	.60	.40
212	Ed Kranepool	1.50	.70	.45
213	Fred Newman	1.25	.60	.40
214	Tommy Harper	1.25	.60	.40
215	N.L. Batting Leaders (Hank Aaron, Bob			
	Clemente, Willie Mays)	20.00	10.00	6.00
216	A.L. Batting Leaders (Vic Davalillo, Tony			
	Oliva, Carl Yastrzemski)	6.00	3.00	1.75
217	N.L. Home Run Leaders (Willie Mays,			
	Willie McCovey, Billy Williams)	5.00	2.50	1.50
218	A.L. Home Run Leaders (Norm Cash,			
	Tony Conigliaro, Willie Horton)	2.50	1.25	.70
219	N.L. RBI Leaders (Deron Johnson, Willie			
	Mays, Frank Robinson)	6.00	3.00	1.75
220	A.L. RBI Leaders (Rocky Colavito, Willie			
	Horton, Tony Oliva)	2.50	1.25	.70
221	N.L. ERA Leaders (Sandy Koufax, Vern			
	Law, Juan Marichal)	6.00	3.00	1.75
222	A.L. ERA Leaders (Eddie Fisher, Sam			
	McDowell, Sonny Siebert)	2.50	1.25	.70
223	N.L. Pitching Leaders (Tony Cloninger,			
	Don Drysdale, Sandy Koufax)	6.00	3.00	1.75
224	A.L. Pitching Leaders (Jim Grant, Jim			
	Kaat, Mel Stottlemyre)	3.00	1.50	.90
225	N.L. Strikeout Leaders (Bob Gibson,			
	Sandy Koufax, Bob Veale)	6.00	3.00	1.75
226	A.L. Strikeout Leaders (Mickey Lolich,			
	Sam McDowell, Denny McLain, Sonny			
	Siebert)	2.50	1.25	.70
227	Russ Nixon	1.25	.60	.40
228	Larry Dierker	1.25	.60	.40
229	Hank Bauer	1.25	.60	.40
230	Johnny Callison	1.25	.60	.40
231	Floyd Weaver	1.25	.60	.40
232	Glenn Beckert	1.50	.70	.45
233	Dom Zanni	1.25	.60	.40
234	Yankees Rookies (Rich Beck, *Roy White*)			
		5.00	2.50	1.50
235	Don Cardwell	1.25	.60	.40
236	Mike Hershberger	1.25	.60	.40
237	Billy O'Dell	1.25	.60	.40
238	Dodgers Team	5.00	2.50	1.50
239	Orlando Pena	1.25	.60	.40
240	Earl Battey	1.25	.60	.40
241	Dennis Ribant	1.25	.60	.40
242	Jesus Alou	1.25	.60	.40
243	Nelson Briles	1.25	.60	.40
244	Astros Rookies (Chuck Harrison, Sonny			
	Jackson)	1.25	.60	.40
245	John Buzhardt	1.25	.60	.40
246	Ed Bailey	1.25	.60	.40
247	Carl Warwick	1.25	.60	.40
248	Pete Mikkelsen	1.25	.60	.40
249	Bill Rigney	1.25	.60	.40
250	Sam Ellis	1.25	.60	.40
251	Ed Brinkman	1.25	.60	.40

		NR MT	EX	VG
252	Denver Lemaster	1.25	.60	.40
253	Don Wert	1.25	.60	.40
254	Phillies Rookies (*Ferguson Jenkins*, Bill			
	Sorrell)	150.00	75.00	45.00
255	Willie Stargell	18.00	9.00	5.50
256	Lew Krausse	1.25	.60	.40
257	Jeff Torborg	1.25	.60	.40
258	Dave Giusti	1.25	.60	.40
259	Red Sox Team	2.50	1.25	.70
260	Bob Shaw	1.25	.60	.40
261	Ron Hansen	1.25	.60	.40
262	Jack Hamilton	1.25	.60	.40
263	Tom Egan	1.25	.60	.40
264	Twins Rookies (Andy Kosco, Ted			
	Uhlaender)	1.25	.60	.40
265	Stu Miller	1.25	.60	.40
266	Pedro Gonzalez	1.25	.60	.40
267	Joe Sparma	1.25	.60	.40
268	John Blanchard	1.25	.60	.40
269	Don Heffner	1.25	.60	.40
270	Claude Osteen	1.25	.60	.40
271	Hal Lanier	1.50	.70	.45
272	Jack Baldschun	1.25	.60	.40
273	Astro Aces (Bob Aspromonte, Rusty			
	Staub)	5.00	2.50	1.50
274	Buster Narum	1.25	.60	.40
275	Tim McCarver	2.50	1.25	.70
276	Jim Bouton	2.50	1.25	.70
277	George Thomas	1.25	.60	.40
278	Calvin Koonce	1.25	.60	.40
279a	Checklist 265-352 (player's cap black)			
		6.00	3.00	1.75
279b	Checklist 265-352 (player's cap red)			
		3.00	1.50	.90
280	Bobby Knoop	1.25	.60	.40
281	Bruce Howard	1.25	.60	.40
282	Johnny Lewis	1.25	.60	.40
283	Jim Perry	1.50	.70	.45
284	Bobby Wine	1.25	.60	.40
285	Luis Tiant	2.50	1.25	.70
286	Gary Geiger	1.25	.60	.40
287	Jack Aker	1.25	.60	.40
288	Dodgers Rookies (*Bill Singer, Don Sutton*)			
		150.00	75.00	45.00
289	Larry Sherry	1.25	.60	.40
290	Ron Santo	5.00	2.50	1.50
291	Moe Drabowsky	1.25	.60	.40
292	Jim Coker	1.25	.60	.40
293	Mike Shannon	1.25	.60	.40
294	Steve Ridzik	1.25	.60	.40
295	Jim Hart	1.25	.60	.40
296	Johnny Keane	1.25	.60	.40
297	Jim Owens	1.25	.60	.40
298	Rico Petrocelli	1.25	.60	.40
299	Lou Burdette	5.00	2.50	1.50
300	Bob Clemente	110.00	55.00	33.00
301	Greg Bollo	1.25	.60	.40
302	Ernie Bowman	1.25	.60	.40
303	Indians Team	2.25	1.25	.70
304	John Herrnstein	1.25	.60	.40
305	Camilo Pascual	1.25	.60	.40
306	Ty Cline	1.25	.60	.40
307	Clay Carroll	1.25	.60	.40
308	Tom Haller	1.25	.60	.40
309	Diego Segui	1.25	.60	.40
310	Frank Robinson	35.00	17.50	10.50
311	Reds Rookies (Tommy Helms, Dick			
	Simpson)	1.25	.60	.40
312	Bob Saverine	1.25	.60	.40
313	Chris Zachary	1.25	.60	.40
314	Hector Valle	1.25	.60	.40
315	Norm Cash	5.00	2.50	1.50
316	Jack Fisher	1.25	.60	.40
317	Dalton Jones	1.25	.60	.40
318	Harry Walker	1.25	.60	.40
319	Gene Freese	1.25	.60	.40
320	Bob Gibson	20.00	10.00	6.00
321	Rick Reichardt	1.25	.60	.40
322	Bill Faul	1.25	.60	.40
323	Ray Barker	1.50	.70	.45
324	John Boozer	1.25	.60	.40
325	Vic Davalillo	1.25	.60	.40
326	Braves Team	2.25	1.25	.70
327	Bernie Allen	1.25	.60	.40
328	Jerry Grote	1.25	.60	.40
329	Pete Charton	1.25	.60	.40
330	Ron Fairly	1.25	.60	.40
331	Ron Herbel	1.25	.60	.40
332	Billy Bryan	1.25	.60	.40
333	Senators Rookies (*Joe Coleman*, Jim			
	French)	1.25	.60	.40

		NR MT	EX	VG			NR MT	EX	VG
334	Marty Keough	1.25	.60	.40	421	Roy McMillan	1.25	.60	.40
335	Juan Pizarro	1.25	.60	.40	422	Ed Charles	1.25	.60	.40
336	Gene Alley	1.25	.60	.40	423	Ernie Broglio	1.25	.60	.40
337	Fred Gladding	1.25	.60	.40	424	Reds Rookies (Lee May, Darrell Osteen)			
338	Dal Maxvill	1.25	.60	.40			2.25	1.25	.70
339	Del Crandall	1.50	.70	.45	425	Bob Veale	1.25	.60	.40
340	Dean Chance	1.25	.60	.40	426	White Sox Team	2.25	1.25	.70
341	Wes Westrum	1.25	.60	.40	427	John Miller	1.25	.60	.40
342	Bob Humphreys	1.25	.60	.40	428	Sandy Alomar	1.25	.60	.40
343	Joe Christopher	1.25	.60	.40	429	Bill Monbouquette	1.25	.60	.40
344	Steve Blass	1.25	.60	.40	430	Don Drysdale	15.00	7.50	4.50
345	Bob Allison	1.50	.70	.45	431	Walt Bond	1.25	.60	.40
346	Mike de la Hoz	1.25	.60	.40	432	Bob Heffner	1.25	.60	.40
347	Phil Regan	1.25	.60	.40	433	Alvin Dark	1.25	.60	.40
348	Orioles Team	5.00	2.50	1.50	434	Willie Kirkland	1.25	.60	.40
349	Cap Peterson	1.25	.60	.40	435	Jim Bunning	6.00	3.00	1.75
350	Mel Stottlemyre	3.00	1.50	.90	436	Julian Javier	1.25	.60	.40
351	Fred Valentine	1.25	.60	.40	437	Al Stanek	1.25	.60	.40
352	Bob Aspromonte	1.25	.60	.40	438	Willie Smith	1.25	.60	.40
353	Al McBean	1.25	.60	.40	439	Pedro Ramos	1.50	.70	.45
354	Smoky Burgess	1.50	.70	.45	440	Deron Johnson	1.25	.60	.40
355	Wade Blasingame	1.25	.60	.40	441	Tommie Sisk	1.25	.60	.40
356	Red Sox Rookies (Owen Johnson, Ken Sanders)	1.25	.60	.40	442	Orioles Rookies (Ed Barnowski, Eddie Watt)	1.25	.60	.40
357	Gerry Arrigo	1.25	.60	.40	443	Bill Wakefield	1.25	.60	.40
358	Charlie Smith	1.25	.60	.40	444a	Checklist 430-506 (456 is R. Sox Rookies)			
359	Johnny Briggs	1.25	.60	.40			3.00	1.50	.90
360	Ron Hunt	1.25	.60	.40	444b	Checklist 430-506 (456 is Red Sox Rookies)			
361	Tom Satriano	1.25	.60	.40			5.00	2.50	1.50
362	Gates Brown	1.25	.60	.40	445	Jim Kaat	6.00	3.00	1.75
363	Checklist 353-429	3.00	1.50	.90	446	Mack Jones	1.25	.60	.40
364	Nate Oliver	1.25	.60	.40	447	Dick Ellsworth (photo actually Ken Hubbs)			
365	Roger Maris	70.00	35.00	23.00			5.00	2.50	1.50
366	Wayne Causey	1.25	.60	.40	448	Eddie Stanky	6.00	3.00	1.75
367	Mel Nelson	1.25	.60	.40	449	Joe Moeller	5.00	2.50	1.50
368	Charlie Lau	1.25	.60	.40	450	Tony Oliva	7.00	3.50	2.00
369	Jim King	1.25	.60	.40	451	Barry Latman	5.00	2.50	1.50
370	Chico Cardenas	1.25	.60	.40	452	Joe Azcue	5.00	2.50	1.50
371	Lee Stange	1.25	.60	.40	453	Ron Kline	5.00	2.50	1.50
372	Harvey Kuenn	5.00	2.50	1.50	454	Jerry Buchek	5.00	2.50	1.50
373	Giants Rookies (Dick Estelle, Jack Hiatt)	1.25	.60	.40	455	Mickey Lolich	6.00	3.00	1.75
374	Bob Locker	1.25	.60	.40	456	Red Sox Rookies (Darrell Brandon, Joe Foy)	5.00	2.50	1.50
375	Donn Clendenon	1.25	.60	.40	457	Joe Gibbon	5.00	2.50	1.50
376	Paul Schaal	1.25	.60	.40	458	Manny Jiminez (Jimenez)	5.00	2.50	1.50
377	Turk Farrell	1.25	.60	.40	459	Bill McCool	5.00	2.50	1.50
378	Dick Tracewski	1.25	.60	.40	460	Curt Blefary	5.00	2.50	1.50
379	Cardinals Team	2.25	1.25	.70	461	Roy Face	6.00	3.00	1.75
380	Tony Conigliaro	5.00	2.50	1.50	462	Bob Rodgers	2.50	1.25	.70
381	Hank Fischer	1.25	.60	.40	463	Phillies Team	6.00	3.00	1.75
382	Phil Roof	1.25	.60	.40	464	Larry Bearnarth	6.00	3.00	1.75
383	Jackie Brandt	1.25	.60	.40	465	Don Buford	6.00	3.00	1.75
384	Al Downing	5.00	2.50	1.50	466	Ken Johnson	5.00	2.50	1.50
385	Ken Boyer	2.50	1.25	.70	467	Vic Roznovsky	5.00	2.50	1.50
386	Gil Hodges	6.00	3.00	1.75	468	Johnny Podres	6.00	3.00	1.75
387	Howie Reed	1.25	.60	.40	469	Yankees Rookies (Bobby Murcer, Dooley Womack)	20.00	10.00	6.00
388	Don Mincher	1.25	.60	.40	470	Sam McDowell	6.00	3.00	1.75
389	Jim O'Toole	1.25	.60	.40	471	Bob Skinner	5.00	2.50	1.50
390	Brooks Robinson	30.00	15.00	9.00	472	Terry Fox	5.00	2.50	1.50
391	Chuck Hinton	1.25	.60	.40	473	Rich Rollins	5.00	2.50	1.50
392	Cubs Rookies (Bill Hands, Randy Hundley)	1.25	.60	.40	474	Dick Schofield	5.00	2.50	1.50
393	George Brunet	1.25	.60	.40	475	Dick Radatz	6.00	3.00	1.75
394	Ron Brand	1.25	.60	.40	476	Bobby Bragan	6.00	3.00	1.75
395	Len Gabrielson	1.25	.60	.40	477	Steve Barber	5.00	2.50	1.50
396	Jerry Stephenson	1.25	.60	.40	478	Tony Gonzalez	5.00	2.50	1.50
397	Bill White	1.50	.70	.45	479	Jim Hannan	5.00	2.50	1.50
398	Danny Cater	1.25	.60	.40	480	Dick Stuart	6.00	3.00	1.75
399	Ray Washburn	1.25	.60	.40	481	Bob Lee	5.00	2.50	1.50
400	Zoilo Versalles	1.25	.60	.40	482	Cubs Rookies (John Boccabella, Dave Dowling)	5.00	2.50	1.50
401	Ken McMullen	1.25	.60	.40	483	Joe Nuxhall	6.00	3.00	1.75
402	Jim Hickman	1.25	.60	.40	484	Wes Covington	5.00	2.50	1.50
403	Fred Talbot	1.25	.60	.40	485	Bob Bailey	5.00	2.50	1.50
404	Pirates Team	2.25	1.25	.70	486	Tommy John	15.00	7.50	4.50
405	Elston Howard	6.00	3.00	1.75	487	Al Ferrara	5.00	2.50	1.50
406	Joe Jay	1.25	.60	.40	488	George Banks	5.00	2.50	1.50
407	John Kennedy	1.25	.60	.40	489	Curt Simmons	6.00	3.00	1.75
408	Lee Thomas	1.25	.60	.40	490	Bobby Richardson	12.00	6.00	3.50
409	Billy Hoeft	1.25	.60	.40	491	Dennis Bennett	5.00	2.50	1.50
410	Al Kaline	25.00	12.50	7.50	492	Athletics Team	5.00	2.50	1.50
411	Gene Mauch	1.25	.60	.40	493	Johnny Klippstein	5.00	2.50	1.50
412	Sam Bowens	1.25	.60	.40	494	Gordon Coleman	5.00	2.50	1.50
413	John Romano	1.25	.60	.40	495	Dick McAuliffe	6.00	3.00	1.75
414	Dan Coombs	1.25	.60	.40	496	Lindy McDaniel	5.00	2.50	1.50
415	Max Alvis	1.25	.60	.40	497	Chris Cannizzaro	5.00	2.50	1.50
416	Phil Ortega	1.25	.60	.40	498	Pirates Rookies (Woody Fryman, Luke Walker)	6.00	3.00	1.75
417	Angels Rookies (Jim McGlothlin, Ed Sukla)	1.25	.60	.40	499	Wally Bunker	5.00	2.50	1.50
418	Phil Gagliano	1.25	.60	.40	500	Hank Aaron	125.00	67.00	37.00
419	Mike Ryan	1.25	.60	.40	501	John O'Donoghue	5.00	2.50	1.50
420	Juan Marichal	8.00	4.00	2.50					

		NR MT	EX	VG
502	Lenny Green	5.00	2.50	1.50
503	Steve Hamilton	6.00	3.00	1.75
504	Grady Hatton	5.00	2.50	1.50
505	Jose Cardenal	5.00	2.50	1.50
506	Bo Belinsky	6.00	3.00	1.75
507	John Edwards	5.00	2.50	1.50
508	*Steve Hargan*	6.00	3.00	1.75
509	Jake Wood	5.00	2.50	1.50
510	Hoyt Wilhelm	15.00	7.50	4.50
511	Giants Rookies (Bob Barton, *Tito Fuentes*)			
		6.00	3.00	1.75
512	Dick Stigman	5.00	2.50	1.50
513	Camilo Carreon	5.00	2.50	1.50
514	Hal Woodeshick	5.00	2.50	1.50
515	Frank Howard	7.00	3.50	2.00
516	Eddie Bressoud	5.00	2.50	1.50
517a	Checklist 507-598 (529 is W. Sox Rookies)			
		9.00	4.50	2.75
517b	Checklist 506-598 (529 is White Sox Rookies)			
		10.00	5.00	3.00
518	Braves Rookies (Herb Hippauf, Arnie Umbach)			
		5.00	2.50	1.50
519	Bob Friend	6.00	3.00	1.75
520	Jim Wynn	6.00	3.00	1.75
521	John Wyatt	5.00	2.50	1.50
522	Phil Linz	5.00	2.50	1.50
523	Bob Sadowski	15.00	7.50	4.50
524	Giants Rookies (Ollie Brown, Don Mason)			
		20.00	10.00	6.00
525	Gary Bell	15.00	7.50	4.50
526	Twins Team	70.00	35.00	20.00
527	Julio Navarro	15.00	7.50	4.50
528	Jesse Gonder	20.00	10.00	6.00
529	White Sox Rookies (*Lee Elia*, Dennis Higgins, Bill Voss)			
		18.00	9.00	5.50
530	Robin Roberts	40.00	20.00	12.00
531	Joe Cunningham	15.00	7.50	4.50
532	Aurelio Monteagudo	15.00	7.50	4.50
533	Jerry Adair	15.00	7.50	4.50
534	Mets Rookies (Dave Eilers, Rob Gardner)			
		18.00	9.00	5.50
535	Willie Davis	50.00	25.00	15.00
536	Dick Egan	15.00	7.50	4.50
537	Herman Franks	15.00	7.50	4.50
538	Bob Allen	15.00	7.50	4.50
539	Astros Rookies (Bill Heath, Carroll Sembera)			
		15.00	7.50	4.50
540	Denny McLain	50.00	25.00	15.00
541	Gene Oliver	15.00	7.50	4.50
542	George Smith	15.00	7.50	4.50
543	Roger Craig	50.00	25.00	15.00
544	Cardinals Rookies (Joe Hoerner, George Kernek, Jimmy Williams)			
		20.00	10.00	6.00
545	Dick Green	20.00	10.00	6.00
546	Dwight Siebler	15.00	7.50	4.50
547	*Horace Clarke*	20.00	10.00	6.00
548	Gary Kroll	20.00	10.00	6.00
549	Senators Rookies (Al Closter, Casey Cox)			
		15.00	7.50	4.50
550	Willie McCovey	125.00	62.00	37.00
551	Bob Purkey	20.00	10.00	6.00
552	Birdie Tebbetts	15.00	7.50	4.50
553	Major League Rookies (Pat Garrett, Jackie Warner)			
		15.00	7.50	4.50
554	Jim Northrup	18.00	9.00	5.50
555	Ron Perranoski	18.00	9.00	5.50
556	Mel Queen	20.00	10.00	6.00
557	Felix Mantilla	15.00	7.50	4.50
558	Red Sox Rookies (Guido Grilli, Pete Magrini, *George Scott*)			
		20.00	10.00	6.00
559	Roberto Pena	15.00	7.50	4.50
560	Joel Horlen	15.00	7.50	4.50
561	Choo Choo Coleman	20.00	10.00	6.00
562	Russ Snyder	15.00	7.50	4.50
563	Twins Rookies (Pete Cimino, Cesar Tovar)			
		18.00	9.00	5.50
564	Bob Chance	15.00	7.50	4.50
565	Jimmy Piersall	35.00	17.50	10.50
566	Mike Cuellar	18.00	9.00	5.50
567	Dick Howser	20.00	10.00	6.00
568	Athletics Rookies (Paul Lindblad, Ron Stone)			
		15.00	7.50	4.50
569	Orlando McFarlane	15.00	7.50	4.50
570	Art Mahaffey	20.00	10.00	6.00
571	Dave Roberts	15.00	7.50	4.50
572	Bob Priddy	15.00	7.50	4.50
573	Derrell Griffith	15.00	7.50	4.50
574	Mets Rookies (Bill Hepler, Bill Murphy)			
		18.00	9.00	5.50
575	Earl Wilson	15.00	7.50	4.50
576	Dave Nicholson	20.00	10.00	6.00

		NR MT	EX	VG
577	Jack Lamabe	15.00	7.50	4.50
578	Chi Chi Olivo	15.00	7.50	4.50
579	Orioles Rookies (Frank Bertaina, Gene Brabender, Dave Johnson)			
		20.00	10.00	6.00
580	Billy Williams	100.00	50.00	30.00
581	Tony Martinez	15.00	7.50	4.50
582	Garry Roggenburk	15.00	7.50	4.50
583	Tigers Team	150.00	75.00	52.00
584	Yankees Rookies (Frank Fernandez, *Fritz Peterson*)			
		18.00	9.00	5.50
585	Tony Taylor	15.00	7.50	4.50
586	Claude Raymond	15.00	7.50	4.50
587	Dick Bertell	15.00	7.50	4.50
588	Athletics Rookies (Chuck Dobson, Ken Suarez)			
		15.00	7.50	4.50
589	Lou Klimchock	18.00	9.00	5.50
590	Bill Skowron	35.00	17.50	10.50
591	N.L. Rookies (*Grant Jackson*, Bart Shirley)			
		20.00	10.00	6.00
592	Andre Rodgers	15.00	7.50	4.50
593	Doug Camilli	20.00	10.00	6.00
594	Chico Salmon	15.00	7.50	4.50
595	Larry Jackson	15.00	7.50	4.50
596	Astros Rookies (*Nate Colbert*, Greg Sims)			
		18.00	9.00	5.50
597	John Sullivan	15.00	7.50	4.50
598	Gaylord Perry	310.00	155.00	93.00

1966 Topps Rub-Offs

Returning to a concept last tried in 1961, Topps tried an expanded version of Rub-Offs in 1966. Measuring 2-1/16" by 3," the Rub-Offs are in vertical format for the 100 players and horizontal for the 20 team pennants. The player Rub-Offs feature a color photo.

		NR MT	EX	VG
Complete Set:		225.00	112.00	67.00
Common Player:		.60	.30	.20
(1)	Hank Aaron	8.00	4.00	2.50
(2)	Jerry Adair	.60	.30	.20
(3)	Richie Allen	1.00	.50	.30
(4)	Jesus Alou	.60	.30	.20
(5)	Max Alvis	.60	.30	.20
(6)	Bob Aspromonte	.60	.30	.20
(7)	Ernie Banks	3.50	1.75	1.00
(8)	Earl Battey	.70	.35	.20
(9)	Curt Blefary	.60	.30	.20
(10)	Ken Boyer	1.00	.50	.30
(11)	Bob Bruce	.60	.30	.20
(12)	Jim Bunning	1.50	.70	.45
(13)	Johnny Callison	.70	.35	.20
(14)	Bert Campaneris	.70	.35	.20
(15)	Jose Cardenal	.60	.30	.20
(16)	Dean Chance	.60	.30	.20
(17)	Ed Charles	.60	.30	.20
(18)	Bob Clemente	7.00	3.50	2.00
(19)	Tony Cloninger	.60	.30	.20
(20)	Rocky Colavito	1.00	.50	.30
(21)	Tony Conigliaro	1.00	.50	.30
(22)	Vic Davalillo	.60	.30	.20
(23)	Willie Davis	.70	.35	.20
(24)	Don Drysdale	3.00	1.50	.90
(25)	Sammy Ellis	.60	.30	.20
(26)	Dick Ellsworth	.60	.30	.20
(27)	Ron Fairly	.70	.35	.20

		NR MT	EX	VG
(28)	Dick Farrell	.60	.30	.20
(29)	Eddie Fisher	.60	.30	.20
(30)	Jack Fisher	.60	.30	.20
(31)	Curt Flood	.70	.35	.20
(32)	Whitey Ford	3.50	1.75	1.00
(33)	Bill Freehan	.70	.35	.20
(34)	Jim Fregosi	.70	.35	.20
(35)	Bob Gibson	3.00	1.50	.90
(36)	Jim Grant	.60	.30	.20
(37)	Jimmie Hall	.60	.30	.20
(38)	Ken Harrelson	.70	.35	.20
(39)	Jim Hart	.60	.30	.20
(40)	Joel Horlen	.60	.30	.20
(41)	Willie Horton	.70	.35	.20
(42)	Frank Howard	1.00	.50	.30
(43)	Deron Johnson	.60	.30	.20
(44)	Al Kaline	4.00	2.00	1.25
(45)	Harmon Killebrew	4.00	2.00	1.25
(46)	Bobby Knoop	.60	.30	.20
(47)	Sandy Koufax	7.00	3.50	2.00
(48)	Ed Kranepool	.60	.30	.20
(49)	Gary Kroll	.60	.30	.20
(50)	Don Landrum	.60	.30	.20
(51)	Vernon Law	.70	.35	.20
(52)	Johnny Lewis	.60	.30	.20
(53)	Don Lock	.60	.30	.20
(54)	Mickey Lolich	1.00	.50	.30
(55)	Jim Maloney	.60	.30	.20
(56)	Felix Mantilla	.60	.30	.20
(57)	Mickey Mantle	40.00	20.00	12.00
(58)	Juan Marichal	3.00	1.50	.90
(59)	Ed Mathews	3.00	1.50	.90
(60)	Willie Mays	8.00	4.00	2.50
(61)	Bill Mazeroski	1.00	.50	.30
(62)	Dick McAuliffe	.60	.30	.20
(63)	Tim McCarver	.70	.35	.20
(64)	Willie McCovey	3.00	1.50	.90
(65)	Sammy McDowell	.70	.35	.20
(66)	Ken McMullen	.60	.30	.20
(67)	Denis Menke	.60	.30	.20
(68)	Bill Monbouquette	.60	.30	.20
(69)	Joe Morgan	2.00	1.00	.60
(70)	Fred Newman	.60	.30	.20
(71)	John O'Donoghue	.60	.30	.20
(72)	Tony Oliva	1.00	.50	.30
(73)	Johnny Orsino	.60	.30	.20
(74)	Phil Ortega	.60	.30	.20
(75)	Milt Pappas	.70	.35	.20
(76)	Dick Radatz	.60	.30	.20
(77)	Bobby Richardson	1.50	.70	.45
(78)	Pete Richert	.60	.30	.20
(79)	Brooks Robinson	4.00	2.00	1.25
(80)	Floyd Robinson	.60	.30	.20
(81)	Frank Robinson	3.50	1.75	1.00
(82)	Cookie Rojas	.60	.30	.20
(83)	Pete Rose	20.00	10.00	6.00
(84)	John Roseboro	.60	.30	.20
(85)	Ron Santo	1.00	.50	.30
(86)	Bill Skowron	.70	.35	.20
(87)	Willie Stargell	3.00	1.50	.90
(88)	Mel Stottlemyre	.70	.35	.20
(89)	Dick Stuart	.60	.30	.20
(90)	Ron Swoboda	.60	.30	.20
(91)	Fred Talbot	.60	.30	.20
(92)	Ralph Terry	.60	.30	.20
(93)	Joe Torre	1.00	.50	.30
(94)	Tom Tresh	.70	.35	.20
(95)	Bob Veale	.60	.30	.20
(96)	Pete Ward	.60	.30	.20
(97)	Bill White	.70	.35	.20
(98)	Billy Williams	2.00	1.00	.60
(99)	Jim Wynn	.70	.35	.20
(100)	Carl Yastrzemski	12.00	6.00	3.50
(101)	Angels Pennant	.60	.30	.20
(102)	Astros Pennant	.60	.30	.20
(103)	Athletics Pennant	.60	.30	.20
(104)	Braves Pennant	.60	.30	.20
(105)	Cards Pennant	.60	.30	.20
(106)	Cubs Pennant	.60	.30	.20
(107)	Dodgers Pennant	.60	.30	.20
(108)	Giants Pennant	.60	.30	.20
(109)	Indians Pennant	.60	.30	.20
(110)	Mets Pennant	.60	.30	.20
(111)	Orioles Pennant	.60	.30	.20
(112)	Phillies Pennant	.60	.30	.20
(113)	Pirates Pennant	.60	.30	.20
(114)	Red Sox Pennant	.60	.30	.20
(115)	Reds Pennant	.60	.30	.20
(116)	Senators Pennant	.60	.30	.20
(117)	Tigers Pennant	.60	.30	.20
(118)	Twins Pennant	.60	.30	.20

		NR MT	EX	VG
(119)	White Sox Pennant	.60	.30	.20
(120)	Yankees Pennant	.60	.30	.20

1967 Topps

This 609-card set of 2-1/2" by 3-1/2" cards marked the largest set up to that time for Topps. Card fronts feature large color photographs bordered by white. The player's name and position are printed at the top with the team at the bottom. Across the front of the card with the exception of #254 (Milt Pappas) there is a facsimile autograph. The backs were the first to be done vertically, although they continued to carry familiar statistical and biographical information. The only subsets are statistical leaders and World Series highlights. Rookie cards are done by team or league with two players per card. The high numbers (#'s 534-609) in '67 are quite scarce, and while it is known that some are even scarcer, by virtue of having been short-printed in relation to the rest of the series, there is no general agreement on which cards are involved.

		NR MT	EX	VG
Complete Set:		5000.00	2500.00	1500.
Common Player: 1-110		1.00	.50	.30
Common Player: 111-370		1.50	.70	.45
Common Player: 371-457		1.25	.60	.40
Common Player: 458-533		5.00	2.50	1.50
Common Player: 534-609		12.00	6.00	3.50
1	The Champs (Hank Bauer, Brooks Robinson, Frank Robinson)	20.00	9.00	5.50
2	Jack Hamilton	1.25	.60	.40
3	Duke Sims	1.00	.50	.30
4	Hal Lanier	1.25	.60	.40
5	Whitey Ford	20.00	10.00	6.00
6	Dick Simpson	1.00	.50	.30
7	Don McMahon	1.00	.50	.30
8	Chuck Harrison	1.00	.50	.30
9	Ron Hansen	1.00	.50	.30
10	Matty Alou	1.25	.60	.40
11	Barry Moore	1.00	.50	.30
12	Dodgers Rookies (Jimmy Campanis, Bill Singer)	1.50	.70	.45
13	Joe Sparma	1.00	.50	.30
14	Phil Linz	1.00	.50	.30
15	Earl Battey	1.50	.70	.45
16	Bill Hands	1.00	.50	.30
17	Jim Gosger	1.00	.50	.30
18	Gene Oliver	1.00	.50	.30
19	Jim McGlothlin	1.00	.50	.30
20	Orlando Cepeda	10.00	5.00	3.00
21	Dave Bristol	1.00	.50	.30
22	Gene Brabender	1.00	.50	.30
23	Larry Elliot	1.50	.70	.45
24	Bob Allen	1.00	.50	.30
25	Elston Howard	5.00	2.50	1.50
26a	Bob Priddy (no trade statement)	15.00	7.50	4.50
26b	Bob Priddy (with trade statement)	1.00	.50	.30
27	Bob Saverine	1.00	.50	.30
28	Barry Latman	1.00	.50	.30
29	Tommy McCraw	1.00	.50	.30
30	Al Kaline	20.00	10.00	6.00

		NR MT	EX	VG
31	Jim Brewer	1.00	.50	.30
32	Bob Bailey	1.00	.50	.30
33	Athletics Rookies (Sal Bando, Randy Schwartz)	1.75	.90	.50
34	Pete Cimino	1.00	.50	.30
35	Rico Carty	1.25	.60	.40
36	Bob Tillman	1.00	.50	.30
37	Rick Wise	1.50	.70	.45
38	Bob Johnson	1.00	.50	.30
39	Curt Simmons	1.25	.60	.40
40	Rick Reichardt	1.00	.50	.30
41	Joe Hoerner	1.00	.50	.30
42	Mets Team	5.00	2.50	1.50
43	Chico Salmon	1.00	.50	.30
44	Joe Nuxhall	1.25	.60	.40
45	Roger Maris	50.00	25.00	15.00
46	Lindy McDaniel	1.00	.50	.30
47	Ken McMullen	1.00	.50	.30
48	Bill Freehan	1.25	.60	.40
49	Roy Face	1.50	.70	.45
50	Tony Oliva	4.00	2.00	1.25
51	Astros Rookies (Dave Adlesh, Wes Bales)	1.00	.50	.30
52	Dennis Higgins	1.00	.50	.30
53	Clay Dalrymple	1.00	.50	.30
54	Dick Green	1.00	.50	.30
55	Don Drysdale	12.00	6.00	3.50
56	Jose Tartabull	1.00	.50	.30
57	Pat Jarvis	1.50	.70	.45
58	Paul Schaal	1.00	.50	.30
59	Ralph Terry	1.25	.60	.40
60	Luis Aparicio	5.00	2.50	1.50
61	Gordy Coleman	1.00	.50	.30
62	Checklist 1-109 (Frank Robinson)	5.00	2.50	1.50
63	Cards' Clubbers (Lou Brock, Curt Flood)	13.00	6.50	4.00
64	Fred Valentine	1.00	.50	.30
65	Tom Haller	1.50	.70	.45
66	Manny Mota	1.25	.60	.40
67	Ken Berry	1.00	.50	.30
68	Bob Buhl	1.50	.70	.45
69	Vic Davalillo	1.50	.70	.45
70	Ron Santo	1.75	.90	.50
71	Camilo Pascual	1.50	.70	.45
72	Tigers Rookies (George Korince, John Matchick)	1.00	.50	.30
73	Rusty Staub	2.50	1.25	.70
74	Wes Stock	1.00	.50	.30
75	George Scott	1.25	.60	.40
76	Jim Barbieri	1.00	.50	.30
77	Dooley Womack	1.25	.60	.40
78	Pat Corrales	1.25	.60	.40
79	Bubba Morton	1.00	.50	.30
80	Jim Maloney	1.50	.70	.45
81	Eddie Stanky	1.50	.70	.45
82	Steve Barber	1.00	.50	.30
83	Ollie Brown	1.00	.50	.30
84	Tommie Sisk	1.00	.50	.30
85	Johnny Callison	1.25	.60	.40
86a	Mike McCormick (no trade statement)	15.00	7.50	4.50
86b	Mike McCormick (with trade statement)	1.50	.70	.45
87	George Altman	1.00	.50	.30
88	Mickey Lolich	2.25	1.25	.70
89	Felix Millan	1.25	.60	.40
90	Jim Nash	1.00	.50	.30
91	Johnny Lewis	1.50	.70	.45
92	Ray Washburn	1.00	.50	.30
93	Yankees Rookies (Stan Bahnsen, Bobby Murcer)	2.50	1.25	.70
94	Ron Fairly	1.25	.60	.40
95	Sonny Siebert	1.50	.70	.45
96	Art Shamsky	1.00	.50	.30
97	Mike Cuellar	1.25	.60	.40
98	Rich Rollins	1.00	.50	.30
99	Lee Stange	1.00	.50	.30
100	Frank Robinson	20.00	10.00	6.00
101	Ken Johnson	1.00	.50	.30
102	Phillies Team	2.00	1.00	.60
103a	Checklist 110-196 (Mickey Mantle) (170 is D McAuliffe)	15.00	7.50	4.50
103b	Checklist 110-196 (Mickey Mantle) (170 is D. McAuliffe)	12.00	6.00	3.50
104	Minnie Rojas	1.00	.50	.30
105	Ken Boyer	2.00	1.00	.60
106	Randy Hundley	1.50	.70	.45
107	Joel Horlen	1.00	.50	.30
108	Alex Johnson	1.00	.50	.30
109	Tribe Thumpers (Rocky Colavito, Leon Wagner)	1.50	.70	.45
110	Jack Aker	1.00	.50	.30
111	John Kennedy	1.50	.70	.45
112	Dave Wickersham	1.50	.70	.45
113	Dave Nicholson	1.50	.70	.45
114	Jack Baldschun	1.50	.70	.45
115	Paul Casanova	1.50	.70	.45
116	Herman Franks	1.50	.70	.45
117	Darrell Brandon	1.50	.70	.45
118	Bernie Allen	1.50	.70	.45
119	Wade Blasingame	1.50	.70	.45
120	Floyd Robinson	1.50	.70	.45
121	Ed Bressoud	1.25	.60	.40
122	George Brunet	1.50	.70	.45
123	Pirates Rookies (Jim Price, Luke Walker)	1.50	.70	.45
124	Jim Stewart	1.50	.70	.45
125	Moe Drabowsky	1.50	.70	.45
126	Tony Taylor	1.50	.70	.45
127	John O'Donoghue	1.50	.70	.45
128	Ed Spiezio	1.50	.70	.45
129	Phil Roof	1.50	.70	.45
130	Phil Regan	1.50	.70	.45
131	Yankees Team	5.00	2.50	1.50
132	Ozzie Virgil	1.50	.70	.45
133	Ron Kline	1.50	.70	.45
134	Gates Brown	1.50	.70	.45
135	Deron Johnson	1.50	.70	.45
136	Carroll Sembera	1.50	.70	.45
137	Twins Rookies (Ron Clark, Jim Ollom)	1.50	.70	.45
138	Dick Kelley	1.50	.70	.45
139	Dalton Jones	1.50	.70	.45
140	Willie Stargell	20.00	10.00	6.00
141	John Miller	1.50	.70	.45
142	Jackie Brandt	1.50	.70	.45
143	Sox Sockers (Don Buford, Pete Ward)	1.25	.60	.40
144	Bill Hepler	1.25	.60	.40
145	Larry Brown	1.50	.70	.45
146	Steve Carlton	125.00	62.00	37.00
147	Tom Egan	1.50	.70	.45
148	Adolfo Phillips	1.50	.70	.45
149	Joe Moeller	1.50	.70	.45
150	Mickey Mantle	200.00	80.00	50.00
151	World Series Game 1 (Moe Mows Down 11)	2.00	1.00	.60
152	World Series Game 2 (Palmer Blanks Dodgers)	3.50	1.75	1.00
153	World Series Game 3 (Blair's Homer Defeats L.A.)	2.00	1.00	.60
154	World Series Game 4 (Orioles Win 4th Straight)	2.00	1.00	.60
155	World Series Summary (The Winners Celebrate)	2.00	1.00	.60
156	Ron Herbel	1.50	.70	.45
157	Danny Cater	1.50	.70	.45
158	Jimmy Coker	1.50	.70	.45
159	Bruce Howard	1.50	.70	.45
160	Willie Davis	1.50	.70	.45
161	Dick Williams	1.50	.70	.45
162	Billy O'Dell	1.50	.70	.45
163	Vic Roznovsky	1.50	.70	.45
164	Dwight Siebler	1.50	.70	.45
165	Cleon Jones	1.25	.60	.40
166	Ed Mathews	12.00	6.00	3.50
167	Senators Rookies (Joe Coleman, Tim Cullen)	1.25	.60	.40
168	Ray Culp	1.50	.70	.45
169	Horace Clarke	1.25	.60	.40
170	Dick McAuliffe	1.25	.60	.40
171	Calvin Koonce	1.50	.70	.45
172	Bill Heath	1.50	.70	.45
173	Cardinals Team	2.00	1.00	.60
174	Dick Radatz	1.25	.60	.40
175	Bobby Knoop	1.50	.70	.45
176	Sammy Ellis	1.50	.70	.45
177	Tito Fuentes	1.50	.70	.45
178	John Buzhardt	1.50	.70	.45
179	Braves Rookies (Cecil Upshaw, Chas. Vaughn)	1.50	.70	.45
180	Curt Blefary	1.50	.70	.45
181	Terry Fox	1.50	.70	.45
182	Ed Charles	1.50	.70	.45
183	Jim Pagliaroni	1.50	.70	.45
184	George Thomas	1.50	.70	.45
185	Ken Holtzman	2.75	1.50	.80
186	Mets Maulers (Ed Kranepool, Ron Swoboda)	1.50	.70	.45
187	Pedro Ramos	1.50	.70	.45
188	Ken Harrelson	1.50	.70	.45
189	Chuck Hinton	1.50	.70	.45

		NR MT	EX	VG
190	Turk Farrell	1.50	.70	.45
191a	Checklist 197-283 (Willie Mays) (214 is Dick Kelley)	12.00	6.00	3.50
191b	Checklist 197-283 (Willie Mays) (214 is Tom Kelley)	12.00	6.00	3.50
192	Fred Gladding	1.50	.70	.45
193	Jose Cardenal	1.25	.60	.40
194	Bob Allison	1.50	.70	.45
195	Al Jackson	1.50	.70	.45
196	Johnny Romano	1.50	.70	.45
197	Ron Perranoski	1.25	.60	.40
198	Chuck Hiller	1.25	.60	.40
199	Billy Hitchcock	1.50	.70	.45
200	Willie Mays	100.00	50.00	30.00
201	Hal Reniff	1.25	.60	.40
202	Johnny Edwards	1.50	.70	.45
203	Al McBean	1.50	.70	.45
204	Orioles Rookies (*Mike Epstein*, Tom Phoebus)	1.50	.70	.45
205	Dick Groat	1.50	.70	.45
206	Dennis Bennett	1.50	.70	.45
207	John Orsino	1.50	.70	.45
208	Jack Lamabe	1.50	.70	.45
209	Joe Nossek	1.50	.70	.45
210	Bob Gibson	18.00	9.00	5.50
211	Twins Team	2.00	1.00	.60
212	Chris Zachary	1.50	.70	.45
213	*Jay Johnstone*	1.75	.90	.50
214	Tom Kelley	1.50	.70	.45
215	Ernie Banks	20.00	10.00	6.00
216	Bengal Belters (Norm Cash, Al Kaline)	5.00	2.50	1.50
217	Rob Gardner	1.25	.60	.40
218	Wes Parker	1.25	.60	.40
219	Clay Carroll	1.25	.60	.40
220	Jim Hart	1.25	.60	.40
221	Woody Fryman	1.25	.60	.40
222	Reds Rookies (Lee May, Darrell Osteen)	1.25	.60	.40
223	Mike Ryan	1.50	.70	.45
224	Walt Bond	1.50	.70	.45
225	Mel Stottlemyre	2.25	1.25	.70
226	Julian Javier	1.25	.60	.40
227	Paul Lindblad	1.50	.70	.45
228	Gil Hodges	5.00	2.50	1.50
229	Larry Jackson	1.50	.70	.45
230	Boog Powell	2.50	1.25	.70
231	John Bateman	1.50	.70	.45
232	Don Buford	1.25	.60	.40
233	A.L. ERA Leaders (Steve Hargan, Joel Horlen, Gary Peters)	2.00	1.00	.60
234	N.L. ERA Leaders (Mike Cuellar, Sandy Koufax, Juan Marichal)	12.00	6.00	3.50
235	A.L. Pitching Leaders (Jim Kaat, Denny McLain, Earl Wilson)	2.50	1.25	.70
236	N.L. Pitching Leaders (Bob Gibson, Sandy Koufax, Juan Marichal, Gaylord Perry)	12.00	6.00	3.50
237	A.L. Strikeout Leaders (Jim Kaat, Sam McDowell, Earl Wilson)	2.50	1.25	.70
238	N.L. Strikeout Leaders (Jim Bunning, Sandy Koufax, Bob Veale)	12.00	6.00	3.50
239	AL 1966 Batting Leaders (Al Kaline, Tony Oliva, Frank Robinson)	12.00	6.00	3.50
240	N.L. Batting Leaders (Felipe Alou, Matty Alou, Rico Carty)	2.00	1.00	.60
241	A.L. RBI Leaders (Harmon Killebrew, Boog Powell, Frank Robinson)	3.50	1.75	1.00
242	N.L. RBI Leaders (Hank Aaron, Richie Allen, Bob Clemente)	12.00	6.00	3.50
243	A.L. Home Run Leaders (Harmon Killebrew, Boog Powell, Frank Robinson)	3.50	1.75	1.00
244	N.L. Home Run Leaders (Hank Aaron, Richie Allen, Willie Mays)	12.00	6.00	3.50
245	Curt Flood	2.50	1.25	.70
246	Jim Perry	1.25	.60	.40
247	Jerry Lumpe	1.25	.60	.40
248	Gene Mauch	1.25	.60	.40
249	Nick Willhite	1.50	.70	.45
250	Hank Aaron	100.00	50.00	30.00
251	Woody Held	1.50	.70	.45
252	Bob Bolin	1.50	.70	.45
253	Indians Rookies (Bill Davis, Gus Gil)	1.50	.70	.45
254	Milt Pappas	1.25	.60	.40
255	Frank Howard	2.50	1.25	.70
256	Bob Hendley	1.50	.70	.45
257	Charley Smith	1.25	.60	.40
258	Lee Maye	1.50	.70	.45
259	Don Dennis	1.50	.70	.45

		NR MT	EX	VG
260	Jim Lefebvre	1.25	.60	.40
261	John Wyatt	1.50	.70	.45
262	Athletics Team	2.00	1.00	.60
263	Hank Aguirre	1.25	.70	.45
264	Ron Swoboda	1.25	.60	.40
265	Lou Burdette	2.50	1.25	.70
266	Pitt Power (Donn Clendenon, Willie Stargell)	3.50	1.75	1.00
267	Don Schwall	1.50	.70	.45
268	John Briggs	1.50	.70	.45
269	Don Nottebart	1.50	.70	.45
270	Zoilo Versalles	1.25	.60	.40
271	Eddie Watt	1.50	.70	.45
272	Cubs Rookies (Bill Connors, Dave Dowling)	1.50	.70	.45
273	Dick Lines	1.50	.70	.45
274	Bob Aspromonte	1.50	.70	.45
275	Fred Whitfield	1.50	.70	.45
276	Bruce Brubaker	1.50	.70	.45
277	Steve Whitaker	1.25	.60	.40
278	Checklist 284-370 (Jim Kaat)	5.00	2.50	1.50
279	Frank Linzy	1.50	.70	.45
280	Tony Conigliaro	2.00	1.00	.60
281	Bob Rodgers	1.50	.70	.45
282	Johnny Odom	1.25	.60	.40
283	Gene Alley	1.25	.60	.40
284	Johnny Podres	5.00	2.50	1.50
285	Lou Brock	25.00	12.50	7.50
286	Wayne Causey	1.50	.70	.45
287	Mets Rookies (Greg Goossen, Bart Shirley)	1.25	.60	.40
288	Denver Lemaster	1.50	.70	.45
289	Tom Tresh	1.75	.90	.50
290	Bill White	1.25	.60	.40
291	Jim Hannan	1.50	.70	.45
292	Don Pavletich	1.50	.70	.45
293	Ed Kirkpatrick	1.50	.70	.45
294	Walt Alston	3.25	1.75	1.00
295	Sam McDowell	1.25	.60	.40
296	Glenn Beckert	1.25	.60	.40
297	Dave Morehead	1.50	.70	.45
298	Ron Davis	1.50	.70	.45
299	Norm Siebern	1.25	.60	.40
300	Jim Kaat	13.00	6.50	4.00
301	Jesse Gonder	1.50	.70	.45
302	Orioles Team	2.00	1.00	.60
303	Gil Blanco	1.50	.70	.45
304	Phil Gagliano	1.50	.70	.45
305	Earl Wilson	1.50	.70	.45
306	*Bud Harrelson*	1.75	.90	.50
307	Jim Beauchamp	1.50	.70	.45
308	Al Downing	1.50	.70	.45
309	Hurlers Beware (Richie Allen, Johnny Callison)	2.00	1.00	.60
310	Gary Peters	1.25	.60	.40
311	Ed Brinkman	1.25	.60	.40
312	Don Mincher	1.25	.60	.40
313	Bob Lee	1.50	.70	.45
314	Red Sox Rookies (*Mike Andrews, Reggie Smith*)	5.00	2.50	1.50
315	Billy Williams	12.00	6.00	3.50
316	Jack Kralick	1.50	.70	.45
317	Cesar Tovar	1.50	.70	.45
318	Dave Giusti	1.50	.70	.45
319	Paul Blair	1.25	.60	.40
320	Gaylord Perry	15.00	7.50	4.50
321	Mayo Smith	1.50	.70	.45
322	Jose Pagan	1.50	.70	.45
323	Mike Hershberger	1.50	.70	.45
324	Hal Woodeshick	1.50	.70	.45
325	Chico Cardenas	1.50	.70	.45
326	Bob Uecker	20.00	10.00	6.00
327	Angels Team	2.00	1.00	.60
328	Clete Boyer	1.50	.70	.45
329	Charlie Lau	1.25	.60	.40
330	Claude Osteen	1.25	.60	.40
331	Joe Foy	1.50	.70	.45
332	Jesus Alou	1.50	.70	.45
333	Ferguson Jenkins	30.00	15.00	9.00
334	Twin Terrors (Bob Allison, Harmon Killebrew)	3.50	1.75	1.00
335	Bob Veale	1.25	.60	.40
336	Joe Azcue	1.50	.70	.45
337	Joe Morgan	25.00	12.50	7.50
338	Bob Locker	1.50	.70	.45
339	Chico Ruiz	1.50	.70	.45
340	Joe Pepitone	2.00	1.00	.60
341	Giants Rookies (*Dick Dietz*, Bill Sorrell)	1.25	.60	.40
342	Hank Fischer	1.50	.70	.45
343	Tom Satriano	1.50	.70	.45

		NR MT	EX	VG
344	Ossie Chavarria	1.50	.70	.45
345	Stu Miller	1.50	.70	.45
346	Jim Hickman	1.25	.60	.40
347	Grady Hatton	1.50	.70	.45
348	Tug McGraw	2.25	1.25	.70
349	Bob Chance	1.50	.70	.45
350	Joe Torre	2.00	1.00	.60
351	Vern Law	1.50	.70	.45
352	Ray Oyler	1.50	.70	.45
353	Bill McCool	1.50	.70	.45
354	Cubs Team	2.00	1.00	.60
355	Carl Yastrzemski	75.00	37.50	23.50
356	Larry Jaster	1.50	.70	.45
357	Bill Skowron	1.50	.70	.45
358	Ruben Amaro	1.25	.60	.40
359	Dick Ellsworth	1.50	.70	.45
360	Leon Wagner	1.25	.60	.40
361	Checklist 371-457 (Bob Clemente)			
		13.00	6.50	4.00
362	Darold Knowles	1.50	.70	.45
363	Dave Johnson	2.00	1.00	.60
364	Claude Raymond	1.50	.70	.45
365	John Roseboro	1.25	.60	.40
366	Andy Kosco	1.50	.70	.45
367	Angels Rookies (Bill Kelso, Don Wallace)			
		1.50	.70	.45
368	Jack Hiatt	1.50	.70	.45
369	Jim Hunter	18.00	9.00	5.50
370	Tommy Davis	1.50	.70	.45
371	Jim Lonborg	1.50	.70	.45
372	Mike de la Hoz	1.25	.60	.40
373	White Sox Rookies (Duane Josephson, Fred Klages)			
		1.25	.60	.40
374	Mel Queen	1.25	.60	.40
375	Jake Gibbs	1.25	.60	.40
376	Don Lock	1.25	.60	.40
377	Luis Tiant	2.25	1.25	.70
378	Tigers Team	5.00	2.50	1.50
379	Jerry May	1.25	.60	.40
380	Dean Chance	1.50	.70	.45
381	Dick Schofield	1.25	.60	.40
382	Dave McNally	1.25	.60	.40
383	Ken Henderson	1.25	.60	.40
384	Cardinals Rookies (Jim Cosman, Dick Hughes)			
		1.25	.60	.40
385	Jim Fregosi	1.50	.70	.45
386	Dick Selma	1.50	.70	.45
387	Cap Peterson	1.25	.60	.40
388	Arnold Earley	1.25	.60	.40
389	Al Dark	1.50	.70	.45
390	Jim Wynn	1.25	.60	.40
391	Wilbur Wood	1.50	.70	.45
392	Tommy Harper	1.50	.70	.45
393	Jim Bouton	2.25	1.25	.70
394	Jake Wood	1.25	.60	.40
395	Chris Short	1.25	.60	.40
396	Atlanta Aces (Tony Cloninger, Denis Menke)			
		1.25	.60	.40
397	Willie Smith	1.25	.60	.40
398	Jeff Torborg	1.50	.70	.45
399	Al Worthington	1.25	.60	.40
400	Bob Clemente	85.00	42.00	26.00
401	Jim Coates	1.25	.60	.40
402	Phillies Rookies (Grant Jackson, Billy Wilson)			
		1.25	.60	.40
403	Dick Nen	1.25	.60	.40
404	Nelson Briles	1.50	.70	.45
405	Russ Snyder	1.25	.60	.40
406	Lee Elia	1.50	.70	.45
407	Reds Team	2.50	1.25	.70
408	Jim Northrup	1.50	.70	.45
409	Ray Sadecki	1.25	.60	.40
410	Lou Johnson	1.25	.60	.40
411	Dick Howser	1.50	.70	.45
412	Astros Rookies (Norm Miller, *Doug Rader*)			
		1.25	.60	.40
413	Jerry Grote	1.50	.70	.45
414	Casey Cox	1.25	.60	.40
415	Sonny Jackson	1.25	.60	.40
416	Roger Repoz	1.25	.60	.40
417	Bob Bruce	1.25	.60	.40
418	Sam Mele	1.25	.60	.40
419	Don Kessinger	1.50	.70	.45
420	Denny McLain	5.00	2.50	1.50
421	Dal Maxvill	1.50	.70	.45
422	Hoyt Wilhelm	15.00	7.50	4.50
423	Fence Busters (Willie Mays, Willie McCovey)			
		25.00	12.50	7.50
424	Pedro Gonzalez	1.25	.60	.40
425	Pete Mikkelsen	1.25	.60	.40
426	Lou Clinton	1.25	.60	.40

		NR MT	EX	VG
427	Ruben Gomez	1.25	.60	.40
428	Dodgers Rookies (Tom Hutton, *Gene Michael*)			
		1.25	.60	.40
429	Garry Roggenburk	1.25	.60	.40
430	Pete Rose	75.00	38.00	23.00
431	Ted Uhlaender	1.25	.60	.40
432	Jimmie Hall	1.25	.60	.40
433	Al Luplow	1.50	.70	.45
434	Eddie Fisher	1.25	.60	.40
435	Mack Jones	1.25	.60	.40
436	Pete Ward	1.25	.60	.40
437	Senators Team	2.25	1.25	.70
438	Chuck Dobson	1.25	.60	.40
439	Byron Browne	1.25	.60	.40
440	Steve Hargan	1.25	.60	.40
441	Jim Davenport	1.25	.60	.40
442	Yankees Rookies (*Bill Robinson*, Joe Verbanic)			
		1.50	.70	.45
443	Tito Francona	1.50	.70	.45
444	George Smith	1.25	.60	.40
445	Don Sutton	30.00	15.00	9.00
446	Russ Nixon	1.25	.60	.40
447	Bo Belinsky	1.25	.60	.40
448	Harry Walker	1.50	.70	.45
449	Orlando Pena	1.25	.60	.40
450	Richie Allen	5.00	2.50	1.50
451	Fred Newman	1.25	.60	.40
452	Ed Kranepool	1.25	.60	.40
453	Aurelio Monteagudo	1.25	.60	.40
454a	Checklist 458-533 (Juan Marichal) (left ear shows)			
		12.00	6.00	3.50
454b	Checklist 458-533 (Juan Marichal) (no left ear)			
		12.00	6.00	3.50
455	Tommie Agee	1.50	.70	.45
456	Phil Niekro	12.00	6.00	3.50
457	Andy Etchebarren	1.25	.60	.40
458	Lee Thomas	5.00	2.50	1.50
459	Senators Rookies (*Dick Bosman*, Pete Craig)			
		12.00	6.00	3.50
460	Harmon Killebrew	50.00	25.00	15.00
461	Bob Miller	5.00	2.50	1.50
462	Bob Barton	5.00	2.50	1.50
463	Tribe Hill Aces (Sam McDowell, Sonny Siebert)			
		12.00	6.00	3.50
464	Dan Coombs	5.00	2.50	1.50
465	Willie Horton	12.00	6.00	3.50
466	Bobby Wine	5.00	2.50	1.50
467	Jim O'Toole	5.00	2.50	1.50
468	Ralph Houk	13.00	6.50	4.00
469	Len Gabrielson	5.00	2.50	1.50
470	Bob Shaw	5.00	2.50	1.50
471	Rene Lachemann	5.00	2.50	1.50
472	Pirates Rookies (John Gelnar, George Spriggs)			
		5.00	2.50	1.50
473	Jose Santiago	5.00	2.50	1.50
474	Bob Tolan	12.00	6.00	3.50
475	Jim Palmer	100.00	50.00	30.00
476	Tony Perez	80.00	40.00	25.00
477	Braves Team	5.50	2.75	1.75
478	Bob Humphreys	5.00	2.50	1.50
479	Gary Bell	5.00	2.50	1.50
480	Willie McCovey	30.00	15.00	9.00
481	Leo Durocher	13.00	6.50	4.00
482	Bill Monbouquette	12.00	6.00	3.50
483	Jim Landis	5.00	2.50	1.50
484	Jerry Adair	5.00	2.50	1.50
485	Tim McCarver	13.00	6.50	4.00
486	Twins Rookies (Rich Reese, Bill Whitby)			
		5.00	2.50	1.50
487	Tom Reynolds	5.00	2.50	1.50
488	Gerry Arrigo	5.00	2.50	1.50
489	Doug Clemens	5.00	2.50	1.50
490	Tony Cloninger	12.00	6.00	3.50
491	Sam Bowens	5.00	2.50	1.50
492	Pirates Team	5.50	2.75	1.75
493	Phil Ortega	5.00	2.50	1.50
494	Bill Rigney	5.00	2.50	1.50
495	Fritz Peterson	12.00	6.00	3.50
496	Orlando McFarlane	5.00	2.50	1.50
497	Ron Campbell	5.00	2.50	1.50
498	Larry Dierker	12.00	6.00	3.50
499	Indians Rookies (George Culver, Jose Vidal)			
		5.00	2.50	1.50
500	Juan Marichal	20.00	10.00	6.00
501	Jerry Zimmerman	5.00	2.50	1.50
502	Derrell Griffith	5.00	2.50	1.50
503	Dodgers Team	13.00	6.50	4.00
504	Orlando Martinez	5.00	2.50	1.50
505	Tommy Helms	5.00	2.50	1.50
506	Smoky Burgess	12.00	6.00	3.50
507	Orioles Rookies (Ed Barnowski, Larry Haney)			
		5.00	2.50	1.50

		NR MT	EX	VG
508	Dick Hall	5.00	2.50	1.50
509	Jim King	5.00	2.50	1.50
510	Bill Mazeroski	13.00	6.50	4.00
511	Don Wert	5.00	2.50	1.50
512	Red Schoendienst	15.00	7.50	4.50
513	Marcelino Lopez	5.00	2.50	1.50
514	John Werhas	5.00	2.50	1.50
515	Bert Campaneris	12.00	6.00	3.50
516	Giants Team	5.50	2.75	1.75
517	Fred Talbot	12.00	6.00	3.50
518	Denis Menke	5.00	2.50	1.50
519	Ted Davidson	5.00	2.50	1.50
520	Max Alvis	5.00	2.50	1.50
521	Bird Bombers (Curt Blefary, Boog Powell)			
		13.00	6.50	4.00
522	John Stephenson	5.00	2.50	1.50
523	Jim Merritt	5.00	2.50	1.50
524	Felix Mantilla	5.00	2.50	1.50
525	Ron Hunt	12.00	6.00	3.50
526	Tigers Rookies (Pat Dobson, George			
	Korince)	12.00	6.00	3.50
527	Dennis Ribant	5.00	2.50	1.50
528	Rico Petrocelli	12.00	6.00	3.50
529	Gary Wagner	5.00	2.50	1.50
530	Felipe Alou	12.00	6.00	3.50
531	Checklist 534-609 (Brooks Robinson)			
		12.00	6.00	3.50
532	Jim Hicks	5.00	2.50	1.50
533	Jack Fisher	5.00	2.50	1.50
534	Hank Bauer	15.00	7.50	4.50
535	Donn Clendenon	12.00	6.00	3.50
536	Cubs Rookies (Joe Niekro, Paul Popovich)			
		40.00	20.00	12.00
537	Chuck Estrada	12.00	6.00	3.50
538	J.C. Martin	15.00	7.50	4.50
539	Dick Egan	12.00	6.00	3.50
540	Norm Cash	35.00	17.50	10.50
541	Joe Gibbon	15.00	7.50	4.50
542	Athletics Rookies (Rick Monday, Tony			
	Pierce)	12.00	6.00	3.50
543	Dan Schneider	15.00	7.50	4.50
544	Indians Team	12.00	6.00	3.50
545	Jim Grant	15.00	7.50	4.50
546	Woody Woodward	15.00	7.50	4.50
547	Red Sox Rookies (Russ Gibson, Bill Rohr)			
		15.00	7.50	4.50
548	Tony Gonzalez	12.00	6.00	3.50
549	Jack Sanford	12.00	6.00	3.50
550	Vada Pinson	12.00	6.00	3.50
551	Doug Camilli	12.00	6.00	3.50
552	Ted Savage	12.00	6.00	3.50
553	Yankees Rookies (Mike Hegan, Thad			
	Tillotson)	18.00	9.00	5.50
554	Andre Rodgers	12.00	6.00	3.50
555	Don Cardwell	15.00	7.50	4.50
556	Al Weis	12.00	6.00	3.50
557	Al Ferrara	12.00	6.00	3.50
558	Orioles Rookies (Mark Belanger, Bill			
	Dillman)	40.00	20.00	12.00
559	Dick Tracewski	12.00	6.00	3.50
560	Jim Bunning	50.00	25.00	15.00
561	Sandy Alomar	15.00	7.50	4.50
562	Steve Blass	12.00	6.00	3.50
563	Joe Adcock	20.00	10.00	6.00
564	Astros Rookies (Alonzo Harris, Aaron			
	Pointer)	15.00	7.50	4.50
565	Lew Krausse	15.00	7.50	4.50
566	Gary Geiger	12.00	6.00	3.50
567	Steve Hamilton	15.00	7.50	4.50
568	John Sullivan	15.00	7.50	4.50
569	A.L. Rookies (Hank Allen, Rod Carew)			
		500.00	250.00	150.00
570	Maury Wills	80.00	40.00	25.00
571	Larry Sherry	12.00	6.00	3.50
572	Don Demeter	12.00	6.00	3.50
573	White Sox Team	18.00	9.00	5.50
574	Jerry Buchek	12.00	6.00	3.50
575	Dave Boswell	12.00	6.00	3.50
576	N.L. Rookies (Norm Gigon, Ramon			
	Hernandez)	18.00	9.00	5.50
577	Bill Short	15.00	7.50	4.50
578	John Boccabella	15.00	7.50	4.50
579	Bill Henry	15.00	7.50	4.50
580	Rocky Colavito	75.00	38.00	23.00
581	Mets Rookies (Bill Denehy, Tom Seaver)			
		1200.00	600.00	350.00
582	Jim Owens	12.00	6.00	3.50
583	Ray Barker	15.00	7.50	4.50
584	Jim Piersall	20.00	10.00	6.00
585	Wally Bunker	15.00	7.50	4.50
586	Manny Jimenez	15.00	7.50	4.50

		NR MT	EX	VG
587	N.L. Rookies (Don Shaw, Gary			
	Sutherland)	18.00	9.00	5.50
588	Johnny Klippstein	12.00	6.00	3.50
589	Dave Ricketts	12.00	6.00	3.50
590	Pete Richert	15.00	7.50	4.50
591	Ty Cline	12.00	6.00	3.50
592	N.L. Rookies (Jim Shellenback, Ron Willis)			
		13.00	6.50	4.00
593	Wes Westrum	15.00	7.50	4.50
594	Dan Osinski	15.00	7.50	4.50
595	Cookie Rojas	12.00	6.00	3.50
596	Galen Cisco	12.00	6.00	3.50
597	Ted Abernathy	12.00	6.00	3.50
598	White Sox Rookies (Ed Stroud, Walt			
	Williams)	13.00	6.50	4.00
599	Bob Duliba	12.00	6.00	3.50
600	Brooks Robinson	225.00	112.00	67.00
601	Bill Bryan	15.00	7.50	4.50
602	Juan Pizarro	15.00	7.50	4.50
603	Athletics Rookies (Tim Talton, Ramon			
	Webster)	15.00	7.50	4.50
604	Red Sox Team	100.00	50.00	30.00
605	Mike Shannon	50.00	25.00	15.00
606	Ron Taylor	15.00	7.50	4.50
607	Mickey Stanley	12.00	6.00	3.50
608	Cubs Rookies (Rich Nye, John Upham)			
		12.00	6.00	3.50
609	Tommy John	125.00	62.00	37.00

1967 Topps Pin-Ups

The 5" by 7" "All Star Pin-ups" were inserts to regular 1967 Topps baseball cards. They feature a full color picture with the player's name, position and team in a circle on the lower left side of the front. The numbered set consists of 32 players (generally big names). Even so, they are rather inexpensive. Because the large paper pin-ups had to be folded several times to fit into the wax packs, they are almost never found in true "Mint" condition.

		NR MT	EX	VG
	Complete Set:	60.00	30.00	18.00
	Common Player:	.25	.13	.08
1	Boog Powell	.40	.20	.12
2	Bert Campaneris	.30	.15	.09
3	Brooks Robinson	3.00	1.50	.90
4	Tommie Agee	.25	.13	.08
5	Carl Yastrzemski	3.50	1.75	1.00
6	Mickey Mantle	12.00	6.00	3.50
7	Frank Howard	.50	.25	.15
8	Sam McDowell	.25	.13	.08
9	Orlando Cepeda	.60	.30	.20
10	Chico Cardenas	.25	.13	.08
11	Bob Clemente	5.00	2.50	1.50
12	Willie Mays	5.00	2.50	1.50
13	Cleon Jones	.25	.13	.08
14	John Callison	.25	.13	.08
15	Hank Aaron	5.00	2.50	1.50
16	Don Drysdale	3.00	1.50	.90
17	Bobby Knoop	.25	.13	.08
18	Tony Oliva	.50	.25	.15
19	Frank Robinson	2.00	1.00	.60
20	Denny McLain	.50	.25	.15
21	Al Kaline	5.00	2.50	1.50
22	Joe Pepitone	.40	.20	.12
23	Harmon Killebrew	5.00	2.50	1.50

		NR MT	EX	VG
24	Leon Wagner	.25	.13	.08
25	Joe Morgan	5.00	2.50	1.50
26	Ron Santo	.40	.20	.12
27	Joe Torre	.60	.30	.20
28	Juan Marichal	2.00	1.00	.60
29	Matty Alou	.25	.13	.08
30	Felipe Alou	.25	.13	.08
31	Ron Hunt	.25	.13	.08
32	Willie McCovey	2.00	1.00	.60

1967 Topps Stand-Ups

Never actually issued, no more than a handful of each of these rare test issues has made their way into the hobby market. Designed so that the color photo of the player's head could be popped out of the black background, and the top folded over to create a stand-up display, examples of these 3-1/8" by 5-1/4" cards can be found either die-cut around the portrait or without the cutting. Blank-backed, there are 24 cards in the set, numbered on the front at bottom left. The cards are popular with advanced superstar collectors.

		NR MT	EX	VG
Complete Set:		6750.00	3375.00	2025.
Common Player:		65.00	32.00	19.50
1	Pete Rose	700.00	350.00	210.00
2	Gary Peters	65.00	32.00	19.50
3	Frank Robinson	200.00	100.00	60.00
4	Jim Lonborg	65.00	32.00	19.50
5	Ron Swoboda	65.00	32.00	19.50
6	Harmon Killebrew	200.00	100.00	60.00
7	Bob Clemente	800.00	400.00	240.00
8	Mickey Mantle	1500.00	750.00	450.00
9	Jim Fregosi	75.00	37.00	22.00
10	Al Kaline	300.00	150.00	90.00
11	Don Drysdale	250.00	125.00	75.00
12	Dean Chance	65.00	32.00	19.50
13	Orlando Cepeda	75.00	37.00	22.00
14	Tim McCarver	75.00	37.00	22.00
15	Frank Howard	75.00	37.00	22.00
16	Max Alvis	65.00	32.00	19.50
17	Rusty Staub	75.00	37.00	22.00
18	Richie Allen	75.00	37.00	22.00
19	Willie Mays	600.00	300.00	175.00
20	Hank Aaron	600.00	300.00	175.00
21	Carl Yastrzemski	600.00	300.00	180.00
22	Ron Santo	75.00	37.00	22.00
23	Jim Hunter	200.00	100.00	60.00
24	Jim Wynn	65.00	32.00	19.50

1967 Topps Stickers Pirates

Considered a "test" issue, this 33-sticker set of 2-1/2" by 3-1/2" stickers is very similar to the Red Sox stickers which were produced the same year. Player stickers have a color picture (often just the player's head) and the player's name in large "comic book" letters. Besides the players, there are other topics such as "I Love the Pirates," "Bob Clemente for Mayor," and a number of similar sentiments. The

stickers have blank backs and are rather scarce.

		NR MT	EX	VG
Complete Set:		250.00	125.00	75.00
Common Player:		3.00	1.50	.90
1	Gene Alley	5.00	2.50	1.50
2	Matty Alou	7.00	3.50	2.00
3	Dennis Ribant	3.00	1.50	.90
4	Steve Blass	5.00	2.50	1.50
5	Juan Pizarro	3.00	1.50	.90
6	Bob Clemente	75.00	38.00	23.00
7	Donn Clendenon	5.00	2.50	1.50
8	Roy Face	7.00	3.50	2.00
9	Woody Fryman	3.00	1.50	.90
10	Jesse Gonder	3.00	1.50	.90
11	Vern Law	7.00	3.50	2.00
12	Al McBean	3.00	1.50	.90
13	Jerry May	3.00	1.50	.90
14	Bill Mazeroski	12.00	6.00	3.50
15	Pete Mikkelsen	3.00	1.50	.90
16	Manny Mota	5.00	2.50	1.50
17	Billy O'Dell	3.00	1.50	.90
18	Jose Pagan	3.00	1.50	.90
19	Jim Pagliaroni	3.00	1.50	.90
20	Johnny Pesky	3.00	1.50	.90
21	Tommie Sisk	3.00	1.50	.90
22	Willie Stargell	40.00	20.00	12.50
23	Bob Veale	5.00	2.50	1.50
24	Harry Walker	3.00	1.50	.90
25	I Love The Pirates	3.00	1.50	.90
26	Let's Go Pirates	3.00	1.50	.90
27	Bob Clemente For Mayor	35.00	17.50	10.50
28	National League Batting Champion (Matty Alou)	4.00	2.00	1.25
29	Happiness Is A Pirate Win	3.00	1.50	.90
30	Donn Clendenon Is My Hero	4.00	2.00	1.25
31	Pirates' Home Run Champion (Willie Stargell)	15.00	7.50	4.50
32	Pirates Logo	3.00	1.50	.90
33	Pirates Pennant	3.00	1.50	.90

1967 Topps Stickers Red Sox

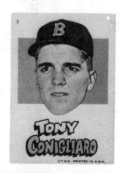

Like the 1967 Pirates Stickers, the Red Sox Stickers were part of the same test procedure. The Red Sox Stickers have the same 2-1/2" by 3-1/2" dimensions, color picture and large player's name on the front. A set is complete at 33 stickers. The majority are players, but themes such as "Let's Go Red Sox" are also included.

		NR MT	EX	VG
	Complete Set:	225.00	112.00	67.00
	Common Player:	3.00	1.50	.90
1	Dennis Bennett	3.00	1.50	.90
2	Darrell Brandon	3.00	1.50	.90
3	Tony Conigliaro	15.00	7.50	4.50
4	Don Demeter	3.00	1.50	.90
5	Hank Fischer	3.00	1.50	.90
6	Joe Foy	3.00	1.50	.90
7	Mike Andrews	3.00	1.50	.90
8	Dalton Jones	3.00	1.50	.90
9	Jim Lonborg	9.00	4.50	2.75
10	Don McMahon	3.00	1.50	.90
11	Dave Morehead	3.00	1.50	.90
12	George Smith	3.00	1.50	.90
13	Rico Petrocelli	6.00	3.00	1.75
14	Mike Ryan	3.00	1.50	.90
15	Jose Santiago	3.00	1.50	.90
16	George Scott	6.00	3.00	1.75
17	Sal Maglie	5.00	2.50	1.50
18	Reggie Smith	10.00	5.00	3.00
19	Lee Stange	3.00	1.50	.90
20	Jerry Stephenson	3.00	1.50	.90
21	Jose Tartabull	3.00	1.50	.90
22	George Thomas	3.00	1.50	.90
23	Bob Tillman	3.00	1.50	.90
24	Johnnie Wyatt	3.00	1.50	.90
25	Carl Yastrzemski	75.00	37.00	22.00
26	Dick Williams	6.00	3.00	1.75
27	I Love The Red Sox	3.00	1.50	.90
28	Let's Go Red Sox	3.00	1.50	.90
29	Carl Yastrzemski For Mayor	35.00	17.50	10.50
30	Tony Conigliaro Is My Hero	7.00	3.50	2.00
31	Happiness Is A Boston Win	3.00	1.50	.90
32	Red Sox Logo	3.00	1.50	.90
33	Red Sox Pennant	3.00	1.50	.90

1968 Topps

In 1968, Topps returned to a 598-card set of 2-1/2" by 3-1/2" cards. It is not, however, more of the same by way of appearance as the cards feature a color photograph on a background of what appears to be a burlap fabric. The player's name is below the photo but on the unusual background. A colored circle on the lower right carries the team and position. Backs were also changed. While retaining the vertical format introduced the previous year, with stats in the middle and cartoon at the bottom, the set features many of the old favorite subsets, including statistical leaders, World Series highlights, multi-player cards, checklists, rookie cards and the return of All-Star cards.

		NR MT	EX	VG
	Complete Set:	3200.00	1600.00	950.00
	Common Player: 1-533	1.00	.50	.30
	Common Player: 534-598	2.50	1.25	.70
1	N.L. Batting Leaders (Matty Alou, Bob Clemente, Tony Gonzalez)	15.00	7.50	4.50
2	A.L. Batting Leaders (Al Kaline, Frank Robinson, Carl Yastrzemski)	4.00	2.00	1.25

		NR MT	EX	VG
3	N.L. RBI Leaders (Hank Aaron, Orlando Cepeda, Bob Clemente)	4.00	2.00	1.25
4	A.L. RBI Leaders (Harmon Killebrew, Frank Robinson, Carl Yastrzemski)	4.00	2.00	1.25
5	N.L. Home Run Leaders (Hank Aaron, Willie McCovey, Ron Santo, Jim Wynn)	4.00	2.00	1.25
6	A.L. Home Run Leaders (Frank Howard, Harmon Killebrew, Carl Yastrzemski)	4.00	2.00	1.25
7	N.L. ERA Leaders (Jim Bunning, Phil Niekro, Chris Short)	2.50	1.25	.70
8	A.L. ERA Leaders (Joe Horlen, Gary Peters, Sonny Siebert)	2.50	1.25	.70
9	N.L. Pitching Leaders (Jim Bunning, Ferguson Jenkins, Mike McCormick, Claude Osteen)	2.50	1.25	.70
10a	A.L. Pitching Leaders (Dean Chance, Jim Lonborg, Earl Wilson) ("Lonberg" on back)	3.50	1.75	1.00
10b	A.L. Pitching Leaders (Dean Chance, Jim Lonborg, Earl Wilson) ("Lonborg" on back)	2.50	1.25	.70
11	N.L. Strikeout Leaders (Jim Bunning, Ferguson Jenkins, Gaylord Perry)	3.00	1.50	.90
12	A.L. Strikeout Leaders (Dean Chance, Jim Lonborg, Sam McDowell)	2.50	1.25	.70
13	Chuck Hartenstein	1.00	.50	.30
14	Jerry McNertney	1.00	.50	.30
15	Ron Hunt	1.00	.50	.30
16	Indians Rookies (Lou Piniella, Richie Scheinblum)	3.50	1.75	1.00
17	Dick Hall	1.00	.50	.30
18	Mike Hershberger	1.00	.50	.30
19	Juan Pizarro	1.00	.50	.30
20	Brooks Robinson	20.00	10.00	6.00
21	Ron Davis	1.00	.50	.30
22	Pat Dobson	1.00	.50	.30
23	Chico Cardenas	1.00	.50	.30
24	Bobby Locke	1.00	.50	.30
25	Julian Javier	1.00	.50	.30
26	Darrell Brandon	1.00	.50	.30
27	Gil Hodges	6.00	3.00	1.75
28	Ted Uhlaender	1.00	.50	.30
29	Joe Verbanic	1.00	.50	.30
30	Joe Torre	3.00	1.50	.90
31	Ed Stroud	1.00	.50	.30
32	Joe Gibbon	1.00	.50	.30
33	Pete Ward	1.00	.50	.30
34	Al Ferrara	1.00	.50	.30
35	Steve Hargan	1.00	.50	.30
36	Pirates Rookies (Bob Moose, Bob Robertson)	1.00	.50	.30
37	Billy Williams	7.00	3.50	2.00
38	Tony Pierce	1.00	.50	.30
39	Cookie Rojas	1.00	.50	.30
40	Denny McLain	3.75	2.00	1.25
41	Julio Gotay	1.00	.50	.30
42	Larry Haney	1.00	.50	.30
43	Gary Bell	1.00	.50	.30
44	Frank Kostro	1.00	.50	.30
45	Tom Seaver	250.00	125.00	75.00
46	Dave Ricketts	1.00	.50	.30
47	Ralph Houk	3.00	1.50	.90
48	Ted Davidson	1.00	.50	.30
49a	Ed Brinkman (yellow team letters)	60.00	30.00	18.00
49b	Ed Brinkman (white team letters)	1.00	.50	.30
50	Willie Mays	70.00	35.00	20.00
51	Bob Locker	1.00	.50	.30
52	Hawk Taylor	1.00	.50	.30
53	Gene Alley	1.00	.50	.30
54	Stan Williams	1.00	.50	.30
55	Felipe Alou	2.50	1.25	.70
56	Orioles Rookies (Dave Leonhard, Dave May)	1.00	.50	.30
57	Dan Schneider	1.00	.50	.30
58	Ed Mathews	10.00	5.00	3.00
59	Don Lock	1.00	.50	.30
60	Ken Holtzman	2.50	1.25	.70
61	Reggie Smith	2.50	1.25	.70
62	Chuck Dobson	1.00	.50	.30
63	Dick Kenworthy	1.00	.50	.30
64	Jim Merritt	1.00	.50	.30
65	John Roseboro	1.00	.50	.30
66a	Casey Cox (yellow team letters)	60.00	30.00	18.00
66b	Casey Cox (white team letters)	1.00	.50	.30
67	Checklist 1-109 (Jim Kaat)	3.00	1.50	.90
68	Ron Willis	1.00	.50	.30
69	Tom Tresh	3.00	1.50	.90
70	Bob Veale	1.00	.50	.30
71	Vern Fuller	1.00	.50	.30
72	Tommy John	5.00	2.50	1.50

		NR MT	EX	VG
73	Jim Hart	1.00	.50	.30
74	Milt Pappas	1.00	.50	.30
75	Don Mincher	1.00	.50	.30
76	Braves Rookies (Jim Britton, *Ron Reed*)	2.50	1.25	.70
77	*Don Wilson*	1.00	.50	.30
78	Jim Northrup	1.00	.50	.30
79	Ted Kubiak	1.00	.50	.30
80	Rod Carew	125.00	67.00	37.00
81	Larry Jackson	1.00	.50	.30
82	Sam Bowens	1.00	.50	.30
83	John Stephenson	1.00	.50	.30
84	Bob Tolan	1.00	.50	.30
85	Gaylord Perry	15.00	7.50	4.50
86	Willie Stargell	10.00	5.00	3.00
87	Dick Williams	2.50	1.25	.70
88	Phil Regan	1.00	.50	.30
89	Jake Gibbs	1.00	.50	.30
90	Vada Pinson	3.00	1.50	.90
91	Jim Ollom	1.00	.50	.30
92	Ed Kranepool	1.00	.50	.30
93	Tony Cloninger	1.00	.50	.30
94	Lee Maye	1.00	.50	.30
95	Bob Aspromonte	1.00	.50	.30
96	Senators Rookies (Frank Coggins, Dick Nold)	1.00	.50	.30
97	Tom Phoebus	1.00	.50	.30
98	Gary Sutherland	1.00	.50	.30
99	Rocky Colavito	2.25	1.25	.70
100	Bob Gibson	25.00	12.50	7.50
101	Glenn Beckert	1.00	.50	.30
102	Jose Cardenal	1.00	.50	.30
103	Don Sutton	8.00	4.00	2.50
104	Dick Dietz	1.00	.50	.30
105	Al Downing	2.50	1.25	.70
106	Dalton Jones	1.00	.50	.30
107	Checklist 110-196 (Juan Marichal)	3.50	1.75	1.00
108	Don Pavletich	1.00	.50	.30
109	Bert Campaneris	2.50	1.25	.70
110	Hank Aaron	80.00	40.00	25.00
111	Rich Reese	1.00	.50	.30
112	Woody Fryman	1.00	.50	.30
113	Tigers Rookies (Tom Matchick, Daryl Patterson)	1.00	.50	.30
114	Ron Swoboda	1.00	.50	.30
115	Sam McDowell	1.00	.50	.30
116	Ken McMullen	1.00	.50	.30
117	Larry Jaster	1.00	.50	.30
118	Mark Belanger	2.50	1.25	.70
119	Ted Savage	1.00	.50	.30
120	Mel Stottlemyre	3.00	1.50	.90
121	Jimmie Hall	1.00	.50	.30
122	Gene Mauch	1.00	.50	.30
123	Jose Santiago	1.00	.50	.30
124	Nate Oliver	1.00	.50	.30
125	Joe Horlen	1.00	.50	.30
126	Bobby Etheridge	1.00	.50	.30
127	Paul Lindblad	1.00	.50	.30
128	Astros Rookies (Tom Dukes, Alonzo Harris)	1.00	.50	.30
129	Mickey Stanley	1.00	.50	.30
130	Tony Perez	6.00	3.00	1.75
131	Frank Bertaina	1.00	.50	.30
132	Bud Harrelson	2.50	1.25	.70
133	Fred Whitfield	1.00	.50	.30
134	Pat Jarvis	1.00	.50	.30
135	Paul Blair	1.00	.50	.30
136	Randy Hundley	1.00	.50	.30
137	Twins Team	3.00	1.50	.90
138	Ruben Amaro	1.00	.50	.30
139	Chris Short	1.00	.50	.30
140	Tony Conigliaro	2.50	1.25	.70
141	Dal Maxvill	1.00	.50	.30
142	White Sox Rookies (Buddy Bradford, Bill Voss)	1.00	.50	.30
143	Pete Cimino	1.00	.50	.30
144	Joe Morgan	15.00	7.50	4.50
145	Don Drysdale	8.00	4.00	2.50
146	Sal Bando	2.50	1.25	.70
147	Frank Linzy	1.00	.50	.30
148	Dave Bristol	1.00	.50	.30
149	Bob Saverine	1.00	.50	.30
150	Bob Clemente	70.00	35.00	23.00
151	World Series Game 1 (Brock Socks 4-Hits In Opener)	3.50	1.75	1.00
152	World Series Game 2 (Yaz Smashes Two Homers)	5.00	2.50	1.50
153	World Series Game 3 (Briles Cools Off Boston)	3.00	1.50	.90
154	World Series Game 4 (Gibson Hurls Shutout!)	3.50	1.75	1.00
155	World Series Game 5 (Lonborg Wins Again!)	2.50	1.25	.70
156	World Series Game 6 (Petrocelli Socks Two Homers)	2.50	1.25	.70
157	World Series Game 7 (St. Louis Wins It!)	3.00	1.50	.90
158	World Series Summary (The Cardinals Celebrate!)	3.00	1.50	.90
159	Don Kessinger	1.00	.50	.30
160	Earl Wilson	1.00	.50	.30
161	Norm Miller	1.00	.50	.30
162	Cardinals Rookies (Hal Gilson, *Mike Torrez*)	2.50	1.25	.70
163	Gene Brabender	1.00	.50	.30
164	Ramon Webster	1.00	.50	.30
165	Tony Oliva	2.50	1.25	.70
166	Claude Raymond	1.00	.50	.30
167	Elston Howard	3.00	1.50	.90
168	Dodgers Team	2.50	1.25	.70
169	Bob Bolin	1.00	.50	.30
170	Jim Fregosi	2.50	1.25	.70
171	Don Nottebart	1.00	.50	.30
172	Walt Williams	1.00	.50	.30
173	John Boozer	1.00	.50	.30
174	Bob Tillman	1.00	.50	.30
175	Maury Wills	3.50	1.75	1.00
176	Bob Allen	1.00	.50	.30
177	Mets Rookies (*Jerry Koosman, Nolan Ryan*)	1600.00	800.00	525.00
178	Don Wert	1.00	.50	.30
179	Bill Stoneman	1.00	.50	.30
180	Curt Flood	2.50	1.25	.70
181	Jerry Zimmerman	1.00	.50	.30
182	Dave Giusti	1.00	.50	.30
183	Bob Kennedy	1.00	.50	.30
184	Lou Johnson	1.00	.50	.30
185	Tom Haller	1.00	.50	.30
186	Eddie Watt	1.00	.50	.30
187	Sonny Jackson	1.00	.50	.30
188	Cap Peterson	1.00	.50	.30
189	Bill Landis	1.00	.50	.30
190	Bill White	2.50	1.25	.70
191	Dan Frisella	1.00	.50	.30
192a	Checklist 197-283 (Carl Yastrzemski) ("To increase the..." on back)	4.50	2.25	1.25
192b	Checklist 197-283 (Carl Yastrzemski) ("To increase your..." on back)	6.00	3.00	1.75
193	Jack Hamilton	1.00	.50	.30
194	Don Buford	1.00	.50	.30
195	Joe Pepitone	3.00	1.50	.90
196	Gary Nolan	1.00	.50	.30
197	Larry Brown	1.00	.50	.30
198	Roy Face	2.50	1.25	.70
199	A's Rookies (Darrell Osteen, Roberto Rodriguez)	1.00	.50	.30
200	Orlando Cepeda	4.00	2.00	1.25
201	*Mike Marshall*	3.00	1.50	.90
202	Adolfo Phillips	1.00	.50	.30
203	Dick Kelley	1.00	.50	.30
204	Andy Etchebarren	1.00	.50	.30
205	Juan Marichal	10.00	5.00	3.00
206	Cal Ermer	1.00	.50	.30
207	Carroll Sembera	1.00	.50	.30
208	Willie Davis	2.50	1.25	.70
209	Tim Cullen	1.00	.50	.30
210	Gary Peters	1.00	.50	.30
211	J.C. Martin	1.00	.50	.30
212	Dave Morehead	1.00	.50	.30
213	Chico Ruiz	1.00	.50	.30
214	Yankees Rookies (Stan Bahnsen, Frank Fernandez)	2.50	1.25	.70
215	Jim Bunning	4.50	2.25	1.25
216	Bubba Morton	1.00	.50	.30
217	Turk Farrell	1.00	.50	.30
218	Ken Suarez	1.00	.50	.30
219	Rob Gardner	1.00	.50	.30
220	Harmon Killebrew	12.00	6.00	3.50
221	Braves Team	3.00	1.50	.90
222	Jim Hardin	1.00	.50	.30
223	Ollie Brown	1.00	.50	.30
224	Jack Aker	1.00	.50	.30
225	Richie Allen	2.25	1.25	.70
226	Jimmie Price	1.00	.50	.30
227	Joe Hoerner	1.00	.50	.30
228	Dodgers Rookies (*Jack Billingham*, Jim Fairey)	.80	.40	.25
229	Fred Klages	1.00	.50	.30
230	Pete Rose	40.00	20.00	12.00
231	Dave Baldwin	1.00	.50	.30
232	Denis Menke	1.00	.50	.30
233	George Scott	1.00	.50	.30

		NR MT	EX	VG
234	Bill Monbouquette	1.00	.50	.30
235	Ron Santo	2.50	1.25	.70
236	Tug McGraw	3.00	1.50	.90
237	Alvin Dark	1.00	.50	.30
238	Tom Satriano	1.00	.50	.30
239	Bill Henry	1.00	.50	.30
240	Al Kaline	20.00	10.00	6.00
241	Felix Millan	1.00	.50	.30
242	Moe Drabowsky	1.00	.50	.30
243	Rich Rollins	1.00	.50	.30
244	John Donaldson	1.00	.50	.30
245	Tony Gonzalez	1.00	.50	.30
246	Fritz Peterson	2.50	1.25	.70
247	Red Rookies (*Johnny Bench*, Ron Tompkins)	225.00	112.00	70.00
248	Fred Valentine	1.00	.50	.30
249	Bill Singer	.80	.40	.25
250	Carl Yastrzemski	30.00	15.00	9.00
251	*Manny Sanguillen*	2.50	1.25	.70
252	Angels Team	3.00	1.50	.90
253	Dick Hughes	1.00	.50	.30
254	Cleon Jones	1.00	.50	.30
255	Dean Chance	1.00	.50	.30
256	Norm Cash	3.00	1.50	.90
257	Phil Niekro	5.00	2.50	1.50
258	Cubs Rookies (Jose Arcia, Bill Schlesinger)	1.00	.50	.30
259	Ken Boyer	3.00	1.50	.90
260	Jim Wynn	1.00	.50	.30
261	Dave Duncan	1.00	.50	.30
262	Rick Wise	1.00	.50	.30
263	Horace Clarke	1.00	.50	.30
264	Ted Abernathy	1.00	.50	.30
265	Tommy Davis	2.50	1.25	.70
266	Paul Popovich	1.00	.50	.30
267	Herman Franks	1.00	.50	.30
268	Bob Humphreys	1.00	.50	.30
269	Bob Tiefenauer	1.00	.50	.30
270	Matty Alou	2.50	1.25	.70
271	Bobby Knoop	1.00	.50	.30
272	Ray Culp	1.00	.50	.30
273	Dave Johnson	3.00	1.50	.90
274	Mike Cuellar	1.00	.50	.30
275	Tim McCarver	3.00	1.50	.90
276	Jim Roland	1.00	.50	.30
277	Jerry Buchek	1.00	.50	.30
278a	Checklist 284-370 (Orlando Cepeda) (copyright at right)	3.00	1.50	.90
278b	Checklist 284-370 (Orlando Cepeda) (copyright at left)	5.00	2.50	1.50
279	Bill Hands	1.00	.50	.30
280	Mickey Mantle	200.00	100.00	60.00
281	Jim Campanis	1.00	.50	.30
282	Rick Monday	2.50	1.25	.70
283	Mel Queen	1.00	.50	.30
284	John Briggs	1.00	.50	.30
285	Dick McAuliffe	.80	.40	.25
286	Cecil Upshaw	1.00	.50	.30
287	White Sox Rookies (Mickey Abarbanel, Cisco Carlos)	1.00	.50	.30
288	Dave Wickersham	1.00	.50	.30
289	Woody Held	1.00	.50	.30
290	Willie McCovey	10.00	5.00	3.00
291	Dick Lines	1.00	.50	.30
292	Art Shamsky	.80	.40	.25
293	Bruce Howard	1.00	.50	.30
294	Red Schoendienst	2.50	1.25	.70
295	Sonny Siebert	1.00	.50	.30
296	Byron Browne	1.00	.50	.30
297	Russ Gibson	1.00	.50	.30
298	Jim Brewer	1.00	.50	.30
299	Gene Michael	2.50	1.25	.70
300	Rusty Staub	3.00	1.50	.90
301	Twins Rookies (George Mitterwald, Rick Renick)	1.00	.50	.30
302	Gerry Arrigo	1.00	.50	.30
303	Dick Green	1.00	.50	.30
304	Sandy Valdespino	1.00	.50	.30
305	Minnie Rojas	1.00	.50	.30
306	Mike Ryan	1.00	.50	.30
307	John Hiller	1.00	.50	.30
308	Pirates Team	3.00	1.50	.90
309	Ken Henderson	1.00	.50	.30
310	Luis Aparicio	5.00	2.50	1.50
311	Jack Lamabe	1.00	.50	.30
312	Curt Blefary	1.00	.50	.30
313	Al Weis	1.00	.50	.30
314	Red Sox Rookies (Bill Rohr, George Spriggs)	1.00	.50	.30
315	Zoilo Versalles	1.00	.50	.30
316	Steve Barber	1.00	.50	.30

		NR MT	EX	VG
317	Ron Brand	1.00	.50	.30
318	Chico Salmon	1.00	.50	.30
319	George Culver	1.00	.50	.30
320	Frank Howard	3.00	1.50	.90
321	Leo Durocher	2.25	1.25	.70
322	Dave Boswell	1.00	.50	.30
323	Deron Johnson	1.00	.50	.30
324	Jim Nash	1.00	.50	.30
325	Manny Mota	1.00	.50	.30
326	Dennis Ribant	1.00	.50	.30
327	Tony Taylor	1.00	.50	.30
328	Angels Rookies (Chuck Vinson, Jim Weaver)	1.00	.50	.30
329	Duane Josephson	1.00	.50	.30
330	Roger Maris	40.00	20.00	12.00
331	Dan Osinski	1.00	.50	.30
332	Doug Rader	1.00	.50	.30
333	Ron Herbel	1.00	.50	.30
334	Orioles Team	3.00	1.50	.90
335	Bob Allison	2.50	1.25	.70
336	John Purdin	1.00	.50	.30
337	Bill Robinson	1.00	.50	.30
338	Bob Johnson	1.00	.50	.30
339	Rich Nye	1.00	.50	.30
340	Max Alvis	1.00	.50	.30
341	Jim Lemon	1.00	.50	.30
342	Ken Johnson	1.00	.50	.30
343	Jim Gosger	1.00	.50	.30
344	Donn Clendenon	1.00	.50	.30
345	Bob Hendley	1.00	.50	.30
346	Jerry Adair	1.00	.50	.30
347	George Brunet	1.00	.50	.30
348	Phillies Rookies (Larry Colton, Dick Thoenen)	1.00	.50	.30
349	Ed Spiezio	1.00	.50	.30
350	Hoyt Wilhelm	6.00	3.00	1.75
351	Bob Barton	1.00	.50	.30
352	Jackie Hernandez	1.00	.50	.30
353	Mack Jones	1.00	.50	.30
354	Pete Richert	1.00	.50	.30
355	Ernie Banks	25.00	12.50	7.50
356	Checklist 371-457 (Ken Holtzman)	2.50	1.25	.70
357	Len Gabrielson	1.00	.50	.30
358	Mike Epstein	1.00	.50	.30
359	Joe Moeller	1.00	.50	.30
360	Willie Horton	1.00	.50	.30
361	Harmon Killebrew AS	5.00	2.50	1.50
362	Orlando Cepeda AS	2.75	1.50	.80
363	Rod Carew AS	12.00	6.00	3.50
364	Joe Morgan AS	3.00	1.50	.90
365	Brooks Robinson AS	6.00	3.00	1.75
366	Ron Santo AS	3.00	1.50	.90
367	Jim Fregosi AS	2.50	1.25	.70
368	Gene Alley AS	2.50	1.25	.70
369	Carl Yastrzemski AS	15.00	7.50	4.50
370	Hank Aaron AS	15.00	7.50	4.50
371	Tony Oliva AS	3.00	1.50	.90
372	Lou Brock AS	6.00	3.00	1.75
373	Frank Robinson AS	8.00	4.00	2.50
374	Bob Clemente AS	15.00	7.50	4.50
375	Bill Freehan AS	2.50	1.25	.70
376	Tim McCarver AS	2.50	1.25	.70
377	Joe Horlen AS	2.50	1.25	.70
378	Bob Gibson AS	7.00	3.50	2.00
379	Gary Peters AS	2.50	1.25	.70
380	Ken Holtzman AS	2.50	1.25	.70
381	Boog Powell	2.50	1.25	.70
382	Ramon Hernandez	1.00	.50	.30
383	Steve Whitaker	1.00	.50	.30
384	Reds Rookies (Bill Henry, *Hal McRae*)	12.00	6.00	3.50
385	Jim Hunter	10.00	5.00	3.00
386	Greg Goossen	1.00	.50	.30
387	Joe Foy	1.00	.50	.30
388	Ray Washburn	1.00	.50	.30
389	Jay Johnstone	1.00	.50	.30
390	Bill Mazeroski	3.00	1.50	.90
391	Bob Priddy	1.00	.50	.30
392	Grady Hatton	1.00	.50	.30
393	Jim Perry	2.50	1.25	.70
394	Tommie Aaron	1.00	.50	.30
395	Camilo Pascual	1.00	.50	.30
396	Bobby Wine	1.00	.50	.30
397	Vic Davalillo	1.00	.50	.30
398	Jim Grant	1.00	.50	.30
399	Ray Oyler	1.00	.50	.30
400a	Mike McCormick (white team letters)	40.00	20.00	12.00
400b	Mike McCormick (yellow team letters)	1.00	.50	.30

		NR MT	EX	VG
401	Mets Team	3.25	1.75	1.00
402	Mike Hegan	2.50	1.25	.70
403	John Buzhardt	1.00	.50	.30
404	Floyd Robinson	1.00	.50	.30
405	Tommy Helms	1.00	.50	.30
406	Dick Ellsworth	1.00	.50	.30
407	Gary Kolb	1.00	.50	.30
408	Steve Carlton	60.00	30.00	18.00
409	Orioles Rookies (Frank Peters, Ron Stone)	1.00	.50	.30
410	Ferguson Jenkins	20.00	10.00	6.00
411	Ron Hansen	1.00	.50	.30
412	Clay Carroll	1.00	.50	.30
413	Tommy McCraw	1.00	.50	.30
414	Mickey Lolich	2.75	1.50	.80
415	Johnny Callison	2.50	1.25	.70
416	Bill Rigney	1.00	.50	.30
417	Willie Crawford	1.00	.50	.30
418	Eddie Fisher	1.00	.50	.30
419	Jack Hiatt	1.00	.50	.30
420	Cesar Tovar	1.00	.50	.30
421	Ron Taylor	1.00	.50	.30
422	Rene Lachemann	1.00	.50	.30
423	Fred Gladding	1.00	.50	.30
424	White Sox Team	3.00	1.50	.90
425	Jim Maloney	1.00	.50	.30
426	Hank Allen	1.00	.50	.30
427	Dick Calmus	1.00	.50	.30
428	Vic Roznovsky	1.00	.50	.30
429	Tommie Sisk	1.00	.50	.30
430	Rico Petrocelli	1.00	.50	.30
431	Dooley Womack	1.00	.50	.30
432	Indians Rookies (Bill Davis, Jose Vidal)	1.00	.50	.30
433	Bob Rodgers	1.00	.50	.30
434	Ricardo Joseph	1.00	.50	.30
435	Ron Perranoski	1.00	.50	.30
436	Hal Lanier	1.00	.50	.30
437	Don Cardwell	1.00	.50	.30
438	Lee Thomas	1.00	.50	.30
439	Luman Harris	1.00	.50	.30
440	Claude Osteen	1.00	.50	.30
441	Alex Johnson	1.00	.50	.30
442	Dick Bosman	1.00	.50	.30
443	Joe Azcue	1.00	.50	.30
444	Jack Fisher	1.00	.50	.30
445	Mike Shannon	1.00	.50	.30
446	Ron Kline	1.00	.50	.30
447	Tigers Rookies (George Korince, Fred Lasher)	1.00	.50	.30
448	Gary Wagner	1.00	.50	.30
449	Gene Oliver	1.00	.50	.30
450	Jim Kaat	6.00	3.00	1.75
451	Al Spangler	1.00	.50	.30
452	Jesus Alou	1.00	.50	.30
453	Sammy Ellis	1.00	.50	.30
454	Checklist 458-533 (Frank Robinson)	4.00	2.00	1.25
455	Rico Carty	2.50	1.25	.70
456	John O'Donoghue	1.00	.50	.30
457	Jim Lefebvre	1.00	.50	.30
458	Lew Krausse	1.00	.50	.30
459	Dick Simpson	1.00	.50	.30
460	Jim Lonborg	2.50	1.25	.70
461	Chuck Hiller	1.00	.50	.30
462	Barry Moore	1.00	.50	.30
463	Jimmie Schaffer	1.00	.50	.30
464	Don McMahon	1.00	.50	.30
465	Tommie Agee	1.00	.50	.30
466	Bill Dillman	1.00	.50	.30
467	Dick Howser	2.50	1.25	.70
468	Larry Sherry	1.00	.50	.30
469	Ty Cline	1.00	.50	.30
470	Bill Freehan	2.50	1.25	.70
471	Orlando Pena	1.00	.50	.30
472	Walt Alston	2.50	1.25	.70
473	Al Worthington	1.00	.50	.30
474	Paul Schaal	1.00	.50	.30
475	Joe Niekro	2.25	1.25	.70
476	Woody Woodward	1.00	.50	.30
477	Phillies Team	3.00	1.50	.90
478	Dave McNally	2.50	1.25	.70
479	Phil Gagliano	1.00	.50	.30
480	Manager's Dream (Chico Cardenas, Bob Clemente, Tony Oliva)	25.00	12.50	7.50
481	John Wyatt	1.00	.50	.30
482	Jose Pagan	1.00	.50	.30
483	Darold Knowles	1.00	.50	.30
484	Phil Roof	1.00	.50	.30
485	Ken Berry	1.00	.50	.30
486	Cal Koonce	1.00	.50	.30

		NR MT	EX	VG
487	Lee May	2.50	1.25	.70
488	Dick Tracewski	1.00	.50	.30
489	Wally Bunker	1.00	.50	.30
490	Super Stars (Harmon Killebrew, Mickey Mantle, Willie Mays)	125.00	67.00	37.00
491	Denny Lemaster	1.00	.50	.30
492	Jeff Torborg	1.00	.50	.30
493	Jim McGlothlin	1.00	.50	.30
494	Ray Sadecki	1.00	.50	.30
495	Leon Wagner	1.00	.50	.30
496	Steve Hamilton	1.00	.50	.30
497	Cards Team	3.50	1.75	1.00
498	Bill Bryan	1.00	.50	.30
499	Steve Blass	1.00	.50	.30
500	Frank Robinson	20.00	10.00	6.00
501	John Odom	1.00	.50	.30
502	Mike Andrews	1.00	.50	.30
503	Al Jackson	1.00	.50	.30
504	Russ Snyder	1.00	.50	.30
505	Joe Sparma	1.00	.50	.30
506	Clarence Jones	1.00	.50	.30
507	Wade Blasingame	1.00	.50	.30
508	Duke Sims	1.00	.50	.30
509	Dennis Higgins	1.00	.50	.30
510	Ron Fairly	1.00	.50	.30
511	Bill Kelso	1.00	.50	.30
512	Grant Jackson	1.00	.50	.30
513	Hank Bauer	1.00	.50	.30
514	Al McBean	1.00	.50	.30
515	Russ Nixon	1.00	.50	.30
516	Pete Mikkelsen	1.00	.50	.30
517	Diego Segui	1.00	.50	.30
518a	Checklist 534-598 (Clete Boyer) (539 is Maj. L. Rookies)	3.00	1.50	.90
518b	Checklist 534-598 (Clete Boyer) (539 is Amer. L. Rookies)	5.00	2.50	1.50
519	Jerry Stephenson	1.00	.50	.30
520	Lou Brock	20.00	10.00	6.00
521	Don Shaw	1.00	.50	.30
522	Wayne Causey	1.00	.50	.30
523	John Tsitouris	1.00	.50	.30
524	Andy Kosco	1.00	.50	.30
525	Jim Davenport	1.00	.50	.30
526	Bill Denehy	1.00	.50	.30
527	Tito Francona	1.00	.50	.30
528	Tigers Team	60.00	30.00	18.00
529	Bruce Von Hoff	1.00	.50	.30
530	Bird Belters (Brooks Robinson, Frank Robinson)	10.00	5.00	3.00
531	Chuck Hinton	1.00	.50	.30
532	Luis Tiant	3.00	1.50	.90
533	Wes Parker	1.00	.50	.30
534	Bob Miller	2.50	1.25	.70
535	Danny Cater	2.50	1.25	.70
536	Bill Short	2.50	1.25	.70
537	Norm Siebern	2.50	1.25	.70
538	Manny Jimenez	2.50	1.25	.70
539	Major League Rookies (Mike Ferraro, Jim Ray)	2.50	1.25	.70
540	Nelson Briles	2.50	1.25	.70
541	Sandy Alomar	2.50	1.25	.70
542	John Boccabella	2.50	1.25	.70
543	Bob Lee	2.50	1.25	.70
544	Mayo Smith	2.50	1.25	.70
545	Lindy McDaniel	2.50	1.25	.70
546	Roy White	2.50	1.25	.70
547	Dan Coombs	2.50	1.25	.70
548	Bernie Allen	2.50	1.25	.70
549	Orioles Rookies (Curt Motton, Roger Nelson)	2.50	1.25	.70
550	Clete Boyer	2.50	1.25	.70
551	Darrell Sutherland	2.50	1.25	.70
552	Ed Kirkpatrick	2.50	1.25	.70
553	Hank Aguirre	2.50	1.25	.70
554	A's Team	3.00	1.50	.90
555	Jose Tartabull	2.50	1.25	.70
556	Dick Selma	2.50	1.25	.70
557	Frank Quilici	2.50	1.25	.70
558	John Edwards	2.50	1.25	.70
559	Pirates Rookies (Carl Taylor, Luke Walker)	2.50	1.25	.70
560	Paul Casanova	2.50	1.25	.70
561	Lee Elia	2.50	1.25	.70
562	Jim Bouton	2.50	1.25	.70
563	Ed Charles	2.50	1.25	.70
564	Eddie Stanky	2.50	1.25	.70
565	Larry Dierker	2.50	1.25	.70
566	Ken Harrelson	3.00	1.50	.90
567	Clay Dalrymple	2.50	1.25	.70
568	Willie Smith	2.50	1.25	.70
569	N.L. Rookies (Ivan Murrell, Les Rohr)	2.50	1.25	.70

		NR MT	EX	VG
570	Rick Reichardt	2.50	1.25	.70
571	Tony LaRussa	3.00	1.50	.90
572	Don Bosch	2.50	1.25	.70
573	Joe Coleman	2.50	1.25	.70
574	Reds Team	3.00	1.50	.90
575	Jim Palmer	60.00	30.00	18.00
576	Dave Adlesh	2.50	1.25	.70
577	Fred Talbot	2.50	1.25	.70
578	Orlando Martinez	2.50	1.25	.70
579	N.L. Rookies (Larry Hisle, Mike Lum)			
		3.00	1.50	.90
580	Bob Bailey	2.50	1.25	.70
581	Garry Roggenburk	2.50	1.25	.70
582	Jerry Grote	2.50	1.25	.70
583	Gates Brown	2.50	1.25	.70
584	Larry Shepard	2.50	1.25	.70
585	Wilbur Wood	2.50	1.25	.70
586	Jim Pagliaroni	2.50	1.25	.70
587	Roger Repoz	2.50	1.25	.70
588	Dick Schofield	2.50	1.25	.70
589	Twins Rookies (Ron Clark, Moe Ogier)			
		2.50	1.25	.70
590	Tommy Harper	2.50	1.25	.70
591	Dick Nen	2.50	1.25	.70
592	John Bateman	2.50	1.25	.70
593	Lee Stange	2.50	1.25	.70
594	Phil Linz	2.50	1.25	.70
595	Phil Ortega	2.50	1.25	.70
596	Charlie Smith	2.50	1.25	.70
597	Bill McCool	2.50	1.25	.70
598	Jerry May	3.00	1.50	.90

1968 Topps
Action All-Star Stickers

Still another of the many Topps test issues of the late 1960s, the Action All-Star stickers were sold in a strip of three, with bubblegum, for 10¢. The strip is comprised of three 3-1/4" by 5-1/4" panels, perforated at the joints for separation. The central panel which is numbered, contains a large color picture of a star player. The top and bottom panels contains smaller pictures of three players each. While there are 16 numbered center panels, only 12 of them are different; panels 13-16 show players previously used. Similarly, the triple-player panels at top and bottom of stickers 13-16 repeat panels from #'s 1-4. Prices below are for stickers which have all three panels still joined. Individual panels are priced significantly lower.

	NR MT	EX	VG
Complete Set:	1300.00	650.00	390.00
Common Player:	18.00	9.00	5.50

		NR MT	EX	VG
1	Orlando Cepeda, Joe Horlen, Al Kaline, Bill Mazeroski, Claude Osteen, Mel Stottlemyre, Carl Yastrzemski	100.00	50.00	30.00
2	Don Drysdale, Harmon Killebrew, Mike McCormick, Tom Phoebus, George Scott, Ron Swoboda, Pete Ward	30.00	15.00	9.00
3	Hank Aaron, Paul Casanova, Jim Maloney, Joe Pepitone, Rick Reichardt, Frank Robinson, Tom Seaver	35.00	17.50	10.50

		NR MT	EX	VG
4	Bob Aspromonte, Johnny Callison, Dean Chance, Jim Lefebvre, Jim Lonborg, Frank Robinson, Ron Santo	25.00	12.50	7.50
5	Bert Campaneris, Al Downing, Willie Horton, Ed Kranepool, Willie Mays, Pete Rose, Ron Santo	200.00	100.00	60.00
6	Max Alvis, Ernie Banks, Al Kaline, Tim McCarver, Rusty Staub, Walt Williams, Carl Yastrzemski	70.00	35.00	21.00
7	Rod Carew, Tony Gonzalez, Steve Hargan, Mickey Mantle, Willie McCovey, Rick Monday, Billy Williams	300.00	150.00	90.00
8	Clete Boyer, Jim Bunning, Tony Conigliaro, Mike Cuellar, Joe Horlen, Ken McMullen, Don Mincher	18.00	9.00	5.50
9	Orlando Cepeda, Bob Clemente, Jim Fregosi, Harmon Killebrew, Willie Mays, Chris Short, Earl Wilson	40.00	20.00	12.00
10	Hank Aaron, Bob Gibson, Bud Harrelson, Jim Hunter, Mickey Mantle, Gary Peters, Vada Pinson	100.00	50.00	30.00
11	Don Drysdale, Bill Freehan, Frank Howard, Ferguson Jenkins, Tony Oliva, Bob Veale, Jim Wynn	30.00	15.00	9.00
12	Richie Allen, Bob Clemente, Sam McDowell, Jim McGlothlin, Tony Perez, Brooks Robinson, Joe Torre	100.00	50.00	30.00
13	Dean Chance, Don Drysdale, Jim Lefebvre, Tom Phoebus, Frank Robinson, George Scott, Carl Yastrzemski	100.00	50.00	30.00
14	Paul Casanova, Orlando Cepeda, Joe Horlen, Harmon Killebrew, Bill Mazeroski, Rick Reichardt, Tom Seaver	35.00	17.50	10.50
15	Bob Aspromonte, Johnny Callison, Jim Lonborg, Mike McCormick, Frank Robinson, Ron Swoboda, Pete Ward	30.00	15.00	9.00
16	Hank Aaron, Al Kaline, Jim Maloney, Claude Osteen, Joe Pepitone, Ron Santo, Mel Stottlemyre	30.00	15.00	9.00

1968 Topps Discs

One of the scarcest of all Topps collectibles, this 28-player set was apparently a never-completed test issue. These full-color, cardboard discs, which measure approximately 2-1/8" in diameter, were apparently intended to be made into a "pin" set, but for some reason, production was never completed and no actual "pins" are known to exist. Uncut sheets of the player discs have been found, however. The discs include a player portrait photo with the name beneath and the city and team nickname along the sides. The set includes eight Hall of Famers.

		NR MT	EX	VG
Complete Set:		3500.00	1750.00	1050.
Common Player:		35.00	17.50	10.50
(1)	Hank Aaron	250.00	125.00	75.00
(2)	Richie Allen	60.00	30.00	18.00
(3)	Gene Alley	35.00	17.50	10.50
(4)	Rod Carew	300.00	150.00	90.00
(5)	Orlando Cepeda	60.00	30.00	18.00
(6)	Dean Chance	35.00	17.50	10.50
(7)	Bob Clemente	350.00	175.00	100.00
(8)	Tommy Davis	35.00	17.50	10.50
(9)	Bill Freehan	35.00	17.50	10.50
(10)	Jim Fregosi	35.00	17.50	10.50
(11)	Steve Hargan	35.00	17.50	10.50
(12)	Frank Howard	60.00	30.00	18.00
(13)	Al Kaline	200.00	100.00	60.00

		NR MT	EX	VG
(14)	Harmon Killebrew	150.00	75.00	45.00
(15)	Mickey Mantle	600.00	300.00	175.00
(16)	Willie Mays	300.00	150.00	90.00
(17)	Mike McCormick	35.00	17.50	10.50
(18)	Rick Monday	35.00	17.50	10.50
(19)	Claude Osteen	35.00	17.50	10.50
(20)	Gary Peters	35.00	17.50	10.50
(21)	Brooks Robinson	200.00	100.00	60.00
(22)	Frank Robinson	150.00	75.00	45.00
(23)	Pete Rose	400.00	200.00	125.00
(24)	Ron Santo	60.00	30.00	18.00
(25)	Rusty Staub	60.00	30.00	18.00
(26)	Joe Torre	60.00	30.00	18.00
(27)	Carl Yastrzemski	150.00	75.00	45.00
(28)	Bob Veale	35.00	17.50	10.50

1968 Topps Game

A throwback to the Red and Blue Back sets of 1951, the 33-cards in the 1968 Topps Game set, inserted into packs of regular '68 Topps cards or purchases as a complete boxed set, enable the owner to play a game of baseball based on the game situations on each card. Also on the 2-1/4" by 3-1/4" cards were a color photograph of a player and his facsimile autograph. One redeeming social value of the set (assuming you're not mesmerized by the game) is that it affords an inexpensive way to get big-name cards as the set is loaded with stars, but not at all popular with collectors.

		NR MT	EX	VG
	Complete Set:	70.00	35.00	21.00
	Common Player:	.30	.15	.09
1	Mateo Alou	.50	.25	.15
2	Mickey Mantle	15.00	7.50	4.50
3	Carl Yastrzemski	3.25	1.75	1.00
4	Henry Aaron	3.00	1.50	.90
5	Harmon Killebrew	1.75	.90	.50
6	Roberto Clemente	3.00	1.50	.90
7	Frank Robinson	1.75	.90	.50
8	Willie Mays	3.00	1.50	.90
9	Brooks Robinson	2.00	1.00	.60
10	Tommy Davis	.50	.25	.15
11	Bill Freehan	.50	.25	.15
12	Claude Osteen	.40	.20	.12
13	Gary Peters	.30	.15	.09
14	Jim Lonborg	.40	.20	.12
15	Steve Hargan	.30	.15	.09
16	Dean Chance	.40	.20	.12
17	Mike McCormick	.30	.15	.09
18	Tim McCarver	.60	.30	.20
19	Ron Santo	.60	.30	.20
20	Tony Gonzalez	.30	.15	.09
21	Frank Howard	.70	.35	.20
22	George Scott	.40	.20	.12
23	Rich Allen	.70	.35	.20
24	Jim Wynn	.40	.20	.12
25	Gene Alley	.40	.20	.12
26	Rick Monday	.40	.20	.12
27	Al Kaline	2.00	1.00	.60
28	Rusty Staub	.70	.35	.20
29	Rod Carew	2.75	1.50	.80
30	Pete Rose	7.50	3.75	2.25
31	Joe Torre	.70	.35	.20
32	Orlando Cepeda	1.00	.50	.30
33	Jim Fregosi	.50	.25	.15

1968 Topps Plaks

Among the scarcest of the Topps test issues of the late 1960s, the "All Star Baseball Plaks" were plastic busts of two dozen stars of the era which came packaged like model airplane parts. The busts had to be snapped off a sprue and could be inserted into a base which carried the player's name. Packed with the plastic plaks was one of two checklist cards which featured six color photos per side. The 2-1/8" by 4" checklist cards are popular with superstar collectors and are considerably easier to find today than the actual plaks.

		NR MT	EX	VG
	Complete Set:	2300.00	1150.00	690.00
	Common Player:	20.00	10.00	6.00
1	Max Alvis	20.00	10.00	6.00
2	Frank Howard	30.00	15.00	9.00
3	Dean Chance	20.00	10.00	6.00
4	Jim Hunter	50.00	25.00	15.00
5	Jim Fregosi	25.00	12.50	7.50
6	Al Kaline	60.00	30.00	18.00
7	Harmon Killebrew	60.00	30.00	18.00
8	Gary Peters	20.00	10.00	6.00
9	Jim Lonborg	20.00	10.00	6.00
10	Frank Robinson	60.00	30.00	18.00
11	Mickey Mantle	800.00	400.00	240.00
12	Carl Yastrzemski	175.00	87.00	52.00
13	Hank Aaron	100.00	50.00	30.00
14	Bob Clemente	100.00	50.00	30.00
15	Richie Allen	30.00	15.00	9.00
16	Tommy Davis	25.00	12.50	7.50
17	Orlando Cepeda	30.00	15.00	9.00
18	Don Drysdale	50.00	25.00	15.00
19	Willie Mays	100.00	50.00	30.00
20	Rusty Staub	30.00	15.00	9.00
21	Tim McCarver	30.00	15.00	9.00
22	Pete Rose	250.00	125.00	75.00
23	Ron Santo	30.00	15.00	9.00
24	Jim Wynn	20.00	10.00	6.00
----	Checklist Card 1-12	250.00	125.00	75.00
----	Checklist Card 13-24	250.00	125.00	75.00

1968 Topps Posters

Yet another innovation from the creative minds at Topps appeared in 1968; a set of color player posters. Measuring 9-3/4" by 18-1/8," each poster was sold separately with its own piece of gum, rather than as an insert. The posters feature a large color photograph with a star at the bottom containing the player's name, position and team. There are 24 different posters which were folded numerous times to fit into the package they were sold in.

		NR MT	EX	VG
Complete Set:		325.00	162.00	97.00
Common Player:		3.00	1.50	.90
1	Dean Chance	3.00	1.50	.90
2	Max Alvis	3.00	1.50	.90
3	Frank Howard	8.00	4.00	2.50
4	Jim Fregosi	7.00	3.50	2.00
5	Jim Hunter	12.00	6.00	3.50
6	Bob Clemente	25.00	12.50	7.50
7	Don Drysdale	12.00	6.00	3.50
8	Jim Wynn	3.00	1.50	.90
9	Al Kaline	25.00	12.50	7.50
10	Harmon Killebrew	20.00	10.00	6.00
11	Jim Lonborg	3.00	1.50	.90
12	Orlando Cepeda	8.00	4.00	2.50
13	Gary Peters	3.00	1.50	.90
14	Hank Aaron	25.00	12.50	7.50
15	Richie Allen	8.00	4.00	2.50
16	Carl Yastrzemski	20.00	10.00	6.00
17	Ron Swoboda	3.00	1.50	.90
18	Mickey Mantle	50.00	25.00	15.00
19	Tim McCarver	7.00	3.50	2.00
20	Willie Mays	25.00	12.50	7.50
21	Ron Santo	7.00	3.50	2.00
22	Rusty Staub	7.00	3.50	2.00
23	Pete Rose	40.00	20.00	12.00
24	Frank Robinson	15.00	7.50	4.50

1968 Topps 3-D

These are very rare pioneer issues on the part of Topps. The cards measure 2-1/4" by 3-1/2" and were specially printed to simulate a three-dimensional effect. Backgrounds are a purposely blurred stadium scene, in front of which was a normally sharp color player photograph. The outer layer is a thin coating of ribbed plastic. The special process gives the picture the illusion of depth when the card is moved or tilted. As this was done two years before Kellogg's began its 3-D cards, this 12-card test issue really was breaking new ground. Unfortunately, production and distribution were limited making the cards very tough to find.

		NR MT	EX	VG
Complete Set:		9000.00	4500.00	2500.
Common Player:		350.00	175.00	105.00
(1)	Bob Clemente	2500.00	1250.00	750.00
(2)	Willie Davis	400.00	200.00	125.00
(3)	Ron Fairly	400.00	200.00	125.00
(4)	Curt Flood	400.00	200.00	125.00
(5)	Jim Lonborg	400.00	200.00	125.00
(6)	Jim Maloney	350.00	175.00	105.00
(7)	Tony Perez	600.00	300.00	175.00

		NR MT	EX	VG
(8)	Boog Powell	500.00	250.00	150.00
(9)	Bill Robinson	350.00	175.00	105.00
(10)	Rusty Staub	450.00	230.00	135.00
(11)	Mel Stottlemyre	400.00	200.00	120.00
(12)	Ron Swoboda	350.00	175.00	105.00

1969 Topps

The 1969 Topps set broke yet another record for quantity as the issue is officially a whopping 664 cards. With substantial numbers of variations, the number of possible cards runs closer to 700. The design of the 2-1/2" by 3-1/2" cards in the set feature a color photo with the team name printed in block letters underneath. A circle contains the player's name and position. Card backs returned to a horizontal format. Despite the size of the set, it contains no teamcards. It does, however, have multi-player cards, All-Stars, statistical leaders, and World Series highlights. Most significant among the varieties are white and yellow letter cards from the run of #'s 440-511. The complete set prices below do not include the scarcer and more expensive "white letter" variations.

	NR MT	EX	VG
Complete Set:	2600.00	1300.00	800.00
Common Player: 1-218	1.00	.50	.30
Common Player: 219-327	1.50	.70	.45
Common Player: 328-512	1.00	.50	.30
Common Player: 513-664	1.00	.50	.30

		NR MT	EX	VG
1	A.L. Batting Leaders (Danny Cater, Tony Oliva, Carl Yastrzemski)	10.00	5.00	3.00
2	N.L. Batting Leaders (Felipe Alou, Matty Alou, Pete Rose)	4.00	2.00	1.25
3	A.L. RBI Leaders (Ken Harrelson, Frank Howard, Jim Northrup)	2.00	1.00	.60
4	N.L. RBI Leaders (Willie McCovey, Ron Santo, Billy Williams)	3.50	1.75	1.00
5	A.L. Home Run Leaders (Ken Harrelson, Willie Horton, Frank Howard)	2.00	1.00	.60
6	N.L. Home Run Leaders (Richie Allen, Ernie Banks, Willie McCovey)	3.50	1.75	1.00
7	A.L. ERA Leaders (Sam McDowell, Dave McNally, Luis Tiant)	2.00	1.00	.60
8	N.L. ERA Leaders (Bobby Bolin, Bob Gibson, Bob Veale)	3.00	1.50	.90
9	A.L. Pitching Leaders (Denny McLain, Dave McNally, Mel Stottlemyre, Luis Tiant)	2.00	1.00	.60
10	N.L. Pitching Leaders (Bob Gibson, Fergie Jenkins, Juan Marichal)	3.50	1.75	1.00
11	A.L. Strikeout Leaders (Sam McDowell, Denny McLain, Luis Tiant)	2.00	1.00	.60
12	N.L. Strikeout Leaders (Bob Gibson, Fergie Jenkins, Bill Singer)	3.00	1.50	.90
13	Mickey Stanley	1.00	.50	.30
14	Al McBean	1.00	.50	.30
15	Boog Powell	2.50	1.25	.70
16	Giants Rookies (Cesar Gutierrez, Rich Robertson)	1.00	.50	.30
17	Mike Marshall	1.50	.70	.45
18	Dick Schofield	1.00	.50	.30
19	Ken Suarez	1.00	.50	.30
20	Ernie Banks	20.00	10.00	6.00
21	Jose Santiago	1.00	.50	.30

		NR MT	EX	VG
22	Jesus Alou	1.00	.50	.30
23	Lew Krausse	1.00	.50	.30
24	Walt Alston	3.00	1.50	.90
25	Roy White	1.50	.70	.45
26	Clay Carroll	1.00	.50	.30
27	Bernie Allen	1.00	.50	.30
28	Mike Ryan	1.00	.50	.30
29	Dave Morehead	1.00	.50	.30
30	Bob Allison	1.00	.50	.30
31	Mets Rookies (Gary Gentry, Amos Otis)			
		1.50	.70	.45
32	Sammy Ellis	1.00	.50	.30
33	Wayne Causey	1.00	.50	.30
34	Gary Peters	1.00	.50	.30
35	Joe Morgan	12.00	6.00	3.50
36	Luke Walker	1.00	.50	.30
37	Curt Motton	1.00	.50	.30
38	Zoilo Versalles	1.00	.50	.30
39	Dick Hughes	1.00	.50	.30
40	Mayo Smith	1.00	.50	.30
41	Bob Barton	1.00	.50	.30
42	Tommy Harper	1.00	.50	.30
43	Joe Niekro	1.50	.70	.45
44	Danny Cater	1.00	.50	.30
45	Maury Wills	2.50	1.25	.70
46	Fritz Peterson	1.00	.50	.30
47a	Paul Popovich (emblem visible thru airbrush)			
		4.00	2.00	1.25
47b	Paul Popovich (helmet emblem completely airbrushed)			
		1.00	.50	.30
48	Brant Alyea	1.00	.50	.30
49a	Royals Rookies (Steve Jones, Eliseo Rodriquez) (Rodriquez on front)			
		6.00	3.00	1.75
49b	Royals Rookies (Steve Jones, Eliseo Rodriguez) (Rodriguez on front)			
		1.00	.50	.30
50	Bob Clemente	55.00	28.00	16.50
51	Woody Fryman	1.00	.50	.30
52	Mike Andrews	1.00	.50	.30
53	Sonny Jackson	1.00	.50	.30
54	Cisco Carlos	1.00	.50	.30
55	Jerry Grote	1.00	.50	.30
56	Rich Reese	1.00	.50	.30
57	Checklist 1-109 (Denny McLain)	3.00	1.50	.90
58	Fred Gladding	1.00	.50	.30
59	Jay Johnstone	1.00	.50	.30
60	Nelson Briles	1.00	.50	.30
61	Jimmie Hall	1.00	.50	.30
62	Chico Salmon	1.25	.60	.40
63	Jim Hickman	1.00	.50	.30
64	Bill Monbouquette	1.00	.50	.30
65	Willie Davis	1.00	.50	.30
66	Orioles Rookies (Mike Adamson, Merv Rettenmund)			
		1.00	.50	.30
67	Bill Stoneman	1.00	.50	.30
68	Dave Duncan	1.00	.50	.30
69	Steve Hamilton	1.00	.50	.30
70	Tommy Helms	1.00	.50	.30
71	Steve Whitaker	1.00	.50	.30
72	Ron Taylor	1.00	.50	.30
73	Johnny Briggs	1.00	.50	.30
74	Preston Gomez	1.00	.50	.30
75	Luis Aparicio	5.00	2.50	1.50
76	Norm Miller	1.00	.50	.30
77a	Ron Perranoski (LA visible thru airbrush)			
		4.50	2.25	1.25
77b	Ron Perranoski (cap emblem completely airbrushed)			
		1.00	.50	.30
78	Tom Satriano	1.00	.50	.30
79	Milt Pappas	1.00	.50	.30
80	Norm Cash	1.75	.90	.50
81	Mel Queen	1.00	.50	.30
82	Pirates Rookies (Rich Hebner, Al Oliver)			
		12.00	6.00	3.50
83	Mike Ferraro	1.25	.60	.40
84	Bob Humphreys	1.00	.50	.30
85	Lou Brock	20.00	10.00	6.00
86	Pete Richert	1.00	.50	.30
87	Horace Clarke	1.00	.50	.30
88	Rich Nye	1.00	.50	.30
89	Russ Gibson	1.00	.50	.30
90	Jerry Koosman	2.50	1.25	.70
91	Al Dark	1.00	.50	.30
92	Jack Billingham	1.00	.50	.30
93	Joe Foy	1.00	.50	.30
94	Hank Aguirre	1.00	.50	.30
95	Johnny Bench	125.00	67.00	37.00
96	Denver Lemaster	1.00	.50	.30
97	Buddy Bradford	1.00	.50	.30
98	Dave Giusti	1.00	.50	.30
99a	Twins Rookies (Danny Morris, Graig Nettles) (black loop above "Twins")	20.00	10.00	6.00

		NR MT	EX	VG
99b	Twins Rookies (Danny Morris, Graig Nettles) (no black loop)	12.00	6.00	3.50
100	Hank Aaron	60.00	30.00	18.00
101	Daryl Patterson	1.00	.50	.30
102	Jim Davenport	1.00	.50	.30
103	Roger Repoz	1.00	.50	.30
104	Steve Blass	1.00	.50	.30
105	Rick Monday	1.25	.60	.40
106	Jim Hannan	1.00	.50	.30
107a	Checklist 110-218 (Bob Gibson) (161 is Jim Purdin)	3.00	1.50	.90
107b	Checklist 110-218 (Bob Gibson) (161 is John Purdin)	6.00	3.00	1.75
108	Tony Taylor	1.00	.50	.30
109	Jim Lonborg	1.25	.60	.40
110	Mike Shannon	1.00	.50	.30
111	Johnny Morris	1.25	.60	.40
112	J.C. Martin	1.00	.50	.30
113	Dave May	1.00	.50	.30
114	Yankees Rookies (Alan Closter, John Cumberland)	1.00	.50	.30
115	Bill Hands	1.00	.50	.30
116	Chuck Harrison	1.00	.50	.30
117	Jim Fairey	1.00	.50	.30
118	Stan Williams	1.00	.50	.30
119	Doug Rader	1.00	.50	.30
120	Pete Rose	35.00	17.50	10.50
121	Joe Grzenda	1.00	.50	.30
122	Ron Fairly	1.25	.60	.40
123	Wilbur Wood	1.25	.60	.40
124	Hank Bauer	1.25	.60	.40
125	Ray Sadecki	1.00	.50	.30
126	Dick Tracewski	1.00	.50	.30
127	Kevin Collins	1.00	.50	.30
128	Tommie Aaron	1.00	.50	.30
129	Bill McCool	1.00	.50	.30
130	Carl Yastrzemski	30.00	15.00	9.00
131	Chris Cannizzaro	1.00	.50	.30
132	Dave Baldwin	1.00	.50	.30
133	Johnny Callison	1.00	.50	.30
134	Jim Weaver	1.00	.50	.30
135	Tommy Davis	1.50	.70	.45
136	Cards Rookies (Steve Huntz, Mike Torrez)			
		1.00	.50	.30
137	Wally Bunker	1.00	.50	.30
138	John Bateman	1.00	.50	.30
139	Andy Kosco	1.00	.50	.30
140	Jim Lefebvre	1.00	.50	.30
141	Bill Dillman	1.00	.50	.30
142	Woody Woodward	1.00	.50	.30
143	Joe Nossek	1.00	.50	.30
144	Bob Hendley	1.00	.50	.30
145	Max Alvis	1.00	.50	.30
146	Jim Perry	1.00	.50	.30
147	Leo Durocher	2.25	1.25	.70
148	Lee Stange	1.00	.50	.30
149	Ollie Brown	1.00	.50	.30
150	Denny McLain	3.00	1.50	.90
151a	Clay Dalrymple (Phillies)	7.00	3.50	2.00
151b	Clay Dalrymple (Orioles)	1.00	.50	.30
152	Tommie Sisk	1.00	.50	.30
153	Ed Brinkman	1.00	.50	.30
154	Jim Britton	1.00	.50	.30
155	Pete Ward	1.00	.50	.30
156	Astros Rookies (Hal Gilson, Leon McFadden)			
		1.00	.50	.30
157	Bob Rodgers	1.00	.50	.30
158	Joe Gibbon	1.00	.50	.30
159	Jerry Adair	1.00	.50	.30
160	Vada Pinson	2.00	1.00	.60
161	John Purdin	1.00	.50	.30
162	World Series Game 1 (Gibson Fans 17; Sets New Record)	3.50	1.75	1.00
163	World Series Game 2 (Tiger Homers Deck The Cards)	2.50	1.25	.70
164	World Series Game 3 (McCarver's Homer Puts St. Louis Ahead)	2.50	1.25	.70
165	World Series Game 4 (Brock's Lead-Off Homer Starts Cards' Romp)	3.50	1.75	1.00
166	World Series Game 5 (Kaline's Key Hit Sparks Tiger Rally)	3.50	1.75	1.00
167	World Series Game 6 (Tiger 10-Run Inning Ties Mark)	2.50	1.25	.70
168	World Series Game 7 (Lolich Series Hero, Outduels Gibson)	2.75	1.50	.80
169	World Series Summary (Tigers Celebrate Their Victory)	2.50	1.25	.70
170	Frank Howard	2.00	1.00	.60
171	Glenn Beckert	1.25	.60	.40
172	Jerry Stephenson	1.00	.50	.30
173	White Sox Rookies (Bob Christian, Gerry Nyman)	1.00	.50	.30

	NR MT	EX	VG
174 Grant Jackson	1.00	.50	.30
175 Jim Bunning	4.00	2.00	1.25
176 Joe Azcue	1.00	.50	.30
177 Ron Reed	1.00	.50	.30
178 Ray Oyler	1.25	.60	.40
179 Don Pavletich	1.00	.50	.30
180 Willie Horton	1.25	.60	.40
181 Mel Nelson	1.00	.50	.30
182 Bill Rigney	1.00	.50	.30
183 Don Shaw	1.00	.50	.30
184 Roberto Pena	1.00	.50	.30
185 Tom Phoebus	1.00	.50	.30
186 John Edwards	1.00	.50	.30
187 Leon Wagner	1.00	.50	.30
188 Rick Wise	1.00	.50	.30
189 Red Sox Rookies (Joe Lahoud, John Thibdeau)	1.00	.50	.30
190 Willie Mays	65.00	33.00	21.00
191 Lindy McDaniel	1.00	.50	.30
192 Jose Pagan	1.00	.50	.30
193 Don Cardwell	1.00	.50	.30
194 Ted Uhlaender	1.00	.50	.30
195 John Odom	1.00	.50	.30
196 Lum Harris	1.00	.50	.30
197 Dick Selma	1.00	.50	.30
198 Willie Smith	1.00	.50	.30
199 Jim French	1.00	.50	.30
200 Bob Gibson	12.00	6.00	3.50
201 Russ Snyder	1.00	.50	.30
202 Don Wilson	1.00	.50	.30
203 Dave Johnson	1.50	.70	.45
204 Jack Hiatt	1.00	.50	.30
205 Rick Reichardt	1.00	.50	.30
206 Phillies Rookies (Larry Hisle, Barry Lersch)	1.25	.60	.40
207 Roy Face	1.50	.70	.45
208a Donn Clendenon (Expos)	7.00	3.50	2.00
208b Donn Clendenon (Houston)	1.00	.50	.30
209 Larry Haney (photo reversed)	1.25	.60	.40
210 Felix Millan	1.00	.50	.30
211 Galen Cisco	1.00	.50	.30
212 Tom Tresh	1.50	.70	.45
213 Gerry Arrigo	1.00	.50	.30
214 Checklist 219-327	2.50	1.25	.70
215 Rico Petrocelli	1.25	.60	.40
216 Don Sutton	5.00	2.50	1.50
217 John Donaldson	1.00	.50	.30
218 John Roseboro	1.00	.50	.30
219 Freddie Patek	2.00	1.00	.60
220 Sam McDowell	1.50	.70	.45
221 Art Shamsky	1.50	.70	.45
222 Duane Josephson	1.50	.70	.45
223 Tom Dukes	1.50	.70	.45
224 Angels Rookies (Bill Harrelson, Steve Kealey)	1.50	.70	.45
225 Don Kessinger	1.50	.70	.45
226 Bruce Howard	1.50	.70	.45
227 Frank Johnson	1.50	.70	.45
228 Dave Leonhard	1.50	.70	.45
229 Don Lock	1.50	.70	.45
230 Rusty Staub	2.50	1.25	.70
231 Pat Dobson	1.50	.70	.45
232 Dave Ricketts	1.50	.70	.45
233 Steve Barber	1.50	.70	.45
234 Dave Bristol	1.50	.70	.45
235 Jim Hunter	10.00	5.00	3.00
236 Manny Mota	1.50	.70	.45
237 Bobby Cox	1.50	.70	.45
238 Ken Johnson	1.50	.70	.45
239 Bob Taylor	1.50	.70	.45
240 Ken Harrelson	2.00	1.00	.60
241 Jim Brewer	1.50	.70	.45
242 Frank Kostro	1.50	.70	.45
243 Ron Kline	1.50	.70	.45
244 Indians Rookies (Ray Fosse, George Woodson)	1.50	.70	.45
245 Ed Charles	1.50	.70	.45
246 Joe Coleman	1.50	.70	.45
247 Gene Oliver	1.50	.70	.45
248 Bob Priddy	1.50	.70	.45
249 Ed Spiezio	1.50	.70	.45
250 Frank Robinson	30.00	15.00	9.00
251 Ron Herbel	1.50	.70	.45
252 Chuck Cottier	1.50	.70	.45
253 Jerry Johnson	1.50	.70	.30
254 Joe Schultz	1.50	.70	.30
255 Steve Carlton	60.00	30.00	18.00
256 Gates Brown	1.50	.70	.30
257 Jim Ray	1.50	.70	.30
258 Jackie Hernandez	1.50	.70	.30
259 Bill Short	1.50	.70	.30
260 Reggie Jackson	800.00	400.00	250.00
261 Bob Johnson	1.50	.70	.30
262 Mike Kekich	1.50	.70	.30
263 Jerry May	1.50	.70	.30
264 Bill Landis	1.50	.70	.30
265 Chico Cardenas	1.50	.70	.30
266 Dodgers Rookies (Alan Foster, Tom Hutton)	1.50	.70	.30
267 Vicente Romo	1.50	.70	.30
268 Al Spangler	1.50	.70	.30
269 Al Weis	1.50	.70	.30
270 Mickey Lolich	3.50	1.75	1.00
271 Larry Stahl	1.50	.70	.30
272 Ed Stroud	1.50	.70	.30
273 Ron Willis	1.50	.70	.30
274 Clyde King	1.50	.70	.30
275 Vic Davalillo	1.50	.70	.30
276 Gary Wagner	1.50	.70	.30
277 Rod Hendricks	1.50	.70	.30
278 Gary Geiger	1.50	.70	.30
279 Roger Nelson	1.50	.70	.30
280 Alex Johnson	1.50	.70	.30
281 Ted Kubiak	1.50	.70	.30
282 Pat Jarvis	1.50	.70	.30
283 Sandy Alomar	1.50	.70	.30
284 Expos Rookies (Jerry Robertson, Mike Wegener)	1.50	.70	.30
285 Don Mincher	1.50	.70	.30
286 Dock Ellis	1.50	.70	.30
287 Jose Tartabull	1.50	.70	.30
288 Ken Holtzman	1.50	.70	.30
289 Bart Shirley	1.50	.70	.30
290 Jim Kaat	4.50	2.25	1.25
291 Vern Fuller	1.50	.70	.30
292 Al Downing	1.50	.70	.45
293 Dick Dietz	1.50	.70	.30
294 Jim Lemon	1.50	.70	.30
295 Tony Perez	10.00	5.00	3.00
296 Andy Messersmith	1.50	.70	.45
297 Deron Johnson	1.50	.70	.30
298 Dave Nicholson	1.50	.70	.30
299 Mark Belanger	1.50	.70	.30
300 Felipe Alou	1.50	.70	.45
301 Darrell Brandon	1.50	.70	.30
302 Jim Pagliaroni	1.50	.70	.30
303 Cal Koonce	1.50	.70	.30
304 Padres Rookies (Bill Davis, Clarence Gaston)	8.00	4.00	2.50
305 Dick McAuliffe	1.50	.70	.30
306 Jim Grant	1.50	.70	.30
307 Gary Kolb	1.50	.70	.30
308 Wade Blasingame	1.50	.70	.30
309 Walt Williams	1.50	.70	.30
310 Tom Haller	1.50	.70	.30
311 Sparky Lyle	12.00	6.00	3.50
312 Lee Elia	1.50	.70	.30
313 Bill Robinson	1.50	.70	.30
314 Checklist 328-425 (Don Drysdale)	3.50	1.75	1.00
315 Eddie Fisher	1.50	.70	.30
316 Hal Lanier	1.50	.70	.30
317 Bruce Look	1.50	.70	.30
318 Jack Fisher	1.50	.70	.30
319 Ken McMullen	1.50	.70	.30
320 Dal Maxvill	1.50	.70	.30
321 Jim McAndrew	1.50	.70	.30
322 Jose Vidal	1.50	.70	.30
323 Larry Miller	1.50	.70	.30
324 Tigers Rookies (Les Cain, Dave Campbell)	1.50	.70	.30
325 Jose Cardenal	1.50	.70	.30
326 Gary Sutherland	1.50	.70	.30
327 Willie Crawford	1.50	.70	.30
328 Joe Horlen	1.00	.50	.30
329 Rick Joseph	1.00	.50	.30
330 Tony Conigliaro	1.50	.70	.45
331 Braves Rookies (Gil Garrido, Tom House)	1.00	.50	.30
332 Fred Talbot	1.25	.60	.40
333 Ivan Murrell	1.00	.50	.30
334 Phil Roof	1.00	.50	.30
335 Bill Mazeroski	1.75	.90	.50
336 Jim Roland	1.00	.50	.30
337 Marty Martinez	1.00	.50	.30
338 Del Unser	1.00	.50	.30
339 Reds Rookies (Steve Mingori, Jose Pena)	1.00	.50	.30
340 Dave McNally	1.25	.60	.40
341 Dave Adlesh	1.00	.50	.30
342 Bubba Morton	1.00	.50	.30
343 Dan Frisella	1.00	.50	.30
344 Tom Matchick	1.00	.50	.30

		NR MT	EX	VG
345	Frank Linzy	1.00	.50	.30
346	Wayne Comer	1.25	.60	.40
347	Randy Hundley	1.00	.50	.30
348	Steve Hargan	1.00	.50	.30
349	Dick Williams	1.25	.60	.40
350	Richie Allen	2.00	1.00	.60
351	Carroll Sembera	1.00	.50	.30
352	Paul Schaal	1.00	.50	.30
353	Jeff Torborg	1.00	.50	.30
354	Nate Oliver	1.25	.60	.40
355	Phil Niekro	7.00	3.50	2.00
356	Frank Quilici	1.00	.50	.30
357	Carl Taylor	1.00	.50	.30
358	Athletics Rookies (George Lauzerique, Roberto Rodriguez)	1.00	.50	.30
359	Dick Kelley	1.00	.50	.30
360	Jim Wynn	1.25	.60	.40
361	Gary Holman	1.00	.50	.30
362	Jim Maloney	1.00	.50	.30
363	Russ Nixon	1.00	.50	.30
364	Tommie Agee	1.25	.60	.40
365	Jim Fregosi	1.00	.50	.30
366	Bo Belinsky	1.00	.50	.30
367	Lou Johnson	1.00	.50	.30
368	Vic Roznovsky	1.00	.50	.30
369	Bob Skinner	1.00	.50	.30
370	Juan Marichal	7.00	3.50	2.00
371	Sal Bando	1.25	.60	.40
372	Adolfo Phillips	1.00	.50	.30
373	Fred Lasher	1.00	.50	.30
374	Bob Tillman	1.00	.50	.30
375	Harmon Killebrew	20.00	10.00	6.00
376	Royals Rookies (Mike Fiore, *Jim Rooker*)	1.00	.50	.30
377	Gary Bell	1.25	.60	.40
378	Jose Herrera	1.00	.50	.30
379	Ken Boyer	1.75	.90	.50
380	Stan Bahnsen	1.25	.60	.40
381	Ed Kranepool	1.25	.60	.40
382	Pat Corrales	1.25	.60	.40
383	Casey Cox	1.00	.50	.30
384	Larry Shepard	1.00	.50	.30
385	Orlando Cepeda	3.50	1.75	1.00
386	Jim McGlothlin	1.00	.50	.30
387	Bobby Klaus	1.00	.50	.30
388	Tom McCraw	1.00	.50	.30
389	Dan Coombs	1.00	.50	.30
390	Bill Freehan	1.00	.50	.30
391	Ray Culp	1.00	.50	.30
392	Bob Burda	1.00	.50	.30
393	Gene Brabender	1.00	.50	.30
394	Pilots Rookies (Lou Piniella, Marv Staehle)	3.00	1.50	.90
395	Chris Short	1.00	.50	.30
396	Jim Campanis	1.00	.50	.30
397	Chuck Dobson	1.00	.50	.30
398	Tito Francona	1.00	.50	.30
399	Bob Bailey	1.00	.50	.30
400	Don Drysdale	8.00	4.00	2.50
401	Jake Gibbs	1.25	.60	.40
402	Ken Boswell	1.00	.50	.30
403	Bob Miller	1.00	.50	.30
404	Cubs Rookies (Vic LaRose, Gary Ross)	1.00	.50	.30
405	Lee May	1.00	.50	.30
406	Phil Ortega	1.00	.50	.30
407	Tom Egan	1.00	.50	.30
408	Nate Colbert	1.00	.50	.30
409	Bob Moose	1.00	.50	.30
410	Al Kaline	18.00	9.00	5.50
411	Larry Dierker	1.00	.50	.30
412	Checklist 426-512 (Mickey Mantle)	7.00	3.50	2.00
413	Roland Sheldon	1.25	.60	.40
414	Duke Sims	1.00	.50	.30
415	Ray Washburn	1.00	.50	.30
416	Willie McCovey AS	3.50	1.75	1.00
417	Ken Harrelson AS	1.00	.50	.30
418	Tommy Helms AS	1.00	.50	.30
419	Rod Carew AS	10.00	7.50	4.50
420	Ron Santo AS	1.00	.50	.30
421	Brooks Robinson AS	4.00	2.00	1.25
422	Don Kessinger AS	1.00	.50	.30
423	Bert Campaneris AS	1.25	.60	.40
424	Pete Rose AS	12.00	6.00	3.50
425	Carl Yastrzemski AS	6.00	3.00	1.75
426	Curt Flood AS	1.00	.50	.30
427	Tony Oliva AS	1.50	.70	.45
428	Lou Brock AS	5.00	2.50	1.50
429	Willie Horton AS	1.25	.60	.40
430	Johnny Bench AS	12.00	6.00	3.50

		NR MT	EX	VG
431	Bill Freehan AS	1.00	.50	.30
432	Bob Gibson AS	5.00	2.50	1.50
433	Denny McLain AS	1.50	.70	.45
434	Jerry Koosman AS	1.00	.50	.30
435	Sam McDowell AS	1.25	.60	.40
436	Gene Alley	1.00	.50	.30
437	Luis Alcaraz	1.00	.50	.30
438	Gary Waslewski	1.00	.50	.30
439	White Sox Rookies (Ed Herrmann, Dan Lazar)	1.00	.50	.30
440a	Willie McCovey (last name in white)	90.00	45.00	27.00
440b	Willie McCovey (last name in yellow)	18.00	9.00	5.50
441a	Dennis Higgins (last name in white)	10.00	5.00	3.00
441b	Dennis Higgins (last name in yellow)	1.00	.50	.30
442	Ty Cline	1.00	.50	.30
443	Don Wert	1.00	.50	.30
444a	Joe Moeller (last name in white)	10.00	5.00	3.00
444b	Joe Moeller (last name in yellow)	1.00	.50	.30
445	Bobby Knoop	1.00	.50	.30
446	Claude Raymond	1.00	.50	.30
447a	Ralph Houk (last name in white)	15.00	7.50	4.50
447b	Ralph Houk (last name in yellow)	1.50	.70	.45
448	Bob Tolan	1.00	.50	.30
449	Paul Lindblad	1.00	.50	.30
450	Billy Williams	6.00	3.00	1.75
451a	Rich Rollins (first name in white)	10.00	5.00	3.00
451b	Rich Rollins (first name in yellow)	1.25	.60	.40
452a	Al Ferrara (first name in white)	10.00	5.00	3.00
452b	Al Ferrara (first name in yellow)	1.00	.50	.30
453	Mike Cuellar	1.25	.60	.40
454a	Phillies Rookies (Larry Colton, *Don Money*) (names in white)	10.00	5.00	3.00
454b	Phillies Rookies (Larry Colton, *Don Money*) (names in yellow)	1.25	.60	.40
455	Sonny Siebert	1.00	.50	.30
456	Bud Harrelson	1.00	.50	.30
457	Dalton Jones	1.00	.50	.30
458	Curt Blefary	1.00	.50	.30
459	Dave Boswell	1.00	.50	.30
460	Joe Torre	1.75	.90	.50
461a	Mike Epstein (last name in white)	10.00	5.00	3.00
461b	Mike Epstein (last name in yellow)	1.00	.50	.30
462	Red Schoendienst	1.50	.70	.45
463	Dennis Ribant	1.00	.50	.30
464a	Dave Marshall (last name in white)	10.00	5.00	3.00
464b	Dave Marshall (last name in yellow)	1.00	.50	.30
465	Tommy John	4.50	2.25	1.25
466	John Boccabella	1.00	.50	.30
467	Tom Reynolds	1.00	.50	.30
468a	Pirates Rookies (Bruce Dal Canton, Bob Robertson) (names in white)	10.00	5.00	3.00
468b	Pirates Rookies (Bruce Dal Canton, Bob Robertson) (names in yellow)	1.00	.50	.30
469	Chico Ruiz	1.00	.50	.30
470a	Mel Stottlemyre (last name in white)	15.00	7.50	4.50
470b	Mel Stottlemyre (last name in yellow)	1.50	.70	.45
471a	Ted Savage (last name in white)	10.00	5.00	3.00
471b	Ted Savage (last name in yellow)	1.00	.50	.30
472	Jim Price	1.00	.50	.30
473a	Jose Arcia (first name in white)	10.00	5.00	3.00
473b	Jose Arcia (first name in yellow)	1.00	.50	.30
474	Tom Murphy	1.00	.50	.30
475	Tim McCarver	1.50	.70	.45
476a	Red Sox Rookies (*Ken Brett*, Gerry Moses) (names in white)	10.00	5.00	3.00
476b	Red Sox Rookies (*Ken Brett*, Gerry Moses) (names in yellow)	1.00	.50	.30
477	Jeff James	1.00	.50	.30
478	Don Buford	1.00	.50	.30
479	Richie Scheinblum	1.00	.50	.30
480	Tom Seaver	160.00	80.00	52.00
481	*Bill Melton*	1.25	.60	.40
482a	Jim Gosger (first name in white)	10.00	5.00	3.00
482b	Jim Gosger (first name in yellow)	1.25	.60	.40
483	Ted Abernathy	1.00	.50	.30
484	Joe Gordon	1.00	.50	.30
485a	Gaylord Perry (last name in white)	75.00	38.00	23.00
485b	Gaylord Perry (last name in yellow)	10.00	5.00	3.00
486a	Paul Casanova (last name in white)	10.00	5.00	3.00

		NR MT	EX	VG
486b	Paul Casanova (last name in yellow)			
		1.00	.50	.30
487	Denis Menke	1.00	.50	.30
488	Joe Sparma	1.00	.50	.30
489	Clete Boyer	1.25	.60	.40
490	Matty Alou	1.00	.50	.30
491a	Twins Rookies (Jerry Crider, George Mitterwald) (names in white)	10.00	5.00	3.00
491b	Twins Rookies (Jerry Crider, George Mitterwald) (names in yellow)	1.00	.50	.30
492	Tony Cloninger	1.00	.50	.30
493a	Wes Parker (last name in white)	10.00	5.00	3.00
493b	Wes Parker (last name in yellow)	1.00	.50	.30
494	Ken Berry	1.00	.50	.30
495	Bert Campaneris	1.50	.70	.45
496	Larry Jaster	1.00	.50	.30
497	Julian Javier	1.00	.50	.30
498	Juan Pizarro	1.00	.50	.30
499	Astros Rookies (Don Bryant, Steve Shea)			
		1.00	.50	.30
500a	Mickey Mantle (last name in white)			
		475.00	190.00	119.00
500b	Mickey Mantle (last name in yellow)			
		175.00	87.00	52.00
501a	Tony Gonzalez (first name in white)			
		10.00	5.00	3.00
501b	Tony Gonzalez (first name in yellow)			
		1.00	.50	.30
502	Minnie Rojas	1.00	.50	.30
503	Larry Brown	1.00	.50	.30
504	Checklist 513-588 (Brooks Robinson)			
		4.00	2.00	1.25
505a	Bobby Bolin (last name in white)	10.00	5.00	3.00
505b	Bobby Bolin (last name in yellow)	1.00	.50	.30
506	Paul Blair	1.00	.50	.30
507	Cookie Rojas	1.00	.50	.30
508	Moe Drabowsky	1.00	.50	.30
509	Manny Sanguillen	1.00	.50	.30
510	Rod Carew	60.00	30.00	18.00
511a	Diego Segui (first name in white)	10.00	5.00	3.00
511b	Diego Segui (first name in yellow)	1.25	.60	.40
512	Cleon Jones	1.25	.60	.40
513	Camilo Pascual	1.00	.50	.30
514	Mike Lum	1.00	.50	.30
515	Dick Green	1.00	.50	.30
516	Earl Weaver	5.00	2.50	1.50
517	Mike McCormick	1.25	.60	.40
518	Fred Whitfield	1.00	.50	.30
519	Yankees Rookies (Len Boehmer, Gerry Kenney)			
		1.00	.50	.30
520	Bob Veale	1.25	.60	.40
521	George Thomas	1.00	.50	.30
522	Joe Hoerner	1.00	.50	.30
523	Bob Chance	1.00	.50	.30
524	Expos Rookies (Jose Laboy, Floyd Wicker)			
		1.00	.50	.30
525	Earl Wilson	1.00	.50	.30
526	Hector Torres	1.00	.50	.30
527	Al Lopez	3.00	1.50	.90
528	Claude Osteen	1.00	.50	.30
529	Ed Kirkpatrick	1.00	.50	.30
530	Cesar Tovar	1.00	.50	.30
531	Dick Farrell	1.00	.50	.30
532	Bird Hill Aces (Mike Cuellar, Jim Hardin, Dave McNally, Tom Phoebus)	1.50	.70	.45
533	Nolan Ryan	600.00	300.00	175.00
534	Jerry McNertney	1.00	.50	.30
535	Phil Regan	1.00	.50	.30
536	Padres Rookies (Danny Breeden, Dave Roberts)	1.25	.60	.40
537	Mike Paul	1.00	.50	.30
538	Charlie Smith	1.00	.50	.30
539	Ted Shows How (Mike Epstein, Ted Williams)	3.25	1.75	1.00
540	Curt Flood	1.50	.70	.45
541	Joe Verbanic	1.00	.50	.30
542	Bob Aspromonte	1.00	.50	.30
543	Fred Newman	1.00	.50	.30
544	Tigers Rookies (Mike Kilkenny, Ron Woods)	1.00	.50	.30
545	Willie Stargell	10.00	5.00	3.00
546	Jim Nash	1.00	.50	.30
547	Billy Martin	5.00	2.50	1.50
548	Bob Locker	1.00	.50	.30
549	Ron Brand	1.00	.50	.30
550	Brooks Robinson	15.00	7.50	4.50
551	Wayne Granger	1.00	.50	.30
552	Dodgers Rookies (Ted Sizemore, Bill Sudakis)	1.25	.60	.40
553	Ron Davis	1.00	.50	.30
554	Frank Bertaina	1.00	.50	.30
555	Jim Hart	1.25	.60	.40
556	A's Stars (Sal Bando, Bert Campaneris, Danny Cater)	1.50	.70	.45
557	Frank Fernandez	1.00	.50	.30
558	Tom Burgmeier	1.25	.60	.40
559	Cards Rookies (Joe Hague, Jim Hicks)			
		1.00	.50	.30
560	Luis Tiant	1.50	.70	.45
561	Ron Clark	1.00	.50	.30
562	Bob Watson	1.00	.50	.30
563	Marty Pattin	1.00	.50	.30
564	Gil Hodges	6.00	3.00	1.75
565	Hoyt Wilhelm	6.00	3.00	1.75
566	Ron Hansen	1.00	.50	.30
567	Pirates Rookies (Elvio Jimenez, Jim Shellenback)	1.00	.50	.30
568	Cecil Upshaw	1.00	.50	.30
569	Billy Harris	1.00	.50	.30
570	Ron Santo	1.75	.90	.50
571	Cap Peterson	1.00	.50	.30
572	Giants Heroes (Juan Marichal, Willie McCovey)	7.00	3.50	2.00
573	Jim Palmer	40.00	20.00	12.00
574	George Scott	1.00	.50	.30
575	Bill Singer	1.25	.60	.40
576	Phillies Rookies (Ron Stone, Bill Wilson)	1.00	.50	.30
577	Mike Hegan	1.00	.50	.30
578	Don Bosch	1.00	.50	.30
579	Dave Nelson	1.25	.60	.40
580	Jim Northrup	1.25	.60	.40
581	Gary Nolan	1.00	.50	.30
582a	Checklist 589-664 (Tony Oliva) (red circle on back)	3.50	1.75	1.00
582b	Checklist 589-664 (Tony Oliva) (white circle on back)	2.50	1.25	.70
583	Clyde Wright	1.25	.60	.40
584	Don Mason	1.00	.50	.30
585	Ron Swoboda	1.00	.50	.30
586	Tim Cullen	1.00	.50	.30
587	Joe Rudi	1.75	.90	.50
588	Bill White	1.00	.50	.30
589	Joe Pepitone	2.00	1.00	.60
590	Rico Carty	1.00	.50	.30
591	Mike Hedlund	1.00	.50	.30
592	Padres Rookies (Rafael Robles, Al Santorini)	1.00	.50	.30
593	Don Nottebart	1.00	.50	.30
594	Dooley Womack	1.00	.50	.30
595	Lee Maye	1.00	.50	.30
596	Chuck Hartenstein	1.00	.50	.30
597	A.L. Rookies (Larry Burchart, Rollie Fingers, Bob Floyd)	150.00	75.00	50.00
598	Ruben Amaro	1.00	.50	.30
599	John Boozer	1.00	.50	.30
600	Tony Oliva	4.00	2.00	1.25
601	Tug McGraw	2.00	1.00	.60
602	Cubs Rookies (Alec Distaso, Jim Qualls, Don Young)	1.00	.50	.30
603	Joe Keough	1.00	.50	.30
604	Bobby Etheridge	1.00	.50	.30
605	Dick Ellsworth	1.00	.50	.30
606	Gene Mauch	1.00	.50	.30
607	Dick Bosman	1.00	.50	.30
608	Dick Simpson	1.00	.50	.30
609	Phil Gagliano	1.00	.50	.30
610	Jim Hardin	1.00	.50	.30
611	Braves Rookies (Bob Didier, Walt Hriniak, Gary Neibauer)	1.00	.50	.30
612	Jack Aker	1.00	.50	.30
613	Jim Beauchamp	1.00	.50	.30
614	Astros Rookies (Tom Griffin, Skip Guinn)	1.00	.50	.30
615	Len Gabrielson	1.00	.50	.30
616	Don McMahon	1.00	.50	.30
617	Jesse Gonder	1.00	.50	.30
618	Ramon Webster	1.00	.50	.30
619	Royals Rookies (Bill Butler, Pat Kelly, Juan Rios)	1.25	.60	.40
620	Dean Chance	1.25	.60	.40
621	Bill Voss	1.00	.50	.30
622	Dan Osinski	1.00	.50	.30
623	Hank Allen	1.00	.50	.30
624	N.L. Rookies (Darrel Chaney, Duffy Dyer, Terry Harmon)	1.25	.60	.40
625	Mack Jones	1.00	.50	.30
626	Gene Michael	1.00	.50	.30
627	George Stone	1.00	.50	.30
628	Red Sox Rookies (Bill Conigliaro, Syd O'Brien, Fred Wenz)	1.00	.50	.30
629	Jack Hamilton	1.00	.50	.30

		NR MT	EX	VG
630	*Bobby Bonds*	40.00	20.00	12.00
631	John Kennedy	1.00	.50	.30
632	Jon Warden	1.00	.50	.30
633	Harry Walker	1.25	.60	.40
634	Andy Etchebarren	1.00	.50	.30
635	George Culver	1.00	.50	.30
636	Woodie Held	1.00	.50	.30
637	Padres Rookies (Jerry DaVanon, *Clay Kirby*, Frank Reberger)	1.25	.60	.40
638	Ed Sprague	1.00	.50	.30
639	Barry Moore	1.00	.50	.30
640	Fergie Jenkins	20.00	10.00	6.00
641	N.L. Rookies (Bobby Darwin, Tommy Dean, John Miller)	1.00	.50	.30
642	John Hiller	1.25	.60	.40
643	Billy Cowan	1.00	.50	.30
644	Chuck Hinton	1.00	.50	.30
645	George Brunet	1.00	.50	.30
646	Expos Rookies (Dan McGinn, *Carl Morton*)	1.00	.50	.30
647	Dave Wickersham	1.00	.50	.30
648	Bobby Wine	1.00	.50	.30
649	Al Jackson	1.00	.50	.30
650	Ted Williams	12.00	6.00	3.50
651	Gus Gil	1.00	.50	.30
652	Eddie Watt	1.00	.50	.30
653	*Aurelio Rodriguez* (photo actually batboy Leonard Garcia)	1.50	.70	.45
654	White Sox Rookies (*Carlos May*, Rich Morales, Don Secrist)	1.00	.50	.30
655	Mike Hershberger	1.00	.50	.30
656	Dan Schneider	1.00	.50	.30
657	Bobby Murcer	2.25	1.25	.70
658	A.L. Rookies (Bill Burbach, Tom Hall, Jim Miles)	1.00	.50	.30
659	Johnny Podres	1.75	.90	.50
660	Reggie Smith	1.75	.90	.50
661	Jim Merritt	1.00	.50	.30
662	Royals Rookies (Dick Drago, Bob Oliver, George Spriggs)	1.25	.60	.40
663	Dick Radatz	1.00	.50	.30
664	Ron Hunt	2.00	.50	.25

1969 Topps Decals

Designed as an insert for 1969 regular issue card packs, these decals are virtually identical in format to the '69 cards. The 48 decals in the set measure 1" by 2-1/2," although they are mounted on white paper backing which measures 1-3/4" by 2-1/8."

		NR MT	EX	VG
Complete Set:		350.00	175.00	105.00
Common Player:		4.00	2.00	1.25
(1)	Hank Aaron	40.00	20.00	12.00
(2)	Richie Allen	4.00	2.00	1.25
(3)	Felipe Alou	4.00	2.00	1.25
(4)	Matty Alou	4.00	2.00	1.25
(5)	Luis Aparicio	4.50	2.25	1.25
(6)	Bob Clemente	50.00	25.00	15.00
(7)	Donn Clendenon	4.00	2.00	1.25
(8)	Tommy Davis	4.00	2.00	1.25
(9)	Don Drysdale	7.00	3.50	2.00
(10)	Joe Foy	4.00	2.00	1.25
(11)	Jim Fregosi	4.00	2.00	1.25
(12)	Bob Gibson	7.00	3.50	2.00
(13)	Tony Gonzalez	4.00	2.00	1.25

		NR MT	EX	VG
(14)	Tom Haller	4.00	2.00	1.25
(15)	Ken Harrelson	4.00	2.00	1.25
(16)	Tommy Helms	4.00	2.00	1.25
(17)	Willie Horton	4.00	2.00	1.25
(18)	Frank Howard	4.00	2.00	1.25
(19)	Reggie Jackson	100.00	50.00	30.00
(20)	Fergie Jenkins	6.00	3.00	1.75
(21)	Harmon Killebrew	6.00	3.00	1.75
(22)	Jerry Koosman	4.00	2.00	1.25
(23)	Mickey Mantle	75.00	38.00	23.00
(24)	Willie Mays	35.00	17.50	10.50
(25)	Tim McCarver	4.00	2.00	1.25
(26)	Willie McCovey	7.00	3.50	2.00
(27)	Sam McDowell	4.00	2.00	1.25
(28)	Denny McLain	4.00	2.00	1.25
(29)	Dave McNally	4.00	2.00	1.25
(30)	Don Mincher	4.00	2.00	1.25
(31)	Rick Monday	4.00	2.00	1.25
(32)	Tony Oliva	4.00	2.00	1.25
(33)	Camilo Pascual	4.00	2.00	1.25
(34)	Rick Reichardt	4.00	2.00	1.25
(35)	Pete Rose	25.00	12.50	7.50
(36)	Frank Robinson	7.00	3.50	2.00
(37)	Ron Santo	4.00	2.00	1.25
(38)	Dick Selma	4.00	2.00	1.25
(39)	Tom Seaver	50.00	25.00	15.00
(40)	Chris Short	4.00	2.00	1.25
(41)	Rusty Staub	4.00	2.00	1.25
(42)	Mel Stottlemyre	4.00	2.00	1.25
(43)	Luis Tiant	4.00	2.00	1.25
(44)	Pete Ward	4.00	2.00	1.25
(45)	Hoyt Wilhelm	6.00	3.00	1.75
(46)	Maury Wills	4.00	2.00	1.25
(47)	Jim Wynn	4.00	2.00	1.25
(48)	Carl Yastrzemski	30.00	15.00	9.00

1969 Topps Deckle Edge

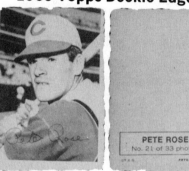

PETE ROSE
No. 21 of 33 photos

These 2-1/4" by 3-1/4" inch cards take their name from their interesting borders which have a scalloped effect. The fronts have a black and white picture of the player along with a blue facsimile autograph. Backs have the player's name and the card number in light blue ink in a small box at the bottom of the card. Technically, there are only 33 numbered cards, but there are actually 35 possible players; both Jim Wynn and Hoyt Wilhelm cards are found as #11 while cards of Joe Foy and Rusty Staub can be found as #22. Many of the players in the set are stars.

		NR MT	EX	VG
Complete Set:		100.00	50.00	30.00
Common Player:		1.00	.50	.30
1	Brooks Robinson	15.00	7.50	4.50
2	Boog Powell	1.00	.50	.30
3	Ken Harrelson	1.00	.50	.30
4	Carl Yastrzemski	15.00	7.50	4.50
5	Jim Fregosi	1.00	.50	.30
6	Luis Aparicio	1.25	.60	.40
7	Luis Tiant	1.00	.50	.30
8	Denny McLain	1.00	.50	.30
9	Willie Horton	1.00	.50	.30
10	Bill Freehan	1.00	.50	.30
11a	Hoyt Wilhelm	10.00	5.00	3.00
11b	Jim Wynn	10.00	5.00	3.00
12	Rod Carew	15.00	7.50	4.50

		NR MT	EX	VG
13	Mel Stottlemyre	1.00	.50	.30
14	Rick Monday	1.00	.50	.30
15	Tommy Davis	1.00	.50	.30
16	Frank Howard	1.00	.50	.30
17	Felipe Alou	1.00	.50	.30
18	Don Kessinger	1.00	.50	.30
19	Ron Santo	1.00	.50	.30
20	Tommy Helms	1.00	.50	.30
21	Pete Rose	10.00	5.00	3.00
22a	Rusty Staub	2.25	1.25	.70
22b	Joe Foy	7.00	3.50	2.00
23	Tom Haller	1.00	.50	.30
24	Maury Wills	1.00	.50	.30
25	Jerry Koosman	1.00	.50	.30
26	Richie Allen	1.00	.50	.30
27	Bob Clemente	15.00	7.50	4.50
28	Curt Flood	1.00	.50	.30
29	Bob Gibson	10.00	5.00	3.00
30	Al Ferrara	1.00	.50	.30
31	Willie McCovey	10.00	5.00	3.00
32	Juan Marichal	7.00	3.50	2.00
33	Willie Mays, Willie Mays	15.00	7.50	4.50

		NR MT	EX	VG
(14)	Red Sox Rookie Stars, World Series Game 7, Gerry Arrigo, Jim Perry	18.00	9.00	5.50
(15)	World Series Game 2, Bill McCool, Roberto Pena, Doug Rader	15.00	7.50	4.50
(16)	Ed Brinkman, Roy Face, Willie Horton, Bob Rodgers	18.00	9.00	5.50
(17)	Dave Baldwin, J.C. Martin, Dave May, Ray Sadecki	15.00	7.50	4.50
(18)	World Series Game 1, Jose Pagan, Tom Phoebus, Mike Shannon	15.00	7.50	4.50
(19)	Pete Rose, Lee Stange, Don Sutton, Ted Uhlaender	275.00	137.00	82.00
(20)	Joe Grzenda, Frank Howard, Dick Tracewski, Jim Weaver	20.00	10.00	6.00
(21)	White Sox Rookie Stars, Joe Azcue, Grant Jackson, Denny McLain	20.00	10.00	6.00
(22)	John Edwards, Jim Fairey, Phillies Rookies, Stan Williams	15.00	7.50	4.50
(23)	World Series Summary, John Bateman, Willie Smith, Leon Wagner	15.00	7.50	4.50
(24)	World Series Game 5, Yankees Rookies, Chris Cannizzaro, Bob Hendley	15.00	7.50	4.50
(25)	Cardinals Rookie Stars, Joe Nossek, Rico Petrocelli, Carl Yastrzemski	175.00	87.00	52.00

1969 Topps 4-On-1 Mini Stickers

Another in the long line of Topps test issues, the 4-on-1s are 2-1/2" by 3-1/2" cards with blank backs featuring a quartet of miniature stickers in the design of the same cards from the 1969 Topps regular set. There are 25 different cards, for a total of 100 different stickers. As they are not common, Mint cards bring fairly strong prices on today's market. As the set was drawn from the 3rd Series of the regular cards, it includes some rookie stickers and World Series highlight stickers.

	NR MT	EX	VG
Complete Set:	950.00	475.00	285.00
Common Player:	15.00	7.50	4.50

		NR MT	EX	VG
(1)	Jerry Adair, Willie Mays, Johnny Morris, Don Wilson	100.00	50.00	30.00
(2)	Tommie Aaron, Jim Britton, Donn Clendenon, Woody Woodward	15.00	7.50	4.50
(3)	World Series Game 4, Tommy Davis, Don Pavletich, Vada Pinson	20.00	10.00	6.00
(4)	Max Alvis, Glenn Beckert, Ron Fairly, Rick Wise	15.00	7.50	4.50
(5)	Johnny Callison, Jim French, Lum Harris, Dick Selma	15.00	7.50	4.50
(6)	World Series Game 3, Bob Gibson, Larry Haney, Rick Reichardt	40.00	20.00	12.00
(7)	Houston Rookie Stars, Wally Bunker, Don Cardwell, Joe Gibbon	15.00	7.50	4.50
(8)	Ollie Brown, Jim Bunning, Andy Kosco, Ron Reed	20.00	10.00	6.00
(9)	Bill Dillman, Jim Lefebvre, John Purdin, John Roseboro	15.00	7.50	4.50
(10)	Bill Hands, Chuck Harrison, Lindy McDaniel, Felix Millan	15.00	7.50	4.50
(11)	Jack Hiatt, Dave Johnson, Mel Nelson, Tommie Sisk	18.00	9.00	5.50
(12)	Clay Dalrymple, Leo Durocher, John Odom, Wilbur Wood	18.00	9.00	5.50
(13)	Hank Bauer, Kevin Collins, Ray Oyler, Russ Snyder	15.00	7.50	4.50

1969 Topps Stamps

Topps continued to refine its efforts at baseball stamps in 1969 with the release of 240 player stamps, each measuring 1" by 1-7/16." Each stamp jsd s color photo along with the player's name, position and team. Unlike prior stamp issues, the 1969 stamps have 24 separate albums (one per team). The stamps were issued in strips of 12.

	NR MT	EX	VG
Complete Sheet Set:	250.00	125.00	75.00
Common Sheet:	1.25	.60	.40
Complete Stamp Album Set:	14.00	7.00	4.25
Single Stamp Album:	.50	.25	.15

		NR MT	EX	VG
(1)	Tommie Agee, Sandy Alomar, Jose Cardenal, Dean Chance, Joe Foy, Jim Grant, Don Kessinger, Mickey Mantle, Jerry May, Bob Rodgers, Cookie Rojas, Gary Sutherland	18.00	9.00	5.50
(2)	Jesus Alou, Mike Andrews, Larry Brown, Moe Drabowsky, Alex Johnson, Lew Krausse, Jim Lefebvre, Dal Maxvill, John Odom, Claude Osteen, Rick Reichardt, Luis Tiant	1.50	.70	.45
(3)	Hank Aaron, Matty Alou, Max Alvis, Nelson Briles, Eddie Fisher, Bud Harrelson, Willie Horton, Randy Hundley, Larry Jaster, Jim Kaat, Gary Peters, Pete Ward	7.00	3.50	2.00
(4)	Don Buford, John Callison, Tommy Davis, Jackie Hernandez, Fergie Jenkins, Lee May, Denny McLain, Bob Oliver, Roberto Pena, Tony Perez, Joe Torre, Tom Tresh	3.00	1.50	.90
(5)	Jim Bunning, Dean Chance, Joe Foy, Sonny Jackson, Don Kessinger, Rick Monday, Gaylord Perry, Roger Repoz, Cookie Rojas, Mel Stottlemyre, Leon Wagner, Jim Wynn	3.00	1.50	.90
(6)	Felipe Alou, Gerry Arrigo, Bob Aspromonte, Gary Bell, Clay Dalrymple, Jim Fregosi, Tony Gonzalez, Duane Josephson, Dick McAuliffe, Tony Oliva, Brooks Robinson, Willie Stargell	6.00	3.00	1.75

	NR MT	EX	VG
(7) Steve Barber, Donn Clendenon, Joe Coleman, Vic Davalillo, Russ Gibson, Jerry Grote, Tom Haller, Andy Kosco, Willie McCovey, Don Mincher, Joe Morgan, Don Wilson 4.00		2.00	1.25
(8) George Brunet, Don Buford, John Callison, Danny Cater, Tommy Davis, Willie Davis, John Edwards, Jim Hart, Mickey Lolich, Willie Mays, Roberto Pena, Mickey Stanley 7.00		3.50	2.00
(9) Ernie Banks, Glenn Beckert, Ken Berry, Horace Clarke, Bob Clemente, Larry Dierker, Len Gabrielson, Jake Gibbs, Jerry Koosman, Sam McDowell, Tom Satriano, Bill Singer 3.50		1.75	1.00
(10) Gene Alley, Lou Brock, Larry Brown, Moe Drabowsky, Frank Howard, Tommie John, Roger Nelson, Claude Osteen, Phil Regan, Rick Reichardt, Tony Taylor, Roy White 4.00		2.00	1.25
(11) Bob Allison, John Bateman, Don Drysdale, Dave Johnson, Harmon Killebrew, Jim Maloney, Bill Mazeroski, Gerry McNertney, Ron Perranoski, Rico Petrocelli, Pete Rose, Billy Williams 18.00		9.00	5.50
(12) Bernie Allen, Jose Arcia, Stan Bahnsen, Sal Bando, Jim Davenport, Tito Francona, Dick Green, Ron Hunt, Mack Jones, Vada Pinson, George Scott, Don Wert 1.50		.70	.45
(13) Gerry Arrigo, Bob Aspromonte, Joe Azcue, Curt Blefary, Orlando Cepeda, Bill Freehan, Jim Fregosi, Dave Giusti, Duane Josephson, Tim McCarver, Jose Santiago, Bob Tolan 2.00		1.00	.60
(14) Jerry Adair, Johnny Bench, Clete Boyer, John Briggs, Bert Campaneris, Woody Fryman, Ron Kline, Bobby Knoop, Ken McMullen, Adolfo Phillips, John Roseboro, Tom Seaver 7.00		3.50	2.00
(15) Norm Cash, Ron Fairly, Bob Gibson, Bill Hands, Cleon Jones, Al Kaline, Paul Schaal, Mike Shannon, Duke Sims, Reggie Smith, Steve Whitaker, Carl Yastrzemski 12.00		6.00	3.50
(16) Steve Barber, Paul Casanova, Dick Dietz, Russ Gibson, Jerry Grote, Tom Haller, Ed Kranepool, Juan Marichal, Denis Menke, Jim Nash, Bill Robinson, Frank Robinson 4.00		2.00	1.25
(17) Bobby Bolin, Ollie Brown, Rod Carew, Mike Epstein, Bud Harrelson, Larry Jaster, Dave McNally, Willie Norton, Milt Pappas, Gary Peters, Paul Popovich, Stan Williams 6.00		3.00	1.75
(18) Ted Abernathy, Bob Allison, Ed Brinkman, Don Drysdale, Jim Hardin, Julian Javier, Hal Lanier, Jim McGlothlin, Ron Perranoski, Rich Rollins, Ron Santo, Billy Williams 3.00		1.50	.90
(19) Richie Allen, Luis Aparicio, Wally Bunker, Curt Flood, Ken Harrelson, Jim Hunter, Denver Lemaster, Felix Millan, Jim Northrop (Northrup), Art Shamsky, Larry Stahl, Ted Uhlaender 3.00		1.50	.90
(20) Bob Bailey, Johnny Bench, Woody Fryman, Jim Hannan, Ron Kline, Al McBean, Camilo Pascual, Joe Pepitone, Doug Rader, Ron Reed, John Roseboro, Sonny Siebert 3.00		1.50	.90
(21) Jack Aker, Tommy Harper, Tommy Helms, Dennis Higgins, Jim Hunter, Don Lock, Lee Maye, Felix Millan, Jim Northrop (Northrup), Larry Stahl, Don Sutton, Zoilo Versalles 3.00		1.50	.90
(22) Norm Cash, Ed Charles, Joe Horlen, Pat Jarvis, Jim Lonborg, Manny Mota, Boog Powell, Dick Selma, Mike Shannon, Duke Sims, Steve Whitaker, Hoyt Wilhelm 3.00		1.50	.90
(23) Bernie Allen, Ray Culp, Al Ferrara, Tito Francona, Dick Green, Ron Hunt, Ray Oyler, Tom Phoebus, Rusty Staub, Bob Veale, Maury Wills, Wilbur Wood 2.00		1.00	.60
(24) Ernie Banks, Mark Belanger, Steve Blass, Horace Clarke, Bob Clemente, Larry Dierker, Dave Duncan, Chico Salmon, Chris Short, Ron Swoboda, Cesar Tovar, Rick Wise 3.50		1.75	1.00

A player's name in *italic* type indicates a rookie card. An (FC) indicates a player's first card for that particular card company.

1969 Topps Super

These 2-1/4" by 3-1/4" cards are not the bigger "Super" cards which would be seen in following years. Rather, what enabled Topps to dub them "Super Baseball Cards" is their high-gloss finish which enhances the bright color photograph used on their fronts. The only other design element on the front is a facsimile autograph. The backs contain a box at the the bottom which carries the player's name, team, position, a copyright line and the card number. Another unusual feature is that the cards have rounded corners. The 66-card set saw limited production, meaning supplies are tight today. Considering the quality of the cards and the fact that many big names are represented, it's easy to understand why the set is quite expensive and desirable.

		NR MT	EX	VG
	Complete Set:	6000.00	3000.00	1800.
	Common Player:	25.00	12.50	7.50
1	Dave McNally	25.00	12.50	7.50
2	Frank Robinson	350.00	175.00	105.00
3	Brooks Robinson	350.00	175.00	105.00
4	Ken Harrelson	25.00	12.50	7.50
5	Carl Yastrzemski	700.00	350.00	210.00
6	Ray Culp	25.00	12.50	7.50
7	James Fregosi	25.00	12.50	7.50
8	Rick Reichardt	25.00	12.50	7.50
9	V. Davalillo	25.00	12.50	7.50
10	Luis Aparicio	35.00	17.50	10.50
11	Pete Ward	25.00	12.50	7.50
12	Joe Horlen	25.00	12.50	7.50
13	Luis Tiant	25.00	12.50	7.50
14	Sam McDowell	25.00	12.50	7.50
15	Jose Cardenal	25.00	12.50	7.50
16	Willie Horton	25.00	12.50	7.50
17	Denny McLain	25.00	12.50	7.50
18	Bill Freehan	25.00	12.50	7.50
19	Harmon Killebrew	275.00	137.00	82.00
20	Tony Oliva	25.00	12.50	7.50
21	Dean Chance	25.00	12.50	7.50
22	Joe Foy	25.00	12.50	7.50
23	Roger Nelson	25.00	12.50	7.50
24	Mickey Mantle	1500.00	750.00	450.00
25	Mel Stottlemyre	25.00	12.50	7.50
26	Roy White	25.00	12.50	7.50
27	Rick Monday	25.00	12.50	7.50
28	Reginald Jackson	750.00	375.00	225.00
29	Dagoberto Campaneris	25.00	12.50	7.50
30	Frank Howard	25.00	12.50	7.50
31	Camilo Pascual	25.00	12.50	7.50
32	Tommy Davis	25.00	12.50	7.50
33	Don Mincher	25.00	12.50	7.50
34	Henry Aaron	500.00	250.00	150.00
35	Felipe Rojas Alou	25.00	12.50	7.50
36	Joseph Torre	25.00	12.50	7.50
37	Fergie Jenkins	25.00	12.50	7.50
38	Ronald Santo	25.00	12.50	7.50
39	Billy Williams	40.00	20.00	12.00
40	Tommy Helms	25.00	12.50	7.50
41	Pete Rose	500.00	250.00	150.00
42	Joe Morgan	275.00	137.00	82.00
43	Jim Wynn	25.00	12.50	7.50
44	Curt Blefary	25.00	12.50	7.50
45	Willie Davis	25.00	12.50	7.50

		NR MT	EX	VG
46	Donald Drysdale	275.00	137.00	82.00
47	Tom Haller	25.00	12.50	7.50
48	Rusty Staub	25.00	12.50	7.50
49	Maurice Wills	25.00	12.50	7.50
50	Cleon Jones	25.00	12.50	7.50
51	Jerry Koosman	25.00	12.50	7.50
52	Tom Seaver	700.00	350.00	210.00
53	Rich Allen	25.00	12.50	7.50
54	Chris Short	25.00	12.50	7.50
55	Cookie Rojas	25.00	12.50	7.50
56	Mateo Alou	25.00	12.50	7.50
57	Steve Blass	25.00	12.50	7.50
58	Roberto Clemente	700.00	350.00	210.00
59	Curt Flood	25.00	12.50	7.50
60	Robert Gibson	90.00	45.00	27.00
61	Tim McCarver	25.00	12.50	7.50
62	Dick Selma	25.00	12.50	7.50
63	Ollie Brown	25.00	12.50	7.50
64	Juan Marichal	90.00	45.00	27.00
65	Willie Mays	500.00	250.00	150.00
66	Willie McCovey	90.00	45.00	27.00

1969 Topps Team Posters

Picking up where the 1968 posters left off, the 1969 poster is larger at about 12" by 20." The posters, 24 in number like the previous year, are very different in style. Each has a team focus with a large pennant carrying the team name, along with nine or ten photos of players. Each of the photos carries a name and a facsimile autograph. Unfortunately, the bigger size of 1969 posters meant they had to be folded to fit in their packages as was the case in 1968. That means that collectors today will have a tough job finding them without fairly heavy creases from the folding.

		NR MT	EX	VG
Complete Set:		900.00	450.00	270.00
Common Poster:		17.00	8.50	5.00

		NR MT	EX	VG
1	Detroit Tigers (Norm Cash, Bill Freehan, Willie Horton, Al Kaline, Mickey Lolich, Dick McAuliffe, Denny McLain, Jim Northrup, Mickey Stanley, Don Wert, Earl Wilson)	40.00	20.00	12.00
2	Atlanta Braves (Hank Aaron, Felipe Alou, Clete Boyer, Rico Carty, Tito Francona, Sonny Jackson, Pat Jarvis, Felix Millan, Phil Niekro, Milt Pappas, Joe Torre)	40.00	20.00	12.00
3	Boston Red Sox (Mike Andrews, Tony Conigliaro, Ray Culp, Russ Gibson, Ken Harrelson, Jim Lonborg, Rico Petrocelli, Jose Santiago, George Scott, Reggie Smith, Carl Yastrzemski)	60.00	30.00	18.00
4	Chicago Cubs (Ernie Banks, Glenn Beckert, Bill Hands, Jim Hickman, Ken Holtzman, Randy Hundley, Fergie Jenkins, Don Kessinger, Adolfo Phillips, Ron Santo, Billy Williams)	35.00	17.50	10.50
5	Baltimore Orioles (Mark Belanger, Paul Blair, Don Buford, Andy Etchebarren, Jim Hardin, Dave Johnson, Dave McNally, Tom Phoebus, Boog Powell, Brooks Robinson, Frank Robinson)	50.00	25.00	15.00
6	Houston Astros (Curt Blefary, Donn Clendenon, Larry Dierker, John Edwards, Denny Lemaster, Denis Menke, Norm Miller, Joe Morgan, Doug Rader, Don Wilson, Jim Wynn)	17.00	8.50	5.00

		NR MT	EX	VG
7	Kansas City Royals (Jerry Adair, Wally Bunker, Mike Fiore, Joe Foy, Jackie Hernandez, Pat Kelly, Dave Morehead, Roger Nelson, Dave Nicholson, Eliseo Rodriguez, Steve Whitaker)	17.00	8.50	5.00
8	Philadelphia Phillies (Richie Allen, Johnny Callison, Woody Fryman, Larry Hisle, Don Money, Cookie Rojas, Mike Ryan, Chris Short, Tony Taylor, Bill White, Rick Wise)	17.00	8.50	5.00
9	Seattle Pilots (Jack Aker, Steve Barber, Gary Bell, Tommy Davis, Jim Gosger, Tommy Harper, Gerry McNertney, Don Mincher, Ray Oyler, Rich Rollins, Chico Salmon)	35.00	17.50	10.50
10	Montreal Expos (John Bailey, John Bateman, Jack Billingham, Jim Grant, Larry Jaster, Mack Jones, Manny Mota, Rusty Staub, Gary Sutherland, Jim Williams, Maury Wills)	17.00	8.50	5.00
11	Chicago White Sox (Sandy Alomar, Luis Aparicio, Ken Berry, Buddy Bradford, Joe Horlen, Tommy John, Duane Josephson, Tom McCraw, Bill Melton, Pete Ward, Wilbur Wood)	17.00	8.50	5.00
12	San Diego Padres (Jose Arcia, Danny Breeden, Ollie Brown, Bill Davis, Ron Davis, Tony Gonzalez, Dick Kelley, Al McBean, Roberto Pena, Dick Selma, Ed Spiezio)	17.00	8.50	5.00
13	Cleveland Indians (Max Alvis, Joe Azcue, Jose Cardenal, Vern Fuller, Lou Johnson, Sam McDowell, Sonny Siebert, Duke Sims, Russ Snyder, Luis Tiant, Zoilo Versalles)	17.00	8.50	5.00
14	San Francisco Giants (Bobby Bolin, Jim Davenport, Dick Dietz, Jim Hart, Ron Hunt, Hal Lanier, Juan Marichal, Willie Mays, Willie McCovey, Gaylord Perry, Charlie Smith)	40.00	20.00	12.00
15	Minnesota Twins (Bob Allison, Chico Cardenas, Rod Carew, Dean Chance, Jim Kaat, Harmon Killebrew, Tony Oliva, Jim Perry, John Roseboro, Cesar Tovar, Ted Uhlaender)	40.00	20.00	12.00
16	Pittsburgh Pirates (Gene Alley, Matty Alou, Steve Blass, Jim Bunning, Bob Clemente, Rich Hebner, Jerry May, Bill Mazeroski, Bob Robertson, Willie Stargell, Bob Veale)	40.00	20.00	12.00
17	California Angels (Ruben Amaro, George Brunet, Bob Chance, Vic Davalillo, Jim Fregosi, Bobby Knoop, Jim McGlothlin, Rick Reichardt, Roger Repoz, Bob Rodgers, Hoyt Wilhelm)	20.00	10.00	6.00
18	St. Louis Cardinals (Nelson Briles, Lou Brock, Orlando Cepeda, Curt Flood, Bob Gibson, Julian Javier, Dal Maxvill, Tim McCarver, Vada Pinson, Mike Shannon, Ray Washburn)	35.00	17.50	10.50
19	New York Yankees (Stan Bahnsen, Horace Clarke, Bobby Cox, Jake Gibbs, Mickey Mantle, Joe Pepitone, Fritz Peterson, Bill Robinson, Mel Stottlemyre, Tom Tresh, Roy White)	90.00	45.00	27.00
20	Cincinnati Reds (Gerry Arrigo, Johnny Bench, Tommy Helms, Alex Johnson, Jim Maloney, Lee May, Gary Nolan, Tony Perez, Pete Rose, Bob Tolan, Woody Woodward)	90.00	45.00	27.00
21	Oakland Athletics (Sal Bando, Bert Campaneris, Danny Cater, Dick Green, Mike Hershberger, Jim Hunter, Reggie Jackson, Rick Monday, Jim Nash, John Odom, Jim Pagliaroni)	60.00	30.00	18.00
22	Los Angeles Dodgers (Willie Crawford, Willie Davis, Don Drysdale, Ron Fairly, Tom Haller, Andy Kosco, Jim Lefebvre, Claude Osteen, Paul Popovich, Bill Singer, Bill Sudakis)	35.00	17.50	10.50
23	Washington Senators (Bernie Allen, Brant Alyea, Ed Brinkman, Paul Casanova, Joe Coleman, Mike Epstein, Jim Hannan, Frank Howard, Ken McMullen, Camilo Pascual, Del Unser)	17.00	8.50	5.00
24	New York Mets (Tommie Agee, Ken Boswell, Ed Charles, Jerry Grote, Bud Harrelson, Cleon Jones, Jerry Koosman, Ed Kranepool, Jim McAndrew, Tom Seaver, Ron Swoboda)	100.00	50.00	30.00

Great Moments
In
Hobby History

From April 30, 1977 Sports Collectors Digest

Bowman vs Topps

THE LEGAL BATTLE AND THE SALES BATTLE

By Marv Porten, 61 Crestwood #28 - Daly City, Calif. 94015

In 1948, Bowman began distributing baseball cards with its gum products. Topps came on the scene in 1951. Soon thereafter, Bowman initiated legal proceedings in an attempt to drive Topps baseball cards off the market. Bowman and Topps were in and out of the courts for two years. Here is the story of that legal battle and the subsequent sales battle for supremacy in the baseball card field.

In the spring of 1950 the Russell Publishing Company contracted with 248 major league baseball players for permission to use their names, pictures and biographical data on flip books and cards. During the same period, Players Enterprises, Inc., contracted with a number of major league baseball players for the right to use their names and pictures in connection with the manufacture and sale of products.

In December 1950, Topps Chewing Gum, Inc., completed a deal with Players Enterprises and acquired the right to use the names, pictures and biographical data of the players who had contracted with Players Enterprises. Topps intended to use these rights in connection with the sale of candy in 1951, and the sale of candy and chewing gum in 1952. (Bubble gum was referred to as "candy" in the early 1950s.) In April 1951 Topps began issuing baseball cards with its "candy."

About the same time, Russell Publishing Company and Players Enterprises merged. As a result, the players under contract with Russell Publishing were made available to Topps. In June 1951, Topps distributed a second series of baseball cards. The second series contained primarily those players who had previously contracted with Russell Publishing.

Beginning in May 1951, Players Enterprises entered into new contracts for the 1952 baseball season with 283 major league baseball players. Topps had plans for a banner year in 1952. But one company did not care much for the turn of events: Bowman Gum, Inc.

Beginning in 1948, Bowman employed Art Flynn Associates to contract with baseball players for the use of their names, pictures and biographical data on cards sold with chewing gum. Until 1951, Bowman paid each player $100, and in 1951 they gave each player a wristwatch for these rights. Some, but not all, of the contracts prohibited the player from selling these rights to other companies. By 1951, Bowman had 340 players under contract. (Cards were not produced during the 1951 season for 16 players under contract with Bowman. This might have been due to their retirement or relegation to the minors after contracts had been signed.)

It was now early 1953. The Federal District Court had a monumental task. Hundreds of players were involved and there were about two thousand contracts to review. Most of the players had signed several contracts: with Bowman, with Topps, with Players Associates and with Russell Publishing. The court had to determine which contract, if any, was binding on each player. (Some of the players had provisions in their contracts which allowed them to appear on both Topps and Bowman cards.) In the meantime Topps and Bowman were already printing 1953 baseball cards.

In March 1953, the Federal District Court announced its decision. It named the players who had binding contracts with Bowman, those who had binding contracts with Topps, and those who had not bound themselves exclusively to one or the other. The court also enjoined Topps and Bowman from attempting to contract with players who already had exclusive contracts with the other company.

Remaining was the problem of what to do about 1953 cards which had already been printed. Topps had printed cards of players who belonged to Bowman and Bowman had printed cards of players who belonged to Topps. The court ordered that cards which were already wrapped in retail packages could be distributed, but if cards had not yet been wrapped (for example, those still on uncut sheets) all cards of players not belonging to that company had to be removed and destroyed. These cards could not be packaged and sold. And, of course, in future printings Topps and Bowman could produce cards only of those players with whom it had valid contracts. This court order may explain why six numbers are completely omitted from the 1953 Topps set, and why some others are scarce. After fighting a two year court battle, Topps had won its place in the baseball card industry. It was able to call its cards "baseball cards" and sell them in connection with gum. It could contract with players who did not sign with Bowman and with those whose contracts with Bowman had expired. More importantly, players were alerted not to sign exclusive contracts with Bowman, but rather to include provisions in their contracts which allowed them to appear on both Bowman and Topps cards.

Following the resolution of the legal matters, Topps and Bowman began a sales competition for baseball card supremacy. Perhaps others have their own explanation of why Topps prevailed, but in my view there is a very simple explanation. I remember as a youngster that each new season Topps cards arrived at the corner candy store a week or two before Bowman cards. We kids had only enough extra pennies to try to complete just one set of cards. Most kids did not have the money to work on two different sets at once. The set we tried to complete, by buying more cards, was the one we started on first: Topps.

In retrospect, after the courts had given Topps the legal go ahead, it was the young card collectors of the early 1950s who made the final decision. For one reason or another they (we) preferred Topps cards over Bowman cards, and this decision led to the demise of Bowman and the ascendancy of Topps.

After viewing Topps' activities in 1951, Bowman accused Topps of wrongful conduct by contracting with some of the same players as Bowman and by copying Bowman's style of using baseball cards in connection with the sale of gum products. Bowman also claimed that the term "baseball" was its registered trademark and Topps should not be permitted to call its cards "baseball" cards. (On 1952 Bowman cards the "registered trademark" symbol appears after the word "baseball" on the back of the cards.) Bowman sued Topps in Federal District Court in New York and sought an injunction to stop Topps from selling baseball cards. If Bowman were successful, Topps would be forced out of business before its 1952 series went on sale.

Bowman's actual legal complaint against Topps charged Topps with trademark infringement, unfair competition, and violation of contract rights. Bowman claimed 1) that it alone had the right to use the trademark "baseball" with the sale of its products; 2) that Topps unfairly copied Bowman's distinctive use of baseball cards to sell gum products; and 3) that it had exclusive baseball card contracts with baseball players and no one else could contract for baseball cards with the same players.

Bowman was represented by Philadelphia lawyers and New York lawyers. Voluminous evidence was presented to the federal judge who heard the case. After considering all the arguments, the judge wrote a lengthy legal decision which found no merit in Bowman's complaint and gave Topps the go ahead to distribute its 1952 baseball card set.

The judge specifically decided that Bowman did not have a monopoly on the term "baseball" to promote its products. The term "baseball" was found to be a descriptive term which was available for use by anyone. Bowman could not get a trademark for "baseball" and prohibit others from making "baseball" cards. The judge also concluded that Topps was not unfairly copying Bowman's idea of distributing baseball cards with gum products. The judge pointed out that Goudey Gum Co. did the same thing beginning in 1933 and Bowman's idea was not original. More importantly, the judge found no evidence which suggested that Topps had been "palming off" its products in 1951 as Bowman products. To quote the judge: "The dress and packaging of Topps' baseball trading card candy is outstandingly different from the dress and packaging of Bowman's baseball picture card gum. Also, though Bowman gives the biographical data of the baseball player on the reverse side, that is not done by Topps. Another item of difference exists between the posturing of the ball players on Bowman's cards and the absence thereof on Topps' cards. There is no proof of any deception that was practiced on any of Bowman's customers; and likewise the record is barren of any proof that there is likely to be any confusion among those who purchase the products of either, or that Topps has offered them as the products of Bowman, directly or through devious means."

Finally, the judge dismissed Bowman's claim that Topps infringed upon contracts between the baseball players and Bowman. The judge interpreted the contracts as giving Bowman the right to use the baseball players' names and pictures in promoting its products without having to worry about being sued by the players for invasion of privacy. The judge said the contract did not prevent the players from granting the same right to others, and nothing at all prevented Topps from seeking contracts with players who had already given Bowman the right to use their names, and pictures.

Bowman accepted the judge's decision that Topps could use the word "baseball" in describing its cards and that Topps was not engaging in unfair business practices. But Bowman disagreed that Topps could make valid contracts with players who already signed "exclusive" contracts with Bowman, and Bowman appealed this part of the decision to the Federal Court of Appeals.

The Court of Appeals reversed this part of the lower court's decision. It agreed with Bowman that Topps could not contract with players who had given Bowman exclusive rights to use their names and pictures on gum cards. The Court of Appeals ordered the case returned to the Federal District Court to determine which players could appear on Topps cards and which could appear on Bowman cards.

Now it was Topps' turn to appeal — to the United States Supreme Court. The Supreme Court declined to review the case. Thus, in effect, it agreed with the decision of the Court of Appeals. The case had to be returned to the lower court and every contract had to be studied.

DOYLE, N. Y. NAT'L

DOYLE, N. Y.

From May 29, 1987 Sports Collectors Digest

Rare T206 variation sells for $10,000

A newly discovered variation in the T206 set was recently sold at auction for an astounding $10,000, making it the second most valuable baseball card in the history of the hobby.

The variation, a very rare version of the Joe Doyle T-206 card, was sold by the House of Cards in Wheaton, Md. Bill Huggins, one of the owners of the shop, said the buyer of the card "wishes to remain anonymous." He was identified only as "a very serious collector."

The card pictures Doyle in a hands-above-the-head pitching pose, but it's the caption at the bottom that contains the variation. The common variety of the card, valued at $11 in Excellent condition, states only "DOYLE, N.Y." The rare variation, however, also contains the league designation "NAT'L." after the name and team. The 77-year-old card was described as being in "Near Excellent" condition.

T206 cards were issued by tobacco companies from 1909-1911, and the backs of the cards contain ads for one of 16 different brands of cigarettes. The rare Doyle card has a "Piedmont" back.

The House of Cards advertised the rare variation in a half-page ad in the May 1 issue of *Sports Collectors*

Digest. The card was sold by "telephone auction," with most of the bids coming in the last 15 minutes. The auction was scheduled to close at 10 p.m., May 11.

Huggins said at 9:45 the high bid stood at $3500, and "then the phone wouldn't stop ringing." Five bidders were still in the running when the bidding jumped over the $5000 level. Three bidders gradually dropped out as the bids continued to climb.

"The phone was ringing every five minutes with a higher bid," Huggins said. "We decided to keep taking bids until the phone was quiet for 10 minutes." The auction finally ended when one of the two remaining bidders raised it to $10,000.

That makes it the second most expensive card in the hobby," Huggins said.

The only card which has sold for more, of course, is the famous T206 Honus Wagner card, which has had documented sales in the $25,000 range and is listed in the *SCD Price Guide* at $34,000 in Near Mint condition.

Huggins said the rare Doyle variation was included in a collection he recently bought, but he wasn't even aware of the card at the time.

"It was kind of a fluke," Huggins said. "We really bought it as just a $5 card."

He said the variation wasn't discovered until the collection was being sorted later. "We didn't really know what it was worth," Huggins said. "We didn't put any specific value on it before the auction."

From November 27, 1987 Sports Collectors Digest

Unopened 1950s cards found

By Vic Knight

Imagine finding over 200 boxes of unopened 1954-55 Topps and Bowman baseball cards. A collector's dream, right?

But wait a minute. Upon closer inspection, you notice that over half of the boxes have been damaged by water or eaten by insects. You pop open the boxes and rip into the wax packs and suddenly your dreams turn sour. Bugs scramble from out of the boxes and packs. Partially-eaten cards abound.

Well-known dealer Alan Rosen recently went through such an emotional roller coaster when he "found" several boxes of 1954-55 Topps and Bowman cards, only to find that many of them had been destroyed or damaged by water and bugs.

Nevertheless, the number of cards that he was able to salvage amounts to one of the largest finds of unopened 1950s material in recent memory.

Like many great "finds," this one started with a phone call. On Saturday evening, Oct. 24, Rosen received a call from a Paris, Tenn., resident.

"He said he had stumbled upon several cases of 'Ball' cards. Since he had followed my ads for several years,

he decided to call me," said Rosen. "At first, I thought it was a prank phone call — who wouldn't?"

Rosen, however, remembered the circumstances surrounding the famous 1952 Topps find and decided to treat this case as the real thing.

"I said to myself, 'Anything could be possible.' I listened to him relate the individual box and pack descriptions and everything seemed to match up," he said. Rosen then contacted hobby friend Brian Morris, who bought over some 1954-55 Bowman and Topps wrappers so they could confirm the descriptions. They checked.

Rosen and Morris immediately flew to Paris, Tenn., where they were met by Dick DeCourcey of Georgia Music and Sports in Riverdale, Ga. Upon their arrival, the trio rented a meeting room at their hotel where individual boxes of 1954 and 1955 Topps and Bowman baseball cards were soon piled — 212 in all.

"The sight was straight out of every baseball card collector's best dream," said Rosen. "When I walked into the room and saw all of those unopened boxes, my knees started shaking."

Then panic set it.

"As I got closer, I could see there was something wrong. There were bugs crawling all over the place," he said.

Many of the boxes, which have been sitting on a dirt floor in the basement of a warehouse for the past 32 years, had become infested with bugs — silverfish to be exact. Water had also contributed to much of the damage found on the cards and boxes.

"We held in our hands packs of 1955 Bowman cards that literally had holes bored right through them as if someone had shot bullets at them," said Rosen. "Many of the boxes were literally filled with bugs and the remnants of 1954 and '55 Bowman and Topps cards. It was a shame."

However, despite the massive amount of destroyed or damaged cards, the discovery was by no means a total loss. Even though nearly half of the boxes and cards had been ruined by water and bugs, many mint cards and boxes remained intact.

All in all, the find consisted of the following undamaged boxes of cards: 24 boxes of 5-cent wax packs of 1954 Bowman baseball, 13 boxes of 1955 Bowman baseball and 11 boxes of 1955 Topps baseball packs.

In addition, there were 61 boxes of 1954 and '55 Bowman baseball cards that were damaged beyond repair, but contained some cards that were salvageable. Incredibly, over 70 boxes of 1954 and '55 Bowman and 1955 Topps baseball had to be thrown away in their entirety.

The history of the cards, as one might expect, is confusing and interesting. It goes something like this:

An oldtime Paris, Tenn., candy wholesaler was the original owner of the boxes. He had recently passed away, and his widow desired to sell the building that had housed the cards for the past 32 years. She had the building emptied and the person cleaning out the property was given the cards for an undisclosed amount. That person, in turn, sold the cards to a candy wholesaler who was the new occupant of the warehouse. He, in turn, was contacted by the individual who called Rosen.

He completed his transaction with the new wholesaler and then contacted Rosen. Upon completion of the deal for the baseball cards, Rosen asked the seller if there was a possibility that more boxes of cards existed. He was told that three cases of football cards were included in the find, but that they had already been purchased by someone else.

"The next morning as we were preparing to leave Paris, I decided to check my messages from home," said Rosen. "Apparently, I had gotten a call from a guy named Randy Scarborough who also happened to live in Paris, Tenn. Randy, who had been a previous customer of mine, had called to see if I was interested in the three cases of football cards, not knowing that I was already in the area."

An hour later, Rosen was at his house.

The football boxes were also damaged in the same manner as the baseball boxes, and once again box after box had to be discarded. They were, however, able to salvage the following football cards: 39 boxes of 1-cent (1 card) wax packs of 1954 Bowmans and 26 boxes of 5-cent wax packs of 1954 Bowmans. A 1954 Bowman 5-cent wax pack contained seven cards plus the traditional gum.

Scarborough also produced 15 heavily damaged boxes of 1960 Topps baseball cards. However, due to heavy water and bug damage, only a small number of cards from three different boxes could be saved.

"Imagine sitting at a table and ripping open 1960 Topps wax packs and getting dozens of Mantles, McCoveys, Aarons and Clementes, but having to throw them away because they were ruined," said Rosen. "What a shame."

Rosen indicated that nearly three-quarters of the salvaged cards were sold to collectors before his recent ad for the cards appeared in *SCD*. The rest will certainly be gobbled up soon. Unopened 1950s material just doesn't pop up every day.

"To me, it's finds like these that makes this business so much fun," said Rosen. "The anticipation, the hunt and the chase all make it exciting."

From October 28, 1988 Sports Collectors Digest

Joshua Evans discovers previous unknown card

By Steve Ellingboe

Allentown, Pa., dealer Joshua Evans stunned the hobby world recently with the startling announcement that he is in possession of a previously unknown card from the scarce 1932 U.S. Caramel set. Advanced collectors consider it among the most significant hobby "finds" in years.

Evans believes the card, which pictures Hall of Famer Fred Lindstrom, is the only one of its kind in existence. The card is #16 in the set, a number previously thought to have been unissued. The 32-card set of "famous athletes" was produced by the U.S. Caramel Co. of East Boston, Mass., in 1932. It features 26 baseball players, almost all of whom are now Hall of Famers, including Babe Ruth, Ty Cobb, Lou Gehrig, Rogers Hornsby and other greats of the day.

Because of its relative scarcity, the obscure set is generally only collected by advanced hobbyists and carries a value of about $10,000 in top condition.

Even "commons" from the set in Near Mint condition command a price of $200 or more.

Until Evans' dramatic revelation last month, it had been assumed by collectors that card #16 in the U.S. Caramel set was never issued — a reasonable assumption considering that during the past 56 years no examples of the card had ever surfaced.

Evans is not disclosing the details regarding his purchase of the Lindstrom card, but said the transaction was completed at the Labor Day weekend show in San Francisco. He declined to comment on the purchase price.

Evans described the card as being in "Excellent" condition, although it is stamped "CANCELLED" on the back and has two punch holes in it.

The trading card set was originally issued as a promotion by the caramel company, and the back of the cards advised youngsters to return one complete set for a baseball (valued at $1) or three complete sets for a fielder's glove (valued at $3).

"Your pictures will be returned with your gifts," the cards promised, which accounts for the punch holes and the "CANCELLED" mark on the Lindstrom card.

For years it has been assumed that the Caramel company purposely withheld card #16 to dupe Depression-era youngsters into buying more caramels, hoping to find a card that didn't exist.

There was additional speculation that card #16 was supposed to picture Joe Kuhel, the Senators and White Sox first baseman, but that the card was never issued. Why Kuhel's name was associated with the missing card has never been fully explained, except that, as advanced collector Lew Lipset points out, Kuhel was #16 in the 1934 Goudey set. "It's just another hobby myth that has been perpetuated through the years," Lipset said.

According to Evans, the Lindstrom card had been owned by a farmer in Illinois, who sold the card to another party, who in turn offered it to Evans. The deal was completed over the Labor Day weekend in San Francisco, but Evans did not publicize the transaction until a couple of weeks later. Evans declined to identify any of the people involved in the sale, saying they wished to remain anonymous.

It is not clear what connection, if any, the Illinois farmer may have had with the Boston-based U.S. Caramel Company, but Evans referred to the card as the company's original "file copy" and said it is "the only one in existence." Evans speculates that the company either made just one copy of the Lindstrom card, or else made more but destroyed the others to insure that no one would be able to win any of the prizes.

Interestingly, the front of the rare card identifies Lindstrom as "Charles" (Lindy) Lindstrom, calling the ball player by his middle name rather than his more familiar first name, "Fred," which appears on the back of the card.

That, too, could explain the card's rarity. If the name "Charles" was printed by mistake, company officials could have considered it a serious enough error that they decided not to issue the card.

Although Evans refused to disclose what he paid for the card, he is not at all shy about disclosing what he hopes to get for it.

"It's a million-dollar card," Evans said confidently, calling it a "one-of-a-kind treasure" and comparing it to a "Rembrandt or Van Gogh that is suddenly discovered in some attic." Evans, who is associated with Leland's auction house in Allenton, Pa., reasons that "if the T206 Honus Wagner card is worth over $100,000, and there are 40 or 50 of them in existence, then this card ought to be worth a million.

"It's like a rare coin," Evans told a reporter. "If you've got the only one, it's priceless."

Other advanced collectors, however, scoff at the million-dollar estimate. In a *New York Daily News* article, Barry Halper, whose impressive collection rivals that of the Hall of Fame, called the million-dollar price tag "crazy." And Alan Rosen, one of the nation's largest dealers asked, "If you paid the million, who would you sell it to?"

Lew Lipset, an authority on older card sets, laughed at the asking price, calling it "imbecilic and moronic."

Lipset and Larry Fritsch, another veteran collector who owns one of the most complete collections in the country and recently established a baseball card museum in Cooperstown, agree that the Lindstrom card is a significant "find," but both suggest that the card may not be the unique, one-of-a-kind example that Evans claims it is. Although no other U.S. Caramel card of Lindstrom has ever turned up, Fritsch takes the position that "if there's one out there, then there are two out there someplace."

Lipset agrees. "It has always been my feeling that if you find one, you'll probably find another."

Fritsch also points out that compared to the T206 set, the 1932 U.S. Caramel set is relatively unpopular and not widely collected. So even if the Lindstrom card is rare, he says, the potential demand for it is small, making the million-dollar asking price unrealistic.

Evans told *SCD* that he has already received some offers for the card, but none of them have been acceptable. "Let's just say that they were for more than a dollar and less than a million," he said.

The real value, of course, remains to be seen. But there's no doubt that Evans's dramatic announcement will send advanced collectors scurrying to find another example of the Lindstrom caramel card, now that a 56-year-old hobby mystery is finally starting to unravel.

From Trader Speaks - February 1990

100-year-old find is hobby's most historically significant

By Bob Lemke
Editor-Publisher

While its dollar value does not approach many of the fabulous baseball card "finds" of the decade, the last great hoard discovery of the 1980s surely ranks as the most historically significant. The true hobbyist will also find considerably more charm in the tale than in the stories associated with more commercially valuable discoveries of recent years.

The box itself is unremarkable. Though obviously of quality manufacture a century ago, this child's wooden lap desk shows the effects of generations of use. The fine oak is dried, cracked and separating. There are gouges

and chips in both the woodwork and the slate center. A heavy black garter, probably cut from an inner tube, holds the 18x12" box together. The top is still firmly held in place by rusting brass hinges.

If you saw the desk at a flea market or antique shop, you would probably not give it a second glance. Unless ... the eye happens to catch the scraps of yellowing newspaper once glued, then partially torn from the top of the desk. Apparently cut from a contemporary issue of *The Sporting News* or *The Sporting Life,* the remnants reveal rosters of baseball teams of the late 1880s.

No real card collector could resist a peek inside.

It is a find, no doubt about it. A find — at least — of cigarette boxes. There must be three dozen "Duke's Cameo" boxes; bright with pastel flowers, feathers and a gaily colored portrait of a Victorian era beauty. There're another 10 or 12 "Dog's Head" boxes, in more somber shades of brown. Boxes like this can bring $100-150 in the tobacco collectors' market.

Inside, the desk top is pasted with more scraps of newsprint; more team rosters, from the National League, American Association, Western Association and other minor leagues. On some of the rosters there is a bold red ink mark to the left of most names. Many of the names have other pencilled marks following.

A scrap of paper in the bottom of the box draws the eye. Neatly inked thereon is "Louisville". Hello! Each of the cigarette boxes has a similar paper strip glued to a side. Some bear a penned notation, some typed: "Washington", "New York", "Hamilton", "Chicago", "Buffalo/Detroit", "Jersey City" ...

Each box bears a label repeating the team names pasted to the desk's lid.

Picking up one of the cigarette boxes, a rattle is heard from inside. Another box, another rattle.

It couldn't be ... could it?

How do these damn things open? Ah! "To open this Box Push this End" reads the printing at one end of the cigarette box. An inner tray slides forward at the other end of the box, along with a small stack of cards inside. A familiar black cartouche is seen at the top: "OLD JUDGE Cigarettes". Underneath, the top of another card is visible. The words "Gypsy Queen" surmount a familiar tombstone-shaped photo of a baseball player with a striped cap and a laced jersey that reads "St. Louis".

At this juncture, most of us would expect to awaken from a pleasant, though frustrating, dream. And while this is no dream, there is a frustrating realization to come.

As each of the cigarette boxes is emptied and piles of Old Judge and Gypsy Queen cards begin to build on the table, there is a gnawing feeling that something is not quite right.

When one of the boxes disgorges a card that seems so much larger than the rest, a terrible realization hits home — these cards are trimmed.

Out of just over 500 Old Judge cards and more than 60 Gypsy Queens, only a handful remain in their original size. All the rest have suffered the application of the razor; cut down on the sides and tops to nearly the borders of the photos, though the cigarette brand names have been left mercifully intact.

Who? When? Why?

Those are just about the only substantive questions for which the current owner of this hoard offers no answers. He is exceedingly well versed on the rest of the history of this collection. It has been in his family for over 100 years.

The current owner, who wishes to remain anonymous, became aware of the cards' existence about four years ago when the lap desk was found in the attic of the ancestral home in Maine.

Judging from the player rosters glued to the lid of the desk, the assembly of the collection appears to have peaked in 1888. At that time, according to the owner, his grandfather would have been 10 years old.

A decade later, the original collector moved into a huge, new house. The lineal descendents of the original owner have inhabited the house since 1898. With some 20,000 square feet of home, and the family never moving, it is not hard to imagine how the desk — and collection — survived intact for a century. The mobility of most American families in the past hundred years created many opportunities for similar collections to have been trashed at least once per generation.

The discovery of so many N-172s (the *American Card Catalog* designation for Old Judge and Gyspy Queen baseball cards) in a collection untouched for 100 years at first glance seemed like it must rewrite the checklist, if not the price guide, for this most popular of 19th century card issues.

Significantly, however, the hoard adds virtually nothing to the existing cataloging done by the Cartophilic Society of Great Britain over the years. According to the cards' owner, there are no new players among the 560+ cards. Cursory comparison of the discovery with the N-172 checklist in the *Standard Catalog of Baseball*

 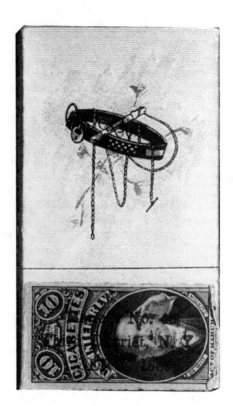

Cards has revealed only a few pose and/or team variations for previously known players. A complete card-by-card analysis of the hoard has yet to be undertaken by a knowledgeable hobbyist.

For the most part, the photos on the cards remain in bright, sharp contrast. Only a small percentage exhibit the characteristic fading exhibited by many Old Judge cards known within the hobby. No doubt the fact the cards were sealed away from damaging light rays for a century contributed to the remarkable state of the images' preservation.

Too bad the cards could not have been preserved from the knife, as well. The owner professes no knowledge of who trimmed the cards, why or when. There does exist several untrimmed cards in the hoard. The characteristic slightly rounded corners on those few undamaged specimens might give a person pause to consider that the cards were only recently trimmed, perhaps to conform to a non-hobbyist's view of baseball card aesthetics. The survival of at least one card in the collection with thumbtack holes in each corner also makes plausible the theory that the cards were later trimmed to remove the holed corners, though none of the trimmed cards exhibit the indentations of the tacks' rounded edge, as is usually seen.

Too, it must be considered that trimming this many N-172s would be no easy task. Essentially photographic prints affixed to stiff, multi-layered cardboard backs, the Old Judge cards are not easily trimmed, especially so as to yield the clean, sharp edges which these cards exhibit.

Despite the fact the cards are housed in cigarette boxes that do not bear the Old Judge or Gypsy Queen brand name, and in the case of the Duke's Cameo boxes are not even of the Goodwin & Co. family, there was no need to trim the cards to fit the boxes. A normal-sized N-172 fits inside with room to spare.

While condition freaks will argue that the trimming has destroyed most of the cards' market value, they would be overlooking the true nature of the Old Judge market.

Part of the historic significance of this find is that in many cases the cards in this hoard double the known examples of a particular N-172. The collector who has been searching in vain for years for a particular player, pose or team designation within this set may have seen the pool of potential specimens available double from its previous level — if he is willing to accept a trimmed card. However, since many collectors of N-172 will accept a card in any condition, unless or until something better comes along, the trimmed nature of these cards may not have all that disastrous an effect on market value.

As of now, however, the market value of this collection is only theoretical because the owner has not determined whether or not he will sell the find. He currently holds the commercial element of the baseball card hobby in little regard, the result of a negative contact made at a show when the cards first came into his possession. The cards' owner visited one of the larger Anaheim shows several years ago and approached a self-proclaimed Old Judge expert with a handful of the cards. He was rudely brushed off by the dealer who, not realizing the extent of the find, told him the cards were worthless in their trimmed state.

It was several years before the owner looked into the matter again, after having purchased a copy of the *SCD Baseball Card Price Guide* annual, and realizing that even in their damaged condition, the cards would have some value.

Whether that value will be enough to induce the owner to part with a collection that has been in his family for three generations is an open question at this point.

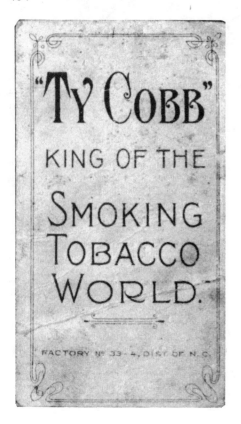

From October 26, 1990 Sports Collectors Digest

California dealer acquires true hobby rarity

One of the rarest cards in the hobby — a T206 Ty Cobb card with a Ty Cobb back — was recently acquired by California hobby dealer David Kohler of SportsCards Plus.

As collectors of tobacco cards are well aware, cards in the T206 set are found with any of 16 different back designs, each advertising a different brand of tobacco. Of the 16 backs available, the Ty Cobb backs are by far the rarest. Only about five T206 cards with Ty Cobb backs are known to exist, making it among the rarest and most valuable cards in the hobby.

The massive T-206 set contains over 500 different players, but because most can be found with several different front/back combinations, there are thousands of potential variations in the set.

Hall of Famer Ty Cobb was pictured on four different cards in the T206 set — two portrait photos and two holding a bat. The Cobb card that Kohler purchased is listed in price guides and catalogs as the "portrait photo with red background."

Kohler purchased the rarity from an unnamed private collector who had received the Cobb card as part of his grandfather's collection, which also included other T206 cards and various tobacco issues.

Kohler, who has been a baseball card dealer since 1979, said it was the first time he had ever seen the rare Cobb card offered for sale. "I can't recall, in the 12 years I've been in this business, ever seeing this card offered for sale, either in an ad, at a show or by auction," he said.

Kohler estimates that no more than five examples of the Cobb card with a Cobb back are known to exist.

Regarding the card's condition, Kohler said that "despite some creasing, the card is extremely eye-appealing." He said the corners are "fairly sharp" and "by no means rounded." He added that the colors of the card are "extremely bright" and the back of the card — which is actually what makes this particular card so valuable — is "very clean and boldly displays the rare green Ty Cobb advertisement."

Kohler plans to eventually sell the card at auction — but will first use it for promotional purposes.

"Once we decide it's time to sell," Kohler said, "we'll definitely make people aware of it," indicating he plans to notify collectors and investors via ads in the hobby press.

Kohler declined to attach a price tag to the rarity, but he said he has already turned down an offer of $50,000.

"With only about five copies known to exist," Kohler said, "this card easily surpasses the rarity of the T206 Wagner, Plank or Magie." Kohler added that the card's value is also enhanced because it belongs to "the most popular Pre-war set ever issued," and it pictures "one of the most popular players in the history of the game."

To ensure its authenticity, Kohler hired paper and documents expert James A. Black of Lake Forest, Calif., to examine the card. Black's examination verified the card's age and confirmed that the composition of the paper, ink, printing and wear are all consistent with other cards from 1910. Black further stated that "no optical brighteners" are present, and concluded that there is no evidence that the card had been altered in any way.

From April 12, 1991 Sports Collectors Digest

Sotheby's sale totals $4.6 million

New York auction sells the Copeland Collection

By Steve Ellingboe

Record-high prices were established on a regular basis in New York last month as more than $4.6 million worth of baseball cards and memorabilia were sold at the Sotheby's auction of the Copeland Collection.

It was, without question, the single most impressive collection of baseball cards and memorabilia ever assembled for one sale. The items offered at the March 22-23 auction were the finest in the hobby — both in terms of completeness and condition.

But what made the auction even more amazing is that everything in the sale was, owned by one individual collector, James Copeland, a California sporting goods retailer who had assembled the vast collection in just four year's time.

Adding to the significance of the event was that it marked the first time that Sotheby's — perhaps the most prestigious and distinguished auction house in the world — had devoted an entire sale to baseball cards and related memorabilia.

And according to a Sotheby's spokesman, the auction attracted more attention than any other sale the firm had ever conducted.

The demand for auction catalogs was the strongest in Sotheby's long history, the spokesman said. The first printing of 8,300 copies sold out early, and a second printing of an additional 6,000 catalogs was ordered to meet the continuing demand. The $30, full-color catalog is expected to become a collectible itself.

The auction attracted nearly 1,000 people to the impressive Sotheby's Galleries on Manhattan's Upper East Side. Several hundred additional bidders were prepared to bid by phone, and hundreds more had already mailed in their bids.

The auction consisted of 873 lots which together comprised the best and most complete collection in the hobby. Copeland's collection was dominated by baseball cards, but also included programs, pins, bats, tickets, statues, autographed baseballs, photographs, yearbooks, scorecards, wrappers, advertising pieces and other substantial pieces of baseball memorabilia. The sports of football, basketball, hockey and boxing were also represented and brought very strong prices.

The Copeland collection included complete runs of virtually every known baseball card set, even dating back to the 19th century. And everything was in the best condition available, most of it Near Mint to Mint.

The auction, which was divided into four sessions over the two-day sale, brought some staggering prices and shattered many previously existing records. The strongest prices were realized for the more popular, frequently-collected material. Post-war material was especially strong, with the Topps and Bowman sets bringing in very high bids.

The popular candy and tobacco cards from earlier years were also strong, although some of the more obscure and esoteric material was relatively soft. The 19th century material was especially weak, with much of it failing to generate even the minimum bid.

The auction attracted major investors, collectors and hobby dealers from across the country. Much of the buying was done by private individuals for their own personal collections. Many of the lots were priced too high for dealers to buy for their inventories, although a few discriminating and patient dealers said they did find a few items that were priced reasonably enough to be purchased and resold at a profit.

Sotheby's had expected the auction to bring in between $5 million and $7 million, based on presale estimates. And although much of the material sold for far more than the presale estimates, the softness of the more esoteric material and the weakness of the 19th century items held down the final tally to just over $4.6 million.

In addition, one of the auction's centerpieces, Copeland's complete run of over 150 World Series press pins — which was expected to bring in as much as $300,000 — failed to attract a buyer.

Still, Copeland and Sotheby's were both very pleased with the final results, according to Bill Mastro, the veteran dealer/collector who was hired by the auction as a special consultant for the sale.

"Some things went higher than expected, some lower," said Mastro. "Overall, we were very satisfied."

Unfortunately, the timing of the sale was not the best from a financial standpoint, Mastro confided, adding that "Had the auction been held 12 months ago, prices would have been even stronger."

But despite a generally weak economy and what many perceive to be a softening collectibles market, interest in the auction was very high, and bidding was spirited and aggressive on many items.

The auction, and the media attention surrounding it — virtually every television station and newspaper in America carried reports — should provide a major boost to the hobby and has the potential to bring in thousands of new collectors and investors.

The highlight of the auction was, of course, the Mint-condition T206 Honus Wagner card, which first stunned the crowd when it sold for a staggering $451,000 (all prices quoted here include the additional 10 percent buyer's fee), and then caused even more excitement when it was revealed several hours later that it was hockey superstar Wayne Gretzky who purchased the treasure.

Just before the famous Wagner card was offered, a nearly complete set of T206 cards (missing only the Wagner, Plank and Magie cards) was sold for $99,000.

The Magie card was sold as a separate lot moments later and commanded a price of $29,700, while the Plank card brought $16,500. Both cards were graded Near Mint to Mint.

To many in attendance, even more surprising than the record sale of the T206 Wagner was the price paid for 1952 Topps Mickey Mantle card. The Mint Mantle, which had a presale estimate of $12,000 to $15,000, sold for a whopping $49,500, by far the highest price ever paid for a Mantle card.

Interestingly, Alan Rosen, the New Jersey dealer who had originally sold Copeland the '52 Mantle card for $4,000 in 1987, was trying to buy it back at the auction and remained in the bidding until prices topped the $40,000 mark.

"I just wanted to have the card back," said Rosen. "It's the best one I ever saw."

Seconds after Rosen dropped out, the card was sold to an unidentified telephone bidder.

The next lot, a complete 1952 Topps set in Near Mint to Mint condition (containing another '52 Mantle) brought $75,900, another record.

Other auction highlights included:

An 1886 St. Louis Browns pendant, a unique example of perhaps the finest piece of baseball jewelry to ever surface in the hobby, was sold for $82,500 to Steve Rotman of Rotman Collectibles.

An autographed baseball from the 1939 Hall of Fame induction ceremonies containing a dozen Hall of Famers' signatures (including Wagner, Ruth and Cobb) sold for $20,900.

An uncut 1934 Goudey sheet that included the scarce '33 Lajoie card commanded $79,750.

A complete 1933 Goudey set (including another #106 Lajoie) sold for $55,000 in Near Mint to Mint condition.

A complete set of T202 Hassan Triple Folders in Near Mint to Mint condition commanded $49,500.

A T204 Ramly set in Near Mint to Mint sold for $46,750.

A T205 Gold Border set in similar condition brought $41,250.

A 1949 Bowman set graded "mostly Mint" sold for $18,700, while a 1951 Bowman set (with the Mantle rookie card) went for $25,300.

A separate '51 Bowman Mantle in Mint condition brought $7,425.

From April 12, 1991 Sports Collectors Digest

Hockey star Gretzky buys $451,000 Wagner card

Although the Sotheby's auction featured enough "glamor" material to fill a museum, clearly the T206 Honus Wagner card was the star attraction.

Scheduled as lot number 196, the sale was beginning its third hour when auctioneer Robert Woolley, sounding more like a circus ringmaster, finally intoned, "and now, The Holy Grail," as the Wagner card was introduced for bidding.

Even though the previous 195 lots had already brought in more than a million dollars, it was the famous Wagner card that had brought in the crowds — including dozens of reporters and television news crews.

Never before had the baseball card hobby enjoyed so much publicity. Lining the aisles of the prestigious auction house were news crews from every major TV network and cable system in America, reporters from every local television affiliate, representatives of every wire service, all the local newspapers, the Wall Street investment journals and, of course, the hobby press.

They, and the hundreds of others in the room — collectors, investors, hobby dealers and curiosity-seekers — were waiting to witness history.

They were not disappointed.

The buzz of anticipation had been present in the room all morning. And as the auction progressed, anxious onlookers began paging ahead in their auction catalogs, silently counting down the number of lots until "the big one."

Not that the previous lots hadn't been big. Quite the contrary. The Friday morning session had included some of the finest material ever offered for sale anywhere and had already established record-high prices for dozens of cards and sets, sometimes shattering previous marks by thousands of dollars.

In fact, the lot immediately prior to the Wagner card, a nearly complete T206 set (missing only the Wagner, Plank and Magie cards) was sold for a cool $99,000!

But that was merely a warm-up for what was to follow.

Copeland's T206 Honus Wagner card, correctly graded as "Mint" and accurately described in the auction catalog as "clean and crisp," is undoubtedly the finest-known example of the most sought-after card in the hobby.

The story of the 1910 Honus Wagner card is legendary: How Wagner, one of the most popular players of his day, objected to his name and likeness being used to promote tobacco products and requested that the card be withdrawn from cigarette packages.

It makes a good story, but whether it's true or not is still open to speculation. Another, perhaps more likely theory, is that Wagner demanded the withdrawal of the card because he was never compensated for it.

In any event, there's no argument regarding the card's scarcity. According to the auction catalog, fewer than 40 T206 Wagners have ever surfaced, and no more than 10 are in a collectible condition of Excellent or better. Furthermore, only one other Wagner card is known to exist with the extremely rare "Piedmont" advertisement on the back. (All other Wagner cards have "Sweet Caporal" backs.)

The auction catalog listed a presale estimate on the valuable Wagner card of between $125,000 and $150,000, and a price within that range would indeed have established a new record price for a baseball card. But it was clearly evident, even long before the card was brought to the floor, that it would command a much higher price.

Not until the bidding actually began, however, did it become immediately apparent just how much higher the card would go.

The crowd was buzzing with excitement when the bidding opened at $228,000 — already twice the presale estimate — but as the bidding quickly escalated in 10 thousand-dollar increments, the crowd grew strangely quiet. As the bidding continued, now between just two bidders — one in the room, the other bidding via telephone — the tension increased. The silence was broken when the bidding reached the $300,000 plateau and the crowd responded with loud applause, but then quickly became quiet again as the price continued to climb.

The bidder in the room, later identified as Mark Friedland, a collectibles dealer from Aspen, Colo., continued to raise his numbered paddle in response to each increase by the phone bidder. The bidding continued at a frantic pace, and within seconds the silence was broken again with another outburst of applause as the phone bidder hit the $400,000 mark.

Friedland immediately countered with a bid of $405,000, and the phone bidder responded instantly, jumping the bid to $410,000.

And then it was over. Friedland, who had been matching the phone bidder at every increase without hesitation, had finally reached his limit, and auctioneer Woolley hammered down the sale at $410,000 "to the bidder on the phone."

The 10 percent buyer's premium, which is automatically added to each lot, brought the final selling price to $451,000 — by far the highest price ever paid for a baseball card, actually three times more than the previous record.

A disappointed Friedland later told reporters that he dropped out of the bidding because it appeared obvious that the phone bidder was prepared to pay whatever price was necessary to obtain the Wagner card, and since Friedland had already exceeded the $330,000 limit he had set for himself before the auction, he thought it was silly to continue to run up the price.

"I gave it my best shot," he said, "but when the phone bidder passed the $400,000 mark, I knew he was prepared to go all the way to a half-million if that's what it took to get the card. At that point I decided to drop out."

That left one final question unanswered: Who was the successful phone bidder who bought the card?

Immediate speculation pointed to a wealthy Texas oilman who was known to be interested in the card and had the money to afford it, but that rumor was dismissed by a Sotheby's spokeswoman who said only that the report was false and that the buyer would remain anonymous — at least for now.

"I may have some news for you later," she told a reporter.

"Later" came within a few hours, and when it did, the news was a blockbuster: The valuable Wagner card had been bought by hockey superstar Wayne Gretzky, who made the purchase in partnership with Bruce McNall, a major Beverly Hills coin dealer and the owner of the team for which Gretzky plays, the Los Angeles Kings.

The revelation further excited the already-stunned crowd who took additional delight in knowing that not only had they witnessed the hobby's most historic sale, but also that the card had been purchased by a super-star athlete of major proportions.

"Gretzky, himself, was on the phone doing the bidding," said Bill Mastro, the longtime collector/dealer who was hired by Sotheby's as a special consultant for the auction.

The Wagner card, which Gretzky called a belated Christmas present to himself, is the most recent in a series of investment purchases. At a major coin auction last May, Gretzky acquired one of the treasures of the numis-matic hobby, an 1873 pattern Trade dollar set that sold for over $137,000. After making that purchase, Gretzky told a reporter that he had "lots of coins" and was originally introduced to coin collecting in 1989 after McNall presented him with 1,851 quarter-ounce gold Eagle coins to commemorate his NHL-record 1,851st point.

The 40-year-old McNall, in addition to owning the Los Angeles Kings hockey team, is also the owner of Numismatic Fine Arts and is a major stockholder in the Superior Stamp & Coin Co., both located in Beverly Hills.

Gretzky and McNall have also been partners in previous investments. Earlier the pair purchased the Toronto Argonauts of the Canadian Football League, and they also jointly own a thoroughbred horse that ran in last year's Kentucky Derby. In addition to the T206 Wagner card, it is also believed that Gretzky later bought some of the hockey collectibles offered in another session of the Sotheby's auction, Mastro said.

INDEX

Six more books for sports collectors

$16⁹⁵

SCD Sportscard Counterfeit Detector, 2nd Edition

240 pages, 6"x9"

Don't get fooled by worthless look-alikes. Save hundreds of dollars with clues and photos that help you identify nearly 200 of the hobby's most dangerous counterfeit cards.

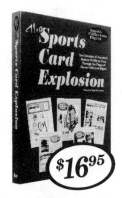

$16⁹⁵

The Sports Card Explosion

304 pages, 8 1/2"x11"

Join the staff of Sports Collectors Digest as they celebrate the last two decades in America's hottest hobby. From one-cent cards to $450,000 investments, it's a fascinating trip down memory lane.

$6⁹⁵

101 Sports Card Investments

220 pages, 5 1/2"x8 1/2"

Which cards should you be investing in? The staff at SCD tells you in this book packed with 101 can't-miss investment tips for baseball, football, basketball and hockey cards.

$6⁹⁵

Getting Started in Card Collecting

208 pages, 5 1/2"x8 1/2"

The ideal primer for beginning collectors. Packed with everything a novice needs to know to start a collection and make the most out of America's #1 hobby.

$5⁹⁵

Baseball Cards Questions & Answers, 2nd Edition

272 pages, 6"x9"

A virtual know-it-all on the subject of sports cards. Featuring answers to more than 500 of the hobby's most frequently-asked questions. Fascinating reading for all levels of collectors.

$14⁹⁵

Mickey Mantle Memorabilia

208 pages, 8 1/2"x11"

The hobby's most extensive chronicle of Mantle cards and memorabilia. Features pricing information and more than 150 photos. The ultimate book for fans and collectors of "The Mick."

Your ultimate collection connection

SPORTS COLLECTORS DIGEST

The premiere publication for advanced collectors. Each weekly issue of **Sports Collectors Digest** features news, articles, card prices, a show calendar, and ads for thousands of sports cards and collectibles.
1/2 year (26 issues)

$26.25

SPORTS CARDS

Month after month, Sports Cards arrives with hobby news, special features, updated card prices, investment tips and plenty of ads for cards and collectibles from all sports and all eras. Terrific reading for beginning, intermediate and advanced collectors.
1 year (12 issues)

$18.95

SPORTS CARD PRICE GUIDE MONTHLY

The hobby's most accurate monthly price guide features today's prices for baseball, football, basketball and hockey cards. Altogether you'll get 45,000 prices in each issue, along with news, articles and valuable investment advice.
1 year (12 issues)

$18.95

Name _____

Address _____

City _____

State _____ Zip _____

( ) Sports Collectors Digest
1/2 year (26 issues) **$26.25**

( ) Sports Cards
1 year (12 issues) **$18.95**

( ) Sports Card Price Guide Monthly
1 year (12 issues) **$18.95**

( ) New subscription

( ) Renewal / extension
(please attach your mailing label)

( ) Check or money order enclosed
(please make check payable to the publication ordered)

( ) MasterCard   ( ) VISA

Credit Card No. _____

Expires: Mo. _____ Yr. _____

Signature _____

Mail with payment to:
**Krause Publications, Circulation Dept.
700 E. State St. • Iola, WI 54990-0001**

MasterCard & VISA Cardholders save time by calling toll-free

800-258-0929 Dept. 7PR

Mon. - Fri. 6:30 a.m. to 8:00 p.m. • Sat. 8:00 a.m. to 2 p.m., CST.